CONNECT PLUS FEATURES

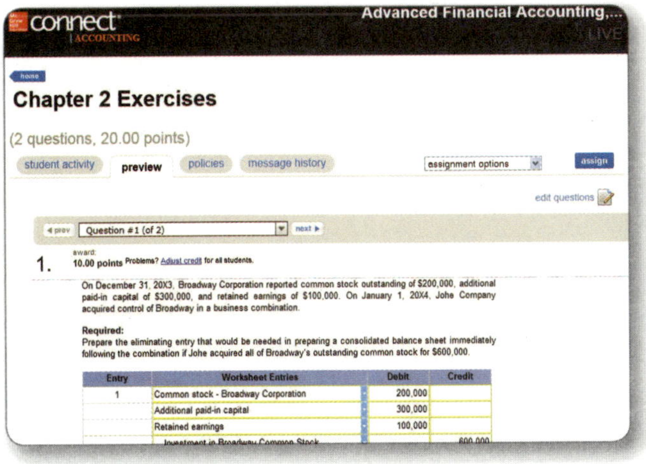

End-of-Chapter Material

McGraw-Hill Education redesigned the student interface for our end-of-chapter assessment content. The new interface provides improved answer acceptance to reduce students' frustration with formatting issues (such as rounding), and, for select questions, provides an expanded table that guides students through the process of solving the problem. Many questions have been redesigned to more fully test students' mastery of the content.

eBook

Connect Plus includes a media-rich eBook that allows you to share your notes with your students. Your students can insert and review their own notes, highlight the text, search for specific information, and interact with media resources. Using an eBook with Connect Plus gives your students a complete digital solution that allows them to access their materials from any computer.

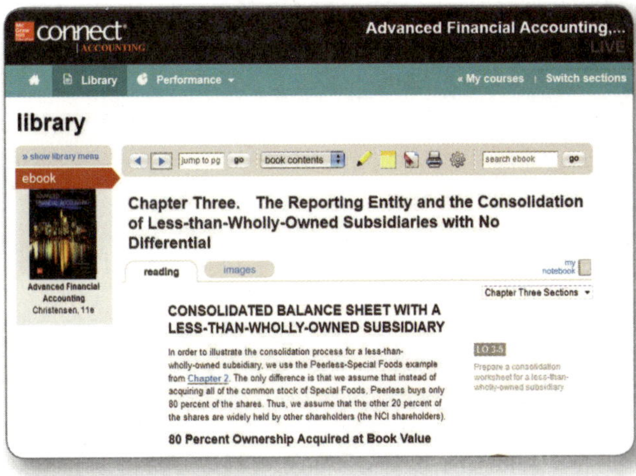

Tegrity

Make your classes available anytime, anywhere. With simple, one-click recording, students can search for a word or phrase and be taken to the exact place in your lecture that they need to review.

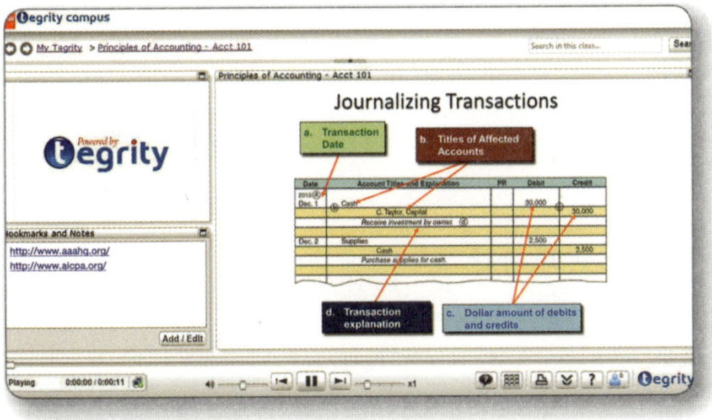

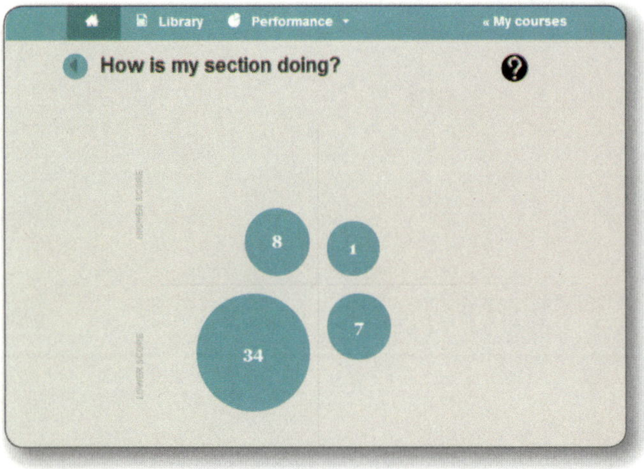

Connect Insight

The first and only analytics tool of its kind, Connect Insight is a series of visual data displays that are each framed by an intuitive question and provide at-a-glance information regarding how an instructor's class is performing. Connect Insight is available through Connect or Connect Plus titles.

EASY TO USE

Learning Management System Integration

McGraw-Hill Campus is a one-stop teaching and learning experience available to use with any learning management system. McGraw-Hill Campus provides single sign-on to faculty and students for all McGraw-Hill material and technology from within the school website. McGraw-Hill Campus also allows instructors instant access to all supplements and teaching materials for all McGraw-Hill products.

Blackboard users also benefit from McGraw-Hill's industry-leading integration, providing single sign-on to access all Connect Plus assignments and automatic feeding of assignment results to the Blackboard grade book.

POWERFUL REPORTING

Connect Plus generates comprehensive reports and graphs that provide instructors with an instant view of the performance of individual students, a specific section, or multiple sections. Since all content is mapped to learning objectives, Connect Plus reporting is ideal for accreditation or other administrative documentation.

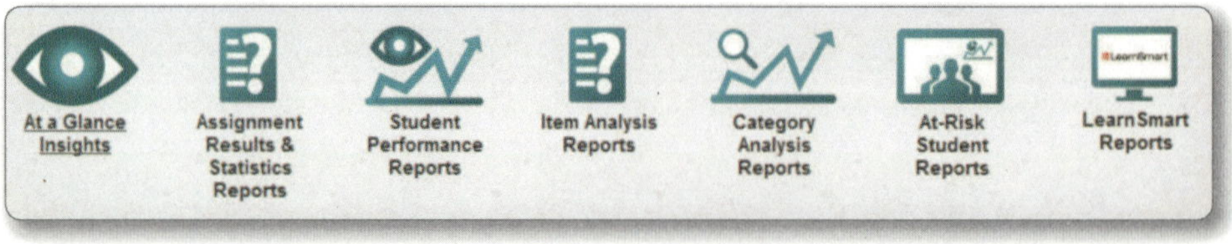

Advanced Financial Accounting

Advanced Financial Accounting

Eleventh Edition

Theodore E. Christensen
Brigham Young University

David M. Cottrell
Brigham Young University

Cassy JH Budd
Brigham Young University

McGraw Hill Education

ADVANCED FINANCIAL ACCOUNTING, ELEVENTH EDITION

Published by McGraw-Hill Education, 2 Penn Plaza, New York, NY 10121.

Some ancillaries, including electronic and print components, may not be available to customers outside the United States.

This book is printed on acid-free paper.

4 5 6 7 8 9 DOW 21 20 19 18 17 16

ISBN 978-0-07-802587-7
MHID 0-07-802587-7

Senior Vice President, Products & Markets: *Kurt L. Strand*
Vice President, General Manager, Products & Markets: *Marty Lange*
Vice President, Content Design & Delivery: *Kimberly Meriwether David*
Managing Director: *Tim Vertovec*
Marketing Director: *Brad Parkins*
Executive Brand Manager: *James Heine*
Director, Product Development: *Rose Koos*
Director of Digital Content: *Patricia Plumb*
Lead Product Developer: *Ann Torbert*
Product Developer: *Danielle Andries*
Marketing Manager: *Kathleen Klehr*
Digital Product Developer: *Kevin Moran*
Digital Product Analyst: *Xin Lin*
Director, Content Design & Delivery: *Linda Avenarius*
Program Manager: *Daryl Horrocks*
Content Project Managers: *Dana M. Pauley/Brian Nacik*
Buyer: *Debra R. Sylvester*
Design: *Matt Diamond*
Cover Image: © *Krzysztof Baranowski/Getty Images*
Compositor: *Laserwords Private Limited*
Printer: *R. R. Donnelley*

Library of Congress Cataloging-in-Publication Data

Christensen, Theodore E.
Advanced financial accounting.—Eleventh edition / Theodore E. Christensen, David M. Cottrell, Cassy Budd.
pages cm
ISBN 978-0-07-802587-7 (alk. paper)
1. Accounting. I. Cottrell, David M. II. Budd, Cassy. III. Title.
HF5636.B348 2016
657'.046—dc23

2014026757

www.mhhe.com

About the Authors

Theodore E. Christensen

Ted Christensen has been a faculty member at Brigham Young University since 2000. Prior to coming to BYU, he was on the faculty at Case Western Reserve University for five years. He received a BS degree in accounting at San Jose State University, a MAcc degree in tax at Brigham Young University, and a PhD in accounting from the University of Georgia. Professor Christensen has authored and coauthored articles published in many journals including *The Accounting Review, Journal of Accounting Research, Journal of Accounting and Economics, Review of Accounting Studies, Contemporary Accounting Research, Accounting Organizations and Society, Journal of Business Finance & Accounting, Accounting Horizons,* and *Issues in Accounting Education.* Professor Christensen has taught financial accounting at all levels, financial statement analysis, both introductory and intermediate managerial accounting, and corporate taxation. He is the recipient of numerous awards for both teaching and research. He has been active in serving on various committees of the American Accounting Association and is a CPA.

David M. Cottrell

Professor Cottrell joined the faculty at Brigham Young University in 1991. He currently serves as the Associate Director of the School of Accountancy. Prior to coming to BYU he spent five years at The Ohio State University, where he earned his PhD. Before pursuing a career in academics he worked as an auditor and consultant for the firm of Ernst & Young in its San Francisco office. At BYU, Professor Cottrell has developed and taught courses in the School of Accountancy, the MBA program, and the Finance program. He has won numerous awards from the alumni and faculty for his teaching and curriculum development. He has received the Outstanding Professor Award in the college of business as selected by the students in the Finance Society; he has received the Outstanding Teaching Award as selected by the Marriott School of Management; and he is a four-time winner of the collegewide Teaching Excellence Award for Management Skills, which is selected by the Alumni Board of the Marriott School of Management at BYU. Professor Cottrell also has authored many articles about accounting and auditing issues. His articles have been published in *Issues in Accounting Education, Journal of Accounting Case Research, Quarterly Review of Distance Education, Journal of Accountancy, The CPA Journal, Internal Auditor, The Tax Executive,* and *Journal of International Taxation,* among others.

Cassy JH Budd

Professor Budd has been a faculty member at Brigham Young University since 2005. Prior to coming to BYU, she was on the faculty at Utah State University for three years. She received a BS degree in accounting at Brigham Young University and a MAcc degree in tax at Utah State University. Before pursuing a career in academics she worked as an auditor for the firm of PricewaterhouseCoopers LLP in its Salt Lake, San Jose, and Phoenix offices and continues to maintain her CPA license. Professor Budd has taught financial accounting at all levels, introductory managerial accounting, undergraduate and graduate auditing, and partnership taxation. She is the recipient of numerous awards for teaching and student advisement, including the Dean Fairbanks Teaching and Learning Faculty Fellowship, Brigham Young University; School of Accountancy Advisor of the

Year, Utah State University; State of Utah Campus Compact Service-Learning Engaged Scholar Award, and the Joe Whitesides Scholar–Athlete Recognition Award from Utah State University. She has been active in serving on various committees of the American Accounting Association, including chairing the annual Conference on Teaching and Learning in Accounting.

Preface

The Eleventh Edition of *Advanced Financial Accounting* is an up-to-date, comprehensive, and highly illustrated presentation of the accounting and reporting principles and procedures used in a variety of business entities. Every day, the business press carries stories about the merger and acquisition mania, the complexities of modern business entities, new organizational structures for conducting business, accounting scandals related to complex business transactions, the foreign activities of multinational firms, the operations of governmental and not-for-profit entities, and bankruptcies of major firms. Accountants must understand and know how to deal with the accounting and reporting ramifications of these issues.

OVERVIEW

This edition continues to provide strong coverage of advanced accounting topics with clarity of presentation and integrated coverage based on continuous case examples. The text is complete with presentations of worksheets, schedules, and financial statements so students can see the development of each topic. Inclusion of all recent FASB and GASB pronouncements and the continuing deliberations of the authoritative bodies provide a current and contemporary text for students preparing for the CPA examination and current practice. This emphasis has become especially important given the recent rapid pace of the authoritative bodies in dealing with major issues having far-reaching implications. The Eleventh Edition covers the following topics:

Multicorporate Entities

Business Combinations

1 Intercorporate Acquisitions and Investments in Other Entities

Consolidation Concepts and Procedures

2 Reporting Intercorporate Investments and Consolidation of Wholly Owned Subsidiaries with No Differential

3 The Reporting Entity and the Consolidation of Less-than-Wholly-Owned Subsidiaries with No Differential

4 Consolidation of Wholly Owned Subsidiaries Acquired at More than Book Value

5 Consolidation of Less-than-Wholly-Owned Subsidiaries Acquired at More than Book Value

Intercompany Transfers

6 Intercompany Inventory Transactions

7 Intercompany Transfers of Services and Noncurrent Assets

8 Intercompany Indebtedness

Additional Consolidation Issues

9 Consolidation Ownership Issues

10 Additional Consolidation Reporting Issues

Multinational Entities

Foreign Currency Transactions

11 Multinational Accounting: Foreign Currency Transactions and Financial Instruments

Translation of Foreign Statements

12 Multinational Accounting: Issues in Financial Reporting and Translation of Foreign Entity Statements

Reporting Requirements

Segment and Interim Reporting

13 Segment and Interim Reporting

SEC Reporting

14 SEC Reporting

NEW FEATURES ADDED IN THE ELEVENTH EDITION

- **Deferred tax coverage.** We have made extensive revisions to Chapter 10 to add more coverage of the deferred tax implications associated with business combinations, including the allocation of deferred taxes related to the book-tax basis differences of acquired assets.
- **New shading of consolidation worksheet entries.** Based on the new two-color shading introduced in the Eleventh Edition, we have revised the shading of consolidation worksheet entries to clearly distinguish between the various types of entries. We have extended this shading not only to the worksheets but also to supporting schedules and calculation boxes so that numbers appearing in consolidation worksheet entries are uniformly shaded in all locations.
- **Presentation of intercompany transactions.** We have significantly revised the three chapters related to intercompany transactions. Based on feedback from instructors, we have revised Chapters 6, 7, and 8 by adding illustrations to better simplify adjustments to the basic consolidation entry.

KEY FEATURES MAINTAINED IN THE ELEVENTH EDITION

The key strengths of this text are the clear and readable discussions of concepts and their detailed demonstrations through illustrations and explanations. The many favorable responses to prior editions from both students and instructors confirm our belief that clear presentation and comprehensive illustrations are essential to learning the sophisticated topics in an advanced accounting course. Key features maintained in the Eleventh Edition include:

- **Callout boxes.** We have updated the "callout boxes" that appear in the left-hand margin to draw attention to important points throughout the chapters. The most common callout boxes are the "FYI" boxes, which often illustrate how real-world companies or entities apply the principles discussed in the various chapters. The "Caution" boxes draw students' attention to common mistakes and explain how to avoid them. The "Stop & Think" boxes help students take a step back and think through the logic of difficult concepts.
- **FASB codification.** All authoritative citations to U.S. GAAP are now exclusively cited based on the FASB codification.
- **Introductory vignettes.** Each chapter begins with a brief story of a well-known company to illustrate why topics covered in that chapter are relevant in current practice.

Short descriptions of the vignettes and the featured companies are included in the Chapter-by-Chapter Changes section on page xvii.

- **A building-block approach to consolidation.** Virtually all advanced financial accounting classes cover consolidation topics. Although this topic is perhaps the most important to instructors, students frequently struggle to gain a firm grasp of consolidation principles. The Eleventh Edition provides students a learning-friendly framework to consolidations by introducing consolidation concepts and procedures more gradually. This is accomplished by a building-block approach that introduces consolidations in Chapters 2 and 3 and continues through chapter 5.
- **IFRS comparisons.** As the FASB and IASB work toward convergence to a single set of global accounting standards, the SEC is debating the wholesale introduction of international financial reporting standards (IFRS). The Eleventh Edition summarizes key differences between current U.S. GAAP and IFRS to make students aware of changes that will likely occur if the SEC adopts IFRS in the near future.
- **AdvancedStudyGuide.com.** See page xv for details.
- **The use of a continuous case for each major subject-matter area.** This textbook presents the complete story of a company, Peerless Products Corporation, from its beginning through its growth to a multinational consolidated entity and finally to its end. At each stage of the entity's development, including the acquisition of a subsidiary, Special Foods Inc., the text presents comprehensive examples and discussions of the accounting and financial reporting issues that accountants face. The discussions tied to the Peerless Products continuous case are easily identified by the company logos in the margin:

  We use the comprehensive case of Peerless Products Corporation and its subsidiary, Special Foods Inc., throughout the for-profit chapters. For the governmental chapters, the Sol City case facilitates the development of governmental accounting and reporting concepts and procedures. Using a continuous case provides several benefits. First, students need become familiar with only one set of data and can then move more quickly through the subsequent discussion and illustrations without having to absorb a new set of data. Second, the case adds realism to the study of advanced accounting and permits students to see the effects of each successive step on an entity's financial reports. Finally, comparing and contrasting alternative methods using a continuous case allows students to evaluate different methods and outcomes more readily.
- **Extensive illustrations of key concepts.** The book is heavily illustrated with complete, not partial, workpapers, financial statements, and other computations and comparisons useful for demonstrating each topic. The illustrations are cross-referenced to the relevant text discussion. In the consolidations portion of the text, the focus is on the fully adjusted equity method of accounting for an investment in a subsidiary, but two other methods—the cost method and the modified equity method—are also discussed and illustrated in chapter appendixes.
- **Comprehensive coverage with significant flexibility.** The subject matter of advanced accounting is expanding at an unprecedented rate. New topics are being added, and traditional topics require more extensive coverage. Flexibility is therefore essential in an advanced accounting text. Most one-term courses are unable to cover all topics included in this text. In recognition of time constraints, this text is structured to provide the most efficient use of the time available. The self-contained units of subject matter allow for substantial flexibility in sequencing the course materials. In addition, individual chapters are organized to allow for going into more depth on some topics

through the use of the "Additional Considerations" sections. Several chapters include appendixes containing discussions of alternative accounting procedures or illustrations of procedures or concepts that are of a supplemental nature.

- **Extensive end-of-chapter materials.** A large number of questions, cases, exercises, and problems at the end of each chapter provide the opportunity to solidify understanding of the chapter material and assess mastery of the subject matter. The end-of-chapter materials progress from simple focused exercises to more complex integrated problems. Cases provide opportunities for extending thought, gaining exposure to different sources of accounting-related information, and applying the course material to real-world situations. These cases include research cases that refer students to authoritative pronouncements and Kaplan CPA Review simulations. The American Institute of CPAs has identified five skills to be examined as part of the CPA exam: (*a*) analysis, (*b*) judgment, (*c*) communication, (*d*) research, and (*e*) understanding. The end-of-chapter materials provide abundant opportunities for students to enhance those skills with realistic and real-world applications of advanced financial accounting topics. Cases and exercises identified with a world globe icon provide special opportunities for students to access real-world data by using electronic databases, Internet search engines, or other inquiry processes to answer the questions presented on the topics in the chapters.

MCGRAW-HILL *CONNECT® ACCOUNTING*

Easy to Use. Proven Effective. Tailored to You.

McGraw-Hill *Connect Accounting* is a digital teaching and learning environment that gives students the means to better connect with their coursework, with their instructors, and with the important concepts that they will need to know for success now and in the future. With *Connect Accounting,* instructors can deliver assignments, quizzes,

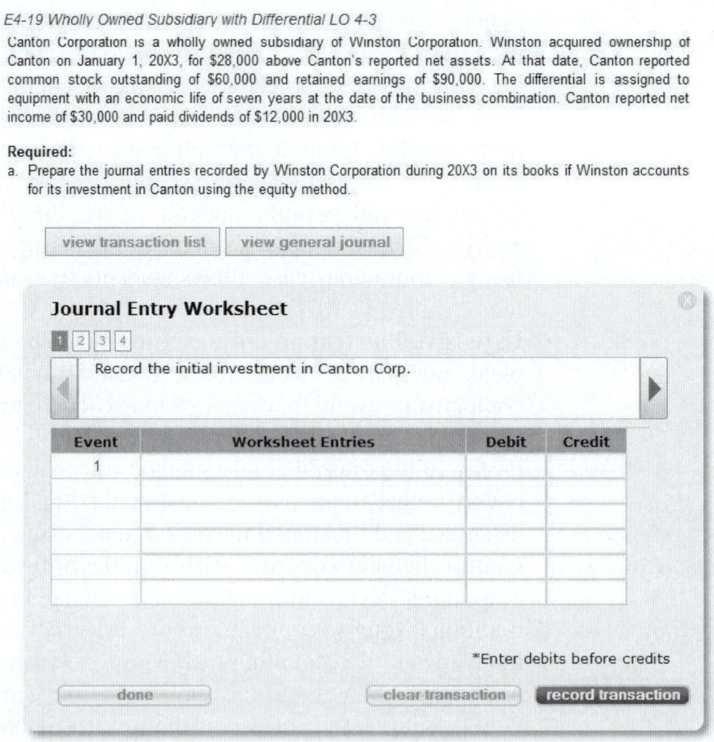

and tests easily online. Students can review course material and practice important skills. *Connect Accounting* provides the following features:

- SmartBook and LearnSmart.
- Auto-graded Online Homework.
- An integrated media-rich eBook, allowing for anytime, anywhere access to the textbook.
- Dynamic links between the problems or questions assigned to the students and the location in the eBook where that concept is covered.
- A powerful search function to pinpoint and connect key concepts to review.

In short, *Connect Accounting* offers students powerful tools and features that optimize their time and energy, enabling them to focus on learning.

For more information about *Connect Accounting,* go to **www.connect.mheducation .com,** or contact your local McGraw-Hill Higher Education representative.

SmartBook, powered by LearnSmart

LearnSmart™ is the market-leading adaptive study resource that is proven to strengthen memory recall, increase class retention, and boost grades. LearnSmart allows students to study more efficiently because they are made aware of what they know and don't know.

SmartBook™, which is powered by LearnSmart, is the first and only adaptive reading experience designed to change the way students read and learn. It creates a personalized reading experience by highlighting the most impactful concepts a student needs to learn at that moment in time. As a student engages with SmartBook, the reading experience continuously adapts by highlighting content based on what the student knows and doesn't know. This ensures that the focus is on the content he or she needs to learn, while simultaneously promoting long-term retention of material. Use SmartBook's real-time reports to quickly identify the concepts that require more attention from individual students—or the entire class. The end result? Students are more engaged with course content, can better prioritize their time, and come to class ready to participate.

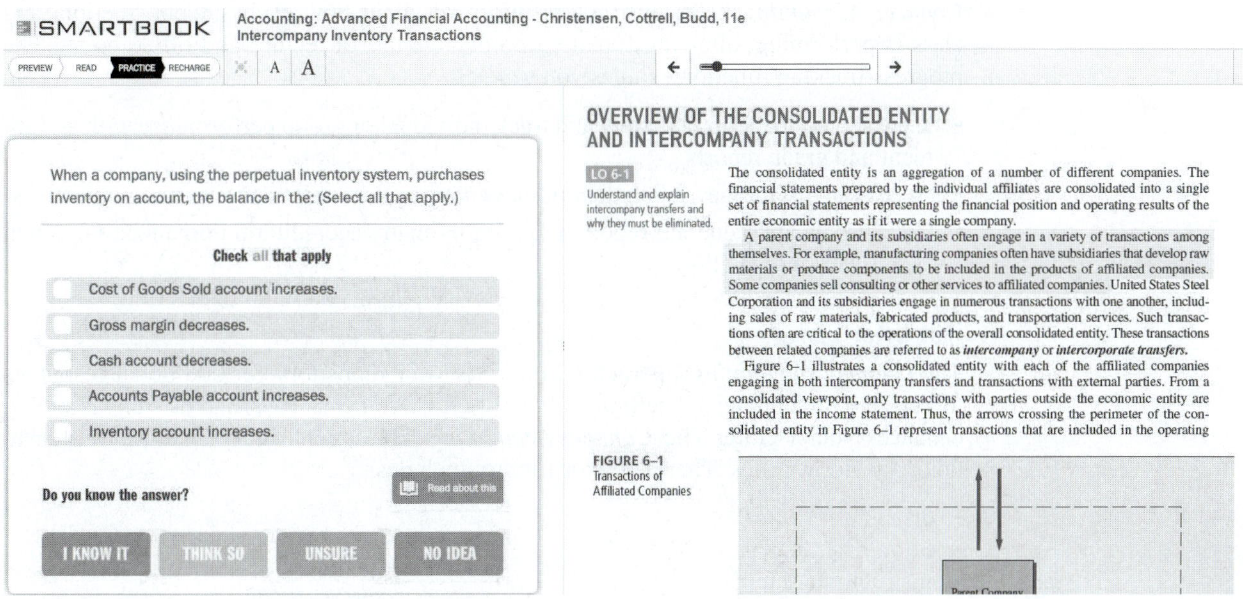

Online Assignments

Connect Accounting helps students learn more efficiently by providing feedback and practice material when they need it, where they need it. *Connect* grades homework automatically and gives immediate feedback on any questions students may have missed. Our assignable, gradable end-of-chapter content includes a general journal application that looks and feels more like what you would find in a general ledger software package. Also, select questions have been redesigned to test students' knowledge more fully. They now include tables for students to work through rather than requiring that all calculations be done offline.

MCGRAW-HILL *CONNECT ACCOUNTING* FEATURES

Connect Accounting offers powerful tools, resources, and features to make managing assignments easier so faculty can spend more time teaching.

Simple Assignment Management and Smart Grading

With *Connect Accounting,* creating assignments is easier than ever, so you can spend more time teaching and less time managing.

- Create and deliver assignments easily with selectable end-of-chapter questions and test bank items.
- Use algorithmically generated numbers for selected problems. This feature allows each student to complete an individualized problem with customized explanations of each calculation.
- Have assignments scored automatically, giving students immediate feedback on their work and side-by-side comparisons with correct answers.
- Access and review each response; manually change grades or leave comments for students to review.
- Reinforce classroom concepts with practice assignments, instant quizzes, and exams.

Powerful Instructor and Student Reports

Connect Accounting keeps instructors informed about how each student, section, and class is performing, allowing for more productive use of lecture and office hours. The progress-tracking function enables you to

- View scored work immediately and track individual or group performance with assignment and grade reports.
- Access an instant view of student or class performance relative to learning objectives.
- Collect data and generate reports required by many accreditation organizations, such as AACSB and AICPA.

Instructor Library

The *Connect Accounting* Instructor Library is your repository for additional resources to improve student engagement in and out of class. You can select and use any asset that enhances your lecture. The *Connect Accounting* Instructor Library also allows you to upload your own files. The Instructor Library includes

- eBook
- Solutions Manual
- Instructor's Manual
- Instructor PowerPoint® Presentations
- Test Bank

Student Resource Library

The *Connect Accounting* Student Resources give students access to additional resources such as recorded lectures, online practice materials, an eBook, and more.

Connect Insight

The first and only analytics tool of its kind, Connect Insight™ is a series of visual data displays—each framed by an intuitive question—to provide at-a-glance information regarding how your class is doing.

Connect Insight provides a quick analysis on five key insights, available at a moment's notice from your tablet device:

1. How are my students doing?
2. How is my section doing?
3. How is this student doing?
4. How are my assignments doing?
5. How is this assignment going?

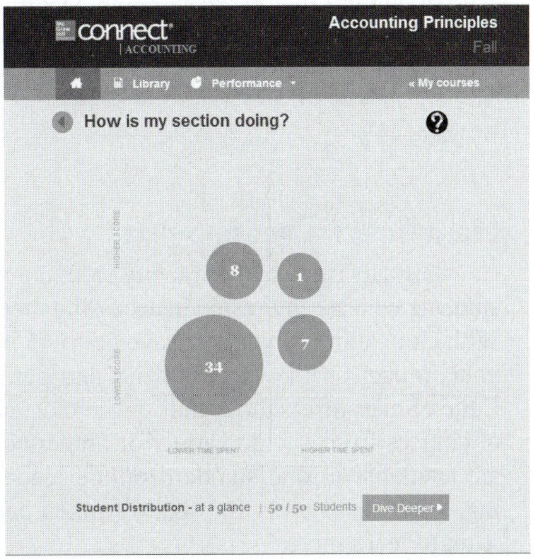

TEGRITY CAMPUS: LECTURES 24/7

Tegrity Campus® is a service that makes class time available 24/7 by automatically capturing every lecture. With a simple one-click start-and-stop process, you capture all computer screens and corresponding audio in a format that is easily searchable, frame by frame. Students can replay any part of any class with easy-to-use browser-based viewing on a PC, Mac, or mobile device.

Help turn your students' study time into learning moments immediately supported by your lecture. With Tegrity Campus, you also increase intent listening and class participation by easing students' concerns about note taking. Lecture Capture will make it more likely you will see students' faces, not the tops of their heads.

To learn more about Tegrity, watch a two-minute Flash demo at **http://tegritycampus.mhhe.com.**

CUSTOM PUBLISHING THROUGH CREATE

McGraw-Hill Create™ is a new, self-service website that allows instructors to create custom course materials by drawing upon McGraw-Hill's comprehensive, cross-disciplinary content. Instructors can add their own content quickly and easily and tap into other rights-secured third-party sources as well, then arrange the content in a way that makes the most sense for their course. Instructors can even personalize their book with the course name and information and choose the best format for their students—color print, black-and-white print, or an eBook.

Through Create, instructors can

- Select and arrange the content in a way that makes the most sense for their course.
- Combine material from different sources and even upload their own content.
- Choose the best format for their students—print or eBook.
- Edit and update their course materials as often as they'd like.
- Begin creating now at **www.mcgrawhillcreate.com.**

MCGRAW-HILL CAMPUS

McGraw-Hill Campus™ is a new one-stop teaching and learning experience available to users of any learning management system. This institutional service allows faculty and students to enjoy single sign-on (SSO) access to all McGraw-Hill Higher Education materials, including the award winning McGraw-Hill *Connect Plus* platform, from directly within the institution's website. To learn more about MH Campus, visit **http:/mhcampus.mhhe.com.**

COURSESMART

Learn Smart. Choose Smart.

CourseSmart is a way for faculty to find and buy eTextbooks. It's also a great option for students who are interested in accessing their course materials digitally and saving money. With CourseSmart, you can save up to 45 percent off the cost of a print textbook, reduce your impact on the environment, and gain access to powerful web tools for learning. CourseSmart offers thousands of the most commonly adopted textbooks across hundreds of courses from a wide variety of higher-education publishers. CourseSmart eTextbooks are available in one standard online reader with full-text search, notes and highlighting, and e-mail tools for sharing notes between classmates. Go to **www.coursesmart.com** to learn more.

EZ TEST ONLINE

The comprehensive test bank includes both conceptual and procedural exercises, problems, multiple-choice, and matching questions. Each test item is tagged by learning objective; topic area; difficulty level; and AACSB, Bloom's, and AICPA categories.

McGraw-Hill's EZ Test Online is a flexible and easy-to-use electronic testing program that allows instructors to create tests from book-specific items. EZ Test Online accommodates a wide range of question types and allows instructors to add their own questions. Multiple versions of the test can be created and any test can be exported for use with course management systems such as BlackBoard/WebCT. EZ Test Online gives instructors a place to easily administer exams and quizzes online. The program is available for Windows and Mac environments.

ASSURANCE OF LEARNING READY

Many educational institutions today focus on the notion of *assurance of learning,* an important element of some accreditation standards. *Advanced Financial Accounting* is designed specifically to support your assurance of learning initiatives with a simple yet powerful solution.

Each test bank question for *Advanced Financial Accounting* maps to a specific chapter learning outcome/objective listed in the text. You can use our test bank software, EZ Test and EZ Test Online, or McGraw-Hill's *Connect Accounting* to easily query for learning outcomes/objectives that directly relate to the learning objectives for your course. You can then use the reporting features of EZ Test to aggregate student results in a similar fashion, making the collection and presentation of assurance of learning data simple and easy.

MCGRAW-HILL CUSTOMER CARE CONTACT INFORMATION

At McGraw-Hill, we understand that getting the most from new technology can be challenging. That's why our services don't stop after you purchase our products. You can contact our Technical Support Analysts 24 hours a day to get product training online. Or you can search our knowledge bank of Frequently Asked Questions on our support website. For Customer Support, call **800-331-5094** or visit **www.mhhe.com/support.** One of our Technical Support Analysts will be able to assist you in a timely fashion.

AACSB STATEMENT

The McGraw-Hill Companies is a proud corporate member of AACSB International. Understanding the importance and value of AACSB accreditation, *Advanced Financial Accounting* Eleventh Edition recognizes the curricula guidelines detailed in the AACSB standards for business accreditation by connecting selected questions in the text and the test bank to the six general knowledge and skill guidelines in the AACSB standards.

The statements contained in *Advanced Financial Accounting* Eleventh Edition are provided only as a guide for the users of this textbook. The AACSB leaves content coverage and assessment within the purview of individual schools, the mission of the school, and the faculty. Although *Advanced Financial Accounting* Eleventh Edition and the teaching package make no claim of any specific AACSB qualification or evaluation, we have within *Advanced Financial Accounting* Eleventh Edition labeled selected questions according to the six general knowledge and skills areas.

HIGH TECH: THE ELEVENTH EDITION ADDS KEY TECHNOLOGY RESOURCES TO BENEFIT BOTH STUDENTS AND INSTRUCTORS

Advanced StudyGuide .com

The Eleventh Edition of *Advanced Financial Accounting* introduces the most cutting-edge technology supplement ever delivered in the advanced accounting market. AdvancedStudyGuide.com is a product created exclusively by the text authors that represents a new generation in study resources available to students as well as a new direction and options in the resources instructors can use to help their students and elevate their classroom experiences.

Traditional study guides offer students a resource similar to the text itself—that is, more discussion like the text accompanied by more problems and exercises like the ones in the text at a fairly high price to give students the same type of materials that have they already received with the text.

At its core, **AdvancedStudyGuide.com** (ASG) offers materials that go beyond what a printed text can possibly deliver. The ASG contains dozens of narrated, animated discussions and explanations of materials aligned to key points in the chapter. Not only that, the ASG also contains animated problems just like key problems in the exercises and problems at the end of each chapter. For the student who would like a little help with *Advanced Financial Accounting,* the ASG is like having private tutoring sessions from the authors who wrote the book (not a class TA) any time, day or night. This also can provide tremendous benefits for instructors, as outlined below.

For Students

The Questions

- Have you ever had to miss a class and were then confused about what the book was trying to say about a topic?
- Even when you were in class, do things sometimes not make as much sense when you are reviewing on your own?
- Do you ever feel stuck when it comes to doing homework problems even though you read the chapter?
- When the exam is a few weeks after you covered the material in class, do you ever wish someone could walk you through a few examples as you review for the exam?
- Have you ever purchased a study guide for a text and found it was very expensive and did not give the additional study help you needed?

The ASG Answer

- The answer, at least in part, is the ASG: a new type of study guide designed for the way you like to study and the way that you learn best.
- It is our attempt as authors to really discuss the material in a way that a text-only approach cannot do.
- AND we can discuss your questions with you 24/7, anytime—day or night, at times when your regular instructor is not around.
- Through the ASG, we will bring you streaming media discussions by the authors of the book (not a class TA) to explain key points of each chapter.
- The ASG will also show, explain, and illustrate for you the approach to solving key homework problems in the text. These explanations are ***Like Problems***; that is, they are problems "just like" some in the text that you were assigned for homework.

The ASG Benefit

AdvancedStudyGuide.com brings you discussion and examples worked out in streaming video. Although traditional study guides can ***Tell*** you what to do, the ASG will ***Show You What to Do AND HOW to Do It.***

See the student page at AdvancedStudyGuide.com.

For Instructors

The Questions

- Have you ever had a student miss class and then come to your office and ask you to go over the topics that were discussed in class the day the student was absent?
- Even when a student is in class, does he or she sometimes come to your office and ask you to repeat the discussion?
- Even when you have discussed the chapter concepts, do you have students who still get stuck when it comes to doing homework problems?
- When exams are approaching, do students sometimes ask you to go back over material you taught days or weeks before?
- Would it be helpful to you if, on occasion, the authors of the text offered to hold "office hours" with your students for you?

The ASG Answer

- The answer, at least in part, is the ASG: the authors' attempt to partner with you in helping to better serve students' needs in some of the common situations where questions arise, without using more of your scarce time.
- The ASG will allow you to refer to streaming media discussions where the authors explain key points of each chapter.

- The ASG will show, explain, and illustrate for students the approach to solving key homework problems in the text. These explanations are ***Like Problems***; that is they are problems "just like" some in the text that you can assign for homework.

The ASG Benefit

AdvancedStudyGuide.com is a great tool to let the authors of the text partner with you, the instructor, in helping students learn *Advanced Financial Accounting*. The ASG will (1) help your students learn more effectively, (2) improve your class discussions, and (3) make your student contact hours more efficient.

See the instructor page at AdvancedStudyGuide.com.

CHAPTER-BY-CHAPTER CHANGES

- **Chapter 1** emphasizes the importance of business acquisitions and combinations. The chapter has been significantly reorganized and updated based on feedback from textbook adopters to provide a clearer and more concise discussion of the accounting treatment of mergers, acquisitions, and other intercorporate investments. We have added new illustrations and updated the beginning-of-chapter vignette and callout boxes to provide real-world examples of the topics discussed in the chapter, most of which provide additional information about the **Kraft Foods Inc.** example in the introductory vignette.

- **Chapter 2** summarizes the different types of intercorporate investments and introduces consolidation in the most straightforward scenario—where the parent company acquires full ownership of the subsidiary for an amount equal to the subsidiary's book value (i.e., no differential). Based on the new two-color shading introduced in the Eleventh Edition, this chapter introduces a new method of shading our consolidation worksheet entries to make them easily distinguishable by the reader. We have updated this chapter to provide a more streamlined and understandable coverage of topics traditionally included in this chapter. Finally, we have updated the "callout boxes" that provide real-world examples of the topics discussed in the chapter, some of which provide additional information about **Berkshire Hathaway's** investments discussed in the introductory vignette.

- **Chapter 3** explores how the basic consolidation process differs when a subsidiary is only partially owned. Moreover, it introduces the notion of special-purpose entities and accounting standards related to variable interest entities by discussing the well-known collapse of **Enron Corporation.** We have streamlined and shortened this chapter based on feedback from adopters to provide a better flow for the material. In addition, we have updated the callout boxes to help students understand the intricacies associated with the consolidation of a partially owned subsidiary and dealing with variable interest entities.

- **Chapter 4** gives a behind-the-scenes look at the work that goes into the consolidation process based on **Disney Corporation.** This chapter introduces consolidation of wholly owned subsidiaries with a differential, which results in situations in which the acquiring company pays more than the book value of the acquired company's net assets. This chapter adds a detailed explanation of the new shading of the consolidation worksheet entries introduced in Chapter 2. Finally, we have added a new illustration based on Disney's recent acquisition of the rights to the well-known "Star Wars" films when it acquired Lucasfilm.

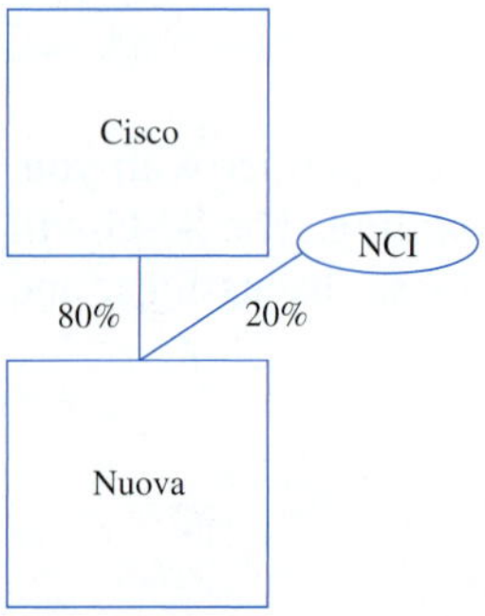

- **Chapter 5** discusses majority ownership of subsidiaries based on the 80 percent acquisition of **Nuova Systems** by **Cisco Systems Inc.** We further the discussion of acquisitions with a differential that has the added complexity of noncontrolling interest shareholders when they purchase less than 100 percent of the outstanding common stock. We have simplified the coverage of some of the topics in this chapter and removed tangential topics to provide more concise coverage of the important material.

- **Chapter 6** introduces intercompany inventory transfers based on **Samsung Electronics** and its subsidiaries. The elimination of intercompany profits can become complicated. In fact, intercompany inventory transactions and the consolidated procedures associated with them represent one of the topics textbook adopters have found most difficult to teach to students. As a result, we have rewritten this chapter extensively. We have added illustrations to better simplify adjustments to the basic consolidation entry and new graphics to illustrate difficult topics. In addition, we have added a series of new callout boxes to draw students' attention to the subtle complexities that our students have frequently struggled to understand.

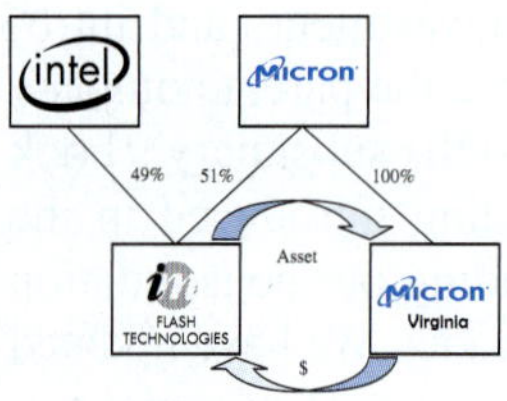

- **Chapter 7** presents a real fixed asset transfer between two of **Micron's** subsidiaries. This chapter explores the accounting for both depreciable and nondepreciable asset transfers among affiliated companies. Continuing the coverage of intercompany transfers from Chapter 6, Chapter 7 is one of the most difficult to teach for many adopters. Therefore, we have spent considerable time revising this chapter. We have reorganized some of the material and have added illustrations to better simplify adjustments to the basic consolidation entry and new graphics to simplify difficult topics.

- **Chapter 8** explains how **Ford Motor Credit Company** was able to survive the economic turmoil of 2008–2009 by wisely using intercompany debt transactions to its advantage. Ford Motor Credit benefited by borrowing funds from its parent company rather than going directly to the capital markets. This chapter was the most extensively rewritten chapter in the Tenth Edition of the book. The original approach of introducing the accounting for debt transfers using the straight-line amortization of discounts and premiums was not representative of real-world accounting treatment. As a result, the Tenth Edition introduced the effective interest method and moved the majority of the original chapter (based on the straight-line method) to the appendix so that instructors can teach this chapter using whichever method they prefer. Based on feedback from adopters, we have made additional revisions in the Eleventh Edition to clarify the effective interest method approach.

Berkshire Hathaway Inc.

- **Chapter 9** resumes the discussion of **Berkshire Hathaway** to demonstrate that, in practice, ownership situations can be complex. The discussion here provides a basic understanding of some of the consolidation problems arising from complex situations commonly encountered in practice including but not limited to changes in the parent's ownership interest and multiple ownership levels. We have revised the chapter to simplify and clarify some of these complex transactions.

- **Chapter 10** uses the example of the rapid growth of **Google Inc.** to explore four additional issues related to consolidated financial statements: the consolidated statement of cash flows, consolidation following an interim acquisition, consolidated tax considerations, and consolidated earnings per share. We have made extensive revisions to add more coverage of the deferred tax implications associated with business combinations, including the allocation of deferred taxes related to the book-tax basis differences of acquired assets.

- **Chapter 11** focuses on foreign currency transactions, financial instruments, and the effects that changes in exchange rates can have on reported results. We provide real-world examples of the topics discussed in the chapter, including the introductory vignette about **Microsoft.** We have revised this chapter extensively based on feedback from adopters to simplify and clarify the illustrations related to the use of forward contracts as hedging instruments.

- **Chapter 12** resumes the discussion of international accounting by exploring **McDonald's** global empire and how differences in accounting standards across countries and jurisdictions can cause significant difficulties for multinational firms. We have made significant revisions based on feedback from students on how the material could be presented in a more straightforward and easy-to-understand manner.

- **Chapter 13** examines segment reporting. We have made minor revisions to more clearly discuss the accounting standards for reporting an entity's operating components, foreign operations, and major customers and have updated the callout boxes illustrating how real companies, including **Walmart** from the introductory vignette, deal with segment reporting issues.

- **Chapter 14** reviews the complex role of the **Securities and Exchange Commission** to regulate trades of securities and to determine the type of financial disclosures that a publicly held company must make. We have made light revisions to update the coverage of recent laws and regulations.

- **Chapter 15** uses the example of **PricewaterhouseCoopers** to summarize the evolution of the original Big 8 accounting firms to today's Big 4 with an emphasis on partnerships. This chapter focuses on the formation and operation of partnerships, including accounting for the addition of new partners and the retirement of a present partner. We have made light revisions to the chapter to better explain partnership accounting.

- **Chapter 16** illustrates the dissolution of partnerships with the example of **Laventhol & Horwath,** the seventh-largest accounting firm in 1990. We have made light revisions to clarify some of the more difficult concepts related to partnership liquidation.

- **Chapter 17** introduces the topic of accounting for governmental entities. The chapter has two parts: the accounting and reporting requirements for state and local governmental units and a comprehensive illustration of accounting for a city's general fund. We have made light revisions to better explain some topics that students have found to be most difficult. Moreover, we have updated the callout boxes (most of which highlight specific examples related to the introductory vignette about **San Diego, California**) to clarify various topics.

- **Chapter 18** resumes the discussion of accounting for governmental entities by specifically examining special funds and governmentwide financial statements. We have lightly revised the chapter topics that are often misunderstood by students and have updated the callout boxes (which highlight specific examples related to the introductory vignette about the state of **Maryland**). Moreover, we have added some additional details related to more recent GASB pronouncements that were not included in the last edition.

- **Chapter 19** introduces accounting for not-for-profit entities using the example of **United Way Worldwide,** the largest charitable organization in the United States. We present the accounting and financial reporting principles used by both governmental and nongovernmental colleges and universities, health care providers, voluntary health and welfare organizations, and other not-for-profit organizations such as professional and fraternal associations. We have made light revisions and updated the callout boxes illustrating the real-world application of topics discussed in the chapter by well-known not-for-profit entities.

- **Chapter 20** introduces our final topic of corporations in financial difficulty by illustrating **General Motors Corporation** and its Chapter 11 bankruptcy protection granted in 2009. GM's experience illustrates that dealing with financial difficulty can be a long and complicated process, especially for large corporations. We present the range of major actions typically used by such a company. We have made minor revisions to the chapter content and have updated the callout boxes to highlight recent well-publicized bankruptcies.

Acknowledgments

This text includes the thoughts and contributions of many individuals, and we wish to express our sincere appreciation to them. First and foremost, we thank all the students in our advanced accounting classes from whom we have learned so much. In many respects, this text is an outcome of the learning experiences we have shared with our students. Second, we wish to thank the many outstanding teachers we have had in our own educational programs from whom we learned the joy of learning. We are indebted to our colleagues in advanced accounting for helping us reach our goal of writing the best possible advanced financial accounting text. We appreciate the many valuable comments and suggestions from the faculty who used recent editions of the text. Their comments and suggestions have contributed to making this text a more effective learning tool. We especially wish to thank Lauren Materne and James Shinners from the University of Michigan, Melissa Larson from Brigham Young University, and Sheldon Smith from Utah Valley State University.

We express our sincere thanks to the following individuals who provided reviews on the previous editions:

Andrea Astill
Indiana University–Bloomington

Jason Bergner
University of Central Missouri

Fatma Cebenoyan
Hunter College

Bobbie Daniels
Jackson State University

Carlos Diaz
Johnson & Wales University

David Doyon
Southern New Hampshire University

Cobby Harmon
University of California–Santa Barbara

Mark Holtzman
Seton Hall University

Charles Lewis
University of Houston–Downtown

Stephani Mason
Hunter College

Mallory McWilliams
University of California–Santa Cruz

Barbara Reeves
Cleary University

Sara Reiter
Binghamton University

Tom Rosengarth
Bridgewater College

Chantal Rowat
Bentley University

Mike Slaubaugh
Indiana University-Purdue University–Fort Wayne

Hannah Wong
William Paterson University

We are grateful for the assistance and direction of the McGraw-Hill team: Tim Vertovec, James Heine, Kathleen Klehr, Danielle Andries, Dana Pauley, Matt Diamond, Brian Nacik, Debra Sylvester, and Alpana Jolly, who all worked hard to champion our book through the production process.

We have permission from the Institute of Certified Management Accountants of the Institute of Management Accountants to use questions and/or unofficial answers from past CMA examinations. We appreciate the cooperation of the American Institute of Certified Public Accountants for providing permission to adapt and use materials from past Uniform CPA Examinations. And we thank Kaplan CPA Review for providing its online framework for *Advanced Financial Accounting* students to gain important experience with the types of simulations that are included on the Uniform CPA Examination.

Above all, we extend our deepest appreciation to our families who continue to provide the encouragement and support necessary for this project.

Theodore E. Christensen
David M. Cottrell
Cassy JH Budd

Brief Table of Contents

Table of Contents

Chapter 14

SEC Reporting 729

Chapter 15

Partnerships: Formation, Operation, and Changes in Membership 757

Chapter 16

Partnerships: Liquidation 811

Chapter 19
Not-for-Profit Entities 974

Chapter 20
Corporations in Financial Difficulty 1044

1 Intercorporate Acquisitions and Investments in Other Entities

Multicorporate Entities

Business Combinations

Consolidation Concepts and Procedures

Intercompany Transfers

Additional Consolidation Issues

Multinational Entities

Reporting Requirements

Partnerships

Governmental and Not-for-Profit Entities

Corporations in Financial Difficulty

KRAFT'S ACQUISITION OF CADBURY

In recent years, as well as during the past several decades, the business world has witnessed many corporate acquisitions and combinations, often involving some of the world's largest and best-known companies. Some of these combinations have captured public attention because of the personalities involved, the daring strategies employed, and the huge sums of money at stake. On February 2, 2010, Kraft Foods Inc. finalized a deal to *acquire* Cadbury PLC for $18.5 billion, forming the second-largest confectionery, food, and beverage company in the world. At the time of the acquisition, Cadbury's net assets were worth only around $4.6 billion. This highly visible transaction was merely the next step in more than a century of regular acquisitions.

In 1903, James L. Kraft started selling cheese door to door from the back of a horse-drawn wagon. Although not immediately successful, he continued operations and was eventually joined by four of his brothers in 1909. By 1914, Kraft & Bros. Company (later Kraft Foods Inc.) had opened its first cheese manufacturing plant and, in 1916, patented a new process for pasteurizing cheese, making the cheese resistant to spoilage and allowing it to be transported over long distances. In 1937, Kraft launched its well-known macaroni and cheese dinners.

Philip Morris acquired General Foods in 1985 and Kraft in 1988. A year later, General Foods and Kraft were *merged* to form Kraft General Foods Inc., which was renamed Kraft Foods Inc. in 1995. In 2000, Philip Morris acquired Nabisco Holdings and began integrating Nabisco and Kraft. In August 2008, the Post Cereal portion of Kraft was *split off* and *merged* with Ralcorp Holdings. The remaining portion of Kraft Foods Inc. is the company that took part in the 2010 acquisition of Cadbury PLC. Of course, this is only half of the story as Cadbury's history includes a unique journey as well. It took 104 years and dozens of *mergers* and *acquisitions* for Cadbury to grow into the company acquired by Kraft in 2010.

In August 2012, a mere two and a half years after acquiring Cadbury, Kraft's board of directors approved a *spin-off* of several of its businesses, including Cadbury. This *spin-off* would separate the high-growth global snack business from the North American grocery business ($18 billion in annual sales), which is focused in more mature markets. Analysts predicted that this *spin-off* would allow Kraft to separate two very distinct businesses that face different opportunities and challenges.

Accordingly, Kraft Foods Inc. was *split* into two separate companies, Kraft Foods Group and Mondelēz International on October 1, 2012. The Kraft Foods Group includes the U.S. and Canadian grocery operations of the Kraft food family including brands like Cheez Whiz, Cool Whip, Jell-O, Kraft Macaroni & Cheese, Oscar Mayer, and Velveeta. Mondelēz International includes brands such as Cadbury, Chips Ahoy!, Nabisco, Oreo, Tang, Teddy Grahams, and Wheat Thins. Mondelēz includes nine brands that generate over $1 billion in revenue annually and Kraft Foods includes 10 brands with over $500 million in annual revenue. With the *division* into two companies complete, each can now focus on its own distinct strategies. For example on July 1, 2013,

Kraft Food Groups *created* two new business units, a meals and desserts unit and an enhancers and snack nuts unit.

The business world is complex and frequent business combinations will continue to increase the complex nature of the business environment in the future. An understanding of the accounting treatment of mergers, acquisitions, and other intercorporate investments is an invaluable asset in our ever-changing markets. This chapter introduces the key concepts associated with business combinations.

LEARNING OBJECTIVES

When you finish studying this chapter, you should be able to:

LO 1-1 Understand and explain the reasons for and different methods of business expansion, the types of organizational structures, and the types of acquisitions.

LO 1-2 Understand the development of standards related to acquisition accounting over time.

LO 1-3 Make calculations and prepare journal entries for the creation of a business entity.

LO 1-4 Understand and explain the differences between different forms of business combinations.

LO 1-5 Make calculations and business combination journal entries in the presence of a differential, goodwill, or a bargain purchase element.

LO 1-6 Understand additional considerations associated with business combinations.

AN INTRODUCTION TO COMPLEX BUSINESS STRUCTURES

LO 1-1

Understand and explain the reasons for and different methods of business expansion, the types of organizational structures, and the types of acquisitions.

The business environment in the United States is perhaps the most dynamic and vibrant in the world, characterized by rapid change and exceptional complexity. In this environment, regulators and standard setters such as the Securities and Exchange Commission (SEC), the Financial Accounting Standards Board (FASB), and the Public Company Accounting Oversight Board (PCAOB) are scrambling to respond to the rapid-paced changes in a manner that ensures the continued usefulness of accounting reports to reflect economic reality. A number of accounting and reporting issues arise when two or more companies join under common ownership or a company creates a complex organizational structure involving new financing or operating entities. The first 10 chapters of this text focus on a number of these issues. Chapter 1 lays the foundation by describing some of the factors that have led to corporate expansion and some of the types of complex organizational structures and relationships that have evolved. Then it describes the accounting and reporting issues related to formal business combinations. Chapter 2 focuses on investments in the common stock of other companies. It also introduces basic concepts associated with the preparation of ***consolidated financial statements*** that portray the related companies as if they were actually a single entity. The next eight chapters systematically explain additional details related to the preparation and use of consolidated financial statements.

Enterprise Expansion

Most business enterprises seek to expand over time in order to survive and become profitable. Both the owners and managers of a business enterprise have an interest in seeing a company grow in size. Increased size often allows economies of scale in both production and distribution. By expanding into new markets or acquiring other companies already in those markets, companies can develop new earning potential and those in cyclical industries can add greater stability to earnings through diversification. For example, in 1997, Boeing, a company very strong in commercial aviation, acquired McDonnell Douglas, a company weak in commercial aviation but very strong in military aviation and other defense and space applications. In the early 2000s when orders for commercial airliners plummeted following a precipitous decline in air travel, increased defense spending helped level out Boeing's earnings.

Business Objectives

Complex organizational structures often evolve to help achieve a business's objectives, such as increasing profitability or reducing risk. For example, many companies establish subsidiaries to conduct certain business activities. A ***subsidiary*** is a corporation that another corporation, referred to as a ***parent company,*** controls, usually through majority ownership of its common stock. Because a subsidiary is a separate legal entity, the parent's risk associated with the subsidiary's activities is limited. There are many reasons for creating or acquiring a subsidiary. For example, companies often transfer their receivables to subsidiaries or special-purpose entities that use the receivables as collateral for bonds issued to other entities (securitization). External parties may hold partial or complete ownership of those entities, allowing the transferring company (i.e., the parent that originally held the receivables) to share its risk associated with the receivables. In some situations, companies can realize tax benefits by conducting certain activities through a separate entity. Bank of America, for example, established a subsidiary to which it transferred bank-originated loans and was able to save $418 million in quarterly taxes.[1]

Frequency of Business Combinations

Very few major companies function as single legal entities in our modern business environment. Virtually all major companies have at least one subsidiary, with more than a few broadly diversified companies having several hundred subsidiaries. In some cases, subsidiaries are created internally to separately incorporate part of the ongoing operations previously conducted within the parent company. Other subsidiaries are acquired externally through business combinations.

Business combinations are a continuing and frequent part of the business environment. For example, a merger boom occurred in the 1960s. This period was characterized by frantic and, in some cases, disorganized merger binges, resulting in creation of a large number of conglomerates, or companies operating in many different industries. Because many of the resulting companies lacked coherence in their operations, they often were less successful than anticipated, and many of the acquisitions of the 1960s have since been sold or abandoned. In the 1980s, the number of business combinations again increased. That period saw many leveraged buyouts or LBOs (when an acquiring company borrows the funds to buy another company), but the resulting debt plagued many of those companies for many years.

Through much of the 1990s, merger activity was fueled by a new phenomenon, the use of *private equity* money. Rather than the traditional merger activity that typically involves one publicly held company acquiring another, groups of investors—such as wealthy individuals, pension and endowment funds, and mutual funds—pooled their money to make acquisitions. Most of these acquisitions did not result in lasting ownership relationships, with the private equity companies usually attempting to realize a return by selling their investments after a relatively short holding period.

The number of business combinations through the 1990s dwarfed previous merger booms, with all records for merger activity shattered. This pace continued into the new century, with a record-setting $3.3 trillion in deals closed in 2000.[2] However, with the downturn in the economy in the early 2000s, the number of mergers declined significantly. Many companies put their expansion plans on hold, and a number of the mergers that did occur were aimed at survival.

[1] "PNC Shakes Up Banking Sector; Investors Exit," *The Wall Street Journal,* January 30, 2002, p. C2.

[2] Dennis K. Berman and Jason Singer, "Big Mergers Are Making a Comeback as Companies, Investors Seek Growth," *The Wall Street Journal,* November 5, 2005, p. A1.

Toward the middle of 2003, merger activity again increased and accelerated significantly through the middle of the decade. During one period of less than 100 hours in 2006, "around $110 billion in acquisition deals were sealed worldwide in sectors ranging from natural gas, to copper, to mouthwash to steel, linking investors and industrialists from India, to Canada, to Luxembourg to the U.S."[3]

This activity was slowed dramatically by the credit crunch of 2007–2008. Nevertheless, business combinations have increased dramatically in the postcrisis period and will continue to be an important business activity into the foreseeable future.

Aside from private equity acquisitions, business combinations have been common in telecommunications, defense, banking and financial services, information technology, energy and natural resources, entertainment, pharmaceuticals, and manufacturing. Some of the world's largest companies and best-known names have been involved in recent major acquisitions, such as Procter & Gamble, Gillette, Citigroup, Bank of America, AT&T, Whirlpool, Sprint, Verizon, Adobe Systems, Chrysler, Daimler, ConocoPhillips, BP, and ExxonMobil.

FYI

Historically, mergers have come in waves as indicated by the following summary:

Period	Name	Facet
1897–1904	First Wave	Horizontal mergers
1916–1929	Second Wave	Vertical mergers
1965–1969	Third Wave	Diversified conglomerate mergers
1981–1989	Fourth Wave	Congeneric mergers; hostile takeovers; corporate raiding, LBOs
1992–2000	Fifth Wave	Cross-border mergers
2003–2008	Sixth Wave	Shareholder activism, private equity, LBOs
2010–2014	Seventh Wave	Global expansion

Sources: Martin Lipton, "Merger Waves in the 19th, 20th and 21st Centuries," *The Davies Lecture*, York University, September 14, 2006."
Michael J. De La Merced and Jeffrey Cane, "Confident Deal Makers Pulled Out Checkbooks in 2010," *The New York Times*, January 3, 2011.

Ethical Considerations

Acquisitions can sometimes lead to ethical challenges for managers. Corporate managers are often rewarded with higher salaries as their companies increase in size. In addition, prestige frequently increases with the size of a company and with a reputation for the successful acquisition of other companies. As a result, corporate managers often find it personally advantageous to increase company size. For instance, Bernard Ebbers started his telecommunications career as the head of a small discount long-distance telephone service company and built it into one of the world's largest corporations, WorldCom. In the process, Ebbers became well known for his acquisition prowess and grew tremendously wealthy—until WorldCom was racked by accounting scandals and declared bankruptcy and Ebbers was sentenced to prison in 2003.

Acquisitions and complex organizational structures have sometimes been used to manipulate financial reporting with the aim of enhancing or enriching managers. Many major corporations, taking advantage of loopholes or laxness in financial reporting requirements, have used subsidiaries or other entities to borrow large amounts of money without reporting the debt on their balance sheets. Some companies have created special entities that have then been used to manipulate profits.

The term *special-purpose entity* has become well known in recent years because of the egregious abuse of these entities by companies such as Enron. A ***special-purpose entity*** (SPE) is, in general, a financing vehicle that is not a substantive operating entity, usually one created for a single specified purpose. An SPE may be in the form of a corporation, trust, or partnership. Enron, one of the world's largest companies prior to its collapse in 2001, established many SPEs, at least some of which were intended to manipulate financial reporting. Some of Enron's SPEs apparently were created primarily to hide debt, and others were used to create fictional transactions or to convert borrowings into reported revenues. The FASB has since clarified the rules around the accounting for SPEs to avoid this issue.

Accounting for mergers and acquisitions is also an area that can lend itself to manipulation. Arthur Levitt, former chairman of the SEC, referred to some of the accounting

[3] Dennis K. Berman and Jason Singer, "Blizzard of Deals Heralds an Era of Megamergers," *The Wall Street Journal*, June 27, 2006, p. A1.

practices that have been used in accounting for mergers and acquisitions as "creative acquisition accounting" or "merger magic." For example, an approach used by many companies in accounting for their acquisitions was to assign a large portion of the purchase price of an acquired company to its in-process research and development, immediately expensing the full amount and freeing financial reporting in future periods from the burden of those costs. The FASB has since eliminated this practice.

The scandals and massive accounting failures at companies such as Enron, WorldCom, and Tyco—causing creditors, investors, employees, and others to suffer heavy losses—focused considerable attention on weaknesses in accounting and the accounting profession. In the past several years, Congress, the SEC, and the FASB have taken actions to strengthen the financial reporting process and to clarify the accounting rules relating to special entities and to acquisitions. However, the frequency and size of business combinations, the complexity of accounting, and the potential impact on financial statements of the accounting methods employed mean that the issues surrounding the accounting for business combinations are still of critical importance.

BUSINESS EXPANSION AND FORMS OF ORGANIZATIONAL STRUCTURE

Historically, businesses have expanded by internal growth through new product development and expansion of existing product lines into new markets. In recent decades, however, many companies have chosen to expand by combining with or acquiring other companies. Either approach may lead to a change in organizational structure.

Internal Expansion: Creating a Business Entity

As companies expand from within, they often find it advantageous to conduct their expanded operations through new subsidiaries or other entities such as partnerships, joint ventures, or special entities. In most of these situations, an identifiable segment of the company's existing assets is transferred to the new entity (Subsidiary), and in exchange, the transferring company (Parent) receives equity ownership.

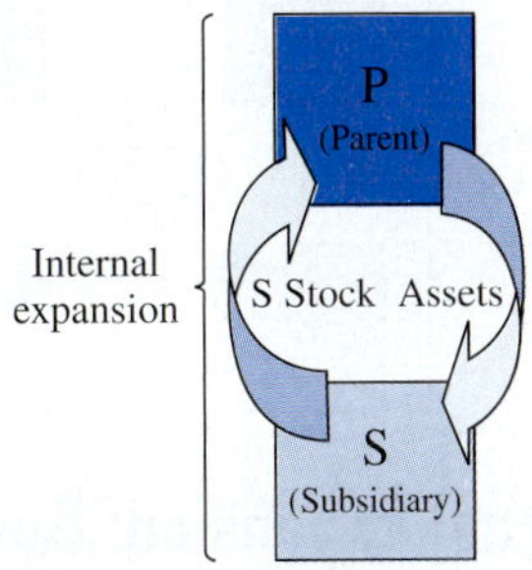

Companies may be motivated to establish new subsidiaries or other entities for a variety of reasons. Broadly diversified companies may place unrelated operations in separate subsidiaries to establish clear lines of control and facilitate the evaluation of operating results. In some cases, an entity that specializes in a particular type of activity or has its operations in a particular country may qualify for special tax incentives. Of particular importance in some industries is the fact that a separate legal entity may be permitted to operate in a regulatory environment without subjecting the entire entity to regulatory control. Also, by creating a separate legal entity, a parent company may be able to protect itself from exposing the entire company's assets to legal liability that may stem from a new product line or entry into a higher-risk form of business activity.

Companies also might establish new subsidiaries or other entities, not as a means of expansion, but as a means of disposing of a portion of their existing operations through outright sale or a transfer of ownership to existing shareholders or others. In some cases, companies have used this approach to dispose of a segment of operations that no longer fits well with the overall

FYI

In October of 2012 Kraft spun off its $32 billion snack business in order to better focus on its grocery business and other strategic goals.

mission of the company. In other cases, this approach has been used as a means of disposing of unprofitable operations or to gain regulatory or shareholder approval of a proposed merger with another company. A ***spin-off*** occurs when the ownership of a newly created or existing subsidiary is distributed to the parent's stockholders without the stockholders surrendering any of their stock in the parent company. Thus, the company divests itself of the subsidiary because it is owned by the company's shareholders after the spin-off.

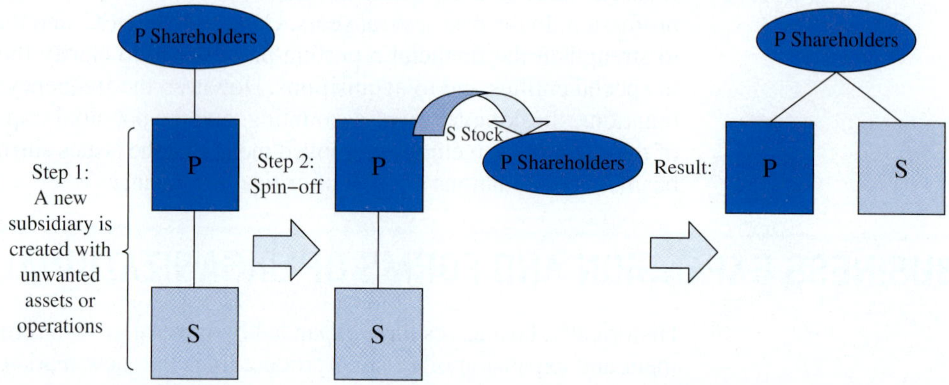

A ***split-off*** occurs when the subsidiary's shares are exchanged for shares of the parent, thereby leading to a reduction in the parent company's outstanding shares. Although the two divestiture types are similar, the split-off could result in one set of the former parent shareholders exchanging their shares for those of the divested subsidiary.

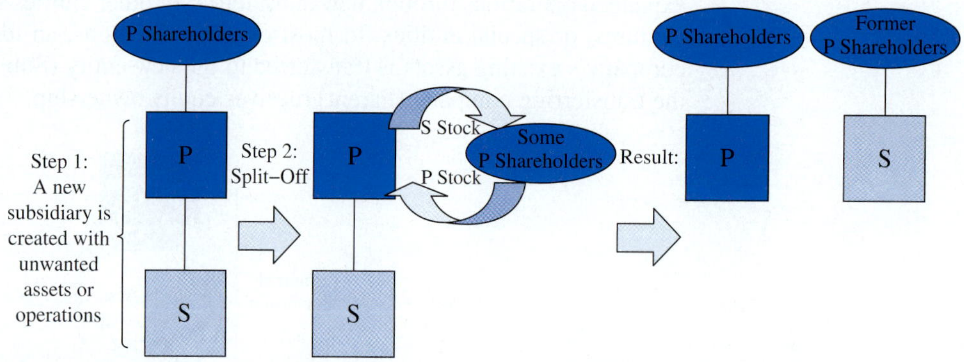

External Expansion: Business Combinations

Many times companies find that entry into new product areas or geographic regions is more easily accomplished by acquiring or combining with other companies than through internal expansion. For example, SBC Communications, a major telecommunications company and one of the "Baby Bells," significantly increased its service area by combining with Pacific Telesis and Ameritech, later acquiring AT&T (and adopting its name), and subsequently combining with BellSouth. Similarly, because the state of Florida has traditionally been very reluctant to issue new bank charters, bank corporations wishing to establish operations in Florida have had to acquire an existing bank to obtain a charter in the state.

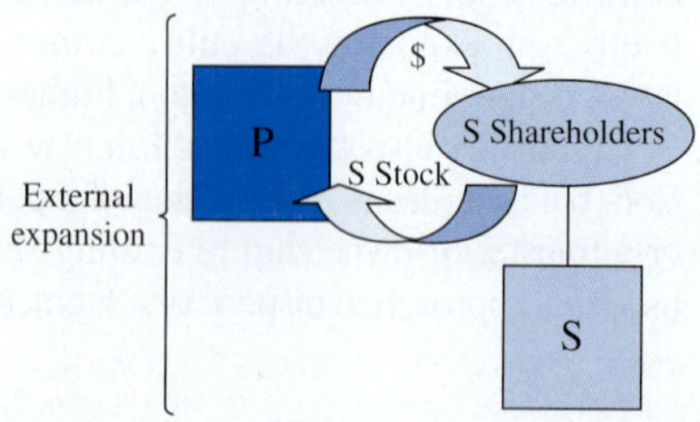

A business can be defined as an organization or enterprise engaged in providing goods or services to customers. However, a business doesn't necessarily have to be a separate legal entity. A ***business combination*** occurs when ". . . an acquirer obtains control of one or more businesses."[4] The diagram on the preceding page illustrates a typical acquisition. The concept of ***control*** relates to the ability to direct policies and management. Traditionally, control over a company has been gained by acquiring a majority of the company's common stock. However, the diversity of financial and operating arrangements employed in recent years also raises the possibility of gaining control with less than majority ownership or, in some cases, with no ownership at all through other contractual arrangements.

FYI

On April 2, 2012, Zynga Inc. purchased its previously leased corporate headquarters building located in San Francisco, California, to support the overall growth of its business. In accordance with **ASC 805,** "Business Combinations," Zynga accounted for the building purchase as a business combination even though it wasn't a stand-alone legal entity because (it argued) the building met the definition of a business.

The types of business combinations found in today's business environment and the terms of the combination agreements are as diverse as the firms involved. Companies enter into various types of formal and informal arrangements that may have at least some of the characteristics of a business combination. Most companies tend to avoid recording informal agreements on their books because of the potential difficulty of enforcing them. In fact, some types of informal arrangements, such as those aimed at fixing prices or apportioning potential customers, are illegal. Formal agreements generally are enforceable and are more likely to be recognized on the books of the participants.

Organizational Structure and Financial Reporting

When companies expand or change organizational structure by acquiring other companies or through internal division, the new structure must be examined to determine the appropriate financial reporting procedures. Several approaches are possible, depending on the circumstances:

1. **Merger** A merger is a business combination in which the acquired business's assets and liabilities are combined with those of the acquiring company. Thus, two companies are merged into a single entity. In essence, the acquiring company "swallows" the acquired business.
2. **Controlling ownership** A business combination in which the acquired company remains as a separate legal entity with a majority of its common stock owned by the purchasing company leads to a parent–subsidiary relationship. Accounting standards normally require that the financial statements of the parent and subsidiary be consolidated for general-purpose reporting so the companies appear as a single entity. The treatment is the same if the subsidiary is created rather than purchased. The treatment is also the same when the other entity is unincorporated and the investor company has control and majority ownership.[5]
3. **Noncontrolling ownership** The purchase of a less-than-majority interest in another corporation does not usually result in a business combination or controlling situation. A similar situation arises when a company creates another entity and holds less than a controlling position in it or purchases a less-than-controlling interest in an existing partnership. In its financial statements, the investor company reports its interest in the investee as an investment with the specific method of accounting (cost method, equity method, consolidation) dictated by the circumstances.
4. **Other beneficial interest** One company may have a beneficial interest in another entity even without a direct ownership interest. The beneficial interest may be defined by the agreement establishing the entity or by an operating or financing agreement. When the beneficial interest is based on contractual arrangements instead of majority stock

[4] **ASC 805-10-65-1.**

[5] Majority ownership is generally a sufficient but not a necessary condition for the indicated treatment. Unlike the corporate case, percentage ownership does not fully describe the nature of a beneficial interest in a partnership. Investments in partnerships are discussed in later chapters.

ownership, the reporting rules may be complex and depend on the circumstances. In general, a company that has the ability to make decisions significantly affecting the results of another entity's activities or is expected to receive a majority of the other entity's profits and losses is considered to be that entity's ***primary beneficiary.*** Normally, that entity's financial statements would be consolidated with those of the primary beneficiary.

These different situations, and the related accounting and reporting procedures, are discussed throughout the first 10 chapters of the text. The primary focus is on the first three situations, especially the purchase of all or part of another company's stock. The discussion of the fourth situation in Chapter 3 is limited because of its complexity and the diversity of these contractual arrangements.

THE DEVELOPMENT OF ACCOUNTING FOR BUSINESS COMBINATIONS

LO 1-2

Understand the development of standards related to acquisition accounting over time.

For more than half a century, accounting for business combinations remained largely unchanged. Two methods of accounting for business combinations, *the purchase method* and the ***pooling-of-interests method,*** were acceptable during that time. However, major changes in accounting for business combinations have occurred over the past 15 years. First, the FASB eliminated the pooling-of-interests method in 2001, leaving only a single method, purchase accounting. Then, in 2007, the FASB issued the revised standard (**ASC 805**) that replaced the purchase method with the *acquisition method,* which is now the only acceptable method of accounting for business combinations.

Although all business combinations must now be accounted for using the acquisition method, many companies' financial statements will continue to include the effects of previous business combinations recorded using the pooling-of-interests and purchase methods. Thus, a general understanding of these methods can be helpful.

The idea behind a pooling of interests was that no change in ownership had actually occurred in the business combination, often a questionable premise. Based on this idea, the book values of the combining companies were carried forward to the combined company and no revaluations to fair value were made. Managers often preferred pooling accounting because it did not result in asset write-ups or goodwill that might burden future earnings with additional depreciation or write-offs. Also, reporting practices often made acquisitions appear better than they would have appeared if purchase accounting had been used.

Purchase accounting treated the purchase of a business much like the purchase of any asset. The acquired company was recorded based on the purchase price that the acquirer paid. Individual assets and liabilities of the acquired company were valued at their fair values, and the difference between the total purchase price and the fair value of the net identifiable assets acquired was recorded as goodwill. All direct costs of bringing about and consummating the combination were included in the total purchase price.

Acquisition accounting is consistent with the FASB's intention to move accounting in general more toward recognizing fair values. Under acquisition accounting, the acquirer in a business combination, in effect, values the acquired company based on the fair value of the consideration given in the combination and the fair value of any noncontrolling interest not acquired by the acquirer.

ACCOUNTING FOR INTERNAL EXPANSION: CREATING BUSINESS ENTITIES[6]

LO 1-3

Make calculations and prepare journal entries for the creation of a business entity.

Companies that choose to conduct a portion of their operations through separate business entities usually do so through corporate subsidiaries, corporate joint ventures, or partnerships. The ongoing accounting and reporting for investments in corporate joint ventures and subsidiaries are discussed in Chapters 2 through 10. This section discusses the origination of these entities when the parent or investor creates them rather than purchases an interest in an existing corporation or partnership.

[6] To view a video explanation of this topic, visit advancedstudyguide.com.

Advanced StudyGuide .com

When a company transfers assets or operations to another entity that it has created, a vast number of variations in the types of entities and the types of agreements between the creating company and the created entity are possible. Accordingly, it is impossible to establish a single set of rules and procedures that will suffice in all situations. We focus on the most straightforward and common cases in which the transferring company creates a subsidiary or partnership that it owns and controls, including cases in which the company intends to transfer ownership to its stockholders through a spin-off or split-off. In simple cases, the company transfers assets, and perhaps liabilities, to an entity that the company has created and controls and in which it holds majority ownership. The company transfers assets and liabilities to the created entity at book value, and the transferring company recognizes an ownership interest in the newly created entity equal to the book value of the net assets transferred. Recognition of fair values of the assets transferred in excess of their carrying values on the books of the transferring company normally is not appropriate in the absence of an arm's-length transaction. Thus, no gains or losses are recognized on the transfer by the transferring company. However, if the value of an asset transferred to a newly created entity has been impaired prior to the transfer and its fair value is less than the carrying value on the transferring company's books, the transferring company should recognize an impairment loss and transfer the asset to the new entity at the lower fair value.

FYI

An "arm's-length transaction" is one in which the parties are completely independent of one another so that they act in their personal best interests or to maximize their own wealth. Thus, there is no chance of collusion between them.

The created entity begins accounting for the transferred assets and liabilities in the normal manner based on their book values at the time of transfer. Subsequent financial reporting involves consolidating the created entity's financial statements with those of the parent company. Overall, the consolidated financial statements appear the same as if the transfer had not taken place.

As an illustration of a created entity, assume that Allen Company creates a subsidiary, Blaine Company, and transfers the following assets to Blaine in exchange for all 100,000 shares of Blaine's $2 par common stock:

Item	Cost	Book Value
Cash		$ 70,000
Inventory	$ 50,000	50,000
Land	75,000	75,000
Building	100,000	80,000
Equipment	250,000	160,000
		$435,000

Allen records the transfer with the following entry:[7]

(1)			
	Investment in Blaine Company Common Stock	435,000	
	Accumulated Depreciation, Building	20,000	
	Accumulated Depreciation, Equipment	90,000	
	Cash		70,000
	Inventory		50,000
	Land		75,000
	Building		100,000
	Equipment		250,000

Record the creation of Blaine Company.

[7] Journal entries used in the text to illustrate the various accounting procedures are numbered sequentially within individual chapters for easy reference. Each journal entry number appears only once in a chapter.

Blaine Company records the transfer of assets and the issuance of stock (at the book value of the assets) as follows:

(2)	Cash	70,000	
	Inventory	50,000	
	Land	75,000	
	Building	100,000	
	Equipment	250,000	
	Accumulated Depreciation, Building		20,000
	Accumulated Depreciation, Equipment		90,000
	Common Stock, $2 par		200,000
	Additional Paid-In Capital		235,000

Record the receipt of assets and the issuance of $2 par common stock.

ACCOUNTING FOR EXTERNAL EXPANSION: BUSINESS COMBINATIONS

LO 1-4

Understand and explain the differences between different forms of business combinations.

Advanced StudyGuide .com

A business combination occurs when one party acquires control over one or more businesses. This usually involves two or more separate businesses being joined together under common control. The acquirer may obtain control by paying cash, transferring other assets, issuing debt, or issuing stock. In rare cases, the acquirer might obtain control by agreement or through other means without an exchange taking place. Business combinations can take one of several different forms and can be effected in different ways.

Legal Forms of Business Combinations

Figure 1–1 illustrates the three primary legal forms of business combinations. A ***statutory merger*** is a type of business combination in which only one of the combining companies survives and the other loses its separate identity. The acquired company's assets and liabilities are transferred to the acquiring company, and the acquired company is dissolved, or ***liquidated.*** The operations of the previously separate companies are carried on in a single legal entity following the merger.

A ***statutory consolidation*** is a business combination in which both combining companies are dissolved and the assets and liabilities of both companies are transferred to a newly created corporation. The operations of the previously separate companies are carried on in a single legal entity, and neither of the combining companies remains in existence after a statutory consolidation. In many situations, however, the resulting corporation is new in form only, and in substance it actually is one of the combining companies reincorporated with a new name.

A ***stock acquisition*** occurs when one company acquires the voting shares of another company and the two companies continue to operate as separate, but related, legal entities. Because neither of the combining companies is liquidated, the acquiring company accounts for its ownership interest in the other company as an investment. In a stock acquisition, the acquiring company need not acquire all the other company's stock to gain control. The relationship that is created in a stock acquisition is referred to as a ***parent–subsidiary relationship.*** A *parent company* is one that controls another company, referred to as a *subsidiary,* usually through majority ownership of common stock. For general-purpose financial reporting, a parent company and its subsidiaries present consolidated financial statements that appear largely as if the companies had actually merged into one.

Sometimes a new corporation is created by two (or more) companies to become their common ***holding company,*** a special case of a stock acquisition. Assuming the shareholders of the two companies approve of the creation of the new holding company, they will exchange their shares in the existing companies for shares of the newly created holding company. The holding company becomes the parent company and the existing companies become the subsidiaries.

FIGURE 1–1
Legal Forms of Business Combinations

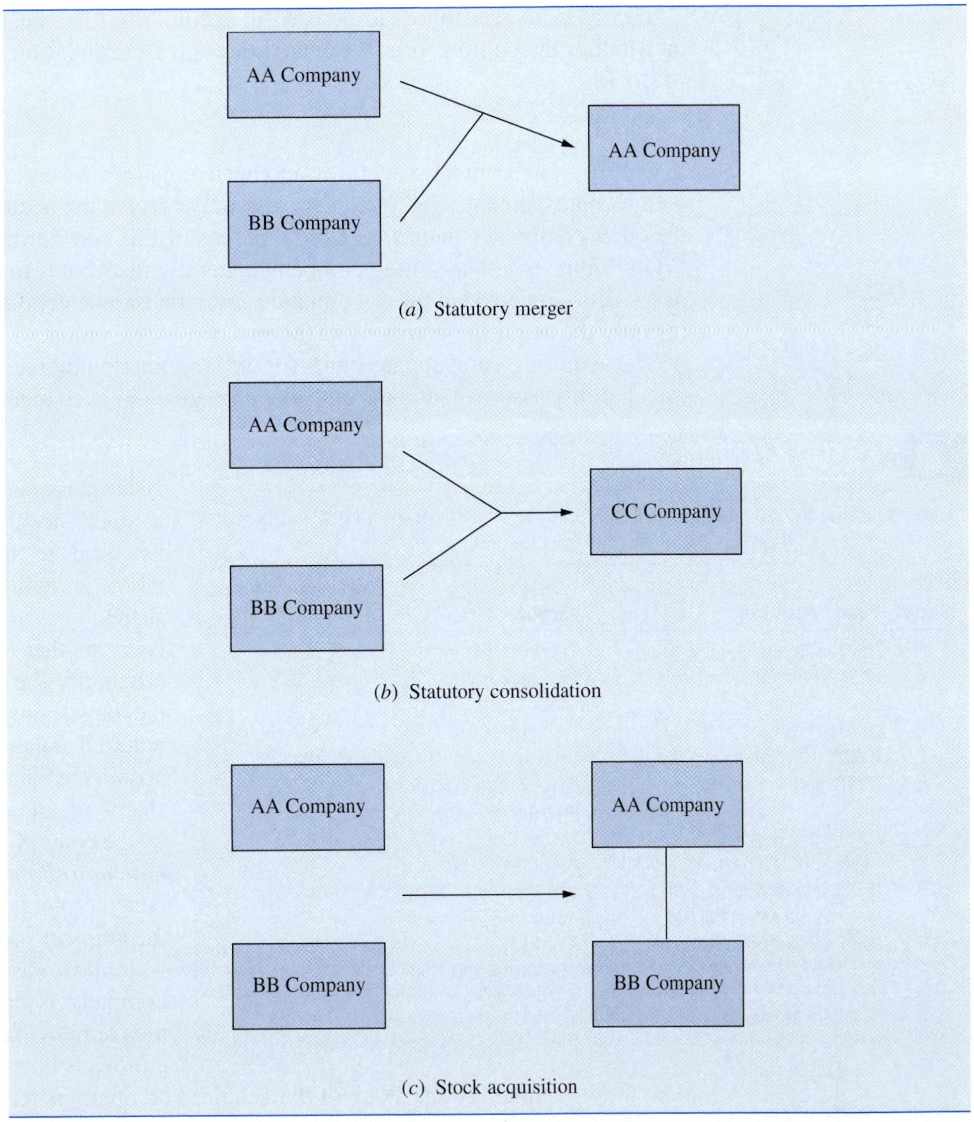

The legal form of a business combination, the substance of the combination agreement, and the circumstances surrounding the combination all affect how the combination is recorded initially and the accounting and reporting procedures used subsequent to the combination.

Methods of Effecting Business Combinations

Business combinations can be characterized as either friendly or unfriendly. In a friendly combination, the managements of the companies involved come to an agreement on the terms of the combination and recommend approval by the stockholders. Such combinations usually are effected in a single transaction involving an exchange of assets or voting shares. In an unfriendly combination, or "hostile takeover," the managements of the companies involved are unable to agree on the terms of a combination, and the management of one of the companies makes a ***tender offer*** directly to the shareholders of the other company to buy their stock at a specified price. A tender offer invites the shareholders of the other company to "tender," or exchange, their shares for securities or assets of the acquiring company. If sufficient shares are tendered, the acquiring company gains voting control of the other company and can install its own management by exercising its voting rights.

The specific procedures to be used in accounting for a business combination depend on whether the combination is effected through an acquisition of assets or an acquisition of stock.

Acquisition of Assets

Sometimes one company acquires another company's assets through direct negotiations with its management. The agreement also may involve the acquiring company's assuming the other company's liabilities. Combinations of this sort normally take form (*a*) or form (*b*) in Figure 1–1. The selling company generally distributes to its stockholders the assets or securities received in the combination from the acquiring company and liquidates, leaving only the acquiring company as the surviving legal entity.

The acquiring company accounts for the combination by recording each asset acquired, each liability assumed, and the consideration given in exchange at fair value.

STOP & THINK

Can you name the 10 largest and best-known North American merger and acquisition transactions? They've all happened in your lifetime!

Rank	Year	Acquirer	Target	Transaction Value (in bil. USD)
1	2000	America Online Inc.	Time Warner Inc.	164.7
2	1999	Pfizer Inc.	Warner-Lambert Co.	89.2
3	1998	Exxon Corp.	Mobil Corp.	78.9
4	2006	AT&T Inc.	BellSouth Corp.	72.7
5	1998	Travelers Group Inc.	Citicorp	72.6
6	2001	Comcast Corp.	AT&T Broadband & Internet Services	72.0
7	2009	Pfizer Inc.	Wyeth Corp.	67.3
8	1998	SBC Communications Inc.	Ameritech Corp.	62.6
9	1998	NationsBank Corp., Charlotte, NC	BankAmerica Corp.	61.6
10	1999	Vodafone Group PLC	AirTouch Communications Inc.	60.3

Source: Institute of Mergers, Acquisitions and Alliances.

Acquisition of Stock

A business combination effected through a stock acquisition does not necessarily have to involve the acquisition of all of a company's outstanding voting shares. For one company to gain control over another through stock ownership, a majority (i.e., more than 50 percent) of the outstanding voting shares usually is required unless other factors lead to the acquirer gaining control. The total of the shares of an acquired company not held by the controlling shareholder is called the ***noncontrolling interest.*** In the past, the noncontrolling interest was referred to as the ***minority interest.***

In those cases when control of another company is acquired and both companies remain in existence as separate legal entities following the business combination, the investment in the stock of the acquired company is recorded on the books of the acquiring company as an asset.

Valuation of Business Entities

All parties involved in a business combination must believe they have an opportunity to benefit before they will agree to participate. Determining whether a particular combination proposal is advantageous can be difficult. Both the value of a company's assets and its future earning potential are important in assessing the value of the company. Tax laws also influence investment decisions. For example, the existence of accumulated net operating losses that can be used under U.S. tax law to shelter future income from taxes increases the value of a potential acquiree.

Value of Individual Assets and Liabilities

The value of a company's individual assets and liabilities is usually determined by appraisal. For some items, the value may be determined with relative ease, such as investments that are traded actively in the securities markets or short-term receivables or payables. For other items, the appraisal may be much more subjective, such as the value of land located in an area where few recent sales have occurred. In addition, certain intangibles typically are not reported on the balance sheet. For example, the costs of developing new ideas, new products, and new production methods normally are expensed as research and development costs in the period incurred.

Current liabilities are often viewed as having fair values equal to their book values because they will be paid at face amount within a short time. Long-term liabilities, however, must be valued based on current interest rates if different from the effective rates at the issue dates of the liabilities. For example, if $100,000 of 10-year, 6 percent bonds, paying interest annually, had been issued at par three years ago, and the current market rate of interest for the same type of security is 10 percent, the value of the liability currently is computed as follows:

Present value for 7 years at 10% of principal payment of $100,000	$51,316
Present value at 10% of 7 interest payments of $6,000	29,211
Present value of bond	$80,527

Although accurate assessments of the value of assets and liabilities may be difficult, they form an important part of the overall determination of the value of an enterprise.

Value of Potential Earnings

In many cases, assets operated together as a group have a value that exceeds the sum of their individual values (i.e., there is unrecorded goodwill). This "going-concern value" makes it desirable to operate the assets as an ongoing entity rather than sell them individually. A company's earning power as an ongoing enterprise is of obvious importance in valuing that company.

There are different approaches to measuring the value of a company's future earnings. Sometimes companies are valued based on a multiple of their current earnings. For example, if Bargain Company reports earnings of $35,000 for the current year, the company's value based on a multiple of 10 times current earnings is $350,000. The appropriate multiple to use is a matter of judgment and is based on factors such as the riskiness and variability of the earnings and the anticipated degree of growth.

Another method of valuing a company is to compute the present value of the anticipated future net cash flows generated by the company. This requires assessing the amount and timing of future cash flows and discounting them back to the present value at the discount rate determined to be appropriate for the type of enterprise. For example, if Bargain Company is expected to generate cash flows of $35,000 for each of the next 25 years, the present value of the firm at a discount rate of 10 percent is $317,696. Estimating the potential for future earnings requires numerous assumptions and estimates. Not surprisingly, the buyer and seller often have difficulty agreeing on the value of a company's expected earnings.

Valuation of Consideration Exchanged

When one company acquires another, the acquiring company must place a value on the consideration given in the exchange. Little difficulty is encountered when the acquiring company gives cash in an acquisition, but valuation may be more difficult when the acquiring company gives securities, particularly new untraded securities or securities with unusual features. For example, General Motors completed an acquisition a number of years ago by issuing a new Series B common stock that paid dividends based on subsequent earnings of the acquired company rather than on the earnings of General Motors as a whole. Some companies have issued non-interest-bearing bonds (zero coupon bonds), which have a fair value sufficiently below par value to compensate the holder for interest. Other companies have issued various types of convertible securities. Unless these securities, or others that are considered equivalent, are being traded in the market, estimates of their value must be made. The approach generally followed is to use the value of some similar security with a determinable market value and adjust for the estimated value of the differences in the features of the two securities.

ACQUISITION ACCOUNTING

LO 1-5

Make calculations and business combination journal entries in the presence of a differential, goodwill, or a bargain purchase element.

Current standards require the use of the ***acquisition method*** of accounting for business combinations. Under the acquisition method, the acquirer recognizes all assets acquired and liabilities assumed in a business combination and measures them at their acquisition-date fair values. If less than 100 percent of the acquiree is acquired, the noncontrolling interest also is measured at its acquisition-date fair value. If the acquiring company already had an ownership interest in the acquiree, that investment is also measured at its acquisition-date fair value. Note that a business combination does not affect the amounts at which the other assets and liabilities of the acquirer are valued.

Advanced StudyGuide .com

Fair Value Measurements

Because accounting for business combinations is now based on fair values, the measurement of fair values takes on added importance. The acquirer must value at fair value (1) the consideration it exchanges in a business combination, (2) each of the individual identifiable assets and liabilities acquired, (3) any noncontrolling interest in the acquiree, and (4) any interest already held in the acquiree. Normally, a business combination involves an arm's-length exchange between two unrelated parties. The value of the consideration given in the exchange is usually the best measure of the value received and, therefore, reflects the value of the acquirer's interest in the acquiree.[8]

Applying the Acquisition Method

For all business combinations, an acquirer must be identified, and that party is the one gaining control over the other. In addition, an acquisition date must be determined. That date is usually the closing date when the exchange transaction actually occurs. However, in rare cases control may be acquired on a different date or without an exchange, so the circumstances must be examined to determine precisely when the acquirer gains control.

Under the acquisition method, the full acquisition-date fair values of the individual assets acquired, both tangible and intangible, and liabilities assumed in a business combination are recognized by the consolidated entity. This is true regardless of the percentage ownership acquired by the controlling entity. If the acquirer acquires all of the assets and liabilities of the acquiree in a merger, these assets and liabilities are recorded on the books of the acquiring company at their acquisition-date fair values. If the acquiring company acquires partial ownership of the acquiree in a stock acquisition, the assets acquired and liabilities assumed appear at their full acquisition-date fair values in a consolidated balance sheet prepared immediately after the combination.

All costs of bringing about and consummating a business combination are charged to an acquisition expense as incurred. Examples of traceable costs include finders' fees, consulting fees, travel costs, and so on. The costs of issuing equity securities used to acquire the acquiree are treated in the same manner as stock issues costs are normally treated, as a reduction in the paid-in capital associated with the securities.

Goodwill

Conceptually, *goodwill* as it relates to business combinations consists of all those intangible factors that allow a business to earn above-average profits. From an accounting perspective, the FASB has stated that ***goodwill*** "is an asset representing the future economic benefits arising from other assets acquired in a business combination that are not individually identified and separately recognized" (**ASC 805-10-65-1**). An asset is considered to

[8] However, the FASB decided in **ASC 805** to focus directly on the value of the consideration given rather than just using it to impute a fair value for the acquiree as a whole. In some cases, the value of the consideration given may be difficult to determine, or there may be no exchange, and valuation is better based on the value of the acquirer's interest in the acquiree or other valuation techniques. **ASC 820** provides a framework for applying fair value measurements in accounting.

be *identifiable,* and therefore must be separately recognized, if it is separable (can be separated from the business) or arises from a contractual or other right.

FYI

Kraft's $18.5 billion acquisition of Cadbury mentioned at the beginning of the chapter resulted in Kraft recording $13.9 billion in goodwill.

Under the acquisition method, an acquirer measures and recognizes goodwill from a business combination based on the difference between the total fair value of the acquired company and the fair value of its net identifiable assets. However, the FASB decided, for several reasons, not to focus directly on the total fair value of the acquiree, but rather on the components that provide an indication of that fair value.

The fair value of the consideration given is compared with the acquisition-date fair value of the acquiree's net identifiable assets, and any excess is *goodwill.*

As an example of the computation of goodwill, assume that Albert Company acquires all of the assets of Zanfor Company for $400,000 when the fair value of Zanfor's net identifiable assets is $380,000. Goodwill is recognized for the $20,000 difference between the total consideration given and the fair value of the net identifiable assets acquired. If, instead of an acquisition of assets, Albert acquires 75 percent of the common stock of Zanfor for $300,000, and the fair value of the noncontrolling interest is $100,000, goodwill is computed as follows:

Fair value of consideration given by Albert	$300,000
+ Fair value of noncontrolling interest	100,000
Total fair value of Zanfor Company	$400,000
− Fair value of net identifiable assets acquired	(380,000)
Goodwill	$ 20,000

Note that the total amount of goodwill is not affected by whether 100 percent of the acquiree or less than that is acquired. However, the fair value of the noncontrolling interest does have an effect on the amount of goodwill recognized. In the example given, the fair values of the controlling and noncontrolling interests are proportional (each is valued at an amount equal to its proportionate ownership share of the total) and imply a total fair value of the acquired company of $400,000. This is frequently the case and will always be assumed throughout the text unless indicated otherwise. However, that may not always be the case in practice. Situations might arise in a stock acquisition, for example, where the per-share value of the controlling interest is higher than that of the noncontrolling interest because of a premium associated with gaining control.

Combination Effected through the Acquisition of Net Assets

Advanced StudyGuide .com

When one company acquires all the net assets of another in a business combination, the acquirer records on its books the individual assets acquired and liabilities assumed in the combination and the consideration given in exchange. Each identifiable asset and liability acquired is recorded by the acquirer at its acquisition-date fair value. The acquiring company records any excess of the fair value of the consideration exchanged over the fair value of the acquiree's net identifiable assets as goodwill.

To illustrate the application of the acquisition method of accounting to a business combination effected through the acquisition of the acquiree's net assets, assume that Point Corporation acquires all of the assets and assumes all of the liabilities of Sharp Company in a statutory merger by issuing 10,000 shares of $10 par common stock to Sharp. The shares issued have a total market value of $610,000. Point incurs legal and appraisal fees of $40,000 in connection with the combination and stock issue costs of $25,000. Figure 1–2 shows the book values and fair values of Sharp's individual assets and liabilities on the date of combination.

FIGURE 1–2
Sharp Company Balance Sheet Information, December 31, 20X0

Assets, Liabilities & Equities	Book Value	Fair Value
Cash & Receivables	$ 45,000	$ 45,000
Inventory	65,000	75,000
Land	40,000	70,000
Buildings & Equipment	400,000	350,000
Accumulated Depreciation	(150,000)	
Patent		80,000
Total Assets	$400,000	$620,000
Current Liabilities	$100,000	110,000
Common Stock ($5 par)	100,000	
Additional Paid-In Capital	50,000	
Retained Earnings	150,000	
Total Liabilities & Equities	$400,000	
Fair Value of Net Assets		$510,000

The relationships among the fair value of the consideration exchanged, the fair value of Sharp's net assets, and the book value of Sharp's net assets are illustrated in the following diagram:

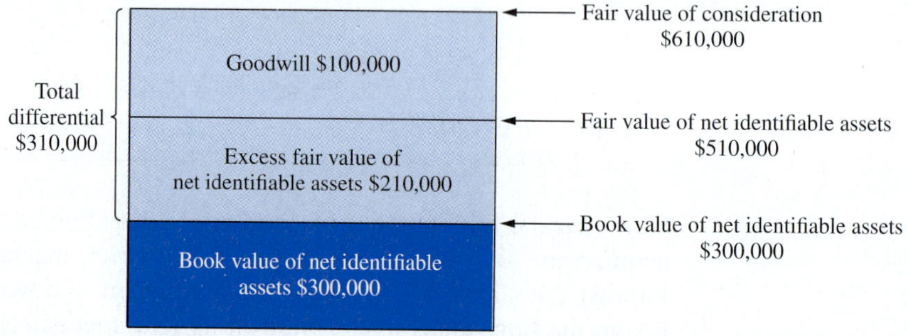

The total difference at the acquisition date between the fair value of the consideration exchanged and the book value of the net identifiable assets acquired is referred to as the ***differential.*** In more complex situations, the differential is equal to the difference between (1) the acquisition-date fair value of the consideration transferred by the acquirer, plus the acquisition-date fair value of any equity interest in the acquiree previously held by the acquirer, plus the fair value of any noncontrolling interest in the acquiree and (2) the acquisition-date book values of the identifiable assets acquired and liabilities assumed.

In the Point/Sharp merger, the total differential of $310,000 reflects the difference between the total fair value of the shares issued by Point and the carrying amount of Sharp's net assets reflected on its books at the date of combination. A portion of that difference ($210,000) is attributable to the increased value of Sharp's net assets over book value. The remainder of the difference ($100,000) is considered to be goodwill.

The $40,000 of acquisition costs incurred by Point in carrying out the acquisition are expensed as incurred:

(3)			
	Acquisition Expense	40,000	
	Cash		40,000
	Record costs related to acquisition of Sharp Company.		

Portions of the $25,000 of stock issue costs related to the shares issued to acquire Sharp may be incurred at various times. To facilitate accumulating these amounts before recording the combination, Point may record them in a separate temporary "suspense" account as incurred:

(4)			
	Deferred Stock Issue Costs	25,000	
	Cash		25,000
	Record costs related to issuance of common stock.		

On the date of combination, Point records the acquisition of Sharp with the following entry:

(5)			
	Cash and Receivables	45,000	
	Inventory	75,000	
	Land	70,000	
	Buildings and Equipment	350,000	
	Patent	80,000	
	Goodwill	100,000	
	Current Liabilities		110,000
	Common Stock		100,000
	Additional Paid-In Capital		485,000
	Deferred Stock Issue Costs		25,000
	Record acquisition of Sharp Company.		

Entry (5) records all of Sharp's individual assets and liabilities, both tangible and intangible, on Point's books at their fair values on the date of combination. The fair value of Sharp's net assets recorded is $510,000 ($620,000 – $110,000). The $100,000 difference between the fair value of the shares given by Point ($610,000) and the fair value of Sharp's net assets is recorded as goodwill.

In recording the business combination, Sharp's book values are not relevant to Point; only the fair values are recorded. Because a change in ownership has occurred, the basis of accounting used by the acquired company is not relevant to the acquirer. Consistent with this view, accumulated depreciation recorded by Sharp on its buildings and equipment is not relevant to Point and is not recorded. (Note that this is different from the way depreciable assets for an internally created subsidiary were handled previously.)

The stock issue costs are treated as a reduction in the proceeds received from the issuance of the stock. Thus, these costs are removed from the temporary account with a credit and decrease to Additional Paid-In Capital. Point records the $610,000 of stock issued at its value minus the stock issue costs, or $585,000. Of this amount, the $100,000 par value is recorded in the Common Stock account and the remainder in Additional Paid-In Capital.

Entries Recorded by Acquired Company

On the date of the combination, Sharp records the following entry to recognize receipt of the Point shares and the transfer of all individual assets and liabilities to Point:

(6)			
	Investment in Point Stock	610,000	
	Current Liabilities	100,000	
	Accumulated Depreciation	150,000	
	Cash and Receivables		45,000
	Inventory		65,000
	Land		40,000
	Buildings and Equipment		400,000
	Gain on Sale of Net Assets		310,000
	Record transfer of assets to Point Corporation.		

Sharp recognizes the fair value of Point Corporation shares at the time of the exchange and records a gain of $310,000. The distribution of Point shares to Sharp shareholders and the liquidation of Sharp are recorded on Sharp's books with the following entry:

(7)			
	Common Stock	100,000	
	Additional Paid-In Capital	50,000	
	Retained Earnings	150,000	
	Gain on Sale of Net Assets	310,000	
	Investment in Point Stock		610,000
	Record distribution of Point Corporation stock.		

Subsequent Accounting for Goodwill by Acquirer

The acquirer records goodwill arising in a merger as the difference between the fair value of the consideration exchanged and the fair value of the identifiable net assets acquired, as illustrated in entry (5). Once the acquirer records goodwill, it must be accounted for in accordance with **ASC 350.** Goodwill is carried forward at the originally recorded amount unless it is determined to be impaired. Goodwill must be reported as a separate line item in the balance sheet. A goodwill impairment loss that occurs subsequent to recording goodwill must be reported as a separate line item within income from continuing operations in the income statement unless the loss relates to discontinued operations, in which case the loss is reported within the discontinued operations section.

Goodwill must be tested for impairment at least annually, at the same time each year, and more frequently if events that are likely to impair the value of the goodwill occur. The process of testing goodwill for impairment is complex. It involves examining potential goodwill impairment by each of the company's reporting units, where a reporting unit is an operating segment[9] or a component of an operating segment that is a business for which management regularly reviews financial information from that component. When goodwill arises in a business combination, it must be assigned to individual reporting units. The goodwill is assigned to units that are expected to benefit from the combination, even if no other assets or liabilities of the acquired company are assigned to those units. To test for goodwill impairment, the fair value of the reporting unit is compared with its carrying amount. If the fair value of the reporting unit exceeds its carrying amount, the goodwill of that reporting unit is considered unimpaired. On the other hand, if the carrying amount of the reporting unit exceeds its fair value, an impairment of the reporting unit's goodwill is implied.

The amount of the reporting unit's goodwill impairment is measured as the excess of the carrying amount of the unit's goodwill over the implied value of its goodwill. The implied value of its goodwill is determined as the excess of the fair value of the reporting unit as a whole over the fair value of its net assets excluding goodwill.[10]

As an example of goodwill impairment, assume that Reporting Unit A is assigned $100,000 of goodwill arising from a recent business combination. The following assets and liabilities are assigned to Reporting Unit A:

[9] An operating segment is defined in **ASC 280-10-50.** Whereas U.S. GAAP assigns goodwill to reporting units, IFRS assigns goodwill to cash-generating units (GCU).

[10] The one-step impairment test for goodwill under IFRS is slightly different. The recoverable amount of the cash-generating unit (GCU) is compared with its carrying amount. Any impairment loss is recognized in operating results as the excess of the carrying amount over the recoverable amount. Impairment losses are recognized in operating results. If the impairment loss exceeds the book value of goodwill, the loss is allocated first to goodwill and then on a pro rata basis to the other assets of the CGU.

Item	Carrying Amount	Fair Value
Cash and Receivables	$ 50,000	$ 50,000
Inventory	80,000	90,000
Equipment	120,000	150,000
Goodwill	100,000	
Total Assets	$350,000	$290,000
Current Payables	(10,000)	(10,000)
Net Assets	$340,000	$280,000

By summing the carrying amounts of the assets and subtracting the carrying amount of the payables, the carrying amount of the reporting unit, including the goodwill, is determined to be $340,000. If the fair value of the reporting unit is estimated to be $360,000, (or any number greater than the carrying amount) there is no evidence of goodwill impairment. On the other hand, if the fair value of the reporting unit is estimated to be $320,000, a second comparison must be made to determine the amount of any impairment loss because the fair value of the reporting unit is lower than its carrying amount. The implied value of Reporting Unit A's goodwill is then determined by deducting the $280,000 fair value of the net assets, excluding goodwill, from the unit's $320,000 fair value. The $40,000 difference ($320,000 − $280,000) represents Reporting Unit A's implied goodwill. The impairment loss is measured as the excess of the carrying amount of the unit's goodwill ($100,000) over the implied value of the goodwill ($40,000), or $60,000. This goodwill impairment loss is combined with any impairment losses from other reporting units to determine the total goodwill impairment loss to be reported by the company as a whole. Goodwill is written down by the amount of the impairment loss. Once written down, goodwill may not be written up for subsequent recoveries.

Bargain Purchase*

Occasionally, the fair value of the consideration given in a business combination, along with the fair value of any equity interest in the acquiree already held and the fair value of any noncontrolling interest in the acquiree, may be less than the fair value of the acquiree's net identifiable assets, resulting in a ***bargain purchase.*** This might occur, for example, with a forced sale.

When a bargain purchase occurs (rarely), the acquirer must take steps to ensure that all acquisition-date valuations are appropriate. If they are, the acquirer recognizes a gain at the date of acquisition for the excess of the amount of the net identifiable assets acquired and liabilities assumed as valued under **ASC 805,** usually at fair value, over the sum of the fair value of the consideration given in the exchange, the fair value of any equity interest in the acquiree held by the acquirer at the date of acquisition, and the fair value of any noncontrolling interest. Along with the amount of the gain, companies must disclose the operating segment where the gain is reported and the factors that led to the gain.

To illustrate accounting for a bargain purchase, assume that in the previous example of Point and Sharp, Point is able to acquire Sharp for $500,000 cash even though the fair value of Sharp's net identifiable assets is estimated to be $510,000. In this simple bargain-purchase case without an equity interest already held or a noncontrolling interest, the fair value of Sharp's net identifiable assets exceeds the consideration exchanged by Point, and, accordingly, a $10,000 gain attributable to Point is recognized.

FYI

On September 22, 2008, at the climax of the global financial crisis, Barclays Bank PLC completed the bargain purchase acquisition of Lehman Brothers' North American businesses. Lehman Brothers was a former U.S.-based investment bank. Barclays is an international banking and financial services firm based in London. Barclays recorded a significant gain on bargain purchase at the time of this acquisition:

		In 1000s of USD
Net Assets Acquired		$6,098[a]
Cash Paid	1,541	
Attributable Costs	75	
Obligation to Be Settled in Shares	301	
Less: Total Consideration		1,917
Gain on Bargain Purchase		$4,181

[a]Selected Information from Barclays Bank PLC Annual Report 2008 Note 40(a), translated to U.S.$ using the GBPUSD Spot Rate 9/22/08 of 1.8483£/$.

* See Chapter 4 for a more detailed discussion of this topic.

In accounting for the bargain purchase (for cash) on Point's books, the following entry replaces previous entry (5):

(8)	Cash and Receivables	45,000	
	Inventory	75,000	
	Land	70,000	
	Buildings and Equipment	350,000	
	Patent	80,000	
	Cash		500,000
	Current Liabilities		110,000
	Gain on Bargain Purchase of Sharp Company		10,000

Record acquisition of Sharp Company.

Combination Effected through Acquisition of Stock

Many business combinations are effected by acquiring the voting stock of another company rather than by acquiring its net assets. When a business combination is effected through a stock acquisition, the acquiree may lose its separate identity and be merged into the acquiring company or it may continue to operate as a separate company. If the acquired company is liquidated and its assets and liabilities are transferred to the acquirer, the dollar amounts recorded are identical to those in entry (5).

If the acquired company continues to exist, the acquirer records an investment in the common stock of the acquiree rather than its individual assets and liabilities. The acquirer records its investment in the acquiree's common stock at the total fair value of the consideration given in exchange. For example, if Point Corporation (*a*) exchanges 10,000 shares of its stock with a total market value of $610,000 for all of Sharp Company's shares and (*b*) incurs merger costs of $40,000 and stock issue costs of $25,000, Point records the following entries upon receipt of the Sharp stock:

(9)	Acquisition Expense	40,000	
	Deferred Stock Issue Costs	25,000	
	Cash		65,000

Record merger and stock issue costs related to acquisition of Sharp Company.

(10)	Investment in Sharp Stock	610,000	
	Common Stock		100,000
	Additional Paid-In Capital		485,000
	Deferred Stock Issue Costs		25,000

Record acquisition of Sharp Company stock.

The details of the accounting and reporting procedures for intercorporate investments in common stock when the acquiree continues in existence are discussed in the next nine chapters.

Financial Reporting Subsequent to a Business Combination

Financial statements prepared subsequent to a business combination reflect the combined entity beginning on the date of combination going forward to the end of the fiscal period. When a combination occurs during a fiscal period, income earned by the acquiree prior to the combination is not reported in the income of the combined enterprise. If the combined company presents comparative financial statements that include statements for periods before the combination, those statements include only the activities and financial position of the acquiring company, not those of the combined entity or the acquiree.

To illustrate financial reporting subsequent to a business combination, assume the following information for Point Corporation and Sharp Company:

	20X0	20X1
Point Corporation:		
Separate Income (excluding any income from Sharp)	$300,000	$300,000
Shares Outstanding, December 31	30,000	40,000
Sharp Company:		
Net Income	$ 60,000	$ 60,000

Point Corporation acquires all of Sharp Company's stock at book value on January 1, 20X1, by issuing 10,000 shares of common stock. Subsequently, Point Corporation presents comparative financial statements for the years 20X0 and 20X1. The net income and earnings per share (EPS) that Point presents in its comparative financial statements for the two years are as follows:

20X0:	
Net Income	$300,000
Earnings per Share ($300,000/30,000 shares)	$10.00
20X1:	
Net Income ($300,000 + $60,000)	$360,000
Earnings per Share ($360,000/40,000 shares)	$9.00

If Point Corporation had acquired Sharp Company in the middle of 20X1 instead of at the beginning, Point would include only Sharp's earnings subsequent to acquisition in its 20X1 income statement. If Sharp earned $25,000 in 20X1 before acquisition by Point and $35,000 after the combination, Point would report total net income for 20X1 of $335,000 ($300,000 + $35,000). Note that if the shares are issued in the middle of the year to effect the acquisition, the weighted-average shares used in the EPS calculation would change as well.

ADDITIONAL CONSIDERATIONS IN ACCOUNTING FOR BUSINESS COMBINATIONS

LO 1-6

Understand additional considerations associated with business combinations.

ASC 805 includes a number of requirements relating to specific items or aspects encountered in business combinations. A discussion of the more common situations follows.

Uncertainty in Business Combinations

Uncertainty affects much of accounting measurement but is especially prevalent in business combinations. Although uncertainty relates to many aspects of business combinations, three aspects of accounting for business combinations deserve particular attention: the measurement period, contingent consideration, and acquiree contingencies.

Measurement Period

One type of uncertainty in business combinations arises from numerous required fair value measurements. Because the acquirer may not have sufficient information available immediately to properly ascertain fair values, **ASC 805** allows for a period of time, called the ***measurement period,*** to acquire the necessary information. The measurement period ends once the acquirer obtains the necessary information about the facts as of the acquisition date, but may not exceed one year beyond the acquisition date.

Assets that have been provisionally recorded as of the acquisition date are retrospectively adjusted in value during the measurement period for new information that clarifies the acquisition-date value. Usually, the offsetting entry is to goodwill. Retrospective adjustments may not be made for changes in value that occur subsequent to the acquisition date, even when those changes occur during the measurement period.

As an illustration, assume that Blaine Company acquires land in a business combination and provisionally records the land at its estimated fair value of $100,000. During the measurement period, Blaine receives a reliable appraisal that the land was worth $110,000 at the acquisition date. Subsequently, during the same accounting period, a change in the zoning of a neighboring parcel of land reduces the value of the land acquired by Blaine to $75,000. Blaine records the clarification of the acquisition-date fair value of the land and the subsequent impairment of value with the following entries:

		Debit	Credit
(11)	Land	10,000	
	Goodwill		10,000
	Adjust acquisition-date value of land acquired in business combination.		
(12)	Impairment Loss	35,000	
	Land		35,000
	Recognize decline in value of land held.		

Contingent Consideration

Sometimes the consideration exchanged by the acquirer in a business combination is not fixed in amount, but rather is contingent on future events. For example, the acquiree and acquirer may enter into a *contingent-share agreement* whereby, in addition to an initial issuance of shares, the acquirer may agree to issue a certain number of additional shares for each percentage point by which the earnings number exceeds a set amount over the next five years. Thus, total consideration exchanged in the business combination is not known within the measurement period because the number of shares to be issued is dependent on future events.

ASC 805 requires contingent consideration in a business combination to be valued at fair value as of the acquisition date (and classified as either a liability or equity). The right to require the return of consideration given that it is dependent on future events is classified as an asset. Contingent consideration classified as an asset or liability is remeasured each period to fair value and the change is recognized in income.[11] Contingent consideration classified as equity is not remeasured.

Acquiree Contingencies

Certain contingencies may relate to an acquiree in a business combination, such as pending lawsuits or loan guarantees made by the acquiree. Certainly, the acquirer considers such contingencies when entering into an acquisition agreement, and the accounting must also consider such contingencies. Under **ASC 805,** the acquirer must recognize all contingencies that arise from contractual rights or obligations and other contingencies if it is more likely than not that they meet the definition of an asset or liability at the acquisition date. The acquirer records these contingencies at acquisition-date fair value.

For all acquired contingencies, the acquirer should provide a description of each, disclose the amount recognized at the acquisition date, and describe the estimated range of possible undiscounted outcomes. Subsequently, the acquirer should disclose changes in the amounts recognized and in the range of possible outcomes. Note that the accounting for acquiree contingencies is no different from the accounting for any other contingency.

In-Process Research and Development

In normal operations, research and development costs are required to be expensed as incurred except under certain limited conditions. When a company acquires valuable ongoing research and development projects from an acquiree in a business combination,

[11] The treatment of contingent consideration under IFRS is slightly different. Although contingent consideration classified as an asset or liability will likely be a financial instrument measured at fair value with gains or losses recognized in profit or loss, if the asset or liability is not a financial instrument, it is accounted for in accordance with the standard provisions for that class of asset or liability (i.e., not necessarily at fair value).

a question arises as to whether these should be recorded as assets. The FASB concluded in **ASC 805** that these projects are assets and should be recorded at their acquisition-date fair values, even if they have no alternative use. These projects should be classified as having indefinite lives and, therefore, should not be amortized until completed and brought to market. They should be tested for impairment in accordance with current standards. Projects that are subsequently abandoned are written off when abandoned. Subsequent expenditures for the previously acquired research and development projects would normally be expensed as incurred.

Noncontrolling Equity Held Prior to Combination

In some cases, an acquirer may hold an equity interest in an acquiree prior to obtaining control through a business combination. The total amount of the acquirer's investment in the acquiree subsequent to the combination is equal to the acquisition-date fair value of the equity interest previously held and the fair value of the consideration given in the business combination. For example, if Lemon Company held 10 percent of Aide Company's stock with a fair value of $500,000 and Lemon acquired the remaining shares of Aide for $4,500,000 cash, Lemon's total investment is considered to be $5,000,000.

An acquirer that held an equity position in an acquiree immediately prior to the acquisition date must revalue that equity position to its fair value at the acquisition date and recognize a gain or loss on the revaluation. Suppose that Lemon's 10 percent investment in Aide has a book value of $300,000 and fair value of $500,000 at the date Lemon acquires the remaining 90 percent of Aide's stock. Lemon revalues its original investment in Aide to its $500,000 fair value and recognizes a $200,000 gain on the revaluation at the date it acquires the remaining shares of Aide. Lemon records the following entries on its books in connection with the acquisition of Aide:

(13)	Investment in Aide Company Stock	200,000	
	Gain on revaluation of Aide Company Stock		200,000
	Revalue Aide Company stock to fair value at date of business combination.		
(14)	Investment in Aide Company Stock	4,500,000	
	Cash		4,500,000
	Acquire controlling interest in Aide Company.		

SUMMARY OF KEY CONCEPTS

Business combinations and complex organizational structures are an important part of the global business scene. Many companies add organizational components by creating new corporations or partnerships through which to carry out a portion of their operations. In other cases, companies may enter into business combinations to acquire other companies through which to further their objectives.

When a company creates another corporation or a partnership through a transfer of assets, the book values of those assets are transferred to the new entity and no gain or loss is recognized. The creating company and the new entity will combine their financial statements for general-purpose financial reporting to appear as if they were a single company as long as the creating company continues to control the new entity.

A business combination occurs when an acquirer obtains control of one or more other businesses. The three legal forms of business combination that are commonly found are (*a*) statutory mergers in which the acquiree loses its separate identity and the acquirer continues with the assets and liabilities of both companies; (*b*) statutory consolidations in which both combining companies join to form a new company; and (*c*) stock acquisitions in which both combining companies maintain their separate identities, with the acquirer owning the stock of the acquiree.

ASC 805 requires that the acquisition method be used to account for business combinations. Under the acquisition method, all of the assets acquired and liabilities assumed by the acquirer in a business combination are valued at their fair values. The excess of the sum of the fair value of the acquirer's consideration transferred, the fair value of any equity interest in the acquiree already held, and the fair value of any noncontrolling interest in the acquiree over the fair value of the net identifiable assets acquired is goodwill. In subsequent financial statements, goodwill must be reported separately. Goodwill is not amortized, but it must be tested for impairment at least annually. If goodwill is impaired, it is written down to its new fair value and a loss recognized for the amount of the impairment. If the fair value of the consideration transferred by the acquirer in a business combination, along with the fair value of an equity interest already held, and the noncontrolling interest is less than the fair value of the acquiree's net identifiable assets, a situation referred to as a bargain purchase, the difference is recognized as a gain attributable to the acquirer.

All costs associated with a business combination are expensed as incurred. Any stock issue costs incurred in connection with a business combination are treated as a reduction in paid-in capital. A business combination is given effect as of the acquisition date for subsequent financial reporting.

KEY TERMS

QUESTIONS

LO 1-1 **Q1-1** What types of circumstances would encourage management to establish a complex organizational structure?

LO 1-1 **Q1-2** How would the decision to dispose of a segment of operations using a split-off rather than a spin-off impact the financial statements of the company making the distribution?

LO 1-1 **Q1-3** Why did companies such as Enron find the use of special-purpose entities to be advantageous?

LO 1-4 **Q1-4** Describe each of the three legal forms that a business combination might take.

LO 1-1 **Q1-5** When does a noncontrolling interest arise in a business combination?

LO 1-5 **Q1-6** How is the amount reported as goodwill determined under the acquisition method?

LO 1-5 **Q1-7** What impact does the level of ownership have on the amount of goodwill reported under the acquisition method?

LO 1-5 **Q1-8** What is a differential?

LO 1-5 **Q1-9** When a business combination occurs after the beginning of the year, the income earned by the acquired company between the beginning of the year and the date of combination is excluded from the net income reported by the combined entity for the year. Why?

LO 1-5 **Q1-10** What is the maximum balance in retained earnings that can be reported by the combined entity immediately following a business combination?

LO 1-5 **Q1-11** How is the amount of additional paid-in capital determined when recording a business combination?

LO 1-5 **Q1-12** Which of the costs incurred in completing a business combination are capitalized under the acquisition method?

LO 1-5 **Q1-13** Which of the costs incurred in completing a business combination should be treated as a reduction of additional paid-in capital?

LO 1-5 **Q1-14** When is goodwill considered impaired following a business combination?

LO 1-5 **Q1-15** When does a bargain purchase occur?

LO 1-6 **Q1-16** Within the measurement period following a business combination, the acquisition-date fair value of buildings acquired is determined to be less than initially recorded. How is the reduction in value recognized?

LO 1-6 **Q1-17** P Company reports its 10,000 shares of S Company at $40 per share. P Company then purchases an additional 60,000 shares of S Company for $65 each and gains control of S Company. What must be done with respect to the valuation of the shares previously owned?

CASES

LO 1-2, 1-5 **C1-1** **Assignment of Acquisition Costs**

Research

Troy Company notified Kline Company's shareholders that it was interested in purchasing controlling ownership of Kline and offered to exchange one share of Troy's common stock for each share of Kline Company submitted by July 31, 20X7. At the time of the offer, Troy's shares were trading for $35 per share and Kline's shares were trading at $28. Troy acquired all of the shares of Kline prior to December 31, 20X7, and transferred Kline's assets and liabilities to its books. In addition to issuing its shares, Troy paid a finder's fee of $200,000, stock registration and audit fees of $60,000, legal fees of $90,000 for transferring Kline's assets and liabilities to Troy, and $370,000 in legal fees to settle litigation brought by Kline's shareholders who alleged that the offering price was below the per-share fair value of Kline's net assets.

Required

Troy Company's vice president of finance has asked you to review the current accounting literature, including authoritative pronouncements, and prepare a memo reporting the required treatment of the additional costs at the time Kline Company was acquired. Support your recommendations with citations and quotations from the authoritative financial reporting standards or other literature.

LO 1-1, 1-3 **C1-2** **Evaluation of Merger**

Research

One company may acquire another for a number of different reasons. The acquisition often has a significant impact on the financial statements. In 2005, 3M Corporation acquired CUNO Incorporated. Obtain a copy of the 3M 10-K filing for 2005. The 10-K reports the annual results for a company and is often available on the Investor Relations section of a company's website. It is also available on the SEC's website at www.sec.gov.

Required

Use the 10-K for 2005 to find the answers to the following questions about 3M's acquisition of CUNO Inc. (*Hint:* You can search for the term CUNO once you have accessed the 10-K online.)

a. Provide at least one reason why 3M acquired CUNO.

b. How was the acquisition funded?

c. What was the impact of the CUNO acquisition on net accounts receivable?

d. What was the impact of the CUNO acquisition on inventories?

LO 1-4 **C1-3** **Business Combinations**

Analysis

A merger boom comparable to those of the 1960s and mid-1980s occurred in the 1990s and into the new century. The merger activity of the 1960s was associated with increasing stock prices and heavy use of pooling-of-interests accounting. The mid-1980s activity was associated with a number of leveraged buyouts and acquisitions involving junk bonds. Merger activity in the early 1990s, on the other hand, appeared to involve primarily purchases with cash and standard debt instruments. By the mid-1990s, however, many business combinations were being effected through exchanges of stock. In the first decade of the new century, the nature of many business acquisitions changed, and by late 2008, the merger boom had slowed dramatically.

a. Which factors do you believe were the most prominent in encouraging business combinations in the 1990s? Which of these was the most important? Explain why.

b. Why were so many of the business combinations in the middle and late 1990s effected through exchanges of stock?

c. What factors had a heavy influence on mergers during the mid-2000s? How did many of the business combinations of this period differ from earlier combinations? Why did the merger boom slow so dramatically late in 2008 and in 2009?

d. If a major review of the tax laws were undertaken, would it be wise or unwise public policy to establish greater tax incentives for corporate mergers? Propose three incentives that might be used.

e. If the FASB were interested in encouraging more mergers, what action should it take with regard to revising or eliminating existing accounting standards? Explain.

LO 1-5

C1-4 Determination of Goodwill Impairment

Research

Plush Corporation purchased 100 percent of Common Corporation's common stock on January 1, 20X3, and paid $450,000. The fair value of Common's identifiable net assets at that date was $430,000. By the end of 20X5, the fair value of Common, which Plush considers to be a reporting unit, had increased to $485,000; however, Plush's external auditor made a passing comment to the company's chief accountant that Plush might need to recognize impairment of goodwill on one or more of its investments.

Required

Prepare a memo to Plush's chief accountant indicating the tests used in determining whether goodwill has been impaired. Include in your discussion one or more possible conditions under which Plush might be required to recognize impairment of goodwill on its investment in Common Corporation. In preparing your memo, review the current accounting literature, including authoritative pronouncements of the FASB and other appropriate bodies. Support your discussion with citations and quotations from the applicable literature.

LO 1-1

C1-5 Risks Associated with Acquisitions

Analysis

Not all business combinations are successful, and many entail substantial risk. Acquiring another company may involve a number of different types of risk. Obtain a copy of the 10-K report for Google Inc. for the year ended December 31, 2006, available at the SEC's website (www.sec.gov). The report also can be accessed through Yahoo! Finance or the company's Investor Relations page.

Required

On page 21 of the 10-K report, Google provides information to investors about its motivation for acquiring companies and the possible risks associated with such acquisitions. Briefly discuss the risks that Google sees inherent in potential acquisitions.

LO 1-1

C1-6 Numbers Game

Communication

Arthur Levitt's speech, "The Numbers Game," is available on the SEC's website at www.sec.gov/news/speech/speecharchive/1998/spch220.txt. Read the speech, and then answer the following questions.

Required

a. Briefly explain what motivations Levitt discusses for earnings management.

b. What specific techniques for earnings management does Levitt discuss?

c. According to Levitt, why is the issue of earnings management important?

LO 1-1, 1-4

C1-7 MCI: A Succession of Mergers

Research

MCI WorldCom Inc. (later MCI), was known as a high-flying company, having had its roots in a small local company and rising to one of the world's largest communications giants. The company's spectacular growth was accomplished through a string of business combinations. However, not all went as planned, and MCI is no longer an independent company.

Required

Provide a brief history of, and indicate subsequent events related to, MCI WorldCom. Include in your discussion the following:

a. Trace the major acquisitions leading to MCI WorldCom and indicate the type of consideration used in the acquisitions.

b. Who is Bernard Ebbers, and where is he now?

c. What happened to MCI WorldCom, and where is it now?

LO 1-4

Analysis

C1-8 Leveraged Buyouts

A type of acquisition that was not discussed in the chapter is the *leveraged buyout.* Many experts argue that a leveraged buyout (LBO) is not a type of business combination but rather just a restructuring of ownership. Yet some would see an LBO as having many of the characteristics of a business combination. The number of LBOs in recent years has grown dramatically and, therefore, accounting for these transactions is of increased importance.

Required

a. What is a leveraged buyout? How does an LBO compare with a management buyout (MBO)?
b. What authoritative pronouncements, if any, deal with leveraged buyouts?
c. Is a leveraged buyout a type of business combination? Explain.
d. What is the major issue in determining the proper basis for an interest in a company purchased through a leveraged buyout?

EXERCISES

LO 1-1, 1-3, 1-5

E1-1 Multiple-Choice Questions on Complex Organizations

Select the correct answer for each of the following questions.

1. Growth in the complexity of the U.S. business environment
   a. Has led to increased use of partnerships to avoid legal liability.
   b. Has led to increasingly complex organizational structures as management has attempted to achieve its business objectives.
   c. Has encouraged companies to reduce the number of operating divisions and product lines so they may better control those they retain.
   d. Has had no particular impact on the organizational structures or the way in which companies are managed.
2. Which of the following is *not* an appropriate reason for establishing a subsidiary?
   a. The parent wishes to protect existing operations by shifting new activities with greater risk to a newly created subsidiary.
   b. The parent wishes to avoid subjecting all of its operations to regulatory control by establishing a subsidiary that focuses its operations in regulated industries.
   c. The parent wishes to reduce its taxes by establishing a subsidiary that focuses its operations in areas where special tax benefits are available.
   d. The parent wishes to be able to increase its reported sales by transferring products to the subsidiary at the end of the fiscal year.
3. Which of the following actions is likely to result in recording goodwill on Randolph Company's books?
   a. Randolph acquires Penn Corporation in a business combination recorded as a merger.
   b. Randolph acquires a majority of Penn's common stock in a business combination and continues to operate it as a subsidiary.
   c. Randolph distributes ownership of a newly created subsidiary in a distribution considered to be a spin-off.
   d. Randolph distributes ownership of a newly created subsidiary in a distribution considered to be a split-off.
4. When an existing company creates a new subsidiary and transfers a portion of its assets and liabilities to the new entity
   a. The new entity records both the assets and liabilities it received at fair values.
   b. The new entity records both the assets and liabilities it received at the carrying values of the original company.
   c. The original company records a gain or loss on the difference between its carrying values and the fair values of the assets transferred to the new entity.
   d. The original company records the difference between the carrying values and the fair values of the assets transferred to the new entity as goodwill.

5. When a company assigns goodwill to a reporting unit acquired in a business combination, it must record an impairment loss if
   a. The fair value of the net identifiable assets held by a reporting unit decreases.
   b. The fair value of the reporting unit decreases.
   c. The carrying value of the reporting unit is less than the fair value of the reporting unit.
   d. The fair value of the reporting unit is less than its carrying value and the carrying value of goodwill is more than the implied value of its goodwill.

LO 1-2, 1-5

E1-2 Multiple-Choice Questions on Recording Business Combinations [AICPA Adapted]

Select the correct answer for each of the following questions.

1. Goodwill represents the excess of the sum of the fair value of the (1) consideration given, (2) shares already owned, and (3) the noncontrolling interest over the
   a. Sum of the fair values assigned to identifiable assets acquired less liabilities assumed.
   b. Sum of the fair values assigned to tangible assets acquired less liabilities assumed.
   c. Sum of the fair values assigned to intangible assets acquired less liabilities assumed.
   d. Book value of an acquired company.
2. In a business combination, costs of registering equity securities to be issued by the acquiring company are a(n)
   a. Expense of the combined company for the period in which the costs were incurred.
   b. Direct addition to stockholders' equity of the combined company.
   c. Reduction of the recorded value of the securities.
   d. Addition to goodwill.
3. Which of the following is the appropriate basis for valuing fixed assets acquired in a business combination carried out by exchanging cash for common stock?
   a. Historical cost.
   b. Book value.
   c. Cost plus any excess of purchase price over book value of assets acquired.
   d. Fair value.
4. In a business combination in which an acquiring company purchases 100 percent of the outstanding common stock of another company, if the fair value of the net identifiable assets acquired exceeds the fair value of the consideration given. The excess should be reported as a
   a. Deferred credit.
   b. Reduction of the values assigned to current assets and a deferred credit for any unallocated portion.
   c. Pro rata reduction of the values assigned to current and noncurrent assets and a deferred credit for any unallocated portion.
   d. No answer listed is correct.
5. A and B Companies have been operating separately for five years. Each company has a minimal amount of liabilities and a simple capital structure consisting solely of voting common stock. In exchange for 40 percent of its voting stock A Company, acquires 80 percent of the common stock of B Company. This is a "tax-free" stock-for-stock exchange for tax purposes. B Company's identifiable assets have a total net fair market value of $800,000 and a total net book value of $580,000. The fair market value of the A stock used in the exchange is $700,000, and the fair value of the noncontrolling interest is $175,000. The goodwill reported following the acquisition would be
   a. Zero.
   b. $60,000.
   c. $75,000.
   d. $295,000.

LO 1-2, 1-5

E1-3 Multiple-Choice Questions on Reported Balances [AICPA Adapted]

Select the correct answer for each of the following questions.

1. On December 31, 20X3, Saxe Corporation was merged into Poe Corporation. In the business combination, Poe issued 200,000 shares of its $10 par common stock, with a market price of

$18 a share, for all of Saxe's common stock. The stockholders' equity section of each company's balance sheet immediately before the combination was:

	Poe	Saxe
Common Stock	$3,000,000	$1,500,000
Additional Paid-In Capital	1,300,000	150,000
Retained Earnings	2,500,000	850,000
	$6,800,000	$2,500,000

In the December 31, 20X3, combined balance sheet, additional paid-in capital should be reported at

a. $950,000.
b. $1,300,000.
c. $1,450,000.
d. $2,900,000.

2. On January 1, 20X1, Rolan Corporation issued 10,000 shares of common stock in exchange for all of Sandin Corporation's outstanding stock. Condensed balance sheets of Rolan and Sandin immediately before the combination follow:

	Rolan	Sandin
Total Assets	$1,000,000	$500,000
Liabilities	$ 300,000	$150,000
Common Stock ($10 par)	200,000	100,000
Retained Earnings	500,000	250,000
Total Liabilities & Equities	$1,000,000	$500,000

Rolan's common stock had a market price of $60 per share on January 1, 20X1. The market price of Sandin's stock was not readily determinable. The fair value of Sandin's net identifiable assets was determined to be $570,000. Rolan's investment in Sandin's stock will be stated in Rolan's balance sheet immediately after the combination in the amount of

a. $350,000.
b. $500,000.
c. $570,000.
d. $600,000.

3. On April 1, 20X2, Jack Company paid $800,000 for all of Ann Corporation's issued and outstanding common stock. Ann's recorded assets and liabilities on April 1, 20X2, were as follows:

Cash	$ 80,000
Inventory	240,000
Property & Equipment (net of accumulated depreciation of $320,000)	480,000
Liabilities	(180,000)

On April 1, 20X2, Ann's inventory was determined to have a fair value of $190,000, and the property and equipment had a fair value of $560,000. What is the amount of goodwill resulting from the business combination?

a. $0.
b. $50,000.
c. $150,000.
d. $180,000.

4. Action Corporation issued nonvoting preferred stock with a fair market value of $4,000,000 in exchange for all the outstanding common stock of Master Corporation. On the date of the exchange, Master had tangible net assets with a book value of $2,000,000 and a fair value of $2,500,000. In addition, Action issued preferred stock valued at $400,000 to an individual as a finder's fee in arranging the transaction. As a result of this transaction, Action should record an increase in net assets of
   a. $2,000,000.
   b. $2,500,000.
   c. $4,000,000.
   d. $4,400,000.

LO 1-2, 1-5

E1-4 Multiple-Choice Questions Involving Account Balances

Select the correct answer for each of the following questions.

1. Topper Company established a subsidiary and transferred equipment with a fair value of $72,000 to the subsidiary. Topper had purchased the equipment with ten-year expected life of four years earlier for $100,000 and has used straight-line depreciation with no expected residual value. At the time of the transfer, the subsidiary should record
   a. Equipment at $72,000 and no accumulated depreciation.
   b. Equipment at $60,000 and no accumulated depreciation.
   c. Equipment at $100,000 and accumulated depreciation of $40,000.
   d. Equipment at $120,000 and accumulated depreciation of $48,000.
2. Lead Corporation established a new subsidiary and transferred to it assets with a cost of $90,000 and a book value of $75,000. The assets had a fair value of $100,000 at the time of transfer. The transfer will result in
   a. A reduction of net assets reported by Lead Corporation of $90,000.
   b. A reduction of net assets reported by Lead Corporation of $75,000.
   c. No change in the reported net assets of Lead Corporation.
   d. An increase in the net assets reported by Lead Corporation of $25,000.
3. Tear Company, a newly established subsidiary of Stern Corporation, received assets with an original cost of $260,000, a fair value of $200,000, and a book value of $140,000 from the parent in exchange for 7,000 shares of Tear's $8 par value common stock. Tear should record
   a. Additional paid-in capital of $0.
   b. Additional paid-in capital of $84,000.
   c. Additional paid-in capital of $144,000.
   d. Additional paid-in capital of $204,000.
4. Grout Company reports assets with a carrying value of $420,000 (including goodwill with a carrying value of $35,000) assigned to an identifiable reporting unit purchased at the end of the prior year. The fair value of the net assets held by the reporting unit is currently $350,000, and the fair value of the reporting unit is $395,000. At the end of the current period, Grout should report goodwill of
   a. $45,000.
   b. $35,000.
   c. $25,000.
   d. $10,000.
5. Twill Company has a reporting unit with the fair value of its net identifiable assets of $500,000. The carrying value of the reporting unit's net assets on Twill's books is $575,000, which includes $90,000 of goodwill. The fair value of the reporting unit is $560,000. Twill should report impairment of goodwill of
   a. $60,000.
   b. $30,000.
   c. $15,000.
   d. $0.

LO 1-3

E1-5 Asset Transfer to Subsidiary

Pale Company was established on January 1, 20X1. Along with other assets, it immediately purchased land for $80,000, a building for $240,000, and equipment for $90,000. On January 1, 20X5, Pale transferred these assets, cash of $21,000, and inventory costing $37,000 to a newly created subsidiary, Bright Company, in exchange for 10,000 shares of Bright's $6 par value stock. Pale uses straight-line depreciation and useful lives of 40 years and 10 years for the building and equipment, respectively, with no estimated residual values.

Required

a. Give the journal entry that Pale recorded when it transferred the assets to Bright.

b. Give the journal entry that Bright recorded for the receipt of assets and issuance of common stock to Pale.

LO 1-3

E1-6 Creation of New Subsidiary

Lester Company transferred the following assets to a newly created subsidiary, Mumby Corporation, in exchange for 40,000 shares of its $3 par value stock:

	Cost	Book Value
Cash	$ 40,000	$ 40,000
Accounts Receivable	75,000	68,000
Inventory	50,000	50,000
Land	35,000	35,000
Buildings	160,000	125,000
Equipment	240,000	180,000

Required

a. Give the journal entry in which Lester recorded the transfer of assets to Mumby Corporation.

b. Give the journal entry in which Mumby recorded the receipt of assets and issuance of common stock to Lester.

LO 1-2, 1-3

E1-7 Balance Sheet Totals of Parent Company

Foster Corporation established Kline Company as a wholly owned subsidiary. Foster reported the following balance sheet amounts immediately before and after it transferred assets and accounts payable to Kline Company in exchange for 4,000 shares of $12 par value common stock:

	Amount Reported			
	Before Transfer		After Transfer	
Cash		$ 40,000		$ 25,000
Accounts Receivable		65,000		41,000
Inventory		30,000		21,000
Investment in Kline Company				66,000
Land		15,000		12,000
Depreciable Assets	$180,000		$115,000	
Accumulated Depreciation	75,000	105,000	47,000	68,000
Total Assets		$255,000		$233,000
Accounts Payable		$ 40,000		$ 18,000
Bonds Payable		80,000		80,000
Common Stock		60,000		60,000
Retained Earnings		75,000		75,000
Total Liabilities & Equities		$255,000		$233,000

Required

a. Give the journal entry that Foster recorded when it transferred its assets and accounts payable to Kline.

b. Give the journal entry that Kline recorded upon receipt of the assets and accounts payable from Foster.

LO 1-2, 1-5

E1-8 Acquisition of Net Assets

Sun Corporation concluded the fair value of Tender Company was $60,000 and paid that amount to acquire its net assets. Tender reported assets with a book value of $55,000 and fair value of $71,000 and liabilities with a book value and fair value of $20,000 on the date of combination. Sun also paid $4,000 to a search firm for finder's fees related to the acquisition.

Required

Give the journal entries to be made by Sun to record its investment in Tender and its payment of the finder's fees.

LO 1-5

E1-9 Reporting Goodwill

Samper Company reported the book value of its net assets at $160,000 when Public Corporation acquired 100 percent of its voting stock for cash. The fair value of Samper's net assets was determined to be $190,000 on that date.

Required

Determine the amount of goodwill to be reported in consolidated financial statements presented immediately following the combination and the amount at which Public will record its investment in Samper if the amount paid by Public is

a. $310,000.

b. $196,000.

c. $150,000.

LO 1-5

E1-10 Stock Acquisition

McDermott Corporation has been in the midst of a major expansion program. Much of its growth had been internal, but in 20X1 McDermott decided to continue its expansion through the acquisition of other companies. The first company acquired was Tippy Inc., a small manufacturer of inertial guidance systems for aircraft and missiles. On June 10, 20X1, McDermott issued 17,000 shares of its $25 par common stock for all 40,000 of Tippy's $10 par common shares. At the date of combination, Tippy reported additional paid-in capital of $100,000 and retained earnings of $350,000. McDermott's stock was selling for $58 per share immediately prior to the combination. Subsequent to the combination, Tippy operated as a subsidiary of McDermott.

Required

Present the journal entry or entries that McDermott would make to record the business combination with Tippy.

LO 1-5

E1-11 Balances Reported Following Combination

Elm Corporation and Maple Company have announced terms of an exchange agreement under which Elm will issue 8,000 shares of its $10 par value common stock to acquire all of Maple Company's assets. Elm shares currently are trading at $50, and Maple $5 par value shares are trading at $18 each. Historical cost and fair value balance sheet data on January 1, 20X2, are as follows:

	Elm Corporation		Maple Company	
Balance Sheet Item	**Book Value**	**Fair Value**	**Book Value**	**Fair Value**
Cash & Receivables	$150,000	$150,000	$ 40,000	$ 40,000
Land	100,000	170,000	50,000	85,000
Buildings & Equipment (net)	300,000	400,000	160,000	230,000
Total Assets	$550,000	$720,000	$250,000	$355,000
Common Stock	$200,000		$100,000	
Additional Paid-In Capital	20,000		10,000	
Retained Earnings	330,000		140,000	
Total Equities	$550,000		$250,000	

Required

What amount will be reported immediately following the business combination for each of the following items in the combined company's balance sheet?

a. Common Stock.

b. Cash and Receivables.

c. Land.
d. Buildings and Equipment (net).
e. Goodwill.
f. Additional Paid-In Capital.
g. Retained Earnings.

LO 1-5

E1-12 Goodwill Recognition

Spur Corporation reported the following balance sheet amounts on December 31, 20X1:

Balance Sheet Item	Historical Cost	Fair Value
Cash & Receivables	$ 50,000	$ 40,000
Inventory	100,000	150,000
Land	40,000	30,000
Plant & Equipment	400,000	350,000
Less: Accumulated Depreciation	(150,000)	
Patent		130,000
Total Assets	$440,000	$700,000
Accounts Payable	$ 80,000	$ 85,000
Common Stock	200,000	
Additional Paid-In Capital	20,000	
Retained Earnings	140,000	
Total Liabilities & Equities	$440,000	

Required

Blanket acquired Spur Corporation's assets and liabilities for $670,000 cash on December 31, 20X1. Give the entry that Blanket made to record the purchase.

LO 1-5

E1-13 Acquisition Using Debentures

Fortune Corporation used debentures with a par value of $625,000 to acquire 100 percent of Sorden Company's net assets on January 1, 20X2. On that date, the fair value of the bonds issued by Fortune was $608,000. The following balance sheet data were reported by Sorden:

Balance Sheet Item	Historical Cost	Fair Value
Cash & Receivables	$ 55,000	$ 50,000
Inventory	105,000	200,000
Land	60,000	100,000
Plant & Equipment	400,000	300,000
Less: Accumulated Depreciation	(150,000)	
Goodwill	10,000	
Total Assets	$480,000	$650,000
Accounts Payable	$ 50,000	$ 50,000
Common Stock	100,000	
Additional Paid-In Capital	60,000	
Retained Earnings	270,000	
Total Liabilities & Equities	$480,000	

Required

Give the journal entry that Fortune recorded at the time of exchange.

LO 1-5

E1-14 Bargain Purchase

Using the data presented in E1-13, determine the amount Fortune Corporation would record as a gain on bargain purchase and prepare the journal entry Fortune would record at the time of the exchange if Fortune issued bonds with a par value of $580,000 and a fair value of $564,000 in completing the acquisition of Sorden.

LO 1-5

E1-15 Impairment of Goodwill

Mesa Corporation purchased Kwick Company's net assets and assigned goodwill of $80,000 to Reporting Division K. The following assets and liabilities are assigned to Reporting Division K:

	Carrying Amount	Fair Value
Cash	$ 14,000	$ 14,000
Inventory	56,000	71,000
Equipment	170,000	190,000
Goodwill	80,000	
Accounts Payable	30,000	30,000

Required

Determine the amount of goodwill to be reported for Division K and the amount of goodwill impairment to be recognized, if any, if Division K's fair value is determined to be

a. $340,000.
b. $280,000.
c. $260,000.

LO 1-5

E1-16 Assignment of Goodwill

Double Corporation acquired all of the common stock of Simple Company for $450,000 on January 1, 20X4. On that date, Simple's identifiable net assets had a fair value of $390,000. The assets acquired in the purchase of Simple are considered to be a separate reporting unit of Double. The carrying value of Double's investment at December 31, 20X4, is $500,000.

Required

Determine the amount of goodwill impairment, if any, that should be recognized at December 31, 20X4, if the fair value of the net assets (excluding goodwill) at that date is $440,000 and the fair value of the reporting unit is determined to be

a. $530,000.
b. $485,000.
c. $450,000.

LO 1-5

Advanced StudyGuide .com

E1-17 Goodwill Assigned to Reporting Units

Groft Company purchased Strobe Company's net assets and assigned them to four separate reporting units. Total goodwill of $186,000 is assigned to the reporting units as indicated:

	Reporting Unit			
	A	B	C	D
Carrying value of investment	$700,000	$330,000	$380,000	$520,000
Goodwill included in carrying value	60,000	48,000	28,000	50,000
Fair value of net identifiable assets at year-end	600,000	300,000	400,000	500,000
Fair value of reporting unit at year-end	690,000	335,000	370,000	585,000

Required

Determine the amount of goodwill that Groft should report at year-end. Show how you computed it.

LO 1-5

E1-18 Goodwill Measurement

Washer Company has a reporting unit resulting from an earlier business combination. The reporting unit's current assets and liabilities are

	Carrying Amount	Fair Value
Cash	$ 30,000	$ 30,000
Inventory	70,000	100,000
Land	30,000	60,000
Buildings	210,000	230,000
Equipment	160,000	170,000
Goodwill	150,000	
Notes Payable	100,000	100,000

Required

Determine the amount of goodwill to be reported and the amount of goodwill impairment, if any, if the fair value of the reporting unit is determined to be

a. $580,000.
b. $540,000.
c. $500,000.
d. $460,000.

LO 1-5

E1-19 Computation of Fair Value

Grant Company acquired all of Bedford Corporation's assets and liabilities on January 1, 20X2, in a business combination. At that date, Bedford reported assets with a book value of $624,000 and liabilities of $356,000. Grant noted that Bedford had $40,000 of capitalized research and development costs on its books at the acquisition date that did not appear to be of value. Grant also determined that patents developed by Bedford had a fair value of $120,000 but had not been recorded by Bedford. Except for buildings and equipment, Grant determined the fair value of all other assets and liabilities reported by Bedford approximated the recorded amounts. In recording the transfer of assets and liabilities to its books, Grant recorded goodwill of $93,000. Grant paid $517,000 to acquire Bedford's assets and liabilities. If the book value of Bedford's buildings and equipment was $341,000 at the date of acquisition, what was their fair value?

LO 1-5

Advanced StudyGuide .com

E1-20 Computation of Shares Issued and Goodwill

Dunyain Company acquired Allsap Corporation on January 1, 20X1, through an exchange of common shares. All of Allsap's assets and liabilities were immediately transferred to Dunyain, which reported total par value of shares outstanding of $218,400 and $327,600 and additional paid-in capital of $370,000 and $650,800 immediately before and after the business combination, respectively.

Required

a. Assuming that Dunyain's common stock had a market value of $25 per share at the time of exchange, what number of shares was issued?
b. What is the par value per share of Dunyain's common stock?
c. Assuming that Allsap's identifiable assets had a fair value of $476,000 and its liabilities had a fair value of $120,000, what amount of goodwill did Dunyain record at the time of the business combination?

LO 1-5

E1-21 Combined Balance Sheet

The following balance sheets were prepared for Adam Corporation and Best Company on January 1, 20X2, just before they entered into a business combination:

	Adam Corporation		Best Company	
Item	**Book Value**	**Fair Value**	**Book Value**	**Fair Value**
Cash & Receivables	$150,000	$150,000	$ 90,000	$ 90,000
Inventory	300,000	380,000	70,000	160,000
Buildings & Equipment	600,000	430,000	250,000	240,000
Less: Accumulated Depreciation	(250,000)		(80,000)	
Total Assets	$800,000	$960,000	$330,000	$490,000
Accounts Payable	$ 75,000	$ 75,000	$ 50,000	$ 50,000
Notes Payable	200,000	215,000	30,000	35,000
Common Stock:				
$8 par value	180,000			
$6 par value			90,000	
Additional Paid-In Capital	140,000		55,000	
Retained Earnings	205,000		105,000	
Total Liabilities & Equities	$800,000		$330,000	

Adam acquired all of Best Company's assets and liabilities on January 1, 20X2, in exchange for its common shares. Adam issued 8,000 shares of stock to complete the business combination.

Required

Prepare a balance sheet of the combined company immediately following the acquisition, assuming Adam's shares were trading at $60 each.

LO 1-5

E1-22 Recording a Business Combination

The following financial statement information was prepared for Blue Corporation and Sparse Company at December 31, 20X2:

Balance Sheets
December 31, 20X2

	Blue Corporation		Sparse Company	
Cash		$ 140,000		$ 70,000
Accounts Receivable		170,000		110,000
Inventory		250,000		180,000
Land		80,000		100,000
Buildings & Equipment	$ 680,000		$ 450,000	
Less: Accumulated Depreciation	(320,000)	360,000	(230,000)	220,000
Goodwill		70,000		20,000
Total Assets		$1,070,000		$700,000
Accounts Payable		$ 70,000		$195,000
Bonds Payable		320,000		100,000
Bond Premium				10,000
Common Stock		120,000		150,000
Additional Paid-In Capital		170,000		60,000
Retained Earnings		390,000		185,000
Total Liabilities & Equities		$1,070,000		$700,000

Blue and Sparse agreed to combine as of January 1, 20X3. To effect the merger, Blue paid finder's fees of $30,000 and legal fees of $24,000. Blue also paid $15,000 of audit fees related to the issuance of stock, stock registration fees of $8,000, and stock listing application fees of $6,000.

At January 1, 20X3, book values of Sparse Company's assets and liabilities approximated market value except for inventory with a market value of $200,000, buildings and equipment with a market value of $350,000, and bonds payable with a market value of $105,000. All assets and liabilities were immediately recorded on Blue's books.

Required

Give all journal entries that Blue recorded assuming Blue issued 40,000 shares of $8 par value common stock to acquire all of Sparse's assets and liabilities in a business combination. Blue common stock was trading at $14 per share on January 1, 20X3.

LO 1-5

E1-23 Reporting Income

On July 1, 20X2, Alan Enterprises merged with Cherry Corporation through an exchange of stock and the subsequent liquidation of Cherry. Alan issued 200,000 shares of its stock to effect the combination. The book values of Cherry's assets and liabilities were equal to their fair values at the date of combination, and the value of the shares exchanged was equal to Cherry's book value. Information relating to income for the companies is as follows:

	20X1	Jan. 1–June 30, 20X2	July 1–Dec. 31, 20X2
Net Income:			
Alan Enterprises	$4,460,000	$2,500,000	$3,528,000
Cherry Corporation	1,300,000	692,000	—

Alan Enterprises had 1,000,000 shares of stock outstanding prior to the combination. Remember that when calculating earnings per share (EPS) for the year of the combination, the shares issued in the combination were not outstanding for the entire year.

Required

Compute the net income and earnings-per-share amounts that would be reported in Alan's 20X2 comparative income statements for both 20X2 and 20X1.

PROBLEMS

LO 1-3

P1-24 Assets and Accounts Payable Transferred to Subsidiary

Tab Corporation decided to establish Collon Company as a wholly owned subsidiary by transferring some of its existing assets and liabilities to the new entity. In exchange, Collon issued Tab 30,000 shares of $6 par value common stock. The following information is provided on the assets and accounts payable transferred:

	Cost	Book Value	Fair Value
Cash	$ 25,000	$ 25,000	$ 25,000
Inventory	70,000	70,000	70,000
Land	60,000	60,000	90,000
Buildings	170,000	130,000	240,000
Equipment	90,000	80,000	105,000
Accounts Payable	45,000	45,000	45,000

Required

a. Give the journal entry that Tab recorded for the transfer of assets and accounts payable to Collon.

b. Give the journal entry that Collon recorded for the receipt of assets and accounts payable from Tab.

LO 1-3

P1-25 Creation of New Subsidiary

Eagle Corporation established a subsidiary to enter into a new line of business considered to be substantially more risky than Eagle's current business. Eagle transferred the following assets and accounts payable to Sand Corporation in exchange for 5,000 shares of $10 par value stock of Sand:

	Cost	Book Value
Cash	$ 30,000	$ 30,000
Accounts Receivable	45,000	40,000
Inventory	60,000	60,000
Land	20,000	20,000
Buildings & Equipment	300,000	260,000
Accounts Payable	10,000	10,000

Required

a. Give the journal entry that Eagle recorded for the transfer of assets and accounts payable to Sand.

b. Give the journal entry that Sand recorded for receipt of the assets and accounts payable from Eagle.

LO 1-3

P1-26 Incomplete Data on Creation of Subsidiary

Thumb Company created New Company as a wholly owned subsidiary by transferring assets and accounts payable to New in exchange for its common stock. New recorded the following entry when it received the assets and accounts payable:

Cash	3,000	
Accounts Receivable	16,000	
Inventory	27,000	
Land	9,000	
Buildings	70,000	
Equipment	60,000	
Accounts Payable		14,000
Accumulated Depreciation—Buildings		21,000
Accumulated Depreciation—Equipment		12,000
Common Stock		40,000
Additional Paid-In Capital		98,000

Required

a. What was Thumb's book value of the total assets (not net assets) transferred to New Company?

b. What amount did Thumb report as its investment in New after the transfer?

c. What number of shares of $5 par value stock did New issue to Thumb?

d. What impact did the transfer of assets and accounts payable have on the amount reported by Thumb as total assets?

e. What impact did the transfer of assets and accounts payable have on the amount that Thumb and the consolidated entity reported as shares outstanding?

LO 1-5

P1-27 Acquisition in Multiple Steps

Deal Corporation issued 4,000 shares of its $10 par value stock with a market value of $85,000 to acquire 85 percent ownership of Mead Company on August 31, 20X3. Mead's fair value was determined to be $100,000 on that date. Deal had earlier purchased 15 percent of Mead's shares for $9,000 and used the cost method in accounting for its investment in Mead. Deal also paid appraisal fees of $3,500 and stock issue costs of $2,000 incurred in completing the acquisition of the additional shares.

Required

Give the journal entries to be recorded by Deal in completing the acquisition of the additional shares of Mead.

LO 1-5

P1-28 Journal Entries to Record a Business Combination

On January 1, 20X2, Frost Company acquired all of TKK Corporation's assets and liabilities by issuing 24,000 shares of its $4 par value common stock. At that date, Frost shares were selling at

Advanced StudyGuide .com

$22 per share. Historical cost and fair value balance sheet data for TKK at the time of acquisition were as follows:

Balance Sheet Item	Historical Cost	Fair Value
Cash & Receivables	$ 28,000	$ 28,000
Inventory	94,000	122,000
Buildings & Equipment	600,000	470,000
Less: Accumulated Depreciation	(240,000)	
Total Assets	$ 482,000	$620,000
Accounts Payable	$ 41,000	$ 41,000
Notes Payable	65,000	63,000
Common Stock ($10 par value)	160,000	
Retained Earnings	216,000	
Total Liabilities & Equities	$ 482,000	

Frost paid legal fees for the transfer of assets and liabilities of $14,000. Frost also paid audit fees of $21,000 and listing application fees of $7,000, both related to the issuance of new shares.

Required

Prepare the journal entries made by Frost to record the business combination.

LO 1-5

P1-29 Recording Business Combinations

Flint Corporation exchanged shares of its $2 par common stock for all of Mark Company's assets and liabilities in a planned merger. Immediately prior to the combination, Mark's assets and liabilities were as follows:

Assets	
Cash & Equivalents	$ 41,000
Accounts Receivable	73,000
Inventory	144,000
Land	200,000
Buildings	1,520,000
Equipment	638,000
Accumulated Depreciation	(431,000)
Total Assets	$2,185,000

Liabilities & Equities	
Accounts Payable	$ 35,000
Short-Term Notes Payable	50,000
Bonds Payable	500,000
Common Stock ($10 par)	1,000,000
Additional Paid-In Capital	325,000
Retained Earnings	275,000
Total Liabilities & Equities	$2,185,000

Immediately prior to the combination, Flint reported $250,000 additional paid-in capital and $1,350,000 retained earnings. The fair values of Mark's assets and liabilities were equal to their book values on the date of combination except that Mark's buildings were worth $1,500,000 and its equipment was worth $300,000. Costs associated with planning and completing the business combination totaled $38,000, and stock issue costs totaled $22,000. The market value of Flint's stock at the date of combination was $4 per share.

Required

Prepare the journal entries that would appear on Flint's books to record the combination if Flint issued 450,000 shares.

LO 1-5

Advanced StudyGuide .com

P1-30 Business Combination with Goodwill

Anchor Corporation paid cash of $178,000 to acquire Zink Company's net assets on February 1, 20X3. The balance sheet data for the two companies and fair value information for Zink immediately before the business combination were:

	Anchor Corporation	Zink Company	
Balance Sheet Item	**Book Value**	**Book Value**	**Fair Value**
Cash	$ 240,000	$ 20,000	$ 20,000
Accounts Receivable	140,000	35,000	35,000
Inventory	170,000	30,000	50,000
Patents	80,000	40,000	60,000
Buildings & Equipment	380,000	310,000	150,000
Less: Accumulated Depreciation	(190,000)	(200,000)	
Total Assets	$ 820,000	$ 235,000	$315,000
Accounts Payable	$ 85,000	$ 55,000	$ 55,000
Notes Payable	150,000	120,000	120,000
Common Stock:			
$10 par value	200,000		
$6 par value		18,000	
Additional Paid-In Capital	160,000	10,000	
Retained Earnings	225,000	32,000	
Total Liabilities & Equities	$ 820,000	$ 235,000	

Required

a. Give the journal entry recorded by Anchor Corporation when it acquired Zink's net assets.

b. Prepare a balance sheet for Anchor immediately following the acquisition.

c. Give the journal entry to be recorded by Anchor if it acquires all of Zink's common stock (instead of Zink's net assets) for $178,000.

LO 1-5

Advanced StudyGuide .com

P1-31 Bargain Purchase

Bower Company purchased Lark Corporation's net assets on January 3, 20X2, for $625,000 cash. In addition, Bower incurred $5,000 of direct costs in consummating the combination. At the time of acquisition, Lark reported the following historical cost and current market data:

Balance Sheet Item	Book Value	Fair Value
Cash & Receivables	$ 50,000	$ 50,000
Inventory	100,000	150,000
Buildings & Equipment (net)	200,000	300,000
Patent	—	200,000
Total Assets	$350,000	$700,000
Accounts Payable	$ 30,000	$ 30,000
Common Stock	100,000	
Additional Paid-In Capital	80,000	
Retained Earnings	140,000	
Total Liabilities & Equities	$350,000	

Required

Give the journal entry or entries with which Bower recorded its acquisition of Lark's net assets.

LO 1-5

P1-32 Computation of Account Balances

Aspro Division is considered to be an individual reporting unit of Tabor Company. Tabor acquired the division by issuing 100,000 shares of its common stock with a market price of $7.60 each. Tabor management was able to identify assets with fair values of $810,000 and liabilities of

$190,000 at the date of acquisition. At the end of the first year, the reporting unit had assets with a fair value of $950,000, and the fair value of the reporting entity was $930,000. Tabor's accountants concluded it must recognize impairment of goodwill in the amount of $30,000 at the end of the first year.

Required

a. Determine the fair value of the reporting unit's liabilities at the end of the first year. Show your computation.

b. If the reporting unit's liabilities at the end of the period had been $70,000, what would the fair value of the reporting unit have to have been to avoid recognizing an impairment of goodwill? Show your computation.

LO 1-5

P1-33 Goodwill Assigned to Multiple Reporting Units

The fair values of assets and liabilities held by three reporting units and other information related to the reporting units owned by Rover Company are as follows:

	Reporting Unit		
	A	B	C
Cash & Receivables	$ 30,000	$ 80,000	$ 20,000
Inventory	60,000	100,000	40,000
Land	20,000	30,000	10,000
Buildings	100,000	150,000	80,000
Equipment	140,000	90,000	50,000
Accounts Payable	40,000	60,000	10,000
Fair Value of Reporting Unit	400,000	440,000	265,000
Carrying Value of Investment	420,000	500,000	290,000
Goodwill Included in Carrying Value	70,000	80,000	40,000

Required

a. Determine the amount of goodwill that Rover should report in its current financial statements.

b. Determine the amount, if any, that Rover should report as impairment of goodwill for the current period.

LO 1-5

P1-34 Journal Entries

On January 1, 20X3, PURE Products Corporation issued 12,000 shares of its $10 par value stock to acquire the net assets of Light Steel Company. Underlying book value and fair value information for the balance sheet items of Light Steel at the time of acquisition follow:

Balance Sheet Item	Book Value	Fair Value
Cash	$ 60,000	$ 60,000
Accounts Receivable	100,000	100,000
Inventory (LIFO basis)	60,000	115,000
Land	50,000	70,000
Buildings & Equipment	400,000	350,000
Less: Accumulated Depreciation	(150,000)	—
Total Assets	$520,000	$695,000
Accounts Payable	$ 10,000	$ 10,000
Bonds Payable	200,000	180,000
Common Stock ($5 par value)	150,000	
Additional Paid-In Capital	70,000	
Retained Earnings	90,000	
Total Liabilities & Equities	$520,000	

Light Steel shares were selling at $18 and PURE Products shares were selling at $50 just before the merger announcement. Additional cash payments made by PURE Products in completing the acquisition were

Finder's fee paid to firm that located Light Steel	$10,000
Audit fee for stock issued by PURE Products	3,000
Stock registration fee for new shares of PURE Products	5,000
Legal fees paid to assist in transfer of net assets	9,000
Cost of SEC registration of PURE Products shares	1,000

Required

Prepare all journal entries to record the business combination on PURE Products' books.

LO 1-5

P1-35 Purchase at More than Book Value

Ramrod Manufacturing acquired all the assets and liabilities of Stafford Industries on January 1, 20X2, in exchange for 4,000 shares of Ramrod's $20 par value common stock. Balance sheet data for both companies just before the merger are given as follows:

	Ramrod Manufacturing		Stafford Industries	
Balance Sheet Items	**Book Value**	**Fair Value**	**Book Value**	**Fair Value**
Cash	$ 70,000	$ 70,000	$ 30,000	$ 30,000
Accounts Receivable	100,000	100,000	60,000	60,000
Inventory	200,000	375,000	100,000	160,000
Land	50,000	80,000	40,000	30,000
Buildings & Equipment	600,000 }	540,000	400,000 }	350,000
Less: Accumulated Depreciation	(250,000) }		(150,000) }	
Total Assets	$ 770,000	$1,165,000	$ 480,000	$630,000
Accounts Payable	$ 50,000	$ 50,000	$ 10,000	$ 10,000
Bonds Payable	300,000	310,000	150,000	145,000
Common Stock:				
$20 par value	200,000			
$5 par value			100,000	
Additional Paid-In Capital	40,000		20,000	
Retained Earnings	180,000		200,000	
Total Liabilities & Equities	$ 770,000		$ 480,000	

Ramrod shares were selling for $150 on the date of acquisition.

Required

Prepare the following:

a. Journal entries to record the acquisition on Ramrod's books.

b. A balance sheet for the combined enterprise immediately following the business combination.

LO 1-5

P1-36 Business Combination

Following are the balance sheets of Boogie Musical Corporation and Toot-Toot Tuba Company as of December 31, 20X5.

BOOGIE MUSICAL CORPORATION
Balance Sheet
December 31, 20X5

Assets		**Liabilities & Equities**	
Cash	$ 23,000	Accounts Payable	$ 48,000
Accounts Receivable	85,000	Notes Payable	65,000
Allowance for Uncollectible Accounts	(1,200)	Mortgage Payable	200,000

(continued)

Inventory	192,000	Bonds Payable	200,000
Plant & Equipment	980,000	Capital Stock ($10 par)	500,000
Accumulated Depreciation	(160,000)	Premium on Capital Stock	1,000
Other Assets	14,000	Retained Earnings	118,800
Total Assets	$1,132,800	Total Liabilities & Equities	$1,132,800

TOOT-TOOT TUBA COMPANY
Balance Sheet
December 31, 20X5

Assets		**Liabilities & Equities**	
Cash	$ 300	Accounts Payable	$ 8,200
Accounts Receivable	17,000	Notes Payable	10,000
Allowance for Uncollectible Accounts	(600)	Mortgage Payable	50,000
Inventory	78,500	Bonds Payable	100,000
Plant & Equipment	451,000	Capital Stock ($50 par)	100,000
Accumulated Depreciation	(225,000)	Premium on Capital Stock	150,000
Other Assets	25,800	Retained Earnings	(71,200)
Total Assets	$347,000	Total Liabilities & Equities	$347,000

In preparation for a possible business combination, a team of experts from Boogie Musical made a thorough examination and audit of Toot-Toot Tuba. They found that Toot-Toot's assets and liabilities were correctly stated except that they estimated uncollectible accounts at $1,400. The experts also estimated the market value of the inventory at $35,000 and the market value of the plant and equipment at $500,000. The business combination took place on January 1, 20X6, and on that date Boogie Musical acquired all the assets and liabilities of Toot-Toot Tuba. On that date, Boogie's common stock was selling for $55 per share.

Required

Record the combination on Boogie's books assuming that Boogie issued 9,000 of its $10 par common shares in exchange for Toot-Toot's assets and liabilities.

LO 1-5

P1-37 Combined Balance Sheet

Bilge Pumpworks and Seaworthy Rope Company agreed to merge on January 1, 20X3. On the date of the merger agreement, the companies reported the following data:

	Bilge Pumpworks		Seaworthy Rope Company	
Balance Sheet Items	**Book Value**	**Fair Value**	**Book Value**	**Fair Value**
Cash & Receivables	$ 90,000	$ 90,000	$ 20,000	$ 20,000
Inventory	100,000	150,000	30,000	42,000
Land	100,000	140,000	10,000	15,000
Plant & Equipment	400,000	300,000	200,000	140,000
Less: Accumulated Depreciation	(150,000)		(80,000)	
Total Assets	$ 540,000	$680,000	$180,000	$217,000
Current Liabilities	$ 80,000	$ 80,000	$ 20,000	$ 20,000
Capital Stock	200,000		20,000	
Capital in Excess of Par Value	20,000		5,000	
Retained Earnings	240,000		135,000	
Total Liabilities & Equities	$ 540,000		$180,000	

Bilge Pumpworks has 10,000 shares of its $20 par value shares outstanding on January 1, 20X3, and Seaworthy has 4,000 shares of $5 par value stock outstanding. The market values of the shares are $300 and $50, respectively.

Required

a. Bilge issues 700 shares of stock in exchange for all of Seaworthy's net assets. Prepare a balance sheet for the combined entity immediately following the merger.

b. Prepare the stockholders' equity section of the combined company's balance sheet, assuming Bilge acquires all of Seaworthy's net assets by issuing

1. 1,100 shares of common.
2. 1,800 shares of common.
3. 3,000 shares of common.

LO 1-5

P1-38 Incomplete Data

On January 1, 20X2, End Corporation acquired all of Cork Corporation's assets and liabilities by issuing shares of its common stock. Partial balance sheet data for the companies prior to the business combination and immediately following the combination are as follows:

	End Corp. Book Value	Cork Corp. Book Value	Combined Entity
Cash	$ 40,000	$ 10,000	$ 50,000
Accounts Receivable	60,000	30,000	88,000
Inventory	50,000	35,000	96,000
Buildings & Equipment (net)	300,000	110,000	430,000
Goodwill			?
Total Assets	$450,000	$185,000	$?
Accounts Payable	$ 32,000	$ 14,000	$ 46,000
Bonds Payable	150,000	70,000	220,000
Bond Premium	6,000		6,000
Common Stock, $5 par	100,000	40,000	126,000
Additional Paid-In Capital	65,000	28,000	247,000
Retained Earnings	97,000	33,000	?
Total Liabilities & Equities	$450,000	$185,000	$?

Required

a. What number of shares did End issue to acquire Cork's assets and liabilities?

b. What was the total market value of the shares issued by End?

c. What was the fair value of the inventory held by Cork at the date of combination?

d. What was the fair value of the identifiable net assets held by Cork at the date of combination?

e. What amount of goodwill, if any, will be reported by the combined entity immediately following the combination?

f. What balance in retained earnings will the combined entity report immediately following the combination?

g. If the depreciable assets held by Cork had an average remaining life of 10 years at the date of acquisition, what amount of depreciation expense will be reported on those assets in 20X2?

LO 1-5

Advanced StudyGuide .com

P1-39 Incomplete Data Following Purchase

On January 1, 20X1, Alpha Corporation acquired all of Bravo Company's assets and liabilities by issuing shares of its $3 par value stock to the owners of Bravo Company in a business combination. Alpha also made a cash payment to Banker Corporation for stock issue costs. Partial balance sheet data for Alpha and Bravo, before the cash payment and issuance of shares, and a combined balance sheet following the business combination are as follows:

	Alpha Corporation	Bravo Company		
	Book Value	Book Value	Fair Value	Combined Entity
Cash	$ 65,000	$ 15,000	$ 15,000	$ 56,000
Accounts Receivable	105,000	30,000	30,000	135,000
Inventory	210,000	90,000	?	320,000
Buildings & Equipment (net)	400,000	210,000	293,000	693,000
Goodwill				?
Total Assets	$780,000	$345,000	$448,000	$?
Accounts Payable	$ 56,000	$ 22,000	$ 22,000	$ 78,000
Bonds Payable	200,000	120,000	120,000	320,000
Common Stock	96,000	70,000		117,000
Additional Paid-In Capital	234,000	42,000		553,000
Retained Earnings	194,000	91,000		?
Total Liabilities & Equities	$780,000	$345,000		$?

Required

a. What number of its $5 par value shares did Bravo have outstanding at January 1, 20X1?

b. Assuming that all of Bravo's shares were issued when the company was started, what was the price per share received at the time of issue?

c. How many shares of Alpha were issued at the date of combination?

d. What amount of cash did Alpha pay as stock issue costs?

e. What was the total market value of Alpha's shares issued at the date of combination?

f. What was the fair value of Bravo's inventory at the date of combination?

g. What was the fair value of Bravo's net assets at the date of combination?

h. What amount of goodwill, if any, will be reported in the combined balance sheet following the combination?

LO 1-5

P1-40 Comprehensive Business Combination

Bigtime Industries Inc. entered into a business combination agreement with Hydrolized Chemical Corporation (HCC) to ensure an uninterrupted supply of key raw materials and to realize certain economies from combining the operating processes and the marketing efforts of the two companies. Under the terms of the agreement, Bigtime issued 180,000 shares of its $1 par common stock in exchange for all of HCC's assets and liabilities. The Bigtime shares then were distributed to HCC's shareholders, and HCC was liquidated.

Immediately prior to the combination, HCC's balance sheet appeared as follows, with fair values also indicated:

	Book Values	Fair Values
Assets		
Cash	$ 28,000	$ 28,000
Accounts Receivable	258,000	251,500
Less: Allowance for Bad Debts	(6,500)	
Inventory	381,000	395,000
Long-Term Investments	150,000	175,000
Land	55,000	100,000
Rolling Stock	130,000	63,000
Plant & Equipment	2,425,000	2,500,000
Less: Accumulated Depreciation	(614,000)	
Patents	125,000	500,000
Special Licenses	95,800	100,000
Total Assets	$3,027,300	$4,112,500

(continued)

	Book Values	Fair Values
Liabilities		
Current Payables	$ 137,200	$ 137,200
Mortgages Payable	500,000	520,000
Equipment Trust Notes	100,000	95,000
Debentures Payable	1,000,000	950,000
Less: Discount on Debentures	(40,000)	
Total Liabilities	$1,697,200	$1,702,200
Stockholders' Equity		
Common Stock ($5 par)	600,000	
Additional Paid-In Capital from Common Stock	500,000	
Additional Paid-In Capital from Retirement of Preferred Stock	22,000	
Retained Earnings	220,100	
Less: Treasury Stock (1,500 shares)	(12,000)	
Total Liabilities & Equity	$3,027,300	

Immediately prior to the combination, Bigtime's common stock was selling for $14 per share. Bigtime incurred direct costs of $135,000 in arranging the business combination and $42,000 of costs associated with registering and issuing the common stock used in the combination.

Required

a. Prepare all journal entries that Bigtime should have entered on its books to record the business combination.

b. Present all journal entries that should have been entered on HCC's books to record the combination and the distribution of the stock received.

2 Reporting Intercorporate Investments and Consolidation of Wholly Owned Subsidiaries with No Differential

Multicorporate Entities

- Business Combinations
- **Consolidation Concepts and Procedures**
- Intercompany Transfers
- Additional Consolidation Issues
- Multinational Entities
- Reporting Requirements
- Partnerships
- Governmental and Not-for-Profit Entities
- Corporations in Financial Difficulty

BERKSHIRE HATHAWAY'S MANY INVESTMENTS

As of this writing (February 2014), Warren Buffett is the fourth-richest man in the world, worth a staggering $58.5 billion. He is also the chairman, CEO, and primary shareholder of Berkshire Hathaway Inc. Over the past 48 years, Berkshire has grown at an average rate of 19.7 percent annually. Warren Buffett has achieved this success through his unparalleled business sense regarding investments and acquisitions of other companies.

Berkshire Hathaway was originally a textile manufacturing company. In 1962, Warren Buffett and his partners began buying large blocks of Berkshire stock. Within five years, Buffett began expanding into the insurance industry, and in 1985 the last of Berkshire's textile operations was shut down. In the late 1970s, Berkshire began acquiring stock in GEICO insurance and in January 1996 bought GEICO outright. While Berkshire has extensive insurance holdings, it has not focused its investment activities solely on insurance. Since Buffett took the helm in the 1960s, Berkshire has made many acquisitions. Look at the list of selected Berkshire holdings as of the end of 2013 (on the next page). Do you recognize any of these companies?

Each item in Berkshire's portfolio has to be accounted for individually. For example, Comdisco Holdings and Graham Holdings Company are accounted for as equity method investments, while Walmart and American Express are classified as available-for-sale investments. Berkshire consolidates the fully owned companies such as Wesco Financial and See's Candies. In addition, companies like GEICO have many subsidiaries of their own. As you can imagine, accounting for investments at Berkshire can be very complex. This chapter focuses on issues related to the accounting for investments.

BERKSHIRE HATHAWAY INC.

BERKSHIRE HATHAWAY SELECTED HOLDINGS (AS OF 12/31/2013)

Examples of fully owned subsidiaries:

Benjamin Moore & Co.
Dairy Queen
GEICO
Fruit of the Loom
H.J. Heinz Company
See's Candies
The Pampered Chef Ltd.

15 largest partially owned companies:	% Owned	Market Value
DIRECTV	4.2	$ 1,536
American Express Company	14.2	13,756
Exxon Mobil Corp.	0.9	4,162
International Business Machines Corporation	6.3	12,778
Moody's Corporation	11.5	1,936
Munich Re Group	11.2	4,415
Phillips 66	3.4	1,594
Sanofi	1.7	2,354
Tesco PLC	3.7	1,666
The Coca-Cola Company	9.1	16,524
The Goldman Sachs Group Inc.	2.8	2,315
Procter & Gamble Co.	1.9	4,272
U.S. Bancorp	5.3	3,883
Wal-Mart Stores Inc.	1.8	4,470
Wells Fargo & Company	9.2	21,950

LEARNING OBJECTIVES

When you finish studying this chapter, you should be able to:

LO 2-1 Understand and explain how ownership and control can influence the accounting for investments in common stock.

LO 2-2 Prepare journal entries using the cost method of accounting for investments.

LO 2-3 Prepare journal entries using the equity method of accounting for investments.

LO 2-4 Understand and explain differences between the cost and equity methods.

LO 2-5 Prepare journal entries using the fair value option.

LO 2-6 Make calculations and prepare basic consolidation entries for a simple consolidation.

LO 2-7 Prepare a consolidation worksheet.

ACCOUNTING FOR INVESTMENTS IN COMMON STOCK

LO 2-1

Understand and explain how ownership and control can influence the accounting for investments in common stock.

Companies acquire ownership interests in other companies for a variety of reasons. For example, some companies invest in other companies simply to earn a favorable return by taking advantage of the future earnings potential of their investees. Other reasons for acquiring interests in other entities include (1) gaining voting control, (2) entering new product markets by purchasing companies already established in those areas, (3) ensuring a supply of raw materials or other production inputs, (4) ensuring a customer for production output, (5) gaining economies associated with greater size, (6) diversifying operations, (7) obtaining new technology, (8) lessening competition, and (9) limiting risk.

The method used to account for investments in common stock depends, in part, on the level of influence or control that the investor is able to exercise over the investee. The investment will normally be reported on the investor's balance sheet using the cost method (adjusted to market value, if appropriate), the equity method, or the fair value option. Note that, while use of the cost or equity method is dictated by the level of influence, the investor can elect the fair value option in place of either method. However, if the investor company acquires more than 50 percent of the investee's voting shares, it is required to consolidate the investee company, in which case, the investment account would not appear on the consolidated balance sheet. Essentially, consolidation replaces the investment account with all of the detail on the subsidiary's balance sheet. Figure 2–1 summarizes how the reporting of intercorporate investments in common stock changes with the investor's level of ownership and influence.

The ***cost method*** is used for reporting investments in equity securities when both consolidation and equity-method reporting are inappropriate. If cost-method equity securities have readily determinable fair values, they must be adjusted to market value at year-end under **ASC 320-10-30-2.**[1] Under the cost method, the investor recognizes income from the investment when the income is distributed by the investee as dividends.

The ***equity method*** is required for external reporting when the investor exercises ***significant influence*** over the operating and financial policies of the investee and consolidation is not appropriate. This method is used most often when one company holds 20 percent or more of another company's common stock. Under the equity method, the investor recognizes income from the investment as the investee earns the income. Instead of combining the individual assets, liabilities, revenues, and expenses of the investee with those of the investor, as in consolidation, the investment is reported as one line in the investor's balance sheet, and income recognized from the investee is reported as one line in the investor's income statement. The investment represents the investor's share of the investee's net assets, and the income recognized is the investor's share of the investee's net income.

For financial reporting, consolidated financial statements that include both the investor and the investee must be presented if the investor can exercise ***control*** over the investee. ***Consolidation*** involves combining for financial reporting the individual assets, liabilities, revenues, and expenses of two or more related companies as if they were part of a single company. This process includes the elimination of all intercompany ownership and activities. Consolidation normally is appropriate when one company, referred to as the ***parent,*** controls another company, referred to as a ***subsidiary.*** We discuss the specific requirements for consolidation later in this chapter. A subsidiary that is not consolidated with the parent is referred to as an ***unconsolidated subsidiary*** and is shown as an

FIGURE 2–1
Financial Reporting Basis by Level of Common Stock Ownership

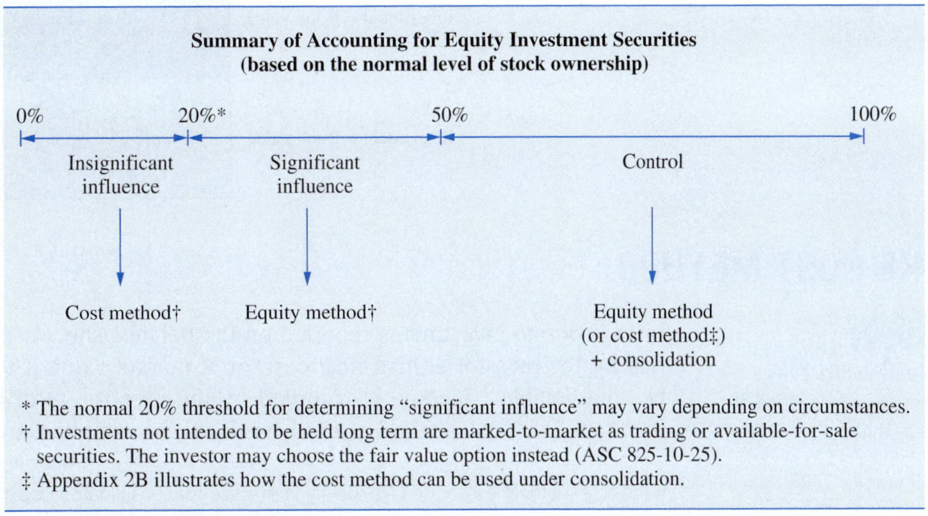

[1] Because the provisions of **ASC 320-10-30-2** are normally discussed in Intermediate Accounting, detailed coverage is not provided here. Note, however, that equity investments accounted for using the cost method are accounted for as discussed in this chapter, with the provisions of **ASC 320-10-30-2** applied as end-of-period adjustments. **ASC 320-10-30-2** is not applicable to equity-method investments.

investment on the parent's balance sheet. Under current accounting standards, most subsidiaries are consolidated. When intercorporate investments are consolidated for financial reporting, the investment and related income accounts are eliminated in preparing the consolidated financial statements. Nevertheless, the parent must still account for the investments on its books. Parent companies have the choice of accounting for investments in consolidated subsidiaries on their books using the cost or equity method.[2]

Under the fair value option **(ASC 825-10-25),** companies have the choice of using traditional methods, such as the cost and equity methods, to report financial assets and liabilities of unconsolidated subsidiaries, or they can elect to report some or all of their financial assets and liabilities at fair value. Under the fair value option, intercorporate investments in common stock are remeasured to fair value at the end of each period, and the unrealized gain or loss is recognized in income. The fair value option does not apply to intercorporate investments that must be consolidated.

This chapter follows Figure 2–1 in summarizing the accounting for investments in other companies. It first discusses the cost and equity methods of accounting for investments. It then summarizes the fair value option. Finally, it introduces the preparation of consolidated financial statements using the most simple consolidation scenario (when a subsidiary is wholly owned and it is either created or purchased for an amount exactly equal to the book value of the subsidiary's net assets). Since consolidation is a major topic of this textbook, we use a building block approach to our coverage of consolidation in Chapters 2 through 5. Chapter 3 explains how the basic consolidation process changes when the parent company owns less than 100 percent of the subsidiary. Chapter 4 shows how the consolidation process differs when the parent company acquires 100 percent of a subsidiary for an amount greater (or less) than the book value of the subsidiary's net assets. Finally, Chapter 5 presents the most complex consolidation scenario (where the parent owns less than 100 percent of the subsidiary's outstanding voting stock and the acquisition price is not equal to the book value of the subsidiary's net assets). Chapters 6 through 10 delve into asset transfers among members of the same consolidated group of companies and additional details related to consolidation.

Summary of Consolidation Coverage in Chapters 2–5

	Wholly Owned Subsidiary	Partially Owned Subsidiary
Investment = Book value	Chapter 2	Chapter 3
Investment > Book value	Chapter 4	Chapter 5

THE COST METHOD

LO 2-2

Prepare journal entries using the cost method of accounting for investments.

Intercorporate investments reported on the balance sheet using the cost method are carried by the investor at historical cost, or at market value if the security is considered to be "marketable." Income is recorded by the investor as dividends are declared by the investee. The cost method is used when the investor lacks the ability either to control

[2] The cost method is also used frequently in practice for consolidated investments since (as explained later in this chapter) the investment account is eliminated in the consolidated financial statements. While both the cost and the equity methods are acceptable in accounting for a consolidated subsidiary, we advocate the use of the equity method because it ensures that the parent company's books accurately reflect everything on the subsidiary's books. Conceptually, the use of the equity method is a useful way to understand the notion of consolidating a controlled subsidiary because the investment account is simply replaced by the detail on the subsidiary's balance sheet.

or to exercise significant influence over the investee. The inability of an investor to exercise either control or significant influence over an investee may result from the size of the investment, usually at common stock ownership levels of less than 20 percent. In some situations, other factors, such as the existence of a majority shareholder, prevent the investor from exercising significant influence regardless of the size of the investment. (See Appendix 2A for a discussion of additional factors that may influence the use of the cost or equity methods.)

Accounting Procedures under the Cost Method

The cost method is consistent with the treatment normally accorded noncurrent assets. At the time of purchase, the investor records its investment in common stock at the total cost incurred in making the purchase. Subsequently, the carrying amount of the investment remains unchanged under the cost method; the investment continues to be carried at its original cost until it is sold. Income from the investment is recognized by the investor as dividends are declared by the investee. Once the investee declares a dividend, the investor has a legal claim against the investee for a proportionate share of the dividend, and realization of the income is considered certain enough to be recognized. Recognition of investment income before a dividend declaration is considered inappropriate because the investee's income is not available to the owners until a dividend is declared.

To illustrate the cost method, assume that ABC Company purchases 20 percent of XYZ Company's common stock for $100,000 at the beginning of the year but does not gain significant influence over XYZ. During the year, XYZ has net income of $60,000 and declares dividends of $20,000. Assuming the dividend is paid later, ABC Company records the following entries relating to its investment in XYZ:

(1)	Investment in XYZ Company Stock	100,000	
	Cash		100,000
	Record purchase of XYZ Company stock.		
(2)	Dividends Receivable	4,000	
	Dividend Income		4,000
	Record dividend declared by XYZ Company ($20,000 × 0.20).		

Note that ABC records only its share of XYZ's distributed earnings and makes no entry for the undistributed portion. The carrying amount of the investment is still the original cost of $100,000.

Declaration of Dividends in Excess of Earnings since Acquisition

A special treatment is required under the cost method in situations in which an investor holds common stock in a company that declares dividends in excess of the cumulative income it has earned since the investor acquired its stock. The dividends received are viewed first as representing earnings of the investee from the purchase date of the investment to the dividend declaration date. All dividends declared by the investee in excess of its earnings since acquisition by the investor are viewed by the investor as ***liquidating dividends.*** The investor's share of these liquidating dividends is treated as a return of capital, and the investment account balance is reduced by that amount. Blocks of an investee's stock acquired at different times should be treated separately for purposes of computing liquidating dividends.

Liquidating Dividends Example

To illustrate the computation of liquidating dividends received by the investor, assume that Investor Company purchases 10 percent of the common stock of Investee Company on January 2, 20X1. The annual income and dividends of Investee, the amount of dividend income recognized by Investor each year under the cost method, and the reduction of the carrying amount of Investor's investment in Investee when appropriate are as follows:

	Investee Company			Investor Company		
Year	**Net Income**	**Dividends**	**Cumulative Undistributed Income**	**Cash Received**	**Dividend Income**	**Reduction of Investment**
20X1	$100,000	$ 70,000	$30,000	$ 7,000	$ 7,000	
20X2	100,000	120,000	10,000	12,000	12,000	
20X3	100,000	120,000	0	12,000	11,000	$1,000
20X4	100,000	120,000	0	12,000	10,000	2,000
20X5	100,000	70,000	30,000	7,000	7,000	

Investor Company records its 10 percent share of Investee's dividend as income in 20X1 because the income of Investee exceeds its dividend. In 20X2, Investee's dividend exceeds earnings for the year, but the cumulative dividends declared since January 2, 20X1, the date Investor acquired Investee's stock, do not exceed Investee's earnings since that date. Hence, Investor again records its 10 percent share of the dividend as income. By the end of 20X3, dividends declared by Investee since January 2, 20X1, total $310,000 while Investee's income since that date totals only $300,000. Thus, from Investor's point of view, $10,000 of the 20X3 dividend represents a return of capital while the remaining $110,000 represents a distribution of earnings. Investor's share of each amount is 10 percent. The entry to record the 20X3 dividend on Investor's books is:

(3)			
	Cash	12,000	
	Investment in Investee		1,000
	Dividend Income		11,000

Record receipt of 20X3 dividend from Investee.
$12,000 = $120,000 × 0.10.
$1,000 = ($310,000 − $300,000) + 0.10.
$11,000 = ($120,000 − $10,000) + 0.10.

Once the investor has recorded a liquidating dividend, the comparison in future periods between cumulative earnings and dividends of the investee should be based on the date of the last liquidating dividend rather than the date the investor acquired the investee's stock. In this example, Investor Company records liquidating dividends in 20X3 and 20X4. In years after 20X4, Investor compares earnings and dividends of Investee from the date of the most recent liquidating dividend in 20X4 rather than comparing from January 2, 20X1. Investor considers the entire dividend paid in 20X5 to be a distribution of earnings.

Acquisition at Interim Date

The acquisition of an investment at a date other than the beginning or end of a fiscal period generally does not create any major problems when the cost method is used to account for the investment. The only potential difficulty involves determining whether some part of the payment received by the investor is a liquidating dividend when the investee declares a dividend soon after the investor purchases stock in the investee. In this situation, the investor must estimate the amount of the investee's earnings for the portion of the period during which the investor held the investee's stock and may record dividend income only on that portion.

Changes in the Number of Shares Held

Changes in the number of investment shares resulting from stock dividends, stock splits, or reverse splits receive no formal recognition in the accounts of the investor. The carrying value of the investment before the stock dividend or split becomes the carrying amount of the new, higher or lower number of shares. Purchases and sales of shares, of course, do require journal entries but do not result in any unusual difficulties under the cost method.

Purchases of Additional Shares

The purchase of additional shares of a company already held is recorded at cost in the same way as an initial purchase of shares. The investor's new percentage ownership of the investee then is calculated, and other evidence, if available, is evaluated to determine whether the total investment still should be carried at cost or if the investor should switch to the equity method. When the additional shares give the investor the ability to exercise significant influence over the investee, the equity method should be applied retroactively from the date of the original investment, as illustrated later in this chapter.

Sales of Shares

If a company sells all or part of an intercorporate investment in stock, the transaction is accounted for in the same manner as the sale of any other noncurrent asset. A gain or loss on the sale is recognized for the difference between the proceeds received and the carrying amount of the investment sold.

If shares of the stock have been purchased at more than one price, a determination must be made at the time of sale as to which of the shares have been sold. The specific shares sold may be identified through segregation, numbered stock certificates, or other means. When specific identification is impractical, either a FIFO or weighted-average cost flow assumption may be used. However, the weighted-average method seldom is used in practice because it is not acceptable for tax purposes.

THE EQUITY METHOD

LO 2-3

Prepare journal entries using the equity method of accounting for investments.

The equity method of accounting for intercorporate investments in common stock is intended to reflect the investor's changing equity or interest in the investee. This method is a rather curious one in that the balance in the investment account generally does not reflect either cost or market value, and it does not necessarily represent a pro rata share of the investee's book value. Instead, the investment is recorded at the initial purchase price and adjusted each period for the investor's share of the investee's profits or losses and the dividends declared by the investee.

Use of the Equity Method

ASC 323-10-30 requires that the equity method be used for reporting investments in common stock of the following:

1. Corporate joint ventures. A ***corporate joint venture*** is a corporation owned and operated by a small group of businesses, none of which owns a majority of the joint venture's common stock.
2. Companies in which the investor's voting stock interest gives the investor the "ability to exercise significant influence over operating and financial policies" of that company.

The second condition is the broader of the two and establishes the "significant influence" criterion. Because assessing the degree of influence may be difficult in some cases, **ASC 323-10-15** establishes a 20 percent rule. In the absence of evidence to the contrary, an investor holding 20 percent or more of an investee's voting stock is presumed to have the ability to exercise significant influence over the investee. On the other hand, an investor holding less than 20 percent of an investee's voting stock is presumed not to have the ability to exercise significant influence in the absence of evidence to the contrary.

In most cases, an investment of 20 percent or more in another company's voting stock is reported under the equity method. Notice, however, that the 20 percent rule does not apply if other evidence is available that provides a better indication of the ability or inability of the investor to significantly influence the investee.

Regardless of the level of ownership, the equity method is not appropriate if the investor's influence is limited by circumstances other than stock ownership, such as the existence of a majority shareholder (i.e., two owners with a 25/75 split) or severe restrictions placed on the availability of a foreign investee's earnings or assets by a foreign government.

Investor's Equity in the Investee

Under the equity method, the investor records its investment at the original cost. This amount is adjusted periodically for changes in the investee's stockholders' equity occasioned by the investee's profits, losses, and dividend declarations. The effect of the investee's income, losses, and dividends on the investor's investment account and other accounts can be summarized as follows:

Reported by Investee	Effect on Investor's Accounts
Net income	Record income from investment Increase investment account
Net loss	Record loss from investment Decrease investment account
Dividend declaration	Record asset (cash or receivable) Decrease investment account

Recognition of Income

Under the equity method, the investor's income statement includes the investor's proportionate share of the investee's income or loss each period. The carrying amount of the investment is adjusted by the same amount to reflect the change in the net assets of the investee resulting from the investee's income.

To illustrate, assume that ABC Company acquires significant influence over XYZ Company by purchasing 20 percent of XYZ's common stock for $100,000 at the beginning of the year.

(4)			
	Investment in XYZ Company Stock	100,000	
	Cash		100,000

Record purchase of XYZ Company stock.

XYZ reports income of $60,000 for the year. ABC records its 20 percent share of XYZ's income ($12,000) in an account called "Income from XYZ Company" as follows:

(5)			
	Investment in XYZ Company Stock	12,000	
	Income from XYZ Company		12,000

Record income from XYZ Company ($60,000 × 0.20).

This entry may be referred to as the ***equity accrual*** and normally is made as an adjusting entry at the end of the period. If the investee reports a loss for the period, the investor recognizes its share of the loss and reduces the carrying amount of the investment by that amount.

Because of the ability to exercise significant influence over the policies of the investee, realization of income from the investment is considered to be sufficiently ensured to warrant recognition by the investor as the investee earns the income. This differs from the case in which the investor does not have the ability to significantly influence the investee and the investment must be reported using the cost method; in that case, income from the investment is recognized only upon declaration of a dividend by the investee.

Recognition of Dividends

Dividends from an investment are not recognized as income under the equity method because the investor's share of the investee's income is recognized as the investee earns it. Instead, the investee's dividends are viewed as distributions of previously recognized income that already has been capitalized in the carrying amount of the investment. The investor must consider investee dividends declared as a reduction in its equity in the investee and, accordingly, reduce the carrying amount of its investment. In effect, all dividends from the investee are treated as liquidating dividends under the equity method. Thus, if ABC Company owns 20 percent of XYZ Company's common stock and XYZ declares a $20,000 dividend, the following entry is recorded on ABC's books to record its share of the dividend:

(6)		Debit	Credit
	Dividends Receivable	4,000	
	Investment in XYZ Company Stock		4,000
	Record dividend from XYZ Company ($20,000 × 0.20).		

The following T-accounts summarize all of the normal equity-method entries (journal entries 4–6) on the investor's books:

	Investment in XYZ Company (Dr)	Investment in XYZ Company (Cr)		Income from XYZ Company (Dr)	Income from XYZ Company (Cr)	
Purchase	100,000					
20% of NI	12,000				12,000	20% of NI
		4,000	20% of Dividend			
Ending Balance	108,000				12,000	Ending Balance

While the Investment in XYZ Company account summarizes ABC's ownership of the net assets of XYZ Company, the Income from XYZ account summarizes ABC's share of XYZ Company's income. The Investment in XYZ Company account appears on ABC's balance sheet and the Income from XYZ Company account appears in ABC's income statement.

Differences in the Carrying Amount of the Investment and Investment Income under the Cost and Equity Methods

Because the investment account on the investor's books under the equity method is adjusted for the investor's share of the investee's income or losses and dividends, the carrying amount of the investment usually is not the same as the original cost to the investor. Only if the investee pays dividends in the exact amount of its earnings will the carrying amount of the investment subsequent to acquisition be equal to its original cost.

To compare the change in the carrying amount of the investment under the equity method relative to the cost method, assume the same facts listed previously for ABC's 20 percent acquisition of XYZ's common stock. The carrying amount of the investment using the equity method at the end of the period is $108,000 ($100,000 + $12,000 − $4,000), compared to the original acquisition price of $100,000 under the cost method.

Investment income under the equity method (the balance in the Income from XYZ account) is $12,000 while investment income under the cost method is equal to dividend income, $4,000.

Acquisition at Interim Date

When a company purchases an investment, the investor begins accruing income from the investee under the equity method at the date of acquisition. The investor may not accrue income earned by the investee before the acquisition date of the investment. When the purchase occurs between balance sheet dates, the amount of income earned by the investee from the date of acquisition to the end of the fiscal period may need to be estimated by the investor in recording the equity accrual. However, since "significant influence" is a requirement for using the equity method, it is likely that the investor will be able to simply ask for the actual post purchase financial results from the investee.

To illustrate, assume that ABC acquires 20 percent of XYZ's common stock on October 1 for $100,000. XYZ earns income of $60,000 uniformly throughout the year and declares dividends of $20,000 on December 20 (paid on December 31). The carrying amount of the investment is increased by $3,000, which represents ABC's share of XYZ's net income earned between October 1 and December 31 (1/4 of the year), and is decreased by $4,000 as a result of dividends declared at year-end (resulting in a net *decrease* of $1,000 since the time of the stock purchase).[3]

	Investment in XYZ Company		
Stock Purchase	100,000		
20% × NI × 1/4	3,000		
		4,000	20% Dividends
Ending Balance	99,000		

Investment in XYZ Company		
	3,000	20% × NI × 1/4

Changes in the Number of Shares Held

Some changes in the number of common shares held by an investor are handled easily under the equity method, but others require a bit more attention. A change resulting from a stock dividend, split, or reverse split is treated in the same way as under the cost method. No formal accounting recognition is required on the books of the investor. On the other hand, purchases and sales of shares do require formal recognition.

> **FYI**
>
> Figure 2–1 indicates that once a company owns more than 50% of the outstanding voting stock of an investee company, the parent company can account for the investment using the cost method on its own books because the investment account is eliminated in the consolidation process. Berkshire Hathaway's 2010 Form 10-K indicates: "As a result of our acquisition of the remaining outstanding stock of BNSF on February 12, 2010, we discontinued the use of the equity method and since that date, BNSF's accounts have been consolidated in our financial statements."

Purchases of Additional Shares

A purchase of additional shares of a common stock already held by an investor and accounted for using the equity method simply involves adding the cost of the new shares to the investment account and applying the equity method in the normal manner from the date of acquisition forward. The new and old investments in the same stock are combined for financial reporting purposes. Income accruing to the new shares can be recognized by the investor only from the date of acquisition forward.

To illustrate, assume that ABC Company purchases 20 percent of XYZ Company's common stock on January 2, 20X1, for $100,000, and another 10 percent on July 1, 20X1, for $51,500, and that the stock purchases represent 20 percent and 10 percent, respectively, of the book value of XYZ's net assets. If XYZ earns income of $25,000 from January 2 to June 30 and earns $35,000 from July 1 to December 31, the total income recognized in 20X1 by ABC from its investment in XYZ is $15,500, computed as follows:

[3] Note that we assume the entire dividend ($20,000) was declared and paid at the end of the year. If dividends had been declared and paid quarterly, we would record dividends declared only after ABC's acquisition of the XYZ shares.

Income, January 2 to June 30: $25,000 × 0.20	$ 5,000
Income, July 1 to December 31: $35,000 × 0.30	10,500
Investment Income, 20X1	$15,500

If XYZ declares and pays a $10,000 dividend on January 15 and again on July 15, ABC reduces its investment account by $2,000 ($10,000 × 0.20) on January 15 and by $3,000 ($10,000 × 0.30) on July 15. Thus, the ending balance in the investment account at the end of the year is $160,500, computed as follows:

	Investment in XYZ Company				Income from XYZ Company		
1/2/X1 Purchase	100,000						
20% NI to 6/30	5,000	2,000	20% Div. to 6/30			5,000	20% NI to 6/30
7/1/X1 Purchase	51,500						
30% NI from 7/1	10,500	3,000	30% Div. from 7/1			10,500	30% NI from 7/1
Ending Balance	162,000					15,500	Ending Balance

When an investment in common stock is carried using the cost method and purchases of additional shares give the investor the ability to significantly influence the investee, a retroactive switch from the cost method to the equity method is required. This change to the equity method must be applied retroactively to the date of the first acquisition of the investee's stock.

To illustrate a change to the equity method, assume that Aron Corporation purchases 15 percent of Zenon Company's common stock on January 2, 20X1, and another 10 percent on January 2, 20X4. Furthermore, assume that Aron switches to the equity method on January 2, 20X4, because it gains the ability to significantly influence Zenon. Given the following income and dividend data for Zenon, and assuming that the purchases of stock are at book value, the investment income figures reported by Aron originally and as restated are as follows:

	Zenon		Aron's Reported Investment Income	
Year	**Net Income**	**Dividends**	**Originally under Cost[a]**	**Restated under Equity[b]**
20X1	$15,000	$10,000	$1,500	$2,250
20X2	18,000	10,000	1,500	2,700
20X3	22,000	10,000	1,500	3,300
	$55,000	$30,000	$4,500	$8,250

[a]15 percent of Zenon's dividends for the year.
[b]15 percent of Zenon's net income for the year.

Thus, in Aron's 20X4 financial report, the comparative statements for 20X1, 20X2, and 20X3 are restated to include Aron's 15 percent share of Zenon's profit and to exclude from income Aron's share of dividends recognized under the cost method. In addition, Aron's investment account and retained earnings are restated as if the equity method had been applied from the date of the original acquisition. This restatement is accomplished on Aron's books with the following journal entry on January 2, 20X4:

(7)	Investment in Zenon Company Stock	3,750	
	Retained Earnings		3,750

Restate investment account from cost to equity method:
$8,250 − $4,500.

In 20X4, if Zenon reports net income of $30,000, Aron's investment income is $7,500 (25 percent of Zenon's net income).

FYI

The summary of Berkshire Hathaway's holdings at the beginning of the chapter lists its stake in Moody's at 12.8%. Its holdings had previously exceeded 20%. However, Berkshire's 2009 10-K indicates: "As a result of a reduction in our ownership of Moody's in July of 2009, we discontinued the use of the equity method as of the beginning of the third quarter of 2009."

Sales of Shares

The sale of all or part of an investment in common stock carried using the equity method is treated the same as the sale of any noncurrent asset. First, the investment account is adjusted to the date of sale for the investor's share of the investee's current earnings. Then a gain or loss is recognized for the difference between the proceeds received and the carrying amount of the shares sold.

If only part of the investment is sold, the investor must decide whether to continue using the equity method to account for the remaining shares or to change to the cost method. The choice is based on evidence available after the sale as to whether the investor still is able to exercise significant influence over the investee. If the equity method no longer is appropriate after the date of sale, the carrying value of the remaining investment is treated as the cost of that investment, and the cost method is applied in the normal manner from the date of sale forward. No retroactive restatement of the investment to actual cost is made.

COMPARISON OF THE COST AND EQUITY METHODS[4]

LO 2-4

Understand and explain differences between the cost and equity methods.

Advanced StudyGuide .com

Figure 2–2 summarizes some of the key features of the cost and equity methods of accounting for intercorporate investments. The cost method is consistent with the historical cost basis for most other assets. This method is subject to the usual criticisms leveled against historical cost. In particular, questions arise as to the relevance of reporting the purchase price of an investment acquired some years earlier. The cost method conforms more closely to the traditional accounting and legal views of the realization of income in that the investee's earnings are not available to the investor until transferred as dividends. However, income based on dividend distributions can sometimes be manipulated. The significant influence criterion required for the equity method considers that the declaration of dividends by the investee can be influenced by the investor. Recognizing

FIGURE 2–2
Summary Comparison of the Cost and Equity Methods

Item	Cost Method	Equity Method
Recorded amount of investment at date of acquisition	Original cost	Original cost
Usual carrying amount of investment subsequent to acquisition	Original cost	Original cost increased (decreased) by investor's share of investee's income (loss) and decreased by investor's share of investee's dividends
Income recognition by investor	Investor's share of investee's dividends declared from earnings since acquisition	Investor's share of investee's earnings since acquisition, whether distributed or not
Investee dividends from earnings since acquisition by investor	Income	Reduction of investment
Investee dividends in excess of earnings since acquisition by investor	Reduction of investment	Reduction of investment

[4] To view a video explanation of this topic, visit advancedstudyguide.com.

equity-method income from the investee without regard to investee dividends provides protection against manipulating the investor's net income by influencing investee dividend declarations. On the other hand, the equity method is sometimes criticized because the asset valuation departs from historical cost but stops short of a market value approach. Instead, the carrying amount of the investment is composed of a number of components and is not similar to the valuation of any other assets.

Over the years, there has been considerable criticism of the use of the equity method as a substitute for the consolidation of certain types of subsidiaries. Although the equity method has been viewed as a ***one-line consolidation,*** the amount of detail reported is considerably different under the equity method than with consolidation. For example, an investor would report the same equity-method income from the following two investees even though their income statements are quite different in composition:

	Investee 1	Investee 2
Sales	$ 50,000	$ 500,000
Operating Expenses	(30,000)	(620,000)
Operating Income (Loss)	$ 20,000	$(120,000)
Gain on Sale of Land		140,000
Net Income	$ 20,000	$ 20,000

Similarly, an investment in the stock of another company is reported under the equity method as a single amount in the investor's balance sheet regardless of the investee's asset and capital structure.

THE FAIR VALUE OPTION

LO 2-5

Prepare journal entries using the fair value option.

ASC 825-10-45 permits, but does not require, companies to measure many financial assets and liabilities at fair value. Companies holding investments in the common stock of other companies have this option for investments that are not required to be consolidated. Thus, rather than using the cost or equity method to report unconsolidated investments in common stock, investors may report those investments at fair value.

Under the fair value option, the investor remeasures the investment to its fair value at the end of each period. The change in value is then recognized in income for the period. Although the FASB does not specify how to account for dividends received from the investment, normally the investor recognizes dividend income in the same manner as under the cost method.

To illustrate the use of the fair value method, assume that Ajax Corporation purchases 40 percent of Barclay Company's common stock on January 1, 20X1, for $200,000. Ajax prepares financial statements at the end of each calendar quarter. On March 1, 20X1, Ajax receives a cash dividend of $1,500 from Barclay. On March 31, 20X1, Ajax determines the fair value of its investment in Barclay to be $207,000. During the first quarter of 20X1, Ajax records the following entries on its books in relation to its investment in Barclay:

(8)	Investment in Barclay Stock	200,000	
	Cash		200,000

Record purchase of Barclay Company stock.

(9)	Cash	1,500	
	Dividend Income		1,500
	Record dividend income from Barclay Company.		

(10)	Investment in Barclay Stock	7,000	
	Unrealized Gain on Barclay Stock		7,000
	Record increase in fair value of Barclay stock.		

OVERVIEW OF THE CONSOLIDATION PROCESS

LO 2-6

Make calculations and prepare basic consolidation entries for a simple consolidation.

Advanced StudyGuide .com

The consolidation process adds together the financial statements of two or more legally separate companies, creating a single set of financial statements. Chapters 2 through 5 discuss the specific procedures used to produce consolidated financial statements in considerable detail. An understanding of the procedures is important because they facilitate the accurate and efficient preparation of consolidated statements. However, the focus should continue to be on the end product—the financial statements. The procedures are intended to produce financial statements that appear as if the consolidated companies are actually a single company.

The separate financial statements of the companies involved serve as the starting point each time consolidated statements are prepared. These separate statements are added together, after some adjustments, to generate consolidated financial statements. The adjustments relate to intercompany transactions and holdings. Although the individual companies within a consolidated entity may legitimately report sales and receivables or payables to one another, the consolidated entity as a whole must report transactions only with parties outside the consolidated entity and receivables from or payables to external parties. Thus, the adjustments required as part of the consolidation process aim at ensuring that the consolidated financial statements are presented as if they were the statements of a single enterprise.

CONSOLIDATION PROCEDURES FOR WHOLLY OWNED SUBSIDIARIES THAT ARE CREATED OR PURCHASED AT BOOK VALUE

We begin preparing consolidated financial statements with the books of the individual companies that are to be consolidated. Because the consolidated entity has no books, all amounts in the consolidated financial statements originate on the books of the parent or a subsidiary or in the consolidation worksheet.

The term *subsidiary* has been defined as "an entity . . . in which another entity, known as its *parent,* holds a controlling financial interest **(ASC 810-10-20).**" A parent company does not need to hold all of a corporate subsidiary's common stock, but at least majority ownership is normally required for the presentation of consolidated financial statements. Most, but not all, corporate subsidiaries are wholly owned by their parents.

Because most subsidiaries are wholly owned, this chapter begins the in-depth examination of consolidation procedures for wholly owned subsidiaries. Moreover, we begin with the most basic consolidation scenario when the subsidiary is either created by the parent or purchased for an amount exactly equal to the book value of the subsidiary's net assets. This assumption simplifies the consolidation because there is no differential. We start with basic consolidation procedures applied to the preparation of a consolidated balance sheet immediately following the establishment of a parent–subsidiary relationship, either through creation or acquisition of the subsidiary. Then we introduce the use of a simple consolidation worksheet for the balance sheet only. The chapter then moves to the preparation of a full set of consolidated financial statements in subsequent periods and the use of a three-part worksheet designed to facilitate the preparation of a consolidated income statement, retained earnings statement, and balance sheet.

CONSOLIDATION WORKSHEETS

LO 2-7

Prepare a consolidation worksheet.

The ***consolidation worksheet*** provides a mechanism for efficiently combining the accounts of the separate companies involved in the consolidation and for adjusting the combined balances to the amounts that would be reported if all consolidating companies were actually a single company. When consolidated financial statements are prepared, the account balances are taken from the separate books of the parent and each subsidiary and placed in the consolidation worksheet. The consolidated statements are prepared, after adjustments, from the amounts in the consolidation worksheet.

Worksheet Format

In practice, companies use several different worksheet formats for preparing consolidated financial statements. One of the most widely used formats is the three-part worksheet, consisting of one part for each of three financial statements: (1) the income statement, (2) the statement of retained earnings, and (3) the balance sheet. In recent years, the retained earnings statement has been dropped by many companies in favor of the statement of changes in stockholders' equity. Nevertheless, the information normally found in a retained earnings statement is included in the statement of stockholders' equity, along with additional information, and so the three-part worksheet still provides a useful format. Figure 2–3 presents the format for the comprehensive three-part consolidation worksheet. Specifically, Figure 2–3 illustrates the basic form of a consolidation worksheet. The titles of the accounts of the consolidating companies are listed in the first column of the worksheet. The account balances from the books or trial balances of the individual companies are listed in the next set of columns, with a separate column for each company included in the consolidation. Entries are made in the columns labeled *Consolidation Entries* to adjust or eliminate balances so that the resulting amounts are those that would appear in the financial statements if all the consolidating companies actually formed a single company. The balances in the last column are obtained by summing all amounts algebraically across the worksheet by account. These are the balances that appear in the consolidated financial statements.

The top portion of the worksheet is used in preparing the consolidated income statement. All income statement accounts are listed in the order they normally appear in an income

FIGURE 2–3
Format for Consolidation Worksheet

	Parent	Subsidiary	Consolidation Entries DR	Consolidation Entries CR	Consolidated
Income Statement					
Revenues					
Expenses					
Net Income					
Statement of Retained Earnings					
Retained Earnings (1/1)					
Add: Net Income					
Less: Dividends					
Retained Earnings (12/31)					
Balance Sheet					
Assets					
Total Assets					
Liabilities					
Equity					
Common Stock					
Retained Earnings					
Total Liabilities & Equity					

statement.[5] When the income statement portion of the worksheet is completed, a total for each column is entered at the bottom of the income statement portion of the worksheet. The bottom line in this part of the worksheet shows the parent's net income, the subsidiary's net income, the totals of the debit and credit adjustments for this section of the worksheet, and consolidated net income. The entire bottom line is carried down to the "net income" line in the retained earnings statement portion of the worksheet immediately below the income statement.

The retained earnings statement section of the worksheet is in the same format as a retained earnings statement, or the retained earnings section of a statement of stockholders' equity. Net income and the other column totals from the bottom line of the income statement portion of the worksheet are brought down from the income statement above. Similarly, the final line in the retained earnings statement section of the worksheet is carried down in its entirety to the retained earnings line in the balance sheet section.

The bottom portion of the worksheet reflects the balance sheet amounts at the end of the period.[6] The retained earnings amounts appearing in the balance sheet section of the worksheet are the totals carried forward from the bottom line of the retained earnings statement section. The examples in the following sections of this chapter demonstrate the use of the comprehensive three-part consolidation worksheet.

! CAUTION

The most common error students commit in preparing the worksheet is forgetting to carry down the adjustments when they carry down net income from the income statement to the statement of retained earnings and when they carry down the retained earnings ending balance in the statement of retained earnings to the balance sheet.

Nature of Consolidation Entries

Consolidation entries are used in the consolidation worksheet to adjust the totals of the individual account balances of the separate consolidating companies to reflect the amounts that would appear if the legally separate companies were actually a single company. Consolidation entries appear only in the consolidation worksheet and do not affect the books of the separate companies. These worksheet entries are sometimes called "elimination" entries.

For the most part, companies that are to be consolidated record their transactions during the period without regard to the consolidated entity. Transactions with related companies tend to be recorded in the same manner as those with unrelated parties, although intercompany transactions may be recorded in separate accounts or other records may be kept to facilitate the later elimination of intercompany transactions. Each of the consolidating companies also prepares its adjusting and closing entries at the end of the period in the normal manner. The resulting balances are entered in the consolidation worksheet and combined to arrive at the consolidated totals. Consolidation entries are used in the worksheet to increase or decrease the combined totals for individual accounts so that only transactions with external parties are reflected in the consolidated amounts.

Some consolidation entries are required at the end of one period but not at the end of subsequent periods. For example, a loan from a parent to a subsidiary in December 20X1, repaid in February 20X2, requires an entry to eliminate the intercompany receivable and payable on December 31, 20X1, but not at the end of 20X2. Some other consolidation entries need to be placed in the consolidation worksheets each time consolidated statements are prepared for a period of years. For example, if a parent company sells land to a subsidiary for $5,000 above the original cost to the parent, a worksheet entry is needed to reduce the basis of the land by $5,000 each time consolidated statements are prepared for as long as an ***affiliate*** (an affiliated company) holds the land.[7] It is important to remember that because consolidation entries are not made on the books of any company, they do not carry over from period to period.

[5] An optional format lists accounts with credit balance accounts first and those having debit balances listed next.

[6] Optionally, accounts can be separated and listed with debits first and then credits.

[7] An affiliated company is one that is related to the company in question. For example, two corporations controlled by the same parent company would be considered affiliates.

CONSOLIDATED BALANCE SHEET WITH WHOLLY OWNED SUBSIDIARY

The simplest consolidation setting occurs when the financial statements of related companies are consolidated immediately after a parent–subsidiary relationship is established through a business combination or the creation of a new subsidiary. We present a series of examples to illustrate the preparation of a consolidated balance sheet. Consolidation procedures are the same whether a subsidiary is created or acquired. We use the case of an acquired subsidiary to illustrate the consolidation procedures in the examples that follow. In each example, Peerless Products Corporation purchases all of the common stock of Special Foods Inc. on January 1, 20X1, and immediately prepares a consolidated balance sheet. Figure 2–4 presents the separate balance sheets of the two companies immediately before the combination.

In the following discussion, we present all journal entries and worksheet consolidation entries in the text of the chapter. To avoid confusing the consolidation entries with journal entries that appear on the separate books of the parent or subsidiary, all worksheet consolidation entries appearing in the text are shaded; journal entries recorded in the books of the parent company are not shaded.

100 Percent Ownership Acquired at Book Value

In the first example, Peerless acquires all of Special Foods' outstanding common stock for $300,000, an amount equal to the fair value of Special Foods as a whole. On the date of combination, the fair values of Special Foods' individual assets and liabilities are equal to their book values shown in Figure 2–4. Because Peerless acquires all of Special Foods' common stock and because Special Foods has only the one class of stock outstanding, the total book value of the shares acquired equals the total stockholders' equity of Special Foods ($200,000 + $100,000). The $300,000 of consideration exchanged is equal to the book value of the shares acquired. This ownership situation can be characterized as follows:

	P	Fair value of consideration		$300,000
1/1/X1 100%	↓	Book value of shares acquired		
		Common stock—Special Foods	$200,000	
		Retained earnings—Special Foods	100,000	
	S			300,000
		Difference between fair value and book value		$ 0

FIGURE 2–4
Balance Sheets of Peerless Products and Special Foods, January 1, 20X1, Immediately before Combination

	Peerless Products	Special Foods
Assets		
Cash	$ 350,000	$ 50,000
Accounts Receivable	75,000	50,000
Inventory	100,000	60,000
Land	175,000	40,000
Buildings & Equipment	800,000	600,000
Accumulated Depreciation	(400,000)	(300,000)
Total Assets	$1,100,000	$500,000
Liabilities & Stockholders' Equity		
Accounts Payable	$ 100,000	$100,000
Bonds Payable	200,000	100,000
Common Stock	500,000	200,000
Retained Earnings	300,000	100,000
Total Liabilities & Equity	$1,100,000	$500,000

Peerless records the stock acquisition on its books with the following entry on the combination date:

(11)	Investment in Special Foods	300,000	
	Cash		300,000
	Record the purchase of Special Foods stock.		

Figure 2–5 presents the separate financial statements of Peerless and Special Foods immediately after the combination. Special Foods' balance sheet in Figure 2–5 is the same as in Figure 2–4, but Peerless' balance sheet has changed to reflect the $300,000 reduction in cash and the recording of the investment in Special Foods stock for the same amount. Note that the $300,000 of cash was paid to the former stockholders of Special Foods, not to the company itself. Accordingly, that cash is no longer in the consolidated entity. Instead, Peerless' balance sheet now reflects a $300,000 Investment in Special Foods Stock account.

Basic Consolidation Entry

The basic consolidation entry removes the Investment in Special Foods Stock account and the subsidiary's stockholders' equity accounts. Although this consolidation entry is very simple, to be consistent with the discussion of more complicated examples later in the chapter, we illustrate the thought process in developing the worksheet entry.

In this example, Peerless' investment is exactly equal to the book value of equity of Special Foods. Therefore, no goodwill is recorded and all assets and liabilities are simply combined from Special Foods' financial statements at their current book values. In Chapters 4 and 5, we will explore situations in which the acquiring company pays more than the book value of the acquired company's net assets (i.e., when there is a positive differential). However, in Chapters 2 and 3, the excess value of identifiable net assets and goodwill will always be equal to zero. To maintain a consistent approach through all four chapters, we always illustrate the components of the acquiring company's investment, even though it will always be exactly equal to its share of the book value of net assets in Chapters 2 and 3. Therefore, the relationship between the fair value of the consideration given to acquire Special Foods, the fair value of

FIGURE 2–5
Balance Sheets of Peerless Products and Special Foods, January 1, 20X1, Immediately after Combination

	Peerless Products	Special Foods
Assets		
Cash	$ 50,000	$ 50,000
Accounts Receivable	75,000	50,000
Inventory	100,000	60,000
Land	175,000	40,000
Buildings & Equipment	800,000	600,000
Accumulated Depreciation	(400,000)	(300,000)
Investment in Special Foods Stock	300,000	
Total Assets	$1,100,000	$500,000
Liabilities & Stockholders' Equity		
Accounts Payable	$ 100,000	$100,000
Bonds Payable	200,000	100,000
Common Stock	500,000	200,000
Retained Earnings	300,000	100,000
Total Liabilities & Equity	$1,100,000	$500,000

Special Foods' net assets, and the book value of Special Foods' net assets can be illustrated as follows:

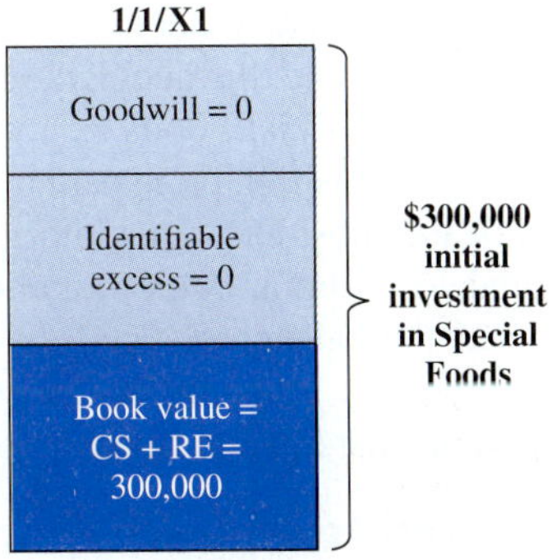

The book value of Special Foods' equity as of the acquisition date is equal to the sum of common stock and retained earnings:

Book Value Calculations:

	Total Investment	=	Common Stock	+	Retained Earnings
Original Book Value	300,000		200,000		100,000

Therefore, the consolidation entry simply credits the Investment in Special Foods Stock account (for the acquisition price, $300,000) from Peerless' balance sheet. In this and all future examples, we use blue highlighting with white drop-out lettering to designate the numbers from the book value analysis that appear in the basic consolidation entry:

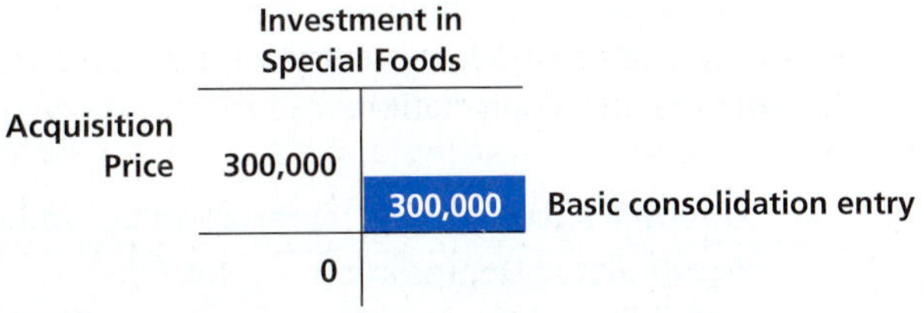

The corresponding debits eliminate the beginning balances in the equity accounts of Special Foods:

Basic Consolidation Entry:

Common Stock	200,000		← Common stock balance
Retained Earnings	100,000		← Beginning balance in ret. earnings
Investment in Special Foods		300,000	← Book value in investment account

Remember that this entry is made in the consolidation worksheet, not on the books of either the parent or the subsidiary, and is presented here in general journal form only for instructional purposes.

The investment account must be eliminated because, from a single entity viewpoint, a company cannot hold an investment in itself. The subsidiary's stockholders' equity accounts must be eliminated because the subsidiary's stock is held entirely within the consolidated entity and none represents claims by outsiders.

From a somewhat different viewpoint, the investment account on the parent's books can be thought of as a single account representing the parent's investment in the net assets of the subsidiary, a so-called *one-line consolidation.* In a full consolidation, the subsidiary's individual assets and liabilities are combined with those of the parent. Including both the net assets of the subsidiary, as represented by the balance in the investment account, and the subsidiary's individual assets and liabilities would double-count the same set of assets. Therefore, the investment account is eliminated and not carried to the consolidated balance sheet.

In this example, the acquisition price of the stock acquired by Peerless is equal to the fair value of Special Foods as a whole. This assumption reflects the normal situation in which the acquisition price paid by the parent is equal to the fair value of its proportionate share of the subsidiary. In addition, this example assumes that the subsidiary's fair value is equal to its book value, a generally unrealistic assumption. Given this assumption, however, the balance of Peerless' investment account is equal to Special Foods' stockholders' equity accounts, so this worksheet entry fully eliminates Peerless' investment account against Special Foods' stockholders' equity accounts.

The Optional Accumulated Depreciation Consolidation Entry

We now introduce a second consolidation entry that is optional but that provides for a more "correct" consolidation. When a company acquires a depreciable asset, it records the asset with a zero balance in accumulated depreciation (i.e., without any accumulated depreciation previously recorded by the seller). Likewise, when a company acquires all of the net assets of another company, the depreciable assets acquired are recorded without any existing accumulated depreciation from the seller's books. The buyer disregards the seller's historical cost and accumulated since they are irrelevant to the acquiring company. For the same reason, when a parent company acquires the stock of a subsidiary, the consolidated financial statements should include the depreciable assets of the subsidiary without the preacquisition accumulated depreciation. However, in a stock acquisition, the consolidation worksheet begins with the book values reflected in the subsidiary's financial statements. Eliminating the old accumulated depreciation of the subsidiary as of the acquisition date and netting it out against the historical cost gives the appearance that the depreciable assets have been newly acquired as of the acquisition date. Special Foods' books indicate accumulated depreciation on the acquisition date of $300,000. Thus, the following consolidation entry will be made to eliminate this acquisition date subsidiary accumulated depreciation.

Optional Accumulated Depreciation Consolidation Entry:

Accumulated Depreciation	**300,000**		
Buildings & Equipment		**300,000**	← Accumulated depreciation at the time of the acquisition netted against cost

Note that this worksheet consolidation entry does not change the net buildings and equipment balance. Netting the preacquisition accumulated depreciation against the cost basis of the corresponding assets merely causes the buildings and equipment to appear in the consolidated financial statements as if they had been acquired without their existing accumulated depreciation.

As explained previously, consolidation entries are not made on the books of any company, so they do not carry over from period to period. Thus, we would make this same accumulated depreciation consolidation entry each succeeding period as long as these depreciable assets remain on Special Foods' books (always based on accumulated depreciation balance as of the acquisition date).

Consolidation Worksheet

We present the worksheet for the preparation of a consolidated balance sheet immediately following the acquisition in Figure 2–6. The first two columns of the worksheet in Figure 2–6 are the account balances taken from the books of Peerless and Special Foods, as shown in Figure 2–5. The balances of like accounts are placed side by side so that they may be added together. If more than two companies were to be consolidated, a separate column would be included in the worksheet for each additional subsidiary.

The accounts are placed in the worksheet in the order they would normally appear in the companies' financial statements. The two columns labeled *Consolidation Entries* in Figure 2–6 are used to adjust the amounts reported by the individual companies to the amounts appropriate for the consolidated statement. All adjustments made in the worksheets are made in double-entry form. Thus, when the worksheet is completed, total debits entered in the Debit Consolidation column must equal total credits entered in the Credit Consolidation column. We highlight all parts of each consolidation entry with the same color so that the reader can identify the individual consolidation entries in the worksheet. After the appropriate consolidation entries have been entered in the Consolidation Entries columns, summing algebraically across the individual accounts provides the consolidated totals.

The consolidated balance sheet presented in Figure 2–7 comes directly from the last column of the consolidation worksheet in Figure 2–6. Because no operations occurred between the date of combination and the preparation of the consolidated balance sheet, the stockholders' equity section of the consolidated balance sheet is identical to that of Peerless in Figure 2–5.

FIGURE 2–6 Worksheet for Consolidated Balance Sheet, January 1, 20X1, Date of Combination; 100 Percent Acquisition at Book Value

	Peerless Products	Special Foods	Consolidation Entries DR	Consolidation Entries CR	Consolidated
Balance Sheet					
Cash	$ 50,000	$ 50,000			$ 100,000
Accounts Receivable	75,000	50,000			125,000
Inventory	100,000	60,000			160,000
Investment in Special Foods	300,000			$300,000	0
Land	175,000	40,000			215,000
Buildings & Equipment	800,000	600,000		300,000	1,100,000
Less: Accumulated Depreciation	(400,000)	(300,000)	300,000		(400,000)
Total Assets	**$1,100,000**	**$500,000**	**$300,000**	**$600,000**	**$1,300,000**
Accounts Payable	100,000	100,000			200,000
Bonds Payable	200,000	100,000			300,000
Common Stock	500,000	200,000	200,000		500,000
Retained Earnings	300,000	100,000	100,000		300,000
Total Liabilities & Equity	**$1,100,000**	**$500,000**	**$300,000**	**$ 0**	**$1,300,000**

FIGURE 2–7 Consolidated Balance Sheet, January 1, 20X1, Date of Combination; 100 Percent Acquisition at Book Value

PEERLESS PRODUCTS CORPORATION AND SUBSIDIARY
Consolidated Balance Sheet
January 1, 20X1

Assets			**Liabilities**	
Cash		$ 100,000	Accounts Payable	$ 200,000
Accounts Receivable		125,000	Bonds Payable	300,000
Inventory		160,000		
Land		215,000	Stockholders' Equity	
Buildings & Equipment	$1,100,000		Common Stock	500,000
Accumulated Depreciation	(400,000)	700,000	Retained Earnings	300,000
Total Assets		$1,300,000	Total Liabilities & Equity	$1,300,000

CONSOLIDATION SUBSEQUENT TO ACQUISITION

The preceding section introduced the procedures used to prepare a consolidated balance sheet as of the acquisition date. However, more than a consolidated balance sheet is needed to provide a comprehensive picture of the consolidated entity's activities following acquisition. As with a single company, the set of basic financial statements for a consolidated entity consists of a balance sheet, an income statement, a statement of changes in retained earnings, and a statement of cash flows.

This section of the chapter presents the procedures used to prepare an income statement, statement of retained earnings, and consolidated balance sheet subsequent to the acquisition date. We discuss the preparation of a consolidated statement of cash flows in Chapter 10.

The following discussion first deals with the important concepts of consolidated net income and consolidated retained earnings, followed by a description of the worksheet format used to facilitate the preparation of a full set of consolidated financial statements. We then discuss the specific procedures used to prepare consolidated financial statements subsequent to the date of combination.

This and subsequent chapters focus on procedures for consolidation when the parent company accounts for its investment in subsidiary stock using the equity method. If the parent accounts for its investment using the cost method, the general approach to the preparation of consolidated financial statements is the same, but the specific consolidation entries differ. Appendix 2B summarizes consolidation procedures using the cost method. Regardless of the method the parent uses to account for its subsidiary investment, the consolidated statements will be the same because the investment and related accounts are eliminated in the consolidation process.

The approach followed to prepare a complete set of consolidated financial statements subsequent to a business combination is quite similar to that used to prepare a consolidated balance sheet as of the date of combination. However, in addition to the assets and liabilities, the consolidating companies' revenues and expenses must be combined. As the accounts are combined, adjustments must be made in the consolidation worksheet so that the consolidated financial statements appear as if they are the financial statements of a single company.

When a full set of consolidated financial statements is prepared subsequent to the date of combination, two of the important concepts affecting the statements are those of consolidated net income and consolidated retained earnings.

Consolidated Net Income

All revenues and expenses of the individual consolidating companies arising from transactions with unaffiliated companies are included in the consolidated financial statements. The consolidated income statement includes 100 percent of the revenues and expenses regardless of the parent's percentage ownership. Similar to single-company financial statements, where the difference between revenues and expenses equals net income, revenues minus expenses in the consolidated financial statements equal consolidated net income. ***Consolidated net income*** is equal to the parent's income from its own operations, excluding any investment income from consolidated subsidiaries, plus the net income from each of the consolidated subsidiaries, adjusted for any differential write-off (which is zero in this chapter). Intercorporate investment income from consolidated subsidiaries included in the parent's net income under either the cost or equity method must be eliminated in computing consolidated net income to avoid double-counting.

Consolidated net income and consolidated net income attributable to the controlling interest are the same when all consolidated subsidiaries are wholly owned. For example, assume that Push Corporation purchases all of the stock of Shove Company at an amount equal to its book value. During 20X1, Shove reports net income of $25,000 while Push reports net income of $125,000, including equity-method income from Shove of $25,000. Consolidated net income for 20X1 is computed as follows:

Push's net income	$125,000
Less: Equity-method income from Shove	(25,000)
Shove's net income	25,000
Consolidated net income	$125,000

Note that when the parent company properly applies the equity method, consolidated net income is always equal to the parent's equity-method net income.

Consolidated Retained Earnings

Consolidated retained earnings, as it appears in the consolidated balance sheet, is that portion of the consolidated enterprise's undistributed earnings accruing to the parent company shareholders. Consolidated retained earnings at the end of the period is equal to the beginning consolidated retained earnings balance, plus consolidated net income attributable to the controlling interest, less dividends declared by the parent company.

Computing Consolidated Retained Earnings

Consolidated retained earnings is computed by adding together the parent's retained earnings from its own operations (excluding any income from consolidated subsidiaries recognized by the parent) and the parent's proportionate share of the net income of each subsidiary since the date of acquisition, adjusted for differential write-off and goodwill impairment. Consolidated retained earnings should be equal to the parent's equity-method retained earnings.

If the parent accounts for subsidiaries using the equity method on its books, the retained earnings of each subsidiary is completely eliminated when the subsidiary is consolidated. This is necessary because (1) retained earnings cannot be purchased, and so subsidiary retained earnings at the date of a business combination cannot be included in the combined company's retained earnings; (2) the parent's share of the subsidiary's income since acquisition is already included in the parent's equity-method retained earnings; and (3) the noncontrolling interest's share (if any) of the subsidiary's retained earnings is not included in consolidated retained earnings.

In the simple example given previously, assume that on the date of combination, January 1, 20X1, Push's retained earnings balance is $400,000 and Shove's is $250,000. During 20X1, Shove reports $25,000 of net income and declares $10,000 of dividends. Push reports $100,000 of separate operating earnings plus $25,000 of equity-method income from its 100 percent interest in Shove; Push declares dividends of $30,000. Based on this information, the retained earnings balances for Push and Shove on December 31, 20X1, are computed as follows:

	Push	Shove
Balance, January 1, 20X1	$400,000	$250,000
Net income, 20X1	125,000	25,000
Dividends declared in 20X1	(30,000)	(10,000)
Balance, December 31, 20X1	$495,000	$265,000

Consolidated retained earnings is computed by first determining the parent's retained earnings from its own operations. This computation involves removing from the parent's retained earnings the $25,000 of subsidiary income since acquisition recognized by the parent, leaving $470,000 ($495,000 − $25,000) of retained earnings resulting from the parent's own operations. The parent's 100 percent share of the subsidiary's net income since the date of acquisition is then added to this number, resulting in consolidated retained earnings of $495,000. We note that because this is the first year since the acquisition, the net income since the date of acquisition is just this year's income. Subsequent examples will illustrate how this calculation differs in later years. We also emphasize that since Push uses the ***fully adjusted equity method,*** this number is the same as the parent's equity-method retained earnings.

CONSOLIDATED FINANCIAL STATEMENTS—100 PERCENT OWNERSHIP, CREATED OR ACQUIRED AT BOOK VALUE

Each of the consolidated financial statements is prepared as if it is taken from a single set of books that is being used to account for the overall consolidated entity. There is, of course, no set of books for the consolidated entity, and as in the preparation of the consolidated balance sheet, the consolidation process starts with the data recorded on the books of the individual consolidating companies. The account balances from the books of the individual companies are placed in the three-part worksheet, and entries are made to eliminate the effects of intercorporate ownership and transactions. The consolidation approach and procedures are the same whether the subsidiary being consolidated was acquired or created.

To understand the process of consolidation subsequent to the start of a parent–subsidiary relationship, assume that on January 1, 20X1, Peerless Products Corporation acquires all of the common stock of Special Foods Inc. for $300,000, an amount equal to Special Foods' book value on that date. At that time, Special Foods has $200,000 of common stock outstanding and retained earnings of $100,000, summarized as follows:

P → S (1/1/X1, 100%)			
	Fair value of consideration		$300,000
	Book value of shares acquired		
	Common stock—Special Foods	$200,000	
	Retained earnings—Special Foods	100,000	
			300,000
	Difference between fair value and book value		$ 0

Peerless accounts for its investment in Special Foods stock using the equity method. Information about Peerless and Special Foods as of the date of combination and for the years 20X1 and 20X2 appears in Figure 2–8.

FIGURE 2–8
Selected Information about Peerless Products and Special Foods on January 1, 20X1, and for the Years 20X1 and 20X2

	Peerless Products	Special Foods
Common Stock, January 1, 20X1	$500,000	$200,000
Retained Earnings, January 1, 20X1	300,000	100,000
20X1:		
Separate Operating Income, Peerless	140,000	
Net Income, Special Foods		50,000
Dividends	60,000	30,000
20X2:		
Separate Operating Income, Peerless	160,000	
Net Income, Special Foods		75,000
Dividends	60,000	40,000

Initial Year of Ownership

On January 1, 20X1, Peerless records its purchase of Special Foods common stock with the following entry:

(12)	Investment in Special Foods	300,000	
	Cash		300,000
	Record the purchase of Special Foods stock.		

During 20X1, Peerless records operating earnings of $140,000, excluding its income from investing in Special Foods, and declares dividends of $60,000. Special Foods reports 20X1 net income of $50,000 and declares dividends of $30,000.

Parent Company Entries

Peerless records its 20X1 income and dividends from Special Foods under the equity method as follows:

(13)	Investment in Special Foods	50,000	
	Income from Special Foods		50,000
	Record Peerless' 100% share of Special Foods' 20X1 income.		

(14)	Cash	30,000	
	Investment in Special Foods		30,000
	Record Peerless' 100% share of Special Foods' 20X1 dividend.		

Consolidation Worksheet—Initial Year of Ownership

Advanced StudyGuide .com

After all appropriate entries have been made on the books of Peerless and Special Foods, including year-end adjustments, a consolidation worksheet is prepared as in Figure 2–9. The adjusted account balances from the books of Peerless and Special Foods are placed in the first two columns of the worksheet. Then all amounts that reflect intercorporate transactions or ownership are eliminated in the consolidation process.

The distinction between journal entries recorded on the books of the individual companies and the consolidation entries recorded only on the consolidation worksheet is an important one. Book entries affect balances on the books and the amounts that are carried to the consolidation worksheet; worksheet consolidation entries affect only those balances carried to the consolidated financial statements in that period. As mentioned previously, the consolidation entries presented in this text are shaded both when presented in journal entry form in the text and in the worksheet.

In this example, the accounts that must be eliminated because of intercorporate ownership are the stockholders' equity accounts of Special Foods, including dividends declared, Peerless' investment in Special Foods stock, and Peerless' income from Special Foods. However, unlike previous examples, the book value portion of Peerless' investment has changed because earnings and dividends have adjusted the investment account balance. The book value portion of the investment account can be summarized as follows:

Book Value Calculations:

	Total Investment	=	Common Stock	+	Retained Earnings
Original Book Value	**300,000**		**200,000**		**100,000**
+ Net Income	**50,000**				**50,000**
– Dividends	**(30,000)**				**(30,000)**
Ending Book Value	**320,000**		**200,000**		**120,000**

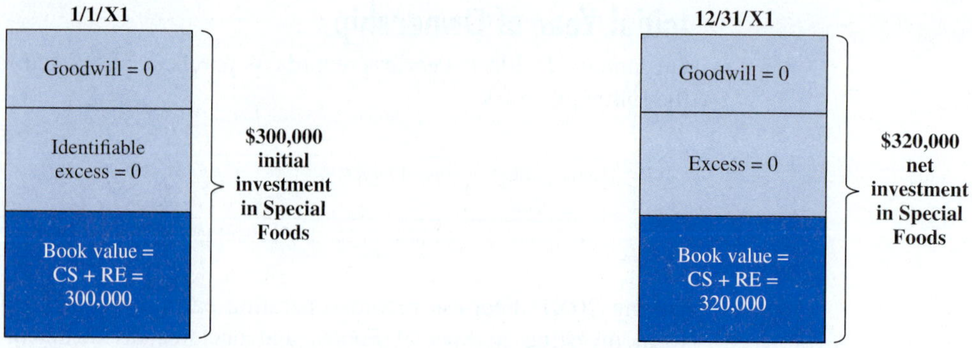

Under the equity method, Peerless recognizes its share (100 percent) of Special Foods' reported income. In the consolidated income statement, however, Special Foods' individual revenue and expense accounts are combined with Peerless' accounts. Peerless' equity method income from Special Foods, therefore, must be eliminated to avoid double-counting. Special Foods' dividends paid to Peerless must be eliminated when consolidated statements are prepared (because the dividend is really just an intercompany cash transfer, not a transfer of wealth to external shareholders) so that only dividend declarations related to the parent's shareholders are reported as dividends of the consolidated entity. Thus, the basic consolidation entry removes both the equity method Income from Special Foods and also all dividends declared by Special Foods during the period:

Basic Consolidation Entry:

Common Stock	200,000		← Common stock balance
Retained Earnings	100,000		← Beginning balance in ret. earnings
Income from Special Foods	50,000		← Special Foods' reported income
Dividends Declared		30,000	← 100% of Special Foods' dividends
Investment in Special Foods		320,000	← Net BV in investment account

The book value calculations in the chart on the previous page help to facilitate preparation of the basic consolidation entry. Thus, the basic consolidation entry removes (1) Special Foods' equity accounts, (2) Special Foods' dividends declared, (3) Peerless' Income from Special Foods account, and (4) Peerless' Investment in Special Foods account. Note that we use blue highlighting with white drop-out numbers in the book value analysis that appear in the basic consolidation entry. Also note that we eliminate the beginning retained earnings balance since income and dividends are eliminated separately. Because there is no differential in this example, the basic consolidation entry completely eliminates the balance in Peerless' investment account on the balance sheet as well as the Income from Special Foods account on the income statement in the worksheet. Additional consolidation entries will be necessary when there is a differential as illustrated in Chapters 4 and 5.

	Investment in Special Foods (Dr)	Investment in Special Foods (Cr)		Income from Special Foods (Dr)	Income from Special Foods (Cr)	
Acquisition Price	300,000					
Net Income	50,000				50,000	Net Income
		30,000	Dividends			
Ending Balance	320,000				50,000	Ending Balance
		320,000	Basic	50,000		
	0				0	

We show the worksheet entry in these T-accounts only to illustrate how these accounts are eliminated in the consolidation worksheet. Consolidation entries do not affect the actual books of either the parent or the subsidiary.

As explained previously, we repeat the accumulated depreciation worksheet entry in each succeeding period for as long as the subsidiary owns these assets. The purpose of this entry is to appropriately present these assets in the consolidated financial statements as if they had been purchased on the date the subsidiary was acquired at their acquisition date book values with no preacquisition accumulated depreciation.

Optional Accumulated Depreciation Consolidation Entry:

Accumulated Depreciation	**300,000**		Accumulated depreciation at the time of the acquisition netted against cost
Buildings & Equipment		**300,000**	←

Worksheet Relationships

Both of the consolidation entries are entered in Figure 2–9 and the amounts are totaled across each row and down each column to complete the worksheet. Some specific points to recognize with respect to the full worksheet are as follows:

1. Because of the normal articulation among the financial statements, the bottom-line number from each of the first two sections of the worksheet carries down to the next

FIGURE 2–9 December 31, 20X1, Equity-Method Worksheet for Consolidated Financial Statements, Initial Year of Ownership; 100 Percent Acquisition at Book Value

	Peerless Products	Special Foods	Consolidation Entries DR	Consolidation Entries CR	Consolidated
Income Statement					
Sales	400,000	200,000			600,000
Less: Cost of Goods Sold (COGS)	(170,000)	(115,000)			(285,000)
Less: Depreciation Expense	(50,000)	(20,000)			(70,000)
Less: Other Expenses	(40,000)	(15,000)			(55,000)
Income from Special Foods	50,000		50,000		0
Net Income	**190,000**	**50,000**	**50,000**	**0**	**190,000**
Statement of Retained Earnings					
Beginning Balance	300,000	100,000	100,000		300,000
Net Income	**190,000**	**50,000**	**50,000**	**0**	190,000
Less: Dividends Declared	(60,000)	(30,000)		30,000	(60,000)
Ending Balance	**430,000**	**120,000**	**150,000**	**30,000**	**430,000**
Balance Sheet					
Cash	210,000	75,000			285,000
Accounts Receivable	75,000	50,000			125,000
Inventory	100,000	75,000			175,000
Investment in Special Foods	320,000			320,000	0
Land	175,000	40,000			215,000
Buildings & Equipment	800,000	600,000		300,000	1,100,000
Less: Accumulated Depreciation	(450,000)	(320,000)	300,000		(470,000)
Total Assets	**1,230,000**	**520,000**	**300,000**	**620,000**	**1,430,000**
Accounts Payable	100,000	100,000			200,000
Bonds Payable	200,000	100,000			300,000
Common Stock	500,000	200,000	200,000		500,000
Retained Earnings	**430,000**	**120,000**	**150,000**	**30,000**	430,000
Total Liabilities & Equity	**1,230,000**	**520,000**	**350,000**	**30,000**	**1,430,000**

financial statement in a logical progression. As part of the normal accounting cycle, net income is closed to retained earnings, and retained earnings is reflected in the balance sheet. Therefore, in the consolidation worksheet, the net income is carried down to the retained earnings statement section of the worksheet, and the ending retained earnings line is carried down to the balance sheet section of the worksheet. Note that in both cases the entire line, including total adjustments, is carried forward.

2. Double-entry bookkeeping requires total debits to equal total credits for any single consolidation entry and for the worksheet as a whole. Because some consolidation entries extend to more than one section of the worksheet, however, the totals of the debit and credit adjustments are not likely to be equal in either of the first two sections of the worksheet. The totals of all debits and credits at the bottom of the balance sheet section are equal because the cumulative balances from the two upper sections are carried forward to the balance sheet section.
3. In the balance sheet portion of the worksheet, total debit balances must equal total credit balances for each company and the consolidated entity.
4. When the parent uses the full equity method of accounting for the investment, consolidated net income should equal the parent's net income, and consolidated retained earnings should equal the parent's retained earnings. This means the existing balance in subsidiary retained earnings must be eliminated to avoid double-counting.
5. Certain other clerical safeguards are incorporated into the worksheet. The amounts reflected in the bottom line of the income statement section, when summed (algebraically) across, must equal the number reported as consolidated net income. Similarly, the amounts in the last line of the retained earnings statement section must equal consolidated retained earnings when summed across.

Second and Subsequent Years of Ownership

The consolidation procedures employed at the end of the second and subsequent years are basically the same as those used at the end of the first year. Adjusted trial balance data of the individual companies are used as the starting point each time consolidated statements are prepared because no separate books are kept for the consolidated entity. An additional check is needed in each period following acquisition to ensure that the beginning balance of consolidated retained earnings shown in the completed worksheet after consolidation entries equals the balance reported at the end of the prior period. In all other respects, the consolidation entries and worksheet are comparable with those shown for the first year.

Parent Company Entries

We illustrate consolidation after two years of ownership by continuing the example of Peerless Products and Special Foods, based on the data in Figure 2–8. Peerless' separate income from its own operations for 20X2 is $160,000, and its dividends total $60,000. Special Foods reports net income of $75,000 in 20X2 and pays dividends of $40,000. Peerless records the following equity-method entries in 20X2:

(15)	Investment in Special Foods	75,000	
	Income from Special Foods		75,000
	Record Peerless' 100% share of Special Foods' 20X2 income.		

(16)	Cash	40,000	
	Investment in Special Foods		40,000
	Record Peerless' 100% share of Special Foods' 20X2 dividend.		

The balance in the investment account reported by Peerless increases from $320,000 on January 1, 20X2, to $355,000 on December 31, 20X2, and reported net income of Peerless totals $235,000 ($160,000 + $75,000).

Advanced StudyGuide .com

Consolidation Worksheet—Second Year of Ownership

Figure 2–10 illustrates the worksheet to prepare consolidated statements for 20X2. The book value of Peerless' investment in Special Foods (which is equal to the book value of Special Foods' equity accounts) can be analyzed and summarized as follows:

Book Value Calculations:

	Total Investment	=	Common Stock	+	Retained Earnings
Beginning Book Value	320,000		200,000		120,000
+ Net Income	75,000				75,000
− Dividends	(40,000)				(40,000)
Ending Book Value	355,000		200,000		155,000

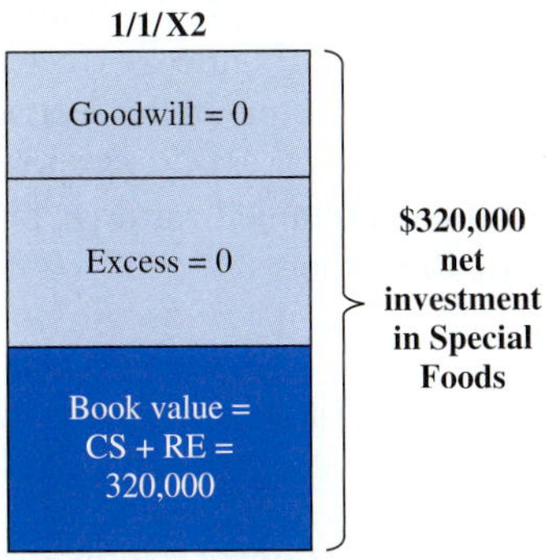

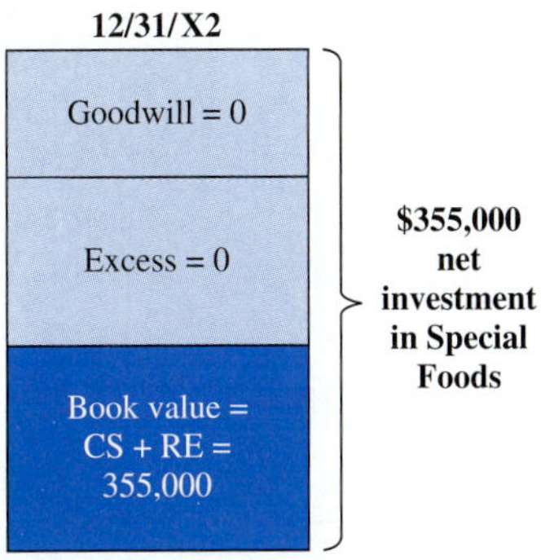

Again, the basic consolidation entry removes (1) Special Foods' equity accounts, (2) Special Foods' dividends declared, (3) Peerless' Income from Special Foods account, and (4) Peerless' Investment in Special Foods account:

Basic Consolidation Entry:

Account	Debit	Credit	
Common Stock	200,000		← Common stock balance
Retained Earnings	120,000		← Beginning balance in RE
Income from Special Foods	75,000		← Special Foods' reported income
Dividends Declared		40,000	← 100% of Special Foods' dividends
Investment in Special Foods		355,000	← Net BV in investment account

Note that the beginning balance in retained earnings in 20X2, $75,000, is different than the balance in 20X1 because of income earned and dividends declared during 20X1. However, it is the beginning balance in retained earnings that is eliminated since income and dividends are eliminated separately. As explained previously, since there is no differential in this example, the basic consolidation entry completely eliminates the balance in Peerless' investment account on the balance sheet as well as the Income from Special Foods account on the income statement in the worksheet.

	Investment in Special Foods (Debit)	Investment in Special Foods (Credit)		Income from Special Foods (Debit)	Income from Special Foods (Credit)	
Beginning Balance	320,000					
Net Income	75,000				75,000	Net Income
		40,000	Dividends			
Ending Balance	355,000				75,000	Ending Balance
		355,000	Basic	75,000		
	0				0	

We again show the worksheet entry in these T-accounts only to illustrate how these accounts are eliminated in the consolidation worksheet. Consolidation entries do not affect the actual books of either the parent or the subsidiary.

In this example, Special Foods had accumulated depreciation of $300,000 on the acquisition date. Thus, we repeat the same accumulated depreciation consolidation entry this year (and every year as long as Special Foods owns the assets) that we used in the initial year.

Optional Accumulated Depreciation Consolidation Entry:

Accumulated Depreciation	**300,000**		
Buildings & Equipment		**300,000**	← Accumulated depreciation at the time of the acquisition netted against cost

After placing the two consolidation entries in the consolidation worksheet, it is completed in the normal manner as illustrated in Figure 2–10. All worksheet relationships discussed in conjunction with Figure 2–9 continue in the second year as well. The beginning consolidated retained earnings balance for 20X2, as shown in Figure 2–10, should be compared with the ending consolidated retained earnings balance for 20X1, as shown in Figure 2–9, to ensure that they are the same.

FIGURE 2–10 December 31, 20X2, Equity-Method Worksheet for Consolidated Financial Statements, Second Year of Ownership; 100 Percent Acquisition at Book Value

	Peerless Products	Special Foods	Consolidation Entries DR	Consolidation Entries CR	Consolidated
Income Statement					
Sales	450,000	300,000			750,000
Less: COGS	(180,000)	(160,000)			(340,000)
Less: Depreciation Expense	(50,000)	(20,000)			(70,000)
Less: Other Expenses	(60,000)	(45,000)			(105,000)
Income from Special Foods	75,000		75,000		0
Net Income	**235,000**	**75,000**	**75,000**	**0**	**235,000**
Statement of Retained Earnings					
Beginning Balance	430,000	120,000	120,000		430,000
Net Income	**235,000**	**75,000**	**75,000**	**0**	235,000
Less: Dividends Declared	(60,000)	(40,000)		40,000	(60,000)
Ending Balance	**605,000**	**155,000**	**195,000**	**40,000**	**605,000**
Balance Sheet					
Cash	245,000	85,000			330,000
Accounts Receivable	150,000	80,000			230,000
Inventory	180,000	90,000			270,000
Investment in Special Foods	355,000			355,000	0
Land	175,000	40,000			215,000
Buildings & Equipment	800,000	600,000		300,000	1,100,000
Less: Accumulated Depreciation	(500,000)	(340,000)	300,000		(540,000)
Total Assets	**1,405,000**	**555,000**	**300,000**	**655,000**	**1,605,000**
Accounts Payable	100,000	100,000			200,000
Bonds Payable	200,000	100,000			300,000
Common Stock	500,000	200,000	200,000		500,000
Retained Earnings	**605,000**	**155,000**	**195,000**	**40,000**	605,000
Total Liabilities & Equity	**1,405,000**	**555,000**	**395,000**	**40,000**	**1,605,000**

Consolidated Net Income and Retained Earnings

In the consolidation worksheets illustrated in Figures 2–9 and 2–10, consolidated net income for 20X1 and 20X2 appear as the last numbers in the income statement section of the worksheets in the Consolidated column on the far right. The numbers can be computed as follows:

	20X1	20X2
Peerless' net income	$190,000	$235,000
Peerless' equity income from Special Foods	(50,000)	(75,000)
Special Foods' net income	50,000	75,000
Consolidated net income	$190,000	$235,000

In this simple illustration, consolidated net income is the same as Peerless' equity-method net income.

In Figures 2–9 and 2–10, the ending consolidated retained earnings number is equal to the beginning balance of consolidated retained earnings plus consolidated net income, less dividends declared on the parent's common stock. It also can be computed as follows:

	20X1	20X2
Peerless' beginning retained earnings from its own operations	$300,000	$380,000
Peerless' income from its own operations	140,000	160,000
Peerless' income from Special Foods since acquisition (cumulative)	50,000	125,000
Peerless' dividends declared	(60,000)	(60,000)
Consolidated retained earnings	$430,000	$605,000

STOP & THINK

Note that Peerless' beginning retained earnings from its own operations in 20X2, $380,000, is calculated as the beginning balance for 20X1 plus Peerless' income from its own operations in 20X1, $140,000, minus its dividends declared in 20X1, $60,000.

As with income, consolidated retained earnings is the same as the parent's equity-method retained earnings if the parent company uses the equity method. We note that the second year of this calculation illustrates how cumulative income from Special Foods (since the acquisition date) can be used to calculate ending retained earnings.

SUMMARY OF KEY CONCEPTS

Companies owning investments in the common stock of other companies generally report those investments by consolidating them or reporting them using the cost method (adjusted to market, if appropriate) or equity method, depending on the circumstances. Consolidation generally is appropriate if one entity controls the investee, usually through majority ownership of the investee's voting stock. The equity method is required when an investor has sufficient stock ownership in an investee to significantly influence the operating and financial policies of the investee but owns less than a majority of the investee's stock. In the absence of other evidence, ownership of 20 percent or more of an investee's voting stock is viewed as giving the investor the ability to exercise significant influence over the investee. The cost method is used when consolidation and the equity method are not appropriate, usually when the investor is unable to exercise significant influence over the investee.

The cost method is similar to the approach used in accounting for other noncurrent assets. The investment is carried at its original cost to the investor. Consistent with the realization concept, income from the investment is recognized when distributed by the investee in the form of dividends.

The equity method is unique in that the carrying value of the investment is adjusted periodically to reflect the investor's changing equity in the underlying investee. Income from the investment is recognized by the investor under the equity method as the investee reports the income rather than when it is distributed.

Companies also have the choice of reporting nonconsolidated investments using the fair value option instead of the cost or equity method. Under the fair value option, the investment is remeasured to fair value at the end of each reporting period and the change in value recognized as an unrealized gain or loss in income.

Consolidated financial statements present the financial position and results of operations of two or more separate legal entities as if they were a single company. A consolidated balance sheet prepared on the date a parent acquires a subsidiary appears the same as if the acquired company had been merged into the parent.

A consolidation worksheet provides a means of efficiently developing the data needed to prepare consolidated financial statements. The worksheet includes a separate column for the trial balance data of each of the consolidating companies, a debit and a credit column for the consolidation entries, and a column for the consolidated totals that appear in the consolidated financial statements. A three-part consolidation worksheet facilitates preparation of a consolidated income statement, retained earnings statement, and balance sheet, and it includes a section for each statement. Consolidation entries are needed in the worksheet to remove the effects of intercompany ownership and intercompany transactions so the consolidated financial statements appear as if the separate companies are actually one.

KEY TERMS

affiliate, *62*
consolidated net income, *68*
consolidated retained earnings, *69*
consolidation, *49*
consolidation entries, *62*
consolidation worksheet, *61*
control, *49*
corporate joint venture, *53*
cost method, *49*
equity accrual, *54*
equity method, *49*
fully adjusted equity method, *70*
liquidating dividends, *51*
modified equity method, *80*
one-line consolidation, *59*
parent, *49*
significant influence, *49*
subsidiary, *49*
unconsolidated subsidiary, *49*

Appendix 2A Additional Considerations Relating to the Equity Method

Determination of Significant Influence

The general rule established in **ASC 323-10-15** is that the equity method is appropriate when the investor, by virtue of its common stock interest in an investee, is able to exercise significant influence, but not control, over the operating and financial policies of the investee. In the absence of other evidence, common stock ownership of 20 percent or more is viewed as indicating that the investor is able to exercise significant influence over the investee. However, the APB also stated a number of factors that could constitute other evidence of the ability to exercise significant influence:

1. Representation on board of directors.
2. Participation in policy making.
3. Material intercompany transactions.
4. Interchange of managerial personnel.
5. Technological dependency.
6. Size of investment in relation to concentration of other shareholdings.

Conversely, the FASB provides in **ASC 323-10-15-10** some examples of evidence where an investor is unable to exercise significant influence over an investee. These situations include legal or regulatory challenges to the investor's influence by the investee, agreement by the investor to give up important shareholder rights, concentration of majority ownership among a small group of owners who disregard the views of the investor, and unsuccessful attempts by the investor to obtain information from the investee or to obtain representation on the investee's board of directors.

Unrealized Intercompany Profits

Only "arms-length" transactions (i.e., those conducted between completely independent parties who act in their own best interests) may be reflected in the consolidated financial statements. Thus, all aspects of intercompany transfers must be eliminated in preparing consolidated financial statements so that the statements appear as if they were those of a single company.

Adjusting for Unrealized Intercompany Profits

An intercompany sale normally is recorded on the books of the selling affiliate in the same manner as any other sale, including the recognition of profit. In applying the equity method, any intercompany profit remaining unrealized at the end of the period must be deducted from the amount of income that otherwise would be reported.

The income recognized from the investment and the carrying amount of the investment are reduced to remove the effects of the unrealized intercompany profits. In future periods when the intercompany profit actually is realized, the entry is reversed.

Unrealized Profit Adjustments Illustrated

To illustrate the adjustment for unrealized intercompany profits under the equity method, assume that Palit Corporation owns 40 percent of the common stock of Label Manufacturing. During 20X1, Palit sells inventory to Label for $10,000; the inventory originally cost Palit $7,000. Label resells one-third of the inventory to outsiders during 20X1 and retains the other two-thirds in its ending inventory. The amount of unrealized profit is computed as follows:

Total intercompany profit	$10,000 − $7,000 = $3,000
Unrealized portion	$3,000 × 2/3 = $2,000

Assuming that Label reports net income of $60,000 for 20X1 and declares no dividends, the following entries are recorded on Palit's books at the end of 20X1:

(17)	Investment in Label Manufacturing	24,000	
	Income from Label Manufacturing		24,000
	Record equity-method income: $60,000 × 0.40.		

(18)	Income from Label Manufacturing	2,000	
	Investment in Label Manufacturing		2,000
	Remove unrealized intercompany profit.		

If all the remaining inventory is sold in 20X2, the following entry is made on Palit's books at the end of 20X2 to record the realization of the previously unrealized intercompany profit:

(19)	Investment in Label Manufacturing Stock	2,000	
	Income from Label Manufacturing		2,000
	Recognize realized intercompany profit.		

Additional Requirements of ASC 323-10

ASC 323-10, the main authoritative guidance on equity-method reporting, includes several additional requirements:

1. The investor's share of the investee's extraordinary items and prior-period adjustments should be reported as such by the investor, if material.
2. If an investor's share of investee losses exceeds the carrying amount of the investment, the equity method should be discontinued once the investment has been reduced to zero. No further losses are to be recognized by the investor unless the investor is committed to provide further financial support for the investee or unless the investee's imminent return to profitability appears assured. If, after the equity method has been suspended, the investee reports net income, the investor again should apply the equity method, but only after the investor's share of net income equals its share of losses not previously recognized.

3. Preferred dividends of the investee should be deducted from the investee's net income if declared or, whether declared or not, if the preferred stock is cumulative, before the investor computes its share of investee earnings.

ASC 323-10-50-3 includes a number of required financial statement disclosures. When using the equity method, the investor must disclose[8] the following:

1. The name and percentage ownership of each investee.
2. The investor's accounting policies with respect to its investments in common stock, including the reasons for any departures from the 20 percent criterion established by **ASC 323-10-15.**
3. The amount and accounting treatment of any differential.
4. The aggregate market value of each identified nonsubsidiary investment where a quoted market price is available.
5. Either separate statements for or summarized information as to assets, liabilities, and results of operations of corporate joint ventures of the investor, if material in the aggregate.

Investor's Share of Other Comprehensive Income

When an investor uses the equity method to account for its investment in another company, the investor's comprehensive income should include its proportionate share of each of the amounts reported as "Other Comprehensive Income" by the investee. For example, assume that Ajax Corporation purchases 40 percent of the common stock of Barclay Company on January 1, 20X1. For the year 20X1, Barclay reports net income of $80,000 and comprehensive income of $115,000, which includes other comprehensive income (in addition to net income) of $35,000. This other comprehensive income (OCI) reflects an unrealized $35,000 gain (net of tax) resulting from an increase in the fair value of an investment in stock classified as available-for-sale under the criteria established by **ASC 320-10-35-1.** In addition to recording the normal equity-method entries, Ajax recognizes its proportionate share of the unrealized gain on available-for-sale securities reported by Barclay during 20X1 with the following entry:

(20)			
	Investment in Barclay Stock	14,000	
	Unrealized Gain on Investee AFS Investments		14,000
	Recognize share of investee's unrealized gain on available-for-sale securities.		

Entry (20) has no effect on Ajax's net income for 20X1, but it does increase Ajax's other comprehensive income, and thus its total comprehensive income, by $14,000. Ajax will make a similar entry at the end of each period for its proportionate share of any increase or decrease in Barclay's accumulated unrealized holding gain on the available-for-sale securities.

Alternative Versions of the Equity Method of Accounting for Investments in Consolidated Subsidiaries

Companies are free to adopt whatever procedures they wish in accounting for investments in controlled subsidiaries on their books. Because investments in consolidated subsidiaries are eliminated when consolidated statements are prepared, the consolidated statements are not affected by the procedures used to account for the investments on the parent's books.

In practice, companies follow three different approaches in accounting for their consolidated subsidiaries:

1. Cost method.
2. Fully adjusted equity method.
3. Modified version of the equity method.

Several modified versions of the equity method are found in practice, and all are usually referred to as the ***modified equity method.*** Some companies apply the equity method without

[8] **ASC 825-10-45** requires most of the same disclosures for investments in common stock reported under the fair value option that otherwise would have been reported using the equity method.

making adjustments for unrealized intercompany profits and the amortization of the differential. Others adjust for the amortization of the differential but omit the adjustments for unrealized intercompany profits. Modified versions of the equity method may provide some clerical savings for the parent if used on the books when consolidation of the subsidiary is required.

Appendix 2B Consolidation and the Cost Method

Advanced StudyGuide .com

Not all parent companies use the equity method to account for their subsidiary investments that are to be consolidated. The choice of the cost or equity method has no effect on the consolidated financial statements. This is true because the balance in the parent's investment account, the parent's income from the subsidiary, and related items are eliminated in preparing the consolidated statements. Thus, the parent is free to use either the cost method or some version of the equity method on its separate books in accounting for investments in subsidiaries that are to be consolidated.

Because the cost method uses different parent company entries than the equity method, it also requires different consolidation entries in preparing the consolidation worksheet. Keep in mind that the consolidated financial statements appear the same regardless of whether the parent uses the cost or the equity method on its separate books.

CONSOLIDATION—YEAR OF COMBINATION

To illustrate the preparation of consolidated financial statements when the parent company carries its subsidiary investment using the cost method, refer again to the Peerless Products and Special Foods example. Assume that Peerless purchases 100 percent of the common stock of Special Foods on January 1, 20X1, for $300,000. At that date, the book value of Special Foods as a whole is $300,000. All other data are the same as presented in Figures 2–4 and 2–5.

Parent Company Cost-Method Entries

When the parent company uses the cost method, Peerless records only two journal entries during 20X1 related to its investment in Special Foods. Entry (21) records Peerless' purchase of Special Foods stock; entry (22) recognizes dividend income based on the $30,000 ($30,000 × 100%) of dividends received during the period:

(21)	Investment in Special Foods	300,000	
	Cash		300,000
	Record the initial investment in Special Foods.		

(22)	Cash	30,000	
	Dividend Income		30,000
	Record Peerless' 100% share of Special Foods' 20X1 dividend.		

No entries are made on the parent's books with respect to Special Foods income in 20X1, as would be done under the equity method.

Consolidation Worksheet—Year of Combination

Figure 2–11 illustrates the worksheet to prepare consolidated financial statements for December 31, 20X1, using the cost method. The trial balance data for Peerless and Special Foods included in the worksheet in Figure 2–11 differ from those presented in Figure 2–9 only by the effects of using the cost method rather than the equity method on Peerless' books. Note that all of the amounts in the Consolidated column are the same as in Figure 2–9 because the method used by the parent to account for its subsidiary investment on its books has no effect on the consolidated financial statements.

When a company uses the cost method, the basic consolidation entry can be divided into two parts. The first eliminates the investment account. The investment consolidation entry eliminates the balances in the stockholders' equity accounts of Special Foods and the balance in Peerless' investment account as of the date of combination. This consolidation entry is the same each year (assuming there is no impairment of the investment account) because it relates to the original acquisition price and the original balances in Special Foods' equity accounts.

FIGURE 2–11 December 31, 20X1, Cost-Method Worksheet for Consolidated Financial Statements, Initial Year of Ownership; 100 Percent Acquisition at Book Value

	Peerless Products	Special Foods	Consolidation Entries DR	Consolidation Entries CR	Consolidated
Income Statement					
Sales	400,000	200,000			600,000
Less: COGS	(170,000)	(115,000)			(285,000)
Less: Depreciation Expense	(50,000)	(20,000)			(70,000)
Less: Other Expenses	(40,000)	(15,000)			(55,000)
Dividend Income	30,000		30,000		0
Net Income	**170,000**	**50,000**	**30,000**	**0**	**190,000**
Statement of Retained Earnings					
Beginning Balance	300,000	100,000	100,000		300,000
Net Income	**170,000**	**50,000**	**30,000**	**0**	190,000
Less: Dividends Declared	(60,000)	(30,000)		30,000	(60,000)
Ending Balance	**410,000**	**120,000**	**130,000**	**30,000**	**430,000**
Balance Sheet					
Cash	210,000	75,000			285,000
Accounts Receivable	75,000	50,000			125,000
Inventory	100,000	75,000			175,000
Investment in Special Foods	300,000			300,000	0
Land	175,000	40,000			215,000
Buildings & Equipment	800,000	600,000		300,000	1,100,000
Less: Accumulated Depreciation	(450,000)	(320,000)	300,000		(470,000)
Total Assets	**1,210,000**	**520,000**	**300,000**	**600,000**	**1,430,000**
Accounts Payable	100,000	100,000			200,000
Bonds Payable	200,000	100,000			300,000
Common Stock	500,000	200,000	200,000		500,000
Retained Earnings	**410,000**	**120,000**	**130,000**	**30,000**	430,000
Total Liabilities & Equity	**1,210,000**	**520,000**	**330,000**	**30,000**	**1,430,000**

Investment Consolidation Entry:

Common Stock	200,000	
Retained Earnings	100,000	
Investment in Special Foods		300,000

The dividend consolidation entry eliminates the dividend income recorded by Peerless during the period along with Special Foods' dividend declaration related to the stockholdings of Peerless.

Dividend Consolidation Entry:

Dividend Income	30,000	
Dividends Declared		30,000

Finally, the accumulated depreciation consolidation entry is the same as under the equity method.

Optional Accumulated Depreciation Consolidation Entry:

Accumulated Depreciation	300,000	
Buildings & Equipment		300,000

As mentioned previously, the amounts in the Consolidated column of the worksheet in Figure 2–11 are the same as those in Figure 2–9 because the method used on the parent's books to account for the subsidiary investment does not affect the consolidated financial statements.

CONSOLIDATION—SECOND YEAR OF OWNERSHIP

Consolidation differences between cost-method accounting and equity-method accounting tend to be more evident in the second year of ownership simply because the equity-method entries change every year while the cost-method entries are generally the same (with the exception of recording the initial investment).

Parent Company Cost-Method Entry

Peerless only records a single entry on its books in 20X2 related to its investment in Special Foods:

(23)			
	Cash	40,000	
	Dividend Income		40,000

Record Peerless' 100% share of Special Foods' 20X2 dividend.

Consolidation Worksheet—Second Year Following Combination

The worksheet consolidation entries are identical to those used in the first year except that the amount of dividends declared by Special Foods in the second year is $40,000 instead of $30,000.

Investment Consolidation Entry:

Common Stock	200,000	
Retained Earnings	100,000	
Investment in Special Foods		300,000

Dividend Consolidation Entry:

Dividend Income	40,000	
Dividends Declared		40,000

Optional Accumulated Depreciation Consolidation Entry:

Accumulated Depreciation	300,000	
Buildings & Equipment		300,000

Under the cost method, Peerless has not recognized any portion of the undistributed earnings of Special Foods on its parent company books. Therefore, Peerless' retained earnings at the beginning of the second year are less than consolidated retained earnings. Also, Peerless' Investment in Special Foods account balance is less than its 100 percent share of Special Foods' net assets at that date. The consolidation worksheet in Figure 2–12 demonstrates how the worksheet entries eliminate the balances reported by Peerless under the cost method.

Note that while the Consolidated column yields identical numbers to those found in Figure 2–10, the cost method does not maintain the favorable properties that exist when the equity method is employed. Specifically, the parent's net income no longer equals consolidated net income, and the parent's retained earnings no longer equals consolidated retained earnings balance. Hence, although the procedures used under the cost method require less work, the parent company does not enjoy some of the favorable relationships among parent and consolidated numbers that exist under the equity method.

QUESTIONS

LO 2-1 **Q2-1** What types of investments in common stock normally are accounted for using *(a)* the equity method and *(b)* the cost method?

LO 2-1 **Q2-2A** How is the ability to significantly influence the operating and financial policies of a company normally demonstrated?

"A" and "B" indicate that the item relates to Appendix 2A and Appendix 2B, respectively.

FIGURE 2–12 December 31, 20X1, Cost-Method Worksheet for Consolidated Financial Statements, Second Year of Ownership; 100 Percent Acquisition at Book Value

	Peerless Products	Special Foods	Consolidation Entries DR	Consolidation Entries CR	Consolidated
Income Statement					
Sales	450,000	300,000			750,000
Less: COGS	(180,000)	(160,000)			(340,000)
Less: Depreciation Expense	(50,000)	(20,000)			(70,000)
Less: Other Expenses	(60,000)	(45,000)			(105,000)
Income from Special Foods	40,000		40,000		0
Net Income	**200,000**	**75,000**	**40,000**	**0**	**235,000**
Statement of Retained Earnings					
Beginning Balance	410,000	120,000	100,000		430,000
Net Income	**200,000**	**75,000**	**40,000**	**0**	235,000
Less: Dividends Declared	(60,000)	(40,000)		40,000	(60,000)
Ending Balance	**550,000**	**155,000**	**140,000**	**40,000**	**605,000**
Balance Sheet					
Cash	245,000	85,000			330,000
Accounts Receivable	150,000	80,000			230,000
Inventory	180,000	90,000			270,000
Investment in Special Foods	300,000			300,000	0
Land	175,000	40,000			215,000
Buildings & Equipment	800,000	600,000		300,000	1,100,000
Less: Accumulated Depreciation	(500,000)	(340,000)	300,000		(540,000)
Total Assets	**1,350,000**	**555,000**	**300,000**	**600,000**	**1,605,000**
Accounts Payable	100,000	100,000			200,000
Bonds Payable	200,000	100,000			300,000
Common Stock	500,000	200,000	200,000		500,000
Retained Earnings	**550,000**	**155,000**	**140,000**	**40,000**	605,000
Total Liabilities & Equity	**1,350,000**	**555,000**	**340,000**	**40,000**	**1,605,000**

LO 2-1 **Q2-3A** When is equity-method reporting considered inappropriate even though sufficient common shares are owned to allow the exercise of significant influence?

LO 2-4 **Q2-4** When will the balance in the intercorporate investment account be the same under the cost method and the equity method?

LO 2-2, 2-3 **Q2-5** Describe an investor's treatment of an investee's prior-period dividends and earnings when the investor acquires significant influence through a purchase of additional stock.

LO 2-2, 2-3 **Q2-6** From the point of view of an investor in common stock, what is a liquidating dividend?

LO 2-2, 2-3 **Q2-7** What effect does a liquidating dividend have on the balance in the investment account under the cost method and the equity method?

LO 2-2, 2-3 **Q2-8** How is the receipt of a dividend recorded under the equity method? Under the cost method?

LO 2-5 **Q2-9** How does the fair value method differ from the cost method and equity method in reporting income from nonsubsidiary investments?

LO 2-3 **Q2-10A** How does the fully adjusted equity method differ from the modified equity method?

LO 2-4 **Q2-11** Explain the concept of a one-line consolidation.

LO 2-3 **Q2-12A** What is the modified equity method? When might a company choose to use the modified equity method rather than the fully adjusted equity method?

LO 2-3 **Q2-13A** How are extraordinary items of the investee disclosed by the investor under equity-method reporting?

LO 2-7 **Q2-14** How does a consolidation entry differ from an adjusting entry?

LO 2-6, 2-7 **Q2-15** What portion of the balances of subsidiary stockholders' equity accounts is included in the consolidated balance sheet?

LO 2-7 **Q2-16** How does the consolidation process change when consolidated statements are prepared after—rather than at—the date of acquisition?

LO 2-7 **Q2-17** What are the three parts of the consolidation worksheet, and what sequence is used in completing the worksheet parts?

LO 2-7 **Q2-18** How are a subsidiary's dividend declarations reported in the consolidated retained earnings statement?

LO 2-7 **Q2-19** How is consolidated net income computed in a consolidation worksheet?

LO 2-7 **Q2-20** Give a definition of *consolidated retained earnings.*

LO 2-7 **Q2-21** How is the amount reported as consolidated retained earnings determined?

LO 2-7 **Q2-22** Why is the beginning retained earnings balance for each company entered in the three-part consolidation worksheet rather than just the ending balance?

CASES

LO 2-2, 2-3 **C2-1A**

Understanding

Choice of Accounting Method

Slanted Building Supplies purchased 32 percent of the voting shares of Flat Flooring Company in March 20X3. On December 31, 20X3, the officers of Slanted Building Supplies indicated they needed advice on whether to use the equity method or cost method in reporting their ownership in Flat Flooring.

Required

a. What factors should be considered in determining whether equity-method reporting is appropriate?

b. Which of the two methods is likely to show the larger reported contribution to Slanted's earnings in 20X4? Explain.

c. Why might the use of the equity method become more appropriate as the percentage of ownership increases?

LO 2-2, 2-3 **C2-2**

Research

Intercorporate Ownership

Most Company purchased 90 percent of the voting common stock of Port Company on January 1, 20X4, and 15 percent of the voting common stock of Adams Company on July 1, 20X4. In preparing the financial statements for Most Company at December 31, 20X4, you discover that Port Company purchased 10 percent of the common stock of Adams Company in 20X2 and continues to hold those shares. Adams Company reported net income of $200,000 for 20X4 and paid a dividend of $70,000 on December 20, 20X4.

Required

Most Company's chief accountant instructs you to review the Accounting Standards Codification and prepare a memo discussing whether the cost or equity method should be used in reporting the investment in Adams Company in Most's consolidated statements prepared at December 31, 20X4. Support your recommendations with citations and quotations from the authoritative financial reporting standards or other literature.

LO 2-2, 2-3 **C2-3A**

Research

Application of the Equity Method

Forth Company owned 85,000 of Brown Company's 100,000 shares of common stock until January 1, 20X2, at which time it sold 70,000 of the shares to a group of seven investors, each of whom purchased 10,000 shares. On December 3, 20X2, Forth received a dividend of $9,000 from Brown. Forth continues to purchase a substantial portion of Brown's output under a contract that runs until the end of 20X9. Because of this arrangement, Forth is permitted to place two of its employees on Brown's board of directors.

Required

Forth Company's controller is not sure whether the company should use the cost or equity method in accounting for its investment in Brown Company. The controller asked you to review the relevant accounting literature and prepare a memo containing your recommendations. Support your recommendations with citations and quotations from the Accounting Standards Codification.

LO 2-6, 2-7 **C2-4** *Communication*

Need for Consolidation Process

At a recent staff meeting, the vice president of marketing appeared confused. The controller had assured him that the parent company and each of the subsidiary companies had properly accounted for all transactions during the year. After several other questions, he finally asked, "If it has been done properly, then why must you spend so much time and make so many changes to the amounts reported by the individual companies when you prepare the consolidated financial statements each month? You should be able to just add the reported balances together."

Required

Prepare an appropriate response to help the controller answer the marketing vice president's question.

LO 2-1 **C2-5** *Research*

Account Presentation

Prime Company has been expanding rapidly and is now an extremely diversified company for its size. It currently owns three companies with manufacturing facilities, two companies primarily in retail sales, a consumer finance company, and two natural gas pipeline companies. This has led to some conflict between the company's chief accountant and its treasurer. The treasurer advocates presenting no more than five assets and three liabilities on its balance sheet. The chief accountant has resisted combining balances from substantially different subsidiaries and has asked for your assistance.

Required

Research the Accounting Standards Codification to see what guidance is provided and prepare a memo to the chief accountant with your findings. Include citations to and quotations from the most relevant references. Include in your memo at least two examples of situations in which it may be inappropriate to combine similar-appearing accounts of two subsidiaries.

LO 2-6, 2-7 **C2-6** *Research*

Consolidating an Unprofitable Subsidiary

Amazing Chemical Corporation's president had always wanted his own yacht and crew and concluded that Amazing Chemical should diversify its investments by purchasing an existing boatyard and repair facility on the lakeshore near his summer home. He could then purchase a yacht and have a convenient place to store it and have it repaired. Although the board of directors was never formally asked to approve this new venture, the president moved forward with optimism and a rather substantial amount of corporate money to purchase full ownership of the boatyard, which had lost rather significant amounts of money each of the five prior years and had never reported a profit for the original owners.

Not surprisingly, the boatyard continued to lose money after Amazing Chemical purchased it, and the losses grew larger each month. Amazing Chemical, a very profitable chemical company, reported net income of \$780,000 in 20X2 and \$850,000 in 20X3 even though the boatyard reported net losses of \$160,000 in 20X2 and \$210,000 in 20X3 and was fully consolidated.

Required

Amazing Chemical's chief accountant has become concerned that members of the board of directors or company shareholders will accuse him of improperly preparing the consolidated statements. The president does not plan to tell anyone about the losses, which do not show up in the consolidated income statement that the chief accountant prepared. You have been asked to prepare a memo to the chief accountant indicating the way to include subsidiaries in the consolidated income statement and to provide citations to or quotations from the Accounting Standards Codification that would assist the chief accountant in dealing with this matter. You have also been asked to search the accounting literature to see whether any reporting requirements require disclosure of the boatyard in notes to the financial statements or in management's discussion and analysis.

EXERCISES

LO 2-2, 2-3

E2-1 Multiple-Choice Questions on Use of Cost and Equity Methods [AICPA Adapted]

Select the correct answer for each of the following questions.

1. Peel Company received a cash dividend from a common stock investment. Should Peel report an **increase** in the investment account if it uses the cost method or equity method of accounting?

	Cost	Equity
a.	No	No
b.	Yes	Yes
c.	Yes	No
d.	No	Yes

2. In 20X0, Neil Company held the following investments in common stock:
   - 25,000 shares of B&K Inc.'s 100,000 outstanding shares. Neil's level of ownership gives it the ability to exercise significant influence over the financial and operating policies of B&K.
   - 6,000 shares of Amal Corporation's 309,000 outstanding shares.

   During 20X0, Neil received the following distributions from its common stock investments:

November 6	$30,000 cash dividend from B&K
November 11	$1,500 cash dividend from Amal
December 26	3 percent common stock dividend from Amal The closing price of this stock was $115 per share.

   What amount of dividend revenue should Neil report for 20X0?

   a. $1,500.
   b. $4,200.
   c. $31,500.
   d. $34,200.

3. An investor uses the equity method to account for an investment in common stock. Assume that (1) the investor owns more than 50 percent of the outstanding common stock of the investee, (2) the investee company reports net income and declares dividends during the year, and (3) the investee's net income is more than the dividends it declares. How would the investor's investment in the common stock of the investee company under the equity method differ at year-end from what it would have been if the investor had accounted for the investment under the cost method?

   a. The balance under the equity method is higher than it would have been under the cost method.
   b. The balance under the equity method is lower than it would have been under the cost method.
   c. The balance under the equity method is higher than it would have been under the cost method, but only if the investee company actually paid the dividends before year-end.
   d. The balance under the equity method is lower than it would have been under the cost method, but only if the investee company actually paid the dividends before year-end.

4. A corporation exercises significant influence over an affiliate in which it holds a 40 percent common stock interest. If its affiliate completed a fiscal year profitably but paid no dividends, how would this affect the investor corporation?

   a. Result in an increased current ratio.
   b. Result in increased earnings per share.
   c. Increase asset turnover ratios.
   d. Decrease book value per share.

5. An investor in common stock received dividends in excess of the investor's share of investee's earnings subsequent to the date of the investment. How will the investor's investment account be affected by those dividends under each of the following methods?

	Cost Method	Equity Method
a.	No effect	No effect
b.	Decrease	No effect
c.	No effect	Decrease
d.	Decrease	Decrease

6. An investor uses the cost method to account for an investment in common stock. A portion of the dividends received this year was in excess of the investor's share of the investee's earnings subsequent to the date of investment. The amount of dividend revenue that should be reported in the investor's income statement for this year would be
   a. Zero.
   b. The total amount of dividends received this year.
   c. The portion of the dividends received this year that was in excess of the investor's share of investee's earnings subsequent to the date of investment.
   d. The portion of the dividends received this year that was not in excess of the investor's share of the investee's earnings subsequent to the date of investment.

LO 2-4

E2-2 Multiple-Choice Questions on Intercorporate Investments

Select the correct answer for each of the following questions.

1. Companies often acquire ownership in other companies using a variety of ownership arrangements. The investor should use equity-method reporting whenever
   a. The investor purchases voting common stock of the investee.
   b. The investor has significant influence over the operating and financing decisions of the investee.
   c. The investor purchases goods and services from the investee.
   d. When there is no differential included in an investment, the carrying value of the investment is less than the market value of the investee's shares held by the investor.
2. The carrying amount of an investment in stock correctly accounted for under the equity method is equal to
   a. The original price paid to purchase the investment.
   b. The original price paid to purchase the investment plus cumulative net income plus cumulative dividends declared by the investee since the date the investment was acquired.
   c. The original price paid to purchase the investment plus cumulative net income minus cumulative dividends declared by the investee since the date the investment was acquired.
   d. The original price paid to purchase the investment minus cumulative net income minus cumulative dividends declared by the investee since the date the investment was acquired.

LO 2-3

E2-3 Multiple-Choice Questions on Applying Equity Method [AICPA Adapted]

Select the correct answer for each of the following questions.

1. On January 2, 20X3, Kean Company purchased a 30 percent interest in Pod Company for \$250,000. Pod reported net income of \$100,000 for 20X3 and declared and paid a dividend of \$10,000. Kean accounts for this investment using the equity method. In its December 31, 20X3, balance sheet, what amount should Kean report as its investment in Pod?
   a. \$160,000.
   b. \$223,000.
   c. \$340,000.
   d. \$277,000.

2. On January 1, 20X8, Mega Corporation acquired 10 percent of the outstanding voting stock of Penny Inc. On January 2, 20X9, Mega gained the ability to exercise significant influence over Penny's financial and operating decisions by acquiring an additional 20 percent of Penny's outstanding stock. The two purchases were made at prices proportionate to the value assigned to Penny's net assets, which equaled their carrying amounts. For the years ended December 31, 20X8 and 20X9, Penny reported the following:

	20X8	20X9
Dividends Paid	$200,000	$300,000
Net Income	600,000	650,000

In 20X9, what amounts should Mega report as current year investment income and as an adjustment, before income taxes, to 20X8 investment income?

	20X9 Investment Income	Adjustment to 20X8 Investment Income
a.	$195,000	$160,000
b.	195,000	100,000
c.	195,000	40,000
d.	105,000	40,000

3. Investor Inc. owns 40 percent of Alimand Corporation. During the calendar year 20X5, Alimand had net earnings of $100,000 and paid dividends of $10,000. Investor mistakenly recorded these transactions using the cost method rather than the equity method of accounting. What effect would this have on the investment account, net earnings, and retained earnings, respectively?

a. Understate, overstate, overstate.
b. Overstate, understate, understate.
c. Overstate, overstate, overstate.
d. Understate, understate, understate.

4. A corporation using the equity method of accounting for its investment in a 40 percent–owned investee, which earned $20,000 and paid $5,000 in dividends, made the following entries:

Investment in Investee	8,000	
Income from Investee		8,000
Cash	2,000	
Dividend Revenue		2,000

What effect will these entries have on the investor's statement of financial position?

a. Financial position will be fairly stated.
b. Investment in the investee will be overstated, retained earnings understated.
c. Investment in the investee will be understated, retained earnings understated.
d. Investment in the investee will be overstated, retained earnings overstated.

LO 2-4

E2-4 Cost versus Equity Reporting

Winston Corporation purchased 40 percent of the stock of Fullbright Company on January 1, 20X2, at underlying book value. The companies reported the following operating results and dividend payments during the first three years of intercorporate ownership:

	Winston Corporation		Fullbright Company	
Year	Operating Income	Dividends	Net Income	Dividends
20X2	$100,000	$ 40,000	$70,000	$30,000
20X3	60,000	80,000	40,000	60,000
20X4	250,000	120,000	25,000	50,000

Required

Compute the net income reported by Winston for each of the three years, assuming it accounts for its investment in Fullbright using (*a*) the cost method and (*b*) the equity method.

LO 2-2, 2-3

E2-5 Acquisition Price

Phillips Company bought 40 percent ownership in Jones Bag Company on January 1, 20X1, at underlying book value. In 20X1, 20X2, and 20X3, Jones Bag reported the following:

Year	Net Income	Dividends
20X1	$ 8,000	$15,000
20X2	12,000	10,000
20X3	20,000	10,000

The balance in Phillips Company's investment account on December 31, 20X3, was $54,000.

Required

In each of the following independent cases, determine the amount that Phillips paid for its investment in Jones Bag stock assuming that Phillips accounted for its investment using the (*a*) cost method and (*b*) equity method.

LO 2-2, 2-3

Advanced StudyGuide .com

E2-6 Investment Income

Ravine Corporation purchased 30 percent ownership of Valley Industries for $90,000 on January 1, 20X6, when Valley had capital stock of $240,000 and retained earnings of $60,000. The following data were reported by the companies for the years 20X6 through 20X9:

			Dividends Declared	
Year	Operating Income, Ravine Corporation	Net Income, Valley Industries	Ravine	Valley
20X6	$140,000	$30,000	$ 70,000	$20,000
20X7	80,000	50,000	70,000	40,000
20X8	220,000	10,000	90,000	40,000
20X9	160,000	40,000	100,000	20,000

Required

a. What net income would Ravine Corporation have reported for each of the years, assuming Ravine accounts for the intercorporate investment using (1) the cost method and (2) the equity method?

b. Give all appropriate journal entries for 20X8 that Ravine made under both the cost and the equity methods.

LO 2-3

E2-7 Investment Value

Port Company purchased 30,000 of the 100,000 outstanding shares of Sund Company common stock on January 1, 20X2, for $180,000. The purchase price was equal to the book value of the shares purchased. Sund reported the following:

Year	Net Income	Dividends
20X2	$40,000	$25,000
20X3	30,000	
20X4	5,000	

Required

Compute the amounts Port Company should report as the carrying values of its investment in Sund Company at December 31, 20X2, 20X3, and 20X4.

LO 2-2, 2-3

E2-8A Income Reporting

Grandview Company purchased 40 percent of the stock of Spinet Corporation on January 1, 20X8, at underlying book value. Spinet recorded the following income for 20X9:

Income before Extraordinary Gain	$60,000
Extraordinary Gain	30,000
Net Income	$90,000

Required

Prepare all journal entries on Grandview's books for 20X9 to account for its investment in Spinet.

LO 2-4, 2-5

E2-9 Fair Value Method

Small Company reported 20X7 net income of $40,000 and paid dividends of $15,000 during the year. Mock Corporation acquired 20 percent of Small's shares on January 1, 20X7, for $105,000. At December 31, 20X7, Mock determined the fair value of the shares of Small to be $121,000. Mock reported operating income of $90,000 for 20X7.

Required

Compute Mock's net income for 20X7 assuming it uses

a. The cost method in accounting for its investment in Small.

b. The equity method in accounting for its investment in Small.

c. The fair value method in accounting for its investment in Small.

LO 2-3, 2-5

E2-10 Fair Value Recognition

Kent Company purchased 35 percent ownership of Lomm Company on January 1, 20X8, for $140,000. Lomm reported 20X8 net income of $80,000 and paid dividends of $20,000. At December 31, 20X8, Kent determined the fair value of its investment in Lomm to be $174,000.

Required

Give all journal entries recorded by Kent with respect to its investment in Lomm in 20X8 assuming it uses

a. The equity method.

b. The fair value method.

LO 2-3, 2-5

E2-11A Investee with Preferred Stock Outstanding

Reden Corporation purchased 45 percent of Montgomery Company's common stock on January 1, 20X9, at underlying book value of $288,000. Montgomery's balance sheet contained the following stockholders' equity balances:

Preferred Stock ($5 par value, 50,000 shares issued and outstanding)	$250,000
Common Stock ($1 par value, 150,000 shares issued and outstanding)	150,000
Additional Paid-In Capital	180,000
Retained Earnings	310,000
Total Stockholders' Equity	$890,000

Montgomery's preferred stock is cumulative and pays a 10 percent annual dividend. Montgomery reported net income of $95,000 for 20X9 and paid total dividends of $40,000.

Required

Give the journal entries recorded by Reden Corporation for 20X9 related to its investment in Montgomery Company common stock.

LO 2-2, 2-3

E2-12A Other Comprehensive Income Reported by Investee

Callas Corporation paid $380,000 to acquire 40 percent ownership of Thinbill Company on January 1, 20X9. The amount paid was equal to Thinbill's underlying book value. During 20X9, Thinbill reported operating income of $45,000 and an increase of $20,000 in the market value of available-for-sale securities held for the year. Thinbill paid dividends of $9,000 on December 10, 20X9.

Required

Give all journal entries that Callas Corporation recorded in 20X9, including closing entries at December 31, 20X9, associated with its investment in Thinbill Company.

LO 2-2, 2-3

Advanced StudyGuide .com

E2-13A Other Comprehensive Income Reported by Investee

Baldwin Corporation purchased 25 percent of Gwin Company's common stock on January 1, 20X8, at underlying book value. In 20X8, Gwin reported a net loss of $20,000 and paid dividends of $10,000, and in 20X9, The company reported net income of $68,000 and paid dividends of $16,000. Gwin also purchased marketable securities classified as available-for-sale on February 8, 20X9, and reported an increase of $12,000 in their fair value at December 31, 20X9. Baldwin reported a balance of $67,000 in its investment in Gwin at December 31, 20X9.

Required

Compute the amount paid by Baldwin Corporation to purchase the shares of Gwin Company.

LO 2-7

E2-14 Basic Consolidation Entry

On December 31, 20X3, Broadway Corporation reported common stock outstanding of $200,000, additional paid-in capital of $300,000, and retained earnings of $100,000. On January 1, 20X4, Johe Company acquired control of Broadway in a business combination.

Required

Give the consolidation entry that would be needed in preparing a consolidated balance sheet immediately following the combination if Johe acquired all of Broadway's outstanding common stock for $600,000.

LO 2-6, 2-7

E2-15 Balance Sheet Worksheet

Blank Corporation acquired 100 percent of Faith Corporation's common stock on December 31, 20X2, for $150,000. Data from the balance sheets of the two companies included the following amounts as of the date of acquisition:

Item	Blank Corporation	Faith Corporation
Cash	$ 65,000	$ 18,000
Accounts Receivable	87,000	37,000
Inventory	110,000	60,000
Buildings & Equipment (net)	220,000	150,000
Investment in Faith Corporation Stock	150,000	
Total Assets	$632,000	$265,000
Accounts Payable	$ 92,000	$ 35,000
Notes Payable	150,000	80,000
Common Stock	100,000	60,000
Retained Earnings	290,000	90,000
Total Liabilities & Stockholders' Equity	$632,000	$265,000

At the date of the business combination, the book values of Faith's net assets and liabilities approximated fair value. Assume that Faith Corporation's accumulated depreciation on buildings and equipment on the acquisition date was $30,000.

Required

a. Give the consolidation entry or entries needed to prepare a consolidated balance sheet immediately following the business combination.

b. Prepare a consolidated balance sheet worksheet.

LO 2-3, 2-7

E2-16 Consolidation Entries for Wholly Owned Subsidiary

Trim Corporation acquired 100 percent of Round Corporation's voting common stock on January 1, 20X2, for $400,000. At that date, the book values and fair values of Round's assets and liabilities were equal. Round reported the following summarized balance sheet data:

Assets	$700,000	Accounts Payable	$100,000
		Bonds Payable	200,000
		Common Stock	120,000
		Retained Earnings	280,000
Total	$700,000	Total	$700,000

Round reported net income of $80,000 for 20X2 and paid dividends of $25,000.

Required

a. Give the journal entries recorded by Trim Corporation during 20X2 on its books if Trim accounts for its investment in Round using the equity method.

b. Give the consolidation entries needed at December 31, 20X2, to prepare consolidated financial statements.

LO 2-3, 2-7

E2-17 Basic Consolidation Entries for Fully Owned Subsidiary

Amber Corporation reported the following summarized balance sheet data on December 31, 20X6:

Assets	$600,000	Liabilities	$100,000
		Common Stock	300,000
		Retained Earnings	200,000
Total	$600,000	Total	$600,000

On January 1, 20X7, Purple Company acquired 100 percent of Amber's stock for $500,000. At the acquisition date, the book values and fair values of Amber's assets and liabilities were equal. Amber reported net income of $50,000 for 20X7 and paid dividends of $20,000.

Required

a. Give the journal entries recorded by Purple on its books during 20X7 if it accounts for its investment in Amber using the equity method.

b. Give the consolidation entries needed on December 31, 20X7, to prepare consolidated financial statements.

PROBLEMS

LO 2-2, 2-3

P2-18 Retroactive Recognition

Idle Corporation has been acquiring shares of Fast Track Enterprises at book value for the last several years. Fast Track provided data including the following:

	20X2	20X3	20X4	20X5
Net Income	$40,000	$60,000	$40,000	$50,000
Dividends	20,000	20,000	10,000	20,000

Fast Track declares and pays its annual dividend on November 15 each year. Its net book value on January 1, 20X2, was $250,000. Idle purchased shares of Fast Track on three occasions:

Date	Percent of Ownership Purchased	Amount Paid
January 1, 20X2	10%	$25,000
July 1, 20X3	5	15,000
January 1, 20X5	10	34,000

Required

Give the journal entries to be recorded on Idle's books in 20X5 related to its investment in Fast Track.

LO 2-4, 2-5

P2-19 Fair Value Method

Advanced StudyGuide .com

Gant Company purchased 20 percent of the outstanding shares of Temp Company for $70,000 on January 1, 20X6. The following results are reported for Temp Company:

	20X6	20X7	20X8
Net Income	$40,000	$35,000	$60,000
Dividends Paid	15,000	30,000	20,000
Fair Value of Shares Held by Gant:			
January 1	70,000	89,000	86,000
December 31	89,000	86,000	97,000

Required

Determine the amounts reported by Gant as income from its investment in Temp for each year and the balance in Gant's investment in Temp at the end of each year assuming that Gant uses the following methods in accounting for its investment in Temp:

a. Cost method.

b. Equity method

c. Fair value method.

LO 2-5

P2-20 Fair Value Journal Entries

Marlow Company acquired 40 percent of the voting shares of Brown Company on January 1, 20X8, for $85,000. The following results are reported for Brown Company:

	20X8	20X9
Net Income	$20,000	$30,000
Dividends Paid	10,000	15,000
Fair Value of Shares Held by Marlow:		
January 1	85,000	97,000
December 31	97,000	92,000

Required

Give all journal entries recorded by Marlow for 20X8 and 20X9 assuming that it uses the fair value method in accounting for its investment in Brown.

LO 2-5

P2-21A Other Comprehensive Income Reported by Investee

Dewey Corporation owns 30 percent of the common stock of Jimm Company, which it purchased at underlying book value on January 1, 20X5. Dewey reported a balance of $245,000 for its investment in Jimm Company on January 1, 20X5, and $276,800 at December 31, 20X5. During 20X5, Dewey and Jimm Company reported operating income of $340,000 and $70,000, respectively. Jimm received dividends from investments in marketable equity securities in the amount of $7,000 during 20X5. It also reported an increase of $18,000 in the market value of its portfolio of trading securities and an increase in the value of its portfolio of securities classified as available-for-sale. Jimm paid dividends of $20,000 in 20X5. Ignore income taxes in determining your solution.

Required

a. Assuming that Dewey uses the equity method in accounting for its investment in Jimm, compute the amount of income from Jimm recorded by Dewey in 20X5.

b. Compute the amount reported by Jimm as other comprehensive income in 20X5.

c. If all of Jimm's other comprehensive income arose solely from its investment in available-for-sale securities purchased on March 10, 20X5, for $130,000, what was the market value of those securities at December 31, 20X5?

LO 2-3, 2-7

P2-22A Equity-Method Income Statement

Wealthy Manufacturing Company purchased 40 percent of the voting shares of Diversified Products Corporation on March 23, 20X4. On December 31, 20X8, Wealthy Manufacturing's controller attempted to prepare income statements and retained earnings statements for the two companies using the following summarized 20X8 data:

	Wealthy Manufacturing	Diversified Products
Net Sales	$850,000	$400,000
Cost of Goods Sold	670,000	320,000
Other Expenses	90,000	25,000
Dividends Declared & Paid	30,000	10,000
Retained Earnings, 1/1/X8	420,000	260,000

Wealthy Manufacturing uses the equity method in accounting for its investment in Diversified Products. The controller was also aware of the following specific transactions for Diversified Products in 20X8, which were not included in the preceding data:

1. On June 30, 20X8, Diversified incurred a $5,000 extraordinary loss from a volcanic eruption near its Greenland facility.
2. Diversified sold its entire Health Technologies division on September 30, 20X8, for $375,000. The book value of Health Technologies division's net assets on that date was $331,000. The division incurred an operating loss of $15,000 in the first nine months of 20X8.
3. During 20X8, Diversified sold one of its delivery trucks after it was involved in an accident and recorded a gain of $10,000.

Required

a. Prepare an income statement and retained earnings statement for Diversified Products for 20X8.

b. Prepare an income statement and retained earnings statement for Wealthy Manufacturing for 20X8.

LO 2-3, 2-6, 2-7

P2-23 Consolidated Worksheet at End of the First Year of Ownership (Equity Method)

Peanut Company acquired 100 percent of Snoopy Company's outstanding common stock for $300,000 on January 1, 20X8, when the book value of Snoopy's net assets was equal to $300,000. Peanut uses the equity method to account for investments. Trial balance data for Peanut and Snoopy as of December 31, 20X8, are as follows:

Advanced StudyGuide .com

	Peanut Company		Snoopy Company	
	Debit	**Credit**	**Debit**	**Credit**
Cash	$ 130,000		$ 80,000	
Accounts Receivable	165,000		65,000	
Inventory	200,000		75,000	
Investment in Snoopy Stock	355,000		0	
Land	200,000		100,000	
Buildings & Equipment	700,000		200,000	
Cost of Goods Sold	200,000		125,000	
Depreciation Expense	50,000		10,000	
S&A Expense	225,000		40,000	
Dividends Declared	100,000		20,000	
Accumulated Depreciation		$ 450,000		$ 20,000
Accounts Payable		75,000		60,000
Bonds Payable		200,000		85,000
Common Stock		500,000		200,000
Retained Earnings		225,000		100,000
Sales		800,000		250,000
Income from Snoopy		75,000		0
Total	$2,325,000	$2,325,000	$715,000	$715,000

Required

a. Prepare the journal entries on Peanut's books for the acquisition of Snoopy on January 1, 20X8, as well as any normal equity-method entry(ies) related to the investment in Snoopy Company during 20X8.

b. Prepare a consolidation worksheet for 20X8 in good form.

LO 2-3, 2-6, 2-7

P2-24 Consolidated Worksheet at End of the Second Year of Ownership (Equity Method)

Peanut Company acquired 100 percent of Snoopy Company's outstanding common stock for $300,000 on January 1, 20X8, when the book value of Snoopy's net assets was equal to $300,000. Problem 2-23 summarizes the first year of Peanut's ownership of Snoopy. Peanut uses the equity method to account for investments. The following trial balance summarizes the financial position and operations for Peanut and Snoopy as of December 31, 20X9:

Advanced StudyGuide .com

	Peanut Company		Snoopy Company	
	Debit	**Credit**	**Debit**	**Credit**
Cash	$ 230,000		$ 75,000	
Accounts Receivable	190,000		80,000	
Inventory	180,000		100,000	
Investment in Snoopy Stock	405,000		0	
Land	200,000		100,000	
Buildings & Equipment	700,000		200,000	
Cost of Goods Sold	270,000		150,000	
Depreciation Expense	50,000		10,000	
Selling & Administrative Expense	230,000		60,000	
Dividends Declared	225,000		30,000	
Accumulated Depreciation		$ 500,000		$ 30,000
Accounts Payable		75,000		35,000
Bonds Payable		150,000		85,000
Common Stock		500,000		200,000
Retained Earnings		525,000		155,000
Sales		850,000		300,000
Income from Snoopy		80,000		0
Total	$2,680,000	$2,680,000	$805,000	$805,000

Required

a. Prepare any equity-method journal entry(ies) related to the investment in Snoopy Company during 20X9.

b. Prepare a consolidation worksheet for 20X9 in good form.

LO 2-3, 2-6, 2-7

P2-25 Consolidated Worksheet at End of the First Year of Ownership (Equity Method) Paper Company acquired 100 percent of Scissor Company's outstanding common stock for $370,000 on January 1, 20X8, when the book value of Scissor's net assets was equal to $370,000. Paper uses the equity method to account for investments. Trial balance data for Paper and Scissor as of December 31, 20X8, are as follows:

	Paper Company		Scissor Company	
	Debit	**Credit**	**Debit**	**Credit**
Cash	$ 122,000		$ 46,000	
Accounts Receivable	140,000		60,000	
Inventory	190,000		120,000	
Investment in Scissor Stock	438,000		0	
Land	250,000		125,000	
Buildings & Equipment	875,000		250,000	
Cost of Goods Sold	250,000		155,000	
Depreciation Expense	65,000		12,000	
Selling & Administrative Expense	280,000		50,000	
Dividends Declared	80,000		25,000	
Accumulated Depreciation		$ 565,000		$ 36,000
Accounts Payable		77,000		27,000
Bonds Payable		250,000		100,000
Common Stock		625,000		250,000
Retained Earnings		280,000		120,000
Sales		800,000		310,000
Income from Scissor		93,000		0
Total	$2,690,000	$2,690,000	$843,000	$843,000

Required

a. Prepare the journal entries on Paper's books for the acquisition of Scissor on January 1, 20X8 as well as any normal equity-method entry(ies) related to the investment in Scissor Company during 20X8.

b. Prepare a consolidation worksheet for 20X8 in good form.

LO 2-3, 2-6, 2-7

P2-26 Consolidated Worksheet at End of the Second Year of Ownership (Equity Method) Paper Company acquired 100 percent of Scissor Company's outstanding common stock for $370,000 on January 1, 20X8, when the book value of Scissor's net assets was equal to $370,000. Problem 2-25 summarizes the first year of Paper's ownership of Scissor. Paper uses the equity method to account for investments. The following trial balance summarizes the financial position and operations for Paper and Scissor as of December 31, 20X9:

	Paper Company		Scissor Company	
	Debit	**Credit**	**Debit**	**Credit**
Cash	$232,000		$116,000	
Accounts Receivable	165,000		97,000	
Inventory	193,000		115,000	
Investment in Scissor Stock	515,000		0	
Land	250,000		125,000	
Buildings & Equipment	875,000		250,000	
Cost of Goods Sold	$278,000		$178,000	
Depreciation Expense	65,000		12,000	
Selling & Administrative Expense	312,000		58,000	
Dividends Declared	90,000		30,000	

(continued)

Accumulated Depreciation		$ 630,000		$ 48,000
Accounts Payable		85,000		40,000
Bonds Payable		150,000		100,000
Common Stock		625,000		250,000
Retained Earnings		498,000		188,000
Sales		880,000		355,000
Income from Scissor		107,000		0
Total	$2,975,000	$2,975,000	$981,000	$981,000

Required

a. Prepare any equity-method journal entry(ies) related to the investment in Scissor Company during 20X9.

b. Prepare a consolidation worksheet for 20X9 in good form.

LO 2-2, 2-6, 2-7

P2-27B Consolidated Worksheet at End of the First Year of Ownership (Cost Method)

Peanut Company acquired 100 percent of Snoopy Company's outstanding common stock for $300,000 on January 1, 20X8, when the book value of Snoopy's net assets was equal to $300,000. Peanut uses the cost method to account for investments. Trial balance data for Peanut and Snoopy as of December 31, 20X8, are as follows:

	Peanut Company		Snoopy Company	
	Debit	**Credit**	**Debit**	**Credit**
Cash	$ 130,000		$ 80,000	
Accounts Receivable	165,000		65,000	
Inventory	200,000		75,000	
Investment in Snoopy Stock	300,000		0	
Land	200,000		100,000	
Buildings & Equipment	700,000		200,000	
Cost of Goods Sold	200,000		125,000	
Depreciation Expense	50,000		10,000	
Selling & Administrative Expense	225,000		40,000	
Dividends Declared	100,000		20,000	
Accumulated Depreciation		$ 450,000		$ 20,000
Accounts Payable		75,000		60,000
Bonds Payable		200,000		85,000
Common Stock		500,000		200,000
Retained Earnings		225,000		100,000
Sales		800,000		250,000
Dividend Income		20,000		0
Total	$2,270,000	$2,270,000	$715,000	$715,000

Required

a. Prepare the journal entries on Peanut's books for the acquisition of Snoopy on January 1, 20X8 as well as any normal cost-method entry(ies) related to the investment in Snoopy Company during 20X8.

b. Prepare a consolidation worksheet for 20X8 in good form.

LO 2-2, 2-6, 2-7

P2-28B Consolidated Worksheet at End of the Second Year of Ownership (Cost Method)

Peanut Company acquired 100 percent of Snoopy Company's outstanding common stock for $300,000 on January 1, 20X8, when the book value of Snoopy's net assets was equal to $300,000.

Problem 2-27 summarizes the first year of Peanut's ownership of Snoopy. Peanut uses the cost method to account for investments. The following trial balance summarizes the financial position and operations for Peanut and Snoopy as of December 31, 20X9:

	Peanut Company		Snoopy Company	
	Debit	**Credit**	**Debit**	**Credit**
Cash	$ 230,000		$ 75,000	
Accounts Receivable	190,000		80,000	
Inventory	180,000		100,000	
Investment in Snoopy Stock	300,000		0	
Land	200,000		100,000	
Buildings & Equipment	700,000		200,000	
Cost of Goods Sold	270,000		150,000	
Depreciation Expense	50,000		10,000	
Selling & Administrative Expense	230,000		60,000	
Dividends Declared	225,000		30,000	
Accumulated Depreciation		$ 500,000		$ 30,000
Accounts Payable		75,000		35,000
Bonds Payable		150,000		85,000
Common Stock		500,000		200,000
Retained Earnings		470,000		155,000
Sales		850,000		300,000
Dividend Income		30,000		0
Total	$2,575,000	$2,575,000	$805,000	$805,000

Required

a. Prepare any cost-method journal entry(ies) related to the investment in Snoopy Company during 20X9.

b. Prepare a consolidation worksheet for 20X9 in good form.

KAPLAN CPA REVIEW

KAPLAN CPA REVIEW

Kaplan CPA Review Simulation on Comprehensive Consolidation Procedures

Please visit the *Connect Library* for the online Kaplan CPA Review task-based simulation.

Situation

For each parent–subsidiary relationship, determine the proper accounting treatment.

Topics Covered in the Simulation

a. Consolidation requirements.

b. Consolidation exceptions.

3 The Reporting Entity and the Consolidation of Less-than-Wholly-Owned Subsidiaries with No Differential

THE COLLAPSE OF ENRON AND THE BIRTH OF A NEW PARADIGM

In February 2001, *Fortune* magazine named Enron the most innovative company in America for the sixth year in a row. Ten months later on December 2, 2001, Enron filed for bankruptcy. At that time, it was the largest bankruptcy in history. What was the cause of this drastic turnaround? Did Enron just throw in the towel after six years of "innovation" and decide to call it quits? Sadly, this was not the case; something much more serious caused Enron's historic fall.

Enron came into being in 1985 when InterNorth acquired Houston Natural Gas. Originally, the company was headquartered in Omaha, but shortly after Kenneth Lay took over as CEO of the company, he moved its headquarters to Houston. Enron was originally in the business of transmitting electricity and natural gas throughout the United States, which it accomplished through its extensive network of pipelines and power plants. These types of services made up the bulk of Enron's revenues until management decided to branch out. In 1990, Enron began to serve as an intermediary for gas contracts.

Energy and gas prices have traditionally been extremely volatile. Companies didn't want to sign long-term contracts because of the large fluctuations in these prices. Enron would buy 30-day gas contracts from a variety of suppliers and then bundle these contracts to offer long-term prices to local utility companies. Basically, Enron accepted the price risk in exchange for a fee. Over time, the wholesale trading of energy contracts became an increasingly important part of Enron's business, as illustrated in the figure on the next page. For the 2000 fiscal year, Enron reported revenues of $93 billion from these "wholesale" activities and only $2.7 billion from its traditional piping business.

Even with these extreme revenues, Enron was forced to file for bankruptcy at the end of 2001. How did this happen? Enron used two clever accounting tricks to inflate its performance. First, managers used special-purpose entities (SPEs) to hide losses and move liabilities and impaired assets off Enron's books. We discuss SPEs in detail in this chapter. Second, Enron "grossed up" its revenues to make its performance look better than it actually was. That is, Enron reported the total value of the trades it facilitated, not just its fee for its wholesale services.

Enron

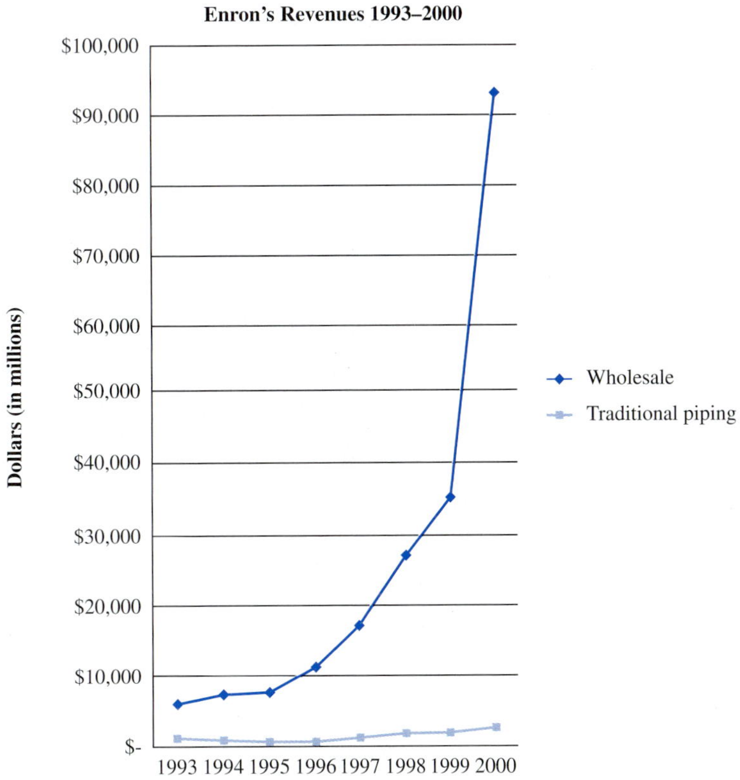

As a result of Enron's bankruptcy and the demise of its auditor, Arthur Andersen, more than 100,000 jobs were lost along with billions of dollars of investors' money. Accounting policies can have a significant influence on the economy. As Enron illustrated, careful manipulation of even a few simple rules can have catastrophic effects on individuals and on the global economy. This chapter introduces accounting rules (resulting from this and other accounting scandals) for determining when a business entity must be consolidated. It also explores how the basic consolidation process differs when a subsidiary is only partially owned instead of wholly owned as discussed in Chapter 2.

LEARNING OBJECTIVES

When you finish studying this chapter, you should be able to:

LO 3-1 Understand and explain the usefulness and limitations of consolidated financial statements.

LO 3-2 Understand and explain how direct and indirect control influence the consolidation of a subsidiary.

LO 3-3 Understand and explain differences in the consolidation process when the subsidiary is not wholly owned.

LO 3-4 Make calculations for the consolidation of a less-than-wholly-owned subsidiary.

LO 3-5 Prepare a consolidation worksheet for a less-than-wholly-owned subsidiary.

LO 3-6 Understand and explain the purpose of combined financial statements and how they differ from consolidated financial statements.

LO 3-7 Understand and explain rules related to the consolidation of variable interest entities.

LO 3-8 Understand and explain differences in consolidation rules under U.S. GAAP and IFRS.

THE USEFULNESS OF CONSOLIDATED FINANCIAL STATEMENTS

LO 3-1

Understand and explain the usefulness and limitations of consolidated financial statements.

Chapter 2 provides an introduction to the consolidation process and introduces an example of a basic consolidation. This chapter expands the consolidation discussion by exploring more complex situations in which the parent company does not have complete ownership of the subsidiary. Companies provide consolidated financial statements primarily for parties having a long-run interest in the parent company, including the parent's shareholders, creditors, and other resource providers. Consolidated statements often provide the only means of obtaining a clear picture of the total resources of the combined entity that are under the parent's control and the results of employing those resources. Especially when the number of related companies is substantial, consolidated statements are the only way to conveniently summarize the vast amount of information relating to the individual companies and how the financial positions and operations of these companies affect the overall consolidated entity.

Current and prospective stockholders of the parent company are usually more interested in the consolidated financial statements than those of the individual companies because the well-being of the parent company is affected by its subsidiaries' operations. When subsidiaries are profitable, profits accrue to the parent. However, the parent cannot escape the ill effects of unprofitable subsidiaries. By examining the consolidated statements, owners and potential owners are better able to assess how effectively management employs all the resources under its control.

The parent's long-term creditors also find the consolidated statements useful because the effects of subsidiary operations on the overall health and future of the parent are relevant to their decisions. In addition, although the parent and its subsidiaries are separate companies, the parent's creditors have an indirect claim on the subsidiaries' assets.

The parent company's management has a continuing need for current information about the combined operations of the consolidated entity in addition to details about the individual companies forming the consolidated entity. For example, some of the individual subsidiaries might have substantial volatility in their operations. As a result, the manager may not be able to fully understand the overall impact of the activities for the period until the operating results and balance sheets are combined into consolidated financial statements. On the other hand, information about individual companies within the consolidated entity also may be useful. For example, it may allow a manager to offset a cash shortfall in one subsidiary with excess cash from another without resorting to costly outside borrowing. The parent company's management may be particularly concerned with the consolidated financial statements because top management generally is evaluated, and sometimes compensated, based on the overall performance of the entity as reflected in the consolidated statements.

LIMITATIONS OF CONSOLIDATED FINANCIAL STATEMENTS

Although consolidated financial statements are useful, their limitations also must be kept in mind. Some information is lost any time data sets are aggregated; this is particularly true when the information involves an aggregation across companies that have substantially different operating characteristics. Some of the more important limitations of consolidated financial statements are:

1. *The masking of poor performance:* Because the operating results and financial position of individual companies included in the consolidation are not disclosed, the poor performance or financial position of one or more companies may be hidden by the good performance and financial position of others.
2. *Limited availability of resources:* Not all of the consolidated retained earnings balance is necessarily available for dividends of the parent because a portion may represent the parent's share of undistributed subsidiary earnings. Similarly, because

the consolidated statements include the subsidiary's assets, not all assets shown are available for dividend distributions of the parent company.

3. *Unrepresentative combined financial ratios:* Because financial ratios based on the consolidated statements are calculated on aggregated information, they are not necessarily representative of any single company in the consolidation, including the parent.
4. *A lack of uniformity:* Similar accounts of different companies that are combined in the consolidation may not be entirely comparable. For example, the length of operating cycles of different companies may vary, causing receivables of similar length to be classified differently.
5. *The lack of detailed disclosures:* Additional information about individual companies or groups of companies included in the consolidation often is necessary for a fair presentation; such additional disclosures may require voluminous footnotes.

SUBSIDIARY FINANCIAL STATEMENTS

Some financial statement users may be interested in the separate financial statements of individual subsidiaries, either instead of or in addition to consolidated financial statements. Although the parent company's management is concerned with the entire consolidated entity as well as individual subsidiaries, the creditors, preferred stockholders, and noncontrolling common stockholders of subsidiary companies are most interested in the separate financial statements of the subsidiaries in which they have an interest. Because subsidiaries are legally separate from their parents, a subsidiary's creditors and stockholders generally have no claim on the parent and the subsidiary's stockholders do not share in the parent's profits unless the parent has provided guarantees or entered into other arrangements for the benefit of the subsidiaries. Therefore, consolidated financial statements usually are of little use to those interested in obtaining information about the assets, capital, or income of individual subsidiaries.

CONSOLIDATED FINANCIAL STATEMENTS: CONCEPTS AND STANDARDS

LO 3-2

Understand and explain how direct and indirect control influence the consolidation of a subsidiary.

Consolidated financial statements are intended to provide a meaningful representation of the overall financial position and activities of a single economic entity comprising a number of related companies. Under current standards, subsidiaries must be consolidated unless the parent is precluded from exercising control. When it is not appropriate to consolidate a subsidiary, it is reported as an intercompany investment **(ASC 810-10-10, 15, 25).**

Traditional View of Control

Over the years, the concept of control has been the single most important criterion for determining when an individual subsidiary should be consolidated. **ASC 810-10-10** indicates that consolidated financial statements normally are appropriate for a group of companies when one company "has a controlling financial interest in the other companies." It also states that "the usual condition for a controlling financial interest is ownership of a majority voting interest. . . ." In practice, control has been determined by the proportion of voting shares of a company's stock owned directly or indirectly by another company. This criterion was formalized by **ASC 810-10-15,** which requires consolidation of all majority-owned subsidiaries unless the parent is unable to exercise control.

Although majority ownership is the most common means of acquiring control, a company may be able to direct the operating and financing policies of another with less than majority ownership, such as when the remainder of the stock is widely held. **ASC 810-10-15** does not preclude consolidation with less than majority ownership, but the consolidation of less-than-majority-owned subsidiaries is very rare in practice.

More directly, **ASC 810-10-55** indicates that control can be obtained without majority ownership of a company's common stock.

Indirect Control[1]

Advanced StudyGuide .com

The traditional view of control includes both direct and indirect control. ***Direct control*** typically occurs when one company owns a majority of another company's common stock. ***Indirect control*** or *pyramiding* occurs when a company's common stock is owned by one or more other companies that are all under common control. In each of the following examples, P Company controls Z Company. However, in each case, P Company does not own a direct interest in Z. Instead, P controls Z indirectly through the ownership of other companies.

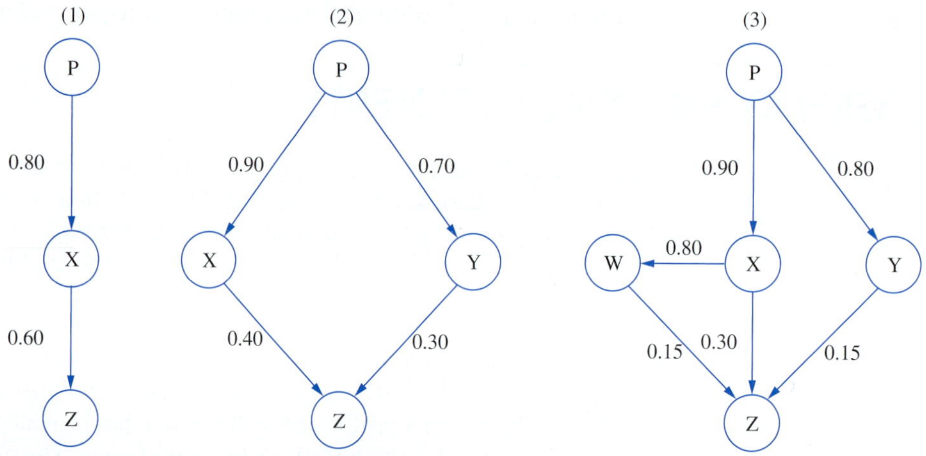

FYI

In 2005, consumer products giant Procter & Gamble completed one of its largest acquisitions in company history when it acquired Gillette for $57 billion. As a result, Procter & Gamble also gained indirect control over the subsidiaries controlled by Gillette, such as Braun.

In (1), P owns 80 percent of X, which owns 60 percent of Z. Because P controls X and X controls Z, P indirectly controls Z. In (2), P owns 90 percent of X and 70 percent of Y; X owns 40 percent of Z; Y owns 30 percent of Z. Because P controls both X and Y and they, in turn, jointly control Z (with a combined ownership of 70 percent), P effectively controls Z through its two subsidiaries. In (3), P owns 90 percent of X and 80 percent of Y; X owns 80 percent of W and 30 percent of Z; Y owns 15 percent of Z; W owns 15 percent of Z. Because P controls both X and Y and they, in turn, jointly control Z (with a combined control of 60 percent—15 percent of which comes through X's subsidiary W), P effectively controls Z through its two subsidiaries. In each case, P controls Z through its subsidiaries.

Ability to Exercise Control

Under certain circumstances, a subsidiary's majority stockholders may not be able to exercise control even though they hold more than 50 percent of its outstanding voting stock. This might occur, for instance, if the subsidiary was in legal reorganization or in bankruptcy; although the parent might hold majority ownership, control would rest with the courts or a court-appointed trustee. Similarly, if the subsidiary were located in a foreign country and that country had placed restrictions on the subsidiary that prevented the remittance of profits or assets back to the parent company, consolidation of that subsidiary would not be appropriate because of the parent's inability to control important aspects of the subsidiary's operations.

[1] To view a video explanation of this topic, visit advancedstudyguide.com.

Differences in Fiscal Periods

A difference in the fiscal periods of a parent and subsidiary should not preclude consolidation of that subsidiary. Often the subsidiary's fiscal period, if different from the parent's, is changed to coincide with that of the parent. Another alternative is to adjust the financial statement data of the subsidiary each period to place the data on a basis consistent with the parent's fiscal period. Both the Securities and Exchange Commission and current accounting standards permit the consolidation of a subsidiary's financial statements without adjusting the fiscal period of the subsidiary if that period does not differ from the parent's by more than three months and if recognition is given to intervening events that have a material effect on financial position or results of operations.

Changing Concept of the Reporting Entity

For nearly three decades beginning in the 1960s, little change was observed in the authoritative literature governing consolidation policies. However, during that time, many changes occurred in the business environment, including widespread diversification of companies and the increased emphasis on financial services by manufacturing and merchandising companies (such as General Electric and Harley-Davidson).

In addition, the criteria used in determining whether to consolidate specific subsidiaries were subject to varying interpretations. Companies exercised great latitude in selecting which subsidiaries to consolidate and which to report as intercorporate investments. The lack of consistency in consolidation policy became of increasing concern as many manufacturing and merchandising companies engaged in "off-balance sheet financing" by borrowing heavily through finance subsidiaries and then excluding those subsidiaries from consolidation.

In 1982, the FASB began a project aimed at developing a comprehensive consolidation policy. The guidance in **ASC 810-10-15** was developed in 1987, requiring the consolidation of all majority-owned subsidiaries. The intent was to eliminate the inconsistencies found in practice until a more comprehensive standard could be issued. Unfortunately, the issues have been more difficult to resolve than anticipated. After grappling with these issues for more than two decades, the FASB has still been unable to provide a comprehensive consolidation policy.

Completion of the FASB's consolidation project has been hampered by, among other things, the inability to resolve issues related to two important concepts: (1) control and (2) the reporting entity. Regarding the first issue, the FASB has attempted to move beyond the traditional notion of control based on majority ownership of common stock to requiring consolidation of entities under ***effective control.*** This idea reflects the ability to direct the policies of another entity even though majority ownership is lacking. Adopting the concept of effective control can lead to the consolidation of companies in which little or even no ownership is held and to the consolidation of entities other than corporations, such as partnerships and trusts. Although the FASB has indicated in **ASC 805-10-55** that control can be achieved without majority ownership, a comprehensive consolidation policy has yet to be achieved.

With respect to the second issue, defining the accounting entity would go a long way toward resolving the issue of when to prepare consolidated financial statements and what entities should be included. Unfortunately, the FASB has found both the entity and control issues so complex that they are not easily resolved and require further study. Accordingly, the FASB issued guidance dealing with selected issues related to consolidated financial statements **(ASC 810),** leaving a comprehensive consolidation policy until a later time.

NONCONTROLLING INTEREST

LO 3-3

Understand and explain differences in the consolidation process when the subsidiary is not wholly owned.

A parent company does not always own 100 percent of a subsidiary's outstanding common stock. The parent may have acquired less than 100 percent of a company's stock in a business combination, or it may originally have held 100 percent but sold or awarded some shares to others. For the parent to consolidate the subsidiary, only a controlling interest is needed. Those shareholders of the subsidiary other than the parent are referred to as "noncontrolling" shareholders. The claim of these shareholders on the income and net assets of the subsidiary is referred to as the ***noncontrolling interest*** (formerly referred to as the ***minority interest***).[2] Throughout this chapter and in subsequent chapters, whenever the acquired company is less than wholly owned, we will frequently refer to the noncontrolling interest shareholders as the "NCI shareholders." The NCI shareholders clearly have a claim on the subsidiary's assets and earnings through their stock ownership. Because 100 percent of a subsidiary's assets, liabilities, and earnings is included in the consolidated financial statements, regardless of the parent's percentage ownership, the NCI shareholders' claim on these items must be reported.

Computation and Presentation of Noncontrolling Interest

In uncomplicated situations, the noncontrolling interest's share of consolidated net income is a simple proportionate share of the subsidiary's net income. For example, if a subsidiary has net income of $150,000 and the NCI shareholders own 10 percent of the subsidiary's common stock, their share of income is $15,000 ($150,000 × 0.10).

The NCI shareholders' claim on the net assets of the subsidiary is based on the acquisition-date fair value of the noncontrolling interest, adjusted over time for a proportionate share of the subsidiary's income and dividends. We discuss the noncontrolling interest in more detail in Chapter 5.

The current standard on reporting noncontrolling interests, **ASC 810-10-50,** requires that the term "consolidated net income" be applied to the income available to all stockholders, with the allocation of that income between the controlling and noncontrolling stockholders included in the consolidated income statement. For example, assume that Parent Company owns 90 percent of Sub Company's stock, acquired without a differential, and that the two companies report revenues and expenses as follows:

	Parent	Sub
Revenues	$300,000	$100,000
Expenses	225,000	65,000

An abbreviated consolidated income statement for Parent and its subsidiary would appear as follows:

Revenues	$ 400,000
Expenses	(290,000)
Consolidated Net Income	$ 110,000
Less: Consolidated Net Income Attributable to the Noncontrolling Interest in Sub Company	(3,500)
Consolidated Net Income Attributable to the Controlling Interest in Sub Company	$ 106,500

Also assume that Parent's beginning retained earnings is $200,500, common stock is $50,000, additional paid-in capital is $700,000, and dividends declared and paid by the parent this period are $27,000. The noncontrolling interest's claim on the net assets of the subsidiary was previously reported in the balance sheet most frequently in the "mezzanine" between liabilities and stockholders' equity. Some companies reported the

[2] Although the term "minority interest" was commonly used in the past, **ASC 805-10-20** replaces this term with "noncontrolling interest." The FASB's intent is that the term "noncontrolling interest" be used going forward. Thus, we use this term consistently throughout this and future chapters.

FYI

In Berkshire Hathaway's 2011 consolidated income statement, the company reported total consolidated net income of $10.75 billion, which included $492 million in earnings attributable to noncontrolling interests. Additionally, Berkshire's 2011 consolidated balance sheet reported total noncontrolling interests in net assets of $4.1 billion.

noncontrolling interest as a liability, although it clearly did not meet the definition of a liability. **ASC 810-10-55** is clear that the noncontrolling interest's claim on net assets is an element of equity, not a liability. It requires reporting the noncontrolling interest in equity in the following manner:

Controlling Interest:	
Common Stock	$ 50,000
Additional Paid-In Capital	700,000
Retained Earnings	280,000
Total Controlling Interest	$1,030,000
Noncontrolling Interest in the Net Assets of Sub Company	75,000
Total Stockholders' Equity	$1,105,000

THE EFFECT OF A NONCONTROLLING INTEREST

LO 3-4

Make calculations for the consolidation of a less-than-wholly-owned subsidiary.

When a subsidiary is less than wholly owned, the general approach to consolidation is the same as discussed in Chapter 2, but the consolidation procedures must be modified slightly to recognize the noncontrolling interest. Thus, the difference between the consolidation procedures illustrated in Chapter 2 and what we will demonstrate here is that we now have to account for the NCI shareholders' ownership in the income and net assets of the acquired company. The following two-by-two matrix indicates that the only difference in consolidation in Chapter 3 relative to Chapter 2 is the separate recognition of the NCI shareholder share of income and net assets.

Before examining the specific procedures used in consolidating a less-than-wholly-owned subsidiary, we discuss the computation of consolidated net income, consolidated retained earnings, and the noncontrolling interest's claim on income and net assets. We also discuss modifications to the consolidation worksheet.

	Wholly owned subsidiary	Partially owned subsidiary
Investment = Book value	Chapter 2	Chapter 3
Investment > Book value	Chapter 4	Chapter 5
	No NCI shareholders	NCI shareholders

Consolidated Net Income

Consolidated net income, as it appears in the consolidated income statement, is the difference between consolidated revenues and expenses. In the absence of transactions between companies included in the consolidation, ***consolidated net income*** is equal to the parent's income from its own operations, excluding any investment income from consolidated subsidiaries, plus the net income from each of the consolidated subsidiaries.

When all subsidiaries are wholly owned, all of the consolidated net income accrues to the parent company, or the controlling interest. If one or more of the consolidated subsidiaries is less than wholly owned, a portion of the consolidated net income accrues to the NCI shareholders. In that case, the income attributable to the subsidiary's noncontrolling interest is deducted from consolidated net income on the face of the income statement to arrive at consolidated net income attributable to the controlling interest.

Income attributable to a noncontrolling interest in a subsidiary is based on a proportionate share of that subsidiary's net income. The subsidiary's net income available to common shareholders is divided between the parent and noncontrolling stockholders based on their relative common stock ownership of the subsidiary. Note that the NCI shareholders in a particular subsidiary have a proportionate claim only on the income of that subsidiary and not on the income of the parent or any other subsidiary.

As an example of the computation and allocation of consolidated net income, assume that Push Corporation purchases 80 percent of the stock of Shove Company for an amount equal to 80 percent of Shove's total book value. During 20X1, Shove reports separate net income of $25,000, while Push reports net income of $120,000, including equity-method income from Shove of $20,000 ($25,000 × 0.80). Consolidated net income for 20X1 is computed and allocated as follows:

Push's net income	$120,000
Less: Equity-method income from Shove	(20,000)
Shove's net income	25,000
Consolidated net income	$125,000
Income attributable to noncontrolling interest	(5,000)
Income attributable to controlling interest	$120,000

Consolidated net income is equal to the separate income of Push from its own operations ($100,000) plus Shove's net income ($25,000). The $20,000 of equity-method income from Shove that had been recognized by Push must be excluded from the computation to avoid double-counting the same income. Consolidated net income is allocated to the noncontrolling stockholders based on their 20 percent share of Shove's net income. The amount of income allocated to the controlling interest is equal to Push's income from its own operations ($100,000) and Push's 80 percent share of Shove's income ($20,000) because Push used the equity method of accounting for its investment in Shove.

Consolidated Retained Earnings

The retained earnings figure reported in the consolidated balance sheet is not entirely consistent with the computation of consolidated net income. Retained earnings in the consolidated balance sheet is that portion of the consolidated entity's undistributed earnings accruing to the parent's stockholders. Assuming the parent company correctly uses the fully adjusted equity method to account for its investments, consolidated retained earnings should equal the parent's retained earnings. It is calculated by adding the parent's share of subsidiary cumulative net income since acquisition to the parent's retained earnings from its own operations (excluding any income from the subsidiary included in the parent's retained earnings) and subtracting the parent's share of any differential write-off. Any retained earnings related to subsidiary NCI shareholders is included in the Noncontrolling Interest in Net Assets of Subsidiary amount reported in the equity section of the consolidated balance sheet.

To illustrate the computation of consolidated retained earnings when a noncontrolling interest exists, assume that Push purchases 80 percent of Shove's stock on January 1, 20X1, and accounts for the investment using the equity method. Assume net income and dividends as follows during the two years following the acquisition:

	Push	Shove
Retained earnings, January 1, 20X1	$400,000	$250,000
Net income, 20X1	120,000	25,000
Dividends, 20X1	(30,000)	(10,000)
Retained earnings, December 31, 20X1	$490,000	$265,000
Net income, 20X2	148,000	35,000
Dividends, 20X2	(30,000)	(10,000)
Retained earnings, December 31, 20X2	$608,000	$290,000

Consolidated retained earnings as of two years after the date of combination is computed as follows:

Push's retained earnings, December 31, 20X2	$608,000
Equity accrual from Shove since acquisition ($25,000 + $35,000) × 0.80	(48,000)
Push's retained earnings from its own operations, December 31, 20X2	$560,000
Push's share of Shove's net income since acquisition ($60,000 × 0.80)	48,000
Consolidated retained earnings, December 31, 20X2	$608,000

We note several important points from the example. First, the subsidiary's retained earnings are not combined with the parent's retained earnings. Only the parent's share of the subsidiary's cumulative net income since the date of combination is included. Second, consolidated retained earnings are equal to the parent's retained earnings because the parent uses the equity method to account for its investment in the subsidiary. If the parent accounted for the investment using the cost method, the parent's retained earnings and consolidated retained earnings would differ. Finally, we note that the consolidated financial statements include the equity accounts of the parent. In the Push and Shove example, Push's shareholders effectively control both Push and Shove. Hence, Push's equity accounts, along with the noncontrolling interest in Shove's net assets, comprise the equity section of the consolidated group of companies. For the same reason, only Push's dividends influence consolidated retained earnings.

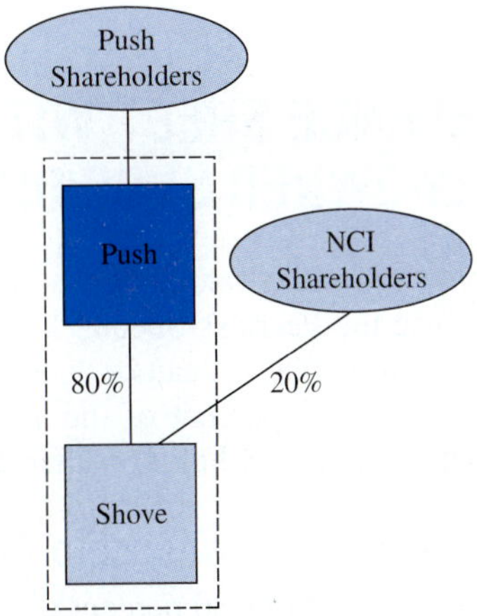

Worksheet Format

The same three-part worksheet described in Chapter 2 can be used when consolidating less-than-wholly-owned subsidiaries, with only minor modifications. The worksheet must allow for including the noncontrolling interest's claim on the income and net assets of the subsidiaries. The noncontrolling interest's claim on the income of a subsidiary is deducted from consolidated net income at the bottom of the worksheet's income statement section in the Consolidated column to arrive at consolidated net income attributable to the controlling interest. The noncontrolling interest's claim on the subsidiary's net assets is placed at the bottom of the worksheet's balance sheet section. The noncontrolling interest's claims on both income and net assets are entered in the worksheet through consolidation entries and then carried over to the Consolidated column. As discussed in Chapter 2, the amounts in the Consolidated column are used to prepare the consolidated financial statements.

	Parent	Subsidiary	Consolidation Entries DR	Consolidation Entries CR	Consolidated
Income Statement					
Revenues					
Expenses					
Consolidated Net Income					
NCI in Net Income					
Controlling interest in Net Income					
Statement of Retained Earnings					
Retained Earnings (1/1)					
Add: Net Income					
Less: Dividends					
Retained Earnings (12/31)					
Balance Sheet					
Assets					
Total Assets					
Liabilities					
Equity					
Common Stock					
Retained Earnings					
NCI in Net Assets of Subsidiary					
Total Liabilities & Equity					

CONSOLIDATED BALANCE SHEET WITH A LESS-THAN-WHOLLY-OWNED SUBSIDIARY

LO 3-5

Prepare a consolidation worksheet for a less-than-wholly-owned subsidiary.

In order to illustrate the consolidation process for a less-than-wholly-owned subsidiary, we use the Peerless-Special Foods example from Chapter 2. The only difference is that we assume that instead of acquiring all of the common stock of Special Foods, Peerless buys only 80 percent of the shares. Thus, we assume that the other 20 percent of the shares are widely held by other shareholders (the NCI shareholders).

80 Percent Ownership Acquired at Book Value

Peerless acquires 80 percent of Special Foods' outstanding common stock for $240,000, an amount equal to 80 percent of the fair value of Special Foods' net assets on January 1, 20X1. On this date, the fair values of Special Foods' individual assets and liabilities are equal to their book values. Thus, there is no differential. Because Peerless acquires only 80 percent of Special Foods' common stock, the Investment in Special Foods equals 80 percent of the total stockholders' equity of Special Foods ($200,000 + $100,000). We can summarize Special Foods' ownership as follows:

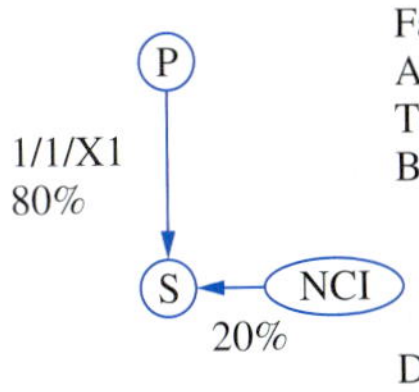

Fair value of Peerless' consideration		$240,000
Add the fair value of the NCI interest		60,000
Total fair value		300,000
Book value of Special Foods' net assets		
Common stock—Special Foods	200,000	
Retained earnings—Special Foods	100,000	
		300,000
Difference between fair value and book value		$ 0

Peerless records the 80 percent stock acquisition on its books with the following entry on January 1, 20X1:

(1)			
	Investment in Special Foods	240,000	
	Cash		240,000
	Record purchase of Special Foods stock.		

Advanced StudyGuide .com

The Basic Investment Consolidation Entry

The basic consolidation entry on the date of acquisition would be the same as the one illustrated in Chapter 2 except that the $300,000 book value of net assets is now jointly owned by Peerless (80 percent) and the NCI shareholders (20 percent). Thus, the original $300,000 credit to the Investment in Special Foods account from the wholly owned example in Chapter 2 is now "shared" with the NCI shareholders as shown in the breakdown of the book value of Special Foods:

Book Value Calculations:

	NCI 20%	+ Peerless 80%	= Common Stock	+ Retained Earnings
Beginning Book Value	60,000	240,000	200,000	100,000

Because the fair value of Special Foods' net assets on the acquisition date is equal to their book value, there is no differential. Thus, the only required consolidation entry (the basic consolidation entry) in the worksheet removes the Investment in Special Foods Stock account and Special Foods' stockholders' equity accounts and records the $60,000 NCI interest in the net assets of Special Foods.

Basic Consolidation Entry:

Common Stock	200,000		← Common stock balance
Retained Earnings	100,000		← Beginning balance in RE
Investment in Special Foods		240,000	← Peerless' share of "book value"
NCI in NA of Special Foods		60,000	← NCI's share of "book value"

In this example, Peerless' investment is exactly equal to its 80 percent share of the book value of Special Foods' net assets. Therefore, goodwill is not recorded and all assets and liabilities are simply combined from Special Foods' financial statements at their current book values. Again, in Chapters 4 and 5, we will explore situations in which the acquiring company pays more than the book value of the acquired company's net assets. However, in Chapters 2 and 3, the excess value of identifiable net assets and goodwill will always be equal to zero. To maintain a consistent approach through all four chapters, we always illustrate the components of the acquiring company's investment, even though the acquiring company's investment will always be exactly equal to its share of the book value of net assets in this chapter. Thus, the relationship between the fair value of the consideration given to acquire Special Foods, the fair value of Special Foods' net assets, and the book value of Special Foods' net assets can be illustrated as follows:

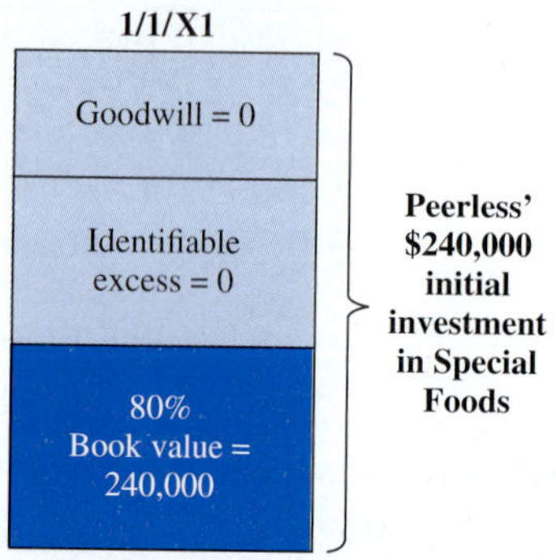

The consolidation entry simply credits the Investment in Special Foods Stock account (for the original acquisition price, $240,000), eliminating this account from Peerless' balance sheet.

	Investment in Special Foods		
Acquisition Price	**240,000**		
		240,000	**Basic consolidation entry**
	0		

Remember that this entry is made in the consolidation worksheet, not on the books of either the parent or the subsidiary, and is presented here in T-account form for instructional purposes only. The investment account must be eliminated in the consolidation process because, as explained in Chapter 2, from a single-entity viewpoint, a company cannot hold an investment in itself. Stated differently, since the Investment in Special Foods account already summarizes Special Foods' entire balance sheet, adding the individual line items on Special Foods' balance sheet together with Peerless' balance sheet items would be equivalent to double counting Special Foods' balance sheet.

As explained in Chapter 2, we first examine situations where a subsidiary is created (hence the parent's book values of transferred assets carry over) or where the acquisition price is exactly equal to the book value of the target company's net assets. When a parent company acquires a subsidiary, the consolidated financial statements should appear as if all of the subsidiary's assets and liabilities were acquired and recorded at their acquisition prices (equal to their former book values). If Peerless had purchased Special Foods' assets instead of its stock with an acquisition price equal to the book value of net assets, the assets would have been recorded in Peerless' books at their acquisition prices (as if they were new assets with zero accumulated depreciation). Following this logic, because Peerless did acquire Special Foods' stock, the consolidated financial statements should present all of Special Foods' assets and liabilities as if they had been recorded at their acquisition prices and then depreciated from that date forward. Thus, eliminating the old accumulated depreciation of the subsidiary as of the acquisition date and netting it out against the historical cost gives the appearance that the depreciable assets have been newly recorded at their acquisition prices (which happen to be equal to Special Foods' book values). In this example, Special Foods had accumulated depreciation on the acquisition date of $300,000. Thus, as explained in Chapter 2, the following consolidation entry nets this accumulated depreciation out against the cost of the building and equipment.

Optional Accumulated Depreciation Consolidation Entry:

Accumulated Depreciation	**300,000**		
Building & Equipment		**300,000**	← Accumulated depreciation at the time of the acquisition netted against cost

Also as explained in Chapter 2, this worksheet consolidation entry does not change the net buildings and equipment balance. Netting the preacquisition accumulated depreciation out against the cost basis of the corresponding assets merely causes the buildings and equipment to appear in the consolidated financial statements as if they had been recorded as new assets (which coincidentally happen to be equal to their former book values) on the acquisition date. In this chapter and in Chapter 2, we assume that the fair values of all assets and liabilities are equal to their book values on the acquisition date. This same entry would be included in each succeeding consolidation as long as the assets remain on Special Foods' books (always based on the accumulated depreciation balance as of the acquisition date).

Consolidation Worksheet

Figure 3–1 presents the consolidation worksheet. As explained previously in Chapter 2, the investment account on the parent's books can be thought of as a single account representing the parent's investment in the net assets of the subsidiary, a *one-line consolidation.* In a full consolidation, the subsidiary's individual assets and liabilities are combined with those of the parent. Including both the net assets of the subsidiary, as represented by the balance in the investment account, and the subsidiary's individual assets and liabilities would double-count the same set of assets. Therefore, the investment account is eliminated, not carried to the consolidated balance sheet.

Figure 3–2 presents the consolidated balance sheet, prepared from the consolidation worksheet, as of the acquisition date. Because no operations occurred between the date of combination and the preparation of the consolidated balance sheet, there is no income statement or statement of retained earnings.

FIGURE 3–1 January 1, 20X1, Worksheet for Consolidated Balance Sheet, Date of Combination; 80 Percent Acquisition at Book Value

	Peerless Products	Special Foods	Consolidation Entries DR	Consolidation Entries CR	Consolidated
Balance Sheet					
Cash	110,000	50,000			160,000
Accounts Receivable	75,000	50,000			125,000
Inventory	100,000	60,000			160,000
Investment in Special Foods	240,000			240,000	0
Land	175,000	40,000			215,000
Buildings & Equipment	800,000	600,000		300,000	1,100,000
Less: Accumulated Depreciation	(400,000)	(300,000)	300,000		(400,000)
Total Assets	**1,100,000**	**500,000**	**$300,000**	**$540,000**	**1,360,000**
Accounts Payable	100,000	100,000			200,000
Bonds Payable	200,000	100,000			300,000
Common Stock	500,000	200,000	200,000		500,000
Retained Earnings	300,000	100,000	100,000		300,000
NCI in NA of Special Foods				60,000	60,000
Total Liabilities & Equity	**1,100,000**	**500,000**	**300,000**	**60,000**	**1,360,000**

FIGURE 3–2 Consolidated Balance Sheet, January 1, 20X1, Date of Combination; 80 Percent Acquisition at Book Value

PEERLESS PRODUCTS CORPORATION AND SUBSIDIARY
Consolidated Balance Sheet
January 1, 20X1

Assets			Liabilities	
Cash		160,000	Accounts Payable	200,000
Accounts Receivable		125,000	Bonds Payable	300,000
Inventory		160,000	Stockholders' Equity	
Land		215,000	Common Stock	500,000
Buildings & Equipment	1,100,000		Retained Earnings	300,000
Accumulated Depreciation	(400,000)	700,000	NCI in NA of Special Foods	60,000
Total Assets		1,360,000	Total Liabilities & Equity	1,360,000

CONSOLIDATION SUBSEQUENT TO ACQUISITION— 80 PERCENT OWNERSHIP ACQUIRED AT BOOK VALUE

Chapter 2 explains the procedures used to prepare a consolidated balance sheet as of the acquisition date. More than a consolidated balance sheet, however, is needed to provide a comprehensive picture of the consolidated entity's activities following acquisition. As with a single company, the set of basic financial statements for a consolidated entity consists of an income statement, a statement of changes in retained earnings, a balance sheet, and a statement of cash flows. Each of the consolidated financial statements is prepared as if it is taken from a single set of books that is being used to account for the overall consolidated entity. There is, of course, no set of books for the consolidated entity. Therefore, as in the preparation of the consolidated balance sheet, the consolidation process starts with the data recorded on the books of the individual consolidating companies. The account balances from the books of the individual companies are placed in the three-part worksheet, and entries are made to eliminate the effects of intercorporate ownership and transactions. The consolidation approach and procedures are the same whether the subsidiary being consolidated was acquired or created.

Initial Year of Ownership

Assume that Peerless already recorded the acquisition on January 1, 20X1, and that during 20X1, Peerless records operating earnings of $140,000, excluding its income from investing in Special Foods, and declares dividends of $60,000. Special Foods reports 20X1 net income of $50,000 and declares dividends of $30,000.

Parent Company Entries

Peerless records its 20X1 income and dividends from Special Foods under the equity method as follows:

(2)			
	Investment in Special Foods	40,000	
	Income from Special Foods		40,000

Record Peerless' 80% share of Special Foods' 20X1 income.

(3)			
	Cash	24,000	
	Investment in Special Foods		24,000

Record Peerless' 80% share of Special Foods' 20X1 dividend.

Consolidation Worksheet—Initial Year of Ownership

Advanced StudyGuide .com

After all appropriate equity method entries have been recorded on Peerless' books, the company can prepare a consolidation worksheet. Peerless begins the worksheet by placing the adjusted account balances from both Peerless' and Special Foods' books in the first two columns of the worksheet. Then all amounts that reflect intercorporate transactions or ownership are eliminated in the consolidation process.

The distinction between journal entries recorded on the books of the individual companies and the consolidation entries recorded only on the consolidation worksheet is an important one. Book entries affect balances on the books and the amounts that are carried to the consolidation worksheet; worksheet consolidation entries affect only those balances carried to the consolidated financial statements in the period. As mentioned previously, the consolidation entries presented in this text are shaded when presented both in journal entry form in the text and in the worksheet.

In this example, the accounts that must be eliminated because of intercorporate ownership are the stockholders' equity accounts of Special Foods, including dividends declared, Peerless' investment in Special Foods stock, and Peerless' income from Special Foods. However, the book value portion of Peerless' investment has changed since the January 1 acquisition date because under the equity method, Peerless has adjusted the investment account balance for its share of earnings and dividends (entries 2 and 3). The book value portion of the investment account can be summarized as follows:

Book Value Calculations:

	NCI 20%	+ Peerless 80%	= Common Stock	+ Retained Earnings
Beginning Book Value	60,000	240,000	200,000	100,000
+ Net Income	10,000	40,000		50,000
− Dividends	(6,000)	(24,000)		(30,000)
Ending Book Value	64,000	256,000	200,000	120,000

Note that we use dark shading with a white drop-out font for the amounts in the book value analysis that appear in the basic consolidation entry.

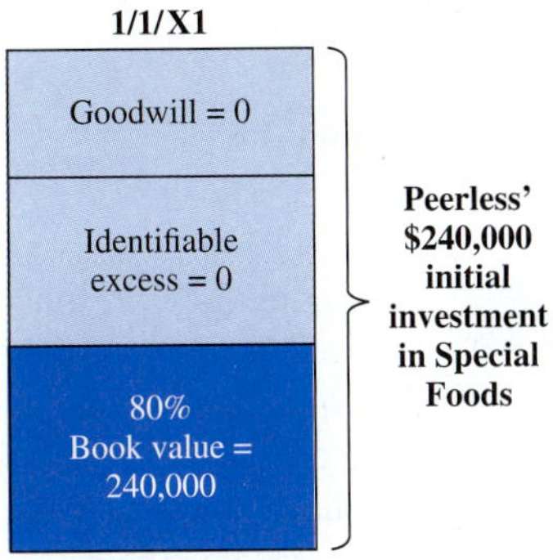

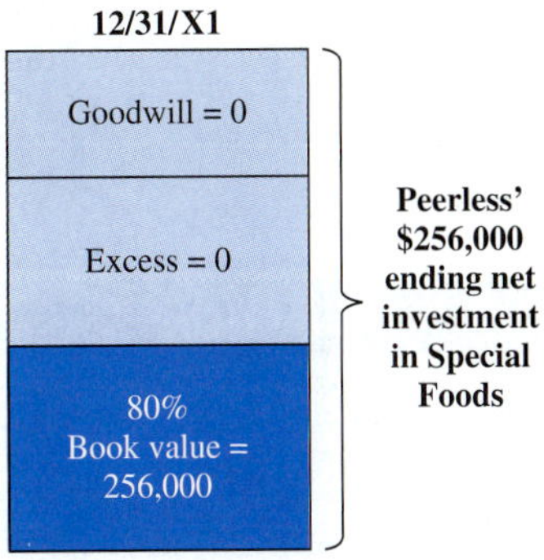

Under the equity method, the parent recognized its share (80 percent) of the subsidiary's income on its separate books. In the consolidated income statement, however, the individual revenue and expense accounts of the subsidiary are combined with those of the parent. Income recognized by the parent from all consolidated subsidiaries, therefore, must be eliminated to avoid double-counting. The subsidiary's dividends must be eliminated when consolidated statements are prepared so that only dividend declarations related to the parent's shareholders are treated as dividends of the consolidated entity. Thus, the basic consolidation entry removes both the investment income reflected in the parent's income statement and any dividends declared by the subsidiary during the period:

Basic Consolidation Entry:

Common Stock	200,000		← Common stock balance
Retained Earnings	100,000		← Beginning RE from trial balance
Income from Special Foods	40,000		← Peerless' share of Special Foods' NI
NCI in NI of Special Foods	10,000		← NCI share of Special Foods' reported NI
Dividends Declared		30,000	← 100% of sub's dividends declared
Investment in Special Foods		256,000	← Peerless' share of BV of net assets
NCI in NA of Special Foods		64,000	← NCI share of BV of net assets

Because there is no differential in this example, the basic consolidation entry completely eliminates the balance in Peerless' investment account on the balance sheet as well as the Income from Special Foods account on the income statement. Note again that the parent's investment in the stock of a consolidated subsidiary never appears in the consolidated balance sheet and the income from subsidiary account never appears on the consolidated income statement.

	Investment in Special Foods		
Acquisition Price	240,000		
80% of Net Income	40,000		
		24,000	80% Dividends
Ending Balance	256,000		
		256,000	Basic entry
	0		

	Income from Special Foods		
		40,000	80% Net Income
		40,000	Ending Balance
Basic entry	40,000		
		0	

As explained previously, we repeat the accumulated depreciation entry in each succeeding period for as long as the subsidiary owns these assets. The purpose of this entry is to appropriately present these assets in the consolidated financial statements as if they had been purchased on the date the subsidiary was acquired at their acquisition date fair values.

Optional Accumulated Depreciation Consolidation Entry:

Accumulated Depreciation	**300,000**		
Building & Equipment		**300,000**	← Accumulated depreciation at the time of the acquisition netted against cost

! CAUTION

Note that the $10,000 debit to NCI in Net Income in the Consolidation Entries column of Figure 3–3 is added to the $40,000 Consolidated Net Income debit subtotal to arrive at the total debit adjustments in the Controlling Interest in the Net Income row. Students sometimes forget that the Consolidation Entries columns simply add total debit and credit adjustments (ignoring the "formula" used in the income calculation). The reason the $10,000 NCI in Net Income is listed with brackets in the Consolidated column is because a debit *decreases* income.

Figure 3–3 presents the consolidation worksheet. We note that there are only two changes on the worksheet when the subsidiary is only partially owned (Chapter 3) relative to when the subsidiary is wholly owned (Chapter 2). First, the income statement calculates the consolidated net income ($190,000 in this example) and then deducts the portion attributable to the NCI shareholders (NCI in Net Income) to arrive at the portion attributable to the parent (controlling interest). In this example, the final line of the income statement presents Peerless' share of the consolidated net income, $180,000. This amount should always equal the parent's net income in the first column of the worksheet if the parent properly accounts for the investment in the subsidiary using the equity method on its own books.[3] Second, since the parent company consolidates the entire balance sheet of the subsidiary, it must disclose the portion of the subsidiary's net assets that belong to the noncontrolling interest (NCI in Net Assets).

Second and Subsequent Years of Ownership

The consolidation procedures employed at the end of the second and subsequent years are basically the same as those used at the end of the first year. Adjusted trial balance data of the individual companies are used as the starting point each time consolidated statements are prepared because no separate books are kept for the consolidated entity. An additional

[3] Note that the "Consolidated Net Income" line properly adds Peerless' reported net income, $180,000, to Special Foods' net income, $50,000, and eliminates Peerless' share of Special Foods' net income such that the total consolidated net income is equal to Peerless' income from separate operations ($140,000) plus Special Foods' reported net income ($50,000). On the other hand, the "Controlling Interest in Net Income" line indicates that Peerless' true income can be calculated in two ways. Either start with total "Consolidated Net Income" and deduct the portion that belongs to the NCI shareholders in the far right column or simply use Peerless' correctly calculated equity method net income, $180,000, which is its income from separate operations ($140,000), plus its share of Special Foods' net income ($40,000). The controlling interest in the Net Income line starts with this correctly calculated number from Peerless' income statement (in the first column) and adds it to Special Foods' reported income (in the second column), but then eliminates Special Foods' reported income in the Consolidation Entries column. Thus, the controlling interest in net income in the Consolidation column equals Peerless' reported net income under the equity method.

FIGURE 3–3 December 31, 20X1, Equity-Method Worksheet for Consolidated Financial Statements, Initial Year of Ownership; 80 percent Acquisition at Book Value

	Peerless Products	Special Foods	Consolidation Entries DR	Consolidation Entries CR	Consolidated
Income Statement					
Sales	400,000	200,000			600,000
Less: COGS	(170,000)	(115,000)			(285,000)
Less: Depreciation Expense	(50,000)	(20,000)			(70,000)
Less: Other Expenses	(40,000)	(15,000)			(55,000)
Income from Special Foods	40,000		40,000		0
Consolidated Net Income	180,000	50,000	40,000	0	190,000
NCI in Net Income			10,000		(10,000)
Controlling Interest in Net Income	**180,000**	**50,000**	**50,000**	**0**	**180,000**
Statement of Retained Earnings					
Beginning Balance	300,000	100,000	100,000		300,000
Net Income	**180,000**	**50,000**	**50,000**	**0**	180,000
Less: Dividends Declared	(60,000)	(30,000)		30,000	(60,000)
Ending Balance	**420,000**	**120,000**	**150,000**	**30,000**	**420,000**
Balance Sheet					
Cash	264,000	75,000			339,000
Accounts Receivable	75,000	50,000			125,000
Inventory	100,000	75,000			175,000
Investment in Special Foods	256,000			256,000	0
Land	175,000	40,000			215,000
Buildings & Equipment	800,000	600,000		300,000	1,100,000
Less: Accumulated Depreciation	(450,000)	(320,000)	300,000		(470,000)
Total Assets	**1,220,000**	**520,000**	**300,000**	**556,000**	**1,484,000**
Accounts Payable	100,000	100,000			200,000
Bonds Payable	200,000	100,000			300,000
Common Stock	500,000	200,000	200,000		500,000
Retained Earnings	**420,000**	**120,000**	**150,000**	**30,000**	420,000
NCI in NA of Special Foods				64,000	64,000
Total Liabilities & Equity	**1,220,000**	**520,000**	**350,000**	**94,000**	**1,484,000**

check is needed in each period following acquisition to ensure that the beginning balance of consolidated retained earnings shown in the completed worksheet equals the balance reported at the end of the prior period. In all other respects, the consolidation entries and worksheet are comparable with those shown for the first year.

Parent Company Entries

Consolidation after two years of ownership is illustrated by continuing the example of Peerless Products and Special Foods. Peerless' separate income from its own operations for 20X2 is $160,000, and its dividends total $60,000. Special Foods reports net income of $75,000 in 20X2 and pays dividends of $40,000. Equity-method entries recorded by Peerless in 20X2 are as follows:

		Dr	Cr
(4)	Investment in Special Foods	60,000	
	Income from Special Foods		60,000
	Record Peerless' 80% share of Special Foods' 20X2 income.		
(5)	Cash	32,000	
	Investment in Special Foods		32,000
	Record Peerless' 80% share of Special Foods' 20X2 dividend.		

Peerless' reported net income totals $220,000 ($160,000 from separate operations + $60,000 from Special Foods).

Advanced StudyGuide .com

Consolidation Worksheet—Second Year of Ownership

In order to complete the worksheet, Peerless must calculate the worksheet consolidation entries using the following process. The book value of equity can be analyzed and summarized as follows:

Book Value Calculations:

	NCI 20% +	Peerless 80% =	Common Stock +	Retained Earnings
Beginning Book Value	64,000	256,000	200,000	120,000
+ Net Income	15,000	60,000		75,000
− Dividends	(8,000)	(32,000)		(40,000)
Ending Book Value	71,000	284,000	200,000	155,000

The book value calculations indicate that the balance in Peerless' Investment in Special Foods account increases from $256,000 to $284,000 in 20X2. Recall that the numbers in the lighter font from the book value calculations appear in the basic consolidation entry. This consolidation entry removes both the investment income reflected in the parent's income statement and any dividends declared by the subsidiary during the period:

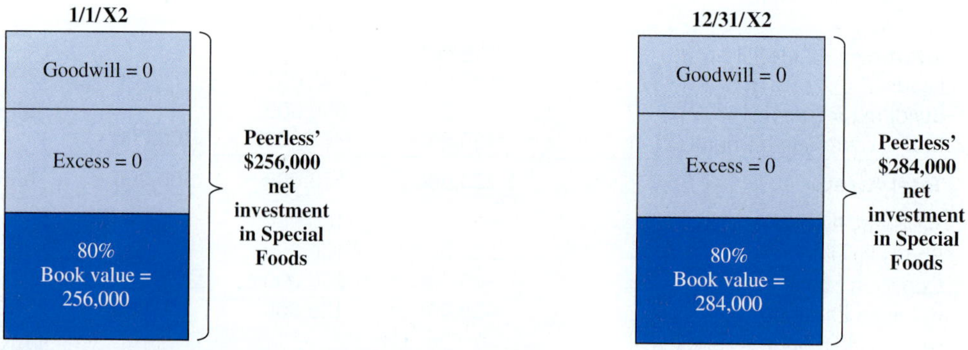

Basic Consolidation Entry:

Common Stock	200,000		← Common stock balance
Retained Earnings	120,000		← Beginning balance in ret. earnings
Income from Special Foods	60,000		← Peerless' share of Special Foods' NI
NCI in NI of Special Foods	15,000		← NCI share of Special Foods' reported NI
Dividends Declared		40,000	← 100% of sub's dividends declared
Investment in Special Foods		284,000	← Peerless' share of BV of net assets
NCI in NA of Special Foods		71,000	← NCI share of BV of net assets

Because there is no differential in this example, the basic consolidation entry completely eliminates the balance in Peerless' investment account on the balance sheet as well as the Income from Special Foods account on the income statement.

	Investment in Special Foods (Dr.)	Investment in Special Foods (Cr.)		Income from Special Foods (Dr.)	Income from Special Foods (Cr.)	
Beginning Balance	256,000					
80% of Net Income	60,000				60,000	80% of Net Income
		32,000	80% Dividends			
Ending Balance	284,000				60,000	Ending Balance
		284,000	Basic entry	60,000		
	0				0	

FIGURE 3–4 December 31, 20X2, Equity-Method Worksheet for Consolidated Financial Statements, Second Year of Ownership; 80 percent Acquisition at Book Value

	Peerless Products	Special Foods	Consolidation Entries DR	Consolidation Entries CR	Consolidated
Income Statement					
Sales	450,000	300,000			750,000
Less: COGS	(180,000)	(160,000)			(340,000)
Less: Depreciation Expense	(50,000)	(20,000)			(70,000)
Less: Other Expenses	(60,000)	(45,000)			(105,000)
Income from Special Foods	60,000		60,000		0
Consolidated Net Income	220,000	75,000	60,000	0	235,000
NCI in Net Income			15,000		(15,000)
Controlling Interest Net Income	**220,000**	**75,000**	**75,000**	**0**	**220,000**
Statement of Retained Earnings					
Beginning Balance	420,000	120,000	120,000		420,000
Net Income	**220,000**	**75,000**	**75,000**	**0**	220,000
Less: Dividends Declared	(60,000)	(40,000)		40,000	(60,000)
Ending Balance	**580,000**	**155,000**	**195,000**	**40,000**	**580,000**
Balance Sheet					
Cash	291,000	85,000			376,000
Accounts Receivable	150,000	80,000			230,000
Inventory	180,000	90,000			270,000
Investment in Special Foods	284,000			284,000	0
Land	175,000	40,000			215,000
Buildings & Equipment	800,000	600,000		300,000	1,100,000
Less: Accumulated Depreciation	(500,000)	(340,000)	300,000		(540,000)
Total Assets	**1,380,000**	**555,000**	**300,000**	**584,000**	**1,651,000**
Accounts Payable	100,000	100,000			200,000
Bonds Payable	200,000	100,000			300,000
Common Stock	500,000	200,000	200,000		500,000
Retained Earnings	**580,000**	**155,000**	**195,000**	**40,000**	580,000
NCI in NA of Special Foods				71,000	71,000
Total Liabilities & Equity	**1,380,000**	**555,000**	**395,000**	**111,000**	**1,651,000**

In this example, Special Foods had accumulated depreciation on the acquisition date of $300,000. Thus, we repeat the same accumulated depreciation consolidation entry this year (and every year as long as Special Foods owns the assets) that we used in the initial year.

Optional Accumulated Depreciation Consolidation Entry:

Accumulated Depreciation	**300,000**		
Building & Equipment		**300,000**	← Accumulated depreciation at the time of the acquisition netted against cost

After placement of the two consolidation entries in the consolidation worksheet, the worksheet is completed in the normal manner as shown in Figure 3–4.

COMBINED FINANCIAL STATEMENTS

LO 3-6

Understand and explain the purpose of combined financial statements and how they differ from consolidated financial statements.

Financial statements are sometimes prepared for a group of companies when no one company in the group owns a majority of the common stock of any other company in the group. Financial statements that include a group of related companies without including the parent company or other owner are referred to as ***combined financial statements.***

Combined financial statements are commonly prepared when an individual, rather than a corporation, owns or controls a number of companies and wishes to include them all in a single set of financial statements. In some cases, a parent company may prepare financial statements that include only its subsidiaries, not the parent. In other cases, a parent may prepare financial statements for its subsidiaries by operating group, with all the subsidiaries engaged in a particular type of operation, or those located in a particular geographical region, reported together.

The procedures used to prepare combined financial statements are essentially the same as those used in preparing consolidated financial statements. All intercompany receivables and payables, intercompany transactions, and unrealized intercompany profits and losses must be eliminated in the same manner as in the preparation of consolidated statements. Although no parent company is included in the reporting entity, any intercompany ownership, and the associated portion of stockholders' equity, must be eliminated in the same way as the parent's investment in a subsidiary is eliminated in preparing consolidated financial statements. The remaining stockholders' equity of the companies in the reporting entity is divided into the portions accruing to the controlling and noncontrolling interests.

SPECIAL-PURPOSE AND VARIABLE INTEREST ENTITIES

LO 3-7

Understand and explain rules related to the consolidation of variable interest entities.

Although consolidation standards pertaining to related corporations have at times lacked clarity and needed updating, consolidation standards relating to partnerships or other types of entities such as trusts have been virtually nonexistent. Even corporate consolidation standards have not been adequate in situations in which other relationships such as guarantees and operating agreements overshadow the lack of a significant ownership element. As a result, companies such as Enron have taken advantage of the lack of standards to avoid reporting debt or losses by hiding them in special entities that were not consolidated. Although many companies have used special entities for legitimate purposes, financial reporting has not always captured the economic substance of the relationships. Only in recent years have consolidation standards for these special entities started to provide some uniformity in the financial reporting for corporations having relationships with such entities.

ASC 810-10-10 establishes consolidation standards in terms of one company controlling another and sets majority voting interest as the usual condition leading to consolidation. Similarly, **ASC 810-10-15** requires consolidation for majority-owned subsidiaries. In recent years, however, new types of relationships have been established between corporations and other entities that often are difficult to characterize in terms of voting, controlling, or ownership interests. Such entities often are structured to provide financing and/or control through forms other than those used by traditional operating companies. Some entities have no governing boards, or they may have boards or managers with only a limited ability to direct the entity's activities. Such entities may be governed instead by their incorporation or partnership documents, or by other agreements or documents. Some entities may have little equity investment, and the equity investors may have little or no control over the entity. For these special types of entities, **ASC 810-10-10** does not provide a clear basis for consolidation.

These special types of entities have generally been referred to as ***special-purpose entities (SPEs).*** In general, SPEs are corporations, trusts, or partnerships created for a single specified purpose. They usually have no substantive operations and are used only for financing purposes. SPEs have been used for several decades for asset securitization, risk sharing, and taking advantage of tax statutes. Prior to 2003, no comprehensive reporting framework had been established for SPEs. Several different pronouncements from various bodies dealt with selected issues or types of SPEs, but the guidance provided by these issuances was incomplete, vague, and not always correctly interpreted in practice.

Variable Interest Entities

In January 2003, the FASB issued guidance on variable interest entities **(ASC 810-10-25)** and updated this guidance later the same year **(ASC 810-10-38C).** For clarification, the interpretation uses the term *variable interest entities* to encompass SPEs and any other entities falling within its conditions.

A ***variable interest entity (VIE)*** is a legal structure used for business purposes, usually a corporation, trust, or partnership, that either (1) does not have equity investors that have voting rights and share in all of the entity's profits and losses or (2) has equity investors that do not provide sufficient financial resources to support the entity's activities. In a variable interest entity, specific agreements may limit the extent to which the equity investors, if any, share in the entity's profits or losses, and the agreements may limit the control that equity investors have over the entity's activities. For the equity investment to be considered sufficient financial support for the entity's activities (condition 2), it must be able to absorb the entity's expected future losses. A total equity investment that is less than 10 percent of the entity's total assets is, in general, considered to be insufficient by itself to allow the entity to finance its activities, and an investment of more than 10 percent might be needed, depending on the circumstances.

A corporation might create (or sponsor) a typical variable interest entity for a particular purpose, such as purchasing the sponsoring company's receivables or leasing facilities to the sponsoring company. The sponsoring company may acquire little or no stock in the VIE. Instead, the sponsoring company may enlist another party to purchase most or all of the common stock. The majority of the VIE's capital, however, normally comes from borrowing. Because lenders may be reluctant to lend (at least at reasonable interest rates) to an entity with only a small amount of equity, the sponsoring company often guarantees the VIE's loans. Thus, the sponsoring company may have little or no equity investment in the VIE, but the loan guarantees represent a type of interest in the VIE.

A corporation having an interest in a VIE cannot simply rely on its percentage stock ownership, if any, to determine whether to consolidate the entity. Instead each party having a variable interest in the VIE must determine the extent to which it shares in the VIE's expected profits and losses. **ASC 810-10-20** defines a *variable interest* in a VIE as a contractual ownership (with or without voting rights), or other money-related interest in an entity that changes with changes in the fair value of the entity's net assets exclusive of variable interests. In other words, variable interests increase with the VIE's profits and decrease with its losses. The VIE's variable interests will absorb portions of the losses, if they occur, or receive portions of the residual returns.

There are several different types of variable interests, some of which can be summarized as follows:

Type of Interest	Variable Interest?
Common stock, with no special features or provisions	Yes
Common stock, with loss protection or other provisions	Maybe
Senior debt	Usually not
Subordinated debt	Yes
Loan or asset guarantees	Yes

STOP & THINK

The following "red flags" often indicate a variable interest:

- Subordinated loans to a VIE.
- Equity interests in a VIE (50% or less).
- Guarantees to a VIE's lenders or equity holders.
- Guarantees of asset recovery values.
- Written put options on a VIE's assets held by a VIE or its lenders or equity holders.
- Forward contracts on purchases and sales.

Common stock that places the owners' investment at risk is a variable interest. In some cases, common stock may have, by agreement, special provisions that protect the investor against losses or provide a fixed return. These special types of shares may not involve significant risk on the part of the investor and might, depending on the provisions, result in an interest that is not a variable interest. Senior debt usually carries a fixed return and is protected against loss by subordinated

! CAUTION

A pending FASB rule change regarding the determination of the primary beneficiary will involve a more qualitative approach requiring both of the following (810-10-25-38A): (a) The power to direct the activities of a VIE that most significantly impact the VIE's economic performance and (b) The obligation to absorb losses of the VIE that could potentially be significant to the VIE or the right to receive benefits from the VIE that could potentially be significant to the VIE.

interests. Subordinated debt represents a variable interest because, if the entity's cash flows are insufficient to pay off the subordinated debt, the holders of that debt will sustain losses. They do not have the same protection against loss that holders of the senior debt have. Parties that guarantee the value of assets or liabilities can sustain losses if they are called on to make good on their guarantees, and, therefore, the guarantees represent variable interests.

The nature of each party's variable interest determines whether consolidation by that party is appropriate. In recent years, an enterprise that absorbs a majority of the VIE's expected losses, receives a majority of the VIE's expected residual returns, or both, is called the ***primary beneficiary*** of the variable interest entity. The primary beneficiary must consolidate the VIE. If the entity's profits and losses are divided differently, the enterprise absorbing a majority of the losses will consolidate the VIE.

As an example of the financial reporting determinations of parties with an interest in a VIE, suppose that Young Company and Zebra Corporation, both financially stable companies, create YZ Corporation to lease equipment to Young and other companies. Zebra purchases all of YZ's common stock. Young guarantees Zebra a 7 percent dividend on its stock, agrees to absorb all of YZ's losses, and guarantees fixed-rate bank loans that are made to YZ. All profits in excess of the 7 percent payout to Zebra are split evenly between Young and Zebra.

In this case, the bank loans are not variable interests because they carry a fixed interest rate and are guaranteed by Young, a company capable of honoring the guarantee. Common stock of a VIE is a variable interest if the investment is at risk. In this case, Zebra's investment is not at risk, but it does share in the profits of YZ, and the amount of profits is not fixed. Therefore, the common stock is a variable interest. However, Zebra will not consolidate YZ because Zebra does not share in the losses, all of which Young will bear. Young will consolidate YZ because Young's guarantees represent a variable interest, and it will absorb a majority (all) of the losses.

If consolidation of a VIE is appropriate, the amounts to be consolidated with those of the primary beneficiary are based on fair values at the date the enterprise first becomes the primary beneficiary. However, assets and liabilities transferred to a VIE by its primary beneficiary are valued at their book values, with no gain or loss recognized on the transfer. Subsequent to the initial determination of consolidation values, a VIE is accounted for in consolidated financial statements in accordance with **ASC 810-10-10** in the same manner as if it were consolidated based on voting interests. Intercompany balances and transactions are eliminated so the resulting consolidated financial statements appear as if there were just a single entity. These procedures are consistent with those used when consolidating parent and subsidiary corporations. Appendix 3A at the end of the chapter presents a simple illustration of the consolidation of a VIE.

FYI

Disney controls Euro Disney and Hong Kong Disneyland as variable interest entities. Disney follows **ASC 810-10-10** by fully consolidating the financial statements of Euro Disney and Hong Kong Disneyland.

LO 3-8

Understand and explain differences in consolidation rules under U.S. GAAP and IFRS.

IFRS Differences in Determining Control of VIEs and SPEs

Although rules under International Financial Reporting Standards (IFRS) for consolidation are generally very similar to those under U.S. GAAP, there are some important differences. Figure 3–5 provides a summary of the main differences in current standards.

FIGURE 3–5 Summary of Differences between IFRS and U.S. GAAP related to Control and VIEs

Topic	U.S. GAAP	IFRS
Determination of Control	• Normally, control is determined by majority ownership of voting shares. • However, majority ownership may not indicate control of a VIE. • Thus, VIE rules must be evaluated first in all situations. • The primary beneficiary must consolidate a VIE. • The majority shareholder consolidates most non-VIEs. • Control is based on direct or indirect voting interests. • An entity with less than 50 percent ownership may have "effective control" through other contractual arrangements.	• Normally, control is determined by majority ownership of voting shares. • In addition to voting shares, convertible instruments and other contractual rights that could affect control are considered. • A parent with less than 50 percent of the voting shares could have control through contractual arrangements allowing control of votes or the board of directors. • Control over SPEs is determined based on judgment and relevant facts. • Substance over is form considered in determining whether an SPE should be consolidated.
Related Parties	• Interests held by related parties and *de facto* agents may be considered in determining control of a VIE.	• There is no specific provision for related parties or *de facto* agents.
Definitions of VIEs versus SPEs	• SPEs can be VIEs. • Consolidation rules focus on whether an entity is a VIE (regardless of whether or not it is an SPE). • U.S. GAAP guidance applies only to legal entities.	• IFRS considers specific indicators of whether an entity has control of an SPE: (1) whether the SPE conducts activities for the entity, (2) whether the entity has decision-making power to obtain majority of benefits from the SPE, (3) whether the entity has the right to majority of benefits from the SPE, and (4) whether the entity has a majority of the SPE's residual or risks. • IFRS guidance applies whether or not conducted by a legal entity.
Disclosure	• Disclosures are required for determining control of a VIE. • Entities must disclose whether or not they are the primary beneficiary of related VIEs.	• There are no SPE-specific disclosure requirements. • There are specific disclosure requirements related to consolidation in general.
Accounting for Joint Ventures	• Owners typically share control (often with 50-50 ownership). • If the joint venture is a VIE, contracts must be considered to determine whether consolidation is required. • If the joint venture is not a VIE, venturers use the equity method. • Proportional consolidation is generally not permitted.	• Joint ventures can be accounted for using either proportionate consolidation or the equity method. • Proportionate consolidation reports the venturer's share of the assets, liabilities, income, and expenses on a line-by-line basis based on the venturer's financial statement line items.

SUMMARY OF KEY CONCEPTS

Consolidated financial statements present the financial position and operating results of a parent and one or more subsidiaries as if they were actually a single company. As a result, the consolidated financial statements portray a group of legally separate companies as a single economic entity. All indications of intercorporate ownership and the effects of all intercompany transactions are excluded from the consolidated statements. The basic approach to the preparation of consolidated financial statements is to combine the separate financial statements of the individual consolidating companies and then to eliminate or adjust those items that would not appear, or that would appear differently, if the companies actually were one.

Current consolidation standards require that the consolidated financial statements include all companies under common control unless control is questionable. Consolidated financial statements are prepared primarily for those with a long-run interest in the parent company, especially the parent's stockholders and long-term creditors. While consolidated financial statements allow interested parties to view a group of related companies as a single economic entity, such statements have some limitations. In particular, information about the characteristics and operations of the individual companies within the consolidated entity is lost in the process of combining financial statements.

New types of business arrangements have proven troublesome in the past for financial reporting. In particular, special types of entities, called *special-purpose entities* and *variable interest entities,* have been used to hide or transform various types of transactions, in addition to being used for many legitimate purposes such as risk sharing. Often these entities were disclosed only through vague notes to the financial statements. Reporting standards now require that the party that is the primary beneficiary of a variable interest entity consolidate that entity.

KEY TERMS

combined financial statements, *119*
consolidated net income, *107*
direct control, *104*
effective control, *105*
indirect control, *104*
minority interest, *106*
noncontrolling interest, *106*
primary beneficiary, *122*
special-purpose entities (SPEs), *120*
variable interest entity (VIE), *121*

Appendix 3A Consolidation of Variable Interest Entities

The standards for determining whether a party with an interest in a variable interest entity (VIE) should consolidate the VIE were discussed earlier in the chapter. Once a party has determined that it must consolidate a VIE, the consolidation procedures are similar to those used when consolidating a subsidiary. As an illustration, assume that Ignition Petroleum Company joins with Mammoth Financial Corporation to create a special corporation, Exploration Equipment Company, that would lease equipment to Ignition and other companies. Ignition purchases 10 percent of Exploration's stock for $1,000,000, and Mammoth purchases the other 90 percent for $9,000,000. Profits are to be split equally between the two owners, but Ignition agrees to absorb the first $500,000 of annual losses. Immediately after incorporation, Exploration borrows $120,000,000 from a syndicate of banks, and Ignition guarantees the loan. Exploration then purchases plant, equipment, and supplies for its own use and equipment for lease to others. The balance sheets of Ignition and Exploration appear as follows just prior to the start of Exploration's operations:

Item	Ignition	Exploration
Cash and Receivables	$100,000,000	$ 23,500,000
Inventory and Supplies	50,000,000	200,000
Equipment Held for Lease		105,000,000
Investment in Exploration Equipment Co.	1,000,000	
Plant & Equipment (net)	180,000,000	1,350,000
Total Assets	$331,000,000	$130,050,000
Accounts Payable	$ 900,000	$ 50,000
Bank Loans Payable	30,000,000	120,000,000
Common Stock Issued & Outstanding	200,000,000	10,000,000
Retained Earnings	100,100,000	
Total Liabilities & Equity	$331,000,000	$130,050,000

FIGURE 3–6
Balance Sheet Consolidating a Variable Interest Entity

IGNITION PETROLEUM COMPANY Consolidated Balance Sheet		
Assets		
Cash & Receivables		$123,500,000
Inventory & Supplies		50,200,000
Equipment Held for Lease		105,000,000
Plant & Equipment (net)		181,350,000
Total Assets		$460,050,000
Liabilities		
Accounts Payable	$ 950,000	
Bank Loans Payable	150,000,000	
Total Liabilities		$150,950,000
Stockholders' Equity		
Common Stock	$200,000,000	
Retained Earnings	100,100,000	
Noncontrolling Interest	9,000,000	
Total Stockholders' Equity		309,100,000
Total Liabilities & Stockholders' Equity		$460,050,000

Both Ignition and Mammoth hold variable interests in Exploration. Ignition's variable interests include both its common stock and its guarantees. Ignition is the primary beneficiary of Exploration because it shares equally in the profits with Mammoth but must absorb a larger share of the expected losses than Mammoth through both its profit-and-loss-sharing agreement with Mammoth and its loan guarantee. Accordingly, Ignition must consolidate Exploration.

Ignition's consolidated balance sheet that includes Exploration appears as in Figure 3–6. The balances in Exploration's asset and liability accounts are added to the balances of Ignition's like accounts. Ignition's $1,000,000 investment in Exploration is eliminated against the common stock of Exploration, and Exploration's remaining $9,000,000 of common stock (owned by Mammoth) is labeled as noncontrolling interest and reported within the equity section of the consolidated balance sheet.

QUESTIONS

LO 3-1 **Q3-1** What is the basic idea underlying the preparation of consolidated financial statements?

LO 3-1 **Q3-2** How might consolidated statements help an investor assess the desirability of purchasing shares of the parent company?

LO 3-1 **Q3-3** Are consolidated financial statements likely to be more useful to the owners of the parent company or to the noncontrolling owners of the subsidiaries? Why?

LO 3-2 **Q3-4** What is meant by *parent company?* When is a company considered to be a parent?

LO 3-1 **Q3-5** Are consolidated financial statements likely to be more useful to the creditors of the parent company or the creditors of the subsidiaries? Why?

LO 3-2 **Q3-6** Why is ownership of a majority of the common stock of another company considered important in consolidation?

LO 3-2 **Q3-7** What major criteria must be met before a company is consolidated?

LO 3-2 **Q3-8** When is consolidation considered inappropriate even though the parent holds a majority of the voting common shares of another company?

LO 3-7 **Q3-9** How has reliance on legal control as a consolidation criterion led to off-balance sheet financing?

LO 3-7 **Q3-10** What types of entities are referred to as *special-purpose entities,* and how have they generally been used?

LO 3-7 **Q3-11** How does a variable interest entity typically differ from a traditional corporate business entity?

LO 3-7 **Q3-12** What characteristics are normally examined in determining whether a company is a primary beneficiary of a variable interest entity?

LO 3-2 **Q3-13** What is meant by *indirect control?* Give an illustration.

LO 3-2 **Q3-14** What means other than majority ownership might be used to gain control over a company? Can consolidation occur if control is gained by other means?

LO 3-4 **Q3-15** Why are subsidiary shares not reported as stock outstanding in the consolidated balance sheet?

LO 3-2 **Q3-16** What must be done if the fiscal periods of the parent and its subsidiary are not the same?

LO 3-3 **Q3-17** What is the noncontrolling interest in a subsidiary?

LO 3-4, 3-6 **Q3-18** What is the difference between consolidated and combined financial statements?

CASES

LO 3-5

C3-1 Computation of Total Asset Values

A reader of Gigantic Company's consolidated financial statements received from another source copies of the financial statements of the individual companies included in the consolidation. The person is confused by the fact that the total assets in the consolidated balance sheet differ rather substantially from the sum of the asset totals reported by the individual companies.

Required

Will this relationship always be true? What factors may cause this difference to occur?

LO 3-3, 3-7

C3-2 Accounting Entity [AICPA Adapted]

The concept of the accounting entity often is considered to be the most fundamental of accounting concepts, one that pervades all of accounting. For each of the following, indicate whether the entity concept is applicable; discuss and give illustrations.

Required

a. A unit created by or under law.
b. The product-line segment of an enterprise.
c. A combination of legal units.
d. All the activities of an owner or a group of owners.
e. The economy of the United States.

LO 3-3, 3-6

C3-3 Joint Venture Investment

Research

Dell Computer Corp. and CIT Group Inc. established Dell Financial Services LP (DFS) as a joint venture to provide financing services for Dell customers. Dell originally purchased 70 percent of the equity of DFS and CIT purchased 30 percent. In the initial agreement, losses were allocated entirely to CIT, although CIT would recoup any losses before any future income was allocated. At the time the joint venture was formed, both Dell and CIT indicated that they had no plans to consolidate DFS.

Required

a. How could both Dell and CIT avoid consolidating DFS?
b. Does Dell currently employ off-balance sheet financing? Explain.

LO 3-1

C3-4 What Company Is That?

Analysis

Many well-known products and names come from companies that may be less well known or may be known for other reasons. In some cases, an obscure parent company may have well-known subsidiaries, and often familiar but diverse products may be produced under common ownership.

Required

a. Viacom is not necessarily a common name easily identified because it operates through numerous subsidiaries, but its brand names are seen every day. What are some of the well-known brand names from Viacom's subsidiaries? What changes occurred in its organizational structure in 2006? Who is Sumner Redstone?

b. ConAgra Foods Inc. is one of the world's largest food processors and distributors. Although it produces many products with familiar names, the company's name generally is not well known. What are some of ConAgra's brand names?

c. What type of company is Yum! Brands Inc.? What are some of its well-known brands? What is the origin of the company, and what was its previous name?

LO 3-1

C3-5 Subsidiaries and Core Businesses

Analysis

During previous merger booms, a number of companies acquired many subsidiaries that often were in businesses unrelated to the acquiring company's central operations. In many cases, the acquiring company's management was unable to manage effectively the many diverse types of operations found in the numerous subsidiaries. More recently, many of these subsidiaries have been sold or, in a few cases, liquidated so the parent companies could concentrate on their core businesses.

Required

a. In 1986, General Electric acquired nearly all of the common stock of the large brokerage firm Kidder, Peabody Inc. Unfortunately, the newly acquired subsidiary's performance was very poor. What ultimately happened to this General Electric subsidiary?

b. What major business has Sears Holdings Corporation been in for many decades? What other businesses was it in during the 1980s and early 1990s? What were some of its best-known subsidiaries during that time? Does Sears still own those subsidiaries? What additional acquisitions have occurred?

c. PepsiCo is best known as a soft-drink company. What well-known subsidiaries did PepsiCo own during the mid-1990s? Does PepsiCo still own them?

d. When a parent company and its subsidiaries are in businesses that are considerably different in nature, such as retailing and financial services, how meaningful are their consolidated financial statements in your opinion? Explain. How might financial reporting be improved in such situations?

LO 3-8

C3-6 International Consolidation Issues

Research

The International Accounting Standards Board (IASB) is charged with developing a set of high-quality standards and encouraging their adoption globally. Standards promulgated by the IASB are called International Financial Reporting Standards (IFRS). The European Union (EU) requires statements prepared using IFRS for all companies that list on the EU stock exchanges. Currently, the SEC allows international companies that list on U.S. exchanges to use IFRS for financial reporting in the United States.

The differences between U.S. GAAP and IFRS are described in many different publications. For example, PricewaterhouseCoopers has a publication available for download on its website (http://www.pwc.com/us/en/issues/ifrs-reporting/publications/ifrs-and-us-gaap-similarities-and-differences.jhtml) entitled "IFRS and U.S. GAAP: Similarities and Differences" that provides a topic-based comparison. Based on the information in this publication or others, answer the following questions about the preparation of consolidated financial statements.

Required

a. Under U.S. GAAP, a two-tiered consolidation model is applied, one focused on voting rights and the second based on a party's exposure to risks and rewards associated with the entity's activities (the VIE model). Upon what is the IFRS framework based?

b. U.S. GAAP requires a two-step process to evaluate goodwill for potential impairment (as discussed in Chapter 1). What is required by IFRS with respect to goodwill impairment?

c. Under U.S. GAAP, noncontrolling interests are measured at fair value. What is required by IFRS?

LO 3-7

C3-7 Off-Balance Sheet Financing and VIEs

Understanding

A variable interest entity (VIE) is a structure frequently used for off-balance sheet financing. VIEs have become quite numerous in recent years and have been the subject of some controversy.

Required

a. Briefly explain what is meant by off-balance sheet financing.

b. What are three techniques used to keep debt off the balance sheet?

c. What are some legitimate uses of VIEs?

d. How can VIEs be used to manage earnings to meet financial reporting goals? How does this relate to the importance of following the intent of the guidelines for consolidations?

LO 3-6

C3-8 Consolidation Differences among Major Companies

Research

A variety of organizational structures are used by major companies, and different approaches to consolidation are sometimes found. Two large and familiar U.S. corporations are Union Pacific and ExxonMobil.

Required

a. Many large companies have tens or even hundreds of subsidiaries. List the significant subsidiaries of Union Pacific Corporation.

b. ExxonMobil Corporation is a major energy company. Does ExxonMobil consolidate all of its majority-owned subsidiaries? Explain. Does ExxonMobil consolidate any entities in which it does not hold majority ownership? Explain. What methods does ExxonMobil use to account for investments in the common stock of companies in which it holds less than majority ownership?

EXERCISES

LO 3-1, 3-2

E3-1 Multiple-Choice Questions on Consolidation Overview [AICPA Adapted]

Select the correct answer for each of the following questions.

1. When a parent–subsidiary relationship exists, consolidated financial statements are prepared in recognition of the accounting concept of
   a. Reliability.
   b. Materiality.
   c. Legal entity.
   d. Economic entity.
2. Consolidated financial statements are typically prepared when one company has a controlling interest in another unless
   a. The subsidiary is a finance company.
   b. The fiscal year-ends of the two companies are more than three months apart.
   c. Circumstances prevent the exercise of control.
   d. The two companies are in unrelated industries, such as real estate and manufacturing.
3. Penn Inc., a manufacturing company, owns 75 percent of the common stock of Sell Inc., an investment company. Sell owns 60 percent of the common stock of Vane Inc., an insurance company. In Penn's consolidated financial statements, should Sell and Vane be consolidated or reported as equity method investments (assuming there are no side agreements)?
   a. Consolidation used for Sell and equity method used for Vane.
   b. Consolidation used for both Sell and Vane.
   c. Equity method used for Sell and consolidation used for Vane.
   d. Equity method used for both Sell and Vane.
4. Which of the following is the best theoretical justification for consolidated financial statements?
   a. In form, the companies are one entity; in substance, they are separate.
   b. In form, the companies are separate; in substance, they are one entity.
   c. In form and substance, the companies are one entity.
   d. In form and substance, the companies are separate.

LO 3-7

E3-2 Multiple-Choice Questions on Variable Interest Entities

Select the correct answer for each of the following questions.

1. Special-purpose entities generally
   a. Have a much larger portion of assets financed by equity shareholders than do companies such as General Motors.
   b. Have relatively large amounts of preferred stock and convertible securities outstanding.

c. Have a much smaller portion of their assets financed by equity shareholders than do companies such as General Motors.
d. Pay out a relatively high percentage of their earnings as dividends to facilitate the sale of additional shares.

2. Variable interest entities may be established as
   a. Corporations.
   b. Trusts.
   c. Partnerships.
   d. All of the above.
3. An enterprise that will absorb a majority of a variable interest entity's expected losses is called the
   a. Primary beneficiary.
   b. Qualified owner.
   c. Major facilitator.
   d. Critical management director.
4. In determining whether or not a variable interest entity is to be consolidated, the FASB focused on
   a. Legal control.
   b. Share of profits and obligation to absorb losses.
   c. Frequency of intercompany transfers.
   d. Proportionate size of the two entities.

LO 3-5

E3-3 Multiple-Choice Questions on Consolidated Balances [AICPA Adapted]

Select the correct answer for each of the following questions.

Items 1 and 2 are based on the following:

On January 2, 20X8, Pare Company acquired 75 percent of Kidd Company's outstanding common stock at an amount equal to its underlying book value. Selected balance sheet data at December 31, 20X8, are as follows:

	Pare Company	Kidd Company
Total Assets	$420,000	$180,000
Liabilities	$120,000	$ 60,000
Common Stock	100,000	50,000
Retained Earnings	200,000	70,000
	$420,000	$180,000

1. In Pare's December 31, 20X8, consolidated balance sheet, what amount should be reported as minority interest in net assets?
   a. $0.
   b. $30,000.
   c. $45,000.
   d. $105,000.
2. In its consolidated balance sheet at December 31, 20X8, what amount should Pare report as common stock outstanding?
   a. $50,000.
   b. $100,000.
   c. $137,500.
   d. $150,000.

3. Consolidated statements are proper for Neely Inc., Randle Inc., and Walker Inc., if
   a. Neely owns 80 percent of the outstanding common stock of Randle and 40 percent of Walker; Randle owns 30 percent of Walker.
   b. Neely owns 100 percent of the outstanding common stock of Randle and 90 percent of Walker; Neely bought the Walker stock one month before the foreign country in which Walker is based imposed restrictions preventing Walker from remitting profits to Neely.
   c. Neely owns 100 percent of the outstanding common stock of Randle and Walker; Walker is in legal reorganization.
   d. Neely owns 80 percent of the outstanding common stock of Randle and 40 percent of Walker; Reeves Inc. owns 55 percent of Walker.

LO 3-2, 3-3

E3-4 Multiple-Choice Questions on Consolidation Overview [AICPA Adapted]

Select the correct answer for each of the following questions.

1. Consolidated financial statements are typically prepared when one company has
   a. Accounted for its investment in another company by the equity method.
   b. Accounted for its investment in another company by the cost method.
   c. Significant influence over the operating and financial policies of another company.
   d. The controlling financial interest in another company.
2. Aaron Inc. owns 80 percent of the outstanding stock of Belle Inc. Compare the total consolidated net earnings of Aaron and Belle (X) and Aaron's operating earnings before considering the income from Belle (Y). Assume that neither company incurs a net loss during the period.
   a. X is more than Y.
   b. X is equal to Y.
   c. X is less than Y.
   d. Cannot be determined.
3. On October 1, X Company acquired for cash all of Y Company's outstanding common stock. Both companies have a December 31 year-end and have been in business for many years. Consolidated net income for the year ended December 31 should include net income of
   a. X Company for three months and Y Company for three months.
   b. X Company for 12 months and Y Company for 3 months.
   c. X Company for 12 months and Y Company for 12 months.
   d. X Company for 12 months, but no income from Y Company until Y Company distributes a dividend.
4. Ownership of 51 percent of the outstanding voting stock of a company would usually result in
   a. The use of the cost method.
   b. The use of the lower-of-cost-or-market method.
   c. The use of the equity method.
   d. A consolidation.

LO 3-5

E3-5 Balance Sheet Consolidation

On January 1, 20X3, Guild Corporation reported total assets of $470,000, liabilities of $270,000, and stockholders' equity of $200,000. At that date, Bristol Corporation reported total assets of $190,000, liabilities of $135,000, and stockholders' equity of $55,000. Following lengthy negotiations, Guild paid Bristol's existing shareholders $44,000 in cash for 80 percent of the voting common shares of Bristol.

Required

Immediately after Guild purchased the Bristol shares

a. What amount of total assets did Guild report in its individual balance sheet?
b. What amount of total assets was reported in the consolidated balance sheet?
c. What amount of total liabilities was reported in the consolidated balance sheet?
d. What amount of stockholders' equity was reported in the consolidated balance sheet?

LO 3-5

E3-6 Balance Sheet Consolidation with Intercompany Transfer

Potter Company acquired 90 percent of the voting common shares of Stately Corporation by issuing bonds with a par value and fair value of $121,500 to Stately's existing shareholders. Immediately prior to the acquisition, Potter reported total assets of $510,000, liabilities of $320,000, and stockholders' equity of $190,000. At that date, Stately reported total assets of $350,000, liabilities of $215,000, and stockholders' equity of $135,000.

Required

Immediately after Potter acquired Stately's shares

a. What amount of total assets did Potter report in its individual balance sheet?

b. What amount of total assets was reported in the consolidated balance sheet?

c. What amount of total liabilities was reported in the consolidated balance sheet?

d. What amount of stockholders' equity was reported in the consolidated balance sheet?

LO 3-5

E3-7 Subsidiary Acquired for Cash

Fineline Pencil Company acquired 80 percent of Smudge Eraser Corporation's stock on January 2, 20X3, for $72,000 cash. Summarized balance sheet data for the companies on December 31, 20X2, are as follows:

	Fineline Pencil Company		Smudge Eraser Corporation	
	Book Value	**Fair Value**	**Book Value**	**Fair Value**
Cash	$200,000	$200,000	$ 50,000	$ 50,000
Other Assets	400,000	400,000	120,000	120,000
Total Debits	$600,000		$170,000	
Current Liabilities	$100,000	100,000	$ 80,000	80,000
Common Stock	300,000		50,000	
Retained Earnings	200,000		40,000	
Total Credits	$600,000		$170,000	

Required

Prepare a consolidated balance sheet immediately following the acquisition.

LO 3-5

E3-8 Subsidiary Acquired with Bonds

Byte Computer Corporation acquired 75 percent of Nofail Software Company's stock on January 2, 20X3, by issuing bonds with a par value of $50,000 and a fair value of $67,500 in exchange for the shares. Summarized balance sheet data presented for the companies just before the acquisition are as follows:

	Byte Computer Corporation		Nofail Software Company	
	Book Value	**Fair Value**	**Book Value**	**Fair Value**
Cash	$200,000	$200,000	$ 50,000	$ 50,000
Other Assets	400,000	400,000	120,000	120,000
Total Debits	$600,000		$170,000	
Current Liabilities	$100,000	100,000	$ 80,000	80,000
Common Stock	300,000		50,000	
Retained Earnings	200,000		40,000	
Total Credits	$600,000		$170,000	

Required

Prepare a consolidated balance sheet immediately following the acquisition.

LO 3-5

E3-9 Subsidiary Acquired by Issuing Preferred Stock

Byte Computer Corporation acquired 90 percent of Nofail Software Company's common stock on January 2, 20X3, by issuing preferred stock with a par value of $6 per share and a market value of $8.10 per share. A total of 10,000 shares of preferred stock was issued. Balance sheet data for the two companies immediately before the business combination are presented in E3-8.

Required

Prepare a consolidated balance sheet for the companies immediately after Byte obtains ownership of Nofail by issuing the preferred stock.

LO 3-4, 3-7

E3-10 Reporting for a Variable Interest Entity

Gamble Company convinced Conservative Corporation that the two companies should establish Simpletown Corporation to build a new gambling casino in Simpletown Corner. Although chances for the casino's success were relatively low, a local bank loaned $140,000,000 to the new corporation, which built the casino at a cost of $130,000,000. Conservative purchased 100 percent of the initial capital stock offering for $5,600,000, and Gamble agreed to supply 100 percent of the management and guarantee the bank loan. Gamble also guaranteed a 20 percent return to Conservative on its investment for the first 10 years. Gamble will receive all profits in excess of the 20 percent return to Conservative. Immediately after the casino's construction, Gamble reported the following amounts:

Cash	$ 3,000,000
Buildings & Equipment	240,600,000
Accumulated Depreciation	10,100,000
Accounts Payable	5,000,000
Bonds Payable	20,300,000
Common Stock	103,000,000
Retained Earnings	105,200,000

The only disclosure that Gamble currently provides in its financial reports about its relationships to Conservative and Simpletown is a brief footnote indicating that a contingent liability exists on its guarantee of Simpletown Corporation's debt.

Required

Prepare a consolidated balance sheet in good form for Gamble immediately following the casino's construction.

LO 3-4, 3-7

E3-11 Consolidation of a Variable Interest Entity

Teal Corporation is the primary beneficiary of a variable interest entity with total assets of $500,000, liabilities of $470,000, and owners' equity of $30,000. Because Teal owns 25 percent of the VIE's voting stock, it reported a $7,500 investment in the VIE in its balance sheet. Teal reported total assets of $190,000 (including its investment in the VIE), liabilities of $80,000, common stock of $15,000, and retained earnings of $95,000 in its balance sheet.

Required

Prepare a consolidated balance sheet in good form for Teal, taking into consideration that it is the primary beneficiary of the variable interest entity.

LO 3-3

E3-12 Computation of Subsidiary Net Income

Frazer Corporation owns 70 percent of Messer Company's stock. In the 20X9 consolidated income statement, the noncontrolling interest was assigned $18,000 of income. There was no differential in the acquisition.

Required

What amount of net income did Messer Company report for 20X9?

LO 3-3, 3-4

E3-13 Incomplete Consolidation

Advanced StudyGuide .com

Belchfire Motors' accountant was called away after completing only half of the consolidated statements at the end of 20X4. The data left behind included the following:

Item	Belchfire Motors	Premium Body Shop	Consolidated
Cash	$ 40,000	$ 20,000	$ 60,000
Accounts Receivable	180,000	30,000	200,000
Inventory	220,000	50,000	270,000
Buildings & Equipment (net)	300,000	290,000	590,000
Investment in Premium Body Shop	150,000		
Total Debits	$890,000	$390,000	$1,120,000
Accounts Payable	$ 30,000	$ 40,000	
Bonds Payable	400,000	200,000	
Common Stock	200,000	100,000	
Retained Earnings	260,000	50,000	
Total Credits	$890,000	$390,000	

Required

a. Belchfire Motors acquired shares of Premium Body Shop at underlying book value on January 1, 20X1. What portion of the ownership of Premium Body Shop does Belchfire apparently hold?

b. Compute the consolidated totals for each of the remaining balance sheet items.

LO 3-3, 3-4

E3-14 Noncontrolling Interest

Sanderson Corporation acquired 70 percent of Kline Corporation's common stock on January 1, 20X7, for $294,000 in cash. At the acquisition date, the book values and fair values of Kline's assets and liabilities were equal, and the fair value of the noncontrolling interest was equal to 30 percent of the total book value of Kline. The stockholders' equity accounts of the two companies at the date of purchase are:

	Sanderson Corporation	Kline Corporation
Common Stock ($10 par value)	$400,000	$180,000
Additional Paid-In Capital	222,000	65,000
Retained Earnings	358,000	175,000
Total Stockholders' Equity	$980,000	$420,000

Required

a. What amount will be assigned to the noncontrolling interest on January 1, 20X7, in the consolidated balance sheet?

b. Prepare the stockholders' equity section of Sanderson and Kline's consolidated balance sheet as of January 1, 20X7.

c. Sanderson acquired ownership of Kline to ensure a constant supply of electronic switches, which it purchases regularly from Kline. Why might Sanderson not feel compelled to purchase all of Kline's shares?

LO 3-3, 3-4

E3-15 Computation of Consolidated Net Income

Ambrose Corporation owns 75 percent of Kroop Company's common stock, acquired at underlying book value on January 1, 20X4. At the acquisition date, the book values and fair values of Kroop's assets and liabilities were equal, and the fair value of the noncontrolling interest was equal to 25 percent of the total book value of Kroop. The income statements for Ambrose and Kroop for 20X4 include the following amounts:

	Ambrose Corporation	Kroop Company
Sales	$528,000	$150,000
Dividend Income	9,000	
Total Income	$537,000	$150,000
Less: Cost of Goods Sold	$380,000	$ 87,000
Depreciation Expense	32,000	20,000
Other Expenses	66,000	23,000
Total Expenses	$478,000	$130,000
Net Income	$ 59,000	$ 20,000

Ambrose uses the cost method in accounting for its ownership of Kroop. Kroop paid dividends of $12,000 in 20X4.

Required

a. What amount would Ambrose report in its income statement as income from its investment in Kroop if Ambrose used equity-method accounting?

b. What amount of income should be assigned to noncontrolling interest in the consolidated income statement for 20X4?

c. What amount should Ambrose report as consolidated net income for 20X4?

d. Why should Ambrose not report consolidated net income of $79,000 ($59,000 + $20,000) for 20X4?

LO 3-4

Advanced StudyGuide .com

E3-16 Computation of Subsidiary Balances

Tall Corporation acquired 75 percent of Light Corporation's voting common stock on January 1, 20X2, at underlying book value. At the acquisition date, the book values and fair values of Light's assets and liabilities were equal, and the fair value of the noncontrolling interest was equal to 25 percent of the total book value of Light. Noncontrolling interest was assigned income of $8,000 in Tall's consolidated income statement for 20X2 and a balance of $65,500 in Tall's consolidated balance sheet at December 31, 20X2. Light reported retained earnings of $70,000 and additional paid-in capital of $40,000 on January 1, 20X2. Light did not pay dividends or issue stock in 20X2.

Required

a. Compute the amount of net income reported by Light for 20X2.

b. Prepare the stockholders' equity section of Light's balance sheet at December 31, 20X2.

LO 3-4, 3-5

E3-17 Subsidiary Acquired at Net Book Value

On December 31, 20X8, Banner Corporation acquired 80 percent of Dwyer Company's common stock for $136,000. At the acquisition date, the book values and fair values of all of Dwyer's assets and liabilities were equal. Banner uses the equity method in accounting for its investment. Balance sheet information provided by the companies at December 31, 20X8, immediately following the acquisition is as follows:

	Banner Corporation	Dwyer Company
Cash	$ 74,000	$ 20,000
Accounts Receivable	120,000	70,000
Inventory	180,000	90,000
Fixed Assets (net)	350,000	240,000
Investment in Dwyer Company Stock	136,000	
Total Debits	$860,000	$420,000
Accounts Payable	$ 65,000	$ 30,000
Notes Payable	350,000	220,000
Common Stock	150,000	90,000
Retained Earnings	295,000	80,000
Total Credits	$860,000	$420,000

Required

Prepare a consolidated balance sheet for Banner at December 31, 20X8.

LO 3-4

E3-18 Acquisition of Majority Ownership

Lang Company reports net assets with a book value and fair value of $200,000. Pace Corporation acquires 75 percent ownership for $150,000. Pace reports net assets with a book value of $520,000 and a fair value of $640,000 at that time, excluding its investment in Lang.

Required

For each of the following, compute the amounts that would be reported immediately after the combination under current accounting practice:

a. Consolidated net identifiable assets.

b. Noncontrolling interest.

PROBLEMS

LO 3-4, 3-6

P3-19 Multiple-Choice Questions on Consolidated and Combined Financial Statements [AICPA Adapted]

Select the correct answer for each of the following questions.

1. What is the theoretically preferred method of presenting a noncontrolling interest in a consolidated balance sheet?
   a. As a separate item within the liability section.
   b. As a deduction from (contra to) goodwill from consolidation, if any.
   c. By means of notes or footnotes to the balance sheet.
   d. As a separate item within the stockholders' equity section.
2. Mr. Cord owns four corporations. Combined financial statements are being prepared for these corporations, which have intercompany loans of $200,000 and intercompany profits of $500,000. What amount of these intercompany loans and profits should be included in the combined financial statements?

	Intercompany	
	Loans	Profits
a.	$200,000	$ 0
b.	$200,000	$500,000
c.	$ 0	$ 0
d.	$ 0	$500,000

LO 3-4

P3-20 Determining Net Income of Parent Company

Tally Corporation and its subsidiary reported consolidated net income of $164,300 for 20X2. Tally owns 60 percent of the common shares of its subsidiary, acquired at book value. Noncontrolling interest was assigned income of $15,200 in the consolidated income statement for 20X2.

Required

Determine the amount of separate operating income reported by Tally for 20X2.

LO 3-7

P3-21 Consolidation of a Variable Interest Entity

On December 28, 20X3, Stern Corporation and Ram Company established S&R Partnership, with cash contributions of $10,000 and $40,000, respectively. The partnership's purpose is to purchase from Stern accounts receivable that have an average collection period of 80 days and hold them to collection. The partnership borrows cash from Midtown Bank and purchases the receivables without recourse but at an amount equal to the expected percent to be collected, less a financing fee of 3 percent of the gross receivables. Stern and Ram hold 20 percent and 80 percent of the ownership of the partnership, respectively, and Stern guarantees both the bank loan made to the partnership and a 15 percent annual return on the investment made by Ram. Stern receives any income in excess of the 15 percent return guaranteed to Ram. The partnership agreement provides Stern total control over the partnership's activities. On December 31, 20X3, Stern sold $8,000,000 of accounts receivable to the partnership. The partnership immediately borrowed $7,500,000 from the bank and paid Stern $7,360,000. Prior to the sale, Stern had established a $400,000 allowance for uncollectibles on the receivables sold to the partnership. The balance sheets of Stern and S&R immediately after the sale of receivables to the partnership contained the following:

	Stern Corporation	S&R Partnership
Cash	$7,960,000	$ 190,000
Accounts Receivable	4,200,000	8,000,000
Allowance for Uncollectible Accounts	(210,000)	(400,000)
Other Assets	5,400,000	
Prepaid Finance Charges	240,000	
Investment in S&R Partnership	10,000	
Accounts Payable	950,000	
Deferred Revenue		240,000
Bank Notes Payable		7,500,000
Bonds Payable	9,800,000	
Common Stock	700,000	
Retained Earnings	6,150,000	
Capital, Stern Corporation		10,000
Capital, Ram Company		40,000

Required

Assuming that Stern is S&R's primary beneficiary, prepare a consolidated balance sheet in good form for Stern at January 1, 20X4.

LO 3-7

P3-22 Reporting for Variable Interest Entities

Purified Oil Company and Midwest Pipeline Corporation established Venture Company to conduct oil exploration activities in North America to reduce their dependence on imported crude oil. Midwest Pipeline purchased all 20,000 shares of the newly created company for $10 each. Purified Oil agreed to purchase all of Venture's output at market price, guarantee up to $5,000,000 of debt for Venture, and absorb all losses if the company proved unsuccessful. Purified and Midwest agreed to share equally the profits up to $80,000 per year and to allocate 70 percent of those in excess of $80,000 to Purified and 30 percent to Midwest.

Venture immediately borrowed $3,000,000 from Second National Bank and purchased land, drilling equipment, and supplies to start its operations. Following these asset purchases, Venture and Purified Oil reported the following balances:

	Venture Company	Purified Oil Company
Cash	$ 230,000	$ 410,000
Drilling Supplies	420,000	
Accounts Receivable		640,000
Equipment (net)	1,800,000	6,700,000
Land	900,000	4,200,000
Accounts Payable	150,000	440,000
Bank Loans Payable	3,000,000	8,800,000
Common Stock	200,000	560,000
Retained Earnings		2,150,000

The only disclosure that Purified Oil currently provides in its financial statements with respect to its relationship with Midwest Pipeline and Venture is a brief note indicating that a contingent liability exists on the guarantee of Venture Company debt.

Required

Assuming that Venture is considered to be a variable interest entity and Purified Oil is the primary beneficiary, prepare a balance sheet in good form for Purified Oil.

LO 3-4

P3-23 Parent Company and Consolidated Amounts

Quoton Corporation acquired 80 percent of Tempro Company's common stock on December 31, 20X5, at underlying book value. The book values and fair values of Tempro's assets and liabilities were equal, and the fair value of the noncontrolling interest was equal to 20 percent of the total book value of Tempro. Tempro provided the following trial balance data at December 31, 20X5:

	Debit	Credit
Cash	$ 28,000	
Accounts Receivable	65,000	
Inventory	90,000	
Buildings & Equipment (net)	210,000	
Cost of Goods Sold	105,000	
Depreciation Expense	24,000	
Other Operating Expenses	31,000	
Dividends Declared	15,000	
Accounts Payable		$ 33,000
Notes Payable		120,000
Common Stock		90,000
Retained Earnings		130,000
Sales		195,000
Total	$568,000	$568,000

Required

a. How much did Quoton pay to purchase its shares of Tempro?

b. If consolidated financial statements are prepared at December 31, 20X5, what amount will be assigned to the noncontrolling interest in the consolidated balance sheet?

c. If Quoton reported income of $143,000 from its separate operations for 20X5, what amount of consolidated net income will be reported for 20X5?

d. If Quoton had purchased its ownership of Tempro on January 1, 20X5, at underlying book value and Quoton reported income of $143,000 from its separate operations for 20X5, what amount of consolidated net income would be reported for 20X5?

LO 3-4

Advanced StudyGuide .com

P3-24 Parent Company and Consolidated Balances

Exacto Company reported the following net income and dividends for the years indicated:

Year	Net Income	Dividends
20X5	$35,000	$12,000
20X6	45,000	20,000
20X7	30,000	14,000

True Corporation acquired 75 percent of Exacto's common stock on January 1, 20X5. On that date, the fair value of Exacto's net assets was equal to the book value. True uses the equity method in accounting for its ownership in Exacto and reported a balance of $259,800 in its investment account on December 31, 20X7.

Required

a. What amount did True pay when it purchased Exacto's shares?

b. What was the fair value of Exacto's net assets on January 1, 20X5?

c. What amount was assigned to the NCI shareholders on January 1, 20X5?

d. What amount will be assigned to the NCI shareholders in the consolidated balance sheet prepared at December 31, 20X7?

LO 3-2, 3-4

P3-25 Indirect Ownership

Purple Corporation recently attempted to expand by acquiring ownership in Green Company. The following ownership structure was reported on December 31, 20X9:

Investor	Investee	Percentage of Ownership Held
Purple Corporation	Green Company	70
Green Company	Orange Corporation	10
Orange Corporation	Blue Company	60
Green Company	Yellow Company	40

The following income from operations (excluding investment income) and dividend payments were reported by the companies during 20X9:

Company	Operating Income	Dividends Paid
Purple Corporation	$ 90,000	$60,000
Green Company	20,000	10,000
Orange Corporation	40,000	30,000
Blue Company	100,000	80,000
Yellow Company	60,000	40,000

Required

Compute the amount reported as consolidated net income for 20X9.

LO 3-4, 3-5

P3-26 Consolidated Worksheet and Balance Sheet on the Acquisition Date (Equity Method)

Advanced StudyGuide .com

Peanut Company acquired 90 percent of Snoopy Company's outstanding common stock for $270,000 on January 1, 20X8, when the book value of Snoopy's net assets was equal to $300,000. Peanut uses the equity method to account for investments. Trial balance data for Peanut and Snoopy as of January 1, 20X8, are as follows:

	Peanut Company	Snoopy Company
Assets		
Cash	55,000	20,000
Accounts Receivable	50,000	30,000
Inventory	100,000	60,000
Investment in Snoopy Stock	270,000	
Land	225,000	100,000
Buildings & Equipment	700,000	200,000
Accumulated Depreciation	(400,000)	(10,000)
Total Assets	1,000,000	400,000
Liabilities & Stockholders' Equity		
Accounts Payable	75,000	25,000
Bonds Payable	200,000	75,000
Common Stock	500,000	200,000
Retained Earnings	225,000	100,000
Total Liabilities & Equity	1,000,000	400,000

Required

a. Prepare the journal entry on Peanut's books for the acquisition of Snoopy on January 1, 20X8.

b. Prepare a consolidation worksheet on the acquisition date, January 1, 20X8, in good form.

c. Prepare a consolidated balance sheet on the acquisition date, January 1, 20X8, in good form.

LO 3-4, 3-5

Advanced StudyGuide .com

P3-27 Consolidated Worksheet at End of the First Year of Ownership (Equity Method)

Peanut Company acquired 90 percent of Snoopy Company's outstanding common stock for $270,000 on January 1, 20X8, when the book value of Snoopy's net assets was equal to $300,000. Peanut uses the equity method to account for investments. Trial balance data for Peanut and Snoopy as of December 31, 20X8, are as follows:

	Peanut Company		Snoopy Company	
	Debit	**Credit**	**Debit**	**Credit**
Cash	158,000		80,000	
Accounts Receivable	165,000		65,000	
Inventory	200,000		75,000	
Investment in Snoopy Stock	319,500		0	
Land	200,000		100,000	
Buildings & Equipment	700,000		200,000	
Cost of Goods Sold	200,000		125,000	
Depreciation Expense	50,000		10,000	
Selling & Administrative Expense	225,000		40,000	
Dividends Declared	100,000		20,000	
Accumulated Depreciation		450,000		20,000
Accounts Payable		75,000		60,000
Bonds Payable		200,000		85,000
Common Stock		500,000		200,000
Retained Earnings		225,000		100,000
Sales		800,000		250,000
Income from Snoopy		67,500		0
Total	2,317,500	2,317,500	715,000	715,000

Required

a. Prepare any equity-method entry(ies) related to the investment in Snoopy Company during 20X8.

b. Prepare a consolidation worksheet for 20X8 in good form.

LO 3-4, 3-5

Advanced StudyGuide .com

P3-28 Consolidated Worksheet at End of the Second Year of Ownership (Equity Method)

Peanut Company acquired 90 percent of Snoopy Company's outstanding common stock for $270,000 on January 1, 20X8, when the book value of Snoopy's net assets was equal to $300,000. Problem 3-34 summarizes the first year of Peanut's ownership of Snoopy. Peanut uses the equity method to account for investments. The following trial balance summarizes the financial position and operations for Peanut and Snoopy as of December 31, 20X9:

	Peanut Company		Snoopy Company	
	Debit	**Credit**	**Debit**	**Credit**
Cash	255,000		75,000	
Accounts Receivable	190,000		80,000	
Inventory	180,000		100,000	
Investment in Snoopy Stock	364,500		0	
Land	200,000		100,000	
Buildings & Equipment	700,000		200,000	
Cost of Goods Sold	270,000		150,000	
Depreciation Expense	50,000		10,000	
Selling & Administrative Expense	230,000		60,000	
Dividends Declared	225,000		30,000	
Accumulated Depreciation		500,000		30,000
Accounts Payable		75,000		35,000
Bonds Payable		150,000		85,000
Common Stock		500,000		200,000

(continued)

Retained Earnings		517,500		155,000
Sales		850,000		300,000
Income from Snoopy		72,000		0
Total	2,664,500	2,664,500	805,000	805,000

Required

a. Prepare any equity-method journal entry(ies) related to the investment in Snoopy Company during 20X9.

b. Prepare a consolidation worksheet for 20X9 in good form.

LO 3-4, 3-5 **P3-29 Consolidated Worksheet and Balance Sheet on the Acquisition Date (Equity Method)**

Paper Company acquired 80 percent of Scissor Company's outstanding common stock for $296,000 on January 1, 20X8, when the book value of Scissor's net assets was equal to $370,000. Paper uses the equity method to account for investments. Trial balance data for Paper and Scissor as of January 1, 20X8, are as follows:

	Paper Company	Scissor Company
Assets		
Cash	109,000	25,000
Accounts Receivable	65,000	37,000
Inventory	125,000	87,000
Investment in Scissor Stock	296,000	
Land	280,000	125,000
Buildings & Equipment	875,000	250,000
Accumulated Depreciation	(500,000)	(24,000)
Total Assets	1,250,000	500,000
Liabilities & Stockholders' Equity		
Accounts Payable	95,000	30,000
Bonds Payable	250,000	100,000
Common Stock	625,000	250,000
Retained Earnings	280,000	120,000
Total Liabilities & Equity	1,250,000	500,000

Required

a. Prepare the journal entry on Paper's books for the acquisition of Scissor Co. on January 1, 20X8.

b. Prepare a consolidation worksheet on the acquisition date, January 1, 20X8, in good form.

c. Prepare a consolidated balance sheet on the acquisition date, January 1, 20X8, in good form.

LO 3-4, 3-5 **P3-30 Consolidated Worksheet at End of the First Year of Ownership (Equity Method)**

Paper Company acquired 80 percent of Scissor Company's outstanding common stock for $296,000 on January 1, 20X8, when the book value of Scissor's net assets was equal to $370,000. Paper uses the equity method to account for investments. Trial balance data for Paper and Scissor as of December 31, 20X8, are as follows:

	Paper Company		Scissor Company	
	Debit	Credit	Debit	Credit
Cash	191,000		46,000	
Accounts Receivable	140,000		60,000	

(continued)

Inventory	190,000		120,000	
Investment in Scissor Stock	350,400		0	
Land	250,000		125,000	
Buildings & Equipment	875,000		250,000	
Cost of Goods Sold	250,000		155,000	
Depreciation Expense	65,000		12,000	
Selling & Administrative Expense	280,000		50,000	
Dividends Declared	80,000		25,000	
Accumulated Depreciation		565,000		36,000
Accounts Payable		77,000		27,000
Bonds Payable		250,000		100,000
Common Stock		625,000		250,000
Retained Earnings		280,000		120,000
Sales		800,000		310,000
Income from Scissor		74,400		0
Total	2,671,400	2,671,400	843,000	843,000

Required

a. Prepare any equity-method entry(ies) related to the investment in Scissor Company during 20X8.

b. Prepare a consolidation worksheet for 20X8 in good form.

LO 3-4, 3-5 **P3-31 Consolidated Worksheet at End of the Second Year of Ownership (Equity Method)**

Paper Company acquired 80 percent of Scissor Company's outstanding common stock for $296,000 on January 1, 20X8, when the book value of Scissor's net assets was equal to $370,000. Problem 3-30 summarizes the first year of Paper's ownership of Scissor. Paper uses the equity method to account for investments. The following trial balance summarizes the financial position and operations for Paper and Scissor as of December 31, 20X9:

	Paper Company		Scissor Company	
	Debit	**Credit**	**Debit**	**Credit**
Cash	295,000		116,000	
Accounts Receivable	165,000		97,000	
Inventory	193,000		115,000	
Investment in Scissor Stock	412,000		0	
Land	250,000		125,000	
Buildings & Equipment	875,000		250,000	
Cost of Goods Sold	278,000		178,000	
Depreciation Expense	65,000		12,000	
Selling & Administrative Expense	312,000		58,000	
Dividends Declared	90,000		30,000	
Accumulated Depreciation		630,000		48,000
Accounts Payable		85,000		40,000
Bonds Payable		150,000		100,000
Common Stock		625,000		250,000
Retained Earnings		479,400		188,000
Sales		880,000		355,000
Income from Scissor		85,600		0
Total	2,935,000	2,935,000	981,000	981,000

Required

a. Prepare any equity-method journal entry(ies) related to the investment in Scissor Company during 20X9.

b. Prepare a consolidation worksheet for 20X9 in good form.

4 Consolidation of Wholly Owned Subsidiaries Acquired at More than Book Value

HOW MUCH WORK DOES IT REALLY TAKE TO CONSOLIDATE? ASK THE PEOPLE WHO DO IT AT DISNEY

Multicorporate Entities
- Business Combinations
- **Consolidation Concepts and Procedures**
- Intercompany Transfers
- Additional Consolidation Issues

Multinational Entities

Reporting Requirements

Partnerships

Governmental and Not-for-Profit Entities

Corporations in Financial Difficulty

DISNEY

The Walt Disney Company, whose history goes back to 1923, is parent company to some of the most well-known businesses in the world. While best known for Walt Disney Studios, world-famous parks and resorts, media operations such as the Disney Channel, and its consumer products, Disney is a widely diversified company. For example, did you know that Disney owns the ABC Television Network and is the majority owner of ESPN? While the consolidation examples you're working on in class usually involve a parent company and a single subsidiary, Disney employs a dedicated staff at its Burbank, California, headquarters each quarter to complete the consolidation of its five segments, each comprising many subsidiaries, in preparation for its quarterly 10-Q and annual 10-K filings with the SEC. Preparation for the actual consolidation begins before the end of the fiscal period. Soon after the end of the period, each segment closes its books, including performing its own subsidiary consolidations, works with the independent auditors, and prepares for the roll-up to the overall company consolidation. The work continues as the finance and accounting staff of approximately 100 men and women at the corporate offices review and analyze the results from the individual segments and work with segment financial staff to prepare what becomes the publicly disclosed set of consolidated financial statements.

However, the work doesn't all take place at the end of the fiscal period. The accounting system also tracks intercompany transactions throughout the period. The consolidation process requires the elimination of intercompany sales and asset transfers among others cost allocations (as discussed in Chapters 6 and 7). Tracking these transactions involves ongoing efforts throughout the period.

One of the reasons Disney has grown and become so diversified over the years is that it frequently acquires other companies. Three of the more notable acquisitions in recent years are Lucasfilm in 2012, Marvel Entertainment in 2009, and Pixar Animation Studios in 2006. In these and other well-known acquisitions, Disney paid more than the book value of each acquired company's net assets. Acquisition accounting rules require Disney to account for the full acquisition price—even though the acquired companies may continue to report their assets and liabilities on their separate books at their historical book values. Thus, acquisition accounting requires Disney to essentially revalue the balance sheets of these companies to their amortized fair values in the consolidation process each period. We provide more details on the Pixar and Lucasfilm acquisitions later in the chapter.

The bottom line is that preparation of Disney's publicly disclosed financial statements is the culmination of a lot of work by the segment and corporate accounting and finance staff. The issues mentioned here illustrate the complexity of a process that requires substantial teamwork and effort to produce audited financial statements that are valuable to an investor or interested accounting student. You'll learn in this chapter about the activities during the consolidation process performed by the accounting staff at any well-known public company. This chapter also introduces differences in the consolidation process when there is a differential (i.e., the acquiring company pays something other than the book value of the acquired company's net assets).

LEARNING OBJECTIVES

When you finish studying this chapter, you should be able to:

LO 4-1 Understand and make equity-method journal entries related to the differential.

LO 4-2 Understand and explain how consolidation procedures differ when there is a differential.

LO 4-3 Make calculations and prepare consolidation entries for the consolidation of a wholly owned subsidiary when there is a complex positive differential at the acquisition date.

LO 4-4 Make calculations and prepare consolidation entries for the consolidation of a wholly owned subsidiary when there is a complex bargain-purchase differential.

LO 4-5 Prepare equity-method journal entries, consolidation entries, and the consolidation worksheet for a wholly owned subsidiary when there is a complex positive differential.

LO 4-6 Understand and explain the elimination of basic intercompany transactions.

LO 4-7 Understand and explain the basics of push-down accounting.

DEALING WITH THE DIFFERENTIAL

This chapter continues to build upon the foundation established in Chapters 2 and 3 related to the consolidation of majority-owned subsidiaries. In Chapters 2 and 3, we focus on relatively simple situations when the acquisition price is exactly equal to the parent's share of the book value of the subsidiary's net assets or where the subsidiary is created by the parent. In Chapter 4, we relax this assumption and allow the acquisition price to differ from book value. As explained in Chapter 1, this allows for a "differential."

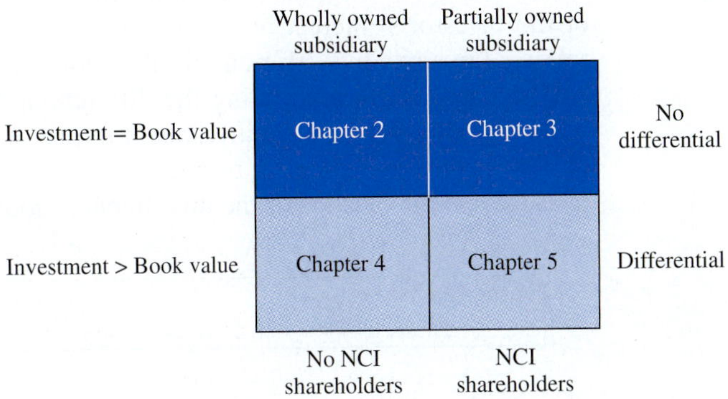

The Difference between Acquisition Price and Underlying Book Value

When an investor purchases the common stock of another company, the purchase price normally is based on the market value of the shares acquired rather than the book value of the investee's assets and liabilities. Not surprisingly, the acquisition price is usually different from the book value of the investor's proportionate share of the investee's net assets. This difference is referred to as a ***differential.*** The differential is frequently positive, meaning the acquiring company pays more than its share of the book value of the subsidiary's net assets. Note that in the case of an equity-method investment, the differential on the parent's books relates only to the parent's share of any difference between total investee's fair value and book value. The differential in the case of an equity-method investment is implicit in the investment account on the parent's books and is not recorded separately.

The cost of an investment might exceed the book value of the underlying net assets, giving rise to a positive differential, for any of several reasons. One reason is that the investee's assets may be worth more than their book values. Another reason could be the existence of unrecorded goodwill associated with the excess earning power of the investee. In either case, the portion of the differential pertaining to each asset of the investee, including goodwill, must be ascertained. When the parent company uses the equity method, for reporting purposes (i.e., the subsidiary remains unconsolidated) that portion of the differential pertaining to limited-life assets of the investee, including identifiable intangibles, must be amortized over the remaining economic lives of those assets. Any portion of the differential that represents goodwill (referred to as *equity-method goodwill* or *implicit goodwill*) is not amortized or separately tested for impairment. However, an impairment loss on the investment itself should be recognized if it suffers a material decline in value that is other than temporary **(ASC 323-10-35-32).**

FYI

In 2009, Bank of America reported one of the largest goodwill balances of all time, $86.3 billion. However, due to large goodwill impairment charges in 2010 and 2011, its 2011 goodwill balance decreased to $69.967 billion.

LO 4-1

Understand and make equity-method journal entries related to the differential.

Advanced StudyGuide .com

Amortization or Write-Off of the Differential[1]

When the equity method is used, each portion of the differential must be treated in the same manner that the investee treats the assets or liabilities to which the differential relates. Thus, any portion of the differential related to depreciable or amortizable assets of the investee should be amortized over the remaining time to which the cost of the related asset is being allocated by the investee. Amortization of the differential associated with depreciable or amortizable assets of the investee is necessary on the investor's books to reflect the decline in the future benefits the investor expects from that portion of the investment cost associated with those assets. The investee recognizes the reduction in service potential of assets with limited lives as depreciation or amortization expense based on the amount it has invested in those assets. This reduction, in turn, is recognized by the investor through its share of the investee's net income. When the acquisition price of the investor's interest in the investee's assets is higher than the investee's cost (as reflected in a positive differential), the additional cost must be amortized.

The approach to amortizing the differential that is most consistent with the idea of reflecting all aspects of the investment in just one line on the balance sheet and one line on the income statement is to reduce the income recognized by the investor from the investee and the balance of the investment account:

Income from Investee	XXXX	
Investment in Common Stock of Investee		XXX

[1] To view a video explanation of this topic, visit advancedstudyguide.com.

The differential represents the amount paid by the investor company in excess of the book value of the net assets of the investee company and is included in the original acquisition price. Hence, the amortization or reduction of the differential involves the reduction of the investment account. At the same time, the investor's net income must be reduced by an equal amount to recognize that a portion of the amount paid for the investment has expired.

Treatment of the Differential Illustrated

To illustrate how to apply the equity method when the cost of the investment exceeds the book value of the underlying net assets, assume that Ajax Corporation purchases 40 percent of the common stock of Barclay Company on January 1, 20X1, for $200,000. Barclay has net assets on that date with a book value of $400,000 and fair value of $465,000. The total differential is equal to the market value of Barclay's common stock, $500,000, ($200,000/40%) minus the book value of its net assets, $400,000. Thus, the entire differential is $100,000.

Ajax's share of the book value of Barclay's net assets at acquisition is $160,000 ($400,000 × 0.40). Thus, Ajax's 40 percent share of the differential is computed as follows:

Cost of Ajax's investment in Barclay's stock	$200,000
Book value of Ajax's share of Barclay's net assets	(160,000)
Ajax's share of the differential	$ 40,000

The portion of the total differential that can be directly traced to specific assets that are undervalued on Barclay's books is the $65,000 excess of the fair value over the book value of Barclay's net assets ($465,000 − $400,000), and the remaining $35,000 of the differential is goodwill. Specifically, an appraisal of Barclay's assets indicates that its land is worth $15,000 more than the recorded value on its books and its equipment is worth $50,000 more than its current book value. Ajax's 40 percent share of the differential is as follows:

	Total Increase	Ajax's 40% Share
Land	$ 15,000	6,000
Equipment	50,000	20,000
Goodwill	35,000	14,000
	$100,000	$40,000

Thus, $26,000 of Ajax's share of the differential is assigned to land and equipment, with the remaining $14,000 attributed to goodwill. The allocation of Ajax's share of the differential can be illustrated as shown in the diagram below:

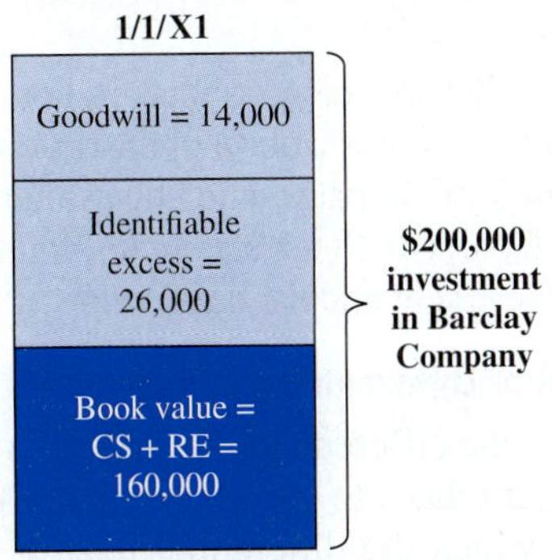

Although the differential relates to Barclay's assets, the additional cost incurred by Ajax to acquire a claim on Barclay's assets is reflected in Ajax's investment in

Barclay. There is no need to establish a separate differential account and separate accounts are not recorded on Ajax's books to reflect the apportionment of the differential to specific assets. Similarly, a separate expense account is not established on Ajax's books. Amortization or write-off of the differential is accomplished by reducing Ajax's investment account and the income Ajax recognizes from its investment in Barclay.

Because land has an unlimited economic life, the portion of the differential related to land is not amortized. Ajax's \$20,000 portion of the differential related to Barclay's equipment is amortized over the equipment's remaining life. If the equipment's remaining life is five years, Ajax's annual amortization of the differential is \$4,000 (\$20,000 ÷ 5) (assuming straight-line depreciation).

Regarding the goodwill in the differential, accounting standards state that equity-method goodwill is not amortized nor is it separately tested for impairment when the equity method is used for reporting purposes. Instead, the entire investment is tested for impairment **(ASC 323-10-35-32).** In this example, the only amortization of the differential is the \$4,000 related to Barclay's equipment.

Barclay reports net income of \$80,000 at year end and declares dividends of \$20,000 during 20X1. Using the equity-method, Ajax records the following entries on its books during 20X1:

(1)	Investment in Barclay Stock	200,000	
	Cash		200,000
	Record purchase of Barclay stock.		
(2)	Investment in Barclay Stock	32,000	
	Income from Barclay Company		32,000
	Record equity-method income: \$80,000 × 0.40.		
(3)	Cash	8,000	
	Investment in Barclay Stock		8,000
	Record dividend from Barclay: \$20,000 × 0.40.		
(4)	Income from Barclay Company	4,000	
	Investment in Barclay Stock		4,000
	Amortize differential related to equipment.		

With these entries, Ajax recognizes \$28,000 of income from Barclay and adjusts its investment in Barclay to an ending balance of \$220,000.

The amortization on Ajax's books of the portion of the differential related to Barclay's equipment is the same (\$4,000) for each of the first five years (20X1 through 20X5). This amortization stops after 20X5 because this portion of the differential is fully amortized after five years.

Notice that special accounts are not established on Ajax's books with regard to the differential or the amortization of the differential. The only two accounts involved are "Income from Barclay Company" and "Investment in Barclay Company Stock." As the Investment in Barclay Company Stock account is amortized, the differential between the carrying amount of the investment and the book value of the underlying net assets decreases.

Disposal of Differential-Related Assets

Although the differential is included on the books of the investor as part of the investment account, it relates to specific assets of the investee. Thus, if the investee disposes of any asset to which the differential relates, that portion of the differential must be removed from the investment account on the investor's books. When this is done, the investor's share of the investee's gain or loss on disposal of the asset must be adjusted to reflect the fact that the investor paid more for its proportionate share of that asset than did the investee.

For example, if in the previous illustration Barclay Company sells the land to which \$6,000 of Ajax's differential relates, Ajax does not recognize a full 40 percent of the gain or loss on the sale. Assume that Barclay originally had purchased the land in 20X0 for \$75,000 and sells the land in 20X2 for \$125,000. Barclay recognizes a gain on the sale of \$50,000, and Ajax's share of that gain is 40 percent, or \$20,000. The portion of the gain actually recognized by Ajax, however, must be adjusted as follows because of the amount in excess of book value paid by Ajax for its investment in Barclay:

Ajax's share of Barclay's reported gain	\$20,000
Portion of Ajax's differential related to the land	(6,000)
Gain to be recognized by Ajax	\$14,000

Thus, if Barclay reports net income (including the gain on the sale of land) of \$150,000 for 20X2, Ajax records the following entries (disregarding dividends and amortization of the differential relating to equipment):

(5)	Investment in Barclay Company	60,000	
	Income from Barclay Company		60,000
	Record equity-method income: \$150,000 × 0.40.		

(6)	Income from Barclay Company	6,000	
	Investment in Barclay Stock		6,000
	Remove differential related to Barclay's land that was sold.		

The same approach applies when dealing with a limited-life asset. The unamortized portion of the original differential relating to the asset sold is removed from the investment account, and the investor's share of the investee's income is adjusted by that amount.

Note that the investor does not separately report its share of ordinary gains or losses included in the investee's net income, such as the gain on the sale of the fixed asset or the write-off of the unamortized differential. Consistent with the idea of using only a single line in the income statement to report the impact of the investee's activities on the investor, all such items are included in the Income from Investee account. Current standards require the investor to report its share of an investee's extraordinary gains and losses, discontinued operations, and elements of other comprehensive income, if material to the investor, as separate items in the same manner as the investor reports its own.

Impairment of Investment Value

As with many assets, accounting standards require that equity-method investments be written down if their value is impaired. If the market value of the investment declines materially below its equity-method carrying amount, and the decline in value is considered other than temporary, the carrying amount of the investment should be written down to the market value and a loss should be recognized. The new lower value serves as a starting point for continued application of the equity-method. Subsequent recoveries in the value of the investment may not be recognized.

ADDITIONAL CONSIDERATIONS

Disney's 2006 Pixar Acquisition

On May 5, 2006, Disney completed an all-stock acquisition of Pixar, a digital animation studio. To purchase Pixar, Disney exchanged 2.3 shares of its common stock for each share of Pixar common stock, resulting in the issuance of 279 million shares of Disney common stock, and converted previously issued vested and unvested Pixar equity-based awards into approximately 45 million Disney equity-based awards.

The acquisition purchase price was $7.5 billion ($6.4 billion, net of Pixar's cash and investments of approximately $1.1 billion). The value of the stock issued was calculated based on the market value of the Company's common stock using the average stock price for the five-day period beginning two days before the acquisition announcement date on January 24, 2006. The fair value of the vested equity-based awards issued at the closing was estimated using the Black-Scholes option pricing model, as the information required to use a binomial valuation model was not reasonably available.

The Company allocated the purchase price to the tangible and identifiable intangible assets acquired and liabilities assumed based on their fair values, which were determined primarily through third-party appraisals. The excess of the purchase price over those fair values was recorded as goodwill, which is not amortizable for tax purposes. The fair values set forth below are subject to adjustment if additional information is obtained prior to the one-year anniversary of the acquisition that would change the fair value allocation as of the acquisition date. The following table summarizes the allocation of the purchase price:

	Estimated Fair Value	Weighted Average Useful Lives (years)
Cash and cash equivalents	$ 11	
Investments	1,073	
Prepaid and other assets	45	
Film costs	538	12
Buildings & equipment	225	16
Intangibles	233	17
Goodwill	5,557	
Total assets acquired	$ 7,682	
Liabilities	64	
Deferred income taxes	123	
Total liabilities assumed	$ 187	
Net assets acquired	$ 7,495	

Disney's 2012 Lucasfilm Acquisition

On October 30, 2012, The Walt Disney Company announced the acquisition of Lucasfilm Ltd. in a stock and cash transaction.* The press release on that date states:

> "For the past 35 years, one of my greatest pleasures has been to see Star Wars passed from one generation to the next," said George Lucas, Chairman and Chief Executive Officer of Lucasfilm. "It's now time for me to pass Star Wars on to a new generation of filmmakers. I've always believed that Star Wars could live beyond me, and I thought it was important to set up the transition during my lifetime ... Disney's reach and experience give Lucasfilm the opportunity to blaze new trails in film, television, interactive media, theme parks, live entertainment, and consumer products."
>
> The acquisition combines two highly compatible family entertainment brands, and strengthens the long-standing beneficial relationship between them that already includes successful integration of Star Wars content into Disney theme parks in Anaheim, Orlando, Paris and Tokyo. Driven by a tremendously talented creative team, Lucasfilm's legendary Star Wars franchise has flourished for more than 35 years, and offers a virtually limitless universe of characters

* *The Walt Disney Company,* "Disney to Acquire Lucasfilm LTD." October 30, 2012, http://thewaltdisneycompany.com/disney-news/press-releases/2012/10/disney-acquire-lucasfilm-ltd.

and stories to drive continued feature film releases and franchise growth over the long term. Star Wars resonates with consumers around the world and creates extensive opportunities for Disney to deliver the content across its diverse portfolio of businesses including movies, television, consumer products, games and theme parks. Star Wars feature films have earned a total of $4.4 billion in global box to date, and continued global demand has made Star Wars one of the world's top product brands, and Lucasfilm a leading product licensor in the United States in 2011 ... The Lucasfilm acquisition follows Disney's very successful acquisitions of Pixar and Marvel, which demonstrated the company's unique ability to fully develop and expand the financial potential of high quality creative content with compelling characters and storytelling through the application of innovative technology and multiplatform distribution on a truly global basis to create maximum value. Adding Lucasfilm to Disney's portfolio of world class brands significantly enhances the company's ability to serve consumers with a broad variety of the world's highest-quality content and to create additional long-term value for our shareholders.

On December 21, 2012, the Walt Disney Company completed the merger transaction in which the company distributed 37.1 million shares and paid $2.2 billion in cash. Based on the $50 per share closing price of Disney shares on December 21, 2012, the transaction had a value of $4.1 billion. The excess of the purchase price over those fair values of assets was allocated to goodwill.

CONSOLIDATION PROCEDURES FOR WHOLLY OWNED SUBSIDIARIES ACQUIRED AT MORE THAN BOOK VALUE

LO 4-2

Understand and explain how consolidation procedures differ when there is a differential.

Advanced StudyGuide .com

Many factors have an effect on the fair value of a company and its stock price, including its asset values, its earning power, and general market conditions. When one company acquires another, the acquiree's fair value usually differs from its book value (differential), and so the consideration given by the acquirer does as well.

The process of preparing a consolidated balance sheet immediately after a business combination is complicated only slightly when 100 percent of a company's stock is acquired at a price that differs from the acquiree's book value. To illustrate the acquisition of a subsidiary when the consideration given is greater than the book value of the net assets of the acquiree, we use the Peerless-Special Foods example from Chapter 2. We assume that Peerless Products acquires all of Special Foods' outstanding stock on January 1, 20X1, by paying $340,000 cash, an amount equal to Special Foods' fair value as a whole. The consideration given by Peerless is $40,000 in excess of Special Foods' book value of $300,000. The resulting ownership situation can be viewed as follows:

(P)	Fair value of consideration		$340,000
1/1/X1 100%	Book value of Special Foods' net assets		
	Common stock—Special Foods	200,000	
	Retained earnings—Special Foods	100,000	
(S)			300,000
	Difference between fair value and book value		$ 40,000

Peerless records the stock acquisition with the following entry:

(7)	Investment in Special Foods	340,000	
	Cash		340,000

Record purchase of Special Foods stock.

In a business combination, and therefore in a consolidation following a business combination, the full amount of the consideration given by the acquirer must be assigned to the individual assets and liabilities acquired and to goodwill. In this example, the fair value of consideration given (the acquisition price) includes an extra $40,000 for appreciation in the value of the land since it was originally acquired by Special Foods. The relationship between the fair value of the consideration given for Special Foods, the fair value of Special Foods' net assets, and the book value of Special Foods' net assets can be illustrated as follows:

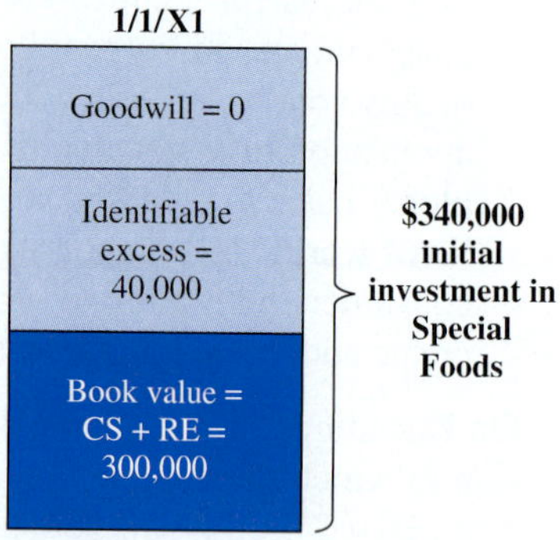

Assume that Peerless prepares a consolidated balance sheet on the date it acquires Special Foods. The consolidation worksheet procedures used in adjusting to the proper consolidated amounts follow a consistent pattern. The first worksheet entry (often referred to as the "basic" consolidation entry) eliminates the book value portion of the parent's investment account and each of the subsidiary's stockholders' equity accounts. It is useful to analyze the investment account and the subsidiary's equity accounts as follows:

Book Value Calculations:

	Total Investment	=	Common Stock	+	Retained Earnings
Book Value at Acquisition	300,000		200,000		100,000

The worksheet entry to eliminate the book value portion of Peerless' investment account and the stockholders' equity accounts of Special Foods is as follows:

Basic Consolidation Entry:

Common Stock	200,000		← Common stock balance
Retained Earnings	100,000		← Beginning balance in RE
Investment in Special Foods		300,000	← Net BV in investment account

When the acquisition-date fair value of the consideration is more than the acquiree's book value at that date, the second consolidation entry reclassifies the excess acquisition price to the specific accounts on the balance sheet for which the book values are not the same as their fair values on the acquisition date.[2] The differential represents (in simple situations involving a 100 percent acquisition) the total difference between the acquisition-date fair value of the consideration given by the acquirer and the acquiree's

[2] Alternatively, a separate clearing account titled "Excess of Acquisition Consideration over Acquiree Book Value" or just "Differential" can be debited for this excess amount. A subsequent entry can be used to reclassify the differential to the various accounts on the balance sheet that need to be revalued to their acquisition date amounts. Note that the Differential account is simply a worksheet clearing account and is not found on the books of the parent or subsidiary and does not appear in the consolidated financial statements.

book value of net assets. In this example, the differential is the additional $40,000 Peerless paid to acquire Special Foods because its land was worth $40,000 more than its book value as of the acquisition date. In preparing a consolidated balance sheet immediately after acquisition (on January 1, 20X1), the second consolidation entry appearing in the consolidation worksheet simply reassigns this $40,000 from the investment account to the land account so that: (*a*) the Land account fully reflects the fair value of this asset as of the acquisition date and (*b*) the investment account is fully eliminated from Peerless' books:

Excess Value Reclassification Entry:

Land	**40,000**		← Excess value assigned to land
Investment in Special Foods		**40,000**	← Reclassify excess acquisition price

Thus, these two consolidation entries completely eliminate the balance in Peerless' investment account and the second entry assigns the differential to the land account.

	Investment in Special Foods		
Acquisition Price	**340,000**		
		300,000	**Basic Consolidation Entry**
		40,000	**Excess Value Reclassification Entry**
	0		

In more complicated examples when the fair values of various balance sheet accounts differ from book values, the excess value reclassification entry reassigns the differential to adjust various account balances to reflect the fair values of the subsidiary's assets and liabilities at the time the parent acquired the subsidiary and to establish goodwill, if appropriate.

Figure 4–1 illustrates the consolidation worksheet reflecting the elimination of Special Foods' equity accounts and the allocation of the differential to the subsidiary's land. As explained previously, the combination of these two worksheet entries also eliminates the investment account.

FIGURE 4–1 January 1, 20X1, Worksheet for Consolidated Balance Sheet, Date of Combination; 100 Percent Acquisition at More than Book Value

	Peerless Products	Special Foods	Consolidation Entries DR	Consolidation Entries CR	Consolidated
Balance Sheet					
Cash	10,000	50,000			60,000
Accounts Receivable	75,000	50,000			125,000
Inventory	100,000	60,000			160,000
Investment in Special Foods	340,000			300,000	0
				40,000	
Land	175,000	40,000	40,000		255,000
Buildings & Equipment	800,000	600,000		300,000	1,100,000
Less: Accumulated Depreciation	(400,000)	(300,000)	300,000		(400,000)
Total Assets	**1,100,000**	**500,000**	**$340,000**	**$640,000**	**1,300,000**
Accounts Payable	100,000	100,000			200,000
Bonds Payable	200,000	100,000			300,000
Common Stock	500,000	200,000	200,000		500,000
Retained Earnings	300,000	100,000	100,000		300,000
Total Liabilities & Equity	**1,100,000**	**500,000**	**300,000**	**0**	**1,300,000**

As usual, we eliminate Special Foods' acquisition date accumulated depreciation against the Buildings and Equipment account balance so that, combined with the excess value reclassification entry it will appear as if these fixed assets were recorded at their acquisition costs.

Optional Accumulated Depreciation Consolidation Entry:

Accumulated Depreciation	**300,000**		← Accumulated depreciation at the time of the acquisition netted against cost
Buildings & Equipment		**300,000**	

The amounts reported externally in the consolidated balance sheet are those in the Consolidated column of the worksheet in Figure 4–1. Land would be included in the consolidated balance sheet at $255,000, the amount carried on Peerless' books ($175,000) plus the amount carried on Special Foods' books ($40,000) plus the differential reflecting the increased value of Special Foods' land ($40,000).

This example is simple enough that the assignment of the differential to land could be made directly in the basic consolidation entry rather than through the use of a separate entry. In practice, however, the differential often relates to more than a single asset, and the allocation of the differential may be considerably more complex than in this example. The possibilities for clerical errors are reduced in complex situations by making two separate entries rather than one complicated entry.

Treatment of a Positive Differential

The fair value, and hence acquisition price, of a subsidiary might exceed the book value for several reasons, such as the following:

1. Errors or omissions on the subsidiary's books.
2. Excess of fair value over the book value of the subsidiary's net identifiable assets.
3. Existence of goodwill.

Errors or Omissions on the Books of the Subsidiary

An examination of an acquired company's books may reveal material errors. In some cases, the acquired company may have expensed rather than capitalized assets or, for other reasons, omitted them from the books. An acquired company that previously had been closely held may not have followed generally accepted accounting principles in maintaining its accounting records. In some cases, the recordkeeping may have simply been inadequate.

Where errors or omissions occur, corrections should be made directly on the subsidiary's books as of the date of acquisition. These corrections are treated as prior-period adjustments in accordance with **ASC 250-10-60.** Once the subsidiary's books are stated in accordance with generally accepted accounting principles, that portion of the differential attributable to errors or omissions will no longer exist.

Excess of Fair Value over Book Value of Subsidiary's Net Identifiable Assets

The fair value of a company's assets is an important factor in the overall determination of the company's fair value. In many cases, the fair value of an acquired company's net assets exceeds the book value. Consequently, the consideration given by an acquirer may exceed the acquiree's book value. The procedures used in preparing the consolidated balance sheet should lead to reporting all of the acquired company's assets and liabilities based on their fair values on the date of combination. This valuation may be accomplished in one of two ways: (1) the subsidiary's assets and liabilities may be revalued directly on the books of the subsidiary or (2) the accounting basis of the subsidiary may be maintained and the revaluations made each period in the consolidation worksheet.

Revaluing the assets and liabilities on the subsidiary's books generally is the simplest approach if all of the subsidiary's common stock is acquired. On the other hand, it generally is not appropriate to revalue the assets and liabilities on the subsidiary's books if there is a significant noncontrolling interest in that subsidiary. From a noncontrolling shareholder's point of view, the subsidiary is a continuing company, and the basis of accounting should not change. More difficult to resolve is the situation in which the parent acquires all of the subsidiary's common stock but continues to issue separate financial statements of the subsidiary to holders of the subsidiary's bonds or preferred stock. Revaluing the assets and liabilities of the subsidiary directly on its books is referred to as ***push-down accounting.*** It is discussed later in this chapter and is illustrated in Appendix 4A.

When the assets and liabilities are revalued directly on the subsidiary's books, that portion of the differential then no longer exists. However, if the assets and liabilities are not revalued on the subsidiary's books, an entry to revalue those assets and allocate the differential is needed in the consolidation worksheet each time consolidated financial statements are prepared for as long as the related assets are held.

Existence of Goodwill

If the acquisition-date fair value of the consideration exchanged for an acquired subsidiary is higher than the total fair value of the subsidiary's net identifiable assets, the difference is considered to be related to the future economic benefits associated with other assets of the subsidiary that are not separately identified and recognized and is referred to as ***goodwill.*** Thus, once a subsidiary's identifiable assets and liabilities are revalued to their fair values, any remaining debit differential is normally allocated to goodwill. For example, assuming that in the Peerless Products and Special Foods illustration, the acquisition-date fair values of Special Foods' assets and liabilities are equal to their book values, then the $40,000 difference between the $340,000 consideration exchanged and the $300,000 fair value of the subsidiary's net identifiable assets should be attributed to goodwill. The following entry to assign the differential is needed in the consolidation worksheet prepared immediately after the combination:

Excess Value Reclassification Entry:

Goodwill	**40,000**		← Excess value assigned to goodwill
Investment in Special Foods		**40,000**	← Reassign excess acquisition price

The consolidation worksheet is similar to Figure 4–1 except that the debit in the excess value reclassification worksheet entry would be to goodwill instead of land. Goodwill, which does not appear on the books of either Peerless or Special Foods, would appear at $40,000 in the consolidated balance sheet prepared immediately after acquisition.

In the past, some companies have included the fair-value increment related to certain identifiable assets of the subsidiary in goodwill rather than separately recognizing those assets. This treatment is not acceptable, and any fair-value increment related to an intangible asset that arises from a contractual or legal right or that is separable from the entity must be allocated to that asset.

Illustration of Treatment of a Complex Differential

LO 4-3

Make calculations and prepare consolidation entries for the consolidation of a wholly owned subsidiary when there is a complex positive differential at the acquisition date.

In many situations, the differential relates to a number of different assets and liabilities. As a means of illustrating the allocation of the differential to various assets and liabilities, assume that the acquisition-date book values and fair values of Special Foods' assets and liabilities are as shown in Figure 4–2. The inventory and land have fair values in excess of their book values, although the buildings and equipment are worth less than their book values.

Bond prices fluctuate as interest rates change. In this example, the value of Special Foods' bonds payable is higher than the book value. This indicates that the nominal interest rate on the bonds is higher than the current market interest rate and, therefore, investors are willing to

FIGURE 4–2
Differences between Book and Fair Values of Special Foods' Identifiable Assets and Liabilities as of January 1, 20X1, the Date of Combination

		Book Value	Fair Value	Difference between Fair Value and Book Value
Cash		$ 50,000	$ 50,000	
Accounts Receivable		50,000	50,000	
Inventory		60,000	75,000	$15,000
Land		40,000	100,000	60,000
Buildings & Equipment	600,000			
Accumulated Depreciation	(300,000)	300,000	290,000	(10,000)
		$500,000	$565,000	
Accounts Payable		$100,000	$100,000	
Bonds Payable		100,000	135,000	(35,000)
Common Stock		200,000		
Retained Earnings		100,000		
		$500,000	$235,000	$30,000

Advanced StudyGuide .com

pay a price higher than par for the bonds. In determining the value of Special Foods, Peerless must recognize that it is assuming a liability that pays an interest rate higher than the current market rate. Accordingly, the fair value of Special Foods' net assets will be less than if the liability had been carried at a lower interest rate. The resulting consolidated financial statements must recognize the acquisition-date fair values of Special Foods' liabilities as well as its assets.

Assume that Peerless Products acquires all of Special Foods' capital stock for $400,000 on January 1, 20X1, by issuing $100,000 of 9 percent bonds, with a fair value of $100,000, and paying cash of $300,000. The resulting ownership situation can be pictured as follows with a $100,000 differential:

P → S (1/1/X1, 100%)			
	Fair value of consideration		$400,000
	Book value of Special Foods' net assets		
	Common stock—Special Foods	200,000	
	Retained earnings—Special Foods	100,000	
			300,000
	Difference between fair value and book value		$100,000

Peerless records the investment on its books with the following entry:

(8)		Debit	Credit
	Investment in Special Foods	400,000	
	Bonds Payable		100,000
	Cash		300,000
	Record purchase of Special Foods stock.		

The fair value of the consideration that Peerless gave to acquire Special Foods' stock ($400,000) can be divided between the fair value of Special Foods' identifiable net assets ($330,000) and goodwill ($70,000), illustrated as follows:

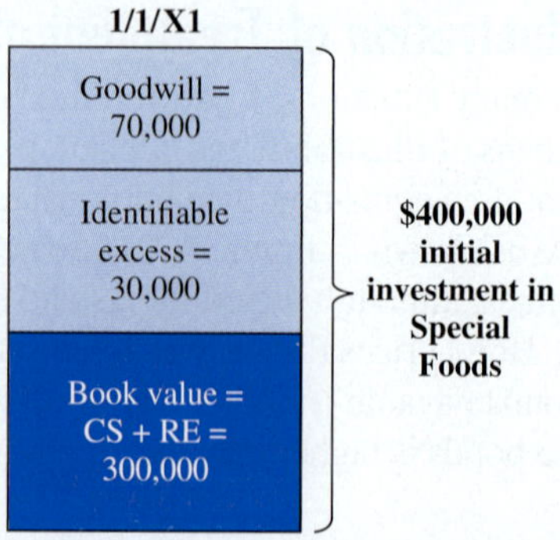

The total $400,000 consideration exceeds the book value of Special Foods' net assets, $300,000 (assets of $500,000 less liabilities of $200,000), by $100,000. Thus, the total differential is $100,000. The total fair value of the net identifiable assets acquired in the combination is $330,000 ($565,000 − $235,000), based on the data in Figure 4–2. The amount by which the total consideration of $400,000 exceeds the $330,000 fair value of the net identifiable assets is $70,000, and that amount is assigned to goodwill in the consolidated balance sheet. Assume that Peerless decides to prepare a consolidated balance sheet as of the date it acquired Special Foods.

The book value portion of the acquisition price is $300,000:

Book Value Calculations:

	Total Investment	=	Common Stock	+	Retained Earnings
Book Value at Acquisition	300,000		200,000		100,000

Thus, the basic consolidation entry is as follows:

Basic Consolidation Entry:

Common Stock	200,000		← Common stock balance
Retained Earnings	100,000		← Beginning balance in RE
Investment in Special Foods		300,000	← Net BV in investment account

The reclassification of the differential to the various accounts that are either over- or undervalued on Special Foods' balance sheet as of the acquisition date is more complicated than in the previous example. Thus, it is helpful to analyze the differential as follows:

Excess Value (Differential) Calculations:

Total Differential	=	Inventory	+	Land	+	Goodwill	+	Building	+	Bonds Payable
100,000		15,000		60,000		70,000		(10,000)		(35,000)

This analysis leads to the following reclassification entry to assign the $100,000 differential to the specific accounts that need to be "revalued" to reflect their fair values as of the acquisition date. Moreover, this entry completes the elimination of the investment account from Peerless' books.

Excess Value (Differential) Reclassification Entry:

Inventory	15,000		← Excess value assigned to inventory
Land	60,000		← Excess value assigned to land
Goodwill	70,000		← Excess value assigned to goodwill
Building		10,000	← Building revalued down to fair value
Bonds Payable		35,000	← Excess liability associated with the bonds
Investment in Special Foods		100,000	← Reassign excess acquisition price

In summary, these two consolidation entries completely eliminate the balance in Peerless' investment account and the second entry assigns the differential to various balance sheet accounts. As in previous examples, it is helpful to visualize how the two consolidation entries "zero out" the investment account:

	Investment in Special Foods		
Acquisition Price	400,000		
		300,000	Basic Consolidation Entry
		100,000	Excess Value Reclassification Entry
	0		

As usual, we eliminate Special Foods' acquisition date accumulated depreciation against the Buildings and Equipment account balance so that, combined with the excess value reclassification entry it will appear as if these fixed assets were recorded at their acquisition costs.

Optional Accumulated Depreciation Consolidation Entry:

Accumulated Depreciation	**300,000**		← Accumulated depreciation at the time
Buildings & Equipment		**300,000**	of the acquisition netted against cost

These entries are reflected in the worksheet in Figure 4–3. Although the reclassification entry is somewhat more complex than in the previous example, the differential allocation is conceptually the same in both cases. In each case, the end result is a consolidated balance sheet with the subsidiary's assets and liabilities valued at their fair values at the date of combination.

FIGURE 4–3 January 1, 20X1, Worksheet for Consolidated Balance Sheet, Date of Combination; 100 Percent Acquisition at More than Book Value

	Peerless Products	Special Foods	Consolidation Entries DR	Consolidation Entries CR	Consolidated
Balance Sheet					
Cash	50,000	50,000			100,000
Accounts Receivable	75,000	50,000			125,000
Inventory	100,000	60,000	15,000		175,000
Investment in Special Foods	400,000			300,000	0
				100,000	
Land	175,000	40,000	60,000		275,000
Buildings & Equipment	800,000	600,000		10,000	1,090,000
				300,000	
Less: Accumulated Depreciation	(400,000)	(300,000)	300,000		(400,000)
Goodwill			70,000		70,000
Total Assets	**1,200,000**	**500,000**	**$445,000**	**$710,000**	**1,435,000**
Accounts Payable	100,000	100,000			200,000
Bonds Payable	300,000	100,000			400,000
Premium on Bonds Payable				35,000	35,000
Common Stock	500,000	200,000	200,000		500,000
Retained Earnings	300,000	100,000	100,000		300,000
Total Liabilities & Equity	**1,200,000**	**500,000**	**300,000**	**35,000**	**1,435,000**

100 Percent Ownership Acquired at Less than Fair Value of Net Assets

LO 4-4

Make calculations and prepare consolidation entries for the consolidation of a wholly owned subsidiary when there is a complex bargain-purchase differential.

Advanced StudyGuide .com

It is not uncommon for companies' stock to trade at prices that are lower than the fair value of their net assets. These companies are often singled out as prime acquisition targets. The acquisition price of an acquired company may be less than the fair value of its net assets because some of the acquiree's assets or liabilities may have been incorrectly valued or because the transaction reflects a forced sale where the seller was required to sell quickly and was unable to fully market the sale.

Obviously, if assets or liabilities acquired in a business combination have been incorrectly valued, the errors must be corrected and the assets and liabilities valued at their fair values. Once this is done, if the fair value of the consideration given is still less than the fair value of the net assets acquired, a gain attributable to the acquirer is recognized for the difference. In general, as discussed in Chapter 1, a business combination in which (1) the sum of the acquisition-date fair values of the consideration given, any equity interest already held by the acquirer, and any noncontrolling interest is less than (2) the amounts at which the identifiable net assets must be valued at the acquisition date (usually fair values) is considered a ***bargain purchase,*** and a gain attributable to the acquirer is recognized for the difference (as specified by **ASC 805-10-20**).

The purpose of the differential is to account for items attributable to the subsidiary company that are not already accounted for by that acquiring entity. Since the gain on bargain purchase is attributed to the parent, it is recorded directly on the records of the parent, in effect increasing the differential, which is the difference between the investment account on the parent records and the book value of the subsidiary. The acquirer will record the gain as part of the acquisition transaction in its individual records.

Illustration of Treatment of Bargain-Purchase

Using the example of Peerless Products and Special Foods, assume that the acquisition-date book values and fair values of Special Foods' assets and liabilities are equal except that the fair value of Special Foods' land is $40,000 more than its book value. On January 1, 20X1, Peerless acquires all of Special Foods' common stock for $310,000, resulting in a bargain purchase. The resulting ownership situation is as follows:

P	Fair value of consideration		$310,000
1/1/X1 100%	Book value of Special Foods' net assets		
	Common stock—Special Foods	200,000	
	Retained earnings—Special Foods	100,000	
S			300,000
	Difference between fair value and book value		$ 10,000

Peerless records its investment in Special Foods with the following entry on its books:

(9)	Investment in Special Foods	340,000	
	Cash		310,000
	Gain on Bargain Purchase		30,000
	Record purchase of Special Foods stock.		

In this example, the acquisition-date fair value of Special Foods' net assets ($340,000) is higher than its book value by $40,000. However, the purchase price ($310,000) exceeds Special Foods' book value by only $10,000 and, thus, is less than the fair value of the net identifiable assets acquired. This business combination, therefore, represents a bargain purchase. All of the acquiree's assets and liabilities must be valued at fair value, which in this case requires only Special Foods' land to be revalued. This revaluation is accomplished in the consolidation worksheet. Assuming

Peerless wants to prepare a consolidated balance sheet on the acquisition date, the book value portion of the acquisition price is $300,000:

Book Value Calculations:

	Total Investment	=	Common Stock	+	Retained Earnings
Book Value at Acquisition	300,000		200,000		100,000

Thus, the basic consolidation entry is the same as in previous examples:

Basic Consolidation Entry:

Common Stock	200,000		← Common stock balance
Retained Earnings	100,000		← Beginning balance in RE
Investment in Special Foods		300,000	← Net BV in investment account

In this example, the total differential relates to the fair value of Special Foods' land, which is $40,000 more than its book value at acquisition. The reclassification of this total differential can be summarized as follows:

Excess Value (Differential) Calculations:

Total Differential	=	Land
40,000		40,000

This analysis leads to the following reclassification entry to assign the $40,000 net differential to the Land.

Excess Value (Differential) Reclassification Entry:

Land	40,000		← Excess value assigned to land
Investment in Special Foods		40,000	← Reclassify excess value portion of the investment account

In summary, these two consolidation entries effectively eliminate the balance in Peerless' investment account and assign the total differential to the Land account. As in previous examples, it is helpful to visualize how the two consolidation entries "zero out" the investment account:

	Investment in Special Foods (Dr.)	Investment in Special Foods (Cr.)	
Acquisition Price	340,000		
		300,000	Basic Consolidation Entry
		40,000	Excess Value Reclassification
	0		

When the consolidation worksheet is prepared at the end of the year, the notion of recognizing a gain for the $30,000 excess of the $340,000 fair value of Special Foods' net assets over the $310,000 fair value of the consideration given by Peerless in the exchange is correct. However, assuming a consolidation worksheet is also prepared on the acquisition date (January 1, 20X1), the gain will already be recorded in the parent's retained earnings account because an income statement is not prepared on the acquisition date, only a balance sheet (because it is the first day of the year).

CONSOLIDATED FINANCIAL STATEMENTS—100 PERCENT OWNERSHIP ACQUIRED AT MORE THAN BOOK VALUE

LO 4-5

Prepare equity-method journal entries, consolidation entries, and the consolidation worksheet for a wholly owned subsidiary when there is a complex positive differential.

Advanced StudyGuide .com

When an investor company accounts for an investment using the equity method, as illustrated in Chapter 2, it records the amount of differential viewed as expiring during the period as a reduction of the income recognized from the investee. In consolidation, the differential is assigned to the appropriate asset and liability balances, and consolidated income is adjusted for the amounts expiring during the period by assigning them to the related expense items (e.g., depreciation expense).

Initial Year of Ownership

As an illustration of the acquisition of 100 percent ownership acquired at an amount higher than book value, assume that Peerless Products acquires all of Special Foods' common stock on January 1, 20X1, for $387,500, an amount $87,500 in excess of the book value. The acquisition price includes cash of $300,000 and a 60-day note for $87,500 (paid at maturity during 20X1). At the date of combination, Special Foods holds the assets and liabilities shown in Figure 4–2. The resulting ownership situation is as follows:

Peerless Products Corporation

Special Foods Inc.

P	Fair value of consideration		$387,500
1/1/X1 100%	Book value of Special Foods' net assets		
	Common stock—Special Foods	200,000	
	Retained earnings—Special Foods	100,000	
S			300,000
	Difference between fair value and book value		$ 87,500

On the acquisition date, all of Special Foods' assets and liabilities have fair values equal to their book values, except as follows:

	Book Value	Fair Value	Fair Value Increment
Inventory	$ 60,000	$ 65,000	$ 5,000
Land	40,000	50,000	10,000
Buildings & Equipment	300,000	360,000	60,000
	$400,000	$475,000	$75,000

Of the $87,500 total differential, $75,000 relates to identifiable assets of Special Foods. The remaining $12,500 is attributable to goodwill. The apportionment of the differential appears as follows: The entire amount of inventory to which the differential relates is sold during 20X1; none is left in ending inventory. The buildings and equipment have a remaining economic life of 10 years from the date of combination, and Special Foods uses straight-line depreciation. At the end of 20X1, in evaluating the Investment in Special Foods account for impairment, Peerless' management determines that the goodwill acquired in the combination with Special Foods has been impaired. Management determines that a $3,000 goodwill impairment loss should be recognized in the consolidated income statement.

For the first year immediately after the date of combination, 20X1, Peerless Products earns income from its own separate operations of $140,000 and pays dividends of $60,000. Special Foods reports net income of $50,000 and pays dividends of $30,000.

Parent Company Entries

During 20X1, Peerless makes the normal equity-method entries on its books to record its purchase of Special Foods stock and its income and dividends from Special Foods:

(10)	Investment in Special Foods	387,500	
	Cash		300,000
	Notes Payable		87,500
	Record the initial investment in Special Foods.		

(11)	Investment in Special Foods	50,000	
	Income from Special Foods		50,000
	Record Peerless' 100% share of Special Foods' 20X1 income.		

(12)	Cash	30,000	
	Investment in Special Foods		30,000
	Record Peerless' 100% share of Special Foods' 20X1 dividend.		

In this case, Peerless paid an amount for its investment that was $87,500 in excess of the book value of the shares acquired. As discussed previously, this difference is a differential that is implicit in the amount recorded in the investment account on Peerless' books. Because Peerless acquired 100 percent of Special Foods' stock, Peerless' differential included in its investment account is equal to the total differential arising from the business combination. However, although the differential arising from the business combination must be allocated to specific assets and liabilities in consolidation, the differential on Peerless' books does not appear separate from the Investment in Special Foods account. A portion of the differential ($5,000) in the investment account on Peerless' books relates to a portion of Special Foods' inventory that is sold during 20X1. Because Special Foods no longer holds the asset to which that portion of the differential relates at year-end, that portion of the differential is written off by reducing the investment account and Peerless' income from Special Foods. An additional $60,000 of the differential is attributable to the excess of the acquisition-date fair value over book value of Special Foods' buildings and equipment. As the service potential of the underlying assets expires, Peerless must amortize the additional cost it incurred because of the higher fair value of those assets. This is accomplished through annual amortization of $6,000 ($60,000 ÷ 10) over the remaining 10-year life beginning in 20X1. Finally, the goodwill is deemed to be impaired by $3,000 and is also adjusted on Peerless' books. Thus, the differential must be written off on Peerless' books to recognize the cost expiration related to the service expiration of Special Foods' assets to which it relates. Under the equity method, the differential is written off periodically from the investment account to Income from Special Foods to reflect these changes in the differential ($5,000 inventory + $6,000 depreciation + $3,000 goodwill impairment = $14,000):

(13)	Income from Special Foods	14,000	
	Investment in Special Foods		14,000
	Record amortization of excess acquisition price.		

Consolidation Worksheet—Year of Combination

The following diagrams illustrate the breakdown of the book value and excess value components of the investment account at the beginning and end of the year.

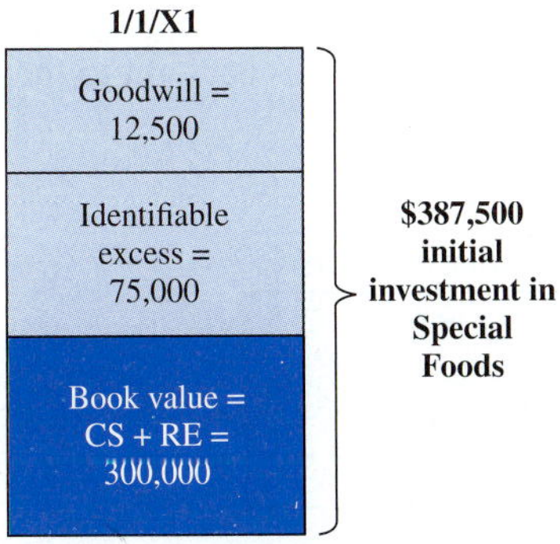

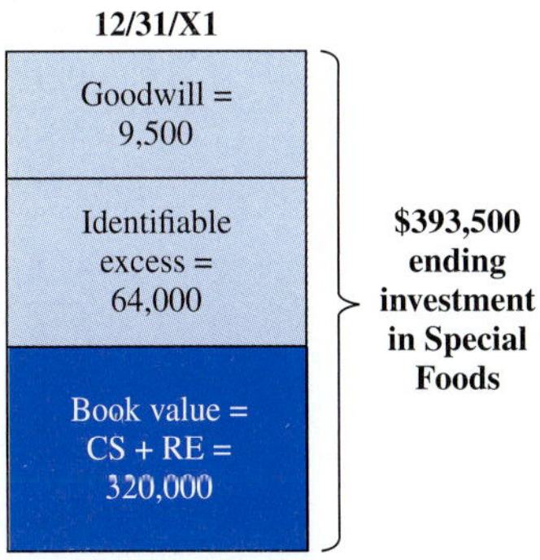

Because a year has passed since the acquisition date, the book value of Special Foods' net assets has changed because it has earned income and declared dividends. The book value component can be summarized as follows:

Book Value Calculations:

	Total Investment	=	Common Stock	+	Retained Earnings
Beginning Book Value	300,000		200,000		100,000
+ Net Income	50,000				50,000
− Dividends	(30,000)				(30,000)
Ending Book Value	320,000		200,000		120,000

This chart leads to the basic consolidation entry. Note that we use a shaded font to distinguish the numbers that appear in the consolidation entry to help the reader see how it should be constructed.

Basic Consolidation Entry:

Common Stock	200,000		← Common stock balance
Retained Earnings	100,000		← Beginning balance in RE
Income from Special Foods	50,000		← Special Foods' reported income
Dividends Declared		30,000	← 100% of Special Foods' dividends
Investment in Special Foods		320,000	← Net BV in investment account

We then analyze the differential and its changes during the period:

Excess Value (Differential) Calculations:

	Total	= Inventory +	Land	+ Building	+ Acc. Depr.	+ Goodwill
Beginning Balance	87,500	5,000	10,000	60,000	0	12,500
− Changes	(14,000)	(5,000)			(6,000)	(3,000)
Ending Balance	73,500	0	10,000	60,000	(6,000)	9,500

The entire differential amount assigned to the inventory already passed through cost of goods sold during the year. The only other amortization item—the excess value assigned to the building—is amortized over a 10-year period ($60,000 ÷ 10 = $6,000 per year). Finally, the goodwill is deemed to be impaired and worth only $9,500. Because the amortization of the differential has already been written off on Peerless' books from the investment account against the Income from Special Foods account, the amortized excess value reclassification entry simply reclassifies these changes in the differential during the period from the Income from the Special Foods account to the various income statement accounts to which they apply:

Amortized Excess Value Reclassification Entry:

Account	Debit	Credit	
Cost of Goods Sold	5,000		← Extra cost of goods sold
Depreciation Expense	6,000		← Depreciation of excess building value
Goodwill Impairment Loss	3,000		← Goodwill impairment
Income from Special Foods		14,000	← See calculation above

Finally, the remaining unamortized differential of $73,500 is reclassified to the correct accounts based on the ending balances (the bottom row) in the excess value calculations chart:

Excess Value (Differential) Reclassification Entry:

Account	Debit	Credit	
Land	10,000		← Excess value at acquisition
Building	60,000		← Excess value at acquisition
Goodwill	9,500		← Calculated value postimpairment
Accumulated Depreciation		6,000	← = 60,000 ÷ 10 years
Investment in Special Foods		73,500	← Remaining balance in differential

Recall that Special Foods reports its balance sheet based on the book values of the various accounts. This consolidation entry essentially reclassifies the differential from the Investment in Special Foods account to the individual accounts that need to be revalued to their amortized fair values as of the balance sheet date.

In sum, these worksheet entries (1) eliminate the balances in the Investment in Special Foods and Income from Special Foods accounts, (2) reclassify the amortization of excess

	Inv. in Special Foods (Dr)	Inv. in Special Foods (Cr)		Inc. from Special Foods (Dr)	Inc. from Special Foods (Cr)	
Acquisition Price	387,500					
Net Income	50,000				50,000	80% Net Income
		30,000	Dividends			
		14,000	Excess Value Amortization	14,000		
Ending Balance	393,500				36,000	Ending Balance
		320,000	Basic	50,000		
		73,500	Excess Reclass.		14,000	Amort. Reclass.
	0				0	

value to the proper income statement accounts, and (3) reclassify the remaining differential to the appropriate balance sheet accounts as of the end of the period.

As usual, we eliminate Special Foods' acquisition date accumulated depreciation against the Buildings and Equipment account balance.

Optional Accumulated Depreciation Consolidation Entry:

Account	Debit	Credit	
Accumulated Depreciation	300,000		← Accumulated depreciation at the time of the acquisition netted against cost
Buildings & Equipment		300,000	

The following T-accounts illustrate how the excess value reclassification entry combined with the accumulated depreciation consolidation entry make the consolidated balances for the Buildings and Equipment and Accumulated Depreciation accounts appear as if these assets had been purchased at the beginning of the year for their acquisition date fair values ($360,000) and that these "new" assets had then been depreciated $26,000 during the first year of their use by the newly purchased company.

	Buildings & Equip.			Accumulated Depr.		
End. Bal.	**600,000**				**320,000**	**End. Bal.**
Excess Reclass.	**60,000**				**6,000**	**Excess Reclass.**
		300,000	**Acc. Depr. Entry**	**300,000**		
	360,000				**26,000**	

After the subsidiary income accruals are entered on Peerless' books, the adjusted trial balance data of the consolidating companies are entered in the three-part consolidation worksheet as shown in Figure 4–4. We note that because all inventory on hand on the date of combination has been sold during the year, the $5,000 of differential applicable

FIGURE 4–4 December 31, 20X1, Equity-Method Worksheet for Consolidated Financial Statements, Initial Year of Ownership; 100 Percent Acquisition at More than Book Value

	Peerless Products	Special Foods	Consolidation Entries DR	Consolidation Entries CR	Consolidated
Income Statement					
Sales	400,000	200,000			600,000
Less: COGS	(170,000)	(115,000)	5,000		(290,000)
Less: Depreciation Expense	(50,000)	(20,000)	6,000		(76,000)
Less: Other Expenses	(40,000)	(15,000)			(55,000)
Less: Impairment Loss			3,000		(3,000)
Income from Special Foods	36,000		50,000	14,000	0
Net Income	**176,000**	**50,000**	**64,000**	**14,000**	**176,000**
Statement of Retained Earnings					
Beginning Balance	300,000	100,000	100,000		300,000
Net Income	**176,000**	**50,000**	**64,000**	**14,000**	176,000
Less: Dividends Declared	(60,000)	(30,000)		30,000	(60,000)
Ending Balance	**416,000**	**120,000**	**164,000**	**44,000**	**416,000**
Balance Sheet					
Cash	122,500	75,000			197,500
Accounts Receivable	75,000	50,000			125,000
Inventory	100,000	75,000			175,000
Investment in Special Foods	393,500			320,000 73,500	0
Land	175,000	40,000	10,000		225,000
Buildings & Equipment	800,000	600,000	60,000	300,000	1,160,000
Less: Accumulated Depreciation	(450,000)	(320,000)	300,000	6,000	(476,000)
Goodwill			9,500		9,500
Total Assets	**1,216,000**	**520,000**	**379,500**	**699,500**	**1,416,000**
Accounts Payable	100,000	100,000			200,000
Bonds Payable	200,000	100,000			300,000
Common Stock	500,000	200,000	200,000		500,000
Retained Earnings	**416,000**	**120,000**	**164,000**	**44,000**	416,000
Total Liabilities & Equity	**1,216,000**	**520,000**	**364,000**	**44,000**	**1,416,000**

to inventory is allocated directly to cost of goods sold. The cost of goods sold recorded on Special Foods' books is correct for that company's separate financial statements. However, the cost of the inventory to the consolidated entity is viewed as being $5,000 higher, and this additional cost must be included in consolidated cost of goods sold. No worksheet entry is needed in future periods with respect to the inventory because it has been expensed and no longer is on the subsidiary's books. The portion of the differential related to the inventory no longer exists on Peerless' books after 20X1 because the second consolidation entry removed it from the investment account.

The differential assigned to depreciable assets must be charged to depreciation expense over the remaining lives of those assets. From a consolidated viewpoint, the acquisition-date fair value increment associated with the depreciable assets acquired becomes part of the assets' depreciation base. Depreciation already is recorded on the subsidiary's books based on the original cost of the assets to the subsidiary, and these amounts are carried to the consolidation worksheet as depreciation expense.

The difference between the $387,500 fair value of the consideration exchanged and the $375,000 fair value of Special Foods' net identifiable assets is assumed to be related to the excess earning power of Special Foods. This difference is entered in the worksheet in Figure 4–4. A distinction must be made between journal entries recorded on the parent's books under equity-method reporting and the consolidation entries needed in the worksheet to prepare the consolidated financial statements. Again, we distinguish between actual equity-method journal entries on the parent's books (not shaded) and worksheet consolidation entries (shaded).

Consolidated Net Income and Retained Earnings

As can be seen from the worksheet in Figure 4–4, consolidated net income for 20X1 is $176,000 and consolidated retained earnings on December 31, 20X1, is $416,000. These amounts can be computed as shown in Figure 4–5.

Second Year of Ownership

The consolidation procedures employed at the end of the second year, and in periods thereafter, are basically the same as those used at the end of the first year. Consolidation two years after acquisition is illustrated by continuing the example used for 20X1. During 20X2, Peerless Products earns income of $160,000 from its own separate operations and pays dividends of $60,000; Special Foods reports net income of $75,000 and pays dividends of $40,000. No further impairment of the goodwill from the business combination occurs during 20X2.

FIGURE 4–5
Consolidated Net Income and Retained Earnings, 20X1; 100 Percent Acquisition at More than Book Value

Consolidated net income, 20X1:	
Peerless' separate operating income	$140,000
Special Foods' net income	50,000
Write-off of differential related to inventory sold during 20X1	(5,000)
Amortization of differential related to buildings & equipment in 20X1	(6,000)
Goodwill impairment loss	(3,000)
Consolidated net income, 20X1	$176,000
Consolidated retained earnings, December 31, 20X1:	
Peerless' retained earnings on date of combination, January 1, 20X1	$300,000
Peerless' separate operating income, 20X1	140,000
Special Foods' 20X1 net income	50,000
Write-off of differential related to inventory sold during 20X1	(5,000)
Amortization of differential related to buildings & equipment in 20X1	(6,000)
Goodwill impairment loss	(3,000)
Dividends declared by Peerless, 20X1	(60,000)
Consolidated retained earnings, December 31, 20X1	$416,000

Parent Company Entries

Peerless Products records the following entries on its separate books during 20X2:

(14)	Investment in Special Foods	75,000	
	Income from Special Foods		75,000
	Record Peerless' 100% share of Special Foods' 20X2 income.		

(15)	Cash	40,000	
	Investment in Special Foods		40,000
	Record Peerless' 100% share of Special Foods' 20X2 dividend.		

(16)	Income from Special Foods	6,000	
	Investment in Special Foods		6,000
	Record amortization of excess acquisition price.		

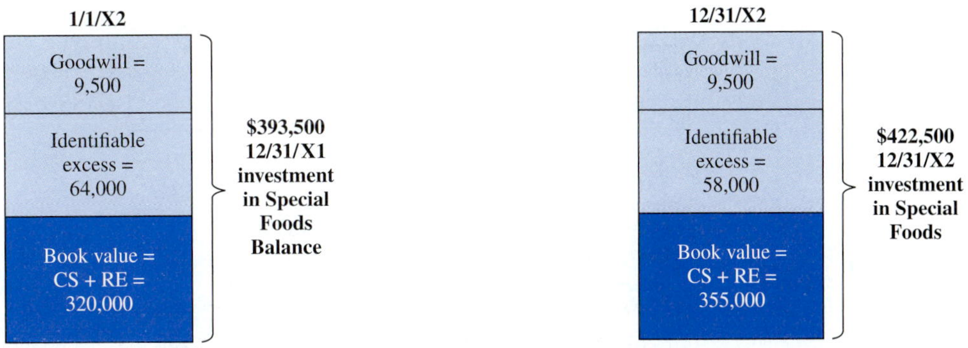

The book value component can be summarized as follows:

Book Value Calculations:

	Total Investment	=	Common Stock	+	Retained Earnings
Beginning Book Value	320,000		200,000		120,000
+ Net Income	75,000				75,000
− Dividends	(40,000)				(40,000)
Ending Book Value	355,000		200,000		155,000

The numbers in this chart in the shaded font determine the basic consolidation entry:

Basic Consolidation Entry:

Common Stock	200,000		← Common stock balance
Retained Earnings	120,000		← Beginning balance in RE
Income from Special Foods	75,000		← Special Foods' reported income
Dividends Declared		40,000	← 100% of Special Foods' dividends
Investment in Special Foods		355,000	← Net BV in investment account

The entire differential amount assigned to the inventory already passed through cost of goods sold during the prior year period. The only other amortization item is the excess value assigned to the building, which continues to be written off over a 10-year period ($60,000 ÷ 10 = $6,000) as illustrated in the following chart. Again, the goodwill is deemed not to be further impaired this year.

Excess Value (Differential) Calculations:

	Total	=	Land	+	Building	+	Acc. Depr.	+	Goodwill
Beginning Balance	73,500		10,000		60,000		(6,000)		9,500
– Changes	(6,000)						(6,000)		
Ending Balance	67,500		10,000		60,000		(12,000)		9,500

Because the amortization of the differential was already written off from the investment account against the Income from Special Foods account, the change to the differential (i.e., the middle row of the chart) is simply reclassified from the Income from Special Foods account to the income statement account to which it applies during the consolidation process. Then, the remaining amount of the differential at year end (i.e., the bottom row of the chart) is reclassified to the various balance sheet accounts to which they apply:

Amortized Excess Value Reclassification Entry:

Depreciation Expense	6,000		← Extra depreciation expense
Income from Special Foods		6,000	← See calculation above.

Excess Value (Differential) Reclassification Entry:

Land	10,000		← Excess value at acquisition
Building	60,000		← Excess value at acquisition
Goodwill	9,500		← Calculated value postimpairment
Accumulated Depreciation		12,000	← = (60,000 ÷ 10 years) × 2 years
Investment in Special Foods		67,500	← Remaining balance in differential

These consolidation entries (1) eliminate the balances in the Investment in Special Foods and Income from Special Foods accounts, (2) reclassify the amortization of excess value to the proper income statement accounts, and (3) reclassify the remaining differential to the appropriate balance sheet accounts as of the end of the accounting period. The following T-accounts illustrate how the three consolidation entries "zero out" the equity-method investment and income accounts:

	Inv. in Special Foods (Dr.)	Inv. in Special Foods (Cr.)		Inc. from Special Foods (Dr.)	Inc. from Special Foods (Cr.)	
Beginning Balance	393,500					
Net Income	75,000				75,000	Net Income
		40,000	Dividends			
		6,000	Excess Price Amortization	6,000		
Ending Balance	422,500				69,000	Ending Balance
		355,000	Basic	75,000		
		67,500	Excess Reclass.		6,000	Amort. Reclass.
	0				0	

Again, we repeat the same accumulated depreciation consolidation entry this year (and every year as long as Special Foods owns the assets) that we used in the initial year.

Optional Accumulated Depreciation Consolidation Entry:

Accumulated Depreciation	300,000		← Accumulated depreciation at the time of the acquisition netted against cost
Building and Equipment		300,000	

FIGURE 4–6 December 31, 20X2, Equity-Method Worksheet for Consolidated Financial Statements, Second Year of Ownership; 100 Percent Acquisition at More than Book Value

	Peerless Products	Special Foods	Consolidation Entries		Consolidated
			DR	CR	
Income Statement					
Sales	450,000	300,000			750,000
Less: COGS	(180,000)	(160,000)			(340,000)
Less: Depreciation Expense	(50,000)	(20,000)	6,000		(76,000)
Less: Other Expenses	(60,000)	(45,000)			(105,000)
Less: Impairment Loss					0
Income from Special Foods	69,000		75,000	6,000	0
Net Income	**229,000**	**75,000**	**81,000**	**6,000**	**229,000**
Statement of Retained Earnings					
Beginning Balance	416,000	120,000	120,000		416,000
Net Income	**229,000**	**75,000**	**81,000**	**6,000**	229,000
Less: Dividends Declared	(60,000)	(40,000)		40,000	(60,000)
Ending Balance	**585,000**	**155,000**	**201,000**	**46,000**	**585,000**
Balance Sheet					
Cash	157,500	85,000			242,500
Accounts Receivable	150,000	80,000			230,000
Inventory	180,000	90,000			270,000
Investment in Special Foods	422,500			355,000	0
				67,500	
Land	175,000	40,000	10,000		225,000
Buildings & Equipment	800,000	600,000	60,000	300,000	1,160,000
Less: Accumulated Depreciation	(500,000)	(340,000)	300,000	12,000	(552,000)
Goodwill			9,500		9,500
Total Assets	**1,385,000**	**555,000**	**379,500**	**734,500**	**1,585,000**
Accounts Payable	100,000	100,000			200,000
Bonds Payable	200,000	100,000			300,000
Common Stock	500,000	200,000	200,000		500,000
Retained Earnings	**585,000**	**155,000**	**201,000**	**46,000**	585,000
Total Liabilities & Equity	**1,385,000**	**555,000**	**401,000**	**46,000**	**1,585,000**

Consolidation Worksheet—Second Year Following Combination

The worksheet for the second year, 20X2, completes the two-year cycle as illustrated in Figure 4–6. Moreover, as can be seen from the worksheet, consolidated net income for 20X2 is $229,000 and consolidated retained earnings on December 31, 20X2, is $585,000 as illustrated in Figure 4–7.

FIGURE 4–7 Consolidated Net Income and Retained Earnings, 20X2; 100 Percent Acquisition at More than Book Value

Consolidated net income, 20X2:	
Peerless' separate operating income	$160,000
Special Foods' net income	75,000
Amortization of differential related to buildings & equipment in 20X2	(6,000)
Consolidated net income, 20X2	$229,000
Consolidated retained earnings, December 31, 20X2:	
Consolidated retained earnings, December 31, 20X1	$416,000
Peerless' separate operating income, 20X2	160,000
Special Foods' 20X2 net income	75,000
Amortization of differential related to buildings & equipment in 20X2	(6,000)
Dividends declared by Peerless, 20X2	(60,000)
Consolidated retained earnings, December 31, 20X2	$585,000

INTERCOMPANY RECEIVABLES AND PAYABLES

LO 4-6

Understand and explain the elimination of basic intercompany transactions.

All forms of intercompany receivables and payables need to be eliminated when consolidated financial statements are prepared. From a single-company viewpoint, a company cannot owe itself money. If a company owes an affiliate $1,000 on account, one company carries a $1,000 receivable on its separate books and the other has a payable for the same amount. When consolidated financial statements are prepared, the following consolidation entry is needed in the consolidation worksheet:

Accounts Payable	1,000	
Accounts Receivable		1,000

Eliminate intercompany receivable/payable.

If no consolidation entry is made, both the consolidated assets and liabilities are overstated by an equal amount.

If the intercompany receivable/payable bears interest, all accounts related to the intercompany claim must be eliminated in the preparation of consolidated statements, including the receivable/payable, interest income, interest expense, and any accrued interest on the intercompany claim. Other forms of intercorporate claims, such as bonds, are discussed in subsequent chapters. In all cases, failure to eliminate these claims can distort consolidated balances. As a result, the magnitude of debt of the combined entity may appear to be greater than it is, working capital ratios may be incorrect, and other types of comparisons may be distorted.

PUSH-DOWN ACCOUNTING

LO 4-7

Understand and explain the basics of push-down accounting.

The term ***push-down accounting*** refers to the practice of revaluing an acquired subsidiary's assets and liabilities to their fair values directly on that subsidiary's books at the date of acquisition. If this practice is followed, the revaluations are recorded once on the subsidiary's books at the date of acquisition and, therefore, are not made in the consolidation worksheets each time consolidated statements are prepared.

Those who favor push-down accounting argue that the change in the subsidiary's ownership in an acquisition is reason for adopting a new basis of accounting for the subsidiary's assets and liabilities, and this new basis of accounting should be reflected directly on the subsidiary's books. This argument is most persuasive when the subsidiary is wholly owned, is consolidated, or has its separate financial statements included with the parent's statements.

On the other hand, when a subsidiary has a significant noncontrolling interest or the subsidiary has bonds or preferred stock held by the public, push-down accounting may be inappropriate. Its use in the financial statements issued to the noncontrolling shareholders or to those holding bonds or preferred stock results in a new basis of accounting even though, from the perspective of those statement users, the entity has not changed. From their viewpoint, push-down accounting results in the revaluation of the assets and liabilities of a continuing enterprise, a practice that normally is not acceptable.

ASC 805-50-S99-2 requires push-down accounting whenever a business combination results in the acquired subsidiary becoming substantially wholly owned, i.e., greater than 95 percent ownership, (but only if it issues separate financial statements). It encourages but does not require the use of push-down accounting in situations in which the subsidiary is less than wholly owned (80 to 95 percent ownership) or the subsidiary has outstanding debt or preferred stock held by the public. Push-down accounting is prohibited when the subsidiary is less than 80 percent owned.

The revaluation of assets and liabilities on a subsidiary's books involves making an entry to debit or credit each asset and liability account to be revalued, with the balancing entry to a revaluation capital account (this amount is usually a credit). The revaluation capital account is part of the subsidiary's stockholders' equity. Once the revaluations are made on the books of the subsidiary, the new book values of the subsidiary's assets, including goodwill, are equal to the acquisition cost of the subsidiary.

Thus, no differential arises in the consolidation process. The investment consolidation entry in a consolidation worksheet prepared immediately after acquisition of a subsidiary and revaluation of its assets on its books might appear as follows:

Capital Stock—Subsidiary	XXX	
Retained Earnings	XXX	
Revaluation Capital	XXX	
Investment in Subsidiary Stock		XXX

Eliminate investment balance.

Note that the Revaluation Capital account, as part of the subsidiary's stockholders' equity, is eliminated in preparing consolidated statements. We provide a more detailed example of push-down accounting in Appendix 4A.

SUMMARY OF KEY CONCEPTS

Worksheet consolidation entries are needed to remove the effects of intercompany ownership and intercompany transactions so the consolidated financial statements appear as if the separate companies are actually one. These worksheet entries are needed to (1) eliminate the book value portion of the parent's subsidiary investment and the subsidiary's stockholders' equity accounts, (2) reclassify the amortization of excess value from the parent's income from subsidiary account to the correct income statement line items, (3) assign any remaining differential to specific assets and liabilities, and (4) net the subsidiary's accumulated depreciation as of the acquisition date against the historical cost of property, plant, and equipment.

Consolidated net income is computed in simple cases for a parent and a wholly owned subsidiary as the total of the parent's income from its own operations and the subsidiary's net income, adjusted for the write-off of differential, if appropriate. In this situation, consolidated retained earnings is computed as the total of the parent's retained earnings, excluding any income from the subsidiary, plus the subsidiary's cumulative net income since acquisition adjusted for the differential amount.

When a subsidiary is acquired for an amount higher than its book value, some parent companies may prefer to assign the differential to individual assets and liabilities directly on the subsidiary's books at the time of acquisition, thereby eliminating the need for revaluation entries in the consolidation worksheet each period. This procedure is called push-down accounting.

KEY TERMS

bargain purchase, *157*
differential, *144*
goodwill, *153*
push-down accounting, *153, 168*

Appendix 4A Push-Down Accounting Illustrated

When a subsidiary is acquired in a business combination, its assets and liabilities must be revalued to their fair values as of the date of combination for consolidated reporting. If *push-down accounting* is employed, the revaluations are made as of the date of combination directly on the books of the subsidiary and no consolidation entries related to the differential are needed in the consolidation worksheets.

The following example illustrates the consolidation process when assets and liabilities are revalued directly on a subsidiary's books rather than using consolidation worksheet entries to accomplish the revaluation. Assume that Peerless Products purchases all of Special Foods' common stock on January 1, 20X1, for $370,000 cash. The purchase price is $70,000 in excess of Special Foods' book value. Of the $70,000 total differential, $10,000 is related to land held by Special Foods and $60,000 is related to buildings and equipment having a 10-year remaining life. Accumulated depreciation on Special Foods' books at the acquisition date is $300,000. Peerless accounts for its investment in Special Foods stock using the equity method.

Peerless records the acquisition of stock on its books with the following entry:

(17)	Investment in Special Foods	370,000	
	Cash		370,000

Record the initial investment in Special Foods.

In contrast to a worksheet revaluation, the use of push-down accounting involves the revaluation of the assets on the separate books of Special Foods and alleviates the need for revaluation entries in the consolidation worksheet each period. If push-down accounting is used to revalue Special Foods' assets, the following entry is made directly on its books:

(18)			
	Land	10,000	
	Buildings & Equipment	60,000	
	Revaluation Capital		70,000

Record the increase in fair value of land and buildings.

This entry increases the amount at which the land and the buildings and equipment are shown in Special Foods' separate financial statements and gives rise to a revaluation capital account that is shown in the stockholders' equity section of Special Foods' balance sheet. Special Foods records $6,000 additional depreciation on its books to reflect the amortization over 10 years of the $60,000 write-up of buildings and equipment.

Entry (19) removes the accumulated depreciation on the acquisition date so that the buildings and equipment appear at their acquisition date fair value with zero accumulated depreciation.

(19)			
	Accumulated Depreciation	300,000	
	Buildings & Equipment		300,000

Assuming Special Foods recorded net income of $44,000 and paid dividends of $30,000 during 20X1, Peerless records the following entries on its parent-company books:

(20)			
	Investment in Special Foods	44,000	
	Income from Special Foods		44,000

Record Peerless' 100% share of Special Foods' 20X1 income.

(21)			
	Cash	30,000	
	Investment in Special Foods		30,000

Record Peerless' 100% share of Special Foods' 20X1 dividend.

Because the revaluation is recorded on the subsidiary's books, Special Foods' book value is then equal to the fair value of the consideration given in the combination. Therefore, no differential exists, and Peerless need not record any amortization associated with the investment. The net amount of income from Special Foods recorded by Peerless is the same regardless of whether or not push-down accounting is employed. The book value portion of the investment account can be summarized as follows:

Book Value Calculations:

	Total Investment	=	Common Stock	+	Retained Earnings	+	Revaluation Capital
Beginning Book Value	**370,000**		**200,000**		**100,000**		**70,000**
+ Net Income	**44,000**				**44,000**		
− Dividends	**(30,000)**				**(30,000)**		
Ending Book Value	**384,000**		**200,000**		**114,000**		**70,000**

The basic consolidation entry is very similar to the original example presented previously except that it must also eliminate Special Foods' revaluation capital account:

Basic Consolidation Entry:

Common Stock	**200,000**	
Retained Earnings	**100,000**	
Revaluation Capital	**70,000**	
Income from Special Foods	**44,000**	
Dividends Declared		**30,000**
Investment in Special Foods		**384,000**

Again, because there is no differential with push-down accounting, the basic consolidation entry completely eliminates the balance in Peerless' investment account on the balance sheet as well as the Income from Special Foods account on the income statement.

	Investment in Special Foods		
Acquisition Price	370,000		
Net Income	44,000		
		30,000	Dividends
Ending Balance	384,000		
		384,000	Basic
	0		

	Income from Special Foods		
		44,000	Net Income
		44,000	Ending Balance
Basic	44,000		
		0	

Figure 4–8 shows the consolidation worksheet prepared at the end of 20X1 and includes the effects of revaluing Special Foods' assets. Note that Special Foods' Land and Buildings and Equipment have been increased by $10,000 and $60,000, respectively. Also note the Revaluation Capital account in Special Foods' stockholders' equity. Because the revaluation was accomplished directly on the books of Special Foods, only the basic consolidation entry is needed in the worksheet illustrated in Figure 4–8.

FIGURE 4–8 December 31, 20X1, Equity-Method Worksheet for Consolidated Financial Statements, Initial Year of Ownership; 100 Percent Acquisition at More than Book Value; Push-Down Accounting

	Peerless Products	Special Foods	Consolidation Entries DR	Consolidation Entries CR	Consolidated
Income Statement					
Sales	400,000	200,000			600,000
Less: COGS	(170,000)	(115,000)			(285,000)
Less: Depreciation Expense	(50,000)	(26,000)			(76,000)
Less: Other Expenses	(40,000)	(15,000)			(55,000)
Income from Special Foods	44,000		44,000		0
Net Income	**184,000**	**44,000**	**44,000**	**0**	**184,000**
Statement of Retained Earnings					
Beginning Balance	300,000	100,000	100,000		300,000
Net Income	**184,000**	**44,000**	**44,000**	**0**	184,000
Less: Dividends Declared	(60,000)	(30,000)		30,000	(60,000)
Ending Balance	**424,000**	**114,000**	**144,000**	**30,000**	**424,000**
Balance Sheet					
Cash	140,000	75,000			215,000
Accounts Receivable	75,000	50,000			125,000
Inventory	100,000	75,000			175,000
Investment in Special Foods	384,000			384,000	0
Land	175,000	50,000			225,000
Buildings & Equipment	800,000	360,000			1,160,000
Less: Accumulated Depreciation	(450,000)	(26,000)			(476,000)
Total Assets	**1,224,000**	**584,000**	**0**	**384,000**	**1,424,000**
Accounts Payable	100,000	100,000			200,000
Bonds Payable	200,000	100,000			300,000
Common Stock	500,000	200,000	200,000		500,000
Retained Earnings	**424,000**	**114,000**	**144,000**	**30,000**	424,000
Revaluation Capital		70,000	70,000		0
Total Liabilities & Equity	**1,224,000**	**584,000**	**414,000**	**30,000**	**1,424,000**

QUESTIONS

LO 4-1 **Q4-1** When is the carrying value of the investment account reduced under equity-method reporting?

LO 4-1 **Q4-2** What is a differential? How is a differential treated by an investor in computing income from an investee under (*a*) cost-method and (*b*) equity-method reporting?

LO 4-1 **Q4-3** Turner Manufacturing Corporation owns 100 percent of the common shares of Straight Lace Company. If Straight Lace reports net income of $100,000 for 20X5, what factors may cause Turner to report less than $100,000 of income from the investee?

LO 4-1 **Q4-4** What is the term *differential* used to indicate?

LO 4-1 **Q4-5** What conditions must exist for a negative differential to occur?

LO 4-2 **Q4-6** What portion of the book value of the net assets held by a subsidiary at acquisition is included in the consolidated balance sheet?

LO 4-2 **Q4-7** What portion of the fair value of a subsidiary's net assets normally is included in the consolidated balance sheet following a business combination?

LO 4-3 **Q4-8** What happens to the differential in the consolidation worksheet prepared as of the date of combination? How is it reestablished so that the proper balances can be reported the following year?

LO 4-2 **Q4-9** Explain why consolidated financial statements become increasingly important when the differential is very large.

LO 4-3 **Q4-10** Give a definition of *consolidated net income.*

LO 4-5 **Q4-11** When Ajax was preparing its consolidation worksheet, the differential was properly assigned to buildings and equipment. What additional entry generally must be made in the worksheet?

LO 4-3, 4-4 **Q4-12** What determines whether the balance assigned to the differential remains constant or decreases each period?

LO 4-7 **Q4-13** What does the term *push-down accounting* mean?

LO 4-7 **Q4-14** Under what conditions is push-down accounting considered appropriate?

LO 4-7 **Q4-15** What happens to the differential when push-down accounting is used following a business combination?

CASES

LO 4-1 **C4-1** **Reporting Significant Investments in Common Stock**

Analysis

The reporting treatment for investments in common stock depends on the level of ownership and the ability to influence the investee's policies. The reporting treatment may even change over time as ownership levels or other factors change. When investees are not consolidated, the investments typically are reported in the Investments section of the investor's balance sheet. However, the investor's income from those investments is not always easy to find in the investor's income statement.

Required

a. Harley-Davidson Inc. holds an investment in the common stock of Buell Motorcycle Company. How did Harley-Davidson report this investment before 1998? How does it report the investment now? Why did Harley change its method of reporting its investment in Buell?

b. How does Chevron Corporation account for its investments in affiliated companies? How does the company account for issuances of additional stock by affiliates that change the company's proportionate dollar share of the affiliates' equity? How does Chevron treat a differential associated with an equity-method investment? How does Chevron account for the impairment of an equity investment?

c. Does Sears have any investments in companies that it accounts for using the equity method? Where are these investments reported in the balance sheet, and where is the income from these investments reported in the income statement?

LO 4-2

C4-2 Assigning an Acquisition Differential

Analysis

Ball Corporation's owners recently offered to sell 100 percent of their ownership to Timber Corporation for $450,000. Timber's business manager was told that Ball's book value was $300,000, and she estimates the fair value of its net assets at approximately $600,000. Ball has relatively old equipment and manufacturing facilities and uses a LIFO basis for inventory valuation of some items and a FIFO basis for others.

Required

If Timber accepts the offer and acquires a controlling interest in Ball, what difficulties are likely to be encountered in assigning the differential?

LO 4-2, 4-3

C4-3 Negative Retained Earnings

Understanding

Although Sloan Company had good earnings reports in 20X5 and 20X6, it had a negative retained earnings balance on December 31, 20X6. Jacobs Corporation purchased 100 percent of Sloan's common stock on January 1, 20X7.

Required

a. Explain how Sloan's negative retained earnings balance is reflected in the consolidated balance sheet immediately following the acquisition.

b. Explain how the existence of negative retained earnings changes the consolidation worksheet entries.

c. Can goodwill be recorded if Jacobs pays more than book value for Sloan's shares? Explain.

LO 4-1, 4-3

C4-4 Balance Sheet Reporting Issues

Judgment

Crumple Car Rentals is planning to expand into the western part of the United States and needs to acquire approximately 400 additional automobiles for rental purposes. Because Crumple's cash reserves were substantially depleted in replacing the bumpers on existing automobiles with new "fashion plate" bumpers, the expansion funds must be acquired through other means. Crumple's management has identified two options:

1. Issue additional debt.
2. Create a wholly owned leasing subsidiary that would borrow the money with a guarantee for payment from Crumple. The subsidiary would then lease the cars to the parent.

The acquisition price of the cars is approximately the same under both alternatives.

Required

a. You have been asked to compare and contrast the two alternatives from the perspective of

(1) The impact on Crumple's consolidated balance sheet.

(2) Their legal ramifications.

(3) The ability to control the maintenance, repair, and replacement of automobiles.

b. What other alternatives might be used in acquiring the required automobiles?

c. Select your preferred alternative and show why it is the better choice.

LO 4-1, 4-2

C4-5 Subsidiary Ownership: AMR Corporation and International Lease

Research

Most subsidiaries are wholly owned, although only majority ownership is usually all that is required for consolidation. The parent's ownership may be direct or indirect. Frequently, a parent's direct subsidiaries have subsidiaries of their own, thus providing the parent with indirect ownership of the subsidiary's subsidiaries.

Required

International Lease Finance Corporation is a very large leasing company. It leases equipment that everyone is familiar with and many have used.

(1) Specifically, what is the principal business of International Lease Finance Corporation?

(2) Who are the direct owners of International Lease?

(3) In what city is International Lease headquartered?

(4) In what state is International Lease incorporated?

(5) Where is International Lease's common stock traded?

(6) What company is the parent in the consolidated financial statements in which International Lease is included, and what is that company's principal business?

EXERCISES

LO 4-1

E4-1 Cost versus Equity Reporting

Roller Corporation purchased 100 percent ownership of Steam Company on January 1, 20X5, for $270,000. On that date, the book value of Steam's reported net assets was $200,000. The excess over book value paid is attributable to depreciable assets with a remaining useful life of 10 years. Net income and dividend payments of Steam in the following periods were

Year	Net Income	Dividends
20X5	$20,000	$ 5,000
20X6	40,000	15,000
20X7	20,000	35,000

Required

Prepare journal entries on Roller Corporation's books relating to its investment in Steam Company for each of the three years, assuming it accounts for the investment using (*a*) the cost method and (*b*) the equity method.

LO 4-1

E4-2 Differential Assigned to Patents

Power Corporation purchased 100 percent of the common stock of Snow Corporation on January 1, 20X2, by issuing 45,000 shares of its $6 par value common stock. The market price of Power's shares at the date of issue was $24. Snow reported net assets with a book value of $980,000 on that date. The amount paid in excess of the book value of Snow's net assets was attributed to the increased value of patents held by Snow with a remaining useful life of eight years. Snow reported net income of $56,000 and paid dividends of $20,000 in 20X2 and reported a net loss of $44,000 and paid dividends of $10,000 in 20X3.

Required

Assuming that Power Corporation uses the equity method in accounting for its investment in Snow Corporation, prepare all journal entries for Power for 20X2 and 20X3.

LO 4-1

E4-3 Differential Assigned to Copyrights

Best Corporation acquired 100 percent of the voting common stock of Flair Company on January 1, 20X7, by issuing bonds with a par value and fair value of $670,000 and making a cash payment of $24,000. At the date of acquisition, Flair reported assets of $740,000 and liabilities of $140,000. The book values and fair values of Flair's net assets were equal except for land and copyrights. Flair's land had a fair value $16,000 higher than its book value. All of the remaining purchase price was attributable to the increased value of Flair's copyrights with a remaining useful life of eight years. Flair Company reported a loss of $88,000 in 20X7 and net income of $120,000 in 20X8. Flair paid dividends of $24,000 each year.

Required

Assuming that Best Corporation uses the equity method in accounting for its investment in Flair Company, prepare all journal entries for Best for 20X7 and 20X8.

LO 4-1

Advanced StudyGuide .com

E4-4 Differential Attributable to Depreciable Assets

Capital Corporation purchased 100 percent of Cook Company's stock on January 1, 20X4, for $340,000. On that date, Cook reported net assets with a historical cost of $300,000 and a fair value of $340,000. The difference was due to the increased value of buildings with a remaining life of 10 years. During 20X4 and 20X5 Cook reported net income of $10,000 and $20,000 and paid dividends of $6,000 and $9,000, respectively.

Required

Assuming that Capital Corporation uses (*a*) the equity method and (*b*) the cost method in accounting for its ownership of Cook Company, give the journal entries that Capital recorded in 20X4 and 20X5.

LO 4-1

E4-5 Investment Income

Brindle Company purchased 100 percent of Monroe Company's voting common stock for $648,000 on January 1, 20X4. At that date, Monroe reported assets of $690,000 and liabilities of $230,000. The book values and fair values of Monroe's assets were equal except for land, which had a fair value $108,000 more than book value, and equipment, which had a fair value $80,000 more than book value. The remaining economic life of all depreciable assets at January 1, 20X4, was five years. Monroe reported net income of $68,000 and paid dividends of $34,000 in 20X4.

Required

Compute the amount of investment income to be reported by Brindle for 20X4.

LO 4-1

E4-6 Determination of Purchase Price

Branch Corporation purchased 100 percent of Hardy Company's common stock on January 1, 20X5, and paid $28,000 above book value. The full amount of the additional payment was attributed to amortizable assets with a life of eight years remaining at January 1, 20X5. During 20X5 and 20X6, Hardy reported net income of $33,000 and $6,000 and paid dividends of $15,000 and $12,000, respectively. Branch uses the equity method in accounting for its investment in Hardy and reported a balance in its investment account of $161,000 on December 31, 20X6.

Required

Compute the amount paid by Branch to purchase Hardy shares.

LO 4-1, 4-2

E4-7 Correction of Error

During review of the adjusting entries to be recorded on December 31, 20X8, Grand Corporation discovered that it had inappropriately been using the cost method in accounting for its investment in Case Products Corporation. Grand purchased 100 percent ownership of Case Products on January 1, 20X6, for $56,000, at which time Case Products reported retained earnings of $10,000 and capital stock outstanding of $30,000. The differential was attributable to patents with a life of eight years. Income and dividends of Case Products were:

Year	Net Income	Dividends
20X6	$16,000	$6,000
20X7	24,000	8,000
20X8	32,000	8,000

Required

Give the correcting entry required on December 31, 20X8, to properly report the investment under the equity method, assuming the books have not been closed. Case Products' dividends were declared in early November and paid in early December each year.

LO 4-1

E4-8 Differential Assigned to Land and Equipment

Rod Corporation purchased 100 percent ownership of Stafford Corporation on January 1, 20X4, for $65,000, which was $10,000 above the underlying book value. Half the additional amount was attributable to an increase in the value of land held by Stafford, and half was due to an increase in the value of equipment. The equipment had a remaining economic life of five years on January 1, 20X4. During 20X4, Stafford reported net income of $12,000 and paid dividends of $4,500.

Required

Give the journal entries that Rod Corporation recorded during 20X4 related to its investment in Stafford Corporation, assuming Rod uses the equity method in accounting for its investment.

LO 4-1, 4-2

E4-9 Equity Entries with Goodwill

Turner Corporation reported the following balances at January 1, 20X9:

Advanced StudyGuide .com

Item	Book Value	Fair Value
Cash	$ 45,000	$ 45,000
Accounts Receivable	60,000	60,000
Inventory	120,000	130,000
Buildings & Equipment	300,000	240,000
Less: Accumulated Depreciation	(150,000)	
Total Assets	$375,000	$475,000
Accounts Payable	$ 75,000	$ 75,000
Common Stock ($10 par value)	100,000	
Additional Paid-In Capital	30,000	
Retained Earnings	170,000	
Total Liabilities & Equities	$375,000	

On January 1, 20X9, Gross Corporation purchased 100 percent of Turner's stock. All tangible assets had a remaining economic life of 10 years at January 1, 20X9. Both companies use the FIFO inventory method. Turner reported net income of $16,000 in 20X9 and paid dividends of $3,200. Gross uses the equity method in accounting for its investment in Turner.

Required

Give all journal entries that Gross recorded during 20X9 with respect to its investment assuming Gross paid $437,500 for the ownership of Turner on January 1, 20X9. The amount of the differential assigned to goodwill is not impaired.

LO 4-1, 4-2, 4-6

E4-10 Multiple-Choice Questions on Consolidation Process

Select the most appropriate answer for each of the following questions.

1. Goodwill is

   a. Seldom reported because it is too difficult to measure.

   b. Reported when more than book value is paid in purchasing another company.

   c. Reported when the fair value of the acquiree is higher than the fair value of the net identifiable assets acquired.

   d. Generally smaller for small companies and increases in amount as the companies acquired increase in size.

2. [AICPA Adapted] Wright Corporation includes several subsidiaries in its consolidated financial statements. In its December 31, 20X2, trial balance, Wright had the following intercompany balances before consolidation entries:

	Debit	Credit
Current receivable due from Main Company	$ 32,000	
Noncurrent receivable from Main Company	114,000	
Cash advance to Corn Corporation	6,000	
Cash advance from King Company		$ 15,000
Intercompany payable to King Company		101,000

   In its December 31, 20X2, consolidated balance sheet, what amount should Wright report as intercompany receivables?

   a. $152,000.

   b. $146,000.

   c. $36,000.

   d. $0.

3. Beni Corporation acquired 100 percent of Carr Corporation's outstanding capital stock for $430,000 cash. Immediately before the purchase, the balance sheets of both corporations reported the following:

	Beni	Carr
Assets	$2,000,000	$750,000
Liabilities	$ 750,000	$400,000
Common Stock	1,000,000	310,000
Retained Earnings	250,000	40,000
Liabilities & Stockholders' Equity	$2,000,000	$750,000

At the date of purchase, the fair value of Carr's assets was $50,000 more than the aggregate carrying amounts. In the consolidated balance sheet prepared immediately after the purchase, the consolidated stockholders' equity should amount to

a. $1,680,000.
b. $1,650,000.
c. $1,600,000.
d. $1,250,000.

Note: Questions 4 and 5 are based on the following information:
Nugget Company's balance sheet on December 31, 20X6, was as follows:

Assets		Liabilities & Stockholders' Equity	
Cash	$ 100,000	Current Liabilities	$ 300,000
Accounts Receivable	200,000	Long-Term Debt	500,000
Inventories	500,000	Common Stock (par $1 per share)	100,000
Property, Plant & Equipment (net)	900,000	Additional Paid-In Capital	200,000
		Retained Earnings	600,000
Total Assets	$1,700,000	Total Liabilities & Stockholders' Equity	$1,700,000

On December 31, 20X6, Gold Company acquired all of Nugget's outstanding common stock for $1,500,000 cash. On that date, the fair (market) value of Nugget's inventories was $450,000, and the fair value of Nugget's property, plant, and equipment was $1,000,000. The fair values of all other assets and liabilities of Nugget were equal to their book values.

4. As a result of Gold's acquisition of Nugget, the consolidated balance sheet of Gold and Nugget should reflect goodwill in the amount of

a. $500,000.
b. $550,000.
c. $600,000.
d. $650,000.

5. Assuming Gold uses the equity method to account for investments and that Gold's (unconsolidated) balance sheet on December 31, 20X6, reflected retained earnings of $2,000,000, what amount of retained earnings should be shown in the December 31, 20X6, consolidated balance sheet of Gold and its new subsidiary, Nugget?

a. $2,000,000.
b. $2,600,000.
c. $2,800,000.
d. $3,150,000.

LO 4-3, 4-6

E4-11 Multiple-Choice Questions on Consolidation [AICPA Adapted]
Select the correct answer for each of the following questions.

1. On January 1, 20X1, Prim Inc. acquired all of Scrap Inc.'s outstanding common shares for cash equal to the stock's book value. The carrying amounts of Scrap's assets and liabilities approximated their fair values, except that the carrying amount of its building was more than fair value. In preparing Prim's 20X1 consolidated income statement, which of the following adjustments would be made?
   a. Decrease depreciation expense and recognize goodwill amortization.
   b. Increase depreciation expense and recognize goodwill amortization.
   c. Decrease depreciation expense and recognize no goodwill amortization.
   d. Increase depreciation expense and recognize no goodwill amortization.
2. The first examination of Rudd Corporation's financial statements was made for the year ended December 31, 20X8. The auditor found that Rudd had acquired another company on January 1, 20X8, and had recorded goodwill of $100,000 in connection with this acquisition. Although a friend of the auditor believes the goodwill will last no more than five years, Rudd's management has found no impairment of goodwill during 20X8. In its 20X8 financial statements, Rudd should report

	Amortization Expense	Goodwill
a.	$ 0	$100,000
b.	$100,000	$ 0
c.	$ 20,000	$ 80,000
d.	$ 0	$ 0

3. Consolidated financial statements are being prepared for a parent and its four wholly owned subsidiaries that have intercompany loans of $100,000 and intercompany profits of $300,000. How much of these intercompany loans and profits should be eliminated?

	Intercompany	
	Loans	Profits
a.	$ 0	$ 0
b.	$ 0	$300,000
c.	$100,000	$ 0
d.	$100,000	$300,000

4. On April 1, 20X8, Plum Inc. paid $1,700,000 for all of Long Corp.'s issued and outstanding common stock. On that date, the costs and fair values of Long's recorded assets and liabilities were as follows:

	Cost	Fair Value
Cash	$ 160,000	$ 160,000
Inventory	480,000	460,000
Property, plant & equipment (net)	980,000	1,040,000
Liabilities	(360,000)	(360,000)
Net assets	$1,260,000	$1,300,000

In Plum's March 31, 20X9, consolidated balance sheet, what amount of goodwill should be reported as a result of this business combination?
a. $360,000.
b. $396,000.
c. $400,000.
d. $440,000.

LO 4-3

Advanced StudyGuide .com

E4-12 Consolidation Entries with Differential

On June 10, 20X8, Tower Corporation acquired 100 percent of Brown Company's common stock. Summarized balance sheet data for the two companies immediately after the stock acquisition are as follows:

	Tower Corp.	Brown Company	
Item		**Book Value**	**Fair Value**
Cash	$ 15,000	$ 5,000	$ 5,000
Accounts Receivable	30,000	10,000	10,000
Inventory	80,000	20,000	25,000
Buildings & Equipment (net)	120,000	50,000	70,000
Investment in Brown Stock	100,000		
Total	$345,000	$85,000	$110,000
Accounts Payable	$ 25,000	$ 3,000	$ 3,000
Bonds Payable	150,000	25,000	25,000
Common Stock	55,000	20,000	
Retained Earnings	115,000	37,000	
Total	$345,000	$85,000	$ 28,000

Required

a. Give the consolidation entries required to prepare a consolidated balance sheet immediately after the acquisition of Brown Company shares.

b. Explain how consolidation entries differ from other types of journal entries recorded in the normal course of business.

LO 4-5

E4-13 Balance Sheet Consolidation

Reed Corporation acquired 100 percent of Thorne Corporation's voting common stock on December 31, 20X4, for $395,000. At the date of combination, Thorne reported the following:

Cash	$120,000	Current Liabilities	$ 80,000
Inventory	100,000	Long-Term Liabilities	200,000
Buildings (net)	420,000	Common Stock	120,000
		Retained Earnings	240,000
Total	$640,000	Total	$640,000

At December 31, 20X4, the book values of Thorne's net assets and liabilities approximated their fair values, except for buildings, which had a fair value of $20,000 less than book value, and inventories, which had a fair value $36,000 more than book value.

Required

Reed Corporation wishes to prepare a consolidated balance sheet immediately following the business combination. Give the consolidation entry or entries needed to prepare a consolidated balance sheet at December 31, 20X4.

LO 4-2, 4-3

E4-14 Acquisition with Differential

Road Corporation acquired all of Conger Corporation's voting shares on January 1, 20X2, for $470,000. At that time Conger reported common stock outstanding of $80,000 and retained earnings of $130,000. The book values of Conger's assets and liabilities approximated fair values, except for land, which had a book value of $80,000 and a fair value of $100,000, and buildings, which had a book value of $220,000 and a fair value of $400,000. Land and buildings are the only noncurrent assets that Conger holds.

Required

a. Compute the amount of goodwill at the date of acquisition.

b. Give the consolidation entry or entries required immediately following the acquisition to prepare a consolidated balance sheet.

LO 4-5

E4-15 Balance Sheet Worksheet with Differential

Blank Corporation acquired 100 percent of Faith Corporation's common stock on December 31, 20X2, for $189,000. Data from the balance sheets of the two companies included the following amounts as of the date of acquisition:

Item	Blank Corporation	Faith Corporation
Cash	$ 26,000	$ 18,000
Accounts Receivable	87,000	37,000
Inventory	110,000	60,000
Buildings & Equipment (net)	220,000	150,000
Investment in Faith Corporation Stock	189,000	
Total Assets	$632,000	$265,000
Accounts Payable	$ 92,000	$ 35,000
Notes Payable	150,000	80,000
Common Stock	100,000	60,000
Retained Earnings	290,000	90,000
Total Liabilities & Stockholders' Equity	$632,000	$265,000

At the date of the business combination, Faith's net assets and liabilities approximated fair value except for inventory, which had a fair value of $84,000, and buildings and equipment (net), which had a fair value of $165,000.

Required

a. Give the consolidation entry or entries needed to prepare a consolidated balance sheet immediately following the business combination.

b. Prepare a consolidation balance sheet worksheet.

LO 4-5

E4-16 Worksheet for Wholly Owned Subsidiary

Gold Enterprises acquired 100 percent of Premium Builders' stock on December 31, 20X4. Balance sheet data for Gold and Premium on January 1, 20X5, are as follows:

	Gold Enterprises	Premium Builders
Cash & Receivables	$ 80,000	$ 30,000
Inventory	150,000	350,000
Buildings & Equipment (net)	430,000	80,000
Investment in Premium Stock	167,000	
Total Assets	$827,000	$460,000
Current Liabilities	$100,000	$110,000
Long-Term Debt	400,000	200,000
Common Stock	200,000	140,000
Retained Earnings	127,000	10,000
Total Liabilities & Stockholders' Equity	$827,000	$460,000

At the date of the business combination, Premium's cash and receivables had a fair value of $28,000, inventory had a fair value of $357,000, and buildings and equipment had a fair value of $92,000.

Required

a. Give all consolidation entries needed to prepare a consolidated balance sheet on January 1, 20X5.

b. Complete a consolidated balance sheet worksheet.

c. Prepare a consolidated balance sheet in good form.

LO 4-3, 4-5

E4-17 Computation of Consolidated Balances

Astor Corporation's balance sheet at January 1, 20X7, reflected the following balances:

Cash & Receivables	$ 80,000	Accounts Payable	$ 40,000
Inventory	120,000	Income Taxes Payable	60,000
Land	70,000	Bonds Payable	200,000
Buildings & Equipment (net)	480,000	Common Stock	250,000
		Retained Earnings	200,000
Total Assets	$750,000	Total Liabilities & Stockholders' Equity	$750,000

Phel Corporation, which had just entered into an active acquisition program, acquired 100 percent of Astor's common stock on January 2, 20X7, for $576,000. A careful review of the fair value of Astor's assets and liabilities indicated the following:

	Book Value	Fair Value
Inventory	$120,000	$140,000
Land	70,000	60,000
Buildings & Equipment (net)	480,000	550,000

Assume the book values of Phel's Inventory, Land, and Buildings and Equipment accounts are $300,000, $85,000, and $1,200,000, respectively.

Required

Compute the appropriate amount to be included in the consolidated balance sheet immediately following the acquisition for each of the following items:

a. Inventory.
b. Land.
c. Buildings and Equipment (net).
d. Goodwill.
e. Investment in Astor Corporation.

LO 4-3

E4-18 Multiple-Choice Questions on Balance Sheet Consolidation

Top Corporation acquired 100 percent of Sun Corporation's common stock on December 31, 20X2. Balance sheet data for the two companies immediately following the acquisition follow:

Item	Top Corporation	Sun Corporation
Cash	$ 49,000	$ 30,000
Accounts Receivable	110,000	45,000
Inventory	130,000	70,000
Land	80,000	25,000
Buildings & Equipment	500,000	400,000
Less: Accumulated Depreciation	(223,000)	(165,000)
Investment in Sun Corporation Stock	198,000	
Total Assets	$844,000	$405,000
Accounts Payable	$ 61,500	$ 28,000
Taxes Payable	95,000	37,000
Bonds Payable	280,000	200,000
Common Stock	150,000	50,000
Retained Earnings	257,500	90,000
Total Liabilities & Stockholders' Equity	$844,000	$405,000

At the date of the business combination, the book values of Sun's net assets and liabilities approximated fair value except for inventory, which had a fair value of $85,000, and land, which had a fair value of $45,000.

Required

For each question, indicate the appropriate total that should appear in the consolidated balance sheet prepared immediately after the business combination.

1. What amount of inventory will be reported?
   a. $70,000.
   b. $130,000.
   c. $200,000.
   d. $215,000.
2. What amount of goodwill will be reported?
   a. $0.
   b. $23,000.
   c. $43,000.
   d. $58,000.
3. What amount of total assets will be reported?
   a. $84,400.
   b. $1,051,000.
   c. $1,109,000.
   d. $1,249,000.
4. What amount of total liabilities will be reported?
   a. $265,000.
   b. $436,500.
   c. $701,500.
   d. $1,249,000.
5. What amount of consolidated retained earnings will be reported?
   a. $547,500.
   b. $397,500.
   c. $347,500.
   d. $257,500.
6. What amount of total stockholders' equity will be reported?
   a. $407,500.
   b. $547,500.
   c. $844,000.
   d. $1,249,000.

LO 4-3

E4-19 Wholly Owned Subsidiary with Differential

Canton Corporation is a wholly owned subsidiary of Winston Corporation. Winston acquired ownership of Canton on January 1, 20X3, for $28,000 above Canton's reported net assets. At that date, Canton reported common stock outstanding of $60,000 and retained earnings of $90,000. The differential is assigned to equipment with an economic life of seven years at the date of the business combination. Canton reported net income of $30,000 and paid dividends of $12,000 in 20X3.

Required

a. Give the journal entries recorded by Winston Corporation during 20X3 on its books if Winston accounts for its investment in Canton using the equity method.

b. Give the consolidation entries needed at December 31, 20X3, to prepare consolidated financial statements.

LO 4-5

E4-20 Basic Consolidation Worksheet

Blake Corporation acquired 100 percent of Shaw Corporation's voting shares on January 1, 20X3, at underlying book value. At that date, the book values and fair values of Shaw's assets and liabilities were equal. Blake uses the equity method in accounting for its investment in Shaw. Adjusted trial balances for Blake and Shaw on December 31, 20X3, are as follows:

	Blake Corporation		Shaw Corporation	
Item	**Debit**	**Credit**	**Debit**	**Credit**
Current Assets	$145,000		$105,000	
Depreciable Assets (net)	325,000		225,000	
Investment in Shaw Corporation Stock	170,000			
Depreciation Expense	25,000		15,000	
Other Expenses	105,000		75,000	
Dividends Declared	40,000		10,000	
Current Liabilities		$ 50,000		$ 40,000
Long-Term Debt		100,000		120,000
Common Stock		200,000		100,000
Retained Earnings		230,000		50,000
Sales		200,000		120,000
Income from Subsidiary		30,000		
	$810,000	$810,000	$430,000	$430,000

Required

a. Give all consolidation entries required on December 31, 20X3, to prepare consolidated financial statements.

b. Prepare a three-part consolidation worksheet as of December 31, 20X3.

LO 4-5

E4-21 Basic Consolidation Worksheet for Second Year

Blake Corporation acquired 100 percent of Shaw Corporation's voting shares on January 1, 20X3, at underlying book value. At that date, the book values and fair values of Shaw's assets and liabilities were equal. Blake uses the equity method in accounting for its investment in Shaw. Adjusted trial balances for Blake and Shaw on December 31, 20X4, are as follows:

	Blake Corporation		Shaw Corporation	
Item	**Debit**	**Credit**	**Debit**	**Credit**
Current Assets	$210,000		$150,000	
Depreciable Assets (net)	300,000		210,000	
Investment in Shaw Corporation Stock	190,000			
Depreciation Expense	25,000		15,000	
Other Expenses	150,000		90,000	
Dividends Declared	50,000		15,000	
Current Liabilities		$ 70,000		$ 50,000
Long-Term Debt		100,000		120,000
Common Stock		200,000		100,000
Retained Earnings		290,000		70,000
Sales		230,000		140,000
Income from Subsidiary		35,000		
	$925,000	$925,000	$480,000	$480,000

Required

a. Give all consolidation entries required on December 31, 20X4, to prepare consolidated financial statements.

b. Prepare a three-part consolidation worksheet as of December 31, 20X4.

LO 4-5

E4-22 Consolidation Worksheet with Differential

Kennelly Corporation acquired all of Short Company's common shares on January 1, 20X5, for $180,000. On that date, the book value of the net assets reported by Short was $150,000. The entire differential was assigned to depreciable assets with a six-year remaining economic life from January 1, 20X5.

The adjusted trial balances for the two companies on December 31, 20X5, are as follows:

	Kennelly Corporation		Short Company	
Item	**Debit**	**Credit**	**Debit**	**Credit**
Cash	$ 15,000		$ 5,000	
Accounts Receivable	30,000		40,000	
Inventory	70,000		60,000	
Depreciable Assets (net)	325,000		225,000	
Investment in Short Company Stock	195,000			
Depreciation Expense	25,000		15,000	
Other Expenses	105,000		75,000	
Dividends Declared	40,000		10,000	
Accounts Payable		$ 50,000		$ 40,000
Notes Payable		100,000		120,000
Common Stock		200,000		100,000
Retained Earnings		230,000		50,000
Sales		200,000		120,000
Income from Subsidiary		25,000		
	$805,000	$805,000	$430,000	$430,000

Kennelly uses the equity method in accounting for its investment in Short. Short declared and paid dividends on December 31, 20X5.

Required

a. Prepare the consolidation entries needed as of December 31, 20X5, to complete a consolidation worksheet.

b. Prepare a three-part consolidation worksheet as of December 31, 20X5.

LO 4-5

E4-23 Consolidation Worksheet for Subsidiary

Land Corporation acquired 100 percent of Growth Company's voting stock on January 1, 20X4, at underlying book value. Land uses the equity method in accounting for its ownership of Growth. On December 31, 20X4, the trial balances of the two companies are as follows:

	Land Corporation		Growth Company	
Item	**Debit**	**Credit**	**Debit**	**Credit**
Current Assets	$ 238,000		$150,000	
Depreciable Assets	500,000		300,000	
Investment in Growth Company Stock	190,000			
Depreciation Expense	25,000		15,000	
Other Expenses	150,000		90,000	
Dividends Declared	50,000		15,000	
Accumulated Depreciation		$ 200,000		$ 90,000
Current Liabilities		70,000		50,000
Long-Term Debt		100,000		120,000
Common Stock		200,000		100,000
Retained Earnings		318,000		70,000
Sales		230,000		140,000
Income from Subsidiary		35,000		
	$1,153,000	$1,153,000	$570,000	$570,000

Required

a. Give all consolidation entries required on December 31, 20X4, to prepare consolidated financial statements.

b. Prepare a three-part consolidation worksheet as of December 31, 20X4.

LO 4-7

E4-24A Push-Down Accounting

Jefferson Company acquired all of Louis Corporation's common shares on January 2, 20X3, for $789,000. At the date of combination, Louis's balance sheet appeared as follows:

Assets		Liabilities	
Cash & Receivables	$ 34,000	Current Payables	$ 25,000
Inventory	165,000	Notes Payable	100,000
Land	60,000	Stockholders' Equity	
Buildings (net)	250,000	Common Stock	200,000
Equipment (net)	320,000	Additional Capital	425,000
		Retained Earnings	79,000
Total	$829,000	Total	$829,000

The fair values of all of Louis's assets and liabilities were equal to their book values except for its fixed assets. Louis's land had a fair value of $75,000; the buildings, a fair value of $300,000; and the equipment, a fair value of $340,000.

Jefferson Company decided to employ push-down accounting for the acquisition of Louis Corporation. Subsequent to the combination, Louis continued to operate as a separate company.

Required

a. Record the acquisition of Louis's stock on Jefferson's books.

b. Present any entries that would be made on Louis's books related to the business combination, assuming push-down accounting is used.

c. Present, in general journal form, all consolidation entries that would appear in a consolidation worksheet for Jefferson and its subsidiary prepared immediately following the combination.

PROBLEMS

LO 4-5

P4-25 Assignment of Differential in Worksheet

Teresa Corporation acquired all the voting shares of Sally Enterprises on January 1, 20X4. Balance sheet amounts for the companies on the date of acquisition were as follows:

	Teresa Corporation	Sally Enterprises
Cash & Receivables	$ 40,000	$ 20,000
Inventory	95,000	40,000
Land	80,000	90,000
Buildings & Equipment	400,000	230,000
Investment in Sally Enterprises	290,000	
Total Debits	$905,000	$380,000
Accumulated Depreciation	$175,000	$ 65,000
Accounts Payable	60,000	15,000
Notes Payable	100,000	50,000
Common Stock	300,000	100,000
Retained Earnings	270,000	150,000
Total Credits	$905,000	$380,000

Sally Enterprises' buildings and equipment were estimated to have a market value of $175,000 on January 1, 20X4. All other items appeared to have market values approximating current book values.

Required

a. Complete a consolidated balance sheet worksheet for January 1, 20X4.

b. Prepare a consolidated balance sheet in good form.

LO 4-3

P4-26 Computation of Consolidated Balances

Retail Records Inc. acquired all of Decibel Studios' voting shares on January 1, 20X2, for $280,000. Retail's balance sheet immediately after the combination contained the following balances:

RETAIL RECORDS INC.
Balance Sheet
January 1, 20X2

Cash & Receivables	$120,000	Accounts Payable	$ 75,000
Inventory	110,000	Taxes Payable	50,000
Land	70,000	Notes Payable	300,000
Buildings & Equipment (net)	350,000	Common Stock	400,000
Investment in Decibel Stock	280,000	Retained Earnings	105,000
Total Assets	$930,000	Total Liabilities & Stockholders' Equity	$930,000

Decibel's balance sheet at acquisition contained the following balances:

DECIBEL STUDIOS
Balance Sheet
January 1, 20X2

Cash & Receivables	$ 40,000	Accounts Payable	$ 90,000
Inventory	180,000	Notes Payable	250,000
Buildings & Equipment (net)	350,000	Common Stock	100,000
Goodwill	30,000	Additional Paid-In Capital	200,000
		Retained Earnings	(40,000)
Total Assets	$600,000	Total Liabilities & Stockholders' Equity	$600,000

On the date of combination, the inventory held by Decibel had a fair value of $170,000, and its buildings and recording equipment had a fair value of $375,000. Goodwill reported by Decibel resulted from a purchase of Sound Stage Enterprises in 20X1. Sound Stage was liquidated and its assets and liabilities were brought onto Decibel's books.

Required

Compute the balances to be reported in the consolidated balance sheet immediately after the acquisition for:

a. Inventory.

b. Buildings and Equipment (net).

c. Investment in Decibel Stock.

d. Goodwill.

e. Common Stock.

f. Retained Earnings.

LO 4-5

P4-27 Balance Sheet Consolidation [AICPA Adapted]

Case Inc. acquired all Frey Inc.'s outstanding $25 par common stock on December 31, 20X3, in exchange for 40,000 shares of its $25 par common stock. Case's common stock closed at

$56.50 per share on a national stock exchange on December 31, 20X3. Both corporations continued to operate as separate businesses maintaining separate accounting records with years ending December 31.

On December 31, 20X4, after year-end adjustments and the closing of nominal accounts, the companies had condensed balance sheet accounts (below).

Additional Information

1. Case uses the equity method of accounting for its investment in Frey.
2. On December 31, 20X3, Frey's assets and liabilities had fair values equal to the book balances with the exception of land, which had a fair value of $550,000. Frey had no land transactions in 20X4.
3. On June 15, 20X4, Frey paid a cash dividend of $4 per share on its common stock.
4. On December 10, 20X4, Case paid a cash dividend totaling $256,000 on its common stock.
5. On December 31, 20X3, immediately before the combination, the stockholders' equity balance was:

	Case Inc.	Frey Inc.
Common Stock	$2,200,000	$1,000,000
Additional Paid-In Capital	1,660,000	190,000
Retained Earnings	3,166,000	820,000
	$7,026,000	$2,010,000

6. The 20X4 net income amounts according to the separate books of Case and Frey were $890,000 (exclusive of equity in Frey's earnings) and $580,000, respectively.

	Case Inc.	Frey Inc.
Assets		
Cash	$ 825,000	$ 330,000
Accounts & Other Receivables	2,140,000	835,000
Inventories	2,310,000	1,045,000
Land	650,000	300,000
Depreciable Assets (net)	4,575,000	1,980,000
Investment in Frey Inc.	2,680,000	
Long-Term Investments & Other Assets	865,000	385,000
Total Assets	$14,045,000	$4,875,000
Liabilities & Stockholders' Equity		
Accounts Payable & Other Current Liabilities	$ 2,465,000	$1,145,000
Long-Term Debt	1,900,000	1,300,000
Common Stock, $25 Par Value	3,200,000	1,000,000
Additional Paid-In Capital	2,100,000	190,000
Retained Earnings	4,380,000	1,240,000
Total Liabilities & Stockholders' Equity	$14,045,000	$4,875,000

Required

Prepare a consolidated balance sheet worksheet for Case and its subsidiary, Frey, for December 31, 20X4. A formal consolidated balance sheet is not required.

LO 4-5

P4-28 Consolidated Balance Sheet

Thompson Company spent $240,000 to acquire all of Lake Corporation's stock on January 1, 20X2. The balance sheets of the two companies on December 31, 20X3, showed the following amounts:

	Thompson Company	Lake Corporation
Cash	$ 30,000	$ 20,000
Accounts Receivable	100,000	40,000
Land	60,000	50,000
Buildings & Equipment	500,000	350,000
Less: Accumulated Depreciation	(230,000)	(75,000)
Investment in Lake Corporation	252,000	
	$712,000	$385,000
Accounts Payable	$ 80,000	$ 10,000
Taxes Payable	40,000	70,000
Notes Payable	100,000	85,000
Common Stock	200,000	100,000
Retained Earnings	292,000	120,000
	$712,000	$385,000

Lake reported retained earnings of $100,000 at the date of acquisition. The difference between the acquisition price and underlying book value is assigned to buildings and equipment with a remaining economic life of 10 years from the date of acquisition. Assume Lake's accumulated depreciation on the acquisition date was $25,000.

Required

a. Give the appropriate consolidation entry or entries needed to prepare a consolidated balance sheet as of December 31, 20X3.

b. Prepare a consolidated balance sheet worksheet as of December 31, 20X3.

LO 4-5, 4-6

P4-29 Comprehensive Problem: Consolidation in Subsequent Period

Thompson Company spent $240,000 to acquire all of Lake Corporation's stock on January 1, 20X2. On December 31, 20X4, the trial balances of the two companies were as follows:

	Thompson Company		Lake Corporation	
Item	**Debit**	**Credit**	**Debit**	**Credit**
Cash	$ 74,000		$ 42,000	
Accounts Receivable	130,000		53,000	
Land	60,000		50,000	
Buildings & Equipment	500,000		350,000	
Investment in Lake Corporation Stock	268,000			
Cost of Services Provided	470,000		130,000	
Depreciation Expense	35,000		18,000	
Other Expenses	57,000		60,000	
Dividends Declared	30,000		12,000	
Accumulated Depreciation		$ 265,000		$ 93,000
Accounts Payable		71,000		17,000
Taxes Payable		58,000		60,000
Notes Payable		100,000		85,000
Common Stock		200,000		100,000
Retained Earnings		292,000		120,000
Service Revenue		610,000		240,000
Income from Subsidiary		28,000		
	$1,624,000	$1,624,000	$715,000	$715,000

Lake Corporation reported retained earnings of $100,000 at the date of acquisition. The difference between the acquisition price and underlying book value is assigned to buildings and equipment with a remaining economic life of 10 years from the date of acquisition. Lake's accumulated depreciation on the acquisition date was $25,000. At December 31, 20X4, Lake owed Thompson $2,500.

Required

a. Give all journal entries recorded by Thompson with regard to its investment in Lake during 20X4.

b. Give all consolidation entries required on December 31, 20X4, to prepare consolidated financial statements.

c. Prepare a three-part consolidation worksheet as of December 31, 20X4.

LO 4-3, 4-4

P4-30 Acquisition at Other than Fair Value of Net Assets

Mason Corporation acquired 100 percent ownership of Best Company on February 12, 20X9. At the date of acquisition, Best Company reported assets and liabilities with book values of $420,000 and $165,000, respectively, common stock outstanding of $80,000, and retained earnings of $175,000. The book values and fair values of Best's assets and liabilities were identical except for land, which had increased in value by $20,000, and inventories, which had decreased by $7,000.

Required

Give the consolidation entries required to prepare a consolidated balance sheet immediately after the business combination assuming Mason acquired its ownership of Best for:

a. $280,000.

b. $251,000.

LO 4-5, 4-6

P4-31 Intercorporate Receivables and Payables

Kim Corporation acquired 100 percent of Normal Company's outstanding shares on January 1, 20X7. Balance sheet data for the two companies immediately after the purchase follow:

	Kim Corporation	Normal Company
Cash	$ 70,000	$ 35,000
Accounts Receivable	90,000	65,000
Inventory	84,000	80,000
Buildings & Equipment	400,000	300,000
Less: Accumulated Depreciation	(160,000)	(75,000)
Investment in Normal Company Stock	305,000	
Investment in Normal Company Bonds	50,000	
Total Assets	$839,000	$405,000
Accounts Payable	$ 50,000	$ 20,000
Bonds Payable	200,000	100,000
Common Stock	300,000	150,000
Capital in Excess of Par		140,000
Retained Earnings	289,000	(5,000)
Total Liabilities & Equities	$839,000	$405,000

As indicated in the parent company balance sheet, Kim purchased $50,000 of Normal's bonds from the subsidiary at par value immediately after it acquired the stock. An analysis of intercompany receivables and payables also indicates that the subsidiary owes the parent $10,000. On the date of combination, the book values and fair values of Normal's assets and liabilities were the same.

Required

a. Give all consolidation entries needed to prepare a consolidated balance sheet for January 1, 20X7.

b. Complete a consolidated balance sheet worksheet.

c. Prepare a consolidated balance sheet in good form.

LO 4-5

P4-32 Balance Sheet Consolidation

On January 2, 20X8, Primary Corporation acquired 100 percent of Street Company's outstanding common stock. In exchange for Street's stock, Primary issued bonds payable with a par and fair value of $650,000 directly to the selling stockholders of Street. The two companies continued to operate as separate entities subsequent to combination.

Immediately prior to the combination, the book values and fair values of the companies' assets and liabilities were as follows:

	Primary Corporation		Street Company	
	Book Value	**Fair Value**	**Book Value**	**Fair Value**
Cash	$ 12,000	$ 12,000	$ 9,000	$ 9,000
Receivables	41,000	39,000	31,000	30,000
Allowance for Bad Debts	(2,000)		(1,000)	
Inventory	86,000	89,000	68,000	72,000
Land	55,000	200,000	50,000	70,000
Buildings & Equipment	960,000	650,000	670,000	500,000
Accumulated Depreciation	(411,000)		(220,000)	
Patent				40,000
Total Assets	$741,000	$990,000	$607,000	$721,000
Current Payables	$ 38,000	$ 38,000	$ 29,000	$ 29,000
Bonds Payable	200,000	210,000	100,000	90,000
Common Stock	300,000		200,000	
Additional Paid-In Capital	100,000		130,000	
Retained Earnings	103,000		148,000	
Total Liabilities & Equity	$741,000		$607,000	

At the date of combination, Street owed Primary $6,000 plus accrued interest of $500 on a short-term note. Both companies have properly recorded these amounts.

Required

a. Record the business combination on the books of Primary Corporation.

b. Present in general journal form all consolidation entries needed in a worksheet to prepare a consolidated balance sheet immediately following the business combination on January 2, 20X8.

c. Prepare and complete a consolidated balance sheet worksheet as of January 2, 20X8, immediately following the business combination.

d. Present a consolidated balance sheet for Primary and its subsidiary as of January 2, 20X8.

LO 4-5

Advanced StudyGuide .com

P4-33 Consolidation Worksheet at End of First Year of Ownership

Mill Corporation acquired 100 percent ownership of Roller Company on January 1, 20X8, for $128,000. At that date, the fair value of Roller's buildings and equipment was $20,000 more than the book value. Buildings and equipment are depreciated on a 10-year basis. Although goodwill is not amortized, Mill's management concluded at December 31, 20X8, that goodwill involved in its acquisition of Roller shares had been impaired and the correct carrying value was $2,500.

Trial balance data for Mill and Roller on December 31, 20X8, are as follows:

	Mill Corporation		Roller Company	
Item	**Debit**	**Credit**	**Debit**	**Credit**
Cash	$ 19,500		$ 21,000	
Accounts Receivable	70,000		12,000	
Inventory	90,000		25,000	
Land	30,000		15,000	
Buildings & Equipment	350,000		150,000	
Investment in Roller Co. Stock	128,500			
Cost of Goods Sold	125,000		110,000	
Wage Expense	42,000		27,000	
Depreciation Expense	25,000		10,000	
Interest Expense	12,000		4,000	
Other Expenses	13,500		5,000	
Dividends Declared	30,000		16,000	
Accumulated Depreciation		$145,000		$ 40,000
Accounts Payable		45,000		16,000
Wages Payable		17,000		9,000
Notes Payable		150,000		50,000
Common Stock		200,000		60,000
Retained Earnings		102,000		40,000
Sales		260,000		180,000
Income from Subsidiary		16,500		
	$935,500	$935,500	$395,000	$395,000

Required

a. Give all consolidation entries needed to prepare a three-part consolidation worksheet as of December 31, 20X8.

b. Prepare a three-part consolidation worksheet for 20X8 in good form.

LO 4-5

Advanced StudyGuide .com

P4-34 Consolidation Worksheet at End of Second Year of Ownership

Mill Corporation acquired 100 percent ownership of Roller Company on January 1, 20X8, for $128,000. At that date, the fair value of Roller's buildings and equipment was $20,000 more than the book value. Buildings and equipment are depreciated on a 10-year basis. Although goodwill is not amortized, Mill's management concluded at December 31, 20X8, that goodwill involved in its acquisition of Roller shares had been impaired and the correct carrying value was $2,500. No additional impairment occurred in 20X9.

Trial balance data for Mill and Roller on December 31, 20X9, are as follows:

	Mill Corporation		Roller Company	
Item	**Debit**	**Credit**	**Debit**	**Credit**
Cash	$ 45,500		$ 32,000	
Accounts Receivable	85,000		14,000	
Inventory	97,000		24,000	
Land	50,000		25,000	
Buildings & Equipment	350,000		150,000	
Investment in Roller Co. Stock	142,500			
Cost of Goods Sold	145,000		114,000	
Wage Expense	35,000		20,000	
Depreciation Expense	25,000		10,000	
Interest Expense	12,000		4,000	
Other Expenses	23,000		16,000	
Dividends Declared	30,000		20,000	

(continued)

Accumulated Depreciation		$ 170,000		$ 50,000
Accounts Payable		51,000		15,000
Wages Payable		14,000		6,000
Notes Payable		150,000		50,000
Common Stock		200,000		60,000
Retained Earnings		131,000		48,000
Sales		290,000		200,000
Income from Subsidiary		34,000		
	$1,040,000	$1,040,000	$429,000	$429,000

Required

a. Give all consolidation entries needed to prepare a three-part consolidation worksheet as of December 31, 20X9.

b. Prepare a three-part consolidation worksheet for 20X9 in good form.

c. Prepare a consolidated balance sheet, income statement, and retained earnings statement for 20X9.

LO 4-5

P4-35 Comprehensive Problem: Wholly Owned Subsidiary

Power Corporation acquired 100 percent ownership of Upland Products Company on January 1, 20X1, for $200,000. On that date, Upland reported retained earnings of $50,000 and had $100,000 of common stock outstanding. Power has used the equity method in accounting for its investment in Upland.

The trial balances for the two companies on December 31, 20X5, appear below.

Additional Information

1. On the date of combination (five years ago), the fair value of Upland's depreciable assets was $50,000 more than the book value. Accumulated depreciation at that date was $10,000. The differential assigned to depreciable assets should be written off over the following 10-year period.
2. There was $10,000 of intercorporate receivables and payables at the end of 20X5.

Required

a. Give all journal entries that Power recorded during 20X5 related to its investment in Upland.

b. Give all consolidation entries needed to prepare consolidated statements for 20X5.

c. Prepare a three-part worksheet as of December 31, 20X5.

	Power Corporation		Upland Products Company	
Item	**Debit**	**Credit**	**Debit**	**Credit**
Cash & Receivables	$ 43,000		$ 65,000	
Inventory	260,000		90,000	
Land	80,000		80,000	
Buildings & Equipment	500,000		150,000	
Investment in Upland Products Stock	235,000			
Cost of Goods Sold	120,000		50,000	
Depreciation Expense	25,000		15,000	
Inventory Losses	15,000		5,000	
Dividends Declared	30,000		10,000	
Accumulated Depreciation		$ 205,000		$105,000
Accounts Payable		60,000		20,000
Notes Payable		200,000		50,000
Common Stock		300,000		100,000
Retained Earnings		318,000		90,000
Sales		200,000		100,000
Income from Subsidiary		25,000		
	$1,308,000	$1,308,000	$465,000	$465,000

LO 4-5

P4-36 Comprehensive Problem: Differential Apportionment

Jersey Corporation acquired 100 percent of Lime Company on January 1, 20X7, for $203,000. The trial balances for the two companies on December 31, 20X7, included the following amounts:

	Jersey Corporation		Lime Company	
Item	**Debit**	**Credit**	**Debit**	**Credit**
Cash	$ 82,000		$ 25,000	
Accounts Receivable	50,000		55,000	
Inventory	170,000		100,000	
Land	80,000		20,000	
Buildings & Equipment	500,000		150,000	
Investment in Lime Company Stock	240,000			
Cost of Goods Sold	500,000		250,000	
Depreciation Expense	25,000		15,000	
Other Expenses	75,000		75,000	
Dividends Declared	50,000		20,000	
Accumulated Depreciation		$ 155,000		$ 75,000
Accounts Payable		70,000		35,000
Mortgages Payable		200,000		50,000
Common Stock		300,000		50,000
Retained Earnings		290,000		100,000
Sales		700,000		400,000
Income from Subsidiary		57,000		
	$1,772,000	$1,772,000	$710,000	$710,000

Additional Information

1. On January 1, 20X7, Lime reported net assets with a book value of $150,000. A total of $20,000 of the acquisition price is applied to goodwill, which was not impaired in 20X7.
2. Lime's depreciable assets had an estimated economic life of 11 years on the date of combination. The difference between fair value and book value of tangible assets is related entirely to buildings and equipment.
3. Jersey used the equity method in accounting for its investment in Lime.
4. Detailed analysis of receivables and payables showed that Lime owed Jersey $16,000 on December 31, 20X7.

Required

a. Give all journal entries recorded by Jersey with regard to its investment in Lime during 20X7.
b. Give all consolidation entries needed to prepare a full set of consolidated financial statements for 20X7.
c. Prepare a three-part consolidation worksheet as of December 31, 20X7.

LO 4-7

P4-37A Push-Down Accounting

On December 31, 20X6, Greenly Corporation and Lindy Company entered into a business combination in which Greenly acquired all of Lindy's common stock for $935,000. At the date of combination, Lindy had common stock outstanding with a par value of $100,000, additional paid-in capital of $400,000, and retained earnings of $175,000. The fair values and book values of all Lindy's assets and liabilities were equal at the date of combination, except for the following:

	Book Value	Fair Value
Inventory	$ 50,000	$ 55,000
Land	75,000	160,000
Buildings	400,000	500,000
Equipment	500,000	570,000

"A" indicates that the item relates to Appendix 4A.

The buildings had a remaining life of 20 years, and the equipment was expected to last another 10 years. In accounting for the business combination, Greenly decided to use push-down accounting on Lindy's books.

During 20X7, Lindy earned net income of $88,000 and paid a dividend of $50,000. All of the inventory on hand at the end of 20X6 was sold during 20X7. During 20X8, Lindy earned net income of $90,000 and paid a dividend of $50,000.

Required

a. Record the acquisition of Lindy's stock on Greenly's books on December 31, 20X6.

b. Record any entries that would be made on December 31, 20X6, on Lindy's books related to the business combination if push-down accounting is employed.

c. Present all consolidation entries that would appear in the worksheet to prepare a consolidated balance sheet immediately after the combination.

d. Present all entries that Greenly would record during 20X7 related to its investment in Lindy if Greenly uses the equity method of accounting for its investment.

e. Present all consolidation entries that would appear in the worksheet to prepare a full set of consolidated financial statements for the year 20X7.

f. Present all consolidation entries that would appear in the worksheet to prepare a full set of consolidated financial statements for the year 20X8.

5 Consolidation of Less-than-Wholly-Owned Subsidiaries Acquired at More than Book Value

Multicorporate Entities

Business Combinations

Consolidation Concepts and Procedures

Intercompany Transfers

Additional Consolidation Issues

Multinational Entities

Reporting Requirements

Partnerships

Governmental and Not-for-Profit Entities

Corporations in Financial Difficulty

CISCO ACQUIRES A CONTROLLING INTEREST IN NUOVA

In many of the examples of corporate acquisitions discussed so far, the acquiring company has purchased 100 percent of the outstanding stock of the acquired company. However, the buyer doesn't always acquire 100 percent ownership of the target company. For example, in 2006 Cisco Systems Inc. acquired 80 percent of Nuova Systems in order to take advantage of Nuova's innovative data center technology. Individual investors still held the remaining 20 percent of the company. Cisco's initial investment in Nuova was $50 million. Accounting for this type of investment can be very complicated. First, Cisco's $50 million investment was not intended solely to purchase Nuova's tangible assets. Cisco also paid for Nuova's potential future earnings capability, for its innovation, and for the fair value (FV) of assets in excess of their book values as of the acquisition date. Because Cisco did not purchase 100 percent of Nuova, the Cisco consolidated financial statements in future years would have to account for the portion of the company owned by the noncontrolling interest (NCI) shareholders. This chapter explores the consolidation of less-than-wholly-owned subsidiaries when there is a positive differential.

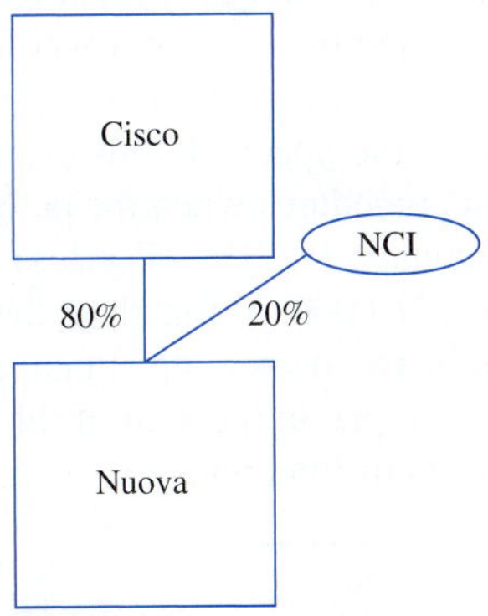

LEARNING OBJECTIVES

When you finish studying this chapter, you should be able to:

LO 5-1 Understand and explain how the consolidation process differs when the subsidiary is less-than-wholly-owned and there is a differential.

LO 5-2 Make calculations and prepare consolidation entries for the consolidation of a partially owned subsidiary when there is a complex positive differential.

LO 5-3 Understand and explain what happens when a parent company ceases to consolidate a subsidiary.

LO 5-4 Make calculations and prepare consolidation entries for the consolidation of a partially owned subsidiary when there is a complex positive differential and other comprehensive income.

A NONCONTROLLING INTEREST IN CONJUNCTION WITH A DIFFERENTIAL

LO 5-1

Understand and explain how the consolidation process differs when the subsidiary is less-than-wholly-owned and there is a differential.

This chapter continues to build upon the foundation established in Chapters 2 through 4 related to the consolidation of majority-owned subsidiaries. In fact, Chapter 5 represents the culmination of our learning process related to procedures associated with the consolidation process. Chapter 5 combines the complexities introduced in Chapters 3 and 4. Specifically, Chapter 5 examines situations in which the acquiring company purchases less than 100 percent of the outstanding stock of the acquired company (similar to Chapter 3) and pays an amount higher than its proportionate share of the book value of net assets (resulting in a differential as introduced in Chapter 4). Once you master Chapter 5, you can handle virtually any consolidation problem!

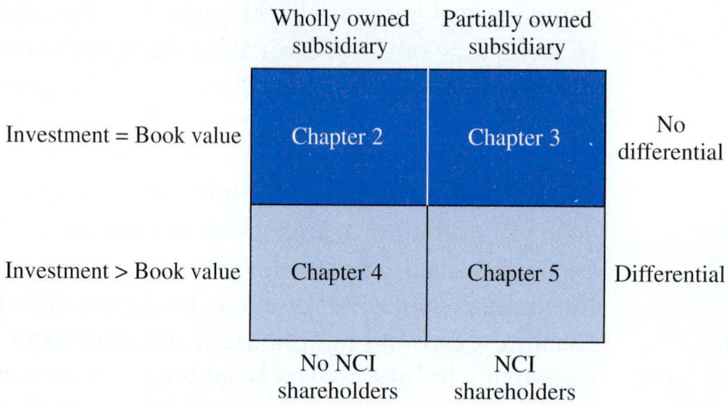

CONSOLIDATED BALANCE SHEET WITH MAJORITY-OWNED SUBSIDIARY

The consolidation process for a less-than-wholly-owned subsidiary with a differential is the same as the process for a wholly owned subsidiary with a differential except that the claims of the noncontrolling interest must be considered. The example of Peerless Products Corporation and Special Foods Inc. from Chapter 4 will serve as a basis for illustrating consolidation procedures when the parent has less than full ownership of a subsidiary. Assume that on January 1, 20X1, Peerless acquires 80 percent of the common stock of Special Foods for $310,000. At that date, the fair value of the noncontrolling interest is estimated to be $77,500. The ownership situation can be viewed as follows, when Special Foods' total fair value is equal to the sum of the fair value of the consideration given and the fair value of the noncontrolling interest:

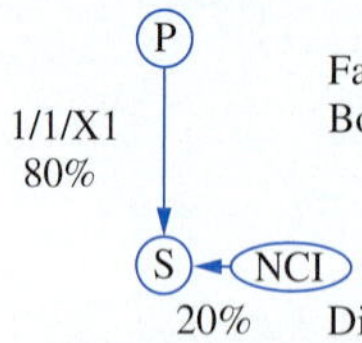

Fair value of Peerless' consideration + FV of the NCI interest		$387,500
Book value of Special Foods' net assets		
Common stock—Special Foods	200,000	
Retained earnings—Special Foods	100,000	
		300,000
Difference between fair value and book value		$ 87,500

Peerless records the acquisition on its books with the following entry:

(1)			
	Investment in Special Foods	310,000	
	Cash		310,000

Record purchase of Special Foods stock.

FIGURE 5–1 Balance Sheets of Peerless Products and Special Foods, January 1, 20X1, Immediately after Combination and Values of Select Assets of Special Foods

		Peerless Products		Special Foods	Special Foods' Fair Value	Fair Value Increment
Assets						
Cash		$ 40,000		$ 50,000		
Accounts Receivable		75,000		50,000		
Inventory		100,000		60,000	$ 65,000	$ 5,000
Land		175,000		40,000	50,000	10,000
Buildings & Equipment	800,000		600,000		360,000	60,000
Accumulated Depreciation	(400,000)		(300,000)			
Net Book Value		400,000		300,000		
Investment in Special Foods Stock		310,000				
Total Assets		$1,100,000		$500,000	$475,000	$75,000
Liabilities & Stockholders' Equity						
Accounts Payable		$ 100,000		$100,000		
Bonds Payable		200,000		100,000		
Common Stock		500,000		200,000		
Retained Earnings		300,000		100,000		
Total Liabilities & Equity		$1,100,000		$500,000		

The balance sheets of Peerless and Special Foods appear immediately after acquisition in Figure 5–1. On the acquisition date, the fair values of all of Special Foods' assets and liabilities are equal to their book values except as shown in Figure 5–1.

The excess of the $387,500 total fair value of the consideration given and the noncontrolling interest on the date of combination over the $300,000 book value of Special Foods is $87,500. Of this total $87,500 differential, $75,000 relates to the excess of the acquisition-date fair value over the book value of Special Foods' net identifiable assets, as presented in Figure 5–1. The remaining $12,500 of the differential, the excess of the consideration given and the noncontrolling interest over the fair value of Special Foods' net identifiable assets, is assigned to goodwill. Because Peerless acquires only 80 percent of Special Foods' outstanding common stock, Peerless' share of the total differential is $70,000 ($87,500 × 0.80). Specifically, Peerless' share of the excess fair value over book value of identifiable net assets (NA) is $60,000 ($75,000 × 0.80) and its share of the goodwill is $10,000 ($12,500 × 0.80). Peerless' share of the book value of Special Foods' net assets is $240,000 (0.80 × [CS $200,000 + RE $100,000]). As a result, Peerless' acquisition price of $310,000 applies to the book value and differential components of Special Foods' fair value as follows:

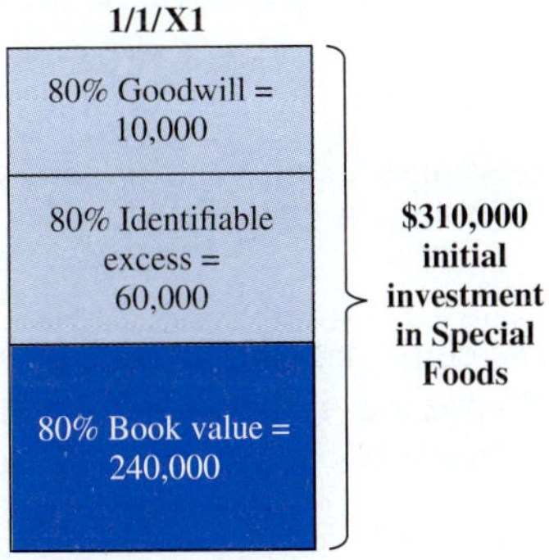

Assuming that Peerless decides to prepare a consolidated balance sheet on the acquisition date, the book value component of the acquisition price is divided between Peerless and the noncontrolling interest as follows:

Book Value Calculations:

	NCI 20%	+	Peerless 80%	=	Common Stock	+	Retained Earnings
Book Value at Acquisition	60,000		240,000		200,000		100,000

This analysis leads to the following basic consolidation entry:

Advanced StudyGuide .com

Basic Consolidation Entry:[1]

Common Stock	200,000		← Common stock balance
Retained Earnings	100,000		← Beginning balance in RE
Investment in Special Foods		240,000	← Peerless' share of Special Foods' BV
NCI in NA of Special Foods		60,000	← NCI's share of BV

The basic consolidation entry here is identical to the entry in Chapter 4 with one small exception: The credit to Investment in Special Foods was $300,000 in Chapter 4 when Peerless purchased 100 percent of Special Foods' common stock. In this example, Peerless purchased only 80 percent of the common stock, so the $300,000 book value of net assets is shared with the NCI shareholders. The differential can be allocated between Peerless and the noncontrolling interest as follows:

Excess Value (Differential) Calculations:

	NCI 20%	+	Peerless 80%	=	Inventory	+	Land	+	Building	+	Acc. Depr.	+	Goodwill
Beginning Balance	17,500		70,000		5,000		10,000		60,000		0		12,500

From this analysis, we can construct the excess value reclassification entry:

Excess Value (Differential) Reclassification Entry:

Inventory	5,000		← Excess value at acquisition
Land	10,000		← Excess value at acquisition
Building	60,000		← Excess value at acquisition
Goodwill	12,500		← Calculated value from acquisition
Investment in Special Foods		70,000	← Peerless' share of differential
NCI in NA of Special Foods		17,500	← NCI's share of differential

Again, this entry is identical to the one in the 100 percent owned Chapter 4 example except that the credit to Investment in Special Foods from the Chapter 4 example is now shared with the NCI shareholders. As explained in Chapter 4, Special Foods had accumulated depreciation on the acquisition date of $300,000. The following consolidation entry nets this accumulated depreciation out against the cost of the buildings and equipment.

Optional Accumulated Depreciation Consolidation Entry:

Accumulated Depreciation	300,000		← Accumulated depreciation at the time of the acquisition netted against cost
Buildings & Equipment		300,000	

The combination of these last two consolidation entries makes the buildings and equipment appear as if they were purchased on the acquisition date for their fair market values and recorded as new assets with zero accumulated depreciation as of that date.

[1] To view a video explanation of this topic, visit advancedstudyguide.com.

FIGURE 5–2 January 1, 20X1, Worksheet for Consolidated Balance Sheet, Date of Combination; 80 Percent Acquisition at More than Book Value

	Peerless Products	Special Foods	Consolidation Entries DR	Consolidation Entries CR	Consolidated
Balance Sheet					
Cash	40,000	50,000			90,000
Accounts Receivable	75,000	50,000			125,000
Inventory	100,000	60,000	5,000		165,000
Investment in Special Foods	310,000			240,000	0
				70,000	
Land	175,000	40,000	10,000		225,000
Buildings & Equipment	800,000	600,000	60,000	300,000	1,160,000
Less: Accumulated Depreciation	(400,000)	(300,000)	300,000		(400,000)
Goodwill			12,500		12,500
Total Assets	1,100,000	500,000	387,500	610,000	1,377,500
Accounts Payable	100,000	100,000			200,000
Bonds Payable	200,000	100,000			300,000
Common Stock	500,000	200,000	200,000		500,000
Retained Earnings	300,000	100,000	100,000		300,000
NCI in NA of Special Foods				60,000	77,500
				17,500	
Total Liabilities & Equity	1,100,000	500,000	300,000	77,500	1,377,500

Advanced StudyGuide .com

Figure 5–2 illustrates Peerless' consolidation worksheet on the date of acquisition at January 1, 20X1. Once the consolidation entries are placed in the worksheet, each row is summed across to get the consolidated totals. Note that the asset amounts included in the Consolidated column, and thus in the consolidated balance sheet, consist of book values for Peerless' assets and liabilities plus acquisition-date fair values for Special Foods' assets and liabilities plus goodwill.

CONSOLIDATED FINANCIAL STATEMENTS WITH A MAJORITY-OWNED SUBSIDIARY

LO 5-2 Make calculations and prepare consolidation entries for the consolidation of a partially owned subsidiary when there is a complex positive differential.

Consolidation subsequent to acquisition involves the preparation of a complete set of consolidated financial statements, as discussed in Chapter 4. To continue the illustration from the previous section beyond the date of acquisition, assume Peerless Products and Special Foods report the income and dividends during 20X1 and 20X2 shown in Figure 5–3. With respect to the assets to which the $87,500 differential relates, assume that the entire inventory is sold during 20X1, the buildings and equipment have a remaining economic life of 10 years from the date of combination, and Special Foods uses straight-line depreciation. Furthermore, assume that management determines at the end of 20X1 that the goodwill is impaired and should be written down by $3,125. Management has determined that the goodwill arising in the acquisition of Special Foods relates proportionately to the controlling and noncontrolling interests, as does the impairment. Finally, assume that Peerless accounts for its investment in Special Foods using the equity method.

Initial Year of Ownership

Advanced StudyGuide .com

The business combination of Peerless Products and Special Foods occurs at the beginning of 20X1. Accordingly, Peerless records the acquisition on January 1, 20X1, as illustrated previously.

Parent Company Entries

During 20X1, Peerless makes the usual equity-method entries to record income and dividends from its subsidiary (see Figure 5–3). Unlike Chapter 4, because Peerless

FIGURE 5–3
Income and Dividend Information about Peerless Products and Special Foods for the Years 20X1 and 20X2

	Peerless Products	Special Foods
20X1:		
Separate operating income, Peerless	$140,000	
Net income, Special Foods		$50,000
Dividends	60,000	30,000
20X2:		
Separate operating income, Peerless	160,000	
Net income, Special Foods		75,000
Dividends	60,000	40,000

purchased only 80 percent of the voting stock, it must share Special Foods' income and dividends with the subsidiary's noncontrolling stockholders. Accordingly, Peerless recognizes only its proportionate share of Special Foods' net income and dividends. Peerless records the following entries during 20X1:

(2)	Investment in Special Foods	40,000	
	Income from Special Foods		40,000
	Record Peerless' 80% share of Special Foods' 20X1 income.		

(3)	Cash	24,000	
	Investment in Special Foods		24,000
	Record Peerless' 80% share of Special Foods' 20X1 dividend.		

In addition, Peerless must write off a portion of the differential with the following entry:

(4)	Income from Special Foods	11,300	
	Investment in Special Foods		11,300
	Record amortization of excess acquisition price.		

Special Foods' undervalued inventory, comprising $5,000 of the total differential, was sold during the year. Therefore, Peerless' $4,000 portion ($5,000 × 80%) must be written off by reducing both the investment account and the parent's income from the subsidiary. Also, Peerless' portion of the excess fair value of Special Foods' buildings and equipment must be amortized at $4,800 per year [($60,000 ÷ 10) × 0.80] over the remaining 10-year life. Finally, Peerless' portion of the goodwill impairment, 2,500 ($3,125 × 0.80), is also included in this adjustment. Thus, the entire write-off of the differential is $11,300 ($4,000 + $4,800 + $2,500). A more detailed calculation of Peerless' share of the differential amortization is illustrated below in the "Excess Value (Differential) Calculations."

The following diagrams illustrate the breakdown of the book value and excess value components of the investment account at the beginning and end of the year.

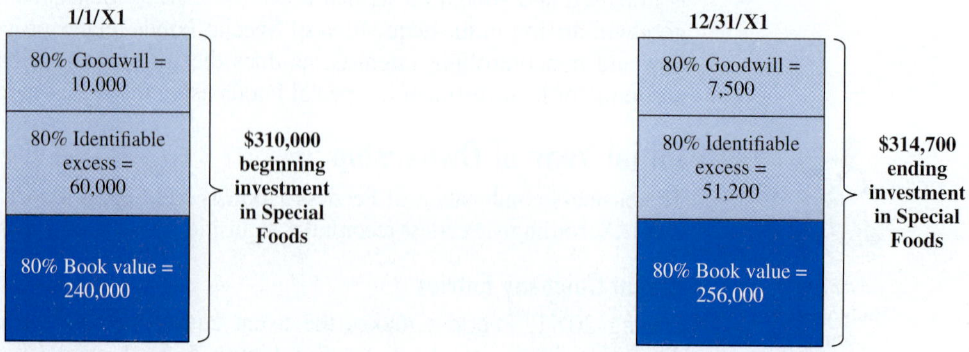

The book value component can be summarized as follows:

Book Value Calculations:

	NCI 20% +	Peerless 80% =	Common Stock +	Retained Earnings
Original Book Value	60,000	240,000	200,000	100,000
+ Net Income	10,000	40,000		50,000
− Dividends	(6,000)	(24,000)		(30,000)
Ending Book Value	64,000	256,000	200,000	120,000

The boxed numbers in the chart above comprise the basic consolidation entry:

Basic Consolidation Entry:

Common Stock	200,000		← Common stock balance
Retained Earnings	100,000		← Beginning balance in RE
Income from Special Foods	40,000		← Peerless' share of Special Foods' NI
NCI in NI of Special Foods	10,000		← NCI's share of Special Foods' NI
Dividends Declared		30,000	← 100% of Special Foods' dividends
Investment in Special Foods		256,000	← Peerless' share of Special Foods' BV
NCI in NA of Special Foods		64,000	← NCI's share of net amount of BV

We then analyze the differential and its changes during the period:

Excess Value (Differential) Calculations:

	NCI 20% +	Peerless 80% =	Inventory +	Land +	Building +	Acc. Depr. +	Goodwill
Beginning Balance	17,500	70,000	5,000	10,000	60,000	0	12,500
Amortization	(2,825)	(11,300)	(5,000)			(6,000)	(3,125)
Ending Balance	14,675	58,700	0	10,000	60,000	(6,000)	9,375

The entire differential amount assigned to the inventory already passed through cost of goods sold during the year. Thus, there is no longer a differential related to inventory at the end of the year. The only other amortization item is the excess value assigned to the building, amortized over a 10-year period ($60,000 ÷ 10 = $6,000 per year). Finally, the goodwill is deemed to be impaired and worth only $9,375.

Because Peerless' share of the amortization of the differential was already written off from the investment account against the Income from Special Foods account on its books, the changes shown in the middle row of this chart are simply reclassified from the Income from Special Foods account to the various income statement accounts to which they apply using the following worksheet entry:

Amortized Excess Value Reclassification Entry:

Cost of Goods Sold	5,000		← Extra cost of goods sold
Depreciation Expense	6,000		← Depreciation of excess building value
Goodwill Impairment Loss	3,125		← Goodwill impairment
Income from Special Foods		11,300	← Peerless' share of amortization
NCI in NI of Special Foods		2,825	← NCI's share of amortization

Finally, the remaining unamortized differential shown in the bottom row of the Excess Value calculations chart is reclassified to the accounts that need to be revalued to their amortized acquisition-date fair values:

Excess Value (Differential) Reclassification Entry:

Account	Debit	Credit	
Land	10,000		← Remaining excess value
Building	60,000		← Remaining excess value
Goodwill	9,375		← Calculated value from acquisition
Accumulated Depreciation		6,000	← Excess building value ÷ 10 years
Investment in Special Foods		58,700	← Peerless' share of differential
NCI in NA of Special Foods		14,675	← NCI's share of differential

In sum, these worksheet entries (1) eliminate the balances in the Investment in Special Foods and Income from Special Foods accounts, (2) reclassify the amortization of excess value to the proper income statement accounts, and (3) reclassify the remaining differential to the appropriate balance sheet accounts as of the end of the accounting period. The following T-accounts illustrate how Peerless' equity method investment-related accounts are eliminated.

Investment in Special Foods

	Debit	Credit	
Acquisition Price	310,000		
80% of NI	40,000		
		24,000	80% of Div.
		11,300	80% of Excess Amortization
Ending Balance	314,700		
		256,000	Basic
		58,700	Excess Value Reclassification
	0		

Income from Special Foods

	Debit	Credit	
		40,000	80% of NI
	11,300		
		28,700	Ending Balance
Basic	40,000		
		11,300	Amort. Reclassification
		0	

Again, we repeat the same accumulated depreciation consolidation entry this year (and every year as long as Special Foods owns the assets) that we used in the initial year.

Optional Accumulated Depreciation Consolidation Entry:

Account	Debit	Credit	
Accumulated Depreciation	300,000		← Accumulated depreciation at the time of the acquisition netted against cost
Buildings & Equipment		300,000	

Consolidation Worksheet—Initial Year of Ownership

After the subsidiary income accruals are entered on Peerless' books, the adjusted trial balance data of the consolidating companies are entered in the three-part consolidation worksheet as shown in Figure 5–4. The last column in the worksheet will serve as a basis for preparing consolidated financial statements at the end of 20X1.

Once the appropriate consolidation entries are placed in the consolidation worksheet in Figure 5–4, the worksheet is completed by summing each row across, taking into consideration the debit or credit effect of the consolidation entries.

Consolidated Net Income and Retained Earnings

Advanced StudyGuide .com

As can be seen from the worksheet in Figure 5–4, total consolidated net income for 20X1 is $175,875 and the amount of that income accruing to the controlling interest, presented as the last number in the income statement section of the worksheet in the Consolidated column, is $168,700. The amount of retained earnings reported in the consolidated balance sheet at December 31, 20X1, shown as the last number in the retained earnings section of the worksheet in the Consolidated column, is $408,700. Figure 5–5 on page 204 illustrates the computation of these amounts.

FIGURE 5–4 December 31, 20X1, Equity-Method Worksheet for Consolidated Financial Statements, Initial Year of Ownership; 80 Percent Acquisition at More than Book Value

	Peerless Products	Special Foods	Consolidation Entries DR	Consolidation Entries CR	Consolidated
Income Statement					
Sales	400,000	200,000			600,000
Less: COGS	(170,000)	(115,000)	5,000		(290,000)
Less: Depreciation Expense	(50,000)	(20,000)	6,000		(76,000)
Less: Other Expenses	(40,000)	(15,000)			(55,000)
Less: Impairment Loss			3,125		(3,125)
Income from Special Foods	28,700		40,000	11,300	0
Consolidated Net Income	168,700	50,000	54,125	11,300	175,875
NCI in Net Income			10,000	2,825	(7,175)
Controlling Interest in Net Income	**168,700**	**50,000**	**64,125**	**14,125**	**168,700**
Statement of Retained Earnings					
Beginning Balance	300,000	100,000	100,000		300,000
Net Income	**168,700**	**50,000**	**64,125**	**14,125**	168,700
Less: Dividends Declared	(60,000)	(30,000)		30,000	(60,000)
Ending Balance	**408,700**	**120,000**	**164,125**	**44,125**	**408,700**
Balance Sheet					
Cash	194,000	75,000			269,000
Accounts Receivable	75,000	50,000			125,000
Inventory	100,000	75,000			175,000
Investment in Special Foods	314,700			256,000 58,700	0
Land	175,000	40,000	10,000		225,000
Buildings & Equipment	800,000	600,000	60,000	300,000	1,160,000
Less: Accumulated Depreciation	(450,000)	(320,000)	300,000	6,000	(476,000)
Goodwill			9,375		9,375
Total Assets	**1,208,700**	**520,000**	**379,375**	**620,700**	**1,487,375**
Accounts Payable	100,000	100,000			200,000
Bonds Payable	200,000	100,000			300,000
Common Stock	500,000	200,000	200,000		500,000
Retained Earnings	**408,700**	**120,000**	**164,125**	**44,125**	408,700
NCI in NA of Special Foods				64,000 14,675	78,675
Total Liabilities & Equity	**1,208,700**	**520,000**	**364,125**	**122,800**	**1,487,375**

Second Year of Ownership

The equity-method and consolidation procedures employed during the second and subsequent years of ownership are the same as those used during the first year and are illustrated by continuing the Peerless Products and Special Foods example through 20X2. No further impairment of the goodwill arising from the business combination occurs in 20X2.

Parent Company Entries

Given the income and dividends as shown in Figure 5–3, Peerless Products records the following entries on its separate books during 20X2:

(5)			
	Investment in Special Foods	60,000	
	Income from Special Foods		60,000
	Record Peerless' 80% share of Special Foods' 20X2 income.		

FIGURE 5–5
Consolidated Net Income and Retained Earnings, 20X1; 80 Percent Acquisition at More than Book Value

Consolidated net income, 20X1:	
Peerless' separate operating income	$140,000
Special Foods' net income	50,000
Write-off of differential related to inventory sold in 20X1	(5,000)
Amortization of differential related to buildings and equipment in 20X1	(6,000)
Goodwill impairment loss	(3,125)
Consolidated net income	$175,875
Income to controlling interest, 20X1:	
Consolidated net income	$175,875
Income to noncontrolling interest	(7,175)
Income to controlling interest	$168,700
Consolidated retained earnings, December 31, 20X1:	
Peerless' retained earnings on date of combination, January 1, 20X1	$300,000
Income to controlling interest, 20X1	168,700
Dividends declared by Peerless, 20X1	(60,000)
Consolidated retained earnings	$408,700

(6)	Cash	32,000	
	Investment in Special Foods		32,000
	Record Peerless' 80% share of Special Foods' 20X2 dividend.		

(7)	Income from Special Foods	4,800	
	Investment in Special Foods		4,800
	Record amortization of excess acquisition price.		

Advanced StudyGuide .com

Consolidation Worksheet—Second Year Following Combination

The consolidation procedures in the second year following the acquisition are very similar to those in the first year. Consistent with the process illustrated in 20X1, we follow the same process for 20X2. In order to determine the worksheet entries for 20X2, we first summarize the changes in the parent's investment account during 20X2 as follows:

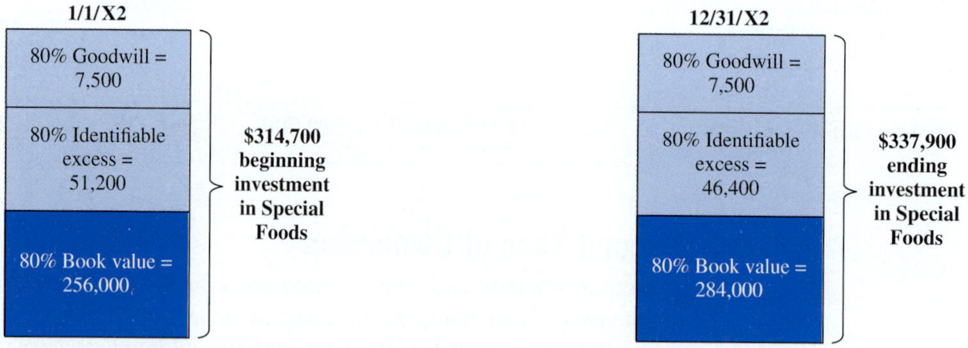

The book value component can be summarized as follows:

Book Value Calculations:

	NCI 20% +	Peerless 80% =	Common Stock +	Retained Earnings
Beginning Book Value	64,000	256,000	200,000	120,000
+ Net Income	15,000	60,000		75,000
− Dividends	(8,000)	(32,000)		(40,000)
Ending Book Value	71,000	284,000	200,000	155,000

The boxed numbers in the preceding chart comprise the basic consolidation entry:

Basic Consolidation Entry:

Common Stock	200,000		← Common stock balance
Retained Earnings	120,000		← Beginning RE from trial balance
Income from Special Foods	60,000		← Peerless' share of reported income
NCI in NI of Special Foods	15,000		← NCI's share of reported income
Dividends Declared		40,000	← 100% of sub's dividends declared
Investment in Special Foods		284,000	← Peerless' share of Special Foods' BV
NCI in NA of Special Foods		71,000	← NCI's share of net amount of BV

The entire differential amount assigned to the inventory already passed through cost of goods sold during the prior year period. The only other amortization item is the excess value assigned to the building, which continues to be written off over a 10-year period ($60,000 ÷ 10 = $6,000).

Excess Value (Differential) Calculations:

	NCI 20%	+ Peerless 80%	= Land	+ Building	+ Acc. Depr.	+ Goodwill
Beginning Balances	14,675	58,700	10,000	60,000	(6,000)	9,375
Amortization	(1,200)	(4,800)			(6,000)	
Ending Balance	13,475	53,900	10,000	60,000	(12,000)	9,375

Because the amortization of the differential was already written off from the investment account against the Income from Special Foods account, the change to the differential presented in the middle row of this chart is simply reclassified from the Income from Special Foods account to the income statement account to which it applies during the consolidation process. Then, the remaining amount of the differential from the last row of this chart is reclassified to the various balance accounts that need to be revalued to their amortized acquisition-date fair values:

Amortized Excess Value Reclassification Entry:

Depreciation Expense	6,000		← Depreciation of excess building value
Income from Special Foods		4,800	← Peerless' share of amortization of diff.
NCI in NI of Special Foods		1,200	← NCI's share of amortization of differential

Excess Value (Differential) Reclassification Entry:

Land	10,000		← Remaining excess value
Building	60,000		← Remaining excess value
Goodwill	9,375		← Calculated value from acquisition
Accumulated Depreciation		12,000	← = (Excess value ÷ 10 years) × 2 years
Investment in Special Foods		53,900	← Peerless' share of excess value
NCI in NA of Special Foods		13,475	← NCI's share of excess value

Again, these worksheet entries (1) eliminate the balances in the Investment in Special Foods and Income from Special Foods accounts, (2) reclassify the amortization of excess value to the proper income statement accounts, and (3) reclassify the remaining differential to the appropriate balance sheet accounts at the end of the accounting period. The following T-accounts illustrate how Peerless' Investment in Special Foods and Income from Special Foods accounts are eliminated.

	Investment in Special Foods (Dr.)	Investment in Special Foods (Cr.)	
Beginning Balance	314,700		
80% of NI	60,000		
		32,000	80% of Div.
		4,800	80% of Excess Amortization
Ending Balance	337,900		
		284,000	Basic
		53,900	Excess Reclass.
	0		

	Income from Special Foods (Dr.)	Income from Special Foods (Cr.)	
		60,000	80% of NI
80% of Excess Amortization	4,800		
		55,200	Ending Balance
Basic	60,000		
		4,800	Amort. Reclassification
		0	

Again, we repeat the same accumulated depreciation consolidation entry this year (and every year as long as Special Foods owns the assets) that we used in the initial year.

Optional Accumulated Depreciation Consolidation Entry:

Accumulated Depreciation	300,000		← Accumulated depreciation at the time of the acquisition netted against cost
Buildings & Equipment		300,000	

Figure 5–6 illustrates the worksheet to prepare a complete set of consolidated financial statements for the year 20X2. Figure 5–7 shows the computation of 20X2 consolidated net income and consolidated retained earnings at the end of 20X2.

Consolidated Financial Statements

Figure 5–8 on page 208 presents a consolidated income statement and retained earnings statement for the year 20X2 and a consolidated balance sheet as of December 31, 20X2.

DISCONTINUANCE OF CONSOLIDATION

LO 5-3

Understand and explain what happens when a parent company ceases to consolidate a subsidiary.

A parent that has been consolidating a subsidiary in its financial statements should exclude that company from future consolidation if the parent can no longer exercise control over it. Control might be lost for a number of reasons, such as (1) the parent sells some or all of its interest in the subsidiary, (2) the subsidiary issues additional common stock, (3) the parent enters into an agreement to relinquish control, or (4) the subsidiary comes under the control of the government or other regulator.

If a parent loses control of a subsidiary and no longer holds an equity interest in the former subsidiary, it recognizes a gain or loss for the difference between any proceeds received from the event leading to loss of control (e.g., sale of interest, expropriation of subsidiary) and the carrying amount of the parent's equity interest. If the parent loses control but maintains a noncontrolling equity interest in the former subsidiary, it must recognize a gain or loss for the difference, at the date control is lost, between (1) the sum of any proceeds received by the parent and the fair value of its remaining equity interest in the former subsidiary and (2) the carrying amount of the parent's total interest in the subsidiary.

As an example, assume that Peerless Products sells three-quarters of its 80 percent interest in Special Foods to an unrelated entity on January 1, 20X2, for $246,000, leaving it holding 20 percent of Special Foods' outstanding stock. On that date, assume that the fair value of Special Foods as a whole is $410,000 and the carrying amount of Peerless' 80 percent share of Special Foods is $314,700 (as shown earlier in the chapter). Assume

FIGURE 5–6 December 31, 20X2, Equity-Method Worksheet for Consolidated Financial Statements, Second Year of Ownership; 80 Percent Acquisition at More than Book Value

	Peerless Products	Special Foods	Consolidation Entries DR	Consolidation Entries CR	Consolidated
Income Statement					
Sales	450,000	300,000			750,000
Less: COGS	(180,000)	(160,000)			(340,000)
Less: Depreciation Expense	(50,000)	(20,000)	6,000		(76,000)
Less: Other Expenses	(60,000)	(45,000)			(105,000)
Less: Impairment Loss					0
Income from Special Foods	55,200		60,000	4,800	0
Consolidated Net Income	215,200	75,000	66,000	4,800	229,000
NCI in Net Income			15,000	1,200	(13,800)
Controlling Interest Net Income	**215,200**	**75,000**	**81,000**	**6,000**	**215,200**
Statement of Retained Earnings					
Beginning Balance	408,700	120,000	120,000		408,700
Net Income	**215,200**	**75,000**	**81,000**	**6,000**	215,200
Less: Dividends Declared	(60,000)	(40,000)		40,000	(60,000)
Ending Balance	**563,900**	**155,000**	**201,000**	**46,000**	**563,900**
Balance Sheet					
Cash	221,000	85,000			306,000
Accounts Receivable	150,000	80,000			230,000
Inventory	180,000	90,000			270,000
Investment in Special Foods	337,900			284,000 53,900	0
Land	175,000	40,000	10,000		225,000
Buildings & Equipment	800,000	600,000	60,000	300,000	1,160,000
Less: Accumulated Depreciation	(500,000)	(340,000)	300,000	12,000	(552,000)
Goodwill			9,375		9,375
Total Assets	**1,363,900**	**555,000**	**379,375**	**649,900**	**1,648,375**
Accounts Payable	100,000	100,000			200,000
Bonds Payable	200,000	100,000			300,000
Common Stock	500,000	200,000	200,000		500,000
Retained Earnings	**563,900**	**155,000**	**201,000**	**46,000**	563,900
NCI in NA of Special Foods				71,000 13,475	84,475
Total Liabilities & Equity	**1,363,900**	**555,000**	**401,000**	**130,475**	**1,648,375**

FIGURE 5–7 Consolidated Net Income and Retained Earnings, 20X2; 80 Percent Acquisition at More than Book Value

Consolidated net income, 20X2:	
Peerless' separate operating income	$160,000
Special Foods' net income	75,000
Amortization of differential related to buildings & equipment in 20X2	(6,000)
Consolidated net income	$229,000
Income to controlling interest, 20X2:	
Consolidated net income	$229,000
Income to noncontrolling interest	(13,800)
Income to controlling interest	$215,200
Consolidated retained earnings, December 31, 20X2:	
Peerless' retained earnings on date of combination, January 1, 20X1	$300,000
Income to controlling interest, 20X1	168,700
Dividends declared by Peerless, 20X1	(60,000)
Consolidated retained earnings, December 31, 20X1	$408,700
Income to controlling interest, 20X2	215,200
Dividends declared by Peerless, 20X2	(60,000)
Consolidated retained earnings, December 31, 20X2	$563,900

FIGURE 5–8 Consolidated Financial Statements for Peerless Products Corporation and Special Foods Inc., 20X2

PEERLESS PRODUCTS CORPORATION AND SUBSIDIARY
Consolidated Income Statement
For the Year Ended December 31, 20X2

Sales		$750,000
Cost of Goods Sold		(340,000)
Gross Margin		$410,000
Expenses:		
Depreciation & Amortization	$ 76,000	
Other Expenses	105,000	
Total Expenses		(181,000)
Consolidated Net Income		$229,000
Income to Noncontrolling Interest		(13,800)
Income to Controlling Interest		$215,200

PEERLESS PRODUCTS CORPORATION AND SUBSIDIARY
Consolidated Retained Earnings Statement
For the Year Ended December 31, 20X2

Retained Earnings, January 1, 20X2	$408,700
Income to Controlling Interest, 20X2	215,200
Dividends Declared, 20X2	(60,000)
Retained Earnings, December 31, 20X2	$563,900

PEERLESS PRODUCTS CORPORATION AND SUBSIDIARY
Consolidated Balance Sheet
December 31, 20X2

Assets			Liabilities		
Cash		$ 306,000	Accounts Payable	$200,000	
Accounts Receivable		230,000	Bonds Payable	300,000	
Inventory		270,000			$500,000
Land		225,000	Stockholders' Equity		
Buildings & Equipment	$1,160,000		Controlling Interest		
Accumulated Depreciation	(552,000)		Common Stock	$500,000	
		608,000	Retained Earnings	563,900	
Goodwill		9,375	Total Controlling Interest		1,063,900
			Noncontrolling Interest		84,475
Total Assets		$1,648,375	Total Liabilities & Equity		$1,648,375

the fair value of Peerless' remaining 20 percent interest in Special Foods is $82,000. Peerless' gain on the sale of Special Foods stock is computed as follows:

Cash proceeds received	$246,000
Fair value of Peerless' remaining equity interest in Special Foods	82,000
	$328,000
Peerless' total interest in Special Foods at date of sale	314,700
Gain on sale of 60 percent interest in Special Foods	$ 13,300

Peerless reports the $13,300 gain in 20X2 income as follows:

(8)	Cash	246,000	
	Investment in Special Foods Stock		232,700
	Gain on sale of investment.		13,300
	Record the sale of 75% of the investment in Special Foods Stock.		

Note that because Peerless no longer has a significant influence, the investment will be accounted for using the cost basis ($82,000) going forward.[2]

[2] As noted in Chapter 2, the cost basis for this type of investment would entail classifying these shares either as trading or available-for-sale securities.

TREATMENT OF OTHER COMPREHENSIVE INCOME

LO 5-4

Make calculations and prepare consolidation entries for the consolidation of a partially owned subsidiary when there is a complex positive differential and other comprehensive income.

ASC 220-10-55 requires that companies separately report ***other comprehensive income (OCI),*** which includes all revenues, expenses, gains, and losses that under generally accepted accounting principles are excluded from net income.[3] ***Comprehensive income*** is the sum of net income and other comprehensive income. **ASC 220-10-55** permits several different options for reporting comprehensive income, but the consolidation process is the same regardless of the reporting format.

Other comprehensive income accounts are temporary accounts that are closed at the end of each period. However, other comprehensive income accounts are closed to a special stockholders' equity account, ***Accumulated Other Comprehensive Income (AOCI),*** not to Retained Earnings as with typical temporary accounts like revenues and expenses.

FYI

Levi Strauss & Co. reported a $69.1 million loss in other comprehensive income (OCI) in 2012. The portion of this loss that accrued to the NCI shareholders was $457,000; the remaining $68.6 million was attributable to the parent company's shareholders.

Modification of the Consolidation Worksheet

When a parent or subsidiary has recorded other comprehensive income, the consolidation worksheet normally includes an additional section for other comprehensive income. This section of the worksheet facilitates computation of the amount of other comprehensive income to be reported; the portion, if any, of other comprehensive income to be assigned to the noncontrolling interest; and the amount of accumulated other comprehensive income to be reported in the consolidated balance sheet. Although this extra section of the worksheet for comprehensive income could be placed after the income statement section of the standard worksheet, the format used here is to place it at the bottom of the worksheet. If neither the parent nor any subsidiary reports other comprehensive income, the section can be omitted from the worksheet. When other comprehensive income is reported, the worksheet is prepared in the normal manner, with the additional section added to the bottom. The only modification within the standard worksheet is an additional stockholders' equity account included in the balance sheet portion of the worksheet for the cumulative effects of the other comprehensive income.

To illustrate the consolidation process when a subsidiary reports other comprehensive income, assume that during 20X2 Special Foods purchases $20,000 of investments classified as available-for-sale. By December 31, 20X2, the fair value of the securities increases to $30,000. Other than the effects of accounting for Special Foods' investment in securities, the financial statement information reported by Peerless Products and Special Foods at December 31, 20X2, is identical to that presented in Figure 5–7.

Adjusting Entry Recorded by Subsidiary

At December 31, 20X2, Special Foods, the subsidiary, recognizes the increase in the fair value of its available-for-sale securities by recording the following adjusting entry:

(9)	Investment in Available-for-Sale Securities	10,000	
	Unrealized Gain on Investments (OCI)		10,000

Record the increase in fair value of available-for sale securities.

The unrealized gain is not included in the subsidiary's net income but is reported by the subsidiary as an element of OCI.

[3] Other comprehensive income elements include foreign currency translation adjustments, unrealized gains and losses on certain derivatives and investments in certain types of securities, and certain minimum pension liability adjustments.

Adjusting Entry Recorded by Parent Company

In 20X2, Peerless records all its normal entries relating to its investment in Special Foods as if the subsidiary had not reported other comprehensive income. In addition, at December 31, 20X2, Peerless Products separately recognizes its proportionate share of the subsidiary's unrealized gain from the increase in the value of the available-for-sale securities:

(10)			
	Investment in Special Foods	8,000	
	Other Comprehensive Income from Special Foods		8,000
	Record share of the increase in value of available-for-sale securities held by subsidiary.		

Consolidation Worksheet—Second Year Following Combination

The worksheet to prepare a complete set of consolidated financial statements for the year 20X2 is illustrated in Figure 5–9. In the worksheet, Peerless' balance in the Investment in Special Foods Stock account is more than the balance in Figure 5–6. Specifically, because of the adjusting entry just mentioned, Peerless' $8,000 proportionate share of Special Foods' unrealized gain is included in the separate section of the worksheet for comprehensive income (Other Comprehensive Income from Subsidiary—Unrealized Gain on Investments). Special Foods' trial balance has been changed to reflect (1) the reduction in the cash balance resulting from the investment acquisition, (2) the investment in available-for-sale securities, and (3) an unrealized gain of $10,000 on the investment.

Consolidation Procedures

The normal consolidation entries (the basic consolidation entry, the amortized excess cost reclassification entry, the differential reclassification entry, and the accumulated depreciation consolidation entry) were used in preparing the consolidation worksheet for 20X2 presented in Figure 5–6.

One additional entry is needed for the treatment of the subsidiary's other comprehensive income. First, the proportionate share of the subsidiary's other comprehensive income recorded by the parent in the adjusting entry previously mentioned must be eliminated to avoid double-counting the subsidiary's other comprehensive income. Thus, the adjusting entry is reversed in the worksheet. Moreover, a proportionate share of the subsidiary's other comprehensive income must be allocated to the noncontrolling interest:

Other Comprehensive Income Entry:

OCI from Special Foods	8,000	
OCI to the NCI	2,000	
Investment in Special Foods		8,000
NCI in NA of Subsidiary		2,000

The amount of consolidated other comprehensive income reported in the consolidated financial statements is equal to the subsidiary's $10,000 amount. The noncontrolling interest's $2,000 proportionate share of the subsidiary's other comprehensive income is deducted to arrive at the $8,000 other comprehensive income allocated to the controlling interest.

Although consolidated net income is the same in Figure 5–9 as in Figure 5–6, the other comprehensive income section of the worksheet in Figure 5–9 gives explicit recognition to the unrealized gain on available-for-sale securities held by Special Foods. This permits recognition in the consolidated financial statements under any of the alternative formats permitted by the FASB. Note that the ***Accumulated Other Comprehensive Income*** row of the balance sheet in the consolidation worksheet is simply carried up from the last row of the separate ***Other Comprehensive Income*** section at the bottom of the worksheet.

FIGURE 5–9 December 31, 20X2, Comprehensive Income Illustration, Second Year of Ownership; 80 Percent Acquisition at More than Book Value

	Peerless Products	Special Foods	Consolidation Entries DR	Consolidation Entries CR	Consolidated
Income Statement					
Sales	450,000	300,000			750,000
Less: COGS	(180,000)	(160,000)			(340,000)
Less: Depreciation Expense	(50,000)	(20,000)	6,000		(76,000)
Less: Other Expenses	(60,000)	(45,000)			(105,000)
Less: Impairment Loss					0
Income from Special Foods	55,200		60,000	4,800	0
Consolidated Net Income	215,200	75,000	66,000	4,800	**229,000**
NCI in Net Income			15,000	1,200	**(13,800)**
Controlling Interest in Net Income	**215,200**	**75,000**	81,000	6,000	**215,200**
Statement of Retained Earnings					
Beginning Balance	408,700	120,000	120,000		408,700
Add Net Income	**215,200**	**75,000**	81,000	6,000	215,200
Less: Dividends Declared	(60,000)	(40,000)		40,000	(60,000)
Ending Balance	**563,900**	**155,000**	201,000	46,000	**563,900**
Balance Sheet					
Cash	221,000	65,000			286,000
Accounts Receivable	150,000	80,000			230,000
Inventory	180,000	90,000			270,000
Investment in Subsidiary	345,900			284,000	0
				53,900	
				8,000	
Investment in AFS Securities		30,000			30,000
Land	175,000	40,000	10,000		225,000
Buildings & Equipment	800,000	600,000	60,000	300,000	1,160,000
Less: Accumulated Depreciation	(500,000)	(340,000)	300,000	12,000	(552,000)
Goodwill			9,375		9,375
Total Assets	**1,371,900**	**565,000**	379,375	657,900	**1,658,375**
Accounts Payable	100,000	100,000			200,000
Bonds Payable	200,000	100,000			300,000
Common Stock	500,000	200,000	200,000		500,000
Retained Earnings	**563,900**	**155,000**	201,000	46,000	563,900
Accumulated Other Comprehensive Income, 12/31/X2	**8,000**	**10,000**	10,000	0	**8,000**
NCI in NA of Special Foods				71,000	86,475
				13,475	
				2,000	
Total Liabilities & Equity	**1,371,900**	**565,000**	411,000	132,475	**1,658,375**
Other Comprehensive Income					
Accumulated Other Comprehensive Income, 1/1/X2	0	0			0
Other Comprehensive Income from Special Foods	8,000		8,000		0
Unrealized Gain on Investments		10,000			10,000
Other Comprehensive Income to NCI			2,000		(2,000)
Accumulated Other Comprehensive Income, 12/31/X2	**8,000**	**10,000**	10,000	0	**8,000**

Consolidated financial statements for the other comprehensive income example are presented in Figure 5–10. Note that consolidated other comprehensive income includes the full $10,000 unrealized gain. The noncontrolling interest's share, $15,800 ($13,800

FIGURE 5–10
Consolidated Financial Statements for Peerless Products Corporation and Special Foods Inc., 20X2, Including Other Comprehensive Income

PEERLESS PRODUCTS CORPORATION AND SUBSIDIARY
Consolidated Income Statement
For the Year Ended December 31, 20X2

Sales		$750,000
Cost of Goods Sold		(340,000)
Gross Margin		$410,000
Expenses:		
Depreciation & Amortization	$ 76,000	
Other Expenses	105,000	
Total Expenses		(181,000)
Consolidated Net Income		$229,000
Income to Noncontrolling Interest		(13,800)
Income to Controlling Interest		$215,200

PEERLESS PRODUCTS CORPORATION AND SUBSIDIARY
Consolidated Statement of Comprehensive Income
For the Year Ended December 31, 20X2

Consolidated Net Income	$229,000
Other Comprehensive Income:	
Unrealized Gain on Investments	10,000
Total Consolidated Comprehensive Income	$239,000
Less: Comprehensive Income Attribute to Noncontrolling Interest	(15,800)
Comprehensive Income Attribute to Controlling Interest	$223,200

PEERLESS PRODUCTS CORPORATION AND SUBSIDIARY
Consolidated Statement of Financial Position
December 31, 20X2

Assets		
Cash		$ 286,000
Accounts Receivable		230,000
Inventory		270,000
Investment in Available-for-Sale Securities		30,000
Land		225,000
Buildings & Equipment	$1,160,000	
Accumulated Depreciation	(552,000)	
		608,000
Goodwill		9,375
Total Assets		$1,658,375
Liabilities		
Accounts Payable	$ 200,000	
Bonds Payable	300,000	
Total Liabilities		$ 500,000
Stockholders' Equity		
Controlling Interest:		
Common Stock	$ 500,000	
Retained Earnings	563,900	
Accumulated Other Comprehensive Income	8,000	
Total Controlling Interest	$1,071,900	
Noncontrolling Interest	86,475	
Total Stockholders' Equity		1,158,375
Total Liabilities & Stockholders' Equity		$1,658,375

income + $2,000 OCI), is then deducted, along with its share of consolidated net income, to arrive at the consolidated comprehensive income allocated to the controlling interest. The amount of other comprehensive income allocated to the controlling interest is carried to the Accumulated Other Comprehensive Income that is reported in the consolidated balance sheet, and the noncontrolling interest's share is included in the Noncontrolling Interest amount in the consolidated balance sheet. The FASB requires that the amount of each other comprehensive income element allocated to the controlling and noncontrolling interests be disclosed in the consolidated statements or notes.

Consolidation Worksheet—Comprehensive Incomc in Subsequent Years

Each year following 20X2, Special Foods will adjust the unrealized gain on investments on its books for the change in fair value of the available-for-sale securities. For example, if Special Foods' investment increased in value by an additional $5,000 during 20X3, Special Foods would increase by $5,000 the carrying amount of its investment in securities and recognize as an element of 20X3's other comprehensive income an unrealized gain of $5,000. Under equity-method recording, Peerless would increase its Investment in Special Foods Stock account and record its $4,000 share of the subsidiary's other comprehensive income.

The consolidation entries required to prepare the consolidation worksheet at December 31, 20X3, would include the normal consolidation entries (the basic consolidation entry, the amortized excess cost reclassification entry, the differential reclassification entry, and the accumulated depreciation consolidation entry). In addition, the basic consolidation entry would be expanded to eliminate the subsidiary's $10,000 beginning Accumulated Other Comprehensive Income balance and to increase the noncontrolling interest by its proportionate share of the subsidiary's beginning Accumulated Other Comprehensive Income amount ($10,000 × 0.20). The Other Comprehensive Income consolidation entry allocates the 20X3 other comprehensive income to the noncontrolling interest:

Other Comprehensive Income Entry:

OCI from Special Foods	4,000	
OCI to the NCI	1,000	
Investment in Special Foods		4,000
NCI in NA of Subsidiary		1,000

SUMMARY OF KEY CONCEPTS

The procedures and worksheet for consolidating less-than-wholly-owned subsidiaries are the same as discussed in Chapter 4 for wholly owned subsidiaries, with several modifications. The worksheet consolidation entries are modified to include the noncontrolling shareholders' claim on the income and assets of the subsidiary. The noncontrolling interest has a claim on subsidiary assets based on its acquisition-date fair value. If the acquisition-date fair value of the consideration given in a business combination, plus the fair value of any noncontrolling interest, exceeds the book value of the subsidiary, the difference is referred to as a *differential* and increases both the controlling and noncontrolling interests. The subsidiary's assets and liabilities are valued in consolidation based on their full acquisition-date fair values, with goodwill recognized at acquisition for the difference between (1) the sum of the fair value of the consideration given in the combination and the fair value of the noncontrolling interest and (2) the fair value of the subsidiary's net identifiable assets. Any subsequent write-off of the differential reduces both the controlling and noncontrolling interests.

Consolidated net income is equal to the parent's income from its own operations plus the subsidiary's net income adjusted for any amortization or write-off of the differential. The amount of consolidated net income attributable to the noncontrolling interest is equal to the noncontrolling interest's proportionate share of the subsidiary's net income less a proportionate share of any differential write-off. The income attributable to the controlling interest is equal to consolidated net income less the income attributable to the noncontrolling interest.

A subsidiary's other comprehensive income for the period must be recognized in consolidated other comprehensive income and allocated between the controlling and noncontrolling interests. The consolidation worksheet is modified to accommodate the other comprehensive income items by adding a special section at the bottom.

KEY TERMS

accumulated other comprehensive income (AOCI), *209, 210*
comprehensive income, *209*
other comprehensive income (OCI), *209, 210*

Appendix 5A Additional Consolidation Details

Chapters 3, 4, and 5 provide a conceptual foundation for preparing consolidated financial statements and a description of the basic procedures used in preparing consolidated statements. Before moving on to intercompany transactions in Chapters 6 through 8, several additional items should be considered to provide completeness and clarity.

NEGATIVE RETAINED EARNINGS OF SUBSIDIARY AT ACQUISITION

A parent company may acquire a subsidiary with a negative or debit balance in its retained earnings account. An accumulated deficit of a subsidiary at acquisition causes no special problems in the consolidation process. The basic investment account consolidation entry is the same in the consolidation worksheet except that the debit balance in the subsidiary's Retained Earnings account is eliminated with a credit entry. Thus, the basic investment account consolidation entry appears as follows:

Basic Investment Account Consolidation Entry:

Common Stock	XX	
Income from Special Foods	XX	
NCI in NI of Special Foods	XX	
Retained Earnings (Accumulated deficit)		XX
Dividends Declared		XX
Investment in Special Foods		XX
NCI in NA of Special Foods		XX

OTHER STOCKHOLDERS' EQUITY ACCOUNTS

The discussion of consolidated statements up to this point has dealt with companies having stockholders' equity consisting only of retained earnings and a single class of capital stock issued at par. Typically, companies have more complex stockholders' equity structures, often including preferred stock and various types of additional contributed capital. In general, all stockholders' equity accounts accruing to the common shareholders receive the same treatment as common stock and are eliminated at the time common stock is eliminated. The treatment of preferred stock in the consolidation process is discussed in Chapter 9.

SUBSIDIARY'S DISPOSAL OF DIFFERENTIAL-RELATED ASSETS

The disposal of an asset usually has income statement implications. If the asset is held by a subsidiary and is one to which a differential is assigned in the consolidation worksheet, both the parent's equity-method income and consolidated net income are affected. On the parent's books, the portion of the differential included in the subsidiary investment account that relates to the asset sold must be written off by the parent under the equity method as a reduction in both the income from the subsidiary and the investment account. In consolidation, the portion of the differential related to the asset sold is treated as an adjustment to consolidated income.

Inventory

Any inventory-related differential is assigned to inventory for as long as the subsidiary holds the inventory units. In the period in which the inventory units are sold, the inventory-related differential is assigned to Cost of Goods Sold, as illustrated previously in Figure 5–4.

The inventory costing method used by the subsidiary determines the period in which the differential cost of goods sold is recognized. When the subsidiary uses FIFO inventory costing, the inventory units on hand on the date of combination are viewed as being the first units sold after the combination. Therefore, the differential normally is assigned to cost of goods sold in the period immediately after the combination. When the subsidiary uses LIFO inventory costing, the inventory units on the date of combination are viewed as remaining in the subsidiary's inventory. Thus, when the subsidiary uses LIFO inventory costing, the differential is not assigned to cost of goods sold unless the inventory level drops below its level at the date of combination.

Fixed Assets

A differential related to land held by a subsidiary is added to the Land balance in the consolidation worksheet each time a consolidated balance sheet is prepared. If the subsidiary sells the land to which the differential relates, the differential is treated in the consolidation worksheet as an adjustment to the gain or loss on the sale of the land in the period of the sale.

To illustrate, assume that on January 1, 20X1, Pluto purchases all the common stock of Star at $10,000 more than book value. All the differential relates to land that Star had purchased earlier for $25,000. So long as Star continues to hold the land, the $10,000 differential is assigned to Land in the consolidation worksheet. If Star sells the land to an unrelated company for $40,000, the following entry is recorded on Star's books:

(11)		Debit	Credit
	Cash	40,000	
	Land		25,000
	Gain on Sale of Land		15,000
	Record sale of land.		

While a gain of $15,000 is appropriate for Star to report, the accounting basis of the land to the consolidated entity is $35,000 ($25,000 + $10,000). Therefore, the consolidated enterprise must report a gain of only $5,000. To reduce the $15,000 gain reported by Star to the $5,000 gain that should be reported by the consolidated entity, the following consolidation entry is included in the worksheet for the year of the sale:

Eliminate Gain on Sale of Land:

	Debit	Credit
Gain on Sale of Land	**10,000**	
Income from Star		**10,000**

If, instead, Star sells the land for $32,000, the $7,000 ($32,000 − $25,000) gain recorded by Star is eliminated, and a loss of $3,000 ($32,000 − $35,000) is recognized in the consolidated income statement. The consolidation entry in this case is

Eliminate Gain and Record Loss on Sale of Land:

	Debit	Credit
Gain on Sale of Land	**7,000**	
Loss on Sale of Land	**3,000**	
Income from Star		**10,000**

When the equity method is used on the parent's books, the parent must adjust the carrying amount of the investment and its equity-method income in the period of the sale to write off the differential, as discussed in Chapter 2. Thereafter, the $10,000 differential no longer exists.

The sale of differential-related equipment is treated in the same manner as land except that the amortization for the current and previous periods must be considered as well as any accumulated depreciation that may have existed at the acquisition date that is being removed from the records. If all of the assets associated with that accumulated depreciation are sold, there is no need for the optional entry after the sale of those assets.

QUESTIONS

LO 5-1 **Q5-1** Where is the balance assigned to the noncontrolling interest reported in the consolidated balance sheet?

LO 5-1 **Q5-2** Why must a noncontrolling interest be reported in the consolidated balance sheet?

LO 5-1 **Q5-3** How does the introduction of noncontrolling shareholders change the consolidation worksheet?

LO 5-1 **Q5-4** How is the amount assigned to the noncontrolling interest normally determined when a consolidated balance sheet is prepared immediately after a business combination?

LO 5-2 **Q5-5** What portion of consolidated retained earnings is assigned to the noncontrolling interest in the consolidated balance sheet?

LO 5-2 **Q5-6** When majority ownership is acquired, what portion of the fair value of assets held by the subsidiary at acquisition is reported in the consolidated balance sheet?

LO 5-2 **Q5-7** When majority ownership is acquired, what portion of the goodwill reported in the consolidated balance sheet is assigned to the noncontrolling interest?

LO 5-2 **Q5-8** How is the income assigned to the noncontrolling interest normally computed?

LO 5-2 **Q5-9** How is income assigned to the noncontrolling interest shown in the consolidation worksheet?

LO 5-2 **Q5-10** How are dividends paid by a subsidiary to noncontrolling shareholders treated in the consolidation worksheet?

LO 5-3 **Q5-11** Under what circumstances would a parent company cease consolidation of a subsidiary? Explain.

LO 5-4 **Q5-12** How do other comprehensive income elements reported by a subsidiary affect the consolidated financial statements?

LO 5-4 **Q5-13** What portion of other comprehensive income reported by a subsidiary is included in the consolidated statement of comprehensive income as accruing to parent company shareholders?

Q5-14A What effect does a negative retained earnings balance on the subsidiary's books have on consolidation procedures?

Q5-15A What type of adjustment must be made in the consolidation worksheet if a differential is assigned to land and the subsidiary disposes of the land in the current period?

CASES

LO 5-2 **C5-1** **Consolidation Worksheet Preparation**

Analysis

The newest clerk in the accounting office recently entered trial balance data for the parent company and its subsidiaries in the company's consolidation program. After a few minutes of additional work needed to eliminate the intercompany investment account balances, he expressed his satisfaction at having completed the consolidation worksheet for 20X5. In reviewing the printout of the consolidation worksheet, other employees raised several questions, and you are asked to respond.

Required

Indicate whether each of the following questions can be answered by looking at the data in the consolidation worksheet (indicate why or why not):

a. Is it possible to tell if the parent is using the equity method in recording its ownership of each subsidiary?

b. Is it possible to tell if the correct amount of consolidated net income has been reported?

c. One of the employees thought the parent company had paid well above the fair value of net assets for a subsidiary purchased on January 1, 20X5. Is it possible to tell by reviewing the consolidation worksheet?

d. Is it possible to determine from the worksheet the percentage ownership of a subsidiary held by the parent?

"A" indicates that the item relates to Appendix 5A.

LO 5-2 **Research**

C5-2 Consolidated Income Presentation

Standard Company has a relatively high profit margin on its sales, and Jewel Company has a substantially lower profit margin. Standard holds 55 percent of Jewel's common stock and includes Jewel in its consolidated statements. Standard and Jewel reported sales of $100,000 and $60,000, respectively, in 20X4. Sales increased to $120,000 and $280,000 for the two companies in 20X5. The average profit margins of the two companies remained constant over the two years at 60 percent and 10 percent, respectively.

Standard's treasurer was aware that the subsidiary was awarded a major new contract in 20X5 and anticipated a substantial increase in net income for the year. She was disappointed to learn that consolidated net income allocated to the controlling interest had increased by only 38 percent even though sales were 2.5 times higher than in 20X4. She is not trained in accounting and does not understand the fundamental processes used in preparing Standard's consolidated income statement. She does know, however, that the earnings per share figures reported in the consolidated income statement are based on income allocated to the controlling interest and she wonders why that number isn't higher.

Required

As a member of the accounting department, you have been asked to prepare a memo to the treasurer explaining how consolidated net income is computed and the procedures used to allocate income to the parent company and to the subsidiary's noncontrolling shareholders. Include in your memo citations to or quotations from the authoritative literature. To assist the treasurer in gaining a better understanding, prepare an analysis showing the income statement amounts actually reported for 20X4 and 20X5.

LO 5-1 **Research**

C5-3 Pro Rata Consolidation

Rose Corporation and Krome Company established a joint venture to manufacture components for both companies' use on January 1, 20X1, and have operated it quite successfully for the past four years. Rose and Krome both contributed 50 percent of the equity when the joint venture was created. Rose purchases roughly 70 percent of the output of the joint venture and Krome purchases 30 percent. Rose and Krome have equal numbers of representatives on the joint venture's board of directors and participate equally in its management. Joint venture profits are distributed at year-end on the basis of total purchases by each company.

Required

Rose has been using the equity method to report its investment in the joint venture; however, Rose's financial vice president believes that each company should use pro rata consolidation. As a senior accountant at Rose, you have been asked to prepare a memo discussing those situations in which pro rata consolidation may be appropriate and to offer your recommendation as to whether Rose should continue to use the equity method or switch to pro rata consolidation. Include in your memo citations of and quotations from the authoritative literature to support your arguments.

LO 5-1 **Communication**

C5-4 Consolidation Procedures

A new employee has been given responsibility for preparing the consolidated financial statements of Sample Company. After attempting to work alone for some time, the employee seeks assistance in gaining a better overall understanding of the way in which the consolidation process works.

Required

You have been asked to provide assistance in explaining the consolidation process.

a. Why must the consolidation entries be entered in the consolidation worksheet each time consolidated statements are prepared?

b. How is the beginning-of-period noncontrolling interest balance determined?

c. How is the end-of-period noncontrolling interest balance determined?

d. Which of the subsidiary's account balances must always be eliminated?

e. Which of the parent company's account balances must always be eliminated?

LO 5-1 **Research**

C5-5 Changing Accounting Standards: Monsanto Company

Monsanto Company, a St. Louis–based company, is a leading provider of agricultural products for farmers. It sells seeds, biotechnology trait products, and herbicides worldwide.

Required

a. How did Monsanto Company report its income to noncontrolling (minority) shareholders of consolidated subsidiaries in its 2007 consolidated income statement?

b. How did Monsanto Company report its subsidiary noncontrolling (minority) interest in its 2007 consolidated balance sheet?

c. Comment on Monsanto's treatment of its subsidiary noncontrolling interest.

d. In 2007, Monsanto had several affiliates that were special-purpose or variable interest entities. What level of ownership did Monsanto have in these entities? Were any of these consolidated? Why?

EXERCISES

LO 5-1, 5-2

E5-1 Multiple-Choice Questions on Consolidation Process

Select the most appropriate answer for each of the following questions.

1. If A Company acquires 80 percent of the stock of B Company on January 1, 20X2, immediately after the acquisition, which of the following is correct?
   a. Consolidated retained earnings will be equal to the combined retained earnings of the two companies.
   b. Goodwill will always be reported in the consolidated balance sheet.
   c. A Company's additional paid-in capital may be reduced to permit the carryforward of B Company retained earnings.
   d. Consolidated retained earnings and A Company retained earnings will be the same.
2. Which of the following is correct?
   a. The noncontrolling shareholders' claim on the subsidiary's net assets is based on the book value of the subsidiary's net assets.
   b. Only the parent's portion of the difference between book value and fair value of the subsidiary's assets is assigned to those assets.
   c. Goodwill represents the difference between the book value of the subsidiary's net assets and the amount paid by the parent to buy ownership.
   d. Total assets reported by the parent generally will be less than total assets reported on the consolidated balance sheet.
3. Which of the following statements is correct?
   a. Foreign subsidiaries do not need to be consolidated if they are reported as a separate operating group under segment reporting.
   b. Consolidated retained earnings do not include the noncontrolling interest's claim on the subsidiary's retained earnings.
   c. The noncontrolling shareholders' claim should be adjusted for changes in the fair value of the subsidiary assets but should not include goodwill.
   d. Consolidation is expected any time the investor holds significant influence over the investee.
4. [AICPA Adapted] At December 31, 20X9, Grey Inc. owned 90 percent of Winn Corporation, a consolidated subsidiary, and 20 percent of Carr Corporation, an investee in which Grey cannot exercise significant influence. On the same date, Grey had receivables of $300,000 from Winn and $200,000 from Carr. In its December 31, 20X9, consolidated balance sheet, Grey should report accounts receivable from its affiliates of
   a. $500,000.
   b. $340,000.
   c. $230,000.
   d. $200,000.

LO 5-1, 5-2

E5-2 Multiple-Choice Questions on Consolidation [AICPA Adapted]

Select the correct answer for each of the following questions.

1. A 70 percent owned subsidiary company declares and pays a cash dividend. What effect does the dividend have on the retained earnings and noncontrolling interest balances in the parent company's *consolidated* balance sheet?
   a. No effect on either retained earnings or noncontrolling interest.
   b. No effect on retained earnings and a decrease in noncontrolling interest.
   c. Decreases in both retained earnings and noncontrolling interest.
   d. A decrease in retained earnings and no effect on noncontrolling interest.
2. How is the portion of consolidated earnings to be assigned to the noncontrolling interest in consolidated financial statements determined?
   a. The parent's net income is subtracted from the subsidiary's net income to determine the noncontrolling interest.
   b. The subsidiary's net income is extended to the noncontrolling interest.
   c. The amount of the subsidiary's earnings recognized for consolidation purposes is multiplied by the noncontrolling interest's percentage of ownership.
   d. The amount of consolidated earnings on the consolidated worksheets is multiplied by the noncontrolling interest percentage on the balance sheet date.
3. On January 1, 20X5, Post Company acquired an 80 percent investment in Stake Company. The acquisition cost was equal to Post's equity in Stake's net assets at that date. On January 1, 20X5, Post and Stake had retained earnings of $500,000 and $100,000, respectively. During 20X5, Post had net income of $200,000, which included its equity in Stake's earnings, and declared dividends of $50,000; Stake had net income of $40,000 and declared dividends of $20,000. There were no other intercompany transactions between the parent and subsidiary. On December 31, 20X5, what should the consolidated retained earnings be?
   a. $650,000.
   b. $666,000.
   c. $766,000.
   d. $770,000.

Note: Items 4 and 5 are based on the following information:

On January 1, 20X8, Ritt Corporation acquired 80 percent of Shaw Corporation's $10 par common stock for $956,000. On this date, the fair value of the noncontrolling interest was $239,000, and the carrying amount of Shaw's net assets was $1,000,000. The fair values of Shaw's identifiable assets and liabilities were the same as their carrying amounts except for plant assets (net) with a remaining life of 20 years, which were $100,000 in excess of the carrying amount. For the year ended December 31, 20X8, Shaw had net income of $190,000 and paid cash dividends totaling $125,000.

4. In the January 1, 20X8, consolidated balance sheet, the amount of goodwill reported should be
   a. $0.
   b. $76,000.
   c. $95,000.
   d. $156,000.
5. In the December 31, 20X8, consolidated balance sheet, the amount of noncontrolling interest reported should be
   a. $200,000.
   b. $239,000.
   c. $251,000.
   d. $252,000.

LO 5-2

Advanced StudyGuide .com

E5-3 Consolidation Entries with Differential

On June 10, 20X8, Game Corporation acquired 60 percent of Amber Company's common stock. The fair value of the noncontrolling interest was $32,800 on that date. Summarized balance sheet data for the two companies immediately after the stock purchase are as follows:

	Game Corp.	Amber Company	
Item	Book Value	Book Value	Fair Value
Cash	$ 25,800	$ 5,000	$ 5,000
Accounts Receivable	30,000	10,000	10,000
Inventory	80,000	20,000	25,000
Buildings & Equipment (net)	120,000	50,000	70,000
Investment in Amber Stock	49,200		
Total	$305,000	$85,000	$110,000
Accounts Payable	$ 25,000	$ 3,000	$ 3,000
Bonds Payable	150,000	25,000	25,000
Common Stock	55,000	20,000	
Retained Earnings	75,000	37,000	
Total	$305,000	$85,000	$ 28,000

Required

a. Give the consolidation entries required to prepare a consolidated balance sheet immediately after the purchase of Amber Company shares.

b. Explain how consolidation entries differ from other types of journal entries recorded in the normal course of business.

LO 5-2

E5-4 Computation of Consolidated Balances

Slim Corporation's balance sheet at January 1, 20X7, reflected the following balances:

Cash & Receivables	$ 80,000	Accounts Payable	$ 40,000
Inventory	120,000	Income Taxes Payable	60,000
Land	70,000	Bonds Payable	200,000
Buildings & Equipment (net)	480,000	Common Stock	250,000
		Retained Earnings	200,000
Total Assets	$750,000	Total Liabilities & Stockholders' Equity	$750,000

Ford Corporation entered into an active acquisition program and acquired 80 percent of Slim's common stock on January 2, 20X7, for $470,000. The fair value of the noncontrolling interest at that date was determined to be $117,500. A careful review of the fair value of Slim's assets and liabilities indicated the following:

	Book Value	Fair Value
Inventory	$120,000	$140,000
Land	70,000	60,000
Buildings & Equipment (net)	480,000	550,000

Goodwill is assigned proportionately to Ford and the noncontrolling shareholders.

Required

Compute the appropriate amount related to Slim to be included in the consolidated balance sheet immediately following the acquisition for each of the following items:

a. Inventory.

b. Land.

c. Buildings and Equipment (net).
d. Goodwill.
e. Investment in Slim Corporation.
f. Noncontrolling Interest.

LO 5-2

E5-5 Balance Sheet Worksheet

Power Company owns 90 percent of Pleasantdale Dairy's stock. The balance sheets of the two companies immediately after the Pleasantdale acquisition showed the following amounts:

	Power Company	Pleasantdale Dairy
Cash & Receivables	$ 130,000	$ 70,000
Inventory	210,000	90,000
Land	70,000	40,000
Buildings & Equipment (net)	390,000	220,000
Investment in Pleasantdale Stock	270,000	
Total Assets	$1,070,000	$420,000
Current Payables	$ 80,000	$ 40,000
Long-Term Liabilities	200,000	100,000
Common Stock	400,000	60,000
Retained Earnings	390,000	220,000
Total Liabilities & Stockholders' Equity	$1,070,000	$420,000

The fair value of the noncontrolling interest at the date of acquisition was determined to be $30,000. The full amount of the increase over book value is assigned to land held by Pleasantdale. At the date of acquisition, Pleasantdale owed Power $8,000 plus $900 accrued interest. Pleasantdale had recorded the accrued interest, but Power had not.

Required

Prepare and complete a consolidated balance sheet worksheet.

LO 5-2

E5-6 Majority-Owned Subsidiary Acquired at Higher than Book Value

Zenith Corporation acquired 70 percent of Down Corporation's common stock on December 31, 20X4, for $102,200. The fair value of the noncontrolling interest at that date was determined to be $43,800. Data from the balance sheets of the two companies included the following amounts as of the date of acquisition:

Item	Zenith Corporation	Down Corporation
Cash	$ 50,300	$ 21,000
Accounts Receivable	90,000	44,000
Inventory	130,000	75,000
Land	60,000	30,000
Buildings & Equipment	410,000	250,000
Less: Accumulated Depreciation	(150,000)	(80,000)
Investment in Down Corporation Stock	102,200	
Total Assets	$692,500	$340,000
Accounts Payable	$152,500	$ 35,000
Mortgage Payable	250,000	180,000
Common Stock	80,000	40,000
Retained Earnings	210,000	85,000
Total Liabilities & Stockholders' Equity	$692,500	$340,000

At the date of the business combination, the book values of Down's assets and liabilities approximated fair value except for inventory, which had a fair value of $81,000, and buildings and equipment, which had a fair value of $185,000. At December 31, 20X4, Zenith reported accounts payable of $12,500 to Down, which reported an equal amount in its accounts receivable.

Required

a. Give the consolidation entry or entries needed to prepare a consolidated balance sheet immediately following the business combination.

b. Prepare a consolidated balance sheet worksheet.

c. Prepare a consolidated balance sheet in good form.

LO 5-2

E5-7 Consolidation with Noncontrolling Interest

Temple Corporation acquired 75 percent of Dynamic Corporation's voting common stock on December 31, 20X4, for $390,000. At the date of combination, Dynamic reported the following:

Current Assets	$220,000	Current Liabilities	$ 80,000
Long-Term Assets (net)	420,000	Long-Term Liabilities	200,000
		Common Stock	120,000
		Retained Earnings	240,000
Total	$640,000	Total	$640,000

At December 31, 20X4, the book values of Dynamic's net assets and liabilities approximated their fair values, except for buildings, which had a fair value of $80,000 more than book value, and inventories, which had a fair value of $36,000 more than book value. The fair value of the noncontrolling interest was determined to be $130,000 at that date.

Required

Temple Corporation wishes to prepare a consolidated balance sheet immediately following the business combination. Give the consolidation entry or entries needed to prepare a consolidated balance sheet at December 31, 20X4.

LO 5-2

E5-8 Multiple-Choice Questions on Balance Sheet Consolidation

Power Corporation acquired 70 percent of Silk Corporation's common stock on December 31, 20X2. Balance sheet data for the two companies immediately following the acquisition follow:

Item	Power Corporation	Silk Corporation
Cash	$ 44,000	$ 30,000
Accounts Receivable	110,000	45,000
Inventory	130,000	70,000
Land	80,000	25,000
Buildings & Equipment	500,000	400,000
Less: Accumulated Depreciation	(223,000)	(165,000)
Investment in Silk Corporation Stock	150,500	
Total Assets	$ 791,500	$405,000
Accounts Payable	$ 61,500	$ 28,000
Taxes Payable	95,000	37,000
Bonds Payable	280,000	200,000
Common Stock	150,000	50,000
Retained Earnings	205,000	90,000
Total Liabilities & Stockholders' Equity	$ 791,500	$405,000

At the date of the business combination, the book values of Silk's net assets and liabilities approximated fair value except for inventory, which had a fair value of $85,000, and land, which had a fair value of $45,000. The fair value of the noncontrolling interest was $64,500 on December 31, 20X2.

Required

For each question below, indicate the appropriate total that should appear in the consolidated balance sheet prepared immediately after the business combination.

1. What amount of inventory will be reported?
   a. $179,000.
   b. $200,000.
   c. $210,500.
   d. $215,000.
2. What amount of goodwill will be reported?
   a. $0.
   b. $28,000.
   c. $40,000.
   d. $52,000.
3. What amount of total assets will be reported?
   a. $1,081,000.
   b. $1,121,000.
   c. $1,196,500.
   d. $1,231,500.
4. What amount of total liabilities will be reported?
   a. $265,000.
   b. $436,500.
   c. $622,000.
   d. $701,500.
5. What amount will be reported as noncontrolling interest?
   a. $42,000.
   b. $52,500.
   c. $60,900.
   d. $64,500.
6. What amount of consolidated retained earnings will be reported?
   a. $295,000.
   b. $268,000.
   c. $232,000.
   d. $205,000.
7. What amount of total stockholders' equity will be reported?
   a. $355,000.
   b. $397,000.
   c. $419,500.
   d. $495,000.

LO 5-2

E5-9 Majority-Owned Subsidiary with Differential

Canton Corporation is a majority-owned subsidiary of West Corporation. West acquired 75 percent ownership on January 1, 20X3, for $133,500. At that date, Canton reported common stock outstanding of $60,000 and retained earnings of $90,000, and the fair value of the noncontrolling interest was $44,500. The differential is assigned to equipment, which had a fair value $28,000 more than book value and a remaining economic life of seven years at the date of the business combination. Canton reported net income of $30,000 and paid dividends of $12,000 in 20X3.

Required

a. Give the journal entries recorded by West during 20X3 on its books if it accounts for its investment in Canton using the equity method.

b. Give the consolidation entries needed at December 31, 20X3, to prepare consolidated financial statements.

LO 5-1, 5-2

E5-10 Differential Assigned to Amortizable Asset

Major Corporation acquired 90 percent of Lancaster Company's voting common stock on January 1, 20X1, for $486,000. At the time of the combination, Lancaster reported common stock outstanding of $120,000 and retained earnings of $380,000, and the fair value of the noncontrolling interest was $54,000. The book value of Lancaster's net assets approximated market value except for patents that had a market value of $40,000 more than their book value. The patents had a remaining economic life of five years at the date of the business combination. Lancaster reported net income of $60,000 and paid dividends of $20,000 during 20X1.

Required

a. What balance did Major report as its investment in Lancaster at December 31, 20X1, assuming Major uses the equity method in accounting for its investment?

b. Give the consolidation entry or entries needed to prepare consolidated financial statements at December 31, 20X1.

LO 5-2

E5-11 Consolidation after One Year of Ownership

Pioneer Corporation purchased 80 percent of Lowe Corporation's stock on January 1, 20X2. At that date, Lowe reported retained earnings of $80,000 and had $120,000 of stock outstanding. The fair value of its buildings was $32,000 more than the book value.

Pioneer paid $190,000 to acquire the Lowe shares. At that date, the noncontrolling interest had a fair value of $47,500. The remaining economic life for all Lowe's depreciable assets was eight years on the date of combination. The amount of the differential assigned to goodwill is not impaired. Lowe reported net income of $40,000 in 20X2 and declared no dividends.

Required

a. Give the consolidation entries needed to prepare a consolidated balance sheet immediately after Pioneer purchased Lowe stock.

b. Give all consolidation entries needed to prepare a full set of consolidated financial statements for 20X2.

LO 5-1, 5-2

E5-12 Consolidation Following Three Years of Ownership

Advanced StudyGuide .com

Knox Corporation purchased 60 percent of Conway Company ownership on January 1, 20X7, for $277,500. Conway reported the following net income and dividend payments:

Year	Net Income	Dividends Paid
20X7	$45,000	$25,000
20X8	55,000	35,000
20X9	30,000	10,000

On January 1, 20X7, Conway had $250,000 of $5 par value common stock outstanding and retained earnings of $150,000, and the fair value of the noncontrolling interest was $185,000. Conway held land with a book value of $22,500 and a market value of $30,000 and equipment with a book value of $320,000 and a market value of $360,000 at the date of combination. The remainder of the differential at acquisition was attributable to an increase in the value of patents, which had a remaining useful life of 10 years. All depreciable assets held by Conway at the date of acquisition had a remaining economic life of eight years.

Required

a. Compute the increase in the fair value of patents held by Conway.

b. Prepare the consolidation entries needed at January 1, 20X7, to prepare a consolidated balance sheet.

c. Compute the balance reported by Knox as its investment in Conway at December 31, 20X8.

d. Prepare the journal entries recorded by Knox with regard to its investment in Conway during 20X9.

e. Prepare the consolidation entries needed at December 31, 20X9, to prepare a three-part consolidation worksheet.

LO 5-2

E5-13 Consolidation Worksheet for Majority-Owned Subsidiary

Proud Corporation acquired 80 percent of Stergis Company's voting stock on January 1, 20X3, at underlying book value. The fair value of the noncontrolling interest was equal to 20 percent of the book value of Stergis at that date. Assume that the accumulated depreciation on depreciable assets was $60,000 on the acquisition date. Proud uses the equity method in accounting for its ownership of Stergis during 20X3. On December 31, 20X3, the trial balances of the two companies are as follows:

	Proud Corporation		Stergis Company	
Item	**Debit**	**Credit**	**Debit**	**Credit**
Current Assets	$173,000		$105,000	
Depreciable Assets	500,000		300,000	
Investment in Stergis Company Stock	136,000			
Depreciation Expense	25,000		15,000	
Other Expenses	105,000		75,000	
Dividends Declared	40,000		10,000	
Accumulated Depreciation		$175,000		$ 75,000
Current Liabilities		50,000		40,000
Long-Term Debt		100,000		120,000
Common Stock		200,000		100,000
Retained Earnings		230,000		50,000
Sales		200,000		120,000
Income from Subsidiary		24,000		
	$979,000	$979,000	$505,000	$505,000

Required

a. Give all consolidation entries required as of December 31, 20X3, to prepare consolidated financial statements.

b. Prepare a three-part consolidation worksheet.

c. Prepare a consolidated balance sheet, income statement, and retained earnings statement for 20X3.

LO 5-2

E5-14 Consolidation Worksheet for Majority-Owned Subsidiary for Second Year

This exercise is a continuation of E5-13. Proud Corporation acquired 80 percent of Stergis Company's voting stock on January 1, 20X3, at underlying book value. The fair value of the noncontrolling interest was equal to 20 percent of the book value of Stergis at that date. Assume that the accumulated depreciation on depreciable assets was $60,000 on the acquisition date. Proud uses the equity method in accounting for its ownership of Stergis. On December 31, 20X4, the trial balances of the two companies are as follows:

	Proud Corporation		Stergis Company	
Item	**Debit**	**Credit**	**Debit**	**Credit**
Current Assets	$ 235,000		$150,000	
Depreciable Assets	500,000		300,000	
Investment in Stergis Company Stock	152,000			
Depreciation Expense	25,000		15,000	
Other Expenses	150,000		90,000	
Dividends Declared	50,000		15,000	

(continued)

	Proud Corporation		Stergis Company	
Item	**Debit**	**Credit**	**Debit**	**Credit**
Accumulated Depreciation		$ 200,000		$ 90,000
Current Liabilities		70,000		50,000
Long-Term Debt		100,000		120,000
Common Stock		200,000		100,000
Retained Earnings		284,000		70,000
Sales		230,000		140,000
Income from Subsidiary		28,000		
	$1,112,000	$1,112,000	$570,000	$570,000

Required

a. Give all consolidation entries required on December 31, 20X4, to prepare consolidated financial statements.

b. Prepare a three-part consolidation worksheet as of December 31, 20X4.

LO 5-4

Advanced StudyGuide .com

E5-15 Preparation of Stockholders' Equity Section with Other Comprehensive Income

Broadmore Corporation acquired 75 percent of Stem Corporation's common stock on January 1, 20X8, for $435,000. At that date, Stem reported common stock outstanding of $300,000 and retained earnings of $200,000, and the fair value of the noncontrolling interest was $145,000. The book values and fair values of Stem's assets and liabilities were equal, except for other intangible assets, which had a fair value $80,000 more than book value and a 10-year remaining life. Broadmore and Stem reported the following data for 20X8 and 20X9:

	Stem Corporation			Broadmore Corporation	
Year	**Net Income**	**Comprehensive Income**	**Dividends Paid**	**Operating Income**	**Dividends Paid**
20X8	$40,000	$50,000	$15,000	$120,000	$70,000
20X9	60,000	65,000	30,000	140,000	70,000

Required

a. Compute consolidated comprehensive income for 20X8 and 20X9.

b. Compute comprehensive income attributable to the controlling interest for 20X8 and 20X9.

c. Assuming that Broadmore reported capital stock outstanding of $320,000 and retained earnings of $430,000 at January 1, 20X8, prepare the stockholders' equity section of the consolidated balance sheet at December 31, 20X8 and 20X9.

LO 5-4

E5-16 Consolidation Entries for Subsidiary with Other Comprehensive Income

Palmer Corporation acquired 70 percent of Krown Corporation's ownership on January 1, 20X8, for $140,000. At that date, Krown reported capital stock outstanding of $120,000 and retained earnings of $80,000, and the fair value of the noncontrolling interest was equal to 30 percent of the book value of Krown. During 20X8, Krown reported net income of $30,000 and comprehensive income of $36,000 and paid dividends of $25,000.

Required

a. Present all equity-method entries that Palmer would have recorded in accounting for its investment in Krown during 20X8.

b. Present all consolidation entries needed at December 31, 20X8, to prepare a complete set of consolidated financial statements for Palmer Corporation and its subsidiary.

E5-17A Consolidation of Subsidiary with Negative Retained Earnings

General Corporation acquired 80 percent of Strap Company's voting common stock on January 1, 20X4, for $138,000. At that date, the fair value of the noncontrolling interest was $34,500. Strap's balance sheet at the date of acquisition contained the following balances:

STRAP COMPANY
Balance Sheet
January 1, 20X4

Cash	$ 20,000	Accounts Payable	$ 35,000
Accounts Receivable	35,000	Notes Payable	180,000
Land	90,000	Common Stock	100,000
Building & Equipment	300,000	Additional Paid-in Capital	75,000
Less: Accumulated Depreciation	(85,000)	Retained Earnings	(30,000)
Total Assets	$360,000	Total Liabilities & Stockholders' Equity	$360,000

At the date of acquisition, the reported book values of Strap's assets and liabilities approximated fair value.

Required

Give the consolidation entry or entries needed to prepare a consolidated balance sheet immediately following the business combination.

E5-18A Complex Assignment of Differential

On December 31, 20X4, Worth Corporation acquired 90 percent of Brinker Inc.'s common stock for $864,000. At that date, the fair value of the noncontrolling interest was $96,000. Of the $240,000 differential, $5,000 related to the increased value of Brinker's inventory, $75,000 related to the increased value of its land, $60,000 related to the increased value of its equipment, and $50,000 was associated with a change in the value of its notes payable due to increasing interest rates. Brinker's equipment had a remaining life of 15 years from the date of combination. Brinker sold all inventory it held at the end of 20X4 during 20X5; the land to which the differential related also was sold during the year for a large gain. The amortization of the differential relating to Brinker's notes payable was $7,500 for 20X5.

At the date of combination, Brinker reported retained earnings of $120,000, common stock outstanding of $500,000, and premium on common stock of $100,000. For the year 20X5, it reported net income of $150,000 but paid no dividends. Worth accounts for its investment in Brinker using the equity method.

Required

a. Present all entries that Worth would have recorded during 20X5 with respect to its investment in Brinker.

b. Present all consolidation entries that would have been included in the worksheet to prepare a full set of consolidated financial statements for the year 20X5.

PROBLEMS

LO 5-1

P5-19 Reported Balances

Roof Corporation acquired 80 percent of the stock of Gable Company by issuing shares of its common stock with a fair value of $192,000. At that time, the fair value of the noncontrolling interest was estimated to be $48,000, and the fair values of Gable's identifiable assets and liabilities were $310,000 and $95,000, respectively. Gable's assets and liabilities had book values of $220,000 and $95,000, respectively.

Required

Compute the following amounts to be reported immediately after the combination

a. Investment in Gable reported by Roof.

b. Goodwill for the combined entity.

c. Noncontrolling interest reported in the consolidated balance sheet.

LO 5-1

P5-20 Acquisition Price

Darwin Company holds assets with a fair value of $120,000 and a book value of $90,000 and liabilities with a book value and fair value of $25,000.

Required

Compute the following amounts if Brad Corporation acquires 60 percent ownership of Darwin:

a. What amount did Brad pay for the shares if no goodwill and no gain on a bargain purchase are reported?

b. What amount did Brad pay for the shares if the fair value of the noncontrolling interest at acquisition is $54,000 and goodwill of $40,000 is reported?

c. What balance will be assigned to the noncontrolling interest in the consolidated balance sheet if Brad pays $73,200 to acquire its ownership and goodwill of $27,000 is reported?

LO 5-1

P5-21 Multiple-Choice Questions on Applying the Equity Method [AICPA Adapted]

Select the correct answer for each of the following questions.

1. On July 1, 20X3, Barker Company purchased 20 percent of Acme Company's outstanding common stock for $400,000 when the fair value of Acme's net assets was $2,000,000. Barker does not have the ability to exercise significant influence over Acme's operating and financial policies. The following data concerning Acme are available for 20X3:

	Twelve Months Ended December 31, 20X3	Six Months Ended December 31, 20X3
Net income	$300,000	$160,000
Dividends declared and paid	190,000	100,000

In its income statement for the year ended December 31, 20X3, how much income should Barker report from this investment?

a. $20,000.
b. $32,000.
c. $38,000.
d. $60,000.

2. On January 1, 20X3, Miller Company purchased 25 percent of Wall Corporation's common stock; no differential resulted from the purchase. Miller appropriately uses the equity method for this investment, and the balance in Miller's investment account was $190,000 on December 31, 20X3. Wall reported net income of $120,000 for the year ended December 31, 20X3, and paid dividends on its common stock totaling $48,000 during 20X3. How much did Miller pay for its 25 percent interest in Wall?

a. $172,000.
b. $202,000.
c. $208,000.
d. $232,000.

3. On January 1, 20X7, Robohn Company purchased for cash 40 percent of Lowell Company's 300,000 shares of voting common stock for $1,800,000 when 40 percent of the underlying equity in Lowell's net assets was $1,740,000. The payment in excess of underlying equity was assigned to amortizable assets with a remaining life of six years. As a result of this transaction, Robohn has the ability to exercise significant influence over Lowell's operating and financial policies. Lowell's net income for the year ended December 31, 20X7, was $600,000. During 20X7, Lowell paid $325,000 in dividends to its shareholders. The income reported by Robohn for its investment in Lowell should be

a. $120,000.
b. $130,000.
c. $230,000.
d. $240,000.

4. In January 20X0, Farley Corporation acquired 20 percent of Davis Company's outstanding common stock for $800,000. This investment gave Farley the ability to exercise significant influence over Davis. The book value of the acquired shares was $600,000. The excess of cost over book

value was attributed to an identifiable intangible asset, which was undervalued on Davis' balance sheet and had a remaining economic life of 10 years. For the year ended December 31, 20X0, Davis reported net income of $180,000 and paid cash dividends of $40,000 on its common stock. What is the proper carrying value of Farley's investment in Davis on December 31, 20X0?

a. $772,000.
b. $780,000.
c. $800,000.
d. $808,000.

LO 5-1

P5-22 Amortization of Differential

Ball Corporation purchased 30 percent of Krown Company's common stock on January 1, 20X5, by issuing preferred stock with a par value of $50,000 and a market price of $120,000. The following amounts relate to Krown's balance sheet items at that date:

	Book Value	Fair Value
Cash & Receivables	$ 200,000	$200,000
Buildings & Equipment	400,000	360,000
Less: Accumulated Depreciation	(100,000)	
Total Assets	$ 500,000	
Accounts Payable	$ 50,000	50,000
Bonds Payable	200,000	200,000
Common Stock	100,000	
Retained Earnings	150,000	
Total Liabilities & Equities	$ 500,000	

Krown purchased buildings and equipment on January 1, 20X0, with an expected economic life of 20 years. No change in overall expected economic life occurred as a result of the acquisition of Ball's stock. The amount paid in excess of the fair value of Krown's reported net assets is attributed to unrecorded copyrights with a remaining useful life of eight years. During 20X5, Krown reported net income of $40,000 and paid dividends of $10,000.

Required

Give all journal entries to be recorded on Ball Corporation's books during 20X5, assuming it uses the equity method in accounting for its ownership of Krown Company.

LO 5-1

P5-23 Computation of Account Balances

Easy Chair Company purchased 40 percent ownership of Stuffy Sofa Corporation on January 1, 20X1, for $150,000. Stuffy Sofa's balance sheet at the time of acquisition was as follows:

STUFFY SOFA CORPORATION
Balance Sheet
January 1, 20X1

Cash		$ 30,000	Current Liabilities	$ 40,000
Accounts Receivable		120,000	Bonds Payable	200,000
Inventory		80,000	Common Stock	200,000
Land		150,000	Additional Paid-In Capital	40,000
Buildings & Equipment	$ 300,000			
Less: Accumulated Depreciation	(120,000)	180,000	Retained Earnings	80,000
Total Assets		$560,000	Total Liabilities & Equities	$560,000

During 20X1 Stuffy Sofa Corporation reported net income of $30,000 and paid dividends of $9,000. The fair values of Stuffy Sofa's assets and liabilities were equal to their book values at the date of acquisition, with the exception of buildings and equipment, which had a fair value $35,000 above book value.

All buildings and equipment had remaining lives of five years at the time of the business combination. The amount attributed to goodwill as a result of its purchase of Stuffy Sofa shares is not impaired.

Required

a. What amount of investment income will Easy Chair Company record during 20X1 under equity-method accounting?

b. What amount of income will be reported under the cost method?

c. What will be the balance in the investment account on December 31, 20X1, under (1) cost-method and (2) equity-method accounting?

LO 5-1, 5-2

P5-24 Complex Differential

Essex Company issued common shares with a par value of $50,000 and a market value of $165,000 in exchange for 30 percent ownership of Tolliver Corporation on January 1, 20X2. Tolliver reported the following balances on that date:

TOLLIVER CORPORATION
Balance Sheet
January 1, 20X2

	Book Value	Fair Value
Assets		
Cash	$ 40,000	$ 40,000
Accounts Receivable	80,000	80,000
Inventory (FIFO basis)	120,000	150,000
Land	50,000	65,000
Buildings & Equipment	500,000	320,000
Less: Accumulated Depreciation	(240,000)	
Patent		25,000
Total Assets	$550,000	$680,000
Liabilities & Equities		
Accounts Payable	$ 30,000	$ 30,000
Bonds Payable	100,000	100,000
Common Stock	150,000	
Additional Paid-In Capital	20,000	
Retained Earnings	250,000	
Total Liabilities & Equities	$550,000	

The estimated economic life of the patents held by Tolliver is 10 years. The buildings and equipment are expected to last 12 more years on average. Tolliver paid dividends of $9,000 during 20X2 and reported net income of $80,000 for the year.

Required

Compute the amount of investment income (loss) reported by Essex from its investment in Tolliver for 20X2 and the balance in the investment account on December 31, 20X2, assuming the equity method is used in accounting for the investment.

LO 5-1

P5-25 Equity Entries with Differential

On January 1, 20X0, Hunter Corporation issued 6,000 of its $10 par value shares to acquire 45 percent of the shares of Arrow Manufacturing. Arrow Manufacturing's balance sheet immediately before the acquisition contained the following items:

ARROW MANUFACTURING
Balance Sheet
January 1, 20X0

	Book Value	Fair Value
Assets		
Cash & Receivables	$ 30,000	$ 30,000
Land	70,000	80,000

(continued)

Buildings & Equipment (net)	120,000	150,000
Patent	80,000	80,000
Total Assets	$300,000	
Liabilities & Equities		
Accounts Payable	$ 90,000	90,000
Common Stock	150,000	
Retained Earnings	60,000	
Total Liabilities & Equities	$300,000	

On the date of the stock acquisition, Hunter's shares were selling at $35, and Arrow Manufacturing's buildings and equipment had a remaining economic life of 10 years. The amount of the differential assigned to goodwill is not impaired.

In the two years following the stock acquisition, Arrow Manufacturing reported net income of $80,000 and $50,000 and paid dividends of $20,000 and $40,000, respectively. Hunter used the equity method in accounting for its ownership of Arrow Manufacturing.

Required

a. Give the entry recorded by Hunter Corporation at the time of acquisition.

b. Give the journal entries recorded by Hunter during 20X0 and 20X1 related to its investment in Arrow Manufacturing.

c. What balance will be reported in Hunter's investment account on December 31, 20X1?

LO 5-1

P5-26 Equity Entries with Differential

Ennis Corporation acquired 35 percent of Jackson Corporation's stock on January 1, 20X8, by issuing 25,000 shares of its $2 par value common stock. Jackson Corporation's balance sheet immediately before the acquisition contained the following items:

JACKSON CORPORATION
Balance Sheet
January 1, 20X8

	Book Value	Fair Value
Assets		
Cash & Receivables	$ 40,000	$ 40,000
Inventory (FIFO basis)	80,000	100,000
Land	50,000	70,000
Buildings & Equipment (net)	240,000	320,000
Total Assets	$410,000	$530,000
Liabilities & Equities		
Accounts Payable	$ 70,000	$ 70,000
Common Stock	130,000	
Retained Earnings	210,000	
Total Liabilities & Equities	$410,000	

Shares of Ennis were selling at $8 at the time of the acquisition. On the date of acquisition, the remaining economic life of buildings and equipment held by Jackson was 20 years. The amount of the differential assigned to goodwill is not impaired. For the year 20X8, Jackson reported net income of $70,000 and paid dividends of $10,000.

Required

a. Give the journal entries recorded by Ennis Corporation during 20X8 related to its investment in Jackson Corporation.

b. What balance will Ennis report as its investment in Jackson at December 31, 20X8?

LO 5-1

P5-27 Additional Ownership Level

Balance sheet, income, and dividend data for Amber Corporation, Blair Corporation, and Carmen Corporation at January 1, 20X3, were as follows:

Account Balances	Amber Corporation	Blair Corporation	Carmen Corporation
Cash	$ 70,000	$ 60,000	$ 20,000
Accounts Receivable	120,000	80,000	40,000
Inventory	100,000	90,000	65,000
Fixed Assets (net)	450,000	350,000	240,000
Total Assets	$740,000	$580,000	$365,000
Accounts Payable	$105,000	$110,000	$ 45,000
Bonds Payable	300,000	200,000	120,000
Common Stock	150,000	75,000	90,000
Retained Earnings	185,000	195,000	110,000
Total Liabilities & Equity	$740,000	$580,000	$365,000
Income from Operations in 20X3	$220,000	$100,000	
Net Income for 20X3			$ 50,000
Dividends Declared & Paid	60,000	30,000	25,000

On January 1, 20X3, Amber Corporation purchased 40 percent of the voting common stock of Blair Corporation by issuing common stock with a par value of $40,000 and fair value of $130,000. Immediately after this transaction, Blair purchased 25 percent of the voting common stock of Carmen Corporation by issuing bonds payable with a par value and market value of $51,500.

On January 1, 20X3, the book values of Blair's net assets were equal to their fair values except for equipment that had a fair value $30,000 more than book value and patents that had a fair value $25,000 more than book value. At that date, the equipment had a remaining economic life of eight years, and the patents had a remaining economic life of five years. The book values of Carmen's assets were equal to their fair values except for inventory that had a fair value $6,000 in excess of book value and was accounted for on a FIFO basis.

Required

a. Compute the net income reported by Amber Corporation for 20X3, assuming Amber and Blair used the equity method in accounting for their intercorporate investments.

b. Give all journal entries recorded by Amber relating to its investment in Blair during 20X3.

LO 5-1

P5-28 Correction of Error

Hill Company paid $164,000 to acquire 40 percent ownership of Dale Company on January 1, 20X2. Net book value of Dale's assets on that date was $300,000. Book values and fair values of net assets held by Dale were the same except for equipment and patents. Equipment held by Dale had a book value of $70,000 and fair value of $120,000. All of the remaining purchase price was attributable to the increased value of patents with a remaining useful life of eight years. The remaining economic life of all depreciable assets held by Dale was five years.

Dale Company's net income and dividends for the three years immediately following the purchase of shares were

Year	Net Income	Dividends
20X2	$40,000	$15,000
20X3	60,000	20,000
20X4	70,000	25,000

The computation of Hill's investment income for 20X4 and entries in its investment account since the date of purchase were as follows:

	20X4 Investment Income	
Pro rata income accrual ($70,000 × 0.40)		$28,000
Amortize patents ($44,000 ÷ 8 years)	$5,500	
Dividends received ($25,000 × 0.40)		10,000
20X4 investment income		$32,500

	Investment in Dale Company	
1/1/X2 purchase price	$164,000	
20X2 income accrual	16,000	
Amortize patents		$5,500
20X3 income accrual	24,000	
Amortize patents		5,500
20X4 income accrual	28,000	
Amortize patents		5,500
12/31/X4 balance	$215,500	

Before making closing entries at the end of 20X4, Hill's new controller reviewed the reports and was convinced that both the balance in the investment account and the investment income that Hill reported for 20X4 were in error.

Required

Prepare a correcting entry, along with supporting computations, to properly state the balance in the investment account and all related account balances at the end of 20X4.

LO 5-2

P5-29 Majority-Owned Subsidiary Acquired at More Than Book Value

Porter Corporation acquired 70 percent of Darla Corporation's common stock on December 31, 20X4, for $102,200. At that date, the fair value of the noncontrolling interest was $43,800. Data from the balance sheets of the two companies included the following amounts as of the date of acquisition:

Item	Porter Corporation	Darla Corporation
Cash	$ 50,300	$ 21,000
Accounts Receivable	90,000	44,000
Inventory	130,000	75,000
Land	60,000	30,000
Buildings & Equipment	410,000	250,000
Less: Accumulated Depreciation	(150,000)	(80,000)
Investment in Darla Corporation Stock	102,200	
Total Assets	$692,500	$340,000
Accounts Payable	$152,500	$ 35,000
Mortgage Payable	250,000	180,000
Common Stock	80,000	40,000
Retained Earnings	210,000	85,000
Total Liabilities & Stockholders' Equity	$692,500	$340,000

At the date of the business combination, the book values of Darla's assets and liabilities approximated fair value except for inventory, which had a fair value of $81,000, and buildings and equipment, which had a fair value of $185,000. At December 31, 20X4, Porter reported accounts payable of $12,500 to Darla, which reported an equal amount in its accounts receivable.

Required

a. Give the consolidation entry or entries needed to prepare a consolidated balance sheet immediately following the business combination.

b. Prepare a consolidated balance sheet worksheet.

c. Prepare a consolidated balance sheet in good form.

LO 5-2 **P5-30** **Balance Sheet Consolidation of Majority-Owned Subsidiary**

On January 2, 20X8, Total Corporation acquired 75 percent of Ticken Tie Company's outstanding common stock. In exchange for Ticken Tie's stock, Total issued bonds payable with a par value of $500,000 and fair value of $510,000 directly to the selling stockholders of Ticken Tie. At that date, the fair value of the noncontrolling interest was $170,000. The two companies continued to operate as separate entities subsequent to the combination.

Immediately prior to the combination, the book values and fair values of the companies' assets and liabilities were as follows:

	Total		Ticken Tie	
	Book Value	**Fair Value**	**Book Value**	**Fair Value**
Cash	$ 12,000	$ 12,000	$ 9,000	$ 9,000
Receivables	41,000	39,000	31,000	30,000
Allowance for Bad Debts	(2,000)		(1,000)	
Inventory	86,000	89,000	68,000	72,000
Land	55,000	200,000	50,000	70,000
Buildings & Equipment	960,000	650,000	670,000	500,000
Accumulated Depreciation	(411,000)		(220,000)	
Patent				40,000
Total Assets	$741,000	$990,000	$607,000	$721,000
Current Payables	$ 38,000	$ 38,000	$ 29,000	$ 29,000
Bonds Payable	200,000	210,000	100,000	100,000
Common Stock	300,000		200,000	
Additional Paid-in Capital	100,000		130,000	
Retained Earnings	103,000		148,000	
Total Liabilities & Equity	$741,000		$607,000	

At the date of combination, Ticken Tie owed Total $6,000 plus accrued interest of $500 on a short-term note. Both companies have properly recorded these amounts.

Required

a. Record the business combination on the books of Total Corporation.

b. Present in general journal form all consolidation entries needed in a worksheet to prepare a consolidated balance sheet immediately following the business combination on January 2, 20X8.

c. Prepare and complete a consolidated balance sheet worksheet as of January 2, 20X8, immediately following the business combination.

d. Present a consolidated balance sheet for Total and its subsidiary as of January 2, 20X8.

LO 5-1, 5-2 **P5-31** **Incomplete Data**

Blue Corporation acquired controlling ownership of Skyler Corporation on December 31, 20X3, and a consolidated balance sheet was prepared immediately. Partial balance sheet data for the two companies and the consolidated entity at that date follow:

BLUE CORPORATION AND SKYLER CORPORATION
Balance Sheet Data
December 31, 20X3

Item	Blue Corporation	Skyler Corporation	Consolidated Entity
Cash	$ 63,650	$ 35,000	$ 98,650
Accounts Receivable	98,000	?	148,000

(continued)

Inventory	105,000	80,000	195,000
Buildings & Equipment	400,000	340,000	640,000
Less: Accumulated Depreciation	(215,000)	(140,000)	(215,000)
Investment in Skyler Corporation Stock	?		
Goodwill			9,000
Total Assets	$620,000	$380,000	$875,650
Accounts Payable	$115,000	$ 46,000	$146,000
Wages Payable	?	?	94,000
Notes Payable	200,000	110,000	310,000
Common Stock	120,000	75,000	?
Retained Earnings	115,000	125,000	?
Noncontrolling Interest			90,650
Total Liabilities & Equities	$?	$380,000	$875,650

During 20X3, Blue provided engineering services to Skyler and has not yet been paid for them. There were no other receivables or payables between Blue and Skyler at December 31, 20X3.

Required

a. What is the amount of unpaid engineering services at December 31, 20X3, on work done by Blue for Skyler?

b. What balance in accounts receivable did Skyler report at December 31, 20X3?

c. What amounts of wages payable did Blue and Skyler report at December 31, 20X3?

d. What was the fair value of Skyler as a whole at the date of acquisition?

e. What percentage of Skyler's shares were purchased by Blue?

f. What amounts of capital stock and retained earnings must be reported in the consolidated balance sheet?

LO 5-2

P5-32 Income and Retained Earnings

Quill Corporation acquired 70 percent of North Company's stock on January 1, 20X9, for $105,000. At that date, the fair value of the noncontrolling interest was equal to 30 percent of the book value of North Company. The companies reported the following stockholders' equity balances immediately after the acquisition:

	Quill Corporation	North Company
Common Stock	$120,000	$ 30,000
Additional Paid-in Capital	230,000	80,000
Retained Earnings	290,000	40,000
Total	$640,000	$150,000

Quill and North reported 20X9 operating incomes of $90,000 and $35,000 and dividend payments of $30,000 and $10,000, respectively.

Required

a. Compute the amount reported as net income by each company for 20X9, assuming Quill uses equity-method accounting for its investment in North.

b. Compute consolidated net income for 20X9.

c. Compute the reported balance in retained earnings at December 31, 20X9, for both companies.

d. Compute consolidated retained earnings at December 31, 20X9.

e. How would the computation of consolidated retained earnings at December 31, 20X9, change if Quill uses the cost method in accounting for its investment in North?

LO 5-2

P5-33 Consolidation Worksheet at End of First Year of Ownership

Power Corporation acquired 75 percent of Best Company's ownership on January 1, 20X8, for $96,000. At that date, the fair value of the noncontrolling interest was $32,000. The book

Advanced StudyGuide .com

value of Best's net assets at acquisition was $100,000. The book values and fair values of Best's assets and liabilities were equal, except for Best's buildings and equipment, which were worth $20,000 more than book value. Accumulated depreciation on the buildings and equipment was $30,000 on the acquisition date. Buildings and equipment are depreciated on a 10-year basis.

Although goodwill is not amortized, the management of Power concluded at December 31, 20X8, that goodwill from its purchase of Best shares had been impaired and the correct carrying amount was $2,500. Goodwill and goodwill impairment were assigned proportionately to the controlling and noncontrolling shareholders.

Trial balance data for Power and Best on December 31, 20X8, are as follows:

	Power Corporation		Best Company	
Item	**Debit**	**Credit**	**Debit**	**Credit**
Cash	$ 47,500		$ 21,000	
Accounts Receivable	70,000		12,000	
Inventory	90,000		25,000	
Land	30,000		15,000	
Buildings & Equipment	350,000		150,000	
Investment in Best Co. Stock	96,375			
Cost of Goods Sold	125,000		110,000	
Wage Expense	42,000		27,000	
Depreciation Expense	25,000		10,000	
Interest Expense	12,000		4,000	
Other Expenses	13,500		5,000	
Dividends Declared	30,000		16,000	
Accumulated Depreciation		$145,000		$ 40,000
Accounts Payable		45,000		16,000
Wages Payable		17,000		9,000
Notes Payable		150,000		50,000
Common Stock		200,000		60,000
Retained Earnings		102,000		40,000
Sales		260,000		180,000
Income from Subsidiary		12,375		
	$931,375	$931,375	$395,000	$395,000

Required

a. Give all consolidation entries needed to prepare a three-part consolidation worksheet as of December 31, 20X8.

b. Prepare a three-part consolidation worksheet for 20X8 in good form.

LO 5-2

P5-34 Consolidation Worksheet at End of Second Year of Ownership

Advanced StudyGuide .com

This problem is a continuation of P5-33. Power Corporation acquired 75 percent of Best Company's ownership on January 1, 20X8, for $96,000. At that date, the fair value of the noncontrolling interest was $32,000. The book value of Best's net assets at acquisition was $100,000. The book values and fair values of Best's assets and liabilities were equal, except for Best's buildings and equipment, which were worth $20,000 more than book value. Accumulated depreciation on the buildings and equipment was $30,000 on the acquisition date. Buildings and equipment are depreciated on a 10-year basis.

Although goodwill is not amortized, the management of Power concluded at December 31, 20X8, that goodwill from its purchase of Best shares had been impaired and the correct carrying amount was $2,500. Goodwill and goodwill impairment were assigned proportionately to the controlling and noncontrolling shareholders. No additional impairment occurred in 20X9.

Trial balance data for Power and Best on December 31, 20X9, are as follows:

Item	Power Corporation Debit	Power Corporation Credit	Best Company Debit	Best Company Credit
Cash	$ 68,500		$ 32,000	
Accounts Receivable	85,000		14,000	
Inventory	97,000		24,000	
Land	50,000		25,000	
Buildings & Equipment	350,000		150,000	
Investment in Best Co. Stock	106,875			
Cost of Goods Sold	145,000		114,000	
Wage Expense	35,000		20,000	
Depreciation Expense	25,000		10,000	
Interest Expense	12,000		4,000	
Other Expenses	23,000		16,000	
Dividends Declared	30,000		20,000	
Accumulated Depreciation		$ 170,000		$ 50,000
Accounts Payable		51,000		15,000
Wages Payable		14,000		6,000
Notes Payable		150,000		50,000
Common Stock		200,000		60,000
Retained Earnings		126,875		48,000
Sales		290,000		200,000
Income from Subsidiary		25,500		
	$1,027,375	$1,027,375	$429,000	$429,000

Required

a. Give all consolidation entries needed to prepare a three-part consolidation worksheet as of December 31, 20X9.

b. Prepare a three-part consolidation worksheet for 20X9 in good form.

c. Prepare a consolidated balance sheet, income statement, and retained earnings statement for 20X9.

LO 5-2

P5-35 Comprehensive Problem: Differential Apportionment

Mortar Corporation acquired 80 percent ownership of Granite Company on January 1, 20X7, for $173,000. At that date, the fair value of the noncontrolling interest was $43,250. The trial balances for the two companies on December 31, 20X7, included the following amounts:

Item	Mortar Corporation Debit	Mortar Corporation Credit	Granite Company Debit	Granite Company Credit
Cash	$ 38,000		$ 25,000	
Accounts Receivable	50,000		55,000	
Inventory	240,000		100,000	
Land	80,000		20,000	
Buildings & Equipment	500,000		150,000	
Investment in Granite Company Stock	202,000			
Cost of Goods Sold	500,000		250,000	
Depreciation Expense	25,000		15,000	
Other Expenses	75,000		75,000	
Dividends Declared	50,000		20,000	
Accumulated Depreciation		$ 155,000		$ 75,000
Accounts Payable		70,000		35,000
Mortgages Payable		200,000		50,000
Common Stock		300,000		50,000
Retained Earnings		290,000		100,000
Sales		700,000		400,000
Income from Subsidiary		45,000		
	$1,760,000	$1,760,000	$710,000	$710,000

Additional Information

1. On January 1, 20X7, Granite reported net assets with a book value of $150,000 and a fair value of $191,250. Accumulated depreciation on Buildings and Equipment was $60,000 on the acquisition date.
2. Granite's depreciable assets had an estimated economic life of 11 years on the date of combination. The difference between fair value and book value of Granite's net assets is related entirely to buildings and equipment.
3. Mortar used the equity method in accounting for its investment in Granite.
4. Detailed analysis of receivables and payables showed that Granite owed Mortar $16,000 on December 31, 20X7.

Required

a. Give all journal entries recorded by Mortar with regard to its investment in Granite during 20X7.
b. Give all consolidation entries needed to prepare a full set of consolidated financial statements for 20X7.
c. Prepare a three-part consolidation worksheet as of December 31, 20X7.

LO 5-2

P5-36 Comprehensive Problem: Differential Apportionment in Subsequent Period

This problem is a continuation of P5-35. Mortar Corporation acquired 80 percent ownership of Granite Company on January 1, 20X7, for $173,000. At that date, the fair value of the noncontrolling interest was $43,250. The trial balances for the two companies on December 31, 20X8, included the following amounts:

	Mortar Corporation		Granite Company	
Item	**Debit**	**Credit**	**Debit**	**Credit**
Cash	$ 59,000		$ 31,000	
Accounts Receivable	83,000		71,000	
Inventory	275,000		118,000	
Land	80,000		30,000	
Buildings & Equipment	500,000		150,000	
Investment in Granite Company Stock	206,200			
Cost of Goods Sold	490,000		310,000	
Depreciation Expense	25,000		15,000	
Other Expenses	62,000		100,000	
Dividends Declared	45,000		25,000	
Accumulated Depreciation		$ 180,000		$ 90,000
Accounts Payable		86,000		30,000
Mortgages Payable		200,000		70,000
Common Stock		300,000		50,000
Retained Earnings		385,000		140,000
Sales		650,000		470,000
Income from Subsidiary		24,200		
	$1,825,200	$1,825,200	$850,000	$850,000

Additional Information

1. On January 1, 20X7, Granite reported net assets with a book value of $150,000 and a fair value of $191,250. The difference between fair value and book value of Granite's net assets is related entirely to Buildings and Equipment. Accumulated depreciation on Buildings and Equipment was $60,000 on the acquisition date. Granite's depreciable assets had an estimated economic life of 11 years on the date of combination.
2. At December 31, 20X8, Mortar's management reviewed the amount attributed to goodwill and concluded goodwill was impaired and should be reduced to $14,000. Goodwill and goodwill impairment were assigned proportionately to the controlling and noncontrolling shareholders.

3. Mortar used the equity method in accounting for its investment in Granite.
4. Detailed analysis of receivables and payables showed that Mortar owed Granite $9,000 on December 31, 20X8.

Required

a. Give all journal entries recorded by Mortar with regard to its investment in Granite during 20X8.

b. Give all consolidation entries needed to prepare a full set of consolidated financial statements for 20X8.

c. Prepare a three-part consolidation worksheet as of December 31, 20X8.

LO 5-4

P5-37 Subsidiary with Other Comprehensive Income in Year of Acquisition

Amber Corporation acquired 60 percent ownership of Sparta Company on January 1, 20X8, at underlying book value. At that date, the fair value of the noncontrolling interest was equal to 40 percent of the book value of Sparta Company. Accumulated depreciation on Buildings and Equipment was $75,000 on the acquisition date. Trial balance data at December 31, 20X8, for Amber and Sparta are as follows:

	Amber Corporation		Sparta Company	
Item	**Debit**	**Credit**	**Debit**	**Credit**
Cash	$ 27,000		$ 8,000	
Accounts Receivable	65,000		22,000	
Inventory	40,000		30,000	
Buildings & Equipment	500,000		235,000	
Investment in Row Company Securities			40,000	
Investment in Sparta Company	108,000			
Cost of Goods Sold	150,000		110,000	
Depreciation Expense	30,000		10,000	
Interest Expense	8,000		3,000	
Dividends Declared	24,000		15,000	
Accumulated Depreciation		$140,000		$ 85,000
Accounts Payable		63,000		20,000
Bonds Payable		100,000		50,000
Common Stock		200,000		100,000
Retained Earnings		208,000		60,000
Other Comprehensive Income from Subsidiary (OCI)—Unrealized Gain on Investments		6,000		
Unrealized Gain on Investments (OCI)				10,000
Sales		220,000		148,000
Income from Subsidiary		15,000		
	$952,000	$952,000	$473,000	$473,000

Additional Information

Sparta purchased stock of Row Company on January 1, 20X8, for $30,000 and classified the investment as available-for-sale securities. The value of Row's securities increased to $40,000 at December 31, 20X8.

Required

a. Give all consolidation entries needed to prepare a three-part consolidation worksheet as of December 31, 20X8.

b. Prepare a three-part consolidation worksheet for 20X8 in good form.

c. Prepare a consolidated balance sheet, income statement, and statement of comprehensive income for 20X8.

LO 5-4

P5-38 Subsidiary with Other Comprehensive Income in Year Following Acquisition

This problem is a continuation of P5-37. Amber Corporation acquired 60 percent ownership of Sparta Company on January 1, 20X8, at underlying book value. At that date, the fair value of the noncontrolling interest was equal to 40 percent of the book value of Sparta Company. Accumulated depreciation on Buildings and Equipment was $75,000 on the acquisition date. Trial balance data at December 31, 20X9, for Amber and Sparta are as follows:

	Amber Corporation		Sparta Company	
Item	**Debit**	**Credit**	**Debit**	**Credit**
Cash	$ 18,000		$ 11,000	
Accounts Receivable	45,000		21,000	
Inventory	40,000		30,000	
Buildings & Equipment	585,000		257,000	
Investment in Row Company Securities			44,000	
Investment in Sparta Company	116,400			
Cost of Goods Sold	170,000		97,000	
Depreciation Expense	30,000		10,000	
Interest Expense	8,000		3,000	
Dividends Declared	40,000		20,000	
Accumulated Depreciation		$ 170,000		$ 95,000
Accounts Payable		75,000		24,000
Bonds Payable		100,000		50,000
Common Stock		200,000		100,000
Retained Earnings		231,000		70,000
Accumulated Other Comprehensive Income		6,000		10,000
Other Comprehensive Income from Subsidiary (OCI)—Unrealized Gain on Investments		2,400		
Unrealized Gain on Investments (OCI)				4,000
Sales		250,000		140,000
Income from Subsidiary		18,000		
	$1,052,400	$1,052,400	$493,000	$493,000

Additional Information

Sparta purchased stock of Row Company on January 1, 20X8, for $30,000 and classified the investment as available-for-sale securities. The value of Row's securities increased to $40,000 and $44,000, respectively, at December 31, 20X8, and 20X9.

Required

a. Give all consolidation entries needed to prepare a three-part consolidation worksheet as of December 31, 20X9.

b. Prepare a three-part consolidation worksheet for 20X9 in good form.

LO 5-2

P5-39 Comprehensive Problem: Majority-Owned Subsidiary

Master Corporation acquired 80 percent ownership of Stanley Wood Products Company on January 1, 20X1, for $160,000. On that date, the fair value of the noncontrolling interest was $40,000, and Stanley reported retained earnings of $50,000 and had $100,000 of common stock outstanding. Master has used the equity method in accounting for its investment in Stanley.

Trial balance data for the two companies on December 31, 20X5, are as follows:

	Master Corporation		Stanley Wood Products Company	
Item	**Debit**	**Credit**	**Debit**	**Credit**
Cash & Receivables	$ 81,000		$ 65,000	
Inventory	260,000		90,000	
Land	80,000		80,000	
Buildings & Equipment	500,000		150,000	
Investment in Stanley Wood Products Stock	188,000			
Cost of Goods Sold	120,000		50,000	
Depreciation Expense	25,000		15,000	
Inventory Losses	15,000		5,000	
Dividends Declared	30,000		10,000	
Accumulated Depreciation		$ 205,000		$105,000
Accounts Payable		60,000		20,000
Notes Payable		200,000		50,000
Common Stock		300,000		100,000
Retained Earnings		314,000		90,000
Sales		200,000		100,000
Income from Subsidiary		20,000		
	$1,299,000	$1,299,000	$465,000	$465,000

Additional Information

1. On the date of combination, the fair value of Stanley's depreciable assets was $50,000 more than book value. The accumulated depreciation on these assets was $10,000 on the acquisition date. The differential assigned to depreciable assets should be written off over the following 10-year period.
2. There was $10,000 of intercorporate receivables and payables at the end of 20X5.

Required

a. Give all journal entries that Master recorded during 20X5 related to its investment in Stanley.
b. Give all consolidation entries needed to prepare consolidated statements for 20X5.
c. Prepare a three-part worksheet as of December 31, 20X5.

6 Intercompany Inventory Transactions

INVENTORY TRANSFERS AT SAMSUNG ELECTRONICS

Most people are familiar with Samsung's products, from cell phones to tablets and flat screens. Samsung was formed in Korea in 1938 as a trading company. However, over the years, the company expanded into various industries, including textiles, food processing, insurance, securities, and retail. It wasn't until the 1960s that Samsung launched into electronics, and in the 1970s it also moved into construction and shipbuilding. While Samsung Heavy Industries is the world's second-largest shipbuilder, the best-known of Samsung's segments is clearly its electronics business.

Samsung Electronics is the world's largest manufacturer of LCD panels, televisions, mobile phones, and memory chips. It is also well known for digital cameras, camcorders, batteries, and storage media. The company has many wholly owned subsidiaries such as World Cyber Games, Samsung Semiconductor, Samsung Electronics Digital Printing, and Samsung Telecommunications America, as well as other majority-owned subsidiaries such as Samsung Display and STECO. While each of its many subsidiaries operates as a stand-alone company, technologies and components are often exchanged via intercompany transactions. For example, Samsung Electronics' 2013 annual report indicates that approximately 59 percent of its total revenues result from intercompany sales transactions. The reason Samsung Electronics sells so much inventory to affiliated companies is because of its vertical integration strategy. According to *Forbes* magazine, "Samsung's strategy underscores a competitive advantage: The South Korean company is able to bring products to the market more quickly than [competitors] because it controls the entire manufacturing process for its smartphones. Samsung makes everything from chips to screens at its own factories, allowing it to change designs and pump out new products at a rapid pace."[1]

Transactions between the affiliated companies are not considered *arm's-length*. These transactions are sometimes called *related-party transactions*. Generally Accepted Accounting Principles only allow companies to recognize sales to third-party buyers outside the consolidated entity. Hence, Samsung Electronics eliminates all within-group sales in calculating consolidated sales revenues. This elimination is required because all companies owned or controlled by Samsung Electronics are, in essence, parts of the same company and a company cannot make a profit by selling inventory to itself. This chapter examines intercompany inventory transactions and the consolidation procedures associated with them.

LEARNING OBJECTIVES

When you finish studying this chapter, you should be able to:

LO 6-1 Understand and explain intercompany transfers and why they must be eliminated.

LO 6-2 Understand and explain concepts associated with inventory transfers and transfer pricing.

[1] Tim Worstall, "Why Samsung Beats Apple or Perhaps Vice Versa," *Forbes*, September 9, 2013; Ian Sherr, Eva Dou, and Lorraine Luk, "Apple Tests iPhone Screens as Large as Six Inches," The *Wall Street Journal*, September 5, 2013.

LO 6-3 Prepare equity-method journal entries and consolidation entries for the consolidation of a subsidiary following downstream inventory transfers.

LO 6-4 Prepare equity-method journal entries and consolidation entries for the consolidation of a subsidiary following upstream inventory transfers.

LO 6-5 Understand and explain additional considerations associated with consolidation.

OVERVIEW OF THE CONSOLIDATED ENTITY AND INTERCOMPANY TRANSACTIONS

LO 6-1

Understand and explain intercompany transfers and why they must be eliminated.

The consolidated entity is an aggregation of a number of different companies. The financial statements prepared by the individual affiliates are consolidated into a single set of financial statements representing the financial position and operating results of the entire economic entity as if it were a single company.

A parent company and its subsidiaries often engage in a variety of transactions among themselves. For example, manufacturing companies often have subsidiaries that develop raw materials or produce components to be included in the products of affiliated companies. Some companies sell consulting or other services to affiliated companies. United States Steel Corporation and its subsidiaries engage in numerous transactions with one another, including sales of raw materials, fabricated products, and transportation services. Such transactions often are critical to the operations of the overall consolidated entity. These transactions between related companies are referred to as ***intercompany*** or ***intercorporate transfers.***

Figure 6–1 illustrates a consolidated entity with each of the affiliated companies engaging in both intercompany transfers and transactions with external parties. From a consolidated viewpoint, only transactions with parties outside the economic entity are included in the income statement. Thus, the arrows crossing the perimeter of the consolidated entity in Figure 6–1 represent transactions that are included in the operating

FIGURE 6–1
Transactions of Affiliated Companies

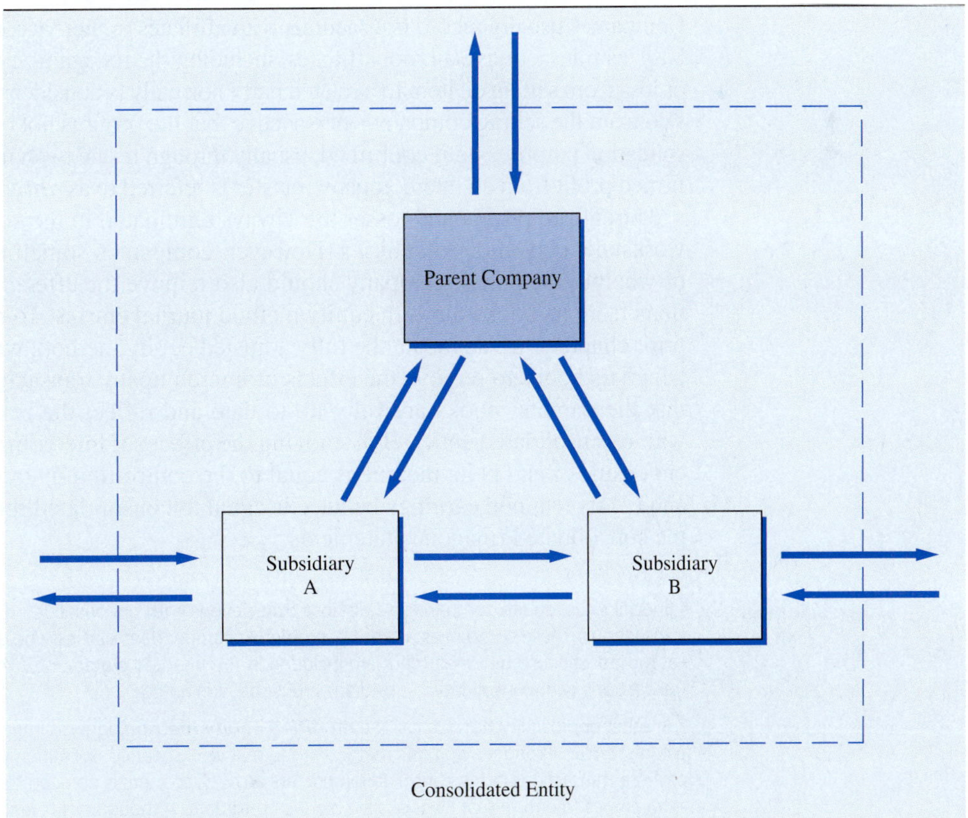

results of the consolidated entity for the period. Transfers between the affiliated companies, shown in Figure 6–1 as those arrows not crossing the boundary of the consolidated entity, are equivalent to transfers between operating divisions of a single company and are not reported in the consolidated statements.

The central idea of consolidated financial statements is that they report on the activities of the consolidating affiliates as if the separate affiliates actually constitute a single company. Because single companies are not permitted to reflect internal transactions in their financial statements, consolidated entities also must exclude the effects of transactions that are totally within the consolidated entity from their financial statements. Building on the basic consolidation procedures presented in earlier chapters, this chapter and the next two deal with the effects of intercompany transfers. This chapter deals with intercompany inventory sales, and Chapters 7 and 8 discuss intercompany services, fixed asset sales, and intercompany debt transfers.

Elimination of Intercompany Transfers

Only *arm's-length* transactions (i.e., those conducted between completely independent parties who act in their own best interests) may be reflected in the consolidated financial statements.[2] Thus, all aspects of intercompany transfers must be eliminated in preparing consolidated financial statements so that the statements appear as if they were those of a single company. **ASC 810-10-45-1** mentions open account balances, security holdings, sales and purchases, and interest and dividends as examples of the intercompany balances and transactions that must be eliminated.

No distinction is made between wholly owned and less-than-wholly-owned subsidiaries with regard to the elimination of intercompany transfers. The focus in consolidation is on the single-entity concept rather than on the percentage of ownership. Once the conditions for consolidation are met, a company becomes part of a single economic entity, and all transactions with consolidated companies become internal transfers that must be eliminated fully, regardless of the level of ownership held.

Elimination of Unrealized Profits and Losses

Companies usually record transactions with affiliates in their accounting records on the same basis as transactions with nonaffiliates, including the recognition of profits and losses. Profit or loss from selling an item to a related party normally is considered realized at the time of the sale from the selling company's perspective, but the profit is not considered realized for consolidation purposes until confirmed, usually through resale to an unrelated party. This unconfirmed profit from an intercompany transfer is referred to as ***unrealized intercompany profit.***

Unrealized profits and losses are always eliminated in the consolidation process using worksheet consolidation entries. However, companies sometimes differ on the question of whether the parent company should also remove the effects of intercompany transactions from its books through equity method journal entries. To maintain consistency with prior chapters, we advocate the fully adjusted equity method, which requires the parent to adjust its books to remove the effects of intercompany transactions. This method ensures that the parents' books are fully up-to-date and reflect the results of operations for the whole consolidated entity. By removing the effects of intercompany transactions, the parent ensures that (1) its income is equal to the controlling interest in consolidated income and (2) its retained earnings balance is equal to consolidated retained earnings amount in the consolidated financial statements.[3]

[2] Special rules require companies to disclose transactions with unconsolidated affiliates as related-party transactions. These companies are not "completely independent parties who act in their own best interests," yet the transactions between them are included in the financial statements. The key difference is that all transactions with consolidated subsidiaries must be eliminated.

[3] Another approach, which we call the ***modified equity method,*** ignores intercompany transactions on the parents' books. Proponents of this method argue that worksheet consolidation entries remove the effects of these transactions in the consolidation process anyway, so there is no need for the parent to record the extra entries to ensure that its books are always up-to-date. Although it is true that the consolidated financial statements are the same either way, when the modified equity method is used, key numbers in the parents' books (such as net income and retained earnings) will no longer equal the balances in the consolidated financial statements. We present this alternative approach in Appendix A.

INVENTORY TRANSACTIONS

LO 6-2

Understand and explain concepts associated with inventory transfers and transfer pricing.

Inventory transactions are the most common form of intercompany exchange. All revenue and expense items recorded by the participants must be eliminated fully in preparing the consolidated income statement, and the recorded value of transferred assets must be adjusted so that they appear in the consolidated balance sheet at the original owner's cost. Moreover, under the fully adjusted equity method, unrealized profits and losses on intercompany transfers are deferred until the items are sold to a nonaffiliate.

The recordkeeping process for intercompany inventory transfers may be more complex than for other forms of transfers. Companies often have many different types of inventory items, and some may be transferred from affiliate to affiliate. Also, the problems of keeping tabs on which items have been resold and which items are still on hand are greater in the case of inventory transactions because part of a shipment may be sold immediately by the purchasing company and other units may remain on hand for one or more accounting periods.[4]

Worksheet Consolidation Entries

The worksheet entries ensure that only the cost of the inventory to the consolidated entity is (1) included in the consolidated balance sheet when the inventory is still on hand and (2) charged to cost of goods sold in the period the inventory is resold to nonaffiliates.

Transfers at Cost

Merchandise is sometimes sold to related companies at the seller's cost or carrying value. When an intercorporate sale includes no profit or loss, the balance sheet inventory amounts at the end of the period require no adjustment for consolidation because the purchasing affiliate's inventory carrying amount is the same as the cost to the transferring affiliate and the consolidated entity. At the time the inventory is resold to a nonaffiliate, the amount recognized as cost of goods sold by the affiliate making the outside sale is the cost to the consolidated entity.

Even when the intercorporate sale includes no profit or loss, however, a worksheet consolidation entry is needed to remove both the revenue and the cost of goods sold recorded by the seller from the intercorporate sale and any unpaid payable or receivable balance that may remain. This worksheet consolidation entry avoids overstating these accounts. The consolidation entry does not affect consolidated net income when the transfer is made at cost because both revenue and cost of goods sold are reduced by the same amount.

FYI

To minimize tax liabilities, companies often transfer inventory at a profit or loss to shift income to jurisdictions with lower tax rates. However, strict federal tax laws limit the transfer of profits outside the United States.

Transfers at a Profit or Loss

Companies use many different approaches in setting intercorporate transfer prices. In some companies, the sale price to an affiliate is the same as the price to any other customer. Some companies routinely mark up inventory transferred to affiliates by a certain percentage of cost. Other companies have elaborate transfer pricing policies designed to encourage internal sales. Regardless of the method used in setting intercorporate transfer prices, the consolidation process must remove the effects of such sales from the consolidated statements.

Calculating Unrealized Profit or Loss

The calculation of unrealized intercompany profit or loss is an important step in eliminating the effects of intercompany transfers. In order to illustrate this calculation, it

[4] Inventory is not typically held for multiple years. However, many companies prepare quarterly consolidated financial statements and each quarter would be considered a unique period. Also, some companies sell large items (like cars, boats, or recreational vehicles) or expensive items (like jewelry), which may remain in inventory for more than one quarterly or annual period. Finally, when companies report LIFO inventories, they may build up LIFO layers, which create a fictional accounting notion that inventory items (long since sold) are still in stock.

FIGURE 6–2
Two Types of Intercompany Inventory Transfers

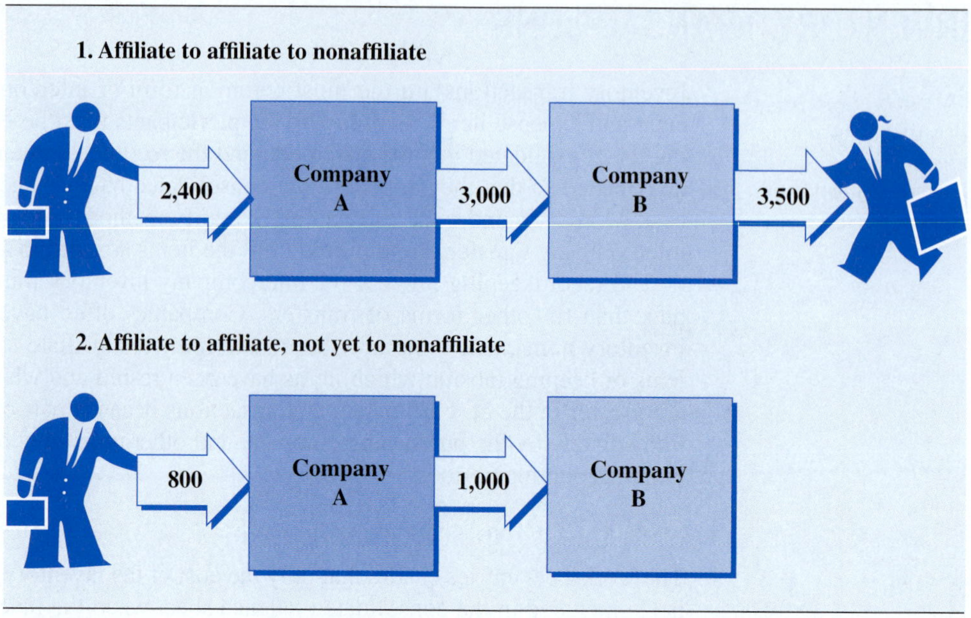

is important to first understand that there are two types of intercompany inventory transfers: (1) a transfer from one affiliate to another, which is then sold to an independent nonaffiliate and (2) a transfer from one affiliate to another, which has not yet been sold to an independent nonaffiliate. Figure 6–2 presents examples of each type of transfer.

In each case, Company A purchases inventory in an arm's-length transaction from an independent party. Company A then transfers the inventory to Company B (an affiliate) at a profit. In case 1, Company B eventually sells the inventory to an unrelated party. However, in case 2, Company B still holds the inventory at the end of the reporting period. The gross profit on the case 2 transfer from Company A to Company B represents unrealized intercompany profit because the inventory has not yet been sold to an independent party. When companies sell to affiliated companies on a regular basis, at the end of a reporting period, some of the inventory is often still on hand awaiting the sale to an independent party. Thus, the two cases in Figure 6–2 could represent intercompany sales between the same two companies (1) during the period and (2) just prior to the end of the period. The following chart summarizes these intercompany inventory transactions:

	Total Intercompany Sales	(1) Resold to Nonaffiliate	(2) Inventory on Hand
Sales	$4,000	$3,000	$1,000
− COGS	3,200	2,400	800
Gross Profit	800	600	200
GP%	20%		

! CAUTION

Note that all numbers in this chart are stated from Company A's perspective. Columns 2 and 3 simply break out the portion of the total column that was (1) resold or (2) still on hand in Company B's ending inventory. For example, the inventory in case 1 was eventually resold to a nonaffiliate for $3,500. However, this chart reports only what happened to Company A's sales.

Company A has total intercompany sales of $4,000 to Company B with total gross profit on these sales of $800. These sales can be divided into two categories: (1) those that Company B eventually resells during the current period, $3,000, and (2) those that are still in Company B's inventory at the end of the accounting period, $1,000. The gross profit on the intercompany sales that have not yet been realized through a sale to an independent third party, $200, should be deferred until this inventory is eventually resold to a nonaffiliate. Under the fully adjusted equity method, this unrealized gross profit is deferred on the parent company's books through an equity method entry (discussed in more detail later). All intercompany sales are eliminated in the consolidated financial statements through a worksheet consolidation entry(ies).

It is sometimes necessary to use the gross profit percentage to estimate the unrealized gross profit on intercompany transfers, assuming that the selling company uses a constant markup percentage on all intercompany transfers. For example, assume that Company A transfers inventory costing $9,000 to Company B, an affiliated company, for $10,000. At the end of the accounting period, Company B still has $3,000 of this inventory on hand in its warehouse. To calculate the unrealized profit given this limited information, first calculate gross profit and gross profit percentage on total intercompany sales.

	Total Intercompany Sales	(1) Resold to Nonaffiliate	(2) Inventory on Hand
Sales	$10,000		$3,000
– COGS	9,000		
Gross Profit			???

Gross profit is $1,000. Thus, the gross profit percentage is 10 percent ($1,000 ÷ $10,000). If we assume the gross profit percentage is the same across all intercompany sales, we can estimate the unrealized gross profit on intercompany sales (lower right-hand corner of the chart) by multiplying the balance on hand in intercompany inventory by the gross profit percentage to calculate the unrealized gross profit of $300 ($3,000 × 10%).

	Total Intercompany Sales	(1) Resold to Nonaffiliate	(2) Inventory on Hand
Sales	$10,000		$3,000
– COGS	9,000		
Gross Profit	1,000		300
GP%	10%		

! CAUTION

Students are sometimes confused when given information about markup on cost. Obviously, markup on cost is not the same ratio as the markup on transfer price. Nevertheless, students often mix them up. Be careful to ensure that you use the markup on transfer price (gross profit percentage) to calculate unrealized gross profit!

Hint:

Markup on cost = Gross Profit / COGS

Markup on transfer price = Gross Profit / Sales = GP%

Inventory transfer problems often use terminology that is unfamiliar. For example, the selling price of the inventory is sometimes called the ***transfer price*** and the gross profit on intercompany sales is often referred to simply as the ***markup***. Based on these definitions, another term for gross profit percentage is simply ***markup on sales***. Similarly, ***markup on cost*** is the ratio of gross profit divided by cost of goods sold. When provided with information about markup on cost, this information must first be used to calculate cost of goods sold. Then calculate gross profit and gross profit percentage to determine unrealized gross profit on intercompany inventory transfers.

As an example, assume that Company A transfers inventory to an affiliate, Company B, for $5,000 with a 25 percent markup on cost and that Company B resells $3,500 of this inventory to nonaffiliates during the accounting period. How much unrealized gross profit from Company A's intercompany sales should be deferred at the end of the period? This information can be summarized as follows:

	Total Intercompany Sales	(1) Resold to Nonaffiliate	(2) Inventory on Hand
Sales	$5,000	$3,500	
− COGS			
Gross Profit			???
GP%			

When the information is given in terms of markup on cost, we must first calculate the cost of goods sold. Because the markup on cost is given as 25 percent, we can express this relationship by defining cost of goods sold as C and then expressing the markup (gross profit) as 0.25C.

	Total Intercompany Sales	(1) Resold to Nonaffiliate	(2) Inventory on Hand
Sales	$5,000	$3,500	
− COGS	C		
Gross Profit	0.25 C		???
GP%			

Thus, we can solve for cost of goods sold algebraically as follows:

$$\text{Sales} - \text{COGS} = \text{Gross Profit}$$
$$\$5{,}000 - C = 0.25C$$
$$\$5{,}000 = 1.25C$$
$$C = \$4{,}000$$

We can then calculate gross profit percentage (markup on transfer price) of 20 percent ($1,000 ÷ $5,000). Moreover, we can solve for Company B's ending inventory balance of $1,500 ($5,000 − $3,500 resold).

	Total Intercompany Sales	(1) Resold to Nonaffiliate	(2) Inventory on Hand
Sales	$5,000	$3,500	$1,500
− COGS	4,000		
Gross Profit	1,000		???
GP%	20%		

Finally, we can calculate the unrealized gross profit of $300 ($1,500 × 20%).

The chart above provides valuable information for two important accounting tasks. First, the number in the lower right-hand corner represents the unrealized profit or loss that must be deferred. The parent company makes an equity method journal entry to defer the portion of the unrealized profits that accrue to the controlling interest. After all the missing numbers in the chart are filled in, it can then be used to prepare consolidation entries to defer unrealized profit and to adjust the recorded value of inventory to reflect the actual purchase price when it was purchased from a nonaffiliate.

Deferring Unrealized Profit or Loss on the Parent's Books

For consolidation purposes, profits recorded on an intercorporate inventory sale are recognized in the period in which the inventory is resold to an unrelated party. Until the point of resale, all intercorporate profits must be deferred. When a parent company sells inventory to a subsidiary, referred to as a ***downstream sale,*** any profit or loss on the transfer accrues to the parent company's stockholders. When a subsidiary sells inventory to its parent, an ***upstream sale,*** any profit or loss accrues to the subsidiary's stockholders. If the subsidiary is wholly owned, all profit or loss ultimately accrues to the parent company as the sole stockholder. If, however, the selling subsidiary is not wholly owned, the profit or loss on the upstream sale is apportioned between the parent company and the noncontrolling shareholders.

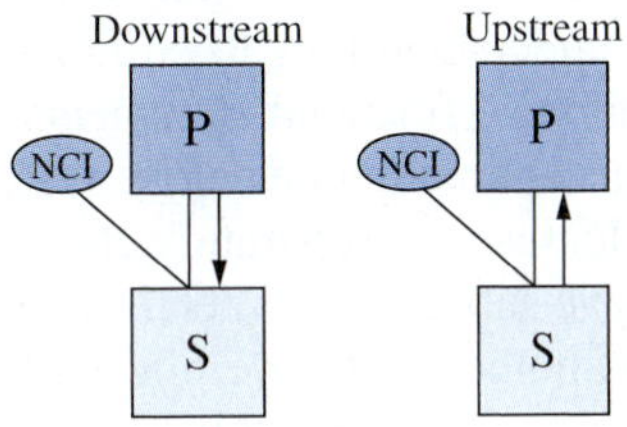

In addition to deferring unrealized profits and losses on the consolidation worksheet, under the fully adjusted equity method, an unrealized profit or loss on intercompany inventory transfers is deferred on the parent's books to ensure that the parent company's (1) net income equals the controlling interest in consolidated income and (2) retained earnings equals consolidated retained earnings. The only question is whether *all* (with downstream transactions) or *the parent's proportionate share* (with upstream transactions) of the unrealized gross profit should be deferred on the parent's books.[5] The journal entry on the parent's books to defer unrealized gross profit follows:

Income from Subsidiary	XXX	
Investment in Subsidiary		XXX

! CAUTION

On downstream transactions, the parent defers *all* (i.e.,100% of) unrealized profits and losses, whether the parent owns 100% or less than 100% of the subsidiary. On upstream transactions, the parent always defers its ownership percentage of unrealized profits and losses.

The unrealized gross profit is calculated as demonstrated in the previous subsection. In downstream transactions, the parent company uses this journal entry to defer the entire amount. In upstream transactions, the parent defers only its proportional share of the unrealized gross profit.

Unrealized profits or losses are deferred only until they are realized. In most cases, inventory on hand at the end of one period is sold in the next period. Once the inventory is sold to an unaffiliated party, the previously deferred amount is recognized in the period of the arm's-length sale by reversing the deferral on the parent's books as follows:

Investment in Subsidiary	XXX	
Income from Subsidiary		XXX

[5] Under the equity method, the parent accounts for all transactions related to its ownership in a subsidiary through the Investment in Subsidiary and Income from Subsidiary accounts. Even though the transaction giving rise to the unrealized profit or loss in this situation relates to an inventory transfer, the parent defers the unrealized profit or loss by making adjustments to the investment and Income from Subsidiary accounts.

Deferring Unrealized Profit or Loss in the Consolidation

When intercompany sales include unrealized profits or losses, the worksheet entry(ies) needed for consolidation in the period of transfer must adjust accounts in both the consolidated income statement and balance sheet:

> **Income statement: Sales and cost of goods sold.** All sales revenue from intercompany transfers and the related cost of goods sold recorded by the transferring affiliate must be removed.
>
> **Balance sheet: Inventory.** The entire unrealized profit or loss on intercompany transfers must be removed from inventory so that it will be reported at the cost to the consolidated entity.

The resulting financial statements appear as if the intercompany transfer had not occurred.

To understand how to eliminate the effects of intercompany inventory transfers in the consolidated financial statements, we refer to the examples illustrated in Figure 6–2 and assume a perpetual inventory system. One way to eliminate intercompany inventory profits or losses is to separately eliminate the effects of (1) sales from one affiliate to another that have subsequently been sold to a nonaffiliated party(ies) and (2) sales from one affiliate to another that have not yet been sold to a nonaffiliated person(s) or entity(ies). To explain how to separately eliminate the effects of these types of inventory transfers, we repeat the summary of the transactions from Figure 6–2 here:

	Total Intercompany Sales	(1) Resold to Nonaffiliate	(2) Inventory on Hand
Sales	$4,000	$3,000	$1,000
– COGS	3,200	2,400	800
Gross Profit	800	600	200

We first focus on Column (1), which summarizes all sales of inventory from Company A to Company B that have eventually been sold to a nonaffiliated party. The inventory was originally purchased in an arm's-length transaction for $2,400. It was then transferred from Company A to Company B for $3,000. Finally, this inventory was sold to an unrelated party for $3,500. The only portion of this transaction that does not involve an unaffiliated party is the $3,000 internal transfer, which needs to be eliminated. In this transaction, it turns out that Company A's transfer price (sales revenue) is $3,000. Company B originally records its inventory at this same amount, but when it is sold, $3,000 is removed from inventory and recorded as cost of goods sold. Thus, the worksheet consolidation entry to remove the effects of this transfer removes Company A's sales revenue and Company B's cost of goods sold related to this intercompany transfer as follows:

Sales	3,000	
Cost of Goods Sold		3,000

We next turn our attention to Column (2), which summarizes all inventory sales from Company A to Company B that are not yet sold to a nonaffiliated party. Company A originally purchased the inventory from an unaffiliated party for $800 and then transferred it to Company B for $1,000. The unrealized gross profit on this transfer is $200. Two problems are associated with this transaction. First, Company A's income is overstated by $200. Second, Company B's inventory is overstated by $200. Although the inventory was purchased in an arm's-length transaction for $800, the intercompany transfer resulted in the recorded value of the inventory being increased by $200. To ensure that the consolidated financial statements will appear as if the inventory had stayed on Company A's books (as if it had not been transferred), we prepare the following worksheet consolidation entry:

Sales	**1,000**	
Cost of Goods Sold		**800**
Inventory		**200**

These two consolidation entries could also be combined. The combined entry would appear as follows:

Sales	**4,000**	
Cost of Goods Sold		**3,800**
Inventory		**200**

After preparing the three-by-three internal inventory transfer summary chart, this elimination "combined" entry can be taken directly from the chart. The debit to sales is always the number in the upper left-hand corner (total intercompany sales). The credit to cost of goods sold is always the sum of the numbers in the middle column of the top row (intercompany sales that are eventually resold to nonaffiliates) and the middle row of the third column (intercompany cost of goods sold on inventory still on hand). Finally, the credit to inventory is the unrealized gross profit number in the lower right column. The purpose of this credit to inventory is to ensure that inventory appears in the consolidated financial statements at the original cost from an arm's-length transaction.

	Total Intercompany Sales	(1) Resold to Nonaffiliate	(2) Inventory on Hand
Sales	**$ 4,000**	**$3,000**	$1,000
– COGS	3,200	2,400	**800**
Gross Profit	800	600	**200**

The net effect of this combined worksheet consolidation entry is to remove the gross profit on *all* intercompany sales and to adjust the ending intercompany-transferred inventory back to its original cost. Thus, one consolidation entry can remove the effects of all intercompany inventory transfers during the accounting period.

We note that the basic consolidation entry is modified slightly when intercompany profits associated with inventory transfers result in unrealized profits. We illustrate this modification later in several examples.

Assuming the inventory in Column (2), which is still on hand at the end of the first year, is subsequently sold in the following year, recognizing the deferred gross profit from the first year in the second year would then be appropriate. The worksheet entry to essentially force this now realized gross profit to be recognized in the consolidated financial statements in year 2 is to credit Cost of Goods Sold and debit the Investment in Subsidiary account as follows:

Investment in Subsidiary	**200**	
Cost of Goods Sold		**200**

Because the overvalued intercompany inventory in beginning inventory is charged to cost of goods sold at the time of the inventory's sale to an unrelated party during the period, the cost of the goods sold is overstated. Thus, a credit to Cost of Goods Sold corrects this account balance and increases income by the amount of gross profit that was deferred in the prior year. The debit goes to Investment in Subsidiary. Note that we prepared an equity-method adjustment in the previous year to defer the unrealized gross profit. We can say that essentially this entry artificially decreased the investment account, so we debit that amount back into the investment account so that the account essentially increases back to its correct balance so that it can be eliminated by the basic consolidation entry. We demonstrate how this works later in the chapter.

Why Adjust the Parent's Books and Make Worksheet Entries?

We defer unrealized intercompany profit or loss to ensure that the parent's books are completely up-to-date. To be consistent with prior chapters, the fully adjusted equity method requires a journal entry to defer intercompany profit/loss to ensure that the parent's net income equals the controlling interest in consolidated net income and that the parent's retained earnings is equal to consolidated retained earnings. However, even though we "fix" the parent's books through an equity-method journal entry, the Investment in Subsidiary account and the Income from Subsidiary accounts are eliminated in the consolidation process. However, without a worksheet consolidation entry, sales and cost of goods sold would be overstated on the income statement, and inventory would be overstated on the balance sheet. Thus, even though we ensure that the parent's books are up-to-date, we still need to remove the effects of intercompany inventory transfers from the consolidated financial statements.

DOWNSTREAM SALE OF INVENTORY[6]

LO 6-3

Prepare equity-method journal entries and consolidation entries for the consolidation of a subsidiary following downstream inventory transfers.

Advanced StudyGuide .com

Consolidated net income must be based on realized income. Because intercompany profits from downstream sales are on the parent's books, consolidated net income and the overall claim of parent company shareholders must be reduced by the full amount of the unrealized profits.

When a company sells an inventory item to an affiliate, one of three situations results: (1) the item is resold to a nonaffiliate during the same period, (2) the item is resold to a nonaffiliate during the next period, or (3) the item is held for two or more periods by the purchasing affiliate.[7] We use the continuing example of Peerless Products Corporation and Special Foods Inc. to illustrate the consolidation process under each of the alternatives. Picking up with the example in Chapter 3, to illustrate more fully the treatment of unrealized intercompany profits, assume the following with respect to the Peerless and Special Foods example used previously:

1. Peerless Products Corporation purchases 80 percent of Special Foods Inc.'s stock on December 31, 20X0, at the stock's book value of $240,000. The fair value of Special Foods' noncontrolling interest on that date is $60,000, the book value of those shares.
2. During 20X1, Peerless reports separate income of $140,000 income from regular operations and declares dividends of $60,000. Special Foods reports net income of $50,000 and declares dividends of $30,000.
3. Peerless accounts for its investment in Special Foods using the equity method under which it records its share of Special Foods' net income and dividends and also adjusts for unrealized intercompany profits using the fully adjusted equity method.

As an illustration of the effects of a downstream inventory sale, assume that on March 1, 20X1, Peerless buys inventory for $7,000 and resells it to Special Foods for $10,000 on April 1. Peerless records the following entries on its books:

	March 1, 20X1		
(1)	Inventory	7,000	
	Cash		7,000
	Record inventory purchase.		

	April 1, 20X1		
(2)	Cash	10,000	
	Sales		10,000
	Record sale of inventory to Special Foods.		

[6] To view a video explanation of this topic, visit advancedstudyguide.com.

[7] As explained previously, inventory is not typically held for multiple periods, but some companies prepare quarterly consolidated financial statements, and some companies sell large or expensive items, which may remain in inventory for more than one period. Moreover, when companies report LIFO inventories, they may build up LIFO layers, which create a fictional accounting notion that inventory items (long since sold) are still in stock.

(3)	Cost of Goods Sold	7,000	
	Inventory		7,000
	Record cost of inventory sold to Special Foods.		

Special Foods records the purchase of the inventory from Peerless with the following entry:

	April 1, 20X1		
(4)	Inventory	10,000	
	Cash		10,000
	Record purchase of inventory from Peerless.		

Resale in Period of Intercorporate Transfer

To illustrate consolidation when inventory is sold to an affiliate and then resold to a nonaffiliate during the same period, assume that on November 5, 20X1, Special Foods sells the inventory purchased from Peerless to a nonaffiliated party for $15,000, as follows:

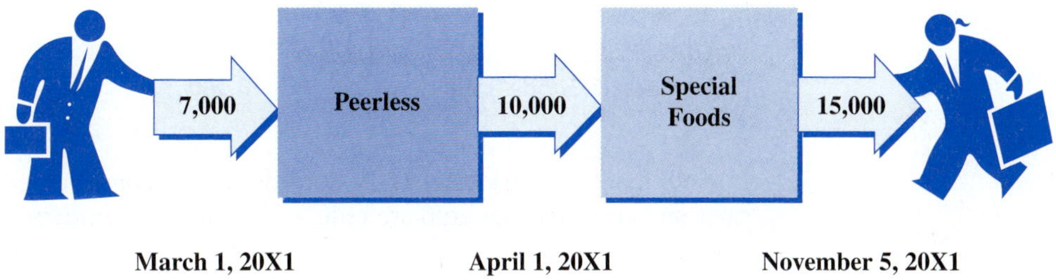

This inventory transfer can be summarized as follows:

	Total Intercompany Sales	(1) Resold to Nonaffiliate	(2) Inventory on Hand
Sales	$10,000	$10,000	0
– COGS	7,000	7,000	0
Gross Profit	3,000	3,000	0

Peerless does not need to defer any intercompany profit on its books because all the intercompany profit has been realized through resale of the inventory to the external party during the current period. Stated differently, the summary chart indicates that there is no intercompany inventory on hand at the end of the period. Thus, there are no unrealized profits to defer.

Special Foods records the sale to a nonaffiliated party with the following entries:

	November 5, 20X1		
(5)	Cash	15,000	
	Sales		15,000
	Record sale of inventory.		

(6)	Cost of Goods Sold	10,000	
	Inventory		10,000
	Record cost of inventory sold.		

A review of all entries recorded by the individual companies indicates that incorrect balances will be reported in the consolidated income statement if the effects of the intercorporate sale are not removed:

Item	Peerless Products	+	Special Foods	=	Unadjusted Totals	≠	Consolidated Amounts
Sales	$10,000		$ 15,000		$ 25,000		$15,000
Cost of Goods Sold	(7,000)		(10,000)		(17,000)		(7,000)
Gross Profit	$ 3,000		$ 5,000		$ 8,000		$ 8,000

Although consolidated gross profit is correct even if no adjustments are made, the totals for sales and cost of goods sold derived by simply adding the amounts on the books of Peerless and Special Foods are overstated for the consolidated entity. The selling price of the inventory in an arm's-length transaction is $15,000, and the original cost to Peerless Products is $7,000. Thus, gross profit of $8,000 is correct from a consolidated viewpoint, but consolidated sales and cost of goods sold should be $15,000 and $7,000, respectively, rather than $25,000 and $17,000. In the consolidation worksheet, the amount of the intercompany sale must be eliminated from both sales and cost of goods sold to correctly state the consolidated totals:

Sales	**10,000**	
Cost of Goods Sold		**10,000**

Note that this worksheet entry does not affect consolidated net income because both sales and cost of goods sold are reduced by the same amount.

Resale in Period Following Intercorporate Transfer

When inventory is sold to an affiliate at a profit but is not resold during the same period, appropriate adjustments are needed to prepare consolidated financial statements in the period of the intercompany sale and in each subsequent period until the inventory is sold to a nonaffiliate. By way of illustration, assume that Peerless Products purchases inventory on March 1, 20X1, for $7,000 and sells the inventory during the year (on April 1) to Special Foods for $10,000. Special Foods sells the inventory to a nonaffiliated party for $15,000 on January 2, 20X2, as follows:

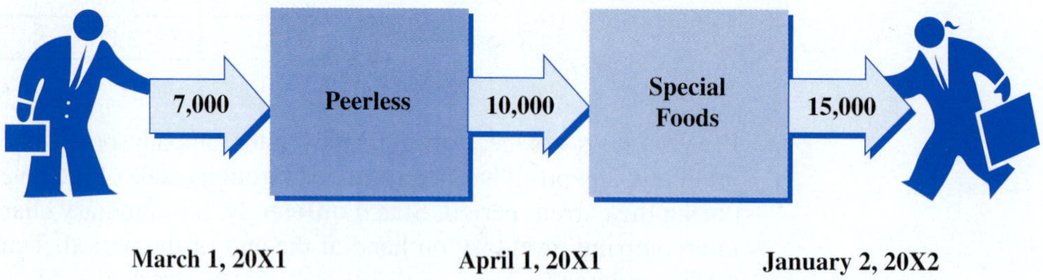

This inventory transfer can be summarized as follows:

	Total Intercompany Sales	(1) Resold to Nonaffiliate	(2) Inventory on Hand
Sales	$ 10,000	0	$ 10,000
– COGS	7,000	0	7,000
Gross Profit	3,000	0	3,000

As of the end of 20X1, the entire intercompany inventory is still on hand in Special Foods' warehouse. In this case, all the intercompany gross profit is unrealized at December 31, 20X1. Thus, Peerless needs to defer the entire intercompany gross profit on its books because none of the intercompany profit has been realized through resale of the inventory to an external party during the current period. In other words, the summary chart indicates that there is $10,000 of intercompany inventory on hand at the end of the period and the unrealized profit of $3,000 must be deferred on Peerless' books as shown in entry (9). During 20X1, Peerless records the purchase of the inventory and the sale to Special Foods with journal entries (1) through (3), given previously; Special Foods records the purchase of the inventory from Peerless with entry (4). In 20X2, Special Foods records the sale of the inventory to Nonaffiliated with entries (5) and (6).

Equity-Method Entries—20X1

Under the equity method, Peerless records its share of Special Foods' income and dividends for 20X1:

(7)	Investment in Special Foods	40,000	
	Income from Special Foods		40,000
	Record Peerless' 80% share of Special Foods' 20X1 income.		

(8)	Cash	24,000	
	Investment in Special Foods		24,000
	Record Peerless' 80% share of Special Foods' 20X1 dividend.		

As a result of these entries, the ending balance in the investment account is currently $256,000 ($240,000 + $40,000 − $24,000). However, because the downstream sale of inventory to Special Foods results in $3,000 of unrealized profits, Peerless defers the unrealized gross profit by making an adjustment in the equity method investment and income accounts to reduce the income from Special Foods on the income statement and Investment in Special Foods on the balance sheet by its share of the unrealized gross profit. Because this is a downstream transaction, the sale (and associated unrealized gross

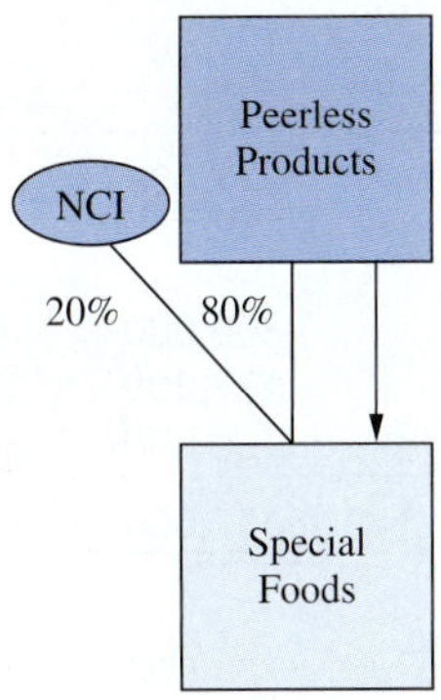

profit) resides on Peerless' income statement. Because we assume the NCI shareholders do not own Peerless stock, they do not share in the deferral of the unrealized profit. Under the fully adjusted equity method, Peerless defers the entire $3,000 using the following equity-method entry:

(9)	Income from Special Foods	3,000	
	Investment in Special Foods		3,000
	Defer unrealized gross profit on inventory sales to Special Foods not yet resold.		

Note that this entry accomplishes two important objectives. First, because Peerless' income is overstated by $3,000, the adjustment to Income from Special Foods offsets this overstatement so that Peerless' bottom-line net income is now correct. Second, Special Foods' inventory is currently overstated by $3,000. Because the Investment in Special Foods account summarizes Peerless' investment in Special Foods' balance sheet, this reduction to the investment account offsets the fact that Special Foods' inventory (and thus entire balance sheet) is overstated by $3,000. Thus, after making this equity-method adjustment to defer the unrealized gross profit, Peerless' financial statements are now correctly stated. Therefore, Peerless' reported income will be exactly equal to the controlling interest in net income on the consolidated financial statements.

Consolidation Worksheet—20X1

We present the consolidation worksheet prepared at the end of 20X1 in Figure 6–3. The first two consolidation entries are the same as we calculated in Chapter 3 with one minor exception. Under the fully adjusted equity method, there is one difference in preparing the basic consolidation entry when unrealized intercompany profits exist. Although the analysis of the "book value" portion of the investment account is the same, in preparing the basic consolidation entry, we reduce the amounts in the Income from Special Foods and Investment in Special Foods by the $3,000 unrealized gross profit deferral.

FIGURE 6–3 December 31, 20X1, Consolidation Worksheet, Period of Intercompany Sale; Downstream Inventory Sale

	Peerless Products	Special Foods	Consolidation Entries DR	Consolidation Entries CR	Consolidated
Income Statement					
Sales	400,000	200,000	10,000		590,000
Less: COGS	(170,000)	(115,000)		7,000	(278,000)
Less: Depreciation Expense	(50,000)	(20,000)			(70,000)
Less: Other Expenses	(40,000)	(15,000)			(55,000)
Income from Special Foods	37,000		37,000		0
Consolidated Net Income	177,000	50,000	47,000	7,000	187,000
NCI in Net Income			10,000		(10,000)
Controlling Interest Net Income	**177,000**	**50,000**	57,000	7,000	**177,000**
Statement of Retained Earnings					
Beginning Balance	300,000	100,000	100,000		300,000
Net Income	**177,000**	**50,000**	57,000	7,000	177,000
Less: Dividends Declared	(60,000)	(30,000)		30,000	(60,000)
Ending Balance	**417,000**	**120,000**	157,000	37,000	**417,000**
Balance Sheet					
Cash	264,000	75,000			339,000
Accounts Receivable	75,000	50,000			125,000
Inventory	100,000	75,000		3,000	172,000
Investment in Special Foods	253,000			253,000	0
Land	175,000	40,000			215,000
Buildings & Equipment	800,000	600,000		300,000	1,100,000
Less: Accumulated Depreciation	(450,000)	(320,000)	300,000		(470,000)
Total Assets	**1,217,000**	**520,000**	300,000	556,000	**1,481,000**
Accounts Payable	100,000	100,000			200,000
Bonds Payable	200,000	100,000			300,000
Common Stock	500,000	200,000	200,000		500,000
Retained Earnings	**417,000**	**120,000**	157,000	37,000	417,000
NCI in NA of Special Foods				64,000	64,000
Total Liabilities & Equity	**1,217,000**	**520,000**	357,000	101,000	**1,481,000**

Calculations for Basic Consolidation Entry:

Book Value Calculations:

	NCI 20% +	Peerless 80%	=	Common Stock	+	Retained Earnings
Original Book Value	60,000	240,000		200,000		100,000
+ Net Income	10,000	40,000				50,000
− Dividends	(6,000)	(24,000)				(30,000)
Ending Book Value	64,000	256,000		200,000		120,000

Adjustment to Basic Consolidation Entry:

	NCI 20%	Peerless 80%
Net Income	10,000	40,000
− Gross profit deferral		(3,000)
Income to be eliminated	10,000	37,000
Ending Book Value	64,000	256,000
− Gross profit deferral		(3,000)
Adjusted Book Value	64,000	253,000

Basic Consolidation Entry:

	Debit	Credit	
Common Stock	200,000		← Common stock balance
Retained Earnings	100,000		← Beginning balance in RE
Income from Special Foods	37,000		← Peerless' % of NI with Adjustment
NCI in NI of Special Foods	10,000		← NCI share of Special Foods' NI
Dividends Declared		30,000	← 100% of sub's dividends declared
Investment in Special Foods		253,000	← Net BV in investment with Adjustment
NCI in NA of Special Foods		64,000	← NCI share of net amount of BV

Advanced StudyGuide .com

The accumulated depreciation entry is the same as in previous chapters. It is always the amount of the subsidiary's accumulated depreciation on the acquisition date.

Optional Accumulated Depreciation Consolidation Entry:

	Debit	Credit	
Accumulated Depreciation	300,000		← Accumulated depreciation at the time of the acquisition netted against cost
Buildings & Equipment		300,000	

Moreover, although Peerless recorded an equity-method entry to defer the unrealized gross profit, both the Income from Special Foods and Investment in Special Foods accounts are eliminated with the basic consolidation entry. Peerless' Sales and Cost of Goods Sold amounts are still overstated (by $10,000 and $7,000, respectively). Moreover, Special Foods' ending inventory is still overstated by $3,000. Simply adding up the Peerless and Special Foods columns of the consolidation worksheet will result in overstated consolidated net income, total assets, and retained earnings. Therefore, we also record a new consolidation entry to correct the unadjusted totals to the appropriate consolidated amounts. In doing so, consolidated income is reduced by $3,000 ($10,000 − $7,000). In addition, ending inventory reported on Special Foods' books is stated at the intercompany exchange price rather than the historical cost to the consolidated entity. Until Special Foods resells it to an external party, the inventory must be reduced by the amount of unrealized intercompany profit each time consolidated statements are prepared.

Elimination of Intercompany Sales to Special Foods (still on hand in ending inventory):

	Debit	Credit
Sales	10,000	
Cost of Goods Sold		7,000
Inventory		3,000

This consolidation entry removes the effects of the intercompany inventory sale. The journal entries recorded by Peerless Products and Special Foods in 20X1 on their separate books will result in an overstatement of consolidated gross profit for 20X1 and the consolidated inventory balance at year-end unless the amounts are adjusted in the consolidation worksheet. The amounts resulting from the intercompany inventory transactions from the separate books of Peerless Products and Special Foods, and the appropriate consolidated amounts, are as follows:

Item	Peerless Products	+	Special Foods	=	Unadjusted Totals	≠	Consolidated Amounts
Sales	$10,000		$ 0		$10,000		$ 0
Cost of Goods Sold	(7,000)		0		(7,000)		0
Gross Profit	$ 3,000		$ 0		$ 3,000		$ 0
Inventory	$ 0		$10,000		$10,000		$7,000

The following T-accounts summarize the effects of all equity-method entries on Peerless' books as well as the basic consolidation entry:

	Investment in Special Foods			Income from Special Foods		
Acquisition	240,000					
80% NI	40,000				40,000	80% NI
		24,000	80% Dividends			
		3,000	Defer GP	3,000		
Ending Balance	253,000				37,000	Ending Balance
		253,000	Basic	37,000		
	0				0	

Consolidated Net Income—20X1

Consolidated net income for 20X1 is shown as $187,000 in the Figure 6–3 worksheet. This amount is computed and allocated as follows:

Peerless' separate income	$140,000
Less: Unrealized intercompany profit on downstream inventory sale	(3,000)
Peerless' separate realized income	$137,000
Special Foods' net income	50,000
Consolidated net income, 20X1	$187,000
Income to noncontrolling interest ($50,000 × 0.20)	(10,000)
Income to controlling interest	$177,000

Equity-Method Entries—20X2

During 20X2, Special Foods receives $15,000 when it sells to an unaffiliated party the inventory that it had purchased for $10,000 from Peerless in 20X1. Also, Peerless records its pro rata portion of Special Foods' net income ($75,000) and dividends ($40,000) for 20X2 with the normal equity-method entries:

(10)	Investment in Special Foods	60,000	
	Income from Special Foods		60,000

Record Peerless' 80% share of Special Foods' 20X2 income.

(11)			
	Cash	32,000	
	Investment in Special Foods		32,000

Record Peerless' 80% share of Special Foods' 20X2 dividend.

Under the fully adjusted equity method, once the inventory is sold to an unaffiliated party, the deferral in the equity-method accounts is no longer necessary (see entry (9) from 20X1) and is reversed as follows:

(12)			
	Investment in Special Foods	3,000	
	Income from Special Foods		3,000

Reverse the 20X1 gross profit deferral on inventory sold to unaffiliated customers.

Consolidation Worksheet—20X2

Figure 6–4 illustrates the consolidation worksheet at the end of 20X2. The first two consolidation entries are the same as those presented in Chapter 3 with one exception to the basic consolidation entry. Whereas we subtracted the deferral of unrealized gross profit in 20X1, we now add back this deferral in the basic consolidation entry for 20X2.

Calculations for Basic Consolidation Entry:

Book Value Calculations:

	NCI 20% +	Peerless 80%	=	Common Stock	+	Retained Earnings
Original Book Value	64,000	256,000		200,000		120,000
+ Net Income	15,000	60,000				75,000
− Dividends	(8,000)	(32,000)				(40,000)
Ending Book Value	71,000	284,000		200,000		155,000

Adjustment to Basic Consolidation Entry:

	NCI 20%	Peerless 80%
Net Income	15,000	60,000
+ Reverse GP deferral		3,000
Income to be eliminated	15,000	63,000
Ending Book Value	71,000	284,000
+ Reverse GP deferral		3,000
Adjusted Book Value	71,000	287,000

Basic Consolidation Entry:

Common Stock	200,000		← Common stock balance
Retained Earnings	120,000		← Beginning balance in RE
Income from Special Foods	63,000		← Peerless' % of NI with Adjustments
NCI in NI of Special Foods	15,000		← NCI share of Special Foods' NI
Dividends Declared		40,000	← 100% of sub's dividends declared
Investment in Special Foods		287,000	← Net investment with Adjustments
NCI in NA of Special Foods		71,000	← NCI share of ending book value

Optional Accumulated Depreciation Consolidation Entry:

Accumulated Depreciation	300,000		← Accumulated depreciation at the time of the acquisition netted against cost
Buildings & Equipment		300,000	

FIGURE 6–4 December 31, 20X2, Consolidation Worksheet, Next Period Following Intercompany Sale; Downstream Inventory Sale

	Peerless Products	Special Foods	Consolidation Entries DR	Consolidation Entries CR	Consolidated
Income Statement					
Sales	450,000	300,000			750,000
Less: COGS	(180,000)	(160,000)		3,000	(337,000)
Less: Depreciation Expense	(50,000)	(20,000)			(70,000)
Less: Other Expenses	(60,000)	(45,000)			(105,000)
Income from Special Foods	63,000		63,000		0
Consolidated Net Income	223,000	75,000	63,000	3,000	238,000
NCI in Net Income			15,000		(15,000)
Controlling Interest Net Income	**223,000**	**75,000**	**78,000**	**3,000**	**223,000**
Statement of Retained Earnings					
Beginning Balance	417,000	120,000	120,000		417,000
Net Income	**223,000**	**75,000**	**78,000**	**3,000**	223,000
Less: Dividends Declared	(60,000)	(40,000)		40,000	(60,000)
Ending Balance	**580,000**	**155,000**	**198,000**	**43,000**	**580,000**
Balance Sheet					
Cash	291,000	85,000			376,000
Accounts Receivable	150,000	80,000			230,000
Inventory	180,000	90,000			270,000
Investment in Special Foods	284,000		3,000	287,000	0
Land	175,000	40,000			215,000
Buildings & Equipment	800,000	600,000		300,000	1,100,000
Less: Accumulated Depreciation	(500,000)	(340,000)	300,000		(540,000)
Total Assets	**1,380,000**	**555,000**	**303,000**	**587,000**	**1,651,000**
Accounts Payable	100,000	100,000			200,000
Bonds Payable	200,000	100,000			300,000
Common Stock	500,000	200,000	200,000		500,000
Retained Earnings	**580,000**	**155,000**	**198,000**	**43,000**	580,000
NCI in NA of Special Foods				71,000	71,000
Total Liabilities & Equity	**1,380,000**	**555,000**	**398,000**	**114,000**	**1,651,000**

An additional consolidation entry is needed to recognize the $3,000 of income that was deferred in 20X1. Whereas the inventory had not yet been sold to an unaffiliated customer in 20X1 and needed to be deferred, that inventory has now been sold in 20X2 and should be recognized in the consolidated financial statements.

Reversal of the 20X1 Gross Profit Deferral:

Investment in Special Foods	**3,000**	
Cost of Goods Sold		**3,000**

Special Foods' unrealized intercompany profit included in beginning inventory was charged to Cost of Goods Sold when Special Foods sold the inventory during the period. Thus, consolidated cost of goods sold will be overstated for 20X2 if it is based on the unadjusted totals from the books of Peerless and Special Foods:

Item	Peerless Products	+	Special Foods	=	Unadjusted Totals	≠	Consolidated Amounts
Sales	$ 0		$ 15,000		$ 15,000		$15,000
Cost of Goods Sold	0		(10,000)		(10,000)		(7,000)
Gross Profit	$ 0		$ 5,000		$ 5,000		$ 8,000

Unlike the period in which the intercompany transfer occurs, no adjustment to sales is required in a subsequent period when the inventory is sold to a nonaffiliate. The amount reported by Special Foods reflects the sale outside the economic entity and is the appropriate amount to be reported for consolidation. By removing the $3,000 of intercorporate profit from Cost of Goods Sold with this consolidation entry, the original acquisition price paid by Peerless Products is reported in Cost of Goods Sold, and $8,000 of gross profit is correctly reported in the consolidated income statement.

Once the sale is made to an external party, the transaction is complete and no adjustments or consolidation entries related to the intercompany transaction are needed in future periods. The following T-accounts illustrate the effects of all equity-method journal entries on Peerless' books as well as the worksheet entries on the consolidation worksheet.

	Investment in Special Foods (Debit)	Investment in Special Foods (Credit)	
Beg. Balance	253,000		
80% NI	60,000		
		32,000	80% Dividends
Reverse 'X1 Deferred GP	3,000		
Ending Balance	284,000		
Worksheet		287,000	Basic
Reversal of 'X1 Deferred GP	3,000		
	0		

	Income from Special Foods (Debit)	Income from Special Foods (Credit)	
		60,000	80% NI
		3,000	Reverse 'X1 Deferred GP
		63,000	Ending Balance
Basic	63,000		
		0	

Consolidated Net Income—20X2

Consolidated net income for 20X2 is shown as $238,000 in the Figure 6–4 worksheet. This amount is verified and allocated as follows:

Peerless' separate income	$160,000
Realization of deferred intercompany profit on downstream inventory sale	3,000
Peerless' separate realized income	$163,000
Special Foods' net income	75,000
Consolidated net income, 20X2	$238,000
Income to noncontrolling interest ($75,000 × 0.20)	(15,000)
Income to controlling interest	$223,000

Inventory Held for Two or More Periods

Companies may carry the cost of inventory purchased from an affiliate for more than one accounting period. For example, the cost of an item may be in a LIFO inventory layer and would be included as part of the inventory balance until the layer is liquidated. Prior to liquidation, a consolidation entry is needed in the consolidation worksheet each time consolidated statements are prepared to restate the inventory to its cost to the consolidated entity. For example, if Special Foods continues to hold the inventory purchased from Peerless Products, the following consolidation entry is needed in the consolidation worksheet each time a consolidated balance sheet is prepared for years following the year of intercompany sale, for as long as the inventory is held:

Investment in Special Foods	**3,000**	
Inventory		**3,000**

This consolidation entry simply corrects the balance in both the Inventory and Investment in Special Foods accounts. Whereas Peerless recorded an equity-method adjustment to defer the $3,000 of unrealized gross profit in the year of the intercompany inventory transfer by artificially decreasing the Investment in Special Foods to offset the overstated inventory balance on Special Foods' books, this entry simply corrects both accounts. No income statement adjustments are needed in the periods following the intercorporate sale until the inventory is resold to parties external to the consolidated entity.

UPSTREAM SALE OF INVENTORY

LO 6-4

Prepare equity-method journal entries and consolidation entries for the consolidation of a subsidiary following upstream inventory transfers.

Advanced StudyGuide .com

When an upstream inventory sale occurs and the parent resells the inventory to a nonaffiliate during the same period, all the parent's equity-method entries and the consolidation entries in the consolidation worksheet are identical to those in the downstream case.

When the inventory is not resold to a nonaffiliate before the end of the period, worksheet entries are different from the downstream case only by the apportionment of the unrealized intercompany profit to both the controlling and noncontrolling interests. In this case because the sale appears on Special Foods' income statement and because the NCI shareholders own 20 percent of Special Foods' outstanding shares, they are entitled to 20 percent of Special Foods' net income. Thus, the deferral of unrealized gross profits accrues to both Peerless and the NCI shareholders. In other words, the intercompany profit in an upstream sale is recognized by the subsidiary and shared between the controlling and noncontrolling stockholders of the subsidiary. Therefore, the consolidation of the unrealized intercompany profit must reduce the interests of both ownership groups each period until the resale of the inventory to a nonaffiliated party confirms the profit.

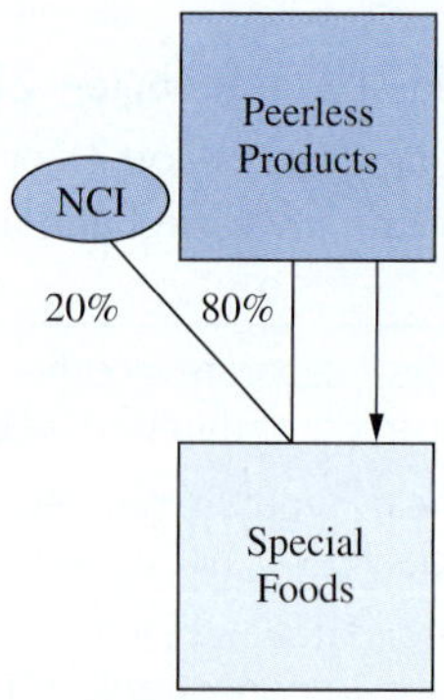

We illustrate an upstream sale using the same example as used for the downstream sale except that Special Foods sells the inventory to Peerless. Assume Special Foods purchases the inventory on March 1, 20X1, for $7,000 and sells it to Peerless for $10,000 during the same year. Peerless holds the inventory until January 2, 20X2, at which time Peerless sells it to a nonaffiliated party for $15,000.

Equity-Method Entries—20X1

Peerless Products records the following equity-method entries in 20X1:

		Debit	Credit
(13)	Investment in Special Foods	40,000	
	Income from Special Foods		40,000
	Record Peerless' 80% share of Special Foods' 20X1 income.		

		Debit	Credit
(14)	Cash	24,000	
	Investment in Special Foods		24,000
	Record Peerless' 80% share of Special Foods' 20X1 dividend.		

These entries are the same as in the illustration of the downstream sale. The only difference is that the fully adjusted equity-method entry to defer the unrealized gross profit is only for Peerless' ownership percentage of Special Foods (80 percent). Thus, the deferral of Peerless' relative share of the unrealized gross profit is \$2,400 (\$3,000 × 80%).

(15)			
	Income from Special Foods	2,400	
	Investment in Special Foods		2,400

Eliminate unrealized gross profit on inventory purchases from Special Foods.

Consolidation Worksheet—20X1

Advanced StudyGuide .com

We present the worksheet for the preparation of the 20X1 consolidated financial statements in Figure 6–5. The first two consolidation entries are the same as we calculated in Chapter 3 with one minor exception. Although the analysis of the book value portion of the investment account is the same, in preparing the basic consolidation entry, we reduce the amounts in Peerless' Income from Special Foods and Investment in Special Foods accounts by Peerless' share of the deferral, \$2,400 (\$3,000 × 80%). We also reduce the NCI in Net Income of Special Foods and NCI in Net Assets of Special Foods by the NCI share of the deferral, \$600 (\$3,000 × 20%).

FIGURE 6–5 December 31, 20X1, Consolidation Worksheet, Period of Intercompany Sale; Upstream Inventory Sale

	Peerless Products	Special Foods	Consolidation Entries		Consolidated
			DR	CR	
Income Statement					
Sales	400,000	200,000	10,000		590,000
Less: COGS	(170,000)	(115,000)		7,000	(278,000)
Less: Depreciation Expense	(50,000)	(20,000)			(70,000)
Less: Other Expenses	(40,000)	(15,000)			(55,000)
Income from Special Foods	37,600		37,600		0
Consolidated Net Income	177,600	50,000	47,600	7,000	187,000
NCI in Net Income			9,400		(9,400)
Controlling Interest Net Income	177,600	50,000	57,000	7,000	177,600
Statement of Retained Earnings					
Beginning Balance	300,000	100,000	100,000		300,000
Net Income	**177,600**	**50,000**	57,000	7,000	177,600
Less: Dividends Declared	(60,000)	(30,000)		30,000	(60,000)
Ending Balance	417,600	120,000	157,000	37,000	417,600
Balance Sheet					
Cash	264,000	75,000			339,000
Accounts Receivable	75,000	50,000			125,000
Inventory	100,000	75,000		3,000	172,000
Investment in Special Foods	253,600			253,600	0
Land	175,000	40,000			215,000
Buildings & Equipment	800,000	600,000		300,000	1,100,000
Less: Accumulated Depreciation	(450,000)	(320,000)	300,000		(470,000)
Total Assets	1,217,600	520,000	300,000	556,600	1,481,000
Accounts Payable	100,000	100,000			200,000
Bonds Payable	200,000	100,000			300,000
Common Stock	500,000	200,000	200,000		500,000
Retained Earnings	**417,600**	**120,000**	157,000	37,000	417,600
NCI in NA of Special Foods				63,400	63,400
Total Liabilities & Equity	1,217,600	520,000	357,000	100,400	1,481,000

Calculations for Basic Consolidation Entry:

Book Value Calculations:

	NCI 20% +	Peerless 80%	=	Common Stock	+ Retained Earnings
Original Book Value	60,000	240,000		200,000	100,000
+ Net Income	10,000	40,000			50,000
− Dividends	(6,000)	(24,000)			(30,000)
Ending Book Value	64,000	256,000		200,000	120,000

Adjustment to Basic Consolidation Entry:

	NCI 20%	Peerless 80%
Net Income	10,000	40,000
− Gross profit deferral	(600)	(2,400)
Income to be eliminated	9,400	37,600
Ending Book Value	64,000	256,000
− Gross profit deferral	(600)	(2,400)
Adjusted Book Value	63,400	253,600

Basic Consolidation Entry:

Account	Debit	Credit	
Common Stock	200,000		← Common stock balance
Retained Earnings	100,000		← Beginning balance in RE
Income from Special Foods	37,600		← Peerless' % of NI with Adjustment
NCI in NI of Special Foods	9,400		← NCI share of NI with Adjustment
Dividends Declared		30,000	← 100% of sub's dividends declared
Investment in Special Foods		253,600	← Net book value with Adjustment
NCI in NA of Special Foods		63,400	← NCI share of BV with Adjustment

Optional Accumulated Depreciation Consolidation Entry:

Account	Debit	Credit	
Accumulated Depreciation	300,000		← Accumulated depreciation at the time of the acquisition netted against cost
Buildings & Equipment		300,000	

The consolidation worksheet entry to remove the effects of the intercompany sale is identical to the downstream case. The only difference is that the overstated Sales and Cost of Goods Sold numbers are now in the Special Foods' column of the consolidation worksheet and the overstated inventory is now in the Peerless column.

Eliminate Inventory Purchases from Special Foods (still on hand):

Account	Debit	Credit
Sales	10,000	
Cost of Goods Sold		7,000
Inventory		3,000

	Investment in Special Foods (Debit)	Investment in Special Foods (Credit)		Income from Special Foods (Debit)	Income from Special Foods (Credit)	
Acquisition	240,000					
80% NI	40,000				40,000	80% NI
		24,000	80% Dividends			
		2,400	Defer 80% GP	2,400		
Ending Balance	253,600				37,600	Ending Balance
		253,600	Basic	37,600		
	0				0	

Consolidated Net Income—20X1

We note that because the unrealized profit consolidation is allocated proportionately between the controlling and noncontrolling interests in the upstream case, the income assigned to the noncontrolling shareholders is $600 ($3,000 × 0.20) less in Figure 6–5 for the upstream case than in Figure 6–3 for the downstream case. Accordingly, the amount of income assigned to the controlling interest is $600 higher. Note that consolidated net income and all other income statement amounts are the same whether the sale is upstream or downstream. The worksheet indicates that consolidated net income for 20X1 is $187,000. Consolidated net income is computed and allocated to the controlling and noncontrolling stockholders as follows:

Peerless' separate income		$140,000
Special Foods' net income	$50,000	
Less: Unrealized intercompany profit on upstream inventory sale	(3,000)	
Special Foods' realized net income		47,000
Consolidated net income, 20X1		$187,000
Income to noncontrolling interest ($47,000 × 0.20)		(9,400)
Income to controlling interest		$177,600

Equity-Method Entries—20X2

Peerless recognizes its share of Special Foods' income ($75,000) and dividends ($40,000) for 20X2 with the normal equity-method entries:

(16)	Investment in Special Foods	60,000	
	Income from Special Foods		60,000
	Record Peerless' 80% share of Special Foods' 20X2 income.		

(17)	Cash	32,000	
	Investment in Special Foods		32,000
	Record Peerless' 80% share of Special Foods' 20X2 dividend.		

Under the fully adjusted equity method, Peerless reverses the deferred gross profit from 20X1 because this inventory has now been sold.

(18)	Investment in Special Foods	2,400	
	Income from Special Foods		2,400
	Reverse the 20X1 gross profit deferral on inventory sold to unaffiliated customers.		

Consolidation Worksheet—20X2

Figure 6–6 illustrates the consolidation worksheet used to prepare consolidated financial statements at the end of 20X2. The first two consolidation entries are the same as we prepared in Chapter 3 with the previously explained exception. Although the analysis of the book value portion of the investment account is the same, in preparing the basic consolidation entry and because the inventory sold to Peerless by Special Foods last year has now been sold to an unaffiliated party, we must now increase the amounts in Peerless' Income from Special Foods and Investment in Special Foods accounts by Peerless' share of the deferral, $2,400 ($3,000 × 80%). We also increase the NCI in Net Income of Special Foods and NCI in Net Assets of Special Foods by the NCI share of the deferral, $600 ($3,000 × 20%).

FIGURE 6–6 December 31, 20X2, Consolidation Worksheet, Next Period following Intercompany Sale; Upstream Inventory Sale

	Peerless Products	Special Foods	Consolidation Entries DR	Consolidation Entries CR	Consolidated
Income Statement					
Sales	450,000	300,000			750,000
Less: COGS	(180,000)	(160,000)		3,000	(337,000)
Less: Depreciation Expense	(50,000)	(20,000)			(70,000)
Less: Other Expenses	(60,000)	(45,000)			(105,000)
Income from Special Foods	62,400		62,400		0
Consolidated Net Income	222,400	75,000	62,400	3,000	238,000
NCI in Net Income			15,600		(15,600)
Controlling Interest Net Income	**222,400**	**75,000**	**78,000**	**3,000**	**222,400**
Statement of Retained Earnings					
Beginning Balance	417,600	120,000	120,000		417,600
Net Income	**222,400**	**75,000**	78,000	3,000	222,400
Less: Dividends Declared	(60,000)	(40,000)		40,000	(60,000)
Ending Balance	**580,000**	**155,000**	**198,000**	**43,000**	**580,000**
Balance Sheet					
Cash	291,000	85,000			376,000
Accounts Receivable	150,000	80,000			230,000
Inventory	180,000	90,000			270,000
Investment in Special Foods	284,000		2,400	286,400	0
Land	175,000	40,000			215,000
Buildings & Equipment	800,000	600,000		300,000	1,100,000
Less: Accumulated Depreciation	(500,000)	(340,000)	300,000		(540,000)
Total Assets	**1,380,000**	**555,000**	**302,400**	**586,400**	**1,651,000**
Accounts Payable	100,000	100,000			200,000
Bonds Payable	200,000	100,000			300,000
Common Stock	500,000	200,000	200,000		500,000
Retained Earnings	**580,000**	**155,000**	198,000	43,000	580,000
NCI in NA of Special Foods			600	71,600	71,000
Total Liabilities & Equity	**1,380,000**	**555,000**	**398,600**	**114,600**	**1,651,000**

Calculations for Basic Consolidation Entry:

Book Value Calculations:

	NCI 20% +	Peerless 80%	=	Common Stock	+ Retained Earnings
Original Book Value	**64,000**	**256,000**		**200,000**	**120,000**
+ Net Income	**15,000**	**60,000**			**75,000**
− Dividends	**(8,000)**	**(32,000)**			**(40,000)**
Ending Book Value	**71,000**	**284,000**		**200,000**	**155,000**

Adjustment to Basic Consolidation Entry:

	NCI 20%	Peerless 80%
Net Income	**15,000**	**60,000**
+ Reverse GP deferral	**600**	**2,400**
Income to be eliminated	**15,600**	**62,400**
Ending Book Value	**71,000**	**284,000**
+ Reverse GP deferral	**600**	**2,400**
Adjusted Book Value	**71,600**	**286,400**

Advanced StudyGuide .com

Basic Consolidation Entry:

Common Stock	200,000		← Common stock balance
Retained Earnings	120,000		← Beginning balance in RE
Income from Special Foods	62,400		← Peerless' % of NI with Adjustment
NCI in NI of Special Foods	15,600		← NCI % of NI with Adjustment
Dividends Declared		40,000	← 100% of sub's dividends declared
Investment in Special Foods		286,400	← Net book value with Adjustment
NCI in NA of Special Foods		71,600	← NCI % of BV with Adjustment

Optional Accumulated Depreciation Consolidation Entry:

Accumulated Depreciation	300,000		← Accumulated depreciation at the time of the acquisition netted against cost
Buildings & Equipment		300,000	

FYI

Recall that Peerless deferred 80 percent of the unrealized gross profit on the upstream inventory sale last year on its books through an equity-method journal entry. Thus, the beginning balance in the Investment account ($253,600) is not equal to Peerless' 80 percent share of Special Foods' equity accounts in the beginning balance line of the Book Value Calculations box above ($256,000). This is why the basic consolidation entry to the Investment in Special Foods account is increased by the amount of last year's deferral.

Similar to the downstream example, the unrealized intercompany profit included in Peerless' beginning inventory was charged to Cost of Goods Sold when Peerless sold the inventory during 20X2. Thus, consolidated cost of goods sold will be overstated for 20X2 if it is reported in the consolidated income statement at the unadjusted total from the books of Peerless and Special Foods. The following consolidation entry corrects Cost of Goods Sold and splits this adjustment proportionately between Peerless' investment account and the NCI in Net Assets of Special Foods.

Reversal of 20X1 Gross Profit Deferral:

Investment in Special Foods	2,400	
NCI in NA of Special Foods	600	
Cost of Goods Sold		3,000

The following T-accounts illustrate the effects of all equity-method journal entries on Peerless' books as well as the worksheet consolidation entries.

	Investment in Special Foods (Dr)	Investment in Special Foods (Cr)		Income from Special Foods (Dr)	Income from Special Foods (Cr)	
Beg. Balance	253,600					
80% NI	60,000				60,000	80% NI
		32,000	80% Dividends			
Reverse 'X1 Deferred GP	2,400				2,400	Reverse 'X1 Deferred GP
Ending Balance	284,000				62,400	Ending Balance
Worksheet		286,400	Basic	62,400		
Reversal of 'X1 Deferred GP	2,400					
	0				0	

Consolidated Net Income—20X2

Consolidated net income for 20X2 is shown as $238,000 in the Figure 6–6 worksheet. This amount is computed and allocated as follows:

Peerless' separate income		$160,000
Special Foods' net income	$75,000	
Realization of deferred intercompany profit on upstream inventory sale	3,000	
Special Foods' realized net income		78,000
Consolidated net income, 20X2		$238,000
Income to noncontrolling interest ($78,000 × 0.20)		(15,600)
Income to controlling interest		$222,400

ADDITIONAL CONSIDERATIONS

LO 6-5

Understand and explain additional considerations associated with consolidation.

The frequency of intercompany inventory transfers and the varied circumstances under which they may occur raise a number of additional implementation issues. We discuss several of these briefly in this section.

Sale from One Subsidiary to Another

Inventory transfers often occur between companies that are under common control or ownership. When one subsidiary sells merchandise to another subsidiary, the consolidation entries are identical to those presented earlier for sales from a subsidiary to its parent. The full amount of any unrealized intercompany profit is eliminated, with the profit elimination allocated proportionately against the selling subsidiary's ownership interests.

As an illustration, assume that Peerless Products owns 90 percent of the outstanding stock of Super Industries in addition to its 80 percent interest in Special Foods. If Special Foods sells inventory at a $3,000 profit to Super Industries for $10,000 and Super Industries holds all of the inventory at the end of the period, the following consolidation entry is among those needed in the consolidation worksheet prepared at the end of the period:

Eliminate Intercompany Inventory Sales (still on hand):

Sales	**10,000**	
Cost of Goods Sold		**7,000**
Inventory		**3,000**

The two shareholder groups of the selling affiliate allocate proportionately the $3,000 deferral of unrealized intercompany profit. Consolidated net income is reduced by the full $3,000 unrealized intercompany profit. The income allocated to the controlling interest is reduced by Peerless' 80 percent share of the intercompany profit, or $2,400, and Special Foods' noncontrolling interest is reduced by its 20 percent share, or $600.

Lower of Cost or Market

A company might write down inventory purchased from an affiliate under the lower-of-cost-or-market rule if the market value at the end of the period is less than the intercompany transfer price. To illustrate this situation, assume that a parent company purchases inventory for $20,000 and sells it to its subsidiary for $35,000. The subsidiary still holds the inventory at year-end and determines that its current market value (replacement cost) is $25,000.

The subsidiary writes the inventory down from $35,000 to its lower market value of $25,000 at the end of the year and records the following entry:

(19)	Loss on Decline in Inventory Value	10,000	
	Inventory		10,000

Write down inventory to market value.

Although this entry revalues the inventory to $25,000 on the subsidiary's books, the appropriate valuation from a consolidated viewpoint is the $20,000 original cost of the inventory to the parent. Therefore, the following consolidation entry is needed in the worksheet:

Eliminate Intercompany Inventory Sales (still on hand):

Sales	35,000	
Cost of Goods Sold		20,000
Inventory		5,000
Loss on Decline in Inventory Value		10,000

The inventory loss recorded by the subsidiary must be eliminated because the $20,000 inventory valuation for consolidation purposes is below the $25,000 market value of the inventory.

Sales and Purchases before Affiliation

Sometimes companies that have sold inventory to one another later join together in a business combination. The consolidation treatment of profits on inventory transfers that occurred before the business combination depends on whether the companies were at that time independent and the sale transaction was the result of arm's-length bargaining. As a general rule, the effects of transactions that are not the result of arm's-length bargaining must be eliminated. However, the combining of two companies does not necessarily mean that their prior transactions with one another were not conducted at arm's length. The circumstances surrounding the prior transactions, such as the price and quantity of units transferred, would have to be examined.

In the absence of evidence to the contrary, companies that have joined together in a business combination are viewed as having been separate and independent prior to the combination. Thus, if the prior sales were the result of arm's-length bargaining, they are viewed as transactions between unrelated parties. Accordingly, no consolidation entry or adjustment is needed in preparing consolidated statements subsequent to the combination, even if an affiliate still holds the inventory.

SUMMARY OF KEY CONCEPTS

Consolidated financial statements are prepared for the consolidated entity as if it were a single company. Therefore, the effects of all transactions between companies within the entity must be eliminated in preparing consolidated financial statements.

Each time consolidated statements are prepared, all effects of intercompany transactions occurring during that period and the effects of unrealized profits from transactions in prior periods must be eliminated. For intercompany inventory transactions, the intercompany sale and cost of goods sold must be eliminated. In addition, the intercompany profit may not be recognized in consolidation until it is confirmed by resale of the inventory to an external party. Unrealized intercompany profits must be eliminated fully and are allocated proportionately against the stockholder groups of the selling affiliate. If inventory containing unrealized intercompany profits is sold during the period, consolidated cost of goods sold must be adjusted to reflect the actual cost to the consolidated entity of the inventory sold; if the inventory is still held at the end of the period, it must be adjusted to its actual cost to the consolidated entity.

KEY TERMS

downstream sale, *249*
intercompany transfers, *243*
intercorporate transfers, *243*
markup, *247*
markup on cost, *247*
markup on sales, *247*
modified equity method, *244*
transfer price, *247*
unrealized intercompany profit, *244*
upstream sale, *249*

Appendix 6A Intercompany Inventory Transactions—Modified Equity Method and Cost Method

This appendix illustrates consolidation procedures under the modified (or sometimes called the basic) equity method and then the cost method. We use the upstream sale example presented earlier to illustrate these alternative methods. Assume that Special Foods purchases inventory for $7,000 in 20X1 and, in the same year, sells the inventory to Peerless Products for $10,000. Peerless Products sells the inventory to external parties in 20X2. Both companies use perpetual inventory control systems.

MODIFIED EQUITY METHOD

The journal entries on Peerless' books and the consolidation entries in the consolidation worksheet are the same under the modified equity method as under the fully adjusted method except for differences related to unrealized intercompany profits. When using the fully adjusted equity method, the parent reduces its income and the balance of the investment account for its share of unrealized intercompany profits that arise during the period. Subsequently, the parent increases its income and the carrying amount of the investment account when the intercompany profits are realized through transactions with external parties. These adjustments related to unrealized gross profit on intercompany sales are omitted under the modified equity method. As a result, the worksheet entry in the second year to recognize the deferred gross profit from the first year is slightly different. Instead of recording a debit to the investment account, this debit goes to beginning retained earnings.

Modified Equity-Method Entries—20X1

In 20X1, Peerless Products records the normal equity-method entries reflecting its share of Special Foods' income and dividends but omits the additional entry to reduce income and the investment account by the parent's share of the unrealized intercompany profit arising during the year:

(20)		Debit	Credit
	Investment in Special Foods	40,000	
	Income from Special Foods		40,000

Record Peerless' 80% share of Special Foods' 20X1 income.

(21)		Debit	Credit
	Cash	24,000	
	Investment in Special Foods		24,000

Record Peerless' 80% share of Special Foods' 20X1 dividend.

Consolidation Entries—20X1

Figure 6–7 illustrates the consolidation worksheet for 20X1 under the modified equity method. The consolidation entries are the same as we presented for the fully adjusted equity method with one minor exception. We do not reduce the amounts in Peerless' Income from Special Foods and Investment in Special Foods accounts by Peerless' share of the deferral, because no adjustment was made to the investment account or income from subsidiary account under the modified equity method, $2,400 ($3,000 × 80%), but we do reduce the NCI in Net Income of Special Foods and NCI in Net Assets of Special Foods by the NCI share of the deferral, $600 ($3,000 × 20%). Thus, the only adjustments to the book value calculations for the basic consolidation entry are made to the NCI amounts for the deferral of unrealized gross profit.

Calculations for Basic Consolidation Entry:

Book Value Calculations:

	NCI 20% +	Peerless 80%	=	Common Stock	+ Retained Earnings
Original Book Value	60,000	240,000		200,000	100,000
+ Net Income	10,000	40,000			50,000
− Dividends	(6,000)	(24,000)			(30,000)
Ending Book Value	64,000	256,000		200,000	120,000

Adjustment to Basic Consolidation Entry:

	NCI	Peerless
Net Income	10,000	40,000
– Gross profit deferral	(600)	(2,400)
Income to be eliminated	9,400	37,600
Ending Book value	64,000	256,000
– Gross profit deferral	(600)	(2,400)
Ending Book Value	63,400	253,600

Basic Consolidation Entry:

Common Stock	200,000		← Common stock balance
Retained Earnings	100,000		← Beginning balance in RE
Income from Special Foods	40,000		← Peerless' % of NI
NCI in NI of Special Foods	9 ,400		← NCI share of NI with Adjustment
Dividends Declared		30,000	← 100% of sub's dividends declared
Investment in Special Foods		256,000	← Net book value
NCI in NA of Special Foods		63,400	← NCI share BV with Adjustment

FIGURE 6–7 December 31, 20X1, Modified Equity-Method Consolidation Worksheet, Period of Intercompany Sale; Upstream Inventory Sale

	Peerless Products	Special Foods	Consolidation Entries DR	Consolidation Entries CR	Consolidated
Income Statement					
Sales	400,000	200,000	10,000		590,000
Less: COGS	(170,000)	(115,000)		7,000	(278,000)
Less: Depreciation Expense	(50,000)	(20,000)			(70,000)
Less: Other Expenses	(40,000)	(15,000)			(55,000)
Income from Special Foods	40,000		40,000		0
Consolidated Net Income	180,000	50,000	50,000	7,000	187,000
NCI in Net Income			9,400		(9,400)
Controlling Interest Net Income	**180,000**	**50,000**	**59,400**	**7,000**	**177,600**
Statement of Retained Earnings					
Beginning Balance	300,000	100,000	100,000		300,000
Net Income	**180,000**	**50,000**	59,400	7,000	177,600
Less: Dividends Declared	(60,000)	(30,000)		30,000	(60,000)
Ending Balance	**420,000**	**120,000**	**159,400**	**37,000**	**417,600**
Balance Sheet					
Cash	264,000	75,000			339,000
Accounts Receivable	75,000	50,000			125,000
Inventory	100,000	75,000		3,000	172,000
Investment in Special Foods	256,000			256,000	0
Land	175,000	40,000			215,000
Buildings & Equipment	800,000	600,000		300,000	1,100,000
Less: Accumulated Depreciation	(450,000)	(320,000)	300,000		(470,000)
Total Assets	**1,220,000**	**520,000**	**300,000**	**559,000**	**1,481,000**
Accounts Payable	100,000	100,000			200,000
Bonds Payable	200,000	100,000			300,000
Common Stock	500,000	200,000	200,000		500,000
Retained Earnings	**420,000**	**120,000**	159,400	37,000	417,600
NCI in NA of Special Foods				63,400	63,400
Total Liabilities & Equity	**1,220,000**	**520,000**	**359,400**	**100,400**	**1,481,000**

Optional Accumulated Depreciation Consolidation Entry:

Accumulated Depreciation	300,000		← Accumulated depreciation at the time of the acquisition netted against cost
Buildings & Equipment		300,000	

Eliminate Inventory Purchases from Special Foods (still on hand):

Sales	10,000	
Cost of Goods Sold		7,000
Inventory		3,000

Investment in Special Foods

	Debit	Credit	
Acquisition	240,000		
80% NI	40,000		
		24,000	80% Dividends
Ending Balance	256,000		
		256,000	Basic
	0		

Income from Special Foods

	Debit	Credit	
		40,000	80% NI
		40,000	Ending Balance
Basic	40,000		
		0	

Modified Equity-Method Entries—20X2

The equity-method journal entries on Peerless' books are the same as illustrated previously, except that the adjustment for Peerless' share of the deferral is omitted:

(22)	Investment in Special Foods	60,000	
	Income from Special Foods		60,000
	Record Peerless' 80% share of Special Foods' 20X2 income.		

(23)	Cash	32,000	
	Investment in Special Foods		32,000
	Record Peerless' 80% share of Special Foods' 20X2 dividend.		

Consolidation Entries—20X2

Figure 6–8 illustrates the consolidation worksheet for 20X2 under the modified equity method. The first two consolidation entries are the same with one exception. Because the inventory sold to Peerless by Special Foods last year has now been sold to an unaffiliated party, we now increase the NCI in Net Income of Special Foods and NCI in Net Assets of Special Foods by the NCI share of the deferral, \$600 (\$3,000 × 20%). However, we do not increase the amounts in Peerless' Income from Special Foods and Investment in Special Foods accounts by Peerless' share of the deferral, \$2,400 (\$3,000 × 80%), because no adjustment was made to the investment account or income account under the modified equity method. Again, the only adjustments to the book value calculations for the basic consolidation entry are made to the NCI amounts for the reversal of last year's unrealized gross profit.

Calculations for Basic Consolidation Entry:

Book Value Calculations:

	NCI 20% +	Peerless 80%	=	Common Stock	+ Retained Earnings
Original Book Value	64,000	256,000		200,000	120,000
+ Net Income	15,000	60,000			75,000
− Dividends	(8,000)	(32,000)			(40,000)
Ending Book Value	71,000	284,000		200,000	155,000

Adjustment to Basic Consolidation Entry:

	NCI	Peerless
Net Income	**15,000**	**60,000**
+ Reverse GP deferral	**(600)**	**(2,400)**
Income to be eliminated	**15,600**	**62,400**
Ending Book Value	**71,000**	**284,000**
+ Reverse GP deferral	**(600)**	**(2,400)**
Ending Book Value	**71,600**	**286,400**

Basic Consolidation Entry:

Common Stock	**200,000**		← Common stock balance
Retained Earnings	**120,000**		← Beginning balance in RE
Income from Special Foods	**60,000**		← Peerless' % of NI
NCI in NI of Special Foods	**15,600**		← NCI % of NI with Adjustment
Dividends Declared		**40,000**	← 100% of sub's dividends declared
Investment in Special Foods		**284,000**	← Net book value
NCI in NA of Special Foods		**71,600**	← NCI % of BV with Adjustment

FIGURE 6–8 December 31, 20X2, Modified Equity-Method Consolidation Worksheet, Next Period Following Intercompany Sale; Upstream Inventory Sale

	Peerless Products	Special Foods	Consolidation Entries DR	Consolidation Entries CR	Consolidated
Income Statement					
Sales	450,000	300,000			750,000
Less: COGS	(180,000)	(160,000)		3,000	(337,000)
Less: Depreciation Expense	(50,000)	(20,000)			(70,000)
Less: Other Expenses	(60,000)	(45,000)			(105,000)
Income from Special Foods	60,000		60,000		0
Consolidated Net Income	220,000	75,000	60,000	3,000	238,000
NCI in Net Income			15,600		(15,600)
Controlling Interest Net Income	**220,000**	**75,000**	**75,600**	**3,000**	**222,400**
Statement of Retained Earnings					
Beginning Balance	420,000	120,000	120,000 2,400		417,600
Net Income	**220,000**	**75,000**	**75,600**	**3,000**	222,400
Less: Dividends Declared	(60,000)	(40,000)		40,000	(60,000)
Ending Balance	**580,000**	**155,000**	**198,000**	**43,000**	**580,000**
Balance Sheet					
Cash	291,000	85,000			376,000
Accounts Receivable	150,000	80,000			230,000
Inventory	180,000	90,000			270,000
Investment in Special Foods	284,000			284,000	0
Land	175,000	40,000			215,000
Buildings & Equipment	800,000	600,000		300,000	1,100,000
Less: Accumulated Depreciation	(500,000)	(340,000)	300,000		(540,000)
Total Assets	**1,380,000**	**555,000**	**300,000**	**584,000**	**1,651,000**
Accounts Payable	100,000	100,000			200,000
Bonds Payable	200,000	100,000			300,000
Common Stock	500,000	200,000	200,000		500,000
Retained Earnings	**580,000**	**155,000**	**198,000**	**43,000**	580,000
NCI in NA of Special Foods			600	71,600	71,000
Total Liabilities & Equity	**1,380,000**	**555,000**	**398,600**	**114,600**	**1,651,000**

Similar to 20X1, the unrealized intercompany profit included in Peerless' beginning inventory was charged to Cost of Goods Sold when Peerless sold the inventory during 20X2. Thus, consolidated cost of goods sold will be overstated for 20X2 if it is reported in the consolidated income statement at the unadjusted total from the books of Peerless and Special Foods. The following consolidation entry corrects Cost of Goods Sold and splits this adjustment proportionately between beginning Retained Earnings and the NCI in Net Assets of Special Foods.

Reversal of 20X1 Gross Profit Deferral:

Retained Earnings	2,400	
NCI in NA of Special Foods	600	
Cost of Goods Sold		3,000

Optional Accumulated Depreciation Consolidation Entry:

Accumulated Depreciation	300,000		← Accumulated depreciation at the time of the acquisition netted against cost
Buildings & Equipment		300,000	

COST METHOD

When using the cost method, the parent records dividends received from the subsidiary as income but makes no adjustments with respect to undistributed income of the subsidiary or unrealized intercompany profits. As an example of consolidation following an upstream intercompany sale of inventory when the parent accounts for its investment in the subsidiary using the cost method, assume the same facts as in previous illustrations dealing with an upstream sale.

Consolidation Entries—20X1

Figure 6–9 illustrates the consolidation worksheet for 20X1 under the cost method. The following consolidation entries are needed in the worksheet used to prepare consolidated financial statements for 20X1 using the cost method:

Investment Consolidation Entry:

Common Stock	200,000		← Common stock balance
Retained Earnings	100,000		← RE on acquisition date
Investment in Special Foods		240,000	← Original cost of investment
NCI in NA of Special Foods		60,000	← NCI share of acquisition date BV

Dividend Consolidation Entry:

Dividend Income	24,000		← Peerless' 80% share of dividends
NCI in NI of Special Foods	6,000		← NCI's 20% share of dividends declared
Dividends Declared		30,000	← 100% of Special Foods' dividends

The amount of undistributed net income assigned to the NCI is adjusted for the NCI's share of the gross profit deferral.

NCI in NI and NCI in NA of Special Foods:

	NCI 20%
Net Income	10,000
− Dividend	(6,000)
− Gross profit deferral	(600)
NCI in NI of Special Foods	3,400

Assign Special Foods' Undistributed Income to NCI:

NCI in NI of Special Foods	3,400		← NCI's 20% share of undistributed NI with Adjustment
NCI in NA of Special Foods		3,400	← NCI's 20% share of undistributed NI with Adjustment

FIGURE 6–9 December 31, 20X1, Cost Method Consolidation Worksheet, Period of Intercompany Sale; Upstream Inventory Sale

	Peerless Products	Special Foods	Consolidation Entries DR	Consolidation Entries CR	Consolidated
Income Statement					
Sales	400,000	200,000	10,000		590,000
Less: COGS	(170,000)	(115,000)		7,000	(278,000)
Less: Depreciation Expense	(50,000)	(20,000)			(70,000)
Less: Other Expenses	(40,000)	(15,000)			(55,000)
Dividend Income	24,000		24,000		0
Consolidated Net Income	164,000	50,000	34,000	7,000	187,000
NCI in Net Income			6,000 3,400		(9,400)
Controlling Interest Net Income	**164,000**	**50,000**	**43,400**	**7,000**	**177,600**
Statement of Retained Earnings					
Beginning Balance	300,000	100,000	100,000		300,000
Net Income	**164,000**	**50,000**	**43,400**	**7,000**	177,600
Less: Dividends Declared	(60,000)	(30,000)		30,000	(60,000)
Ending Balance	**404,000**	**120,000**	**143,400**	**37,000**	**417,600**
Balance Sheet					
Cash	264,000	75,000			339,000
Accounts Receivable	75,000	50,000			125,000
Inventory	100,000	75,000		3,000	172,000
Investment in Special Foods	240,000			240,000	0
Land	175,000	40,000			215,000
Buildings & Equipment	800,000	600,000		300,000	1,100,000
Less: Accumulated Depreciation	(450,000)	(320,000)	300,000		(470,000)
Total Assets	**1,204,000**	**520,000**	**300,000**	**543,000**	**1,481,000**
Accounts Payable	100,000	100,000			200,000
Bonds Payable	200,000	100,000			300,000
Common Stock	500,000	200,000	200,000		500,000
Retained Earnings	**404,000**	**120,000**	**143,400**	**37,000**	417,600
NCI in NA of Special Foods				60,000 3,400	63,400
Total Liabilities & Equity	**1,204,000**	**520,000**	**343,400**	**100,400**	**1,481,000**

Optional Accumulated Depreciation Consolidation Entry:

Accumulated Depreciation	**300,000**		← Accumulated depreciation at the time of the acquisition netted against cost
Buildings & Equipment		**300,000**	

Eliminate Inventory Purchases from Special Foods (still on hand):

Sales	**10,000**	
Cost of Goods Sold		**7,000**
Inventory		**3,000**

The investment consolidation entry eliminates the original balances in Special Foods' equity section accounts as of the acquisition date. It simultaneously eliminates the Investment in Special Foods account and establishes the NCI in Net Assets account (for the NCI share of the Special Foods' net assets as of the acquisition date). The dividend consolidation entry eliminates Special Foods' declared dividends and Peerless' dividend income and establishes the NCI in net income with the NCI share of dividends declared. Although Peerless uses the cost method to account for its investment, the consolidated financial statements still must report the NCI shareholders' share of Special Foods' reported net income, and a portion of that income is allocated in the form of a dividend. Nevertheless, the NCI in net income should report the NCI share of reported income (adjusted for the deferred gross profit on upstream intercompany sales). Thus, the third consolidation entry assigns the NCI shareholders' 20 percent of the undistributed income (adjusted for 20 percent of the deferred gross profit) to both the NCI in Net Income of Special Foods and NCI in Net Assets of Special Foods. The optional accumulated depreciation and deferred gross profit consolidation entries are the same as those explained for the fully adjusted equity method.

Consolidation Entries—20X2

Figure 6–10 illustrates the consolidation worksheet for 20X2 under the cost method. Consolidation entries needed in the consolidation worksheet prepared at the end of 20X2 are as follows:

Investment Consolidation Entry:

Common Stock	200,000		← Common stock balance
Retained Earnings	100,000		← RE on acquisition date
Investment in Special Foods		240,000	← Original cost of investment
NCI in NA of Special Foods		60,000	← NCI share of acquisition date BV

Dividend Consolidation Entry:

Dividend Income	32,000		← Peerless' 80% share of dividends
NCI in NI of Special Foods	8,000		← NCI's 20% share of dividends declared
Dividends Declared		40,000	← 100% of Special Foods' dividends

NCI in NI and NCI in NA of Special Foods:

	NCI 20%
Net Income	15,000
− Dividend	(8,000)
+ Reverse GP deferral	(600)
NCI in NI of Special Foods	7,600
Undistributed from prior year	4,000
NCI in NA of Special Foods	11,600

Assign Special Foods' Undistributed Income to NCI:

NCI in NI of Special Foods	7,600		← NCI's 20% share of 20X2 undistributed NI with Adjustment
Retained Earnings*	4,000		← NCI's 20% share of undistributed 20X1 income from Special Foods
NCI in NA of Special Foods		11,600	← NCI's 20% share of cumulative undistributed NI with Adjustment

*Note that these entries adjust for the subsidiary's retained earnings balance. The subsidiary does not adjust for the deferral of unrealized gross profit because this adjustment is made on the consolidation worksheet, not in the records of the subsidiary.

Optional Accumulated Depreciation Consolidation Entry:

Accumulated Depreciation	300,000		← Accumulated depreciation at the time of the acquisition netted against cost
Buildings & Equipment		300,000	

The investment and dividend consolidation entries are the same as in 20X1. The third entry assigns cumulative undistributed net income from Special Foods. It assigns 20 percent of the 20X2 net income to the NCI shareholders and 20 percent of the 20X1 net income to retained earnings for the prior year. The accumulated depreciation consolidation entry is the same as in 20X1. However, the last entry is identical to the entry under the modified equity method.

Similar to 20X1, the unrealized intercompany profit included in Peerless' beginning inventory was charged to Cost of Goods Sold when Peerless sold the inventory during 20X2. Thus, consolidated cost of goods sold will be overstated for 20X2 if it is reported in the consolidated income statement at the unadjusted total from the books of Peerless and Special Foods. The following

FIGURE 6–10 December 31, 20X2, Cost Method Consolidation Worksheet, Next Period Following Intercompany Sale; Upstream Inventory Sale

	Peerless Products	Special Foods	Consolidation Entries DR	Consolidation Entries CR	Consolidated
Income Statement					
Sales	450,000	300,000			750,000
Less: COGS	(180,000)	(160,000)		3,000	(337,000)
Less: Depreciation Expense	(50,000)	(20,000)			(70,000)
Less: Other Expenses	(60,000)	(45,000)			(105,000)
Dividend Income	32,000		32,000		0
Consolidated Net Income	192,000	75,000	32,000	3,000	238,000
NCI in Net Income			8,000 7,600		(15,600)
Controlling Interest Net Income	**192,000**	**75,000**	47,600	3,000	**222,400**
Statement of Retained Earnings					
Beginning Balance	404,000	120,000	100,000 4,000 2,400		417,600
Net Income	**192,000**	**75,000**	47,600	3,000	222,400
Less: Dividends Declared	(60,000)	(40,000)		40,000	(60,000)
Ending Balance	**536,000**	**155,000**	154,000	43,000	**580,000**
Balance Sheet					
Cash	291,000	85,000			376,000
Accounts Receivable	150,000	80,000			230,000
Inventory	180,000	90,000			270,000
Investment in Special Foods	240,000			240,000	0
Land	175,000	40,000			215,000
Buildings & Equipment	800,000	600,000		300,000	1,100,000
Less: Accumulated Depreciation	(500,000)	(340,000)	300,000		(540,000)
Total Assets	**1,336,000**	**555,000**	300,000	540,000	**1,651,000**
Accounts Payable	100,000	100,000			200,000
Bonds Payable	200,000	100,000			300,000
Common Stock	500,000	200,000	200,000		500,000
Retained Earnings	**536,000**	**155,000**	154,000	43,000	580,000
NCI in NA of Special Foods			600	60,000 11,600	71,000
Total Liabilities & Equity	**1,336,000**	**555,000**	354,600	114,600	**1,651,000**

consolidation entry corrects Cost of Goods Sold and splits this adjustment proportionately between beginning Retained Earnings and the NCI in Net Assets of Special Foods.

Reversal of 20X1 Gross Profit Deferral:

Retained Earnings*	**2,400**	
NCI in NA of Special Foods	**600**	
Cost of Goods Sold		**3,000**

*Note that these entries adjust for the subsidiary's retained earnings balance. The subsidiary does not adjust for the deferral of unrealized gross profit because this adjustment is made in the consolidation worksheet, not in the records of the subsidiary.

QUESTIONS

LO 6-1 **Q6-1** Why must inventory transfers to related companies be eliminated in preparing consolidated financial statements?

LO 6-2 **Q6-2** Why is there a need for a consolidation entry when an intercompany inventory transfer is made at cost?

LO 6-3 **Q6-3** Distinguish between an upstream sale of inventory and a downstream sale. Why is it important to know whether a sale is upstream or downstream?

LO 6-3 **Q6-4** How do unrealized intercompany profits on a downstream sale of inventory made during the current period affect the computation of consolidated net income and income to the controlling interest?

LO 6-4 **Q6-5** How do unrealized intercompany profits on an upstream sale of inventory made during the current period affect the computation of consolidated net income and income to the controlling interest?

LO 6-3, 6-4 **Q6-6** Will the consolidation of unrealized intercompany profits on an upstream sale or on a downstream sale in the current period have a greater effect on income assigned to the noncontrolling interest? Why?

LO 6-3 **Q6-7** What consolidation entry is needed when inventory is sold to an affiliate at a profit and is resold to an unaffiliated party before the end of the reporting period? (Assume both affiliates use perpetual inventory systems.)

LO 6-3 **Q6-8** What consolidation entry is needed when inventory is sold to an affiliate at a profit and is not resold before the end of the period? (Assume both affiliates use perpetual inventory systems.)

LO 6-3, 6-4 **Q6-9** How is the amount to be reported as cost of goods sold by the consolidated entity determined when there have been intercorporate sales during the period?

LO 6-3, 6-4 **Q6-10** How is the amount to be reported as consolidated retained earnings determined when there have been intercorporate sales during the period?

LO 6-3, 6-4 **Q6-11** How is the amount of consolidated retained earnings assigned to the noncontrolling interest affected by unrealized inventory profits at the end of the year?

LO 6-3, 6-4 **Q6-12** How do unrealized intercompany inventory profits from a prior period affect the computation of consolidated net income when the inventory is resold in the current period? Is it important to know whether the sale was upstream or downstream? Why, or why not?

LO 6-3, 6-4 **Q6-13** How will the elimination of unrealized intercompany inventory profits recorded on the parent's books affect consolidated retained earnings?

LO 6-3, 6-4 **Q6-14** How will the elimination of unrealized intercompany inventory profits recorded on the subsidiary's books affect consolidated retained earnings?

LO 6-5 **Q6-15*** Is an inventory sale from one subsidiary to another treated in the same manner as an upstream sale or a downstream sale? Why?

LO 6-5 **Q6-16*** Par Company regularly purchases inventory from Eagle Company. Recently, Par Company purchased a majority of the voting shares of Eagle Company. How should Par Company treat inventory profits recorded by Eagle Company before the day of acquisition? Following the day of acquisition?

CASES

LO 6-2 **C6-1 Measuring Cost of Goods Sold**

Judgment

Shortcut Charlie usually manages to develop some simple rule to handle even the most complex situations. In providing for the elimination of the effects of inventory transfers between the parent company and a subsidiary or between subsidiaries, Shortcut started with the following rules:

1. When the buyer continues to hold the inventory at the end of the period, credit Cost of Goods Sold for the amount recorded as cost of goods sold by the company that made the intercompany sale.
2. When the buyer resells the inventory before the end of the period, credit Cost of Goods Sold for the amount recorded as cost of goods sold by the company that made the intercompany sale plus the profit recorded by that company.
3. Debit Sales for the total amount credited in rule 1 or 2 above.

One of the new employees is seeking some assistance in understanding how the rules work and why.

Required

a. Explain why rule 1 is needed when consolidated statements are prepared.

b. Explain what is missing from rule 1, and prepare an alternative or additional statement for the elimination of unrealized profit when the purchasing affiliate does not resell to an unaffiliated company in the period in which it purchases inventory from an affiliate.

*Indicates that the item relates to "Additional Considerations."

c. Does rule 2 lead to the correct result? Explain your answer.

d. The rules do not provide assistance in determining how much profit either of the two companies recorded. Where should the employee look to determine the amount of profit referred to in rule 2?

LO 6-1, 6-2

C6-2 Inventory Values and Intercompany Transfers

Research

Water Products Corporation has been supplying high-quality bathroom fixtures to its customers for several decades and uses a LIFO inventory system. Rapid increases in the cost of fixtures have resulted in inventory values substantially below current replacement cost. To bring its inventory carrying costs up to more reasonable levels, Water Products sold its entire inventory to Plumbers Products Corporation and purchased an entirely new supply of inventory items from Growinkle Manufacturing. Water Products owns common stock of both Growinkle and Plumbers Products.

Water Products' external auditor immediately pointed out that under some ownership levels of these two companies, Water Products could accomplish its goal and under other levels it could not.

Required

Prepare a memo to Water Products' president describing the effects of intercompany transfers on the valuation of inventories and discuss the effects that different ownership levels of Growinkle and Plumbers Products would have on the success of Water Products' plan. Include citations to or quotations from the authoritative accounting literature to support your position.

LO 6-1

C6-3 Unrealized Inventory Profits

Understanding

Morrison Company owns 80 percent of Bloom Corporation's stock, acquired when Bloom's fair value as a whole was equal to its book value. The companies frequently engage in intercompany inventory transactions.

Required

Name the conditions that would make it possible for each of the following statements to be true. Treat each statement independently.

a. Income assigned to the noncontrolling interest in the consolidated income statement for 20X3 is higher than a pro rata share of Bloom's reported net income.

b. Income assigned to the noncontrolling interest in the consolidated income statement for 20X3 is higher than a pro rata share of Bloom's reported net income, but consolidated net income is reduced as a result of the elimination of intercompany inventory transfers.

c. Cost of goods sold reported in the income statement of Morrison is higher than consolidated cost of goods sold for 20X3.

d. Consolidated inventory is higher than the amounts reported by the separate companies.

LO 6-3, 6-4

C6-4 Eliminating Inventory Transfers

Analysis

Ready Building Products has six subsidiaries that sell building materials and supplies to the public and to the parent and other subsidiaries. Because of the invoicing system Ready uses, it is not possible to keep track of which items have been purchased from related companies and which have been bought from outside sources. Due to the nature of the products purchased, there are substantially different profit margins on different product groupings.

Required

a. If no effort is made to eliminate intercompany sales for the period or unrealized profits at year-end, what elements of the financial statements are likely to be misstated?

b. What type of control system would you recommend to Ready's controller to provide the information needed to make the required consolidation entries?

c. Would it matter if the buyer and seller used different inventory costing methods (FIFO, LIFO, or weighted average)? Explain.

d. Assume you believe that the adjustments for unrealized profit would be material. How would you go about determining what amounts must be eliminated at the end of the current period?

LO 6-1, 6-2

C6-5 Intercompany Profits and Transfers of Inventory

Analysis

Many companies transfer inventories from one affiliate to another. Often the companies have integrated operations in which one affiliate provides the raw materials, another manufactures finished products, another distributes the products, and perhaps another sells the products at retail. In other cases, various affiliates may be established for selling the company's products in different geographic locations, especially in different countries. Often tax considerations also have an effect on intercompany transfers.

Required

a. Are Xerox Corporation's intercompany transfers significant? How does Xerox treat intercompany transfers for consolidation purposes?

b. How does ExxonMobil Corporation price its products for intercompany transfers? Are these transfers significant? How does ExxonMobil treat intercompany profits for consolidation purposes?

c. What types of intercompany and intersegment sales does Ford Motor Company have? Are they significant? How are they treated for consolidation?

EXERCISES

LO 6-3, 6-4

E6-1 Multiple-Choice Questions on Intercompany Inventory Transfers [AICPA Adapted]

Select the correct answer for each of the following questions:

1. Perez Inc. owns 80 percent of Senior Inc. During 20X2, Perez sold goods with a 40 percent gross profit to Senior. Senior sold all of these goods in 20X2. For 20X2 consolidated financial statements, how should the summation of Perez and Senior income statement items be adjusted?
   a. Sales and Cost of Goods Sold should be reduced by the intercompany sales amount.
   b. Sales and Cost of Goods Sold should be reduced by 80 percent of the intercompany sales amount.
   c. Net income should be reduced by 80 percent of the gross profit on intercompany sales amount.
   d. No adjustment is necessary.

2. Parker Corporation owns 80 percent of Smith Inc.'s common stock. During 20X1, Parker sold inventory to Smith for $250,000 on the same terms as sales made to third parties. Smith sold all of the inventory purchased from Parker in 20X1. The following information pertains to Smith's and Parker's sales for 20X1:

	Parker	Smith
Sales	$1,000,000	$ 700,000
Cost of Sales	(400,000)	(350,000)
Gross Profit	$ 600,000	$ 350,000

   What amount should Parker report as cost of sales in its 20X1 consolidated income statement?
   a. $750,000.
   b. $680,000.
   c. $500,000.
   d. $430,000.

Note: Items 3 and 4 are based on the following information:
Nolan owns 100 percent of the capital stock of both Twill Corporation and Webb Corporation. Twill purchases merchandise inventory from Webb at 140 percent of Webb's cost. During 20X0, Webb sold merchandise that had cost it $40,000 to Twill. Twill sold all of this merchandise to unrelated customers for $81,200 during 20X0. In preparing combined financial statements for 20X0, Nolan's bookkeeper disregarded the common ownership of Twill and Webb.

3. What amount should be eliminated from cost of goods sold in the combined income statement for 20X0?
   a. $56,000.
   b. $40,000.
   c. $24,000.
   d. $16,000.

4. By what amount was unadjusted revenue overstated in the combined income statement for 20X0?
   a. $16,000.
   b. $40,000.
   c. $56,000.
   d. $81,200.

5. Clark Company had the following transactions with affiliated parties during 20X2:
   - Sales of $60,000 to Dean Inc., with $20,000 gross profit. Dean had $15,000 of this inventory on hand at year-end. Clark owns a 15 percent interest in Dean and does not exert significant influence.
   - Purchases of raw materials totaling $240,000 from Kent Corporation, a wholly owned subsidiary. Kent's gross profit on the sales was $48,000. Clark had $60,000 of this inventory remaining on December 31, 20X2.

   Before consolidation entries, Clark had consolidated current assets of $320,000. What amount should Clark report in its December 31, 20X2, consolidated balance sheet for current assets?
   a. $320,000.
   b. $317,000.
   c. $308,000.
   d. $303,000.

6. Selected data for two subsidiaries of Dunn Corporation taken from the December 31, 20X8, preclosing trial balances are as follows:

	Banks Co. (Debits)	Lamm Co. (Credits)
Shipments to Banks		$150,000
Shipments from Lamm	$ 200,000	
Intercompany Inventory Profit on Total Shipments		50,000

   Additional data relating to the December 31, 20X8, inventory are as follows:

Inventory acquired by Banks from outside parties	$175,000
Inventory acquired by Lamm from outside parties	250,000
Inventory acquired by Banks from Lamm	60,000

   At December 31, 20X8, the inventory reported on the combined balance sheet of the two subsidiaries should be:
   a. $425,000.
   b. $435,000.
   c. $470,000.
   d. $485,000.

LO 6-3

E6-2 Multiple-Choice Questions on the Effects of Inventory Transfers [AICPA Adapted]

Select the correct answer for each of the following questions.

1. During 20X3, Park Corporation recorded sales of inventory for $500,000 to Small Company, its wholly owned subsidiary, on the same terms as sales made to third parties. At December 31, 20X3, Small held one-fifth of these goods in its inventory. The following information pertains to Park's and Small's sales for 20X3:

	Park	Small
Sales	$2,000,000	$1,400,000
Cost of Sales	(800,000)	(700,000)
Gross Profit	$1,200,000	$ 700,000

In its 20X3 consolidated income statement, what amount should Park report as cost of sales?

a. $1,000,000.
b. $1,060,000.
c. $1,260,000.
d. $1,500,000.

Note: Items 2 through 6 are based on the following information:
Selected information from the separate and consolidated balance sheets and income statements of Power Inc. and its subsidiary, Spin Company, as of December 31, 20X8, and for the year then ended is as follows:

	Power	Spin	Consolidated
Balance Sheet Accounts			
Accounts Receivable	$ 26,000	$ 19,000	$ 39,000
Inventory	30,000	25,000	52,000
Investment in Spin	53,000		
Patents			20,000
NCI in NA of Spin			14,000
Stockholders' Equity	154,000	50,000	154,000
Income Statement Accounts			
Revenues	$200,000	$140,000	$308,000
Cost of Goods Sold	150,000	110,000	231,000
Gross Profit	$ 50,000	$ 30,000	$ 77,000
Income from Spin	7,400		
Amortization of Patents			2,000
Net Income	$ 33,000	$ 15,000	$ 40,000

Additional Information

During 20X8, Power sold goods to Spin at the same markup that Power uses for all sales. At December 31, 20X8, Spin had not paid for all of these goods and still held 37.5 percent of them in inventory.

Power acquired its interest in Spin on January 2, 20X5, when the book values and fair values of the assets and liabilities of Spin were equal, except for patents, which had a fair value of $28,000. The fair value of the noncontrolling interest was equal to a proportionate share of fair value of Spin's net assets.

2. What was the amount of intercompany sales from Power to Spin during 20X8?

a. $3,000.
b. $6,000.
c. $29,000.
d. $32,000.

3. At December 31, 20X8, what was the amount of Spin's payable to Power for intercompany sales?

a. $3,000.
b. $6,000.
c. $29,000.
d. $32,000.

4. In Power's consolidated balance sheet, what was the carrying amount of the inventory that Spin purchased from Power?

a. $3,000.
b. $6,000.
c. $9,000.
d. $12,000.

5. What is the percent of noncontrolling interest ownership of Spin?

a. 10 percent.
b. 20 percent.
c. 25 percent.
d. 45 percent.

6. Over how many years has Power chosen to amortize patents?

   a. 10 years.
   b. 14 years.
   c. 23 years.
   d. 40 years.

LO 6-3

E6-3 Multiple-Choice Questions—Consolidated Income Statement

Select the correct answer for each of the following questions.

Blue Company purchased 60 percent ownership of Kelly Corporation in 20X1. On May 10, 20X2, Kelly purchased inventory from Blue for $60,000. Kelly sold all of the inventory to an unaffiliated company for $86,000 on November 10, 20X2. Blue produced the inventory sold to Kelly for $47,000. The companies had no other transactions during 20X2.

1. What amount of sales will be reported in the 20X2 consolidated income statement?

   a. $51,600.
   b. $60,000.
   c. $86,000.
   d. $146,000.

2. What amount of cost of goods sold will be reported in the 20X2 consolidated income statement?

   a. $36,000.
   b. $47,000.
   c. $60,000.
   d. $107,000.

3. What amount of consolidated net income will be assigned to the controlling shareholders for 20X2?

   a. $13,000.
   b. $26,000.
   c. $28,600.
   d. $39,000.

LO 6-4

E6-4 Multiple-Choice Questions—Consolidated Balances

Select the correct answer for each of the following questions.

Lorn Corporation purchased inventory from Dresser Corporation for $120,000 on September 20, 20X1, and resold 80 percent of the inventory to unaffiliated companies prior to December 31, 20X1, for $140,000. Dresser produced the inventory sold to Lorn for $75,000. Lorn owns 70 percent of Dresser's voting common stock. The companies had no other transactions during 20X1.

1. What amount of sales will be reported in the 20X1 consolidated income statement?

   a. $98,000.
   b. $120,000.
   c. $140,000.
   d. $260,000.

2. What amount of cost of goods sold will be reported in the 20X1 consolidated income statement?

   a. $60,000.
   b. $75,000.
   c. $96,000.
   d. $120,000.
   e. $171,000.

3. What amount of consolidated net income will be assigned to the controlling interest for 20X1?

   a. $20,000.
   b. $30,800.
   c. $44,000.
   d. $45,000.

e. $69,200.
f. $80,000.

4. What inventory balance will be reported by the consolidated entity on December 31, 20X1?
   a. $15,000.
   b. $16,800.
   c. $24,000.
   d. $39,000.

LO 6-3

E6-5 Multiple-Choice Questions—Consolidated Income Statement

Select the correct answer for each of the following questions.

Amber Corporation holds 80 percent of the stock of Movie Productions Inc. During 20X4, Amber purchased an inventory of snack bar items for $40,000 and resold $30,000 to Movie Productions for $48,000. Movie Productions Inc. reported sales of $67,000 in 20X4 and had inventory of $16,000 on December 31, 20X4. The companies held no beginning inventory and had no other transactions in 20X4.

1. What amount of cost of goods sold will be reported in the 20X4 consolidated income statement?
   a. $20,000.
   b. $30,000.
   c. $32,000.
   d. $52,000.
   e. $62,000.
2. What amount of net income will be reported in the 20X4 consolidated income statement?
   a. $12,000.
   b. $18,000.
   c. $40,000.
   d. $47,000.
   e. $53,000.
3. What amount of income will be assigned to the noncontrolling interest in the 20X4 consolidated income statement?
   a. $7,000.
   b. $8,000.
   c. $9,400.
   d. $10,200.
   e. $13,400.

LO 6-3

E6-6 Realized Profit on Intercompany Sale

Nordway Corporation acquired 90 percent of Olman Company's voting shares of stock in 20X1. During 20X4, Nordway purchased 40,000 Playday doghouses for $24 each and sold 25,000 of them to Olman for $30 each. Olman sold all of the doghouses to retail establishments prior to December 31, 20X4, for $45 each. Both companies use perpetual inventory systems.

Required

a. Give the journal entries Nordway recorded for the purchase of inventory and resale to Olman Company in 20X4.
b. Give the journal entries Olman recorded for the purchase of inventory and resale to retail establishments in 20X4.
c. Give the worksheet consolidation entry(ies) needed in preparing consolidated financial statements for 20X4 to remove all effects of the intercompany sale.

LO 6-3

E6-7 Sale of Inventory to Subsidiary

Nordway Corporation acquired 90 percent of Olman Company's voting shares of stock in 20X1. During 20X4, Nordway purchased 40,000 Playday doghouses for $24 each and sold 25,000 of them to Olman for $30 each. Olman sold 18,000 of the doghouses to retail establishments prior to December 31, 20X4, for $45 each. Both companies use perpetual inventory systems.

Required

a. Give all journal entries Nordway recorded for the purchase of inventory and resale to Olman Company in 20X4.

b. Give the journal entries Olman recorded for the purchase of inventory and resale to retail establishments in 20X4.

c. Give the worksheet consolidation entry(ies) needed in preparing consolidated financial statements for 20X4 to remove the effects of the intercompany sale.

LO 6-3

Advanced StudyGuide .com

E6-8 Inventory Transfer between Parent and Subsidiary

Karlow Corporation owns 60 percent of Draw Company's voting shares. During 20X3, Karlow produced 25,000 computer desks at a cost of $82 each and sold 10,000 of them to Draw for $94 each. Draw sold 7,000 of the desks to unaffiliated companies for $130 each prior to December 31, 20X3, and sold the remainder in early 20X4 for $140 each. Both companies use perpetual inventory systems.

Required

a. What amounts of cost of goods sold did Karlow and Draw record in 20X3?

b. What amount of cost of goods sold must be reported in the consolidated income statement for 20X3?

c. Give the worksheet consolidation entry or entries needed in preparing consolidated financial statements at December 31, 20X3, relating to the intercorporate sale of inventory.

d. Give the worksheet consolidation entry or entries needed in preparing consolidated financial statements at December 31, 20X4, relating to the intercorporate sale of inventory.

e. Give the worksheet consolidation entry or entries needed in preparing consolidated financial statements at December 31, 20X4, relating to the intercorporate sale of inventory if the sales were upstream. Assume that Draw produced the computer desks at a cost of $82 each and sold 10,000 desks to Karlow for $94 each in 20X3, with Karlow selling 7,000 desks to unaffiliated companies in 20X3 and the remaining 3,000 in 20X4.

LO 6-4

E6-9 Income Statement Effects of Unrealized Profit

Holiday Bakery owns 60 percent of Farmco Products Company's stock. During 20X8, Farmco produced 100,000 bags of flour, which it sold to Holiday Bakery for $900,000. On December 31, 20X8, Holiday had 20,000 bags of flour purchased from Farmco Products on hand. Farmco prices its sales at cost plus 50 percent of cost for profit. Holiday, which purchased all its flour from Farmco in 20X8, had no inventory on hand on January 1, 20X8.

Holiday Bakery reported income from its baking operations of $400,000, and Farmco Products reported net income of $150,000 for 20X8.

Required

a. Compute the amount reported as cost of goods sold in the 20X8 consolidated income statement.

b. Give the worksheet consolidation entry or entries required to remove the effects of the intercompany sale in preparing consolidated statements at the end of 20X8.

c. Compute the amounts reported as consolidated net income and income assigned to the controlling interest in the 20X8 consolidated income statement.

LO 6-4

E6-10 Prior-Period Unrealized Inventory Profit

Holiday Bakery owns 60 percent of Farmco Products Company's stock. On January 1, 20X9, inventory reported by Holiday included 20,000 bags of flour purchased from Farmco at $9 per bag. By December 31, 20X9, all the beginning inventory purchased from Farmco Products had been baked into products and sold to customers by Holiday. There were no transactions between Holiday and Farmco during 20X9.

Both Holiday Bakery and Farmco Products price their sales at cost plus 50 percent markup for profit. Holiday reported income from its baking operations of $300,000, and Farmco reported net income of $250,000 for 20X9.

Required

a. Compute the amount reported as cost of goods sold in the 20X9 consolidated income statement for the flour purchased from Farmco in 20X8.

b. Give the consolidation entry or entries required to remove the effects of the unrealized profit in beginning inventory in preparing the consolidation worksheet as of December 31, 20X9.

c. Compute the amounts reported as consolidated net income and income assigned to the controlling interest in the 20X9 consolidated income statement.

LO 6-3, 6-4

E6-11 Computation of Consolidated Income Statement Data

Advanced StudyGuide .com

Prem Company acquired 60 percent ownership of Cooper Company's voting shares on January 1, 20X2. During 20X5, Prem purchased inventory for $20,000 and sold the full amount to Cooper Company for $30,000. On December 31, 20X5, Cooper's ending inventory included $6,000 of items purchased from Prem. Also in 20X5, Cooper purchased inventory for $50,000 and sold the units to Prem for $80,000. Prem included $20,000 of its purchase from Cooper in ending inventory on December 31, 20X5.

Summary income statement data for the two companies revealed the following:

	Prem Company	Cooper Company
Sales	$ 400,000	$ 200,000
Income from Cooper	20,500	
	$ 420,500	$ 200,000
Cost of Goods Sold	$ 250,000	$ 120,000
Other Expenses	70,000	35,000
Total Expenses	$(320,000)	$(155,000)
Net Income	$ 100,500	$ 45,000

Required

a. Compute the amount to be reported as sales in the 20X5 consolidated income statement.

b. Compute the amount to be reported as cost of goods sold in the 20X5 consolidated income statement.

c. What amount of income will be assigned to the noncontrolling shareholders in the 20X5 consolidated income statement?

d. What amount of income will be assigned to the controlling interest in the 20X5 consolidated income statement?

LO 6-3, 6-4

E6-12 Intercompany Sales

Hollow Corporation acquired 70 percent of Surg Corporation's voting stock on May 18, 20X1. The companies reported the following data with respect to intercompany sales in 20X4 and 20X5:

Year	Purchased by	Purchase Price	Sold to	Sale Price	Unsold at End of Year	Year Sold to Unaffiliated Co.
20X4	Surg Corp.	$120,000	Hollow Corp.	$180,000	$ 45,000	20X5
20X5	Surg Corp.	90,000	Hollow Corp.	135,000	30,000	20X6
20X5	Hollow Corp.	140,000	Surg Corp.	280,000	110,000	20X6

Hollow reported operating income (excluding income from its investment in Surg) of $160,000 and $220,000 in 20X4 and 20X5, respectively. Surg reported net income of $90,000 and $85,000 in 20X4 and 20X5, respectively.

Required

a. Compute consolidated net income for 20X4.

b. Compute the inventory balance reported in the consolidated balance sheet at December 31, 20X5, for the transactions shown.

c. Compute the amount included in consolidated cost of goods sold for 20X5 relating to the transactions shown.

d. Compute the amount of income assigned to the controlling interest in the 20X5 consolidated income statement.

LO 6-3, 6-4 **E6-13** **Consolidated Balance Sheet Worksheet**

The December 31, 20X8, balance sheets for Doorst Corporation and its 70 percent-owned subsidiary Hingle Company contained the following summarized amounts:

DOORST CORPORATION AND HINGLE COMPANY
Balance Sheets
December 31, 20X8

	Doorst Corporation	Hingle Company
Cash & Receivables	$ 98,000	$ 40,000
Inventory	150,000	100,000
Buildings & Equipment (net)	310,000	280,000
Investment in Hingle Company Stock	242,000	
Total Assets	$800,000	$420,000
Accounts Payable	$ 70,000	$ 20,000
Common Stock	200,000	150,000
Retained Earnings	530,000	250,000
Total Liabilities & Equity	$800,000	$420,000

Doorst acquired the shares of Hingle Company on January 1, 20X7. On December 31, 20X8, assume Doorst sold inventory to Hingle during 20X8 for $100,000 and Hingle sold inventory to Doorst for $300,000. Doorst's balance sheet contains inventory items purchased from Hingle for $95,000. The items cost Hingle $55,000 to produce. In addition, Hingle's inventory contains goods it purchased from Doorst for $25,000 that Doorst had produced for $15,000. Assume Hingle reported net income of $70,000 and dividends of $14,000.

Required

a. Prepare all consolidation entries needed to complete a consolidated balance sheet worksheet as of December 31, 20X8.

b. Prepare a consolidated balance sheet worksheet as of December 31, 20X8.

LO 6-5 **E6-14*** **Multiple Transfers between Affiliates**

Klon Corporation owns 70 percent of Brant Company's stock and 60 percent of Torkel Company's stock. During 20X8, Klon sold inventory purchased in 20X7 for $100,000 to Brant for $150,000. Brant then sold the inventory at its cost of $150,000 to Torkel. Prior to December 31, 20X8, Torkel sold $90,000 of inventory to a nonaffiliate for $120,000 and held $60,000 in inventory at December 31, 20X8.

Required

a. Give the journal entries recorded by Klon, Brant, and Torkel during 20X8 relating to the intercorporate sale and resale of inventory.

b. What amount should be reported in the 20X8 consolidated income statement as cost of goods sold?

c. What amount should be reported in the December 31, 20X8, consolidated balance sheet as inventory?

d. Give the consolidation entry needed at December 31, 20X8, to remove the effects of the inventory transfers.

LO 6-4 **E6-15** **Inventory Sales**

Herb Corporation holds 60 percent ownership of Spice Company. Each year, Spice purchases large quantities of a gnarl root used in producing health drinks. Spice purchased $150,000 of roots in 20X7 and sold $40,000 of these purchases to Herb for $60,000. By the end of 20X7, Herb had resold all but $15,000 of its purchase from Spice. Herb generated $90,000 on the sale of roots to various health stores during the year.

Required

a. Give the journal entries recorded by Herb and Spice during 20X7 relating to the initial purchase, intercorporate sale, and resale of gnarl roots.

b. Give the worksheet consolidation entries needed as of December 31, 20X7, to remove all effects of the intercompany transfer in preparing the 20X7 consolidated financial statements.

LO 6-4

E6-16 Prior-Period Inventory Profits

Home Products Corporation, which sells a broad line of home detergent products, owns 75 percent of the stock of Level Brothers Soap Company. During 20X8, Level Brothers sold soap products to Home Products for $180,000, which it had produced for $120,000. Home Products sold $150,000 of its purchase from Level Brothers in 20X8 and the remainder in 20X9. In addition, Home Products purchased $240,000 of inventory from Level Brothers in 20X9 and resold $90,000 of the items before year-end. Level Brothers' cost to produce the items sold to Home Products in 20X9 was $160,000.

Required

a. Give all worksheet consolidation entries needed for December 31, 20X9, to remove the effects of the intercompany inventory transfers in 20X8 and 20X9.

b. Compute the amount of income assigned to noncontrolling shareholders in the 20X8 and 20X9 consolidated income statements if Level Brothers reported net income of $350,000 for 20X8 and $420,000 for 20X9.

PROBLEMS

LO 6-4

P6-17 Consolidated Income Statement Data

Sweeny Corporation owns 60 percent of Bitner Company's shares. Partial 20X2 financial data for the companies and consolidated entity were as follows:

	Sweeny Corporation	Bitner Company	Consolidated Totals
Sales	$550,000	$450,000	$820,000
Cost of Goods Sold	310,000	300,000	420,000
Inventory, Dec. 31	180,000	210,000	375,000

On January 1, 20X2, Sweeny's inventory contained items purchased from Bitner for $75,000. The cost of the units to Bitner was $50,000. All intercorporate sales during 20X2 were made by Bitner to Sweeny.

Required

a. What amount of intercorporate sales occurred in 20X2?

b. How much unrealized intercompany profit existed on January 1, 20X2? On December 31, 20X2?

c. Give the worksheet consolidation entries relating to inventory and cost of goods sold needed to prepare consolidated financial statements for 20X2.

d. If Bitner reports net income of $90,000 for 20X2, what amount of income is assigned to the noncontrolling interest in the 20X2 consolidated income statement?

LO 6-4

P6-18 Unrealized Profit on Upstream Sales

Carroll Company sells all its output at 25 percent above cost. Pacific Corporation purchases all its inventory from Carroll. Selected information on the operations of the companies over the past three years is as follows:

	Carroll Company		Pacific Corporation	
Year	Sales to Pacific Corp.	Net Income	Inventory, Dec. 31	Operating Income
20X2	$200,000	$100,000	$ 70,000	$150,000
20X3	175,000	90,000	105,000	240,000
20X4	225,000	160,000	120,000	300,000

Pacific acquired 60 percent of the ownership of Carroll on January 1, 20X1, at underlying book value.

Required

Compute consolidated net income and income assigned to the controlling interest for 20X2, 20X3, and 20X4.

LO 6-3, 6-4

P6-19 Net Income of Consolidated Entity

Master Corporation acquired 70 percent of Crown Corporation's voting stock on January 1, 20X2, for $416,500. The fair value of the noncontrolling interest was $178,500 at the date of acquisition. Crown reported common stock outstanding of $200,000 and retained earnings of $350,000. The differential is assigned to buildings with an expected life of 15 years at the date of acquisition.

On December 31, 20X4, Master had $25,000 of unrealized profits on its books from inventory sales to Crown, and Crown had $40,000 of unrealized profit on its books from inventory sales to Master. All inventory held at December 31, 20X4, was sold during 20X5.

On December 31, 20X5, Master had $14,000 of unrealized profit on its books from inventory sales to Crown, and Crown had unrealized profit on its books of $55,000 from inventory sales to Master.

Master reported income from its separate operations (excluding income on its investment in Crown and amortization of purchase differential) of $118,000 in 20X5, and Crown reported net income of $65,000.

Required

Compute consolidated net income and income assigned to the controlling interest in the 20X5 consolidated income statement.

LO 6-4

Advanced StudyGuide .com

P6-20 Correction of Consolidation Entries

In preparing the consolidation worksheet for Bolger Corporation and its 60 percent–owned subsidiary, Feldman Company, the following consolidation entries were proposed by Bolger's bookkeeper:

Cash	80,000	
Accounts Payable		80,000

To eliminate the unpaid balance for intercorporate inventory sales in 20X5.

Cost of Goods Sold	12,000	
Income from Subsidiary		12,000

To eliminate unrealized inventory profits at December 31, 20X5.

Income from Subsidiary	140,000	
Sales		140,000

To eliminate intercompany sales for 20X5.

Bolger's bookkeeper recently graduated from Oddball University, and although the dollar amounts recorded are correct, he had some confusion in determining which accounts needed adjustment. All intercorporate sales in 20X5 were from Feldman to Bolger, and Feldman sells inventory at cost plus 40 percent of cost. Bolger uses the fully adjusted equity method in accounting for its ownership in Feldman.

Required

a. What percentage of the intercompany inventory transfer was resold prior to the end of 20X5?

b. Give the appropriate consolidation entries needed at December 31, 20X5, to prepare consolidated financial statements.

LO 6-3, 6-4

P6-21 Incomplete Data

Lever Corporation acquired 75 percent of the ownership of Tropic Company on January 1, 20X1. The fair value of the noncontrolling interest at acquisition was equal to its proportionate share of the fair value of the net assets of Tropic. The full amount of the differential at acquisition was attributable to buildings and equipment, which had a remaining useful life of eight years.

Financial statement data for the two companies and the consolidated entity at December 31, 20X6, are as follows:

LEVER CORPORATION AND TROPIC COMPANY
Balance Sheet Data
December 31, 20X6

Item	Lever Corporation	Tropic Company	Consolidated Entity
Cash	$ 67,000	$ 45,000	$112,000
Accounts Receivable	?	55,000	145,000
Inventory	125,000	90,000	211,000
Buildings & Equipment	400,000	240,000	680,000
Less: Accumulated Depreciation	(180,000)	(110,000)	(?)
Investment in Tropic Company	?		
Total Assets	$?	$320,000	$?
Accounts Payable	$ 86,000	$ 20,000	$ 89,000
Other Payables	?	8,000	?
Notes Payable	250,000	120,000	370,000
Common Stock	120,000	60,000	120,000
Retained Earnings	172,500	112,000	172,500
Noncontrolling Interest			44,500
Total Liabilities & Equity	$?	$320,000	$?

LEVER CORPORATION AND TROPIC COMPANY
Income Statement Data
For the Year Ended December 31, 20X6

Item	Lever Corporation	Tropic Company	Consolidated Entity
Sales	$420,000	$260,000	$650,000
Income from Subsidiary	32,250		
Total Income	$452,250	$260,000	$650,000
Cost of Goods Sold	$310,000	$170,000	$445,000
Depreciation Expense	20,000	25,000	50,000
Interest Expense	25,000	9,500	34,500
Other Expenses	22,000	15,500	37,500
Total Expenses	($377,000)	($220,000)	($567,000)
Consolidated Net Income			$ 83,000
Income to Noncontrolling Interest			(7,750)
Controlling Interest in Net Income	$ 75,250	$ 40,000	$ 75,250

All unrealized profit on intercompany inventory sales on January 1, 20X6, were eliminated on Lever's books. All unrealized inventory profits at December 31, 20X6, were eliminated on Tropic's books. Assume Lever uses the fully adjusted equity method and that Lever does not make the optional depreciation consolidation worksheet entry.

Required

a. For the buildings and equipment held by Tropic when Lever acquired it and still on hand on December 31, 20X6, by what amount had buildings and equipment increased in value from their acquisition to the date of combination with Lever?

b. What amount should be reported as accumulated depreciation for the consolidated entity at December 31, 20X6 (assuming Lever does not make the optional accumulated depreciation consolidation entry)?

c. If Tropic reported capital stock outstanding of $60,000 and retained earnings of $30,000 on January 1, 20X1, what amount did Lever pay to acquire its ownership of Tropic?

d. What balance does Lever report as its investment in Tropic at December 31, 20X6?

e. What amount of intercorporate sales of inventory occurred in 20X6?

f. What amount of unrealized inventory profit exists at December 31, 20X6?

g. Give the consolidation entry used in eliminating intercompany inventory sales during 20X6.

h. What was the amount of unrealized inventory profit at January 1, 20X6?

i. What balance in accounts receivable did Lever report at December 31, 20X6?

LO 6-4

Advanced StudyGuide .com

P6-22 Eliminations for Upstream Sales

Clean Air Products owns 80 percent of the stock of Superior Filter Company, which it acquired at underlying book value on August 30, 20X6. At that date, the fair value of the noncontrolling interest was equal to 20 percent of the book value of Superior Filter. Summarized trial balance data for the two companies as of December 31, 20X8, are as follows:

	Clean Air Products		Superior Filter Company	
	Debit	**Credit**	**Debit**	**Credit**
Cash and Accounts Receivable	$ 145,000		$ 90,000	
Inventory	220,000		110,000	
Buildings & Equipment (net)	270,000		180,000	
Investment in Superior Filter Stock	268,000			
Cost of Goods Sold	175,000		140,000	
Depreciation Expense	30,000		20,000	
Current Liabilities		$ 150,000		$ 30,000
Common Stock		200,000		90,000
Retained Earnings		472,000		220,000
Sales		250,000		200,000
Income from Subsidiary		36,000		
Total	$1,108,000	$1,108,000	$540,000	$540,000

On January 1, 20X8, Clean Air's inventory contained filters purchased for $60,000 from Superior Filter, which had produced the filters for $40,000. In 20X8, Superior Filter spent $100,000 to produce additional filters, which it sold to Clean Air for $150,000. By December 31, 20X8, Clean Air had sold all filters that had been on hand January 1, 20X8, but continued to hold in inventory $45,000 of the 20X8 purchase from Superior Filter.

Required

a. Prepare all consolidation entries needed to complete a consolidation worksheet for 20X8.

b. Compute consolidated net income and income assigned to the controlling interest in the 20X8 consolidated income statement.

c. Compute the balance assigned to the noncontrolling interest in the consolidated balance sheet as of December 31, 20X8.

LO 6-3, 6-4

P6-23 Multiple Inventory Transfers

Ajax Corporation purchased at book value 70 percent of Beta Corporation's ownership and 90 percent of Cole Corporation's ownership in 20X5. At the dates the ownership was acquired, the fair value of the noncontrolling interest was equal to a proportionate share of book value. There are frequent intercompany transfers among the companies. Activity relevant to 20X8 follows:

Year	Producer	Production Cost	Buyer	Transfer Price	Unsold at End of Year	Year Sold
20X7	Beta Corporation	$24,000	Ajax Corporation	$30,000	$10,000	20X8
20X7	Cole Corporation	60,000	Beta Corporation	72,000	18,000	20X8
20X8	Ajax Corporation	15,000	Beta Corporation	35,000	7,000	20X9
20X8	Beta Corporation	63,000	Cole Corporation	72,000	12,000	20X9
20X8	Cole Corporation	27,000	Ajax Corporation	45,000	15,000	20X9

For the year ended December 31, 20X8, Ajax reported $80,000 of income from its separate operations (excluding income from intercorporate investments), Beta reported net income of $37,500, and Cole reported net income of $20,000.

Required

a. Compute the amount to be reported as consolidated net income for 20X8.

b. Compute the amount to be reported as inventory in the December 31, 20X8, consolidated balance sheet for the preceding items.

c. Compute the amount to be reported as income assigned to noncontrolling shareholders in the 20X8 consolidated income statement.

LO 6-3, 6-4 **P6-24**
Consolidation with Inventory Transfers and Other Comprehensive Income

On January 1, 20X1, Priority Corporation purchased 90 percent of Tall Corporation's common stock at underlying book value. At that date, the fair value of the noncontrolling interest was equal to 10 percent of Tall Corporation's book value. Priority uses the equity method in accounting for its investment in Tall. The stockholders' equity section of Tall at January 1, 20X5, contained the following balances:

Common Stock ($5 par)	$ 400,000
Additional Paid-in Capital	200,000
Retained Earnings	790,000
Accumulated Other Comprehensive Income	10,000
Total	$1,400,000

During 20X4, Tall sold goods costing $30,000 to Priority for $45,000, and Priority resold 60 percent of them prior to year-end. It sold the remainder in 20X5. Also in 20X4, Priority sold inventory items costing $90,000 to Tall for $108,000. Tall resold $60,000 of its purchases in 20X4 and the remaining $48,000 in 20X5.

In 20X5, Priority sold additional inventory costing $30,000 to Tall for $36,000, and Tall resold $24,000 of it prior to year-end. Tall sold inventory costing $60,000 to Priority in 20X5 for $90,000, and Priority resold $48,000 of its purchase by December 31, 20X5.

Priority reported 20X5 income of $240,000 from its separate operations and paid dividends of $150,000. Tall reported 20X5 net income of $90,000 and comprehensive income of $110,000. Tall reported other comprehensive income of $10,000 in 20X4. In both years, other comprehensive income arose from an increase in the market value of securities classified as available-for-sale. Tall paid dividends of $60,000 in 20X5.

Required

a. Compute the balance in the investment account reported by Priority at December 31, 20X5.

b. Compute the amount of investment income reported by Priority on its investment in Tall for 20X5.

c. Compute the amount of income assigned to noncontrolling shareholders in the 20X5 consolidated income statement.

d. Compute the balance assigned to noncontrolling shareholders in the consolidated balance sheet prepared at December 31, 20X5.

e. Priority and Tall report inventory balances of $120,000 and $100,000, respectively, at December 31, 20X5. What amount should be reported as inventory in the consolidated balance sheet at December 31, 20X5?

f. Compute the amount reported as consolidated net income for 20X5.

g. Prepare the consolidation entries needed to complete a consolidation worksheet as of December 31, 20X5.

LO 6-3, 6-4 **P6-25**
Multiple Inventory Transfers between Parent and Subsidiary

Proud Company and Slinky Company both produce and purchase equipment for resale each period and frequently sell to each other. Since Proud Company holds 60 percent ownership of Slinky Company, Proud's controller compiled the following information with regard to intercompany transactions between the two companies in 20X5 and 20X6:

			Percent Resold to Nonaffiliate in			
Year	**Produced by**	**Sold to**	**20X5**	**20X6**	**Cost to Produce**	**Sale Price to Affiliate**
20X5	Proud Company	Slinky Company	60%	40%	$100,000	$150,000
20X5	Slinky Company	Proud Company	30	50	70,000	100,000
20X6	Proud Company	Slinky Company		90	40,000	60,000
20X6	Slinky Company	Proud Company		25	200,000	240,000

Required

a. Give the consolidation entries required at December 31, 20X6, to eliminate the effects of the inventory transfers in preparing a full set of consolidated financial statements.

b. Compute the amount of cost of goods sold to be reported in the consolidated income statement for 20X6.

LO 6-3, 6-4

P6-26 Consolidation Following Inventory Transactions

Bell Company purchased 60 percent ownership of Troll Corporation on January 1, 20X1, for $82,800. On that date, the noncontrolling interest had a fair value of $55,200 and Troll reported common stock outstanding of $100,000 and retained earnings of $20,000. The full amount of the differential is assigned to land to be used as a future building site. Bell uses the fully adjusted equity method in accounting for its ownership of Troll. On December 31, 20X2, the trial balances of the two companies are as follows:

	Bell Company		Troll Corporation	
Item	**Debit**	**Credit**	**Debit**	**Credit**
Cash and Accounts Receivable	$ 69,400		$ 51,200	
Inventory	60,000		55,000	
Land	40,000		30,000	
Buildings & Equipment	520,000		350,000	
Investment in Troll Corporation Stock	103,780			
Cost of Goods Sold	99,800		61,000	
Depreciation Expense	25,000		15,000	
Interest Expense	6,000		14,000	
Dividends Declared	40,000		10,000	
Accumulated Depreciation		$175,000		$ 75,000
Accounts Payable		68,800		41,200
Bonds Payable		80,000		200,000
Bond Premium		1,200		
Common Stock		200,000		100,000
Retained Earnings		227,960		50,000
Sales		200,000		120,000
Income from Subsidiary		11,020		
	$963,980	$963,980	$586,200	$586,200

Troll sold inventory costing $25,500 to Bell for $42,500 in 20X1. Bell resold 80 percent of the purchase in 20X1 and the remainder in 20X2. Troll sold inventory costing $21,000 to Bell in 20X2 for $35,000, and Bell resold 70 percent of it prior to December 31, 20X2. In addition, Bell sold inventory costing $14,000 to Troll for $28,000 in 20X2, and Troll resold all but $13,000 of its purchase prior to December 31, 20X2.

Assume both companies use straight-line depreciation and that no property, plant, and equipment has been purchased since the acquisition.

Required

a. Record the journal entry or entries for 20X2 on Bell's books related to its investment in Troll Corporation, using the equity method.

b. Prepare the consolidation entries needed to complete a consolidated worksheet for 20X2.

c. Prepare a three-part consolidation worksheet for 20X2.

LO 6-3, 6-4 **P6-27** **Consolidation Worksheet**

Crow Corporation purchased 70 percent of West Company's voting common stock on January 1, 20X5, for $291,200. On that date, the noncontrolling interest had a fair value of $124,800 and the book value of West's net assets was $380,000. The book values and fair values of West's assets and liabilities were equal except for land that had a fair value $14,000 higher than book value. The amount attributed to goodwill as a result of the acquisition is not amortized and has not been impaired.

CROW CORPORATION AND WEST COMPANY
Trial Balance Data
December 31, 20X9

Item	Crow Corporation Debit	Crow Corporation Credit	West Company Debit	West Company Credit
Cash and Receivables	$ 81,300		$ 85,000	
Inventory	200,000		110,000	
Land, Buildings, & Equipment (net)	270,000		250,000	
Investment in West Company Stock	290,200			
Cost of Goods & Services	200,000		150,000	
Depreciation Expense	40,000		30,000	
Dividends Declared	35,000		5,000	
Sales & Service Revenue		$ 300,000		$200,000
Income from Subsidiary		24,500		
Accounts Payable		60,000		30,000
Common Stock		200,000		150,000
Retained Earnings		532,000		250,000
Total	$1,116,500	$1,116,500	$630,000	$630,000

On January 1, 20X9, Crow's inventory contained $30,000 of unrealized intercompany profits recorded by West. West's inventory on that date contained $15,000 of unrealized intercompany profits recorded on Crow's books. Both companies sold their ending 20X8 inventories to unrelated companies in 20X9.

During 20X9, West sold inventory costing $37,000 to Crow for $62,000. Crow held all inventory purchased from West during 20X9 on December 31, 20X9. Also during 20X9, Crow sold goods costing $54,000 to West for $90,000. West continues to hold $20,000 of its purchase from Crow on December 31, 20X9. Assume Crow uses the fully adjusted equity method.

Required

a. Prepare all consolidation entries needed to complete a consolidation worksheet as of December 31, 20X9.

b. Prepare a consolidation worksheet as of December 31, 20X9.

LO 6-3, 6-4 **P6-28** **Computation of Consolidated Totals**

Bunker Corporation owns 80 percent of Harrison Company's stock. At the end of 20X8, Bunker and Harrison reported the following partial operating results and inventory balances:

Advanced StudyGuide .com

	Bunker Corporation	Harrison Company
Total sales	$660,000	$510,000
Sales to Harrison Company	140,000	
Sales to Bunker Corporation		240,000
Net income		20,000
Operating income (excluding investment income from Harrison)	70,000	
Inventory on hand, December 31, 20X8, purchased from:		
Harrison Company	48,000	
Bunker Corporation		42,000

Bunker regularly prices its products at cost plus a 40 percent markup for profit. Harrison prices its sales at cost plus a 20 percent markup. The total sales reported by Bunker and Harrison include both intercompany sales and sales to nonaffiliates.

Required

a. What amount of sales will be reported in the consolidated income statement for 20X8?

b. What amount of cost of goods sold will be reported in the 20X8 consolidated income statement?

c. What amount of consolidated net income and income to controlling interest will be reported in the 20X8 consolidated income statement?

d. What balance will be reported for inventory in the consolidated balance sheet for December 31, 20X8?

LO 6 3, 6-4 **P6-29**

Intercompany Transfer of Inventory

Pine Corporation acquired 70 percent of Bock Company's voting common shares on January 1, 20X2, for $108,500. At that date, the noncontrolling interest had a fair value of $46,500 and Bock reported $70,000 of common stock outstanding and retained earnings of $30,000. The differential is assigned to buildings and equipment, which had a fair value $20,000 higher than book value and a remaining 10-year life, and to patents, which had a fair value $35,000 higher than book value and a remaining life of five years at the date of the business combination. Trial balances for the companies as of December 31, 20X3, are as follows:

	Pine Corporation		Bock Company	
Item	**Debit**	**Credit**	**Debit**	**Credit**
Cash & Accounts Receivable	$ 15,400		$ 21,600	
Inventory	165,000		35,000	
Land	80,000		40,000	
Buildings & Equipment	340,000		260,000	
Investment in Bock Company Stock	109,600			
Cost of Goods Sold	186,000		79,800	
Depreciation Expense	20,000		15,000	
Interest Expense	16,000		5,200	
Dividends Declared	30,000		15,000	
Accumulated Depreciation		$140,000		$ 80,000
Accounts Payable		92,400		35,000
Bonds Payable		200,000		100,000
Bond Premium				1,600
Common Stock		120,000		70,000
Retained Earnings		127,900		60,000
Sales		260,000		125,000
Other Income		13,600		
Income from Subsidiary		8,100		
	$962,000	$962,000	$471,600	$471,600

On December 31, 20X2, Bock purchased inventory for $32,000 and sold it to Pine for $48,000. Pine resold $27,000 of the inventory (i.e., $27,000 of the $48,000 acquired from Bock) during 20X3 and had the remaining balance in inventory at December 31, 20X3.

During 20X3, Bock sold inventory purchased for $60,000 to Pine for $90,000, and Pine resold all but $24,000 of its purchase. On March 10, 20X3, Pine sold inventory purchased for $15,000 to Bock for $30,000. Bock sold all but $7,600 of the inventory prior to December 31, 20X3. Assume Pine uses the fully adjusted equity method, that both companies use straight-line depreciation, and that no property, plant, and equipment has been purchased since the acquisition.

Required

a. Give all consolidation entries needed to prepare a full set of consolidated financial statements at December 31, 20X3, for Pine and Bock.

b. Prepare a three-part consolidation worksheet for 20X3.

LO 6-3, 6-4 **P6-30**

Consolidation Using Financial Statement Data

Bower Corporation acquired 60 percent of Concerto Company's stock on January 1, 20X3, for $24,000 in excess of book value. On that date, the book values and fair values of Concerto's assets and liabilities were equal and the fair value of the noncontrolling interest was $16,000 in excess of book value. The full amount of the differential at acquisition was assigned to goodwill of $40,000. At December

31, 20X6, Bower management reviewed the amount assigned to goodwill and concluded it had been impaired. They concluded the correct carrying value at that date should be $30,000 and the impairment loss should be assigned proportionately between the controlling and noncontrolling interests.

Balance sheet data for January 1, 20X6, and December 31, 20X6, and income statement data for 20X6 for the two companies are as follows:

BOWER CORPORATION AND CONCERTO COMPANY
Balance Sheet Data
January 1, 20X6

Item	Bower Corporation		Concerto Company	
Cash	$ 9,800		$ 10,000	
Accounts Receivable	60,000		50,000	
Inventory	100,000		80,000	
Total Current Assets		$169,800		$140,000
Land		70,000		20,000
Buildings & Equipment	$300,000		$200,000	
Less: Accumulated Depreciation	(140,000)	160,000	(70,000)	130,000
Investment in Concerto Company Stock		135,200		
Total Assets		$535,000		$290,000
Accounts Payable		$ 30,000		$ 20,000
Bonds Payable		120,000		70,000
Common Stock	$100,000		$ 50,000	
Retained Earnings	285,000	385,000	150,000	200,000
Total Liabilities & Stockholders' Equity		$535,000		$290,000

BOWER CORPORATION AND CONCERTO COMPANY
Balance Sheet Data
December 31, 20X6

Item	Bower Corporation		Concerto Company	
Cash	$ 26,800		$ 35,000	
Accounts Receivable	80,000		40,000	
Inventory	120,000		90,000	
Total Current Assets		$226,800		$165,000
Land		70,000		20,000
Buildings & Equipment	$340,000		$200,000	
Less: Accumulated Depreciation	(165,000)	175,000	(85,000)	115,000
Investment in Concerto Company Stock		139,600		
Total Assets		$611,400		$300,000
Accounts Payable		$ 80,000		$ 15,000
Bonds Payable		120,000		70,000
Common Stock	$100,000		$ 50,000	
Retained Earnings	311,400	411,400	165,000	215,000
Total Liabilities & Stockholders' Equity		$611,400		$300,000

BOWER CORPORATION AND CONCERTO COMPANY
Income Statement Data
Year Ended December 31, 20X6

Item	Bower Corporation		Concerto Company	
Sales		$400,000		$200,000
Income from Subsidiary		16,400		
		$416,400		$200,000
Cost of Goods Sold	$280,000		$120,000	
Depreciation & Amortization Expense	25,000		15,000	
Other Expenses	35,000	(340,000)	30,000	(165,000)
Net Income		$ 76,400		$ 35,000

On January 1, 20X6, Bower held inventory purchased from Concerto for $48,000. During 20X6, Bower purchased an additional $90,000 of goods from Concerto and held $54,000 of its purchases on December 31, 20X6. Concerto sells inventory to the parent at 20 percent above cost.

Concerto also purchases inventory from Bower. On January 1, 20X6, Concerto held inventory purchased from Bower for $14,000, and on December 31, 20X6, it held inventory purchased from Bower for $7,000. Concerto's total purchases from Bower were $22,000 in 20X6. Bower sells items to Concerto at 40 percent above cost.

During 20X6, Bower paid dividends of $50,000, and Concerto paid dividends of $20,000. Assume that Bower uses the fully adjusted equity method that both companies use straight-line depreciation, and that no property, plant, and equipment has been purchased since the acquisition.

Required

a. Prepare all consolidation entries needed to complete a consolidation worksheet as of December 31, 20X6.

b. Prepare a three-part consolidation worksheet as of December 31, 20X6.

LO 6-3, 6-4 **P6-31** **Intercorporate Transfer of Inventory**

Block Corporation was created on January 1, 20X0, to develop computer software. On January 1, 20X5, Foster Company purchased 90 percent of Block's common stock at underlying book value. At that date, the fair value of the noncontrolling interest was equal to 10 percent of Block's book value. Trial balances for Foster and Block on December 31, 20X9, are as follows:

	20X9 Trial Balance Data			
	Foster Company		Block Corporation	
Item	Debit	Credit	Debit	Credit
Cash	$ 187,000		$ 57,400	
Accounts Receivable	80,000		90,000	
Other Receivables	40,000		10,000	
Inventory	137,000		130,000	
Land	80,000		60,000	
Buildings & Equipment	500,000		250,000	
Investment in Block Corporation Stock	234,900			
Cost of Goods Sold	593,000		270,000	
Depreciation Expense	45,000		15,000	
Other Expenses	95,000		75,000	
Dividends Declared	40,000		20,000	
Accumulated Depreciation		$ 155,000		$ 75,000
Accounts Payable		63,000		35,000
Other Payables		95,000		20,000
Bonds Payable		250,000		200,000
Bond Premium				2,400
Common Stock		210,000		50,000
Additional Paid-in Capital		110,000		
Retained Earnings		235,000		165,000
Sales		815,000		415,000
Other Income		26,000		15,000
Income from Subsidiary		72,900		
Total	$2,031,900	$2,031,900	$977,400	$977,400

During 20X9, Block produced inventory for $20,000 and sold it to Foster for $30,000. Foster resold 60 percent of the inventory in 20X9. Also in 20X9, Foster sold inventory purchased from Block in 20X8. It had cost Block $60,000 to produce the inventory, and Foster purchased it for $75,000. Assume Foster uses the fully adjusted equity method.

Required

a. What amount of cost of goods sold will be reported in the 20X9 consolidated income statement?

b. What inventory balance will be reported in the December 31, 20X9, consolidated balance sheet?

c. What amount of income will be assigned to noncontrolling shareholders in the 20X9 consolidated income statement?

d. What amount will be assigned to noncontrolling interest in the consolidated balance sheet prepared at December 31, 20X9?

e. What amount of retained earnings will be reported in the consolidated balance sheet at December 31, 20X9?

f. Give all consolidation entries required to prepare a three-part consolidation worksheet at December 31, 20X9.

g. Prepare a three-part consolidation worksheet at December 31, 20X9.

LO 6-3

P6-32 Consolidated Balance Sheet Worksheet [AICPA Adapted]

The December 31, 20X6, condensed balance sheets of Pine Corporation and its 90 percent–owned subsidiary, Slim Corporation, are presented in the accompanying worksheet.

Additional Information

1. Pine's investment in Slim was acquired for $1,170,000 cash on January 1, 20X6, and is accounted for by the equity method. The fair value of the noncontrolling interest at that date was $130,000.
2. At January 1, 20X6, Slim's retained earnings amounted to $600,000, and its common stock amounted to $200,000.
3. Slim declared a $1,000 cash dividend in December 20X6, payable in January 20X7.
4. Slim borrowed $100,000 from Pine on June 30, 20X6, with the note maturing on June 30, 20X7, at 10 percent interest. Correct interest accruals have been recorded by both companies.
5. During 20X6, Pine sold merchandise to Slim at an aggregate invoice price of $300,000, which included a profit of $60,000. At December 31, 20X6, Slim had not paid Pine for $90,000 of these purchases, and 5 percent of the total merchandise purchased from Pine still remained in Slim's inventory. Assume Pine uses the fully adjusted equity method.
6. Pine's excess cost over book value of its investment in Slim has appropriately been identified as goodwill. At December 31, 20X6, Pine's management reviewed the amount attributed to goodwill and found no evidence of impairment.

Required

Complete the accompanying worksheet for Pine and its subsidiary, Slim, at December 31, 20X6.

PINE CORPORATION AND SUBSIDIARY
Consolidated Balance Sheet Worksheet
December 31, 20X6

	Pine Corporation	Slim Corporation	Consolidation Entries Debit	Consolidation Entries Credit	Consolidated
Assets					
Cash	$ 105,000	$ 15,000			
Accounts & Other Current Receivables	410,000	120,000			
Merchandise Inventory	920,000	670,000			
Plant & Equipment, Net	1,000,000	400,000			
Investment in Slim	1,257,000				
Totals	$3,692,000	$1,205,000			
Liabilities & Stockholders' Equity:					
Accounts Payable & Other Current Liabilities	$ 140,000	$ 305,000			
Common Stock ($10 par)	500,000	200,000			
Retained Earnings	3,052,000	700,000			
Totals	$3,692,000	$1,205,000			

LO 6-4

P6-33 Comprehensive Consolidation Worksheet; Fully Adjusted Equity Method [AICPA Adapted]

Fran Corporation acquired all outstanding $10 par value voting common stock of Brey Inc. on January 1, 20X9, in exchange for 25,000 shares of its $20 par value voting common stock. On December 31, 20X8, Fran's common stock had a closing market price of $30 per share on a national stock exchange. The acquisition was appropriately accounted for under the acquisition method. Both companies continued to operate as separate business entities maintaining separate accounting records with years ending December 31. Fran accounts for its investment in Brey stock using the fully adjusted equity method (i.e., adjusting for unrealized intercompany profits).

On December 31, 20X9, the companies had condensed financial statements as follows:

	Fran Corporation Dr (Cr)	Brey Inc. Dr (Cr)
Income Statement		
Net Sales	$(3,800,000)	$(1,500,000)
Income from Brey	(128,000)	
Gain on Sale of Warehouse	(30,000)	
Cost of Goods Sold	2,360,000	870,000
Operating Expenses (including depreciation)	1,100,000	440,000
Net Income	$ (498,000)	$ (190,000)
Retained Earnings Statement		
Balance, 1/1/X9	$ (440,000)	$ (156,000)
Net Income	(498,000)	(190,000)
Dividends Paid		40,000
Balance, 12/31/X9	$ (938,000)	$ (306,000)
Balance Sheet		
Assets:		
Cash	$ 570,000	$ 150,000
Accounts Receivable (net)	860,000	350,000
Inventories	1,060,000	410,000
Land, Plant, & Equipment	1,320,000	680,000
Accumulated Depreciation	(370,000)	(210,000)
Investment in Brey	838,000	
Total Assets	$ 4,278,000	$ 1,380,000
Liabilities & Stockholders' Equity:		
Accounts Payable & Accrued Expenses	$(1,340,000)	$ (594,000)
Common Stock	(1,700,000)	(400,000)
Additional Paid-in Capital	(300,000)	(80,000)
Retained Earnings	(938,000)	(306,000)
Total Liabilities & Equity	$(4,278,000)	$(1,380,000)

Additional Information

No changes occurred in the Common Stock and Additional Paid-in Capital accounts during 20X9 except the one necessitated by Fran's acquisition of Brey.

At the acquisition date, the fair value of Brey's machinery exceeded its book value by $54,000. The excess cost will be amortized over the estimated average remaining life of six years. The fair values of all of Brey's other assets and liabilities were equal to their book values. At December 31, 20X9, Fran's management reviewed the amount attributed to goodwill as a result of its purchase of Brey's common stock and concluded an impairment loss of $35,000 should be recognized in 20X9.

During 20X9, Fran purchased merchandise from Brey at an aggregate invoice price of $180,000, which included a 100 percent markup on Brey's cost. At December 31, 20X9, Fran owed Brey $86,000 on these purchases, and $36,000 of this merchandise remained in Fran's inventory.

Required

Develop and complete a consolidation worksheet that would be used to prepare a consolidated income statement and a consolidated retained earnings statement for the year ended December 31, 20X9, and a consolidated balance sheet as of December 31, 20X9. List the accounts in the worksheet in the same order as they are listed in the financial statements provided. Formal consolidated statements are not required. Ignore income tax considerations. Supporting computations should be in good form.

LO 6-3, 6-4 **P6-34 Comprehensive Worksheet Problem**

Randall Corporation acquired 80 percent of Sharp Company's voting shares on January 1, 20X4, for $280,000 in cash and marketable securities. At that date, the noncontrolling interest had a fair value of $70,000 and Sharp reported net assets of $300,000. Assume Randall uses the fully adjusted equity method. Trial balances for the two companies on December 31, 20X7, are as follows:

	Randall Corporation		Sharp Company	
Item	**Debit**	**Credit**	**Debit**	**Credit**
Cash	$ 130,300		$ 10,000	
Accounts Receivable	80,000		70,000	
Inventory	170,000		110,000	
Buildings & Equipment	600,000		400,000	
Investment in Sharp Company Stock	293,000			
Cost of Goods Sold	416,000		202,000	
Depreciation Expense	30,000		20,000	
Other Expenses	24,000		18,000	
Dividends Declared	50,000		25,000	
Accumulated Depreciation		$ 310,000		$120,000
Accounts Payable		100,000		15,200
Bonds Payable		300,000		100,000
Bond Premium				4,800
Common Stock		200,000		100,000
Additional Paid-in Capital				20,000
Retained Earnings		337,500		215,000
Sales		500,000		250,000
Other Income		20,400		30,000
Income from Sharp Company		25,400		
	$1,793,300	$1,793,300	$855,000	$855,000

Additional Information

1. The full amount of the differential at acquisition was assigned to buildings and equipment with a remaining 10-year economic life.
2. Randall and Sharp regularly purchase inventory from each other. During 20X6, Sharp Company sold inventory costing $40,000 to Randall Corporation for $60,000, and Randall resold 60 percent of the inventory in 20X6 and 40 percent in 20X7. Also in 20X6, Randall sold inventory costing $20,000 to Sharp for $26,000. Sharp resold two-thirds of the inventory in 20X6 and one-third in 20X7.
3. During 20X7, Sharp sold inventory costing $30,000 to Randall for $45,000, and Randall sold items purchased for $9,000 to Sharp for $12,000. Before the end of the year, Randall resold one-third of the inventory it purchased from Sharp in 20X7. Sharp continues to hold all the units purchased from Randall during 20X7.
4. Sharp owes Randall $10,000 on account on December 31, 20X7.
5. Assume that both companies use straight-line depreciation and that no property, plant, and equipment has been purchased since the acquisition.

Required

a. Prepare the 20X7 journal entries recorded on Randall's books related to its investment in Sharp if Randall uses the equity method.

b. Prepare all consolidation entries needed to complete a consolidation worksheet as of December 31, 20X7.

c. Prepare a three-part consolidation worksheet as of December 31, 20X7.

d. Prepare, in good form, a consolidated income statement, balance sheet, and retained earnings statement for 20X7.

P6-35A Modified Equity Method

Advanced StudyGuide .com

On December 31, 20X7, Randall Corporation recorded the following entry on its books to adjust from the fully adjusted equity method to the modified equity method for its investment in Sharp Company stock:

Investment in Sharp Company Stock	11,000	
Retained Earnings		8,400
Income from Sharp Company		2,600

Required

a. Adjust the data reported by Randall in the trial balance contained in P6-33 for the effects of the preceding adjusting entry.

b. Prepare the journal entries that would have been recorded on Randall's books during 20X7 under the modified equity method.

c. Prepare all consolidation entries needed to complete a consolidation worksheet at December 31, 20X7, assuming Randall has used the modified equity method.

d. Complete a three-part consolidation worksheet as of December 31, 20X7.

P6-36A Cost Method

The trial balance data presented in Problem P6-34 can be converted to reflect use of the cost method by inserting the following amounts in place of those presented for Randall Corporation:

Investment in Sharp Company Stock	$280,000
Retained Earnings	329,900
Income from Subsidiary	0
Dividend Income	20,000

Required

a. Prepare the journal entries that would have been recorded on Randall's books during 20X7 under the cost method.

b. Prepare all consolidation entries needed to complete a consolidation worksheet as of December 31, 20X7, assuming Randall uses the cost method.

c. Complete a three-part consolidation worksheet as of December 31, 20X7.

"A" indicates that the item relates to Appendix 6A.

7 Intercompany Transfers of Services and Noncurrent Assets

Multicorporate Entities

Business Combinations

Consolidation Concepts and Procedures

Intercompany Transfers

Additional Consolidation Issues

Multinational Entities

Reporting Requirements

Partnerships

Governmental and Not-for-Profit Entities

Corporations in Financial Difficulty

MICRON'S INTERCOMPANY FIXED ASSET SALE

Micron Technology Inc., ranked number 318 in the 2013 Fortune 500 listing, was founded in Boise, Idaho, in 1978 and specializes in the fabrication of DRAM, SDRAM, flash memory, SSD, and CMOS semiconductor chips. Through a long series of acquisitions, Micron now owns many subsidiaries both in the United States and internationally. Micron also has several joint ventures with other companies. For example, in January 2006, Micron and Intel Corporation formed a new company called IM Flash Technologies LLC, located in Lehi, Utah. A few years earlier in 2002, Micron acquired Toshiba's commodity DRAM operations located in Manassas, Virginia. This wholly owned subsidiary is now called Micron Technology Virginia.

In June 2009, IM Flash Technologies sold underutilized semiconductor manufacturing equipment to Micron Technology Virginia. The equipment originally cost \$3,673,962 and had been assigned a five-year useful life. Because it had been depreciated for only approximately 25 months of its expected 60-month useful life, IM Flash Technologies determined that the equipment had a book value of \$2,439,888 at the time of the transfer. Given the agreed-upon fair market value and selling price of \$1,500,000, IM Flash Technologies realized a loss of \$939,888 on this intercompany asset sale. Because Micron Technology Inc. owns more than 50 percent of IM Flash Technologies and 100 percent of Micron Technology Virginia, it consolidates both companies. Therefore, the loss on this sale between affiliated companies had to be eliminated in the consolidation process. This chapter explores the accounting for both depreciable and nondepreciable asset transfers among affiliated companies.

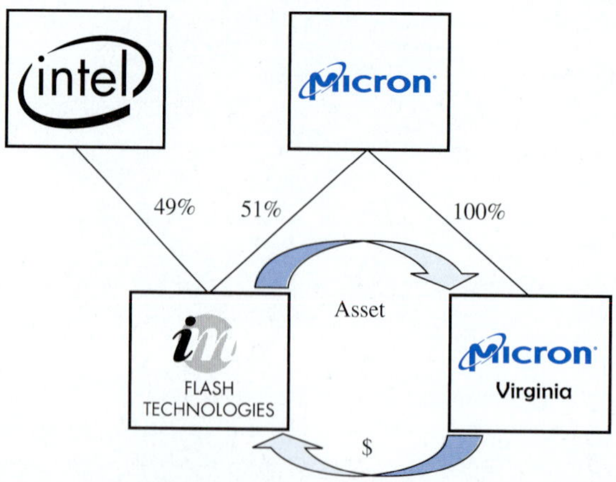

LEARNING OBJECTIVES

When you finish studying this chapter, you should be able to:

LO 7-1 Understand and explain concepts associated with transfers of services and long-term assets.

LO 7-2 Prepare simple equity-method journal entries related to an intercompany land transfer.

LO 7-3 Prepare equity-method journal entries and consolidation entries for the consolidation of a subsidiary following a downstream land transfer.

LO 7-4 Prepare equity-method journal entries and consolidation entries for the consolidation of a subsidiary following an upstream land transfer.

LO 7-5 Prepare equity-method journal entries and consolidation entries for the consolidation of a subsidiary following a downstream depreciable asset transfer.

LO 7-6 Prepare equity-method journal entries and consolidation entries for the consolidation of a subsidiary following an upstream depreciable asset transfer.

INTERCOMPANY TRANSFERS OF SERVICES

LO 7-1

Understand and explain concepts associated with transfers of services and long-term assets.

Related companies frequently purchase services from one another. These services may be of many different types; intercompany purchases of consulting, engineering, marketing, and maintenance services are common.

When one company purchases services from a related company, the purchaser typically records an expense and the seller records revenue. When consolidated financial statements are prepared, both the revenue and the expense must be eliminated. For example, if the parent sells consulting services to the subsidiary for $50,000, the parent would recognize $50,000 of consulting revenue on its books and the subsidiary would recognize $50,000 of consulting expense. In the consolidation worksheet, a consolidation entry would be needed to reduce both consulting revenue (debit) and consulting expense (credit) by $50,000. Because the revenue and expense are equal and both are eliminated, income is unaffected by the consolidation. Even though income is not affected, the consolidation is still important, however, because otherwise both revenues and expenses are overstated.

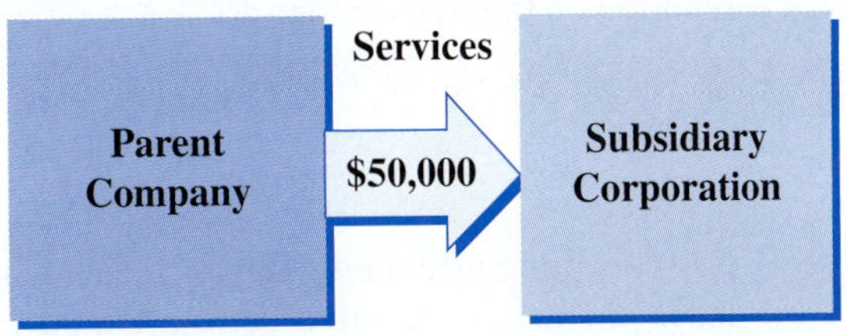

Generally, a simplistic approach is appropriate in eliminating intercompany transfers of services by assuming that the services benefit the current period and, therefore, any intercompany profit on the services becomes realized within the period of transfer. Accordingly, no consolidation entries relating to the current period's transfer of services are needed in future periods because the intercompany profit is considered realized in the transfer period.

Usually the assumption that the profit on intercompany sales of services is realized in the period of sale is realistic. In some cases, however, realization of intercompany profit on the services does not occur in the period the services are provided, and the amounts are significant. For example, if the parent company charges a subsidiary for architectural services to design a new manufacturing facility for the subsidiary, the subsidiary would include that cost in the capitalized cost of the new facility. From a consolidated point of view, however, any profit the parent recognized on the intercompany sale of services (revenue over the cost of providing the service) would have to be eliminated from the reported cost of the new facility until the intercompany profit became realized. Realization would be viewed as occurring over the life of the facility. Thus, consolidation entries would be needed each year similar to those illustrated later in the chapter for intercompany fixed asset transfers.

INTERCOMPANY LONG-TERM ASSET TRANSFERS

The following illustrations provide an overview of the intercompany sale process using land as an example. Figure 7–1 presents a series of transactions involving a parent company and its subsidiary. First, Parent Company purchases land from an unrelated party. Then Parent Company sells the land to a subsidiary. Finally, the subsidiary sells the land to an unrelated party. The three transactions, and the amounts, are

T1—Parent Company purchases land from an independent third party for $10,000.

T2—Parent Company sells the land to Subsidiary Corporation for $15,000.

T3—Subsidiary Corporation sells the land to an independent third party for $25,000.

As illustrated in the following independent cases, the amount of gain reported by each of the individual companies and by the consolidated entity in each accounting period depends on which transactions actually occur during that period.

Case A

Assume that all three transactions are completed in the same accounting period. The gain amounts reported on the transactions are

Parent Company	$ 5,000 ($15,000 − $10,000)
Subsidiary Corporation	10,000 ($25,000 − $15,000)
Consolidated Entity	15,000 ($25,000 − $10,000)

The gain on the sale of the land is considered to be realized because it is resold to an unrelated party during the period. The total gain that the consolidated entity reports is the difference between the $10,000 price it paid to an unaffiliated seller and the $25,000 price at which it sells the land to an unaffiliated buyer. This $15,000 gain is reported in the consolidated income statement. From a consolidated viewpoint, the sale from Parent Company to Subsidiary Corporation, transaction T2, is an internal transaction and is not reported in the consolidated financial statements.

Case B

Assume that only transaction T1 is completed during the current period. The gain amounts reported on the transactions are

Parent Company	$0
Subsidiary Corporation	0
Consolidated Entity	0

Neither of the affiliated companies has made a sale, and no gains are reported or realized. The land is reported both in Parent Company's balance sheet and in the consolidated balance sheet at its cost to Parent, which also is the cost to the consolidated entity.

FIGURE 7–1
Intercompany Sales

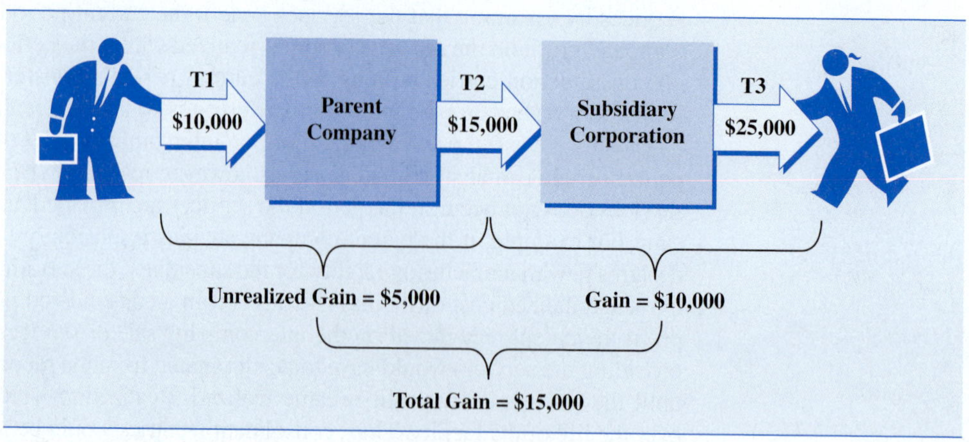

Case C

Assume that only transactions T1 and T2 are completed during the current period. The gain amounts reported on the transactions are

Parent Company	$5,000	($15,000 − $10,000)
Subsidiary Corporation	0	
Consolidated Entity	0	

The $5,000 gain reported by Parent Company is considered unrealized from a consolidated point of view and is not reported in the consolidated income statement because the land has not been resold to a party outside the consolidated entity. Subsidiary Corporation's books carry the land at $15,000, the cost to Subsidiary. From a consolidated viewpoint, the land is overvalued by $5,000 and must be reduced to its $10,000 cost to the consolidated entity.

Case D

Assume that only transaction T3 is completed during the current period and that T1 and T2 occurred in a prior period. The gain amounts reported on the transactions in the current period are

Parent Company	$ 0	
Subsidiary Corporation	10,000	($25,000 − $15,000)
Consolidated Entity	15,000	($25,000 − $10,000)

Subsidiary recognizes a gain equal to the difference between its selling price, $25,000, and cost, $15,000, and the consolidated entity reports a gain equal to the difference between its selling price of $25,000 and the cost to the consolidated entity from an outsider of $10,000.

From a consolidated viewpoint, the sale of an asset wholly within the consolidated entity involves only a change in the technical owner of the asset and possibly its location and does not represent the culmination of the earning process. To culminate the earning process with respect to the consolidated entity, it must make a sale to a party external to the consolidated entity. The key to deciding when to report a transaction in the consolidated financial statements is to visualize the consolidated entity and determine whether a particular transaction (1) occurs totally within the consolidated entity, in which case its effects must be excluded from the consolidated statements or (2) involves outsiders and thus constitutes a transaction of the consolidated entity.

INTERCOMPANY LAND TRANSFERS[1]

LO 7-2

Prepare simple equity-method journal entries related to an intercompany land transfer.

When intercompany transfers of noncurrent assets occur, the parent company must make adjustments in the preparation of consolidated financial statements for as long as the acquiring company holds the assets. The simplest example of an intercompany asset transfer is the intercompany sale of land.

Overview of the Profit Consolidation Process

When related companies transfer land at book value, no special adjustments are needed in preparing the consolidated statements. If, for example, a company purchases land for $10,000 and sells it to its subsidiary for $10,000, the asset continues to be valued at the $10,000 original cost to the consolidated entity:

Advanced StudyGuide .com

Parent			Subsidiary		
Cash	10,000		Land	10,000	
Land		10,000	Cash		10,000

[1] To view a video explanation of this topic, visit advancedstudyguide.com.

Because the seller records no gain or loss, both income and assets are stated correctly from a consolidated viewpoint.

Land transfers at more or less than book value require special treatment. Under the fully adjusted equity method, the parent company must defer any unrealized gains or losses until the assets are eventually sold to unrelated parties. Moreover, in the consolidation process, the selling entity's gain or loss must be eliminated because the consolidated entity still holds the land, and no gain or loss may be reported in the consolidated financial statements until the land is sold to a party outside the consolidated entity. Likewise, the land must be reported at its original cost in the consolidated financial statements as long as it is held within the consolidated entity, regardless of which affiliate holds the land.

As an illustration, assume that Peerless Products Corporation acquires land for $20,000 on January 1, 20X1, and sells the land to its subsidiary, Special Foods Incorporated, on July 1, 20X1, for $35,000, as follows:

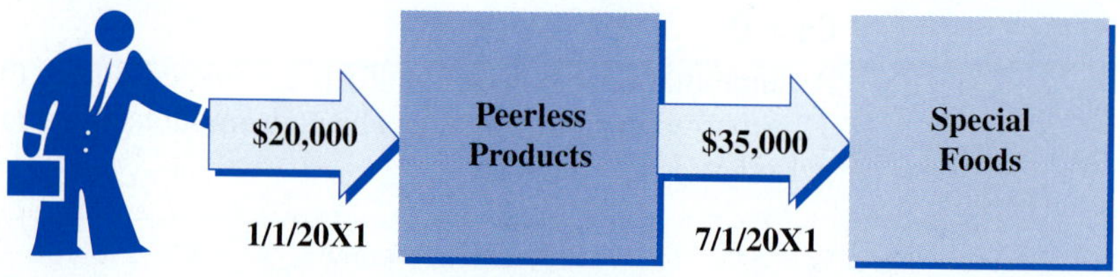

Peerless records the purchase of the land and its sale to Special Foods with the following entries:

	January 1, 20X1		
(1)	Land	20,000	
	Cash		20,000
	Record land purchase.		

	July 1, 20X1		
(2)	Cash	35,000	
	Land		20,000
	Gain on Sale of Land		15,000
	Record sale of land to Special Foods.		

Special Foods records the purchase of the land from Peerless as follows:

	July 1, 20X1		
(3)	Land	35,000	
	Cash		35,000
	Record purchase of land from Peerless.		

The intercompany transfer leads to a $15,000 gain on Peerless' books, and the carrying value of the land increases by the same amount on Special Foods' books. Neither of these amounts may be reported in the consolidated financial statements because the $15,000 intercompany gain is unrealized from a consolidated viewpoint. The land has not been sold to a party outside the consolidated entity but has only been transferred within it; consequently, the land must still be reported in the consolidated financial statements at its original cost to the consolidated entity.

When intercompany gains or losses on asset transfers occur, the parent company can choose to use the fully adjusted equity method, which requires it to adjust its investment and income from subsidiary accounts to remove the unrealized gain.

	July 1, 20X1		
(4)	Income from Special Foods	15,000	
	Investment in Special Foods Stock		15,000
	Defer gain on intercompany land sale to Special Foods.		

FYI

Students sometimes ask if this entry "double-counts" the deferral of the gain because the gain is also eliminated in the consolidation worksheet. Note that this equity-method entry defers the gain on the parent's books to ensure that the parent's net income is accurate and equal to the parent's share of consolidated net income. Although the parent company records this deferral in its books, the investment in subsidiary and income from subsidiary accounts are eliminated in the consolidation process (i.e., they do not show up in the consolidated financial statements). Thus, a worksheet entry is still necessary to ensure that the gain is removed from the consolidated financial statements. This explanation will be clearer in subsequent examples where we present the full consolidation worksheet.

This equity-method entry ensures that the parent company's income is exactly equal to the controlling interest in consolidated income on the consolidated financial statements. Chapter 6 explains that the deferral of unrealized gross profit on intercompany inventory transfers is reversed in the subsequent accounting period if the inventory is sold to an outside party. Similarly, the deferral of gain on an intercompany asset transfer is reversed in the period in which the asset is sold to an outsider (which may or may not be in the very next period).

We use the fully adjusted equity method in all subsequent examples in the chapter. Another option is to ignore this unrealized gain on the parent company's books and adjust for it in the consolidation worksheet only under the modified equity method. We illustrate this approach in the appendix.

In the consolidation process, the gain should be eliminated and the land restated from the $35,000 recorded on Special Foods' books to its original cost of $20,000. This is accomplished with the following entry in the consolidation worksheet prepared at the end of 20X1:

Gain on Sale of Land	**15,000**	
Land		**15,000**

Assignment of Unrealized Profit Consolidation

Unrealized intercompany gains and losses must be eliminated fully when preparing consolidated financial statements. Regardless of the parent's percentage ownership of a subsidiary, the full amount of any unrealized gains and losses must be eliminated and must be excluded from consolidated net income. Although the full amount of an unrealized gain or loss is excluded from consolidated net income, a question arises when the parent owns less than 100 percent of a subsidiary as to whether the unrealized profit consolidation should reduce the controlling or noncontrolling interest, or both.

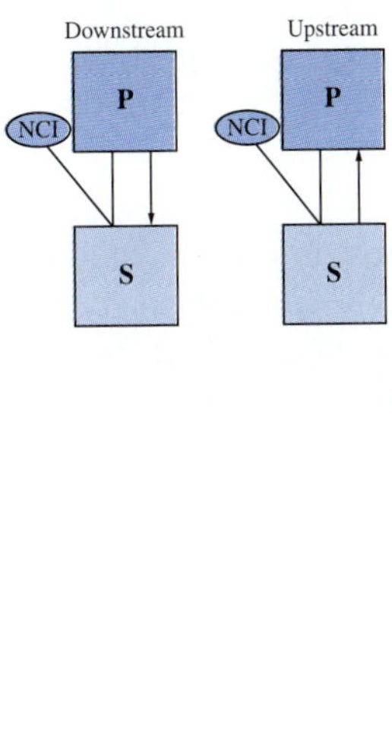

A gain or loss on an intercompany transfer is recognized by the selling affiliate and ultimately accrues to the stockholders of that affiliate. When a parent sells to a subsidiary, referred to as a ***downstream sale,*** any gain or loss on the transfer accrues to the parent company's stockholders. When a subsidiary sells to its parent, an ***upstream sale,*** any gain or loss accrues to the subsidiary's stockholders. If the subsidiary is wholly owned, all gain or loss ultimately accrues to the parent company as the sole stockholder. If, however, the selling subsidiary is not wholly owned, the gain or loss on the upstream sale is apportioned between the parent company and the noncontrolling shareholders.

Generally, the consolidated entity does not consider gains and losses realized until a sale is made to an unrelated, external party. Unrealized gains and losses are eliminated in preparing consolidated financial statements against the interests of those shareholders who recognized the gains and losses in the first place: the shareholders of the selling affiliate. Therefore, the direction of the sale determines which shareholder group absorbs the consolidation of unrealized intercompany gains and losses. Thus, unrealized intercompany gains and losses are eliminated in consolidation in the following ways:

Sale	Consolidation
Downstream (parent to subsidiary)	Against controlling interest
Upstream (subsidiary to parent):	
Wholly owned subsidiary	Against controlling interest
Majority-owned subsidiary	Proportionately against controlling and noncontrolling interests

As an illustration, assume that Purity Company owns 75 percent of the common stock of Southern Corporation. Purity reports operating income of $100,000 from its own activities, excluding any investment income from or transactions with Southern; Southern reports operating income of $50,000, exclusive of any gains or losses on asset transfers. In each example, assume the selling affiliate has a separate unrealized gain of $10,000 on the intercompany transfer of an asset. In the case of a downstream transfer, all unrealized profit is eliminated from the controlling interest's share of income when consolidated statements are prepared. Thus, the controlling interest in consolidated net income is computed as follows:

Southern's reported net income	$ 50,000
Purity's ownership percentage	× 0.75
Purity's share of Southern's reported income	37,500
Less: Purity's 100% deferral of the unrealized downstream intercompany gain	(10,000)
Purity's income from Southern	27,500
Purity's separate income (including downstream intercompany gain)	110,000
Income to controlling interest	$137,500

If, instead, the intercompany transfer is upstream from subsidiary to parent, the unrealized profit on the upstream sale is eliminated proportionately from the interests of the controlling and noncontrolling shareholders. In this situation, the controlling interest in consolidated net income is computed as follows:

Southern's operating income	$ 50,000
Upstream intercompany gain	10,000
Southern's reported net income	60,000
Purity's ownership percentage	× 0.75
Purity's share of Southern's reported income	45,000
Less: Purity's 75% deferral of the upstream unrealized intercompany gain	(7,500)
Purity's income from Southern	37,500
Purity's separate income	100,000
Income to controlling interest	$137,500

Consolidated net income ($150,000) and the controlling interest in consolidated net income ($137,500) are the same whether the intercompany sale is upstream or downstream, but the allocation of the deferral differs. Because Purity recognized all the gain in the downstream case, the controlling interest's share of income is reduced by the full unrealized gain consolidation. In the upstream case, the intercompany gain was recognized by Southern and shared proportionately by Southern's controlling and noncontrolling interests. Therefore, the consolidation is made proportionately against the controlling and noncontrolling interests' share of income.

Note that unrealized intercompany gains and losses are always fully eliminated in preparing consolidated financial statements. The existence of a noncontrolling interest in a selling subsidiary only affects the allocation of the deferral of the unrealized gain or loss, not the amount deferred.

Income to the Noncontrolling Interest

The income assigned to the noncontrolling interest is the noncontrolling interest's proportionate share of the subsidiary's reported net income realized in transactions with parties external to the consolidated entity. Income assigned to the noncontrolling interest in the downstream example is computed as follows:

Southern's reported net income	$50,000
NCI's percentage	× 0.25
Income to NCI	$12,500

Income assigned to the noncontrolling interest in the upstream example is computed as follows:

Southern's reported income (including intercompany gain)	$60,000
NCI's ownership percentage	× 0.25
NCI's share of Southern's reported income	$15,000
Less: NCI's 25% deferral of the upstream unrealized intercompany gain	(2,500)
Income to NCI	$12,500

In the downstream example, the $10,000 of unrealized intercompany profit is recognized on the parent company's books; therefore, the noncontrolling interest is not affected by the unrealized gain on the downstream intercompany transaction. The entire $50,000 of the subsidiary's income is realized in transactions with parties external to the consolidated entity. In the upstream example, the subsidiary's income includes $10,000 of unrealized intercompany profit. The amount of the subsidiary's income realized in transactions with external parties is only $50,000 ($60,000 less $10,000 of unrealized intercompany profit).

LO 7-3

Prepare equity-method journal entries and consolidation entries for the consolidation of a subsidiary following a downstream land transfer.

Downstream Sale of Land (Year of Sale)

As in Chapter 6, assume that Peerless Products purchases 80 percent of the common stock of Special Foods on December 31, 20X0, for its book value of $240,000, and that the fair value of Special Foods' noncontrolling interest on that date is equal to its book value of $60,000. Assume that during 20X1, Peerless reports separate income of $140,000 income from regular operations and declares dividends of $60,000. Special Foods reports net income of $50,000 and declares dividends of $30,000. In addition, on July 1, 20X1, Peerless sells land to Special Foods for $35,000. Peerless had originally purchased the land on January 1, 20X1, for $20,000, resulting in an unrealized gain of $15,000. Special Foods continues to hold the land through 20X1 and subsequent years.

Fully Adjusted Equity-Method Entries—20X1

During 20X1, Peerless records its share of Special Foods' income and dividends with the usual fully adjusted equity-method entries:

(5)	Investment in Special Foods	40,000	
	Income from Special Foods		40,000

Record Peerless' 80% share of Special Foods' 20X1 income.

(6)	Cash	24,000	
	Investment in Special Foods		24,000

Record Peerless' 80% share of Special Foods' 20X1 dividend.

Advanced StudyGuide .com

Under the fully adjusted equity method, because the downstream sale of land to Special Foods results in a $15,000 unrealized gain, Peerless makes an adjustment in the equity-method accounts to reduce Income from Special Foods on the income statement and Investment in Special Foods on the balance sheet by its share of the unrealized gain. Because this is a downstream transaction, the sale (and associated unrealized gain) resides on Peerless' income statement. Because we assume the NCI shareholders do not own Peerless stock, they do not share in the deferral of the unrealized gain.

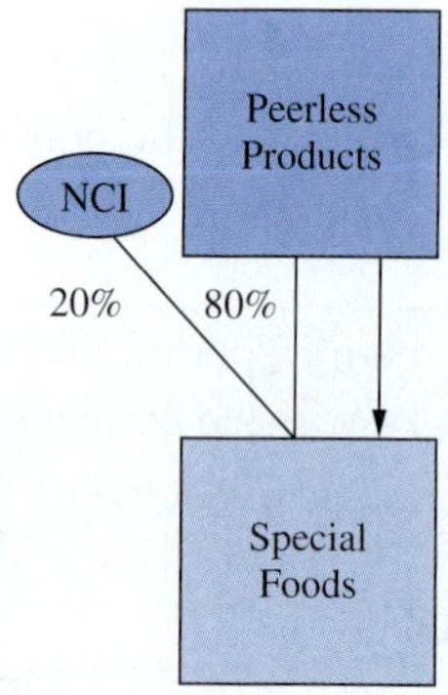

Under the fully adjusted equity method, Peerless Inc. defers the entire $15,000 using the following equity-method entry:

(7)	Income from Special Foods	15,000	
	Investment in Special Foods		15,000
	Defer gain on intercompany land sale to Special Foods.		

Note that this entry accomplishes two important objectives. First, because Peerless' income is overstated by $15,000, the adjustment to Income from Special Foods offsets this overstatement so that Peerless' bottom-line net income is now correct. Second, Special Foods' land account is currently overstated by $15,000 (because the land was originally acquired by Peerless for $20,000, but it is now recorded at $35,000 on Special Foods' books). Because the Investment in Special Foods account summarizes Peerless' investment in Special Foods' balance sheet, this reduction to the investment account offsets the fact that Special Foods' land (and thus entire balance sheet) is overstated by $15,000. Thus, after making this equity-method adjustment to defer the unrealized gain on the sale of land, Peerless' financial statements are now correctly stated. Therefore, Peerless' reported income will be exactly equal to the controlling interest in net income on the consolidated financial statements.

On December 31, 20X1, the Peerless' equity-method accounts appear as follows:

	Investment in Special Foods (Dr.)	Investment in Special Foods (Cr.)		Income from Special Foods (Dr.)	Income from Special Foods (Cr.)	
Acquisition	240,000					
80% of NI	40,000				40,000	80% of NI
		24,000	80% of Dividends			
		15,000	Defer Gain	15,000		
Ending Balance	241,000				25,000	Ending Balance

In summary, when Peerless defers the unrealized gain in the equity method accounts, the $15,000 decrease in the Income from Special Foods account offsets the gain on Peerless' books so that Peerless' income is correct (and equal to the controlling interest in consolidated net income). Moreover, because the Investment in Special Foods account summarizes the entire balance sheet of Special Foods, the $15,000 decrease in the investment account offsets the fact that the land account is overstated by $15,000 on Special Foods' books. The following illustration shows how the internal sale of the land and the deferral on Peerless' books affect the accounting equation.

Peerless Products			Special Foods		
Assets	= *Liabilities*	+ *Equity*	*Assets*	= *Liabilities*	+ *Equity*
Investment −15,000		Gain +15,000	Land +15,000		
		Income from Sub −15,000			

Consolidation Worksheet—20X1

We present the consolidation worksheet prepared at the end of 20X1 in Figure 7–2. The first two consolidation entries are the same as originally presented in Chapter 3 with one minor exception. Although the analysis of the "book value" portion of the investment account is the same, in preparing the basic consolidation entry, we reduce the amounts in the Income from Special Foods and Investment in Special Foods accounts by the $15,000 gain deferral.

FIGURE 7–2 December 31, 20X1, Consolidation Worksheet, Period of Intercompany Sale; Downstream Sale of Land

	Peerless Products	Special Foods	Consolidation Entries DR	Consolidation Entries CR	Consolidated
Income Statement					
Sales	400,000	200,000			600,000
Less: COGS	(170,000)	(115,000)			(285,000)
Less: Depreciation Expense	(50,000)	(20,000)			(70,000)
Less: Other Expenses	(40,000)	(15,000)			(55,000)
Gain on Sale of Land	15,000		15,000		0
Income from Special Foods	25,000		25,000		0
Consolidated Net Income	180,000	50,000	40,000	0	190,000
NCI in Net Income			10,000		(10,000)
Controlling Interest Net Income	**180,000**	**50,000**	**50,000**	**0**	**180,000**
Statement of Retained Earnings					
Beginning Balance	300,000	100,000	100,000		300,000
Net Income	**180,000**	**50,000**	**50,000**	**0**	180,000
Less: Dividends Declared	(60,000)	(30,000)		30,000	(60,000)
Ending Balance	**420,000**	**120,000**	**150,000**	**30,000**	**420,000**
Balance Sheet					
Cash	299,000	40,000			339,000
Accounts Receivable	75,000	50,000			125,000
Inventory	100,000	75,000			175,000
Investment in Special Foods	241,000			241,000	0
Land	155,000	75,000		15,000	215,000
Buildings & Equipment	800,000	600,000		300,000	1,100,000
Less: Accumulated Depreciation	(450,000)	(320,000)	300,000		(470,000)
Total Assets	**1,220,000**	**520,000**	**300,000**	**556,000**	**1,484,000**
Accounts Payable	100,000	100,000			200,000
Bonds Payable	200,000	100,000			300,000
Common Stock	500,000	200,000	200,000		500,000
Retained Earnings	**420,000**	**120,000**	**150,000**	**30,000**	420,000
NCI in NA of Special Foods				64,000	64,000
Total Liabilities & Equity	**1,220,000**	**520,000**	**350,000**	**94,000**	**1,484,000**

Calculations for Basic Consolidation Entry:

Book Value Calculations:

	NCI 20% +	Peerless 80%	= Common Stock	+ Retained Earnings
Original Book Value	60,000	240,000	200,000	100,000
+ Net Income	10,000	40,000		50,000
− Dividends	(6,000)	(24,000)		(30,000)
Ending Book Value	64,000	256,000	200,000	120,000

Adjustment to Basic Consolidation Entry:

	NCI 20%	Peerless 80%
Net Income	10,000	40,000
− Gain on Land Deferral		(15,000)
Income to be Eliminated	10,000	25,000
Ending Book Value	64,000	256,000
− Gain on Land Deferral		(15,000)
Adjusted Book Value	64,000	241,000

Basic Consolidation Entry:

	Debit	Credit	
Common Stock	200,000		← Common stock balance
Retained Earnings	100,000		← Beginning RE from trial balance
Income from Special Foods	25,000		← Peerless' % of NI with Adjustments
NCI in NI of Special Foods	10,000		← NCI share of reported NI
Dividends Declared		30,000	← 100% of sub's dividends declared
Investment in Special Foods		241,000	← Net BV with Adjustments
NCI in NA of Special Foods		64,000	← NCI share of net book value

Optional Accumulated Depreciation Consolidation Entry:

	Debit	Credit	
Accumulated Depreciation	300,000		← Accumulated depreciation at the time of the acquisition netted against cost
Buildings & Equipment		300,000	

Moreover, although Peerless recorded an equity-method entry to defer the unrealized gain on the sale of land, both the Income from Special Foods and Investment in Special Foods accounts are eliminated with the basic consolidation entry. Therefore, based on the remaining numbers appearing in the trial balance, Peerless' income is overstated by the gain ($15,000). Moreover, Special Foods' land account is still overstated by $15,000. Simply adding up the Peerless and Special Foods columns of the consolidation worksheet will result in overstated consolidated net income, total assets, and retained earnings. Therefore, we also record an entry to correct the unadjusted totals to the appropriate consolidated amounts. In doing so, consolidated income is reduced by $15,000 when the gain is eliminated. In addition, land reported on Special Foods' books is stated at the intercompany sale price rather than the historical cost to the consolidated entity. Until the land is resold to an external party by Special Foods, its carrying value must be reduced by the amount of unrealized intercompany gain each time consolidated statements are prepared.

Eliminate Gain on Sale of Land to Special Foods:

	Debit	Credit
Gain on Sale of Land	15,000	
Land		15,000

In sum, because the land is still held within the consolidated entity, the $15,000 gain recognized on Peerless' books must be eliminated in the consolidation worksheet so that it does not appear in the consolidated income statement. Similarly, the land must appear in the consolidated balance sheet at its $20,000 original cost to the consolidated entity and, therefore, must be reduced from the $35,000 amount carried on Special Foods' books.

Consolidated Net Income

The 20X1 consolidated net income is computed and allocated as follows:

Peerless' separate income	$155,000
Less: Unrealized intercompany gain on downstream land sale	(15,000)
Peerless' separate realized income	$140,000
Special Foods' net income	50,000
Consolidated net income, 20X1	$190,000
Income to noncontrolling interest ($50,000 × 0.20)	(10,000)
Income to controlling interest	$180,000

Noncontrolling Interest

The noncontrolling stockholders' share of consolidated net income is limited to their proportionate share of the subsidiary's income. Special Foods' net income for 20X1 is $50,000, and the noncontrolling stockholders' ownership interest is 20 percent. Therefore, income of $10,000 ($50,000 × 0.20) is allocated to the noncontrolling interest.

As shown in Figure 7–2, the total noncontrolling interest in net assets at the end of 20X1 is $64,000. Normally the noncontrolling interest's claim on the subsidiary's net assets at a particular date is equal to a proportionate share of the subsidiary's book value and remaining differential at that date. In this example, the subsidiary's acquisition-date fair value and book value are equal, and, thus, no differential is associated with the combination. Accordingly, the noncontrolling interest on December 31, 20X1, is equal to a proportionate share of Special Foods' book value:

Book value of Special Foods, December 31, 20X1:	
Common stock	$200,000
Retained earnings	120,000
Total book value	$320,000
Noncontrolling stockholders' proportionate share	× 0.20
Noncontrolling interest, December 31, 20X1	$ 64,000

The noncontrolling interest is unaffected by the unrealized gain on the downstream sale.

Downstream Sale of Land

Eliminating the Downstream Unrealized Gain after the First Year

In the period in which unrealized profits arise from an intercompany sale, worksheet entries are used in the consolidation process to remove the gain or loss recorded by the seller and to adjust the reported amount of the asset back to the price the selling affiliate originally paid.

When Peerless deferred the gain on its books in the year of the internal asset sale, the decrease in Income from Special Foods offset the gain on sale on its own books. When the gain and the Income from Special Foods accounts were closed out to retained earnings, the gain was offset against the artificially low Income from Special Foods balance. Hence, Peerless' retained earnings at the end of the year of the internal land sale is correct. The following illustration shows that Special Foods' land account is still overvalued and Peerless' investment account is still artificially low by the $15,000 deferral.

Peerless Products			Special Foods		
Assets =	*Liabilities* +	*Equity*	*Assets* =	*Liabilities* +	*Equity*
Investment −15,000			Land +15,000		

Each period thereafter while the purchasing affiliate holds the asset, the reported asset balance and the shareholder claims of the selling affiliate are adjusted to remove the effects of the unrealized gain or loss. Income in those subsequent periods is not affected. For example, if Special Foods continues to hold the land purchased from Peerless Products, the following consolidation entry is needed in the consolidation worksheet each time a consolidated balance sheet is prepared for years following the year of intercompany sale, for as long as the land is held:

Investment in Special Foods	**15,000**	
Land		**15,000**

This consolidation entry simply corrects the balance in both the Land and Investment in Special Foods accounts. Whereas Peerless recorded an equity-method adjustment to defer the $15,000 of unrealized gain on the sale of land in the year of the intercompany land transfer by artificially decreasing the Investment in Special Foods to offset the overstated land balance on Special Foods' books, this entry simply corrects both accounts. No income statement adjustments are needed in the periods following the intercompany sale until the land is resold to parties external to the consolidated entity.

Subsequent Disposition of the Asset

Unrealized profits on intercompany sales of assets are viewed as being realized at the time the assets are resold to external parties. When a transferred asset is subsequently sold to an external party, the gain or loss recognized by the affiliate selling to the external party must be adjusted for consolidated reporting by the amount of the previously unrealized (and deferred) intercompany gain or loss. Although the seller's reported profit on the external sale is based on that affiliate's cost, the gain or loss reported by the consolidated entity is based on the cost of the asset to the consolidated entity, which is the cost incurred by the affiliate that purchased the asset originally from an outside party.

When previously unrealized intercompany profits are realized, the effects of the profit deferral must be reversed. At the time of realization, the full amount of the deferred intercompany profit is added back into the consolidated income computation and assigned to the shareholder interests from which it originally was eliminated.

To illustrate the treatment of unrealized intercompany profits once the transferred asset is resold, assume that Peerless purchases land from an outside party for $20,000 on January 1, 20X1, and sells the land to Special Foods on July 1, 20X1, for $35,000. Special Foods subsequently sells the land to an outside party on March 1, 20X5, for $45,000, as follows:

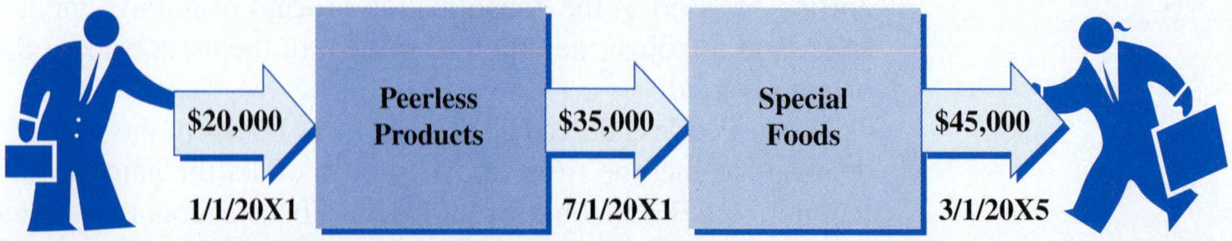

Special Foods recognizes a gain on the sale to the outside party of $10,000 ($45,000 − $35,000). From a consolidated viewpoint, however, the gain is $25,000, the difference between the price at which the land left the consolidated entity ($45,000) and the price at which the land entered the consolidated entity ($20,000) when it was originally purchased by Peerless. Peerless would record an equity-method entry on its books to reverse the original deferral entry (7).

(8)			
	Investment in Special Foods	15,000	
	Income from Special Foods		15,000

Reverse the deferred profit on the sale of land.

In the consolidation worksheet, the land no longer needs to be reduced by the unrealized intercompany gain because the gain now is realized and the consolidated entity no longer holds it. Instead, the $10,000 gain recognized by Special Foods on the sale of the land to an outsider must be adjusted to reflect a total gain for the consolidated entity of $25,000. Thus, the following consolidation entry is made in the consolidation worksheet prepared at the end of 20X5:

Investment in Special Foods	**15,000**	
Gain on Sale of Land		**15,000**

All other consolidation entries are the same as if there were no unrealized intercompany profits at the beginning of the period. No additional consideration need be given to the intercompany transfer in periods subsequent to the external sale. From a consolidated viewpoint, all aspects of the transaction are complete, and the profit is realized once the sale to an external party occurs.

Upstream Sale of Land (Year of Sale)

LO 7-4

Prepare equity-method journal entries and consolidation entries for the consolidation of a subsidiary following an upstream land transfer.

Advanced StudyGuide .com

Assume an upstream sale of land results in the recording of an intercompany gain on the subsidiary's books. If the gain is unrealized from a consolidated viewpoint, it must not be included in the consolidated financial statements. Unrealized intercompany gains are eliminated from the consolidation worksheet in the same manner as in the downstream case. However, the gain consolidation reduces both the controlling and the noncontrolling interests in proportion to their ownership.

When an upstream asset sale occurs and the parent resells the asset to a nonaffiliate during the same period, all the parent's equity-method entries and the consolidation entries in the consolidation worksheet are identical to those in the downstream case. When the asset is not resold to a nonaffiliate before the end of the period, worksheet consolidation entries are different from the downstream case only by the apportionment of the unrealized intercompany gain to both the controlling and noncontrolling interests. In this case, because the sale appears on Special Foods' income statement and because the NCI shareholders own 20 percent of Special Foods' outstanding shares, they are entitled to 20 percent of Special Foods' net income. Thus, the deferral of the unrealized gain accrues to both the Peerless and the NCI shareholders. In other words,

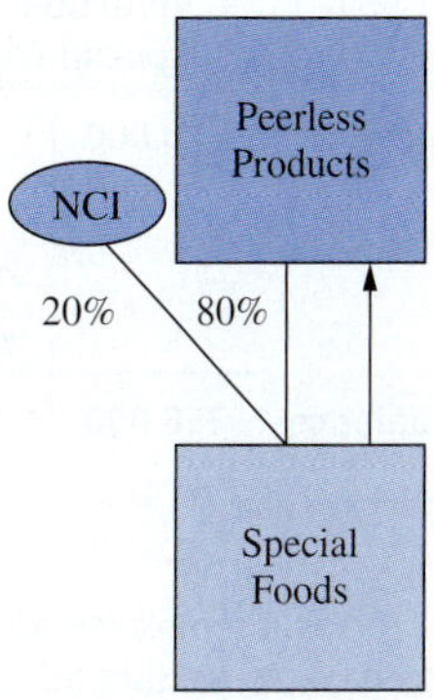

the intercompany gain on an upstream sale is recognized by the subsidiary and shared between the controlling and noncontrolling stockholders of the subsidiary. Therefore, the consolidation of the unrealized intercompany profit must reduce the interests of both ownership groups each period until the profit is realized by resale of the asset to a nonaffiliated party.

The treatment of an upstream sale may be illustrated with the same example used to illustrate a downstream sale. In this case, Special Foods recognizes a $15,000[2] gain from selling the land to Peerless in addition to the $50,000 of income earned from its regular operations; thus, Special Foods' net income for 20X1 is $65,000. Peerless' separate income is $140,000 and comes entirely from its normal operations.

The upstream sale from Special Foods to Peerless is as follows:

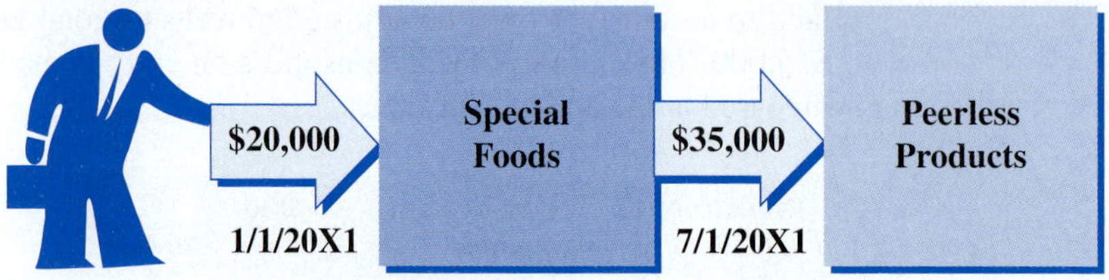

Fully Adjusted Equity-Method Entries—20X1

During 20X1, Peerless records the normal entries under the fully adjusted equity method, reflecting its share of Special Foods' income and dividends:

		Debit	Credit
(9)	Investment in Special Foods	52,000	
	Income from Special Foods		52,000
	Record Peerless' 80% share of Special Foods' 20X1 income.		
(10)	Cash	24,000	
	Investment in Special Foods		24,000
	Record Peerless' 80% share of Special Foods' 20X1 dividend.		

These entries are the same as in the illustration of the downstream sale. The only difference is in the fully adjusted equity-method entry to defer the unrealized gain. The difference is that deferral is only for Peerless' ownership percentage of Special Foods (80 percent). Thus, the deferral of Peerless' relative share of the unrealized gross profit is $12,000 ($15,000 × 0.80).

		Debit	Credit
(11)	Income from Special Foods	12,000	
	Investment in Special Foods		12,000
	Defer Peerless' 80% share of the unrealized gain on the sale of land to Peerless.		

Peerless' equity-method accounts appear as follows at the end of 20X1:

	Investment in Special Foods (Dr)	Investment in Special Foods (Cr)		Income from Special Foods (Dr)	Income from Special Foods (Cr)	
Acquisition	240,000					
80% of NI	52,000				52,000	80% of NI
		24,000	80% of Dividends			
		12,000	Defer 80% of Gain	12,000		
Ending Balance	256,000				40,000	Ending Balance

[2] To avoid additional complexity, we assume the land's fair value is equal to its book value on the business combination date. As a result, there is no differential related to the land.

In summary, when Peerless defers its 80 percent share of Special Foods' unrealized gain in the equity-method accounts, the $12,000 decrease in the Income from Special Foods' account offsets Peerless' 80 percent share of the $15,000 gain on Special Foods' income statement so that Peerless' income is correct (and equal to the controlling interest in consolidated net income). Moreover, the $12,000 decrease in the investment account offsets the fact that its land account is overstated.

Consolidation Worksheet—20X1

Figure 7–3 illustrates the consolidation worksheet prepared at the end of 20X1. The first two consolidation entries are the same as we prepared in Chapter 3 with one minor exception. Although the analysis of the "book value" portion of the investment account is the same, in preparing the basic consolidation entry, we reduce the amounts in Peerless' Income from Special Foods and Investment in Special Foods accounts by Peerless' share of the gain deferral, $12,000 ($15,000 × 0.80). We also reduce the NCI in Net Income of Special Foods and NCI in Net Assets of Special Foods by the NCI's share of the deferral, $3,000 ($15,000 × 0.20).

FIGURE 7–3 December 31, 20X1, Consolidation Worksheet, Period of Intercompany Sale; Upstream Sale of Land

	Peerless Products	Special Foods	Consolidation Entries DR	Consolidation Entries CR	Consolidated
Income Statement					
Sales	400,000	200,000			600,000
Less: COGS	(170,000)	(115,000)			(285,000)
Less: Depreciation Expense	(50,000)	(20,000)			(70,000)
Less: Other Expenses	(40,000)	(15,000)			(55,000)
Gain on Sale of Land		15,000	15,000		0
Income from Special Foods	40,000		40,000		0
Consolidated Net Income	180,000	65,000	55,000	0	190,000
NCI in Net Income			10,000		(10,000)
Controlling Interest Net Income	**180,000**	**65,000**	**65,000**	**0**	**180,000**
Statement of Retained Earnings					
Beginning Balance	300,000	100,000	100,000		300,000
Net Income	**180,000**	**65,000**	**65,000**	**0**	180,000
Less: Dividends Declared	(60,000)	(30,000)		30,000	(60,000)
Ending Balance	**420,000**	**135,000**	**165,000**	**30,000**	**420,000**
Balance Sheet					
Cash	229,000	110,000			339,000
Accounts Receivable	75,000	50,000			125,000
Inventory	100,000	75,000			175,000
Investment in Special Foods	256,000			256,000	0
Land	210,000	20,000		15,000	215,000
Buildings & Equipment	800,000	600,000		300,000	1,100,000
Less: Accumulated Depreciation	(450,000)	(320,000)	300,000		(470,000)
Total Assets	**1,220,000**	**535,000**	**300,000**	**571,000**	**1,484,000**
Accounts Payable	100,000	100,000			200,000
Bonds Payable	200,000	100,000			300,000
Common Stock	500,000	200,000	200,000		500,000
Retained Earnings	**420,000**	**135,000**	**165,000**	**30,000**	420,000
NCI in NA of Special Foods				64,000	64,000
Total Liabilities & Equity	**1,220,000**	**535,000**	**365,000**	**94,000**	**1,484,000**

Calculations for Basic Consolidation Entry:

Book Value Calculations:

	NCI 20% +	Peerless 80%	=	Common Stock	+	Retained Earnings
Original Book Value	60,000	240,000		200,000		100,000
+ Net Income	13,000	52,000				65,000
− Dividends	(6,000)	(24,000)				(30,000)
Ending Book Value	67,000	268,000		200,000		135,000

Adjustment to Basic Consolidation Entry:

	NCI 20%	Peerless 80%
Net Income	13,000	52,000
− Gain on Land Deferral	(3,000)	(12,000)
Income to be Eliminated	10,000	40,000
Ending Book Value	67,000	268,000
− Gain on Land Deferral	(3,000)	(12,000)
Adjusted Book Value	64,000	256,000

Basic Consolidation Entry:

	Debit	Credit	
Common Stock	200,000		← Common stock balance
Retained Earnings	100,000		← Beginning RE from trial balance
Income from Special Foods	40,000		← Peerless' % of NI with Adjustments
NCI in NI of Special Foods	10,000		← NCI share of NI with Adjustments
Dividends Declared		30,000	← 100% of sub's dividends declared
Investment in Special Foods		256,000	← Net BV with Adjustments
NCI in NA of Special Foods		64,000	← NCI share of BV with Adjustments

Optional Accumulated Depreciation Consolidation Entry:

	Debit	Credit	
Accumulated Depreciation	300,000		← Accumulated depreciation at the time of the acquisition netted against cost
Buildings & Equipment		300,000	

The consolidation worksheet entry to correct for the intercompany sale is identical to the downstream case. The only difference is that the unrealized gain (and overstated income) is now in Special Foods' column of the consolidation worksheet and the overstated land is now in Peerless' column.

Eliminate Gain on Purchase of Land from Special Foods:

	Debit	Credit
Gain on Sale of Land	15,000	
Land		15,000

Consolidated Net Income

When intercompany profits that are unrealized from a consolidated point of view are included in a subsidiary's income, both consolidated net income and the noncontrolling stockholders' share of income must be adjusted for the unrealized profits. Consolidated net income for 20X1 is computed and allocated as follows:

Peerless' separate income		$140,000
Special Foods' net income	$65,000	
Less: Unrealized intercompany gain on upstream land sale	(15,000)	
Special Foods' realized net income		50,000
Consolidated net income, 20X1		$190,000
Income to noncontrolling interest ($50,000 × 0.20)		(10,000)
Income to controlling interest		$180,000

Consolidated net income in this year is the same whether or not there is an intercompany sale because the gain is unrealized. The unrealized gain must be eliminated fully, with consolidated net income based only on the realized income of the two affiliates.

Noncontrolling Interest

The income assigned to the noncontrolling shareholders is computed as their proportionate share of the realized income of Special Foods, as follows:

Special Foods' net income	$65,000
Less: Unrealized intercompany profit on upstream land sale	(15,000)
Special Foods' realized income	$50,000
Proportionate share to noncontrolling interest	× 0.20
Income to noncontrolling interest	$10,000

The total noncontrolling interest in the net assets of Special Foods is computed, in the absence of a differential, as the noncontrolling stockholders' proportionate share of the stockholders' equity of Special Foods, excluding unrealized gains and losses. On December 31, 20X1, the noncontrolling interest totals $64,000, computed as follows:

Book value of Special Foods, December 31, 20X1:	
Common stock	$200,000
Retained earnings	135,000
Total book value	$335,000
Unrealized intercompany gain on upstream land sale	(15,000)
Realized book value of Special Foods	$320,000
Noncontrolling stockholders' proportionate share	× 0.20
Noncontrolling interest, December 31, 20X1	$ 64,000

Eliminating the Upstream Unrealized Gain after the First Year

As explained previously, in the period in which unrealized profits arise from an intercompany sale, worksheet entries remove the gain or loss recorded by the seller and adjust the reported amount of the asset back to the price the selling affiliate originally paid. Each period thereafter while the purchasing affiliate holds the asset, the reported asset balance and the shareholder claims are adjusted to remove the effects of the unrealized gain or loss. Income in those subsequent periods is not affected. For example, if Peerless continues to hold the land purchased from Special Foods, the unrealized intercompany gain is eliminated from the reported balance of the land and proportionately from the subsidiary ownership interests with the following entry:

Investment in Special Foods	**12,000**	
NCI in NA of Special Foods	**3,000**	
Land		**15,000**

Recall that in the upstream case, Peerless deferred only its 80 percent share of the unrealized gain. As a result, the Investment in Special Foods account is "artificially low" by $12,000. Thus, it make sense that the consolidation entry can only increase the investment account by the amount that was deferred. All other consolidation entries are made as if there is no unrealized intercompany gain.

Subsequent Disposition of the Asset

As explained earlier, when previously unrealized intercompany profits are realized, the effects of the profit deferral must be reversed. At the time of realization, the full amount of the deferred intercompany profit is added back into the consolidated income computation and assigned to the shareholder interests from which it originally was eliminated. In this example, if Peerless had sold the land to the external party following an upstream intercompany transfer from Special Foods, the worksheet treatment would be the same as in the case of the downstream transfer except that the debit would be prorated between Investment in Special Foods ($12,000) and NCI in Net Assets of Special Foods ($3,000) based on the relative ownership interests.

Account	Debit	Credit
Investment in Special Foods	12,000	
NCI in NA of Special Foods	3,000	
Gain on Sale of Land		15,000

INTERCOMPANY TRANSFERS OF DEPRECIABLE ASSETS

Unrealized intercompany profits on a depreciable or amortizable asset are viewed as being realized gradually over the remaining economic life of the asset as it is used by the purchasing affiliate in generating revenue from unaffiliated parties. In effect, a portion of the unrealized gain or loss is realized each period as benefits are derived from the asset and its service potential expires.

The amount of depreciation recognized on a company's books each period on an asset purchased from an affiliate is based on the intercompany transfer price. From a consolidated viewpoint, however, depreciation must be based on the cost of the asset to the consolidated entity, which is the asset's cost to the affiliate company that originally purchased it from an outsider. Consolidation entries are needed in the consolidation worksheet to restate the asset, the associated accumulated depreciation, and the depreciation expense to the amounts that would have appeared in the financial statements if there had been no intercompany transfer. Because the intercompany sale takes place totally within the consolidated entity, the consolidated financial statements must appear as if the intercompany transfer had never occurred.

Downstream Sale

LO 7-5

Prepare equity-method journal entries and consolidation entries for the consolidation of a subsidiary following a downstream depreciable asset transfer.

We now modify the Peerless Products and Special Foods example to illustrate the downstream sale of a depreciable asset. Assume that Peerless sells equipment to Special Foods on December 31, 20X1, for $7,000, as follows:

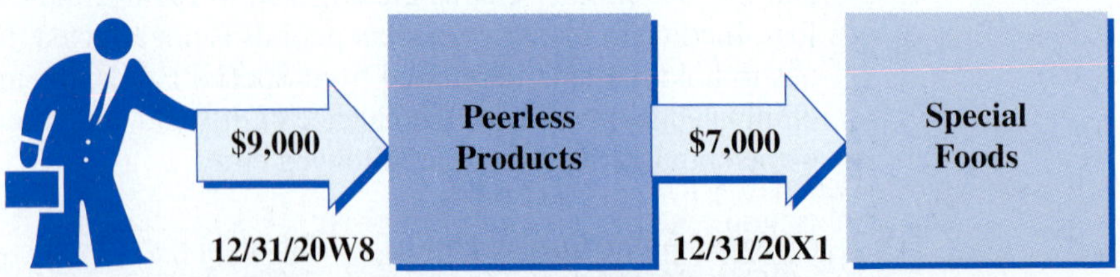

Advanced StudyGuide .com

The equipment originally cost Peerless $9,000 when purchased on December 31, 20W8, three years before the December 31, 20X1, sale to Special Foods. Assume that the equipment has been depreciated based on an estimated useful life of 10 years using the straight-line method with no residual value. The book value of the equipment immediately before the sale by Peerless is computed as follows:

Original cost to Peerless		$9,000
Accumulated depreciation on December 31, 20X1:		
Annual depreciation ($9,000 ÷ 10 years)	$900	
Number of years	× 3	
		(2,700)
Book value on December 31, 20X1		$6,300

Buildings & Equipment		Accumulated Depreciation	
9,000			2,700

Book Value = 6,300

The gain recognized by Peerless on the intercompany sale of the equipment is

Sale price of the equipment	$7,000
Less: Book value of the equipment	(6,300)
Gain on sale of the equipment	$ 700

Separate-Company Entries—20X1

Special Foods records the purchase of the equipment at its cost:

	December 31, 20X1		
(12)	Equipment	7,000	
	Cash		7,000
	Record purchase of equipment.		

Special Foods does not depreciate the equipment during 20X1 because it purchased the equipment at the very end of 20X1. However, Peerless does record depreciation expense on the equipment for 20X1 because it holds the asset until the end of the year (and the 20X1 depreciation expense is recorded prior to calculating the gain on sale shown above):

	December 31, 20X1		
(13)	Depreciation Expense	900	
	Accumulated Depreciation		900
	Record 20X1 depreciation expense on equipment sold.		

Peerless also records the sale of the equipment at the end of 20X1 and recognizes the $700 ($7,000 − $6,300) gain on the sale:

	December 31, 20X1		
(14)	Cash	7,000	
	Accumulated Depreciation	2,700	
	Equipment		9,000
	Gain on Sale of Equipment		700
	Record sale of equipment.		

In addition, Peerless records the normal fully adjusted equity-method entries to recognize its share of Special Foods' income and dividends for 20X1:

(15)	Investment in Special Foods Stock	40,000	
	Income from Special Foods		40,000
	Record equity-method income: $50,000 × 0.80.		

(16)			
	Cash	24,000	
	Investment in Special Foods Stock		24,000
	Record dividends from Special Foods: $30,000 × 0.80.		

To ensure that its income for 20X1 is correct, under the fully adjusted equity method, Peerless also defers 100 percent of the gain on the downstream intercompany sale of equipment as follows:

(17)			
	Income from Special Foods	700	
	Investment in Special Foods		700
	Defer unrealized gain on asset sale to Special Foods.		

Thus, Peerless' equity-method accounts appear as follows at the end of 20X1:

	Investment in Special Foods (Dr.)	Investment in Special Foods (Cr.)		Income from Special Foods (Dr.)	Income from Special Foods (Cr.)	
Acquisition	240,000					
80% of NI	40,000				40,000	80% of NI
		24,000	80% of Dividends			
		700	Defer Gain	700		
Ending Balance	255,300				39,300	Ending Balance

Consolidation Worksheet—20X1

Figure 7–4 illustrates the worksheet to prepare consolidated financial statements at the end of 20X1. To prepare the basic consolidation entry, we first analyze the book value of Special Foods and allocate each component to Peerless and the NCI shareholders:

Calculations for Basic Consolidation Entry:

Book Value Calculations:

	NCI 20% +	Peerless 80%	= Common Stock	+ Retained Earnings
Original Book Value	60,000	240,000	200,000	100,000
+ Net Income	10,000	40,000		50,000
− Dividends	(6,000)	(24,000)		(30,000)
Ending Book Value	64,000	256,000	200,000	120,000

Adjustment to Basic Consolidation Entry:

	NCI 20%	Peerless 80%
Net Income	10,000	40,000
− Gain on Equipment Deferral		(700)
Income to be Eliminated	10,000	39,300
Ending Book Value	64,000	256,000
− Gain on Equipment Deferral		(700)
Adjusted Book Value	64,000	255,300

The basic consolidation entry is the same as illustrated in Chapter 3 except that we adjust the entries to the Investment in Special Foods and Income from Special Foods accounts for the gain that has been deferred on the intercompany asset sale ($700):

FIGURE 7–4 December 31, 20X1, Consolidation Worksheet, Period of Intercompany Sale; Downstream

	Peerless Products	Special Foods	Consolidation Entries DR	Consolidation Entries CR	Consolidated
Income Statement					
Sales	400,000	200,000			600,000
Less: COGS	(170,000)	(115,000)			(285,000)
Less: Depreciation Expense	(50,000)	(20,000)			(70,000)
Less: Other Expenses	(40,000)	(15,000)			(55,000)
Gain on sale of fixed asset	700		700		0
Income from Special Foods	39,300		39,300		0
Consolidated Net Income	180,000	50,000	40,000	0	190,000
NCI in Net Income			10,000		(10,000)
Controlling Interest Net Income	**180,000**	**50,000**	50,000	0	**180,000**
Statement of Retained Earnings					
Beginning Balance	300,000	100,000	100,000		300,000
Net Income	**180,000**	**50,000**	50,000	0	180,000
Less: Dividends Declared	(60,000)	(30,000)		30,000	(60,000)
Ending Balance	**420,000**	**120,000**	150,000	30,000	**420,000**
Balance Sheet					
Cash	271,000	68,000			339,000
Accounts Receivable	75,000	50,000			125,000
Inventory	100,000	75,000			175,000
Investment in Special Foods	255,300			255,300	0
Land	175,000	40,000			215,000
Buildings & Equipment	791,000	607,000	2,000	300,000	1,100,000
Less: Accumulated Depreciation	(447,300)	(320,000)	300,000	2,700	(470,000)
Total Assets	**1,220,000**	**520,000**	302,000	558,000	**1,484,000**
Accounts Payable	100,000	100,000			200,000
Bonds Payable	200,000	100,000			300,000
Common Stock	500,000	200,000	200,000		500,000
Retained Earnings	**420,000**	**120,000**	150,000	30,000	420,000
NCI in NA of Special Foods				64,000	64,000
Total Liabilities & Equity	**1,220,000**	**520,000**	350,000	94,000	**1,484,000**

Basic Consolidation Entry:

	DR	CR	
Common Stock	200,000		← Common stock balance
Retained Earnings	100,000		← Beginning RE from trial balance
Income from Special Foods	39,300		← Peerless' % of NI with Adjustments
NCI in NI of Special Foods	10,000		← NCI share of reported NI
Dividends Declared		30,000	← 100% of sub's dividends declared
Investment in Special Foods		255,300	← Net BV with Adjustments
NCI in NA of Special Foods		64,000	← NCI share of net amount of BV

Optional Accumulated Depreciation Consolidation Entry:

	DR	CR	
Accumulated Depreciation	300,000		← Accumulated depreciation at the time of the acquisition netted against cost
Buildings & Equipment		300,000	

Although Peerless recorded an equity-method entry to defer the unrealized gain on the equipment sale, both the Income from Special Foods and Investment in Special Foods accounts are eliminated with the basic consolidation entry. Peerless' income is overstated by the gain ($700). Moreover, Special Foods' Buildings and Equipment account is overstated by the same amount. Therefore, we need an additional consolidation entry to remove the gain that appears in Peerless' income statement and to correct the basis of the equipment on Special Foods' books to make it appear as if the asset had not been sold within the consolidated group. One way to calculate this consolidation entry is to compare what actually happened (as recorded on the individual financial statements of the two companies) with how the accounts would have appeared in the consolidated financial statements if the transfer had not occurred. Whereas the equipment currently resides on Special Foods' books (valued at the acquisition price of $7,000 with no accumulated depreciation), we want it to appear in the consolidated financial statements as if it had not been transferred from Peerless to Special Foods (historical cost of $9,000 with accumulated depreciation of $2,700 as explained previously). The following T-accounts illustrate how to determine the correct consolidation entry to defer the gain and correct the basis of the asset:

	Buildings & Equipment (Dr)	Buildings & Equipment (Cr)	Accumulated Depreciation (Dr)	Accumulated Depreciation (Cr)	Gain on Sale (Dr)	Gain on Sale (Cr)
Actual (Special Foods):	7,000			0		700
	2,000			2,700	700	
As if (Peerless):	9,000			2,700		0

Note that the consolidation entry comprises the adjustments to convert each account from "actual" to "as if" the transfer had not taken place.

Eliminate Gain on the Equipment Sold to Special Foods and Correct the Asset's Basis:

Account	Debit	Credit
Gain on Sale	700	
Buildings & Equipment	2,000	
Accumulated Depreciation		2,700

Separate-Company Entries—20X2

During 20X2, Special Foods begins depreciating its $7,000 cost of the equipment acquired from Peerless Products over its remaining life of seven years using straight-line depreciation. The resulting depreciation is $1,000 per year ($7,000 ÷ 7 years):

	Account	Debit	Credit
(18)	Depreciation Expense	1,000	
	Accumulated Depreciation		1,000

Record depreciation expense for 20X2.

Peerless records its normal equity-method entries for 20X2 to reflect its share of Special Foods' $74,000 income and dividends of $40,000. Note that Special Foods' net income is only $74,000 in 20X2 because it has been reduced by the $1,000 of depreciation on the transferred asset. Accordingly, Peerless' share of that income is $59,200 ($74,000 × 0.80).

	Account	Debit	Credit
(19)	Investment in Special Foods	59,200	
	Income from Subsidiary		59,200

Record equity-method income: $74,000 × 0.80.

	Account	Debit	Credit
(20)	Cash	32,000	
	Investment in Special Foods		32,000

Record dividends from Special Foods: $40,000 × 0.80.

Peerless must record one additional equity-method entry related to the transferred asset. Because the equipment was recorded at the time of the December 31, 20X1, sale on Special

Foods' balance sheet at $7,000 (rather than the $6,300 book value at which it had been recorded on Peerless' books), Special Foods will record "extra" depreciation expense each year over the asset's seven-year life. Special Foods' annual depreciation ($7,000 ÷ 7 years = $1,000 per year) is $100 higher per year than it would have been if Peerless had kept the equipment ($900 per year).

Gain = 700	÷ 7 =	100	Extra depreciation
BV = 6,300	÷ 7 =	900	Peerless' depreciation
		1,000	Special Foods' total depreciation

Special Foods' extra depreciation essentially cancels out one-seventh of the unrealized gain. As a result, over the asset's seven-year life, the unrealized gain is offset by the $700 of extra depreciation expense. Thus, in 20X2 (and each of the next six years) Peerless adjusts for the "extra depreciation" by reversing one-seventh of the gain deferral in its equity-method accounts as follows:

(21)	Investment in Special Foods	100	
	Income from Special Foods		100

Reverse one-seventh of the deferred gain on fixed asset sold to Special Foods.

Consolidation Worksheet—20X2

Figure 7–5 presents the consolidation worksheet for 20X2. The trial balance amounts from the Chapter 3 example have been adjusted to reflect the intercompany asset sale. To prepare the basic consolidation entry, we again analyze the updated book value of Special Foods and examine the allocation of each component to Peerless and the NCI shareholders. Thus, to present the consolidated financial statements as if the equipment had not been transferred to Special Foods, we need to decrease depreciation expense to the amount Peerless would have recorded had the equipment stayed on its books.

Calculations for Basic Consolidation Entry:

Book Value Calculations:

	NCI 20% +	Peerless 80% =	Common Stock +	Retained Earnings
Original Book Value	64,000	256,000	200,000	120,000
+ Net Income	14,800	59,200		74,000
− Dividends	(8,000)	(32,000)		(40,000)
Ending Book Value	70,800	283,200	200,000	154,000

Adjustment to Basic Consolidation Entry:

	NCI 20%	Peerless 80%
Net Income	14,800	59,200
+ Extra Depreciation		100
Income to be Eliminated	14,800	59,300
Ending Book Value	70,800	283,200
+ Extra Depreciation		100
Adjusted Book Value	70,800	283,300

FIGURE 7–5 December 31, 20X2, Consolidation Worksheet, Next Period Following Intercompany Sale; Downstream Sale of Equipment

	Peerless Products	Special Foods	Consolidation Entries DR	Consolidation Entries CR	Consolidated
Income Statement					
Sales	450,000	300,000			750,000
Less: COGS	(180,000)	(160,000)			(340,000)
Less: Depreciation Expense	(49,100)	(21,000)		100	(70,000)
Less: Other Expenses	(60,000)	(45,000)			(105,000)
Income from Special Foods	59,300		59,300		0
Consolidated Net Income	220,200	74,000	59,300	100	235,000
NCI in Net Income			14,800		(14,800)
Controlling Interest Net Income	**220,200**	**74,000**	74,100	100	**220,200**
Statement of Retained Earnings					
Beginning Balance	420,000	120,000	120,000		420,000
Net Income	**220,200**	**74,000**	74,100	100	220,200
Less: Dividends Declared	(60,000)	(40,000)		40,000	(60,000)
Ending Balance	**580,200**	**154,000**	194,100	40,100	**580,200**
Balance Sheet					
Cash	298,000	78,000			376,000
Accounts Receivable	150,000	80,000			230,000
Inventory	180,000	90,000			270,000
Investment in Special Foods	282,600		700	283,300	0
Land	175,000	40,000			215,000
Buildings & Equipment	791,000	607,000	2,000	300,000	1,100,000
Less: Accumulated Depreciation	(496,400)	(341,000)	300,000 100	2,700	(540,000)
Total Assets	**1,380,200**	**554,000**	302,800	586,000	**1,651,000**
Accounts Payable	100,000	100,000			200,000
Bonds Payable	200,000	100,000			300,000
Common Stock	500,000	200,000	200,000		500,000
Retained Earnings	**580,200**	**154,000**	194,100	40,100	580,200
NCI in NA of Special Foods				70,800	70,800
Total Liabilities & Equity	**1,380,200**	**554,000**	394,100	110,900	**1,651,000**

The basic consolidation entry is the same as illustrated in Chapter 3 except that we adjust the entries to the Investment in Special Foods and Income from Special Foods accounts for the extra $100 of depreciation for 20X2 associated with the asset transfer:

Basic Consolidation Entry:

Common Stock	200,000		← Common stock balance
Retained Earnings	120,000		← Beginning RE from trial balance
Income from Special Foods	59,300		← Peerless' % of NI with Adjustments
NCI in NI of Special Foods	14,800		← NCI share of reported NI
Dividends Declared		40,000	← 100% of sub's dividends declared
Investment in Special Foods		283,300	← Net BV with Adjustments
NCI in NA of Special Foods		70,800	← NCI share of net amount of BV

Optional Accumulated Depreciation Consolidation Entry:

Accumulated Depreciation	**300,000**		← Accumulated depreciation at the time of the acquisition netted against cost
Buildings & Equipment		**300,000**	

In the 20X2 worksheet, two consolidation entries are necessary. The first corrects depreciation expense by adjusting it to what it would have been if the asset had stayed on Peerless' books. The second revalues the asset from its current book value on Special Foods' books to what its book value would have been if it had stayed on Peerless' books. Again, T-accounts can be a helpful tool in figuring out the consolidation entries. We find it useful to calculate the consolidation of the extra depreciation expense first because the debit to Accumulated Depreciation affects the calculation of the credit to this account in the second entry.

	Buildings & Equipment (Dr)	Buildings & Equipment (Cr)	Accumulated Depreciation (Dr)	Accumulated Depreciation (Cr)
Actual (Special Foods):	7,000			1,000
	2,000		100	2,700
As if (Peerless):	9,000			3,600

The actual amounts in these accounts are based on Special Foods' acquisition price ($7,000) and its first year's accumulated depreciation ($1,000). The "as if" amounts are Peerless' original cost when it acquired the equipment from an unrelated party and the accumulated depreciation it would have reflected had the asset stayed on Peerless' books in the absence of the transfer, $3,600 ($2,700 prior year's accumulated depreciation + $900 current year's depreciation). The second consolidation entry is calculated as the amounts needed to adjust from actual to as if the asset had stayed on Peerless' books (after entering the debit to Accumulated Depreciation from the first consolidation entry).

Entries to Adjust Equipment and Accumulated Depreciation as if Still on Parent's Books:

Accumulated Depreciation	**100**	
Depreciation Expense		**100**

Investment in Special Foods	**700**	
Buildings & Equipment	**2,000**	
Accumulated Depreciation		**2,700**

Note that the first consolidation entry backs out the extra depreciation expense from Special Foods' income statement. Again, the debit to the investment account in the second consolidation entry is equal to the amount of unrealized gain at the beginning of the year. Given the gain deferral entry in 20X1 under the fully adjusted equity method, the investment account is "artificially low" by $700. Thus, the basic consolidation entry would "overeliminate" this account. Therefore, the debit of $700 helps to eliminate the investment account. The debit to Buildings and Equipment in this consolidation entry is simply the difference between Special Foods' cost ($7,000) and peerless' historical cost ($9,000). The credit to accumulated depreciation in this consolidation entry represents the difference between what accumulated depreciation would have been if the asset had stayed on Peerless' books, $3,600 ($900 × 4 years), and the amount Special Foods actually recorded, $1,000, plus the extra depreciation.

The following T-accounts illustrate how the worksheet entries eliminate the Investment in Special Foods and Income from Special Foods accounts:

	Investment in Special Foods (Debit)	Investment in Special Foods (Credit)	
Beg. Balance	255,300		
80% of NI	59,200		
		32,000	80% of Dividends
Realize 1/7 of Deferred Gain	100		
Ending Balance	282,600		
		283,300	Basic
Worksheet Adjustment	700		
	0		

	Income from Special Foods (Debit)	Income from Special Foods (Credit)	
		59,200	80% of NI
		100	Realize 1/7 of Deferred Gain
		59,300	Ending Balance
Basic	59,300		
		0	

Once all the consolidation entries have been made in the worksheet, the adjusted balances exclude the effects of the intercompany transfer:

	Subsidiary Trial Balance	Consolidation	Consolidated Amounts
Buildings & Equipment	$7,000	$2,000	$9,000
Accumulated Depreciation	(1,000)	(2,600)	(3,600)
Depreciation Expense	1,000	(100)	900

Consolidated Net Income and Retained Earnings

Computation of consolidated net income for 20X2 must include an adjustment for the realization of profit on the 20X1 sale of equipment to Special Foods:

Peerless' separate income	$160,900
Partial realization of intercompany gain on downstream sale of equipment	100
Peerless' separate realized income	$161,000
Special Foods' net income	74,000
Consolidated net income, 20X2	$235,000
Income to noncontrolling interest ($74,000 × 0.20)	(14,800)
Income to controlling interest	$220,200

Because Peerless adjusts its investment income from Special Foods for unrealized gains and losses under the fully adjusted equity method, Peerless' Retained Earnings account equals the amount that should be reported as consolidated retained earnings. This is one of the advantages of using the fully adjusted equity method. Appendix 7A illustrates procedures for the modified equity method.

Noncontrolling Interest

Income allocated to the noncontrolling stockholders in 20X2 is equal to their proportionate share of the subsidiary's realized and reported income. Special Foods' net income for 20X2 is $74,000, and the noncontrolling interest's 20 percent share is $14,800 ($74,000 × 0.20).

The total noncontrolling interest in the net assets of Special Foods at the end of 20X2 is $70,800, equal to the noncontrolling stockholders' proportionate share of the total book value of the subsidiary:

Book value of Special Foods, December 31, 20X2:	
Common stock	$200,000
Retained earnings	154,000
Total book value	$354,000
Noncontrolling stockholders' proportionate share	× 0.20
Noncontrolling interest, December 31, 20X2	$ 70,800

Normally the noncontrolling interest at a particular date is equal to a proportionate share of the subsidiary's book value plus the noncontrolling interest's share of the remaining differential at that date. In this example, however, no differential was recognized at the date of combination.

Consolidation in Subsequent Years

The consolidation procedures in subsequent years are quite similar to those in 20X2. As long as Special Foods continues to hold and depreciate the equipment (i.e., until the asset is fully depreciated), consolidation procedures include two objectives each year:

1. Restating the asset and accumulated depreciation balances from actual to as if the asset had stayed on Peerless' books.
2. Adjusting depreciation expense for the year from actual to as if the asset had stayed on Peerless' books.

Figure 7–6 summarizes the worksheet consolidation entries at December 31 of each year from 20X1 to 20X8. Observation of the consolidation entries from 20X2–20X8 illustrates a clear pattern. The first consolidation entry to back out the extra depreciation is the same each year. Because the extra depreciation recorded each year by Special Foods effectively cancels out one-seventh of the unrealized gain and because Peerless continues to record an equity method adjustment to recognize this "canceling" of the unrealized gain as shown in entry (21), the debit to the Investment in Special Foods account and the credit to Accumulated Depreciation in the second consolidation entry each decreases by $100 each year until the asset is fully depreciated and the intercompany gain is fully recognized. After 20X8, once the transferred asset is fully depreciated no further equity-method entries are required on Peerless' books and only one consolidation entry is required in consolidation related to this asset transfer. The consolidation entry in all subsequent years (for as long as Special Foods owns the transferred asset) would simply debit Buildings and Equipment for $2,000 (to increase the basis from Special Foods acquisition price of $7,000 to Peerless' original purchase price of $9,000) and credit Accumulated Depreciation for $2,000.

Change in Estimated Life of Asset upon Transfer

When a depreciable asset is transferred between companies, a change in the remaining estimated economic life may be appropriate. For example, the acquiring company may use the asset in a different type of production process, or the frequency of use may change. When a change in the estimated life of a depreciable asset occurs at the time of an intercompany transfer, the treatment is no different than if the change had occurred while the asset remained on the books of the transferring affiliate. The new remaining useful life is used as a basis for depreciation both by the purchasing affiliate and for purposes of preparing consolidated financial statements. Thus, the as if calculation assumes the asset stayed on the transferring company's books but that the transferring company decided to revise its depreciation estimate to the useful life adopted by the new asset owner.

Upstream Sale

LO 7-6

Prepare equity-method journal entries and consolidation entries for the consolidation of a subsidiary following an upstream depreciable asset transfer.

The treatment of unrealized profits arising from upstream intercompany sales is identical to that of downstream sales except that the unrealized profit, and subsequent realization, must be allocated between the controlling and noncontrolling interests. We illustrate an upstream sale using the same example we demonstrated previously for the downstream sale. Assume that Special Foods sells equipment to Peerless Products for $7,000 on December 31, 20X1, and reports total income for 20X1 of $50,700 ($50,000 + $700), including the $700 gain on the sale of the equipment. Special Foods originally purchased the equipment for $9,000 three years before the intercompany sale.[3]

[3] To avoid additional complexity, we assume the equipment's fair value is equal to its book value on the business combination date. As a result, there is no differential related to the equipment.

FIGURE 7–6 Summary of Worksheet Consolidation Entries over the Life of the Transferred Asset (Downstream Transfer)

20X1:

Entry	Debit	Credit
Gain on Sale	700	
Buildings & Equipment	2,000	
Accumulated Depreciation		2,700

Note: This is the acquisition date, so Special Foods has not recorded any depreciation.

	Build. & Equip. (Dr.)	Build. & Equip. (Cr.)	Acc. Depr. (Dr.)	Acc. Depr. (Cr.)
Actual (Special Foods):	7,000			0
	2,000			2,700
As if (Peerless):	9,000			2,700

20X2:

Entry	Debit	Credit
Accumulated Depreciation	100	
Depreciation Expense		100

Entry	Debit	Credit
Investment in Special Foods	700	
Buildings & Equipment	2,000	
Accumulated Depreciation		2,700

	Build. & Equip. (Dr.)	Build. & Equip. (Cr.)	Acc. Depr. (Dr.)	Acc. Depr. (Cr.)
Actual (Special Foods):	7,000			1,000
	2,000		100	2,700
As if (Peerless):	9,000			3,600

20X3:

Entry	Debit	Credit
Accumulated Depreciation	100	
Depreciation Expense		100

Entry	Debit	Credit
Investment in Special Foods	600	
Buildings & Equipment	2,000	
Accumulated Depreciation		2,600

	Build. & Equip. (Dr.)	Build. & Equip. (Cr.)	Acc. Depr. (Dr.)	Acc. Depr. (Cr.)
Actual (Special Foods):	7,000			2,000
	2,000		100	2,600
As if (Peerless):	9,000			4,500

20X4:

Entry	Debit	Credit
Accumulated Depreciation	100	
Depreciation Expense		100

Entry	Debit	Credit
Investment in Special Foods	500	
Buildings & Equipment	2,000	
Accumulated Depreciation		2,500

	Build. & Equip. (Dr.)	Build. & Equip. (Cr.)	Acc. Depr. (Dr.)	Acc. Depr. (Cr.)
Actual (Special Foods):	7,000			3,000
	2,000		100	2,500
As if (Peerless):	9,000			5,400

20X5:

Entry	Debit	Credit
Accumulated Depreciation	100	
Depreciation Expense		100

Entry	Debit	Credit
Investment in Special Foods	400	
Buildings & Equipment	2,000	
Accumulated Depreciation		2,400

	Build. & Equip. (Dr.)	Build. & Equip. (Cr.)	Acc. Depr. (Dr.)	Acc. Depr. (Cr.)
Actual (Special Foods):	7,000			4,000
	2,000		100	2,400
As if (Peerless):	9,000			6,300

20X6:

Entry	Debit	Credit
Accumulated Depreciation	100	
Depreciation Expense		100

Entry	Debit	Credit
Investment in Special Foods	300	
Buildings & Equipment	2,000	
Accumulated Depreciation		2,300

	Build. & Equip. (Dr.)	Build. & Equip. (Cr.)	Acc. Depr. (Dr.)	Acc. Depr. (Cr.)
Actual (Special Foods):	7,000			5,000
	2,000		100	2,300
As if (Peerless):	9,000			7,200

20X7:

Entry	Debit	Credit
Accumulated Depreciation	100	
Depreciation Expense		100

Entry	Debit	Credit
Investment in Special Foods	200	
Buildings & Equipment	2,000	
Accumulated Depreciation		2,200

	Build. & Equip. (Dr.)	Build. & Equip. (Cr.)	Acc. Depr. (Dr.)	Acc. Depr. (Cr.)
Actual (Special Foods):	7,000			6,000
	2,000		100	2,200
As if (Peerless):	9,000			8,100

20X8:

Entry	Debit	Credit
Accumulated Depreciation	100	
Depreciation Expense		100

Entry	Debit	Credit
Investment in Special Foods	100	
Buildings & Equipment	2,000	
Accumulated Depreciation		2,100

	Build. & Equip. (Dr.)	Build. & Equip. (Cr.)	Acc. Depr. (Dr.)	Acc. Depr. (Cr.)
Actual (Special Foods):	7,000			
	2,000		100	2,100
As if (Peerless):	9,000			9,000

After 20X8:

Entry	Debit	Credit
Buildings & Equipment	2,000	
Accumulated Depreciation		2,000

	Build. & Equip. (Dr.)	Build. & Equip. (Cr.)	Acc. Depr. (Dr.)	Acc. Depr. (Cr.)
Actual (Special Foods):	7,000			7,000
	2,000			2,000
As if (Peerless):	9,000			9,000

The book value of the equipment at the date of sale is as follows:

Original cost to Special Foods		$9,000
Accumulated depreciation on December 31, 20X1:		
Annual depreciation ($9,000 ÷ 10 years)	$900	
Number of years	× 3	
		(2,700)
Book value on December 31, 20X1		$6,300

Separate-Company Entries—20X1

Special Foods records depreciation on the equipment for the year and the sale of the equipment to Peerless on December 31, 20X1, with the following entries:

December 31, 20X1

(22)	Depreciation Expense	900	
	Accumulated Depreciation		900

Record 20X1 depreciation expense on equipment sold.

December 31, 20X1

(23)	Cash	7,000	
	Accumulated Depreciation	2,700	
	Equipment		9,000
	Gain on Sale of Equipment		700

Record sale of equipment.

Peerless records the purchase of the equipment from Special Foods with the following entry:

December 31, 20X1

(24)	Equipment	7,000	
	Cash		7,000

Record purchase of equipment.

In addition, Peerless records the following equity-method entries on December 31, 20X1, to recognize its share of Special Foods' reported income and dividends:

(25)	Investment in Special Foods	40,560	
	Income from Special Foods		40,560

Record Peerless' 80% share of Special Foods' 20X1 income: $50,700 × 0.80

(26)	Cash	24,000	
	Investment in Special Foods		24,000

Record Peerless' 80% share of Special Foods' 20X1 dividend: $30,000 × 0.80

Finally, under the fully adjusted equity method, Peerless records its share of the gain deferral from the purchase of the equipment from Special Foods:

(27)	Income from Special Foods	560	
	Investment in Special Foods		560

Defer 80% of the unrealized gain on equipment purchase from Special Foods: $700 × 0.80.

These entries result in the following balances in the Investment in Special Foods and Income from Special Foods equity-method accounts:

	Investment in Special Foods (Dr.)	Investment in Special Foods (Cr.)		Income from Special Foods (Dr.)	Income from Special Foods (Cr.)	
Acquisition	**240,000**					
80% of NI	**40,560**				**40,560**	**80% of NI**
		24,000	**80% of Dividends**			
		560	**Defer 80% Gain**	**560**		
Ending Balance	**256,000**				**40,000**	**Ending Balance**

Consolidation Worksheet—20X1

Figure 7–7 on page 334 illustrates the consolidation worksheet for 20X1. It is the same as the worksheet presented in Figure 7–5 except for minor modifications to reflect the upstream sale of the equipment. As usual, to prepare the basic consolidation entry, we first analyze the book value of Special Foods and allocate each component to Peerless and the NCI shareholders:

Calculations for Basic Consolidation Entry:

Book Value Calculations:

	NCI 20% +	Peerless 80%	= Common Stock	+ Retained Earnings
Original Book Value	60,000	240,000	200,000	100,000
+ Net Income	10,140	40,560		50,700
− Dividends	(6,000)	(24,000)		(30,000)
Ending Book Value	64,140	256,560	200,000	120,700

Adjustment to Basic Consolidation Entry:

	NCI 20%	Peerless 80%
Net Income	10,140	40,560
− Gain on Equipment Deferral	(140)	(560)
Income to be Eliminated	10,000	40,000
Ending Book Value	64,140	256,560
− Gain on Equipment Deferral	(140)	(560)
Adjusted Book Value	64,000	256,000

The basic consolidation entry is the same as illustrated in Chapter 3 except that we adjust both the controlling and noncontrolling interests in Special Foods' income and net assets by their respective shares of the gain that has been deferred on the intercompany asset sale:

Basic Consolidation Entry:

	Debit	Credit	
Common Stock	200,000		← Common stock balance
Retained Earnings	100,000		← Beginning RE from trial balance
Income from Special Foods	40,000		← Peerless' % of NI with Adjustments
NCI in NI of Special Foods	10,000		← NCI share of NI with Adjustments
Dividends Declared		30,000	← 100% of sub's dividends declared
Investment in Special Foods		256,000	← Net BV with Adjustments
NCI in NA of Special Foods		64,000	← NCI share of net BV with Adjustments

Optional Accumulated Depreciation Consolidation Entry:

	Debit	Credit	
Accumulated Depreciation	300,000		← Accumulated depreciation at the time of the acquisition netted against cost
Buildings & Equipment		300,000	

As illustrated previously, one way to calculate the gain consolidation entry is to compare what actually happened (as recorded on the individual financial statements of the two companies) with how the transaction would appear in the consolidated financial statements if the asset transfer had not taken place. Whereas the equipment currently resides on Peerless' books (valued at the acquisition price of $7,000 with no accumulated depreciation), we want it to appear in the consolidated financial statements as if it had not been transferred from Special Foods to Peerless (historical cost of $9,000 with accumulated depreciation of $2,700, as explained previously). The following T-accounts illustrate how to determine the correct consolidation entry to defer the gain and correct the basis of the asset:

	Buildings & Equipment (Dr)	Buildings & Equipment (Cr)	Accumulated Depreciation (Dr)	Accumulated Depreciation (Cr)	Gain on Sale (Dr)	Gain on Sale (Cr)
Actual (Peerless):	7,000			0		700
	2,000			2,700	700	
As if (Special Foods):	9,000			2,700		0

Eliminate Gain on the Equipment Sold to Peerless and Correct the Asset's Basis:

Gain on Sale	700	
Buildings & Equipment	2,000	
Accumulated Depreciation		2,700

As it turns out, the consolidation entry for the upstream sale is exactly the same as the downstream example for 20X1.

As illustrated in Figure 7–7, the income assigned to the noncontrolling shareholders based on their share of Special Foods' realized income is computed as follows:

Net income of Special Foods for 20X1	$50,700
Unrealized gain on intercompany sale	(700)
Realized net income of Special Foods for 20X1	$50,000
Noncontrolling stockholders' proportionate share	× 0.20
Income to noncontrolling interest, 20X1	$10,000

In the upstream case, as in the downstream case, consolidated net income is reduced by the amount of the current period's unrealized gain on the intercompany transfer. However, in the upstream case, the unrealized gain reduces both the controlling and noncontrolling interests proportionately because both are owners of Special Foods and share in the gain. The allocation of Special Foods' income to the controlling and noncontrolling interests is based on Special Foods' realized net income after having deducted the unrealized gain. The computation and allocation of 20X1 consolidated net income is as follows:

Peerless' separate income		$140,000
Special Foods' net income	$50,700	
Less: Unrealized intercompany gain on upstream sale of equipment	(700)	
Special Foods' realized net income		50,000
Consolidated net income, 20X1		$190,000
Income to noncontrolling interest ($50,000 × 0.20)		(10,000)
Income to controlling interest		$180,000

Separate-Company Books—20X2

In the year following the intercompany transfer, Special Foods reports net income of $75,900 (because the $900 of depreciation expense on the transferred asset is now on

FIGURE 7–7 December 31, 20X1, Consolidation Worksheet, Period of Intercompany Sale; Upstream Sale of Equipment

	Peerless Products	Special Foods	Consolidation Entries DR	Consolidation Entries CR	Consolidated
Income Statement					
Sales	400,000	200,000			600,000
Less: COGS	(170,000)	(115,000)			(285,000)
Less: Depreciation Expense	(50,000)	(20,000)			(70,000)
Less: Other Expenses	(40,000)	(15,000)			(55,000)
Gain on Sale of Fixed Asset		700	700		0
Income from Special Foods	40,000		40,000		0
Consolidated Net Income	180,000	50,700	40,700	0	190,000
NCI in Net Income			10,000		(10,000)
Controlling Interest Net Income	**180,000**	**50,700**	**50,700**	**0**	**180,000**
Statement of Retained Earnings					
Beginning Balance	300,000	100,000	100,000		300,000
Net Income	**180,000**	**50,700**	**50,700**	**0**	180,000
Less: Dividends Declared	(60,000)	(30,000)		30,000	(60,000)
Ending Balance	**420,000**	**120,700**	**150,700**	**30,000**	**420,000**
Balance Sheet					
Cash	257,000	82,000			339,000
Accounts Receivable	75,000	50,000			125,000
Inventory	100,000	75,000			175,000
Investment in Special Foods	256,000			256,000	0
Land	175,000	40,000			215,000
Buildings & Equipment	807,000	591,000	2,000	300,000	1,100,000
Less: Accumulated Depreciation	(450,000)	(317,300)	300,000	2,700	(470,000)
Total Assets	**1,220,000**	**520,700**	**302,000**	**558,700**	**1,484,000**
Accounts Payable	100,000	100,000			200,000
Bonds Payable	200,000	100,000			300,000
Common Stock	500,000	200,000	200,000		500,000
Retained Earnings	**420,000**	**120,700**	**150,700**	**30,000**	420,000
NCI in NA of Special Foods				64,000	64,000
Total Liabilities & Equity	**1,220,000**	**520,700**	**350,700**	**94,000**	**1,484,000**

Peerless' income statement). In the upstream example, the extra $100 of depreciation expense now appears in Peerless' income statement:

Gain = 700	**÷ 7 =**	**100**	**Extra depreciation**
BV = 6,300	**÷ 7 =**	**900**	**Special Foods' depreciation**
		1,000	**Peerless' total depreciation**

Peerless records the normal fully adjusted equity-method entries on its books to recognize its share of Special Foods' 20X2 income and dividends. Moreover, it recognizes 80 percent of the deferred gain, $80 (($700 ÷ 7 years) × 0.80).

Peerless' extra depreciation essentially cancels out one-seventh of the unrealized gain. As a result, over the seven-year life of the asset, Peerless recognizes one-seventh of the gain deferral each year in its equity-method accounts:

(28)			
	Investment in Special Foods	80	
	Income from Special Foods		80

Recognize 80% of 1/7 of the deferred gain on fixed asset purchased from Special Foods.

At the end of 20X2, the Investment in Special Foods and Income from Special Foods accounts on Peerless' books appear as follows:

	Investment in Special Foods (Dr.)	Investment in Special Foods (Cr.)			Income from Special Foods (Dr.)	Income from Special Foods (Cr.)	
Beg. Balance	256,000						
80% of NI	60,720					60,720	80% of NI
		32,000	80% of Dividends				
Realize 80% of 1/7 Deferred Gain	80					80	Realize 80% of 1/7 Deferred Gain
Ending Balance	284,800					60,800	Ending Balance

Consolidation Entries—20X2

Figure 7–8 presents the consolidation worksheet for 20X2. We again analyze the updated book value of Special Foods and examine the allocation of each component to Peerless and the NCI shareholders. Also, to present the consolidated financial statements as if the equipment had not been transferred to Peerless, we need to decrease depreciation expense to the amount Special Foods would have recorded had the equipment stayed on its books.

Calculations for Basic Consolidation Entry:

Book Value Calculations:

	NCI 20%	+	Peerless 80%	=	Common Stock	+	Retained Earnings
Original Book Value	64,140		256,560		200,000		120,700
+ Net Income	15,180		60,720				75,900
− Dividends	(8,000)		(32,000)				(40,000)
Ending Book Value	71,320		285,280		200,000		156,600

Adjustment to Basic Consolidation Entry:

	NCI 20%	Peerless 80%
Net Income	15,180	60,720
+ Excess Depreciation	20	80
Income to be Eliminated	15,200	60,800
Ending Book Value	71,320	285,280
+ Excess Depreciation	20	80
Adjusted Book Value	71,340	285,360

The basic consolidation entry is the same as illustrated in Chapter 3 except that we adjust the entries to the Investment in Special Foods and Income from Special Foods accounts for their 80 percent share of the extra $100 of depreciation for 20X2 associated with the asset transfer. Moreover, we add back 20 percent of the $100 of extra depreciation to the NCI in NI of Special Foods and NCI in NA of Special Foods:

FIGURE 7–8 December 31, 20X2, Consolidation Worksheet, Next Period Following Intercompany Sale; Upstream Sale of Equipment

	Peerless Products	Special Foods	Consolidation Entries DR	Consolidation Entries CR	Consolidated
Income Statement					
Sales	450,000	300,000			750,000
Less: COGS	(180,000)	(160,000)			(340,000)
Less: Depreciation Expense	(51,000)	(19,100)		100	(70,000)
Less: Other Expenses	(60,000)	(45,000)			(105,000)
Income from Special Foods	60,800		60,800		0
Consolidated Net Income	219,800	75,900	60,800	100	235,000
NCI in Net Income			15,200		(15,200)
Controlling Interest Net Income	**219,800**	**75,900**	76,000	100	**219,800**
Statement of Retained Earnings					
Beginning Balance	420,000	120,700	120,700		420,000
Net Income	**219,800**	**75,900**	76,000	100	219,800
Less: Dividends Declared	(60,000)	(40,000)		40,000	(60,000)
Ending Balance	**579,800**	**156,600**	196,700	40,100	**579,800**
Balance Sheet					
Cash	284,000	92,000			376,000
Accounts Receivable	150,000	80,000			230,000
Inventory	180,000	90,000			270,000
Investment in Special Foods	284,800		560	285,360	0
Land	175,000	40,000			215,000
Buildings & Equipment	807,000	591,000	2,000	300,000	1,100,000
Less: Accumulated Depreciation	(501,000)	(336,400)	300,000 100	2,700	(540,000)
Total Assets	**1,379,800**	**556,600**	302,660	588,060	**1,651,000**
Accounts Payable	100,000	100,000			200,000
Bonds Payable	200,000	100,000			300,000
Common Stock	500,000	200,000	200,000		500,000
Retained Earnings	**579,800**	**156,600**	196,700	40,100	579,800
NCI in NA of Special Foods			140	71,340	71,200
Total Liabilities & Equity	**1,379,800**	**556,600**	396,840	111,440	**1,651,000**

Basic Consolidation Entry:

	DR	CR	
Common Stock	**200,000**		← Common stock balance
Retained Earnings	**120,700**		← Beginning RE from trial balance
Income from Special Foods	**60,800**		← Peerless' % of NI with Adjustments
NCI in NI of Special Foods	**15,200**		← NCI share of NI with Adjustments
Dividends Declared		**40,000**	← 100% of sub's dividends declared
Investment in Special Foods		**285,360**	← Net BV with Adjustments
NCI in NA of Special Foods		**71,340**	← NCI share of BV with Adjustments

Optional Accumulated Depreciation Consolidation Entry:

	DR	CR	
Accumulated Depreciation	**300,000**		← Accumulated depreciation at the time of the acquisition netted against cost
Buildings & Equipment		**300,000**	

In the 20X2 worksheet, the same two consolidation entries discussed in the downstream example are necessary. The only difference from the downstream example is that the amount of deferred gain on Special Foods' equipment sale to Peerless at the beginning of the period ($700) is allocated between Peerless and the NCI shareholders based on their relative ownership percentages. Again, T-accounts can be a helpful tool in figuring out the consolidation entries. It is helpful to calculate the consolidation of the extra depreciation expense first because the debit to Accumulated Depreciation affects the calculation of the credit to this account in the second entry.

	Buildings & Equipment (Dr)	Buildings & Equipment (Cr)	Accumulated Depreciation (Dr)	Accumulated Depreciation (Cr)
Actual (Peerless):	7,000			1,000
	2,000		100	2,700
As if (Special Foods):	9,000			3,600

Accumulated Depreciation	**100**	
Depreciation Expense		**100**

The actual amounts in these accounts are based on Peerless' acquisition price ($7,000) and its first year's accumulated depreciation ($1,000). The as if amounts are Special Foods' original cost when it acquired the equipment from an unrelated party and the accumulated depreciation it would have reflected had the asset stayed on Special Foods' books in the absence of the transfer, $3,600 ($2,700 prior-year accumulated depreciation + $900 current-year depreciation). The second consolidation entry is calculated as the amounts needed to adjust from actual to as if the asset had stayed on Special Foods' books.

Entries to Adjust Equipment and Accumulated Depreciation as if Still on Subsidiary's Books:

Investment in Special Foods	**560**	
NCI in NA of Special Foods	**140**	
Buildings & Equipment	**2,000**	
Accumulated Depreciation		**2,700**

As explained in the downstream example, the key to understanding these consolidation entries is that the debit to the investment account in the first consolidation entry is equal to Peerless' share of the unrealized gain at the beginning of the year. Given the gain deferral entry in 20X1 under the fully adjusted equity method, the investment account is "artificially low" by $560. Thus, the basic consolidation entry would "over-eliminate" this account. For this reason, the debit of $560 helps to eliminate the investment account. The rest of the deferral, $140, is allocated to the noncontrolling interest.

Consolidated Net Income

Peerless Products' separate income for 20X2 is $159,000 after deducting an additional $1,000 for the depreciation on the transferred asset. Consolidated net income for 20X2 is computed and allocated as follows:

Peerless' separate income		$159,000
Special Foods' net income	$75,900	
Partial realization of intercompany gain on upstream sale of equipment	100	
Special Foods' realized net income		76,000
Consolidated net income, 20X2		$235,000
Income to noncontrolling interest ($76,000 × 0.20)		(15,200)
Income to controlling interest		$219,800

Note that the partial realization of intercompany gain on the asset transfer is the extra depreciation recorded this year by Peerless.

Noncontrolling Interest

The noncontrolling interest's share of income is $15,200 for 20X2, computed as the noncontrolling stockholders' proportionate share of the realized income of Special Foods ($76,000 × 0.20). Total noncontrolling interest in the absence of a differential is computed as the noncontrolling stockholders' proportionate share of the stockholders' equity of Special Foods, excluding unrealized gains and losses. On December 31, 20X2, the noncontrolling interest totals $71,200, computed as follows:

Book value of Special Foods, December 31, 20X2:	
Common Stock	$200,000
Retained earnings ($120,700 + $75,900 − $40,000)	156,600
Total book value	$356,600
Unrealized 20X1 intercompany gain on upstream sale	(700)
Intercompany gain realized in 20X2	100
Realized book value of Special Foods	$356,000
Noncontrolling stockholders' share	× 0.20
Noncontrolling interest, December 31, 20X2	$ 71,200

Consolidation in Subsequent Years

The consolidation procedures in subsequent years are quite similar to those in 20X2. Figure 7–9 summarizes the worksheet consolidation entries at December 31 of each year from 20X2 to 20X8. We omit 20X1 because it is identical to the downstream entry reported in Figure 7–6. Observation of the consolidation entries from 20X2–20X8 again illustrates a clear pattern. The first consolidation entry to back out the extra depreciation is the same each year. Because the extra depreciation recorded each year by Peerless effectively cancels out one-seventh of the unrealized gain and because Peerless continues to record an equity-method adjustment to recognize this acknowledgment of the unrealized gain (entry 28), the sum of the debits to the Investment and NCI in NA of Special Foods accounts, and the credit to accumulated depreciation in the second consolidation entry each decreases by $100 each year until the asset is fully depreciated and the intercompany gain is fully recognized. After 20X8, no further equity-method entries are required on Peerless' books, and only one consolidation entry is required in consolidation related to this asset transfer. The consolidation entry in all subsequent years (for as long as Peerless owns the transferred asset) would simply debit Buildings and Equipment for $2,000 (to increase the basis from Peerless' acquisition price of $7,000 to Special Foods' original purchase price of $9,000) and credit Accumulated Depreciation for $2,000.

Asset Transfers before Year-End

In cases in which an intercompany asset transfer occurs during a period rather than at its end, a portion of the intercompany gain or loss is considered to be realized in the period of the transfer. When this occurs, the worksheet consolidation entries at year-end must include an adjustment of depreciation expense and accumulated depreciation. The amount of this adjustment is equal to the difference between the depreciation recorded by the purchaser and that which would have been recorded by the seller during the portion of the year elapsing after the intercompany sale.

For example, if the upstream equipment sale from Special Foods to Peerless had occurred on January 1, 20X1, rather than on December 31, 20X1, an additional consolidation entry (the second entry listed for every other year) would be needed in the consolidation worksheet on December 31, 20X1, to eliminate the "extra" depreciation.

FIGURE 7–9 Summary of Worksheet Consolidation Entries over the Life of the Transferred Asset (Upstream Transfer)

20X2:

Account	Debit	Credit
Accumulated Depreciation	100	
Depreciation Expense		100
Investment in Special Foods	560	
NCI in NA of Special Foods	140	
Buildings & Equipment	2,000	
Accumulated Depreciation		2,700

	Build. & Equip. (Dr)	Build. & Equip. (Cr)	Acc. Depr. (Dr)	Acc. Depr. (Cr)
Actual (Peerless):	7,000			1,000
	2,000		100	2,700
As if (Special Foods):	9,000			3,600

20X3:

Account	Debit	Credit
Accumulated Depreciation	100	
Depreciation Expense		100
Investment in Special Foods	480	
NCI in NA of Special Foods	120	
Buildings & Equipment	2,000	
Accumulated Depreciation		2,600

	Build. & Equip. (Dr)	Build. & Equip. (Cr)	Acc. Depr. (Dr)	Acc. Depr. (Cr)
Actual (Peerless):	7,000			2,000
	2,000		100	2,600
As if (Special Foods):	9,000			4,500

20X4:

Account	Debit	Credit
Accumulated Depreciation	100	
Depreciation Expense		100
Investment in Special Foods	400	
NCI in NA of Special Foods	100	
Buildings & Equipment	2,000	
Accumulated Depreciation		2,500

	Build. & Equip. (Dr)	Build. & Equip. (Cr)	Acc. Depr. (Dr)	Acc. Depr. (Cr)
Actual (Peerless):	7,000			3,000
	2,000		100	2,500
As if (Special Foods):	9,000			5,400

20X5:

Account	Debit	Credit
Accumulated Depreciation	100	
Depreciation Expense		100
Investment in Special Foods	320	
NCI in NA of Special Foods	80	
Buildings & Equipment	2,000	
Accumulated Depreciation		2,400

	Build. & Equip. (Dr)	Build. & Equip. (Cr)	Acc. Depr. (Dr)	Acc. Depr. (Cr)
Actual (Peerless):	7,000			4,000
	2,000		100	2,400
As if (Special Foods):	9,000			6,300

20X6:

Account	Debit	Credit
Accumulated Depreciation	100	
Depreciation Expense		100
Investment in Special Foods	240	
NCI in NA of Special Foods	60	
Buildings & Equipment	2,000	
Accumulated Depreciation		2,300

	Build. & Equip. (Dr)	Build. & Equip. (Cr)	Acc. Depr. (Dr)	Acc. Depr. (Cr)
Actual (Peerless):	7,000			5,000
	2,000		100	2,300
As if (Special Foods):	9,000			7,200

20X7:

Account	Debit	Credit
Accumulated Depreciation	100	
Depreciation Expense		100
Investment in Special Foods	160	
NCI in NA of Special Foods	40	
Buildings & Equipment	2,000	
Accumulated Depreciation		2,200

	Build. & Equip. (Dr)	Build. & Equip. (Cr)	Acc. Depr. (Dr)	Acc. Depr. (Cr)
Actual (Peerless):	7,000			6,000
	2,000		100	2,200
As if (Special Foods):	9,000			8,100

20X8:

Account	Debit	Credit
Accumulated Depreciation	100	
Depreciation Expense		100
Investment in Special Foods	80	
NCI in NA of Special Foods	20	
Buildings & Equipment	2,000	
Accumulated Depreciation		2,100

	Build. & Equip. (Dr)	Build. & Equip. (Cr)	Acc. Depr. (Dr)	Acc. Depr. (Cr)
Actual (Peerless):	7,000			7,000
	2,000		100	2,100
As if (Special Foods):	9,000			9,000

After 20X8:

Account	Debit	Credit
Buildings & Equipment	2,000	
Accumulated Depreciation		2,000

	Build. & Equip. (Dr)	Build. & Equip. (Cr)	Acc. Depr. (Dr)	Acc. Depr. (Cr)
Actual (Peerless):	7,000			7,000
	2,000			2,000
As if (Special Foods):	9,000			9,000

INTERCOMPANY TRANSFERS OF AMORTIZABLE ASSETS

Production rights, patents, and other types of intangible assets may be sold to affiliated enterprises. Accounting for intangible assets usually differs from accounting for tangible assets in that amortizable intangibles normally are reported at the remaining unamortized balance without the use of a contra account for accumulated amortization. Other than netting the accumulated amortization on an intangible asset against the asset cost, the intercompany sale of intangibles is treated in the same way in consolidation as the intercompany sale of tangible assets.

SUMMARY OF KEY CONCEPTS

Transactions between affiliated companies within a consolidated entity must be viewed as if they occurred within a single company. Under generally accepted accounting principles, the effects of transactions that are internal to an enterprise may not be included in external accounting reports. Therefore, the effects of all transactions between companies within the consolidated entity must be eliminated in preparing consolidated financial statements.

The treatment of intercompany noncurrent asset transfers is similar to the treatment of intercompany inventory transfers discussed in Chapter 6. The consolidation of intercompany transactions must include the removal of unrealized intercompany profits. When one company sells an asset to an affiliate within the consolidated entity, any intercompany profit is not considered realized until confirmed by subsequent events. If the asset has an unlimited life, as with land, the unrealized intercompany gain or loss is realized at the time the asset is resold to a party outside the consolidated entity. If the asset has a limited life, the unrealized intercompany gain or loss is considered to be realized over the remaining life of the asset as the asset is used and depreciated or amortized.

Consolidation procedures relating to unrealized gains and losses on intercompany transfers of assets involve worksheet adjustments to restate the assets and associated accounts, such as accumulated depreciation, to the balances that would be reported if there had been no intercompany transfer. In the period of transfer, the income assigned to the shareholders of the selling affiliate must be reduced by their share of the unrealized intercompany profit. If the sale is a downstream sale, the unrealized intercompany gain or loss is eliminated against the controlling interest. When an upstream sale occurs, the unrealized intercompany gain or loss is eliminated proportionately against the controlling and noncontrolling interests.

KEY TERMS

downstream sale, *307* upstream sale, *307*

Appendix 7A Intercompany Noncurrent Asset Transactions—Modified Equity Method and Cost Method

A parent company may account for a subsidiary using any of several methods. So long as the subsidiary is to be consolidated, the method of accounting for it on the parent's books will have no impact on the consolidated financial statements. Although the primary focus of this chapter is on consolidation using the fully adjusted equity method on the parent's books, two other methods are used in practice with some frequency as well. These methods are the modified equity method and the cost method.

MODIFIED EQUITY METHOD

A company that chooses to account for an investment using the modified equity method records its proportionate share of subsidiary income and dividends in the same manner as under the fully adjusted equity method. However, it does not defer its share of any unrealized profits from intercompany transactions using equity-method entries. Instead, these unrealized gains and losses are removed from the parent's retained earnings in the period after the intercompany sale. In the absence of these equity-method adjustments, the parent's net income is usually not equal to the amount of consolidated net income allocated to the controlling interest.

As an illustration, assume the same facts as in the upstream sale of equipment discussed previously and reflected in the worksheets presented in Figures 7–7 and 7–8. Special Foods sells equipment to Peerless Products for $7,000 on December 31, 20X1, and reports total income of $50,700 for 20X1, including the $700 gain on the sale of the equipment. Special Foods originally purchased the equipment for $9,000 three years before the intercompany sale. Both companies use straight-line depreciation.

As illustrated previously, Special Foods records 20X1 depreciation on the equipment and the gain on the December 31, 20X1, sale of the equipment to Peerless with the following entries:

	December 31, 20X1		
(29)	Depreciation Expense	900	
	Accumulated Depreciation		900
	Record 20X1 depreciation expense on equipment sold.		

	December 31, 20X1		
(30)	Cash	7,000	
	Accumulated Depreciation	2,700	
	Equipment		9,000
	Gain on Sale of Equipment		700
	Record sale of equipment.		

Peerless records the purchase of the equipment from Special Foods with the following entry:

	December 31, 20X1		
(31)	Equipment	7,000	
	Cash		7,000
	Record purchase of equipment.		

Modified Equity-Method Entries—20X1

In addition, Peerless records the following modified equity-method entries on December 31, 20X1, to recognize its share of Special Foods' reported income and dividends:

(32)	Investment in Special Foods	40,560	
	Income from Special Foods		40,560
	Record Peerless' 80% share of Special Foods' 20X1 income: $50,700 × 0.80.		

(33)	Cash	24,000	
	Investment in Special Foods		24,000
	Record Peerless' 80% share of Special Foods' 20X1 dividend: $30,000 × 0.80.		

However, Peerless does not record an equity-method entry for its share of the gain deferral from the purchase of the asset from Special Foods.

Consolidation Entries—20X1

The consolidation worksheet consolidation entries under the modified equity method are almost identical to those used under the fully adjusted equity method for 20X1 with one minor exception. We go through the exact same analysis of the book value of Special Foods and allocate each component to Peerless and the NCI shareholders:

Calculations for Basic Consolidation Entry:

Book Value Calculations:

	NCI 20% +	Peerless 80%	=	Common Stock	+ Retained Earnings
Original Book Value	**60,000**	**240,000**		**200,000**	**100,000**
+ Net Income	**10,140**	**40,560**			**50,700**
− Dividends	**(6,000)**	**(24,000)**			**(30,000)**
Ending Book Value	**64,140**	**256,560**		**200,000**	**120,700**

(continued)

Adjustment to Basic Consolidation Entry:

	NCI	Peerless
Net Income	10,140	40,560
− Gain Deferral	(140)	(560)
Income to be Eliminated	10,000	40,000
Ending Book Value	64,140	256,560
− Gain Deferral	(140)	(560)
Adjusted Book Value	64,000	256,000

The basic consolidation entry under the modified equity method is almost identical to the basic consolidation entry under the fully adjusted equity method with one minor exception. Because we don't make equity-method adjustments for the unrealized gain in Peerless' books, we no longer adjust the entries to the Investment in Special Foods and Income from Special Foods accounts for the gain that has been deferred on the intercompany asset sale. Note that we continue to adjust the NCI shareholders' share of Special Foods' income and their share of Special Foods' book value of net assets:

Basic Consolidation Entry:

Common Stock	200,000		← Common stock balance
Retained Earnings	100,000		← Beginning RE from trial balance
Income from Special Foods	40,560		← Peerless' % of reported NI
NCI in NI of Special Foods	10,000		← NCI share of NI with Adjustments
Dividends Declared		30,000	← 100% of sub's dividends declared
Investment in Special Foods		256,560	← Net BV left in the invest. acct.
NCI in NA of Special Foods		64,000	← NCI share of net BV with Adjustments

Optional Accumulated Depreciation Consolidation Entry:

Accumulated depreciation	300,000		← Accumulated depreciation at the time of the acquisition netted against cost
Buildings & equipment		300,000	

The following T-accounts illustrate that we arrive at the exact same answer in 20X1 for eliminating the intercompany gain on the sale of equipment from Special Foods to Peerless Products:

	Buildings & Equipment (Dr)	Buildings & Equipment (Cr)	Accumulated Depreciation (Dr)	Accumulated Depreciation (Cr)	Gain on Sale (Dr)	Gain on Sale (Cr)
Actual (Special Foods):	7,000			0		700
	2,000			2,700	700	
As if (Peerless):	9,000			2,700		0

Eliminate Gain on the Equipment Sold to Special Foods and Correct the Assets' Basis:

Gain on Sale	700	
Buildings & Equipment	2,000	
Accumulated Depreciation		2,700

Figure 7–10 illustrates the consolidation worksheet for 20X1.

Modified Equity-Method Entries—20X2

In 20X2, Peerless records its share of Special Foods' $75,900 income and $40,000 of dividends as follows:

(34)	Investment in Special Foods	60,720	
	Income from Special Foods		60,720

Record Peerless' 80% share of Special Foods' 20X2 income: $75,900 × 0.80.

(35)	Cash	32,000	
	Investment in Special Foods		32,000

Record Peerless' 80% share of Special Foods' 20X2 dividend: $40,000 × 0.80.

Peerless does not make an entry under the modified equity method to increase income for the partial realization of the unrealized intercompany gain.

Consolidation Entries—20X2

To derive the consolidation entries for the 20X2 worksheet, we again analyze the updated book value of Special Foods and examine the allocation of each component to Peerless and the NCI shareholders. Also, to present the consolidated financial statements as if the equipment had not been transferred to Peerless, we need to decrease depreciation expense to the amount Special Foods would have recorded had the equipment stayed on its books.

FIGURE 7–10 December 31, 20X1, Modified Equity Method Consolidation Worksheet, Period of Intercompany Sale; Upstream Sale of Equipment

	Peerless Products	Special Foods	Consolidation Entries DR	Consolidation Entries CR	Consolidated
Income Statement					
Sales	400,000	200,000			600,000
Less: COGS	(170,000)	(115,000)			(285,000)
Less: Depreciation Expense	(50,000)	(20,000)			(70,000)
Less: Other Expenses	(40,000)	(15,000)			(55,000)
Gain on Sale of Fixed Asset		700	700		0
Income from Special Foods	40,560		40,560		0
Consolidated Net Income	180,560	50,700	41,260	0	190,000
NCI in Net Income			10,000		(10,000)
Controlling Interest Net Income	**180,560**	**50,700**	**51,260**	**0**	**180,000**
Statement of Retained Earnings					
Beginning Balance	300,000	100,000	100,000		300,000
Net Income	**180,560**	**50,700**	**51,260**	**0**	180,000
Less: Dividends Declared	(60,000)	(30,000)		30,000	(60,000)
Ending Balance	**420,560**	**120,700**	**151,260**	**30,000**	**420,000**
Balance Sheet					
Cash	257,000	82,000			339,000
Accounts Receivable	75,000	50,000			125,000
Inventory	100,000	75,000			175,000
Investment in Special Foods	256,560			256,560	0
Land	175,000	40,000			215,000
Buildings & Equipment	807,000	591,000	2,000	300,000	1,100,000
Less: Accumulated Depreciation	(450,000)	(317,300)	300,000	2,700	(470,000)
Total Assets	**1,220,560**	**520,700**	**302,000**	**559,260**	**1,484,000**
Accounts Payable	100,000	100,000			200,000
Bonds Payable	200,000	100,000			300,000
Common Stock	500,000	200,000	200,000		500,000
Retained Earnings	**420,560**	**120,700**	**151,260**	**30,000**	420,000
NCI in NA of Special Foods				64,000	64,000
Total Liabilities & Equity	**1,220,560**	**520,700**	**351,260**	**94,000**	**1,484,000**

Calculations for Basic Consolidation Entry:

Book Value Calculations:

	NCI 20% +	Peerless 80%	=	Common Stock	+	Retained Earnings
Original Book Value	64,140	256,560		200,000		120,700
+ Net Income	15,180	60,720				75,900
− Dividends	(8,000)	(32,000)				(40,000)
Ending Book Value	71,320	285,280		200,000		156,600

Adjustment to Basic Consolidation Entry:

	NCI	Peerless
Net Income	15,180	60,720
+ Excess Depreciation	20	80
Income to be Eliminated	15,200	60,800
Ending Book Value	71,320	285,280
+ Excess Depreciation	20	80
Adjusted Book Value	71,340	285,360

The basic consolidation entry is the same as illustrated for the fully adjusted equity method except that we no longer adjust the entries to the Investment in Special Foods and Income from Special Foods accounts for their 80 percent share of the extra $100 of depreciation for 20X2 associated with the asset transfer. However, we continue to add back 20 percent of the $100 of extra depreciation to the NCI in NI of Special Foods and NCI in NA of Special Foods:

Basic Consolidation Entry:

	Debit	Credit	
Common Stock	200,000		← Common stock balance
Retained Earnings	120,700		← Beginning RE from trial balance
Income from Special Foods	60,720		← Peerless' share of reported NI
NCI in NI of Special Foods	15,200		← NCI share of NI with Adjustments
Dividends Declared		40,000	← 100% of sub's dividends declared
Investment in Special Foods		285,280	← Net BV left in the invest. acct.
NCI in NA of Special Foods		71,340	← NCI share of BV with Adjustments

Optional Accumulated Depreciation Consolidation Entry:

	Debit	Credit	
Accumulated Depreciation	300,000		← Accumulated depreciation at the time of the acquisition netted against cost
Buildings & Equipment		300,000	

In the 20X2 worksheet, the only difference from the fully adjusted equity-method example is that although the amount of deferred gain on Special Foods' equipment sale to Peerless at the beginning of the period ($700) is still allocated between Peerless and the NCI shareholders based on their relative ownership percentages, the amount accruing to Peerless is recorded as a decrease to beginning Retained Earnings rather than as a debit to the Investment in Special Foods account. The reason the consolidation entry affects the Retained Earnings account instead of the Investment in Special Foods account is that no adjustments have been made under the equity method to ensure that Peerless' books are up-to-date. T-accounts can be a helpful tool in figuring out the consolidation entries:

	Buildings & Equipment (Dr)	Buildings & Equipment (Cr)	Accumulated Depreciation (Dr)	Accumulated Depreciation (Cr)
Actual (Special Foods):	7,000			1,000
	2,000		100	2,700
As if (Peerless):	9,000			3,600

Accumulated Depreciation	**100**	
Depreciation Expense		**100**

Entries to Adjust Equipment and Accumulated Depreciation as if Still on Parent's Books:

Retained Earnings	**560**	
NCI in NA of Special Foods	**140**	
Buildings & Equipment	**2,000**	
Accumulated Depreciation		**2,700**

Again, these consolidation entries related to the intercompany asset sale are identical to those used under the fully adjusted equity method with the one exception that the debit for $560 in the second consolidation entry goes to Retained Earnings rather than the Investment in Special Foods account. In all cases, the entries under the modified equity method are identical to those illustrated in Figure 7-9 except that the entries to the Investment in Special Foods account are replaced with entries to Retained Earnings.

Figure 7–11 illustrates the consolidation worksheet for 20X2.

FIGURE 7–11 December 31, 20X2, Modified Equity-Method Consolidation Worksheet, Next Period Following Intercompany Sale; Upstream Sale of Equipment

	Peerless Products	Special Foods	Consolidation Entries DR	Consolidation Entries CR	Consolidated
Income Statement					
Sales	450,000	300,000			750,000
Less: COGS	(180,000)	(160,000)			(340,000)
Less: Depreciation Expense	(51,000)	(19,100)		100	(70,000)
Less: Other Expenses	(60,000)	(45,000)			(105,000)
Income from Special Foods	60,720		60,720		0
Consolidated Net Income	219,720	75,900	60,720	100	235,000
NCI in Net Income			15,200		(15,200)
Controlling Interest Net Income	**219,720**	**75,900**	75,920	100	**219,800**
Statement of Retained Earnings					
Beginning Balance	420,560	120,700	120,700 560		420,000
Net Income	**219,720**	**75,900**	75,920	100	219,800
Less: Dividends Declared	(60,000)	(40,000)		40,000	(60,000)
Ending Balance	**580,280**	**156,600**	197,180	40,100	**579,800**
Balance Sheet					
Cash	284,000	92,000			376,000
Accounts Receivable	150,000	80,000			230,000
Inventory	180,000	90,000			270,000
Investment in Special Foods	285,280			285,280	0
Land	175,000	40,000			215,000
Buildings & Equipment	807,000	591,000	2,000	300,000	1,100,000
Less: Accumulated Depreciation	(501,000)	(336,400)	300,000 100	2,700	(540,000)
Total Assets	**1,380,280**	**556,600**	302,100	587,980	**1,651,000**
Accounts Payable	100,000	100,000			200,000
Bonds Payable	200,000	100,000			300,000
Common Stock	500,000	200,000	200,000		500,000
Retained Earnings	**580,280**	**156,600**	197,180	40,100	579,800
NCI in NA of Special Foods			140	71,340	71,200
Total Liabilities & Equity	**1,380,280**	**556,600**	397,320	111,440	**1,651,000**

COST METHOD

When using the cost method of accounting for an investment in a subsidiary, the parent records dividends received from the subsidiary during the period as income. No entries are made under the cost method to record the parent's share of undistributed subsidiary earnings, amortize differential, or remove unrealized intercompany profits.

To illustrate consolidation following an intercompany sale of equipment when the parent accounts for its subsidiary investment using the cost method, assume the same facts as in the previous illustrations of an upstream sale.

Consolidation Entries—20X1

The following consolidation entries would appear in the worksheet used to consolidate Peerless and Special Foods at the end of 20X1, assuming Peerless uses the cost method to account for its investment:

Investment Consolidation Entry:

Common Stock	200,000	
Retained Earnings	100,000	
Investment in Special Foods		240,000
NCI in NA of Special Foods		60,000

Dividend Consolidation Entry:

Dividend Income	24,000	
NCI in NI of Special Foods	6,000	
Dividends Declared		30,000

The amount of undistributed net income assigned to the NCI is adjusted for the NCI's share of the gain deferral.

NCI in NI and NCI in NA of Special Foods:

	NCI 20%
Net Income	10,140
+ Dividend	(6,000)
− Gain on Equipment Deferral	(140)
NCI in NI of Special Foods	4,000

Assign Undistributed Income to NCI:

NCI in NI of Special Foods	4,000		← NCI's 20% share of undistributed NI with Adjustments
NCI in NA of Special Foods		4,000	← NCI's 20% share of undistributed NI with Adjustments

Optional Accumulated Depreciation Consolidation Entry:

Accumulated Depreciation	300,000		← Accumulated depreciation at the time of the acquisition netted against cost
Buildings & Equipment		300,000	

Eliminate Asset Purchase from Special Foods:

Buildings & Equipment	2,000	
Gain on Sale	700	
Accumulated Depreciation		2,700

The first four consolidation entries are identical to those illustrated in Appendix 6A. They (1) eliminate the book value of Special Foods' equity accounts against the original investment account, (2) eliminate Special Foods' 20X1 dividends declared, (3) assign undistributed realized income to the NCI shareholders, and (4) eliminate accumulated depreciation recorded by Special Foods on fixed assets prior to Peerless' acquisition. Finally, the consolidation entry related to the fixed asset transfer is identical to the one used under both the fully adjusted and modified equity methods.

Figure 7–12 illustrates the consolidation worksheet for 20X1.

Consolidation Entries—20X2

The following consolidation entries would appear in the worksheet used to consolidate Peerless and Special Foods at the end of 20X2, assuming Peerless uses the cost method to account for its investment:

Investment Consolidation Entry:

Common Stock	200,000	
Retained Earnings	100,000	
Investment in Special Foods		240,000
NCI in NA of Special Foods		60,000

FIGURE 7–12 December 31, 20X1, Cost Method Consolidation Worksheet, Period of Intercompany Sale; Upstream Sale of Equipment

	Peerless Products	Special Foods	Consolidation Entries DR	Consolidation Entries CR	Consolidated
Income Statement					
Sales	400,000	200,000			600,000
Less: COGS	(170,000)	(115,000)			(285,000)
Less: Depreciation Expense	(50,000)	(20,000)			(70,000)
Less: Other Expenses	(40,000)	(15,000)			(55,000)
Gain on Sale of Fixed Asset		700	700		0
Dividend Income	24,000		24,000		0
Consolidated Net Income	164,000	50,700	24,700	0	190,000
NCI in Net Income			6,000 4,000		(10,000)
Controlling Interest Net Income	**164,000**	**50,700**	**34,700**	**0**	**180,000**
Statement of Retained Earnings					
Beginning Balance	300,000	100,000	100,000		300,000
Net Income	**164,000**	**50,700**	**34,700**	**0**	180,000
Less: Dividends Declared	(60,000)	(30,000)		30,000	(60,000)
Ending Balance	**404,000**	**120,700**	**134,700**	**30,000**	**420,000**
Balance Sheet					
Cash	257,000	82,000			339,000
Accounts Receivable	75,000	50,000			125,000
Inventory	100,000	75,000			175,000
Investment in Special Foods	240,000			240,000	0
Land	175,000	40,000			215,000
Buildings & Equipment	807,000	591,000	2,000	300,000	1,100,000
Less: Accumulated Depreciation	(450,000)	(317,300)	300,000	2,700	(470,000)
Total Assets	**1,204,000**	**520,700**	**302,000**	**542,700**	**1,484,000**
Accounts Payable	100,000	100,000			200,000
Bonds Payable	200,000	100,000			300,000
Common Stock	500,000	200,000	200,000		500,000
Retained Earnings	**404,000**	**120,700**	**134,700**	**30,000**	420,000
NCI in NA of Special Foods				60,000 4,000	64,000
Total Liabilities & Equity	**1,204,000**	**520,700**	**334,700**	**94,000**	**1,484,000**

Dividend Consolidation Entry:

Dividend Income	32,000	
NCI in NI of Special Foods	8,000	
Dividends Declared		40,000

NCI in NI and NCI in NA of Special Foods

	NCI 20%
Net Income	15,180
− Dividend	(8,000)
+ Reverse GP Deferral	20
NCI in NI of Special Foods	7,200
Undistributed from Prior Years	4,140
NCI in NA of Special Foods	11,340

Assign Prior Undistributed Income to NCI:

NCI in NI of Special Foods	7,200		← NCI's 20% share of 20X2 undistributed NI with Adjustments
Retained Earnings*	4,140		← NCI's 20% share of 20X1 undistributed NI
NCI in NA of Special Foods		11,340	← NCI's 20% share of cumulative undistributed NI with Adjustments

Optional Accumulated Depreciation Consolidation Entry:

Accumulated Depreciation	300,000		← Accumulated depreciation at the time of the acquisition netted against cost
Buildings & Equipment		300,000	

Entries to Adjust Equipment and Accumulated Depreciation as if Still on Subsidiary's Books:

Accumulated Depreciation	100	
Depreciation Expense		100

Retained Earnings†	560	
NCI in NA of Special Foods	140	
Buildings & Equipment	2,000	
Accumulated Depreciation		2,700

Again, the first four consolidation entries are essentially identical to those illustrated in Appendix 6A. They (1) eliminate the book value of Special Foods' equity accounts against the original investment account, (2) eliminate Special Foods' 20X1 dividends declared, (3) assign undistributed income to the NCI shareholders, and (4) eliminate accumulated depreciation recorded by Special Foods on fixed assets prior to Peerless' acquisition. Finally, the consolidation entries related to the fixed asset transfer is identical to the one used under the modified equity method.

Figure 7–13 illustrates the consolidation worksheet for 20X2.

* Note that this is the subsidiary's retained earnings balance. The subsidiary does not adjust for the deferral of unrealized gain because this adjustment is made on the consolidation worksheet, not in the records of the subsidiary.

† Note that this is the subsidiary's retained earnings balance. The subsidiary does not adjust for the deferral of the remaining unrealized gain because this adjustment is made on the consolidation worksheet, not in the records of the subsidiary.

FIGURE 7–13 December 31, 20X2, Cost Method Consolidation Worksheet, Next Period Following Intercompany Sale; Upstream Sale of Equipment

	Peerless Products	Special Foods	Consolidation Entries DR	Consolidation Entries CR	Consolidated
Income Statement					
Sales	450,000	300,000			750,000
Less: COGS	(180,000)	(160,000)			(340,000)
Less: Depreciation Expense	(51,000)	(19,100)		100	(70,000)
Less: Other Expenses	(60,000)	(45,000)			(105,000)
Dividend Income	32,000		32,000		0
Consolidated Net Income	191,000	75,900	32,000	100	235,000
			8,000		
NCI in Net Income			7,200		(15,200)
Controlling Interest Net Income	**191,000**	**75,900**	47,200	100	**219,800**
Statement of Retained Earnings					
Beginning Balance	404,000	120,700	100,000		420,000
			4,140		
			560		
Net Income	**191,000**	**75,900**	**47,200**	100	219,800
Less: Dividends Declared	(60,000)	(40,000)		40,000	(60,000)
Ending Balance	**535,000**	**156,600**	**151,900**	**40,100**	**579,800**
Balance Sheet					
Cash	284,000	92,000			376,000
Accounts Receivable	150,000	80,000			230,000
Inventory	180,000	90,000			270,000
Investment in Special Foods	240,000			240,000	0
Land	175,000	40,000			215,000
Buildings & Equipment	807,000	591,000	2,000	300,000	1,100,000
Less: Accumulated Depreciation	(501,000)	(336,400)	300,000	2,700	(540,000)
			100		
Total Assets	**1,335,000**	**556,600**	302,100	542,700	**1,651,000**
Accounts Payable	100,000	100,000			200,000
Bonds Payable	200,000	100,000			300,000
Common Stock	500,000	200,000	200,000		500,000
Retained Earnings	**535,000**	**156,600**	**151,900**	**40,100**	579,800
NCI in NA of Special Foods			140	60,000	71,200
				11,340	
Total Liabilities & Equity	**1,335,000**	**556,600**	352,040	111,440	**1,651,000**

QUESTIONS

LO 7-1 **Q7-1** When are profits on intercompany sales considered to be realized? Explain.

LO 7-2 **Q7-2** What is an upstream sale? Which company may have unrealized profits on its books in an upstream sale?

LO 7-1 **Q7-3** What dollar amounts in the consolidated financial statements will be incorrect if intercompany services are not eliminated?

LO 7-1 **Q7-4** How are unrealized profits on current-period intercompany sales treated in preparing the income statement for (*a*) the selling company and (*b*) the consolidated entity?

LO 7-1 **Q7-5** How are unrealized profits treated in the consolidated income statement if the intercompany sale occurred in a prior period and the transferred item is sold to a nonaffiliate in the current period?

LO 7-1 **Q7-6** How are unrealized intercompany profits treated in the consolidated statements if the intercompany sale occurred in a prior period and the profits have not been realized by the end of the current period?

LO 7-2 **Q7-7** What is a downstream sale? Which company may have unrealized profits on its books in a downstream sale?

LO 7-2, 7-3, 7-4 **Q7-8** What portion of the unrealized intercompany profit is eliminated in a downstream sale? In an upstream sale?

LO 7-2 **Q7-9** How is the effect of unrealized intercompany profits on consolidated net income different between an upstream and a downstream sale?

LO 7-4 **Q7-10** Unrealized profits from a prior-year upstream sale were realized in the current period. What effect will this event have on income assigned to the noncontrolling interest in the consolidated income statement for the current period?

LO 7-6 **Q7-11** A subsidiary sold a depreciable asset to the parent company at a gain in the current period. Will the income assigned to the noncontrolling interest in the consolidated income statement for the current period be more than, less than, or equal to a proportionate share of the reported net income of the subsidiary? Why?

LO 7-6 **Q7-12** A subsidiary sold a depreciable asset to the parent company at a profit of $1,000 in the current period. Will the income assigned to the noncontrolling interest in the consolidated income statement for the current period be more if the intercompany sale occurs on January 1 or on December 31? Why?

LO 7-5 **Q7-13** If a company sells a depreciable asset to its subsidiary at a profit on December 31, 20X3, what account balances must be eliminated or adjusted in preparing the consolidated income statement for 20X3?

LO 7-5 **Q7-14** If the sale in the preceding question occurs on January 1, 20X3, what additional account will require adjustment in preparing the consolidated income statement?

LO 7-5, 7-6 **Q7-15** In the period in which an intercompany sale occurs, how do the consolidation entries differ when unrealized profits pertain to an intangible asset rather than a tangible asset?

LO 7-3, 7-5 **Q7-16** When is unrealized profit on an intercompany sale of land considered realized? When is profit on an intercompany sale of equipment considered realized? Why do the treatments differ?

LO 7-5, 7-6 **Q7-17** In the consolidation of a prior-period unrealized intercompany gain on depreciable assets, why does the debit to the Investment account decrease over time?

LO 7-2, 7-5, 7-6 **Q7-18A** A parent company may use on its books one of several different methods of accounting for its ownership of a subsidiary: (*a*) cost method, (*b*) modified equity method, or (*c*) fully adjusted equity method. How will the choice of method affect the reported balance in the investment account when there are unrealized intercompany profits on the parent's books at the end of the period?

CASES

LO 7-6 **C7-1** **Correction of Consolidation Procedures**

Research

Plug Corporation purchased 60 percent of Coy Company's common stock approximately 10 years ago. On January 1, 20X2, Coy sold equipment to Plug for $850,000 and recorded a $150,000 loss on the sale. Coy had purchased the equipment for $1,200,000 on January 1, 20X0, and was depreciating it on a straight-line basis over 12 years with no assumed residual value.

In preparing Plug's consolidated financial statements for 20X2, its chief accountant increased the reported amount of the equipment by $150,000 and eliminated the loss on the sale of equipment recorded by Coy. No other consolidations or adjustments related to the equipment were made.

Required

As a member of the audit firm Gotcha and Gotcha, you have been asked, after reviewing Plug's consolidated income statement, to prepare a memo to Plug's controller detailing the consolidation procedures that should be followed in transferring equipment between subsidiary and parent. Include citations to or quotations from the authoritative literature to support your recommendations. Your memo should include the correct consolidation entry and explain why each debit and credit is needed.

"A" indicates that the item relates to Appendix 7A.

LO 7-1, 7-2

Research

C7-2 Consolidation of Intercompany Services

Dream Corporation owns 90 percent of Classic Company's common stock and 70 percent of Plain Company's stock. Dream provides legal services to each subsidiary and bills it for 150 percent of the cost of the services provided. During 20X3, Classic recorded legal expenses of $80,000 when it paid Dream for legal assistance in an unsuccessful patent infringement suit against another company, and Plain recorded legal expenses of $150,000 when it paid Dream for legal work associated with the purchase of additional property in Montana to expand an existing strip mine owned by Plain. In preparing the consolidated statements at December 31, 20X3, no consolidation entries were made for intercompany services. When asked why no entries had been made to eliminate the intercompany services, Dream's chief accountant replied that intercompany services are not mentioned in the company accounting manual and can be ignored.

Required

Prepare a memo detailing the appropriate treatment of legal services provided by Dream to Plain and Classic during 20X3. Include citations to or quotations from authoritative accounting standards to support your recommendations. In addition, provide the consolidation entries at December 31, 20X3 and 20X4, needed as a result of the services provided in 20X3, and explain why each debit or credit is necessary.

LO 7-2, 7-5

Understanding

C7-3 Noncontrolling Interest

Current reporting standards require the consolidated entity to include all the revenues, expenses, assets, and liabilities of the parent and its subsidiaries in the consolidated financial statements. When the parent does not own all of a subsidiary's shares, various rules and procedures exist with regard to the assignment of income and net assets to noncontrolling shareholders and the way in which the noncontrolling interest is to be reported.

Required

a. How is the amount of income assigned to noncontrolling shareholders in the consolidated income statement computed if there are no unrealized intercompany profits on the subsidiary's books?

b. How is the amount reported for the noncontrolling interest in the consolidated balance sheet computed if there are no unrealized intercompany profits on the subsidiary's books?

c. What effect do unrealized intercompany profits have on the computation of income assigned to the noncontrolling interest if the profits arose from a transfer of (1) land or (2) equipment?

d. Are the noncontrolling shareholders of a subsidiary likely to find the amounts assigned to them in the consolidated financial statements useful? Explain.

LO 7-1, 7-4

Analysis

C7-4 Intercompany Sale of Services

Diamond Manufacturing Company regularly purchases janitorial and maintenance services from its wholly owned subsidiary, Schwartz Maintenance Services Inc. Schwartz bills Diamond monthly at its regular rates for the services provided, with the services consisting primarily of cleaning, grounds keeping, and small repairs. The cost of providing the services that Schwartz sells consists mostly of salaries and associated labor costs that total about 60 percent of the amount billed. Diamond issues consolidated financial statements annually.

Required

a. When Diamond prepares consolidated financial statements, what account balances of Diamond and Schwartz related to the intercompany sale of services must be adjusted or eliminated in the consolidation worksheet? What impact do these adjustments have on consolidated net income?

b. In the case of intercompany sales of services at a profit, at what point in time are the intercompany profits considered to be realized? Explain.

LO 7-1

Analysis

C7-5 Intercompany Profits

Companies have many different practices for pricing transfers of goods and services from one affiliate to another. Regardless of the approaches used for internal decision making and performance evaluation or for tax purposes, all intercompany profits, unless immaterial, are supposed to be eliminated when preparing consolidated financial statements until confirmed through transactions with external parties.

Required

Verizon Communications is in the telephone business, although it is larger and more diversified than many smaller telecommunications companies. How does it treat intercompany profits for consolidation?

EXERCISES

LO 7-5, 7-6

E7-1 Multiple-Choice Questions on Intercompany Transfers [AICPA Adapted]

For each question, select the single best answer.

1. Water Company owns 80 percent of Fire Company's outstanding common stock. On December 31, 20X9, Fire sold equipment to Water at a price in excess of Fire's carrying amount but less than its original cost. On a consolidated balance sheet at December 31, 20X9, the carrying amount of the equipment should be reported at
   a. Water's original cost.
   b. Fire's original cost.
   c. Water's original cost less Fire's recorded gain.
   d. Water's original cost less 80 percent of Fire's recorded gain.
2. Company J acquired all of Company K's outstanding common stock in exchange for cash. The acquisition price exceeds the fair value of net assets acquired. How should Company J determine the amounts to be reported for the plant and equipment and long-term debt acquired from Company K?

	Plant and Equipment	Long-Term Debt
a.	K's carrying amount	K's carrying amount
b.	K's carrying amount	Fair value
c.	Fair value	K's carrying amount
d.	Fair value	Fair value

3. Port Inc. owns 100 percent of Salem Inc. On January 1, 20X2, Port sold delivery equipment to Salem at a gain. Port had owned the equipment for two years and used a five-year straight-line depreciation rate with no residual value. Salem is using a three-year straight-line depreciation rate with no residual value for the equipment. In the consolidated income statement, Salem's recorded depreciation expense on the equipment for 20X2 will be decreased by
   a. 20 percent of the gain on the sale.
   b. $33^1/_3$ percent of the gain on the sale.
   c. 50 percent of the gain on the sale.
   d. 100 percent of the gain on the sale.
4. On January 1, 20X0, Poe Corporation sold a machine for $900,000 to Saxe Corporation, its wholly owned subsidiary. Poe paid $1,100,000 for this machine, which had accumulated depreciation of $250,000. Poe estimated a $100,000 salvage value and depreciated the machine using the straight-line method over 20 years, a policy that Saxe continued. In Poe's December 31, 20X0, consolidated balance sheet, this machine should be included in fixed-asset cost and accumulated depreciation as

	Cost	Accumulated Depreciation
a.	$1,100,000	$300,000
b.	$1,100,000	$290,000
c.	$ 900,000	$ 40,000
d.	$ 850,000	$ 42,500

5. Scroll Inc., a wholly owned subsidiary of Pirn Inc., began operations on January 1, 20X1. The following information is from the condensed 20X1 income statements of Pirn and Scroll:

	Pirn	Scroll
Sales	$500,000	$300,000
Cost of Goods Sold	(350,000)	(270,000)
Gross Profit	$150,000	$ 30,000
Depreciation	(40,000)	(10,000)
Other Expenses	(60,000)	(15,000)
Income from Operations	$ 50,000	$ 5,000
Gain on Sale of Equipment to Scroll	12,000	
Income before Taxes	$ 62,000	$ 5,000

Scroll purchased equipment from Pirn for $36,000 on January 1, 20X1, that is depreciated using the straight-line method over four years. What amount should be reported as depreciation expense in Pirn's 20X1 consolidated income statement?

a. $50,000.
b. $47,000.
c. $44,000.
d. $41,000.

LO 7-2, 7-6

E7-2 Multiple-Choice Questions on Intercompany Transactions

Select the correct answer for each of the following questions.

1. Upper Company holds 60 percent of Lower Company's voting shares. During the preparation of consolidated financial statements for 20X5, the following consolidation entry was made:

Investment in Lower	10,000	
Land		10,000

Which of the following statements is correct?

a. Upper Company purchased land from Lower Company during 20X5.
b. Upper Company purchased land from Lower Company before January 1, 20X5.
c. Lower Company purchased land from Upper Company during 20X5.
d. Lower Company purchased land from Upper Company before January 1, 20X5.

2. Middle Company holds 60 percent of Bottom Corporation's voting shares. Bottom has developed a new type of production equipment that appears to be quite marketable. It spent $40,000 in developing the equipment; however, Middle agreed to purchase the production rights for the machine for $100,000. If the intercompany sale occurred on January 1, 20X2, and the production rights are expected to have value for five years, at what amount should the rights be reported in the consolidated balance sheet for December 31, 20X2?

a. $0.
b. $32,000.
c. $80,000.
d. $100,000.

Note: Questions 3 through 6 are based on the following information:
On January 1, 20X4, Gold Company purchased a computer with an expected economic life of five years. On January 1, 20X6, Gold sold the computer to TLK Corporation and recorded the following entry:

Cash	39,000	
Accumulated Depreciation	16,000	
Computer Equipment		40,000
Gain on Sale of Equipment		15,000

TLK Corporation holds 60 percent of Gold's voting shares. Gold reported net income of $45,000 including the gain on the sale of equipment, and TLK reported income from its own operations of $85,000 for 20X6. There is no change in the estimated economic life of the equipment as a result of the intercompany transfer.

3. In the preparation of the 20X6 consolidated income statement, depreciation expense will be

a. Debited for $5,000 in the consolidation entries.
b. Credited for $5,000 in the consolidation entries.
c. Debited for $13,000 in the consolidation entries.
d. Credited for $13,000 in the consolidation entries.

4. In the preparation of the 20X6 consolidated balance sheet, computer equipment will be

a. Debited for $1,000.
b. Debited for $15,000.
c. Credited for $24,000.
d. Debited for $40,000.

5. Income assigned to the noncontrolling interest in the 20X6 consolidated income statement will be
   a. $12,000.
   b. $14,000.
   c. $18,000.
   d. $52,000.
6. Consolidated net income for 20X6 will be
   a. $106,000.
   b. $112,000.
   c. $120,000.
   d. $130,000.

LO 7-3

E7-3 Consolidation Entries for Land Transfer

Huckster Corporation purchased land on January 1, 20X1, for $20,000. On June 10, 20X4, it sold the land to its subsidiary, Lowly Corporation, for $30,000. Huckster owns 60 percent of Lowly's voting shares.

Required

a. Give the worksheet consolidation entries needed to remove the effects of the intercompany sale of land in preparing the consolidated financial statements for 20X4 and 20X5.

b. Give the worksheet consolidation entries needed on December 31, 20X4 and 20X5, if Lowly had initially purchased the land for $20,000 and then sold it to Huckster on June 10, 20X4, for $30,000.

LO 7-1, 7-2

E7-4 Intercompany Services

Power Corporation owns 75 percent of Swift Company's stock. Swift provides health care services to its employees and those of Power. During 20X2, Power recorded $45,000 as health care expense for medical care given to its employees by Swift. Swift's costs incurred in providing the services to Power were $32,000.

Required

a. By what amount will consolidated net income change when the intercompany services are eliminated in preparing Power's consolidated statements for 20X2?

b. What would be the impact of eliminating the intercompany services on consolidated net income if Power owned 100 percent of Swift's stock rather than 75 percent? Explain.

c. If in its consolidated income statement for 20X2 Power had reported total health care costs of $70,000, what was the cost to Swift of providing health care services to its own employees?

LO 7-1, 7-2

E7-5 Consolidation Entries for Intercompany Services

On January 1, 20X5, Block Corporation started using a wholly owned subsidiary to deliver all its sales overnight to its customers. During 20X5, Block recorded delivery service expense of $76,000 and made payments of $58,000 to the subsidiary.

Required

Give the worksheet consolidation entries related to the intercompany services needed on December 31, 20X5, to prepare consolidated financial statements.

LO 7-6

E7-6 Consolidation Entries for Depreciable Asset Transfer: Year-End Sale

Pam Corporation holds 70 percent ownership of Northern Enterprises. On December 31, 20X6, Northern paid Pam $40,000 for a truck that Pam had purchased for $45,000 on January 1, 20X2. The truck was considered to have a 15-year life from January 1, 20X2, and no residual value. Both companies depreciate equipment using the straight-line method.

Required

a. Give the worksheet consolidation entry or entries needed on December 31, 20X6, to remove the effects of the intercompany sale.

b. Give the worksheet consolidation entry or entries needed on December 31, 20X7, to remove the effects of the intercompany sale.

LO 7-4

E7-7 Transfer of Land

Bowen Corporation owns 70 percent of Roan Corporation's voting common stock. On March 12, 20X2, Roan sold land it had purchased for $140,000 to Bowen for $185,000. Bowen plans to build a new warehouse on the property in 20X3.

Required

a. Give the worksheet consolidation entries to remove the effects of the intercompany sale of land in preparing the consolidated financial statements at December 31, 20X2 and 20X3.

b. Give the worksheet consolidation entries needed at December 31, 20X3 and 20X4, if Bowen had initially purchased the land for $150,000 and sold it to Roan on March 12, 20X2, for $180,000.

LO 7-5

E7-8 Transfer of Depreciable Asset at Year-End

Frazer Corporation purchased 60 percent of Minnow Corporation's voting common stock on January 1, 20X1. On December 31, 20X5, Frazer received $210,000 from Minnow for a truck Frazer had purchased on January 1, 20X2, for $300,000. The truck is expected to have a 10-year useful life and no salvage value. Both companies depreciate trucks on a straight-line basis.

Required

a. Give the worksheet consolidation entry or entries needed at December 31, 20X5, to remove the effects of the intercompany sale.

b. Give the worksheet consolidation entry or entries needed at December 31, 20X6, to remove the effects of the intercompany sale.

LO 7-5

E7-9 Transfer of Depreciable Asset at Beginning of Year

Frazer Corporation purchased 60 percent of Minnow Corporation's voting common stock on January 1, 20X1. On January 1, 20X5, Frazer received $245,000 from Minnow for a truck Frazer had purchased on January 1, 20X2, for $300,000. The truck is expected to have a 10-year useful life and no salvage value. Both companies depreciate trucks on a straight-line basis.

Required

a. Give the worksheet consolidation entry or entries needed at December 31, 20X5, to remove the effects of the intercompany sale.

b. Give the worksheet consolidation entry or entries needed at December 31, 20X6, to remove the effects of the intercompany sale.

LO 7-5

E7-10 Sale of Equipment to Subsidiary in Current Period

On January 1, 20X7, Wainwrite Corporation sold to Lance Corporation equipment it had purchased for $150,000 and used for eight years. Wainwrite recorded a gain of $14,000 on the sale. The equipment has a total useful life of 15 years and is depreciated on a straight-line basis. Wainwrite holds 70 percent of Lance's voting common shares.

Required

a. Give the journal entry made by Wainwrite on January 1, 20X7, to record the sale of equipment.

b. Give the journal entries recorded by Lance during 20X7 to record the purchase of equipment and year-end depreciation expense.

c. Give the consolidation entry or entries related to the intercompany sale of equipment needed at December 31, 20X7, to prepare a full set of consolidated financial statements.

d. Give the consolidation entry or entries related to the equipment required at January 1, 20X8, to prepare a consolidated balance sheet only.

LO 7-6

E7-11 Upstream Sale of Equipment in Prior Period

Baywatch Industries has owned 80 percent of Tubberware Corporation for many years. On January 1, 20X6, Baywatch paid Tubberware $270,000 to acquire equipment that Tubberware had purchased on January 1, 20X3, for $300,000. The equipment is expected to have no scrap value and is depreciated over a 15-year useful life.

Baywatch reported operating earnings of $100,000 for 20X8 and paid dividends of $40,000. Tubberware reported net income of $40,000 and paid dividends of $20,000 in 20X8.

Required

a. Compute the amount reported as consolidated net income for 20X8.

b. By what amount would consolidated net income change if the equipment sale had been a downstream sale rather than an upstream sale?

c. Give the consolidation entry or entries required to eliminate the effects of the intercompany sale of equipment in preparing a full set of consolidated financial statements at December 31, 20X8.

LO 7-5

E7-12 Consolidation Entries for Midyear Depreciable Asset Transfer

Kline Corporation holds 90 percent ownership of Andrews Company. On July 1, 20X3, Kline sold equipment that it had purchased for $30,000 on January 1, 20X1, to Andrews for $28,000. The equipment's original six-year estimated total economic life remains unchanged. Both companies use straight-line depreciation. The equipment's residual value is considered negligible.

Required

a. Give the consolidation entry or entries in the consolidation worksheet prepared as of December 31, 20X3, to remove the effects of the intercompany sale.

b. Give the consolidation entry or entries in the consolidation worksheet prepared as of December 31, 20X4, to remove the effects of the intercompany sale.

LO 7-2

E7-13 Consolidated Net Income Computation

Verry Corporation owns 75 percent of Spawn Corporation's voting common stock. Verry reported income from its separate operations of $90,000 and $110,000 in 20X4 and 20X5, respectively. Spawn reported net income of $60,000 and $40,000 in 20X4 and 20X5, respectively.

Required

a. Compute consolidated net income and the income assigned to the controlling interest for 20X4 and 20X5 if Verry sold land with a book value of $95,000 to Spawn for $120,000 on June 30, 20X4.

b. Compute consolidated net income and the amount of income assigned to the controlling interest in the consolidated statements for 20X4 and 20X5 if Spawn sold land with a book value of $95,000 to Verry for $120,000 on June 30, 20X4.

LO 7-2, 7-3, 7-4

Advanced StudyGuide .com

E7-14 Consolidation Entries for Intercompany Transfers

Grand Delivery Service acquired at book value 80 percent of the voting shares of Acme Real Estate Company. On that date, the fair value of the noncontrolling interest was equal to 20 percent of Acme's book value. Acme Real Estate reported common stock of $300,000 and retained earnings of $100,000. During 20X3 Grand Delivery provided courier services for Acme Real Estate in the amount of $15,000. Also during 20X3, Acme Real Estate purchased land for $1,000. It sold the land to Grand Delivery Service for $26,000 so that Grand Delivery could build a new transportation center. Grand Delivery reported $65,000 of operating income from its delivery operations in 20X3. Acme Real Estate reported net income of $40,000 and paid dividends of $10,000 in 20X3.

Required

a. Compute consolidated net income for 20X3.

b. Give all journal entries recorded by Grand Delivery Service related to its investment in Acme Real Estate assuming Grand uses the fully adjusted equity method in accounting for the investment.

c. Give all consolidation entries required in preparing a consolidation worksheet as of December 31, 20X3.

LO 7-6

E7-15 Sale of Building to Parent in Prior Period

Turner Company purchased 70 percent of Split Company's stock approximately 20 years ago. On December 31, 20X8, Turner purchased a building from Split for $300,000. Split had purchased the building on January 1, 20X1, at a cost of $400,000 and used straight-line depreciation on an expected life of 20 years. The asset's total estimated economic life is unchanged as a result of the intercompany sale.

Advanced StudyGuide .com

Required

a. What amount of depreciation expense on the building will Turner report for 20X9?

b. What amount of depreciation expense would Split have reported for 20X9 if it had continued to own the building?

c. Give the consolidation entry or entries needed to eliminate the effects of the intercompany building transfer in preparing a full set of consolidated financial statements at December 31, 20X9.

d. What amount of income will be assigned to the noncontrolling interest in the consolidated income statement for 20X9 if Split reports net income of $40,000 for 20X9?

e. Split reports assets with a book value of $350,000 and liabilities of $150,000 at January 1, 20X9, and reports net income of $40,000 and dividends of $15,000 for 20X9. What amount will be assigned to the noncontrolling interest in the consolidated balance sheet at December 31, 20X9, assuming the fair value of the noncontrolling interest at the date of acquisition was equal to 30 percent of Split Company's book value?

LO 7-5

E7-16 Intercompany Sale at a Loss

Parent Company holds 90 percent of Sunway Company's voting common shares. On December 31, 20X8, Parent recorded a loss of $16,000 on the sale of equipment to Sunway. At the time of the sale, the equipment's estimated remaining economic life was eight years.

Required

a. Will consolidated net income be increased or decreased when consolidation entries associated with the sale of equipment are made at December 31, 20X8? By what amount?

b. Will consolidated net income be increased or decreased when consolidation entries associated with the sale of equipment are made at December 31, 20X9? By what amount?

LO 7-6

E7-17 Consolidation Entries Following Intercompany Sale at a Loss

Brown Corporation holds 70 percent of Transom Company's voting common stock. On January 1, 20X2, Transom paid $300,000 to acquire a building with a 15-year expected economic life. Transom uses straight-line depreciation for all depreciable assets. On December 31, 20X7, Brown purchased the building from Transom for $144,000. Brown reported income, excluding investment income from Transom, of $125,000 and $150,000 for 20X7 and 20X8, respectively. Transom reported net income of $15,000 and $40,000 for 20X7 and 20X8, respectively.

Required

a. Give the appropriate consolidation entry or entries needed to eliminate the effects of the intercompany sale of the building in preparing consolidated financial statements for 20X7.

b. Compute the amount to be reported as consolidated net income for 20X7 and the income to be allocated to the controlling interest.

c. Give the appropriate consolidation entry or entries needed to eliminate the effects of the intercompany sale of the building in preparing consolidated financial statements for 20X8.

d. Compute consolidated net income and the amount of income assigned to the controlling shareholders in the consolidated income statement for 20X8.

LO 7-4

E7-18 Multiple Transfers of Asset

Swanson Corporation purchased land from Clayton Corporation for $240,000 on December 20, 20X3. This purchase followed a series of transactions between Swanson-controlled subsidiaries. On February 7, 20X3, Sullivan Corporation purchased the land from a nonaffiliate for $145,000. It sold the land to Kolder Company for $130,000 on October 10, 20X3, and Kolder sold the land to Clayton for $180,000 on November 27, 20X3. Swanson has control of the following companies:

Subsidiary	Level of Ownership	20X3 Net Income
Sullivan Corporation	80 percent	$120,000
Kolder Company	70 percent	60,000
Clayton Corporation	90 percent	80,000

Swanson reported income from its separate operations of $150,000 for 20X3.

Required

a. At what amount should the land be reported in the consolidated balance sheet as of December 31, 20X3?

b. What amount of gain or loss on sale of land should be reported in the consolidated income statement for 20X3?

c. What amount of income should be assigned to the controlling shareholders in the consolidated income statement for 20X3?

d. Give any consolidation entry related to the land that should appear in the worksheet used to prepare consolidated financial statements for 20X3.

LO 7-6

E7-19 Consolidation Entry in Period of Transfer

Blank Corporation owns 60 percent of Grand Corporation's voting common stock. On December 31, 20X4, Blank paid Grand $276,000 for dump trucks Grand had purchased on January 1, 20X2. Both companies use straight-line depreciation. The consolidation entry included in preparing consolidated financial statements at December 31, 20X4, was

Trucks	24,000	
Gain on Sale of Trucks	36,000	
Accumulated Depreciation		60,000

Required

a. What amount did Grand pay to purchase the trucks on January 1, 20X2?

b. What was the economic life of the trucks on January 1, 20X2?

c. Give the worksheet consolidation entry needed in preparing the consolidated financial statements at December 31, 20X5.

LO 7-6

E7-20 Consolidation Entry Computation

Stern Manufacturing purchased an ultrasound drilling machine with a remaining 10-year economic life from a 70 percent-owned subsidiary for $360,000 on January 1, 20X6. Both companies use straight-line depreciation. The subsidiary recorded the following entry when it sold the machine to Stern:

Cash	360,000	
Accumulated Depreciation	150,000	
Equipment		450,000
Gain on Sale of Equipment		60,000

Required

Give the worksheet consolidation entry or entries needed to remove the effects of the intercompany sale of equipment when consolidated financial statements are prepared as of (*a*) December 31, 20X6, and (*b*) December 31, 20X7.

LO 7-6

E7-21 Using the Consolidation Entry to Determine Account Balances

Pastel Corporation acquired a controlling interest in Somber Corporation in 20X5 for an amount equal to its underlying book value. At the date of acquisition, the fair value of the noncontrolling interest was equal to its proportionate share of the book value of Somber Corporation. In preparing a consolidated balance sheet worksheet at January 1, 20X9, Pastel's controller included the following consolidation entry:

Equipment	53,500	
Investment in Somber Corp.	9,450	
NCI in NA of Somber	1,050	
Accumulated Depreciation		64,000

A note at the bottom of the consolidation worksheet at January 1, 20X9, indicates the equipment was purchased from a nonaffiliate on January 1, 20X1, for $120,000 and was sold to an affiliate on December 31, 20X8. The equipment is being depreciated on a 15-year straight-line basis. Somber reported stock outstanding of $300,000 and retained earnings of $200,000 at January 1, 20X9. Somber reported net income of $25,000 and paid dividends of $6,000 for 20X9.

Required

a. What percentage ownership of Somber Corporation does Pastel hold?

b. Was the parent or subsidiary the owner prior to the intercompany sale of equipment? Explain.

c. What was the intercompany transfer price of the equipment on December 31, 20X8?

d. What amount of income will be assigned to the noncontrolling interest in the consolidated income statement for 20X9?

e. Assuming Pastel and Somber report depreciation expense of $15,000 and $9,000, respectively, for 20X9, what depreciation amount will be reported in the consolidated income statement for 20X9?

f. Give all remaining consolidation entries needed at December 31, 20X9, to prepare a complete set of consolidated financial statements.

LO 7-1, 7-2 **E7-22**

Intercompany Sale of Services

Norgaard Corporation purchased management consulting services from its 75 percent-owned subsidiary, Bline Inc. During 20X3, Norgaard paid Bline $123,200 for its services. For the year 20X4, Bline billed Norgaard $138,700 for such services and collected all but $6,600 by year-end. Bline's labor cost and other associated costs for the employees providing services to Norgaard totaled $91,000 in 20X3 and $112,000 in 20X4. Norgaard reported $2,342,000 of income from its own separate operations for 20X4, and Bline reported net income of $631,000.

Required

a. Present all consolidation entries related to the intercompany sale of services that would be needed in the consolidation worksheet used to prepare a complete set of consolidated financial statements for 20X4.

b. Compute consolidated net income for 20X4 and the amount of income assigned to the controlling interest.

LO 7-3, 7-6 **E7-23A**

Modified Equity Method and Cost Method

Newtime Products purchased 65 percent of TV Sales Company's stock at underlying book value on January 1, 20X3. At that date, the fair value of the noncontrolling interest was equal to 35 percent of the book value of TV Sales. TV Sales reported shares outstanding of $300,000 and retained earnings of $100,000. During 20X3, TV Sales reported net income of $50,000 and paid dividends of $5,000. In 20X4, TV Sales reported net income of $70,000 and paid dividends of $20,000.

The following transactions occurred between Newtime Products and TV Sales in 20X3 and 20X4:

1. TV Sales sold camera equipment to Newtime for a $40,000 profit on December 31, 20X3. The equipment had a five-year estimated economic life remaining at the time of intercompany transfer and is depreciated on a straight-line basis.
2. Newtime sold land costing $30,000 to TV Sales on June 30, 20X4, for $41,000.

Required

a. Assuming that Newtime uses the modified equity method to account for its investment in TV Sales:

(1) Give the journal entries recorded on Newtime's books in 20X4 related to its investment in TV Sales.

(2) Give all consolidation entries needed to prepare a consolidation worksheet for 20X4.

b. Assuming that Newtime uses the cost method to account for its investment in TV Sales:

(1) Give the journal entries recorded on Newtime's books in 20X4 related to its investment in TV Sales.

(2) Give all consolidation entries needed to prepare a consolidation worksheet for 20X4.

PROBLEMS

LO 7-3, 7-4 **P7-24**

Computation of Consolidated Net Income

Petime Corporation acquired 90 percent ownership of United Grain Company on January 1, 20X4, for $108,000 when the fair value of United's net assets was $10,000 higher than its $110,000 book value. The increase in value was attributed to amortizable assets with a remaining life of 10 years. At that date, the fair value of the noncontrolling interest was equal to $12,000.

During 20X4, United sold land to Petime at a $7,000 profit. United Grain reported net income of $19,000 and paid dividends of $4,000 in 20X4. Petime reported income, exclusive of its income from United Grain, of $34,000 and paid dividends of $15,000 in 20X4.

Advanced StudyGuide .com

Required

a. Compute the amount of income assigned to the controlling interest in the consolidated income statement for 20X4.

b. By what amount will the 20X4 income assigned to the controlling interest increase or decrease if the sale of land had been from Petime to United Grain, the gain on the sale of land had been included in Petime's $34,000 income, and the $19,000 was income from operations of United Grain?

LO 7-6

P7-25 Subsidiary Net Income

Bold Corporation acquired 75 percent of Toll Corporation's voting common stock on January 1, 20X4, for $348,000, when the fair value of its net identifiable assets was $464,000 and the fair value of the noncontrolling interest was $116,000. Toll reported common stock outstanding of $150,000 and retained earnings of $270,000. The excess of fair value over book value of Toll's net assets was attributed to amortizable assets with a remaining life of 10 years. On December 31, 20X4, Toll sold a building to Bold and recorded a gain of $20,000. Income assigned to the noncontrolling shareholders in the 20X4 consolidated income statement was $17,500.

Required

a. Compute the amount of net income Toll reported for 20X4.

b. Compute the amount reported as consolidated net income if Bold reported operating income of $234,000 for 20X4.

c. Compute the amount of income assigned to the controlling interest in the 20X4 consolidated income statement.

LO 7-6

P7-26 Transfer of Asset from One Subsidiary to Another

Pelts Company holds a total of 70 percent of Bugle Corporation and 80 percent of Cook Products Corporation stock. Bugle purchased a warehouse with an expected life of 20 years on January 1, 20X1, for $40,000. On January 1, 20X6, it sold the warehouse to Cook Products for $45,000.

Required

Complete the following table showing selected information that would appear in the separate 20X6 income statements and balance sheets of Bugle Corporation and Cook Products Corporation and in the 20X6 consolidated financial statements.

	Bugle Corporation	Cook Products Corporation	Consolidated Entity
Depreciation expense			
Fixed assets—warehouse			
Accumulated depreciation			
Gain on sale of warehouse			

LO 7-6

P7-27 Consolidation Entry

In preparing its consolidated financial statements at December 31, 20X7, the following consolidation entries were included in the consolidation worksheet of Master Corporation:

Buildings	140,000	
Gain on Sale of Building	28,000	
Accumulated Depreciation		168,000

Accumulated Depreciation	2,000	
Depreciation Expense		2,000

Advanced StudyGuide .com

Master owns 60 percent of Rakel Corporation's voting common stock. On January 1, 20X7, Rakel sold Master a building it had purchased for $600,000 on January 1, 20X1, and depreciated on a 20-year straight-line basis. Master recorded depreciation for 20X7 using straight-line depreciation and the same useful life and residual value as Rakel.

Required

a. What amount did Master pay Rakel for the building?
b. What amount of accumulated depreciation did Rakel report at January 1, 20X7, prior to the sale?
c. What annual depreciation expense did Rakel record prior to the sale?
d. What expected residual value did Rakel use in computing its annual depreciation expense?
e. What amount of depreciation expense did Master record in 20X7?
f. If Rakel reported net income of $80,000 for 20X7, what amount of income will be assigned to the noncontrolling interest in the consolidated income statement for 20X7?
g. If Rakel reported net income of $65,000 for 20X8, what amount of income will be assigned to the noncontrolling interest in the consolidated income statement for 20X8?

LO 7-4, 7-6

P7-28 Multiple-Choice Questions

Select the correct answer for each of the following questions.

1. In the preparation of a consolidated income statement:
   a. Income assigned to noncontrolling shareholders always is computed as a pro rata portion of the reported net income of the consolidated entity.
   b. Income assigned to noncontrolling shareholders always is computed as a pro rata portion of the reported net income of the subsidiary.
   c. Income assigned to noncontrolling shareholders in the current period is likely to be less than a pro rata portion of the reported net income of the subsidiary in the current period if the subsidiary had an unrealized gain on an intercompany sale of depreciable assets in the preceding period. Assume the depreciable asset was subsequently sold in the current period.
   d. Income assigned to noncontrolling shareholders in the current period is likely to be more than a pro rata portion of the reported net income of the subsidiary in the current period if the subsidiary had an unrealized gain on an intercompany sale of depreciable assets in the preceding period. Assume the depreciable asset was subsequently sold in the current period.
2. When a 90 percent-owned subsidiary records a gain on the sale of land to an affiliate during the current period and the land is not resold before the end of the period:
   a. Ninety percent of the gain will be excluded from consolidated net income.
   b. Consolidated net income will be increased by the full amount of the gain.
   c. A proportionate share of the unrealized gain will be excluded from income assigned to noncontrolling interest.
   d. The full amount of the unrealized gain will be excluded from income assigned to noncontrolling interest.
3. Minor Company sold land to Major Company on November 15, 20X4, and recorded a gain of $30,000 on the sale. Major owns 80 percent of Minor's common shares. Which of the following statements is correct?
   a. A proportionate share of the $30,000 must be treated as a reduction of income assigned to the noncontrolling interest in the consolidated income statement unless the land is resold to a nonaffiliate in 20X4.
   b. The $30,000 will not be treated as an adjustment in computing income assigned to the noncontrolling interest in the consolidated income statement in 20X4 unless the land is resold to a nonaffiliate in 20X4.
   c. In computing consolidated net income, it does not matter whether the land is or is not resold to a nonaffiliate before the end of the period; the $30,000 will not affect the computation of consolidated net income in 20X4 because the profits are on the subsidiary's books.
   d. Minor's trial balance as of December 31, 20X4, should be adjusted to remove the $30,000 gain because the gain is not yet realized.
4. Lewis Company owns 80 percent of Tomassini Corporation's stock. You are told that Tomassini has sold equipment to Lewis and that the following consolidation entries are needed to prepare consolidated statements for 20X9:

Equipment	20,000	
Gain on Sale of Equipment	40,000	
Accumulated Depreciation		60,000

Accumulated Depreciation	5,000	
Depreciation Expense		5,000

Which of the following is incorrect?

a. The parent paid $40,000 in excess of the subsidiary's carrying amount to acquire the asset.

b. From a consolidated viewpoint, depreciation expense as Lewis recorded it is overstated.

c. The asset transfer occurred in 20X9 before the end of the year.

d. Consolidated net income will be reduced by $40,000 when these consolidation entries are made.

LO 7-1, 7-2 **P7-29 Intercompany Services Provided to Subsidiary**

During 20X4, Plate Company paid its employees $80,000 for work done in helping its wholly owned subsidiary build a new office building that was completed on December 31, 20X4. Plate recorded the $110,000 payment from the subsidiary for the work done as service revenue. The subsidiary included the payment in the cost of the building and is depreciating the building over 25 years with no assumed residual value. Plate uses the fully adjusted equity method.

Required

Present the consolidation entries needed at December 31, 20X4 and 20X5, to prepare Plate's consolidated financial statements.

LO 7-4, 7-5 **P7-30 Consolidated Net Income with Intercompany Transfers**

Advanced StudyGuide .com

In its 20X7 consolidated income statement, Bower Development Company reported consolidated net income of $961,000 and $39,000 of income assigned to the 30 percent noncontrolling interest in its only subsidiary, Subsidence Mining Inc. During the year, Subsidence had sold a previously mined parcel of land to Bower for a new housing development; the sales price to Bower was $500,000, and the land had a carrying amount at the time of sale of $560,000. At the beginning of the previous year, Bower had sold excavation and grading equipment to Subsidence for $240,000; the equipment had a remaining life of six years as of the date of sale and a book value of $210,000. The equipment originally had cost $350,000 when Bower purchased it on January 2, 20X2. The equipment never was expected to have any salvage value.

Bower had acquired 70 percent of the voting shares of Subsidence eight years earlier when the fair value of its net assets was $200,000 higher than book value, and the fair value of the noncontrolling interest was $60,000 more than a proportionate share of the book value of Subsidence's net assets. All the excess over the book value was attributable to intangible assets with a remaining life of 10 years from the date of combination. Both parent and subsidiary use straight-line amortization and depreciation. Assume Bower uses the fully adjusted equity method.

Required

a. Present the journal entry made by Bower to record the sale of equipment in 20X6 to Subsidence.

b. Present all consolidation entries related to the intercompany transfers of land and equipment that should appear in the consolidation worksheet used to prepare a complete set of consolidated financial statements for 20X7.

c. Compute Subsidence's 20X7 reported net income.

d. Compute Bower's 20X7 income from its own separate operations, excluding any investment income from its investment in Subsidence Mining.

LO 7-4, 7-5 **P7-31 Preparation of Consolidated Balance Sheet**

Lofton Company owns 60 percent of Temple Corporation's voting shares, purchased on May 17, 20X1, at book value. At that date, the fair value of the noncontrolling interest was equal to 40 percent of the book value of Temple Corporation. The companies' permanent accounts on December 31, 20X6, contained the following balances:

	Lofton Company	Temple Corporation
Cash and Receivables	$101,000	$ 20,000
Inventory	80,000	40,000
Land	150,000	90,000
Buildings & Equipment	400,000	300,000
Investment in Temple Corporation Stock	141,000	
	872,000	$450,000
Accumulated Depreciation	$135,000	$ 85,000
Accounts Payable	90,000	25,000
Notes Payable	200,000	90,000
Common Stock	100,000	200,000
Retained Earnings	347,000	50,000
	$872,000	$450,000

On January 1, 20X2, Lofton paid $100,000 for equipment with a 10-year expected total economic life. The equipment was depreciated on a straight-line basis with no residual value. Temple purchased the equipment from Lofton on December 31, 20X4, for $91,000. Assume Temple did not change the remaining estimated useful life of the equipment.

Temple sold land it had purchased for $30,000 on February 23, 20X4, to Lofton for $20,000 on October 14, 20X5. Assume Lofton uses the fully adjusted equity method.

Required

a. Prepare a consolidated balance sheet worksheet in good form as of December 31, 20X6.

b. Prepare a consolidated balance sheet as of December 31, 20X6.

LO 7-4, 7-5 **P7-32** **Consolidation Worksheet in Year of Intercompany Transfer**

Prime Company holds 80 percent of Lane Company's stock, acquired on January 1, 20X2, for $160,000. On the acquisition date, the fair value of the noncontrolling interest was $40,000. Lane reported retained earnings of $50,000 and had $100,000 of common stock outstanding. Prime uses the fully adjusted equity method in accounting for its investment in Lane.

Trial balance data for the two companies on December 31, 20X6, are as follows:

Advanced StudyGuide .com

	Prime Company		Lane Company	
Item	**Debit**	**Credit**	**Debit**	**Credit**
Cash & Accounts Receivable	$ 113,000		$ 35,000	
Inventory	260,000		90,000	
Land	80,000		80,000	
Buildings & Equipment	500,000		150,000	
Investment in Lane Company Stock	191,600			
Cost of Goods Sold	140,000		60,000	
Depreciation & Amortization	25,000		15,000	
Other Expenses	15,000		5,000	
Dividends Declared	30,000		5,000	
Accumulated Depreciation		$ 205,000		$ 45,000
Accounts Payable		60,000		20,000
Bonds Payable		200,000		50,000
Common Stock		300,000		100,000
Retained Earnings		322,000		95,000
Sales		240,000		130,000
Gain on Sale of Equipment		20,000		
Income from Subsidiary		7,600		
Total	$1,354,600	$1,354,600	$440,000	$440,000

Additional Information

1. At the date of combination, the book values and fair values of all separately identifiable assets and liabilities of Lane were the same. At December 31, 20X6, the management of Prime reviewed the amount attributed to goodwill as a result of its purchase of Lane stock and concluded an impairment loss of $18,000 should be recognized in 20X6 and shared proportionately between the controlling and noncontrolling shareholders.
2. On January 1, 20X5, Lane sold land that had cost $8,000 to Prime for $18,000.
3. On January 1, 20X6, Prime sold to Lane equipment that it had purchased for $75,000 on January 1, 20X1. The equipment has a total economic life of 15 years and was sold to Lane for $70,000. Both companies use straight-line depreciation.
4. There was $7,000 of intercompany receivables and payables on December 31, 20X6.

Required

a. Give all consolidation entries needed to prepare a consolidation worksheet for 20X6.

b. Prepare a three-part worksheet for 20X6 in good form.

c. Prepare a consolidated balance sheet, income statement, and retained earnings statement for 20X6.

LO 7-4, 7-5 **P7-33 Consolidation Worksheet in Year Following Intercompany Transfer**

Prime Company holds 80 percent of Lane Company's stock, acquired on January 1, 20X2, for $160,000. On the date of acquisition, Lane reported retained earnings of $50,000 and $100,000 of common stock outstanding, and the fair value of the noncontrolling interest was $40,000. Prime uses the fully adjusted equity method in accounting for its investment in Lane.

Trial balance data for the two companies on December 31, 20X7, are as follows:

	Prime Company		Lane Company	
Item	**Debit**	**Credit**	**Debit**	**Credit**
Cash & Accounts Receivable	$ 151,000		$ 55,000	
Inventory	240,000		100,000	
Land	100,000		80,000	
Buildings & Equipment	500,000		150,000	
Investment in Lane Company Stock	201,600			
Cost of Goods Sold	160,000		80,000	
Depreciation & Amortization	25,000		15,000	
Other Expenses	20,000		10,000	
Dividends Declared	60,000		35,000	
Accumulated Depreciation		$ 230,000		$ 60,000
Accounts Payable		60,000		25,000
Bonds Payable		200,000		50,000
Common Stock		300,000		100,000
Retained Earnings		379,600		140,000
Sales		250,000		150,000
Income from Subsidiary		38,000		
Total	$1,457,600	$1,457,600	$525,000	$525,000

Additional Information

1. At the date of combination, the book values and fair values of Lane's separately identifiable assets and liabilities were equal. The full amount of the increased value of the entity was attributed to goodwill. At December 31, 20X6, the management of Prime reviewed the amount attributed to goodwill as a result of its purchase of Lane stock and recognized an impairment loss of $18,000. No further impairment occurred in 20X7.
2. On January 1, 20X5, Lane sold land for $18,000 that had cost $8,000 to Prime.
3. On January 1, 20X6, Prime sold to Lane equipment that it had purchased for $75,000 on January 1, 20X1. The equipment has a total 15-year economic life and was sold to Lane for $70,000. Both companies use straight-line depreciation.
4. Intercompany receivables and payables total $4,000 on December 31, 20X7.

Required

a. Prepare a reconciliation between the balance in Prime's Investment in Lane Company Stock account reported on December 31, 20X7, and Lane's book value.

b. Prepare all worksheet consolidation entries needed as of December 31, 20X7, and complete a three-part consolidation worksheet for 20X7.

LO 7-4, 7-5

P7-34 Intercompany Sales in Prior Years

On January 1, 20X5, Pond Corporation acquired 80 percent of Skate Company's stock by issuing common stock with a fair value of $180,000. At that date, Skate reported net assets of $150,000. The fair value of the noncontrolling interest was $45,000. Assume Pond uses the fully adjusted equity method. The balance sheets for Pond and Skate at January 1, 20X8, and December 31, 20X8, and income statements for 20X8 were reported as follows:

20X8 Balance Sheet Data

	Pond Corporation		Skate Company	
	January 1	**December 31**	**January 1**	**December 31**
Cash	$ 40,400	$ 68,400	$ 10,000	$ 47,000
Accounts Receivable	120,000	130,000	60,000	65,000
Interest & Other Receivables	40,000	45,000	8,000	10,000
Inventory	100,000	140,000	50,000	50,000
Land	50,000	50,000	22,000	22,000
Buildings & Equipment	400,000	400,000	240,000	240,000
Accumulated Depreciation	(150,000)	(185,000)	(70,000)	(94,000)
Investment in Skate Company Stock	185,600	200,100		
Investment in Tin Co. Bonds	135,000	134,000		
Total Assets	921,000	982,500	$320,000	$340,000
Accounts Payable	$ 60,000	$ 65,000	$ 16,500	$ 11,000
Interest & Other Payables	40,000	45,000	7,000	12,000
Bonds Payable	300,000	300,000	100,000	100,000
Bond Discount			(3,500)	(3,000)
Common Stock	150,000	150,000	30,000	30,000
Additional Paid-in Capital	155,000	155,000	20,000	20,000
Retained Earnings	216,000	267,500	150,000	170,000
Total Liabilities & Equities	921,000	982,500	$320,000	$340,000

20X8 Income Statement Data

	Pond Corporation		Skate Company	
Sales		$450,000		$250,000
Income from Subsidiary		22,500		
Interest Income		14,900		
Total Revenue		487,400		$250,000
Cost of Goods Sold	$285,000		$136,000	
Other Operating Expenses	50,000		40,000	
Depreciation Expense	35,000		24,000	
Interest Expense	24,000		10,500	
Miscellaneous Expenses	11,900	(405,900)	9,500	(220,000)
Net Income		$ 81,500		$ 30,000

Additional Information

1. In 20X2, Skate developed a patent for a high-speed drill bit that Pond planned to market extensively. In accordance with generally accepted accounting standards, Skate charges all research and development costs to expense in the year the expenses are incurred. At January 1, 20X5, the market value of the patent rights was estimated to be $50,000. Pond believes the patent will

be of value for the next 20 years. The remainder of the differential is assigned to buildings and equipment, which also had a 20-year estimated economic life at January 1, 20X5. All of Skate's other assets and liabilities identified by Pond at the date of acquisition had book values and fair values that were relatively equal.

2. On December 31, 20X7, Pond sold a building to Skate for $65,000 that it had purchased for $125,000 and depreciated on a straight-line basis over 25 years. At the time of sale, Pond reported accumulated depreciation of $75,000 and a remaining life of 10 years.
3. On July 1, 20X6, Skate sold land that it had purchased for $22,000 to Pond for $35,000. Pond is planning to build a new warehouse on the property prior to the end of 20X9.
4. Both Pond and Skate paid dividends in 20X8.

Required

a. Give all consolidation entries required to prepare a three-part consolidation working paper at December 31, 20X8.

b. Prepare a three-part worksheet for 20X8 in good form.

LO 7-3, 7-6

P7-35 Intercompany Sale of Land and Depreciable Asset

Topp Corporation acquired 70 percent of Morris Company's voting common stock on January 1, 20X3, for $158,900. Morris reported common stock outstanding of $100,000 and retained earnings of $85,000. The fair value of the noncontrolling interest was $68,100 at the date of acquisition. Buildings and equipment held by Morris had a fair value $25,000 higher than book value. The remainder of the differential was assigned to a copyright held by Morris. Buildings and equipment had a 10-year remaining life and the copyright had a 5-year life at the date of acquisition.

Trial balances for Topp and Morris on December 31, 20X5, are as follows:

	Topp Corporation		Morris Company	
	Debit	Credit	Debit	Credit
Cash	$ 15,850		$ 58,000	
Accounts Receivable	65,000		70,000	
Interest & Other Receivables	30,000		10,000	
Inventory	150,000		180,000	
Land	80,000		60,000	
Buildings & Equipment	315,000		240,000	
Bond Discount			15,000	
Investment in Morris Company Stock	157,630			
Cost of Goods Sold	375,000		110,000	
Depreciation Expense	25,000		10,000	
Interest Expense	24,000		33,000	
Other Expense	28,000		17,000	
Dividends Declared	30,000		5,000	
Accumulated Depreciation—Buildings & Equipment		$ 120,000		$ 60,000
Accounts Payable		61,000		28,000
Other Payables		30,000		20,000
Bonds Payable		250,000		300,000
Common Stock		150,000		100,000
Additional Paid-in Capital		30,000		
Retained Earnings		165,240		100,000
Sales		450,000		190,400
Other Income		28,250		
Gain on Sale of Equipment				9,600
Income from Subsidiary		10,990		
Total	$1,295,480	$1,295,480	$808,000	$808,000

Topp sold land it had purchased for $21,000 to Morris on September 20, 20X4, for $32,000. Morris plans to use the land for future plant expansion. On January 1, 20X5, Morris sold equipment to Topp for $91,600. Morris purchased the equipment on January 1, 20X3, for $100,000 and depreciated it on a 10-year basis, including an estimated residual value of $10,000. The residual value and estimated economic life of the equipment remained unchanged as a result of the transfer and both companies use straight-line depreciation. Assume Topp uses the fully adjusted equity method.

Required

a. Compute the amount of income assigned to the noncontrolling interest in the consolidated income statement for 20X5.

b. Prepare a reconciliation between the balance in the Investment in Morris Company Stock account reported by Topp at December 31, 20X5, and the underlying book value of net assets reported by Morris at that date.

c. Give all consolidation entries needed to prepare a full set of consolidated financial statements at December 31, 20X5, for Topp and Morris.

d. Prepare a three-part worksheet for 20X5 in good form.

LO 7-3, 7-6

P7-36 Incomplete Data

Partial trial balance data for Mound Corporation, Shadow Company, and the consolidated entity at December 31, 20X7, are as follows:

Item	Mound Corporation	Shadow Company	Consolidated Entity
Cash	$ 65,300	$ 25,000	$ 90,300
Accounts Receivable	(d)	35,000	126,000
Inventory	160,000	75,000	235,000
Buildings & Equipment	345,000	150,000	(i)
Land	70,000	90,000	153,000
Investment in Shadow Company Stock	(f)		
Cost of Goods Sold	230,000	195,000	425,000
Depreciation Expense	45,000	10,000	52,000
Amortization Expense			(e)
Miscellaneous Expense	18,000	15,000	33,000
Dividends Declared	25,000	20,000	25,000
Income to Noncontrolling Interest			(l)
Copyrights			9,000
Total Debits	$1,180,900	$615,000	$1,674,200
Accumulated Depreciation	$ 180,000	$ 80,000	$ (j)
Accounts Payable	25,000	85,000	101,000
Common Stock	100,000	50,000	(a)
Additional Paid-in Capital	(b)	70,000	140,000
Retained Earnings	375,800	80,000	(k)
Income from Subsidiary	10,100		
Sales	343,000	(c)	593,000
Gain on Sale of Land	(g)		(h)
Noncontrolling Interest			86,400
Total Credits	$1,180,900	$615,000	$1,674,200

Additional Information

1. Mound Corporation acquired 60 percent ownership of Shadow Company on January 1, 20X4, for $106,200. Shadow reported net assets of $150,000 at that date, and the fair value of the noncontrolling interest was estimated to be $70,800. The full amount of the differential at acquisition is assigned to copyrights that are being amortized over a six-year life.
2. On August 13, 20X7, Mound sold land to Shadow for $28,000. Mound also has accounts receivable from Shadow on services performed prior to the end of 20X7.
3. Shadow sold equipment it had purchased for $60,000 on January 1, 20X4, to Mound on for $45,000 January 1, 20X6. The equipment is depreciated on a straight-line basis and had a total expected useful life of five years when Shadow purchased it. No change in life expectancy resulted from the intercompany transfer. Assume Mound uses the fully adjusted equity method.
4. Assume Mound Corp. does not use the optional accumulation depreciation consolidation entry.

Required

Compute the dollar amount for each of the balances identified by a letter.

LO 7-6

P7-37 Intercompany Sale of Equipment at a Loss in Prior Period

Block Corporation was created on January 1, 20X0, to develop computer software. On January 1, 20X5, Foster Company acquired 90 percent of Block's common stock at its underlying book value. At that date, the fair value of the noncontrolling interest was equal to 10 percent of the book value of Block Corporation. Trial balances for Foster and Block on December 31, 20X9, follow:

	Foster Company		Block Corporation	
	Debit	Credit	Debit	Credit
Cash	$ 82,000		$ 32,400	
Accounts Receivable	80,000		90,000	
Other Receivables	40,000		10,000	
Inventory	200,000		130,000	
Land	80,000		60,000	
Buildings & Equipment	500,000		250,000	
Investment in Block Corporation Stock	229,500			
Cost of Goods Sold	500,000		250,000	
Depreciation Expense	45,000		15,000	
Other Expense	95,000		75,000	
Dividends Declared	40,000		20,000	
Accumulated Depreciation		$ 155,000		$ 75,000
Accounts Payable		63,000		35,000
Other Payables		95,000		20,000
Bonds Payable		250,000		200,000
Bond Premium				2,400
Common Stock		210,000		50,000
Additional Paid-in Capital		110,000		
Retained Earnings		251,200		150,000
Sales		680,000		385,000
Other Income		26,000		15,000
Income from Subsidiary		51,300		
Total	$1,891,500	$1,891,500	$932,400	$932,400

On January 1, 20X7, Block sold equipment to Foster for $48,000. Block had purchased the equipment for $90,000 on January 1, 20X5, and was depreciating it on a straight-line basis with a 10-year expected life and no anticipated scrap value. The equipment's total expected life is unchanged as a result of the intercompany sale. Assume Foster uses the fully adjusted equity method.

Required

a. Give all consolidation entries required to prepare a three-part consolidated working paper at December 31, 20X9.

b. Prepare a three-part worksheet for 20X9 in good form.

LO 7-1, 7-2, 7-3, 7-6

P7-38 Comprehensive Problem: Intercompany Transfers

Rossman Corporation holds 75 percent of the common stock of Schmid Distributors Inc., purchased on December 31, 20X1, for $2,340,000. At the date of acquisition, Schmid reported common stock with a par value of $1,000,000, additional paid-in capital of $1,350,000, and retained earnings of $620,000. The fair value of the noncontrolling interest at acquisition was $780,000. The differential at acquisition was attributable to the following items:

Inventory (sold in 20X2)	$ 30,000
Land	56,000
Goodwill	64,000
Total Differential	$150,000

During 20X2, Rossman sold a plot of land that it had purchased several years before to Schmid at a gain of $23,000; Schmid continues to hold the land. In 20X6, Rossman and Schmid entered into a five-year contract under which Rossman provides management consulting services to Schmid on a continuing basis; Schmid pays Rossman a fixed fee of $80,000 per year for these services. At December 31, 20X8, Schmid owed Rossman $20,000 as the final 20X8 quarterly payment under the contract.

On January 2, 20X8, Rossman paid $250,000 to Schmid to purchase equipment that Schmid was then carrying at $290,000. Schmid had purchased that equipment on December 27, 20X2, for $435,000. The equipment is expected to have a total 15-year life and no salvage value. The amount of the differential assigned to goodwill has not been impaired.

At December 31, 20X8, trial balances for Rossman and Schmid appeared as follows:

	Rossman Corporation		Schmid Distributors Inc.	
Item	**Debit**	**Credit**	**Debit**	**Credit**
Cash	$ 50,700		$ 38,000	
Current Receivables	101,800		89,400	
Inventory	286,000		218,900	
Investment in Schmid Stock	2,974,000			
Land	400,000		1,200,000	
Buildings & Equipment	2,400,000		2,990,000	
Cost of Goods Sold	2,193,000		525,000	
Depreciation & Amortization	202,000		88,000	
Other Expenses	1,381,000		227,000	
Dividends Declared	50,000		20,000	
Accumulated Depreciation		$ 1,105,000		$ 420,000
Current Payables		86,200		76,300
Bonds Payable		1,000,000		200,000
Common Stock		100,000		1,000,000
Additional Paid-in Capital		1,272,000		1,350,000
Retained Earnings, January 1		1,474,800		1,400,000
Sales		4,801,000		985,000
Other Income or Loss		90,000	35,000	
Income from Schmid		109,500		
Total	$10,038,500	$10,038,500	$5,431,300	$5,431,300

As of December 31, 20X8, Schmid had declared but not yet paid its fourth-quarter dividend of $5,000. Both companies use straight-line depreciation and amortization. Rossman uses the fully adjusted equity method to account for its investment in Schmid.

Required

a. Compute the amount of the differential as of January 1, 20X8.

b. Verify the balance in Rossman's Investment in Schmid Stock account as of December 31, 20X8.

c. Present all consolidation entries that would appear in a three-part consolidation worksheet as of December 31, 20X8.

d. Prepare and complete a three-part worksheet for the preparation of consolidated financial statements for 20X8.

LO 7-4, 7-5 P7-39A Modified Equity Method Computation of Retained Earnings Following Multiple Transfers

Great Company acquired 80 percent of Meager Corporation's common stock on January 1, 20X4, for $280,000. The fair value of the noncontrolling interest was $70,000 at the date of acquisition. Great's corporate controller has lost the consolidation files for the past three years and has asked you to compute the proper retained earnings balances for the consolidated entity at January 1, 20X8, and December 31, 20X8. The controller has been able to determine the following:

1. The book value of Meager's net assets at January 1, 20X4, was $290,000, and the fair value of its net assets was $325,000. This difference was due to an increase in the value of equipment. All depreciable assets had a remaining life of 10 years at the date of combination. At December 31, 20X8, Great's management reviewed the amount attributed to goodwill as a result of its purchase

of Meager common stock and concluded that an impairment loss of $17,500 should be recognized in 20X8 and shared proportionately between the controlling and noncontrolling shareholders.

2. Great uses the modified equity method in accounting for its investment in Meager.
3. Meager has reported net income of $30,000 and paid dividends of $20,000 each year since Great purchased its ownership.
4. Great reported retained earnings of $450,000 in its December 31, 20X7, balance sheet. For 20X8, Great reported operating income of $65,000 and paid dividends of $45,000.
5. Meager sold land costing $40,000 to Great for $56,000 on December 31, 20X7.
6. On January 1, 20X6, Great sold depreciable assets with a remaining useful life of 10 years to Meager and recorded a $22,000 gain on the sale.

Required

Compute the appropriate amounts to be reported as consolidated retained earnings at January 1, 20X8, and December 31, 20X8.

LO 7-1, 7-3, 7-6

P7-40A Consolidation Worksheet with Intercompany Transfers (Modified Equity Method)

Mist Company acquired 65 percent of Blank Corporation's voting common stock on June 20, 20X2, at underlying book value. At that date, the fair value of the noncontrolling interest was equal to 35 percent of the book value of Blank Corporation. The balance sheets and income statements for the companies at December 31, 20X4, are as follows:

MIST COMPANY AND BLANK CORPORATION
Balance Sheets
December 31, 20X4

Item	Mist Company	Blank Corp.
Cash	$ 32,500	$ 22,000
Accounts Receivable	62,000	37,000
Inventory	95,000	71,000
Land	40,000	15,000
Buildings & Equipment (net)	200,000	125,000
Investment in Blank Corp. Stock	110,500	
Total Assets	$540,000	$270,000
Accounts Payable	$ 35,000	$ 20,000
Bonds Payable	180,000	80,000
Common Stock, $5 par value	100,000	60,000
Retained Earnings	225,000	110,000
Total Liabilities & Stockholders' Equity	$540,000	$270,000

MIST COMPANY AND BLANK CORPORATION
Combined Income and Retained Earnings Statements
Year Ended December 31, 20X4

Item	Mist Company		Blank Corp.	
Sales and Service Revenue		$286,500		$128,500
Gain on Sale of Land		4,000		
Gain on Sale of Building				13,200
Income from Subsidiary		19,500		
		$310,000		$141,700
Cost of Goods & Services Sold	$160,000		$75,000	
Depreciation Expense	22,000		19,000	
Other Expenses	76,000	(258,000)	17,700	(111,700)
Net Income		$ 52,000		$ 30,000
Dividends Paid		(25,000)		(5,000)
Change in Retained Earnings		$ 27,000		$ 25,000

Additional Information

1. Mist uses the modified equity method in accounting for its investment in Blank.
2. During 20X4, Mist charged Blank $24,000 for consulting services provided to Blank during the year. The services cost Mist $17,000.
3. On January 1, 20X4, Blank sold Mist a building for $13,200 above its carrying value on Blank's books. The building had a 12-year remaining economic life at the time of transfer.
4. On June 14, 20X4, Mist sold land it had purchased for $3,000 to Blank for $7,000. Blank continued to hold the land at December 31, 20X4.

Required

a. Give all consolidation entries needed to prepare a full set of consolidated financial statements for 20X4.

b. Prepare a consolidation worksheet for 20X4.

c. Prepare the 20X4 consolidated balance sheet, income statement, and retained earnings statement.

LO 7-6

P7-41A Modified Equity Method

Using the data in P7-33, on December 31, 20X7, Prime Company recorded the following entry on its books to adjust its investment in Lane Company from the fully adjusted equity method to the modified equity method:

Income from Lane Company	2,000	
Investment in Lane Company Stock	38,400	
Retained Earnings		40,400

Required

a. Adjust the data reported by Prime in the trial balance in Problem P7-33 for the effects of the adjusting entry presented above.

b. Prepare the journal entries that would have been recorded on Prime's books during 20X7 if it had always used the modified equity method.

c. Prepare all consolidation entries needed to complete a consolidation worksheet as of December 31, 20X7, assuming Prime has used the modified equity method.

d. Complete a three-part consolidation worksheet as of December 31, 20X7.

LO 7-6

P7-42A Cost Method

The trial balance data presented in P7-33 can be converted to reflect use of the cost method by inserting the following amounts in place of those presented for Prime Company:

Investment in Lane Company Stock	$160,000
Beginning Retained Earnings	348,000
Income from Subsidiary	0
Dividend Income	28,000

Required

a. Prepare the journal entries that would have been recorded on Prime's books during 20X7 under the cost method.

b. Prepare all consolidation entries needed to complete a consolidation worksheet as of December 31, 20X7, assuming Prime has used the cost method.

c. Complete a three-part consolidation worksheet as of December 31, 20X7.

8 Intercompany Indebtedness

Multicorporate Entities

Business Combinations

Consolidation Concepts and Procedures

Intercompany Transfers

Additional Consolidation Issues

Multinational Entities

Reporting Requirements

Partnerships

Governmental and Not-for-Profit Entities

Corporations in Financial Difficulty

FORD'S DEBT TRANSFERS

An advantage when one corporation controls another is that the controlling entity's management has the ability to transfer resources between the two legal entities as needed. For example, the controlling corporation may make loans to or borrow from the other entity when cash is short. The borrower often benefits from lower borrowing rates, less-restrictive credit terms, and the informality and lower debt issue costs of intercompany borrowing relative to public debt offerings. The lending affiliate may benefit by being able to invest excess funds in a company about which it has considerable knowledge, perhaps allowing it to earn a given return on the funds invested while incurring less risk than if it invested in unrelated companies. Also, the combined entity may find it advantageous for the parent company or another affiliate to borrow funds for the entire enterprise rather than having each affiliate going directly to the capital markets. Ford exercised this option in 2009.

Between January 2003 and January 2008, the U.S. economy underwent one of the biggest booms in its history. The NASDAQ, S&P 500, and Dow Jones Industrial Average all increased by at least 60 percent, with the NASDAQ jumping almost 100 percent. However, such unprecedented growth could not continue indefinitely. Beginning in early 2008 and continuing through 2009, the economy made a complete turnaround. The housing bubble burst, Lehman Brothers closed its doors, and the great behemoth, General Motors, was forced into bankruptcy. However, during this time of economic turmoil, Ford was able to wisely use intercompany debt transactions to its advantage.

During the first quarter of 2009, Ford Motor Credit (a wholly owned subsidiary of Ford Motor Company) paid $1.1 billion to purchase a portion of Ford Motor Company's senior secured term loan debt. Ford Motor Credit then distributed the debt to its immediate parent, Ford Holdings LLC, which in turn forgave the debt. By carefully managing its business, in part through a savvy application of debt transfers, Ford was able to avoid much of the turmoil many other companies experienced during this turbulent period. This chapter introduces accounting for debt transfers.

LEARNING OBJECTIVES

When you finish studying this chapter, you should be able to:

LO 8-1 Understand and explain concepts associated with intercompany debt transfers.

LO 8-2 Prepare journal entries and consolidation entries related to direct intercompany debt transfers.

LO 8-3 Prepare journal entries and consolidation entries related to an affiliate's debt purchased from a nonaffiliate at an amount less than book value.

LO 8-4 Prepare journal entries and consolidation entries related to an affiliate's debt purchased from a nonaffiliate at an amount more than book value.

CONSOLIDATION OVERVIEW

LO 8-1

Understand and explain concepts associated with intercompany debt transfers.

Figure 8–1 illustrates two types of intercompany debt transfers. A ***direct intercompany debt transfer*** involves a loan from one affiliate to another without the participation of an unrelated party, as in Figure 8–1(a). Examples include a trade receivable/payable arising from an intercompany sale of inventory on credit and the issuance of a note payable by one affiliate to another in exchange for operating funds.

An ***indirect intercompany debt transfer*** involves the issuance of debt to an unrelated party and the subsequent purchase of the debt instrument by an affiliate of the issuer. For example, in Figure 8–1(b), Special Foods borrows funds by issuing a debt instrument, such as a note or a bond, to a nonaffiliated investor. Special Foods' parent, Peerless Products, subsequently purchased the debt instrument from the nonaffiliated investor. Thus, Peerless Products acquires the debt of Special Foods indirectly through the nonaffiliated investor.

All account balances arising from intercorporate financing arrangements must be eliminated when consolidated statements are prepared. The consolidated financial statements portray the consolidated entity as a single company. Therefore, in Figure 8–1, transactions that do not cross the boundary of the consolidated entity are not reported in the consolidated financial statements. Although in illustration (a) Special Foods borrows funds from Peerless, the consolidated entity as a whole does not borrow, and the intercompany loan is not reflected in the consolidated financial statements.

In illustration (b), Special Foods borrows funds from the nonaffiliated investor. Because this transaction is with an unrelated party and crosses the boundary of the consolidated entity (denoted by the dashed line), it is reflected in the consolidated financial statements.

FIGURE 8–1 Intercompany Debt Transactions

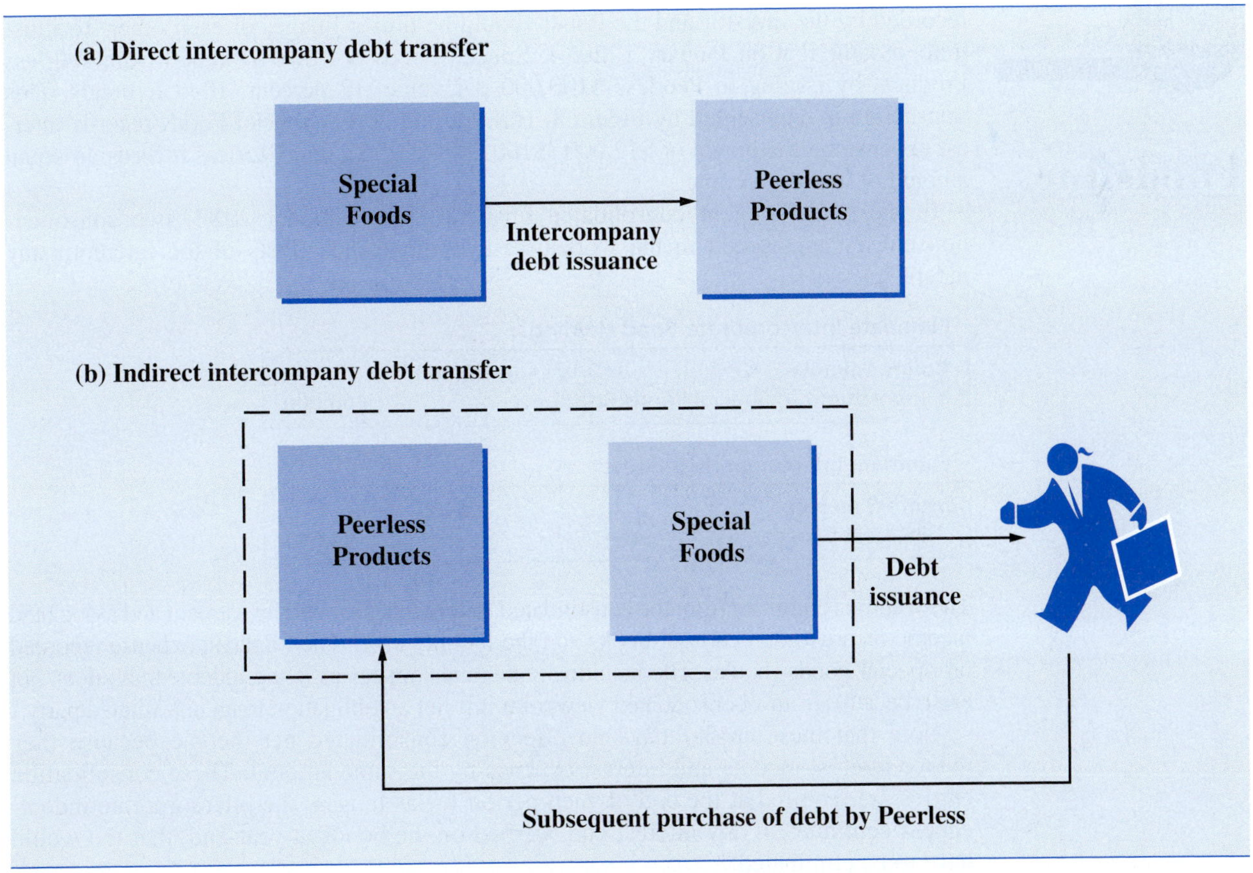

In effect, the consolidated entity is borrowing from an outside party, and the liability is included in the consolidated balance sheet. When Peerless purchases Special Foods' debt instrument from the nonaffiliated investor, this transaction also crosses the boundary of the consolidated entity. In effect, the consolidated entity repurchases its debt, which it reports as a debt retirement. As with most retirements of debt before maturity, a purchase of an affiliate's bonds usually gives rise to a gain or loss on the retirement; the gain or loss is reported in the consolidated income statement even though it does not appear in the separate income statement of either affiliate.

This chapter discusses the procedures used to prepare consolidated financial statements when intercorporate indebtedness arises from either direct or indirect debt transfers. Although the discussion focuses on bonds, the same concepts and procedures also apply to notes and other types of intercorporate indebtedness.

BOND SALE DIRECTLY TO AN AFFILIATE

LO 8-2

Prepare journal entries and consolidation entries related to direct intercompany debt transfers.

When one company sells bonds directly to an affiliate, all effects of the intercompany indebtedness must be eliminated in preparing consolidated financial statements. A company cannot report an investment in its own bonds or a bond liability to itself. Thus, when the consolidated entity is viewed as a single company, all amounts associated with the intercorporate indebtedness must be eliminated, including the investment in bonds, the bonds payable, any unamortized discount or premium on the bonds, the interest income and expense on the bonds, and any accrued interest receivable and payable.

Transfer at Par Value

When a note or bond payable is sold directly to an affiliate at par value, the entries recorded by the investor and the issuer should be mirror images of each other. To illustrate, assume that on January 1, 20X1, Special Foods borrows \$100,000 from Peerless Products by issuing to Peerless \$100,000 par value, 12 percent, 10-year bonds. This transaction is represented by Figure 8–1(a). During 20X1, Special Foods records interest expense on the bonds of \$12,000 (\$100,000 × 0.12), and Peerless records an equal amount of interest income.

In the preparation of consolidated financial statements for 20X1, two consolidation entries are needed in the worksheet to remove the effects of the intercompany indebtedness:

Eliminate Intercorporate Bond Holdings:

Bonds Payable	100,000	
Investment in Special Foods Bonds		100,000

Eliminate Intercompany Interest:

Interest Income	12,000	
Interest Expense		12,000

These entries eliminate from the consolidated statements the bond investment and associated income recorded on Peerless' books and the liability and related interest expense recorded on Special Foods' books. The resulting statements appear as if the indebtedness does not exist, because from a consolidated viewpoint it is not an obligation to an unaffiliated party.

Note that these entries have no effect on consolidated net income because they reduce interest income and interest expense by the same amount. These consolidation entries are required at the end of each period for as long as the intercorporate indebtedness continues. If any interest had accrued on the bonds at year-end, that too would have to be eliminated.

Transfer at a Discount or Premium

When the coupon or nominal interest rate on a bond is different from the yield demanded by those who lend funds, a bond sells at a discount or premium. In these cases, the amount of bond interest income or expense recorded no longer equals the cash interest payments. Instead, interest income and expense amounts are adjusted for the amortization of the discount or premium.

As an illustration of the treatment of intercompany bond transfers at other than par, assume that on January 1, 20X1, Peerless Products purchases $100,000 par value, 12 percent, 10-year bonds from Special Foods when the market interest rate is 13 percent. In order to yield a 13 percent return, Special Foods issues the bonds at a discount for $94,490.75. Interest on the bonds is payable on January 1 and July 1. The interest expense recognized by Special Foods and the interest income recognized by Peerless each period based on effective interest amortization of the discount over the life of the bonds (straight-line amortization is illustrated in Appendix A) can be summarized as follows:

Bond Discount Amortization Table

Payment Number	Period End	Interest Payment (Face × 0.12 × 6/12)	Interest Expense (Carrying Value × 0.13 × 6/12)	Amortization of Discount	Discount	Bonds Payable Face Value	Carrying Value of Bonds
					(5,509.25)	100,000	94,490.75
1	7/1/20X1	6,000	6,141.90	141.90	(5,367.36)	100,000	94,632.64
2	1/1/20X2	6,000	6,151.12	151.12	(5,216.23)	100,000	94,783.77
3	7/1/20X2	6,000	6,160.94	160.94	(5,055.29)	100,000	94,944.71
4	1/1/20X3	6,000	6,171.41	171.41	(4,883.88)	100,000	95,116.12
5	7/1/20X3	6,000	6,182.55	182.55	(4,701.33)	100,000	95,298.67
6	1/1/20X4	6,000	6,194.41	194.41	(4,506.92)	100,000	95,493.08
7	7/1/20X4	6,000	6,207.05	207.05	(4,299.87)	100,000	95,700.13
8	1/1/20X5	6,000	6,220.51	220.51	(4,079.36)	100,000	95,920.64
9	7/1/20X5	6,000	6,234.84	234.84	(3,844.52)	100,000	96,155.48
10	1/1/20X6	6,000	6,250.11	250.11	(3,594.42)	100,000	96,405.58
11	7/1/20X6	6,000	6,266.36	266.36	(3,328.05)	100,000	96,671.95
12	1/1/20X7	6,000	6,283.68	283.68	(3,044.38)	100,000	96,955.62
13	7/1/20X7	6,000	6,302.12	302.12	(2,742.26)	100,000	97,257.74
14	1/1/20X8	6,000	6,321.75	321.75	(2,420.51)	100,000	97,579.49
15	7/1/20X8	6,000	6,342.67	342.67	(2,077.84)	100,000	97,922.16
16	1/1/20X9	6,000	6,364.94	364.94	(1,712.90)	100,000	98,287.10
17	7/1/20X9	6,000	6,388.66	388.66	(1,324.24)	100,000	98,675.76
18	1/1/20Y0	6,000	6,413.92	413.92	(910.31)	100,000	99,089.69
19	7/1/20Y0	6,000	6,440.83	440.83	(469.48)	100,000	99,530.52
20	1/1/20Y1	6,000	6,469.48	469.48	0.00	100,000	100,000.00
		120,000	125,509.25	5,509.25			

Entries by the Debtor

Special Foods records the issuance of the bonds on January 1 at a discount of $5,509. It recognizes interest expense on July 1, when the first semiannual interest payment is made, and on December 31, when interest is accrued for the second half of the year. The amortization of the bond discount causes interest expense to be higher than the cash interest payment and causes the balance of the discount to decrease. Special Foods records the following entries related to the bonds during 20X1:[1]

	January 1, 20X1		
(1)	Cash	94,491	
	Discount on Bonds Payable	5,509	
	Bonds Payable		100,000
	Issue bonds to Peerless Products.		

	July 1, 20X1		
(2)	Interest Expense	6,142	
	Discount on Bonds Payable		142
	Cash		6,000
	Pay semiannual interest.		

	December 31, 20X1		
(3)	Interest Expense	6,151	
	Discount on Bonds Payable		151
	Interest Payable		6,000
	Accrue interest expense at year-end.		

Entries by the Bond Investor

Peerless Products records the purchase of the bonds and the interest income derived from the bonds during 20X1 with the following entries:

	January 1, 20X1		
(4)	Investment in Special Foods Bonds	94,491	
	Cash		94,491
	Purchase bonds from Special Foods.		

	July 1, 20X1		
(5)	Cash	6,000	
	Investment in Special Foods Bonds	142	
	Interest Income		6,142
	Receive interest on bond investment.		

	December 31, 20X1		
(6)	Interest Receivable	6,000	
	Investment in Special Foods Bonds	151	
	Interest Income		6,151
	Accrue interest income at year-end.		

The amortization of the discount by Peerless increases interest income to an amount higher than the cash interest payment and causes the balance of the bond investment account to increase.

Consolidation Entries at Year-End[2]

The December 31, 20X1, bond-related amounts taken from the books of Peerless Products and Special Foods and the appropriate consolidated amounts are as follows:

Advanced StudyGuide .com

Item	Peerless Products	+	Special Foods	=	Unadjusted Totals	≠	Consolidated Amounts
Bonds Payable	0		$(100,000)		$(100,000)		0
Discount on Bonds Payable	0		5,216		5,216		0
Interest Payable	0		(6,000)		(6,000)		0
Investment in Bonds	$ 94,784		0		94,784		0
Interest Receivable	6,000		0		6,000		0
Interest Expense	0		$ 12,293		$ 12,293		0
Interest Income	$(12,293)		0		(12,293)		0

[1] For convenience, we round all journal and worksheet entries to the nearest whole dollar.
[2] To view a video explanation of this topic, visit advancedstudyguide.com.

All account balances relating to the intercorporate bond holdings must be eliminated in the preparation of consolidated financial statements. Toward that end, the consolidation worksheet prepared on December 31, 20X1, includes the following consolidation entries related to the intercompany bond holdings:

Eliminate Intercorporate Bond Holdings:

Bonds Payable	100,000	
Investment in Special Foods Bonds		94,784
Discount on Bonds Payable		5,216

Eliminate Intercompany Interest:

Interest Income	12,293	
Interest Expense		12,293

Eliminate Intercompany Interest Receivable/Payable:

Interest Payable	6,000	
Interest Receivable		6,000

The first entry eliminates the bonds payable and associated discount against the investment in bonds. The book value of the bond liability on Special Foods' books and the investment in bonds on Peerless' books will be the same as long as both companies amortize the discount in the same way.

The second entry eliminates the bond interest income recognized by Peerless during 20X1 against the bond interest expense recognized by Special Foods. Because the interest for the second half of 20X1 was accrued but not paid, an intercompany receivable/payable exists at the end of the year. The third entry eliminates the interest receivable against the interest payable.

Consolidation at the end of 20X2 requires consolidation entries similar to those at the end of 20X1. Under the effective interest method, an increasing portion of the discount is amortized each period. By the end of the second year (i.e., the fourth interest payment), the carrying value of the bond investment on Peerless' books increases to \$95,116 (\$94,491 issue price + discount amortization of \$142 + \$151 + \$161 + 171). Similarly, the bond discount on Special Foods' books decreases to \$4,884, resulting in an effective bond liability of \$95,116. The consolidation entries related to the bonds at the end of 20X2 are as follows:

Eliminate Intercorporate Bond Holdings:

Bonds Payable	100,000	
Investment in Special Foods Bonds		95,116
Discount on Bonds Payable		4,884

Eliminate Intercompany Interest:

Interest Income	12,332	
Interest Expense		12,332

Eliminate Intercompany Interest Receivable/Payable:

Interest Payable	6,000	
Interest Receivable		6,000

BONDS OF AFFILIATE PURCHASED FROM A NONAFFILIATE

A more complex situation occurs when an affiliate of the issuer later acquires bonds that were issued to an unrelated party. From the viewpoint of the consolidated entity, an acquisition of an affiliate's bonds retires the bonds at the time they are purchased. The bonds no longer are held outside the consolidated entity once another company within the consolidated entity purchases them, and they must be treated as if repurchased by the debtor. Acquisition of an affiliate's bonds by another company within the consolidated entity is referred to as ***constructive retirement***. Although the bonds actually are not retired, they are treated as if they were retired in preparing consolidated financial statements.

When a constructive retirement occurs, the consolidated income statement for the period reports a gain or loss on debt retirement based on the difference between the carrying value of the bonds on the books of the debtor and the purchase price paid by the affiliate in acquiring the bonds. Neither the bonds payable nor the purchaser's investment in the bonds is reported in the consolidated balance sheet because the bonds are no longer considered outstanding.

Purchase at Book Value

In the event that a company purchases an affiliate's debt from an unrelated party at a price equal to the liability reported by the debtor, the consolidation entries required in preparing the consolidated financial statements are identical to those used in eliminating a direct intercorporate debt transfer. In this case, the total of the bond liability and the related premium or discount reported by the debtor equal the balance in the investment account shown by the bondholder, and the interest income reported by the bondholder each period equals the interest expense reported by the debtor. All these amounts need to be eliminated to avoid misstating the accounts in the consolidated financial statements.

Purchase at an Amount Less than Book Value

LO 8-3

Prepare journal entries and consolidation entries related to an affiliate's debt purchased from a nonaffiliate at an amount less than book value.

Continuing movement in the level of interest rates and the volatility of other factors influencing the securities markets make it unlikely that a company's bonds will sell after issuance at a price identical to their book value. When the price paid to acquire an affiliate's bonds differs from the liability reported by the debtor, a gain or loss is reported in the consolidated income statement in the period of constructive retirement. In addition, the bond interest income and interest expense reported by the two affiliates subsequent to the purchase must be eliminated in preparing consolidated statements. Interest income reported by the investing affiliate and interest expense reported by the debtor are not equal in this case because of the different bond carrying amounts on the books of the two companies. The difference in the bond carrying amounts is reflected in the amortization of the discount or premium and, in turn, causes interest income and expense to differ.

As an example of consolidation following the purchase of an affiliate's bonds at less than book value, assume that Peerless Products Corporation purchases 80 percent of the common stock of Special Foods Inc. on December 31, 20X0, for its underlying book value of $240,000. At that date, the fair value of the noncontrolling interest is equal to its book value of $60,000. In addition, the following conditions occur:

1. On January 1, 20X1, Special Foods issues 10-year, 12 percent bonds payable with a par value of $100,000; the bonds are issued at a premium, $105,975.19, to yield the current market interest rate of 11 percent. A nonaffiliated investor purchases the bonds from Special Foods.
2. The bonds pay interest on June 30 and December 31.
3. Both Peerless Products and Special Foods amortize bond discounts and premiums using the effective interest method.
4. On December 31, 20X1, Peerless Products purchases the bonds from the nonaffiliated investor for $94,823.04 when the bonds' carrying value on Special Foods' books is $105,623.04, resulting in a gain of $10,800 on the constructive retirement of the bonds. Note that Peerless' purchase price reflects the current market interest rate of 12.992186% when the bonds have 18 payments left to maturity.
5. Special Foods reports net income of $50,152 for 20X1 and $75,192 for 20X2 and declares dividends of $30,000 in 20X1 and $40,000 in 20X2.
6. Peerless earns $140,000 in 20X1 and $160,000 in 20X2 from its own separate operations. Peerless declares dividends of $60,000 in both 20X1 and 20X2.

The bond transactions of Special Foods and Peerless appear as follows:

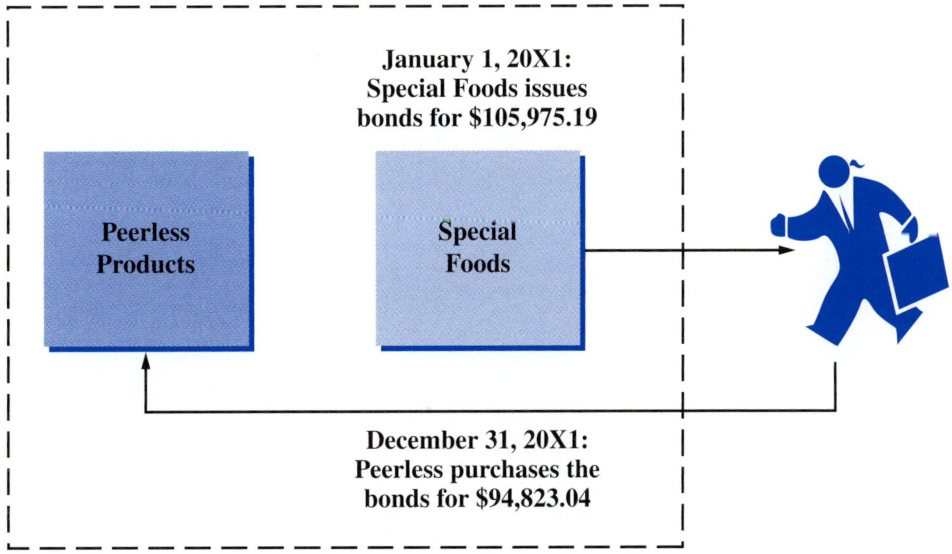

In addition, the interest expense recognized by Special Foods each period based on effective interest amortization of the premium over the life of the bonds can be summarized as follows:

Bond Premium Amortization Table

Payment Number	Period End	Interest Payment (Face × 0.12 × 6/12)	Interest Expense (Carrying Value × 0.11 × 6/12)	Amortization of Premium	Premium	Bonds Payable Face Value	Carrying Value of Bonds
	1/1/20X1				5,975.19	100,000.00	105,975.19
1	6/30/20X1	6,000.00	5,828.64	(171.36)	5,803.83	100,000.00	105,803.83
2	12/31/20X1	6,000.00	5,819.21	(180.79)	5,623.04	100,000.00	105,623.04
3	6/30/20X2	6,000.00	5,809.27	(190.73)	5,432.30	100,000.00	105,432.30
4	12/31/20X2	6,000.00	5,798.78	(201.22)	5,231.08	100,000.00	105,231.08
5	6/30/20X3	6,000.00	5,787.71	(212.29)	5,018.79	100,000.00	105,018.79
6	12/31/20X3	6,000.00	5,776.03	(223.97)	4,794.82	100,000.00	104,794.82
7	6/30/20X4	6,000.00	5,763.72	(236.28)	4,558.54	100,000.00	104,558.54
8	12/31/20X4	6,000.00	5,750.72	(249.28)	4,309.26	100,000.00	104,309.26
9	6/30/20X5	6,000.00	5,737.01	(262.99)	4,046.27	100,000.00	104,046.27
10	12/31/20X5	6,000.00	5,722.54	(277.46)	3,768.81	100,000.00	103,768.81
11	6/30/20X6	6,000.00	5,707.28	(292.72)	3,476.10	100,000.00	103,476.10
12	12/31/20X6	6,000.00	5,691.19	(308.81)	3,167.28	100,000.00	103,167.28
13	6/30/20X7	6,000.00	5,674.20	(325.80)	2,841.48	100,000.00	102,841.48
14	12/31/20X7	6,000.00	5,656.28	(343.72)	2,497.77	100,000.00	102,497.77
15	6/30/20X8	6,000.00	5,637.38	(362.62)	2,135.14	100,000.00	102,135.14
16	12/31/20X8	6,000.00	5,617.43	(382.57)	1,752.58	100,000.00	101,752.58
17	6/30/20X9	6,000.00	5,596.39	(403.61)	1,348.97	100,000.00	101,348.97
18	12/31/20X9	6,000.00	5,574.19	(425.81)	923.16	100,000.00	100,923.16
19	6/30/20Y0	6,000.00	5,550.77	(449.23)	473.93	100,000.00	100,473.93
20	12/31/20Y0	6,000.00	5,526.07	(473.93)	0.00	100,000.00	100,000.00
		120,000.00	114,024.81	(5,975.19)			

Bond Liability Entries—20X1

Special Foods records the following entries related to its bonds during 20X1:

	January 1, 20X1		
(7)	Cash	105,975	
	Bonds Payable		100,000
	Premium on Bonds Payable		5,975
	Sale of bonds to nonaffiliated investor.		

	June 30, 20X1		
(8)	Interest Expense	5,829	
	Premium on Bonds Payable	171	
	Cash		6,000
	Semiannual payment of interest (see amortization table).		

	December 31, 20X1		
(9)	Interest Expense	5,819	
	Premium on Bonds Payable	181	
	Cash		6,000
	Semiannual payment of interest.		

Entry (7) records the issuance of the bonds to a nonaffiliated investor for $105,975. Entries (8) and (9) record the payment of interest and the amortization of the bond premium at each of the two interest payment dates during 20X1. Total interest expense for 20X1 is $11,648 ($5,829 + $5,819), and the book value of the bonds on December 31, 20X1, is $105,623 as shown in the amortization table.

Bond Investment Entries—20X1

Peerless Products records the purchase of Special Foods' bonds from the nonaffiliated party with the following entry:

	December 31, 20X1		
(10)	Investment in Special Foods Bonds	94,823	
	Cash		94,823
	Purchase of Special Foods bonds from a nonaffiliated investor.		

Advanced StudyGuide .com

This entry is the same as if the bonds purchased were those of an unrelated company. Peerless purchases the bonds at the very end of the year after payment of the interest to the nonaffiliated investor; therefore, Peerless earns no interest on the bonds during 20X1, nor is there any interest accrued on the bonds at the date of purchase.

Computation of Gain on Constructive Retirement of Bonds

From a consolidated viewpoint, the purchase of Special Foods' bonds by Peerless is considered a retirement of the bonds by the consolidated entity. Therefore, in the preparation of consolidated financial statements, a gain or loss must be recognized for the difference between the book value of the bonds on the date of repurchase and the amount paid by the consolidated entity in reacquiring the bonds:

Book value of Special Foods' bonds, December 31, 20X1	$105,623
Price paid by Peerless to purchase bonds	(94,823)
Gain on constructive retirement of bonds	$ 10,800

This gain is included in the consolidated income statement as a gain on the retirement of bonds.

Assignment of Gain on Constructive Retirement

Four approaches have been used in practice for assigning the gain or loss on the constructive retirement of an affiliate's bonds to the shareholders of the participating companies.

Depending upon the method selected, the gain or loss may be assigned to any of the following:

1. The affiliate issuing the bonds.
2. The affiliate purchasing the bonds.
3. The parent company.
4. The issuing and purchasing companies based on the difference between the carrying amounts of the bonds on their books at the date of purchase and the par value of the bonds.

No compelling reasons seem to exist for choosing one of these methods over the others, and in practice the choice often is based on expediency and lack of materiality. The FASB's approach is to assign the gain or loss to the issuing company (approach 1). In previous chapters, gains and losses on intercompany transactions were viewed as accruing to the shareholders of the selling affiliate. When this approach is applied in the case of intercorporate debt transactions, gains and losses arising from the intercompany debt transactions are viewed as accruing to the shareholders of the selling or issuing affiliate. In effect, the purchasing affiliate is viewed as acting on behalf of the issuing affiliate by acquiring the bonds.

An important difference exists between the intercompany gains and losses discussed in previous chapters and the gains and losses arising from intercorporate debt transactions. Gains and losses from intercorporate transfers of assets are recognized by the individual affiliates and are eliminated in consolidation. Gains and losses from intercorporate debt transactions are not recognized by the individual affiliates but must be included in consolidation.

When the subsidiary is the issuing affiliate, the gain or loss on constructive retirement of the bonds is viewed as accruing to the subsidiary's shareholders. Thus, the gain or loss is apportioned between the controlling and noncontrolling interests based on the relative ownership interests in the common stock (similar to upstream inventory or asset transfers). If the parent is the issuing affiliate, the entire gain or loss on the constructive retirement accrues to the controlling interest and none is apportioned to the noncontrolling interest (similar to downstream inventory or asset transfers).

As a result of the interest income and expense entries recorded annually by the companies involved, the constructive gain or loss is recognized over the remaining term of the bond issue; accordingly, the total amount of the unrecognized gain or loss decreases each period and is fully amortized at the time the bond matures. Thus, no permanent gain or loss is assigned to the debtor company's shareholders.

Fully Adjusted Equity-Method Entries—20X1

In addition to recording the bond investment with entry (10), Peerless records the following equity-method entries during 20X1 to account for its investment in Special Foods stock:

(11)	Investment in Special Foods Stock	40,122	
	Income from Special Foods		40,122
	Record equity-method income: $50,152 × 0.80.		

(12)	Cash	24,000	
	Investment in Special Foods Stock		24,000
	Record dividends from Special Foods: $30,000 × 0.80.		

The full gain on constructive retirement is included in consolidated net income. That gain is attributed to the shareholders of the issuing company, Special Foods. Therefore, Peerless records its proportionate share of the gain, $8,640 ($10,800 × 0.80) under the fully adjusted equity method.

(13)	Investment in Special Foods	8,640	
	Income from Special Foods		8,640
	Record Peerless' 80% share of the gain on the constructive retirement of Special Foods' bonds.		

We note that a proportionate share of the gain is also assigned to the noncontrolling interest when the consolidation entries are made in preparing the worksheet. If Peerless had been the issuing affiliate, all of the gain would have been included in its share of consolidated net income and none would have been allocated to the noncontrolling interest. These entries result in a $264,762 balance in the investment account at the end of 20X1.

	Inv. in Special Foods			Inc. from Special Foods		
Acquisition	240,000					
80% Net Income	40,122				40,122	80% Net Income
		24,000	80% Dividends			
	8,640		80% of Bond Retirement Gain		8,640	
Ending Balance	264,762				48,762	Ending Balance

Consolidation Worksheet—20X1

Figure 8–2 on page 384 illustrates the consolidation worksheet prepared at the end of 20X1. The first two consolidation entries are the same as we prepared in Chapter 3 with one minor exception. Although the analysis of the "book value" portion of the investment account is the same, in preparing the basic consolidation entry, we increase the amounts in Peerless' Income from Special Foods and Investment in Special Foods accounts by Peerless' share of the gain on bond retirement, $8,640 ($10,800 × 80%). We also increase the NCI in Net Income of Special Foods and NCI in Net Assets of Special Foods by the NCI share of the gain, $2,160 ($10,800 × 20%).

Calculations for Basic Consolidation Entry:

Book Value Calculations:

	NCI 20%	+	Peerless 80%	=	Common Stock	+	Retained Earnings
Original Book Value	60,000		240,000		200,000		100,000
+ Net Income	10,030		40,122				50,152
− Dividends	(6,000)		(24,000)				(30,000)
Ending Book Value	64,030		256,122		200,000		120,152

Adjustment to Basic Consolidation Entry:

	NCI 20%	Peerless 80%
Net Income	10,030	40,122
+ Gain on Bond Retirement	2,160	8,640
Income to be Eliminated	12,190	48,762
Ending Book Value	64,030	256,122
+ Gain on Bond Retirement	2,160	8,640
Adjusted Book Value	66,190	264,762

Basic Consolidation Entry:

Common Stock	200,000		← Common stock balance
Retained Earnings	100,000		← Beg. RE from trial balance
Income from Special Foods	48,762		← Peerless' % of NI with Adjustment
NCI in NI of Special Foods	12,190		← NCI share of NI with Adjustment
Dividends Declared		30,000	← 100% of sub's dividends
Investment in Special Foods		264,762	← Net BV with Adjustment
NCI in NA of Special Foods		66,190	← NCI share of BV with Adjustment

Optional Accumulated Depreciation Consolidation Entry:

Accumulated Depreciation	**300,000**	
Buildings & Equipment		**300,000**

← Accumulated depreciation at the time of the acquisition netted against cost

Special Foods' bonds payable and Peerless' investment in Special Foods' bonds cannot appear in the consolidated balance sheet because the bond holdings involve parties totally within the single economic entity. Note that the gain recognized on the constructive retirement of the bonds does not appear on the books of either Peerless or Special Foods because the bonds still are outstanding from the perspective of the separate companies. From the viewpoint of the consolidated entity, the bonds are retired at the end of 20X1, and a gain must be entered in the consolidation worksheet so that it appears in the consolidated income statement.

Item	Peerless Products	+	Special Foods	=	Unadjusted Totals	≠	Consolidated Amounts
Bonds Payable	0		$(100,000)		$(100,000)		0
Premium on Bonds Payable	0		(5,623)		(5,623)		0
Investment in Bonds	$94,823		0		94,823		0
Interest Expense	0		$ 11,648		$ 11,648		$11,648
Interest Income	0		0		0		0
Gain on Bond Retirement	0		0		0		(10,800)

Thus, the consolidation worksheet entry to eliminate intercompany bond holdings eliminates the bond payable and its associated premium accounts from Special Foods' financial statements. It also removes the investment in Special Foods Bonds from Peerless' financial statements. Finally, it records the bond retirement gain.

Eliminate Intercorporate Bond Holdings:

Bonds Payable	**100,000**	
Premium on Bonds Payable	**5,623**	
Investment in Special Foods Bonds		**94,823**
Gain on Bond Retirement		**10,800**

No consolidations are needed with respect to interest income or interest expense in preparing the consolidated statements for December 31, 20X1. Because Peerless purchased the bonds at the end of the year, Peerless records no interest income until 20X2. The interest expense of $11,648 ($5,829 + 5,819) recorded by Special Foods is viewed appropriately as interest expense of the consolidated entity because an unrelated party held the bonds during all of 20X1.

Consolidated Net Income—20X1

Consolidated net income of $200,952 (Figure 8–2) is computed and allocated as follows:

Peerless' separate income		$140,000
Special Foods' net income	$50,152	
Gain on constructive retirement of bonds	10,800	
Special Foods' realized net income		60,952
Consolidated net income, 20X1		$200,952
Income to noncontrolling interest ($60,952 × 0.20)		(12,190)
Income to controlling interest		$188,762

Advanced StudyGuide .com

Consolidated net income is $10,800 higher than it would have been had Peerless not purchased the bonds.

FIGURE 8–2 December 31, 20X1, Consolidation Worksheet; Repurchase of Bonds at Less than Book Value

	Peerless Products	Special Foods	Consolidation Entries DR	Consolidation Entries CR	Consolidated
Income Statement					
Sales	400,000	200,000			600,000
Less: COGS	(170,000)	(115,000)			(285,000)
Less: Depreciation Expense	(50,000)	(20,000)			(70,000)
Less: Other Expenses	(20,000)	(3,200)			(23,200)
Less: Interest Expense	(20,000)	(11,648)			(31,648)
Income from Special Foods	48,762		48,762		0
Gain from Bond Retirement				10,800	10,800
Consolidated Net Income	**188,762**	**50,152**	**48,762**	**10,800**	**200,952**
NCI in Net Income			12,190		(12,190)
Controlling Interest Net Income	**188,762**	**50,152**	**60,952**	**10,800**	**188,762**
Statement of Retained Earnings					
Beginning Balance	300,000	100,000	100,000		300,000
Net Income	**188,762**	**50,152**	**60,952**	**10,800**	188,762
Less: Dividends Declared	(60,000)	(30,000)		30,000	(60,000)
Ending Balance	**428,762**	**120,152**	**160,952**	**40,800**	**428,762**
Balance Sheet					
Cash	169,177	80,775			249,952
Accounts Receivable	75,000	50,000			125,000
Inventory	100,000	75,000			175,000
Investment in Special Foods Stock	264,762			264,762	0
Investment in Special Foods Bonds	94,823			94,823	0
Land	175,000	40,000			215,000
Buildings & Equipment	800,000	600,000		300,000	1,100,000
Less: Accumulated Depreciation	(450,000)	(320,000)	300,000		(470,000)
Total Assets	**1,228,762**	**525,775**	**300,000**	**659,585**	**1,394,952**
Accounts Payable	100,000	100,000			200,000
Bonds Payable	200,000	100,000	100,000		200,000
Premium on Bonds Payable		5,623	5,623		0
Common Stock	500,000	200,000	200,000		500,000
Retained Earnings	**428,762**	**120,152**	**160,952**	**40,800**	428,762
NCI in NA of Special Foods				66,190	66,190
Total Liabilities & Equity	**1,228,762**	**525,775**	**466,575**	**106,990**	**1,394,952**

Noncontrolling Interest—December 31, 20X1

Total noncontrolling interest on December 31, 20X1, in the absence of a differential, includes a proportionate share of both the reported book value of Special Foods and the gain on constructive bond retirement. The balance of the noncontrolling interest on December 31, 20X1, is computed as follows:

Book value of Special Foods' net assets, December 31, 20X1:	
Common stock	$200,000
Retained earnings	120,152
Total reported book value	$320,152
Gain on constructive retirement of bonds	10,800
Realized book value of Special Foods' net assets	$330,952
Noncontrolling stockholders' share	× 0.20
Noncontrolling interest in net assets, December 31, 20X1	$ 66,190

Bond Liability Entries—20X2

Special Foods records interest on its bonds during 20X2 with the following entries:

	June 30, 20X2		
(14)	Interest Expense	5,809	
	Premium on Bonds Payable	191	
	Cash		6,000
	Semiannual payment of interest.		

	December 31, 20X2		
(15)	Interest Expense	5,799	
	Premium on Bonds Payable	201	
	Cash		6,000
	Semiannual payment of interest.		

Bond Investment Entries—20X2

Peerless Products accounts for its investment in Special Foods' bonds in the same way as if the bonds were those of a nonaffiliate. The $94,823 purchase price paid by Peerless reflects a $5,177 ($100,000 − $94,823) discount from the par value of the bonds. This discount is amortized over the nine-year remaining term of the bonds based on the amortization table (partially presented below) for each six-month interest payment period.

Bond Discount Amortization Table

Payment Number	Period End	Interest Receipt (Face × 0.12 × 6/12)	Interest Income (Carrying Value × 0.12992186 × 6/12)	Amortization of Discount	Discount	Bond Investment Face Value	Carrying Value of Investment
	12/31/20X1				(5,176.96)	100,000.00	94,823.04
1	6/30/20X2	6,000	6,159.79	159.79	(5,017.17)	100,000.00	94,982.83
2	12/31/20X2	6,000	6,170.17	170.17	(4,847.00)	100,000.00	95,153.00
3	6/30/20X3	6,000	6,181.23	181.23	(4,665.77)	100,000.00	95,334.23
4	12/31/20X3	6,000	6,193.00	193.00	(4,472.77)	100,000.00	95,527.23

Peerless' entries to record interest income for 20X2 are as follows:

	June 30, 20X2		
(16)	Cash	6,000	
	Investment in Special Foods Bonds	160	
	Interest Income		6,160
	Record receipt of bond interest.		

	December 31, 20X2		
(17)	Cash	6,000	
	Investment in Special Foods Bonds	170	
	Interest Income		6,170
	Record receipt of bond interest.		

Peerless earns this $12,330 ($6,160 + $6,170) of interest income in addition to its $160,000 of separate operating income for 20X2.

Advanced StudyGuide .com

Subsequent Recognition of Gain on Constructive Retirement

In the year of the constructive bond retirement, 20X1, the entire $10,800 gain on the retirement is recognized in the consolidated income statement but not on the books of either Peerless or Special Foods. The total gain on the constructive bond retirement in

20X1 is equal to the sum of Peerless' discount on the bond investment and Special Foods' premium on the bond liability at the time of the constructive retirement (12/31/20X1):

Peerless' discount on bond investment	$ 5,177
Special Foods' premium on bond liability	5,623
Total gain on constructive retirement of bonds	$10,800

This concept can be illustrated as follows:

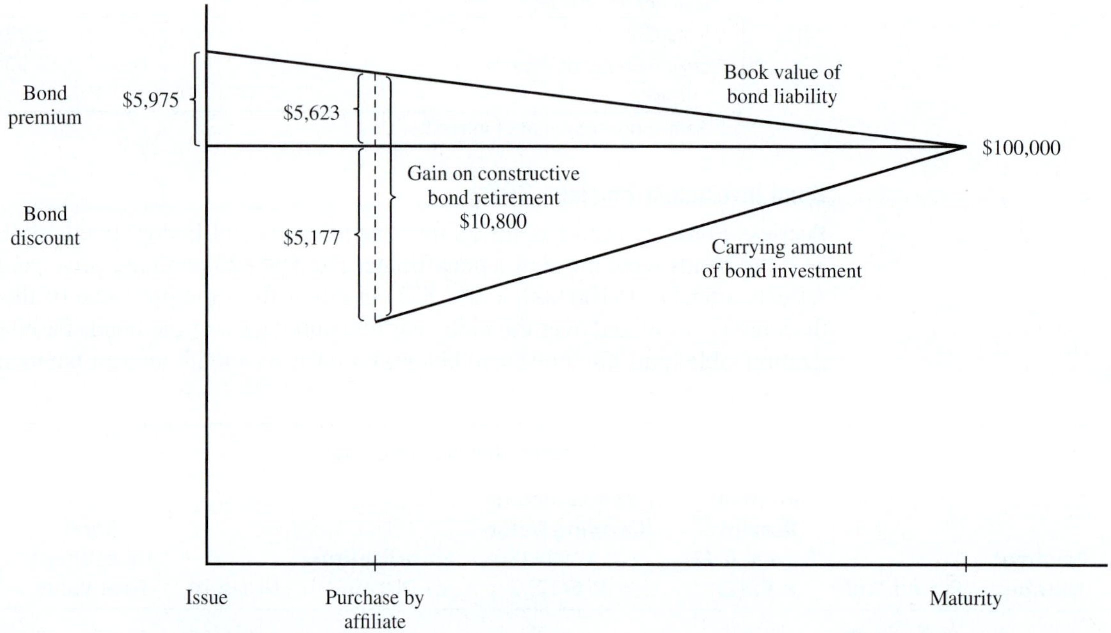

In each year subsequent to 20X1, both Peerless and Special Foods recognize a portion of the constructive gain as they amortize the discount on the bond investment and the premium on the bond liability (based on their respective amortization tables). Thus, the $10,800 gain on constructive bond retirement, previously recognized in the consolidated income statement, is recognized on the books of Peerless and Special Foods over the remaining nine-year term of the bonds.

Fully Adjusted Equity-Method Entries—20X2

Peerless recognizes its share of Special Foods' income ($75,192) and dividends ($40,000) for 20X2 with the normal equity-method entries:

(18)	Investment in Special Foods	60,154	
	Income from Special Foods		60,154

Record Peerless' 80% share of Special Foods' 20X2 income.

(19)	Cash	32,000	
	Investment in Special Foods		32,000

Record Peerless' 80% share of Special Foods' 20X2 dividend.

Under the fully adjusted equity method, Peerless records its proportionate 80 percent share of the constructive gain recognition.

(20)	Income from Special Foods	578	
	Investment in Special Foods		578

Recognize 80% share of amortization of premium and discount [0.80 × (191 + 201 + 160 + 170)].

Whereas neither Peerless nor Special Foods recognized any of the gain from the constructive bond retirement on its separate books in 20X1, Peerless adjusted its equity-method income from Special Foods for its 80 percent share of the $10,800 gain, $8,640. Therefore, as Peerless and Special Foods recognize the gain over the remaining term of the bonds, Peerless must reverse its 20X1 entry for its share of the gain. This adjustment is needed to avoid double-counting Peerless' share of the gain. Thus, the original adjustment of $8,640 is reversed by the 80 percent portion of the combined amortization of Special Foods' premium and Peerless' discount each year.

Consolidation Worksheet—20X2

Figure 8–3 on page 390 presents the consolidation worksheet for December 31, 20X2. The first two consolidation entries are the same as we prepared in Chapter 3 with the previously explained exception. Although the analysis of the "book value" portion of the investment account is the same, in preparing the basic consolidation entry, a portion of the constructive gain is recognized and shared between Peerless (80 percent) and the NCI shareholders (20 percent). Thus, the basic consolidation entry subtracts the proportionate share of the constructive gain recognition from the Income from Special Foods, Investment in Special Foods' stock, NCI in net income of Special Foods, and NCI in net assets of Special Foods accounts.

Calculations for Basic Consolidation Entry:

Book Value Calculations:

	NCI 20%	+	Peerless 80%	=	Common Stock	+	Retained Earnings
Original Book Value	64,030		256,122		200,000		120,152
+ Net Income	15,038		60,154				75,192
− Dividends	(8,000)		(32,000)				(40,000)
Ending Book Value	71,068		284,276		200,000		155,344

Adjustment to Basic Consolidation Entry:

	NCI 20%	Peerless 80%
Net Income	15,038	60,154
− 20X2 Constructive Gain Rec.	(144)	(578)
Income to be Eliminated	14,894	59,576
Ending Book Value	71,068	284,276
− 20X2 Constructive Gain Rec.	(144)	(578)
Adjusted Book Value	70,924*	283,698*

*Rounding difference

Basic Consolidation Entry:

Account	Debit	Credit	
Common Stock	200,000		← Common stock balance
Retained Earnings	120,152		← Beg. RE from trial balance
Income from Special Foods	59,576		← Peerless' % of NI with Adjustment
NCI in NI of Special Foods	14,894		← NCI % of NI with Adjustment
Dividends Declared		40,000	← 100% of sub's dividends declared
Investment in Special Foods Stock		283,698	← Net BV with Adjustment
NCI in NA of Special Foods		70,924	← NCI % of BV with Adjustment

Optional Accumulated Depreciation Consolidation Entry:

Account	Debit	Credit	
Accumulated Depreciation	300,000		← Accumulated depreciation at the time of the acquisition netted against cost
Buildings & Equipment		300,000	

The worksheet entry to eliminate the intercompany bond holdings credits the constructive gain on the bond retirement amount between the NCI interest in net assets of Special Foods and Peerless' Investment in Special Foods Common Stock account. In other words, the worksheet entry credits the Investment in Special Foods Common Stock account for $8,640 ($10,800 × 0.80) to eliminate the remaining balance in the account. Similarly, the noncontrolling interest is increased by $2,160 ($10,800 × 0.20), its proportionate share of the constructive gain on the bond retirement.

The intercompany bond holdings consolidation entry also eliminates all aspects of the intercorporate bond holdings, including (1) Peerless' investment in bonds, $95,153, (2) Special Foods' bonds payable, $100,000, and the associated premium, $5,231, (3) Peerless' bond interest income, $12,338, and (4) Special Foods' bond interest expense, $12,330 ($6,160 + $6,170). The amounts related to the bonds from the books of Peerless and Special Foods and the appropriate consolidated amounts are as follows:

Item	Peerless Products	+	Special Foods	=	Unadjusted Totals	≠	Consolidated Amounts
Bonds Payable	0		$(100,000)		$(100,000)		0
Premium on Bonds Payable	0		(5,231)		(5,231)		0
Investment in Bonds	$95,153		0		95,153		0
Interest Expense	0		$ 11,608		$ 11,608		0
Interest Income	$(12,330)		0		(12,330)		0

This analysis leads to the following worksheet entry to eliminate intercompany bond holdings.

Eliminate Intercompany Bond Holdings:

	Debit	Credit
Bonds Payable	**100,000**	
Premium on Bonds Payable	**5,231**	
Interest Income	**12,330**	
Investment in Special Foods Bonds		**95,153**
Interest Expense		**11,608**
Investment in Special Foods Stock		**8,640**
NCI in NA of Special Foods		**2,160**

Investment Account—20X2

The following T-accounts illustrate Peerless' Investment in the common stock of Special Foods and Income from Special Foods accounts at the end of 20X2 and how the consolidation entries zero out their balances on the worksheet:

	Inv. in Special Foods (Dr.)	Inv. in Special Foods (Cr.)		Inc. from Special Foods (Dr.)	Inc. from Special Foods (Cr.)	
Beg. Balance	**264,762**					
80% Net Income	**60,154**				**60,154**	**80% Net Income**
		32,000	**80% Dividends**			
		578	**Recognize 80% of Constructive Gain Recognized**	**578**		
Ending Balance	**292,338**				**59,576**	**Ending Balance**
		283,698	**Basic**	**59,576**		
		8,640				
	0				**0**	

Consolidated Net Income—20X2

Consolidated net income of $246,800 in Figure 8–3 is computed and allocated as follows:

Peerless' separate income		$172,330
Special Foods' net income	$75,192	
Peerless' amortization of bond discount	(330)	
Special Foods' amortization of bond premium	(392)	
Special Foods' realized net income		74,470
Consolidated net income, 20X1		$246,800
Income to noncontrolling interest ($74,470 × 0.20)		(14,894)
Income to controlling interest		$231,906

Noncontrolling Interest—December 31, 20X2

Total noncontrolling interest in the Net Assets of Special Foods account on December 31, 20X2, includes a proportionate share of both the reported book value of Special Foods and the portion of the gain on constructive bond retirement not yet recognized by the affiliates:

Book value of Special Foods' net assets, December 31, 20X2:		
Common stock		$200,000
Retained earnings		155,344
Total book value of net assets		$355,344
Gain on constructive retirement of bonds	$10,800	
Less: Portion recognized by affiliates during 20X2	(722)	
Constructive gain not yet recognized by affiliates		10,078
Realized book value of Special Foods net assets		$365,422
Noncontrolling stockholders' share		× 0.20
Noncontrolling interest in net assets, December 31, 20X2		$ 73,084

Bond Consolidation Entry in Subsequent Years

In years after 20X2, the worksheet entry to eliminate the intercompany bonds and to adjust for the gain on constructive retirement of the bonds is similar to the entry to eliminate intercompany bond holdings in 20X2. The unamortized bond discount and premium decrease each year based on the amortization table. As of the beginning of 20X3, $10,078 of the gain on the constructive retirement of the bonds remains unrecognized by the affiliates, computed as follows:

Gain on constructive retirement of bonds		$10,800
Less: Portion recognized by affiliates during 20X2:		
Peerless' amortization of bond discount	$330	
Special Foods' amortization of bond premium	392	
Total gain recognized by affiliates		(722)
Unrecognized gain on constructive retirement of bonds, January 1, 20X3		$10,078

The remaining unrecognized gain, $10,078, can be allocated between Peerless ($8,062) and the noncontrolling interest ($2,016) based on their respective ownership interests (80% and 20%). The intercompany bond holdings consolidation entry also eliminates all aspects of the intercorporate bond holdings, including (1) Peerless' investment in bonds, $95,527, (2) Special Foods' bonds payable, $100,000, and the associated premium, $4,795, (3) Peerless' bond interest income, $12,374, and (4) Special Foods' bond interest expense, $11,564 ($5,788 + $5,776). The amounts related to the bonds from the books of Peerless and Special Foods and the appropriate consolidated amounts are as follows:

Item	Peerless Products	+	Special Foods	=	Unadjusted Totals	≠	Consolidated Amounts
Bonds Payable	0		$(100,000)		$(100,000)		0
Premium on Bonds Payable	0		(4,795)		(4,795)		0
Investment in Bonds	$95,527		0		95,527		0
Interest Expense	0		$ 11,564		$ 11,564		0
Interest Income	$(12,374)		0		(12,374)		0

Based on these numbers, the bond consolidation entry at the end of 20X3 would be as follows:

Eliminate Intercompany Bond Holdings:

Account	DR	CR
Bonds Payable	**100,000**	
Premium on Bonds Payable	**4,795**	
Interest Income	**12,374**	
Investment in Special Foods Bonds		**95,527**
Interest Expense		**11,564**
Investment in Special Foods Stock		**8,062**
NCI in NA of Special Foods		**2,016**

FIGURE 8–3 December 31, 20X2, Consolidation Worksheet; Next Year Following Repurchase of Bonds at Less than Book Value

	Peerless Products	Special Foods	Consolidation Entries DR	Consolidation Entries CR	Consolidated
Income Statement					
Sales	450,000	300,000			750,000
Less: COGS	(180,000)	(160,000)			(340,000)
Less: Depreciation Expense	(50,000)	(20,000)			(70,000)
Less: Other Expenses	(40,000)	(33,200)			(73,200)
Less: Interest Expense	(20,000)	(11,608)		11,608	(20,000)
Interest Income	12,330		12,330		0
Income from Special Foods	59,576		59,576		0
Consolidated Net Income	**231,906**	**75,192**	**71,906**	**11,608**	**246,800**
NCI in Net Income			14,894		(14,894)
Controlling Interest Net Income	**231,906**	**75,192**	**86,800**	**11,608**	**231,906**
Statement of Retained Earnings					
Beginning Balance	428,762	120,152	120,152		428,762
Net Income	**231,906**	**75,192**	**86,800**	**11,608**	231,906
Less: Dividends Declared	(60,000)	(40,000)		40,000	(60,000)
Ending Balance	**600,668**	**155,344**	**206,952**	**51,608**	**600,668**
Balance Sheet					
Cash	208,177	90,575			298,752
Accounts Receivable	150,000	80,000			230,000
Inventory	180,000	90,000			270,000
Investment in Special Foods Stock	292,338			283,698	0
				8,640	
Investment in Special Foods Bonds	95,153			95,153	0
Land	175,000	40,000			215,000
Buildings & Equipment	800,000	600,000		300,000	1,100,000
Less: Accumulated Depreciation	(500,000)	(340,000)	300,000		(540,000)
Total Assets	**1,400,668**	**560,575**	**300,000**	**687,491**	**1,573,752**
Accounts Payable	100,000	100,000			200,000
Bonds Payable	200,000	100,000	100,000		200,000
Premium on Bonds Payable		5,231	5,231		
Common Stock	500,000	200,000	200,000		500,000
Retained Earnings	**600,668**	**155,344**	**206,952**	**51,608**	600,668
NCI in NA of Special Foods				70,924	73,084
				2,160	
Total Liabilities & Equity	**1,400,668**	**560,575**	**512,183**	**124,692**	**1,573,752**

LO 8-4

Prepare journal entries and consolidation entries related to an affiliate's debt purchased from a nonaffiliate at an amount more than book value.

Purchase at an Amount Higher than Book Value

When an affiliate's bonds are purchased from a nonaffiliate at an amount greater than their book value, the consolidation procedures are virtually the same as previously illustrated except that a loss is recognized on the constructive retirement of the debt. For example, assume that Special Foods issues 10-year, 12 percent bonds on January 1, 20X1, at par of $100,000. The bonds are purchased from Special Foods by a nonaffiliate, which sells the bonds to Peerless Products on December 31, 20X1, for $104,500.

The bond transactions of Special Foods and Peerless appear as follows:

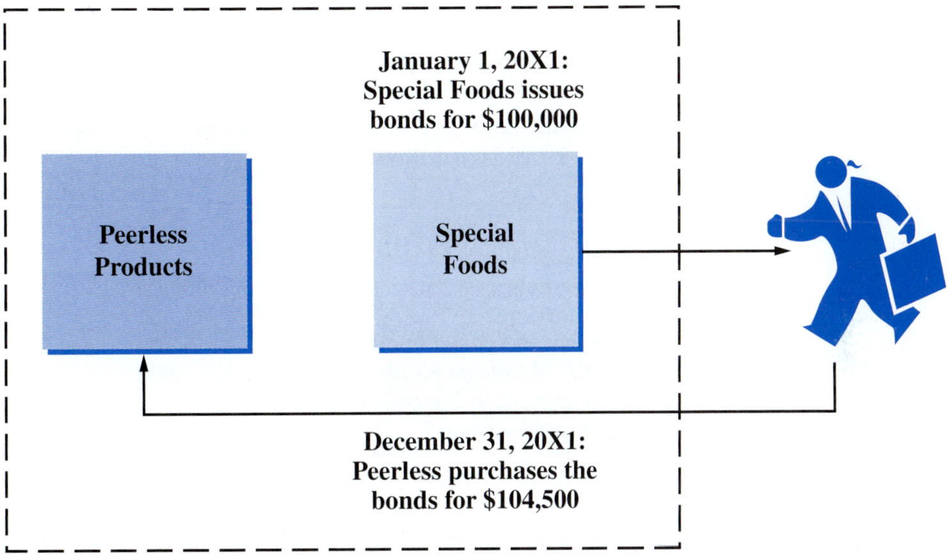

Special Foods recognizes $12,000 ($100,000 × 0.12) of interest expense each year. Peerless recognizes interest income based on the following amortization table:

Bond Premium Amortization Table

Payment Number	Period End	Interest Receipt (Face × 0.12 × 6/12)	Interest Income (Carrying Value × 0.11193771 × 6/12)	Amortization of Premium	Premium	Bond Investment Face Value	Carrying Value of Investment
	12/31/20X1				4,500.00	100,000.00	104,500.00
1	6/30/20X2	6,000	5,848.75	(151.25)	4,348.75	100,000.00	104,348.75
2	12/31/20X2	6,000	5,840.28	(159.72)	4,189.03	100,000.00	104,189.03
3	6/30/20X3	6,000	5,831.34	(168.66)	4,020.37	100,000.00	104,020.37
4	12/31/20X3	6,000	5,821.90	(178.10)	3,842.27	100,000.00	103,842.27

Because the bonds were issued at par, the carrying amount on Special Foods' books remains at $100,000. Thus, once Peerless purchases the bonds from a nonaffiliate for $104,500, a loss on the constructive retirement must be recognized in the consolidated income statement for $4,500 ($104,500 − $100,000). The bond consolidation entry in the worksheet prepared at the end of 20X1 removes the bonds payable and the bond investment and recognizes the loss on the constructive retirement:

Eliminate Intercorporate Bond Holdings:

Bonds Payable	100,000	
Loss on Bond Retirement	4,500	
Investment in Special Foods Bonds		104,500

In subsequent years, Peerless amortizes the premium on the bond investment, reducing interest income and the bond investment balance by the amount the premium is amortized each year. This, in effect, recognizes a portion of the loss on the constructive retirement. When consolidated statements are prepared, the amount of the loss on constructive retirement that has not been recognized by the separate affiliates at the beginning of the period is allocated proportionately against the ownership interests of the issuing affiliate. The bond consolidation entry needed in the worksheet prepared at the end of 20X2 is as follows:

Eliminate Intercompany Bond Holdings:

Bonds Payable	100,000	
Interest Income	11,689	
Investment in Special Foods Stock	3,600	
NCI in NA of Special Foods	900	
Investment in Special Foods Bonds		104,189
Interest Expense		12,000

$11,689 = $5,849 + $5,840 from amortization table

$3,600 = $4,500 × 0.80 (Peerless' share of the premium)

$900 = $4,500 × 0.20 (NCI's share of the premium)

$104,189 = $104,500 − $151 − $160 (amortized premium)

$12,000 = $100,000 × 0.12

Similarly, the following worksheet entry is needed in the consolidation worksheet at the end of 20X3:

Eliminate Intercompany Bond Holdings:

Bonds Payable	100,000	
Interest Income	11,653	
Investment in Special Foods Stock	3,351	
NCI in NA of Special Foods	838	
Investment in Special Foods Bonds		103,842
Interest Expense		12,000

$11,653 = $5,831 + $5,822 from amortization table

$3,351 = $4,189 × 0.80 (Peerless' share of the premium)

$838 = $4,189 × 0.20 (NCI's share of the premium)

$103,842 = $104,189 − $169 − $178 (amortized premium)

$12,000 = $100,000 × 0.12

SUMMARY OF KEY CONCEPTS

The effects of intercompany debt transactions must be eliminated completely in preparing consolidated financial statements, just as with other types of intercompany transactions. Only debt transactions between the consolidated entity and unaffiliated parties are reported in the consolidated statements.

When one affiliate issues bonds that are purchased directly by another affiliate, the bonds are viewed from a consolidated point of view as never having been issued. Thus, all aspects of the intercompany bond holding are eliminated in consolidation. Items requiring consolidation include (1) the bond investment from the purchasing affiliate's books, (2) the bond liability and any associated discount or premium from the issuer's books, (3) the interest income recognized by the investing affiliate and the interest expense recognized by the issuer, and (4) any intercompany interest receivable/payable as of the date of the consolidated statements.

When a company purchases the bonds of an affiliate from a nonaffiliate, it treats the bonds in consolidation as if they had been issued and subsequently repurchased by the consolidated entity. If the price paid by the purchasing affiliate is different from the issuer's book value of the bonds, a gain or loss from retirement of the bonds is recognized in the consolidated income statement. In addition, all aspects of the intercompany bond holding are eliminated because the bonds are treated as if the consolidated entity had retired them.

KEY TERMS

constructive retirement, *378*

direct intercompany debt transfer, *373*

indirect intercompany debt transfer, *373*

Appendix 8A Intercompany Indebtedness—Fully Adjusted Equity Method Using Straight-Line Interest Amortization

LO 8-2

Prepare journal entries and consolidation entries related to direct intercompany debt transfers.

This appendix repeats the main examples in the chapter but assumes that the companies amortize interest using the straight-line method for amortizing discounts and premiums on bonds payable.

TRANSFER AT A DISCOUNT OR PREMIUM

When the coupon or nominal interest rate on a bond is different from the yield demanded by those who lend funds, a bond sells at a discount or premium. In such cases, the amount of bond interest income or expense recorded no longer equals the cash interest payments. Instead, interest income and expense amounts are adjusted for the amortization of the discount or premium.

As an illustration of the treatment of intercompany bond transfers at other than par, assume that on January 1, 20X1, Peerless Products purchases $100,000 par value, 12 percent, 10-year bonds from Special Foods for $90,000. Interest on the bonds is payable on January 1 and July 1. The interest expense recognized by Special Foods and the interest income recognized by Peerless each year include straight-line amortization of the discount, as follows:

Cash interest ($100,000 × 0.12)	$12,000
Amortization of discount ($10,000 ÷ 20 semiannual interest periods) × 2 periods	1,000
Interest expense or income	$13,000

Half of these amounts are recognized in each of the two interest payment periods during a year. Although the effective interest method of amortization usually is required for amortizing discounts and premiums, the straight-line method is acceptable when it does not depart materially from the effective interest method and when transactions are between parent and subsidiary companies or between subsidiaries of a common parent.

Entries by the Debtor

Special Foods records the issuance of the bonds on January 1 at a discount of $10,000. It recognizes interest expense on July 1 when the first semiannual interest payment is made, and on December 31, when interest is accrued for the second half of the year. The amortization of the bond discount causes interest expense to be higher than the cash interest payment and causes the balance of the discount to decrease. Special Foods records the following entries related to the bonds during 20X1:

	January 1, 20X1		
(1A)	Cash	90,000	
	Discount on Bonds Payable	10,000	
	Bonds Payable		100,000
	Issue bonds to Peerless Products.		

	July 1, 20X1		
(2A)	Interest Expense	6,500	
	Discount on Bonds Payable		500
	Cash		6,000
	Make semiannual interest payment.		

	December 31, 20X1		
(3A)	Interest Expense	6,500	
	Discount on Bonds Payable		500
	Interest Payable		6,000
	Accrue interest expense at year-end.		

Entries by the Bond Investor

Peerless Products records the purchase of the bonds and the interest income derived from the bonds during 20X1 with the following entries:

	January 1, 20X1		
(4A)	Investment in Special Foods Bonds	90,000	
	Cash		90,000
	Purchase bonds from Special Foods.		

	July 1, 20X1		
(5A)	Cash	6,000	
	Investment in Special Foods Bonds	500	
	Interest Income		6,500
	Receive interest on bond investment.		

	December 31, 20X1		
(6A)	Interest Receivable	6,000	
	Investment in Special Foods Bonds	500	
	Interest Income		6,500
	Accrue interest income at year-end.		

The amortization of the discount by Peerless increases interest income to an amount higher than the cash interest payment and causes the balance of the bond investment account to increase.

Consolidation Entries at Year-End

The December 31, 20X1, bond-related amounts taken from the books of Peerless Products and Special Foods and the appropriate consolidated amounts are as follows:

Item	Peerless Products	+	Special Foods	=	Unadjusted Totals	≠	Consolidated Amounts
Bonds Payable	0		$(100,000)		$(100,000)		0
Discount on Bonds Payable	0		9,000		9,000		0
Interest Payable	0		(6,000)		(6,000)		0
Investment in Bonds	$ 91,000		0		91,000		0
Interest Receivable	6,000		0		6,000		0
Interest Expense	0		$ 13,000		$ 13,000		0
Interest Income	$(13,000)		0		(13,000)		0

All account balances relating to the intercorporate bond holdings must be eliminated in the preparation of consolidated financial statements. Toward that end, the consolidation worksheet prepared on December 31, 20X1, includes the following consolidation entries related to the intercompany bond holdings:

Eliminate Intercorporate Bond Holdings:

Bonds Payable	100,000	
Investment in Special Foods Bonds		91,000
Discount on Bonds Payable		9,000

Eliminate Intercompany Interest:

Interest Income	13,000	
Interest Expense		13,000

Eliminate Intercompany Interest Receivable/Payable:

Interest Payable	6,000	
Interest Receivable		6,000

The first entry eliminates the bonds payable and associated discount against the investment in bonds. The book value of the bond liability on Special Foods' books and the investment in bonds on Peerless' books will be the same as long as both companies amortize the discount in the same way.

The second entry eliminates the bond interest income recognized by Peerless during 20X1 against the bond interest expense recognized by Special Foods. Because the interest for the second half of 20X1 was accrued but not paid, an intercompany receivable/payable exists at the end of the year. The third entry eliminates the interest receivable against the interest payable.

Consolidation at the end of 20X2 requires consolidation entries similar to those at the end of 20X1. Because $1,000 of the discount is amortized each year, the bond investment balance on Peerless' books increases to $92,000 ($90,000 + $1,000 + $1,000). Similarly, the bond discount on Special Foods' books decreases to $8,000, resulting in an effective bond liability of $92,000. The consolidation entries related to the bonds at the end of 20X2 are as follows:

Eliminate Intercorporate Bond Holdings:

Bonds Payable	100,000	
Investment in Special Foods Bonds		92,000
Discount on Bonds Payable		8,000

Eliminate Intercompany Interest:

Interest Income	13,000	
Interest Expense		13,000

Eliminate Intercompany Interest Receivable/Payable:

Interest Payable	6,000	
Interest Receivable		6,000

BONDS OF AFFILIATE PURCHASED FROM A NONAFFILIATE

A more complex situation occurs when an affiliate of the issuer later acquires bonds that were issued to an unrelated party. From the viewpoint of the consolidated entity, an acquisition of an affiliate's bonds retires the bonds at the time they are purchased. The bonds no longer are held outside the consolidated entity once another company within the consolidated entity purchases them, and they must be treated as if repurchased by the debtor. Acquisition of an affiliate's bonds by another company within the consolidated entity is referred to as ***constructive retirement.*** Although the bonds actually are not retired, they are treated as if they were retired in preparing consolidated financial statements.

When a constructive retirement occurs, the consolidated income statement for the period reports a gain or loss on debt retirement based on the difference between the carrying value of the bonds on the books of the debtor and the purchase price paid by the affiliate in acquiring the bonds. Neither the bonds payable nor the purchaser's investment in the bonds is reported in the consolidated balance sheet because the bonds are no longer considered outstanding.

Purchase at Book Value

In the event that a company purchases an affiliate's debt from an unrelated party at a price equal to the liability reported by the debtor, the consolidation entries required in preparing the consolidated financial statements are identical to those used in eliminating a direct intercorporate debt transfer. In this case, the total of the bond liability and the related premium or discount reported by the debtor equal the balance in the investment account shown by the bondholder, and the interest income reported by the bondholder each period equals the interest expense reported by the debtor. All of these amounts need to be eliminated to avoid misstating the accounts in the consolidated financial statements.

LO 8-3

Prepare journal entries and consolidation entries related to an affiliate's debt purchased from a nonaffiliate at an amount less than book value.

Purchase at an Amount Less than Book Value

Continuing movement in the level of interest rates and the volatility of other factors influencing the securities markets make it unlikely that a company's bonds will sell after issuance at a price identical to their book value. When the price paid to acquire an affiliate's bonds differs from the liability reported by the debtor, a gain or loss is reported in the consolidated income statement in the period of constructive retirement. In addition, the bond interest income and interest expense reported by the two affiliates subsequent to the purchase must be eliminated in preparing consolidated statements. Interest income reported by the investing affiliate and interest expense reported by the debtor are not equal in this case because of the different bond carrying amounts on the books of the two companies. The difference in the bond carrying amounts is reflected in the amortization of the discount or premium and, in turn, causes interest income and expense to differ.

As an example of consolidation following the purchase of an affiliate's bonds at less than book value, assume that Peerless Products Corporation purchases 80 percent of the common stock of Special Foods Inc. on December 31, 20X0, for its underlying book value of $240,000. At that date, the fair value of the noncontrolling interest is equal to its book value of $60,000. In addition, the following conditions occur:

1. On January 1, 20X1, Special Foods issues 10-year, 12 percent bonds payable with a par value of $100,000; the bonds are issued at 102. The nonaffiliated investor purchases the bonds from Special Foods.
2. The bonds pay interest on June 30 and December 31.
3. Both Peerless Products and Special Foods amortize bond discount and premium using the straight-line method.
4. On December 31, 20X1, Peerless Products purchases the bonds from the nonaffiliated investor for $91,000.
5. Special Foods reports net income of $50,000 for 20X1 and $75,000 for 20X2 and declares dividends of $30,000 in 20X1 and $40,000 in 20X2.
6. Peerless earns $140,000 in 20X1 and $160,000 in 20X2 from its own separate operations. Peerless declares dividends of $60,000 in both 20X1 and 20X2.

The bond transactions of Special Foods and Peerless appear as follows:

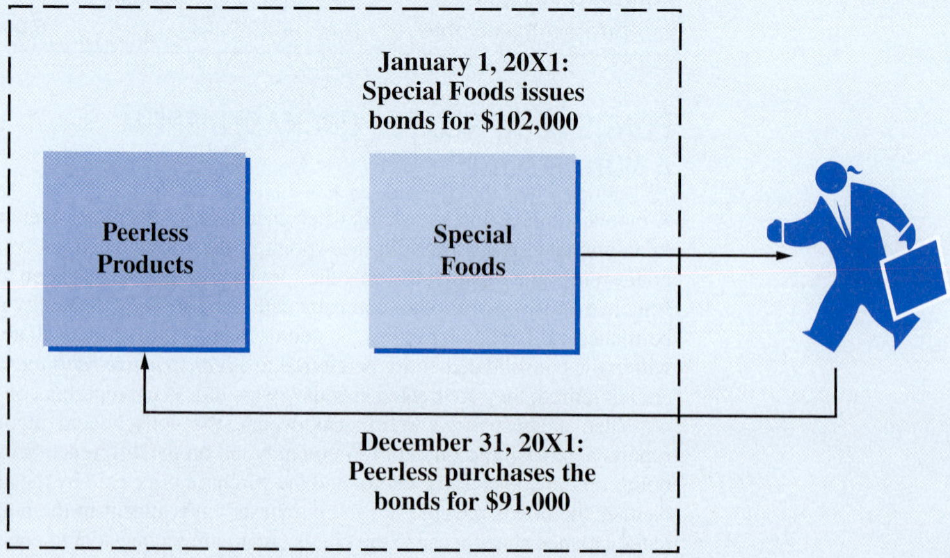

Bond Liability Entries—20X1

Special Foods records the following entries related to its bonds during 20X1:

	January 1, 20X1		
(7A)	Cash	102,000	
	Bonds Payable		100,000
	Premium on Bonds Payable		2,000
	Sale of bonds to the nonaffiliated investor.		

	June 30, 20X1		
(8A)	Interest Expense	5,900	
	Premium on Bonds Payable	100	
	Cash		6,000
	Semiannual payment of interest: $5,900 = $6,000 − $100 $100 = $2,000 ÷ 20 interest periods $6,000 = $100,000 × 0.12 × 6/12.		

	December 31, 20X1		
(9A)	Interest Expense	5,900	
	Premium on Bonds Payable	100	
	Cash		6,000
	Semiannual payment of interest.		

Entry (7A) records the issuance of the bonds to the nonaffiliated investor for $102,000. Entries (8A) and (9A) record the payment of interest and the amortization of the bond premium at each of the two interest payment dates during 20X1. Total interest expense for 20X1 is $11,800 ($5,900 × 2), and the book value of the bonds on December 31, 20X1, is as follows:

Book value of bonds at issuance	$102,000
Amortization of premium, 20X1	(200)
Book value of bonds, December 31, 20X1	$101,800

Bond Investment Entries—20X1

Peerless Products records the purchase of Special Foods' bonds from the nonaffiliated investor with the following entry:

	December 31, 20X1		
(10A)	Investment in Special Foods Bonds	91,000	
	Cash		91,000
	Purchase of Special Foods bonds from a nonaffiliated investor.		

This entry is the same as if the bonds purchased were those of an unrelated company. Peerless purchases the bonds at the very end of the year after payment of the interest to a nonaffiliated investor; therefore, Peerless earns no interest on the bonds during 20X1, nor is there any interest accrued on the bonds at the date of purchase.

Computation of Gain on Constructive Retirement of Bonds

Advanced StudyGuide .com

From a consolidated viewpoint, the purchase of Special Foods' bonds by Peerless is considered a retirement of the bonds by the consolidated entity. Therefore, in the preparation of consolidated financial statements, a gain or loss must be recognized for the difference between the book value of the bonds on the date of repurchase and the amount paid by the consolidated entity in reacquiring the bonds:

Book value of Special Foods' bonds, December 31, 20X1	$101,800
Price paid by Peerless to purchase bonds	(91,000)
Gain on constructive retirement of bonds	$ 10,800

This gain is included in the consolidated income statement as a gain on the retirement of bonds.

Assignment of Gain on Constructive Retirement

Four approaches have been used in practice for assigning the gain or loss on the constructive retirement of an affiliate's bonds to the shareholders of the participating companies. Depending upon the method selected, the gain or loss may be assigned to any of the following:

1. The affiliate issuing the bonds.
2. The affiliate purchasing the bonds.
3. The parent company.
4. The issuing and purchasing companies based on the difference between the carrying amounts of the bonds on their books at the date of purchase and the par value of the bonds.

No compelling reasons seem to exist for choosing one of these methods over the others, and in practice, the choice often is based on expediency and lack of materiality. The FASB's approach is to assign the gain or loss to the issuing company. In previous chapters, gains and losses on intercompany transactions were viewed as accruing to the shareholders of the selling affiliate. When this approach is applied in the case of intercorporate debt transactions, gains and losses arising from the intercompany debt transactions are viewed as accruing to the shareholders of the selling or issuing affiliate. In effect, the purchasing affiliate is viewed as acting on behalf of the issuing affiliate by acquiring the bonds.

An important difference exists between the intercompany gains and losses discussed in previous chapters and the gains and losses arising from intercorporate debt transactions. Gains and losses from intercorporate transfers of assets are recognized by the individual affiliates and are eliminated in consolidation. Gains and losses from intercorporate debt transactions are not recognized by the individual affiliates but must be included in consolidation.

When the subsidiary is the issuing affiliate, the gain or loss on constructive retirement of the bonds is viewed as accruing to the subsidiary's shareholders. Thus, the gain or loss is apportioned between the controlling and noncontrolling interests based on the relative ownership interests in the common stock (similar to upstream inventory or asset transfers). If the parent is the issuing affiliate, the entire gain or loss on the constructive retirement accrues to the controlling interest and none is apportioned to the noncontrolling interest (similar to downstream inventory or asset transfers).

As a result of the interest income and expense entries recorded annually by the companies involved, the constructive gain or loss is recognized over the remaining term of the bond issue; accordingly, the total amount of the unrecognized gain or loss decreases each period and is fully amortized at the time the bond matures. Thus, no permanent gain or loss is assigned to the debtor company's shareholders.

Fully Adjusted Equity-Method Entries—20X1

In addition to recording the bond investment with entry (10A), Peerless records the following equity-method entries during 20X1 to account for its investment in Special Foods stock:

(11A)	Investment in Special Foods Stock	40,000	
	Income from Special Foods		40,000

Record equity-method income: $50,000 × 0.80.

(12A)	Cash	24,000	
	Investment in Special Foods Stock		24,000

Record dividends from Special Foods: $30,000 × 0.80.

The full gain on constructive retirement is included in consolidated net income. That gain is attributed to the shareholders of the issuing company, Special Foods. Therefore, Peerless records its proportionate share of the gain, $8,640 ($10,800 × 0.80), under the fully adjusted equity method.

(13A)	Investment in Special Foods Stock	8,640	
	Income from Special Foods		8,640

Record Peerless' 80% share of the gain on the constructive retirement of Special Foods' bonds.

We note that a proportionate share of the gain is also assigned to the noncontrolling interest when the consolidation entries are made in preparing the worksheet. If Peerless had been the issuing affiliate, all of the gain would have been included in its share of consolidated net income and none would have been allocated to the noncontrolling interest. These entries result in a $264,640 balance in the investment account at the end of 20X1.

Inv. in Special Foods

	Debit	Credit	
Acquisition	240,000		
80% Net Income	40,000		
		24,000	80% Dividends
	8,640		80% of Bond Retirement Gain
Ending Balance	264,640		

Inc. from Special Foods

Debit	Credit	
	40,000	80% Net Income
	8,640	
	48,640	Ending Balance

Consolidation Worksheet—20X1

Figure 8A–1 illustrates the consolidation worksheet prepared at the end of 20X1. The first two consolidation entries are the same as we prepared in Chapter 3 with one minor exception. Although the analysis of the "book value" portion of the investment account is the same, in preparing the basic consolidation entry, we increase the amounts in Peerless' Income from Special Foods and Investment in Special Foods Stock accounts by Peerless' share of the gain on bond retirement, $8,640 ($10,800 × 0.80). We also increase the NCI in Net Income of Special Foods and NCI in Net Assets of Special Foods by the NCI share of the gain, $2,160 ($10,800 × 0.20).

Calculations for Basic Consolidation Entry:

Book Value Calculations:

	NCI 20%	+	Peerless 80%	=	Common Stock	+	Retained Earnings
Original Book Value	60,000		240,000		200,000		100,000
+ Net Income	10,000		40,000				50,000
− Dividends	(6,000)		(24,000)				(30,000)
Ending Book Value	64,000		256,000		200,000		120,000

Adjustment to Basic Consolidation Entry:

	NCI 20%	Peerless 80%
Net Income	10,000	40,000
+ Gain on Bond Retirement	2,160	8,640
Income to be Eliminated	12,160	48,640
Ending Book Value	64,000	256,000
+ Gain on Bond Retirement	2,160	8,640
Adjusted Book Value	66,160	264,640

Basic Consolidation Entry:

	Debit	Credit	
Common Stock	200,000		← Common stock balance
Retained Earnings	100,000		← Beg. RE from trial balance
Income from Special Foods	48,640		← Peerless' % of NI with Adjustment
NCI in NI of Special Foods	12,160		← NCI share of NI with Adjustment
Dividends Declared		30,000	← 100% of sub's dividends
Investment in Special Foods Stock		264,640	← Net BV with Adjustment
NCI in NA of Special Foods		66,160	← NCI share of BV with Adjustment

Optional Accumulated Depreciation Consolidation Entry:

	Debit	Credit	
Accumulated Depreciation	300,000		← Accumulated depreciation at the time of the acquisition netted against cost
Buildings & Equipment		300,000	

Special Foods' bonds payable and Peerless' investment in Special Foods' bonds cannot appear in the consolidated balance sheet because the bond holdings involve parties totally within the single

FIGURE 8A–1 December 31, 20X1, Consolidation Worksheet; Repurchase of Bonds at Less than Book Value

	Peerless Products	Special Foods	Consolidation Entries DR	Consolidation Entries CR	Consolidated
Income Statement					
Sales	400,000	200,000			600,000
Less: COGS	(170,000)	(115,000)			(285,000)
Less: Depreciation Expense	(50,000)	(20,000)			(70,000)
Less: Other Expenses	(20,000)	(3,200)			(23,200)
Less: Interest Expense	(20,000)	(11,800)			(31,800)
Income from Special Foods	48,640		48,640		0
Gain from Bond Retirement				10,800	10,800
Consolidated Net Income	**188,640**	**50,000**	**48,640**	**10,800**	**200,800**
NCI in Net Income			12,160		(12,160)
Controlling Interest Net Income	**188,640**	**50,000**	**60,800**	**10,800**	**188,640**
Statement of Retained Earnings					
Beginning Balance	300,000	100,000	100,000		300,000
Net Income	**188,640**	**50,000**	**60,800**	**10,800**	188,640
Less: Dividends Declared	(60,000)	(30,000)		30,000	(60,000)
Ending Balance	**428,640**	**120,000**	**160,800**	**40,800**	**428,640**
Balance Sheet					
Cash	173,000	76,800			249,800
Accounts Receivable	75,000	50,000			125,000
Inventory	100,000	75,000			175,000
Investment in Special Foods Stock	264,640			264,640	0
Investment in Special Foods Bonds	91,000			91,000	0
Land	175,000	40,000			215,000
Buildings & Equipment	800,000	600,000		300,000	1,100,000
Less: Accumulated Depreciation	(450,000)	(320,000)	300,000		(470,000)
Total Assets	**1,228,640**	**521,800**	**300,000**	**655,640**	**1,394,800**
Accounts Payable	100,000	100,000			200,000
Bonds Payable	200,000	100,000	100,000		200,000
Premium on Bonds Payable		1,800	1,800		0
Common Stock	500,000	200,000	200,000		500,000
Retained Earnings	**428,640**	**120,000**	**160,800**	**40,800**	428,640
NCI in NA of Special Foods				66,160	66,160
Total Liabilities & Equity	**1,228,640**	**521,800**	**462,600**	**106,960**	**1,394,800**

economic entity. Note that the gain recognized on the constructive retirement of the bonds does not appear on the books of either Peerless or Special Foods because the bonds still are outstanding from the perspective of the separate companies. From the viewpoint of the consolidated entity, the bonds are retired at the end of 20X1, and a gain must be entered in the consolidation worksheet so that it appears in the consolidated income statement.

Item	Peerless Products	+	Special Foods	=	Unadjusted Totals	≠	Consolidated Amounts
Bonds Payable	0		$(100,000)		$(100,000)		0
Premium on Bonds Payable	0		(1,800)		(1,800)		0
Investment in Bonds	$91,000		0		91,000		0
Interest Expense	0		$ 11,800		$ 11,800		$11,800
Interest Income	0		0		0		0
Gain on Bond Retirement	0		0		0		(10,800)

Thus, the consolidation worksheet entry to eliminate intercompany bond holdings eliminates the bond payable and its associated premium accounts from Special Foods' financial statements. It also removes the investment in Special Foods Bonds from Peerless' financial statements. Finally, it records the bond retirement gain.

Eliminate Intercorporate Bond Holdings:

Bonds Payable	**100,000**	
Premium on Bonds Payable	**1,800**	
Investment in Special Foods Bonds		**91,000**
Gain on Bond Retirement		**10,800**

No consolidations are needed with respect to interest income or interest expense in preparing the consolidated statements for December 31, 20X1. Because Peerless purchased the bonds at the end of the year, Peerless records no interest income until 20X2. The interest expense of $11,800 ($12,000 − $200) recorded by Special Foods is viewed appropriately as interest expense of the consolidated entity because an unrelated party held the bonds during all of 20X1.

Consolidated Net Income—20X1

Consolidated net income of $200,800 (in Figure 8A–1) is computed and allocated as follows:

Peerless' separate income		$140,000
Special Foods' net income	$50,000	
Gain on constructive retirement of bonds	10,800	
Special Foods' realized net income		60,800
Consolidated net income, 20X1		$200,800
Income to noncontrolling interest ($60,800 × 0.20)		(12,160)
Income to controlling interest		$188,640

Consolidated net income is $10,800 higher than it would have been had Peerless not purchased the bonds.

Noncontrolling Interest—December 31, 20X1

Total noncontrolling interest on December 31, 20X1, in the absence of a differential, includes a proportionate share of both the reported book value of Special Foods and the gain on constructive bond retirement. The balance of the noncontrolling interest on December 31, 20X1, is computed as follows:

Book value of Special Foods' net assets, December 31, 20X1:	
Common stock	$200,000
Retained earnings	120,000
Total reported book value	$320,000
Gain on constructive retirement of bonds	10,800
Realized book value of Special Foods' net assets	$330,800
Noncontrolling stockholders' share	× 0.20
Noncontrolling interest, in net assets December 31, 20X1	$ 66,160

Bond Liability Entries—20X2

Special Foods records interest on its bonds during 20X2 with the following entries:

	June 30, 20X2		
(14A)	Interest Expense	5,900	
	Premium on Bonds Payable	100	
	Cash		6,000
	Semiannual payment of interest.		
	December 31, 20X2		
(15A)	Interest Expense	5,900	
	Premium on Bonds Payable	100	
	Cash		6,000
	Semiannual payment of interest.		

Bond Investment Entries—20X2

Peerless Products accounts for its investment in Special Foods' bonds in the same way as if the bonds were those of a nonaffiliate. The $91,000 purchase price paid by Peerless reflects a $9,000 ($100,000 − $91,000) discount from the par value of the bonds. This discount is amortized over the nine-year remaining term of the bonds at $1,000 per year ($9,000 ÷ 9 years), or $500 per six-month interest payment period. Peerless' entries to record interest income for 20X2 are as follows:

	June 30, 20X2		
(16A)	Cash	6,000	
	Investment in Special Foods Bonds	500	
	Interest Income		6,500
	Record receipt of bond interest.		
	December 31, 20X2		
(17A)	Cash	6,000	
	Investment in Special Foods Bonds	500	
	Interest Income		6,500
	Record receipt of bond interest.		

Peerless earns this $13,000 of interest income in addition to its $160,000 of separate operating income for 20X2.

Subsequent Recognition of Gain on Constructive Retirement

In the year of the constructive bond retirement, 20X1, the entire $10,800 gain on the retirement was recognized in the consolidated income statement but not on the books of either Peerless or Special Foods. The total gain on the constructive bond retirement in 20X1 was equal to the sum of the discount on Peerless' bond investment and the premium on Special Foods' bond liability at the time of the constructive retirement:

Peerless' discount on bond investment	$ 9,000
Special Foods' premium on bond liability	1,800
Total gain on constructive retirement of bonds	$10,800

In each year subsequent to 20X1, both Peerless and Special Foods recognize a portion of the constructive gain as they amortize the discount on the bond investment and the premium on the bond liability:

Peerless' amortization of discount on bond investment ($9,000 ÷ 9 years)	$1,000
Special Foods' amortization of premium on bonds payable ($1,800 ÷ 9 years)	200
Annual increase in combined incomes of separate companies	$1,200

Thus, the $10,800 gain on constructive bond retirement, previously recognized in the consolidated income statement, is recognized on the books of Peerless and Special Foods at the rate of $1,200 each year. Over the remaining nine-year term of the bonds, Peerless and Special Foods will recognize the full $10,800 gain ($1,200 × 9). This concept can be illustrated as follows:

Fully Adjusted Equity-Method Entries—20X2

Peerless recognizes its share of Special Foods' income ($75,000) and dividends ($40,000) for 20X2 with the normal equity-method entries:

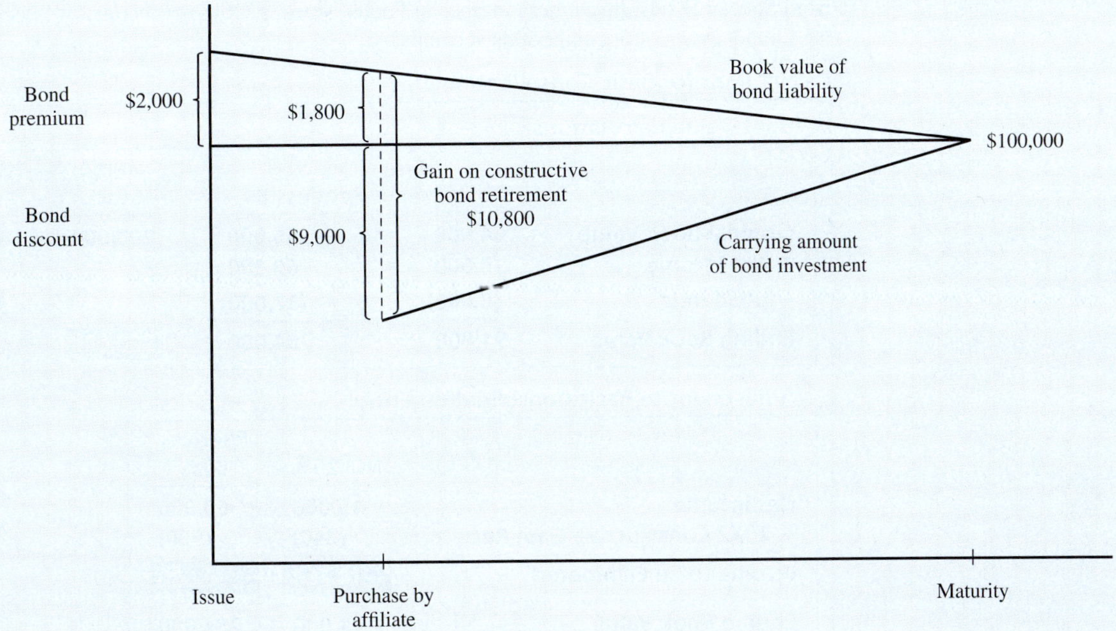

(18A)	Investment in Special Foods Stock	60,000	
	Income from Special Foods		60,000

Record Peerless' 80% share of Special Foods' 20X2 income.

(19A)	Cash	32,000	
	Investment in Special Foods Stock		32,000

Record Peerless' 80% share of Special Foods' 20X2 dividend.

Under the fully adjusted equity method, Peerless records its proportionate 80 percent share of the constructive gain recognition.

(20A)	Income from Special Foods	960	
	Investment in Special Foods Stock		960

Recognize 80% share of ⅑ of constructive gain: 0.80 × ⅑ × $10,800.

Whereas neither Peerless nor Special Foods recognized any of the gain from the constructive bond retirement on its separate books in 20X1, Peerless adjusts its equity-method income from Special Foods for its 80 percent share of the $10,800 gain, $8,640. Therefore, as Peerless and Special Foods recognize the gain over the remaining term of the bonds, Peerless must reverse its 20X1 equity-method entry for its share of the gain amortization each year. Thus, the original adjustment of $8,640 is reversed by $960 ($8,640 ÷ 9 years) each year.

Consolidation of Peerless' interest income	$13,000
Consolidation of Special Foods' interest expense	(11,800)
Net reduction in consolidated net income	$ 1,200
Peerless' proportionate share	× 0.80
Reduction in Peerless' share of consolidated net income	$ 960

Consolidation Worksheet—20X2

Figure 8A–2 presents the consolidation worksheet for December 31, 20X2. The first two consolidation entries are the same as we prepared in Chapter 3 with the previously explained exception. Although the analysis of the "book value" portion of the investment account is the same, in preparing the basic consolidation entry, one-ninth of the constructive gain is recognized and shared between Peerless (80 percent) and the NCI shareholders (20 percent). Thus, the basic consolidation entry subtracts the proportionate share of the constructive gain recognition from the Income from Special Foods, Investment in Special Foods' stock, NCI in net income of Special Foods, and NCI in net assets of Special Foods accounts.

Calculations for Basic Consolidation Entry:

Book Value Calculations:

	NCI 20%	+	Peerless 80%	=	Common Stock	+	Retained Earnings
Original Book Value	64,000		256,000		200,000		120,000
+ Net Income	15,000		60,000				75,000
− Dividends	(8,000)		(32,000)				(40,000)
Ending Book Value	71,000		284,000		200,000		155,000

Adjustment to Basic Consolidation Entry:

	NCI 20%	Peerless 80%
Net Income	15,000	60,000
− 20X2 Constructive Gain Rec.	(240)	(960)
Income to be Eliminated	14,760	59,040
Ending Book Value	71,000	284,000
− 20X2 Constructive Gain Rec.	(240)	(960)
Adjusted Book Value	70,760	283,040

Basic Consolidation Entry:

Common Stock	200,000		← Common stock balance
Retained Earnings	120,000		← Beg. RE from trial balance
Income from Special Foods	59,040		← % of NI with Adjustment
NCI in NI of Special Foods	14,760		← NCI % of NI with Adjustment
Dividends Declared		40,000	← 100% of sub's dividends
Investment in Special Foods Stock		283,040	← Net BV with Adjustment
NCI in NA of Special Foods		70,760	← NCI % of BV with Adjustment

Optional Accumulated Depreciation Consolidation Entry:

Accumulated Depreciation	300,000		← Accumulated depreciation at the time of the acquisition netted against cost
Buildings & Equipment		300,000	

The worksheet entry to eliminate the intercompany bond holdings credits the constructive gain on the bond retirement amount between the NCI interest in net assets of Special Foods and Peerless' Investment in Special Foods Common Stock account. In other words, the worksheet entry credits the Investment in Special Foods Common Stock account for $8,640 ($10,800 × 0.80) to eliminate the remaining balance in the account. Similarly, the noncontrolling interest is increased by $2,160 ($10,800 × 0.20), its proportionate share of the constructive gain on the bond retirement.

The intercompany bond holdings consolidation entry also eliminates all aspects of the intercorporate bond holdings, including (1) Peerless' investment in bonds, (2) Special Foods' bonds payable and the associated premium, (3) Peerless' bond interest income, and (4) Special Foods' bond interest expense. The amounts related to the bonds from the books of Peerless and Special Foods and the appropriate consolidated amounts are as follows:

Item	Peerless Products	+	Special Foods	=	Unadjusted Totals	≠	Consolidated Amounts
Bonds Payable	0		$(100,000)		$(100,000)		0
Premium on Bonds Payable	0		(1,600)		(1,600)		0
Investment in Bonds	$92,000		0		92,000		0
Interest Expense	0		$ 11,800		$ 11,800		0
Interest Income	$(13,000)		0		(13,000)		0

FIGURE 8A–2 December 31, 20X2, Consolidation Worksheet; Next Year Following Repurchase of Bonds at Less than Book Value

	Peerless Products	Special Foods	Consolidation Entries DR	Consolidation Entries CR	Consolidated
Income Statement					
Sales	450,000	300,000			750,000
Less: COGS	(180,000)	(160,000)			(340,000)
Less: Depreciation Expense	(50,000)	(20,000)			(70,000)
Less: Other Expenses	(40,000)	(33,200)			(73,200)
Less: Interest Expense	(20,000)	(11,800)		11,800	(20,000)
Interest Income	13,000		13,000		0
Income from Special Foods	59,040		59,040		0
Consolidated Net Income	**232,040**	**75,000**	**72,040**	**11,800**	**246,800**
NCI in Net Income			14,760		(14,760)
Controlling Interest Net Income	**232,040**	**75,000**	**86,800**	**11,800**	**232,040**
Statement of Retained Earnings					
Beginning Balance	428,640	120,000	120,000		428,640
Net Income	**232,040**	**75,000**	**86,800**	**11,800**	232,040
Less: Dividends Declared	(60,000)	(40,000)		40,000	(60,000)
Ending Balance	**600,680**	**155,000**	**206,800**	**51,800**	**600,680**
Balance Sheet					
Cash	212,000	86,600			298,600
Accounts Receivable	150,000	80,000			230,000
Inventory	180,000	90,000			270,000
Investment in Special Foods Stock	291,680			283,040	0
				8,640	
Investment in Special Foods Bonds	92,000			92,000	0
Land	175,000	40,000			215,000
Buildings & Equipment	800,000	600,000		300,000	1,100,000
Less: Accumulated Depreciation	(500,000)	(340,000)	300,000		(540,000)
Total Assets	**1,400,680**	**556,600**	**300,000**	**683,680**	**1,573,600**
Accounts Payable	100,000	100,000			200,000
Bonds Payable	200,000	100,000	100,000		200,000
Premium on Bonds Payable		1,600	1,600		
Common Stock	500,000	200,000	200,000		500,000
Retained Earnings	**600,680**	**155,000**	**206,800**	**51,800**	600,680
NCI in NA of Special Foods				70,760	72,920
				2,160	
Total Liabilities & Equity	**1,400,680**	**556,600**	**508,400**	**124,720**	**1,573,600**

This analysis leads to the following worksheet entry to eliminate intercompany bond holdings:

Eliminate Intercompany Bond Holdings:

Bonds Payable	100,000	
Premium on Bonds Payable	1,600	
Interest Income	13,000	
Investment in Special Foods Bonds		92,000
Interest Expense		11,800
Investment in Special Foods Stock		8,640
NCI in NA of Special Foods		2,160

Investment Account—20X2

The following T-accounts illustrate Peerless' Investment in the Common Stock of Special Foods and Income from Special Foods accounts at the end of 20X2 and how the consolidation entries zero out their balances on the worksheet:

	Inv. in Special Foods (Dr)	Inv. in Special Foods (Cr)		Inc. from Special Foods (Dr)	Inc. from Special Foods (Cr)	
Beg. Balance	264,640					
80% Net Income	60,000				60,000	**80% Net Income**
		32,000	**80% Dividends**			
		960	**Recognize 80% of $\frac{1}{9}$ of Constructive Gain**	960		
Ending Balance	291,680				59,040	**Ending Balance**
		283,040	**Basic**	59,040		
		8,640				
	0				0	

Consolidated Net Income—20X2

Consolidated net income of $246,800 in Figure 8A–2 is computed and allocated as follows:

Peerless' separate income		$173,000
Special Foods' net income	$75,000	
Peerless' amortization of bond discount	(1,000)	
Special Foods' amortization of bond premium	(200)	
Special Foods' realized net income		73,800
Consolidated net income, 20X2		$246,800
Income to noncontrolling interest ($73,800 × 0.20)		(14,760)
Income to controlling interest		$232,040

Net income assigned to the noncontrolling interest can be computed as follows:

Net income of Special Foods, 20X2	$75,000
Less: 20X1 gain on constructive retirement of debt recognized in 20X2 by affiliates:	
Amortization of Peerless' bond discount	(1,000)
Amortization of Special Foods' bond premium	(200)
Special Foods' realized net income	$73,800
Noncontrolling interest's proportionate share	× 0.20
Noncontrolling interest's share of income	$14,760

Noncontrolling Interest—December 31, 20X2

Total noncontrolling interest in the net assets of Special Foods on December 31, 20X2, includes a proportionate share of both the reported book value of Special Foods and the portion of the gain on constructive bond retirement not yet recognized by the affiliates:

Book value of Special Foods' net assets, December 31, 20X2:		
Common stock		$200,000
Retained earnings		155,000
Total book value		$355,000
Gain on constructive retirement of bonds	$10,800	
Less: Portion recognized by affiliates during 20X2	(1,200)	
Constructive gain not yet recognized by affiliates		9,600
Realized book value of Special Foods' net assets		$364,600
Noncontrolling stockholders' share		× 0.20
Noncontrolling interest net assets, December 31, 20X2		$ 72,920

Bond Consolidation Entry in Subsequent Years

In years after 20X2, the worksheet entry to eliminate the intercompany bonds and to adjust for the gain on constructive retirement of the bonds is similar to the entry to eliminate intercompany bond holdings in 20X2. The unamortized bond discount and premium decrease each year by $1,000 and $200, respectively. As of the beginning of 20X3, $9,600 of the gain on the constructive retirement of the bonds remains unrecognized by the affiliates, computed as follows:

Gain on constructive retirement of bonds		$10,800
Less: Portion recognized by affiliates during 20X2:		
Peerless' amortization of bond discount	$1,000	
Special Foods' amortization of bond premium	200	
Total gain recognized by affiliates		(1,200)
Unrecognized gain on constructive retirement of bonds, January 1, 20X3		$ 9,600

The bond consolidation entry at the end of 20X3 would be as follows:

Eliminate Intercompany Bond Holdings:

Bonds Payable	**100,000**	
Premium on Bonds Payable	**1,400**	
Interest Income	**13,000**	
Investment in Special Foods Bonds		**93,000**
Interest Expense		**11,800**
Investment in Special Foods Stock		**7,680**
NCI in NA of Special Foods		**1,920**

LO 8-4

Prepare journal entries and consolidation entries related to an affiliate's debt purchased from a nonaffiliate at an amount more than book value.

Purchase at an Amount Higher than Book Value

When an affiliate's bonds are purchased from a nonaffiliate at an amount greater than their book value, the consolidation procedures are virtually the same as previously illustrated except that a loss is recognized on the constructive retirement of the debt. For example, assume that Special Foods issues 10-year, 12 percent bonds on January 1, 20X1, at par of $100,000. The bonds are purchased from Special Foods by a nonaffiliated investor, which sells the bonds to Peerless Products on December 31, 20X1, for $104,500. Special Foods recognizes $12,000 ($100,000 × 0.12) of interest expense each year. Peerless recognizes interest income of $11,500 in each year after 20X1, computed as follows:

Annual cash interest payment ($100,000 × 0.12)	$12,000
Less: Amortization of premium on bond investment ($4,500 ÷ 9 years)	(500)
Interest income	$11,500

Because the bonds were issued at par, the carrying amount on Special Foods' books remains at $100,000. Thus, once Peerless purchases the bonds from the nonaffiliated investor for $104,500, a loss on the constructive retirement must be recognized in the consolidated income statement for $4,500 ($104,500 − $100,000). The bond consolidation entry in the worksheet prepared at the end of 20X1 removes the bonds payable and the bond investment and recognizes the loss on the constructive retirement:

Eliminate Intercorporate Bond Holdings:

Bonds Payable	**100,000**	
Loss on Bond Retirement	**4,500**	
Investment in Special Foods Bonds		**104,500**

In subsequent years, Peerless amortizes the premium on the bond investment, reducing interest income and the bond investment balance by $500 each year. This, in effect, recognizes a portion of the loss on the constructive retirement. When consolidated statements are prepared, the amount of the loss on constructive retirement that has not been recognized by the separate affiliates at the beginning of the period is allocated proportionately against the ownership interests of the issuing affiliate. The bond consolidation entry needed in the worksheet prepared at the end of 20X2 is as follows:

Eliminate Intercorporate Bond Holdings:

Bonds Payable	100,000	
Interest Income	11,500	
Investment in Special Foods Stock	3,600	
NCI in NA of Special Foods	900	
Investment in Special Foods Bonds		104,000
Interest Expense		12,000

$11,500 = ($100,000 × 0.12) − $500
$3,600 = $4,500 × 0.80
$900 = $4,500 × 0.20
$104,000 = $104,500 − $500
$12,000 = $100,000 × 0.12

Similarly, the following entry is needed in the consolidation worksheet at the end of 20X3:

Eliminate Intercorporate Bond Holdings:

Bonds Payable	100,000	
Interest Income	11,500	
Investment in Special Foods Stock	3,200	
NCI in NA of Special Foods	800	
Investment in Special Foods Bonds		103,500
Interest Expense		12,000

$3,200 = ($4,500 − $500) × 0.80
$800 = ($4,500 − $500) × 0.20
$103,500 = $104,500 − $500 − $500

Appendix 8B Intercompany Indebtedness—Modified Equity Method and Cost Method

This appendix illustrates consolidation procedures under the modified equity method and then the cost method using the straight-line example of the intercompany bond transaction presented earlier in Appendix 8A. Assume that Special Foods issues bonds with a par value of $100,000 and a term of 10 years to a nonaffiliated investor for $102,000 on January 1, 20X1. Peerless Products purchases the bonds from the nonaffiliated investor on December 31, 20X1, for $91,000.

MODIFIED EQUITY METHOD

The accounting procedures under the modified equity method are the same as under the fully adjusted equity method except that the parent (1) does not adjust its income and the investment account by its proportionate share of the gain or loss on the constructive retirement of the bonds in the year of repurchase and (2) does not adjust for the implicit recognition of the gain or loss by it and its subsidiary as they amortize the discount and premium in subsequent years. The 20X1 gain on the constructive retirement in this illustration is $10,800, computed as follows:

Book value of Special Foods' bonds, December 31, 20X1 ($102,000 − $200)	$101,800
Price paid by Peerless to purchase bonds	(91,000)
Gain on constructive retirement of bonds	$ 10,800

Modified Equity-Method Entries—20X1

Peerless records the following entries under the modified equity method during 20X1:

(1B)	Investment in Special Foods Stock	40,000	
	Income from Special Foods		40,000

Record Peerless' 80% share of Special Foods' 20X1 income.

(2B)			
	Cash	24,000	
	Investment in Special Foods Stock		24,000

Record Peerless' 80% share of Special Foods' 20X1 dividend.

The difference is that this method does not adjust equity-method net income for Peerless' proportionate share of the gain on the constructive retirement of Special Foods' bonds. Because Peerless does not adjust its equity-method income for its share of the constructive retirement gain, Peerless' net income will not equal the controlling interest in consolidated net income.

Consolidation Entries—20X1

Figure 8B–1 illustrates the 20X1 worksheet under the modified equity method. The 20X1 worksheet to prepare consolidated financial statements for Peerless Products and Special Foods contains the following consolidation entries. The book value calculations for the basic consolidation entry are essentially the same as those presented in the chapter except that only the NCI accounts are adjusted for the 20 percent portion of the retirement gain (i.e., the Income from Special Foods and Investment in Special Foods common stock are not adjusted):

Calculations for Basic Consolidation Entry:

Book Value Calculations:

	NCI 20%	+	Peerless 80%	=	Common Stock	+	Retained Earnings
Original Book Value	60,000		240,000		200,000		100,000
+ Net Income	10,000		40,000				50,000
− Dividends	(6,000)		(24,000)				(30,000)
Ending Book Value	64,000		256,000		200,000		120,000

Adjustment to Basic Consolidation Entry:

	NCI	Peerless
Net Income	10,000	40,000
+ Gain on Bond Retirement	2,160	8,640
Income to be Eliminated	12,160	48,640
Ending Book Value	64,000	256,000
+ Gain on Bond Retirement	2,160	8,640
Adjusted Book Value	66,160	264,640

Basic Consolidation Entry:

Common Stock	200,000		← Common stock balance
Retained Earnings	100,000		← Beg. RE from trial balance
Income from Special Foods	40,000		← Peerless' share of Special Foods' NI
NCI in NI of Special Foods	12,160		← NCI share of NI with Adjustment
Dividends Declared		30,000	← 100% of sub's dividends
Investment in Special Foods stock		256,000	← Net BV left in inv. acct.
NCI in NA of Special Foods		66,160	← NCI share of BV with Adjustment

Optional Accumulated Depreciation Consolidation Entry:

Accumulated Depreciation	300,000		← Accumulated depreciation at the time of the acquisition netted against cost
Buildings & Equipment		300,000	

Eliminate Intercorporate Bond Holdings:

Bonds Payable	100,000	
Premium on Bonds Payable	1,800	
Investment in Special Foods Bonds		91,000
Gain on Bond Retirement		10,800

FIGURE 8B–1 December 31, 20X1, Consolidation Worksheet; Repurchase of Bonds at Less than Book Value, Modified Equity Method

	Peerless Products	Special Foods	Consolidation Entries DR	Consolidation Entries CR	Consolidated
Income Statement					
Sales	400,000	200,000			600,000
Less: COGS	(170,000)	(115,000)			(285,000)
Less: Depreciation Expense	(50,000)	(20,000)			(70,000)
Less: Other Expenses	(20,000)	(3,200)			(23,200)
Less: Interest Expense	(20,000)	(11,800)			(31,800)
Income from Special Foods	40,000		40,000		0
Gain from Bond Retirement				10,800	10,800
Consolidated Net Income	180,000	50,000	40,000	10,800	200,800
NCI in Net Income			12,160		(12,160)
Controlling Interest Net Income	**180,000**	**50,000**	**52,160**	**10,800**	**188,640**
Statement of Retained Earnings					
Beginning Balance	300,000	100,000	100,000		300,000
Net Income	**180,000**	**50,000**	**52,160**	**10,800**	188,640
Less: Dividends Declared	(60,000)	(30,000)		30,000	(60,000)
Ending Balance	**420,000**	**120,000**	**152,160**	**40,800**	**428,640**
Balance Sheet					
Cash	173,000	76,800			249,800
Accounts Receivable	75,000	50,000			125,000
Inventory	100,000	75,000			175,000
Investment in Special Foods Stock	256,000			256,000	0
Investment in Special Foods Bonds	91,000			91,000	0
Land	175,000	40,000			215,000
Buildings & Equipment	800,000	600,000		300,000	1,100,000
Less: Accumulated Depreciation	(450,000)	(320,000)	300,000		(470,000)
Total Assets	**1,220,000**	**521,800**	**300,000**	**647,000**	**1,394,800**
Accounts Payable	100,000	100,000			200,000
Bonds Payable	200,000	100,000	100,000		200,000
Premium on Bonds Payable		1,800	1,800		0
Common Stock	500,000	200,000	200,000		500,000
Retained Earnings	**420,000**	**120,000**	**152,160**	**40,800**	428,640
NCI in NA of Special Foods				66,160	66,160
Total Liabilities & Equity	**1,220,000**	**521,800**	**453,960**	**106,960**	**1,394,800**

Modified Equity-Method Entries—20X2

In addition to the entries related to its investment in Special Foods' bonds, Peerless records the following entries during 20X2 under the modified equity method:

(3B)	Investment in Special Foods Stock	60,000	
	Income from Special Foods		60,000

Record Peerless' 80% share of Special Foods' 20X1 income.

(4B)	Cash	32,000	
	Investment in Special Foods Stock		32,000

Record Peerless' 80% share of Special Foods 20X1 dividend.

Consolidation Entries—20X2

Figure 8B–2 illustrates the consolidation worksheet for 20X2 under the modified equity method. The following consolidation entries are needed in the worksheet to prepare consolidated financial statements for 20X2. Again, the book value calculations for the basic consolidation entry are essentially the same as those presented in the chapter except that only the NCI accounts are adjusted for the 20 percent portion of the retirement gain recognition in the basic consolidation entry (i.e., the Income from Special Foods and Investment in Special Foods Common Stock accounts are not adjusted).

Calculations for Basic Consolidation Entry:

Book Value Calculations:

	NCI 20%	+	Peerless 80%	=	Common Stock	+	Retained Earnings
Original Book Value	64,000		256,000		200,000		120,000
+ Net Income	15,000		60,000				75,000
− Dividends	(8,000)		(32,000)				(40,000)
Ending Book Value	71,000		284,000		200,000		155,000

Adjustment to Basic Consolidation Entry:

	NCI	Peerless
Net Income	15,000	60,000
− 20X2 Constructive Gain Rec.	(240)	(960)
Income to be Eliminated	14,760	59,040
Ending Book Value	71,000	284,000
− 20X2 Constructive Gain Rec.	(240)	(960)
Adjusted Book Value	70,760	283,040

Basic Consolidation Entry:

	Debit	Credit	
Common Stock	200,000		← Common stock balance
Retained Earnings	120,000		← Beg. RE from trial balance
Income from Special Foods	60,000		← Peerless' share of Special Foods' NI
NCI in NI of Special Foods	14,760		← NCI % of NI with Adjustment
Dividends Declared		40,000	← 100% of sub's dividends
Investment in Special Foods stock		284,000	← Net BV left in the inv. acct.
NCI in NA of Special Foods		70,760	← NCI % of BV with Adjustment

Optional Accumulated Depreciation Consolidation Entry:

	Debit	Credit	
Accumulated Depreciation	300,000		← Accumulated depreciation at the time of the acquisition netted against cost
Buildings & Equipment		300,000	

Eliminate Intercompany Bond Holdings:

	Debit	Credit
Bonds Payable	100,000	
Premium on Bonds Payable	1,600	
Interest Income	13,000	
Investment in Special Foods Bonds		92,000
Interest Expense		11,800
Retained Earnings, January 1		8,640
NCI in NA of Special Foods		2,160

FIGURE 8B–2 December 31, 20X2, Consolidation Worksheet; Next Year Following Repurchase of Bonds at Less than Book Value, Modified Equity Method

	Peerless Products	Special Foods	Consolidation Entries DR	Consolidation Entries CR	Consolidated
Income Statement					
Sales	450,000	300,000			750,000
Less: COGS	(180,000)	(160,000)			(340,000)
Less: Depreciation Expense	(50,000)	(20,000)			(70,000)
Less: Other Expenses	(40,000)	(33,200)			(73,200)
Less: Interest Expense	(20,000)	(11,800)		11,800	(20,000)
Interest Income	13,000		13,000		0
Income from Special Foods	60,000		60,000		0
Consolidated Net Income	**233,000**	**75,000**	**73,000**	**11,800**	**246,800**
NCI in Net Income			14,760		(14,760)
Controlling Interest Net Income	**233,000**	**75,000**	**87,760**	**11,800**	**232,040**
Statement of Retained Earnings					
Beginning Balance	420,000	120,000	120,000	8,640	428,640
Net Income	**233,000**	**75,000**	**87,760**	**11,800**	232,040
Less: Dividends Declared	(60,000)	(40,000)		40,000	(60,000)
Ending Balance	**593,000**	**155,000**	**207,760**	**60,440**	**600,680**
Balance Sheet					
Cash	212,000	86,600			298,600
Accounts Receivable	150,000	80,000			230,000
Inventory	180,000	90,000			270,000
Investment in Special Foods Stock	284,000			284,000	0
Investment in Special Foods Bonds	92,000			92,000	0
Land	175,000	40,000			215,000
Buildings & Equipment	800,000	600,000		300,000	1,100,000
Less: Accumulated Depreciation	(500,000)	(340,000)	300,000		(540,000)
Total Assets	**1,393,000**	**556,600**	**300,000**	**676,000**	**1,573,600**
Accounts Payable	100,000	100,000			200,000
Bonds Payable	200,000	100,000	100,000		200,000
Premium on Bonds Payable		1,600	1,600		
Common Stock	500,000	200,000	200,000		500,000
Retained Earnings	**593,000**	**155,000**	**207,760**	**60,440**	600,680
NCI in NA of Special Foods				70,760 2,160	72,920
Total Liabilities & Equity	**1,393,000**	**556,600**	**509,360**	**133,360**	**1,573,600**

COST METHOD

Preparation of consolidated financial statements when the cost method has been used is illustrated with the same example employed for the modified equity method. Peerless recognizes dividend income of $24,000 ($30,000 × 0.80) in 20X1 and $32,000 ($40,000 × 0.80) in 20X2 under the cost method. Peerless makes no adjustments with respect to Special Foods' undistributed earnings or the gain on the constructive bond retirement.

Consolidation Entries—20X1

Figure 8B–3 illustrates the consolidation worksheet for 20X1 under the cost method. The following consolidation entries are needed in the worksheet used to prepare consolidated financial statements for 20X1 using the cost method:

FIGURE 8B–3 December 31, 20X1, Consolidation Worksheet; Repurchase of Bonds at Less than Book Value, Cost Method

	Peerless Products	Special Foods	Consolidation Entries DR	Consolidation Entries CR	Consolidated
Income Statement					
Sales	400,000	200,000			600,000
Less: COGS	(170,000)	(115,000)			(285,000)
Less: Depreciation Expense	(50,000)	(20,000)			(70,000)
Less: Other Expenses	(20,000)	(3,200)			(23,200)
Less: Interest Expense	(20,000)	(11,800)			(31,800)
Dividend Income	24,000		24,000		0
Gain on Bond Retirement				10,800	10,800
Consolidated Net Income	**164,000**	**50,000**	24,000	10,800	**200,800**
NCI in Net Income			6,000 6,160		(12,160)
Controlling Interest Net Income	**164,000**	**50,000**	36,160	10,800	**188,640**
Statement of Retained Earnings					
Beginning Balance	300,000	100,000	100,000		300,000
Net Income	**164,000**	**50,000**	36,160	10,800	188,640
Less: Dividends Declared	(60,000)	(30,000)		30,000	(60,000)
Ending Balance	**404,000**	**120,000**	136,160	40,800	**428,640**
Balance Sheet					
Cash	173,000	76,800			249,800
Accounts Receivable	75,000	50,000			125,000
Inventory	100,000	75,000			175,000
Investment in Special Foods Stock	240,000			240,000	0
Investment in Special Foods Bonds	91,000			91,000	
Land	175,000	40,000			215,000
Buildings & Equipment	800,000	600,000		300,000	1,100,000
Less: Accumulated Depreciation	(450,000)	(320,000)	300,000		(470,000)
Total Assets	**1,204,000**	**521,800**	300,000	631,000	**1,394,800**
Accounts Payable	100,000	100,000			200,000
Bonds Payable	200,000	100,000	100,000		200,000
Premium on Bonds Payable		1,800	1,800		
Common Stock	500,000	200,000	200,000		500,000
Retained Earnings	**404,000**	**120,000**	136,160	40,800	428,640
NCI in NA of Special Foods				60,000 6,160	66,160
Total Liabilities & Equity	**1,204,000**	**521,800**	437,960	106,960	**1,394,800**

Investment Consolidation Entry:

Common Stock	200,000		← Original amount invested (100%)
Retained Earnings	100,000		← RE on acquisition date
Investment in Special Foods stock		240,000	← Original cost of investment
NCI in NA of Special Foods		60,000	← NCI share of acquisition date BV

Dividend Consolidation Entry:

Dividend Income	24,000		← Peerless' 80% share of dividends declared
NCI in NI of Special Foods	6,000		← NCI's 20% share of dividends declared
Dividends Declared		30,000	← 100% of Special Foods' dividends declared

The amount of undistributed net income assigned to the NCI is adjusted for the NCI's share of the gross profit deferral.

NCI in NI and NCI in NA of Special Foods:

	NCI 20%
Net Income	10,000
− Dividend	(6,000)
+ Gain on Bond Retirement	2,160
NCI in NI of Special Foods	6,160

Assign Undistributed Income to NCI:

NCI in NI of Special Foods	6,160		← NCI's 20% share of undistributed income from Special Foods with Adjustment
NCI in NA of Special Foods		6,160	← NCI's 20% share of undistributed income from Special Foods with Adjustment

Optional Accumulated Depreciation Consolidation Entry:

Accumulated Depreciation	300,000		← Accumulated depreciation at the time of the acquisition netted against cost
Buildings & Equipment		300,000	

Eliminate Intercorporate Bond Holdings:

Bonds Payable	100,000	
Premium on Bonds Payable	1,800	
Investment in Special Foods Bonds		91,000
Gain on Bond Retirement		10,800

Consolidation Entries—20X2

Figure 8B–4 illustrates the consolidation worksheet for 20X2 under the cost method. Consolidation entries needed in the consolidation worksheet prepared at the end of 20X2 are as follows:

Investment Consolidation Entry:

Common Stock	200,000		← Original amount invested (100%)
Retained Earnings	100,000		← RE on acquisition date
Investment in Special Foods stock		240,000	← Original cost of investment
NCI in NA of Special Foods		60,000	← NCI share of acquisition date BV

Dividend Consolidation Entry:

Dividend Income	32,000		← Peerless' 80% share of dividends declared
NCI in NI of Special Foods	8,000		← NCI's 20% share of dividends declared
Dividends Declared		40,000	← 100% of Special Foods' dividends declared

The amount of undistributed net income assigned to the NCI is adjusted for the NCI's share of the gross profit deferral.

NCI in NI and NCI in NA of Special Foods:

	NCI 20%
Net Income	15,000
− Dividend	(8,000)
− 20X2 Constructive Gain Rec.	(240)
NCI in NI of Special Foods	6,760
Undistributed from Prior Years	4,000
NCI in NA of Special Foods	10,760

FIGURE 8B–4 December 31, 20X2, Consolidation Worksheet; Next Year Following Repurchase of Bonds at Less than Book Value, Cost Method

	Peerless Products	Special Foods	Consolidation Entries DR	Consolidation Entries CR	Consolidated
Income Statement					
Sales	450,000	300,000			750,000
Less: COGS	(180,000)	(160,000)			(340,000)
Less: Depreciation Expense	(50,000)	(20,000)			(70,000)
Less: Other Expenses	(40,000)	(33,200)			(73,200)
Less: Interest Expense	(20,000)	(11,800)		11,800	(20,000)
Interest Income	13,000		13,000		
Dividend Income	32,000		32,000		0
Consolidated Net Income	**205,000**	**75,000**	**45,000**	**11,800**	**246,800**
NCI in Net Income			8,000 6,760		(14,760)
Controlling Interest Net Income	**205,000**	**75,000**	**59,760**	**11,800**	**232,040**
Statement of Retained Earnings					
Beginning Balance	404,000	120,000	100,000 4,000	8,640	428,640
Net Income	**205,000**	**75,000**	**59,760**	**11,800**	232,040
Less: Dividends Declared	(60,000)	(40,000)		40,000	(60,000)
Ending Balance	**549,000**	**155,000**	**163,760**	**60,440**	**600,680**
Balance Sheet					
Cash	212,000	86,600			298,600
Accounts Receivable	150,000	80,000			230,000
Inventory	180,000	90,000			270,000
Investment in Special Foods Stock	240,000			240,000	0
Investment in Special Foods Bonds	92,000			92,000	0
Land	175,000	40,000			215,000
Buildings & Equipment	800,000	600,000		300,000	1,100,000
Less: Accumulated Depreciation	(500,000)	(340,000)	300,000		(540,000)
Total Assets	**1,349,000**	**556,600**	**300,000**	**632,000**	**1,573,600**
Accounts Payable	100,000	100,000			200,000
Bonds Payable	200,000	100,000	100,000		200,000
Discount on Bonds Payable		1,600	1,600		0
Common Stock	500,000	200,000	200,000		500,000
Retained Earnings	**549,000**	**155,000**	**163,760**	**60,440**	600,680
NCI in NA of Special Foods				60,000 10,760 2,160	72,920
Total Liabilities & Equity	**1,349,000**	**556,600**	**465,360**	**133,360**	**1,573,600**

Assign Undistributed Income to NCI:

NCI in NI of Special Foods	6,760		← NCI's 20% share of 20X2 undistributed income from Special Foods with Adjustment
Retained Earnings	4,000*		← NCI's 20% share of undistributed 20X1 NI
NCI in NA of Special Foods		10,760	← NCI's 20% share of cumulative undistributed income from Special Foods with Adjustment

* Note that these entries adjust for the subsidiary's retained earnings balance. The subsidiary does not adjust for the gain on bond retirement because this adjustment is made in the consolidation worksheet, not in the records of the subsidiary.

Optional Accumulated Depreciation Consolidation Entry:

Accumulated Depreciation	300,000	
Buildings & Equipment		300,000

← Accumulated depreciation at the time of the acquisition netted against cost

Eliminate Intercompany Bond Holdings:

Bonds Payable	100,000	
Premium on Bonds Payable	1,600	
Interest Income	13,000	
Investment in Special Foods Bonds		92,000
Interest Expense		11,800
Retained Earnings		8,640
NCI in NA of Special Foods		2,160

QUESTIONS

LO 8-1 **Q8-1** When is a gain or loss on bond retirement included in the consolidated income statement?

LO 8-2 **Q8-2** What is meant by a constructive bond retirement in a multicorporate setting? How does a constructive bond retirement differ from an actual bond retirement?

LO 8-2 **Q8-3** When a bond issue has been placed directly with an affiliate, what account balances will be stated incorrectly in the consolidated statements if the intercompany bond ownership is not eliminated in preparing the consolidation worksheet?

LO 8-3, 8-4 **Q8-4** When an affiliate's bonds are purchased from a nonaffiliate during the period, what balances will be stated incorrectly in the consolidated financial statements if the intercompany bond ownership is not eliminated in preparing the consolidation worksheet?

LO 8-1, 8-2 **Q8-5** For a multicorporate entity, how is the recognition of gains or losses on bond retirement changed when emphasis is placed on the economic entity rather than the legal entity?

LO 8-2, 8-3 **Q8-6** When a parent company sells land to a subsidiary at more than book value, the consolidation entries at the end of the period include a debit to the gain on the sale of land. When a parent purchases the bonds of a subsidiary from a nonaffiliate at less than book value, the consolidation entries at the end of the period contain a credit to a gain on bond retirement. Why are these two situations not handled in the same manner in the consolidation worksheet?

LO 8-2 **Q8-7** What is the effect of eliminating intercompany interest income and interest expense on consolidated net income when bonds have been sold directly to an affiliate? Why?

LO 8-2 **Q8-8** What is the effect of eliminating intercompany interest income and interest expense on consolidated net income when a loss on bond retirement has been reported in a prior year's consolidated financial statements as a result of a constructive retirement of an affiliate's bonds? Why?

LO 8-3, 8-4 **Q8-9** If an affiliate's bonds are purchased from a nonaffiliate at the beginning of the current year, how can the amount of the gain or loss on constructive retirement be computed by looking at the two companies' year-end trial balances?

LO 8-4 **Q8-10** When the parent company purchases a subsidiary's bonds from a nonaffiliate for more than book value, what income statement accounts will be affected in preparing consolidated financial statements? What will be the effect on income assigned to the controlling interest in the consolidated income statement?

LO 8-3 **Q8-11** When a subsidiary purchases the bonds of its parent from a nonaffiliate for less than book value, what will be the effect on consolidated net income and income to the controlling interest?

LO 8-2 **Q8-12** How is the amount of income assigned to the noncontrolling interest affected by the direct placement of a subsidiary's bonds with the parent company?

LO 8-3 **Q8-13** How is the amount of income assigned to the noncontrolling interest affected when the parent purchases the bonds of its subsidiary from an unaffiliated company for less than book value?

LO 8-2, 8-3, 8-4 **Q8-14** How would the relationship between interest income recorded by a subsidiary and interest expense recorded by the parent be expected to change when comparing a direct placement of the parent's bonds with the subsidiary to a constructive retirement in which the subsidiary purchases the bonds of the parent from a nonaffiliate?

LO 8-3 **Q8-15** A subsidiary purchased bonds of its parent company from a nonaffiliate in the preceding period, and a gain on bond retirement was reported in the consolidated income statement as a result of the purchase. What effect will that event have on the amount of consolidated net income and income to the noncontrolling interest reported in the current period?

LO 8-4 **Q8-16** A parent company purchased its subsidiary's bonds from a nonaffiliate in the preceding year, and a loss on bond retirement was reported in the consolidated income statement. How will income assigned to the noncontrolling interest be affected in the year following the constructive retirement?

LO 8-3, 8-4 **Q8-17** A parent purchases a subsidiary's bonds directly from it. The parent later sells the bonds to a nonaffiliate. From a consolidated viewpoint, what occurs when the parent sells the bonds? Is a gain or loss reported in the consolidated income statement when the parent sells the bonds? Why?

LO 8-3, 8-4 **Q8-18** Shortly after a parent company purchased its subsidiary's bonds from a nonaffiliate, the subsidiary retired the entire issue. How is the gain or loss on bond retirement reported by the subsidiary treated for consolidation purposes?

CASES

LO 8-4

C8-1 Recognition of Retirement Gains and Losses

Analysis

Bradley Corporation sold bonds to Flood Company in 20X2 at 90. At the end of 20X4, Century Corporation purchased the bonds from Flood at 105. Bradley then retired the full bond issue on December 31, 20X7, at 101. Century holds 80 percent of Bradley's voting stock. Neither Century nor Bradley owns stock of Flood Company.

Required

a. Indicate how each of the three bond transactions should be recorded by the companies involved.

b. Indicate when, if at all, the consolidated entity headed by Century should recognize a gain or loss on bond retirement, and indicate whether a gain or a loss should be recognized.

c. Will income assigned to Bradley's noncontrolling shareholders be affected by the bond transactions? If so, in which years?

LO 8-2

C8-2 Borrowing by Variable Interest Entities

Research

Hydro Corporation needed to build a new production facility. Because it already had a relatively high debt ratio, the company decided to establish a joint venture with Rich Corner Bank. This arrangement permitted the joint venture to borrow $30 million for 20 years on a fixed-interest-rate basis at a rate nearly 2 percent less than Hydro would have paid if it had borrowed the money. Rich Corner Bank purchased 100 percent of the joint venture's equity for $200,000, and Hydro provided a guarantee of the debt to the bondholders and a guarantee to Rich Corner Bank that it would earn a 20 percent annual return on its investment.

On completion of the production facility, Hydro entered into a 10-year lease with the joint venture for use of the new facility. Due to the lease agreement terms, Hydro has reported the lease as an operating lease. Hydro does not report an investment in the joint venture because it holds no equity interest.

Required

As a senior member of Hydro's accounting staff, you have been asked to investigate the financial reporting standards associated with accounting for variable interest entities and determine whether Hydro's reporting is appropriate. Prepare a memo to Hydro's president stating your findings and conclusions and analyzing the impact on Hydro's financial statements if the current reporting procedures are inappropriate. Include citations to or quotations from the authoritative accounting literature in support of your findings and conclusions.

LO 8-3

C8-3 Subsidiary Bond Holdings

Farflung Corporation has in excess of 60 subsidiaries worldwide. It owns 65 percent of the voting common stock of Micro Company and 80 percent of the shares of Eagle Corporation. Micro sold

Research

$400,000 par value first mortgage bonds at par value on January 2, 20X0, to Independent Company. No intercorporate ownership exists between Farflung and its subsidiaries and Independent.

On December 31, 20X4, Independent determined the need for cash for other purposes and sold the Micro bonds to Eagle for $424,000. Farflung's accounting department was not aware of Eagle's bond purchase and included the Micro Company bonds among its long-term liabilities in the consolidated balance sheet prepared at December 31, 20X4.

Required

In reviewing the financial statements of Farflung and its subsidiaries at December 31, 20X5, you discovered Eagle Corporation's investment in Micro's bonds and immediately brought it to the attention of Farflung's financial vice president. You have been asked to prepare a memo to the financial vice president detailing the appropriate reporting treatment when intercorporate bond ownership occurs in this way and to provide recommendations as to the actions, if any, Farflung should take in preparing its consolidated statements at December 31, 20X5. Include in your memo citations to or quotations from applicable authoritative accounting standards in support of your position.

LO 8-4

C8-4 Interest Income and Expense

Understanding

Snerd Corporation's controller is having difficulty explaining the impact of several of the company's intercorporate bond transactions.

Required

a. Snerd receives interest payments in excess of the amount of interest income it records on its investment in Snort bonds. Did Snerd purchase the bonds at par value, at a premium, or at a discount? How can you tell?

b. The 20X3 consolidated income statement reported a gain on the retirement of a subsidiary's bonds. If Snerd purchased the bonds from a nonaffiliate at par value:

(1) Were the subsidiary's bonds originally sold at a premium or a discount? How can you tell?

(2) Will the annual interest payments received by Snerd be more or less than the interest expense recorded by the subsidiary? Explain.

(3) How is the difference between the interest income recorded by Snerd and the interest expense recorded by the subsidiary treated in preparing consolidated financial statements at the end of each period?

LO 8-1, 8-2

C8-5 Intercompany Debt

Analysis

Intercompany debt, both long term and short term, arises frequently. In some cases, intercorporate borrowings may arise because one affiliate can borrow at a cheaper rate than others, and lending to other affiliates may reduce the overall cost of borrowing. In other cases, intercompany receivables/payables arise because of intercompany sales of goods or services or other types of intercompany transactions.

Required

a. What major problem might arise with intercompany debt between a domestic parent and a foreign subsidiary or between subsidiaries in different countries? How has The Hershey Company dealt with this problem?

b. Did The Hershey Company's intercompany loans arise because of direct loans or because of intercompany sales of goods and services on credit?

EXERCISES

LO 8-2

E8-1 Bond Sale from Parent to Subsidiary (Effective Interest Method)

Lamar Corporation owns 60 percent of Humbolt Corporation's voting shares. On January 1, 20X2, Lamar Corporation sold $150,000 par value, 6 percent first mortgage bonds to Humbolt for $156,000. The bonds mature in 10 years and pay interest semiannually on January 1 and July 1.

Required

a. Prepare the journal entries for 20X2 for Humbolt related to its ownership of Lamar's bonds.

b. Prepare the journal entries for 20X2 for Lamar related to the bonds.

c. Prepare the worksheet consolidation entries needed on December 31, 20X2, to remove the effects of the intercorporate ownership of bonds.

LO 8-2

E8-1A Bond Sale from Parent to Subsidiary (Straight-Line Method)

Assume the same facts as in E8-1 and prepare entries using straight-line amortization of bond discount or premium.

LO 8-2

E8-2 Computation of Transfer Price (Effective Interest Method)

Nettle Corporation sold $100,000 par value, 10-year first mortgage bonds to Timberline Corporation on January 1, 20X5. The bonds, which bear a nominal interest rate of 12 percent, pay interest semiannually on January 1 and July 1. The current market interest rate is 11 percent. Timberline Corporation owns 65 percent of the voting stock of Nettle Corporation, and consolidated statements are prepared on December 31, 20X7.

Required

a. What was the original purchase price of the bonds to Timberline Corporation?

b. What is the balance in Timberline's bond investment account on December 31, 20X7?

c. Give the worksheet consolidation entry or entries needed to remove the effects of the intercompany ownership of bonds in preparing consolidated financial statements for 20X7.

LO 8-2

E8-2A Computation of Transfer Price (Straight-line Method)

Nettle Corporation sold $100,000 par value, 10-year first mortgage bonds to Timberline Corporation on January 1, 20X5. The bonds, which bear a nominal interest rate of 12 percent, pay interest semiannually on January 1 and July 1. The entry to record interest income by Timberline Corporation on December 31, 20X7, was as follows:

Interest Receivable	6,000	
Interest Income		5,750
Investment in Nettle Corporation Bonds		250

Timberline Corporation owns 65 percent of the voting stock of Nettle Corporation, and consolidated statements are prepared on December 31, 20X7.

Required

a. What was the original purchase price of the bonds to Timberline Corporation?

b. What is the balance in Timberline's bond investment account on December 31, 20X7?

c. Give the worksheet consolidation entry or entries needed to remove the effects of the intercompany ownership of bonds in preparing consolidated financial statements for 20X7.

LO 8-2

E8-3 Bond Sale at Discount (Effective Interest Method)

Wood Corporation owns 70 percent of Carter Company's voting shares. On January 1, 20X3, Carter sold bonds with a par value of $600,000 at 98. Wood purchased $400,000 par value of the bonds; the remainder was sold to nonaffiliates. The bonds mature in five years and pay an annual interest rate of 8 percent. Interest is paid semiannually on January 1 and July 1.

Required

a. What amount of interest expense should be reported in the 20X4 consolidated income statement?

b. Give the journal entries Wood recorded during 20X4 with regard to its investment in Carter bonds.

c. Give all worksheet consolidation entries needed to remove the effects of the intercorporate bond ownership in preparing consolidated financial statements for 20X4.

LO 8-2

E8-3A Bond Sale at Discount (Straight-line Method)

Assume the same facts as in E8-3 but prepare entries using straight-line amortization of bond discount or premium.

"A" indicates that the item relates to Appendix 8A.

LO 8-3, 8-4

E8-4 Evaluation of Intercorporate Bond Holdings (Effective Interest Method)

Stellar Corporation purchased bonds of its subsidiary from a nonaffiliate during 20X6. Although Stellar purchased the bonds at par value, a loss on bond retirement is reported in the 20X6 consolidated income statement as a result of the purchase.

Required

a. Were the bonds originally sold by the subsidiary at a premium or a discount? Explain.

b. Will the annual interest payments Stellar receives be more or less than the interest expense the subsidiary records each period? Explain.

c. As a result of the entry recorded at December 31, 20X7, to eliminate the effects of the intercompany bond holding, will consolidated net income be increased or decreased? Explain.

LO 8-2, 8-3, 8-4

E8-5 Multiple-Choice Questions (Effective Interest Method)

Select the correct answer for each of the following questions.

1. **[AICPA Adapted]** Wagner, a holder of a $1,000,000 Palmer Inc. bond, collected the interest due on March 31, 20X8, and then sold the bond to Seal Inc. for $975,000. On that date, Palmer, a 75 percent owner of Seal, had a $1,075,000 carrying amount for this bond. What was the effect of Seal's purchase of Palmer's bond on the retained earnings and noncontrolling interest amounts reported in Palmer's March 31, 20X8, consolidated balance sheet?

	Retained Earnings	Noncontrolling Interest
a.	$100,000 increase	No effect
b.	$75,000 increase	$25,000 increase
c.	No effect	$25,000 increase
d.	No effect	$100,000 increase

2. **[AICPA Adapted]** P Company purchased term bonds at a premium on the open market. These bonds represented 20 percent of the outstanding class of bonds issued at a discount by S Company, P's wholly owned subsidiary. P intends to hold the bonds to maturity. In a consolidated balance sheet, the difference between the bond carrying amounts of the two companies would be

   a. Included as a decrease to retained earnings.

   b. Included as an increase in retained earnings.

   c. Reported as a deferred debit to be amortized over the remaining life of the bonds.

   d. Reported as a deferred credit to be amortized over the remaining life of the bonds.

Note: The following information relates to questions 3–6:
Kruse Corporation holds 60 percent of the voting common shares of Gary's Ice Cream Parlors. On January 1, 20X6, Gary's purchased $50,000 par value, 10 percent first mortgage bonds of Kruse from Cane for $58,000. Kruse originally issued the bonds to Cane on January 1, 20X4, for $53,000 (assuming a market interest rate of 9.074505 percent). The bonds have a 10-year maturity from the date of issue and pay interest semiannually on June 30th and December 31st.

Gary's reported net income of $20,000 for 20X6, and Kruse reported income (excluding income from ownership of Gary's stock) of $40,000.

3. What amount of interest expense does Kruse record for 20X6?

   a. $4,777.

   b. $4,767.

   c. $4,756.

   d. $4,805.

4. What amount of interest income does Gary's Ice Cream Parlors record for 20X6?

   a. $4,233.

   b. $5,000.

   c. $4,145.

   d. $6,000.

5. What gain or loss on the retirement of bonds should be reported in the 20X6 consolidated income statement?

   a. $2,423 gain.
   b. $5,617 gain.
   c. $5,408 loss.
   d. $8,004 loss.

6. What amount of consolidated net income should be reported for 20X6?

   a. $47,253.
   b. $54,410.
   c. $55,126.
   d. $60,256.

LO 8-2, 8-3, 8-4

E8-5A Multiple-Choice Questions (Straight-line Method)

Kruse Corporation holds 60 percent of the voting common shares of Gary's Ice Cream Parlors. On January 1, 20X6, Gary's purchased $50,000 par value, 10 percent first mortgage bonds of Kruse from Cane for $58,000. Kruse originally issued the bonds to Cane on January 1, 20X4, for $53,000. The bonds have a 10-year maturity from the date of issue and pay interest semiannually. The bonds are accounted for using straight-line amortization of premiums and discounts.

Gary's reported net income of $20,000 for 20X6, and Kruse reported income (excluding income from ownership of Gary's stock) of $40,000.

Required

Select the correct answer for each of the following questions.

1. What amount of interest expense does Kruse record 20X6?

   a. $4,000.
   b. $4,700.
   c. $5,000.
   d. $10,000.

2. What amount of interest income does Gary's Ice Cream Parlors record for 20X6?

   a. $4,000.
   b. $5,000.
   c. $9,000.
   d. $10,000.

3. What gain or loss on the retirement of bonds should be reported in the 20X6 consolidated income statement?

   a. $2,400 gain.
   b. $5,600 gain.
   c. $5,600 loss.
   d. $8,000 loss.

4. What amount of consolidated net income should be reported for 20X6?

   a. $47,100.
   b. $54,400.
   c. $55,100.
   d. $60,000.

LO 8-2

E8-6 Multiple-Choice Questions (Effective Interest Method)

On January 1, 20X4, Passive Heating Corporation paid $104,000 for $100,000 par value, 9 percent bonds of Solar Energy Corporation. Solar had issued $300,000 of the 10-year bonds on January 1, 20X2, for $360,000. The bonds pay interest semiannually. Passive previously had purchased 80 percent of the common stock of Solar on January 1, 20X1, at underlying book value.

Passive reported operating income (excluding income from subsidiary) of $50,000, and Solar reported net income of $30,000 for 20X4.

Required

Select the correct answer for each of the following questions.

1. What amount of interest expense should be included in the 20X4 consolidated income statement?
   a. $14,626.
   b. $18,415.
   c. $21,678.
   d. $27,112.
2. What amount of gain or loss on bond retirement should be included in the 20X4 consolidated income statement?
   a. $4,243 gain.
   b. $4,243 loss.
   c. $12,923 gain.
   d. $16,115 loss.
3. Income assigned to the noncontrolling interest in the 20X4 consolidated income statement should be
   a. $6,534.
   b. $8,321.
   c. $8,388.
   d. $16,826.

LO 8-2

E8-6A Multiple-Choice Questions (Straight-Line Method)

Assume the same facts as in E8-6 except that the company uses straight-line amortization.

Required

Select the correct answer for each of the following questions.

1. What amount of interest expense should be included in the 20X4 consolidated income statement?
   a. $14,000.
   b. $18,000.
   c. $21,000.
   d. $27,000.
2. What amount of gain or loss on bond retirement should be included in the 20X4 consolidated income statement?
   a. $4,000 gain.
   b. $4,000 loss.
   c. $12,000 gain.
   d. $16,000 loss.
3. Income assigned to the noncontrolling interest in the 20X4 consolidated income statement should be
   a. $6,000.
   b. $8,100.
   c. $8,400.
   d. $16,000.

LO 8-2

E8-7 Constructive Retirement at End of Year (Effective Interest Method)

Able Company issued $600,000 of 9 percent first mortgage bonds on January 1, 20X1, at 103. The bonds mature in 20 years and pay interest semiannually on January 1 and July 1. Prime Corporation purchased $400,000 of Able's bonds from the original purchaser on December 31, 20X5, for $397,000. Prime owns 60 percent of Able's voting common stock.

Required

a. Prepare the worksheet consolidation entry or entries needed to remove the effects of the intercorporate bond ownership in preparing consolidated financial statements for 20X5.

b. Prepare the worksheet consolidation entry or entries needed to remove the effects of the intercorporate bond ownership in preparing consolidated financial statements for 20X6.

LO 8-2

E8-7A Constructive Retirement at End of Year (Straight-Line Method)

Assume the same facts as in E8-7 but prepare entries using straight-line amortization of bond discount or premium.

LO 8-2

E8-8 Constructive Retirement at Beginning of Year (Effective Interest Method)

Able Company issued $600,000 of 9 percent first mortgage bonds on January 1, 20X1, at 103. The bonds mature in 20 years and pay interest semiannually on January 1 and July 1. Prime Corporation purchased $400,000 of Able's bonds from the original purchaser on January 1, 20X5, for $396,800. Prime owns 60 percent of Able's voting common stock.

Required

a. Prepare the worksheet consolidation entry or entries needed to remove the effects of the intercorporate bond ownership in preparing consolidated financial statements for 20X5.

b. Prepare the worksheet consolidation entry or entries needed to remove the effects of the intercorporate bond ownership in preparing consolidated financial statements for 20X6.

LO 8-2

E8-8A Constructive Retirement at Beginning of Year (Straight-Line Method)

Assume the same facts as in E8-8 but prepare entries using straight-line amortization of bond discount or premium.

LO 8-3

E8-9 Retirement of Bonds Sold at a Discount (Effective Interest Method)

Farley Corporation owns 70 percent of Snowball Enterprises' stock. On January 1, 20X1, Farley sold $1 million par value, 7 percent (paid semiannually), 20-year, first mortgage bonds to Kling Corporation at 97. On January 1, 20X8, Snowball purchased $300,000 par value of the Farley bonds directly from Kling for $296,880.

Required

Prepare the consolidation entry needed at December 31, 20X8, to remove the effects of the intercorporate bond ownership in preparing consolidated financial statements.

LO 8-3

E8-9A Retirement of Bonds Sold at a Discount (Straight-Line Method)

Assume the same facts as in E8-9 but prepare entries using straight-line amortization of bond discount or premium.

LO 8-2

E8-10 Loss on Constructive Retirement (Effective Interest Method)

Apple Corporation holds 60 percent of Shortway Publishing Company's voting shares. Apple issued $500,000 of 10 percent (paid semiannually) bonds with a 10-year maturity on January 1, 20X2, at 90. On January 1, 20X8, Shortway purchased $100,000 of the Apple bonds for $106,000. Partial trial balances for the two companies on December 31, 20X8, are as follows:

	Apple Corporation	Shortway Publishing Company
Investment in Shortway Publishing Company Stock	$141,000	
Investment in Apple Corporation Bonds		$104,676
Bonds Payable	500,000	
Discount on Bonds Payable	21,289	
Interest Expense	55,626	
Interest Income		8,676
Interest Payable	25,000	
Interest Receivable		5,000

Required

Prepare the worksheet consolidation entry or entries needed on December 31, 20X8, to remove the effects of the intercorporate bond ownership in preparing consolidated financial statements.

LO 8-2

E8-10A Loss on Constructive Retirement (Straight-Line Method)

Apple Corporation holds 60 percent of Shortway Publishing Company's voting shares. Apple issued $500,000 of 10 percent bonds with a 10-year maturity on January 1, 20X2, at 90. On January 1, 20X8, Shortway purchased $100,000 of the Apple bonds for $106,000. Partial trial balances for the two companies on December 31, 20X8, are as follows:

	Apple Corporation	Shortway Publishing Company
Investment in Shortway Publishing Company Stock	$132,000	
Investment in Apple Corporation Bonds		$106,000
Bonds Payable	500,000	
Discount on Bonds Payable	15,000	
Interest Expense	55,000	
Interest Income		8,000
Interest Payable	25,000	
Interest Receivable		5,000

Required

Prepare the worksheet consolidation entry or entries needed on December 31, 20X8, to remove the effects of the intercorporate bond ownership in preparing consolidated financial statements.

LO 8-2

Advanced StudyGuide .com

E8-11 Determining the Amount of Retirement Gain or Loss (Effective Interest Method)

Online Enterprises owns 95 percent of Downlink Corporation. On January 1, 20X1, Downlink issued $200,000 of five-year bonds at 115. Annual interest of 12 percent is paid semiannually on January 1 and July 1. Online purchased $100,000 of the bonds on July 1, 20X3, at par value. The following balances are taken from the separate 20X3 financial statements of the two companies:

	Online Enterprises	Downlink Corporation
Investment in Downlink Corporation Bonds	$100,000	
Interest Income	6,000	
Interest Receivable	6,000	
Bonds Payable		$200,000
Bond Premium		13,475
Interest Expense		18,039
Interest Payable		12,000

Required

a. Compute the amount of interest expense that should be reported in the consolidated income statement for 20X3.

b. Compute the gain or loss on constructive bond retirement that should be reported in the 20X3 consolidated income statement.

c. Prepare the consolidation worksheet consolidation entry or entries as of December 31, 20X3, to remove the effects of the intercorporate bond ownership.

LO 8-2

E8-11A Determining the Amount of Retirement Gain or Loss (Straight-Line Method)

Online Enterprises owns 95 percent of Downlink Corporation. On January 1, 20X1, Downlink issued $200,000 of five-year bonds at 115. Annual interest of 12 percent is paid semiannually on January 1 and July 1. Online purchased $100,000 of the bonds on August 31, 20X3, at par value. The following balances are taken from the separate 20X3 financial statements of the two companies:

Advanced StudyGuide .com

	Online Enterprises	Downlink Corporation
Investment in Downlink Corporation Bonds	$105,700	
Interest Income	4,000	
Interest Receivable	6,000	
Bonds Payable		$200,000
Bond Premium		12,000
Interest Expense		18,000
Interest Payable		12,000

Required

a. Compute the amount of interest expense that should be reported in the consolidated income statement for 20X3.

b. Compute the gain or loss on constructive bond retirement that should be reported in the 20X3 consolidated income statement.

c. Prepare the consolidation worksheet consolidation entry or entries as of December 31, 20X3, to remove the effects of the intercorporate bond ownership.

LO 8-3

E8-12 Evaluation of Bond Retirement (Effective Interest Method)

Bundle Company issued $500,000 par value, 10-year bonds at 104 on January 1, 20X3, which Mega Corporation purchased. The coupon rate on the bonds is 11 percent. Interest payments are made semiannually on July 1 and January 1. On July 1, 20X6, Parent Company purchased $200,000 par value of the bonds from Mega for $192,200. Parent owns 70 percent of Bundle's voting shares.

Required

a. What amount of gain or loss will be reported in Bundle's 20X6 income statement on the retirement of bonds?

b. Will a gain or loss be reported in the 20X6 consolidated financial statements for Parent for the constructive retirement of bonds? What amount will be reported?

c. How much will Parent's purchase of the bonds change consolidated net income for 20X6?

d. Prepare the worksheet consolidation entry or entries needed to remove the effects of the intercorporate bond ownership in preparing consolidated financial statements at December 31, 20X6.

e. Prepare the worksheet consolidation entry or entries needed to remove the effects of the intercorporate bond ownership in preparing consolidated financial statements at December 31, 20X7.

f. If Bundle reports net income of $50,000 for 20X7, what amount of income will be assigned to the noncontrolling interest in the consolidated income statement?

LO 8-3

E8-12A Loss on Constructive Retirement (Straight-Line Method)

Assume the same facts as in E8-12 but prepare entries using straight-line amortization of bond discount or premium.

LO 8-4

E8-13 Consolidation of Intercorporate Bond Holdings (Effective Interest Method)

Stang Corporation issued to Bradley Company $400,000 par value, 10-year bonds with a coupon rate of 12 percent on January 1, 20X5, at 105. The bonds pay interest semiannually on July 1 and January 1. On January 1, 20X8, Purple Corporation purchased $100,000 of the bonds from Bradley for $104,900. Purple owns 65 percent of the voting common shares of Stang and prepares consolidated financial statements.

Advanced StudyGuide .com

Required

a. Prepare the worksheet consolidation entry or entries needed to remove the effects of the intercorporate bond ownership in preparing consolidated financial statements for 20X8.

b. Assuming that Stang reports net income of $20,000 for 20X8, compute the amount of income assigned to noncontrolling shareholders in the 20X8 consolidated income statement.

c. Prepare the worksheet consolidation entry or entries needed to remove the effects of the intercorporate bond ownership in preparing consolidated financial statements for 20X9.

LO 8-4

E8-13A Loss on Constructive Retirement (Straight-Line Method)

Assume the same facts as in E8-13 but prepare entries using straight-line amortization of bond discount or premium.

PROBLEMS

Note: Since the nature of this chapter is quite technical and since in many of the problems, the original stock acquisition took place at a date that is not specified, these problems skip the optional accumulated depreciation worksheet entry.

LO 8-2

P8-14 Consolidation Worksheet with Sale of Bonds to Subsidiary (Effective Interest Method)

Porter Company purchased 60 percent ownership of Temple Corporation on January 1, 20X1, at underlying book value. At that date, the fair value of the noncontrolling interest was equal to 40 percent of Temple's book value. On January 1, 20X1, Porter sold $80,000 par value, 8 percent, five-year bonds directly to Temple when the market interest rate was 7 percent. The bonds pay interest annually on December 31. Porter uses the fully adjusted equity method in accounting for its ownership of Temple. On December 31, 20X2, the trial balances of the two companies are as follows:

	Porter Company		Temple Corporation	
Item	**Debit**	**Credit**	**Debit**	**Credit**
Cash & Accounts Receivable	$ 81,480		$ 38,720	
Inventory	120,000		65,000	
Buildings & Equipment	500,000		300,000	
Investment in Temple Corporation Stock	101,772			
Investment in Porter Company Bonds			82,100	
Cost of Goods Sold	99,800		61,000	
Depreciation Expense	25,000		15,000	
Interest Expense	5,790		14,000	
Dividends Declared	40,000		10,000	
Accumulated Depreciation		$175,000		$ 75,000
Accounts Payable		68,800		41,200
Bonds Payable		80,000		200,000
Bond Premium		2,100		
Common Stock		200,000		100,000
Retained Earnings		230,068		49,830
Sales		200,000		114,000
Interest Income				5,790
Income from Temple Corp.		17,874		
Total	$973,842	$973,842	$585,820	$585,820

Required

a. Record the journal entry or entries for 20X2 on Porter's books related to its investment in Temple.

b. Record the journal entry or entries for 20X2 on Porter's books related to its bonds payable.

c. Record the journal entry or entries for 20X2 on Temple's books related to its investment in Porter's bonds.

d. Prepare the consolidation entries needed to complete a consolidated worksheet for 20X2.

e. Prepare a three-part consolidated worksheet for 20X2.

LO 8-2

P8-14A Consolidation Worksheet with Sale of Bonds to Subsidiary (Straight-Line Method)

Assume the same facts as in E8-14 except for the changes in the trial balances and assuming the bonds were sold for $82,000, but prepare entries using straight-line amortization of bond discount or premium.

Item	Porter Company Debit	Porter Company Credit	Temple Corporation Debit	Temple Corporation Credit
Cash and Accounts Receivable	$ 80,200		$ 40,000	
Inventory	120,000		65,000	
Buildings & Equipment	500,000		300,000	
Investment in Temple Corporation Stock	102,000			
Investment in Porter Company Bonds			81,200	
Cost of Goods Sold	99,800		61,000	
Depreciation Expense	25,000		15,000	
Interest Expense	6,000		14,000	
Dividends Declared	40,000		10,000	
Accumulated Depreciation		$175,000		$ 75,000
Accounts Payable		68,800		41,200
Bonds Payable		80,000		200,000
Bond Premium		1,200		
Common Stock		200,000		100,000
Retained Earnings		230,000		50,000
Sales		200,000		114,000
Interest Income				6,000
Income from Subsidiary		18,000		
	$973,000	$973,000	$586,200	$586,200

LO 8-2

P8-15 Consolidation Worksheet with Sale of Bonds to Parent (Effective Interest Method)

Mega Corporation purchased 90 percent of Tarp Company's voting common shares on January 1, 20X2, at underlying book value. At that date, the fair value of the noncontrolling interest was equal to 10 percent of the book value of Tarp Company. Mega also purchased $100,000 of 6 percent, five-year bonds directly from Tarp on January 1, 20X2, for $104,000. The bonds pay interest annually on December 31. The trial balances of the companies as of December 31, 20X4, are as follows:

Item	Mega Corporation Debit	Mega Corporation Credit	Tarp Company Debit	Tarp Company Credit
Cash & Receivables	$ 22,000		$ 36,600	
Inventory	165,000		75,000	
Buildings & Equipment	400,000		240,000	
Investment in Tarp Company Stock	121,392			
Investment in Tarp Company Bonds	101,720			
Cost of Goods Sold	86,000		79,800	
Depreciation Expense	20,000		15,000	
Interest Expense	16,000		5,202	
Dividends Declared	30,000		20,000	
Accumulated Depreciation		$140,000		$ 80,000
Current Payables		92,400		35,000
Bonds Payable		200,000		100,000
Bond Premium				1,720
Common Stock		120,000		80,000
Retained Earnings		242,012		49,882
Sales		140,000		125,000
Interest Income		5,202		
Income from Subsidiary		22,498		
	$962,112	$962,112	$471,602	$471,602

Required

a. Record the journal entry or entries for 20X4 on Mega's books related to its investment in Tarp Common stock.

b. Record the journal entry or entries for 20X4 on Mega's books related to its investment in Tarp Company bonds.

c. Record the journal entry or entries for 20X4 on Tarp's books related to its bonds payable.

d. Prepare the consolidation entries needed to complete a consolidated worksheet for 20X4.

e. Prepare a three-part consolidated worksheet for 20X4.

LO 8-2

P8-15A Consolidation Worksheet with Sale of Bonds to Parent (Straight-Line Method)

Assume the same facts as in E8-15 except for the changes in the trial balances, but prepare entries using straight-line amortization of bond discount or premium.

	Mega Corporation		Tarp Company	
Item	**Debit**	**Credit**	**Debit**	**Credit**
Cash & Receivables	$ 22,000		$ 36,600	
Inventory	165,000		75,000	
Buildings & Equipment	400,000		240,000	
Investment in Tarp Company Stock	121,500			
Investment in Tarp Company Bonds	101,600			
Cost of Goods Sold	86,000		79,800	
Depreciation Expense	20,000		15,000	
Interest Expense	16,000		5,200	
Dividends Declared	30,000		20,000	
Accumulated Depreciation		$140,000		$ 80,000
Current Payables		92,400		35,000
Bonds Payable		200,000		100,000
Bond Premium				1,600
Common Stock		120,000		80,000
Retained Earnings		242,000		50,000
Sales		140,000		125,000
Interest Income		5,200		
Income from Tarp Co.		22,500		
Total	$962,100	$962,100	$471,600	$471,600

Required

a. Record the journal entry or entries for 20X4 on Mega's books related to its investment in Tarp Company stock.

b. Record the journal entry or entries for 20X4 on Mega's books related to its investment in Tarp Company bonds.

c. Record the journal entry or entries for 20X4 on Tarp's books related to its bonds payable.

d. Prepare the consolidation entries needed to complete a consolidated worksheet for 20X4.

e. Prepare a three-part consolidated worksheet for 20X4.

LO 8-2

P8-16 Direct Sale of Bonds to Parent (Effective Interest Method)

On January 1, 20X1, Fern Corporation paid Morton Advertising $116,200 to acquire 70 percent of Vincent Company's stock. Fern also paid $45,000 to acquire $50,000 par value 8 percent, 10-year bonds directly from Vincent on that date. This purchase represented ½ of the bonds that were originally issued. Interest payments are made on January 1 and July 1. The fair value of the noncontrolling interest at January 1, 20X1, was $49,800, and book value of Vincent's net assets was $110,000. The book values and fair values of Vincent's assets and liabilities were equal except for buildings and equipment, which had a fair value $56,000 higher than book value and a remaining economic life of 14 years at January 1, 20X1.

The trial balances for the two companies as of December 31, 20X3, are as follows:

	Fern Corporation		Vincent Company	
Item	**Debit**	**Credit**	**Debit**	**Credit**
Cash & Current Receivables	$ 30,300		$ 46,000	
Inventory	170,000		70,000	
Land, Buildings, & Equipment (net)	320,000		180,000	
Investment in Vincent Bonds	46,046			
Investment in Vincent Stock	144,835			
Discount on Bonds Payable			7,908	
Operating Expenses	198,500		161,000	
Interest Expense	27,000		8,764	
Dividends Declared	60,000		10,000	
Current Liabilities		$ 35,000		$ 33,000
Bonds Payable		300,000		100,000
Common Stock		100,000		50,000
Retained Earnings		238,934		100,672
Sales		300,000		200,000
Interest Income		4,382		
Income from Subsidiary		18,365		
Total	$996,681	$996,681	$483,672	$483,672

On July 1, 20X2, Vincent sold land that it had purchased for $17,000 to Fern for $25,000. Fern continues to hold the land at December 31, 20X3. Assume Fern Corporation uses the fully adjusted equity method.

Required

a. Record the journal entries for 20X3 on Fern's books related to its investment in Vincent's stock and bonds.

b. Record the entries for 20X3 on Vincent's books related to its bond issue.

c. Prepare consolidation entries needed to complete a worksheet for 20X3.

d. Prepare a three-part consolidation worksheet for 20X3.

LO 8-2

P8-16A Direct Sale of Bonds to Parent (Straight-Line Method)

On January 1, 20X1, Fern Corporation paid Morton Advertising $116,200 to acquire 70 percent of Vincent Company's stock. Fern also paid $45,000 to acquire $50,000 par value 8 percent, 10-year bonds directly from Vincent on that date. Interest payments are made on January 1 and July 1. The fair value of the noncontrolling interest at January 1, 20X1, was $49,800, and book value of Vincent's net assets was $110,000. The book values and fair values of Vincent's assets and liabilities were equal except for buildings and equipment, which had a fair value $56,000 greater than book value and a remaining economic life of 14 years at January 1, 20X1.

The trial balances for the two companies as of December 31, 20X3, are as follows:

	Fern Corporation		Vincent Company	
Item	**Debit**	**Credit**	**Debit**	**Credit**
Cash & Current Receivables	$ 30,300		$ 46,000	
Inventory	170,000		70,000	
Land, Buildings, & Equipment (net)	320,000		180,000	
Investment in Vincent Bonds	46,500			
Investment in Vincent Stock	144,200			
Discount on Bonds Payable			7,000	
Operating Expenses	198,500		161,000	
Interest Expense	27,000		9,000	
Dividends Declared	60,000		10,000	

(continued)

Current Liabilities		$ 35,000		$ 33,000
Bonds Payable		300,000		100,000
Common Stock		100,000		50,000
Retained Earnings		238,800		100,000
Sales		300,000		200,000
Interest Income		4,500		
Income from Vincent Co.		18,200		
Total	$996,500	$996,500	$483,000	$483,000

On July 1, 20X2, Vincent sold land that it had purchased for $17,000 to Fern for $25,000. Fern continues to hold the land at December 31, 20X3. Assume Fern Corporation uses the fully adjusted equity method.

Required

a. Record the journal entries for 20X3 on Fern's books related to its investment in Vincent's stock and bonds.

b. Record the entries for 20X3 on Vincent's books related to its bond issue.

c. Prepare consolidation entries needed to complete a worksheet for 20X3.

d. Prepare a three-part consolidation worksheet for 20X3.

LO 8-3

P8-17 Information Provided in Consolidation Entry (Effective Interest Method)

Gross Corporation issued $500,000 par value, 10-year bonds at 104 on January 1, 20X1, which Independent Corporation purchased. On January 1, 20X5, Rupp Corporation purchased $200,000 of Gross bonds from Independent for $196,700. The bonds pay 9 percent interest annually on December 31. The preparation of consolidated financial statements for Gross and Rupp at December 31, 20X7, required the following consolidation entry:

Bonds Payable	200,000	
Premium on Bonds Payable	3,105	
Interest Income	18,520	
Investment in Gross Corporation Bonds		198,130
Interest Expense		17,121
Retained Earnings, January 1		4,780
Noncontrolling Interest		1,594

Required

With the information given, answer each of the following questions. Show how you derived your answer.

a. Is Gross or Rupp the parent company? How do you know?

b. What percentage of the subsidiary's ownership does the parent hold?

c. If 20X7 consolidated net income of $70,000 would have been reported without the preceding consolidation entry, what amount will actually be reported?

d. Will income to the noncontrolling interest reported in 20X7 increase or decrease as a result of the preceding consolidation entry? By what amount?

e. Prepare the consolidation entry needed to remove the effects of the intercorporate bond ownership in completing a three-part consolidation worksheet at December 31, 20X8.

LO 8-3

P8-17A Information Provided in Consolidation Entry (Straight-Line Method)

Gross Corporation issued $500,000 par value 10-year bonds at 104 on January 1, 20X1, which Independent Corporation purchased. On July 1, 20X5, Rupp Corporation purchased $200,000 of Gross bonds from Independent. The bonds pay 9 percent interest annually on December 31. The preparation of consolidated financial statements for Gross and Rupp at December 31, 20X7, required the following consolidation entry:

Bonds Payable	200,000	
Premium on Bonds Payable	2,400	
Interest Income	18,600	
Investment in Gross Corporation Bonds		198,200
Interest Expense		17,200
Investment in Gross Corporation Stock		4,200
NCI in NA of Gross Corporation		1,400

Required

With the information given, answer each of the following questions. Show how you derived your answer.

a. Is Gross or Rupp the parent company? How do you know?

b. What percentage of the subsidiary's ownership does the parent hold?

c. If 20X7 consolidated net income of $70,000 would have been reported without the preceding consolidation, what amount will actually be reported?

d. Will income to the noncontrolling interest reported in 20X7 increase or decrease as a result of the preceding consolidation entry? By what amount?

e. Prepare the consolidation entry needed to remove the effects of the intercorporate bond ownership in completing a three-part consolidation worksheet at December 31, 20X8.

LO 8-4

P8-18 Prior Retirement of Bonds (Effective Interest Method)

Amazing Corporation purchased $100,000 par value bonds of its subsidiary, Broadway Company, on December 31, 20X5, from Lemon Corporation for $102,800. The 10-year bonds bear a 9 percent coupon rate, and Broadway originally sold them on January 1, 20X3, to Lemon at 95. Interest is paid annually on December 31. Amazing owns 85 percent of the stock of Broadway.

In preparing the consolidation worksheet at December 31, 20X6, Amazing's controller made the following entry to eliminate the effects of the intercorporate bond ownership:

Bonds Payable	100,000	
Interest Income	8,691	
Retained Earnings, January 1	5,741	
Noncontrolling Interest	1,013	
Investment in Broadway Company Bonds		102,491
Discount on Bonds Payable		3,535
Interest Expense		9,419

Required

With the information given, answer the following questions:

a. Prepare the journal entry made by Amazing in 20X6 to record its interest income on the Broadway bonds that it holds.

b. Prepare the consolidation entry to remove the effects of the intercorporate bond ownership in completing a three-part consolidation worksheet at December 31, 20X5.

c. Broadway reported net income of $60,000 and $80,000 for 20X5 and 20X6, respectively. Amazing reported income from its separate operations of $120,000 and $150,000 for 20X5 and 20X6, respectively. What amount of consolidated net income and income to the controlling interest will be reported in the consolidated income statements for 20X5 and 20X6?

LO 8-4

P8-18A Prior Retirement of Bonds (Straight-Line Method)

Amazing Corporation purchased $100,000 par value bonds of its subsidiary, Broadway Company, on December 31, 20X5, from Lemon Corporation. The 10-year bonds bear a 9 percent coupon rate, and Broadway originally sold them on January 1, 20X3, to Lemon. Interest is paid annually on December 31. Amazing owns 85 percent of the stock of Broadway.

In preparing the consolidation worksheet at December 31, 20X6, Amazing's controller made the following entry to eliminate the effects of the intercorporate bond ownership:

Bonds Payable	100,000	
Interest Income	8,600	
Investment in Broadway Company Stock	5,355	
NCI in NA of Broadway Company	945	
Investment in Broadway Company Bonds		102,400
Discount on Bonds Payable		3,000
Interest Expense		9,500

Required

With the information given, answer the following questions:

a. What amount did Amazing pay when it purchased Broadway's bonds?

b. Prepare the journal entry made by Broadway in 20X6 to record its interest expense for the year.

c. Prepare the journal entry made by Amazing in 20X6 to record its interest income on the Broadway bonds that it holds.

d. Prepare the consolidation entry to remove the effects of the intercorporate bond ownership in completing a three-part consolidation worksheet at December 31, 20X5.

e. Broadway reported net income of $60,000 and $80,000 for 20X5 and 20X6, respectively. Amazing reported income from its separate operations of $120,000 and $150,000 for 20X5 and 20X6, respectively. What amount of consolidated net income and income to the controlling interest will be reported in the consolidated income statements for 20X5 and 20X6?

LO 8-2

P8-19A Incomplete Data (Straight-Line Method)

Advanced StudyGuide .com

Ballard Corporation purchased 70 percent of Condor Company's voting shares on January 1, 20X4, at underlying book value. On that date it also purchased $100,000 par value 12 percent Condor bonds, which had been issued on January 1, 20X1, with a 10-year maturity.

During preparation of the consolidated financial statements for December 31, 20X4, the following consolidation entry was made in the worksheet:

Bonds Payable	100,000	
Bond Premium	6,000	
Loss on Bond Retirement	3,500	
Interest Income	?	
Investment in Condor Company Bonds		109,000
Interest Expense		?

Required

a. What price did Ballard pay to purchase the Condor bonds?

b. What was the carrying amount of the bonds on Condor's books on the date of purchase?

c. If Condor reports net income of $30,000 in 20X5, what amount of income should be assigned to the noncontrolling interest in the 20X5 consolidated income statement?

LO 8-4

P8-20 Balance Sheet Consolidations (Effective Interest Method)

Advanced StudyGuide .com

Bath Corporation acquired 80 percent of Stang Brewing Company's stock on January 1, 20X1, at underlying book value. At that date, the fair value of the noncontrolling interest was equal to 20 percent of Stang's book value. On January 1, 20X1, Stang issued $300,000 par value, 8 percent, 10-year bonds to Sidney Malt Company for $360,000. Bath subsequently purchased $100,000 of the bonds from Sidney Malt for $102,000 on January 1, 20X3. Interest is paid semiannually on January 1 and July 1.

Summarized balance sheets for Bath and Stang as of December 31, 20X4, follow:

BATH CORPORATION
Balance Sheet
December 31, 20X4

Cash & Receivables	$122,500	Accounts Payable	$ 40,000
Inventory	200,000	Bonds Payable	400,000
Buildings & Equipment (net)	320,000	Common Stock	200,000
Investment in Stang Brewing:		Retained Earnings	309,627
Bonds	101,607		
Stock	205,520		
Total Assets	$949,627	Total Liabilities & Owners' Equity	$949,627

STANG BREWING COMPANY
Balance Sheet
December 31, 20X4

Cash & Receivables	$124,000	Accounts Payable	$ 28,000
Inventory	150,000	Bonds Payable	300,000
Buildings & Equipment (net)	360,000	Bond Premium	39,739
		Common Stock	100,000
		Retained Earnings	166,261
Total Assets	$634,000	Total Liabilities & Owners' Equity	$634,000

At December 31, 20X4, Stang holds $42,000 of inventory purchased from Bath, and Bath holds $26,000 of inventory purchased from Stang. Stang and Bath sell inventory to each other at cost plus markups of 30 percent and 40 percent, respectively. Assume total sales from Bath to Stang were $100,000 and from Stang to Bath were $50,000.

Required

a. Prepare all consolidation entries needed on December 31, 20X4, to complete a consolidated balance sheet worksheet. Assume Stang earned $74,476 and paid $10,000 in dividends during the year.

b. Prepare a consolidated balance sheet worksheet.

c. Prepare a consolidated balance sheet in good form.

LO 8-4 **P8-20A Balance Sheet Consolidations (Straight-Line Method)**

Advanced StudyGuide .com

Bath Corporation acquired 80 percent of Stang Brewing Company's stock on January 1, 20X1, at underlying book value. At that date, the fair value of the noncontrolling interest was equal to 20 percent of Stang's book value. On January 1, 20X1, Stang issued $300,000 par value, 8 percent, 10-year bonds to Sidney Malt Company. Bath subsequently purchased $100,000 of the bonds from Sidney Malt for $102,000 on January 1, 20X3. Interest is paid semiannually on January 1 and July 1. Assume Bath Corporation uses the fully adjusted equity method.

Summarized balance sheets for Bath and Stang as of December 31, 20X4, follow:

BATH CORPORATION
Balance Sheet
December 31, 20X4

Cash & Receivables	$122,500	Accounts Payable	$ 40,000
Inventory	200,000	Bonds Payable	400,000
Buildings & Equipment (net)	320,000	Common Stock	200,000
Investment in Stang Brewing:		Retained Earnings	311,600
Bonds	101,500		
Stock	207,600		
Total Assets	$951,600	Total Liabilities & Owners' Equity	$951,600

STANG BREWING COMPANY
Balance Sheet
December 31, 20X4

Cash & Receivables	$124,000	Accounts Payable	$ 28,000
Inventory	150,000	Bonds Payable	300,000
Buildings & Equipment (net)	360,000	Bond Premium	36,000
		Common Stock	100,000
		Retained Earnings	170,000
Total Assets	$634,000	Total Liabilities & Owners' Equity	$634,000

At December 31, 20X4, Stang holds $42,000 of inventory purchased from Bath, and Bath holds $26,000 of inventory purchased from Stang. Stang and Bath sell at cost plus markups of 30 percent and 40 percent, respectively. Assume total sales from Bath to Stang were $100,000 and from Stang to Bath were $50,000.

Required

a. Prepare all consolidation entries needed on December 31, 20X4, to complete a consolidated balance sheet worksheet. Assume Stang earned $75,000 and paid $10,000 in dividends during the year.

b. Prepare a consolidated balance sheet worksheet.

c. Prepare a consolidated balance sheet in good form.

LO 8-4

P8-21 Computations Relating to Bond Purchase from Nonaffiliate (Effective Interest Method)

Bliss Perfume Company issued $300,000 of 10 percent bonds on January 1, 20X2, at 110. The bonds mature 10 years from issue and have semiannual interest payments on January 1 and July 1. Parsons Corporation owns 80 percent of Bliss Perfume stock. On January 1, 20X4, Parsons purchased $100,000 par value of Bliss Perfume bonds in the securities markets for $106,200.

Partial trial balances for the two companies on December 31, 20X4, are as follows:

	Parsons Corporation	Bliss Perfume Company
Investment in Bliss Perfume Company Bonds	$105,640	
Interest Income	9,440	
Interest Receivable	5,000	
Bonds Payable		$300,000
Bond Premium		23,447
Interest Expense		27,632
Interest Payable		15,000

Required

Prepare the necessary worksheet consolidation entries as of December 31, 20X4, to remove the effects of the intercorporate bond ownership.

LO 8-4

P8-21A Computations Relating to Bond Purchase from Nonaffiliate (Straight-Line Method)

Bliss Perfume Company issued $300,000 of 10 percent bonds on January 1, 20X2, at 110. The bonds mature 10 years from issue and have semiannual interest payments on January 1 and July 1. Parsons Corporation owns 80 percent of Bliss Perfume stock. On April 1, 20X4, Parsons purchased $100,000 par value of Bliss Perfume bonds in the securities markets.

Partial trial balances for the two companies on December 31, 20X4, are as follows:

	Parsons Corporation	Bliss Perfume Company
Investment in Bliss Perfume Company Bonds	$105,600	
Interest Income	6,900	
Interest Receivable	5,000	
Bonds Payable		$300,000
Bond Premium		21,000
Interest Expense		27,000
Interest Payable		15,000

Required

a. What was the purchase price of the Bliss Perfume bonds to Parsons?

b. What amount of gain or loss on bond retirement should be reported in the consolidated income statement for 20X4?

c. Prepare the necessary worksheet consolidation entries as of December 31, 20X4, to remove the effects of the intercorporate bond ownership assuming Parsons uses the fully adjusted equity method.

LO 8-2

P8-22B Computations Following Parent's Acquisition of Subsidiary Bonds (Effective Interest Method)

Offenberg Company issued $100,000 of 10 percent bonds on January 1, 20X1, at 120. The bonds mature in 10 years and pay 10 percent interest annually on December 31. Mainstream Corporation holds 80 percent of Offenberg's voting shares, acquired on January 1, 20X1, at underlying book value. On January 1, 20X4, Mainstream purchased Offenberg bonds with a par value of $40,000 from the original purchaser for $44,000. Mainstream uses the modified equity method in accounting for its ownership in Offenberg. Partial balance sheet data for the two companies on December 31, 20X5, are as follows:

	Mainstream Corporation	Offenberg Company
Investment in Offenberg Company Stock	$120,000	
Investment in Offenberg Company Bonds	43,069	
Interest Income	3,517	
Bonds Payable		$100,000
Bond Premium		11,706
Interest Expense		8,105
Common Stock	300,000	100,000
Retained Earnings, December 31, 20X5	500,000	50,000

Required

a. Compute the gain or loss on bond retirement reported in the 20X4 consolidated income statement.

b. Prepare the consolidation entry needed to remove the effects of the intercorporate bond ownership in completing the consolidation worksheet for 20X5.

c. What balance should be reported as consolidated retained earnings on December 31, 20X5?

LO 8-2

P8-22A Computations Following Parent's Acquisition of Subsidiary Bonds (Straight-Line Method)

Mainstream Corporation holds 80 percent of Offenberg Company's voting shares, acquired on January 1, 20X1, at underlying book value. On January 1, 20X4, Mainstream purchased Offenberg bonds with a par value of $40,000. The bonds pay 10 percent interest annually on December 31 and mature on December 31, 20X8. Mainstream uses the fully adjusted equity method in accounting for its ownership in Offenberg. Partial balance sheet data for the two companies on December 31, 20X5, are as follows:

	Mainstream Corporation	Offenberg Company
Investment in Offenberg Company Stock	$121,680	
Investment in Offenberg Company Bonds	42,400	
Interest Income	3,200	
Bonds Payable		$100,000
Bond Premium		11,250
Interest Expense		6,250
Common Stock	300,000	100,000
Retained Earnings, December 31, 20X5	501,680	50,000

Required

a. Compute the gain or loss on bond retirement reported in the 20X4 consolidated income statement.

b. What equity method entry would Mainstream make on its books related to the bond retirement in 20X5?

c. Prepare the consolidation entry needed to remove the effects of the intercorporate bond ownership in completing the consolidation worksheet for 20X5.

d. What balance should be reported as consolidated retained earnings on December 31, 20X5?

LO 8-2

P8-23 Consolidation Worksheet—Year of Retirement (Effective Interest Method)

Tyler Manufacturing purchased 60 percent of the ownership of Brown Corporation stock on January 1, 20X1, at underlying book value. At that date, the fair value of the noncontrolling interest was equal to 40 percent of the book value of Brown Corporation. Tyler also purchased $50,000 of Brown bonds at par value on December 31, 20X3. Brown sold the 10-year bonds on January 1, 20X1, at 120; they have a stated interest rate of 12 percent. Interest is paid semiannually on June 30 and December 31. Assume Tyler uses the fully adjusted equity method.

On December 31, 20X1, Brown sold a building with a remaining life of 15 years to Tyler for $30,000. Brown had purchased the building 10 years earlier for $40,000. It is being depreciated based on a 25-year expected life.

Trial balances for the two companies on December 31 20X3, are as follows:

	Tyler Manufacturing		Brown Corporation	
Item	**Debit**	**Credit**	**Debit**	**Credit**
Cash	$ 68,000		$ 55,000	
Accounts Receivable	100,000		75,000	
Inventory	120,000		110,000	
Investment in Brown Bonds	50,000			
Investment in Brown Stock	101,545			
Depreciable Assets (net)	360,000		210,000	
Interest Expense	20,000		20,884	
Operating Expenses	302,200		150,000	
Dividends Declared	40,000		10,000	
Accounts Payable		$ 94,200		$ 52,000
Bonds Payable		200,000		200,000
Bond Premium				31,413
Common Stock		300,000		100,000
Retained Earnings		145,123		47,471
Sales		400,000		200,000
Income from Brown Corp.		22,422		
Total	$1,161,745	$1,161,745	$630,884	$630,884

Required

a. Prepare a consolidation worksheet for 20X3 in good form.

b. Prepare a consolidated balance sheet, income statement, and statement of changes in retained earnings for 20X3.

LO 8-2

P8-23A Consolidation Worksheet—Year of Retirement (Straight-Line Method)

Tyler Manufacturing purchased 60 percent of the ownership of Brown Corporation stock on January 1, 20X1, at underlying book value. At that date, the fair value of the noncontrolling interest was equal to 40 percent of the book value of Brown Corporation. Tyler also purchased $50,000 of Brown bonds at par value on December 31, 20X3. Brown sold the bonds on January 1, 20X1, at 120; they have a stated interest rate of 12 percent. Interest is paid semiannually on June 30 and December 31. Assume Tyler uses the fully adjusted equity method.

On December 31, 20X1, Brown sold a building with a remaining life of 15 years to Tyler for $30,000. Brown had purchased the building 10 years earlier for $40,000. It is being depreciated based on a 25-year expected life.

Trial balances for the two companies on December 31 20X3, are as follows:

	Tyler Manufacturing		Brown Corporation	
Item	**Debit**	**Credit**	**Debit**	**Credit**
Cash	$ 68,000		$ 55,000	
Accounts Receivable	100,000		75,000	
Inventory	120,000		110,000	
Investment in Brown Bonds	50,000			
Investment in Brown Stock	103,080			

(continued)

Item	Tyler Manufacturing Debit	Tyler Manufacturing Credit	Brown Corporation Debit	Brown Corporation Credit
Depreciable Assets (net)	360,000		210,000	
Interest Expense	20,000		20,000	
Operating Expenses	302,200		150,000	
Dividends Declared	40,000		10,000	
Accounts Payable		$ 94,200		$ 52,000
Bonds Payable		200,000		200,000
Bond Premium				28,000
Common Stock		300,000		100,000
Retained Earnings		146,640		50,000
Sales		400,000		200,000
Income from Brown Corp.		22,440		
Total	$1,163,280	$1,163,280	$630,000	$630,000

Required

a. Prepare a consolidation worksheet for 20X3 in good form.

b. Prepare a consolidated balance sheet, income statement, and statement of changes in retained earnings for 20X3.

LO 8-4

P8-24 Consolidation Worksheet—Year after Retirement (Effective Interest Method)

Bennett Corporation owns 60 percent of the stock of Stone Container Company, which it acquired at book value in 20X1. At that date, the fair value of the noncontrolling interest was equal to 40 percent of Stone's book value. On December 31, 20X3, Bennett purchased $100,000 par value bonds of Stone for $107,000. Stone originally issued the 10-year bonds at par value on January 1, 20X1. The bonds' coupon rate is 9 percent. Interest is paid semiannually on June 30 and December 31. Trial balances for the two companies on December 31, 20X4, are as follows:

Item	Bennett Corporation Debit	Bennett Corporation Credit	Stone Container Company Debit	Stone Container Company Credit
Cash	$ 61,600		$ 20,000	
Accounts Receivable	100,000		80,000	
Inventory	120,000		110,000	
Other Assets	340,000		250,000	
Investment in Stone Container Bonds	106,212			
Investment in Stone Container Stock	122,273			
Interest Expense	20,000		18,000	
Other Expenses	368,600		182,000	
Dividends Declared	40,000		10,000	
Accounts Payable		$ 80,000		$ 50,000
Bonds Payable		200,000		200,000
Common Stock		300,000		100,000
Retained Earnings		210,000		70,000
Sales		450,000		250,000
Interest Income		8,212		
Income from Stone Container Co.		30,473		
Total	$1,278,685	$1,278,685	$670,000	$670,000

All interest income recognized by Bennett is related to its investment in Stone bonds.

Required

a. Prepare a consolidation worksheet for 20X4 in good form.

b. Prepare a consolidated balance sheet, income statement, and retained earnings statement for 20X4.

LO 8-4

P8-24A Consolidation Worksheet—Year after Retirement (Straight-Line Method)

Bennett Corporation owns 60 percent of the stock of Stone Container Company, which it acquired at book value in 20X1. At that date, the fair value of the noncontrolling interest was equal to 40 percent of Stone's book value. On December 31, 20X3, Bennett purchased $100,000 par value of Stone bonds. Stone originally issued the bonds at par value. The bonds' coupon rate is 9 percent. Interest is paid semiannually on June 30 and December 31. Trial balances for the two companies on December 31, 20X4, are as follows:

	Bennett Corporation		Stone Container Company	
Item	**Debit**	**Credit**	**Debit**	**Credit**
Cash	$ 61,600		$ 20,000	
Accounts Receivable	100,000		80,000	
Inventory	120,000		110,000	
Other Assets	340,000		250,000	
Investment in Stone Container Bonds	106,000			
Investment in Stone Container Stock	122,400			
Interest Expense	20,000		18,000	
Other Expenses	368,600		182,000	
Dividends Declared	40,000		10,000	
Accounts Payable		$ 80,000		$ 50,000
Bonds Payable		200,000		200,000
Common Stock		300,000		100,000
Retained Earnings		210,000		70,000
Sales		450,000		250,000
Interest Income		8,000		
Income from Stone Container Co.		30,600		
Total	$1,278,600	$1,278,600	$670,000	$670,000

All interest income recognized by Bennett is related to its investment in Stone bonds. Assume Bennett uses the fully adjusted equity method.

Required

a. Prepare a consolidation worksheet for 20X4 in good form.

b. Prepare a consolidated balance sheet, income statement, and retained earnings statement for 20X4.

LO 8-3

P8-25 Intercorporate Inventory and Debt Transfers (Effective Interest Method)

Lance Corporation purchased 75 percent of Avery Company's common stock at underlying book value on January 1, 20X3. At that date, the fair value of the noncontrolling interest was equal to 25 percent of Avery's book value. Trial balances for Lance and Avery on December 31, 20X7, are as follows:

20X7 Trial Balance Data

	Lance Corporation		Avery Company	
Item	**Debit**	**Credit**	**Debit**	**Credit**
Cash	$ 37,900		$ 48,800	
Accounts Receivable	110,000		105,000	
Other Receivables	30,000		15,000	
Inventory	167,000		120,000	
Land	90,000		40,000	
Buildings & Equipment	500,000		250,000	
Investment in Avery Company:				
Bonds	78,709			
Stock	176,109			
Cost of Goods Sold	620,000		240,000	
Depreciation Expense	45,000		15,000	
Interest & Other Expenses	35,000		22,096	
Dividends Declared	50,000		24,000	

(continued)

20X7 Trial Balance Data

	Lance Corporation		Avery Company	
Item	**Debit**	**Credit**	**Debit**	**Credit**
Accumulated Depreciation		$ 155,000		$ 75,000
Accounts Payable		118,000		35,000
Other Payables		40,000		20,000
Bonds Payable		250,000		200,000
Bond Premium				5,464
Common Stock		250,000		50,000
Additional Paid-In Capital		40,000		
Retained Earnings		282,911		169,432
Sales		750,000		320,000
Interest & Other Income		15,961		5,000
Income from Avery Co.		37,846		
Total	$1,939,718	$1,939,718	$879,896	$879,896

During 20X7, Lance resold inventory purchased from Avery in 20X6. It had cost Avery $44,000 to produce the inventory, and Lance had purchased it for $59,000. In 20X7, Lance had purchased inventory for $40,000 and sold it to Avery for $60,000. At December 31, 20X7, Avery continued to hold $27,000 of the inventory.

Avery had issued $200,000 of 8 percent, 10-year bonds on January 1, 20X4, at 104. Lance had purchased $80,000 of the bonds from one of the original owners for $78,400 on December 31, 20X5. Interest is paid annually on December 31. Assume Lance uses the fully adjusted equity method.

Required

a. What amount of cost of goods sold will be reported in the 20X7 consolidated income statement?

b. What inventory balance will be reported in the December 31, 20X7, consolidated balance sheet?

c. Prepare the journal entry to record interest expense for Avery for 20X7.

d. Prepare the journal entry to record interest income for Lance for 20X7.

e. What amount will be assigned to the noncontrolling interest in the consolidated balance sheet prepared at December 31, 20X7?

f. Prepare all consolidation entries needed at December 31, 20X7, to complete a three-part consolidation worksheet.

g. Prepare a consolidation worksheet for 20X7 in good form.

LO 8-3

P8-25A Intercorporate Inventory and Debt Transfers (Straight-Line Method)
Lance Corporation purchased 75 percent of Avery Company's common stock at underlying book value on January 1, 20X3. At that date, the fair value of the noncontrolling interest was equal to 25 percent of Avery's book value. Trial balances for Lance and Avery on December 31, 20X7, are as follows:

20X7 Trial Balance Data

	Lance Corporation		Avery Company	
Item	**Debit**	**Credit**	**Debit**	**Credit**
Cash	$ 37,900		$ 48,800	
Accounts Receivable	110,000		105,000	
Other Receivables	30,000		15,000	
Inventory	167,000		120,000	
Land	90,000		40,000	
Buildings & Equipment	500,000		250,000	
Investment in Avery Company:				
Bonds	78,800			
Stock	176,340			
Cost of Goods Sold	620,000		240,000	
Depreciation Expense	45,000		15,000	
Interest & Other Expenses	35,000		22,000	
Dividends Declared	50,000		24,000	

(continued)

Accumulated Depreciation		$ 155,000		$ 75,000
Accounts Payable		118,000		35,000
Other Payables		40,000		20,000
Bonds Payable		250,000		200,000
Bond Premium				4,800
Common Stock		250,000		50,000
Additional Paid-In Capital		40,000		
Retained Earnings		283,180		170,000
Sales		750,000		320,000
Interest & Other Income		16,000		5,000
Income from Avery Co.		37,860		
Total	$1,940,040	$1,940,040	$879,800	$879,800

During 20X7, Lance resold inventory purchased from Avery in 20X6. It had cost Avery $44,000 to produce the inventory, and Lance had purchased it for $59,000. In 20X7, Lance had purchased inventory for $40,000 and sold it to Avery for $60,000. At December 31, 20X7, Avery continued to hold $27,000 of the inventory.

Avery had issued $200,000 of 8 percent, 10-year bonds on January 1, 20X4, at 104. Lance had purchased $80,000 of the bonds from one of the original owners for $78,400 on December 31, 20X5. Both companies use straight-line write-off of premiums and discounts. Interest is paid annually on December 31. Assume Lance uses the fully adjusted equity method.

Required

a. What amount of cost of goods sold will be reported in the 20X7 consolidated income statement?

b. What inventory balance will be reported in the December 31, 20X7, consolidated balance sheet?

c. Prepare the journal entry to record interest expense for Avery for 20X7.

d. Prepare the journal entry to record interest income for Lance for 20X7.

e. What amount will be assigned to the noncontrolling interest in the consolidated balance sheet prepared at December 31, 20X7?

f. Prepare all consolidation entries needed at December 31, 20X7, to complete a three-part consolidation worksheet.

g. Prepare a consolidation worksheet for 20X7 in good form.

LO 8-4

P8-26 Intercorporate Bond Holdings and Other Transfers (Effective Interest Method)

On January 1, 20X5, Pond Corporation purchased 75 percent of Skate Company's stock at underlying book value. At that date, the fair value of the noncontrolling interest was equal to 25 percent of Skate's book value. The balance sheets for Pond and Skate at January 1, 20X8, and December 31, 20X8, and income statements for 20X8 were reported as follows:

	20X8 Balance Sheets			
	Pond Corporation		Skate Company	
	January 1	December 31	January 1	December 31
Cash	$ 57,600	$ 53,100	$ 10,000	$ 47,000
Accounts Receivable	130,000	176,000	60,000	65,000
Interest & Other Receivables	40,000	45,000	8,000	10,000
Inventory	100,000	140,000	50,000	50,000
Land	50,000	50,000	22,000	22,000
Buildings & Equipment	400,000	400,000	240,000	240,000
Accumulated Depreciation	(150,000)	(185,000)	(70,000)	(94,000)
Investment in Skate Company:				
Stock	122,327	139,248		
Bonds	42,800	42,494		
Investment in Tin Co. Bonds	135,000	134,000		
Total Assets	$927,727	$994,842	$320,000	$340,000

(continued)

20X8 Balance Sheets

	Pond Corporation		Skate Company	
	January 1	December 31	January 1	December 31
Accounts Payable	$ 60,000	$ 65,000	$ 16,500	$ 11,000
Interest & Other Payables	40,000	45,000	7,000	12,000
Bonds Payable	300,000	300,000	100,000	100,000
Bond Discount			(4,005)	(3,597)
Common Stock	150,000	150,000	30,000	30,000
Additional Paid-In Capital	155,000	155,000	20,000	20,000
Retained Earnings	222,727	279,842	150,505	170,597
Total Liabilities & Equities	$927,727	$994,842	$320,000	$340,000

20X8 Income Statements

	Pond Corporation		Skate Company	
Sales		$450,000		$250,000
Income from Subsidiary		24,421		
Interest Income		18,594		
Total Revenue		$493,015		$250,000
Cost of Goods Sold	$285,000		$136,000	
Other Operating Expenses	50,000		40,000	
Depreciation Expense	35,000		24,000	
Interest Expense	24,000		10,408	
Miscellaneous Expenses	11,900	405,900	9,500	219,908
Net Income		$ 87,115		$ 30,092

Additional Information

1. Pond sold a building to Skate for $65,000 on December 31, 20X7. Pond had purchased the building for $125,000 and was depreciating it on a straight-line basis over 25 years. At the time of sale, Pond reported accumulated depreciation of $75,000 and a remaining life of 10 years.
2. On July 1, 20X6, Skate sold land that it had purchased for $22,000 to Pond for $35,000. Pond is planning to build a new warehouse on the property prior to the end of 20X9.
3. Skate issued $100,000 par value, 10-year bonds with a coupon rate of 10 percent on January 1, 20X5, at $95,000. On December 31, 20X7, Pond purchased $40,000 par value of Skate's bonds for $42,800. Interest payments are made on July 1 and January 1.
4. Pond and Skate paid dividends of $30,000 and $10,000, respectively, in 20X8.

Required

a. Prepare all consolidation entries needed at December 31, 20X8, to complete a three-part consolidation worksheet.

b. Prepare a three-part worksheet for 20X8 in good form.

LO 8-4

P8-26A Intercorporate Bond Holdings and Other Transfers (Straight-Line Method)

On January 1, 20X5, Pond Corporation purchased 75 percent of Skate Company's stock at underlying book value. At that date, the fair value of the noncontrolling interest was equal to 25 percent of Skate's book value. The balance sheets for Pond and Skate at January 1, 20X8, and December 31, 20X8, and income statements for 20X8 were reported as follows:

20X8 Balance Sheets	Pond Corporation		Skate Company	
	January 1	December 31	January 1	December 31
Cash	$ 57,600	$ 53,100	$ 10,000	$ 47,000
Accounts Receivable	130,000	176,000	60,000	65,000
Interest & Other Receivables	40,000	45,000	8,000	10,000
Inventory	100,000	140,000	50,000	50,000
Land	50,000	50,000	22,000	22,000
Buildings & Equipment	400,000	400,000	240,000	240,000
Accumulated Depreciation	(150,000)	(185,000)	(70,000)	(94,000)
Investment in Skate Company:				
Stock	122,100	139,050		
Bonds	42,800	42,400		
Investment in Tin Co. Bonds	135,000	134,000		
Total Assets	$927,250	$994,550	$320,000	$340,000
Accounts Payable	$ 60,000	$ 65,000	$ 16,500	$ 11,000
Interest & Other Payables	40,000	45,000	7,000	12,000
Bonds Payable	300,000	300,000	100,000	100,000
Bond Discount			(3,500)	(3,000)
Common Stock	150,000	150,000	30,000	30,000
Additional Paid-In Capital	155,000	155,000	20,000	20,000
Retained Earnings	222,500	279,550	150,000	170,000
Total Liabilities & Equities	$927,500	$994,550	$320,000	$340,000

20X8 Income Statements	Pond Corporation		Skate Company	
Sales		$450,000		$250,000
Income from Skate Co.		24,450		
Interest Income		18,500		
Total Revenue		$492,950		$250,000
Cost of Goods Sold	$285,000		$136,000	
Other Operating Expenses	50,000		40,000	
Depreciation Expense	35,000		24,000	
Interest Expense	24,000		10,500	
Miscellaneous Expenses	$ 11,900	405,900	$ 9,500	220,000
Net Income		$ 87,050		$ 30,000

Additional Information

1. Pond sold a building to Skate for $65,000 on December 31, 20X7. Pond had purchased the building for $125,000 and was depreciating it on a straight-line basis over 25 years. At the time of sale, Pond reported accumulated depreciation of $75,000 and a remaining life of 10 years. Assume Pond uses the fully adjusted equity method.
2. On July 1, 20X6, Skate sold land that it had purchased for $22,000 to Pond for $35,000. Pond is planning to build a new warehouse on the property prior to the end of 20X9.
3. Skate issued $100,000, par value 10-year bonds with a coupon rate of 10 percent on January 1, 20X5, at $95,000. On December 31, 20X7, Pond purchased $40,000 par value of Skate's bonds for $42,800. Both companies amortize bond premiums and discounts on a straight-line basis. Interest payments are made on July 1 and January 1.
4. Pond and Skate paid dividends of $30,000 and $10,000, respectively, in 20X8.

Required

a. Prepare all consolidation entries needed at December 31, 20X8, to complete a three-part consolidation worksheet.

b. Prepare a three-part worksheet for 20X8 in good form.

LO 8-3, 8-4

P8-27B Comprehensive Multiple-Choice Questions (Modified Equity Method)

Panther Enterprises owns 80 percent of Grange Corporation's voting stock. Panther acquired the shares on January 1, 20X4, for $234,500. On that date, the fair value of the noncontrolling interest was $58,625, and Grange reported common stock outstanding of $200,000 and retained earnings of $50,000. The book values and fair values of Grange's assets and liabilities were equal except for buildings with a fair value $30,000 more than book value at the time of combination. The buildings had an expected 10-year remaining economic life from the date of combination. On December 31, 20X6, Panther's management reviewed the amount attributed to goodwill as a result of the acquisition of Grange and concluded an impairment loss of $7,500 should be recorded in 20X6, with the loss shared proportionately between the controlling and noncontrolling interests.

The following trial balances were prepared by the companies on December 31, 20X6:

	Panther Enterprises		Grange Corporation	
Item	Debit	Credit	Debit	Credit
Cash	$ 194,220		$183,000	
Inventory	200,000		180,000	
Buildings & Equipment	500,000		400,000	
Investment in Grange Corporation Bonds	106,400			
Investment in Grange Corporation Stock	287,300			
Cost of Goods Sold	220,000		140,000	
Depreciation & Amortization	50,000		30,000	
Interest Expense	24,000		16,000	
Other Expenses	16,000		14,000	
Dividends Declared	20,000		15,000	
Accumulated Depreciation		$ 250,000		$180,000
Current Liabilities		100,000		50,000
Bonds Payable		400,000		200,000
Bond Premium				8,000
Common Stock		300,000		200,000
Retained Earnings		202,400		100,000
Sales		300,000		240,000
Other Income		35,920		
Income from Grange Corp.		29,600		
Total	$1,617,920	$1,617,920	$978,000	$978,000

Panther purchases much of its inventory from Grange. The inventory Panther held on January 1, 20X6, contained $2,000 of unrealized intercompany profit. During 20X6, Grange had sold goods costing $50,000 to Panther for $70,000. Panther had resold the inventory held at the beginning of the year and 70 percent of the inventory it purchased in 20X6 prior to the end of the year. The inventory remaining at the end of 20X6 was sold in 20X7.

On January 1, 20X6, Panther purchased from Kirkwood Corporation $100,000 par value bonds of Grange Corporation. Kirkwood had purchased the 10-year bonds on January 1, 20X1. The coupon rate is 9 percent and interest is paid annually on December 31. Assume Panther uses the modified equity method.

"B" indicates that the item relates to Appendix 8B.

Required

Select the correct answer for each of the following questions.

1. What should be the total amount of inventory reported in the consolidated balance sheet as of December 31, 20X6?
   a. \$360,000.
   b. \$374,000.
   c. \$375,200.
   d. \$380,000.
2. What amount of cost of goods sold should be reported in the 20X6 consolidated income statement?
   a. \$288,000.
   b. \$294,000.
   c. \$296,000.
   d. \$360,000.
3. What amount of interest income did Panther Enterprises record from its investment in Grange Corporation bonds during 20X6?
   a. \$7,400.
   b. \$7,720.
   c. \$9,000.
   d. \$10,600.
4. What amount of interest expense should be reported in the 20X6 consolidated income statement?
   a. \$24,000.
   b. \$32,000.
   c. \$33,000.
   d. \$40,000.
5. What amount of goodwill would be reported by the consolidated entity at January 1, 20X4?
   a. \$10,500.
   b. \$13,125.
   c. \$34,500.
   d. \$43,125.
6. What amount of depreciation and amortization expense should be reported in the 20X6 consolidated income statement?
   a. \$77,000.
   b. \$80,000.
   c. \$82,400.
   d. \$83,000.
7. What amount of gain or loss on bond retirement should be included in the 20X6 consolidated income statement?
   a. \$2,400.
   b. \$3,000.
   c. \$4,000.
   d. \$6,400.
8. What amount of income should be assigned to the noncontrolling interest in the 20X6 consolidated income statement?
   a. \$4,620.
   b. \$6,120.
   c. \$6,720.
   d. \$8,000.

9. What amount should be assigned to the noncontrolling interest in the consolidated balance sheet as of December 31, 20X6?
   a. $60,000.
   b. $63,320.
   c. $65,000.
   d. $68,645.

10. What amount of goodwill, if any, should be reported in the consolidated balance sheet as of December 31, 20X6?
   a. $0.
   b. $5,625.
   c. $10,500.
   d. $13,125.

LO 8-2, 8-3

P8-28 Comprehensive Problem: Intercorporate Transfers (Effective Interest Method)

Topp Manufacturing Company acquired 90 percent of Bussman Corporation's outstanding common stock on December 31, 20X5, for $1,152,000. At that date, the fair value of the noncontrolling interest was $128,000, and Bussman reported common stock outstanding of $500,000, premium on common stock of $280,000, and retained earnings of $420,000. The book values and fair values of Bussman's assets and liabilities were equal except for land, which was worth $30,000 more than its book value.

On April 1, 20X6, Topp issued at par $200,000 of 10 percent bonds directly to Bussman; interest on the bonds is payable March 31 and September 30. On January 1, 20X7, Topp purchased all of Bussman's outstanding 10-year 12 percent bonds from an unrelated institutional investor at 98. The bonds originally had been issued on January 1, 20X1, for 101. Interest on the bonds is payable December 31 and June 30.

Since the date it was acquired by Topp Manufacturing, Bussman has sold inventory to Topp on a regular basis. The amount of such intercompany sales totaled $64,000 in 20X6 and $78,000 in 20X7, including a 30 percent gross profit. All inventory transferred in 20X6 had been resold by December 31, 20X6, except inventory for which Topp had paid $15,000 and did not resell until January 20X7. All inventory transferred in 20X7 had been resold at December 31, 20X7, except merchandise for which Topp had paid $18,000.

At December 31, 20X7, trial balances for Topp and Bussman appeared as follows:

	Topp Manufacturing		Bussman Corporation	
Item	**Debit**	**Credit**	**Debit**	**Credit**
Cash	$ 39,500		$ 29,000	
Current Receivables	112,500		85,100	
Inventory	301,000		348,900	
Investment in Bussman Stock	1,240,631			
Investment in Bussman Bonds	984,121			
Investment in Topp Bonds			200,000	
Land	1,231,000		513,000	
Buildings & Equipment	2,750,000		1,835,000	
Cost of Goods Sold	2,009,000		430,000	
Depreciation & Amortization	195,000		85,000	
Other Expenses	643,000		205,874	
Dividends Declared	50,000		40,000	
Accumulated Depreciation		$1,210,000		$ 619,000
Current Payables		98,000		79,000
Bonds Payable		200,000		1,000,000
Premium on Bonds Payable				4,268
Common Stock		1,000,000		500,000
Premium on Common Stock		700,000		280,000
Retained Earnings, January 1		3,027,695		468,606
Sales		3,101,000		790,000
Other Income		134,121		31,000
Income from Bussman Corp.		84,936		
Total	$9,555,752	$9,555,752	$3,771,874	$3,771,874

As of December 31, 20X7, Bussman had declared but not yet paid its fourth-quarter dividend of $10,000. Both Topp and Bussman use the effective interest method for the amortization of bond discount and premium. On December 31, 20X7, Topp's management reviewed the amount attributed to goodwill as a result of its purchase of Bussman common stock and concluded that an impairment loss in the amount of $25,000 had occurred during 20X7 and should be shared proportionately between the controlling and noncontrolling interests. Topp uses the fully adjusted equity method to account for its investment in Bussman.

Required

a. Compute the amount of the goodwill as of January 1, 20X7.

b. Compute the balance of Topp's Investment in Bussman Stock account as of January 1, 20X7.

c. Compute the gain or loss on the constructive retirement of Bussman's bonds that should appear in the 20X7 consolidated income statement.

d. Compute the income that should be assigned to the noncontrolling interest in the 20X7 consolidated income statement.

e. Compute the total noncontrolling interest as of December 31, 20X6.

f. Present all consolidation entries that would appear in a three-part consolidation worksheet as of December 31, 20X7.

g. Prepare and complete a three-part worksheet for the preparation of consolidated financial statements for 20X7.

LO 8-3, 8-4

P8-28A Comprehensive Problem: Intercorporate Transfers (Straight-Line Method)

Topp Manufacturing Company acquired 90 percent of Bussman Corporation's outstanding common stock on December 31, 20X5, for $1,152,000. At that date, the fair value of the noncontrolling interest was $128,000, and Bussman reported common stock outstanding of $500,000, premium on common stock of $280,000, and retained earnings of $420,000. The book values and fair values of Bussman's assets and liabilities were equal except for land, which was worth $30,000 more than its book value.

On April 1, 20X6, Topp issued at par $200,000 of 10 percent bonds directly to Bussman; interest on the bonds is payable March 31 and September 30. On January 2, 20X7, Topp purchased all of Bussman's outstanding 10-year, 12 percent bonds from an unrelated institutional investor at 98. The bonds originally had been issued on January 2, 20X1, for 101. Interest on the bonds is payable December 31 and June 30.

Since the date it was acquired by Topp Manufacturing, Bussman has sold inventory to Topp on a regular basis. The amount of such intercompany sales totaled $64,000 in 20X6 and $78,000 in 20X7, including a 30 percent gross profit. All inventory transferred in 20X6 had been resold by December 31, 20X6, except inventory for which Topp had paid $15,000 and did not resell until January 20X7. All inventory transferred in 20X7 had been resold at December 31, 20X7, except merchandise for which Topp had paid $18,000.

At December 31, 20X7, trial balances for Topp and Bussman appeared as follows:

	Topp Manufacturing		Bussman Corporation	
Item	**Debit**	**Credit**	**Debit**	**Credit**
Cash	$ 39,500		$ 29,000	
Current Receivables	112,500		85,100	
Inventory	301,000		348,900	
Investment in Bussman Stock	1,239,840			
Investment in Bussman Bonds	985,000			
Investment in Topp Bonds			200,000	
Land	1,231,000		513,000	
Buildings & Equipment	2,750,000		1,835,000	
Cost of Goods Sold	2,009,000		430,000	
Depreciation & Amortization	195,000		85,000	
Other Expenses	643,000		206,000	
Dividends Declared	50,000		40,000	

(continued)

	Topp Manufacturing		Bussman Corporation	
Item	**Debit**	**Credit**	**Debit**	**Credit**
Accumulated Depreciation		$1,210,000		$ 619,000
Current Payables		98,000		79,000
Bonds Payable		200,000		1,000,000
Premium on Bonds Payable				3,000
Common Stock		1,000,000		500,000
Premium on Common Stock		700,000		280,000
Retained Earnings, January 1		3,028,950		470,000
Sales		3,101,000		790,000
Other Income		135,000		31,000
Income from Bussman Corp.		82,890		
Total	$9,555,840	$9,555,840	$3,772,000	$3,772,000

As of December 31, 20X7, Bussman had declared but not yet paid its fourth-quarter dividend of $10,000. Both Topp and Bussman use straight-line depreciation and amortization, including the amortization of bond discount and premium. On December 31, 20X7, Topp's management reviewed the amount attributed to goodwill as a result of its purchase of Bussman common stock and concluded that an impairment loss in the amount of $25,000 had occurred during 20X7 and should be shared proportionately between the controlling and noncontrolling interests. Topp uses the fully adjusted equity method to account for its investment in Bussman.

Required

a. Compute the amount of the goodwill as of January 1, 20X7.

b. Compute the balance of Topp's Investment in Bussman Stock account as of January 1, 20X7.

c. Compute the gain or loss on the constructive retirement of Bussman's bonds that should appear in the 20X7 consolidated income statement.

d. Compute the income that should be assigned to the noncontrolling interest in the 20X7 consolidated income statement.

e. Compute the total noncontrolling interest as of December 31, 20X6.

f. Present all consolidation entries that would appear in a three-part consolidation worksheet as of December 31, 20X7.

g. Prepare and complete a three-part worksheet for the preparation of consolidated financial statements for 20X7.

LO 8-2, 8-3

P8-29B Comprehensive Problem: Intercorporate Transfers (Modified Equity Method)

Topp Manufacturing Company acquired 90 percent of Bussman Corporation's outstanding common stock on December 31, 20X5, for $1,152,000. At that date, the fair value of the noncontrolling interest was $128,000, and Bussman reported common stock outstanding of $500,000, premium on common stock of $280,000, and retained earnings of $420,000. The book values and fair values of Bussman's assets and liabilities were equal except for land, which was worth $30,000 more than its book value.

On April 1, 20X6, Topp issued at par $200,000 of 10 percent bonds directly to Bussman; interest on the bonds is payable March 31 and September 30. On January 2, 20X7, Topp purchased all of Bussman's outstanding 10-year, 12 percent bonds from an unrelated institutional investor at 98. The bonds originally had been issued on January 2, 20X1, for 101. Interest on the bonds is payable December 31 and June 30.

Since the date it was acquired by Topp Manufacturing, Bussman has sold inventory to Topp on a regular basis. The amount of such intercompany sales totaled $64,000 in 20X6 and $78,000 in 20X7, including a 30 percent gross profit. All inventory transferred in 20X6 had been resold by December 31, 20X6, except inventory for which Topp had paid $15,000 and did not resell until January 20X7. All inventory transferred in 20X7 had been resold at December 31, 20X7, except merchandise for which Topp had paid $18,000.

At December 31, 20X7, trial balances for Topp and Bussman appeared as follows:

	Topp Manufacturing		Bussman Corporation	
Item	**Debit**	**Credit**	**Debit**	**Credit**
Cash	$ 39,500		$ 29,000	
Current Receivables	112,500		85,100	
Inventory	301,000		348,900	
Investment in Bussman Stock	1,251,000			
Investment in Bussman Bonds	985,000			
Investment in Topp Bonds			200,000	
Land	1,231,000		513,000	
Buildings & Equipment	2,750,000		1,835,000	
Cost of Goods Sold	2,009,000		430,000	
Depreciation & Amortization	195,000		85,000	
Other Expenses	643,000		206,000	
Dividends Declared	50,000		40,000	
Accumulated Depreciation		$1,210,000		$ 619,000
Current Payables		98,000		79,000
Bonds Payable		200,000		1,000,000
Premium on Bonds Payable				3,000
Common Stock		1,000,000		500,000
Premium on Common Stock		700,000		280,000
Retained Earnings, January 1		3,033,000		470,000
Sales		3,101,000		790,000
Other Income		135,000		31,000
Income from Bussman		90,000		
Total	$9,567,000	$9,567,000	$3,772,000	$3,772,000

As of December 31, 20X7, Bussman had declared but not yet paid its fourth-quarter dividend of $10,000. Both Topp and Bussman use straight-line depreciation and amortization, including the amortization of bond discount and premium. On December 31, 20X7, Topp's management reviewed the amount attributed to goodwill as a result of its purchase of Bussman common stock and concluded that an impairment loss in the amount of $25,000 had occurred during 20X7 and should be shared proportionately between the controlling and noncontrolling interests. Topp uses the modified equity method to account for its investment in Bussman.

Required

a. Compute the amount of the goodwill as of January 1, 20X7.

b. Compute the balance of Topp's Investment in Bussman Stock account as of January 1, 20X7.

c. Compute the gain or loss on the constructive retirement of Bussman's bonds that should appear in the 20X7 consolidated income statement.

d. Compute the income that should be assigned to the noncontrolling interest in the 20X7 consolidated income statement.

e. Compute the total noncontrolling interest as of December 31, 20X6.

f. Present all consolidation entries that would appear in a three-part consolidation worksheet as of December 31, 20X7.

g. Prepare and complete a three-part worksheet for the preparation of consolidated financial statements for 20X7.

P8-30B Cost Method

The trial balance data presented in P8–24 can be converted to reflect use of the cost method by inserting the following amounts in place of those presented for Bennett Corporation:

Investment in Stone Container Stock	$ 75,000
Retained Earnings	187,200
Income from Subsidiary	0
Dividend Income	6,000

Stone reported retained earnings of $25,000 on the date Bennett purchased 60 percent of the stock.

Required

a. Prepare the journal entries that would have been recorded on Bennett's books during 20X4 under the cost method.

b. Prepare all consolidation entries needed to complete a consolidation worksheet as of December 31, 20X4, assuming Bennett uses the cost method.

c. Complete a three-part consolidation worksheet as of December 31, 20X4.

9 Consolidation Ownership Issues

Multicorporate Entities

Business Combinations

Consolidation Concepts and Procedures

Intercompany Transfers

Additional Consolidation Issues

Multinational Entities

Reporting Requirements

Partnerships

Governmental and Not-for-Profit Entities

Corporations in Financial Difficulty

BERKSHIRE HATHAWAY'S VARIED INVESTMENTS

Chapter 2 provides an overview of the rise of one of the most successful investment companies in modern history, Berkshire Hathaway, under the direction of Warren Buffett. We do not repeat that history here, but we note that although Berkshire Hathaway owns common stock in many well-known companies, it also has various other investments that might surprise you. For example, did you know that during 2013, Berkshire Hathaway acquired $8 billion of Heinz preferred stock? Did you know that over the past several years, Berkshire also purchased preferred stock in Wrigley, Goldman Sachs, and General Electric (GE) totaling $14.5 billion?

In previous chapters, we have focused on simple ownership situations in which the controlling entity has owned common stock (CS) in other controlled entities. In practice, however, relatively complex ownership structures are frequent. For example, until recently, Berkshire held both common and preferred shares of GE. Other times, one or more subsidiaries may acquire stock of the parent or of other related companies. Sometimes the parent's ownership claim on a subsidiary may change through its purchase or sale of subsidiary shares or through stock transactions of the subsidiary.

The discussion in this chapter provides a basic understanding of some of the consolidation problems arising from complex ownership situations commonly encountered in practice. Specifically, this chapter discusses

1. Subsidiary preferred stock (PS) outstanding.
2. Changes in the parent's ownership interest in the subsidiary.
3. Multiple ownership levels.
4. Reciprocal or mutual ownership.
5. Subsidiary stock dividends.

BERKSHIRE HATHAWAY INC.

LEARNING OBJECTIVES

When you finish studying this chapter, you should be able to:

LO 9-1 Understand and explain how the consolidation process differs when the subsidiary has preferred stock outstanding.

LO 9-2 Make calculations and prepare consolidation entries for a partially owned subsidiary when the subsidiary has preferred stock outstanding.

LO 9-3 Make calculations and explain how consolidation procedures differ when the parent's ownership interest changes during the accounting period.

LO 9-4 Make calculations and prepare consolidation entries for a partially owned subsidiary when the subsidiary has a complex ownership structure.

LO 9-5 Understand and explain how consolidation procedures differ when the subsidiary pays stock dividends.

SUBSIDIARY PREFERRED STOCK OUTSTANDING

LO 9-1

Understand and explain how the consolidation process differs when the subsidiary has preferred stock outstanding.

Many companies have more than one type of stock outstanding. Each type of security typically serves a particular function, and each has a different set of rights and features. Preferred stockholders normally have preference over common shareholders with respect to dividends and the distribution of assets in a liquidation. The right to vote usually is withheld from preferred shareholders, so preferred stock ownership normally does not convey control, regardless of the number of shares owned.

Because a subsidiary's preferred shareholders do have a claim on the net assets of the subsidiary, special attention must be given to that claim in the preparation of consolidated financial statements.

Consolidation with Subsidiary Preferred Stock Outstanding

During the preparation of consolidated financial statements, the amount of subsidiary stockholders' equity accruing to preferred shareholders must be determined before dealing with the elimination of the intercompany common stock ownership. If the parent holds some of the subsidiary's preferred stock, its portion of the preferred stock interest must be eliminated. Any portion of the subsidiary's preferred stock interest not held by the parent is assigned to the noncontrolling interest.

As an illustration of the preparation of consolidated financial statements with subsidiary preferred stock outstanding, recall the following information from the example of Peerless Products Corporation and Special Foods Incorporated used in previous chapters:

1. Peerless Products purchases 80 percent of Special Foods' common stock on January 1, 20X1, at its book value of $240,000. At the date of combination, the fair value of Special Foods' common stock held by the noncontrolling shareholders is equal to its book value of $60,000.
2. Peerless Products earns income from its own operations of $140,000 in 20X1 and declares dividends of $60,000.
3. Special Foods reports net income of $50,000 in 20X1 and declares common dividends of $30,000.

Also assume that on January 1, 20X1, immediately after the combination, Special Foods issues $100,000 of 12 percent preferred stock at par value, none of which Peerless purchased. The regular $12,000 preferred dividend is paid in 20X1.

4. Assume that accumulated depreciation on Special Foods' books on the acquisition date is $200,000.

LO 9-2

Make calculations and prepare consolidation entries for a partially owned subsidiary when the subsidiary has preferred stock outstanding.

Allocation of Special Foods' Net Income

Of the total $50,000 of net income reported by Special Foods for 20X1, $12,000 ($100,000 × 0.12) is assigned to the preferred shareholders as their current dividend. Peerless Products records its share of the remaining amount, computed as follows:

Special Foods' net income, 20X1	$50,000
Less: Preferred dividends ($100,000 × 0.12)	(12,000)
Special Foods' income accruing to common shareholders	$38,000
Peerless' proportionate share	× 0.80
Peerless' income from Special Foods	$30,400

Income assigned to the noncontrolling interest for 20X1 is the total of Special Foods' preferred dividends and the noncontrolling common stockholders' 20 percent share of Special Foods' $38,000 of income remaining after preferred dividends are deducted:

Preferred dividends of Special Foods	$12,000
Income assigned to Special Foods' noncontrolling common shareholders ($38,000 × 0.20)	7,600
Income to noncontrolling interest	$19,600

Although consolidated net income is unaffected by preferred dividends, the amount allocated to the controlling interest is affected because the income allocated to the non-controlling interest is deducted to arrive at the amount allocated to the controlling interest. In this example, the computation and allocation of consolidated net income is as follows:

Peerless' separate operating income	$140,000
Special Foods' net income	50,000
Consolidated net income	$190,000
Income to the noncontrolling interest	(19,600)
Income attributed to the controlling interest	$170,400

Consolidation Worksheet[1]

Advanced StudyGuide .com

Figure 9–1 presents the 20X1 consolidation worksheet. To prepare the consolidation worksheet, we first analyze the book value of common equity to prepare the basic consolidation entry. Because Special Foods was purchased for an amount equal to the book value of net assets, there is no differential in this example. In consolidation, the $12,000 preferred dividend is treated as income assigned to the noncontrolling interest. Because Peerless holds none of Special Foods' preferred stock, the entire $12,000 is allocated to the noncontrolling interest.

Book Value Calculations:

	NCI 20%	+	Investment 80%	=	Preferred Stock	+	Common Stock	+	Retained Earnings
Beginning Book Value	160,000		240,000		100,000		200,000		100,000
+ Net Income	19,600		30,400						50,000
− Preferred Dividends	(12,000)		0						(12,000)
− Common Dividends	(6,000)		(24,000)						(30,000)
Ending Book Value	161,600		246,400		100,000		200,000		108,000

An analysis of these book value calculations leads to the following basic consolidation entry. Note that the numbers highlighted in dark blue with a white drop-out font are the figures that appear in the basic consolidation entry.

Basic Consolidation Entry:

Preferred Stock	100,000		←Balance in PS account
Common Stock	200,000		←Balance in CS account
Retained Earnings	100,000		←Beginning balance in RE
Income from Special Foods	30,400		←Peerless' share of NI
NCI in NI of Special Foods	19,600		←NCI share of NI
Dividends Declared, Preferred		12,000	←100% of sub's pref. div.
Dividends Declared, Common		30,000	←100% of common div.
Investment in Special Foods		246,400	←Peerless' share of Special Foods' BV
NCI in NA of Special Foods		161,600	←NCI share of Special Foods' book value

[1] To view a video explanation of this topic, visit advancedstudyguide.com.

In addition to closing out Special Foods' equity accounts, this consolidation entry also eliminates Peerless' Investment in Special Foods and Income from Special Foods accounts:

	Investment in Special Foods			Income from Special Foods		
Acquisition	**240,000**					
80% Net Income	**30,400**				**30,400**	**80% Net Income**
		24,000	**80% of Common Dividends**			
Ending Balance	**246,400**				**30,400**	**Ending Balance**
		246,400	**Basic**	**30,400**		
	0				**0**	

FIGURE 9–1 December 31, 20X1, Consolidation Worksheet, First Year Following Combination; 80 Percent Purchase at Book Value

	Peerless Products	Special Foods	Consolidation Entries DR	Consolidation Entries CR	Consolidated
Income Statement					
Sales	400,000	200,000			600,000
Less: COGS	(170,000)	(115,000)			(285,000)
Less: Depreciation Expense	(50,000)	(20,000)			(70,000)
Less: Other Expenses	(40,000)	(15,000)			(55,000)
Income from Special Foods	30,400		30,400		0
Consolidated Net Income	170,400	50,000	30,400	0	190,000
NCI in Net Income			19,600		(19,600)
Controlling Interest Net Income	**170,400**	**50,000**	50,000	0	**170,400**
Statement of Retained Earnings					
Beginning Balance	300,000	100,000	100,000		300,000
Net Income	**170,400**	**50,000**	**50,000**	**0**	170,400
Less: Dividends Declared, Preferred		(12,000)		12,000	0
Less: Dividends Declared, Common	(60,000)	(30,000)		30,000	(60,000)
Ending Balance	**410,400**	**108,000**	**150,000**	**42,000**	**410,400**
Balance Sheet					
Cash	264,000	163,000			427,000
Accounts Receivable	75,000	50,000			125,000
Inventory	100,000	75,000			175,000
Investment in Subsidiary	246,400			246,400	0
Land	175,000	40,000			215,000
Buildings & Equipment	800,000	600,000		200,000	1,200,000
Less: Accumulated Depreciation	(250,000)	(220,000)	200,000		(270,000)
Total Assets	**1,410,400**	**708,000**	**200,000**	**446,400**	**1,872,000**
Accounts Payable	100,000	100,000			200,000
Bonds Payable	400,000	200,000			600,000
Preferred Stock		100,000	100,000		0
Common Stock	500,000	200,000	200,000		500,000
Retained Earnings	**410,400**	**108,000**	**150,000**	**42,000**	410,400
NCI in NA of Special Foods				161,600	161,600
Total Liabilities & Equity	**1,410,400**	**708,000**	**450,000**	**203,600**	**1,872,000**

The only other consolidation entry is the optional accumulated depreciation consolidation entry:

Optional Accumulated Depreciation Consolidation Entry:

Accumulated Depreciation	**200,000**		← Accumulated depreciation at the time of the acquisition
Buildings & Equipment		**200,000**	

These consolidation entries lead to the consolidation worksheet shown in Figure 9–1.

Subsidiary Preferred Stock Held by Parent

Occasionally a parent company holds preferred stock of a subsidiary in addition to its investment in the subsidiary's common stock (similar to the Berkshire investment in Heinz mentioned previously). The preferred stock is eliminated along with the subsidiary's other equity accounts in the consolidation process. In addition, any dividend income from the subsidiary's preferred stock recorded by the parent must be eliminated because it is income from an affiliated company.

As an illustration of the treatment of subsidiary preferred stock held by the parent, assume that Peerless Products purchases 60 percent of Special Foods' $100,000 par value, 12 percent preferred stock for $60,000 when issued on January 1, 20X1. During 20X1, dividends of $12,000 are declared on the preferred stock. Peerless recognizes $7,200 ($12,000 × 0.60) of dividend income from its investment in Special Foods' preferred stock, and the remaining $4,800 ($12,000 × 0.40) is paid to the holders of the other preferred shares.

In consolidation, the total income assigned to the noncontrolling interest includes the portion of the preferred dividend paid on the shares not held by Peerless:

Noncontrolling interest's share of preferred dividends ($12,000 × 0.40)	$ 4,800
Income assigned to Special Foods' noncontrolling common shareholders ($38,000 × 0.20)	7,600
Income to noncontrolling interest	$12,400

To prepare the basic consolidation entry, we first analyze the book value of equity and the related investment accounts in Peerless' common and preferred stock, the noncontrolling interest, and preferred dividend income accounts at the end of 20X1 as follows:

Book Value Calculations:

	NCI 40%/20%	+ Inv. PS 60%	+ Pref. Div. Income 60%	+ Inv. CS 80%	= Preferred Stock	+ Common Stock	+ Retained Earnings
Beginning Book Value	100,000	60,000		240,000	100,000	200,000	100,000
+ Net Income	12,400		7,200	30,400			50,000
− Preferred Dividends	(4,800)		(7,200)				(12,000)
− Common Dividends	(6,000)			(24,000)			(30,000)
Ending Book Value	101,600	60,000	0	246,400	100,000	200,000	108,000

We note that although a dividend on common shares represents a return of capital under the equity method, a dividend on preferred shares is dividend income, which is not a return of capital. Therefore, it is recorded as income, not a reduction to the Investment in Special Foods' Preferred Stock account. This is why the preferred dividend income is listed in a separate column from the Investment in Special Foods' Preferred Stock account in this book value analysis. We also note that although Peerless maintains separate accounts for its Investment in Special Foods' Common and Preferred Stock, it is not necessary to keep separate columns in this analysis for the NCI shareholders' share of each. Therefore, the NCI column actually includes 40 percent of the equity accruing to preferred shareholders and 20 percent of the equity accruing to the common shareholders. Finally, because this example has no differential, the basic consolidation entry will eliminate all of these accounts. Therefore, based on this analysis, we prepare the basic consolidation entry as follows:

Account	Debit	Credit	
Preferred Stock	100,000		←Balance in PS account
Common Stock	200,000		←Balance in CS account
Retained Earnings	100,000		←Beginning balance in RE
Income from Special Foods	30,400		←Peerless' % of NI to common interest.
Dividends Income—Preferred	7,200		←Peerless' share of pref. div.
NCI in NI of Special Foods	12,400		←NCI share of NI
Dividends Declared, Preferred		12,000	←100% of sub's pref. div.
Dividends Declared, Common		30,000	←100% of common div.
Investment in Special Foods CS		246,400	←Net BV in inv. CS acct.
Investment in Special Foods PS		60,000	←Net BV in inv. PS acct.
NCI in NA of Special Foods		101,600	←NCI share of Special Foods' book value

Although the "basic" consolidation entry began as a very simple entry back in Chapter 2, this particular example has grown to a more complex entry. The following T-accounts illustrate how this entry achieves the objectives of (1) closing out all of Special Food's equity and dividend accounts, (2) closing out the Investment in Special Foods CS and Income from Special Foods accounts, and (3) closing out the Investment in Special Foods' PS and Dividend Income from Preferred Stock accounts.

	Investment in Special Foods CS (Dr)	Investment in Special Foods CS (Cr)		Income from Special Foods (Dr)	Income from Special Foods (Cr)	
Acquisition	240,000					
80% Com. NI	30,400				30,400	80% Com. NI
		24,000	80% of Common Dividends			
Ending Balance	246,400				30,400	Ending Balance
		246,400	Basic	30,400		
	0				0	

	Investment in Special Foods PS (Dr)	Investment in Special Foods PS (Cr)		Dividend Income, PS (Dr)	Dividend Income, PS (Cr)	
Acquisition	60,000				7,200	60% Pref. Div
		60,000	Basic	7,200		
	0				0	

Note also that the optional accumulated depreciation consolidation entry also applies:

Optional Accumulated Depreciation Consolidation Entry:

Account	Debit	Credit	
Accumulated Depreciation	200,000		← Accumulated depreciation at the time of the acquisition
Buildings & Equipment		200,000	

Subsidiary Preferred Stock with Special Provisions

Many different preferred stock features are found in practice. For example, most preferred stocks are cumulative, a few are participating, and many are callable at some price other than par value. When a subsidiary with preferred stock outstanding is consolidated, the provisions of the preferred stock agreement must be examined to determine the portion of the subsidiary's stockholders' equity to be assigned to the preferred stock interest.

A cumulative dividend provision provides some degree of protection for preferred shareholders by requiring the company to pay both current and omitted past preferred dividends before any dividend can be given to common shareholders. If a subsidiary has cumulative preferred stock outstanding, an amount of income equal to the current year's preferred dividend is assigned to the preferred stock interest in consolidation whether or not the preferred dividend is declared. When dividends are in arrears on a subsidiary's cumulative preferred stock, recognition is given in consolidation to the claim of the preferred shareholders by assigning to the preferred stock interest an amount of subsidiary retained earnings equal to the dividends in arrears. On the other hand, when a subsidiary's preferred stock is noncumulative, the subsidiary has no obligation to pay undeclared dividends. Consequently, no special consolidation procedures are needed with respect to undeclared dividends on noncumulative subsidiary preferred stock.

Preferred stock participation features allow the preferred stockholders to receive a share of income distribution that exceeds the preferred stock base dividend rate. Although few preferred stocks are participating, many different types of participation arrangements are possible. Once the degree of participation has been determined, the appropriate share of subsidiary income and net assets is assigned to the preferred stock interest in the consolidated financial statements.

FYI

Berkshire Hathaway purchased GE callable preferred stock in 2008 for $110,000. On October 17, 2011, GE fully redeemed all of Berkshire Hathaway's 30,000 preferred shares for a total of $3.3 billion.

Many preferred stocks are callable, often at prices that exceed the par value. The amount to be paid to retire a subsidiary's callable preferred stock under the preferred stock agreement is viewed as the preferred stockholders' claim on the subsidiary's assets, and that amount of subsidiary stockholders' equity is assigned to the preferred stock interest in preparing the consolidated balance sheet.

Illustration of Subsidiary Preferred Stock with Special Features

To examine the consolidation treatment of subsidiary preferred stock with the most common special features, assume that Special Foods issues $100,000 par value, 12 percent preferred stock on January 1, 20X0, and that the stock is cumulative, nonparticipating, and callable at 105. No dividends are declared on the preferred stock during 20X0. On January 1, 20X1, Peerless Products purchases 80 percent of Special Foods' common stock for $240,000 when the fair value of the noncontrolling interest in Special Foods' common stock is $60,000. Also on January 1, 20X1, Peerless purchases 60 percent of the preferred stock for $61,000. The fair values of the identifiable assets and liabilities of Special Foods were equal to their book values at the date of acquisition. The following are the stockholders' equity accounts of Special Foods on January 1, 20X1:

Preferred Stock	$100,000
Common Stock	200,000
Retained Earnings	100,000
Total Stockholders' Equity	$400,000

The amount assigned to the preferred stock interest in the preparation of a consolidated balance sheet on January 1, 20X1, is computed as follows:

Par value of Special Foods' preferred stock	$100,000
Call premium	5,000
Dividends in arrears for 20X0	12,000
Total preferred stock interest, January 1, 20X1	$117,000

This amount is apportioned between Peerless and the noncontrolling shareholders:

Peerless' share of preferred stock interest ($117,000 × 0.60)	$ 70,200
Noncontrolling stockholders' share of preferred stock interest ($117,000 × 0.40)	46,800
Total preferred stock interest, January 1, 20X1	$117,000

Because the preferred stock interest exceeds the par value of the preferred stock by $17,000, the portion of Special Foods' retained earnings accruing to the common shareholders is reduced by that amount. Therefore, Special Foods' common stockholders have a total claim on the company's net assets as follows:

Common stock	$200,000
Retained earnings ($100,000 − $17,000)	83,000
Total common stock interest, January 1, 20X1	$283,000

The total common interest in Special Foods should be allocated between Peerless and the noncontrolling interest based on their respective ownership amounts:

Peerless' share of the common stock interest ($283,000 × 0.80)	$ 226,400
Noncontrolling stockholders' share of common interest ($283,000 × 0.20)	56,600
Total common stock interest, January 3, 20X1	$283,000

Because the book value of Special Foods' common stockholders' claim on assets is only $283,000 on January 1, 20X1, Peerless' acquisition of 80 percent of Special Foods' common stock results in the following differential:

Consideration given by Peerless Products	$ 240,000
Fair value of noncontrolling interest in Special Foods' common stock	60,000
	$ 300,000
Book value of Special Foods' common stock	(283,000)
Differential	$ 17,000

Because the fair values of the identifiable assets and liabilities of Special Foods equal the book values, the entire differential will be allocated to goodwill at the date of acquisition.

To prepare consolidation entries, we first allocate the book value of Special Foods' net assets and the associated amounts in Peerless' investment accounts as well as the NCI ownership interest in Special Foods as previously calculated. Remember that the total noncontrolling interest on January 1, 20X1, consists of both preferred and common stock interests as follows:

Preferred stock interest ($117,000 × 0.40)	$ 46,800
Common stock interest	60,000
Total noncontrolling interest, January 1, 20X1	$106,800

Book Value Calculations:

	NCI 40%/20%	+	Inv. PS 60%	+	Inv. CS 80%	=	Preferred Stock	+	Common Stock	+	Retained Earnings
Beginning Book Value	103,400		70,200		226,400		100,000		200,000		100,000

This analysis leads to the following basic consolidation entry:

Basic Consolidation Entry:

Preferred Stock	100,000		← Balance in PS account
Common Stock	200,000		← Balance in CS account
Retained Earnings	100,000		← Beginning balance in RE
Investment in Special Foods CS		226,400	← Net BV in inv. in CS
Investment in Special Foods PS		70,200	← Net BV in inv. in PS
NCI in NA of Special Foods		103,400	← NCI share of net book value

The next consolidation entry assigns the differential to goodwill, removes the remaining investment in Special Foods' common stock, and increases the noncontrolling interest for its 20 percent share of the goodwill:

Excess Value (Differential) Reclassification Entry:

Goodwill	17,000	
Investment in Special Foods CS		13,600
NCI in NA of Special Foods		3,400

The final consolidation entry eliminates the credit balance of $9,200 in the Investment in Special Foods' preferred stock ($61,000 original investment – $70,200 from the basic elimination entry). The NCI shareholders sold 60 percent of the preferred shares to Peerless at an amount lower than their actual value after considering dividends in arrears and the claim associated with the call option.

Claim on Special Foods' net assets ($117,000 × 0.60)	$70,200
Proceeds from sale of preferred stock to Peerless	(61,000)
"Loss" on sale of preferred shares to Peerless	$ 9,200

From a consolidated viewpoint, Peerless' purchase of the preferred stock is considered a retirement of a noncontrolling ownership interest by the consolidated entity. Because this retirement occurred at less than book value and gains and losses are not recognized on capital transactions, this excess is considered to be additional paid-in capital.

This consolidation entry properly classifies the $9,200 gain as additional paid-in-capital:

Investment in Special Foods PS	9,200	
Additional Paid-In-Capital		9,200

CHANGES IN PARENT COMPANY OWNERSHIP

LO 9-3

Make calculations and explain how consolidation procedures differ when the parent's ownership interest changes during the accounting period.

Although preceding chapters have treated the parent company's subsidiary ownership interest as remaining constant over time, in actuality, ownership levels sometimes vary. Changes in ownership levels may result from either the parent's or the subsidiary's actions. The parent company can change ownership ratios by purchasing or selling shares of the subsidiary in transactions with unaffiliated companies. A subsidiary can change the parent's ownership percentage by selling additional shares to or repurchasing shares from unaffiliated parties or through stock transactions with the parent (if the subsidiary is less than wholly owned).

Parent's Purchase of Additional Shares from Nonaffiliate

A parent company may purchase the common stock of a subsidiary at different points in time. Until control is achieved, the intercorporate investment is accounted for as discussed in Chapter 2. Once control is achieved, the entire investment is valued based on fair values at the date control is achieved, and subsequently consolidated financial statements must be presented.

Purchases of additional shares of an investee's stock were discussed in Chapters 1 and 2. Additional effects of multiple purchases of a subsidiary's stock on the consolidation process are illustrated in the following example.

FYI

Prior to 2010, Berkshire Hathaway owned shares of BNSF Railway Corporation, but did not control it. On February 12, 2010, Berkshire purchased the remaining shares to achieve 100% control and now consolidates BNSF.

Assume that on January 1, 20X0, Special Foods has $200,000 of common stock outstanding and retained earnings of $60,000. During 20X0, 20X1, and 20X2, Special Foods reports the following information:

Period	Net Income	Dividends	Ending Book Value
20X0	$40,000	0	$300,000
20X1	50,000	$30,000	320,000
20X2	75,000	40,000	355,000

Peerless Products purchases its 80 percent interest in Special Foods in several blocks, as follows:

Purchase Date	Ownership Percentage Acquired	Cost	Book Value	Differential
January 1, 20X0	20	$ 56,000	$ 52,000	$4,000
December 31, 20X0	10	35,000	30,000	5,000
January 1, 20X2	50	185,000	160,000	
	80			

The entire differential relates to land held by Special Foods. Note that Peerless does not gain control of Special Foods until January 1, 20X2.

The investment account on Peerless' books includes the following amounts through 20X1:

	Investment in Special Foods		
Purchase 20% CS	**56,000**		
20% Net Income	**8,000**		
Purchase 10% CS	**35,000**		
12/31/X0 Balance	**99,000**		
30% Net Income	**15,000**		
		9,000	**30% of Dividend**
12/31/X1 Balance	**105,000**		

When Peerless gains control of Special Foods on January 1, 20X2, assume that the fair value of the 30 percent equity interest it already holds in Special Foods is $111,000 and the fair value of Special Foods' 20 percent remaining noncontrolling interest is $74,000. The book value of Special Foods as a whole on that date is $320,000. Under **ASC 805,** the differential on the combination date is computed as follows:

Fair value of consideration exchanged	$185,000
Fair value of equity interest already held	111,000
Fair value of noncontrolling interest	74,000
	$370,000
Book value of Special Foods	(320,000)
Differential	$ 50,000

Because the entire differential relates to land in this example, it is not amortized or written off either on Peerless' books or for consolidation.

Under the requirements of **ASC 805,** Peerless must remeasure the equity interest it already held in Special Foods to its fair value at the date of combination and recognize a gain or loss for the difference between the fair value and its carrying amount:

Fair value of equity interest already held	$111,000
Carrying amount of investment, December 31, 20X1	(105,000)
Gain on increase in value of investment in Special Foods	$ 6,000

Peerless recognizes the $6,000 gain (with a credit) in income and increases the investment balance (with a debit) on its books by that amount. The total balance of the investment account on Peerless' books immediately after the combination is as follows:

Carrying amount of investment, December 31, 20X1	$105,000
Increase in value of investment in Special Foods	6,000
Cost of January 1, 20X2, shares acquired	185,000
Peerless' total recorded amount of investment	$296,000

Because Peerless Products gains control of Special Foods on January 1, 20X2, consolidated statements are prepared for the year 20X2. The ending balance in the Investment in Special Foods account at the end of 20X2 is calculated as follows:

	Investment in Special Foods (Dr)	Investment in Special Foods (Cr)	
12/31/X1 Balance	105,000		
Fair Value Adjustment	6,000		
Purchase 50% CS	185,000		
1/1/X2 Balance	296,000		
80% Net Income	60,000		
		32,000	80% of Dividend
12/31/X2 Balance	324,000		

To prepare the consolidation worksheet at the end of the year, we first analyze the book value component to construct the basic consolidation entry:

Book Value Calculations:

	NCI 20%	+ Peerless 80%	=	Common Stock	+	Retained Earnings
Beginning Book Value	64,000	256,000		200,000		120,000
+ Net Income	15,000	60,000				75,000
− Dividends	(8,000)	(32,000)				(40,000)
Ending Book Value	71,000	284,000		200,000		155,000

Basic Consolidation Entry:

Common Stock	200,000		← Common stock balance
Retained Earnings	120,000		← Beginning balance in RE
Income from Special Foods	60,000		← Peerless' share of reported NI
NCI in NI of Special Foods	15,000		← NCI share of reported NI
Dividends Declared		40,000	← 100% of dividends
Investment in Special Foods		284,000	← Net amount of BV in inv. acct.
NCI in NA of Special Foods		71,000	← NCI's share of net BV

We then analyze the differential and its changes during the period:

Excess Value (Differential) Calculations:

	NCI 20% +	Peerless 80% =	Land
Beginning Balance	10,000	40,000	50,000
Amortization	0	0	0
Ending Balance	10,000	40,000	50,000

Land	50,000		← Excess value from undervalued land
Investment in Special Foods		40,000	← Peerless' share of excess value
NCI in NA of Special Foods		10,000	← NCI's share of excess value

Parent's Sale of Subsidiary Shares to Nonaffiliate

Peerless Products Corporation

Special Foods Inc.

A gain or loss normally occurs and is recorded on the seller's books when a company disposes of all or part of an investment. **ASC 323** deals explicitly with sales of stock of an investee, requiring recognition of a gain or loss on the difference between the selling price and the carrying amount of the stock. What happens, however, when the shares sold are those of a subsidiary and the subsidiary continues to qualify for consolidation? This question caused difficulty in practice for many years, but **ASC 810** resolves the issue. When a parent sells some shares of a subsidiary but continues to hold a controlling interest, **ASC 810** makes clear that this is considered to be an equity transaction and no gain or loss may be recognized in consolidated net income. Under **ASC 810,** changes in a parent's ownership interest in a subsidiary while the parent retains control require an adjustment to the amount assigned to the noncontrolling interest to reflect its change in ownership of the subsidiary. The difference between the fair value of the consideration received or paid in the equity transaction and the adjustment to the noncontrolling interest results in an adjustment to the stockholders' equity attributable to the controlling interest, through an adjustment to additional paid-in-capital.

As an illustration of the sale of subsidiary stock to a nonaffiliate, assume that on December 31, 20X0, Special Foods has 20,000 common shares outstanding with a total par value of $200,000 and retained earnings of $100,000. On that date, Peerless acquires an 80 percent interest in Special Foods by purchasing 16,000 shares of its $10 par common stock at book value of $240,000 ($300,000 × 0.80). The noncontrolling interest in Special Foods has a fair value equal to its book value of $60,000 at that time. Special Foods reports net income of $50,000 for 20X1 and pays dividends of $30,000. On January 1, 20X2, Peerless sells 1,000 shares of its Special Foods common stock to a nonaffiliate for $19,000, leaving it with a 75 percent interest (15,000 ÷ 20,000) in Special Foods. On the date of sale, Special Foods has total stockholders' equity of $320,000, consisting of common stock of $200,000 and retained earnings of $120,000.

Recognition of Sale on Parent Company Books

The equity-method carrying amount of Peerless' investment in Special Foods on the date Peerless sells 1,000 shares reflects Peerless' share of Special Foods' 20X1 net income and dividends, as follows:

Cost of investment, December 31, 20X0	$240,000
Peerless' share of Special Foods' 20X1 net income ($50,000 × 0.80)	40,000
Peerless' share of Special Foods' 20X1 dividends ($30,000 × 0.80)	(24,000)
Investment balance, January 1, 20X2	$256,000

Because this example has no differential, the balance of the investment account equals 80 percent of the total stockholders' equity of Special Foods on January 1, 20X2. Likewise, the noncontrolling interest is $64,000, equal to 20 percent of Special Foods' total stockholders' equity.

ASC 810 does not permit a gain or loss on the sale of the shares to be reported in consolidated net income. Peerless realizes a gain of $3,000 on the sale for the difference between the $16,000 carrying amount of the shares ($256,000 × 1/16) and the selling price of $19,000. Because the gain cannot be reported in the consolidated financial statements, Peerless will recognize an increase in additional paid-in capital:

	January 1, 20X2		
(1)	Cash	19,000	
	Investment in Special Foods Stock		16,000
	Additional Paid-In Capital		3,000

Consolidation Worksheet 20X2

From a consolidation perspective, **ASC 810** requires that the difference between the proceeds received from the sale of subsidiary stock and the adjustment to the noncontrolling interest from the change in its ownership of the subsidiary be recognized in the parent's equity. Upon Peerless' sale of the Special Foods stock, the noncontrolling interest increases from $64,000 ($320,000 × 0.20) to $80,000 ($320,000 × 0.25), an increase of $16,000. The difference between the $19,000 of proceeds received and the $16,000 increase in the noncontrolling interest is $3,000, and this amount is recognized in consolidation as additional paid-in capital attributable to the parent.

Because Peerless recorded the sale of Special Foods shares on its books with entry (1), consolidated net income and additional paid-in capital in consolidated equity are correctly stated without further adjustment.

The balance in Peerless' investment account at December 31, 20X2, is $266,250. This amount is the result of the following entries in the investment account:

	Investment in Special Foods		
Purchase 80% CS	**240,000**		
80% Net Income	**40,000**		
		24,000	**80% of Dividend**
12/31/X1 Balance	**256,000**		
		16,000	**Sale of 1,000 Shares to NCI**
75% Net Income	**56,250**		
		30,000	**75% of Dividend**
12/31/X2 Balance	**266,250**		
		266,250	**Basic Consolidation Entry**
	0		

To calculate the basic consolidation entry shown in the T-account, we analyze the book value component of the investment:

Book Value Calculations:

	NCI 25%	+ Peerless 75%	=	Common Stock	+	Retained Earnings
Beginning Book Value	80,000	240,000		200,000		120,000
+ Net Income	18,750	56,250				75,000
− Dividends	(10,000)	(30,000)				(40,000)
Ending Book Value	88,750	266,250		200,000		155,000

This analysis leads to the following basic consolidation entry:

Basic Consolidation Entry:

Common Stock	200,000		← Common stock balance
Retained Earnings	120,000		← Beginning balance in RE
Income from Special Foods	56,250		← Peerless' share of reported NI
NCI in NI of Special Foods	18,750		← NCI's share of reported NI
Dividends Declared		40,000	← 100% of dividends declared
Investment in Special Foods		266,250	← Net BV in investment account
NCI in NA of Special Foods		88,750	← NCI's share of net BV

Consolidation Subsequent to 20X2

In preparing consolidated financial statements each year after 20X2, no special consolidation entries are needed with respect to the 20X2 sale of subsidiary shares since Peerless has already properly recorded the realized gain as additional paid-in-capital.

Subsidiary's Sale of Additional Shares to Nonaffiliate

The consolidated enterprise can generate additional funds when a subsidiary sells new shares to parties outside the economic entity. A sale of additional shares to an unaffiliated party increases the total stockholders' equity of the consolidated entity by the amount received by the subsidiary from the sale. Such a sale increases the subsidiary's total shares outstanding and, consequently, reduces the percentage ownership held by the parent company. At the same time, the dollar amount assigned to the noncontrolling interest in the consolidated financial statements increases. The resulting amounts of the controlling and noncontrolling interests are affected by two factors:

1. The number of shares sold to nonaffiliates.
2. The price at which the shares are sold to nonaffiliates.

Difference between Book Value and Sale Price of Subsidiary Shares

If the sale price of new shares equals the book value of outstanding shares, there is no change in the existing shareholders' claim. If the subsidiary's stockholders' equity is viewed as a pie, the overall size of the pie increases. The parent's share of the pie decreases, but the size of the parent's slice remains the same because of the increase in the overall size of the pie. The consolidation entries used simply are changed to recognize the increase in the claim of the noncontrolling shareholders and the corresponding increase in the stockholders' equity balances of the subsidiary.

Most sales, however, do not occur at book value. When the sale price and book value are not the same, all common shareholders are assigned a pro rata portion of the difference. In this situation, the book value of the subsidiary's shares held by the parent changes even though the number remains constant. The size of both the pie and the parent's share of it change; the size of the parent's slice changes because the increase in the pie's size and the decrease in the parent's share do not exactly offset each other.

The issuance of additional shares by a subsidiary to unaffiliated parties is viewed as an equity transaction from a consolidated perspective. Even though the parent is not directly involved in the transaction, the book value of its subsidiary shares changes as a result of the additional shares being issued. The parent recognizes this change in the book value of the controlling interest in the subsidiary by adjusting the carrying amount of its investment in the subsidiary and additional paid-in capital. The parent's additional paid-in capital is then carried to the worksheet in consolidation.

From a consolidated viewpoint, a subsidiary's sale of additional shares to unaffiliated parties and a parent's sale of subsidiary shares are similar transactions: In both cases, the consolidated entity sells shares to the noncontrolling interest. Because the participants in a consolidation are regarded as members of a single economic entity, the sale of subsidiary shares to the noncontrolling interest should be treated in the same way regardless of whether the parent or the subsidiary sells the shares. The recognition of a gain or loss on such a transaction is inappropriate because the sale of stock to unaffiliated parties by the consolidated entity is a capital transaction from a single-entity viewpoint.

Illustration of Subsidiary's Sale of Stock to Nonaffiliate

To examine the sale of additional shares by a subsidiary to a nonaffiliate, assume that Peerless Products acquires an 80 percent interest in Special Foods by purchasing 16,000 shares of Special Foods' $10 par common stock on December 31, 20X0, at book value of $240,000. Special Foods only has common stock outstanding. All other information is the same as that used previously. Therefore, by December 31, 20X1, the equity-method carrying amount of the investment on Peerless' books is $256,000. On January 1, 20X2, Special Foods issues 5,000 additional shares of stock to nonaffiliates for $20 per share, a total of $100,000. After the sale, Special Foods has 25,000 shares outstanding, and Peerless has a 64 percent interest (16,000 ÷ 25,000) in Special Foods.

The January 1, 20X2, issuance of additional shares results in the following change in Special Foods' balance sheet:

	Before Sale	Following Sale
Common Stock, $10 par value	$200,000	$250,000
Additional Paid-In Capital (PIC)		50,000
Retained Earnings	120,000	120,000
Total Stockholders' Equity	$320,000	$420,000

The book value of Peerless' investment in Special Foods changes as a result of the sale of additional shares as follows:

	Before Sale	Following Sale
Special Foods' Total Stockholders' Equity	$320,000	$420,000
Peerless' Proportionate Share	× 0.80	× 0.64
Book Value of Peerless' Investment in Special Foods	$256,000	$268,800

Note that, although Peerless' ownership percentage decreases from 80 percent to 64 percent, the book value of Peerless' investment increases by $12,800. The increase in book value occurs because the $20 issue price of the additional shares exceeds the $16 ($320,000÷20,000 shares) book value of the outstanding shares before the sale:

Issue price of additional shares	$ 20
Book value of shares before sale ($320,000 ÷ 20,000 shares)	(16)
Excess of issue price over book value	$ 4
Number of shares issued	× 5,000
Excess book value added	$20,000
Peerless' proportionate share	× 0.64
Increase in Peerless' interest	$12,800

Peerless records the increase in its equity in the net assets of Special Foods with the following entry:

(2)	Investment in Special Foods Stock	12,800	
	Additional Paid-In Capital		12,800
	Record increase in equity in subsidiary resulting from subsidiary issue of shares.		

The following T-account summarizes the activity in Peerless' investment in Special Foods:

	Investment in Special Foods CS (Debit)	Investment in Special Foods CS (Credit)	
Purchase 80% CS	240,000		
80% Net Income	40,000		
		24,000	80% of Dividend
12/31/X1 Balance	256,000		
New Shares Issued	12,800		
Balance 1/1/20X2	268,800		
		268,800	Basic Consolidation Entry
	0		

To calculate the basic consolidation entry shown in the T-account, we analyze the book value component of the investment:

Book Value Calculations:

	NCI 20%/36%	+	Peerless 80%/64%	=	Common Stock	+	Additional Paid-In Capital	+	Retained Earnings
Book Value on 12/31/20X1	64,000		256,000		200,000				120,000
New Shares Issued (5,000 × 20)	87,200		12,800		50,000		50,000		
Book Value on 1/1/20X2	151,200		268,800		250,000		50,000		120,000

This analysis leads to the following basic consolidation entry:

Basic Consolidation Entry:

Common Stock	250,000		← Ending balance in common stock
Additional Paid-In Capital	50,000		← Ending balance in additional PIC
Retained Earnings	120,000		← Beginning balance in RE
Investment in Special Foods		268,800	← Net book value in invest. acct.
NCI in NA of Special Foods		151,200	← NCI share of net amount of BV

Additional paid-in capital recorded by Special Foods from the sale of the additional shares is eliminated in the preparation of consolidated financial statements, as are all of the subsidiary's stockholders' equity accounts. The noncontrolling interest's share of the increase in the book value of Special Foods' stock resulting from the sale of additional shares is reflected in the balance of the noncontrolling interest in the consolidated balance sheet. The $151,200 balance of the noncontrolling interest is 36 percent of the $420,000 total book value of Special Foods after the sale of the additional shares. Peerless' $12,800 share of the increase in Special Foods' book value is included in the consolidated balance sheet by carrying over the additional paid-in capital recorded by Peerless.

Subsidiary's Sale of Stock at Less than Book Value

A sale of stock by a subsidiary to a nonaffiliate at less than existing book value has an effect opposite to that illustrated in the preceding example. The parent company's claim is diminished as a result of the subsidiary selling additional shares at less than existing book value. A reduction in the book value of the shares held by the parent normally is treated as a debit to Additional Paid-In Capital and a credit to the investment account. In the absence of the Additional Paid-In Capital account, retained earnings decreases.

Subsidiary's Sale of Additional Shares to Parent

A sale of additional shares directly from a less-than-wholly-owned subsidiary to its parent increases the parent's ownership percentage. If the sale is at a price equal to the book value of the existing shares, the increase in the parent's investment account equals the increase in the stockholders' equity of the subsidiary. The net book value assigned to the noncontrolling interest remains unchanged. In preparing consolidated financial statements, the normal consolidation entries are made based on the parent's new ownership percentage.

When a parent purchases a subsidiary's shares directly from the subsidiary at an amount other than book value, it increases the carrying amount of its investment by the fair value of the consideration given. In consolidation, the amount of the noncontrolling interest must be adjusted to reflect the change in its interest in the subsidiary occasioned by the parent's purchase of additional subsidiary shares. **ASC 810** then requires an adjustment to consolidated additional paid-in capital for the difference between any consideration given or received by the consolidated entity and the amount of the adjustment to the noncontrolling interest. In the case of a parent purchasing additional shares from a less-than-wholly-owned subsidiary, no consideration is given or received from a consolidated perspective, so the amount of the adjustment to equity is equal to the change in the noncontrolling interest and total consolidated stockholders' equity is unchanged.

As an illustration of the sale of additional shares from a subsidiary to its parent, assume that in the example of Peerless Products and Special Foods, Peerless purchases 16,000 shares of Special Foods $10 par common stock at book value on the open market for $240,000 on December 31, 20X0, giving Peerless an 80 percent interest. Special Foods has only common stock outstanding. All other information is the same as that used previously. Therefore, by December 31, 20X1, the equity-method carrying amount of the investment on Peerless' books is $256,000. On January 1, 20X2, Peerless purchases an additional 5,000 shares of common directly from Special Foods for $20 per share. This additional $100,000 investment gives Peerless an ownership interest in Special Foods totaling 84 percent (21,000 ÷ 25,000).

Special Foods' sale of additional shares to Peerless results in the following changes:

	Before Sale	Following Sale
Common Stock, $10 par value	$200,000	$250,000
Additional Paid-In Capital		50,000
Retained Earnings	120,000	120,000
Total Stockholders' Equity	$320,000	$420,000

The book value of Peerless' investment in Special Foods changes as a result of the sale of additional shares, as follows:

	Before Sale	Following Sale
Special Foods' Total Stockholders' Equity	$320,000	$420,000
Peerless' Proportionate Share	× 0.80	× 0.84
Book Value of Peerless' Investment in Special Foods	$256,000	$352,800

If Special Foods' stockholders' equity is viewed as a pie, the size of both the pie and Peerless' percentage share of it increase. The size of Peerless' slice of the pie increases by $96,800 ($352,800 − $256,000).

The new book value per share of Special Foods' stock is $16.80 ($420,000 ÷ 25,000 shares) compared to the $16.00 ($320,000 ÷ 20,000 shares) book value before the sale of additional shares. The book value is higher because the price Peerless paid for the additional shares is more than the stock's previous book value. The excess of the amount paid by Peerless for Special Foods' stock ($100,000) over the increase in the book value of the shares held by Peerless ($96,800) is $3,200.

The book value of the shares held by the noncontrolling interest, which is only 16 percent following Peerless' purchase, also increases, as follows:

Noncontrolling interest after sale of additional shares to Peerless ($420,000 × 0.16)	$67,200
Noncontrolling interest before sale of additional shares to Peerless ($320,000 × 0.20)	(64,000)
Increase in book value of noncontrolling interest	$ 3,200

From a consolidated perspective, **ASC 810** requires an adjustment to the parent's equity (consolidated additional paid-in capital) for the amount of the difference between the consideration paid or received by the consolidated entity and the change in the noncontrolling interest. Because no consideration was paid or received by the consolidated entity overall, the required decrease in the parent's equity is equal to the amount of change in the noncontrolling interest, $3,200.

Peerless would record its purchase of additional shares of Special Foods stock as follows:

(3)			
	Investment in Special Foods Stock	96,800	
	Additional Paid-In Capital	3,200	
	Cash		100,000

Record the purchase of additional Special Foods shares.

The following T-account summarizes the activity in Peerless' investment in Special Foods:

	Investment in Special Foods CS		
Purchase 80% CS	240,000		
80% Net Income	40,000		
		24,000	80% of Dividend
12/31/X1 Balance	256,000		
Shares Purchased	96,800		
Balance 1/1/20X2	352,800		
		352,800	Basic Consolidation Entry
	0		

To calculate the basic consolidation entry shown in the T-account, we analyze the book value component of the investment:

Book Value Calculations:

	NCI 20%/16%	+	Peerless 80%/84%	=	Common Stock	+	Additional Paid-In Capital	+	Retained Earnings
Book Value on 12/31/20X1	64,000		256,000		200,000				120,000
New Shares Issued (5,000 × 20)	3,200		96,800		50,000		50,000		
Book Value on 1/1/20X2	67,200		352,800		250,000		50,000		120,000

This analysis leads to the following basic consolidation entry:

Basic Consolidation Entry:

	Debit	Credit	
Common Stock	250,000		← Ending balance in CS account
Additional Paid-In Capital	50,000		← EB in additional PIC
Retained Earnings	120,000		← Beginning balance in RE
Investment in Special Foods		352,800	← Net BV in investment acct.
NCI in NA of Special Foods		67,200	← NCI's share of net amount of BV

The balance eliminated from Peerless' investment account equals the previous balance of $256,000 plus the $100,000 cost of the additional shares, minus the reduction in additional paid-in capital, $3,200. The amount of the noncontrolling interest is established at 16 percent of the $420,000 book value of Special Foods.

Subsidiary's Purchase of Shares from Nonaffiliate

Sometimes a subsidiary purchases treasury shares from noncontrolling shareholders. Noncontrolling shareholders frequently find they have little opportunity for input into the subsidiary's activities and operations and often are willing sellers. The parent company may prefer not to be concerned with outside shareholders and may direct the subsidiary to reacquire any noncontrolling shares that become available.

Although the parent is not a direct participant when a subsidiary purchases treasury stock from noncontrolling shareholders, the parent's equity in the net assets of the subsidiary may change as a result of the transaction. When this occurs, the amount of the change must be recognized in preparing the consolidated statements.

For example, assume that Peerless Products owns 80 percent of Special Foods' 20,000 shares of $10 par common stock, which it purchased on January 1, 20X1, at book value of $240,000. On January 1, 20X2, Special Foods purchases 1,000 treasury shares from a nonaffiliate for $20 per share. Peerless' interest in Special Foods increases to 84.21 percent (16,000 ÷ 19,000) as a result of Special Foods' reacquisition of shares, and the noncontrolling interest decreases to 15.79 percent (3,000 ÷ 19,000). The stockholders' equity of Special Foods before and after the reacquisition of shares is as follows:

	Before Purchase	Following Purchase
Common Stock, $10 par value	$200,000	$200,000
Retained Earnings	120,000	120,000
Total	$320,000	$320,000
Less: Treasury Stock		(20,000)
Total Stockholders' Equity	$320,000	$300,000

The underlying book value of Special Foods' shares held by Peerless changes as a result of the stock reacquisition, as follows:

	Before Purchase	Following Purchase
Special Foods' Total Stockholders' Equity	$320,000	$300,000
Peerless' Proportionate Share	× 0.80	× 0.8421
Book Value of Peerless' Investment in Special Foods	$256,000	$252,630

The reacquisition of shares by Special Foods at an amount higher than book value results in a decrease in the book value of Peerless' investment of $3,370 ($256,000 − $252,630). Peerless recognizes the decrease with the following entry:

(4)		Debit	Credit
	Retained Earnings	3,370	
	Investment in Special Foods Stock		3,370
	Record decrease in equity in subsidiary from subsidiary stock reacquisition		

Because Peerless' equity in Special Foods decreases as a result of the transaction between Special Foods and the noncontrolling shareholders, Peerless recognizes that decrease in equity through entry (4). Peerless reduces its retained earnings because it has no additional paid-in capital on its books (where the reduction would normally take place).

From a consolidated perspective, the subsidiary's acquisition of treasury shares is considered an equity transaction with the noncontrolling shareholders. **ASC 810** requires that the parent's equity be adjusted for the difference between the consideration paid or received by the consolidated entity and the change in the noncontrolling interest. In this case, the stock repurchase by Special Foods reduces the noncontrolling interest as follows:

Noncontrolling interest before repurchase of shares by Special Foods ($320,000 × 0.20)	$64,000
Noncontrolling interest after repurchase of shares by Special Foods ($300,000 × 0.1579)	(47,370)
Decrease in book value of noncontrolling interest	$16,630

The difference between the $20,000 consideration given by Special Foods to repurchase its shares and the $16,630 decrease in the noncontrolling interest is $3,370, and the parent's equity must be reduced by this amount in the consolidated balance sheet. This effect has been accomplished on Peerless' separate books with entry (4) and will carry over to the consolidated financial statements.

The following T-account summarizes the activity in Peerless' investment in Special Foods:

	Investment in Special Foods CS		
Purchase 80% CS	**240,000**		
80% Net Income	**40,000**		
		24,000	**80% of Dividend**
12/31/X1 Balance	**256,000**		
		3,370	**Shares Purchased from NCI**
Balance 1/1/20X2	**252,630**		
		252,630	**Basic Consolidation Entry**
	0		

To calculate the basic consolidation entry shown in the T-account, we analyze the book value component of the investment:

Book Value Calculations:

	NCI 20%/15.79%	+	Peerless 80%/84.21%	=	Common Stock	+	Treasury Stock	+	Retained Earnings
Book Value on 12/31/X1	64,000		256,000		200,000				120,000
Shares Repurchased (1,000 × 20)	(16,630)		(3,370)				(20,000)		
Book Value on 1/1/20X2	47,370		252,630		200,000		(20,000)		120,000

This analysis leads to the following basic consolidation entry:

Basic Consolidation Entry:

Common Stock	200,000		← Ending balance in CS account
Retained Earnings	120,000		← Beginning balance in RE
Treasury Stock		20,000	← Shares reacquired from NCI
Investment in Special Foods		252,630	← Net BV in investment account
NCI in NA of Special Foods		47,370	← NCI's share of net BV

Note that this entry eliminates all the common stockholders' equity balances of the subsidiary, including the treasury stock. A consolidation entry is not needed to reduce equity by the $3,370 change resulting from the repurchase because entry (4) accomplished that on Peerless' books and Peerless' retained earnings amount carries over to the consolidation worksheet.

Subsidiary's Purchase of Shares from Parent

A subsidiary can reduce the number of shares it has outstanding through purchases from the parent as well as from noncontrolling shareholders. In practice, stock repurchases from the parent occur infrequently. A parent reducing its ownership interest in a subsidiary usually does so by selling some of its holdings to nonaffiliates to generate additional funds.

When a subsidiary reacquires some of its shares from its parent, the parent has traditionally recognized a gain or loss on the difference between the selling price and the change in the carrying amount of its investment. Some question exists as to whether a transaction of this type between a parent and its subsidiary can be regarded as arm's length; consequently, reporting the gain or loss in the parent's income statement can be questioned. From a consolidated viewpoint, when a subsidiary reacquires its shares from the parent, the transaction represents an internal transfer and does not give rise to a gain or loss. Because recognizing a gain or loss on the parent's books is questionable and the gain or loss would have to be eliminated in consolidation anyway, a better approach is for the parent to adjust additional paid-in capital rather than record a gain or loss on the transaction.

As an example of the reacquisition of a subsidiary's shares from its parent, assume that Peerless Products purchases 16,000 of Special Foods' 20,000 shares of $10 par common stock on December 31, 20X0, at book value of $240,000. On January 1, 20X2, Special Foods repurchases 4,000 shares from Peerless at $20 per share, leaving Peerless with a 75 percent interest (12,000 ÷ 16,000) in Special Foods. The stockholders' equity of Special Foods before and after the reacquisition of shares is as follows:

	Before Purchase	Following Purchase
Common Stock, $10 par value	$200,000	$200,000
Retained Earnings	120,000	120,000
Total	$320,000	$320,000
Less: Treasury Stock		(80,000)
Total Stockholders' Equity	$320,000	$240,000

The carrying amount of Peerless' investment in Special Foods' stock equals the underlying book value of the shares in this example. The book value of the shares changes as a result of the reacquisition, as follows:

	Before Purchase	Following Purchase
Special Foods' Total Stockholders' Equity	$320,000	$240,000
Peerless' Proportionate Share	× 0.80	× 0.75
Book Value of Peerless' Investment in Special Foods	$256,000	$180,000

Peerless records the sale of 25 percent (4,000 ÷ 16,000) of its investment in Special Foods with the following entry:

	January 1, 20X2		
(5)	Cash	80,000	
	Investment in Special Foods Stock		76,000
	Additional Paid-In Capital		4,000

Record sale of investment:
$80,000 = $20 × 4,000 shares
$76,000 = $256,000 − $180,000
$4,000 = $80,000 − $76,000.

The new carrying value of the investment is $180,000 ($256,000 − $76,000). Because there is no differential in this case, this amount equals 75 percent of Special Foods' total stockholders' equity of $240,000 following the reacquisition. The $76,000 decrease in the carrying value includes both the reduction resulting from the decrease in the number of shares held and the reduction in the book value of those shares still held.

The subsidiary's repurchase of shares from the parent also affects the noncontrolling interest, as follows:

Noncontrolling interest before repurchase of shares by Special Foods ($320,000 × 0.20)	$64,000
Noncontrolling interest after repurchase of shares by Special Foods ($240,000 × 0.25)	(60,000)
Decrease in book value of noncontrolling interest	$ 4,000

From a consolidated perspective, **ASC 810** requires an adjustment to the parent's equity for the difference between the consideration paid or received and the change in the non-controlling interest resulting from the subsidiary's repurchase of shares. In this example, the consolidated entity as a whole paid or received no consideration, so the required adjustment to equity is $4,000, the amount of the change in the noncontrolling interest. The parent's equity has already been increased for the $4,000 difference with entry (5) on the parent's books, and this amount carries into the consolidation worksheet. Thus, no adjustments to equity other than the basic consolidation entry are required.

The following T-account summarizes the activity in Peerless' investment in Special Foods:

	Investment in Special Foods CS		
Purchase 80% CS	**240,000**		
80% Net Income	**40,000**		
		24,000	**80% of Dividend**
12/31/X1 Balance	**256,000**		
		76,000	**Shares Purchased by Special Foods**
Balance 1/1/20X2	**180,000**		
		180,000	**Basic Consolidation Entry**
	0		

To calculate the basic consolidation entry shown in the T-account, we analyze the book value component of the investment:

Book Value Calculations:

	NCI 20%/25%	+	Peerless 80%/75%	=	Common Stock	+	Treasury Stock	+	Retained Earnings
Book Value on 12/31/20X1	64,000		256,000		200,000				120,000
Shares Repurchased (4,000 × 20)	(4,000)		(76,000)				(80,000)		
Book Value on 1/1/20X2	60,000		180,000		200,000		(80,000)		120,000

This analysis leads to the following basic consolidation entry:

Basic Consolidation Entry:

	Debit	Credit	
Common Stock	200,000		← Ending balance in common stock
Retained Earnings	120,000		← Beginning balance in RE
Treasury Stock		80,000	← Shares reacquired from Peerless
Investment in Special Foods		180,000	← Net BV in investment account
NCI in NA of Special Foods		60,000	← NCI share of net BV

COMPLEX OWNERSHIP STRUCTURES

LO 9-4

Make calculations and prepare consolidation entries for a partially owned subsidiary when the subsidiary has a complex ownership structure.

Current reporting standards call for preparing consolidated financial statements when one company has direct or indirect control over another. The discussion to this point has focused on a simple, direct parent–subsidiary relationship. Many companies, however, have substantially more complex organizational schemes.

Figure 9–2 shows three different types of ownership structures. A ***direct ownership*** situation of the type discussed in preceding chapters is shown in Figure 9–2(a); the parent has a controlling interest in each of the subsidiaries. In the ***multilevel ownership*** case shown in Figure 9–2(b), the parent has only ***indirect control*** over the company controlled by its subsidiary. The consolidation entries used in preparing the worksheet in this situation are similar to those used in a simple ownership situation, but careful attention must be given to the sequence in which the data are brought together.

Figure 9–2(c) reflects ***reciprocal ownership*** or ***mutual holdings.*** With reciprocal ownership, the parent owns a majority of the subsidiary's common stock and the subsidiary holds some of the parent's common shares. If mutual shareholdings are ignored in the preparation of consolidated financial statements, some reported amounts may be materially overstated.

FYI

In 2007, Berkshire acquired Boat America Corporation, which owns Seaworthy Insurance Company. Berkshire has indirect control over Seaworthy Insurance and therefore has consolidated both Boat America Corporation and Seaworthy Insurance.

Multilevel Ownership and Control

Advanced StudyGuide .com

In many cases, companies establish multiple corporate levels through which they carry out diversified operations. For example, a company may have a number of subsidiaries, one of which is a retailer. The retail subsidiary may in turn have a finance subsidiary, a real estate subsidiary, an insurance subsidiary, and perhaps other subsidiaries. This means that when consolidated statements are prepared, they include companies in which the parent has only an indirect investment along with those in which it holds direct ownership. The complexity of the consolidation process increases as additional ownership levels are included. The amount of income and net assets to be assigned to the controlling and

FIGURE 9–2 Alternative Ownership Structures

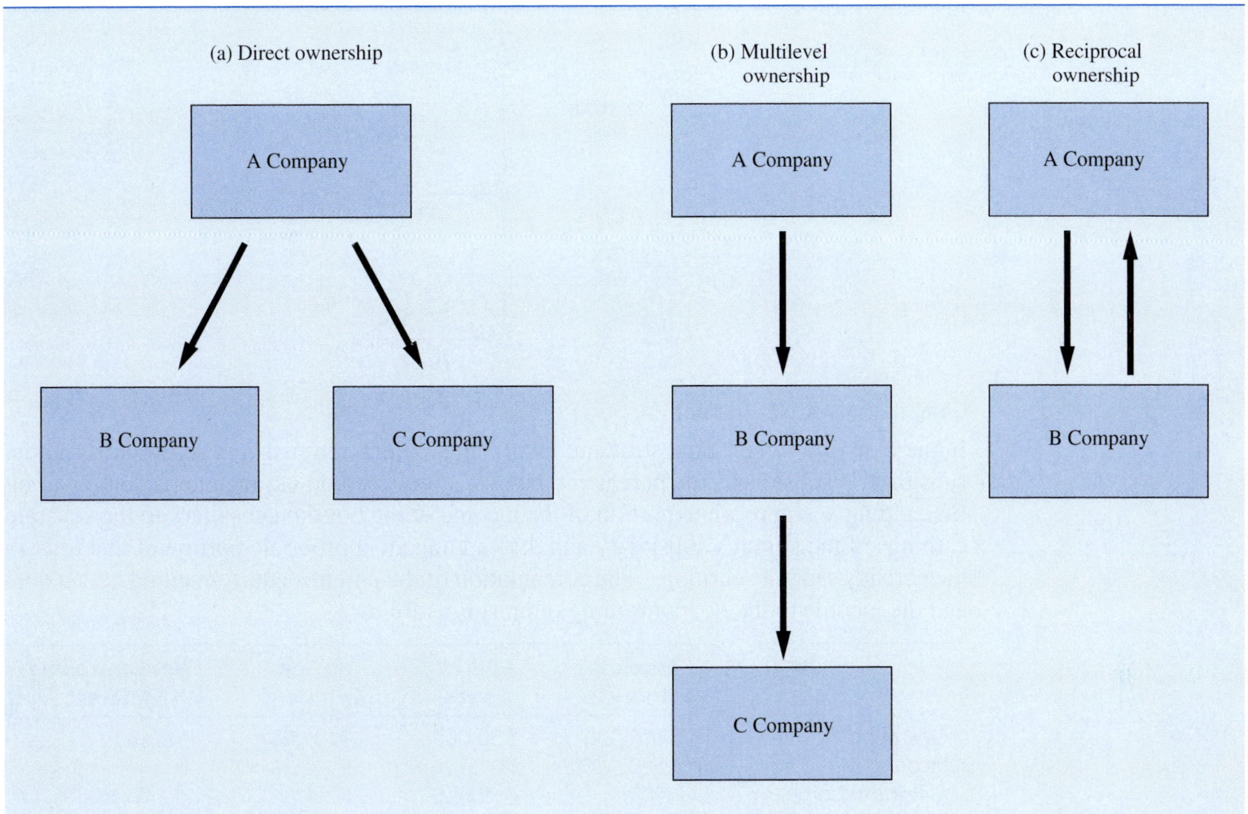

noncontrolling shareholders, and the amount of unrealized profits and losses to be eliminated, must be determined at each level of ownership.

When a number of different levels of ownership exist, the first step normally is to consolidate the bottom, or most remote, subsidiaries with the companies at the next higher level. This sequence is continued up through the ownership structure until the subsidiaries owned directly by the parent company are consolidated with it. Income is apportioned between the controlling and noncontrolling shareholders of the companies at each level.

As an illustration of consolidation when multiple ownership levels exist, assume the following:

1. Peerless Products purchases 80 percent of Special Foods' common stock on December 31, 20X0, at book value of $240,000. On that date, Special Foods' 20 percent noncontrolling interest has a fair value of $60,000.
2. Special Foods purchases 90 percent of Bottom Company's common stock on January 1, 20X1, at book value of $162,000. At that time, Bottom Company's 10 percent noncontrolling interest has a fair value of $18,000. On the date of acquisition, Bottom has common stock of $100,000 and retained earnings of $80,000.
3. During 20X1, Bottom reports net income of $10,000 and declares dividends of $8,000; Special Foods reports separate operating income of $50,000 and declares dividends of $30,000.
4. Assume that accumulated depreciation balances for Special Foods and Bottom Company are $200,000 and $15,000, respectively, on the acquisition dates.

All other data are the same as in the Peerless Products–Special Foods examples used throughout previous chapters. The ownership structure is as follows:

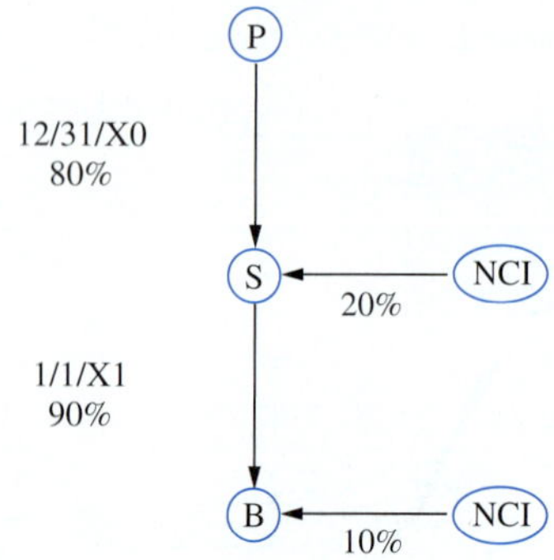

Computation of Net Income

In the case of a three-tiered structure involving a parent company, its subsidiary, and the subsidiary's subsidiary, the parent company's equity-method net income is computed by first adding an appropriate portion of the income of the bottom subsidiary to the separate earnings of the parent's subsidiary and then adding an appropriate portion of that total to the parent's separate earnings. The computation of the parent's equity-method net income and the income to the noncontrolling interest is as follows:

	Peerless Products	Special Foods	Bottom Company	Noncontrolling Interest
Operating income	$140,000	$50,000	$10,000	
Income from:				
Bottom Company		9,000		$ 1,000
Special Foods	47,200			11,800
Net income	$187,200	$59,000	$10,000	$12,800

The computation of consolidated net income and the allocation of that income are as follows:

Operating income:		
Peerless Products		$140,000
Special Foods		50,000
Bottom Company		10,000
Consolidated net income		$200,000
Noncontrolling interest in:		
Bottom Company ($10,000 × 0.10)	$ 1,000	
Special Foods ($59,000 × 0.20)	11,800	
Income to noncontrolling interest		(12,800)
Income to controlling interest		$187,200

Consolidation Worksheet

To prepare the consolidation worksheet, we begin with Special Foods' consolidation of Bottom Company. We first analyze the equity accounts of Bottom Company and the corresponding book value components of the Investment in Bottom Company and NCI accounts.

Book Value Calculations:

	NCI 10%	+ Special Foods 90%	= Common Stock	+ Retained Earnings
Beginning Book Value	**18,000**	**162,000**	**100,000**	**80,000**
+ Net Income	**1,000**	**9,000**		**10,000**
− Dividends	**(800)**	**(7,200)**		**(8,000)**
Ending Book Value	**18,200**	**163,800**	**100,000**	**82,000**

This analysis leads to the basic consolidation entry for Special Foods to consolidate Bottom Company:

Basic Consolidation Entry:

Common Stock	100,000		← Common stock balance
Retained Earnings	80,000		← Beginning balance in RE
Income from Bottom Co.	9,000		← Special Foods' share of NI
NCI in NI of Bottom Co.	1,000		← NCI share of Bottom's NI
Dividends Declared		8,000	← 100% of sub's dividends declared
Investment in Bottom Co.		163,800	← Net BV in investment account
NCI in NA of Bottom Co.		18,200	← NCI share of net BV

We also include the optional accumulated depreciation consolidation entry:

Optional Accumulated Depreciation Consolidation Entry:

Accumulated Depreciation	15,000		← Accumulated depreciation at the time of the acquisition netted against cost
Buildings & Equipment		15,000	

The following T-accounts illustrate how the basic consolidation entry closes out Special Foods' equity-method accounts:

Investment in Bottom Co.

	Debit	Credit	
Acquisition	162,000		
90% Net Income	9,000		
		7,200	90% Dividends
Ending Balance	163,800		
		163,800	Basic
	0		

Income from Bottom Co.

	Debit	Credit	
		9,000	90% Net Income
		9,000	Ending Balance
Basic	9,000		
		0	

Next we prepare Peerless' book value calculations in preparation for its consolidation of Special Foods Inc.:

Book Value Calculations:

	NCI 20%	+ Peerless 80%	= Common Stock	+ Retained Earnings
Beginning Book Value	60,000	240,000	200,000	100,000
+ Net Income	11,800	47,200		59,000
− Dividends	(6,000)	(24,000)		(30,000)
Ending Book Value	65,800	263,200	200,000	129,000

This analysis leads to the basic consolidation entry for Peerless to consolidate Special Foods:

Basic Consolidation Entry:

Common Stock	200,000		← Common stock balance
Retained Earnings	100,000		← Beginning balance in RE
Income from Special Foods	47,200		← Peerless' share of Special Foods' NI
NCI in NI of Special Foods	11,800		← NCI share of Special Foods' NI
Dividends Declared		30,000	← 100% of sub's dividends declared
Investment in Special Foods		263,200	← Net BV in investment account
NCI in NA of Special Foods		65,800	← NCI share of net BV

We also include the optional accumulated depreciation consolidation entry:

Optional Accumulated Depreciation Consolidation Entry:

Accumulated Depreciation	200,000		← Accumulated depreciation at the time of the acquisition netted against cost
Buildings & Equipment		200,000	

The following T-accounts illustrate how the basic consolidation entry closes out Special Foods' equity-method accounts:

	Investment in Special Foods			Income from Special Foods		
Acquisition	240,000					
80% Net Income	47,200				47,200	80% Net Income
		24,000	80% Dividends			
Ending Balance	263,200				47,200	Ending Balance
		263,200	Basic	47,200		
	0				0	

Figure 9–3 presents the 20X1 consolidation worksheet for Peerless Products, Special Foods, and Bottom Company.

Unrealized Intercompany Profits

When intercompany sales occur between multilevel affiliates, unrealized intercompany profits must be eliminated against the appropriate ownership interests. The most convenient way of doing this is to compute the amount of realized income each company contributes before apportioning income between controlling and noncontrolling interests.

For example, the realized income accruing to the ownership interests of each affiliate is computed in the following manner given the unrealized profit amounts indicated:

	Peerless Products	Special Foods	Bottom Company	Noncontrolling Interest
Operating income	$140,000	$50,000	$10,000	
Unrealized profit	(5,000)	(10,000)	(3,000)	
Realized operating profit	$135,000	$40,000	$ 7,000	
Income from:				
Bottom Company		6,300		$ 700
Special Foods	37,040			9,260
Realized net income	$172,040	$46,300	$ 7,000	$9,960

Consolidated net income of $182,000 equals the sum of the realized operating profit numbers of each of the individual companies ($135,000 + $40,000 + $7,000). The income attributable to the controlling interest is $172,040, equal to consolidated net income less the income attributable to the noncontrolling interest ($182,000 − $9,960). The normal worksheet entries to eliminate unrealized intercompany profits, as discussed in Chapters 6 and 7, are entered in the worksheet for each company involved.

Reciprocal or Mutual Ownership

A reciprocal relationship exists when two companies hold stock in each other. Reciprocal relationships are relatively rare in practice. The method of dealing with reciprocal relationships found most often in practice is the ***treasury stock method.*** Under the treasury stock method, purchases of a parent's stock by a subsidiary are treated in the same way as if the parent had repurchased its own stock and was holding it in the treasury. The subsidiary normally accounts for the investment in the parent's stock using the cost method because such investments usually are small and almost never confer the ability to significantly influence the parent.

Income assigned to the noncontrolling interest in the subsidiary should be based on the subsidiary's separate income excluding the dividend income from the investment

FIGURE 9–3 December 31, 20X1, Consolidation Worksheet, First Year Following Combination; Direct and Indirect Holdings

	Peerless Products	Special Foods	Bottom Company	Consolidation Entries DR	Consolidation Entries CR	Consolidated
Income Statement						
Sales	400,000	200,000	150,000			750,000
Less: COGS	(170,000)	(115,000)	(80,000)			(365,000)
Less: Depreciation Expense	(50,000)	(20,000)	(5,000)			(75,000)
Less: Other Expenses	(40,000)	(15,000)	(55,000)			(110,000)
Income from Bottom Company		9,000		9,000		0
Income from Special Foods	47,200			47,200		0
Consolidated Net Income	187,200	59,000	10,000	56,200	0	200,000
NCI in Net Income of Bottom Co.				1,000		(1,000)
NCI in Net Income of Special Foods				11,800		(11,800)
Controlling Interest Net Income	**187,200**	**59,000**	**10,000**	**69,000**	**0**	**187,200**
Statement of Retained Earnings						
Beginning Balance	300,000	100,000	80,000	100,000		300,000
				80,000		
Net Income	**187,200**	**59,000**	**10,000**	**69,000**	**0**	187,200
Less: Dividends Declared	(60,000)	(30,000)	(8,000)		30,000	(60,000)
					8,000	
Ending Balance	**427,200**	**129,000**	**82,000**	**249,000**	**38,000**	**427,200**
Balance Sheet						
Cash	264,000	20,200	25,000			309,200
Accounts Receivable	75,000	50,000	30,000			155,000
Inventory	100,000	75,000	40,000			215,000
Investment in Bottom Company		163,800			163,800	0
Investment in Special Foods	263,200				263,200	0
Land	175,000	40,000	50,000			265,000
Buildings & Equipment	800,000	600,000	75,000		200,000	1,260,000
					15,000	
Less: Accumulated Depreciation	(250,000)	(220,000)	(20,000)	200,000		(275,000)
				15,000		
Total Assets	**1,427,200**	**729,000**	**200,000**	**215,000**	**642,000**	**1,929,200**
Accounts Payable	100,000	100,000	18,000			218,000
Bonds Payable	400,000	300,000				700,000
Common Stock	500,000	200,000	100,000	200,000		500,000
				100,000		
Retained Earnings	**427,200**	**129,000**	**82,000**	**249,000**	**38,000**	427,200
NCI in NA of Bottom Company					18,200	18,200
NCI in NA of Special Foods					65,800	65,800
Total Liabilities & Equity	**1,427,200**	**729,000**	**200,000**	**549,000**	**122,000**	**1,929,200**

in the parent. Similarly, the parent normally bases its equity-method share of the subsidiary's income on the subsidiary's income excluding the dividend income from the parent.

As an example of the treasury stock method, assume the following:

1. Peerless Products purchases 80 percent of Special Foods' common stock on December 31, 20X0, at book value of $240,000. The fair value of the noncontrolling interest on that date is $60,000.

2. Special Foods purchases 10 percent of Peerless' common stock on January 1, 20X1, at book value of $80,000.
3. For 20X1, the two companies report the following separate operating income and dividends:

	Operating Income	Dividends
Peerless Products	$140,000	$60,000
Special Foods	50,000	30,000
Total operating income	$190,000	

The reciprocal ownership relationship between Peerless and Special Foods is as follows:

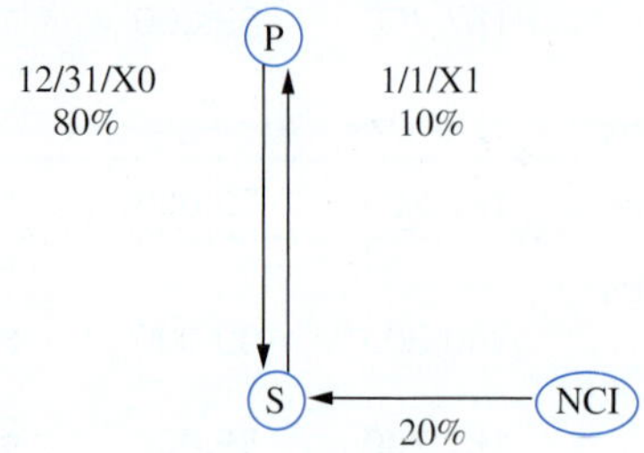

Special Foods records the purchase of its investment in Peerless' common stock with the following entry:

January 1, 20X1

(6)	Investment in Peerless Products Stock	80,000	
	Cash		80,000

Record purchase of Peerless Products stock.

Because it does not gain the ability to significantly influence Peerless, Special Foods accounts for the investment using the cost method. During 20X1, Special Foods records the receipt of dividends from Peerless with the following entry:

(7)	Cash	6,000	
	Dividend Income		6,000

Record dividend income from Peerless: $60,000 × 0.10.

To prepare the consolidation worksheet at the end of 20X1, shown in Figure 9–4, we analyze Special Foods' equity accounts and the corresponding book value components of the Investment in Special Foods and NCI accounts.

Book Value Calculations:

	NCI 20% +	Peerless 80% =	Common Stock +	Retained Earnings
Beginning Book Value	**60,000**	**240,000**	**200,000**	**100,000**
+ Net Income	**10,000**	**40,000**		**50,000**
− Dividends	**(6,000)**	**(24,000)**		**(30,000)**
Ending Book Value	**64,000**	**256,000**	**200,000**	**120,000**

This analysis produces the basic consolidation entry for Peerless to consolidate Special Foods:

Basic Consolidation Entry:

Common Stock	200,000		← Common stock balance
Retained Earnings	100,000		← Beginning balance in RE
Income from Special Foods	40,000		← Peerless' share of Special Foods' NI
NCI in NI of Special Foods	10,000		← NCI share of Special Foods' NI
Dividends Declared		30,000	← 100% of sub's dividends declared
Investment in Special Foods		256,000	← Net BV in investment account
NCI in NA of Special Foods		64,000	← NCI share of net BV

Two worksheet entries eliminate Special Foods' investment in Peerless and Special Foods' dividend income from Peerless:

Eliminate Special Foods' Investment in Peerless:

Treasury Stock	80,000	
Investment in Peerless Stock		80,000

Eliminate Special Foods' Dividend Income from Peerless:

Dividend Income	6,000	
Dividends Declared		6,000

The first of these consolidation entries reclassifies Special Foods' investment in Peerless stock as if it were treasury stock. All of Peerless' common stock is shown in the consolidated balance sheet as outstanding. The treasury stock is shown at cost as an $80,000 deduction from total stockholders' equity, just as treasury stock is shown in a single company's balance sheet at cost. Note that the second of these consolidation entries reduces the amount shown in the consolidated retained earnings statement as dividends paid to those outside the consolidated entity. We also include the optional accumulated depreciation consolidation entry:

Optional Accumulated Depreciation Consolidation Entry:

Accumulated Depreciation	200,000	
Buildings & Equipment		200,000

← Accumulated depreciation at the time of the acquisition netted against cost

The following T-accounts illustrate how the basic consolidation entry closes out Special Foods' equity-method accounts:

	Investment in Special Foods		
Acquisition	240,000		
80% Net Income	40,000		
		24,000	80% Dividends
Ending Balance	256,000		
		256,000	Basic
	0		

	Income from Special Foods		
		40,000	80% Net Income
		40,000	Ending Balance
Basic	40,000		
		0	

The remaining entries needed in the 20X1 consolidation worksheet are the normal entries to eliminate Peerless' investment in Special Foods and income from Special Foods that Peerless recognizes. The income from Special Foods recognized by Peerless is based on Special Foods' separate income, excluding dividend income from Peerless. Therefore, the income elimination is for $40,000, Peerless' 80 percent share of Special Foods' separate operating income of $50,000.

Consolidated net income is $190,000, as can be seen in Figure 9–4. This amount can be computed and is allocated as follows:

Peerless' separate operating income		$140,000
Special Foods' separate operating income		50,000
Consolidated net income		$190,000
Less income to noncontrolling interest:		
Special Foods' separate income ($50,000)	$50,000	
Noncontrolling stockholders' share	× 0.20	
		(10,000)
Income to controlling interest		$180,000

Note that the amount of net income allocated to the noncontrolling interest is based on Special Foods' operating income of $50,000 and excludes the dividends received from

FIGURE 9–4 December 31, 20X1, Treasury Stock Method Worksheet for First Year Following Combination; 80 Percent Purchase at Book Value

	Peerless Products	Special Foods	Consolidation Entries DR	Consolidation Entries CR	Consolidated
Income Statement					
Sales	400,000	200,000			600,000
Less: COGS	(170,000)	(115,000)			(285,000)
Less: Depreciation Expense	(50,000)	(20,000)			(70,000)
Less: Other Expenses	(40,000)	(15,000)			(55,000)
Income from Special Foods	40,000		40,000		0
Dividend Income		6,000	6,000		0
Consolidated Net Income	180,000	56,000	46,000	0	190,000
NCI in Net Income			10,000		(10,000)
Controlling Interest Net Income	**180,000**	**56,000**	**56,000**	**0**	**180,000**
Statement of Retained Earnings					
Beginning Balance	300,000	100,000	100,000		300,000
Net Income	**180,000**	**56,000**	56,000	0	180,000
Less: Dividends Declared	(60,000)	(30,000)		30,000 6,000	(54,000)
Ending Balance	**420,000**	**126,000**	**156,000**	**36,000**	**426,000**
Balance Sheet					
Cash	264,000	1,000			265,000
Accounts Receivable	75,000	50,000			125,000
Inventory	100,000	75,000			175,000
Investment in Subsidiary	256,000			256,000	0
Investment in Peerless Products		80,000		80,000	0
Land	175,000	40,000			215,000
Buildings & Equipment	800,000	600,000		200,000	1,200,000
Less: Accumulated Depreciation	(450,000)	(320,000)	200,000		(570,000)
Total Assets	**1,220,000**	**526,000**	**200,000**	**536,000**	**1,410,000**
Accounts Payable	100,000	100,000			200,000
Bonds Payable	200,000	100,000			300,000
Common Stock	500,000	200,000	200,000		500,000
Retained Earnings	**420,000**	**126,000**	**156,000**	36,000	426,000
Treasury Stock			80,000		(80,000)
NCI in NA of Special Foods				64,000	64,000
Total Liabilities & Equity	**1,220,000**	**526,000**	**436,000**	**100,000**	**1,410,000**

Peerless. A question arises in practice as to whether the income assigned to the noncontrolling interest should be based on the subsidiary's entire net income or only the portion derived from unrelated parties. Although the noncontrolling interest certainly has a claim on its share of the subsidiary's entire income, the approach most consistent with the FASB's entity view of consolidated financial statements is to exclude from the computation of the noncontrolling shareholders' income the dividends from the parent.

SUBSIDIARY STOCK DIVIDENDS

LO 9-5

Understand and explain how consolidation procedures differ when the subsidiary pays stock dividends.

Subsidiary dividends payable in shares of the subsidiary's common stock require slight changes in the consolidation entries used in preparing consolidated financial statements. Because stock dividends are issued proportionally to all common stockholders, the relative interests of the controlling and noncontrolling stockholders do not change as a result of the stock dividend. The investment's carrying amount on the parent's books also is unaffected by a stock dividend. On the other hand, the stockholders' equity accounts of the subsidiary do change, although total stockholders' equity does not. The stock dividend represents a permanent capitalization of retained earnings, thus decreasing retained earnings and increasing capital stock and, perhaps, additional paid-in capital.

In the preparation of consolidated financial statements for the period in which a stock dividend is declared by the subsidiary, the stock dividend declaration must be eliminated along with the increased common stock and increased additional paid-in capital, if any. The stock dividend declared cannot appear in the consolidated retained earnings statement because only the parent's dividends are viewed as dividends of the consolidated entity.

In subsequent years, the balances in the subsidiary's stockholders' equity accounts are eliminated in the normal manner. Keep in mind that stock dividends do not change the total stockholders' equity of a company; they only realign the individual accounts within stockholders' equity. Therefore, the full balances of all the subsidiary's stockholders' equity accounts must be eliminated in consolidation, as is the usual procedure, even though amounts have been shifted from one account to another.

Illustration of Subsidiary Stock Dividends

As an illustration of the treatment of a subsidiary's stock dividend, assume that in the Peerless Products and Special Foods example, Special Foods declares a 25 percent stock dividend in 20X1 on its $200,000 of common stock and elects to capitalize the par value of the shares. Special Foods records the stock dividend with the following entry:

(8)			
	Stock Dividends Declared	50,000	
	Common Stock		50,000

Record 25 percent stock dividend: $200,000 × 0.25.

The investors make only a memo entry to record the receipt of the stock dividend. When Peerless prepares consolidated financial statements at the end of 20X1, the normal consolidation entries are made in the worksheet. If Special Foods had not declared a stock dividend in 20X1, the basic entry would have been calculated as follows:

Book Value Calculations:

	NCI 20% +	Peerless 80% =	Common Stock +	Retained Earnings
Book Value on 12/31/20X1	60,000	240,000	200,000	100,000
+ Net Income	10,000	40,000		50,000
− Dividends	(6,000)	(24,000)		(30,000)
Book Value on 1/1/20X2	64,000	256,000	200,000	120,000

Basic Consolidation Entry:

Common Stock	200,000		← Common stock balance
Retained Earnings	100,000		← Beginning balance in RE
Income from Special Foods	40,000		← Peerless' share of Special Foods' NI
NCI in NI of Special Foods	10,000		← NCI share of Special Foods' NI
Dividends Declared		30,000	← 100% of sub's dividends declared
Investment in Special Foods		256,000	← Net BV in investment account
NCI in NA of Special Foods		64,000	← NCI share of net BV

However, if Special Foods did declare a stock dividend, the basic consolidation entry would be the same except for one minor modification as follows:

Book Value Calculations:

	NCI 20%	+ Peerless 80%	=	Common Stock	+	Retained Earnings
Book Value on 12/31/20X1	60,000	240,000		200,000		100,000
+ Net Income	10,000	40,000				50,000
− Dividends	(6,000)	(24,000)				(30,000)
25% Stock Dividend				50,000		(50,000)
Book Value on 1/1/20X2	64,000	256,000		250,000		70,000

Basic Consolidation Entry:

Common Stock	250,000		← Common stock balance
Retained Earnings	100,000		← Beginning balance in RE
Income from Special Foods	40,000		← Peerless' share of Special Foods' NI
NCI in NI of Special Foods	10,000		← NCI share of Special Foods' NI
Dividends Declared		30,000	← 100% of sub's dividends declared
Stock dividends Declared		50,000	← 100% of sub's stock dividends
Investment in Special Foods		256,000	← Net BV in investment account
NCI in NA of Special Foods		64,000	← NCI share of net BV

Note that although the common stock balance has increased by the $50,000 stock dividend, the elimination of retained earnings is not changed in the year of the stock dividend because dividends declared have not been closed to retained earnings; only the beginning balance of retained earnings is eliminated. Just as with other dividends of the subsidiary, stock dividends must be eliminated because they are not viewed as dividends of the consolidated entity.

Impact on Subsequent Periods

At the end of 20X1, the stock dividend declaration is closed into the subsidiary's Retained Earnings account and does not separately appear in the financial statements of future periods. The stock dividend results in a common stock balance $50,000 higher and a retained earnings balance $50,000 lower on the subsidiary's books than if there had been no stock dividend. The investment consolidation entry in the worksheet must reflect these changed balances.

If Special Foods hadn't declared a stock dividend in 20X1, the basic consolidation entry on December 31, 20X2, would be calculated as follows:

Book Value Calculations:

	NCI 20%	+ Peerless 80%	=	Common Stock	+	Retained Earnings
Book Value on 12/31/20X1	64,000	256,000		200,000		120,000
+ Net Income	15,000	60,000				75,000
− Dividends	(8,000)	(32,000)				(40,000)
Book Value on 1/1/20X2	71,000	284,000		200,000		155,000

Basic Consolidation Entry:

Common Stock	200,000		← Common stock balance
Retained Earnings	120,000		← Beginning balance in RE
Income from Special Foods	60,000		← Peerless' share of Special Foods' NI
NCI in NI of Special Foods	15,000		← NCI share of Special Foods' NI
Dividends Declared		40,000	← 100% of sub's dividends declared
Investment in Special Foods		284,000	← Net BV in investment account
NCI in NA of Special Foods		71,000	← NCI share of net BV

If Special Foods had declared the stock dividend during 20X1, the basic consolidation entry in the worksheet prepared as of December 31, 20X2, would be as follows:

Book Value Calculations:

	NCI 20%	+ Peerless 80%	= Common Stock	+ Retained Earnings
Book Value on 12/31/20X1	64,000	256,000	250,000	70,000
+ Net Income	15,000	60,000		75,000
− Dividends	(8,000)	(32,000)		(40,000)
Book Value on 1/1/20X2	71,000	284,000	250,000	105,000

Basic Consolidation Entry:

	Debit	Credit	
Common Stock	250,000		← Common stock balance
Retained Earnings	70,000		← Beginning balance in RE
Income from Special Foods	60,000		← Peerless' share of Special Foods' NI
NCI in NI of Special Foods	15,000		← NCI share of Special Foods' NI
Dividends Declared		40,000	← 100% of sub's dividends declared
Investment in Special Foods		284,000	← Net BV in investment account
NCI in NA of Special Foods		71,000	← NCI's share of net BV

Note that these two versions of the basic consolidation entry are identical except that the elimination of common stock is $50,000 higher and the elimination of retained earnings is $50,000 lower, reflecting the differences in the balances of those accounts due to the stock dividend.

SUMMARY OF KEY CONCEPTS

A number of stockholders' equity issues arise in the preparation of consolidated financial statements. When subsidiaries have preferred stock outstanding, any of the preferred stock held by the parent must be eliminated because it is held within the consolidated entity. The remaining preferred stock is treated as part of the noncontrolling interest. In the assessment of the preferred shareholders' claim, consideration must be given to all the features of the preferred stock, including cumulative dividends in arrears, dividend participation features, and retirement premiums.

Transactions involving a subsidiary's common stock include purchase or sale transactions involving the parent or parties outside of the consolidated entity (noncontrolling interest). These transactions may affect the carrying amounts of both the controlling and noncontrolling interests. So long as the parent continues to maintain a controlling financial interest in the subsidiary, these transactions are viewed as equity transactions and, from a consolidated perspective, no gain or loss may be recognized. In consolidation, the parent's equity is adjusted for the difference between any consideration paid or received by the consolidated entity and the change in the carrying amount of the noncontrolling interest resulting from the transaction.

The organizational structure of some consolidated entities may be more complex than just a parent and one or more subsidiaries. In some cases, subsidiaries hold controlling interests in other companies, thus giving the parent an indirect controlling interest. Consolidation proceeds from the lowest level to the highest in these cases. In a relatively few cases, a subsidiary may own common shares of its parent. Those common shares are treated as treasury stock in consolidated financial statements.

Stock dividends declared by a subsidiary result in only minor changes in the eliminations needed to prepare consolidated financial statements. In the year the stock dividend is declared, the stock dividend declaration and the higher balance of the common stock must be eliminated in preparing consolidated statements. In subsequent years, the investment elimination entry reflects the higher amount of the subsidiary's common stock and the lower amount of retained earnings.

KEY TERMS

direct ownership, *472*
indirect control, *472*
multilevel ownership, *472*
mutual holdings, *472*
reciprocal ownership, *472*
treasury stock method, *476*

QUESTIONS

LO 9-1 **Q9-1** How does the consolidation process deal with a subsidiary's preferred stock?

LO 9-1 **Q9-2** What portion of subsidiary preferred stock outstanding is reported as part of the noncontrolling interest in the consolidated balance sheet?

LO 9-1, 9-2 **Q9-3** Why are subsidiary preferred dividends that are paid to nonaffiliates normally deducted from earnings in arriving at consolidated net income? When is it not appropriate to deduct subsidiary preferred dividends in computing consolidated net income?

LO 9-2 **Q9-4** How does a call feature on subsidiary preferred stock affect the claim of the noncontrolling interest reported in the consolidated balance sheet?

LO 9-3 **Q9-5** A parent company sells common shares of one of its subsidiaries to a nonaffiliate for more than their carrying value on the parent's books. How should the parent company report the sale? How should the sale be reported in the consolidated financial statements?

LO 9-3 **Q9-6** A subsidiary sells additional shares of its common stock to a nonaffiliate at a price that is higher than the previous book value per share. How does the sale benefit the existing shareholders?

LO 9-3 **Q9-7** A parent company purchases additional common shares of one of its subsidiaries from the subsidiary at $10 per share above underlying book value. Explain how this purchase is reflected in the consolidated financial statements for the year.

LO 9-3 **Q9-8** How are treasury shares held by a subsidiary reported in the consolidated financial statements?

LO 9-4 **Q9-9** What is indirect ownership? How does one company gain control of another through indirect ownership?

LO 9-4 **Q9-10** Explain how a reciprocal ownership arrangement between two subsidiaries could lead the parent company to overstate its income if no adjustment is made for the reciprocal relationship.

LO 9-4 **Q9-11** How will parent company shares held by a subsidiary be reflected in the consolidated balance sheet when the treasury stock method is used?

LO 9-4 **Q9-12** Parent Company holds 80 percent ownership of Subsidiary Company, and Subsidiary Company owns 90 percent of the stock of Tiny Corporation. What effect will $100,000 of unrealized intercompany profits on Tiny's books on December 31, 20X5, have on the amounts reported as consolidated net income and income assigned to the controlling interest?

LO 9-4 **Q9-13** Snapper Corporation holds 70 percent ownership of Bit Company, and Bit holds 60 percent ownership of Slide Company. Should Slide be consolidated with Snapper Corporation? Why?

LO 9-5 **Q9-14** What effect will a subsidiary's 15 percent stock dividend have on the consolidated financial statements?

LO 9-5 **Q9-15** What effect will a subsidiary's 15 percent stock dividend have on the consolidation entries used in preparing a consolidated balance sheet at the end of the year in which the dividend is distributed?

LO 9-4 **Q9-16** When multilevel affiliations exist, explain why it is generally best to prepare consolidated financial statements by completing the consolidation entries for companies furthest from parent company ownership first and completing the consolidation entries for those owned directly by the parent company last.

CASES

LO 9-1

C9-1 Effect of Subsidiary Preferred Stock

Analysis

Snow Corporation issued common stock with a par value of $100,000 and preferred stock with a par value of $80,000 on January 1, 20X5, when the company was created. Klammer Corporation acquired a controlling interest in Snow on January 1, 20X6.

Required

What does Klammer's controller need to know about the preferred stock to determine the proper allocation of consolidated net income to the controlling and noncontrolling interests?

LO 9-2, 9-3

C9-2 Consolidated Stockholders' Equity: Theory vs. Practice

Research

Companies sometimes employ accounting practices that are not necessarily in accordance with accounting theory or even current standards. In some cases, companies may be following industry practices rather than generally accepted practices. In other cases, the practices may be justified as expedient because the amounts may be immaterial.

Required

a. How did Xerox Corporation report the sale of stock of a subsidiary in its consolidated financial statements prior to 2008? How must such sales (assuming Xerox maintains control of the subsidiary) be reported under current standards?

b. How does Occidental Petroleum Corporation treat subsidiary preferred stock? How should subsidiary preferred stock be reported in the consolidated financial statements?

LO 9-3

C9-3 Sale of Subsidiary Shares

Research

Book Corporation purchased 90,000 shares of Lance Company at underlying book value of $3 per share on June 30, 20X1. On January 1, 20X5, Lance reported its net book value as $400,000 and continued to have 100,000 shares of common stock outstanding. On that date, Book sold 30,000 shares of Lance to Triple Corporation for $5.60 per share. Book uses the equity method in accounting for its investment in Lance and recorded a gain on sale of investments of $48,000 in its consolidated income statement for 20X5.

Required

Book's vice president of finance, Robert Reader, has asked you to prepare a memo addressed to him presenting the alternative ways to record the difference between the carrying value and sale price of the shares that are sold and your recommendations on the preferred reporting alternative. Citations to or quotations from the relevant authoritative accounting literature should be included in providing the basis of support for your recommendations.

LO 9-3

C9-4 Sale of Subsidiary Shares

Analysis

Hardcore Mining Company acquired 88 percent of the common stock of Mountain Trucking Company on January 1, 20X2, at a cost of $30 per share. On December 31, 20X7, when the book value of Mountain Trucking stock was $70 per share, Hardcore sold one-quarter of its investment in Mountain Trucking to Basic Manufacturing Company for $90 per share.

Required

What effect will the sale have on the 20X7 consolidated financial statements of Hardcore Mining if (*a*) Basic Manufacturing is an unrelated company or (*b*) Hardcore Mining holds 60 percent of Basic's voting shares?

LO 9-4

C9-5 Reciprocal Ownership

Judgment

Strong Manufacturing Company holds 94 percent ownership of Thorson Farm Products and 68 percent ownership of Kenwood Distributors. Thorson has excess cash at the end of 20X4 and is considering buying shares of its own stock, shares of Strong, or shares of Kenwood.

Required

If Thorson wishes to take the action that will be best for the consolidated entity, what factors must it consider in making its decision? How can it maximize consolidated net income?

LO 9-4

C9-6 Complex Organizational Structures

Analysis

Major companies often have very complex organizational structures, sometimes consisting of different types of entities. Some organizational structures include combinations of corporations, partnerships, and perhaps other types of entities. Complex organizational structures often present challenges for financial reporting.

Required

a. What type of entity is Atlas America Inc. (i.e., corporation, partnership, trust)? What is the company's business?

b. Atlas America lists a number of subsidiaries in its Form 10-K filed with the SEC (in a separate exhibit). What types of entities are included among the subsidiaries? How does the company report its subsidiaries and interests in energy partnerships?

c. Atlas America lists subsidiaries with the names Atlas Pipeline Partners and Atlas Pipeline Holdings. What is the relationship between these companies?

d. What type of entity is Atlas Pipeline Partners LP? What types of entities are its subsidiaries? What arrangement is there for the management of Atlas Pipeline Partners?

e. Does Atlas Pipeline Partners present separate or consolidated financial statements? What type of entity is NOARK Pipeline System, and what is Atlas Pipeline's relationship to NOARK? How is NOARK reflected in Atlas Pipeline's financial statements?

EXERCISES

LO 9-2

E9-1 Multiple-Choice Questions on Preferred Stock Ownership

Blank Corporation prepared the following summarized balance sheet on January 1, 20X1:

Assets	$150,000	Liabilities	$ 20,000
		Preferred Stock	30,000
		Common Stock	40,000
		Retained Earnings	60,000
Total Assets	$150,000	Total Liabilities & Equities	$150,000

Shepard Company acquires 80 percent of Blank Corporation's common stock on January 1, 20X1, for $80,000. At that date, the fair value of the common shares held by the noncontrolling interest is $20,000.

Required

Select the correct answer for each of the following questions.

1. The amount reported as noncontrolling interest in the consolidated balance sheet is
   a. $20,000.
   b. $26,000.
   c. $30,000.
   d. $50,000.
2. In addition to the common shares, Shepard Company purchases 70 percent of Blank's preferred shares for $21,000. The amount reported as noncontrolling interest in Shepard's consolidated balance sheet is
   a. $9,000.
   b. $20,000.
   c. $29,000.
   d. $50,000.
3. In addition to the common shares, Shepard Company purchases 70 percent of Blank's preferred shares for $21,000 on January 1, 20X1. If Shepard's retained earnings are $150,000 on December 31, 20X0, the consolidated retained earnings reported immediately after the stock purchases are
   a. $48,000.
   b. $150,000.
   c. $198,000.
   d. $210,000.
4. In addition to the common shares, Shepard Company purchases 70 percent of Blank's preferred shares for $21,000 on January 1, 20X1. Shepard has no preferred shares outstanding.

The amount of preferred stock reported in the consolidated balance sheet immediately after the stock purchases is

a. $0.
b. $9,000.
c. $21,000.
d. $30,000.

LO 9-4

E9-2 Multiple-Choice Questions on Multilevel Ownership

Musical Corporation acquires 80 percent of Dustin Corporation's common shares on January 1, 20X2. On January 2, 20X2, Dustin acquires 60 percent of Rustic Corporation's common stock. Information on company book values on the date of purchase and operating results for 20X2 is as follows:

Company	Book Value	Purchase Price	20X2 Operating Income
Musical Corporation	$800,000		$100,000
Dustin Corporation	300,000	$240,000	80,000
Rustic Corporation	200,000	120,000	50,000

The fair values of the noncontrolling interests of Dustin and Rustic at the dates of acquisition were $60,000 and $80,000, respectively.

Required

Select the correct answer for each of the following questions.

1. Consolidated net income assigned to the controlling interest for 20X2 is
   a. $180,000.
   b. $188,000.
   c. $194,000.
   d. $234,000.
2. The amount of 20X2 income assigned to the noncontrolling interest of Rustic Corporation is
   a. $0.
   b. $20,000.
   c. $30,000.
   d. $50,000.
3. The amount of 20X2 income assigned to the noncontrolling interest of Dustin Corporation is
   a. $10,000.
   b. $16,000.
   c. $22,000.
   d. $26,000.
4. The amount of income assigned to the noncontrolling interest in the 20X2 consolidated income statement is
   a. $20,000.
   b. $22,000.
   c. $42,000.
   d. $46,000.
5. Assume that Dustin pays $150,000, rather than $120,000, to purchase 60 percent of Rustic's common stock, and the fair value of the noncontrolling interest is $100,000 at the date of acquisition. If the differential is amortized over 10 years, the effect on 20X2 income assigned to the controlling shareholders will be a decrease of
   a. $0.
   b. $2,400.
   c. $3,000.
   d. $5,000.

LO 9-2

E9-3 Acquisition of Preferred Shares

The summarized balance sheet of Separate Company on January 1, 20X3, contained the following amounts:

Advanced StudyGuide .com

Total Assets	$350,000	Total Liabilities	$ 50,000
		Preferred Stock	100,000
		Common Stock	50,000
		Retained Earnings	150,000
Total Assets	$350,000	Total Liabilities & Equities	$350,000

On January 1, 20X3, Joint Corporation acquired 70 percent of the common shares and 60 percent of the preferred shares of Separate Company at underlying book value. At that date, the fair value of the noncontrolling interest in Separate's common stock was equal to 30 percent of the book value of its common stock.

Required

Give the worksheet consolidation entries needed to prepare a consolidated balance sheet immediately following Joint's purchase of shares.

LO 9-4

E9-4 Reciprocal Ownership [AICPA Adapted]

Pride Corporation owns 80 percent of Simba Corporation's outstanding common stock. Simba, in turn, owns 10 percent of Pride's outstanding common stock.

Required

a. What percent of the dividends paid by Simba is reported as dividends declared in the consolidated financial statements?

b. What percent of the dividends paid by Pride is reported as dividends declared in the consolidated retained earnings statement?

LO 9-2

E9-5 Subsidiary with Preferred Stock Outstanding

Clayton Corporation purchased 75 percent of Topple Corporation common stock and 40 percent of its preferred stock on January 1, 20X6, for $270,000 and $80,000, respectively. At the time of purchase, the fair value of the common shares of Topple held by the noncontrolling interest was $90,000. Topple's balance sheet contained the following balances:

Preferred Stock ($10 par value)	$200,000
Common Stock ($5 par value)	150,000
Retained Earnings	210,000
Total Stockholders' Equity	$560,000

Required

Give the consolidation entries needed to prepare a consolidated balance sheet immediately after Clayton purchased the Topple shares.

LO 9-2

E9-6 Subsidiary with Preferred Stock Outstanding

Clayton Corporation purchased 75 percent of Topple Company common stock and 40 percent of its preferred stock on January 1, 20X6, for $270,000 and $80,000, respectively. At the time of purchase, the fair value of Topple's common shares held by the noncontrolling interest was $90,000. Topple's balance sheet contained the following balances:

Preferred Stock ($10 par value)	$200,000
Common Stock ($5 par value)	150,000
Retained Earnings	210,000
Total Stockholders' Equity	$560,000

For the year ended December 31, 20X6, Topple reported net income of $70,000 and paid dividends of $50,000 (which includes the preferred dividend). The preferred stock is cumulative and pays an annual dividend of 8 percent.

Required

a. Prepare the journal entries recorded by Clayton for its investments in Topple during 20X6.

b. Present the consolidation entries needed to prepare the consolidated financial statements for Clayton Corporation as of December 31, 20X6.

LO 9-2

E9-7 Preferred Dividends and Call Premium

On January 1, 20X2, Fischer Corporation purchased 90 percent of Culbertson Company common shares and 60 percent of its preferred shares at underlying book value. At that date, the fair value of the noncontrolling interest in Culbertson's common stock was equal to 10 percent of the book value of its common stock. Culbertson's balance sheet at the time of purchase contained the following balances:

Total Assets	$860,000	Total Liabilities	$ 80,000
		Preferred Stock	100,000
		Common Stock	300,000
		Retained Earnings	380,000
Total Assets	$860,000	Total Liabilities & Equities	$860,000

The preferred shares, which are cumulative with regard to dividends, have a 12 percent annual dividend rate and are five years in arrears on January 1, 20X2. All of the $10 par value preferred shares are callable at $12 per share after December 31, 20X0. During 20X2, Culbertson reported net income of $70,000 and paid no dividends.

Required

a. Compute Culbertson's contribution to consolidated net income for 20X2.

b. Compute the amount of income to be assigned to the noncontrolling interest in the 20X2 consolidated income statement.

c. Compute the portion of Culbertson's retained earnings assignable to its preferred shareholders on January 1, 20X2.

d. Compute the book value assigned to the common shareholders on January 1, 20X2.

e. Compute the amount to be reported as the noncontrolling interest in the consolidated balance sheet on January 1, 20X2.

LO 9-4

E9-8 Multilevel Ownership

Grasper Corporation owns 70 percent of Latent Corporation's common stock and 25 percent of Dally Corporation's common stock. In addition, Latent owns 40 percent of Dally's stock. In 20X6, Grasper, Latent, and Dally reported operating income of $90,000, $60,000, and $40,000 and paid dividends of $45,000, $30,000, and $10,000, respectively.

Required

a. What amount of consolidated net income will Grasper report for 20X6?

b. What amount of income will be assigned to the noncontrolling interest in the 20X6 consolidated income statement?

c. What amount of income will be assigned to the controlling interest in the 20X6 income statement?

d. What amount will be reported as dividends declared in Grasper's 20X6 consolidated retained earnings statement?

LO 9-4

E9-9 Consolidation Entries for Multilevel Ownership

Promise Enterprises acquired 90 percent of Brown Corporation's voting common stock on January 1, 20X3, for $315,000. At that date, the fair value of the noncontrolling interest of Brown Corporation was $35,000. Immediately after Promise acquired its ownership, Brown purchased 60 percent of Tann Company's stock for $120,000. The fair value of the noncontrolling interest of Tann Company was $80,000 at that date. During 20X3, Promise reported operating income of $200,000 and paid dividends of $80,000. Brown reported operating income of $120,000 and paid dividends of $50,000. Tann reported net income of $40,000 and paid dividends of $15,000. At January 1, 20X3, the stockholders' equity sections of the balance sheets of the companies were as follows:

	Promise Enterprises	Brown Corporation	Tann Company
Common Stock	$200,000	$150,000	$100,000
Additional Paid-In Capital	160,000	60,000	60,000
Retained Earnings	360,000	140,000	40,000
Total Stockholders' Equity	$720,000	$350,000	$200,000

Required

a. Prepare the journal entries recorded by Brown for its investment in Tann during 20X3.

b. Prepare the journal entries recorded by Promise for its investment in Brown during 20X3.

c. Prepare the consolidation entries related to Brown's investment in Tann and Promise's investment in Brown that are needed in preparing consolidated financial statements for Promise and its subsidiaries at December 31, 20X3.

LO 9-4

E9-10 Reciprocal Ownership

Grower Supply Corporation holds 85 percent of Schultz Company's voting common stock. At the end of 20X4, Schultz purchased 30 percent of Grower Supply's stock. Schultz records dividends received from Grower Supply as nonoperating income. In 20X5, Grower Supply and Schultz reported operating income (excluding any dividend income or income from subsidiaries) of $112,000 and $50,000 and paid dividends of $70,000 and $30,000, respectively.

Required

Compute the amounts reported as consolidated net income and income assigned to the controlling interest for 20X5 under the treasury stock method.

LO 9-4

Advanced StudyGuide .com

E9-11 Consolidated Balance Sheet with Reciprocal Ownership

Talbott Company purchased 80 percent of Short Company's stock on January 1, 20X8, at underlying book value. At that date, the fair value of the noncontrolling interest was equal to 20 percent of Short's book value. On December 31, 20X9, Short purchased 10 percent of Talbott's stock. Balance sheets for the two companies on December 31, 20X9, are as follows:

TALBOTT COMPANY
Condensed Balance Sheet
December 31, 20X9

Cash	$ 78,000	Accounts Payable	$ 90,000
Accounts Receivable	120,000	Bonds Payable	400,000
Inventory	150,000	Common Stock	300,000
Buildings & Equipment (net)	400,000	Retained Earnings	310,000
Investment in Short Company Common Stock	352,000		
Total Assets	$1,100,000	Total Liabilities & Equities	$1,100,000

SHORT COMPANY
Condensed Balance Sheet
December 31, 20X9

Cash	$ 39,000	Accounts Payable	$ 60,000
Accounts Receivable	80,000	Bonds Payable	100,000
Inventory	120,000	Common Stock	200,000
Buildings & Equipment (net)	300,000	Retained Earnings	240,000
Investment in Talbott Company Common Stock	61,000		
Total Assets	$600,000	Total Liabilities & Equities	$600,000

Required

Assuming that the treasury stock method is used in reporting Talbott's shares held by Short, prepare a consolidated balance sheet worksheet and consolidated balance sheet for December 31, 20X9.

LO 9-5

E9-12 Subsidiary Stock Dividend

Lake Company reported the following summarized balance sheet data as of December 31, 20X2:

Cash	$ 30,000	Accounts Payable	$ 50,000
Accounts Receivable	80,000	Common Stock	100,000
Inventory	90,000	Retained Earnings	200,000
Buildings & Equipment	270,000		
Less: Accumulated Depreciation	(120,000)		
Total Assets	$350,000	Total Liabilities & Equities	$350,000

Lake issues 4,000 additional shares of its $10 par value stock to its shareholders as a stock dividend on April 20, 20X3. The market price of Lake's shares at the time of the stock dividend is $40. Lake reports net income of $25,000 and pays a $10,000 cash dividend in 20X3. Lindale Company acquired 70 percent of Lake's common shares at book value on January 1, 20X1. At that date, the fair value of the noncontrolling interest was equal to 30 percent of Lake's book value. Lindale uses the equity method in accounting for its investment in Lake.

Required

a. Give the journal entries recorded by Lake and Lindale at the time the stock dividend is declared and distributed.

b. Give the worksheet consolidation entries needed to prepare consolidated financial statements for 20X3.

c. Give the worksheet consolidation entry needed to prepare a consolidated balance sheet on January 1, 20X4.

LO 9-3

E9-13 Sale of Subsidiary Shares by Parent

Stable Home Builders Inc. acquired 80 percent of Acme Concrete Works stock on January 1, 20X3, for $360,000. At that date, the fair value of the noncontrolling interest was $90,000. Acme Concrete's balance sheet contained the following amounts at the time of the combination:

Cash	$ 30,000	Accounts Payable	$ 50,000
Accounts Receivable	65,000	Bonds Payable	300,000
Inventory	15,000	Common Stock	200,000
Construction Work in Progress	470,000	Retained Earnings	250,000
Other Assets (net)	220,000		
Total Assets	$800,000	Total Liabilities & Equities	$800,000

During each of the next three years, Acme reported net income of $50,000 and paid dividends of $20,000. On January 1, 20X5, Stable sold 4,000 of the Acme $10 par value shares for $120,000 in cash. Stable used the equity method in accounting for its ownership of Acme.

Required

a. Compute the balance in the investment account reported by Stable on January 1, 20X5, before its sale of shares.

b. Prepare the entry recorded by Stable when it sold the Acme shares.

c. Prepare the appropriate consolidation entries to complete a full worksheet for 20X5.

LO 9-3

E9-14 Purchase of Additional Shares from Nonaffiliate

Weal Corporation purchased 60 percent of Modern Products Company's shares on December 31, 20X7, for $210,000. At that date, the fair value of the noncontrolling interest was $140,000. On January 1, 20X9, Weal purchased an additional 20 percent of Modern's common stock for $96,000. Summarized balance sheets for Modern on the dates indicated are as follows:

	December 31		
	20X7	20X8	20X9
Cash	$ 40,000	$ 70,000	$ 90,000
Accounts Receivable	50,000	90,000	120,000
Inventory	70,000	100,000	160,000
Buildings & Equipment (net)	340,000	320,000	300,000
Total Assets	$500,000	$580,000	$670,000
Accounts Payable	$ 50,000	$100,000	$140,000
Bonds Payable	100,000	100,000	100,000
Common Stock	150,000	150,000	150,000
Retained Earnings	200,000	230,000	280,000
Total Liabilities & Equities	$500,000	$580,000	$670,000

Modern paid dividends of $20,000 in each of the three years. Weal uses the equity method in accounting for its investment in Modern and amortizes all differentials over 10 years against the related investment income. All differentials are assigned to patents in the consolidated financial statements.

Required

a. Compute the balance in Weal's Investment in Modern Products Company Stock account on December 31, 20X8.

b. Compute the balance in Weal's Investment in Modern Products Company Stock account on December 31, 20X9.

c. Prepare the consolidation entries needed as of December 31, 20X9, to complete a worksheet.

LO 9-3

E9-15 Repurchase of Shares by Subsidiary from Nonaffiliate

Blatant Advertising Corporation acquired 60 percent of Quinn Manufacturing Company's shares on December 31, 20X1, at underlying book value of $180,000. At that date, the fair value of the noncontrolling interest was equal to 40 percent of the book value of Quinn Manufacturing. Quinn's balance sheet on January 1, 20X7, contained the following balances:

Cash	$ 80,000	Accounts Payable	$ 60,000
Accounts Receivable	100,000	Bonds Payable	240,000
Inventory	160,000	Common Stock	100,000
Buildings & Equipment	700,000	Additional Paid-In Capital	150,000
Less: Accumulated Depreciation	(240,000)	Retained Earnings	250,000
Total Assets	$800,000	Total Liabilities & Equities	$800,000

On January 1, 20X7, Quinn purchased 2,000 of its own $10 par value common shares from Nonaffiliated Corporation for $42 per share.

Required

a. Compute the change in the book value of the parent's equity as a result of the repurchase of shares by Quinn Manufacturing.

b. Give the entry to be recorded on Blatant Advertising's books to recognize the change in the book value of the shares it holds.

c. Give the consolidation entry needed in preparing a consolidated balance sheet immediately following the purchase of shares by Quinn.

LO 9-3

E9-16 Sale of Shares by Subsidiary to Nonaffiliate

Browne Corporation purchased 11,000 shares of Schroeder Corporation on January 1, 20X3, at book value. At that date, the fair value of the noncontrolling interest was equal to 26.6̄ percent of Schroeder's book value. On December 31, 20X8, Schroeder reported these balance sheet amounts:

Cash	$ 80,000	Accounts Payable	$ 50,000
Accounts Receivable	120,000	Bonds Payable	100,000
Inventory	200,000	Common Stock	150,000
Buildings & Equipment	600,000	Additional Paid-In Capital	50,000
Less: Accumulated Depreciation	(250,000)	Retained Earnings	400,000
Total Assets	$750,000	Total Liabilities & Equities	$750,000

On January 1, 20X9, Schroeder issued an additional 5,000 shares of its $10 par value common stock to Nonaffiliated Company for $80 per share.

Required

a. Compute the change in book value of the shares held by Browne as a result of Schroeder's issuance of additional shares.

b. Give the entry to be recorded on Browne's books to recognize the change in book value of the shares it holds, assuming the change in book value is to be treated as an adjustment to additional paid-in capital.

c. Record the consolidation entry needed to prepare a consolidated balance sheet immediately after Schroeder's issuance of additional shares.

PROBLEMS

LO 9-1, 9-2

P9-17 Multiple-Choice Questions on Preferred Stock Ownership

Stacey Corporation owns 80 percent of the common shares and 70 percent of the preferred shares of Upland Company, all purchased at underlying book value on January 1, 20X2. At that date, the fair value of the noncontrolling interest in Upland's common stock was equal to 20 percent of the book value of its common stock. The balance sheets of Stacey and Upland immediately after the acquisition contained these balances:

	Stacey Corporation	Upland Company
Cash & Receivables	$150,000	$ 80,000
Inventory	200,000	100,000
Buildings & Equipment (net)	250,000	220,000
Investment in Upland Preferred Stock	70,000	
Investment in Upland Common Stock	200,000	
Total Assets	$870,000	$400,000

(continued)

	Stacey Corporation	Upland Company
Liabilities	$220,000	$ 50,000
Preferred Stock		100,000
Common Stock	300,000	200,000
Retained Earnings	350,000	50,000
Total Liabilities & Equities	$870,000	$400,000

The preferred stock issued by Upland pays a 10 percent dividend and is cumulative. For 20X2, Upland reports net income of $30,000 and pays no dividends. Stacey reports income from its separate operations of $100,000 and pays dividends of $40,000 during 20X2.

Required

Select the correct answer for each of the following questions.

1. Total noncontrolling interest reported in the consolidated balance sheet as of January 1, 20X2, is
   a. $30,000.
   b. $50,000.
   c. $70,000.
   d. $80,000.

2. Income assigned to the noncontrolling interest in the 20X2 consolidated income statement is
   a. $6,000.
   b. $7,000.
   c. $9,000.
   d. $14,000.

3. What amount of income is attributable to the controlling interest for 20X2?
   a. $116,000.
   b. $123,000.
   c. $124,000.
   d. $130,000.

4. Total stockholders' equity reported in the consolidated balance sheet as of January 1, 20X2, is
   a. $650,000.
   b. $700,000.
   c. $730,000.
   d. $1,000,000.

5. Preferred stock outstanding reported in the consolidated balance sheet as of January 1, 20X2, is
   a. $0.
   b. $30,000.
   c. $70,000.
   d. $100,000.

LO 9-4

P9-18 Multilevel Ownership with Differential

Purple Corporation owns 80 percent of Corn Corporation's common stock. It purchased the shares on January 1, 20X1, for $520,000. At the date of acquisition, the fair value of the noncontrolling interest was $130,000, and Corn reported common stock outstanding of $400,000 and retained earnings of $200,000. The differential is assigned to a trademark with a life of five years. Each year since acquisition, Corn has reported income from operations of $60,000 and paid dividends of $25,000.

Corn purchased 70 percent ownership of Bark Company on January 1, 20X3, for $406,000. At that date, the fair value of the noncontrolling interest was $174,000, and Bark reported common stock outstanding of $250,000 and retained earnings of $300,000. In 20X3, Bark reported net income of $30,000 and paid dividends of $20,000. The differential is assigned to buildings and equipment with an economic life of 10 years at the date of acquisition.

Required

a. Prepare the journal entries recorded by Corn for its investment in Bark during 20X3.

b. Prepare the journal entries recorded by Purple for its investment in Corn during 20X3.

c. Prepare the consolidation entries related to Corn's investment in Bark and Purple's investment in Corn needed to prepare consolidated financial statements for Purple and its subsidiaries at December 31, 20X3.

LO 9-5

P9-19 Subsidiary Stock Dividend

Pound Manufacturing Corporation prepared the following balance sheet as of January 1, 20X8:

Cash	$ 40,000	Accounts Payable	$ 50,000
Accounts Receivable	90,000	Bonds Payable	200,000
Inventory	180,000	Common Stock	100,000
Buildings & Equipment	500,000	Additional Paid-In Capital	70,000
Less: Accumulated Depreciation	(110,000)	Retained Earnings	280,000
Total Assets	$700,000	Total Liabilities & Equities	$700,000

The company is considering a 2-for-1 stock split, a stock dividend of 4,000 shares, or a stock dividend of 1,500 shares on its $10 par value common stock. The current market price per share of Pound stock on January 1, 20X8, is $50. Quick Sales Corporation acquired 68 percent of Pound's common shares on January 1, 20X4, at underlying book value. At that date, the fair value of the noncontrolling interest was equal to 32 percent of Pound's book value.

Required

Give the investment consolidation entry required to prepare a consolidated balance sheet at the close of business on January 1, 20X8, for each of the alternative transactions under consideration by Pound.

LO 9-2

P9-20 Subsidiary Preferred Stock Outstanding

Advanced StudyGuide .com

Emerald Corporation acquired 10,500 shares of the common stock and 800 shares of the 8 percent preferred stock of Pert Company on December 31, 20X4, at the book value of the underlying stock interests. At that date, the fair value of the noncontrolling interest in Pert's common stock was equal to 30 percent of the book value of its common stock interest. Pert reported the following balance sheet amounts on January 1, 20X5:

Cash	$ 30,000	Accounts Payable	$ 20,000
Accounts Receivable	70,000	Bonds Payable	100,000
Inventory	120,000	Preferred Stock	200,000
Buildings & Equipment	600,000	Common Stock	150,000
Less: Accumulated Depreciation	(150,000)	Retained Earnings	200,000
Total Assets	$670,000	Total Liabilities & Equities	$670,000

Pert's preferred stock is $100 par value, and its common stock is $10 par value. The preferred dividends are cumulative and are two years in arrears on January 1, 20X5. Pert reports net income of $34,000 for 20X5 and pays no dividends.

Required

a. Present the worksheet consolidation entries needed to prepare a consolidated balance sheet on January 1, 20X5.

b. Assuming that Emerald reported income from its separate operations of $80,000 in 20X5, compute the amount of consolidated net income and the amount of income to be assigned to the controlling shareholders in the 20X5 consolidated income statement.

LO 9-2

P9-21 Ownership of Subsidiary Preferred Stock

Presley Pools Inc. acquired 60 percent of the common stock of Jacobs Jacuzzi Company on December 31, 20X6, for $1,800,000. At that date, the fair value of the noncontrolling interest was $1,200,000. The full amount of the differential was assigned to goodwill. On December 31, 20X7, Presley Pools management reviewed the amount attributed to goodwill and concluded an impairment loss of $26,000 should be recognized in 20X7. On January 2, 20X7, Presley purchased 20 percent of the outstanding preferred shares of Jacobs for $42,000.

In its 20X6 annual report, Jacobs reported the following stockholders' equity balances at the end of the year:

Preferred Stock (10 percent, $100 par)	$ 200,000
Premium on Preferred Stock	5,000
Common Stock	500,000
Additional Paid-In Capital—Common	800,000
Retained Earnings	1,650,000
Total Stockholders' Equity	$3,155,000

The preferred stock is cumulative and has a liquidation value equal to its call price of $101 per share. Because of cash flow problems, Jacobs declared no dividends during 20X6, the first time it had missed a preferred dividend. With the improvement in operations during 20X7, Jacobs declared the current stated preferred dividend as well as preferred dividends in arrears; Jacobs also declared a common dividend for 20X7 of $10,000. Jacobs' reported net income for 20X7 was $280,000.

Required

a. Compute the amount of the preferred stockholders' claim on Jacobs Jacuzzi's assets on December 31, 20X6.

b. Compute the December 31, 20X6, book value of the Jacobs common shares purchased by Presley.

c. Compute the amount of goodwill associated with Presley's acquisition of Jacobs common stock.

d. Compute the amount of income that should be assigned to the noncontrolling interest in the 20X7 consolidated income statement.

e. Compute the amount of income from its subsidiary that Presley should have recorded during 20X7 using the fully adjusted equity method.

f. Compute the total amount that should be reported as noncontrolling interest in the December 31, 20X7, consolidated balance sheet.

g. Present all consolidation entries that should appear in a worksheet to prepare a complete set of 20X7 consolidated financial statements for Presley Pools and its subsidiary.

LO 9-2

P9-22 Consolidation Worksheet with Subsidiary Preferred Stock

Brown Company owns 90 percent of the common stock and 60 percent of the preferred stock of White Corporation, both acquired at underlying book value on January 1, 20X1. At that date, the fair value of the noncontrolling interest in White common stock was equal to 10 percent of the book value of its common stock. Trial balances for the companies on December 31, 20X6, are as follows:

	Brown Company		White Corporation	
	Debit	Credit	Debit	Credit
Cash	$ 58,000		$100,000	
Accounts Receivable	80,000		120,000	
Dividends Receivable	9,000			
Inventory	100,000		200,000	
Buildings & Equipment (net)	360,000		270,000	
Investment in White Corporation:				
Preferred Stock	120,000			
Common Stock	364,500			

(continued)

Cost of Goods Sold	280,000		170,000	
Depreciation & Amortization	40,000		30,000	
Other Expenses	131,000		20,000	
Dividends Declared:				
Preferred Stock			15,000	
Common Stock	60,000		10,000	
Accounts Payable		$ 100,000		$ 70,000
Bonds Payable		300,000		
Dividends Payable				15,000
Preferred Stock				200,000
Common Stock		200,000		100,000
Retained Earnings		435,000		250,000
Sales		500,000		300,000
Dividend Income		9,000		
Income from White Corporation		58,500		
Total	$1,602,500	$1,602,500	$935,000	$935,000

White preferred shares pay a 7.5 percent annual dividend and are cumulative. Preferred dividends for 20X6 were declared on December 31, 20X6, and are to be paid January 1, 20X7.

Required

a. Prepare the consolidation entries needed to complete a worksheet for 20X6.

b. Prepare a consolidation worksheet as of December 31, 20X6.

LO 9-3

P9-23 Subsidiary Stock Transactions

Apex Corporation acquired 75 percent of Beta Company's common stock on May 15, 20X3, at underlying book value. Beta's balance sheet on December 31, 20X6, contained these amounts:

Cash	$ 75,000	Accounts Payable	$ 30,000
Accounts Receivable	50,000	Bonds Payable	200,000
Inventory	125,000	Common Stock ($10 par)	100,000
Buildings & Equipment	700,000	Additional Paid-In Capital	80,000
Less: Accumulated Depreciation	(220,000)	Retained Earnings	320,000
Total Assets	$730,000	Total Liabilities & Equities	$730,000

During 20X7, Apex earned operating income of $90,000, and Beta reported net income of $45,000. Neither company declared any dividends during 20X7. Assume Apex Corporation has only no-par stock outstanding.

Beta is considering repurchasing 1,000 of its outstanding shares as treasury stock for $68 each.

Required

a. Assuming Beta purchases the shares from Nonaffiliated Company on January 1, 20X7:

(1) Compute the effect on the book value of the shares held by Apex.

(2) Give the entry on Apex's books to record the change in the book value of its investment in Beta's shares.

(3) Prepare the consolidation entries needed on December 31, 20X7, to complete a worksheet.

b. Assuming Beta purchases the shares directly from Apex on January 1, 20X7:

(1) Compute the effect on the book value of the shares held by Apex.

(2) Give the entry on Apex's books to record its sale of Beta shares to Beta.

(3) Prepare the consolidation entries needed on December 31, 20X7, to complete a worksheet.

LO 9-3

P9-24 Sale of Subsidiary Common Shares

Penn Corporation purchased 80 percent ownership of ENC Company on January 1, 20X2, at underlying book value. At that date, the fair value of the noncontrolling interest was equal to 20 percent of the book value of ENC. On January 1, 20X4, Penn sold 2,000 shares of ENC's stock for $60,000 to American School Products and recorded a $10,000 increase in additional paid-in capital. Trial balances for the companies on December 31, 20X4, contain the following data:

	Penn Corporation		ENC Company	
	Debit	**Credit**	**Debit**	**Credit**
Cash	$ 30,000		$ 35,000	
Accounts Receivable	70,000		50,000	
Inventory	120,000		100,000	
Buildings & Equipment	650,000		230,000	
Investment in ENC Company	162,000			
Cost of Goods Sold	210,000		100,000	
Depreciation Expense	20,000		15,000	
Other Expenses	21,000		25,000	
Dividends Declared	15,000		10,000	
Accumulated Depreciation		$ 170,000		$ 95,000
Accounts Payable		50,000		20,000
Bonds Payable		200,000		30,000
Common Stock ($10 par)		200,000		100,000
Additional Paid-In Capital		60,000		20,000
Retained Earnings		320,000		130,000
Sales		280,000		170,000
Income from ENC		18,000		
Total	$1,298,000	$1,298,000	$565,000	$565,000

ENC's net income was earned evenly throughout the year. Both companies declared and paid their dividends on December 31, 20X4. Penn uses the equity method in accounting for its investment in ENC.

Required

a. Prepare the consolidation entries needed to complete a worksheet for 20X4.

b. Prepare a consolidation worksheet for 20X4.

LO 9-3

P9-25 Sale of Shares by Subsidiary to Nonaffiliate

Craft Corporation held 80 percent of Delta Corporation's outstanding common shares on December 31, 20X2, which it had acquired at underlying book value. When the shares were acquired, the fair value of the noncontrolling interest was equal to 20 percent of Delta's book value. Balance sheets for the two companies on that date follow:

CRAFT CORPORATION
Balance Sheet
December 31, 20X2

Cash	$ 50,000	Accounts Payable	$ 70,000
Accounts Receivable	90,000	Mortgages Payable	250,000
Inventory	180,000	Common Stock	300,000
Buildings & Equipment	700,000	Additional Paid-In Capital	180,000
Less: Accumulated Depreciation	(200,000)	Retained Earnings	500,000
Investment in Delta Corporation	480,000		
Total Assets	$1,300,000	Total Liabilities & Equities	$1,300,000

DELTA CORPORATION
Balance Sheet
December 31, 20X2

Cash	$ 50,000	Accounts Payable	$ 70,000
Accounts Receivable	120,000	Taxes Payable	80,000
Inventory	200,000	Common Stock	200,000
Buildings & Equipment	600,000	Additional Paid-In Capital	50,000
Less: Accumulated Depreciation	(220,000)	Retained Earnings	350,000
Total Assets	$ 750,000	Total Liabilities & Equities	$750,000

On January 1, 20X3, Delta issued 4,000 additional shares of its $10 par value common stock to Nonaffiliated Corporation for $45 per share. Craft recorded the change in the book value of its Delta shares as an adjustment to its investment in Delta and an adjustment to its additional paid-in capital.

Required

a. Give the worksheet consolidation entry needed in preparing a consolidated balance sheet as of January 1, 20X3, immediately following the sale of shares by Delta.

b. Prepare a consolidated balance sheet worksheet as of the close of business on January 1, 20X3.

c. Prepare a consolidated balance sheet as of the close of business on January 1, 20X3.

LO 9-3

P9-26 Sale of Additional Shares to Parent

Lane Manufacturing Company acquired 75 percent of Tin Corporation stock at underlying book value. At the date of acquisition, the fair value of the noncontrolling interest was equal to 25 percent of Tin's book value. The balance sheets of the two companies for January 1, 20X1, are as follows:

LANE MANUFACTURING COMPANY
Balance Sheet
January 1, 20X1

Cash	$ 227,500	Accounts Payable	$ 50,000
Accounts Receivable	60,000	Bonds Payable	400,000
Inventory	100,000	Common Stock	200,000
Buildings & Equipment	600,000	Additional Paid-In Capital	50,000
Less: Accumulated Depreciation	(150,000)	Retained Earnings	400,000
Investment in Tin Products	262,500		
Total Assets	$1,100,000	Total Liabilities & Equities	$1,100,000

TIN CORPORATION
Balance Sheet
January 1, 20X1

Cash	$ 60,000	Accounts Payable	$ 50,000
Accounts Receivable	100,000	Bonds Payable	300,000
Inventory	180,000	Common Stock ($10 par)	100,000
Buildings & Equipment	600,000	Additional Paid-In Capital	50,000
Less: Accumulated Depreciation	(240,000)	Retained Earnings	200,000
Total Assets	$700,000	Total Liabilities & Equities	$700,000

On January 2, 20X1, Lane purchased an additional 2,500 shares of common stock directly from Tin for $150,000.

Required

a. Prepare the consolidation entry needed to complete a consolidated balance sheet worksheet immediately following the issuance of additional shares to Lane.

b. Prepare a consolidated balance sheet worksheet immediately following the issuance of additional shares to Lane.

LO 9-4

P9-27 Complex Ownership Structure

First Boston Corporation acquired 80 percent of Gulfside Corporation common stock on January 1, 20X5. Gulfside holds 60 percent of the voting shares of Paddock Company, and Paddock owns 10 percent of the stock of First Boston. All acquisitions were made at underlying book value. The fair value of the noncontrolling interest in Gulfside was equal to 20 percent of the book value of Gulfside when acquired by First Boston, and the fair value of the noncontrolling interest in Paddock was equal to 40 percent of its book value when control was acquired by Gulfside. During 20X7, income from the separate operations of First Boston, Gulfside, and Paddock was $44,000, $34,000, and $50,000, respectively, and dividends of $30,000, $20,000, and $10,000, respectively, were paid. The companies use the cost method of accounting for intercorporate investments and, accordingly, record dividends received as other (nonoperating) income.

Required

Compute the amount of consolidated net income and the income to be assigned to the noncontrolling shareholders of Gulfside and Paddock for 20X7 using the treasury stock method.

10 Additional Consolidation Reporting Issues

Multicorporate Entities

Business Combinations

Consolidation Concepts and Procedures

Intercompany Transfers

Additional Consolidation Issues

Multinational Entities

Reporting Requirements

Partnerships

Governmental and Not-for-Profit Entities

Corporations in Financial Difficulty

ADVANCED CONSOLIDATION ISSUES AT GOOGLE

Larry Page and Sergey Brin founded Google Inc. while they were doctoral students at Stanford University in the mid-1990s. Google began, of course, as an Internet search engine. The company was incorporated in September 1998 and went public in August 2004. Although Google is best known for its search engine, the company has expanded into various online tools and products. Some of its better-known products are its Gmail e-mail software; its web browser, Google Chrome; and its satellite map program, Google Earth. During its relatively short existence, Google has become one of the most well-known high-tech companies in the world.

Google Inc. has acquired a relatively large number of companies in just over a decade. In fact, between 2001 and 2012, Google was involved in 116 separate acquisitions. Three of the most visible of these acquisitions were Applied Semantics in 2003, YouTube Inc. in 2006, and Motorola in 2012.

Due to its rapid growth, Google went from a small start-up company with relatively simple accounting to a global company with fairly complex accounting in just a few years. Although prior chapters have introduced the preparation of consolidated income statements, statements of retained earnings, and balance sheets, Google also prepares a consolidated statement of cash flows. Moreover, although prior chapters have assumed that all acquisitions used in the illustration have taken place at the beginning or the end of the fiscal year, none of Google's acquisitions took place at the turn of a new fiscal year. Finally, although prior chapters have ignored taxes and earnings per share (EPS) calculations, Google's consolidated financial statements include complex accounting for income taxes and earnings per share. Therefore, this chapter explores four additional issues related to consolidated financial statements:

1. The consolidated statement of cash flows.
2. Consolidation following an interim acquisition.
3. Consolidation tax considerations.
4. Consolidated earnings per share.

Google

LEARNING OBJECTIVES

When you finish studying this chapter, you should be able to:

LO 10-1 Prepare a consolidated statement of cash flows.

LO 10-2 Make calculations and record journal and worksheet entries related to an interim acquisition.

LO 10-3 Make basic calculations and journal entries related to income taxes in the consolidated financial statements.

LO 10-4 Make calculations related to consolidated earnings per share.

CONSOLIDATED STATEMENT OF CASH FLOWS

LO 10-1

Prepare a consolidated statement of cash flows.

Consolidated entities, as with individual companies, must present a ***statement of cash flows*** when they issue a complete set of financial statements. A consolidated statement of cash flows is similar to a statement of cash flows prepared for a single-corporate entity and is prepared in basically the same manner.

Preparation of a Consolidated Cash Flow Statement

A consolidated statement of cash flows is typically prepared after the consolidated income statement, retained earnings statement, and balance sheet. Rather than being included in the three-part consolidation worksheet, the consolidated cash flow statement is prepared from the information in the other three consolidated statements. When an indirect approach is used in preparing the statement with consolidated net income as the starting point, consolidated net income must be adjusted for all items that affect consolidated net income and the cash of the consolidated entity differently.

As in the other consolidated financial statements, all transfers between affiliates should be eliminated in preparing the consolidated statement of cash flows. Although the payment of dividends from a subsidiary to a parent is a source or use of cash to an individual company, this transfer occurs within the consolidated entity and should not be included in the statement of cash flows. Unrealized profits on intercompany transfers are eliminated in preparing the consolidated balance sheet and income statement, and therefore no additional elimination of unrealized intercompany profits is needed in preparing the statement of cash flows.

The existence of a noncontrolling interest typically does not cause any special problems. In and of itself, the noncontrolling interest neither generates nor uses cash. Receipts from and payments to noncontrolling shareholders usually are included in the consolidated cash flow statement as cash flows related to financing activities. For example, dividend payments to noncontrolling shareholders normally are included as a use of cash. A sale of additional shares to noncontrolling shareholders or a repurchase of shares from them is considered to be a transaction with a nonaffiliate and is reported as a source or use of cash.

Consolidated Cash Flow Statement Illustrated[1]

Advanced StudyGuide .com

As an example of the preparation of a consolidated cash flow statement, assume the following:

1. Peerless Products purchases 80 percent of Special Foods common stock on December 31, 20X0, for $66,000 above book value. At the acquisition date, the noncontrolling interest has a fair value $16,500 in excess of its book value. The total differential at the acquisition date is $82,500 ($66,000 + $16,500).
2. Of the $82,500 total differential, $10,000 is assigned to land, $60,000 to equipment with a 10-year remaining life, and $12,500 to goodwill. Management determines that the goodwill is impaired and writes it down by $3,125 at the end of 20X1; the value of the goodwill remains constant thereafter.
3. During 20X2, Peerless pays dividends of $60,000; Special Foods reports net income of $75,000 and pays dividends of $40,000.
4. During 20X2, Peerless sells land that it had purchased in 20X1 for $40,000 to a nonaffiliate for $70,000.
5. Special Foods purchases additional equipment from an unrelated company at the end of 20X2 for $100,000.

[1] To view a video explanation of this topic, visit advancedstudyguide.com.

Consolidated balance sheet information as of December 31, 20X1 and 20X2, follows:

	December 31	
	20X1	20X2
Cash	$ 269,000	$ 276,000
Accounts Receivable	125,000	230,000
Inventories	175,000	270,000
Land	225,000	185,000
Buildings & Equipment	1,460,000	1,560,000
Goodwill	9,375	9,375
Total Debits	$2,263,375	$2,530,375
Accumulated Depreciation	$ 776,000	$ 852,000
Accounts Payable	200,000	230,000
Bonds Payable	300,000	300,000
Common Stock	500,000	500,000
Retained Earnings	408,700	563,900
Noncontrolling Interest	78,675	84,475
Total Credits	$2,263,375	$2,530,375

The consolidated income statement for 20X2 is as follows:

Sales		$720,000
Gain on Sale of Land		30,000
		$750,000
Less: Cost of Goods Sold	$340,000	
Depreciation Expense	76,000	
Other Expenses	105,000	(521,000)
Consolidated Net Income		$229,000
Income to Noncontrolling Interest		(13,800)
Income to Controlling Interest		$215,200

Figure 10–1 presents a worksheet to prepare a consolidated statement of cash flows. Although a number of different worksheet formats may be used in preparing statements of cash flows, the worksheet for preparing a consolidated statement of cash flows is no different from that used for a single-corporate entity. See Figure 10–1 for the essential worksheet entries. The consolidated statement of cash flows is prepared from the bottom portion of the worksheet.

Figure 10–2 illustrates Peerless' consolidated statement of cash flows for 20X2. The statement is similar to one that would be prepared for a single company. The only item that is different from what would be found in the cash flow statement of a single company relates to subsidiary dividends. The dividends paid to subsidiary noncontrolling shareholders result in an outflow of cash from the consolidated entity even though they are not shown as dividends declared in the consolidated retained earnings statement. Although not viewed as distributions of consolidated retained earnings, dividends to the noncontrolling shareholders use cash in reducing the noncontrolling interest.

STOP & THINK

Why is the cash flow statement so important? One reason is that companies can more easily manipulate income than they can cash flows. Operating cash flows can serve as a "reality check" for operating income. For example, in the first six months of 2012, Adidas recognized net income of $625 million. By examining Adidas' consolidated statement of cash flows, a potential investor could understand more about Adidas' operations than is available on the income statement. Adidas' cash flow from operations for the same period was –$70 million, which portrays a very different picture of operating performance. The difference stems primarily from a large increase in receivables ($459 million). This increase could indicate that Adidas is loosening its credit terms with its customers to maintain sales levels or that it is struggling to collect its receivables. Because operating cash flow tells a different story than the reported operating income number on the income statement, investors learn that they may want to investigate more closely.

FIGURE 10–1 Worksheet for Peerless Products and Subsidiary Consolidated Statement of Cash Flows, 20X2

Item	Balance 1/1/X2	Debits	Credits	Balance 12/31/X2
Cash	269,000	7,000 (*a*)		276,000
Accounts Receivable	125,000	105,000 (*b*)		230,000
Inventory	175,000	95,000 (*c*)		270,000
Land	225,000		40,000 (*d*)	185,000
Buildings & Equipment	1,460,000	100,000 (*e*)		1,560,000
Goodwill	9,375			9,375
	2,263,375			2,530,375
Accumulated Depreciation	776,000		76,000 (*f*)	852,000
Accounts Payable	200,000		30,000 (*g*)	230,000
Bonds Payable	300,000			300,000
Common Stock	500,000			500,000
Retained Earnings	408,700	60,000 (*h*)	215,200 (*i*)	563,900
Noncontrolling Interest in Net Assets	78,675	8,000 (*j*)	13,800 (*i*)	84,475
	2,263,375	375,000	375,000	2,530,375
Cash Flows from Operating Activities:				
Consolidated Net Income		229,000 (*i*)		
Depreciation Expense		76,000 (*f*)		
Gain on Sale of Land			30,000 (*d*)	
Increase in Accounts Receivable			105,000 (*b*)	
Increase in Inventory			95,000 (*c*)	
Increase in Accounts Payable		30,000 (*g*)		
Cash Flows from Investing Activities:				
Acquisition of Equipment			100,000 (*e*)	
Sale of Land		70,000 (*d*)		
Cash Flows from Financing Activities:				
Dividends to Parent Company Shareholders			60,000 (*h*)	
Dividends to Noncontrolling Shareholders			8,000 (*j*)	
Increase in Cash			7,000 (*a*)	
		405,000	405,000	

(*a*) Increase in cash balance.
(*b*) Increase in accounts receivable.
(*c*) Increase in inventory.
(*d*) Sale of land.
(*e*) Purchase of buildings and equipment.
(*f*) Depreciation charges for 20X2.
(*g*) Increase in accounts payable.
(*h*) Peerless dividends, $60,000.
(*i*) Consolidated net income, $229,000.
(*j*) Special Foods dividends to noncontrolling interest ($40,000 × 0.20).

Consolidated Cash Flow Statement—Direct Method

Although nearly all major companies use the indirect method of presenting a cash flow statement as illustrated in the previous example, critics have argued that the direct method is less confusing to the reader and more useful. Authoritative bodies have generally expressed a preference for the direct method, even though they have not required its use.

Using the same information as in the illustration of the indirect method, Figure 10–3 shows a worksheet for the preparation of a consolidated cash flow statement using the direct method. The only section of the cash flow statement affected by the difference in approaches is the operating activities section. Under the indirect approach, as in Figure 10–2, the operating activities section starts with net income and, to derive cash provided by operating activities, adjusts for all items affecting cash and net income differently.

FIGURE 10–2
Consolidated Statement of Cash Flows for the Year Ended December 31, 20X2

PEERLESS PRODUCTS CORPORATION AND SUBSIDIARY
Consolidated Statement of Cash Flows
For the Year Ended December 31, 20X2

Cash Flows from Operating Activities:		
Consolidated Net Income	$ 229,000	
Noncash Expenses, Revenues, Losses, & Gains Included in Income:		
Depreciation Expense	76,000	
Gain on Sale of Land	(30,000)	
Changes in Operating Assets and Liabilities:		
Increase in Accounts Receivable	(105,000)	
Increase in Inventory	(95,000)	
Increase in Accounts Payable	30,000	
Net Cash Provided by Operating Activities		$105,000
Cash Flows from Investing Activities:		
Acquisition of Equipment	$(100,000)	
Sale of Land	70,000	
Net Cash Used in Investing Activities		(30,000)
Cash Flows from Financing Activities:		
Dividends Paid:		
To Parent Company Shareholders	$ (60,000)	
To Noncontrolling Shareholders	(8,000)	
Net Cash Used in Financing Activities		(68,000)
Net Increase in Cash		$ 7,000
Cash at Beginning of Year		269,000
Cash at End of Year		$276,000

Under the direct approach in Figure 10–3, the operating activities section of the statement shows the actual cash flows. In this example, the only cash flows related to operations are as follows:

Cash Flows from Operating Activities:	
Cash Received from Customers	$615,000
Cash Paid to Suppliers	(510,000)
Net Cash Provided by Operating Activities	$105,000

The final number in this section is the same under both approaches, but this method provides a clearer picture of cash flows related to operations than does the indirect approach. Cash received from customers equals the sales revenue ($720,000) from the consolidated income statement minus the increase in accounts receivable ($105,000). Cash paid to suppliers equals cost of goods sold ($340,000), plus other expenses ($105,000), plus the increase in inventory ($95,000), minus the increase in accounts payable ($30,000). The remainder of the cash flow statement is the same under both approaches except that a separate reconciliation of operating cash flows and net income is required under the direct approach. This reconciliation is the same as for the operating section of the cash flow statement under the indirect method.

Advanced StudyGuide .com

CONSOLIDATION FOLLOWING AN INTERIM ACQUISITION

LO 10-2
Make calculations and record journal and worksheet entries related to an interim acquisition.

When one company purchases another company's common stock, the subsidiary is viewed as being part of the consolidated entity only from the time the stock is acquired. Consequently, when a subsidiary is acquired during a fiscal period rather than at the beginning or end, the results of the subsidiary's operations are included in the consolidated statements only for the portion of the year that the parent owned the stock. The subsidiary's revenues, expenses, gains, and losses for the portion of the fiscal period prior

FIGURE 10–3 Worksheet for Peerless Products and Subsidiary Consolidated Statement of Cash Flows—Direct Method, 20X2

Item	Balance 1/1/X2	Debits	Credits	Balance 12/31/X2
Cash	269,000	7,000 (*a*)		276,000
Accounts Receivable	125,000	105,000 (*b*)		230,000
Inventory	175,000	95,000 (*c*)		270,000
Land	225,000		40,000 (*d*)	185,000
Buildings & Equipment	1,460,000	100,000 (*e*)		1,560,000
Goodwill	9,375			9,375
	2,263,375			2,530,375
Accumulated Depreciation	776,000		76,000 (*f*)	852,000
Accounts Payable	200,000		30,000 (*c*)	230,000
Bonds Payable	300,000			300,000
Common Stock	500,000			500,000
Retained Earnings	408,700	60,000 (*g*)	215,200 (*h*)	563,900
Noncontrolling Interest in Net Assets	78,675	8,000 (*i*)	13,800 (*h*)	84,475
	2,263,375	375,000	375,000	2,530,375
Sales	720,000		720,000 (*b*)	
Gain on Sale of Land	30,000		30,000 (*d*)	
	750,000			
Cost of Goods Sold	340,000	340,000 (*c*)		
Depreciation Expense	76,000	76,000 (*f*)		
Other Expenses	105,000	105,000 (*c*)		
	521,000			
Consolidated Net Income	229,000	229,000 (*h*)		
		750,000	750,000	
Cash Flows from Operating Activities:				
Cash Received from Customers		615,000 (*b*)		
Cash Paid to Suppliers			510,000 (*c*)	
Cash Flows from Investing Activities:				
Acquisition of Equipment			100,000 (*e*)	
Sale of Land		70,000 (*d*)		
Cash Flows from Financing Activities:				
Dividends to Parent Company Shareholders			60,000 (*g*)	
Dividends to Noncontrolling Shareholders			8,000 (*i*)	
Increase in Cash			7,000 (*a*)	
		685,000	685,000	

(*a*) Increase in cash balance.
(*b*) Payments received from customers.
(*c*) Payments to suppliers.
(*d*) Sale of land.
(*e*) Acquisition of equipment.
(*f*) Depreciation charges for 20X2.
(*g*) Peerless dividends, $60,000.
(*h*) Consolidated net income, $229,000.
(*i*) Special Foods dividends to noncontrolling interest ($40,000 × 0.20).

to the time at which the parent acquired its controlling financial interest in the subsidiary is excluded from the consolidated financial statements.

To better understand consolidation following an interim acquisition, assume that on July 1, 20X1, Peerless Products purchases 80 percent of Special Foods' common stock for its underlying book value of $246,400. At the time of acquisition, the $61,600 fair value of Special Foods' noncontrolling interest is equal to its book value. Special Foods' Common Stock and Retained Earnings balances as of January 1, 20X1, were $200,000 and $100,000, respectively.

For the year 20X1, Special Foods reports the following items:

	Before Combination (1/1 to 6/30)	After Combination (7/1 to 12/31)	Full Year
Sales	80,000	120,000	200,000
Less: COGS	(46,000)	(69,000)	(115,000)
Less: Depreciation Expense	(8,000)	(12,000)	(20,000)
Less: Other Expenses	(6,000)	(9,000)	(15,000)
Net Income	20,000	30,000	50,000
Dividends declared	12,000	18,000	30,000

The book value of Special Foods' stock that Peerless acquired on July 1, 20X1, is computed as follows:

Book value of Special Foods on January 1, 20X1:	
Common stock	$200,000
Retained earnings	100,000
	$300,000
Net income, January 1 to June 30, 20X1	20,000
Dividends, January 1 to June 30, 20X1	(12,000)
Book value of Special Foods on July 1, 20X1	$308,000
Peerless' ownership interest	× 0.80
Book value on July 1, 20X1, of shares acquired by Peerless	$246,400

The ownership situation on July 1, 20X1, is as follows:

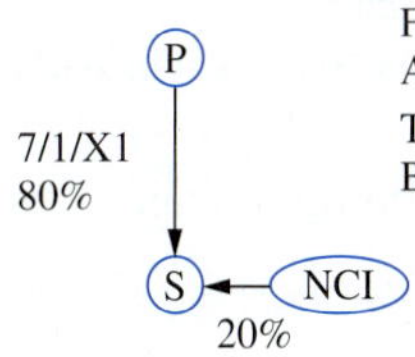

Fair value of Peerless' consideration		246,400
Add: Fair value of the NCI interest		61,600
Total fair value of consideration		308,000
Book value of shares acquired:		
Common stock—Special Foods	200,000	
Retained earnings—Special Foods	108,000	
		308,000
Differential		$ 0

Parent Company Entries

Peerless records the purchase of Special Foods stock with the following entry:

	July 1, 20X1		
(1)	Investment in Special Foods Stock	246,400	
	Cash		246,400
	Record purchase of Special Foods stock.		

During the second half of 20X1, Peerless records its share of Special Foods' income and dividends under the equity method:

(2)	Investment in Special Foods Stock	24,000	
	Income from Special Foods		24,000
	Record equity-method income: $30,000 × 0.80.		

(3)	Cash	14,400	
	Investment in Special Foods Stock		14,400
	Record dividends from Special Foods: $18,000 × 0.80.		

Consolidation Worksheet

Special Foods' trial balance for 20X1 is essentially the same as the trial balance presented previously in Figure 5–5. Specifically, the preconsolidation financial statements for Peerless are the same as in Figure 5–5 except that Peerless' cash reflects the interim purchase as does the income from Special Foods recognized by Peerless. Because the Special Foods' income and dividends earned and declared, respectively, during the first half of the year belong to the previous owners of the Special Foods' stock, the normal consolidation process would attribute earnings and dividends belonging to the former owners to Peerless. Therefore, in the acquisition year, prior to preparing the basic elimination entry, we include an additional consolidation entry to essentially "close out" the income and dividends from the first half of the year (prior to the acquisition) to retained earnings as follows:

Preacquisition Income and Dividend Consolidation Entry:

Sales	80,000		← Close preacquisition sales to RE
COGS		46,000	← Close preacquisition COGS to RE
Depreciation Expense		8,000	← Close preacquisition depr. exp. to RE
Other Expense		6,000	← Close preacquisition other expenses to RE
Dividends Declared		12,000	← Close preacquisition dividends to RE
Retained Earnings		8,000	← Preacquisition net increase in RE

After making this worksheet entry to close the preacquisition earnings and dividends to the Retained Earnings account, the beginning balance in Retained Earnings as of the acquisition date is $108,000.

Retained Earnings		
	100,000	Balance 1/1/20X1
	8,000	
	108,000	Balance 6/30/20X1

Based on this acquisition date beginning balance, we calculate the postacquisition changes in book value as follows:

Book Value Calculations:

	NCI 20%	+	Peerless 80%	=	Common Stock	+	Retained Earnings
July 1, 20X1, Balances	61,600		246,400		200,000		108,000
+ Net Income	6,000		24,000				30,000
− Dividends	(3,600)		(14,400)				(18,000)
December 31, 20X1, Balances	64,000		256,000		200,000		120,000

This leads to the basic consolidation entry, following the normal procedure (but based on postacquisition earnings and dividends):

Basic Consolidation Entry:

Common Stock	200,000		← Common stock balance
Retained Earnings	108,000		← Beginning balance in RE
Income from Special Foods	24,000		← Peerless' share of reported NI
NCI in NI of Special Foods	6,000		← NCI's share of reported NI
Dividends Declared		18,000	← 100% of sub's dividends declared
Investment in Special Foods		256,000	← Net amount of BV in inv. acct.
NCI in NA of Special Foods		64,000	← NCI's share of net BV

The following T-accounts illustrate how the basic consolidation entry zeros out the balances in the Investment in Special Foods and Income from Special Foods accounts:

	Investment in Special Foods (Dr)	Investment in Special Foods (Cr)		Income from Special Foods (Dr)	Income from Special Foods (Cr)	
Acquisition	246,400					
80% Net Income	24,000				24,000	80% Net Income
		14,400	80% Dividends			
Balance 12/31/X1	256,000				24,000	Balance 12/31/X1
		256,000	Basic	24,000		
	0				0	

Again, we include the optional accumulated depreciation consolidation entry for $308,000 (based on the balance in Special Foods' Accumulated Depreciation account as of the acquisition date = $320,000 ending balance − $12,000 depreciation expense for the second half of the year):

Optional Accumulated Depreciation Consolidation Entry:

Accumulated Depreciation	**308,000**		← Accumulated depreciation at the time of the acquisition netted against cost
Buildings & Equipment		**308,000**	

See Figure 10–4 for the consolidation worksheet reflecting the interim acquisition of Special Foods' stock during 20X1.

FIGURE 10–4 December 31, 20X1, Equity-Method Worksheet for Consolidated Financial Statements, Year of Combination; 80 Percent Purchase at Book Value; Interim Acquisition

	Peerless Products	Special Foods	Consolidation Entries DR	Consolidation Entries CR	Consolidated
Income Statement					
Sales	400,000	200,000	80,000		520,000
Less: COGS	(170,000)	(115,000)		46,000	(239,000)
Less: Depreciation Expense	(50,000)	(20,000)		8,000	(62,000)
Less: Other Expenses	(40,000)	(15,000)		6,000	(49,000)
Income from Special Foods	24,000		24,000		0
Consolidated Net Income	164,000	50,000	104,000	60,000	170,000
NCI in Net Income			6,000		(6,000)
Controlling Interest Net Income	**164,000**	**50,000**	**110,000**	**60,000**	**164,000**
Statement of Retained Earnings					
Beginning Balance	300,000	100,000	108,000	8,000	300,000
Net Income	**164,000**	**50,000**	**110,000**	**60,000**	164,000
Less: Dividends Declared	(60,000)	(30,000)		**18,000**	(60,000)
				12,000	
Ending Balance	**404,000**	**120,000**	**218,000**	**98,000**	**404,000**
Balance Sheet					
Cash	248,000	75,000			323,000
Accounts Receivable	75,000	50,000			125,000
Inventory	100,000	75,000			175,000
Investment in Subsidiary	256,000			256,000	0
Land	175,000	40,000			215,000
Buildings & Equipment	800,000	600,000		308,000	1,092,000
Less: Accumulated Depreciation	(450,000)	(320,000)	308,000		(462,000)
Total Assets	**1,204,000**	**520,000**	**308,000**	**564,000**	**1,468,000**
Accounts Payable	100,000	100,000			200,000
Bonds Payable	200,000	100,000			300,000
Common Stock	500,000	200,000	200,000		500,000
Retained Earnings	**404,000**	**120,000**	**218,000**	**98,000**	404,000
NCI in NA of Special Foods				64,000	64,000
Total Liabilities & Equity	**1,204,000**	**520,000**	**418,000**	**162,000**	**1,468,000**

The consolidated income statement prepared for the year of the interim acquisition reflects the inclusion of Special Foods in the consolidated entity only from July 1, the date of acquisition. All of Special Foods' revenues and expenses prior to the date of acquisition are excluded, and the statement appears as follows:

PEERLESS PRODUCTS CORPORATION AND SUBSIDIARY
Consolidated Income Statement
For the Year Ended December 31, 20X1

Sales		$520,000
Cost of Goods Sold		(239,000)
Gross Margin		$281,000
Expenses:		
Depreciation & Amortization	$62,000	
Other Expenses	49,000	
Total Expenses		(111,000)
Consolidated Net Income		$170,000
Income Attributable to the Noncontrolling Interest		(6,000)
Income Attributable to the Controlling Interest		$164,000

Consolidated net income is the same following the procedures illustrated as if Special Foods' books had been closed immediately before the combination and a new fiscal period had started on the date of combination.

CONSOLIDATION INCOME TAX ISSUES

LO 10-3

Make basic calculations and journal entries related to income taxes in the consolidated financial statements.

Allocating the Basis of Assets Acquired in a Business Combination

The legal structure of an acquisition can result in a taxable or nontaxable transaction. In a taxable transaction, the assets acquired and liabilities assumed will generally have tax bases equal to their fair market values because the subsidiary is required to recognize all inherent gains and losses on those assets and liabilities for tax purposes. In order to avoid this treatment, many acquisitions are structured to avoid classification as a taxable transaction. The details of structuring a nontaxable acquisition are beyond the scope of this text; however, it is important to understand the financial reporting implications of this type of transaction.

In a nontaxable acquisition, the tax bases of the assets acquired and liabilities assumed will remain unchanged as a result of the acquisition. The acquiree's basis is referred to as *carryover basis.* At the time of the acquisition, the acquiring company is required to identify all assets and liabilities acquired and their respective fair market values. **ASC 805-740-30-1** requires that the acquiring company record deferred tax assets or liabilities that arise from the difference between fair market value and tax basis when allocating the purchase price.

As an illustration, assume that Peerless acquires 100 percent of Special Foods' outstanding stock on December 31, 20X1, by issuing 10,000 shares of its own no par stock to Special Foods' shareholders. Also assume the no par stock has a market value of $34 per share on the acquisition date and that that this deal is structured as a nontaxable transaction. Thus, the acquisition price is $340,000 (10,000 shares × $34 per share). Special Foods' assets and liabilities will retain their carryover bases for tax purposes in the consolidated entity. Additionally, assume that Special Foods has a current and future effective tax rate of 30 percent. The following table summarizes Special Foods' information at the acquisition date:

	Special Foods		
	Book Value	Fair Value	Tax Basis
Cash	47,000	47,000	47,000
Accounts Receivable, net	50,000	50,000	60,000
Inventory	60,000	60,000	60,000
Deferred Tax Asset	3,000	?	
Land	40,000	55,000	40,000
Buildings & Equipment	600,000	320,000	600,000
Less: Accumulated Depreciation	(300,000)		(400,000)
Patent		20,000	
Total Assets	**500,000**		
Accounts Payable	70,000	70,000	70,000
Deferred Tax Liability	30,000	?	
Bonds Payable	100,000	100,000	100,000
Common Stock	200,000		
Retained Earnings	100,000		
Total Liabilities & Equity	**500,000**		

Using this information, Peerless allocates the $340,000 acquisition price to the identifiable assets and liabilities, including any deferred tax assets and liabilities that may exist as a result of the differences between the fair values and tax bases of the identifiable assets and liabilities. Peerless must first review the differences for each item and the impact of these differences on the deferred tax elements of the acquisition individually before determining if the transaction results in goodwill or a gain.

Accounts Receivable, Net

While U.S. GAAP requires that bad debts be estimated to properly record accounts receivable at their net realizable value, bad debts may only be deducted under the tax law when they are actually written off. The tax basis of the accounts receivable is $10,000 higher than the book value because Special Foods has a $10,000 allowance for doubtful accounts. This book-tax difference results in a $3,000 ($10,000 × 30%) deferred tax asset because the company has already reduced book income with an expense that will be deductible for tax purposes in the future. This future deduction will reduce future taxable income and the tax owed in the year of the deduction. This is a probable future benefit, or in other words, an asset. Since there is no difference between the book value and fair value of accounts receivable, the fair value of the deferred tax asset associated with the allowance is also $3,000.

Land

Because land is not depreciated for US GAAP or for tax purposes, the book basis and the tax basis for the land are the same. However, the land has appreciated in value since the time it was purchased by Special Foods. Since the book value of the land will be revalued to the fair market value of $55,000 in the consolidation process, a book-tax difference of $15,000 ($55,000 FMV less $40,000 original cost) results from the Special Foods acquisition by Peerless. Consequently, a deferred tax liability of $4,500 ($15,000 × 30%) must be recorded as part of the acquisition. The future sale of the land will result in a larger gain (or smaller loss) for tax purposes than for book purposes due to the lower tax basis of the land. This larger gain (or smaller loss) will increase future taxable income and the tax owed in the year of sale. This future tax is a liability to the company, hence the need for a deferred tax liability at the time of the acquisition.

Buildings and Equipment

Special Foods' book value of the buildings and equipment at the time of the acquisition is $300,000 ($600,000 cost less $300,000 accumulated depreciation) compared to a tax basis of $200,000 ($600,000 cost less $400,000 accumulated depreciation). This existing book-tax difference of $100,000 is the source of the $30,000 deferred tax liability ($100,000 × 30%) recorded on Special Foods' balance sheet. The fair value of the buildings and equipment at the time of acquisition is $320,000, which means there is a larger book-tax difference for the consolidated entity of $120,000 ($320,000 FMV less $200,000 tax basis). As a result, the fair value of the related deferred tax liability is $36,000 ($120,000 × 30%). The future depreciation of the buildings and equipment will be higher for book purposes than for tax purposes due to the lower tax basis of the buildings and equipment. This higher book depreciation will never be deductible and will increase future taxable income and the tax owed. This future tax is a liability to the company, hence the need for a deferred tax liability at the time of the acquisition.

Patent

Finally, Peerless has identified a patent worth $20,000 as part of the acquisition which has not previously been recognized on the Special Foods' accounting records. Additionally, the patent does not have a significant tax basis. As a result, the whole fair market value of $20,000 represents a book-tax difference for the consolidated entity, which generates a $6,000 ($20,000 × 30%) deferred tax liability on acquisition date. The patent will be amortized for book purposes; however, there will never be any corresponding tax deduction for the patent because its tax basis is zero. This higher book amortization will increase future taxable income and the tax owed. This future tax is a liability to the company, hence the need for a deferred tax liability at the time of the acquisition.

Deferred Tax Assets and Liabilities

After reviewing all of the book-tax differences at the acquisition date, the fair market value of the deferred tax asset is $3,000 (accounts receivable) and the fair market value of the deferred tax liability is $46,500 (land, buildings & equipment, and patent) at the date of acquisition. These assets and liabilities are considered part of the identifiable assets acquired and liabilities assumed during the acquisition.

	Special Foods		
	Book Value	Fair Value	Differential
Cash	47,000	47,000	
Accounts Receivable, net	50,000	50,000	
Inventory	60,000	60,000	
Deferred Tax asset	3,000	3,000	
Land	40,000	55,000	15,000
Buildings & Equipment, net	300,000	320,000	20,000
Patent		20,000	20,000
	500,000	555,000	
Accounts Payable	70,000	70,000	
Deferred Tax Liability	30,000	46,000	(16,500)
Bonds Payable	100,000	100,000	
Common Stock	200,000		
Retained Earnings	100,000		
	500,000	216,500	38,500

The fair value of the consideration given to acquire Special Foods' stock ($340,000) can be divided between the fair value of Special Foods' identifiable net assets ($338,500) and goodwill ($1,500), illustrated as follows:

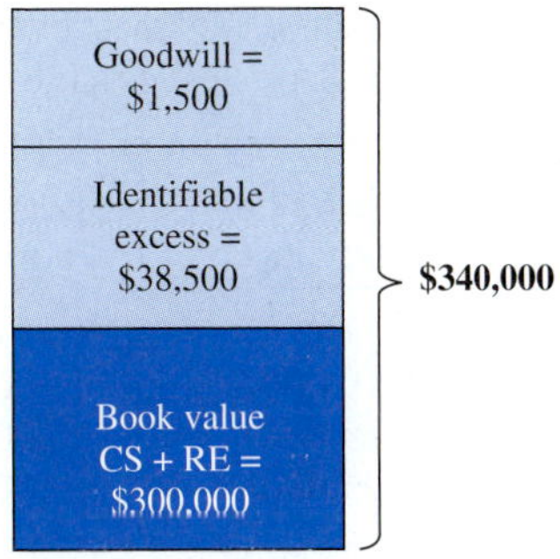

The book value portion of the acquisition price is $300,000.

Book Value Calculations:

	Total Investment	=	Common Stock	+	Retained Earnings
Book Value at Acquisition	300,000		200,000		100,000

The basic elimination entry at the acquisition date is:

Basic Consolidation Entry:

Common Stock	200,000	
Retained Earnings	100,000	
Investment in Special Foods		300,000

The excess value can be summarized as follows:

Excess Value (Differential) Reclassification Entry:

Total Differential	=	Land	+	Buildings & Equip.	+	Patent	+	Def. Tax Liab.	+	Goodwill
40,000		15,000		20,000		20,000		(16,500)		1,500

The following entry is required to assign the $40,000 differential to the specific accounts that need to be revalued to reflect their fair values as of the acquisition date and complete the elimination of the investment account from Special Foods' balance sheet.

Excess Value (Differential) Reclassification Entry:

Land	15,000	
Building	20,000	
Patent	20,000	
Goodwill	1,500	
Deferred Tax Liability		16,500
Investment in Special Foods		40,000

As usual, we eliminate Special Foods' acquisition date accumulated depreciation against the Buildings and Equipment account balance.

Optional Accumulated Depreciation Entry:

Accumulated Depreciation	300,000	
Buildings & Equipment		300,000

All of these consolidation entries are reflected in the worksheet in Figure 10–5.

The differential allocated to the deferred tax assets and liabilities would be amortized to consolidated deferred tax expense or benefit as the excess book-tax differences related

FIGURE 10–5 December 31, 20X1, Equity-Method Worksheet for the Consolidated Balance Sheet, Year of Combination, 100 Percent Purchase with Differential and Book-Tax Differences.

	Peerless Products	Special Foods	Consolidation Entries		Consolidated
			DR	CR	
Balance Sheet					
Cash	10,000	47,000			57,000
Accounts Receivable	75,000	50,000			125,000
Inventory	96,000	60,000			156,000
Deferred Tax Asset	4,000	3,000			7,000
Investment in Special Foods	340,000			300,000	0
				40,000	
Land	175,000	40,000	15,000		230,000
Buildings & Equipment	800,000	600,000	20,000	300,000	1,120,000
Less: Accumulated Depreciation	(400,000)	(300,000)	300,000		(400,000)
Patent			20,000		20,000
Goodwill			1,500		1,500
Total Assets	**1,100,000**	**500,000**	$356,000	**$640,000**	**1,316,500**
Accounts Payable	65,000	70,000			135,000
Deferred Tax Liability	35,000	30,000			81,500
Bonds Payable	200,000	100,000		16,500	300,000
Common Stock	500,000	200,000	200,000		500,000
Retained Earnings	300,000	100,000	100,000		300,000
Total Liabilities & Equity	**1,100,000**	**500,000**	300,000	16,500	**1,316,500**

to the Land, Buildings and Equipment, and Patent are reduced either through depreciation or as the related assets are sold to unrelated parties.

Because there is no tax goodwill in this acquisition, there is a book-tax difference related to the goodwill of $1,500. **ASC 805-740-25-9** indicates that no deferred tax liability is recorded for this particular book-tax difference for the consolidated entity.

Tax Allocation Procedures When Separate Tax Returns Are Filed

We next briefly introduce the concept of tax allocation and the reporting of tax expense under the cost and equity methods when the companies in the consolidated group file separate tax returns. We then discuss tax allocation when the group files a consolidated tax return.

Intercompany income accruals and dividend transfers must be considered in computing income tax expense for the period. The impact depends on the level of ownership and the filing status of the companies. Because corporations generally are permitted to deduct 80 percent of the dividends received (100 percent if at least 80 percent of all voting stock is owned), they are taxed at relatively low effective tax rates (20 percent times the marginal tax rate) on those dividends.

STOP & THINK

How does the dividends received deduction affect the implied tax rate on dividends received from a subsidiary corporation?

Percent Ownership	Dividends Received Deduction	Implied Tax Rate on Dividends[a]
< 20%	70%	10.5% = 35% × (1 − 70%)
20% − 80%	80%	7% = 35% × (1 − 80%)
> 80%	100%	0% = 35% × (1 − 100%)

[a] Assuming a 35% tax rate on dividends received.

When an investor and an investee file a consolidated tax return, intercompany dividends and income accruals are eliminated in determining taxable income. Deferred tax accruals, therefore, are not needed, even though ***temporary differences*** occur between the recognition of investment income by the investor and realization through dividend transfers from the investee. Note that temporary "timing differences" between the recognition of revenues, expenses, gains, and losses under book (GAAP) and tax accounting rules lead to situations in which tax expense can be shifted from one year to another. This shifting of taxes from one period to another is referred to as ***interperiod tax allocation***. Consolidated tax returns may be filed when an investor owns at least 80 percent of a subsidiary's stock and elects to file a consolidated return. Otherwise, an investor and investee must file separate returns.

If an investor and an investee file separate tax returns, the investor is taxed on the dividends received from the investee rather than on the amount of investment income reported. The amount of tax expense reported in the investor's income statement each period should be based on income from its own operations as well as on income recognized from its intercompany investments. **ASC 740** specifies those situations in which additional deferred tax accruals are required as a result of temporary differences in the recognition of income for financial reporting purposes and that used in determining taxable income.

Tax Expense under the Equity Method

If the investment is reported using the equity method and separate tax returns are filed, the investor reports its share of the investee's income in the income statement but reports only its share of the investee's dividends in the tax return. When the amount of the investee's dividends is different from its earnings, a temporary difference arises and interperiod tax allocation is required for the investor. In this situation, deferred income taxes must be recognized on the difference between the equity-method income reported by the investor in its income statement and the dividend income reported in its tax return. Current accounting standards generally require that the investor's reported income tax expense be computed as if all the investment income the investor recognized under the equity method actually had been received. Thus, the investor's tax expense is recorded in excess of the taxes actually paid when the investee's earnings are higher than its dividends and normally is recorded at less than taxes actually paid when dividends are higher than earnings.

Tax Expense under the Cost Method

If the investor reports its investment using the cost method, income tax expense recorded by the investor on the investment income and the amount of taxes actually paid are both based on dividends received from the investee. No interperiod income tax allocation is required under the cost method because the income is recognized in the same period for both financial reporting and tax purposes; there are no temporary differences.

Refer to Figure 10–5 for a summary of the requirements for computing the investor's income tax expense on income from intercorporate investments in common stock.

Allocation of Tax Expense When a Consolidated Return Is Filed

A parent company and its subsidiaries may file a ***consolidated income tax return,*** or they may choose to file separate returns. For a subsidiary to be eligible to be included in a consolidated tax return, at least 80 percent of its stock must be held by the parent company or another company, or combination of companies, included in the consolidated return.

A major advantage of filing a consolidated return is the ability to offset the losses of one company against the profits of another. In addition, dividends and other transfers between the affiliated companies are not taxed. Thus, tax payments on profits from

FIGURE 10–5
Investor Income Tax Expense Computation

Type of Investee	Computation of Investor's Income Tax Expense Related to Income from Investee
Equity-method investees	Ordinary tax rate × (Investor's share of investee net income − Dividend deduction)[a]
Cost-method investees	Ordinary tax rate × (Dividends received − Dividend deduction)

[a] Need not accrue taxes if the earnings will be distributed in a tax-free transfer or if there is evidence that the earnings of a foreign subsidiary or foreign corporate joint venture are to be reinvested permanently.

FYI

Although consolidated entities can elect to file as a consolidated entity or separately, some state laws require separate income tax returns. For example, in 2013, Google Inc. filed a consolidated federal income tax return. However, it filed state and international income tax returns separately, combined, and on a consolidated basis, in accordance with relevant state and international laws and regulations.

intercompany transfers can be delayed until the intercompany profits are realized through transactions with nonaffiliates. When separate returns are filed, the selling company is required to pay tax on the intercompany profits it has recognized whether or not the profits are realized from a consolidated viewpoint. Filing a consolidated return also may make it possible to avoid limits on the use of certain items such as foreign tax credits and charitable contributions.

An election to file a consolidated income tax return carries with it some limitations. Once an election is made to include a subsidiary in the consolidated return, the company cannot file separate tax returns in the future unless it receives approval from the Internal Revenue Service. The subsidiary's tax year also must be brought into conformity with the parent's tax year. In addition, preparing a consolidated tax return can become quite difficult when numerous companies are involved and complex ownership arrangements exist between the companies. A consolidated tax return portrays the companies included in the return as if they actually were a single legal entity. All intercorporate transfers of goods and services and intercompany dividends are eliminated and a single income tax figure is assessed when a consolidated return is prepared.

Consolidated companies sometimes need to prepare separate financial statements for noncontrolling shareholders and creditors. Because only a single income tax amount is determined for the consolidated entity when a consolidated tax return is filed, income tax expense must be assigned to the individual companies included in the return in some manner. The way in which the consolidated income tax amount is allocated to the individual companies can affect the amounts reported in the income statements of both the separate companies and the consolidated entity. When a subsidiary is less than 100 percent owned by the parent, income tax expense assigned to the subsidiary reduces proportionately the subsidiary income assigned to the parent and the noncontrolling interest.

Although no authoritative pronouncements specify the assignment of consolidated income tax expense to the individual companies included in the consolidated tax return, a reasonable approach is to allocate consolidated income tax expense among the companies on the basis of their relative contributions to income before taxes. As an example, assume that Peerless Products owns 80 percent of the stock of Special Foods, purchased at book value, and the two companies elect to file a consolidated tax return for 20X1. Peerless Products reports operating earnings before taxes of $140,000, excluding income from Special Foods, and Special Foods reports income before taxes of $50,000. If the corporate tax rate is 40 percent, consolidated income taxes are $76,000 ($190,000 × 0.40). Tax expense of $56,000 is assigned to Peerless Products, and $20,000 is assigned to Special Foods, determined as follows:

Peerless Products:	($140,000/$190,000) × $76,000 =	$56,000
Special Foods:	($50,000/$190,000) × $76,000 =	20,000
Consolidated tax expense		$76,000

Income assigned to the noncontrolling interest is computed as follows:

Special Foods' income before tax	$50,000
Income tax expense assigned to Special Foods	(20,000)
Special Foods' net income	$30,000
Noncontrolling stockholders' proportionate share	× 0.20
Income assigned to noncontrolling interest	$ 6,000

Advanced StudyGuide .com

The consolidated income statement for 20X1 shows the following amounts:

Consolidated Operating Income	$190,000
Less: Income Tax Expense	(76,000)
Consolidated Net Income	$114,000
Income Attributed to Noncontrolling Interest	(6,000)
Income Attributed to Controlling Interest	$108,000

Other allocation methodologies may be preferred when affiliates have significantly different tax characteristics, such as when only one of the companies qualifies for special tax exemptions or credits.

Tax Effects of Unrealized Intercompany Profit Eliminations

The income tax effects of unrealized intercompany profit eliminations depend on whether the companies within the consolidated entity file a consolidated tax return or separate tax returns.

Unrealized Profits When a Consolidated Return Is Filed

Intercompany transfers are eliminated in computing both consolidated net income and taxable income when a consolidated tax return is filed. Only sales outside the consolidated entity are recognized both for tax and for financial reporting purposes. Because profits are taxed in the same period they are recognized for financial reporting purposes, no temporary differences arise, and no additional tax accruals are needed in preparing the consolidated financial statements.

Unrealized Profits When Separate Returns Are Filed

When each company within a consolidated entity files a separate income tax return, that company is taxed individually on the profits from intercompany sales. The focus in separate tax returns is on the transactions of the separate companies, and no consideration is given to whether the intercompany profits are realized from a consolidated viewpoint. Thus, the profit from an intercompany sale is taxed when the intercompany transfer occurs without waiting for confirmation through sale to a nonaffiliate. For consolidated financial reporting purposes, however, unrealized intercompany profits must be eliminated. Although the separate company may pay income taxes on the unrealized intercompany profit, the tax expense must be eliminated when the unrealized intercompany profit is eliminated in the preparation of consolidated financial statements. This difference in the timing of the income tax expense recognition results in recording ***deferred income taxes.***

For example, if Special Foods sells inventory costing $23,000 to Peerless Products for $28,000, and none is resold before year-end, the entry to eliminate the intercorporate transfer in the consolidated statements is:

Sales	**28,000**	
Cost of Goods Sold		**23,000**
Inventory		**5,000**

Eliminate intercompany upstream sale of inventory.

Income assigned to Special Foods' shareholders is reduced by $5,000 as a result of this entry. An adjustment to tax expense also is required in preparing consolidated statements if Special Foods files a separate tax return. With a 40 percent corporate income tax rate, the following consolidation entry adjusts income tax expense of the consolidated entity downward by $2,000 ($5,000 × 0.40) to reflect the reduction of reported profits:

Deferred Tax Asset	**2,000**	
Deferred Tax Expense		**2,000**

Eliminate tax expense on unrealized intercompany profit.

The debit to the Deferred Tax Asset account reflects the tax effect of a temporary difference between the income reported in the consolidated income statement and that reported in the separate tax returns of the companies within the consolidated entity. Consistent with the treatment accorded to other temporary differences, this tax effect normally is carried to the consolidated balance sheet as an asset. If the intercompany profit is expected to be recognized in the consolidated income statement in the next year, the deferred taxes are classified as current.

Unrealized Profit in Separate Tax Return Illustrated

For purposes of illustrating the treatment of income taxes when Peerless and Special Foods file separate tax returns, assume the following information:

1. Peerless owns 80 percent of Special Foods' common stock, purchased at book value.
2. During 20X1, Special Foods purchases inventory for $23,000 and sells it to Peerless for $28,000. Peerless continues to hold the entire inventory at the end of 20X1.
3. The effective combined federal and state tax rate for both Peerless and Special Foods is 40 percent.
4. Special Foods pays a $30,000 dividend during 20X1.

Although Special Foods' trial balance includes $50,000 of income before taxes and tax expense of $20,000 ($50,000 × 0.40), consolidated net income and income assigned to the controlling and noncontrolling shareholders are based on realized net income of $27,000, computed as follows:

Special Foods' net income	$30,000
Add back income tax expense	20,000
Special Foods' income before taxes	$50,000
Unrealized profit on upstream sale	(5,000)
Special Foods' realized income before taxes	$45,000
Income taxes on realized income (40%)	(18,000)
Special Foods' realized net income	$27,000
Special Foods' realized net income assigned to	
Controlling interest ($27,000 × 0.80)	$21,600
Noncontrolling interest ($27,000 × 0.20)	5,400
Special Foods' realized net income	$27,000

If Peerless accounts for its investment in Special Foods using the fully adjusted equity method, Peerless would make the following journal entries on its books:

(4)	Investment in Special Foods	24,000	
	Income from Special Foods		24,000
	Record Peerless' 80 percent share of Special Foods' 20X1 reported income.		

(5)	Cash	24,000	
	Investment in Special Foods		24,000
	Record Peerless' 80 percent share of Special Foods' 20X1 dividend.		

Peerless also defers its 80 percent share of the unrealized profit on intercompany upstream sales (net of taxes). Thus, the $5,000 of unrealized profit ($28,000 − $23,000) net of 40 percent taxes is $3,000 ($5,000 × 0.60). Thus, the deferral of Peerless' relative share of the unrealized gross profit is $2,400 ($3,000 × 0.80).

(6)	Income from Special Foods	2,400	
	Investment in Special Foods		2,400
	Eliminate unrealized gross profit (net of taxes) on inventory purchases from Special Foods.		

To prepare the basic consolidation entry, we first analyze the book value of Special Foods' equity accounts and the related 80 percent share belonging to Peerless and the 20 percent share belonging to the NCI shareholders:

Calculations for Basic Consolidation Entry:

Book Value Calculations:

	NCI 20% +	Peerless 80%	=	Common Stock	+	Retained Earnings
Original Book Value	60,000	240,000		200,000		100,000
+ Net Income	6,000	24,000				30,000
− Dividends	(6,000)	(24,000)				(30,000)
Ending Book Value	60,000	240,000		200,000		100,000

Adjustment to Basic Consolidation Entry:

	NCI 20%	Peerless 80%
Net Income	6,000	24,000
− Deferred Gross Profit	(1,000)	(4,000)
+ Deferred Tax on Deferred Profit	400	1,600
Income to be Eliminated	5,400	21,600
Ending Book Value	60,000	240,000
− Deferred Gross Profit	(1,000)	(4,000)
+ Deferred Tax on Deferred Profit	400	1,600)
Adjusted Book Value	59,000	237,600

We note that the book value calculations form the basis for the basic consolidation entry, but Peerless' share of income and its investment account must be adjusted for the equity-method entry previously made for $2,400. In addition, the NCI share of income and net assets is adjusted for the 20 percent share of the unrealized gross profit (net of 40 percent taxes), $600.

Basic Investment Account Consolidation Entry:

	Debit	Credit	
Common Stock	200,000		← Common stock balance
Retained Earnings	100,000		← Beginning balance in RE
Income from Special Foods	21,600		← Peerless' % of NI with Adjustments
NCI in NI of Special Foods	5,400		← NCI % of NI with Adjustments
Dividends Declared		30,000	← 100% of sub's dividends declared
Investment in Special Foods		237,600	← Net BV with Adjustments
NCI in NA of Special Foods		59,400	← NCI % of BV with Adjustments

The following T-accounts illustrate how this entry eliminates the balances in the Investment in Special Foods and Income from Special Foods accounts:

Investment in Special Foods

	Debit	Credit	
Acquisition	240,000		
80% Net Income	24,000		
		24,000	80% Dividends
		2,400	Defer GP (net of tax)
Ending Balance	237,600		
		237,600	Basic
	0		

Income from Special Foods

	Debit	Credit	
		24,000	80% Net Income
Defer GP (net of tax)	2,400		
		21,600	Ending Balance
Basic	21,600		
		0	

The consolidation worksheet entry to correct for the intercompany sale is identical to the preceding entry.

Eliminate Inventory Purchases from Special Foods

Sales	28,000	
Cost of Goods Sold		23,000
Inventory		5,000

With a 40 percent income tax rate, the following consolidation entry adjusts income tax expense of the consolidated entity downward by $2,000 ($5,000 × 0.40) to reflect the reduction of reported profits:

Deferred Tax Asset	2,000	
Deferred Tax Expense		2,000

A temporary difference would normally be included in the consolidated balance sheet and in the computation of consolidated income tax expense. In addition to temporary differences arising from unrealized profits, differences generally exist between subsidiary net income and dividend distributions. Peerless pays income taxes for the period based on its reported dividends from Special Foods but includes in consolidated net income for financial reporting its proportionate share of Special Foods' realized net income. This difference between the amount of income reported in the consolidated income statement and the amount reported in the tax return is considered a temporary difference, and deferred taxes normally must be recognized on this difference. In this example, Special Foods distributes all of its income as dividends, and the only temporary difference relates to the unrealized intercompany profit.

Finally, we include the optional depreciation consolidation entry, assuming accumulated depreciation on the date of acquisition was $300,000:

Optional Accumulated Depreciation Consolidation Entry:

Accumulated Depreciation	300,000	
Buildings & Equipment		300,000

← Accumulated depreciation at the time of the acquisition netted against cost

Subsequent Profit Realization When Separate Returns Are Filed

When unrealized intercompany profits at the end of one period subsequently are recognized in another period, the tax effects of the temporary difference must again be considered.

If income taxes were ignored, the following consolidation entry would be used in preparing consolidated statements as of December 31, 20X2, assuming that Special Foods had $5,000 of unrealized inventory profit on its books on January 1, 20X2, and the inventory was resold in 20X2:

Investment in Special Foods	4,000	
NCI in NA of Special Foods	1,000	
Cost of Goods Sold		5,000

Eliminate beginning inventory profit.

On the other hand, when the 40 percent tax rate is considered, the consolidation entry would be modified as follows:

Investment in Special Foods	2,400	
NCI in NA of Special Foods	600	
Deferred Tax Expense	2,000	
Cost of Goods Sold		5,000

Eliminate beginning inventory profit:
$2,400 = ($5,000 − $2,000) × 0.80
$600 = ($5,000 − $2,000) × 0.20
$2,000 = $5,000 × 0.40.

Unrealized profit of $3,000 rather than $5,000 is apportioned between the controlling and noncontrolling shareholders in this case. Deferred tax expense of $2,000 is recognized for financial reporting purposes in 20X2 even though the $5,000 of intercompany profit was reported on Special Foods' separate tax return and the $2,000 of taxes was paid on the profit in 20X1. This entry recognizes the tax expense in the consolidated income statement in the same year as the income is recognized from a consolidated viewpoint. No worksheet adjustment to the Deferred Tax Asset account is needed at the end of 20X2 because the deferred tax asset was entered only in the consolidation worksheet at the end of 20X1, but not on the books of either company; it does not carry over to 20X2.

CONSOLIDATED EARNINGS PER SHARE

LO 10-4

Make calculations related to consolidated earnings per share.

In general, ***consolidated earnings per share*** is calculated in the same way as earnings per share is calculated for a single corporation. Consolidated earnings per share is based on the income attributable to the controlling interest and available to the parent's common stockholders. Basic consolidated EPS is calculated by deducting income to the noncontrolling interest and any preferred dividend requirement of the parent company from consolidated net income. The resulting amount is then divided by the weighted-average number of the parent's common shares outstanding during the period.

The computation of diluted consolidated EPS is more complicated. A subsidiary's contribution to the diluted EPS number may be different from its contribution to consolidated net income because of different underlying assumptions. Both the percentage of ownership held within the consolidated entity and the total amount of subsidiary income available to common shareholders may be different. In the computation of EPS, the parent's percentage of ownership frequently is changed when a subsidiary's convertible bonds and preferred stock are treated as common stock and the subsidiary's options and warrants are treated as if they had been exercised. In addition, income available to the subsidiary's common shareholders changes when bonds and preferred stock are treated as common stock for purposes of computing EPS. Interest expense or preferred dividends, if already deducted, must be added back in computing income available to common shareholders when the securities are considered to be common stock.

Computation of Diluted Consolidated Earnings per Share

The parent's share of consolidated net income normally is the starting point in the computation of diluted consolidated EPS. It then is adjusted for the effects of parent and subsidiary dilutive securities. The following formulation can be used in computing diluted consolidated EPS:

$$\text{Diluted consolidated EPS} = \frac{\begin{array}{c}\text{Parent's share of}\\\text{consolidated}\\\text{net income}\end{array} \pm \begin{array}{c}\text{Adjustment}\\\text{for parent}\\\text{securities}\end{array} - \left(\begin{array}{c}\text{Percent}\\\text{ownership}\\\text{held by}\\\text{parent}\end{array} \times \begin{array}{c}\text{Income}\\\text{available to}\\\text{common}\\\text{shareholders}\\\text{of}\\\text{subsidiary}\end{array}\right) + \left(\begin{array}{c}\text{Shares}\\\text{held}\\\text{by}\\\text{parent}\end{array} \times \begin{array}{c}\text{Subsidiary}\\\text{diluted}\\\text{EPS}\end{array}\right)}{\begin{array}{c}\text{Weighted average of}\\\text{parent company shares}\\\text{outstanding}\end{array} + \begin{array}{c}\text{Shares of parent to be}\\\text{issued if dilutive}\\\text{securities are converted}\\\text{and options exercised}\end{array}}$$

This formula shows the adjustments to the parent's share of consolidated net income and its common shares outstanding that are needed in computing diluted consolidated EPS. In general, the parent company's securities that are convertible or exercisable into parent company shares must be included as shares outstanding if they are dilutive. When convertible bonds are treated as common stock and the additional shares are added in the denominator, the after-tax interest savings must be added back into the numerator.

FYI

When Google went public in 2004, its consolidated diluted EPS was only $1.46. In 2013, its diluted EPS had increased to $38.13.

Google Diluted EPS

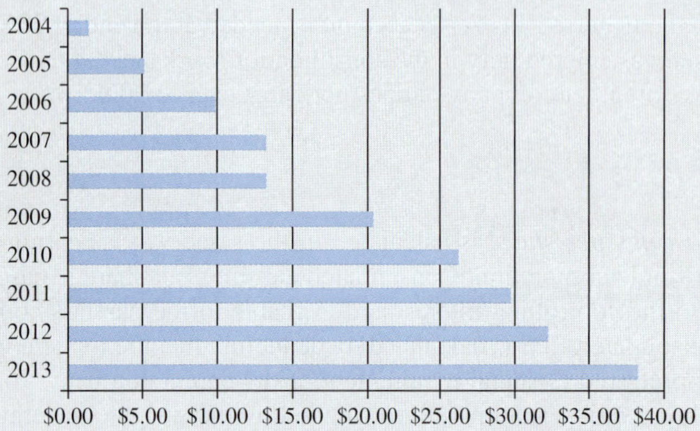

Dividends on preferred stock that continue to be classified as preferred stock are deducted from the numerator, and no deduction is made for dividends on preferred stock considered to be common stock.

The two other adjustments in the numerator relate to the amount of subsidiary income to be included in computing diluted consolidated EPS. First, the parent's portion of the subsidiary's income available to common shareholders is deducted so that an adjusted income number can be substituted. The amount deducted is computed by multiplying the parent's ownership percentage of subsidiary common shares outstanding times the subsidiary's income after preferred dividends have been deducted. The subsidiary's contribution to diluted consolidated EPS is determined by multiplying the subsidiary's number of shares held by the parent and other affiliates (or the number of shares that would be held after exercise or conversion of other subsidiary securities held) times the diluted EPS computed for the subsidiary. In this way, the effect of the subsidiary's dilutive securities is considered in computing diluted consolidated EPS.

Occasionally, a subsidiary is permitted to issue rights, warrants, or options to purchase the parent's common stock or to issue a security convertible into the parent's common stock. Such rights, warrants, and options of the subsidiary are treated in the same way as if the parent had issued them.

Subsidiary bonds or preferred stock convertible into the parent's common stock are treated in a slightly different manner. If the securities are treated as if converted, income available to common shareholders of the subsidiary is increased as a result of the reduction in interest expense, net of tax, or preferred dividends. The parent's portion of the earnings increase is included in the diluted consolidated EPS computation through the subsidiary EPS component. The number of parent company shares into which the security is convertible is added to the denominator of the diluted consolidated EPS computation.

Computation of Consolidated Earnings per Share Illustrated

As an illustration of the computation of consolidated earnings per share for Peerless Products and Special Foods, assume the following:

1. Peerless Products purchases 80 percent of the stock of Special Foods on December 31, 20X0, at book value. On the date of acquisition, the fair value of Special Foods' noncontrolling interest is equal to its book value.
2. Both Special Foods and Peerless Products have effective income tax rates of 40 percent and file a consolidated tax return.
3. Special Foods has 20X1 income before taxes of $50,000, an allocated share of consolidated income taxes of $20,000, and net income of $30,000.
4. Consolidated net income for 20X1 is computed and allocated as follows:

Peerless' separate operating income	$140,000
Special Foods' income before taxes	50,000
Consolidated income before taxes	$190,000
Consolidated income taxes (40%)	(76,000)
Consolidated net income	$114,000
Income to noncontrolling shareholders ($30,000 × 0.20)	(6,000)
Income to controlling interest	$108,000

5. Peerless' capital structure consists of 100,000 shares of $5 par value common stock and 10,000 shares of $10 par 10 percent convertible preferred stock. The preferred stock is convertible into 25,000 shares of Peerless' common.
6. Special Foods has 20,000 shares of $10 par value common stock and $100,000 of 6 percent convertible bonds outstanding. The bonds, issued at par, are convertible into 4,000 shares of Special Foods' common stock.
7. On January 1, 20X1, Special Foods grants its officers options to purchase 9,000 shares of Peerless Products' common stock at $26 per share at any time during the five years following the date of the grant. None is exercised during 20X1. The average market price of Peerless' common stock during 20X1 is $29 per share. (These options originated from Peerless and were given to Special Foods to be used in compensating its officers.)

Special Foods' Earnings per Share

Before consolidated EPS can be calculated, the EPS total for the subsidiary must be computed. Basic and diluted EPS for Special Foods for 20X1 differ because Special Foods has dilutive convertible bonds outstanding.

Basic and diluted EPS for Special Foods for 20X1 are computed as follows:

	Basic	Diluted
Special Foods' net income	$30,000	$30,000
Interest effect of assumed conversion of bonds, net of taxes ($100,000 × 0.06) × (1 − 0.40)		3,600
Income accruing to common shares	$30,000	$33,600
Weighted-average common shares outstanding in 20X1	20,000	20,000
Additional shares from assumed bond conversion		4,000
Weighted-average shares and share equivalents	20,000	24,000
Earnings per share:		
$30,000/20,000 shares	$ 1.50	
$33,600/24,000 shares		$ 1.40

The assumed conversion of the bonds reduces Special Foods' diluted EPS from $1.50 to 1.40.

Consolidated Earnings per Share

Consolidated earnings per share for 20X1 is $0.98 based on weighted-average common shares outstanding and $0.84, assuming full dilution. The computations are shown in Figure 10–6 with diluted EPS based on the formula presented earlier.

For diluted EPS, the parent's $108,000 share of consolidated net income is reduced by Peerless' $24,000 ($30,000 × 0.80) proportionate share of Special Foods' net income. Special Foods' contribution to diluted earnings per share is then added back. A total of $22,400 ($1.40 × 16,000 shares) is added for diluted EPS. If Peerless also had purchased a portion of Special Foods' convertible bonds, an equivalent number of shares would be added to Peerless' holdings in computing the amount added back for diluted EPS. The amount of subsidiary earnings added back into the numerator also can be computed by multiplying the revised ownership ratio times the revised earnings contribution. Earnings available to Special Foods' common shareholders in computing diluted EPS increases to $33,600 ($30,000 + $3,600) with the assumed bond conversion, and the number of shares outstanding increases by 4,000. As a result, the revised ownership ratio is reduced to 66⅔ percent (16,000 shares ÷ 24,000 shares). The earnings contribution computed in this manner is $22,400 (33,600 × 0.66667).

Peerless' preferred stock is treated as preferred stock in computing basic EPS, and preferred dividends are deducted in determining the income accruing to common shareholders in the numerator. In computing diluted EPS, the preferred stock is treated as common stock outstanding because it is convertible and dilutive. Therefore, no dividends

FIGURE 10–6
Computation of Peerless Products and Subsidiary Consolidated Earnings per Share for 20X1

	Basic Earnings per Share	Diluted Earnings per Share
Numerator		
Consolidated net income attributable to parent	$108,000	$108,000
Less: Peerless' share of Special Foods' net income ($30,000 × 0.80)		(24,000)
Add: Peerless' share of Special Foods' income-based on separate diluted EPS ($1.40 × 16,000 shares)		22,400
Less: Preferred dividends	(10,000)	
Total	$ 98,000	$106,400
Denominator		
Weighted-average shares outstanding	100,000	100,000
Assumed exercise of stock options[a]		931
Preferred stock assumed converted		25,000
Total	100,000	125,931
Earnings per Share		
$98,000/100,000 shares	$ 0.98	
$106,400/125,931 shares		$ 0.84

[a]Treasury stock method of assuming exercise of stock options:

Shares issued		9,000
Shares repurchased:		
Proceeds from issuing shares (9,000 shares × $26)	$234,000	
Repurchase price per share	÷ $29	
Shares repurchased		(8,069)
Increase in shares outstanding		931

are deducted in the numerator, and 25,000 shares of common stock are added into the denominator.

Stock options for 9,000 shares of parent company stock can be exercised at any time and must be reflected in the computation of diluted EPS. As computed in Figure 10–6 using the treasury stock method, an additional 931 shares are added to the denominator in computing diluted EPS.

SUMMARY OF KEY CONCEPTS

In addition to an income statement, balance sheet, and statement of retained earnings, a full set of consolidated financial statements must include a consolidated statement of cash flows. The consolidated statement of cash flows is prepared from the other three consolidated statements in the same way as the statement of cash flows is prepared for a single company. Also, dividends to noncontrolling shareholders must be included as a financing use of cash because they do require the use of cash even though they are not viewed as dividends of the consolidated entity.

When a subsidiary is purchased at an interim date during the year, the consolidation procedures must ensure that the subsidiary's operating results are included in the consolidated financial statements for only that portion of the year during which the parent held a controlling financial interest in the subsidiary. All of the subsidiary's revenues, expenses, gains, and losses for the portion of the year prior to the subsidiary's entry into the consolidated entity must be excluded along with its dividends declared before acquisition.

Two major financial reporting issues related to income taxes arise in consolidation. The first is concerns how to allocate income tax expense to individual companies included in a consolidated income tax return. One approach is to allocate the total tax based on the contributions of the individual companies to the total entity income. The issue is important because the allocation impacts the separate financial statements and the amounts assigned to the noncontrolling interests in the consolidated statements. The second tax issue involves the income tax effects of intercorporate transactions. For consolidating companies filing separate tax returns, income tax expense is recognized in the consolidated income statement when the consolidated entity recognizes the associated transaction, not necessarily when an individual company reports it. If an intercompany gain or loss is included in an individual company's tax return in a different period than the one in which it is included in the consolidated income statement, deferred income taxes should be recognized on the temporary difference.

Consolidated earnings per share is calculated largely in the same way it is for a single company. The numerator of the basic EPS computation is based on earnings available to the holders of the parent's common stock, and the denominator is the weighted-average number of the parent's common shares outstanding during the period. Diluted consolidated EPS assumes both the parent's and subsidiary's dilutive securities are converted, and special adjustments to income may be needed to reflect the effect of the assumed conversion on the amount of subsidiary income to include in the EPS numerator.

KEY TERMS

consolidated earnings per share, *521*
consolidated income tax return, *515*
deferred income taxes, *517*
interperiod tax allocation, *515*
statement of cash flows, *502*
temporary differences, *514*

QUESTIONS

LO 10-1 **Q10-1** Why not simply add a fourth part to the three-part consolidation worksheet to permit preparation of a consolidated cash flow statement?

LO 10-1 **Q10-2** Why are dividend payments to noncontrolling shareholders treated as an outflow of cash in the consolidated cash flow statement but not included as dividends paid in the consolidated retained earnings statement?

LO 10-1 **Q10-3** Why are payments to suppliers not shown in the statement of cash flows when the indirect method is used in presenting cash flows from operating activities?

LO 10-1 **Q10-4** Why are changes in inventory balances not shown in the statement of cash flows when the direct method is used in presenting the cash flows from operating activities?

LO 10-1 **Q10-5** Are sales included in the consolidated cash flows worksheet in computing cash flows from operating activities under (*a*) the indirect method or (*b*) the direct method?

LO 10-1 **Q10-6** How is an increase in inventory included in the amounts reported as cash flows from operating activities under (*a*) the indirect method and (*b*) the direct method?

LO 10-2 **Q10-7** What portion of the sales of an acquired company is included in the consolidated income statement following a midyear acquisition?

LO 10-2 **Q10-8** How are dividends declared by an acquired company prior to the date of a midyear acquisition treated in the consolidated financial statements?

LO 10-2 **Q10-9** How do the consolidation entries at the end of the year change when an acquisition occurs at midyear rather than at the beginning of the year?

LO 10-3 **Q10-10** What factors would cause an acquirer to include deferred tax assets and liabilities in the net identifiable assets acquired?

LO 10-3 **Q10-11** Are there any book-tax differences that arise in an acquisition that do not require the inclusion of a deferred tax asset or liability in the net identifiable assets acquired?

LO 10-3 **Q10-12** Why do companies that file consolidated tax returns often choose to allocate tax expense to the individual affiliates?

LO 10-3 **Q10-13** How do unrealized profits on intercompany transfers affect the amount reported as income tax expense in the consolidated financial statements?

LO 10-3 **Q10-14** How do interperiod income tax allocation procedures affect consolidation entries in the period in which unrealized intercompany profits arise?

LO 10-3 **Q10-15** How do interperiod income tax allocation procedures affect consolidation entries in the period in which intercompany profits unrealized as of the beginning of the period are realized?

LO 10-3 **Q10-16** How does the use of interperiod tax allocation procedures affect the amount of income assigned to noncontrolling shareholders in the period in which the subsidiary records unrealized intercompany profits?

LO 10-4 **Q10-17** Why is it not possible simply to add the separately computed EPS amounts of individual affiliates in deriving consolidated EPS?

LO 10-4 **Q10-18** How are dividends that are paid to the parent's preferred shareholders and to the subsidiary's preferred shareholders treated in computing consolidated EPS?

LO 10-4 **Q10-19** What factors may cause a subsidiary's income contribution to consolidated EPS to be different from its contribution to consolidated net income?

LO 10-4 **Q10-20** When a subsidiary's convertible bond is treated as common stock in computing the subsidiary's diluted EPS, how is the interest on the bond treated in computing diluted consolidated EPS?

LO 10-4 **Q10-21** How are rights, warrants, and options of subsidiary companies treated in the computation of consolidated EPS?

LO 10-4 **Q10-22** What effect does the presence of a noncontrolling interest have on the computation of consolidated EPS?

CASES

LO 10-4 **C10-1**

Judgment

The Effect of Security Type on Earnings per Share

Stage Corporation has both convertible preferred stock and convertible debentures outstanding at the end of 20X3. The annual cash payment to the preferred shareholders and to the bondholders is the same, and the two issues convert into the same number of common shares.

Required

a. If both issues are dilutive and are converted into common stock, which issue will cause the larger reduction in basic EPS when converted? Why?

b. If both issues are converted into common stock, which issue will cause the larger increase in consolidated net income when converted?

c. If the preferred shares remain outstanding, what conditions must exist for them to be excluded entirely from the computation of basic EPS?

d. If Stage is a subsidiary of Prop Company, how will these securities affect the EPS reported for the consolidated enterprise?

LO 10-1 **C10-2**

Research

Evaluating Consolidated Statements

Cowl Company, a public company, has been reporting losses for the last three years and has been unable to pay its bills from cash generated from its operations. On December 31, 20X4, Cowl's president instructed its treasurer to transfer a large amount of cash to Cowl from Plum Corporation, which is 80 percent owned by Cowl. It appears Cowl will not return to profitability in the near future and may never be able to repay Plum. Cowl's treasurer is concerned that, although cash will appear to be unchanged in the consolidated financial statements, the subsidiary has much less cash than it previously held and Plum's noncontrolling shareholders might learn about the transfer and initiate a lawsuit or other action against Cowl's management.

Required

As a member of Cowl's accounting department, you have been asked to determine whether information on the transfer will be shown in the consolidated cash flow statement or other financial statements and to search the FASB's pronouncements and those of other authoritative bodies to see whether information germane to the noncontrolling shareholders of a subsidiary must be disclosed in cases such as this. Prepare a memo indicating your findings, and include citations to or quotations from relevant authoritative pronouncements.

LO 10-3 **C10-3**

Understanding

Income Tax Expense

Johnson Corporation purchased 100 percent ownership of Freelance Company at book value on March 3, 20X2. Johnson, which makes frequent inventory purchases from Freelance, uses the equity method in accounting for its investment in Freelance. Both companies are subject to 40 percent income tax rates and file separate tax returns.

Required

a. When will an inventory transfer cause consolidated income tax expense to be higher than the amount paid?

b. When tax payments are higher than tax expense, how is the overpayment reported in the consolidated financial statements?

c. What types of transfers other than inventory transfers will cause consolidated income tax expense to be less than income taxes paid?

d. What types of transfers other than inventory transfers will cause consolidated income tax expense to be more than income taxes paid?

LO 10-1

C10-4 Consolidated Cash Flows

Analysis

The consolidated cash flows from operations of Jones Corporation and its subsidiary Short Manufacturing for 20X2 decreased quite substantially from 20X1 despite the fact that consolidated net income increased slightly in 20X2.

Required

a. What factors included in the computation of consolidated net income may explain this difference between cash flows from operations and net income?

b. How might a change in credit terms extended by Short Manufacturing explain a part of the difference?

c. How would an inventory write-off affect cash flows from operations?

d. How would a write-off of uncollectible accounts receivable affect cash flows from operations?

e. How does the preparation of a statement of cash flows differ for a consolidated entity compared with that of a single corporate entity?

EXERCISES

LO 10-1

E10-1 Analysis of Cash Flows

In its consolidated cash flow statement for the year ended December 31, 20X2, Lamb Corporation reported operating cash inflows of $284,000, financing cash outflows of $230,000, $80,000 for investing cash outflows, and an ending cash balance of $57,000. Lamb purchased 70 percent of Mint Company's common stock on March 12, 20X1, at book value. Mint reported net income of $30,000, paid dividends of $10,000 in 20X2, and is included in Lamb's consolidated statements. Lamb paid dividends of $45,000 in 20X2. The indirect method is used in computing cash flow from operations.

Required

a. What was the consolidated cash balance at January 1, 20X2?

b. What amount was reported as dividends paid in the cash flow from financing activities section of the statement of cash flows?

c. If the other adjustments to reconcile consolidated net income and cash provided by operations resulted in a $77,000 increase over net income, what amount was reported as consolidated net income for 20X2?

LO 10-1

E10-2 Statement of Cash Flows

Becon Corporation's controller has just finished preparing a consolidated balance sheet, income statement, and statement of changes in retained earnings for the year ended December 31, 20X4. Becon owns 60 percent of Handy Corporation's stock, which it acquired at underlying book value on May 7, 20X1. At that date, the fair value of the noncontrolling interest was equal to 40 percent of Handy Corporation's book value. You have been provided the following information:

Consolidated net income for 20X4 was $271,000.

Handy reported net income of $70,000 for 20X4.

Becon paid dividends of $25,000 in 20X4.

Handy paid dividends of $15,000 in 20X4.

Becon issued common stock on April 7, 20X4, for a total of $150,000.

Consolidated wages payable increased by $7,000 in 20X4.

Consolidated depreciation expense for the year was $21,000.

Consolidated accounts receivable decreased by $32,000 in 20X4.

Bonds payable of Becon with a book value of $204,000 were retired for $200,000 on December 31, 20X4.

Consolidated amortization expense on patents was $13,000 for 20X4.

Becon sold land that it had purchased for $142,000 to a nonaffiliate for $134,000 on June 10, 20X4.

Consolidated accounts payable decreased by $12,000 during 20X4.

Total purchases of equipment by Becon and Handy during 20X4 were $295,000.

Consolidated inventory increased by $16,000 during 20X4.

There were no intercompany transfers between Becon and Handy in 20X4 or prior years except for Handy's payment of dividends. Becon uses the indirect method in preparing its cash flow statement.

Required

a. What amount of dividends was paid to the noncontrolling interest during 20X4?

b. What amount will be reported as net cash provided by operating activities for 20X4?

c. What amount will be reported as net cash used in investing activities for 20X4?

d. What amount will be reported as net cash used in financing activities for 20X4?

e. What was the change in cash balance for the consolidated entity for 20X4?

LO 10-1

E10-3 Computation of Operating Cash Flows

Toggle Company reported sales of $310,000 and cost of goods sold of $180,000 for 20X2. During 20X2, Toggle's accounts receivable increased by $17,000, inventory decreased by $8,000, and accounts payable decreased by $21,000.

Required

Compute the amounts to be reported by Toggle as cash received from customers, cash payments to suppliers, and cash flows from operating activities for 20X2, assuming there were no other cash flows from operations.

LO 10-1

E10-4 Consolidated Operating Cash Flows

Power Corporation owns 75 percent of Turk Company's stock; no intercompany purchases or sales were made in 20X4. For the year, Power and Turk reported sales of $300,000 and $200,000 and cost of goods sold of $160,000 and $95,000, respectively. Power's inventory increased by $35,000, but Turk's decreased by $15,000. Power's accounts receivable increased by $28,000 and its accounts payable decreased by $17,000 during 20X4. Turk's accounts receivable decreased by $10,000 and its accounts payable increased by $4,000.

Required

Using the direct method of computing cash flows from operating activities, compute the following:

a. Cash received from customers.

b. Cash payments to suppliers.

c. Cash flows from operating activities, assuming there were no other cash flows from operations.

LO 10-1

E10-5 Preparation of Statement of Cash Flows

The accountant for Consolidated Enterprises Inc. has just finished preparing a consolidated balance sheet, income statement, and statement of changes in retained earnings for 20X3. The accountant has asked for assistance in preparing a statement of cash flows for the consolidated entity. Consolidated Enterprises holds 80 percent of the stock of Separate Way Manufacturing. The following items are proposed for inclusion in the consolidated cash flow statement:

Decrease in accounts receivable	$ 23,000
Increase in accounts payable	5,000
Increase in inventory	15,000
Increase in bonds payable	120,000
Equipment purchased	380,000
Common stock repurchased	35,000
Depreciation reported for current period	73,000
Gain recorded on sale of equipment	8,000
Book value of equipment sold	37,000
Goodwill impairment loss	3,000
Sales	900,000
Cost of goods sold	368,000
Dividends paid by parent	60,000
Dividends paid by subsidiary	30,000
Consolidated net income for the year	464,000
Income assigned to the noncontrolling interest	14,000

Required

Prepare in good form a statement of cash flows for Consolidated Enterprises Inc. using the indirect method of computing cash flows from operations.

LO 10-1

E10-6 Direct Method Cash Flow Statement

Using the data presented in E10-5, prepare a statement of cash flows for Consolidated Enterprises Inc. using the direct method of computing cash flows from operating activities.

LO 10-1

Advanced StudyGuide .com

E10-7 Analysis of Consolidated Cash Flow Statement

The following 20X2 consolidated statement of cash flows is presented for Acme Printing Company and its subsidiary, Jones Delivery:

ACME PRINTING COMPANY AND SUBSIDIARY
Consolidated Statement of Cash Flows
For the Year Ended December 31, 20X2

Cash Flows from Operating Activities:		
Consolidated Net Income	$ 130,000	
Noncash Items Included in Income:		
Depreciation Expense	45,000	
Amortization of Patents	1,000	
Amortization of Bond Premium	(2,000)	
Loss on Sale of Equipment	23,000	
Changes in operating assets and liabilities:		
Decrease in Inventory	20,000	
Increase in Accounts Receivable	(12,000)	
Net Cash Provided by Operating Activities		$205,000
Cash Flows from Investing Activities:		
Purchase of Buildings	$(150,000)	
Sale of Equipment	60,000	
Net Cash Used in Investing Activities		(90,000)
Cash Flows from Financing Activities:		
Dividends Paid:		
To Acme Printing Shareholders	$ (50,000)	
To Noncontrolling Shareholders	(6,000)	
Sale of Bonds	100,000	
Repurchase of Acme Printing Stock	(120,000)	
Net Cash Used in Financing Activities		(76,000)
Net Increase in Cash		$ 39,000

Acme Printing acquired 60 percent of the voting shares of Jones in 20X1 at underlying book value. At that date, the fair value of the noncontrolling interest was equal to 40 percent of the book value of Jones Delivery.

Required

a. Determine the amount of dividends paid by Jones in 20X2.

b. Explain why the amortization of bond premium is treated as a deduction from net income in arriving at net cash flows from operating activities.

c. Explain why an increase in accounts receivable is treated as a deduction from net income in arriving at net cash flows from operating activities.

d. Explain why dividends to noncontrolling stockholders are not shown as a dividend payment in the retained earnings statement but are shown as a distribution of cash in the consolidated cash flow statement.

e. Did the loss on the sale of equipment included in the consolidated statement of cash flows result from a sale to an affiliate or a nonaffiliate? How do you know?

LO 10-2

E10-8 Midyear Acquisition

Advanced StudyGuide .com

Yarn Manufacturing Corporation issued stock with a par value of $67,000 and a market value of $503,500 to acquire 95 percent of Spencer Corporation's common stock on August 30, 20X1. At that date, the fair value of the noncontrolling interest was $26,500. On January 1, 20X1, Spencer reported the following stockholders' equity balances:

Common Stock ($10 par value)	$150,000
Additional Paid-In Capital	50,000
Retained Earnings	300,000
Total Stockholders' Equity	$500,000

Spencer reported net income of $60,000 in 20X1, earned uniformly throughout the year, and declared and paid dividends of $10,000 on June 30 and $25,000 on December 31, 20X1. Yarn accounts for its investment in Spencer Corporation using the equity method.

Yarn reported retained earnings of $400,000 on January 1, 20X1, and had 20X1 income of $140,000 from its separate operations. Yarn paid dividends of $80,000 on December 31, 20X1.

Required

a. Compute consolidated retained earnings as of January 1, 20X1, as it would appear in comparative consolidated financial statements presented at the end of 20X1.

b. Compute consolidated net income and income to the controlling interest for 20X1.

c. Compute consolidated retained earnings as of December 31, 20X1.

d. Give the December 31, 20X1, balance of Yarn Manufacturing's investment in Spencer Corporation.

LO 10-2

E10-9 Purchase of Shares at Midyear

Highbeam Corporation paid $319,500 to acquire 90 percent ownership of Copper Company on April 1, 20X2. At that date, the fair value of the noncontrolling interest was $35,500. On January 1, 20X2, Copper reported these stockholders' equity balances:

Common Stock	$160,000
Additional Paid-In Capital	40,000
Retained Earnings	150,000
Total Stockholders' Equity	$350,000

Copper's operating results and dividend payments for 20X2 were as follows:

	January 1 to March 31	April 1 to December 31
Sales	$90,000	$250,000
Total expenses	(80,000)	(220,000)
Net income	$10,000	$ 30,000
Dividends paid	$ 5,000	$ 15,000

Highbeam uses the equity method in recording its investment in Copper.

Required

a. Prepare the journal entries that Highbeam recorded in 20X2 for its investment in Copper.

b. Give the worksheet consolidation entries needed at December 31, 20X2, to prepare consolidated financial statements.

LO 10-3

E10-10 Deferred Tax Assets and Liabilities Arising in Acquisition

Power Corporation acquired 100 percent of Light Corporation in a nontaxable transaction. The following selected information is available for Light Corporation at the acquisition date:

	Light Corporation		
	Book Values	**Fair Values**	**Tax Basis**
Accounts Receivable, net	$30,000	$28,000	$30,000
Land	10,000	40,000	10,000
Equipment	20,000	15,000	5,000
Bond Payable	120,000	115,000	120,000

Light Corporation has never recorded an allowance for doubtful accounts; however, upon review of the accounts receivable detail, Power has determined that approximately $2,000 of the receivables are uncollectible.

Several years ago, Light purchased a small plot of land for an expanded parking area that has never been developed. An outside party has recently offered to purchase the land for $40,000.

Power estimated the value of the equipment acquired with Light to be $15,000.

Light issued $120,000 in bonds (at par) two years ago. Since that time, interest rates have changed, which has been reflected in the fair value of those bonds at the date of acquisition.

The current and future tax rate for Power Light Consolidated is 40 percent.

Required

Compute the amounts to be included in the consolidated balance sheet as deferred tax assets and/or liabilities as a result of the Light acquisition.

LO 10-3

Advanced StudyGuide .com

E10-11 Tax Deferral on Gains and Losses

Springdale Corporation holds 75 percent of the voting shares of Holiday Services Company. Assume Springdale accounts for this investment using the equity method. During 20X7, Springdale sold inventory costing $60,000 to Holiday Services for $90,000, and Holiday Services resold one-third of the inventory in 20X7. Also in 20X7, Holiday Services sold land with a book value of $140,000 to Springdale for $240,000, and Springdale continues to hold the land. The companies file separate tax returns and are subject to a 40 percent tax rate.

Required

Give the consolidation entries relating to the intercorporate sale of inventories and land to be entered in the consolidation worksheet prepared at the end of 20X7.

LO 10-3

E10-12 Unrealized Profits in Prior Year

Springdale Corporation holds 75 percent of the voting shares of Holiday Services Company. During 20X7, Springdale sold inventory costing $60,000 to Holiday Services for $90,000, and Holiday Services resold one-third of the inventory in 20X7. The remaining inventory was resold in 20X8. Also in 20X7, Holiday Services sold land with a book value of $140,000 to Springdale for $240,000. Springdale continues to hold the land at the end of 20X8. The companies file separate tax returns and are subject to a 40 percent tax rate.

Required

Give the consolidation entries relating to the intercorporate sale of inventories and land needed in the consolidation worksheet at the end of 20X8. Assume that Springdale uses the equity method in accounting for its investment in Holiday Services.

LO 10-3

E10-13 Allocation of Income Tax Expense

Winter Corporation owns 80 percent of Ray Guard Corporation's stock and 90 percent of Block Company's stock. The companies file a consolidated tax return each year and in 20X5 paid a total tax of $80,000. Each company is involved in a number of intercompany inventory transfers each period. Information on the companies' activities for 20X5 is as follows:

Company	20X5 Reported Operating Income	20X4 Intercompany Profit Realized in 20X5	20X5 Intercompany Profit Not Realized in 20X5
Winter Corporation	$100,000	$40,000	$10,000
Ray Guard Corporation	50,000		20,000
Block Company	30,000	20,000	10,000

Required

a. Determine the amount of income tax expense that should be assigned to each company.

b. Compute consolidated net income and income to the controlling interest for 20X5. (*Note:* Winter Corporation does not record income tax expense on income from subsidiaries because a consolidated tax return is filed.)

LO 10-4

E10-14 Effect of Preferred Stock on Earnings per Share

Amber Corporation holds 70 percent of Newtop Company's voting common shares but none of its preferred shares. Summary balance sheets for the companies on December 31, 20X1, are as follows:

	Amber Corporation	Newtop Company
Cash	$ 14,000	$ 30,000
Accounts Receivable	40,000	50,000
Inventory	110,000	80,000
Buildings & Equipment	280,000	200,000
Less: Accumulated Depreciation	(130,000)	(60,000)
Investment in Newtop Company	126,000	
Total Assets	$440,000	$300,000
Accounts Payable	$ 70,000	$ 70,000
Wages Payable	40,000	
Preferred Stock	100,000	50,000
Common Stock ($10 par value)	120,000	100,000
Retained Earnings	110,000	80,000
Total Liabilities & Owners' Equity	$440,000	$300,000

Neither of the preferred issues is convertible. Amber's preferred pays a 9 percent annual dividend and Newtop's preferred pays a 10 percent dividend. Newtop reported net income of $45,000 and paid a total of $20,000 of dividends in 20X1. Amber reported $59,000 of income from its separate operations and paid total dividends of $45,000 in 20X1.

Required

Compute 20X1 consolidated EPS. Ignore any tax consequences.

LO 10-4

E10-15 Effect of Convertible Bonds on Earnings per Share

Crystal Corporation owns 60 percent of Evans Company's common shares. Balance sheet data for the companies on December 31, 20X2, are as follows:

	Crystal Corporation	Evans Company
Cash	$ 85,000	$ 30,000
Accounts Receivable	80,000	50,000
Inventory	120,000	100,000
Buildings & Equipment	700,000	400,000
Less: Accumulated Depreciation	(240,000)	(80,000)
Investment in Evans Company Stock	150,000	
Total Assets	$895,000	$500,000

(continued)

Accounts Payable	$145,000	$ 50,000
Bonds Payable	250,000	200,000
Common Stock ($10 par value)	300,000	100,000
Retained Earnings	200,000	150,000
Total Liabilities & Owners' Equity	$895,000	$500,000

The bonds of Crystal Corporation and Evans Company pay annual interest of 8 percent and 10 percent, respectively. Crystal's bonds are not convertible. Evans' bonds can be converted into 10,000 shares of its company stock any time after January 1, 20X1. An income tax rate of 40 percent is applicable to both companies. Evans reports net income of $30,000 for 20X2 and pays dividends of $15,000. Crystal reports income from its separate operations of $45,000 and pays dividends of $25,000.

Required

Compute basic and diluted EPS for the consolidated entity for 20X2.

LO 10-4 **E10-16 Effect of Convertible Preferred Stock on Earnings per Share**

Eagle Corporation holds 80 percent of Standard Company's common shares. The companies report the following balance sheet data for December 31, 20X1:

	Eagle Corporation	Standard Company
Cash	$ 50,000	$ 40,000
Accounts Receivable	80,000	60,000
Inventory	140,000	90,000
Buildings & Equipment	700,000	300,000
Less: Accumulated Depreciation	(280,000)	(140,000)
Investment in Standard Company Stock	160,000	
Total Assets	$850,000	$350,000
Accounts Payable	$120,000	$ 50,000
Taxes Payable	80,000	
Preferred Stock ($10 par value)	200,000	100,000
Common Stock:		
$10 par value	100,000	
$5 par value		50,000
Retained Earnings	350,000	150,000
Total Liabilities & Owners' Equity	$850,000	$350,000

An 8 percent annual dividend is paid on the Eagle preferred stock and a 12 percent dividend is paid on the Standard preferred stock. Eagle's preferred shares are not convertible. Standard's preferred shares can be converted into 15,000 shares of common stock at any time. For 20X1, Standard reports $45,000 of net income and pays total dividends of $20,000, and Eagle reports $60,000 of income from its separate operations and pays total dividends of $35,000.

Required

Compute basic and diluted EPS for the consolidated entity for 20X1.

PROBLEMS

LO 10-1 **P10-17 Direct Method Computation of Cash Flows**

Car Corporation owns 70 percent of the voting common stock of Bus Company. At December 31, 20X1, the companies reported the following:

	Car Corporation	Bus Company
Sales, 20X1	$400,000	$240,000
Cost of goods sold, 20X1	235,000	105,000
Increase (decrease) in 20X1:		
Inventory	(22,000)	16,000
Accounts receivable	9,000	(2,000)
Accounts payable	(31,000)	15,000

During 20X1, Bus sold inventory costing $70,000 to Car for $100,000, and Car resold 40 percent of the inventory prior to December 31, 20X1. No intercompany inventory transactions occurred prior to 20X1, nor did intercompany receivables and payables exist at December 31, 20X1.

Required

Using the direct method, prepare the cash flows from the operating activities section of the consolidated statement of cash flows for 20X1 in good form.

LO 10-1

P10-18 Preparing a Statement of Cash Flows

Metal Corporation acquired 75 percent ownership of Ocean Company on January 1, 20X1, at underlying book value. At that date, the fair value of the noncontrolling interest was equal to 25 percent of the book value of Ocean Company. Consolidated balance sheets at January 1, 20X3, and December 31, 20X3, are as follows:

Item	Jan. 1, 20X3	Dec. 31, 20X3
Cash	$ 68,500	$100,500
Accounts Receivable	82,000	97,000
Inventory	115,000	123,000
Land	45,000	55,000
Buildings & Equipment	515,000	550,000
Less: Accumulated Depreciation	(186,500)	(223,000)
Patents	5,000	4,000
Total Assets	$644,000	$706,500
Accounts Payable	$ 61,000	$ 66,000
Wages Payable	26,000	20,000
Notes Payable	250,000	265,000
Common Stock ($10 par value)	150,000	150,000
Retained Earnings	130,000	174,500
Noncontrolling Interest	27,000	31,000
Total Liabilities & Owners' Equity	$644,000	$706,500

The consolidated income statement for 20X3 contained the following amounts:

Sales		$490,000
Cost of Goods Sold	$259,000	
Wage Expense	55,000	
Depreciation Expense	36,500	
Interest Expense	16,000	
Amortization Expense	1,000	
Other Expenses	39,000	(406,500)
Consolidated Net Income		$ 83,500
Income to Noncontrolling Interest		(9,000)
Income to Controlling Interest		$ 74,500

Metal and Ocean paid dividends of $30,000 and $20,000, respectively, in 20X3.

Required

a. Prepare a worksheet to develop a consolidated statement of cash flows for 20X3 using the indirect method of computing cash flows from operations.

b. Prepare a consolidated statement of cash flows for 20X3.

LO 10-1

P10-19 Preparing a Statement of Cash Flows—Direct Method

Required

Using the data presented in P10-18:

a. Prepare a worksheet to develop a consolidated statement of cash flows for 20X3 using the direct method of computing cash flows from operations.

b. Prepare a consolidated statement of cash flows for 20X3.

LO 10-1

P10-20 Consolidated Statement of Cash Flows

Traper Company holds 80 percent ownership of Arrow Company. The consolidated balance sheets as of December 31, 20X3, and December 31, 20X4, are as follows:

	Dec. 31, 20X3	Dec. 31, 20X4
Cash	$ 83,000	$ 181,000
Accounts Receivable	210,000	175,000
Inventory	320,000	370,000
Land	190,000	160,000
Buildings & Equipment	850,000	980,000
Less: Accumulated Depreciation	(280,000)	(325,000)
Goodwill	40,000	28,000
Total Assets	$1,413,000	$1,569,000
Accounts Payable	$ 52,000	$ 74,000
Interest Payable	45,000	30,000
Bonds Payable	400,000	500,000
Bond Premium	18,000	16,000
Noncontrolling Interest	40,000	44,000
Common Stock	300,000	300,000
Additional Paid-In Capital	70,000	70,000
Retained Earnings	488,000	535,000
Total Liabilities & Owners' Equity	$1,413,000	$1,569,000

The 20X4 consolidated income statement contained the following amounts:

Sales		$600,000
Cost of Goods Sold	$375,000	
Depreciation Expense	45,000	
Interest Expense	69,000	
Loss on Sale of Land	20,000	
Goodwill Impairment Loss	12,000	(521,000)
Consolidated Net Income		$ 79,000
Income to Noncontrolling Interest		(7,000)
Income to Controlling Interest		$ 72,000

Traper acquired its investment in Arrow on January 1, 20X2, for $176,000. At that date, the fair value of the noncontrolling interest was $44,000, and Arrow reported net assets of $150,000. A total of $40,000 of the differential was assigned to goodwill. The remainder of the differential was assigned to equipment with a remaining life of 20 years from the date of combination.

Traper sold $100,000 of bonds on December 31, 20X4, to assist in generating additional funds. Arrow reported net income of $35,000 for 20X4 and paid dividends of $15,000. Traper reported 20X4 equity-method net income of $80,000 and paid dividends of $25,000.

Required

a. Prepare a worksheet to develop a consolidated statement of cash flows for 20X4 using the indirect method of computing cash flows from operations.

b. Prepare a consolidated statement of cash flows for 20X4.

LO 10-1

P10-21 Consolidated Statement of Cash Flows—Direct Method

Required

Using the data presented in P10-20:

a. Prepare a worksheet to develop a consolidated statement of cash flows for 20X4 using the direct method of computing cash flows from operations.

b. Prepare a consolidated statement of cash flows for 20X4.

LO 10-1

P10-22 Consolidated Statement of Cash Flows

Sun Corporation was created on January 1, 20X2, and quickly became successful. On January 1, 20X6, its owner sold 80 percent of the stock to Weatherbee Company at underlying book value. At the date of that sale, the fair value of the remaining shares was equal to 20 percent of the book value of Weatherbee. Weatherbee continued to operate the subsidiary as a separate legal entity and used the equity method in accounting for its investment in Sun. The following consolidated financial statements have been prepared:

WEATHERBEE COMPANY AND SUBSIDIARY
Consolidated Balance Sheets

	January 1, 20X6	December 31, 20X6
Cash	$ 54,000	$ 75,000
Accounts Receivable	121,000	111,000
Inventory	230,000	360,000
Land	95,000	100,000
Buildings & Equipment	800,000	650,000
Less: Accumulated Depreciation	(290,000)	(230,000)
Total Assets	$1,010,000	$1,066,000
Accounts Payable	$ 90,000	$ 105,000
Bonds Payable	300,000	250,000
Noncontrolling Interest	30,000	38,000
Common Stock	300,000	300,000
Retained Earnings	290,000	373,000
Total Liabilities & Owners' Equity	$1,010,000	$1,066,000

WEATHERBEE COMPANY AND SUBSIDIARY
Consolidated Income Statement
Year Ended December 31, 20X6

Sales	$1,070,000
Gain on Sale of Equipment	30,000
	$1,100,000
Cost of Goods Sold	$ 750,000
Depreciation Expense	40,000
Other Expenses	150,000
Total Expenses	$ (940,000)
Consolidated Net Income	$ 160,000
Income to Noncontrolling Interest	(12,000)
Income to Controlling Interest	$ 148,000

WEATHERBEE COMPANY AND SUBSIDIARY
Consolidated Retained Earnings Statement
Year Ended December 31, 20X6

Balance, January 1, 20X6	$290,000
Income to Controlling Interest	148,000
	$438,000
Dividends Declared, 20X6	(65,000)
Balance, December 31, 20X6	$373,000

During 20X6, Sun reported net income of $60,000 and paid dividends of $20,000; Weatherbee reported net income of $148,000 and paid dividends of $65,000. There were no intercompany transfers during the period.

Required

Prepare a worksheet for a consolidated statement of cash flows for 20X6 using the indirect method of computing cash flows from operations.

LO 10-1

P10-23 Consolidated Statement of Cash Flows—Direct Method

Required

Using the data presented in P10-22, prepare a worksheet to develop a consolidated statement of cash flows using the direct method for computing cash flows from operations.

LO 10-1

P10-24 Consolidated Statement of Cash Flows [AICPA Adapted]

Following are the consolidated balance sheet accounts of Brimer Inc. and its subsidiary, Dore Corporation, as of December 31, 20X6 and 20X5.

	20X6	20X5	Net Increase (Decrease)
Assets			
Cash	$ 313,000	$ 195,000	$118,000
Marketable Equity Securities, at cost	175,000	175,000	0
Allowance to Reduce Marketable Equity Securities to Market	(13,000)	(24,000)	11,000
Accounts Receivable, net	418,000	440,000	(22,000)
Inventories	595,000	525,000	70,000
Land	385,000	170,000	215,000
Plant & Equipment	755,000	690,000	65,000
Accumulated Depreciation	(199,000)	(145,000)	(54,000)
Goodwill, net	57,000	60,000	(3,000)
Total Assets	$2,486,000	$2,086,000	$400,000
Liabilities & Stockholders' Equity			
Current Portion of Long-Term Note	$ 150,000	$ 150,000	$ 0
Accounts Payable and Accrued Liabilities	595,000	474,000	121,000
Note Payable, Long-Term	300,000	450,000	(150,000)
Deferred Income Taxes	44,000	32,000	12,000
Minority Interest in Net Assets of Subsidiary	179,000	161,000	18,000
Common Stock, par $10	580,000	480,000	100,000
Additional Paid-In Capital	303,000	180,000	123,000
Retained Earnings	335,000	195,000	140,000
Treasury Stock, at cost	0	(36,000)	36,000
Total Liabilities & Stockholders' Equity	$2,486,000	$2,086,000	$400,000

Additional Information

1. On January 20, 20X6, Brimer issued 10,000 shares of its common stock for land having a fair value of $215,000.
2. On February 5, 20X6, Brimer reissued all of its treasury stock for $44,000.

3. On May 15, 20X6, Brimer paid a $58,000 cash dividend on its common stock.
4. On August 8, 20X6, Brimer purchased equipment for $127,000.
5. On September 30, 20X6, Brimer sold equipment for $40,000. The equipment cost $62,000 and had a carrying amount of $34,000 on the date of sale.
6. On December 15, 20X6, Dore paid a cash dividend of $50,000 on its common stock.
7. A Dore recognized goodwill impairment loss of $3,000 in 20X6.
8. Deferred income taxes represent temporary differences relating to the use of accelerated depreciation methods for income tax reporting and the straight-line method for financial reporting.
9. Net income for 20X6 was as follows:

Consolidated net income	$231,000
Dore Corporation	110,000

10. Brimer owns 70 percent of its subsidiary, Dore. No change in the ownership interest in Dore occurred during 20X5 and 20X6. No intercompany transactions occurred other than the dividend paid to Brimer Inc. by its subsidiary.

Required

Prepare a consolidated statement of cash flows for Brimer Inc. and its subsidiary for the year ended December 31, 20X6, using the indirect method.

LO 10-1

P10-25 Statement of Cash Flows Prepared from Consolidation Worksheet

Detecto Corporation purchased 60 percent of Strand Company's outstanding shares on January 1, 20X1, for $24,000 more than book value. At that date, the fair value of the noncontrolling interest was $16,000 more than 40 percent of Strand's book value. The full amount of the differential is considered related to patents and is being amortized over an eight-year period. In 20X1, Strand purchased a piece of land for $35,000 and later in the year sold it to Detecto for $45,000. Detecto is still holding the land as an investment. During 20X3, Detecto bonds with a value of $100,000 were exchanged for equipment valued at $100,000.

On January 1, 20X3, Detecto held inventory purchased previously from Strand for $48,000. During 20X3, Detecto purchased an additional $90,000 of goods from Strand and held $54,000 of this inventory on December 31, 20X3. Strand sells merchandise to the parent at cost plus a 20 percent markup.

Strand also purchases inventory items from Detecto. On January 1, 20X3, Strand held inventory it had previously purchased from Detecto for $14,000, and on December 31, 20X3, it held goods it had purchased from Detecto for $7,000 during 20X3. Strand's total purchases from Detecto in 20X3 were $22,000. Detecto sells inventory to Strand at cost plus a 40 percent markup.

The consolidated balance sheet at December 31, 20X2, contained the following amounts:

	Debit	Credit
Cash	$ 92,000	
Accounts Receivable	135,000	
Inventory	140,000	
Land	75,000	
Buildings & Equipment	400,000	
Patents	30,000	
Accumulated Depreciation		$210,000
Accounts Payable		114,200
Bonds Payable		90,000
Noncontrolling Interest		84,800
Common Stock		100,000
Retained Earnings		273,000
Totals	$872,000	$872,000

The following consolidation worksheet was prepared on December 31, 20X3. All consolidation entries and adjustments have been entered properly in the worksheet. Detecto accounts for its investment in Strand using the fully adjusted equity method.

Required

a. Prepare a worksheet for a consolidated statement of cash flows for 20X3 using the indirect method.

b. Prepare a consolidated statement of cash flows for 20X3.

DETECTO CORPORATION AND STRAND COMPANY
Consolidation Worksheet
December 31, 20X3

	Detecto Corporation	Strand Company	Consolidation Entries		Consolidated
			DR	CR	
Income Statement					
Sales	400,000	200,000	**90,000** **22,000**		488,000
Less: Cost of Goods Sold	(280,000)	(120,000)		**8,000** **81,000** **4,000** **20,000**	(287,000)
Less: Depreciation Expense	(25,000)	(15,000)			(40,000)
Less: Amortization Expense			**5,000**		(5,000)
Less: Other Expense	(35,000)	(30,000)			(65,000)
Income from Strand Co.	19,400		**22,400**	**3,000**	0
Consolidated Net Income	**79,400**	**35,000**	139,400	116,000	**91,000**
NCI in Net Income of Strand			**13,600**	**2,000**	(11,600)
Controlling Interest in Net Income	**79,400**	**35,000**	**153,000**	**118,000**	**79,400**
Statement of Retained Earnings					
Beginning Balance	273,000	150,000	**150,000**		273,000
Net Income	**79,400**	**35,000**	**153,000**	**118,000**	79,400
Less: Dividends Declared	(50,000)	(20,000)		**20,000**	(50,000)
Ending Balance	**302,400**	**165,000**	**303,000**	**138,000**	**302,400**
Balance Sheet					
Cash	26,800	35,000			61,800
Accounts Receivable	80,000	40,000			120,000
Inventory	120,000	90,000		**9,000** **2,000**	199,000
Patent			**25,000**		25,000
Investment in Subsidiary	130,600		**6,000** **4,800** **4,000**	**130,400** **15,000**	0
Land	70,000	20,000		**10,000**	80,000
Buildings & Equipment	340,000	200,000		**20,000**	520,000
Less: Accumulated Depreciation	(165,000)	(85,000)	**20,000**		(230,000) 0
Total Assets	**602,400**	**300,000**	**59,800**	**186,400**	**775,800**
Accounts Payable	80,000	15,000			95,000
Bonds Payable	120,000	70,000			190,000
Common Stock	100,000	50,000	**50,000**		100,000
Retained Earnings	**302,400**	**165,000**	**303,000**	**138,000**	**302,400**
NCI in NA of Strand			**4,000** **3,200**	**85,600** **10,000**	88,400
Total Liabilities & Equity	**602,400**	**300,000**	**360,200**	**233,600**	**775,800**

LO 10-2

P10-26 Midyear Purchase of Controlling Interest

Blase Company operates on a calendar-year basis, reporting its results of operations quarterly. For the first quarter of 20X1, Blase reported sales of $240,000 and operating expenses of $180,000 and paid dividends of $10,000. On April 1, 20X1, Mega Theaters Inc. acquired 85 percent of Blase's common stock for $765,000. At that date, the fair value of the noncontrolling interest was $135,000, and Blase had 100,000 outstanding shares of $1 par common stock, originally issued at $6 per share. The differential is related to goodwill. On December 31, 20X1, the management of Mega Theaters reviewed the amount attributed to goodwill as a result of its purchase of Blase common stock and concluded that goodwill was not impaired.

Blase's retained earnings statement for the full year 20X1 appears as follows:

Retained Earnings, January 1, 20X1	$150,000
Net Income	175,000
Dividends	(40,000)
Retained Earnings, December 31, 20X1	$285,000

Mega Theaters accounts for its investment in Blase using the equity method.

Required

a. Present all entries that Mega Theaters would have recorded in accounting for its investment in Blase during 20X1.

b. Present all consolidation entries needed in a worksheet to prepare a complete set of consolidated financial statements for the year 20X1.

LO 10-2

P10-27 Consolidation Involving a Midyear Purchase

Famous Products Corporation acquired 90 percent ownership of Sanford Company on October 20, 20X2, through an exchange of voting shares. Famous Products issued 8,000 shares of its $10 par stock to acquire 27,000 shares of Sanford's $5 par stock. The market value of shares issued by Famous Products was $247,500. At that date, the fair value of the noncontrolling interest was $27,500. Trial balances of the two companies on December 31, 20X2, are as follows:

	Famous Products Corporation		Sanford Company	
	Debit	**Credit**	**Debit**	**Credit**
Cash	$ 85,000		$ 50,000	
Accounts Receivable	100,000		60,000	
Inventory	150,000		100,000	
Buildings & Equipment	400,000		340,000	
Investment in Sanford Stock	252,000			
Cost of Goods Sold	305,000		145,000	
Depreciation Expense	25,000		20,000	
Other Expense	14,000		25,000	
Dividends Declared	40,000		30,000	
Accumulated Depreciation		$ 105,000		$ 65,000
Accounts Payable		40,000		50,000
Taxes Payable		70,000		55,000
Bonds Payable		250,000		100,000
Common Stock		200,000		150,000
Additional Paid-In Capital		167,500		
Retained Earnings		135,000		100,000
Sales		390,000		250,000
Income from Sanford Co.		13,500		
Totals	$1,371,000	$1,371,000	$770,000	$770,000

For 20X2, before acquisition, Sanford reported sales of $205,000, cost of goods sold of $126,000, depreciation of $16,000, and other expenses of $18,000. Sanford paid dividends of $20,000 in

April and $10,000 in November 20X2. Famous Products, which paid dividends of $40,000 in 20X2, uses the equity method in accounting for its investment in Sanford.

Required

a. Give all journal entries recorded by Famous Products during 20X2 that relate to its investment in Sanford.

b. Give the worksheet consolidation entries needed on December 31, 20X2, to prepare consolidated financial statements.

c. Prepare a three-part consolidation worksheet as of December 31, 20X2.

LO 10-3

P10-28 Deferred Tax Assets and Liabilities in a Consolidated Balance Sheet

Peace Corporation acquired 100 percent of Harmony Inc. in a nontaxable transaction on December 31, 20X1. The following balance sheet information is available immediately following the transaction:

	Peace Corporation		Harmony Inc.	
	Book Value	Fair Values	Book Value	Fair Value
Cash	$ 30,000	$ 30,000	$ 8,000	$ 8,000
Accounts Receivable, net	50,000	50,000	12,000	12,000
Inventory	75,000	82,000	7,000	10,000
Deferred Tax Asset	8,000		1,000	?
Investment in Harmony	60,000	60,000		
Equipment, net	160,000	195,000	25,000	40,000
Patent			0	20,000
Total Assets	$383,000		$53,000	
Accounts Payable	$ 62,000	$ 62,000	$13,000	$13,000
Accrued Vacation Payable	15,000	15,000		
Deferred Tax Liability	6,000		2,000	?
Long-Term Debt	100,000	110,000	8,000	8,000
Common Stock	150,000		20,000	
Retained Earnings	50,000		10,000	
Total Liabilities & Equity	$383,000		$53,000	

Additional Information

1. The current and future effective tax rate for both Peace and Harmony is 40 percent.
2. The recorded deferred tax asset for Peace relates to the book-tax differences arising from the allowance for doubtful accounts and the accrued vacation payable. The expenses associated with each of these amounts will not be deductible for tax purposes until the related accounts receivable are written off or until the employee vacation is actually paid out.
3. The recorded deferred tax asset for Harmony is related solely to the book-tax differences arising from the allowance for doubtful accounts.
4. The recorded deferred tax liability in both Peace and Harmony relates solely to the book-tax differences arising from the depreciation of their respective equipment.
5. Accumulated depreciation on the financial accounting records of Peace and Harmony is $40,000 and $10,000, respectively.
6. The Harmony patent was identified by Peace in the due diligence process and has not previously been recorded in the accounting records of Harmony.
7. The book and tax bases of all other assets and liabilities of Peace and Harmony are the same.

Required

a. Compute the tax bases of the assets and liabilities for Peace and Harmony, where different from the amounts recorded in the respective accounting records.

b. Compute the fair value of the deferred tax assets and deferred tax liabilities for Harmony.

c. Prepare all of the consolidation entries needed to prepare the worksheet for Peace and Harmony at the date of acquisition.

d. Prepare the consolidation worksheet for Peace and Harmony at the date of acquisition.

LO 10-3

P10-29 Tax Allocation in Consolidated Balance Sheet

Acme Powder Corporation acquired 70 percent of Brown Company's stock on December 31, 20X7, at underlying book value. At that date, the fair value of the noncontrolling interest was equal to 30 percent of Brown Company's book value. The two companies' balance sheets on December 31, 20X9, are as follows:

ACME POWDER CORPORATION AND BROWN COMPANY
Balance Sheets
December 31, 20X9

	Acme Powder Corporation	Brown Company
Cash	$ 44,400	$ 20,000
Accounts Receivable	120,000	60,000
Inventory	170,000	120,000
Land	90,000	30,000
Buildings & Equipment	500,000	300,000
Less: Accumulated Depreciation	(180,000)	(80,000)
Investment in Brown Company Stock	235,600	
Total Assets	$980,000	$450,000
Accounts Payable	$ 70,000	$ 20,000
Wages Payable	80,000	30,000
Bonds Payable	200,000	
Common Stock	100,000	150,000
Retained Earnings	530,000	250,000
Total Liabilities & Equity	$980,000	$450,000

On December 31, 20X9, Acme Powder holds inventory purchased from Brown for $70,000. Brown's cost of producing the merchandise was $50,000. Brown also had purchased inventory from Acme. Brown's ending inventory contains $85,000 of purchases that had cost Acme Powder $60,000 to produce.

On December 30, 20X9, Brown sells equipment to Acme Powder for $90,000. Brown had purchased the equipment for $120,000 several years earlier. At the time of sale to Acme, the equipment had a book value of $40,000. The two companies file separate tax returns and are subject to a 40 percent tax rate. Acme Powder does not record tax expense on its share of Brown's undistributed earnings.

Required

a. Complete a consolidated balance sheet worksheet as of December 31, 20X9.

b. Prepare a consolidated balance sheet as of December 31, 20X9.

LO 10-3

P10-30 Computations Involving Tax Allocation

Broom Manufacturing used cash to acquire 75 percent of the voting stock of Satellite Industries on January 1, 20X3, at underlying book value. At that date, the fair value of the noncontrolling interest was equal to 25 percent of Satellite's book value. Broom accounts for its investment in Satellite using the equity method.

Broom had no inventory on hand on January 1, 20X5. During 20X5, Broom purchased $300,000 of goods from Satellite and had $100,000 remaining on hand at the end of 20X5. Satellite normally prices its items so that their cost is 70 percent of sale price. On January 1, 20X5, Satellite held inventory that it had purchased from Broom for $50,000. Broom's cost of producing the items was $30,000. Satellite sold all of the merchandise in 20X5 and made no inventory purchases from Broom during 20X5.

On July 15, 20X5, Satellite sold land that it had purchased for $240,000 to Broom for $360,000. The companies file separate tax returns and have a 40 percent income tax rate. Broom does not record tax expense on its portion of Satellite's undistributed earnings. Tax expense recorded by Broom in 20X5 with regard to its investment in Satellite is based on dividends received from Satellite in 20X5. In computing taxable income, 80 percent of intercorporate dividend payments are exempt from tax.

Satellite reported net income of $190,000 for 20X5 and net assets of $900,000 on December 31, 20X5. Broom's reported income before investment income from Satellite and income tax expense of $700,000 for 20X5. Satellite and Broom paid dividends of $150,000 and $400,000, respectively, in 20X5.

Required

a. Give the journal entries recorded on Broom's books during 20X5 to reflect its ownership of Satellite.

b. Compute the income assigned to the noncontrolling interests in the 20X5 consolidated income statement.

c. Compute consolidated net income and income to the controlling interest for 20X5.

d. Compute the amount assigned to the noncontrolling interest in the consolidated balance sheet prepared as of December 31, 20X5.

LO 10-3

P10-31 Worksheet Involving Tax Allocation

Hardtack Bread Company holds 70 percent of the common shares of Custom Pizza Corporation. Trial balances for the two companies on December 31, 20X7, are as follows:

	Hardtack Bread Company		Custom Pizza Corporation	
Item	**Debit**	**Credit**	**Debit**	**Credit**
Cash	$ 35,800		$ 56,000	
Accounts Receivable	130,000		40,000	
Inventory	220,000		60,000	
Land	60,000		20,000	
Buildings & Equipment	450,000		400,000	
Patents	70,000			
Investment in Custom Pizza Common Stock	138,700			
Cost of Goods Sold	435,000		210,000	
Depreciation & Amortization	40,000		20,000	
Tax Expense	44,000		24,000	
Other Expenses	11,400		10,000	
Dividends Declared	20,000		10,000	
Accumulated Depreciation		$ 150,000		$160,000
Accounts Payable		40,000		30,000
Wages Payable		70,000		20,000
Bonds Payable		200,000		100,000
Deferred Income Taxes		120,000		40,000
Common Stock ($10 par value)		100,000		50,000
Retained Earnings		370,000		150,000
Sales		580,000		300,000
Income from Custom Pizza		9,900		
Gain on Sale of Equipment		15,000		
Total	$1,654,900	$1,654,900	$850,000	$850,000

At the beginning of 20X7, Hardtack held inventory purchased from Custom Pizza containing unrealized profits of $10,000. During 20X7, Hardtack purchased $120,000 of inventory from Custom Pizza and on December 31, 20X7, had goods on hand containing $25,000 of unrealized intercompany profit. On December 31, 20X7, Hardtack sold equipment to Custom Pizza for $65,000. Hardtack had purchased the equipment for $150,000 and had accumulated depreciation of $100,000 on it at the time of sale. The companies file separate tax returns and are subject to a 40 percent income tax rate on all taxable income. Intercompany dividends are 80 percent exempt from taxation.

Required

a. Prepare all consolidation entries needed as of December 31, 20X7, to prepare consolidated financial statements for Hardtack Bread Company and its subsidiary.

b. Prepare a consolidation worksheet for 20X7.

LO 10-4

P10-32 Earnings per Share with Convertible Securities

Branch Manufacturing Corporation owns 80 percent of the common shares of Short Retail Stores. The companies' balance sheets as of December 31, 20X4, were as follows:

	Branch Manufacturing Corporation	Short Retail Stores
Cash	$ 50,000	$ 30,000
Accounts Receivable	100,000	80,000
Inventory	260,000	120,000
Land	90,000	60,000
Buildings & Equipment	500,000	300,000
Less: Accumulated Depreciation	(220,000)	(120,000)
Investment in Short Retail Stores Stock	120,000	
Total Assets	$900,000	$470,000
Accounts Payable	$ 40,000	$ 20,000
Bonds Payable	300,000	200,000
Preferred Stock ($10 par value)	200,000	100,000
Common Stock:		
$10 par value	150,000	
$5 par value		100,000
Retained Earnings	210,000	50,000
Total Liabilities & Equity	$900,000	$470,000

Short Retail's 8 percent preferred stock is convertible into 12,000 shares of common stock, and its 10 percent bonds are convertible into 8,000 shares of common stock. Short reported net income of $49,200 for 20X4 and paid dividends of $30,000.

Branch Manufacturing has 11 percent preferred stock and 12 percent bonds outstanding, neither of which is convertible. Branch reported after-tax income, excluding investment income from Short, of $100,000 in 20X4 and paid dividends of $60,000. The companies file separate tax returns and are subject to a 40 percent income tax.

Required

Compute basic and diluted EPS for the consolidated entity.

LO 10-4

P10-33 Comprehensive Earnings per Share

Mighty Corporation holds 80 percent of Longfellow Company's common stock. The following balance sheet data are presented for December 31, 20X7:

	Mighty Corporation	Longfellow Company
Cash	$ 100,000	$ 90,000
Accounts Receivable	150,000	220,000
Inventory	300,000	300,000
Land	100,000	290,000
Buildings & Equipment	2,250,000	900,000
Less: Accumulated Depreciation	(850,000)	(250,000)
Investment in Longfellow Company Stock	600,000	
Total Assets	$2,650,000	$1,550,000

(continued)

Accounts Payable	$ 200,000	$ 100,000
Bonds Payable	800,000	500,000
Preferred Stock ($100 par value)		200,000
Common Stock ($10 par value)	1,000,000	400,000
Retained Earnings	650,000	350,000
Total Liabilities & Equities	$2,650,000	$1,550,000

Longfellow reported net income of $115,000 in 20X7 and paid dividends of $60,000. Its bonds have an annual interest rate of 8 percent and are convertible into 30,000 common shares. Its preferred shares pay an 11 percent annual dividend and convert into 20,000 shares of common stock. In addition, Longfellow has warrants outstanding for 10,000 shares of common stock at $8 per share. The 20X7 average price of Longfellow common shares was $40.

Mighty reported income of $300,000 from its own operations for 20X7 and paid dividends of $200,000. Its 10 percent bonds convert into 25,000 shares of its common stock. The companies file separate tax returns and are subject to income taxes of 40 percent.

Required

Compute basic and diluted EPS for the consolidated entity for 20X7.

11 Multinational Accounting: Foreign Currency Transactions and Financial Instruments

- Multicorporate Entities
- **Multinational Entities**
  - **Foreign Currency Transactions**
  - Translation of Foreign Statements
- Reporting Requirements
- Partnerships
- Governmental and Not-for-Profit Entities
- Corporations in Financial Difficulty

MICROSOFT'S MULTINATIONAL BUSINESS

Microsoft was founded in 1975 by Bill Gates (a Harvard dropout) and Paul Allen (a Washington State University dropout). In 1980, Microsoft teamed up with IBM, and in 1981, the company released the first version of MS DOS for IBM PCs. The year 1983 was another big year for Microsoft with the release of Multi-Tool Word (later Microsoft Word). The first version of Microsoft Windows (Windows 1.0) was released two years later in 1985. When Microsoft went public in 1986, its shares began trading at $21 and closed that first day at $28. Interestingly, each of those original shares issued in 1986 would be worth approximately $11,300 today. At its peak, Microsoft was worth approximately $600 billion and Bill Gates was personally worth close to $90 billion.

Since Microsoft's IPO in 1986, it has continued to update Windows. For most of its history, Microsoft has dominated the PC operating system industry. However, Satya Nadella, Microsoft's new CEO, stated in 2014 that Microsoft must learn how to thrive in a mobile and cloud first world. In order to compete in the ever-growing "mobile-first, cloud-first" world, Microsoft launched Windows 8 on October 26, 2012, an operating system designed to power both personal computers and tablet computers. To go along with Windows 8, Microsoft also launched the Microsoft Surface, a tablet-computer hybrid, the first computer in the company's history to have its hardware made by Microsoft. Three days later Microsoft released Windows Phone 8 and on September 3, 2013, Microsoft agreed to buy Nokia's mobile unit for $7 billion, signaling Microsoft's complete move into the mobile computing world. Finally, on March 27, 2014, Microsoft released its Microsoft Office Suite for the iPad.

Right from the start, Microsoft saw the international market as an important part of its expansion. In fact, the company opened its first international office in Tokyo in 1978 and by 2013 more than 56 percent of Microsoft's total revenues came from international sales and services. Because such a large portion of Microsoft's business comes from foreign markets, the company necessarily engages in hedging activities to protect itself from the risks associated with fluctuations in foreign currency exchange rates. Microsoft's 2013 10-K report indicates that the principal currencies hedged include the euro, Japanese yen, British pound, and Canadian dollar. As of June 30, 2013, and June 30, 2012, the total notional amounts (face values) of these foreign exchange contracts were $5.1 billion and $6.7 billion, respectively. Thus, it is clear that managing foreign currency exchange risks is an integral part of Microsoft's business. This chapter explores the accounting for foreign currencies and introduces the tools that companies such as Microsoft use to alleviate the risks associated with constantly changing foreign currency exchange rates.

LEARNING OBJECTIVES

When you finish studying this chapter, you should be able to:

LO 11-1 Understand how to make calculations using foreign currency exchange rates.

LO 11-2 Understand the accounting implications of and be able to make calculations related to foreign currency transactions.

LO 11-3 Understand how to hedge international currency risk using foreign currency forward exchange financial instruments.

LO 11-4 Know how to measure hedge effectiveness, make interperiod tax allocations for foreign currency transactions, and hedge net investments in a foreign entity.

DOING BUSINESS IN A GLOBAL MARKET

LO 11-1

Understand how to make calculations using foreign currency exchange rates.

Many companies, large and small, depend on international markets for acquiring goods and for selling their products and services. Every day, the business press carries stories about the effects of export and import activity on the U.S. economy and the large flows of capital among the world's major countries. These reports often mention changes in the exchange rates of the major currencies of the world, such as, "The dollar weakened today against the yen." This chapter and Chapter 12 discuss the accounting issues affecting companies with international operations.

A company operating in international markets is subject to normal business risks such as lack of demand for its products in the foreign marketplace, labor strikes, and transportation delays in getting its products to the foreign customer. In addition, the U.S. entity could incur foreign currency risks whenever it conducts transactions in other currencies. For example, if a U.S. company acquires a machine on credit from an Italian manufacturer, the Italian company could require payment in euros. This means the U.S. company must eventually use a foreign currency broker or a bank to exchange U.S. dollars for euros to pay for the machine. In the process, the U.S. company may experience foreign currency gains or losses from fluctuations in the value of the U.S. dollar relative to the euro.

Foreign exchange markets are among the most important and often misunderstood subjects in international business. Multinational enterprises (MNEs) entering into international transactions must agree with customers and suppliers on the currencies in which these transactions will be executed. Factors that affect this decision include familiarity with the foreign currency, the potential for gains and losses from changes in exchange rates, nationalistic pride, and practicality.

STOP & THINK

How big is the foreign currency exchange market? It has grown into one of the largest financial markets in the world. The average daily volume in global foreign exchange transactions is estimated at $5.3 trillion in April 2013, a growth of approximately 61 percent over the $3.3 trillion daily volume in April 2007. This growth has exposed companies to abundant risk and opportunity, which will become an even larger part of the global economy in the future.

MNEs transact in a variety of currencies as a result of their export and import activities. There are approximately 150 different currencies around the world, but most international trade has been settled in six major currencies that have shown stability and general acceptance over time: the U.S. dollar, the British pound, the Canadian dollar, the Japanese yen, the Swiss franc, and the European euro.

The European euro (symbol €) is a relatively new currency introduced in 1999 to members of the European Union (EU) that wished to participate in a common currency. By 2002, euro notes and coins were introduced to be used in everyday trade. The EU is an organization of democratic member states from the European continent. The Union has grown over time and as of 2014 comprises 28 member countries: Austria, Belgium, Bulgaria, Croatia, Cyprus, Czech Republic, Denmark,

Estonia, Finland, France, Germany, Greece, Hungary, Ireland, Italy, Latvia, Lithuania, Luxembourg, Malta, the Netherlands, Poland, Portugal, Romania, Slovakia, Slovenia, Spain, Sweden, and the United Kingdom. In addition, Iceland, Montenegro, Serbia, the former Yugoslav Republic of Macedonia, and Turkey have applied for accession. The EU is a dominant economic force, rivaling the United States, and the euro is now as familiar to companies doing international business as the U.S. dollar. Currently, 18 of the 28 members of the EU use the euro.

The EU is one of several regional groupings, and these groupings are becoming increasingly important. The North American Free Trade Agreement (NAFTA) was approved by the U.S. Congress and came into force on January 1, 1994. It created a free trade area of Canada, Mexico, and the United States, a market that exceeds 460 million people as of November 2013. Over time, the agreement will result in the elimination of tariffs (taxes) on goods shipped between these three countries. The agreement on the South Asian Free Trade Area, or SAFTA, was created on January 1, 2006, and is operational following ratification of the agreement by the seven governments. SAFTA creates a framework for the creation of a free trade zone covering nearly 2 billion people in Bangladesh, Bhutan, India, the Maldives, Nepal, Pakistan, and Sri Lanka. The Association of Southeast Asian Nations (ASEAN) created the ASEAN Free Trade Area (AFTA), which is a trade bloc agreement. The goal of AFTA is to increase ASEAN's competitive edge as a production base in the world market through the elimination, within ASEAN, of tariffs and nontariff barriers. AFTA currently is composed of Brunei, Cambodia, Indonesia, Laos, Malaysia, Myanmar, Philippines, Singapore, Thailand, and Vietnam. AFTA has a population of approximately 600 million. The Greater Arab Free Trade Area (also referred to as GAFTA) came into existence in 1997, founded by 14 countries: Bahrain, Egypt, Iraq, Kuwait, Lebanon, Libya, Morocco, Oman, Qatar, Saudi Arabia, Sudan, Syria, Tunisia, and the United Arab Emirates. It is a pact made by the Arab League to achieve a complete Arab economic bloc that can compete internationally. GAFTA is relatively similar to ASEAN.

Currency names and symbols often reflect a country's nationalistic pride and history. For example, the U.S. dollar receives its name from a variation of the German word *Taler,* the name of a silver piece that was first minted in 1518 and became the chief coin of Europe and the New World. Some historians suggest that the dollar symbol ($) is derived from a capital letter *U* superimposed over a capital letter *S.* The "greenback" as we know it today was first printed in 1862 during the Civil War, and now is issued by the 12 Federal Reserve banks scattered across the United States. The U.S. dollar can be identified in virtually every corner of the world because it has become one of the most widely traded currencies.

THE ACCOUNTING ISSUES

Accountants must be able to record and report transactions involving exchanges of U.S. dollars and foreign currencies. ***Foreign currency transactions*** of a U.S. company include sales, purchases, and other transactions giving rise to a transfer of foreign currency or the recording of receivables or payables that are *denominated*—that is, numerically specified to be settled—in a foreign currency. Because financial statements of virtually all U.S. companies are prepared using the U.S. dollar as the reporting currency, transactions denominated in other currencies must be restated to their U.S. dollar equivalents before they can be recorded in the U.S. company's books and included in its financial statements. This process of restating foreign currency transactions to their U.S. dollar–equivalent values is termed *translation.*

In addition, many large U.S. corporations have multinational operations such as foreign-based subsidiaries or branches. For example, a U.S. auto manufacturer may have manufacturing subsidiaries in Canada, Mexico, Spain, and Great Britain. The foreign subsidiaries prepare their financial statements in their home currencies. For example, the Mexican subsidiary reports its operations in pesos. The foreign currency amounts in the financial statements of these subsidiaries have to be translated, that is, restated, into their U.S. dollar equivalents before they can be consolidated with the financial statements of the U.S. parent company that uses the U.S. dollar as its reporting currency unit.

This chapter presents the accounting procedures for recording and reporting foreign transactions. Chapter 12 presents the procedures for combining or consolidating a foreign entity with a U.S. parent company. **ASC 830** serves as the primary guide for accounting for accounts receivable and accounts payable transactions that require payment or receipt of foreign currency. **ASC 815** guides the accounting for financial instruments specified as derivatives for the purpose of hedging certain items.

FOREIGN CURRENCY EXCHANGE RATES

Before 1972, most major currencies were valued on the basis of a gold standard whereby their international values were fixed per ounce of gold. However, in 1972, most countries signed an agreement to permit the values of their currencies to "float" based on the supply and demand for them. The resulting ***foreign currency exchange rates*** between currencies are established daily by foreign exchange brokers who serve as agents for individuals or countries wishing to deal in foreign currencies. Some countries, such as China, maintain an official fixed rate of currency exchange and have established fixed exchange rates for dividends remitted outside the country. These official rates may be changed at any time, and companies doing business abroad should contact the foreign country's government to ensure that the companies are in compliance with any currency exchange restrictions.

The Determination of Exchange Rates

A country's currency is much like any other commodity, and exchange rates change because of a number of economic factors affecting the supply of and demand for a nation's currency. For example, if a nation is experiencing high levels of inflation, the purchasing power of its currency decreases. This reduction in the value of a currency is reflected by a decrease in the positioning of that country's currency relative to other nations' currencies. Other factors causing exchange rate fluctuations are a nation's balance of payments, changes in a country's interest rate and investment levels, and the stability and process of governance. For example, if the United States had a higher average interest rate than that in Great Britain, the international investment community might seek to invest in the United States, thus increasing the demand for U.S. dollars relative to British pounds. The dollar would increase in value relative to the pound because of the increased demand. Exchange rates are determined daily and published in several sources, including *The Wall Street Journal,* most business publications, many metropolitan newspapers, and websites such as Yahoo! Finance. Figure 11–1 presents an example of a typical daily business press report for selected foreign exchange rates as of May 1, 2014.

Direct versus Indirect Exchange Rates

As indicated in Figure 11–1, the relative value of one currency to another may be expressed in two different ways: either *directly* or *indirectly.*

Direct Exchange Rate

The direct exchange rate (DER) is the number of ***local currency units (LCUs)*** needed to acquire one ***foreign currency unit (FCU).*** From the viewpoint of a U.S. entity, the direct exchange rate can be viewed as the U.S. dollar cost of one foreign currency unit. The direct exchange rate ratio is expressed as follows, with the LCU, the U.S. dollar, in the numerator:

$$\text{DER} = \frac{\text{U.S. dollar} - \text{equivalent value}}{1\,\text{FCU}}$$

FIGURE 11–1 Foreign Exchange Rates for Selected Major Currencies as of May 1, 2014

Country	Currency	Direct Exchange Rate (U.S. Dollar Equivalent)	Indirect Exchange Rate (Currency per U.S. Dollar)
Argentina	Peso	0.1250	8.0001
Australia	Dollar	0.9274	1.0783
Bahrain	Dinar	2.6527	0.3770
Canada	Dollar	0.9126	1.0958
Chile	Peso	0.0018	564.0000
China	Yuan	0.1598	6.2590
Colombia	Peso	0.0005	1,934.5000
Czech Republic	Koruna	0.0505	19.8000
Denmark	Krone	0.1858	5.3816
Ecuador	US dollar	1.0000	1.0000
Euro Area	Euro	1.3869	0.7210
Egypt	Pound	0.1427	7.0081
Hong Kong	Dollar	0.1290	7.7528
Hungary	Forint	0.0045	221.0600
India	Rupee	0.0166	60.1500
Indonesia	Rupiah	0.0001	11,555.0000
Israel	Shekel	0.2896	3.4528
Japan	Yen	0.0098	102.3200
1-mo forward		0.0098	102.3100
3-mo forward		0.0098	102.2700
6-mo forward		0.0098	102.2100
Jordan	Dinar	1.4123	0.7081
Kenya	Shilling	0.0115	86.9500
Kuwait	Dinar	3.5606	0.2809
Lebanon	Pound	0.0007	1,516.1000
Malaysia	Ringgit	0.3062	3.2659
Mexico	Peso	0.0767	13.0434
New Zealand	Dollar	0.8633	1.1584
Norway	Krone	0.1683	5.9433
Pakistan	Rupee	0.0101	98.6450
Peru	New Sol	0.3561	2.8081
Philippines	Peso	0.0224	44.6100
Poland	Zloty	0.3306	3.0246
Romania	Leu	0.3127	3.1978
Russia	Ruble	0.0281	35.6200
Saudi Arabia	Riyal	0.2666	3.7507
Singapore	Dollar	0.7982	1.2528
South Korea	Won	0.0010	1,032.8000
Sweden	Krona	0.1537	6.5068
Switzerland	Franc	1.1373	0.8793
1-mo forward		1.1376	0.8791
3-mo forward		1.1381	0.8786
6-mo forward		1.1391	0.8779
Taiwan	Dollar	0.0331	30.2560
Thailand	Baht	0.0309	32.3670
Turkey	Lira	0.4749	2.1057
UAE	Dirham	0.2723	3.6731
UK	Pound	1.6893	0.5920
1-mo forward		1.6889	0.5921
3-mo forward		1.6881	0.5924
6-mo forward		1.6867	0.5929
Uruguay	Peso	0.0438	22.8355
Venezuela	Bolivar Fuerte	0.1575	6.3500
Vietnam	Dong	0.0001	21,090.0000

The direct exchange rate is used most often in accounting for foreign operations and transactions because the foreign currency–denominated accounts must be translated to their U.S. dollar–equivalent values. For example, if \$1.20 can acquire €1 (1 European euro), the direct exchange rate of the dollar versus the European euro is \$1.20, as follows:

$$\frac{\$1.20}{€1} = \$1.20$$

Indirect Exchange Rate

The indirect exchange rate (IER) is the reciprocal of the direct exchange rate. From the viewpoint of a U.S. entity, the indirect exchange rate is

$$\text{IER} = \frac{1\text{ FCU}}{\text{U.S. dollar} - \text{equivalent value}}$$

For the European euro example, the indirect exchange rate is

$$\frac{€1}{\$1.20} = €0.8333$$

Another way to express this is

$$\text{IER} = \frac{\text{Number of foreign currency units}}{\$1}$$

$$= \frac{€0.8333}{\$1}$$

Thus, the indirect exchange rate of €0.8333 = \$1 shows the number of foreign currency units that may be obtained for 1 U.S. dollar. People who travel outside the United States often use the indirect exchange rate.

Note that the direct and indirect rates are inversely related and that both state the same economic relationships between two currencies. For example, if the indirect exchange rate is given, the direct exchange rate may be computed by simply inverting the indirect exchange rate. If the indirect exchange rate is €0.8333 (€0.8333/\$1), the direct exchange rate can be computed as (\$1/€0.8333) = \$1.20. If the direct exchange rate is \$1.20, the indirect exchange rate can be computed as (€1/\$1.20) = €0.8333. Again, the currency in the numerator identifies the direction of the exchange rate. In practice, a slight difference might exist in the inverse relationship because of brokers' commissions or small differences in demand for the two currencies.

Some persons identify the direct exchange rate as *American terms* to indicate that it is U.S. dollar–based and represents an exchange rate quote from the perspective of a person in the United States. The indirect exchange rate is sometimes identified as *European terms* to indicate the direct exchange rate from the perspective of a person in Europe, which means the exchange rate shows the number of units of the European's local currency units per one U.S. dollar. A guide to help remember the difference in exchange rates is to note that the U.S. dollar is the numerator for the direct rate or American terms (the foreign currency unit is in the denominator), and the foreign currency unit is in the numerator for the indirect rate or European terms (with the U.S. dollar in the denominator). The *terms currency* is the numerator and the *base currency* is the denominator in the exchange rate ratio. The numerator is the key to the identification of the rate.

Changes in Exchange Rates[1]

Advanced StudyGuide .com

A change in an exchange rate is referred to as a *strengthening* or *weakening* of one currency against another. During the first decade of the new century, the relationship between the dollar and the euro was often volatile. For example, the exchange rate of the U.S. dollar versus the euro changed as follows during 2011 and 2012:

	January 2011	July 2011	January 2012	July 2012
Direct exchange rate (U.S. dollar equivalent of 1 euro)	\$1.33	\$1.45	\$1.29	\$1.26
Indirect exchange rate (euro per 1 U.S. dollar)	€0.75	€0.69	€0.78	€0.79

Weakening of the U.S. Dollar—Direct Exchange Rate Increases

Between January 1, 2011, and July 1, 2011, the direct exchange rate increased from \$1.33 = €1 to \$1.45 = €1, indicating that it took more U.S. currency (\$) to acquire 1 European euro (€). In other words, the cost of 1 euro was \$1.33 on January 1 but increased to \$1.45 on July 1. This means that the value of the U.S. currency declined relative to the euro. This is termed a *weakening* of the dollar versus the euro. Alternatively, looking at the indirect exchange rate, 1 U.S. dollar could acquire 0.75 European euro on January 1, but it could acquire fewer euros, 0.69, on July 1. Thus, the relative value of the dollar versus the euro was lower on July 1 than on January 1.

Think of the weakening of the U.S. dollar as

- Taking more U.S. currency to acquire one foreign currency unit.
- One U.S. dollar acquiring fewer foreign currency units.

Imports from Europe were more expensive for U.S. consumers on July 1 than on January 1 because of the weakening of the dollar. For example, assume that a European manufacturer is selling a German-made automobile for €25,000. To determine the U.S. dollar–equivalent value of the €25,000 on January 1, the following equation is used:

U.S. dollar – equivalent value	=	**Foreign currency units**	×	**Direct exchange rate**
\$33,250	=	€25,000	×	\$1.33

Between January 1 and July 1, the direct exchange rate increased as the dollar weakened relative to the euro. On July 1, the U.S. dollar–equivalent value of the €25,000 is

U.S. dollar – equivalent value	=	**Foreign currency units**	×	**Direct exchange rate**
\$36,250	=	€25,000	×	\$1.45

Although a weakening of the dollar is unfavorable for U.S. companies purchasing goods from another country, it favorably affects U.S. companies selling products in that country. Following a weakening of the dollar, U.S. exports to Europe are less expensive for European customers. For example, assume a U.S. manufacturer is selling a U.S.-made machine for \$10,000. To determine the foreign currency (euro) equivalent value of the \$10,000 on January 1, the following equation is used:

Foreign currency equivalent value	=	**U.S. dollar units**	×	**Indirect exchange rate**
€7,500	=	\$10,000	×	€0.75

[1] To view a video explanation of this topic, visit advancedstudyguide.com.

On July 1, after a weakening of the dollar, the machine would cost the European customer €6,900, as follows:

Foreign currency equivalent value	=	**U.S. dollar units**	×	**Indirect exchange rate**
€6,900	=	$10,000	×	€0.69

This substantial decrease in cost could lead the European customer to decide to acquire the machine from the U.S. company. Thus, a U.S. company's international sales can be significantly affected by changes in foreign currency exchange rates.

Strengthening of the U.S. Dollar—Direct Exchange Rate Decreases

Between July 1, 2011, and July 1, 2012, the direct exchange rate decreased from $1.45 = €1 to $1.26 = €1, indicating that it took less U.S. currency to acquire 1 euro. On July 1, 2011, a euro cost $1.45, but on July 1, 2012, the relative cost for 1 euro decreased to $1.26. This means that the value of the U.S. currency increased relative to the euro, termed a *strengthening* of the dollar against the euro. Another way to view this change is to note that the indirect exchange rate increased, indicating that on July 1, 2012, 1 dollar acquired more euros than it did on July 1, 2011. On July 1, 2011, 1 U.S. dollar could acquire 0.69 euro, but on July 1, 2012, 1 U.S. dollar could acquire more euros, 0.79, indicating that the relative value of the dollar increased between July 1, 2011, and July 1, 2012.

Think of the strengthening of the U.S. dollar as

- Taking less U.S. currency to acquire one foreign currency unit.
- One U.S. dollar acquiring more foreign currency units.

Figure 11–2 summarizes the relationships between currencies, imports, and exports.

During the latter part of the 1970s, the dollar consistently weakened against other major currencies because of several factors, including the high inflation the United States experienced. This weakening did help the U.S. balance of trade because it reduced the quantity of then more expensive imports while causing U.S.-made goods to be less expensive in other countries. In the first half of the 1980s, the dollar consistently strengthened relative to other currencies. Not only was the U.S. economy strong and producing goods

FIGURE 11–2
Relationships between Currencies and Exchange Rates

	January 2011	July 2011	July 2012
Direct exchange rate ($/€)	$1.33	$1.45	$1.26
Indirect exchange rate (€/$)	€0.75	€0.69	€0.79

Between January 1, 2011, and July 1, 2011—weakening of the U.S. dollar:
- Direct rate increases
  - Dollar weakens (takes more U.S. currency to acquire 1 euro)
- Indirect rate decreases
  - Euro strengthens (takes fewer euros to acquire 1 U.S. dollar)
- Imports into United States normally decrease in quantity
  - Foreign goods imported into United States more expensive in dollars
- Exports from United States normally increase in quantity
  - U.S.-made exports less expensive in euros

Between July 1, 2011, and July 1, 2012—strengthening of the U.S. dollar:
- Direct rate decreases
  - Dollar strengthens (takes less U.S. currency to acquire 1 euro)
- Indirect rate increases
  - Euro weakens (takes more euros to acquire 1 U.S. dollar)
- Imports into United States normally increase in quantity
  - Foreign goods imported into United States less expensive in dollars ($1 can acquire more)
- Exports from United States normally decrease in quantity
  - U.S.-made exports more expensive (takes more euros to acquire goods)

more efficiently but also high interest rates attracted large foreign investment in the U.S. capital markets. A stronger dollar added to the foreign trade deficit by making imports less expensive and U.S.-made goods more expensive on the world market. Beginning in 1986 and continuing through the early 1990s, the dollar again weakened relative to the major international currencies. In the latter 1990s, the dollar generally strengthened because of the robustness of the U.S. economy, but in the early 2000s, the dollar again weakened because of the high trade deficit and the sluggish U.S. economy.

These changes in the international value of the dollar affect any consumer acquiring imported goods. A weakening dollar means that imports become more expensive whereas a strengthening dollar means that imports become less expensive. One reason the U.S. government may let the dollar weaken is to reduce the trade deficits. U.S. exporters can sell their goods more easily overseas, thus boosting their profitability. Imports should decrease because of the higher relative prices of the foreign-made goods, thus enhancing the demand for domestic-made goods within the United States. If the dollar weakens too far, overseas investors reduce their demand for dollar-dominated U.S. assets such as U.S. stocks and bonds. The reduced investment demand may require an increase in bond interest rates to offset overseas investors' reduction in bond returns caused by the weakening dollar. An increase in interest rates may reduce economic investment within the United States. Finally, a weakening dollar means that foreign travel becomes more expensive because of the reduction in the dollar's purchasing power. Thus, the U.S. government's management of the value of the dollar is a balancing act to achieve the needs of both U.S. businesses and U.S. consumers.

Spot Rates versus Current Rates

ASC 830 refers to the use of both spot rates and current rates for measuring the currency used in international transactions. The ***spot rate*** is the exchange rate for immediate delivery of currencies. The ***current rate*** is defined simply as the spot rate on the entity's balance sheet date.

Forward Exchange Rates

A third exchange rate is the rate on future, or forward, exchanges of currencies. Figure 11–1 shows these exchange rates for selected major international currencies for one month, three months, and six months forward. Active dealer markets in ***forward exchange contracts*** are maintained for companies wishing to either receive or deliver major international currencies. The forward rate on a given date is not the same as the spot rate on the same date. Expectations about the relative value of currencies are built into the forward rate. The difference between the forward rate and the spot rate on a given date is called the ***spread.*** The spread gives information about the perceived strengths or weaknesses of currencies. For instance, assume the spot rate for the Swiss franc is $1.1574 and the 30-day forward rate is $1.0576. The spread is the difference between these two numbers, or $0.0998. Because the forward rate is less than the spot rate, the expectation is that the dollar will strengthen against the franc in the next 30 days. The actual spot rate when the contract is due in 30 days may be higher or lower than the forward rate. By entering into the forward contract, the U.S. company gives up the chance of receiving a better exchange rate but also avoids the possibility of an exchange rate loss. This reduces the risk for the U.S. company.

For example, a U.S. company may have a liability in British pounds due in 30 days. Rather than wait 30 days to buy the pounds and risk having the dollar weaken in value relative to the pound, the company can go to a foreign exchange dealer and enter into a one-month forward exchange contract at the forward exchange rate in effect on the contract date. The United States has approximately 2,000 foreign exchange dealer institutions, of which about 200 are market-making, large banks such as Citibank, JPMorgan Chase, and Bank of America, which do the highest volume of foreign exchange activity. The contract enables the buyer to receive British pounds from an exchange broker 30 days from the contract date at a price fixed now by the contract.

The next section of the chapter presents the accounting for import and export transactions and for forward exchange contracts.

FOREIGN CURRENCY TRANSACTIONS

LO 11-2

Understand the accounting implications of and be able to make calculations related to foreign currency transactions.

As defined earlier, *foreign currency transactions* are economic activities denominated in a currency other than the entity's recording currency. These transactions include the following:

1. Purchases or sales of goods or services (imports or exports), the prices of which are stated in a foreign currency.
2. Loans payable or receivable in a foreign currency.
3. Purchase or sale of foreign currency forward exchange contracts.
4. Purchase or sale of foreign currency units.

One party in a foreign exchange transaction must exchange its own currency for another country's currency. Some persons use a shorthand to refer to foreign exchange transactions by using just the letters FX. This book uses the longer, more generally used description, which is *foreign exchange.*

For financial statement purposes, transactions denominated in a foreign currency must be translated into the currency the reporting company uses. Additionally, at each balance sheet date—interim as well as annual—account balances denominated in a currency other than the entity's reporting currency must be adjusted to reflect changes in exchange rates during the period since the last balance sheet date or since the foreign currency transaction date if it occurred during the period. This adjustment restates the foreign currency–denominated accounts to their U.S. dollar–equivalent values as of the balance sheet date. The adjustment in equivalent U.S. dollar values is a ***foreign currency transaction gain or loss*** for the entity when exchange rates have changed. For example, assume that a U.S. company acquires €5,000 from its bank on January 1, 20X1, for use in future purchases from German companies. The direct exchange rate is \$1.20 = €1; thus the company pays the bank \$6,000 for €5,000, as follows:

U.S. dollar – Equivalent value	**=**	**Foreign currency units**	**×**	**Direct exchange rate**
\$6,000	=	€5,000	×	\$1.20

The following entry records this exchange of currencies:

	January 1, 20X1		
(1)	Foreign Currency Units (€)	6,000	
	Cash		6,000

The parenthetical notation (€) is used here after the debit account to indicate that the asset is European euros, but for accounting purposes, it is recorded and reported at its U.S. dollar–equivalent value. This translation to the U.S. equivalent value is required in order to add the value of the foreign currency units to all of the company's other accounts that are reported in dollars.

On July 1, 20X1, the exchange rate is \$1.100 = €1 as represented in the following time line:

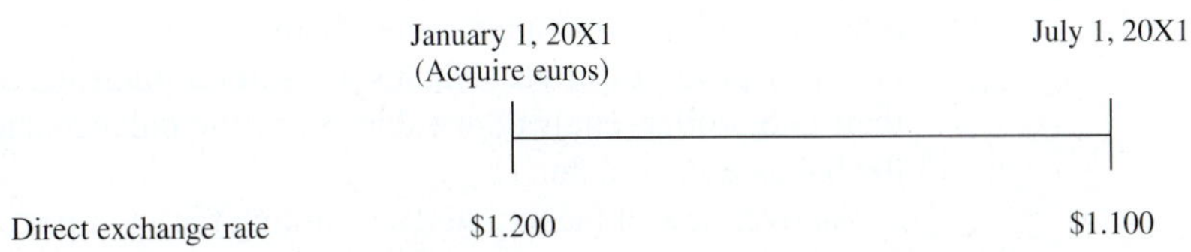

The direct exchange rate has decreased, reflecting that the U.S. dollar has strengthened. On July 1, it takes less U.S. currency to acquire 1 euro than it did on January 1. If the dollar has strengthened, the euro has weakened. By holding the euros during a weakening of the euro relative to the dollar, the company experiences a foreign currency transaction loss, as follows:

Equivalent dollar value of € 5,000 on January 1:	
€ 5,000 × $1.200	$6,000
Equivalent dollar value of € 5,000 on July 1:	
€ 5,000 × $1.100	5,500
Foreign currency transaction loss	$ 500

If the U.S. company prepares financial statements on July 1, the following adjusting entry is required:

	July 1, 20X1		
(2)	Foreign Currency Transaction Loss	500	
	Foreign Currency Units (€)		500

The foreign currency transaction loss is the result of a foreign currency transaction and is included in this period's income statement, usually as a separate item under "Other Income or Loss." Some accountants use the account title Exchange Loss instead of the longer title Foreign Currency Transaction Loss. In this book, the longer, more descriptive account title is used to communicate fully the source of the loss. The Foreign Currency Units account is reported on the balance sheet at a value of $5,500, its equivalent U.S. dollar value on that date.

In the previous examples, the U.S. company used the U.S. dollar as its primary currency for performing its major financial and operating functions, that is, as its ***functional currency.*** Also, the U.S. company prepared its financial statements in U.S. dollars, its ***reporting currency.*** Any transactions denominated in currencies other than the U.S. dollar require translation to their equivalent U.S. dollar values. Generally, the majority of a business's cash transactions take place in the ***local currency*** of the country in which the entity operates. The U.S. dollar is the functional currency for virtually all companies based in the United States. A company operating in Germany would probably use the euro as its functional currency. *In this chapter, the local currency is assumed to be the entity's functional and reporting currency.* The few exceptions to this general case are discussed in Chapter 12.

FYI

Losses on foreign currency transactions can be substantial. For example, Nike reported a $40 million pretax loss on its fiscal 2014 third quarter financial statements related to foreign currency transactions.

Illustrations of various types of foreign currency transactions are given in the sections that follow. Note that different exchange rates are used to value selected foreign currency transactions, depending on a number of factors such as management's reason for entering the foreign currency transaction, the nature of the transaction, and the timing of the transaction.

Foreign Currency Import and Export Transactions

Advanced StudyGuide .com

Payables and receivables that arise from transactions with foreign-based entities and that are denominated in a foreign currency must be measured and recorded by the U.S. entity in the currency used for its accounting records—the U.S. dollar. The relevant exchange rate for settlement of a transaction denominated in a foreign currency is the spot exchange rate on the date of settlement. At the time the transaction is settled, payables or receivables denominated in foreign currency units must be adjusted to their current U.S. dollar–equivalent value. If financial statements are prepared before the foreign currency payables or receivables are settled, their account balances must be adjusted to their U.S. dollar–equivalent values as of the balance sheet date, using the current rate on the balance sheet date.

An overview of the required accounting for an import or export transaction denominated in a foreign currency, assuming the company does *not* use forward contracts, is as follows:

1. *Transaction date.* Record the purchase or sale transaction at the U.S. dollar–equivalent value using the spot direct exchange rate on this date.

2. *Balance sheet date.* Adjust the payable or receivable to its U.S. dollar–equivalent, end-of-period value using the current direct exchange rate. Recognize any exchange gain or loss for the change in rates between the transaction and balance sheet dates.
3. *Settlement date.* First adjust the foreign currency payable or receivable for any changes in the exchange rate between the balance sheet date (or transaction date if transaction occurs after the balance sheet date) and the settlement date, recording any exchange gain or loss as required. Then record the settlement of the foreign currency payable or receivable.

This adjustment process is required because the FASB adopted what is called the *two-transaction approach,* which views the purchase or sale of an item as a separate transaction from the foreign currency commitment. By adopting the two-transaction approach to foreign currency transactions, the FASB established the general rule that foreign currency exchange gains or losses resulting from the revaluation of assets or liabilities denominated in a foreign currency must be recognized currently in the income statement of the period in which the exchange rate changes. A few exceptions to this general rule are allowed and are discussed later in this chapter.

Illustration of Foreign Purchase Transaction

Figure 11–3 illustrates the journal entries used to measure and record a purchase of goods from a foreign supplier denominated either in the entity's local currency or in a foreign currency. On the left side of Figure 11–3, the transaction is denominated in U.S. dollars, the recording and reporting currency of the U.S. company; on the right side, the transaction is denominated in Japanese yen (¥). The U.S. company is subject to a foreign currency transaction gain or loss only if the transaction is denominated in the foreign currency. If the foreign transaction is denominated in U.S. dollars, no special accounting problems exist and no currency rate adjustments are necessary.

The following information describes the case:

1. On October 1, 20X1, Peerless Products, a U.S. company, acquired goods on account from Tokyo Industries, a Japanese company, for $14,000, or 2,000,000 yen.
2. Peerless Products prepared financial statements at its year-end of December 31, 20X1.
3. Settlement of the payable was made on April 1, 20X2.

The direct spot exchange rates of the U.S. dollar–equivalent value of 1 yen were as follows:

Peerless Products Corporation

Date	Direct Exchange Rate
October 1, 20X1 (transaction date)	$0.0070
December 31, 20X1 (balance sheet date)	0.0080
April 1, 20X2 (settlement date)	0.0076

The following timeline may help to clarify the relationships between the dates and the economic events:

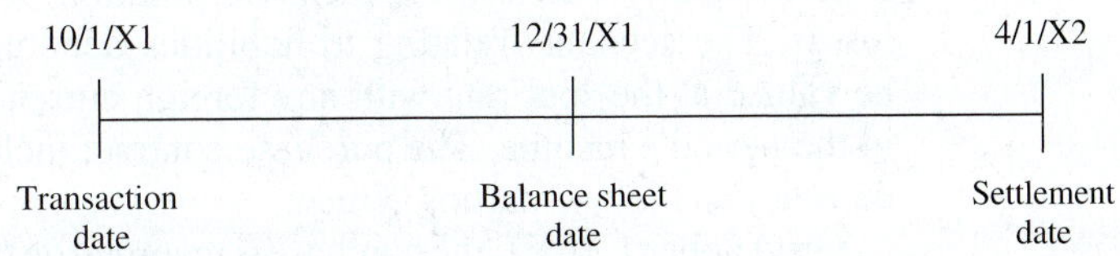

Accounts relating to transactions denominated in yen are noted by the parenthetical symbol for the yen (¥) after the account title. As you proceed through the example, you should especially note the assets and liabilities denominated in the foreign currency and the adjustment needed to reflect their current values by use of the U.S. dollar–equivalent rate of exchange.

FIGURE 11–3 Comparative U.S. Company Journal Entries for Foreign Purchase Transaction Denominated in Dollars versus Foreign Currency Units

If Denominated in U.S. Dollars			If Denominated in Japanese Yen		
October 1, 20X1 (Date of Purchase)					
Inventory	14,000		Inventory	14,000	
Accounts Payable		14,000	Accounts Payable (¥)		14,000
			$14,000 = ¥2,000,000 × $0.0070 spot rate		
December 31, 20X1 (Balance Sheet Date)					
No entry			Foreign Currency Transaction Loss	2,000	
			Accounts Payable (¥)		2,000
			Adjust payable denominated in foreign currency to current U.S. dollar equivalent and recognize exchange loss: $ 16,000 = ¥2,000,000 × $0.0080 Dec. 31 spot rate −14,000 = ¥2,000,000 × $0.0070 Oct. 1 spot rate $ 2,000 = ¥2,000,000 × ($0.0080 − $0.0070).		
April 1, 20X2 (Settlement Date)					
			Accounts Payable (¥)	800	
			Foreign Currency Transaction Gain		800
			Adjust payable denominated in foreign currency to current U.S. dollar equivalent and recognize exchange gain: $ 15,200 = ¥2,000,000 × $0.0076 Apr. 1 spot rate −16,000 = ¥2,000,000 × $0.0080 Dec. 31 spot rate $ 800 = ¥2,000,000 × ($0.0076 − $0.0080).		
			Foreign Currency Units (¥)	15,200	
			Cash		15,200
			Acquire FCU to settle debt: $15,200 = ¥2,000,000 × $0.0076 April 1 spot rate.		
Accounts Payable	14,000		Accounts Payable (¥)	15,200	
Cash		14,000	Foreign Currency Units (¥)		15,200

Key Observations from Illustration

If the purchase contract is denominated in dollars, the foreign entity (Tokyo Industries) bears the foreign currency exchange risk. If the transaction is denominated in yen, the U.S. company (Peerless Products Corporation) is exposed to exchange rate gains and losses. The accounts relating to liabilities denominated in foreign currency units must be valued at the spot rate with any foreign currency transaction gain or loss recognized in the period's income. The purchase contract includes specification of the denominated currency as the two parties agreed.

On October 1, 20X1, the purchase is recorded on the books of Peerless Products. The U.S. dollar–equivalent value of 2,000,000 yen on this date is $14,000 (¥2,000,000 × $0.0070).

On December 31, 20X1, the balance sheet date, the payable denominated in foreign currency units must be adjusted to its current U.S. dollar–equivalent value. The direct exchange rate has increased since the date of purchase, indicating that the U.S. dollar has weakened relative to the yen. Therefore, on December 31, 20X1, $16,000 is required to acquire 2,000,000 yen (¥2,000,000 × $0.0080), whereas, on October 1, 20X1, only

$14,000 was required to obtain 2,000,000 yen (¥2,000,000 × $0.0070). This increase in the exchange rate requires the recognition of a $2,000 foreign currency transaction loss if the transaction is denominated in yen, the foreign currency unit. No entry is made if the transaction is denominated in U.S. dollars because Peerless has a liability for $14,000 regardless of the changes in exchange rates.

The payable is settled on April 1, 20X2. If the payable is denominated in U.S. dollars, no adjustment is necessary and the liability is extinguished by payment of $14,000. However, assets and liabilities denominated in foreign currency units must again be adjusted to their present U.S. dollar–equivalent values. The dollar has strengthened between December 31, 20X1, and April 1, 20X2, as shown by the decrease in the direct exchange rate. In other words, fewer dollars are needed to acquire 2,000,000 yen on April 1, 20X2, than on December 31, 20X1. Accounts Payable is adjusted to its current dollar value, and an $800 foreign currency transaction gain [¥2,000,000 × ($0.0076 − $0.0080)] is recognized for the change in rates since the balance sheet date. Peerless acquires 2,000,000 yen, paying an exchange broker the spot exchange rate of $15,200 (¥2,000,000 × $0.0076). Finally, Peerless extinguishes its liability denominated in yen by paying Tokyo Industries the ¥2,000,000.

Understanding the revaluations may be easier by viewing the process within the perspective of a T-account. The following T-account posts the entries in Figure 11–3:

Accounts Payable (¥)

Debit		Credit
		20X1
		Oct. 1 14,000 (¥2,000,000 × $0.0070)
		Dec. 31 2,000 [¥2,000,000 × ($0.0080 − $0.0070)]
		Dec. 31 16,000 Balance (¥2,000,000 × $0.0080)
20X2		
Apr. 1		
[¥2,000,000 × ($0.0076 − $0.0080)]	800	
Apr. 1 settlement		
(¥2,000,000 × $0.0076)	15,200	
		Apr. 2 0 Balance

Some accountants combine the revaluation and settlement entries into one entry. Under this alternative approach, the following entries would be made on April 1, 20X2, the settlement date, instead of the entries presented for that date in Figure 11–3:

	April 1, 20X2		
(3)	Foreign Currency Units (¥)	15,200	
	Cash		15,200
	Acquire foreign currency.		
(4)	Accounts Payable (¥)	16,000	
	Foreign Currency Transaction Gain		800
	Foreign Currency Units (¥)		15,200
	Settle foreign currency payable and recognize gain from change in exchange rates since December 31, 20X1.		

The final account balances resulting from the preceding one-entry approach and the two-entry approach used in Figure 11–3 are the same.

In summary, if the transaction is denominated in U.S. dollars, Peerless Products has no foreign currency exchange exposure; Tokyo Industries bears the risk of foreign currency exposure. If the transaction is denominated in yen, however, Peerless has a foreign currency exchange risk. The assets and liabilities denominated in foreign currency units must be valued at their U.S. dollar–equivalent values, and a foreign currency transaction gain or loss must be recognized on that period's income statement.

MANAGING INTERNATIONAL CURRENCY RISK WITH FOREIGN CURRENCY FORWARD EXCHANGE FINANCIAL INSTRUMENTS

LO 11-3

Understand how to hedge international currency risk using foreign currency forward exchange financial instruments.

Companies need to manage business risks. Derivative instruments are important tools in managing risk. Companies operating internationally are subject not only to normal business risks but also to additional risks from changes in currency exchange rates. Therefore, multinational enterprises (MNEs) often use derivative instruments, including foreign currency–denominated forward exchange contracts, foreign currency options, and foreign currency futures, to manage risk associated with foreign currency transactions.

The accounting for derivatives and hedging activities is guided by **ASC 815.** A ***financial instrument*** is cash, evidence of ownership, or a contract that both (1) imposes on one entity a contractual obligation to deliver cash or another instrument and (2) conveys to the second entity that contractual right to receive cash or another financial instrument. Examples include cash, stock, notes payable and receivable, and many financial contracts.

A ***derivative*** is a financial instrument or other contract whose value is "derived from" some other item that has a variable value over time. An example of a derivative is a foreign currency forward exchange contract whose value is derived from changes in the foreign currency exchange rate over the contract's term. Note that not all financial instruments are derivatives.

The specific definition of a *derivative* is a financial instrument or contract possessing all of the following characteristics:

1. The financial instrument must contain one or more underlyings and one or more notional amounts, which specify the terms of the financial instrument.
   a. An ***underlying*** is any financial or physical variable that has observable or objectively verifiable changes. Currency exchange rates, commodity prices, indexes of prices or rates, days of winter warming, or other variables including the occurrence or nonoccurrence of a specified event such as the scheduled payment under a contract are examples of an underlying.
   b. A ***notional amount*** is the number of currency units, shares, bushels, pounds, or other units specified in the financial instrument. The notional amount is usually expressed in U.S. dollars.
2. The financial instrument or other contract requires no initial net investment or an initial net investment that is smaller than required for other types of contracts expected to have a similar response to changes in market factors. Many derivative instruments require no initial net investment or only a small investment for the time value of the contract (as discussed later in this chapter).
3. The contract terms: (*a*) require or permit net settlement, (*b*) provide for the delivery of an asset that puts the recipient in an economic position not substantially different from net settlement, or (*c*) allow for the contract to be readily settled net by a market or other mechanism outside the contract. For example, a forward contract requires the delivery of a specified number of shares of stock, but there is an option market mechanism that offers a ready opportunity to sell the contract or to enter into an offsetting contract.

Occasionally, a financial instrument may have an embedded derivative that must be separated, or bifurcated, from its host contract. An example of an embedded derivative is a company's issuing debt that includes regular interest as well as a potential premium payment based on the future price of a commodity such as crude oil. In this case, the contingent payment feature is a derivative. Another example is the debt agreement that specifies a principal, but whose interest rate is based on the U.S. LIBOR (London Interbank Offered Rate), which is a variable rate. In this case, the interest is the embedded derivative because its value, which is derived from the market, is variable.

Advanced StudyGuide .com

Derivatives Designated as Hedges

Derivatives may be designated to hedge or reduce risks. Some companies obtain derivatives that are not designated as hedges but as speculative financial instruments. For example, a company may enter into a forward exchange contract that does not have any offsetting intent. In this case, the gain or loss on the derivative is recorded in periodic earnings.

ASC 815 provides specific requirements for classifying a derivative as a hedge. Hedge accounting offsets the gain (loss) on the hedged item with the loss (gain) on the hedging instrument. Hedges are applicable to (1) foreign currency exchange risk in which currency exchange rates change over time; (2) interest-rate risks, particularly for companies owing variable-rate debt instruments; and (3) commodity risks whose future commodity prices may be quite different from spot prices.

For a derivative instrument to qualify as a hedging instrument, it must meet the following two criteria:

1. Sufficient documentation must be provided at the beginning of the hedge term to identify the objective and strategy of the hedge, the hedging instrument, and the hedged item, and how the hedge's effectiveness will be assessed on an ongoing basis.
2. The hedge must be highly effective throughout its term. Effectiveness is measured by evaluating the hedging instrument's ability to generate changes in fair value that offset the changes in value of the hedged item. This effectiveness must be tested at the time the hedge is entered into, every three months thereafter, and each time financial statements are prepared. Effectiveness is viewed as the derivative instrument's ability to offset changes in the fair value or cash flows of the hedged item within the range between 80 and 125 percent of the change in value of the hedged item.

Derivatives that meet the requirements for a hedge and are designated as such by the company's management are accounted for in accordance with **ASC 815** and as follows:

1. ***Fair value hedges*** are designated to hedge the exposure to potential changes in the fair value of (*a*) a recognized asset or liability such as available-for-sale investments or (*b*) an unrecognized firm commitment for which a binding agreement exists, such as to buy or sell inventory. Because the purpose of the hedging instrument is to hedge against changes in the fair value of the hedged item, the initial valuation of the hedging instrument is zero. The hedging instrument will only take on value if the fair value of the hedged item changes. The following table summarizes the two possible outcomes: (1) a decrease in the fair value of the hedged item or (2) an increase in the fair value of the hedged item.

Scenario	Hedged Item: Asset, Liability, or Firm Commitment	Hedging Instrument	Net Impact on Current Earnings
	(reported at fair value)		
Initial Valuation	Zero	Zero	Zero
Decrease in Fair Value	Loss	Gain	Zero
Increase in Fair Value	Gain	Loss	Zero

A key point in the accounting for fair value hedges is that both the hedged item and the hedging instrument are reported on the balance sheet at their respective fair values. A second key point is that the hedging instrument has been structured so that in any scenario, whether the fair value of the hedged item results in a loss or a gain, the movement in fair value of the hedging instrument will result in an offsetting gain or loss. Therefore, net gains and losses on the hedged asset or liability and the hedging instrument are recognized in current earnings, and since they are always offsetting, there will be no net impact on earnings. Appendix 11B presents an example of a fair value hedge using an option contract to hedge available-for-sale securities.

2. ***Cash flow hedges*** are designated to hedge the exposure to potential changes in the anticipated cash flows, either into or out of the company, for (*a*) a recognized asset or liability such as future interest payments on variable-interest debt or (*b*) a forecasted cash transaction such as a forecasted purchase or sale. A *forecasted cash transaction* is a transaction that is expected to occur but for which there is not yet a firm commitment. Thus, a forecasted transaction has no present rights to future benefits or a present liability for future obligations. **ASC 815** specifies that a derivative must be valued at its current fair market value. For cash flow hedges, changes in the fair market value of a derivative are separated into an effective portion and an ineffective portion. The net gain or loss on the effective portion of the hedging instrument should be reported in other comprehensive income. The gain or loss on the ineffective portion is reported in current earnings on the income statement.

   The *effective portion* is defined as the part of the gain (or loss) on the hedging instrument that offsets a loss (or gain) on the hedged item. This portion of the change in the derivative's fair market value is related to the intrinsic value from changes in the underlying. Any remaining gain (or loss) on the hedging instrument is defined as the *ineffective portion*. This portion of the change in the derivative's fair market value is related to the time value of the derivative and reduces to zero at the derivative's expiration date. For example, focusing on the effective portion of a cash flow hedge, the purpose of the hedging instrument is to hedge against potential changes in fair value in a specific anticipated cash flow. Therefore, the initial valuation of the hedging instrument is zero because no changes have occurred. The hedging instrument will only take on value if there is a change in the underlying, which signals a change to the specific anticipated cash flow. The following table summarizes the two possible outcomes: (1) an increase in the fair value of the anticipated cash flow or (2) a decrease in the fair value of the anticipated cash flow.

Scenario	Change in Anticipated Cash Flow (not reported)	Hedging Instrument (reported at fair value)	Other Comprehensive Income	Net Impact on Current Earnings
Initial Valuation	No change	Zero	Zero	Zero
Increase in Fair Value	Increase	Loss	Decrease	Zero
Decrease in Fair Value	Decrease	Gain	Increase	Zero

When a company uses a cash flow hedge, the hedging instrument is reported at fair value on the balance sheet, similar to the accounting for a fair value hedge. However, since the hedged item is an anticipated cash flow, which is not yet on the balance sheet, the gain or loss is recorded in other comprehensive income (OCI). By recording the gain or loss in OCI, it is effectively deferred from the income statement until the hedged transaction culminates. Therefore, the change in an anticipated cash flow, and the corresponding gain or loss on the hedging instrument, will not affect current earnings.

When the hedged transaction is culminated, and assuming the actual cash flow received is the amount that was anticipated after the last related entry was recorded to OCI, then the gain or loss that was previously recorded in OCI is reversed from OCI to current income. This reversal will offset the current earnings impact of the difference between the actual cash flow and the original hedged cash flow. Thus, the net effect on current earnings is zero as illustrated in the following table:

Scenario	Actual Cash Flow	Other Comprehensive Income	Net Impact on Current Earnings
Increase in Cash Flow	Increase (gain or revenue)	Reverse Prior Decrease (a decrease to current earnings)	Zero
Decrease in Cash Flow	Decrease (loss or expense)	Reverse Prior Increase (an increase to current earnings)	Zero

Appendix 11B presents an example of how to determine the effective versus the ineffective portion of a change in the value of a derivative designed as a cash flow hedge of an anticipated inventory purchase.

3. ***Foreign currency hedges*** are hedges in which the hedged item is denominated in a foreign currency. Note that the incremental risk being hedged in a foreign currency hedge is the change in fair value or the change in cash flows attributable to the changes in the foreign currency exchange rates. The following types of hedges of foreign currency risk may be designated by the entity:

   a. A *fair value hedge* of a firm commitment to enter into a foreign currency transaction, such as a binding agreement to purchase equipment from a foreign manufacturer with the payable due in the foreign currency or a recognized foreign currency–denominated asset or liability (including an available-for-sale security). Just as with hedge accounting for firm commitments not involving foreign currency commitments in item (1) above, the gain or loss on the foreign currency hedging derivative and the offsetting loss or gain on the foreign currency–hedged item are recognized currently in earnings on the income statement.

   b. A *cash flow hedge* of a forecasted foreign currency transaction, such as a probable future foreign currency sale, the forecasted functional currency–equivalent cash flows associated with a recognized asset or liability, or a forecasted intercompany transaction. Just as with accounting for hedges of forecasted transactions not involving foreign currency commitments in item (2) above, the effective portion of the gain or loss on the foreign currency hedging derivative instrument is recognized as a component of other comprehensive income. The ineffective portion of the gain or loss is recognized currently in earnings.

   Cash flow hedges are used when all variability in the hedged item's functional currency–equivalent cash flows are eliminated by the effect of the hedge. Cash flow hedges with a derivative based only on changes in the exchange rates cannot be designated, for example, for a variable-rate foreign currency–denominated asset or liability because some of the cash flow variability is not covered with that specific hedge. However, foreign currency–denominated forward contracts can be used as cash flow hedges of foreign currency–denominated assets or liabilities that are fixed in terms of the number of foreign currency units.

   c. A hedge of a net investment in a foreign operation. A derivative designated as hedging this type of foreign currency exposure has its gain or loss reported in Other Comprehensive Income as part of the cumulative translation adjustment, as will be discussed in Chapter 12.

Forward Exchange Contracts

According to the Bank for International Settlements, foreign-exchange trading has increased to an average of $5.3 trillion a day (as of January 2014). To put this into perspective, this averages out to be $220 billion per hour. The foreign-exchange market's $5.3 trillion per day in trading volume dwarfs the equities and futures markets. In fact, it would take days of trading on the New York Stock Exchange to equal one day of foreign-exchange trading.

The foreign exchange market is largely made up of institutional investors, corporations, governments, banks, as well as currency speculators. Roughly 90 percent of this volume is generated by currency speculators capitalizing on intraday price movements. Unlike the stock and futures market that are housed in central physical exchanges, the foreign exchange market is an over-the-counter, decentralized market completely housed electronically. Though most investors are familiar with the stock market, they are unaware how small in volume it is in relation to the foreign-exchange market.[2]

Companies operating internationally often enter into forward exchange contracts with foreign currency brokers for the exchange of different currencies at specified future dates at specified rates. Forward exchange contracts are acquired from foreign currency brokers. Typically, these contracts are written for one of the major international currencies. They are available for virtually any time period up to 12 months forward, but most are for relatively shorter time periods, usually between 30 and 180 days. Forward exchange contracts can be entered into to receive foreign currency or to deliver foreign currency at a specified date in the future (the expiration date). The forward exchange rate differs from the spot rate because of the different economic factors involved in determining a future versus spot rate of exchange. For hedging transactions, if the forward rate is more than the spot rate, the difference between the forward and spot rate is termed *premium on the forward exchange contract;* that is, the foreign currency is selling at a premium in the forward market. If the forward rate is less than the spot rate, the difference is a *discount on the forward exchange contract;* that is, the foreign currency is selling at a discount in the forward market.

ASC 815 establishes a basic rule of fair value for accounting for forward exchange contracts. Changes in the fair value are recognized in the accounts, but the specific accounting for the change depends on the purpose of the hedge. For forward exchange contracts, the basic rule is to use the forward exchange rate to value the forward contract.

Multinational entities often use foreign currency forward contract derivatives. These contracts may be designated as hedging instruments or may not fulfill all the requirements for a hedge and would thus not be hedging instruments. The cases discussed in the next sections of this chapter illustrate the following:

Case 1: This case presents the most common use of foreign currency forward contracts, which is to manage a part of the foreign currency exposure from accounts payable or accounts receivable denominated in a foreign currency. Note that the company has entered into a foreign currency forward contract but that the contract does not qualify for or the company does not designate the forward contract as a hedging instrument. Thus, the forward contract is not a designated hedge but can offset most, if not all, foreign currency risks. The forward contract is valued using the forward rate, and changes in the market value of the forward contract are recognized currently in earnings on the income statement. The foreign currency account payable or account receivable is revalued using the spot rate in accordance with **ASC 830.**

Case 2: This case presents the accounting for an unrecognized firm commitment to enter into a foreign currency transaction, which is accounted for as a fair value hedge. A firm commitment exists because of a binding agreement for the future transaction that meets all requirements for a firm commitment. The hedge is against the possible changes in fair value of the firm commitment (e.g., the inventory to be purchased or the equipment to be acquired) from changes in the foreign currency exchange rates.

Case 3: This case presents the accounting for a forecasted foreign currency–denominated transaction, which is accounted for as a cash flow hedge of the possible changes in future cash flows. The forecasted transaction is *probable* but not a *firm*

[2] Robert Mackenzie Smith, "FX Now a $5.3 Trillion per Day Market, Says BIS," September 6, 2013, http://www.risk.net/risk-magazine/news/2293080/fx-now-a-usd53-trillion-per-day-market-says-bis.

commitment. Thus, the transaction has not yet occurred nor is it assured; the company is *anticipating* a *possible* future foreign currency transaction. Because the foreign currency hedge is against the impact of changes in the foreign currency exchange rates used to predict the possible future foreign currency–denominated cash flows, it is accounted for as a cash flow hedge. **ASC 815** allows for the continuation of a cash flow hedge after the purchase or sale transaction occurs until settlement of the foreign currency–denominated account payable or receivable arising from the transaction. Alternatively, at the time the company enters into a binding agreement for the transaction that had been forecasted, the hedge can be changed to a fair value hedge, but any other comprehensive income recognized on the cash flow hedge to that date is not reclassified to the income statement until the earnings process is completed.

Case 4: This case presents the accounting for foreign currency forward contracts used to speculate in foreign currency markets. These transactions are not hedging transactions. The foreign currency forward contract is revalued periodically to its fair value using the forward exchange rate for the remainder of the contract term. The gain or loss on the revaluation is recognized currently in earnings on the income statement.

A time line of the possible points at which a company uses foreign currency contracts follows. Note that a company may use just one foreign currency forward contract during the time between each event and the final settlement of the foreign currency payable or receivable or may use more than one foreign currency forward contract during the time span presented. For example, a company could use one forward contract between the time of the forecast of the future transaction and the time it signs a binding agreement, or it could just continue with one forward contract the entire time between the date of the forecast and the final settlement.

Thus, the accounting for the hedge is based on the purpose for which the hedge, in this case a foreign currency forward contract, is entered into.

The following four cases illustrate the accounting for the major uses of forward exchange contracts.

Forecast expected future transaction. Enter into designated foreign currency forward contract.	Sign binding agreement for transaction. Enter into designated foreign currency forward contract.	Receive goods or services from transaction. Enter into undesignated foreign currency forward contract.	Settlement of foreign currency denominated payable or receivable.
Cash flow hedge of possible future foreign currency cash flow.	Fair value hedge of changes in value of goods or services due to possible changes in exchange rates.	Manage exposed position by entering into foreign currency forward contract.	Settle foreign currency payable or receivable.
(Case 3)	(Case 2)	(Case 1)	

Case 1: Managing an Exposed Foreign Currency Net Asset or Liability Position: Not a Designated Hedging Instrument

A company that has more trade receivables or other assets denominated in a foreign currency than liabilities denominated in that currency incurs a foreign currency risk from its *exposed net asset position.* Alternatively, the company has an *exposed net liability position* if liabilities denominated in a foreign currency exceed receivables denominated in that currency.

The most common use of forward exchange contracts is for ***managing an exposed foreign currency position, either a net asset or a net liability position.*** Entering into a foreign currency forward contract balances a foreign exchange payable with a receivable in the same foreign currency, thus offsetting the risk of foreign exchange fluctuations. For example, a U.S. company acquiring goods from a Swiss company may be required to make payment in Swiss francs. If the transaction is denominated in Swiss francs, the U.S. company is exposed to the effects of changes in exchange rates between the dollar and the Swiss franc. To protect itself from fluctuations in the value of the Swiss franc, the U.S. company can enter into a forward exchange contract to receive francs at the future settlement date. The U.S. company then uses these francs to settle its foreign currency commitment arising from the foreign purchase transaction.

Alternatively, a U.S. company could have a receivable denominated in a foreign currency that it also could manage with a forward exchange contract. In this case, the U.S. company contracts to *deliver* foreign currency units to the forward exchange broker at a future date in exchange for U.S. dollars.

ASC 815 specifies the general rule that the relevant exchange rate for measuring the fair value of a forward exchange contract is the *forward exchange rate* at each valuation date. Note that **ASC 830** specifies that the foreign currency–denominated account receivable or account payable from the exchange transaction is valued by using the *spot rate* at the valuation date. Forward contracts must be adjusted for changes in the fair value of the forward contract. Because of the two different currency exchange rates used—the spot and the forward—a difference normally exists between the amount of gain and loss. This difference should not be large but does create some volatility in the income stream.

Time Value of Future Cash Flows from Forward Contracts

One other item of note is that **ASC 815** requires the recognition of an interest factor if interest is significant. Thus, when interest is significant, companies should use the *present value* of the expected future net cash flows to value the forward contract. By using the present value, the company explicitly recognizes the time value of money. For the examples that follow and to focus on the main points of accounting for the hedges, interest was not considered to be significant. A comprehensive example using the time value of money to value a forward contract is presented in Appendix 11A.

Illustration of Managing an Exposed Net Liability Position

The following example shows the accounting for the management of an exposed foreign currency position with a forward exchange contract. For purposes of this example, assume the following:

1. On October 1, 20X1, Peerless Products purchases goods on account from Tokyo Industries in the amount of 2,000,000 yen.
2. This transaction is denominated in yen, and Peerless Products offsets its exposed foreign currency liability with a forward exchange contract for the receipt of 2,000,000 yen from a foreign exchange broker.
3. The term of the forward exchange contract equals the six-month credit period extended by Tokyo Industries.
4. December 31 is the year-end of Peerless Products, and the payable is settled on April 1, 20X2.

The relevant direct exchange rates are as follows:

	U.S. Dollar–Equivalent Value of 1 Yen	
Date	**Spot Rate**	**Forward Exchange Rate**
October 1, 20X1 (transaction date)	$0.0070	$0.0075 (180 days)
December 31, 20X1 (balance sheet date)	0.0080	0.0077 (90 days)
April 1, 20X2 (settlement date)	0.0076	

The following timeline summarizes these transactions:

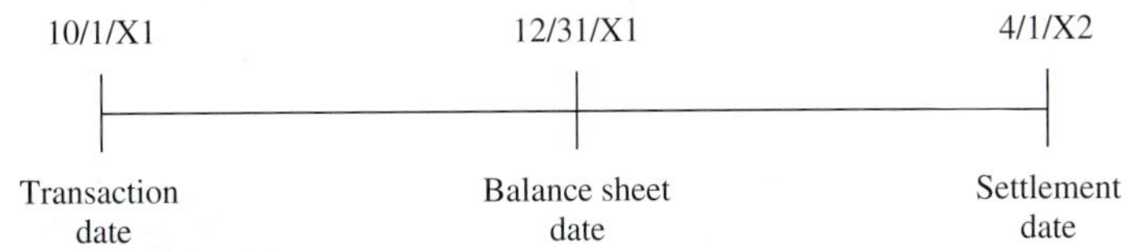

- Incur liability denominated in yen.
- Sign 180-day forward exchange contract to receive yen.

- Obtain yen by settling forward exchange contract.
- Pay yen to settle account payable.

The following entries record the events for this illustration.

October 1, 20X1

(5)	Inventory	14,000	
	Accounts Payable (¥)		14,000

Purchase inventory on account:
$14,000 = ¥2,000,000 × $0.0070 Oct. 1 spot rate.

(6)	Foreign Currency Receivable from Exchange Broker (¥)	15,000	
	Dollars Payable to Exchange Broker ($)		15,000

Purchase forward contract to receive 2,000,000 yen:
$15,000 = ¥2,000,000 × $0.0075 forward rate.

These entries record the purchase of inventory on credit, which is denominated in yen, and the signing of a six-month forward exchange contract to receive 2,000,000 yen in exchange for $15,000 (¥2,000,000 × $0.0075 forward rate). The amount payable to the exchange broker is denominated in U.S. dollars whereas the receivable from the broker is denominated in yen.

The two line items in entry (6) can be thought of together as a forward exchange contract on a net basis. On October 1, the day the contract is purchased, the forward exchange contract has zero net value. A mini trial balance on October 1 after all entries have been recorded would appear as follows:

As of October 1, 20X1

	Case 1
Forward Exchange Contract (Net)	
Foreign Currency Receivable from Broker (¥)	**15,000**
Dollars Payable to Exchange Broker ($)	**(15,000)**
	0
Inventory	**14,000**
Accounts Payable (¥)	**(14,000)**

The entries for the transaction, the adjusting journal entries for the balance sheet date valuations, and the settlements of the forward contract and the accounts payable are posted to T-accounts in Figure 11–4.

The required adjusting entries on December 31, 20X1, Peerless' fiscal year-end, are

(7)	Foreign Currency Receivable from Exchange Broker (¥)	400	
	Foreign Currency Transaction Gain		400

Adjust receivable denominated in yen to current U.S. dollar–equivalent value using the forward rate:
$ 15,400 = ¥2,000,000 × $0.0077 Dec. 31 90-day forward rate
−15,000 = ¥2,000,000 × $0.0075 Oct. 1 180-day forward rate
$ 400 = ¥2,000,000 × ($0.0077 − $0.0075).

FIGURE 11–4
T-Accounts for the Illustration of the Management of an Exposed Net Liability

Foreign Currency Receivable from Broker (¥)

(6)	15,000		
(7)	400		
Bal. 12/31	15,400		
		(9)	200
		(12)	15,200
Bal. 4/1	0		

Accounts Payable (¥)

		(5)	14,000
		(8)	2,000
		Bal. 12/31	16,000
(10)	800		
(13)	15,200		
		Bal. 4/1	0

Foreign Currency Units (¥)

(12)	15,200	(13)	15,200
Bal. 4/1	0		

Dollars Payable to Exchange Broker ($)

		(6)	15,000
		Bal. 12/31	15,000
(11)	15,000		
		Bal 4/1	0

(8)	Foreign Currency Transaction Loss	2,000	
	Accounts Payable (¥)		2,000

Adjust payable denominated in yen to current U.S. dollar–equivalent value using the spot rate:

$ 16,000 = ¥2,000,000 × $0.0080 Dec. 31, spot rate
−14,000 = ¥2,000,000 × $0.0070 Oct. 1, spot rate
$ 2,000 = ¥2,000,000 × ($0.0080 − $0.0070).

Note that the foreign currency–denominated account payable is valued by using the spot rate. This is the valuation requirement specified in **ASC 830.** The forward exchange contract is valued using the forward exchange rate for the remainder of the forward contract. This valuation basis is required by **ASC 815.** The direct exchange spot rate has increased between October 1, 20X1, the date of the foreign currency transaction, and December 31, 20X1, the balance sheet date. As previously illustrated, this means that the U.S. dollar has weakened relative to the yen because it takes more U.S. currency to acquire 1 yen at year-end (¥1 = $0.0080) than at the initial date of the purchase transaction (¥1 = $0.0070), and a U.S. company with a liability in yen experiences an exchange loss. The U.S. dollar–equivalent values of the foreign currency–denominated accounts at October 1, 20X1, and December 31, 20X1, follow:

	U.S. Dollar–Equivalent Values of Foreign Currency–Denominated Accounts		Foreign Currency Transaction Gain (Loss)
Accounts	**October 1, 20X1 (transaction date)**	**December 31, 20X1 (balance sheet date)**	
Foreign Currency Receivable from Exchange Broker (¥)	$15,000 (*a*)	$15,400 (*b*)	$ 400
Accounts Payable (¥)	14,000 (*c*)	16,000 (*d*)	(2,000)

(*a*) ¥2,000,000 × $0.0075 October 1, 180-day forward rate
(*b*) ¥2,000,000 × $0.0077 December 31, 90-day forward rate
(*c*) ¥2,000,000 × $0.0070 October 1, spot rate
(*d*) ¥2,000,000 × $0.0080 December 31, spot rate

On October 1, the U.S. dollar–equivalent value of the foreign currency receivable from the broker is $15,000. Because of the increase in the forward exchange rate of the yen relative to the dollar (i.e., the weakening of the dollar versus the yen), the U.S. dollar–equivalent value of the foreign currency receivable on December 31, 20X1, increases to $15,400, resulting in a foreign currency transaction gain of $400. For the U.S. company, the U.S. dollar–equivalent value of the liability has increased to $16,000, resulting in a $2,000 foreign currency transaction loss. Because of the differing valuation requirements of the forward contract and the exposed liability, the exchange gain of the accounts payable (¥) is not necessarily an exact offset of the exchange loss on the foreign currency receivable (¥).

The required entries on April 1, 20X2, the settlement date, are

(9)	Foreign Currency Transaction Loss	200	
	Foreign Currency Receivable from Exchange Broker (¥)		200

Adjust receivable to spot rate on settlement date:
$ 15,200 = ¥2,000,000 × $0.0076 Apr. 1, 20X2, spot rate
−15,400 = ¥2,000,000 × $0.0077 Dec. 31, 20X1, 90-day forward rate
$ 200 = ¥2,000,000 × ($0.0076 − $0.0077).

(10)	Accounts Payable (¥)	800	
	Foreign Currency Transaction Gain		800

Adjust payable denominated in yen to spot rate on settlement date:
¥2,000,000 × ($0.0076 − $0.0080).

(11)	Dollars Payable to Exchange Broker ($)	15,000	
	Cash		15,000

Deliver U.S. dollars to currency broker as specified in forward contract.

(12)	Foreign Currency Units (¥)	15,200	
	Foreign Currency Receivable from Exchange Broker (¥)		15,200

Receive ¥2,000,000 from exchange broker; valued at Apr. 1, 20X2, spot rate:
$15,200 = ¥2,000,000 × $0.0076.

(13)	Accounts Payable (¥)	15,200	
	Foreign Currency Units (¥)		15,200

Pay 2,000,000 yen to Tokyo Industries Inc. in settlement of liability denominated in yen.

The direct exchange spot rate has decreased from the $0.0080 rate on the balance sheet date to $0.0076 on April 1, 20X2, the settlement date, indicating that the U.S. dollar has strengthened relative to the yen. Fewer dollars are needed to acquire the same number of yen on the settlement date than were needed on the balance sheet date. The forward exchange contract becomes due on April 1, 20X2, and is now valued at the current spot rate. The difference between the 90-day forward rate on December 31, 20X1, and the spot rate at the date of the completion of the forward rate results in the loss of $200. The U.S. dollar–equivalent values of the foreign currency–denominated accounts on December 31, 20X1, and April 1, 20X2, follow:

	U.S. Dollar–Equivalent Values of Foreign Currency–Denominated Accounts		**Foreign Currency Transaction Gain (Loss)**
Accounts	**December 31, 20X1 (balance sheet date)**	**April 1, 20X2 (settlement date)**	
Foreign Currency Receivable from Exchange Broker (¥)	$15,400 (*a*)	$15,200 (*b*)	$(200)
Accounts Payable (¥)	16,000 (c)	15,200 (*d*)	800

(*a*) ¥2,000,000 × $0.0077 December 31, 90-day forward rate
(*b*) ¥2,000,000 × $0.0076 April 1, 20X2, spot rate
(*c*) ¥2,000,000 × $0.0080 December 31, spot rate
(*d*) ¥2,000,000 × $0.0076 April 1, 20X2 spot rate

On December 31, 20X1, the U.S. dollar–equivalent value of the foreign currency receivable from the broker is $15,400. Because the yen weakened relative to the dollar, the foreign currency receivable on April 1, 20X2, is lower in U.S. dollar–equivalent value, and an exchange loss of $200 is recognized. The U.S. dollar–equivalent value of the foreign currency account payable is $16,000 on December 31, 20X1, but because the yen weakened (i.e., the dollar strengthened) during the period from December 31, 20X1, to April 1, 20X2, the U.S. dollar–equivalent value of the payable decreases to $15,200 on April 1, 20X2. This results in an $800 foreign currency transaction gain during this period.

Note that the total net foreign exchange transaction loss for the two years combined is $1,000 [20X1: $(2,000) plus $400; 20X2: $800 less $(200)]. This is the effect of the forward contract premium on October 1, 20X1, being taken into the earnings stream. Note the premium was for the difference between the forward rate ($0.0075) and the spot rate ($0.0070) at the date the forward contract was signed. At the April 1, 20X2, completion date, both of the foreign currency–denominated accounts are valued at the spot rate. Thus, the ¥2,000,000 × ($0.0070 − $0.0075) premium is the net effect on earnings over the term of the forward contract. The two accounts denominated in foreign currency start at different valuations but end using the same spot rate at the end of the term of the forward contract.

The forward exchange contract offsets the foreign currency liability position. On April 1, 20X2, Peerless pays the $15,000 forward contract price to the exchange broker and receives the 2,000,000 yen, which it then uses to extinguish its account payable to Tokyo Industries. Note that after settlement, all account balances in Figure 11–4 are reduced to zero.

If Peerless Products had a foreign currency receivable, it also could manage its exposed net asset position by acquiring a forward exchange contract to deliver foreign currency to the exchange broker. In this case, the forward currency payable to the exchange broker is denominated in the foreign currency. The forward exchange contract is settled when Peerless gives the broker the foreign currency units it has received from its customer. The foreign currency is then exchanged for U.S. dollars at the agreed-upon contractual rate from the forward exchange contract. The assets and liabilities denominated in foreign currency units must be revalued to their U.S. dollar–equivalent values in the same manner as for the import illustration. Recall that, for valuation purposes, **ASC 815** requires the use of the forward exchange rate for forward contracts and **ASC 830** requires the use of spot rates for exposed net asset or liability accounts arising from foreign currency transactions.

Formal Balance Sheets Reporting Net Amounts for Forward Exchange Contracts

ASC 815 requires the recognition of all derivatives in the statement of financial position (the balance sheet) at net fair value. This means that the balance sheet presents the net of the forward contract receivable from the exchange broker against the dollars payable to the exchange broker. Some companies account for the forward exchange contract with only memorandum entries, using the philosophy that the contract is simply for the exchange of one currency for another. The underlying exposed accounts receivable or accounts payable denominated in foreign currency units are still presented. For example, a formal balance sheet prepared on October 1, 20X1, after the transactions recorded in entries (5) and (6) reports the following net amounts:

Assets		Liabilities	
Inventory	$14,000	Accounts Payable (¥)	$14,000

Under the net method of reporting the forward exchange contract, the gain or loss on the change in the value of the forward exchange contract must be recorded and reported in the balance sheet. The balance sheet prepared on December 31, 20X1, after posting entries (7) and (8) includes the following:

Assets		Liabilities and Equity	
Forward Exchange Contract (¥) (at net fair value)	$400	Accounts Payable (¥)	$16,000
		Retained Earnings (for net exchange loss)	(1,600)

Note that under the net approach to reporting, the forward exchange contract is valued at net fair value. The $2,000 foreign currency transaction loss on the account payable denominated in yen is partially offset with the $400 foreign currency transaction gain for the forward contract receivable in yen.

The net balance sheet presented on April 1, 20X2, immediately after entry (10) but before the settlement of the forward exchange contract and the accounts payable is

Assets		Liabilities and Equity	
Forward Exchange Contract (¥) (at net fair value)	$200	Accounts Payable (¥)	$15,200
		Retained Earnings (for amount of the premium)	(1,000)

The forward exchange contract is then settled by paying the exchange broker the $15,000 in U.S. dollars as initially contracted for in the forward exchange contract, receiving the 2,000,000 yen now valued at $15,200, and closing the net forward exchange contract for the difference of the $200.

The net approach is required for reporting derivative forward exchange contracts on the balance sheet. Nevertheless, we believe that recording both sides of the forward exchange contracts in the account maintains a full record of each side of the transaction.

Case 2: Hedging an Unrecognized Foreign Currency Firm Commitment: A Foreign Currency Fair Value Hedge

A company may expose itself to foreign currency risk *before* a purchase or sale transaction occurs. For example, a company may sign a noncancelable order to purchase goods from a foreign entity in the future to be paid for in the foreign currency. By agreeing to a purchase price in the present for a future purchase, the company has accepted an *identifiable foreign currency commitment* although the purchase has not yet occurred; that is, the purchase contract is still executory (unrecognized). The company will not have a liability obligation until after delivery of the goods, but it is exposed to changes in currency exchange rates before the transaction date (the date of delivery of the goods).

ASC 815 specified the accounting requirements for the use of forward exchange contracts ***hedging unrecognized foreign currency firm commitments.*** The company can separate the commitment into its financial instrument (the obligation to pay yen) and nonfinancial asset (the right to receive inventory) aspects. The forward contract taken out is then a hedge of the changes in the fair value of the firm commitment for the foreign currency risk being hedged. A hedge of a firm commitment comes under the accounting for fair value hedges, and the forward contract is to be valued at its fair value.

It is interesting to note the different accounting treatment of a hedge of a forecasted transaction (cash flow hedge) versus that for a hedge of an unrecognized foreign currency firm commitment (fair value hedge). A *forecasted* transaction is *anticipated* but not *guaranteed.* The forecasted transaction may actually occur as anticipated, but a hedge of a forecasted transaction is accounted for as a cash flow hedge with the effective portion of the change in the hedge's fair value recognized in Other Comprehensive Income. On the other hand, a firm commitment is an agreement with an unrelated party that is binding and usually legally enforceable. The agreement has the following characteristics:

1. The agreement specifies all significant terms such as the quantity, the fixed price, and the timing of the transaction. The price may be denominated in either the entity's functional currency or in a foreign currency.
2. The agreement must contain a penalty provision sufficiently large to make performance of the agreement probable.

A forecasted transaction may become a firm commitment if an agreement having these listed characteristics is made between the parties. Any cash flow hedge of the forecasted transaction may be changed to a fair value hedge when the firm commitment agreement is made. However, any amounts recorded in Other Comprehensive Income under the cash flow hedge are not reclassified into earnings until the initially forecasted transaction impacts earnings.

ASC 815 provides for management of an enterprise to select the basis by which the effectiveness of the hedge will be measured. Management may select the forward exchange rate, the spot rate, or the intrinsic value for measuring effectiveness. The examples used in this chapter use the forward rate, which is consistent with the general rule of valuing forward exchange contracts as specified in **ASC 815.** The measure of the change in fair value of the forward contract uses the forward exchange rate for the remainder of the term and then, if interest is significant, the change in the forward rates is discounted to reflect the time value of money. The entries for a hedge of an identifiable foreign currency commitment are presented in the following illustration.

Illustration of Hedging an Unrecognized Foreign Currency Firm Commitment

Advanced StudyGuide .com

For illustration purposes, the import transaction between Peerless Products and Tokyo Industries used throughout this chapter is extended with the following information:

1. On August 1, 20X1, Peerless contracts to purchase special-order goods from Tokyo Industries. Their manufacture and delivery will take place in 60 days (on October 1, 20X1). The contract price is 2,000,000 yen, to be paid by April 1, 20X2, which is 180 days after delivery.
2. On August 1, Peerless hedges its foreign currency payable commitment with a forward exchange contract to receive 2,000,000 yen in 240 days (the 60 days until delivery plus 180 days of credit period). The future rate for a 240-day forward contract is \$0.0073 to 1 yen. The purpose of this 240-day forward exchange contract is twofold. First, for the 60 days from August 1, 20X1, until October 1, 20X1, the forward exchange contract is a hedge of an identifiable foreign currency commitment. For the 180-day period from October 1, 20X1, until April 1, 20X2, the forward exchange contract is a hedge of a foreign currency exposed net liability position.

The relevant exchange rates for this example are as follows:

	U.S. Dollar–Equivalent Value of 1 Yen	
Date	**Spot Rate**	**Forward Exchange Rate**
August 1, 20X1	\$0.0065	\$0.0073 (240 days)
October 1, 20X1	0.0070	0.0075 (180 days)

A time line for the transactions follows:

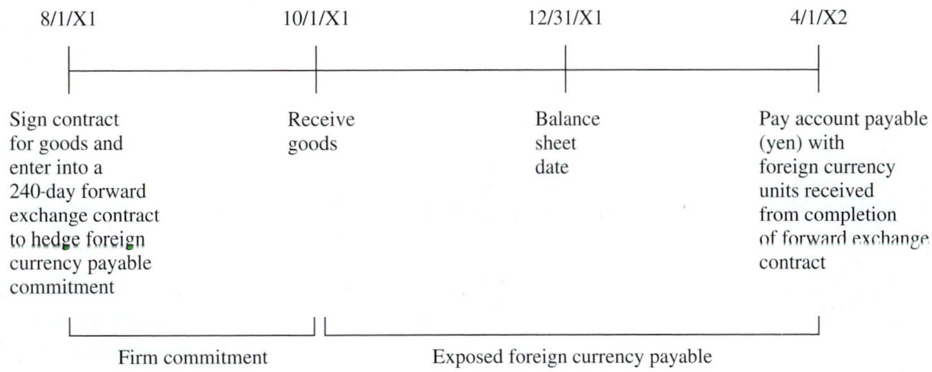

On August 1, 20X1, the company determines the value of its commitment to pay yen for the future accounts payable using the forward exchange rate. However, as summarized in Figure 11–5A, the payable is not recorded on August 1 because the exchange transaction has not yet occurred; the payable is maintained in memorandum form only. The forward exchange contract must be valued at its fair value. At the time the company enters into the forward exchange contract, the contract has no net fair value because the \$14,600 foreign currency receivable equals the \$14,600 dollars payable under the contract. The subsequent changes in the fair value of the forward contract are measured using the forward rate and then, if interest is significant, discounted to reflect the time value of money. For purposes of this illustration, we assume that interest is not significant and that hedge effectiveness is measured with reference to the change in the forward exchange rates.

August 1, 20X1

		Debit	Credit
(14)	Foreign Currency Receivable from Exchange Broker (¥)	14,600	
	Dollars Payable to Exchange Broker (\$)		14,600

Sign forward exchange contract for receipt of 2,000,000 yen in 240 days:
\$14,600 = ¥2,000,000 × \$0.0073 Aug. 1, 240-day forward rate.

On October 1, 20X1, the forward exchange contract is revalued to its fair value. The accounts payable in yen are recorded at the time the inventory is received.

October 1, 20X1

		Debit	Credit
(15)	Foreign Currency Receivable from Exchange Broker (¥)	400	
	Foreign Currency Transaction Gain		400

Adjust forward contract to fair value, using the forward rate at this date, and recognize gain:
\$ 15,000 = ¥2,000,000 × \$0.0075 Oct. 1, 180-day forward rate
−14,600 = ¥2,000,000 × \$0.0073 Aug. 1, 240-day forward rate
\$ 400 = ¥2,000,000 × (\$0.0075 − \$0.0073).

		Debit	Credit
(16)	Foreign Currency Transaction Loss	400	
	Firm Commitment		400

To record the loss on the financial instrument aspect of the firm commitment:
\$ 15,000 = ¥2,000,000 × \$0.0075 Oct. 1, 180-day forward rate
−14,600 = ¥2,000,000 × \$0.0073 Aug. 1, 240-day forward rate
\$ 400 = ¥2,000,000 × (\$0.0075 − \$0.0073).

The Firm Commitment account is a temporary account for the term of the unrecognized firm commitment. If it has a debit balance, it is shown in the assets section of the balance sheet; when it has a credit balance, as in this example, it is shown in the liability section of the balance sheet:

Assets		Liabilities and Equity	
Forward Exchange Contract (¥) (at net fair value)	\$400	Firm Commitment	\$400

Note that the \$400 foreign currency transaction gain is offset against the \$400 foreign currency transaction loss, resulting in no net effect on earnings.

FIGURE 11–5A Journal Entries: Hedge of an Unrecognized Firm Commitment

Forward Exchange Contract (Use forward exchange rate)				Hedge of an Unrecognized Firm Commitment (Use forward exchange rate)		
August 1, 20X1. Recognize forward exchange contract valued at forward rate.						
(14) Foreign Currency Receivable (¥)	14,600					
Dollars Payable to Exchange Broker		14,600				
October 1, 20X1. Revalue foreign currency receivable and firm commitment hedge using forward rate.						
(15) Foreign Currency Receivable (¥)	400			(16) Foreign Currency Transaction Loss	400	
Foreign Currency Transaction Gain		400		Firm Commitment		400
				Economic Management of an Exposed Foreign Currency Payable (Use spot exchange rate)		
October 1, 20X1. Receive inventory, close firm commitment, and recognize foreign currency accounts payable.						
				(17) Inventory	13,600	
				Firm Commitment	400	
				Accounts Payable (¥)		14,000

The next entry records the receipt of the inventory and the recognition of the accounts payable in yen. Note that the temporary account, Firm Commitment, is closed against the purchase price of the inventory. The accounts payable are valued at the spot exchange rate at the purchase date **(ASC 830).**

(17)	Inventory	13,600	
	Firm Commitment	400	
	Accounts Payable (¥)		14,000

Record accounts payable at spot rate and record inventory purchase:
$14,000 = ¥2,000,000 × $0.0070 Oct. 1, spot rate.

Key Observations from Illustration

The August 1, 20X1, entry records the signing of the forward exchange contract that is used to hedge the identifiable foreign currency commitment arising from the noncancelable purchase agreement. At the date of signing, this forward exchange contract has a zero net value as shown in the following table. In entries (15) and (16), the forward contract and the underlying hedged foreign currency payable commitment are both revalued to their current values, and the $400 gain on the forward contract offsets the $400 loss on the foreign currency payable commitment. Entry (17) records the accounts payable in yen at the current spot rate and records the $400 net change in the inventory that results from the recognition of the $400 loss on the financial instrument aspect of the firm commitment in entry (16).

	Case 2 As of Aug 1	Case 2 As of Oct 1	Case 2 As of Oct 1	Case 1 As of Oct 1
Forward Exchange Contract (Net)		Before Inventory Purchase	After Inventory Purchase	
Foreign Currency Receivable from Broker (¥)	14,600	15,000	15,000	15,000
Dollars Payable to Exchange Broker ($)	(14,600)	(14,600)	(14,600)	(15,000)
	0	400	400	0
Inventory			13,600	14,000
Accounts Payable (¥)			(14,000)	(14,000)
Firm Commitment	0	(400)	0	
Foreign Currency Transaction Gain		(400)	(400)	
Foreign Currency Transaction Loss		400	400	

At this point, the company has an exposed net liability position, which is hedged with a forward exchange contract. The Accounts Payable of (¥)14,000 and the Foreign Currency

FIGURE 11–5B Journal Entries: Management of an Exposed Net Liability Using a Forward Exchange Contract

	Forward Exchange Contract (Use forward exchange rate)				Exposed Foreign Currency Position (Use spot rate)		
December 31, 20X1. Revalue forward contract using forward rate, and accounts payable in yen using spot rate.							
(7)	Foreign Currency Receivable (¥)	400		(8)	Foreign Currency Transaction Loss	2000	
	Foreign Currency Transaction Gain		400		Accounts Payable (¥)		2000
April 1, 20X2. Revalue forward contract at its termination to spot rate, and accounts payable in yen to spot rate.							
(9)	Foreign Currency Transaction Loss	200		(10)	Accounts Payable (¥)	800	
	Foreign Currency Receivable (¥)		200		Foreign Currency Transadion Gain		800
April 1, 20X2. Deliver $14,600 in U.S. dollars to exchange broker, receiving yen. Use yen to settle accounts payable.							
(11)	Dollars Payable to Exchange Broker	14,600					
	Cash		14,600				
(12)	Foreign Currency Units (¥)	15,200		(13)	Accounts Payable (¥)	15,200	
	Foreign Currency Receivable (¥)		15,200		Foreign Currency Units (¥)		15,200

Receivable from Broker of (¥)15,000 are exactly the same as in Case 1. Therefore, the subsequent accounting follows the accounting for an exposed foreign currency liability position as presented previously in Case 1. Figure 11–5B presents a side-by-side comparison of the journal entries for the forward contract, which is valued at the forward exchange rate, and the exposed foreign currency–denominated account payable. This payable is recognized at the time the company receives the inventory and is valued using the spot exchange rate at the purchase date.

Advanced StudyGuide .com

Case 3: Hedging a Forecasted Foreign Currency Transaction: A Foreign Currency Cash Flow Hedge

It is interesting to note the different accounting treatment of a hedge of a forecasted transaction as a cash flow hedge versus that of an identifiable foreign currency commitment as a fair value hedge. A forecasted transaction is anticipated but not guaranteed. The forecasted transaction may actually occur as anticipated, but a hedge of a forecasted transaction is accounted for as a cash flow hedge with the effective portion of the change in fair value of the hedging instrument recognized in Other Comprehensive Income. This type of hedge is against the changes in possible future cash flow that may result from changes in the foreign currency exchange rate. A forecasted transaction may become a firm commitment if the parties make a binding agreement. Prior to **ASC 815,** an entity could designate a forward foreign currency contract as a cash flow hedge if the contract's purpose was offsetting forecasted cash flows, including transactions such as forecasted purchases or sales. Changes in the fair value of the cash flow hedge would be recognized as part of other comprehensive income. When the forecasted transaction became a firm commitment, the forward contract would be redesignated as a fair value hedge, and changes in the fair value contract would then be recognized in earnings. Any amount recorded in Other Comprehensive Income under the cash flow hedge would not be reclassified into earnings until the initially forecasted transaction impacted earnings. If the forecasted foreign currency transaction did not occur and was not expected to occur in the future, the amount recorded in Other Comprehensive Income would be reclassified into earnings. The forward rate was used to value the forward contract, and the spot rate was used to value the account receivable or payable resulting from the transaction.

ASC 815 allows management the additional option of designating the forward contract as a cash flow hedge from the time the contract is initially made until the final settlement of the payable or receivable rather than requiring that the contract be redesignated as a fair value hedge when the forecasted transaction becomes a firm commitment. Changes in the value of the forward contract are measured using the forward exchange rate whereas changes in the account payable or receivable are measured using the spot exchange rate. However, **ASC 815** requires that other comprehensive income from the forward contract revaluation be offset for any foreign exchange gain or loss on the account receivable or payable. Any remaining component of other comprehensive income is taken into the earnings stream only on final completion of the earnings process. Note that the forward contract must meet the requirements of a hedging instrument under the provisions of **ASC 815,** including the designation and tests of effectiveness.

ASC 815 allows management to (1) designate the forward contract as a cash flow hedge while it is a forecasted transaction and then redesignate it as a fair value hedge for the remainder of the contract or (2) designate the forward contract as a cash flow hedge for the entire period of time from the initial forecasting of the transaction through the eventual settlement of the receivable or payable. However, most companies regularly hedge their foreign currency receivables and payables and are likely to declare the forward contract as a continuing cash flow hedge in order to fully offset any gains or losses on changes in the fair value of the forward contract.

The following example is based on the data in Case 2 but adds the following assumption: The purchase of inventory is forecasted in August, but there is not a binding agreement for this purchase. Peerless Products Corporation enters into the 240-day forward exchange contract as a designated hedge against the future cash flows from the forecasted transaction, including the foreign currency–denominated accounts payable that would result from the purchase. Figure 11–6 presents the entries for this

FIGURE 11–6 Journal Entries for Cash Flow Hedge Redesignated as Fair Value Hedge When a Forecasted Transaction Becomes a Transaction

Entries for Forward Contract (Use forward exchange rate)				Entries for Foreign Currency Account Payable (Use spot rate)			
August 1, 20X1. Acquire forward exchange contract valued at forward rate.							
(14)	Foreign Currency Receivable (¥)	14,600					
	Dollars Payable to Exchange Broker		14,600				
October 1, 20X1. Receive inventory that was a forecasted transaction and recognize the foreign currency accounts payable at the spot rate. Change designation from a cash flow hedge to a fair value hedge; bring the forward contract to fair value as of this date.							
(15C)	Foreign Currency Receivable (¥)	400		(17C)	Inventory	14,000	
	Other Comprehensive Income		400		Accounts Payable (¥)		14,000
	¥2,000,000 × ($0.0075 − $0.0073).						
December 31, 20X1. Revalue the forward contract to year-end fair values using the change in the forward rate since October 1 and recognize gain or loss in net income. Revalue accounts payable in yen using the spot rate.							
(7)	Foreign Currency Receivable (¥)	400		(8)	Foreign Currency Transaction Loss	2,000	
	Foreign Currency Transaction Gain		400		Accounts Payable (¥)		2,000
	¥2,000,000 × ($0.0077 − $0.0075).						
April 1, 20X2. Revalue the forward contract using the spot rate at the termination of the contract and accounts payable in yen using the spot rate.							
(9)	Foreign Currency Transaction Loss	200		(10)	Accounts Payable (¥)	800	
	Foreign Currency Receivable (¥)		200		Foreign Currency Transaction Gain		800
	¥2,000,000 × ($0.0076 − $0.0077).						
April 1, 20X2. Deliver $14,600 in U.S. dollars to the exchange broker and receive yen. Use yen to settle accounts payable.							
(11)	Dollars Payable to Exchange Broker	14,600					
	Cash		14,600				
(12)	Foreign Currency Units (¥)	15,200		(13)	Accounts Payable (¥)	15,200	
	Foreign Currency Receivable (¥)		15,200		Foreign Currency Units (¥)		15,200
Assumed sale of inventory and culmination of earnings process of other comprehensive income from forward contract.							
	Other Comprehensive Income	400			Cost of Goods Sold	14,000	
	Cost of Goods Sold		400		Inventory		14,000

FIGURE 11–7 Journal Entries for Cash Flow Hedge of a Forecasted Transaction

Entries for Forward Contract (Use forward exchange rate)				Entries for Foreign Currency Account Payable (Use spot rate)			
August 1, 20X1. Acquire forward exchange contract valued at forward rate.							
(14)	Foreign Currency Receivable (¥)	14,600					
	Dollars Payable to Exchange Broker		14,600				
October 1, 20X1. Receive inventory that was a forecasted transaction and recognize the foreign currency accounts payable at the spot rate.							
	(No revaluation of foreign currency receivable required at this date)			(17C)	Inventory	14,000	
					Accounts Payable (¥)		14,000
December 31, 20X1. Revalue the forward contract to year-end fair value using the change in the forward rate since August 1 and recognize the effective portion of the change in value as other comprehensive income. Revalue accounts payable in yen using the spot rate. Then, in accordance with **ASC 815,** reclassify a portion of the other comprehensive income to equally offset the foreign currency transaction loss recognized on the foreign currency payable that was remeasured using the spot exchange rate in accordance with **ASC 830.**							
(7C)	Foreign Currency Receivable (¥)	800		(8)	Foreign Currency Transaction Loss	2,000	
	Other Comprehensive Income		800		Accounts Payable (¥)		2,000
	[¥2,000,000 × ($0.0077 − $0.0073)]						
(C)	Other Comprehensive Income	2,000					
	Foreign Currency Transaction Gain		2,000				
	To offset loss on account payable.						
April 1, 20X2. Revalue the forward contract at its termination using the spot rate and accounts payable in yen using the spot rate. Offset transaction gain on payable against other comprehensive income.							
(9C)	Other Comprehensive Income	200		(10)	Accounts Payable (¥)	800	
	Foreign Currency Receivable (¥)		200		Foreign Currency Transaction Gain		800
(C)	Foreign Currency Transaction Loss	800					
	Other Comprehensive Income		800				
	To offset gain on account payable.						
April 1, 20X2. Deliver $14,600 in U.S. dollars to the exchange broker and receive yen. Use yen to settle accounts payable.							
(11)	Dollars Payable to Exchange Broker	14,600					
	Cash		14,600				
(12)	Foreign Currency Units (¥)	15,200		(13)	Accounts Payable (¥)	15,200	
	Foreign Currency Receivable (¥)		15,200		Foreign Currency Units (¥)		15,200
Assumed sale of inventory and culmination of earnings process of other comprehensive income from forward contract.							
	Cost of Goods Sold	600			Cost of Goods Sold	14,000	
	Other Comprehensive Income		600		Inventory		14,000

case, assuming that the hedge is designated as a cash flow hedge when the transaction is forecasted and then redesignated as a fair value hedge when the transaction occurs and the inventory is purchased. Figure 11–6 presents the entries for this case by bringing into the illustration Case 1 entries that would not change and noting the entries that would change with a *C* after the entry number. Note that the entry on October 1 records the effect of the change in value of the forward contract as a component of Other Comprehensive Income.

Figure 11–7 presents the entries for this case assuming the hedge is designated as a cash flow hedge and remains as such between inception in August and final settlement in April. Figure 11–7 presents the entries for this case by bringing into the illustration

Case 1 entries that would not change and noting the entries that would change with a letter *C* after the entry number. Note the major differences in accounting for the forward contract as a cash flow hedge here versus as a fair value hedge in Case 2 are (1) the effective portion of the revaluation of the forward exchange contract is recorded in Other Comprehensive Income, (2) no firm commitment account exists under a forecasted transaction, (3) no revaluation of the forward contract receivable is required on October 1 and the inventory is recorded at its equivalent U.S. dollar cost determined at the spot rate, (4) there is an offset against Other Comprehensive Income to fully match the foreign currency transaction gain or loss recognized on the exposed foreign currency account payable, and (5) the $600 remaining balance in Other Comprehensive Income after the foreign currency payable is paid on April 1, 20X2, is finally reclassified into cost of goods sold at the time the inventory is sold, which is the culmination of the earnings process related to the cash flow hedge.

Case 4: Speculation in Foreign Currency Markets

An entity also may decide to speculate in foreign currency as with any other commodity. For example, a U.S. company expects that the dollar will strengthen against the Swiss franc, that is, that the direct exchange rate will decrease. In this case, the U.S. company might ***speculate with a forward exchange contract*** to sell francs for future delivery, expecting to be able to purchase them at a lower price at the time of delivery.

The economic substance of this foreign currency speculation is to expose the investor to foreign exchange risk for which the investor expects to earn a profit. The exchange rate for valuing accounts related to speculative foreign exchange contracts is the forward rate for the remaining term of the forward contract. The gain or loss on a speculative forward contract is computed by determining the difference between the forward exchange rate on the contract date of (or on the date of a previous valuation) and the forward exchange rate available for the remaining term of the contract. The forward exchange rate is used to value the forward contract.

Illustration of Speculation with Forward Contract

The following example illustrates the accounting for a U.S. company entering into a speculative forward exchange contract in Swiss francs (SFr), a currency in which the company has no receivables, payables, or commitments.

1. On October 1, 20X1, when the spot rate was $0.73 = SFr 1, Peerless Products entered into a 180-day forward exchange contract to deliver SFr 4,000 at a forward rate of $0.74 = SFr 1. Thus, the forward contract was to deliver SFr 4,000 and receive $2,960 (SFr 4,000 × $0.74).
2. On December 31, 20X1, the balance sheet date, the forward rate for a 90-day forward contract was $0.78 = SFr 1, and the spot rate for francs was $0.75 = SFr 1.
3. On April 1, 20X2, the company acquired SFr 4,000 in the open market and delivered the francs to the broker, receiving the agreed-upon forward contract price of $2,960. At this date, the spot rate was $0.77 = SFr 1.

A summary of the direct exchange rates for this illustration follows.

	U.S. Dollar–Equivalent of 1 Franc	
Date	**Spot Rate**	**Forward Rate**
October 1, 20X1	$0.73	$0.74 (180 days)
December 31, 20X1	0.75	0.78 (90 days)
April 1, 20X2	0.77	

A time line of the economic events is as follows:

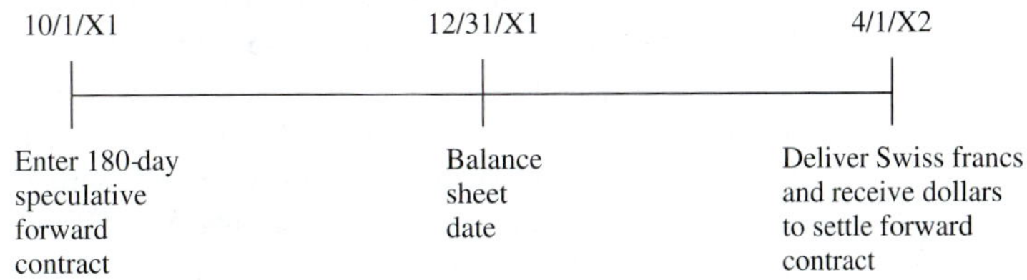

The entries for these transactions are as follows:

October 1, 20X1

(18)	Dollars Receivable from Exchange Broker ($)	2,960	
	Foreign Currency Payable to Exchange Broker (SFr)		2,960

Enter into speculative forward exchange contract:
$2,960 = SFr 4,000 × $0.74, the 180-day forward rate.

December 31, 20X1

(19)	Foreign Currency Transaction Loss	160	
	Foreign Currency Payable to Exchange Broker (SFr)		160

Recognize speculation loss on forward contract for difference between initial 180-day forward rate and forward rate for remaining term to maturity of contract of 90 days:
$160 = SFr 4,000 × ($0.78 − $0.74).

April 1, 20X2

(20)	Foreign Currency Payable to Exchange Broker (SFr)	40	
	Foreign Currency Transaction Gain		40

Revalue foreign currency payable to spot rate at end of term of forward contract:
$40 = SFr 4,000 × ($0.78 − $0.77).

(21)	Foreign Currency Units (SFr)	3,080	
	Cash		3,080

Acquire foreign currency units (SFr) in open market when spot rate is $0.77 = SFr1:
$3,080 = SFr 4,000 × $0.77 spot rate.

(22)	Foreign Currency Payable to Exchange Broker (SFr)	3,080	
	Foreign Currency Units (SFr)		3,080

Deliver foreign currency units to exchange broker in settlement of forward contract:
$3,080 = SFr 4,000 × $0.77 spot rate.

(23)	Cash	2,960	
	Dollars Receivable from Exchange Broker ($)		2,960

Receive U.S. dollars from exchange broker as contracted.

Key Observations from Illustration

The October 1 entry records the forward contract payable of 4,000 Swiss francs to the exchange broker. The payables are denominated in a foreign currency but must be translated into U.S. dollars (because dollars are Peerless Products' reporting currency.). For speculative contracts, the forward exchange contract accounts are valued to fair value by using the forward exchange rate for the remaining contract term.

The December 31 entry adjusts the payable denominated in foreign currency to its appropriate balance at the balance sheet date. The payable, Foreign Currency Payable to Exchange Broker, is adjusted for the increase in the forward exchange rate from October 1, 20X1. The foreign currency transaction loss is reported on the income statement, usually under Other Income (Loss).

Entry (20), the first April 1 entry, revalues the foreign currency payable to its current U.S. dollar–equivalent value using the spot rate of exchange and recognizes the speculation gain. Entry (21) shows the acquisition of the 4,000 francs in the open market at the spot rate of $0.77 = SFr 1. These francs will be used to settle the foreign currency payable to the exchange broker. The next two entries on this date, (22) and (23), recognize the settlement of the forward contract with the delivery of the 4,000 francs to the exchange broker and the receipt of the $2,960 agreed to when the contract was signed on October 1, 20X1. The $40 foreign currency transaction gain is the difference between the value of the foreign currency contract on December 31 using the forward rate and the value of the foreign currency units on April 1 using the spot rate.

Note that the company has speculated and lost because the dollar actually weakened against the Swiss franc. The net loss on the speculative forward contract was $120, which is the difference between the $160 loss recognized in 20X1 and the $40 gain recognized in 20X2.

Although this example shows a delivery of foreign currency units with a forward exchange contract, a company also may arrange a future contract for the receipt of foreign currency units. In this case, the October 1 entry is as follows:

	October 1, 20X1		
(24)	Foreign Currency Receivable from Exchange Broker (SFr)	2,960	
	Dollars Payable to Exchange Broker ($)		2,960
	Sign forward exchange contract for future receipt of foreign currency units: $2,960 = SFr 4,000 × $0.74.		

The remainder of the accounting is similar to that of a delivery contract except that the company records an exchange gain on December 31 because it has a receivable denominated in a foreign currency that has now strengthened relative to the dollar.

Foreign Exchange Matrix

The relationships between changes in exchange rates and the resulting exchange gains and losses are summarized in Figure 11–8. For example, if a company has an account receivable denominated in a foreign currency, the exposed net monetary asset position results in the recognition of an exchange gain if the direct exchange rate increases but an

FIGURE 11–8 Foreign Exchange Matrix

Transactions or Accounts Denominated in Foreign Currency Units	Direct Exchange Rate Changes: Exchange Rate Increases (dollar has weakened)	Direct Exchange Rate Changes: Exchange Rate Decreases (dollar has strengthened)
Net monetary asset position, for example: (1) Foreign Currency Units (2) Accounts Receivable (3) Foreign Currency Receivable from Exchange Broker	EXCHANGE GAIN	EXCHANGE LOSS
Net monetary liability position, for example: (1) Accounts Payable (2) Bonds Payable (3) Foreign Currency Payable to Exchange Broker	EXCHANGE LOSS	EXCHANGE GAIN

exchange loss if the exchange rate decreases. If a company offsets an asset denominated in a foreign currency with a liability also denominated in that currency, the company has protected itself from any changes in the exchange rate because any gain is offset by an equal exchange loss.

ADDITIONAL CONSIDERATIONS

LO 11-4

Know how to measure hedge effectiveness, make interperiod tax allocations for foreign currency transactions, and hedge net investments in a foreign entity.

A Note on Measuring Hedge Effectiveness

ASC 815 states that, at the beginning of each hedging transaction, a company must define the method it will use to measure the effectiveness of the hedge. *Effectiveness* means that there will be an approximate offset, within the range of 80 to 125 percent, of the changes in the fair value of the cash flows or changes in fair value to the risk being hedged. Effectiveness must be assessed at least every three months and when the company reports financial statements or earnings. A company may elect to choose from several different measures for assessing hedge effectiveness. The examples to this point in the chapter use the change in forward rates, but a company may use the change in spot prices or change in intrinsic value. The ***intrinsic value of a derivative*** is the value related to the changes in value of the underlying item. The ***time value of a derivative*** is related to the value assigned to the opportunity to hold the derivative open for a period of time. The time value expires over the term of the derivative and is zero at the derivative's maturity date. If the company uses spot prices for measuring hedge effectiveness, any difference between the spot price and the forward price is excluded from the assessment of hedge effectiveness and is included currently in earnings.

Interperiod Tax Allocation for Foreign Currency Gains (Losses)

Temporary differences in the recognition of foreign currency gains or losses between tax accounting and GAAP accounting require interperiod tax allocation. Generally, the accrual method of recognizing the effects of changes in exchange rates in the period of change differs from the general election for recognizing exchange gains for tax purposes in the period of actual conversion of the foreign currency–denominated item. The temporary difference is recognized in accordance with **ASC 740** as a deferred tax asset or liability.

Hedges of a Net Investment in a Foreign Entity

In the earlier discussions of the use of forward exchange contracts as a hedging instrument, the exchange risks from transactions denominated in a foreign currency could be offset. This same concept is applied by U.S. companies that view a net investment in a foreign entity as a long-term commitment that exposes them to foreign currency risk. A number of balance sheet management tools are available for a U.S. company to hedge its net investment in a foreign affiliate. Management may use forward exchange contracts, other foreign currency commitments, or certain intercompany financing arrangements, including intercompany transactions. For example, a U.S. parent company could borrow 10,000 British pounds to hedge against an equivalent net asset position of its British subsidiary. Any effects of exchange rate fluctuations between the pound and the dollar would be offset by the investment in the British subsidiary and the loan payable.

ASC 815 specifies that for derivative financial instruments designated as a hedge of the foreign currency exposure of a net investment in a foreign operation, the portion of the change in fair value equivalent to a foreign currency transaction gain or loss should be reported in Other Comprehensive Income. That part of other comprehensive income resulting from a hedge of a net investment in a foreign operation then becomes part of the cumulative translation adjustment in accumulated other comprehensive income. Chapter 12 presents both the translation adjustment portion of other comprehensive income and accumulated other comprehensive income.

SUMMARY OF KEY CONCEPTS

Virtually all companies have foreign transactions. The general rule is that accounts resulting from transactions denominated in foreign currency units must be valued and reported at their equivalent U.S. dollar values. Forward exchange contracts typically use the forward rate for determining current fair value. These accounts must be adjusted to recognize the effects of changes in the exchange rates. For fair value hedges, the gain or loss is taken into current earnings. For cash flow hedges, the gain or loss is taken into other comprehensive income for the period.

KEY TERMS

cash flow hedges, *562*
current rate, *554*
derivative, *560*
fair value hedges, *561*
financial instrument, *560*
foreign currency exchange rate, *549*
foreign currency hedges, *563*
foreign currency transaction gain or loss, *555*
foreign currency transactions, *548*
foreign currency unit (FCU), *549*
forward exchange contract, *554*
functional currency, *556*
hedging unrecognized foreign currency firm commitments, *571*
intrinsic value of a derivative, *581*
local currency, *556*
local currency unit (LCU), *549*
managing an exposed foreign currency position, either a net asset or a net liability position, *565*
notional amount, *560*
reporting currency, *556*
speculate with a forward exchange contract, *578*
spot rate, *554*
spread, *554*
time value of a derivative, *581*
underlying, *560*

Appendix 11A Illustration of Valuing Forward Exchange Contracts with Recognition for the Time Value of Money

This illustration uses the example of a hedge of an identifiable, unrecognized foreign currency commitment from the chapter (Case 2) to illustrate the present value of the forward exchange contract and hedge.

1. On August 1, 20X1, Peerless Products Corporation contracts to purchase special-order goods from Tokyo Industries. The manufacture and delivery of the goods will take place in 60 days (on October 1, 20X1). The contract price is ¥2,000,000 to be paid by April 1, 20X2, which is 180 days after delivery.
2. On August 1, 20X1, Peerless Products hedges its foreign currency payable commitment with a forward exchange contract to receive ¥2,000,000 in 240 days (the 60 days until delivery plus 180 days of credit period). The future rate for a 240-day forward contract is $0.0073 to ¥1. The purpose of this 240-day forward exchange contract is twofold. First, for the 60 days from August 1, 20X1, until October 1, 20X1, the forward exchange contract is a hedge of an identifiable foreign currency commitment. For the 180-day period from October 1, 20X1, until April 1, 20X2, the forward exchange contract is a hedge of a foreign currency–exposed net liability position.
3. Peerless uses a discount rate of 10 percent to calculate the present value of the expected future cash flows from forward exchange contracts.
4. Peerless measures the effectiveness of hedges of identifiable, unrecognized firm commitments based on changes in the forward exchange rate.

The relevant exchange rates for this example are as follows:

U.S. Dollar–Equivalent Value of 1 Yen		
Date	**Spot Rate**	**Forward Exchange Rate**
August 1, 20X1	$0.0065	$0.0073 (240 days)
October 1, 20X1	0.0070	0.0075 (180 days)
December 31, 20X1 (balance sheet date)	0.0080	0.0077 (90 days)
April 1, 20X2 (settlement date)	0.0076	

The following timeline summarizes these transactions.

8/1/X1	10/1/X1	12/31/X1	4/1/X2
Sign contract for goods and enter into a 240-day forward exchange contract to hedge foreign currency payable commitment	Receive goods	Balance sheet date	Pay account payable (yen) with foreign currency units received from completion of forward exchange contract

The computation of hedge effectiveness is performed using the changes in the forward exchange rate in accordance with the general requirements of **ASC 815** and the company's specific policies regarding measurement of effectiveness of the hedge by using the forward exchange rates.

	Change in the Fair Value of		
	Forward Contract Based on Changes in Forward Rate Gain (Loss)	Firm Commitment Based on Changes in Forward Rate Gain (Loss)	Effectiveness Ratio for the Period
October 1, 20X1	\$380 (*a*)	\$(380)	1.00
December 31, 20X1	400 (*b*)	No longer applicable because firm commitment was completed on October 1, 20X1.	
April 1, 20X2	(180) (*c*)		

(a) \$380 = [(\$0.0075 − \$0.0073) × ¥2,000,000] for the \$400 cumulative, undiscounted gain from the change in the forward rates and then discounted at a 10 percent annual rate for the six-month period from October 1, 20X1, to April 1, 20X2, the completion date of the forward contract: NPV(0.05, 400) = \$380.95, rounded.
(*b*) \$400 = [(\$0.0077 − \$0.0073) × ¥2,000,000] for the \$800 cumulative, undiscounted gain from the change in the forward rates since entering the forward contract and then (1) discounted at a 10 percent annual rate for the three-month period from December 31, 20X1, to April 1, 20X2, NPV(0.025, 800) = \$780.49, rounded; and then (2) subtract prior recognition of \$380 reported for October 1, 20X1, in (a).
(*c*) \$(180) = [(\$0.0076 − \$0.0073) × ¥2,000,000] for the \$600 cumulative gain from the change in the forward rate since entering the forward contract on August 1, 20X1, to the spot rate on April 1, 20X2, the completion of the forward contract; then subtract the prior recognition of \$780 gain recognized previously in (a) and (b). This results in a loss of \$(180) in the current period.

The amounts in the following entry on August 1, 20X1, are not present valued because the entry is a memorandum-type entry and because the interest factor will be taken into earnings through the changes in the fair value of the forward contract. Note that at the date of signing the forward contract, the net fair value of the forward contract is zero because the receivable and payable are equal to each other.

	August 1, 20X1		
(25)	Foreign Currency Receivable from Exchange Broker (¥)	14,600	
	Dollars Payable to Exchange Broker (\$)		14,600

Sign forward exchange contract for receipt of 2,000,000 yen in 240 days:
\$14,600 = ¥2,000,000 × \$0.0073 Aug. 1, 240-day forward rate.

On October 1, 20X1, the forward exchange contract will be revalued to its net fair value, recognizing the time value of money by using the present value of the expected future net cash flow from the forward contract. The temporary liability account, Firm Commitment, is also recorded at this time. Net present values can easily be computed using an electronic spreadsheet such as Excel and the net present value (NPV) function.

	October 1, 20X1		
(26)	Foreign Currency Receivable from Exchange Broker (¥)	380	
	Foreign Currency Transaction Gain		380

Adjust forward contract to net fair value, using the present value of the change in the forward rates. [Item (*a*) in the hedge effectiveness illustration.]

(27)	Foreign Currency Transaction Loss	380	
	Firm Commitment		380

To record the loss on the financial instrument aspect of the firm commitment using the present value of the change in the forward exchange rates. [Same amount as item (*a*) for this example because the effectiveness of the hedge on the firm commitment is assessed using the change in the forward exchange rates.]

On October 1, 20X1, the discounted net fair value of the forward contract is $380.

The next entry is to record the receipt of the inventory and the recognition of the accounts payable in yen. Note that the temporary account, Firm Commitment, is closed against the purchase price of the inventory.

(28)	Inventory	13,620	
	Firm Commitment	380	
	Accounts Payable (¥)		14,000

Record accounts payable at spot rate and the inventory purchase, closing the temporary liability account:
$14,000 = ¥2,000,000 × $0.0070 Oct. 1 spot rate.

The required adjusting entries on December 31, 20X1, Peerless' fiscal year-end, are

(29)	Foreign Currency Receivable from Exchange Broker (¥)	400	
	Foreign Currency Transaction Gain		400

Adjust forward contract to net fair value, using the present value of the change in the forward rates. [Item (*b*) in the hedge effectiveness illustration.]

(30)	Foreign Currency Transaction Loss	2,000	
	Accounts Payable (¥)		2,000

Adjust payable denominated in yen to current U.S. dollar–equivalent value: $2,000 = ¥2,000,000 × ($0.0080 − $0.0070). No interest factor is used for this revaluation; thus, no present value computation is made.

On December 31, 20X1, the discounted net fair value of the forward contract is $780.

The first required entry on April 1, 20X2, the settlement date, is

(31)	Foreign Currency Transaction Loss	180	
	Foreign Currency Receivable from Exchange Broker (¥)		180

Adjust forward contract for the change in the forward rate to the spot rate on settlement date: [Item (*c*) in the hedge effectiveness illustration.]

$0.0076 spot rate on 4/1/X2, the end of the forward contract
−0.0073 forward rate on 8/1/X1, the beginning of the forward contract
$0.0003 × ¥2,000,000 = $ 600 cumulative change from 8/1/X1
−780 gains previously recognized
$(180) reduction (loss) this period.

Note that at this point, the net foreign currency transaction gain on just the forward contract is $600. This is the difference between the time value of the forward contract (the $1,600 premium on the forward contract—$0.0073 forward rate less $0.0065 spot rate—when the forward contract was signed on August 1, 20X1, which is taken into earnings over the term of the forward contract) and the intrinsic value of the forward contract (the $2,200 difference between the spot rate of $0.0065 on August 1, 20X1, and the spot rate of $0.0076 on the forward contract completion date of April 1, 20X2). Another way to compute the net gain over the term of the forward contract is to compare the forward rate at the date the contract is signed ($0.0073) and the spot rate at the date the contract is completed ($0.0076). The net gain is $600 [¥2,000,000 × ($0.0073 − $0.0076)].

The following April 1, 20X2, entries complete the forward contract and the payment of the accounts payable that was denominated as ¥2,000,000.

(32)	Accounts Payable (¥)	800	
	Foreign Currency Transaction Gain		800

Adjust payable denominated in yen to spot rate on settlement date.
No interest factor for this item.
$800 = ¥2,000,000 × ($0.0076 − $0.0080).

(33)	Dollars Payable to Exchange Broker ($)	14,600	
	Cash		14,600

Deliver U.S. dollars to currency broker as specified in forward contract.

(34)	Foreign Currency Units (¥)	15,200	
	Foreign Currency Receivable from Exchange Broker (¥)		15,200

Receive ¥2,000,000 from exchange broker; valued at Apr. 1, 20X2, spot rate:
$15,200 = ¥2,000,000 × $0.0076.

(35)	Accounts Payable (¥)	15,200	
	Foreign Currency Units (¥)		15,200

Pay 2,000,000 yen to Tokyo Industries Inc. in settlement of liability denominated in yen.

Appendix **11B** Use of Other Financial Instruments by Multinational Companies

This chapter details the accounting for forward exchange contracts that are used to hedge exposed asset or liability positions or to hedge foreign currency commitments, or that are entered into for speculative purposes. Many multinational enterprises (MNEs) typically use financial instruments other than forward contracts to manage the risks associated with international transactions. A general definition of a *financial instrument* is that it is cash, stock, or a contract that imposes a contractual obligation to deliver or receive cash or another financial instrument to/from another entity. Examples of financial instruments are receivables/payables, bonds, shares of stock, foreign currency forward contracts, futures contracts, options, and financial swaps. A derivative financial instrument is the value of a financial instrument derived from some other item such as a contract valued on an index of stock values or futures contracts in which the value is determined by contemporary and predicted economic events. The other derivative financial instruments most often used by MNEs are futures, options, and swaps.

This appendix supplements the chapter by presenting a brief overview of futures, options, and swaps. It first gives brief definitions and descriptions. Next, it presents several examples of accounting for a hedge with a futures contract, a hedge with an option contract, and an interest-rate swap. Finally, it describes the disclosure requirements that apply currently. A discussion of the detailed mechanics and risk ramifications of transactions that utilize these instruments is beyond the coverage of an advanced financial accounting textbook.

DEFINITIONS AND DESCRIPTIONS

A *derivative financial instrument* is an instrument whose value is based on or "derived from" the value of something else (an underlying). That underlying can be the value of another financial instrument, a commodity, an index, an asset, or a debt instrument. Because the derivative financial instrument has a value that is linked to the underlying, it makes the derivative a useful hedging instrument to offset the change in value of the hedged item. Examples of derivative financial instruments include futures, forward, swap, and option contracts.

Forward and Futures Contracts

A forward contract is an agreement between a buyer and a seller that requires the delivery of some commodity at a specified future date at a price agreed to today (the exercise price). As presented in the chapter, foreign currency forward contracts are typically made with dealers of foreign exchange, and the contract is fulfilled at the end of the contract term by the exchanges of the currencies between the company and the dealer. Changes in the underlying market value of the foreign currency are recognized by the company holding the forward contract. The net fair value of a forward contract when it is written is zero because neither party pays anything and neither party receives anything. The contract is executory at this point. During the term of the forward contract, the net fair value changes based on the difference between a newly written forward contract for the remaining term and the original forward contract. At expiration, the forward contract's net fair value is the difference between the spot price and the original forward rate.

Futures are very similar to forward contracts except futures have standardized contract terms, they are traded on organized exchanges, and traders must realize any losses or gains on each and every trading day. Futures are contracts between two parties—a buyer and a seller—to buy or sell something at a specified future date, which is termed the *expiration date.* The contract trades on a futures exchange such as the Chicago Board of Trade (CBOT) or the Chicago Mercantile Exchange (CME). Futures contracts are actively traded in a number of commodities including grains and oilseeds, livestock and meat, food and fiber, and metals and energy. It is even possible to enter into futures contracts on foreign currencies. Companies trading in futures contracts are normally required to place cash in their margin accounts held by the brokerage exchange or a *clearing house,* and the gain (loss) on the futures contract is then added (subtracted) from the company's margin account. This margin account is settled daily for the changes in contract value. Margin accounts are maintained at some percentage (typically 2 to 5 percent) of the contract amount. Most investors do not expect to actually exchange the futures contract for the optioned item—the futures contract is simply an investment vehicle to ride the value curve of the optioned item—and they use a *closing transaction* to settle the futures contract. If a company is the purchaser of a futures contract, it is said to "go long" in a position. If a company contracts to sell with a futures contract, it is said to "go short." Futures contracts are sometimes referred to as *liquid forward contracts* because futures trade separately. The accounting for futures contracts is quite similar to accounting for foreign currency forward contracts.

Both futures and forward contracts are obligations to deliver a specified amount at a specified point in time. There is a potential for a gain under favorable circumstances and a potential for a loss under unfavorable circumstances. As presented in this Chapter, not only the losses but also the gains are minimized by using foreign currency forward contracts. Forward contracts are commonly used for hedging foreign currency transactions because the forward contracts can be customized as to duration and amounts. Futures contracts are standardized as to duration and amount but are more readily accessible because of their wide acceptance in a futures exchange arena.

Option Contracts

An option contract between two parties—the buyer and the seller—gives the buyer (option holder) the right, but not the obligation, to purchase from or sell something to the option seller (option writer) at a date in the future at a price agreed to at the time the option contract is exchanged. Options can be written on a large variety of commodities such as grains, food and fibers, petroleum, livestock, metals, interest rates, and various foreign currencies. The option buyer pays the seller some amount of money, typically termed the "premium," for this right. An option to buy something is referred to as a "call"; an option to sell something is called a "put." Options trade on organized markets similar to the stock market. Exchanges on which options trade are the Chicago Board Options Exchange (CBOE), the Philadelphia Stock Exchange (PHLX), the American Stock Exchange (AMEX), and the Pacific Stock Exchange (PSE).

An option contract can give the buyer future control over a large number of shares or other items at the nominal cost of the option. This ability of the option for future control is the *time value* of the option. Over the option's term, the time value decreases to zero at the option's expiration date. Changes in the time value of the option are always taken to current earnings. The party selling the right is the writer; the party buying the right is the holder. The option holder has the right to exercise or not exercise the option. The holder of the option would not exercise the right embedded in the option if by doing so it would result in a loss. The option writer, however, is subject to risk because the option holder could exercise the option, forcing the writer to deliver under terms that are not favorable to the writer. An option's *intrinsic value* is directly related to the change in value of the underlying. If the option is designated as a hedge, the change in intrinsic value of a fair value hedge is taken to current earnings. The change in the effective portion of intrinsic value of a cash flow hedge is taken to other comprehensive income. An example of an option used as a hedge is presented later in this appendix.

The option is sold with a *strike price,* the price at which the holder has the option to buy or sell the item. If an investor holds a call option to purchase one share of Peerless Products stock for $5 a share from the writer, the holder may exercise that option when the market share price exceeds the strike price. If the market price is $6 a share, the holder will save $1 by exercising the option and purchasing the stock for $5. If the holder wishes to turn the savings into a cash profit, the investor would sell the share of stock, purchased for $5, on the market for $6. Alternatively, the holder of the option could directly sell the option for $1, its intrinsic value. When the market price is more than the strike price, the option to buy is "in the money." When the market price is less than the strike price, the option to buy is "out of the money."

If an investor is the holder of a put option to sell one share of Peerless Products for $5 a share to the writer, the holder will exercise that option when the share price is below the strike price. If the market price is $4 a share, the holder will make $1 by exercising the sell option at $5 per share rather than selling the share on the open market at $4 per share. When the market price is less than the option price, the option to sell is "in the money."

For the Peerless Products stock example, a summary of the relationship between the option type and the term used to describe the difference between the current market price of the underlying and the option's strike price is as follows:

Option	Current Market Price Equals the Option's Strike Price ($5 = $5)	Current Market Price Is More than the Option's Strike Price ($6 > $5)	Current Market Price Is Less than the Option's Strike Price ($4 < $5)
Call (buy)	At the money	In the money	Out of the money
Put (sell)	At the money	Out of the money	In the money

Options are typically purchased for a fee that is usually a small percentage of the optioned item's current value (e.g., 1 to 7 percent). The option's terms stipulate whether the option can be exercised at any time during the option period or only at the end of the exercise period. The minimum value of an option is zero because an option need not be exercised. Therefore, an option can never have a negative value (a liability), and the maximum loss of the holder of an option can incur is the premium initially paid for the option.

Figure 11–9 presents an overview of the major features of forwards, futures, and options.

Swaps

A *swap* is an arrangement by which two parties exchange cash flows over a period of time. Swaps can be designed to swap currencies, interest rates, or commodities. The two most common types of financial swaps used by companies are (1) currency swaps and (2) interest-rate swaps. An example of a currency swap is Peerless Products Corporation's sale of products in Great Britain for which it receives pounds sterling. Another company located in London, England, sells products in the United States for which it receives U.S. dollars. A currency swap would occur, for example, if Peerless (a U.S. company) agrees that the periodic currency flows in pounds sterling from its Great Britain operations will be forwarded to its counterparty in Great Britain, and the dollar sales in the United States by the London company will be forwarded to Peerless, the U.S. company. At the end of each period, the two companies agree to settle up for any differences in the notional amount of the swap at the end of the period. Thus, both parties to this currency swap avoid dealing in other than their local currencies and avoid foreign currency exchange costs.

Another example of a swap is an interest-rate swap in which two parties agree to exchange the interest payments on a stated amount of principal (also called the "notional amount"). Typically, the swap is an exchange of a variable (floating) rate interest and a fixed-rate interest. For example, Peerless may issue variable-rate debt but wish to fix its interest rates because it believes the variable rate may increase. Peerless may enter into a contract with a counterparty that has a fixed-rate bond but is looking for a variable-rate interest because that company assumes the interest rates may decrease. Often the contract includes a financial intermediary to which net settlement payments are made and that charges a nominal fee for its services. Sometimes the counterparty

FIGURE 11–9
Features of Forwards, Futures, and Options

Type of Derivative	Features
Forwards	• Contracted through a dealer, usually a bank • Possibly customized to meet contracting company's terms and needs • Typically no margin deposit required • Must be completed either with the underlying's future delivery or net cash settlement
Futures	• Traded on an exchange and acquired through an exchange broker • Cannot be customized; for a specific amount at a specific date • Often company required to open a margin account with a small deposit so daily changes in futures value can be posted to the account • Usually settled with a net cash amount prior to maturity date; not expected to be completed by the underlying's future delivery
Options	• Traded on a variety of exchanges • Acquired on a large variety of commodities and major foreign currencies • Issued in two types: put (sell) and call (buy) • Option premium (fee) paid by the option holder to the writer (counterparty) for that right • Taker's or holder's loss limited to a maximum of the premium paid but virtually unlimited potential profit if underlying market moves in the option holder's desired direction • Grantor (counterparty or writer) offered potential to earn a maximum of the option premium and to lose a virtually unlimited amount if underlying market moves in the opposite direction than desired

is a dealer—a bank or an investment banking firm—that makes a market in swaps and other interest-rate derivatives. The notional amount (principal) is specified as the same for both parties, and Peerless fixes the interest rate on its notional amount whereas the counterparty obtains the variable rate it was seeking. Note that the debt is not being extinguished and any fees paid to arrange the swap should be treated as debt issuance costs that are amortized over the term of the debt. Each company is still responsible for its actual interest payment to its creditor. The swap is merely an agreement for the net periodic settlement of the difference between the two interest rates and is done solely between the two companies that contracted for the interest swap. The simple swap of fixed- versus variable-interest rates is sometimes referred to as a *plain vanilla swap* or a *generic swap.* An interest-rate swap is presented later in this appendix.

An overview of the accounting for the three major types of hedges is presented in Figure 11–10. Review this figure before proceeding to the examples.

EXAMPLE OF THE USE OF AN OPTION TO HEDGE AN ANTICIPATED PURCHASE OF INVENTORY: A CASH FLOW HEDGE

Assume that Peerless Products plans in 90 days to purchase 30,000 bushels of wheat that currently have a value of $75,000 (30,000 bushels × $2.50 spot price per bushel). Also assume that Peerless wants to lock in the value of the anticipated future purchase.

Peerless purchases a call option on wheat futures to hedge against a price change in the anticipated purchase of the inventory. If the price of wheat increases, the profit on the purchased call option will offset the higher price that Peerless would have to pay for the wheat. If the price of wheat decreases, Peerless loses the premium it paid for the call option but can then buy the wheat at a lower price.

On November 1, 20X1, Peerless purchases call options for a February 1, 20X2, call (90 days in the future) at a call price of $2.50. Peerless pays a premium of $0.05 per bushel, for a total cost of $1,500 (30,000 bushels × $0.05). The call options are for a notional amount of 30,000 bushels of wheat. Peerless specifies that the derivative qualifies for cash flow hedge accounting. It is a cash flow hedge because the option is hedging a forecasted, or planned, future transaction involving cash flows. Note that this example shows the entire $1,500 as the time value of the option; in other words, it sets a futures price equal to the current market price. This type of contract is

FIGURE 11–10 Overview of Three Types of Hedges

Type of Hedge	Basic Criteria	Recognition and Measurement
Fair value hedge	A hedge of the derivative instrument's exposure to changes in the fair value of an asset or liability, or of an unrecognized firm commitment.	Gain or loss on the hedging instrument, as well as the related loss or gain on the hedged item, should be recognized currently in earnings.
Cash flow hedge	Hedge the derivative instrument's exposure to variability in expected future cash flows of a recognized asset or liability, or of a forecasted transaction, that is attributable to a particular risk.	Gain or loss on the effective portion of hedge (e.g., the intrinsic value) is deferred and reported as a component of other comprehensive income. Any gain or loss on the derivative that is not offset by cash flow losses and gains on the hedged forecasted transaction (i.e., ineffective, including the time value of the option) is recognized currently in earnings.
Foreign currency hedge	A hedge of the foreign currency exposure of	The recognition and measurement differ by type of hedge:
	1. An unrecognized firm commitment.	1. This is a foreign currency fair value hedge.
	2. An available-for-sale security.	2. This is a foreign currency cash flow hedge.
	3. A forecasted transaction.	3. The gain or loss on the effective portion of the hedging derivative on a net investment in a foreign operative shall be reported as part of the translation adjustment component of other comprehensive income.
	4. A net investment in a foreign operation.	

sometimes termed "at the money," meaning it specifies the futures price of the underlying at the current market price. Thus, the value of the contract when it is signed is only with regard to the *time value* of the expectation that the actual future price of the commodity will differ from the current market price.

An overview of this hedge follows:

Hedging instrument	Call option on wheat futures
Hedged item	Forecasted purchase of wheat
Type of hedge	Cash flow hedge
Underlying	Price of a bushel of wheat
Notional amount	30,000 bushels of wheat
Time value at origin of hedge	$1,500, at the money
Valuation of call option	Fair value
If underlying increases in value	Call option increases in value
If underlying decreases in value	Call option decreases in value

Gain or loss on hedge:

Effective portion	To other comprehensive income; related to change in intrinsic value of hedge
Ineffective portion	To current earnings; related to change in time value of hedge

The entry to record the purchase of the call options is as follows:

	November 1, 20X1		
(36)	Purchased Call Options	1,500	
	Cash		1,500

To record the purchase of call options for 30,000 bushels of wheat at $2.50 per bushel in 90 days. The options are at the money; therefore, the $1,500 is all time value.

The fair market information for this example follows:

Fair Value Computations			
	November 1, 20X1	December 31, 20X1	February 1, 20X2
Bushel of wheat	$ 2.50	$ 2.60	$ 2.58
Total: 30,000 bushels			
Call Option:			
Option market value (from market information)	$1,500	$3,700	$2,400
Less: Intrinsic value: [Number of bushels × (Market price − Strike price)]			
[30,000 bushels × ($2.50 − $2.50)]	0		
[30,000 bushels × ($2.60 − $2.50)]		(3,000)	
[30,000 bushels × ($2.58 − $2.50)]			(2,400)
Time value remaining	$1,500	$ 700	$ 0

Note that for a cash flow hedge, the change in the intrinsic value (effective portion) is recognized in Other Comprehensive Income, and the change in the time value (ineffective portion) is recognized in current earnings.

At December 31, 20X1, the price of wheat increases to $2.60 per bushel. The *intrinsic value* is the change in value of the options due to the change in market value of the underlying. For cash flow hedges, the change in a derivative's intrinsic value is recorded in other comprehensive income. On December 31, the intrinsic value of the options is $3,000 (30,000 bushels × $0.10 increase).

ASC 815 requires that hedging instruments be revalued to fair value at each balance sheet date. The change in value of the options is due to two factors: the change in the intrinsic value and the reduction of the time value. An option's time value decreases over its term and is zero when the options expire. At December 31, 20X1, the fair market value of the options is $3,700, meaning that the options' remaining time value is valued by the market at $700 ($3,700 fair value less $3,000 intrinsic value). **ASC 815** specifies that the $800 ($1,500 initial amount − $700 remaining) reduction in the time value portion of a derivative is recognized as part of current earnings. Entry (37) records the change in the value of the options to value them at their fair value at the balance sheet date.

	December 31, 20X1		
(37)	Purchased Call Options	2,200	
	Loss on Hedge Activity	800	
	Other Comprehensive Income		3,000

To revalue the options to their fair market value, recognizing the reduction in time value and the increase in intrinsic value:
$2,200 = $3,700 current fair value of options less $1,500 balance on November 1
$800 = ($1,500 − $700 remaining) reduction in time value of options
$3,000 = 30,000 bushels × $0.10 increase in intrinsic value.

Note that the increase in intrinsic value is recorded in Other Comprehensive Income pending the completion of the forecasted inventory transaction. The Other Comprehensive Income account is used to "store" the intrinsic value gains or losses on cash flow hedges until they are reclassified into earnings when the hedged transaction affects earnings.

At February 1, 20X2, the end of the 90 days, the price of wheat is $2.58 per bushel. The decrease in the intrinsic value of the call options is recorded as follows:

	February 1, 20X2		
(38)	Other Comprehensive Income	600	
	Purchased Call Options		600

To record the other comprehensive income, deferring the earning recognition of the loss on the purchased call options:
$600 = 30,000 bushels × ($2.58 − $2.60).

The next entry (39) recognizes the expiration of the remaining amount ($700) of the time value of the purchased call option because the option has now expired. The change in the time value portion of a derivative is recognized in current earnings.

	February 1, 20X2		
(39)	Loss on Hedge Activity	700	
	Purchased Call Options		700
	To recognize the loss of the $700 remaining time value of the purchased call options that have now expired.		

Peerless now decides to sell the contracts for their intrinsic value of $2,400 [30,000 bushels × ($2.58 − $2.50 call price)]. In addition, Peerless acquires the 30,000 bushels of wheat at the current market price of $2.58 per bushel. The next entry records the sale of the purchased call options at their current market price.

	February 1, 20X2		
(40)	Cash	2,400	
	Purchased Call Options		2,400
	To record the sale of the call options.		

Peerless now purchases the 30,000 bushels of wheat at the current market price of $2.58 per bushel.

	February 1, 20X2		
(41)	Wheat Inventory	77,400	
	Cash		77,400

Finally, Peerless later sells the wheat at a price of $100,000 and records the sale as well as the reclassification of the other comprehensive income resulting from the purchased call options. Note that the other comprehensive income is taken into income only when the underlying item enters the income stream.

(42)	Cash	100,000	
	Sale		100,000
	To record the sale of the 30,000 bushels of wheat.		

(43)	Cost of Goods Sold	77,400	
	Wheat Inventory		77,400
	To recognize the cost of the wheat sold.		

(44)	Other Comprehensive Income—Reclassification	2,400	
	Cost of Goods Sold		2,400
	To reclassify into earnings the other comprehensive income from the cash flow hedge.		

The reduction of the cost of goods sold increases net income for the period. The earning process for the other comprehensive income was the sale of the wheat. The hedge was successful. Peerless has a gain of $2,400 less the $1,500 it paid for the time value of the call options.

EXAMPLE OF AN OPTION CONTRACT TO HEDGE AVAILABLE-FOR-SALE SECURITIES: A FAIR VALUE HEDGE

Assume that on January 1, 20X1, Peerless purchases 100 shares of Special Foods stock at a cost of $25 per share. The company classifies these as available-for-sale securities because it does not intend to sell them in the near term. To protect itself from a decrease in the value of the investment, on December 31, 20X1, the company purchases, for a $300 premium, an at-the-money put option (i.e., option price is current market price), which gives it the right but not the obligation to sell 100 shares of Special Foods at $30 per share. The option expires on December 31, 20X3. The fair values of the investment and the option follow:

Fair Value Computations

	December 31		
	20X1	**20X2**	**20X3**
Special Foods shares:			
Per share	$ 30	$ 29	$ 26
Total (100 shares)	3,000	2,900	2,600
Put option:			
Market value (*a*)	$ 300	$ 340	$ 400
Less: Intrinsic value (*b*)	(0)	(100)	(400)
Time value (*c*)	$ 300	$ 240	$ 0

(*a*) Market value is obtained from the current market price. There is a variety of option pricing models, such as the Black-Scholes model, to estimate the value of these options.
(*b*) Intrinsic value is the difference between the current market price and the option price times the number of shares. It is easy to compute at any point in the life of the option. For example, the intrinsic value on December 31, 20X2, is ($30 option price − $29 current market price) × 100 shares.
(*c*) The time value of the option reflects the effect of discounting the expected future cash flows and a portion for the expected volatility in the price of the underlying asset. A simple way to compute the value is by calculating the difference between the option's market value and its intrinsic value.

Note that the time value at December 31, 20X1, is for the entire option price because the option was purchased for the current market price. The time value decreases to zero at the end of the option because no time element remains at that expiration point and the market value of the option is then based solely on its intrinsic value. Peerless exercises the option just before its expiration on December 31, 20X3, and delivers the Special Foods shares to the option writer.

Peerless determines the hedge effectiveness based on the changes in the option's intrinsic value. This is an acceptable method for determining effectiveness using options because of the ultimate value of the option being based on the price of the underlying asset in this example, the stock of Special Foods.

Hedge Effectiveness Analysis

Date	Change in Option's Intrinsic Value (Gain) Loss	Change in Value of Special Foods Shares (Gain) Loss	Effectiveness Ratio for Period
December 31, 20X2	$(100)	$100	1.00
December 31, 20X3	$(300)	$300	1.00

An overview of this hedge is

Hedging instrument	Put option on Special Foods stock
Hedged item	100 shares of Special Foods stock
Type of hedge	Fair value hedge
Underlying	Price of a share of Special Foods stock
Notional amount	100 shares of Special Foods stock
Time value at origin of hedge	$300, at the money
Valuation of put option	Fair value
If underlying increases in value	Put option decreases in value
If underlying decreases in value	Put option increases in value

A gain or loss on this hedge is

Effective portion	To current earnings; related to change in intrinsic value of hedge
Ineffective portion	To current earnings; related to change in time value of hedge

The entries for this example follow:

	January 1, 20X1		
(45)	Available-for-Sale Securities	2,500	
	Cash		2,500
	Acquire 100 shares of Special Foods stock at a price of $25 per share.		

December 31, 20X1

(46)	Available-for-Sale Securities	500	
	Other Comprehensive Income		500

Marked-to-market value of $30 the Special Foods stock and recognize the other comprehensive income in accordance with **ASC 320:** $500 = ($30 − $25) × 100 shares.

(47)	Put Option	300	
	Cash		300

Purchase put option, at the money, to sell 100 shares of Special Foods at $30. This $300 is the time value of the option.

Note that **ASC 815** amends **ASC 320** and requires the gain or loss on an available-for-sale security designated as a hedged item to be recognized in current earnings during the period. In entry (46), the marked-to-market value for the available-for-sale securities was recognized in other comprehensive income, in accordance with **ASC 320.** As can be seen in entry (48), once available-for-sale securities are hedged in a fair value hedge, the gain or loss on marking to market must be taken to earnings for the period.

December 31, 20X2

(48)	Loss on Hedge Activity	100	
	Available-for-Sale Securities		100

Record decrease in fair value for the Special Foods stock in accordance with **ASC 815:** $100 = ($30 − $29) × 100 shares.

ASC 815 specifies that the change in intrinsic value of fair value hedges be recognized currently in net earnings of the period. This is different from cash flow hedges in which the changes in intrinsic value were taken to other comprehensive income. Therefore, entry (49) recognizes the increase in the intrinsic value of this fair value hedge as a gain that will be closed to Retained Earnings.

December 31, 20X2

(49)	Put Option	100	
	Gain on Hedge Activity		100

Record increase in the intrinsic value of the put option.

(50)	Loss on Hedge Activity	60	
	Put Option		60

To record in earnings the ineffective portion of the change in the fair value of the put options (i.e., the change in the time value). $60 = $300 initial time value − $240 remaining time value.

The entries for December 31, 20X3, continue the valuation process.

December 31, 20X3

(51)	Loss on Hedge Activity	300	
	Available-for-Sale Securities		300

Marked-to-market value of $26 the Special Foods stock and recognize the loss in earnings: $300 = ($26 − $29) × 100 shares.

(52)	Put Option	300	
	Gain on Hedge Activity		300

Record the increase in the intrinsic value of the put option.

(53)	Loss on Hedge Activity	240	
	Put Option		240

Record in earnings the ineffective portion of the change in fair value of the put option (i.e., the change in the time value).

Entry (53) eliminates the remainder of the option's time value, which was initially $300. Entry (50) took $60 of the time value of the option against earnings of 20X2. Entry (53) takes the remainder

FIGURE 11–11 Journal Entries for a Fair Value Hedge of Available-for-Sale Securities

Entries for Available-for-Sale Securities (hedged item)				Entries for Put Option Contract (hedging instrument)			
January 1, 20X1. Acquire 100 shares of Special Foods stock as available-for-sale security.							
(45)	Available-for-Sale Securities	2,500					
	Cash		2,500				
December 31, 20X1. Revalue available-for-sale securities to market value in accordance with **ASC 320** and purchase put option for current market price of underlying.							
(46)	Available-for-Sale Securities	500		(47)	Put Option	300	
	Other Comprehensive Income		500		Cash		300
December 31, 20X2. Revalue available-for-sale securities in accordance with **ASC 815** and adjust put option to current market value for increases in $100 intrinsic value and $60 reduction in time value of option.							
(48)	Loss on Hedge Activity	100		(49)	Put Option	100	
	Available-for-Sale Securities		100		Gain on Hedge Activity		100
				(50)	Loss on Hedge Activity	60	
					Put Option		60
December 31, 20X3. Revalue available-for-sale securities and adjust put option to current market value for the $300 increase in intrinsic value and the $240 reduction in time value of the option.							
(51)	Loss on Hedge Activity	300		(52)	Put Option	300	
	Available-for-Sale Securities		300		Gain on Hedge Activity		300
				(53)	Loss on Hedge Activity	240	
					Put Option		240
December 31, 20X3. Exercise put option and deliver 100 shares of stock at a $30 per share price. Reclassify other comprehensive income recognized in (46) on available-for-sale securities now sold.							
(54)	Cash	3,000					
	Put Option		400				
	Available-for-Sale Securities		2,600				
(55)	Other Comprehensive Income	500					
	Realized Gain on Sale of Securities		500				

into earnings of 20X3 because at the end of the option period, no time value remains. The only value of the put option at its term date is its intrinsic value.

(54)	Cash	3,000	
	Put Option		400
	Available-for-Sale Securities		2,600

Exercise the put option and delivery of the securities at a price of $30 per share.

(55)	Other Comprehensive Income	500	
	Realized Gain on Sale of Securities		500

Reclassify the other comprehensive income on Special Foods' stock that was recorded on Dec. 31, 20X1, to earnings because the securities have now been sold.
$100 = ($30 − $29) × 100 shares.

It is also important to note that **ASC 815** does not permit hedge accounting for hedges of trading securities. **ASC 320** requires that trading securities be marked to market with the gain or loss reported in net earnings for the period. Therefore, any gains or losses on financial instruments that are planned to hedge the risks of holding trading securities are always taken to net earnings for the period. See Figure 11–11 for an overview of the journal entries made for the hedged available-for-sale securities and for the hedging put option.

EXAMPLE OF AN INTEREST-RATE SWAP TO HEDGE VARIABLE-RATE DEBT: A CASH FLOW HEDGE

Advanced StudyGuide .com

Assume that on June 30, 20X1, Peerless borrows $5,000,000 of three-year, variable-rate debt with interest payments equal to the six-month US$ LIBOR (London Interbank Offered Rate) for the prior six months. The debt is not prepayable. The company then enters into a three-year interest-rate swap with First Bank to convert the debt's variable rate to a fixed rate. The swap agreement specifies that Peerless will pay interest at a fixed rate of 7.5 percent and receive interest at a variable rate equal to the six-month US$ LIBOR rate based on the notional amount of $5,000,000. Both the debt and the swap require interest to be paid semiannually on June 30 and December 31. Peerless specifies the swap as a cash flow hedge. Refer to Figure 11–12 for a schematic of the swap relationships.

The six-month US$ LIBOR rate and the market value of the swap agreement, as determined by a swap broker, follow for the first year of the swap agreement:

Date	Six-Month US$ LIBOR Rate	Swap Agreement Fair Value Asset (Liability)
June 30, 20X1	6.0%	$ 0
December 31, 20X1	7.0	165,000
June 30, 20X2	5.5	(70,000)

Note that Peerless must still pay the variable interest to the holders of the $5,000,000 debt. The interest-rate swap is just between Peerless and First Bank. The estimate of the fair value of the swap agreement was obtained from a broker-dealer of interest-rate swap agreements. Note that the value of the swap agreement to Peerless is positive if it believes that the variable rate will rise to higher than the fixed rate, but the swap agreement's value to Peerless is negative if it believes that the variable rate will remain lower than the fixed rate. Peerless' payments on the variable-rate debt and the net payments to First Bank on the interest-rate swap agreement are presented for the initial two semiannual periods:

	Interest Payments	
	December 31, 20X1	June 30, 20X2
Variable-rate interest payment	$150,000 (*a*)	$175,000 (*b*)
Interest-rate swap net payment	37,500 (*c*)	12,500
Total cash payment	$187,500 (*d*)	$187,500

(*a*) $150,000 = 5,000,000 × 0.06 × 6/12 months
(*b*) $175,000 = 5,000,000 × 0.07 × 6/12 months
(*c*) $37,500 = net payment required to First Bank for difference between variable and fixed interest rates
(*d*) $187,500 = 5,000,000 × 0.075 fixed rate × 6/12 months

FIGURE 11–12
Fixed for Variable Interest-Rate Swap on $5,000,000 Notional Amount

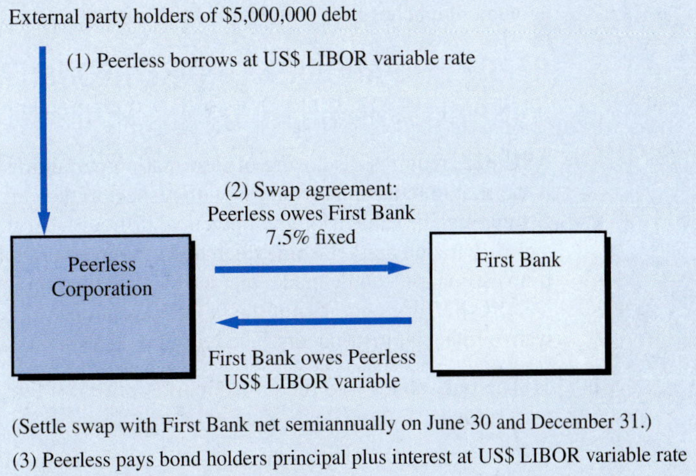

Peerless recognizes interest expense based on the two factors of the variable rate plus the net payment or receipt from the swap agreement. In essence, Peerless has an interest expense equal to 7.5 percent of the notional amount of $5,000,000.

The entries to account for the first year of the interest-rate swap follow:

	June 30, 20X1		
(56)	Cash	5,000,000	
	Debt Payable		5,000,000
	Issue variable-rate debt.		
	December 31, 20X1		
(57)	Interest Expense	150,000	
	Cash		150,000
	Pay debt holder's semiannual interest at a variable rate of 6.0 percent [from (*a*) in preceding table].		
(58)	Interest Expense	37,500	
	Cash		37,500
	Payment to First Bank for semiannual net settlement of swap agreement [from (*c*) in preceding table].		
(59)	Swap Agreement	165,000	
	Other Comprehensive Income		165,000
	Recognize change in fair value of swap agreement to Other Comprehensive Income because the swap is a cash flow hedge.		
	June 30, 20X2		
(60)	Interest Expense	175,000	
	Cash		175,000
	Pay debt holder's semiannual interest at a variable rate of 7.0 percent [from (*b*) in preceding table].		
(61)	Interest Expense	12,500	
	Cash		12,500
	Payment to First Bank for semiannual net settlement of swap agreement.		
(62)	Other Comprehensive Income	235,000	
	Swap Agreement		235,000
	Recognize decrease in fair value of swap agreement from $165,000 asset to $(70,000) liability to Other Comprehensive Income because the swap is a cash flow hedge.		

The swap agreement is reported on the balance sheet at its fair value. The amounts accumulated in Other Comprehensive Income are indirectly recognized in Peerless' earnings as periodic settlements of the payments required under the swap agreement are made, and the fair value of the swap agreement reaches zero at the end of the term of the agreement.

REPORTING AND DISCLOSURE REQUIREMENTS: DISCLOSURES ABOUT FAIR VALUE OF FINANCIAL INSTRUMENTS

ASC 825, requires disclosure of information pertaining to all financial instruments. This standard is the first to require information with respect to the current fair value of the financial instruments. Estimating fair value is of great practical difficulty because many financial instruments do not have a readily traded market from which to determine their value. Estimation methods are permitted, but if no estimation can be made, the reasons for the impracticality must be disclosed.

ASC 825 does not permit the fair values of derivatives to be netted or aggregated with nonderivative financial instruments. The required disclosures are as follows:

1. The fair value based on quoted market prices. If fair value is not quoted, a practical estimation is allowed.
2. Information relevant to the fair value such as carrying value, effective interest rate, maturity, and reasons why it is not practical to estimate, if such is the case.
3. Distinction between instruments held for trading or nontrading purposes.

ASC 815 adds a number of disclosures regarding derivatives and financial instruments. The company holding or issuing derivatives must disclose both its objectives for holding or issuing the instruments and the face or contract amount of the derivatives. The company also must distinguish between derivatives designated as fair value hedges, as cash flow hedges, as hedges of the foreign currency exposure of a net investment in a foreign operation, and all other derivatives. Specific disclosures are required for each type of hedge, but generally the company must disclose the purpose of the activity, the amount of any gains or losses recognized during the period (either in earnings or in other comprehensive income), and where those gains or losses and related assets and liabilities are reported in the income statement and statement of financial position.

Companies operating internationally have increased risks when transacting in more than one currency. For that reason, a number of financial instruments are used in order to manage the increased risk. This chapter has presented the most commonly used financial instrument, the foreign currency forward exchange contract. This appendix briefly discussed several of the other major financial instruments used by multinational companies. It is certain that increased sophistication of the types of risk management tools will continue to occur in the business arena, and accountants must continue their efforts to understand and account for these instruments.

QUESTIONS

LO 11-1 **Q11-1** Explain the difference between indirect and direct exchange rates.

LO 11-1 **Q11-2** What is the direct exchange rate if a U.S. company receives $1.3623 in Canadian currency in exchange for $1.00 in U.S. currency?

LO 11-1 **Q11-3** The U.S. dollar strengthened against the European euro. Will imports from Europe into the United States be more expensive or less expensive in U.S. dollars? Explain.

LO 11-1 **Q11-4** Differentiate between a foreign transaction and a foreign currency transaction. Give an example of each.

LO 11-1 **Q11-5** What types of economic factors affect currency exchange rates? Give an example of a change in an economic factor that results in a weakening of the local currency unit versus a foreign currency unit.

LO 11-2 **Q11-6** How are assets and liabilities denominated in a foreign currency measured on the transaction date? On the balance sheet date?

LO 11-2 **Q11-7** When are foreign currency transaction gains or losses recognized in the financial statements? Where are these gains or losses reported in the financial statements?

LO 11-2 **Q11-8** Sun Company, a U.S. corporation, has an account payable of $200,000 denominated in Canadian dollars. If the direct exchange rate increases, will Sun experience a foreign currency transaction gain or loss on this payable?

LO 11-3 **Q11-9** What are some ways a U.S. company can manage the risk of changes in the exchange rates for foreign currencies?

LO 11-3 **Q11-10** Distinguish between an exposed net asset position and an exposed net liability position.

LO 11-1 **Q11-11** Explain why a difference usually exists between a currency's spot rate and forward rate. Give two reasons this difference is usually positive when a company enters into a contract to receive foreign currency at a future date.

LO 11-3 **Q11-12** A forward exchange contract may be used (*a*) to manage an exposed foreign currency position, (*b*) to hedge an identifiable foreign currency commitment, (*c*) to hedge a forecasted foreign currency transaction, or (*d*) to speculate in foreign currency markets. What are the main differences in accounting for these four uses?

CASES

LO 11-1, 11-2 **C11-1** **Effects of Changing Exchange Rates**

Analysis

Since the early 1970s, the U.S. dollar has both increased and decreased in value against other currencies such as the Japanese yen, the Swiss franc, and the British pound. The value of the U.S. dollar, as well as the value of currencies of other countries, is determined by the balance between the demand for and the supply of the currency on the foreign exchange markets. A drop in the value of the U.S. dollar has a widespread impact not only on consumers and businesses that deal with their counterparts overseas but also on consumers and businesses that operate solely within the United States.

Required

a. Identify the factors that influence the demand for and supply of the U.S. dollar on the foreign exchange markets.

b. Explain the effect a drop in value of the U.S. dollar in relation to other currencies on the foreign exchange markets has on

(1) The sales of a U.S. business firm that exports part of its output to foreign countries.

(2) The costs of a U.S. business firm that imports from foreign countries part of the inputs used in the manufacture of its products.

c. Explain why and how consumers and business firms are affected by the drop in value of the U.S. dollar in relation to other currencies on the foreign exchange markets.

LO 11-2 **C11-2**

Reporting a Foreign Currency Transaction on the Financial Statements [AICPA Adapted]

Judgment

On November 30, 20X5, Bow Company received goods with a cost denominated in pounds. During December 20X5, the dollar's value declined relative to the pound. Bow believes that the original exchange rate will be restored by the time payment is due in 20X6.

Required

a. State how Bow should report the impact, if any, of the changes in the exchange rate of the dollar and the pound on its 20X5 financial statements.

b. Explain why the reporting is appropriate.

LO 11-1 **C11-3**

Changing Exchange Rates

Research

Search online to obtain and or prepare charts of the monthly average direct exchange rates for the past two years for the U.S. dollar versus (1) the Japanese yen, (2) the European euro, (3) the British pound, and (4) the Mexican peso. Your four charts should each have time on the horizontal axis and the direct exchange rate on the horizontal axis.

Questions for Discussion

a. Has the dollar strengthened or weakened during this time against each of the currencies?

b. What major economic or political factors could have caused the changes in the four foreign currencies' exchange rates versus the U.S. dollar?

c. Select one major factor from part (*b*) for each currency and present an argument showing how a change in that factor could cause the change in the exchange rate.

LO 11-2 **C11-4**

Accounting for Foreign Currency–Denominated Accounts Payable

Research

Mardi Gras Corporation operates a group of specialty shops throughout the southeastern United States. The shops have traditionally stocked and sold kitchen and bath products manufactured in the United States. This year, Mardi Gras established a business relationship with a manufacturing company in Lucerne, Switzerland, to purchase a line of luxury bath products to sell in its shops. As part of the business arrangement, payments by Mardi Gras are due 30 days after receipt of the merchandise, whose cost is quoted and payable in Swiss francs.

Mardi Gras records the purchases in inventory when it receives the merchandise and records a liability to the Swiss company, using the exchange rate for Swiss francs on the date the inventory purchase is recorded. When payment is made, Mardi Gras debits or credits to inventory any difference between the liability previously recorded and the dollar amount required to settle the liability in Swiss francs. Mardi Gras uses a perpetual inventory system and the FIFO method of inventory costing and can easily trace these adjustments to the specific inventory purchased.

Required

Obtain the most current accounting standards on accounting for foreign currency transactions. You can obtain access to accounting standards through the FASB codification. As a staff accountant with the public accounting firm that audits Mardi Gras's annual financial statements, write a memo to Marie Lamont, the manager in charge of the audit, discussing the client's accounting for its transactions with the Swiss company. Support any recommendations with citations and quotations from the authoritative financial reporting standards.

LO 11-3

C11-5 Accounting for Foreign Currency Forward Contracts

Research

Avanti Corporation is a small Midwestern company that manufactures wooden furniture. Tim Martin, Avanti's president, has decided to expand operations significantly and has entered into a contract with a German company to purchase specialty equipment for the expansion in manufacturing capacity. The contract fixes the price of the equipment at 4.5 million euros, and the equipment will be delivered in five months with payment due 30 days after delivery.

Tim is concerned that the value of the euro versus the U.S. dollar could increase during the six months between the date of the contract and the date of payment, thus increasing the effective price of the equipment to Avanti. Lindsay Williams, Avanti's treasurer, has suggested that the company enter into a forward contract to purchase 4.5 million euros in six months, thereby locking in an exchange rate for euros. Tim likes the idea of eliminating the uncertainty over the exchange rate for euros but is concerned about the effects of the forward contract on Avanti's financial statements. Because Avanti has not had previous experience with foreign currency transactions, Lindsay is unsure of what the financial statement effects are.

Required

Obtain the most current accounting standards on accounting for foreign currency forward contracts. You can obtain access to accounting standards through the FASB codification. Lindsay has asked you, as her assistant, to research the accounting for a foreign currency forward contract. Write a memo to her reporting on the results of your research. Support your recommendations with citations and quotations from the authoritative financial reporting standards.

LO 11-3

C11-6 Accounting for Hedges of Available-for-Sale Securities

Research

Rainy Day Insurance Company maintains an extensive portfolio of bond investments classified as available-for-sale securities under **ASC 320.** The bond investments have a variety of fixed interest rates and have maturity dates ranging from 1 to 15 years. Rainy Day acquired the bonds with the expectation that it could hold them until maturity or sell them any time that funds are required for unusually high insurance claims.

Because of the large dollar amount invested, Rainy Day is concerned about fluctuations in interest rates that affect the fair value of its bond portfolio. One of Rainy Day's investment professionals has proposed that the company invest in an interest rate futures contract to hedge its exposure to interest rate changes. Changes in the fair value of the futures contract would offset changes in the bond portfolio's fair value. If Rainy Day applies hedge accounting under **ASC 815,** the income statement effect of changes in the fair value of the derivative would be offset by recording in earnings the changes in the fair value of the bond portfolio attributable to the hedged (interest rate) risk.

Required

Obtain the most current accounting standards on accounting for hedges of available-for-sale securities. You can obtain access to accounting standards through the FASB codification. Rainy Day's CFO, Mark Becker, has asked you, as an accountant in Rainy Day's investment division, to determine whether hedge accounting can be used in the scenario proposed. Write a memo to Mark, reporting on the results of your research. Support your recommendations with citations and quotations from the authoritative financial reporting standards.

EXERCISES

LO 11-1

E11-1 Exchange Rates

Suppose the direct foreign exchange rates in U.S. dollars are

1 British pound = $1.60

1 Canadian dollar = $0.74

Required

a. What are the indirect exchange rates for the British pound and the Canadian dollar?

b. How many pounds must a British company pay to purchase goods costing $8,000 from a U.S. company?

c. How many U.S. dollars must be paid for a purchase costing 4,000 Canadian dollars?

LO 11-1

E11-2 Changes in Exchange Rates

Upon arrival at the international airport in the country of Canteberry, Charles Alt exchanged $200 of U.S. currency into 1,000 florins, the local currency unit. Upon departure from Canteberry's international airport on completion of his business, he exchanged his remaining 100 florins into $15 of U.S. currency.

Required

a. Determine the currency exchange rates for each of the cells in the following matrix for Charles Alt's business trip to Canteberry.

b. Discuss and illustrate whether the U.S. dollar strengthened or weakened relative to the florin during Charles's stay in Canteberry.

c. Did Charles experience a foreign currency transaction gain or a loss on the 100 florins he held during his visit to Canteberry and converted to U.S. dollars at the departure date? Explain your answer.

	Arrival Date	**Departure Date**
Direct exchange rate		
Indirect exchange rate		

LO 11-2

E11-3 Basic Understanding of Foreign Exposure

The Hi-Stakes Company has a number of importing and exporting transactions. Importing activities result in payables and exporting activities result in receivables. (LCU represents the local currency unit of the foreign entity.)

Required

a. If the direct exchange rate increases, does the dollar weaken or strengthen relative to the other currency? If the indirect exchange rate increases, does the dollar weaken or strengthen relative to the other currency?

b. Indicate in the following table whether Hi-Stakes will have a foreign currency transaction gain (G), loss (L), or not be affected (NA) by changes in the direct or indirect exchange rates for each of the four situations presented.

		Direct Exchange Rate		Indirect Exchange Rate	
Transaction	**Settlement Currency**	**Increases**	**Decreases**	**Increases**	**Decreases**
Importing	Dollar	______	______	______	______
Importing	LCU	______	______	______	______
Exporting	Dollar	______	______	______	______
Exporting	LCU	______	______	______	______

LO 11-2

E11-4 Account Balances

Merchant Company had the following foreign currency transactions:

1. On November 1, 20X6, Merchant sold goods to a company located in Munich, Germany. The receivable was to be settled in European euros on February 1, 20X7, with the receipt of €250,000 by Merchant Company.
2. On November 1, 20X6, Merchant purchased machine parts from a company located in Berlin, Germany. Merchant is to pay €125,000 on February 1, 20X7.

The direct exchange rates are as follows:

November 1, 20X6	€1 = $0.60
December 31, 20X6	€1 = $0.62
February 1, 20X7	€1 = $0.58

Required

a. Prepare T-accounts for the following five accounts related to these transactions: Foreign Currency Units (€), Accounts Receivable (€), Accounts Payable (€), Foreign Currency Transaction Loss, and Foreign Currency Transaction Gain.

b. Within the T-accounts you have prepared, appropriately record the following items:

1. The November 1, 20X6, export transaction (sale).
2. The November 1, 20X6, import transaction (purchase).
3. The December 31, 20X6, year-end adjustment required of the foreign currency–denominated receivable of €250,000.
4. The December 31, 20X6, year-end adjustment required of the foreign currency–denominated payable of €125,000.
5. The February 1, 20X7, adjusting entry to determine the U.S. dollar–equivalent value of the foreign currency receivable on that date.
6. The February 1, 20X7, adjusting entry to determine the U.S. dollar–equivalent value of the foreign currency payable on that date.
7. The February 1, 20X7, settlement of the foreign currency receivable.
8. The February 1, 20X7, settlement of the foreign currency payable.

LO 11-2

E11-5 Determining Year-End Account Balances for Import and Export Transactions

Delaney Inc. has several transactions with foreign entities. Each transaction is denominated in the local currency unit of the country in which the foreign entity is located. For each of the following independent cases, determine the December 31, 20X2, year-end balance in the appropriate accounts for the case. Write "NA" for "not applicable" in the space provided in the following chart if that account is not relevant to the specific case.

Case 1. On November 12, 20X2, Delaney purchased goods from a foreign company at a price of LCU 40,000 when the direct exchange rate was 1 LCU = $0.45. The account has not been settled as of December 31, 20X2, when the exchange rate has decreased to 1 LCU = $0.40.

Case 2. On November 28, 20X2, Delaney sold goods to a foreign entity at a price of LCU 20,000 when the direct exchange rate was 1 LCU = $1.80. The account has not been settled as of December 31, 20X2, when the exchange rate has increased to 1 LCU = $1.90.

Case 3. On December 2, 20X2, Delaney purchased goods from a foreign company at a price of LCU 30,000 when the direct exchange rate was 1 LCU = $0.80. The account has not been settled as of December 31, 20X2, when the exchange rate has increased to 1 LCU = $0.90.

Case 4. On December 12, 20X2, Delaney sold goods to a foreign entity at a price of LCU 2,500,000 when the direct exchange rate was 1 LCU = $0.003. The account has not been settled as of December 31, 20X2, when the exchange rate has decreased to 1 LCU = $0.0025.

Required

Provide the December 31, 20X2, year-end balances on Delaney's records for each of the following applicable items:

	Accounts Receivable	Accounts Payable	Foreign Currency Transaction Exchange Loss	Foreign Currency Transaction Exchange Gain
Case 1	______	______	______	______
Case 2	______	______	______	______
Case 3	______	______	______	______
Case 4	______	______	______	______

LO 11-2

E11-6 Transactions with Foreign Companies

Harris Inc. had the following transactions:

1. On May 1, Harris purchased parts from a Japanese company for a U.S. dollar equivalent value of $8,400 to be paid on June 20. The exchange rates were

May 1	1 yen = $0.0070
June 20	1 yen = 0.0075

2. On July 1, Harris sold products to a Brazilian customer for a U.S. dollar equivalent of $10,000, to be received on August 10. Brazil's local currency unit is the real. The exchange rates were

July 1	1 real = $0.20
August 10	1 real = 0.22

Required

a. Assume that the two transactions are denominated in U.S. dollars. Prepare the entries required for the dates of the transactions and their settlement in U.S. dollars.

b. Assume that the two transactions are denominated in the applicable LCUs of the foreign entities. Prepare the entries required for the dates of the transactions and their settlement in the LCUs of the Japanese company (yen) and the Brazilian customer (real).

LO 11-2

Advanced StudyGuide .com

E11-7 Foreign Purchase Transaction

On December 1, 20X1, Rone Imports, a U.S. company, purchased clocks from Switzerland for 15,000 francs (SFr) to be paid on January 15, 20X2. Rone's fiscal year ends on December 31, and its reporting currency is the U.S. dollar. The exchange rates are

December 1, 20X1	1 SFr = $0.70
December 31, 20X1	1 SFr = 0.66
January 15, 20X2	1 SFr = 0.68

Required

a. In which currency is the transaction denominated?

b. Prepare journal entries for Rone to record the purchase, the adjustment on December 31, and the settlement.

LO 11-2

E11-8 Adjusting Entries for Foreign Currency Balances

Chocolate De-lites imports and exports chocolate delicacies. Some transactions are denominated in U.S. dollars and others in foreign currencies. A summary of accounts receivable and accounts payable on December 31, 20X6, before adjustments for the effects of changes in exchange rates during 20X6, follows:

Accounts receivable:	
In U.S. dollars	$164,000
In 475,000 Egyptian pounds (E£)	$ 73,600
Accounts payable:	
In U.S. dollars	$ 86,000
In 21,000,000 yen (¥)	$175,300

The spot rates on December 31, 20X6, were

E£1 = $0.176

¥1 = $0.0081

The average exchange rates during the collection and payment period in 20X7 are

E£1 = $0.18
¥1 = $0.0078

Required

a. Prepare the adjusting entries on December 31, 20X6.
b. Record the collection of the accounts receivable in 20X7.
c. Record the payment of the accounts payable in 20X7.
d. What was the foreign currency gain or loss on the accounts receivable transaction denominated in E£ for the year ended December 31, 20X6? For the year ended December 31, 20X7? Overall for this transaction?
e. What was the foreign currency gain or loss on the accounts receivable transaction denominated in ¥? For the year ended December 31, 20X6? For the year ended December 31, 20X7? Overall for this transaction?
f. What was the combined foreign currency gain or loss for both transactions? What could Chocolate De-lites have done to reduce the risk associated with the transactions denominated in foreign currencies?

LO 11-3

E11-9 Purchase with Forward Exchange Contract

Merit & Family purchased engines from Canada for 30,000 Canadian dollars on March 10 with payment due on June 8. Also, on March 10, Merit acquired a 90-day forward contract to purchase 30,000 Canadian dollars at C$1 = $0.58. The forward contract was acquired to manage Merit & Family's exposed net liability position in Canadian dollars, but it was not designated as a hedge. The spot rates were

March 10	C$1 = $0.57
June 8	C$1 = $0.60

Required

Prepare journal entries for Merit & Family to record the purchase of the engines, entries associated with the forward contract, and entries for the payment of the foreign currency payable.

LO 11-3

E11-10 Purchase with Forward Exchange Contract and Intervening Fiscal Year-End

Pumped Up Company purchased equipment from Switzerland for 140,000 francs on December 16, 20X7, with payment due on February 14, 20X8. On December 16, 20X7, Pumped Up also acquired a 60-day forward contract to purchase francs at a forward rate of SFr 1 = $0.67. On December 31, 20X7, the forward rate for an exchange on February 14, 20X8, is SFr 1 = $0.695. The spot rates were

December 16, 20X7	1 SFr = $0.68
December 31, 20X7	1 SFr = 0.70
February 14, 20X8	1 SFr = 0.69

Part I

Assume that the forward contract is not designated as a hedge but is entered into to manage the company's foreign currency–exposed accounts payable.

a. Prepare journal entries for Pumped Up to record the purchase of equipment; all entries associated with the forward contract; the adjusting entries on December 31, 20X7; and entries to record the revaluations and payment on February 14, 20X8.
b. What was the effect of the foreign currency transactions on the income statement, including both the accounts payable and the forward contract, for the year ended December 31, 20X7?
c. What was the overall effect of these transactions on the income statement from December 16, 20X7, to February 14, 20X8?

Part II

Now assume the forward contract is designated as a cash flow hedge of the variability of the future cash flows from the foreign currency account payable. The company uses the forward exchange rate to assess effectiveness.

Required

Prepare journal entries for Pumped Up to record the purchase of equipment; all entries associated with the forward contract; the adjusting and reclassification entries on December 31, 20X7; and entries to record the revaluations and payment on February 14, 20X8.

LO 11-2

E11-11 Foreign Currency Transactions [AICPA Adapted]

Select the correct answer for each of the following questions.

1. Dale Inc., a U.S. company, bought machine parts from a German company on March 1, 20X1, for €30,000, when the spot rate for euros was $0.4895. Dale's year-end was March 31, when the spot rate was $0.4845. On April 20, 20X1, Dale paid the liability with €30,000 acquired at a rate of $0.4945. Dale's income statements should report a foreign exchange gain or loss for the years ended March 31, 20X1 and 20X2 of

	20X1	20X2
a.	$0	$0
b.	$0	$150 loss
c.	$150 loss	$0
d.	$150 gain	$300 loss

2. Marvin Company's receivable from a foreign customer is denominated in the customer's local currency. This receivable of 900,000 LCUs has been translated into $315,000 on Marvin's December 31, 20X5, balance sheet. On January 15, 20X6, the receivable was collected in full when the exchange rate was 3 LCU to $1. The journal entry Marvin should make to record the collection of this receivable is

		Debit	Credit
a.	Foreign Currency Units	300,000	
	Accounts Receivable		300,000
b.	Foreign Currency Units	300,000	
	Exchange Loss	15,000	
	Accounts Receivable		315,000
c.	Foreign Currency Units	300,000	
	Deferred Exchange Loss	15,000	
	Accounts Receivable		315,000
d.	Foreign Currency Units	315,000	
	Accounts Receivable		315,000

3. On July 1, 20X1, Black Company lent $120,000 to a foreign supplier, evidenced by an interest-bearing note due on July 1, 20X2. The note is denominated in the borrower's currency and was equivalent to 840,000 LCUs on the loan date. The note principal was appropriately included at $140,000 in the receivables section of Black's December 31, 20X1, balance sheet. The note principal was repaid to Black on the July 1, 20X2, due date when the exchange rate was 8 LCUs to $1. In its income statement for the year ended December 31, 20X2, what amount should Black include as a foreign currency transaction gain or loss on the note principal?

   a. $0.
   b. $15,000 loss.
   c. $15,000 gain.
   d. $35,000 loss.

4. If 1 Canadian dollar can be exchanged for 90 cents of U.S. currency, what fraction should be used to compute the indirect quotation of the exchange rate expressed in Canadian dollars?
   a. 1.10/1.
   b. 1/1.10.
   c. 1/.90.
   d. 0.90/1.
5. On July 1, 20X4, Bay Company borrowed 1,680,000 local currency units (LCUs) from a foreign lender evidenced by an interest-bearing note due on July 1, 20X5, which is denominated in the currency of the lender. The U.S. dollar equivalent of the note principal was as follows:

Date	Amount
7/1/X4 (date borrowed)	$210,000
12/31/X4 (Bay's year-end)	240,000
7/1/X5 (date repaid)	280,000

   In its income statement for 20X5, what amount should Bay include as a foreign exchange gain or loss on the note principal?
   a. $70,000 gain.
   b. $70,000 loss.
   c. $40,000 gain.
   d. $40,000 loss.
6. An entity denominated a sale of goods in a currency other than its functional currency. The sale resulted in a receivable fixed in terms of the amount of foreign currency to be received. The exchange rate between the functional currency and the currency in which the transaction was denominated changed. The effect of the change should be included as a
   a. Separate component of stockholders' equity whether the change results in a gain or a loss.
   b. Separate component of stockholders' equity if the change results in a gain and as a component of income if the change results in a loss.
   c. Component of income if the change results in a gain and as a separate component of stockholders' equity if the change results in a loss.
   d. Component of income whether the change results in a gain or a loss.
7. An entity denominated a December 15, 20X6, purchase of goods in a currency other than its functional currency. The transaction resulted in a payable fixed in terms of the amount of foreign currency and was paid on the settlement date, January 20, 20X7. The exchange rates between the functional currency and the currency in which the transaction was denominated changed at December 31, 20X6, resulting in a loss that should
   a. Not be reported until January 20, 20X7, the settlement date.
   b. Be included as a separate component of stockholders' equity at December 31, 20X6.
   c. Be included as a deferred charge at December 31, 20X6.
   d. Be included as a component of income from continuing operations for 20X6.

LO 11-2

E11-12 Sale in Foreign Currency

Marko Company sold spray paint equipment to Spain for 5,000,000 pesetas (P) on October 1, with payment due in six months. The exchange rates were

October 1, 20X6	1 peseta = $0.0068
December 31, 20X6	1 peseta = 0.0078
April 1, 20X7	1 peseta = 0.0076

Required

a. Did the dollar strengthen or weaken relative to the peseta during the period from October 1 to December 31? Did it strengthen or weaken between January 1 and April 1 of the next year?

b. Prepare all required journal entries for Marko as a result of the sale and settlement of the foreign transaction, assuming that its fiscal year ends on December 31.

c. Did Marko have an overall net gain or net loss from its foreign currency exposure?

LO 11-3

E11-13 Sale with Forward Exchange Contract

Advanced StudyGuide .com

Alman Company sold pharmaceuticals to a Swedish company for 200,000 kronor (SKr) on April 20, with settlement to be in 60 days. On the same date, Alman entered into a 60-day forward contract to sell 200,000 SKr at a forward rate of 1 SKr = \$0.167 in order to manage its exposed foreign currency receivable. The forward contract is not designated as a hedge. The spot rates were

April 20	SKr 1 = \$0.170
June 19	SKr 1 = 0.165

Required

a. Record all necessary entries related to the foreign transaction and the forward contract.

b. Compare the effects on net income of Alman's use of the forward exchange contract versus the effects if Alman had not used a forward exchange contract.

LO 11-2

E11-14 Foreign Currency Transactions [AICPA Adapted]

Choose the correct answer for each of the following questions.

1. On November 15, 20X3, Chow Inc., a U.S. company, ordered merchandise FOB shipping point from a German company for €200,000. The merchandise was shipped and invoiced on December 10, 20X3. Chow paid the invoice on January 10, 20X4. The spot rates for euros on the respective dates were

November 15, 20X3	\$0.4955
December 10, 20X3	0.4875
December 31, 20X3	0.4675
January 10, 20X4	0.4475

In Chow's December 31, 20X3, income statement, the foreign exchange gain is

a. \$9,600.
b. \$8,000.
c. \$4,000.
d. \$1,600.

2. Stees Corporation had the following foreign currency transactions during 20X2. First, it purchased merchandise from a foreign supplier on January 20, 20X2, for the U.S. dollar equivalent of \$90,000. The invoice was paid on March 20, 20X2, at the U.S. dollar equivalent of \$96,000. Second, on July 1, 20X2, Stees borrowed the U.S. dollar equivalent of \$500,000 evidenced by a note that was payable in the lender's local currency on July 1, 20X4. On December 31, 20X2, the U.S. dollar equivalents of the principal amount and accrued interest were \$520,000 and \$26,000, respectively. Interest on the note is 10 percent per annum. In Stees's 20X2 income statement, what amount should be included as a foreign exchange loss?

a. \$0.
b. \$6,000.
c. \$21,000.
d. \$27,000.

3. On September 1, 20X1, Cott Corporation received an order for equipment from a foreign customer for 300,000 LCUs when the U.S. dollar equivalent was \$96,000. Cott shipped the equipment on October 15, 20X1, and billed the customer for 300,000 LCUs when the U.S. dollar equivalent was \$100,000. Cott received the customer's remittance in full on November 16, 20X1, and sold the 300,000 LCUs for \$105,000. In its income statement for the year ended December 31, 20X1, Cott should report a foreign exchange gain of

a. \$0.
b. \$4,000.
c. \$5,000.
d. \$9,000.

4. On April 8, 20X3, Trul Corporation purchased merchandise from an unaffiliated foreign company for 10,000 units of the foreign company's local currency. Trul paid the bill in full on March 1, 20X4, when the spot rate was $0.45. The spot rate was $0.60 on April 8, 20X3, and was $0.55 on December 31, 20X3. For the year ended December 31, 20X4, Trul should report a transaction gain of
   a. $1,500.
   b. $1,000.
   c. $500.
   d. $0.
5. On October 1, 20X5, Stevens Company, a U.S. company, contracted to purchase foreign goods requiring payment in pesos one month after their receipt in Stevens's factory. Title to the goods passed on December 15, 20X5. The goods were still in transit on December 31, 20X5. Exchange rates were 1 dollar to 22 pesos, 20 pesos, and 21 pesos on October 1, December 15, and December 31, 20X5, respectively. Stevens should account for the exchange rate fluctuations in 20X5 as
   a. A loss included in net income before extraordinary items.
   b. A gain included in net income before extraordinary items.
   c. An extraordinary gain.
   d. An extraordinary loss.
6. On October 2, 20X5, Louis Co., a U.S. company, purchased machinery from Stroup, a German company, with payment due on April 1, 20X6. If Louis's 20X5 operating income included no foreign exchange gain or loss, the transaction could have
   a. Resulted in an extraordinary gain.
   b. Been denominated in U.S. dollars.
   c. Caused a foreign currency gain to be reported as a contra account against machinery.
   d. Caused a foreign currency translation gain to be reported as a separate component of stockholders' equity.
7. Cobb Co. purchased merchandise for 300,000 pounds from a vendor in London on November 30, 20X5. Payment in British pounds (£) was due on January 30, 20X6. The exchange rates to purchase 1 pound were as follows:

	November 30, 20X5	December 31, 20X5
Spot rate	$1.65	$1.62
30-day rate	1.64	1.59
60-day rate	1.63	1.56

   In its December 31, 20X5, income statement, what amount should Cobb report as a foreign exchange gain?
   a. $12,000.
   b. $9,000.
   c. $6,000.
   d. $0.

LO 11-3

E11-15 Sale with Forward Contract and Fiscal Year-End

Jerber Electronics Inc. sold electrical equipment to a Dutch company for 50,000 guilders (G) on May 14, with collection due in 60 days. On the same day, Jerber entered into a 60-day forward contract to sell 50,000 guilders at a forward rate of G1 = $0.541. The forward contract is not designated as a hedge. Jerber's fiscal year ends on June 30. The forward rate on June 30 for an exchange on July 13 is G1 = $0.530. The spot rates follow:

May 14	G1 = $0.530
June 30	G1 = 0.534
July 13	G1 = 0.525

Required

a. Prepare journal entries for Jerber to record (1) the sale of equipment, (2) the forward contract, (3) the adjusting entries on June 30, (4) the July 13 collection of the receivable, and (5) the July settlement of the forward contract.

b. What was the effect on the income statement in the fiscal year ending June 30?

c. What was the overall effect of this transaction on the income statement?

d. What would have been the overall effect on income if the forward contract had not been acquired?

LO 11-3

E11-16A Hedge of a Purchase (Commitment without and with Time Value of Money Considerations)

On November 1, 20X6, Smith Imports Inc. contracted to purchase teacups from England for £30,000. The teacups were to be delivered on January 30, 20X7, with payment due on March 1, 20X7. On November 1, 20X6, Smith entered into a 120-day forward contract to receive 30,000 pounds at a forward rate of £1 = $1.59. The forward contract was acquired to hedge the financial component of the foreign currency commitment.

Additional Information for the Exchange Rate

1. Assume the company uses the forward rate in measuring the forward exchange contract and for measuring hedge effectiveness.
2. Spot and exchange rates follow:

Date	Spot Rate	Forward Rate for March 1, 20X7
November 1, 20X6	£1 = $1.61	£1 = $1.59
December 31, 20X6	£1 = 1.65	£1 = 1.62
January 30, 20X7	£1 = 1.59	£1 = 1.60
March 1, 20X7	£1 = 1.585	

Required

a. What is Smith's net exposure to changes in the exchange rate of pounds for dollars between November 1, 20X6, and March 1, 20X7?

b. Prepare all journal entries from November 1, 20X6, through March 1, 20X7, for the purchase of the teacups, the forward exchange contract, and the foreign currency transaction. Assume Smith's fiscal year ends on December 31, 20X6.

Note: Requirement (*c*) requires information from Appendix 11A.

c. Assume that interest is significant and the time value of money is considered in valuing the forward contract and hedged commitment. Use a 12 percent annual interest rate. Prepare all journal entries from November 1, 20X6, through March 1, 20X7, for the purchase of the teacups, the forward exchange contract, and the foreign currency transaction. Assume Smith's fiscal year ends on December 31, 20X7.

LO 11-3

E11-17 Gain or Loss on Speculative Forward Exchange Contract

Advanced StudyGuide .com

On December 1, 20X1, Sycamore Company acquired a 90-day speculative forward contract to sell €120,000 at a forward rate of €1 = $0.58. The rates are as follows:

Date	SpotRate	Forward Rate for March 1
December 1, 20X1	€1 = $0.60	€1 = $0.58
December 31, 20X1	€1 = 0.59	€1 = 0.56
March 1, 20X2	€1 = 0.57	

Required

a. Prepare a schedule showing the effects of this speculation on 20X1 income before income taxes.

b. Prepare a schedule showing the effects of this speculation on 20X2 income before income taxes.

"A" indicates that the item relates to Appendix 11A.

LO 11-3

E11-18 Speculation in a Foreign Currency

Nick Andros of Streamline Company suggested that the company speculate in foreign currency as a partial hedge against its operations in the cattle market, which fluctuates like a commodity market. On October 1, 20X1, Streamline bought a 180-day forward contract to purchase 50,000,000 yen (¥) at a forward rate of ¥1 = $0.0075 when the spot rate was $0.0070. Other exchange rates were as follows:

Date	Spot Rate	Forward Rate for March 31, 20X2
December 31, 20X1	$0.0073	$0.0076
March 31, 20X2	0.0072	

Required

a. Prepare all journal entries related to Streamline Company's foreign currency speculation from October 1, 20X1, through March 31, 20X2, assuming the fiscal year ends on December 31, 20X1.

b. Did Streamline Company gain or lose on its purchase of the forward contract? Explain.

LO 11-2, 11-3

E11-19 Forward Exchange Transactions [AICPA Adapted]

Select the correct answer for each of the following questions.

1. The following information applies to Denton Inc.'s sale of 10,000 foreign currency units under a forward contract dated November 1, 20X5, for delivery on January 31, 20X6:

	11/1/X5	12/31/X5
Spot rates	$0.80	$0.83
30-day forward rate	0.79	0.82
90-day forward rate	0.78	0.81

Denton entered into the forward contract to speculate in the foreign currency. In its income statement for the year ended December 31, 20X5, what amount of loss should Denton report from this forward contract?

a. $400.
b. $300.
c. $200.
d. $0.

2. On September 1, 20X5, Johnson Inc. entered into a foreign exchange contract for speculative purposes by purchasing €50,000 for delivery in 60 days. The rates to exchange U.S. dollars for euros follow:

	9/1/X5	9/30/X5
Spot rate	$0.75	$0.70
30-day forward rate	0.73	0.72
60-day forward rate	0.74	0.73

In its September 30, 20X5, income statement, what amount should Johnson report as foreign exchange loss?

a. $2,500.
b. $1,500.
c. $1,000.
d. $500.

Note: Items 3 through 5 are based on the following:

On December 12, 20X5, Dahl Company entered into three forward exchange contracts, each to purchase 100,000 francs in 90 days. The relevant exchange rates are as follows:

	Spot Rate	Forward Rate for March 12, 20X6
December 12, 20X5	$0.88	$0.90
December 31, 20X5	0.98	0.93

3. Dahl entered into the first forward contract to manage the foreign currency risk from a purchase of inventory in November 20X5, payable in March 20X6. The forward contract is not designated as a hedge. At December 31, 20X5, what amount of foreign currency transaction gain should Dahl include in income from this forward contract?

   a. $0.
   b. $3,000.
   c. $5,000.
   d. $10,000.

4. Dahl entered into the second forward contract to hedge a commitment to purchase equipment being manufactured to Dahl's specifications. At December 31, 20X5, what amount of foreign currency transaction gain should Dahl include in income from this forward contract?

   a. $0.
   b. $3,000.
   c. $5,000.
   d. $10,000.

5. Dahl entered into the third forward contract for speculation. At December 31, 20X5, what amount of foreign transaction gain should Dahl include in income from this forward contract?

   a. $0.
   b. $3,000.
   c. $5,000.
   d. $10,000.

PROBLEMS

LO 11-2, 11-3 P11-20 Multiple-Choice Questions on Foreign Currency Transactions

Jon-Jan Restaurants purchased green rice, a special variety of rice, from China for 100,000 renminbi on November 1, 20X8. Payment is due on January 30, 20X9. On November 1, 20X8, the company also entered into a 90-day forward contract to purchase 100,000 renminbi. The forward contract is not designated as a hedge. The rates were as follows:

Date	Spot Rate	Forward Rate
November 1, 20X8	$0.120	$0.126 (90 days)
December 31, 20X8	0.124	0.129 (30 days)
January 30, 20X9	0.127	

Required

Select the correct answer for each of the following questions.

1. The entry on November 1, 20X8, to record the forward contract includes a

   a. Debit to Foreign Currency Receivable from Exchange Broker, 100,000 renminbi.
   b. Debit to Foreign Currency Receivable from Exchange Broker, $12,600.
   c. Credit to Premium on Forward Contract, $600.
   d. Credit to Dollars Payable to Exchange Broker, $12,600.

2. The entries on December 31, 20X8, include a
   a. Debit to Financial Expense, $300.
   b. Credit to Foreign Currency Payable to Exchange Broker, $300.
   c. Debit to Foreign Currency Receivable from Exchange Broker, $300.
   d. Debit to Foreign Currency Receivable from Exchange Broker, $12,600.
3. The entries on January 30, 20X9, include a
   a. Debit to Dollars Payable to Exchange Broker, $12,000.
   b. Credit to Cash, $12,600.
   c. Credit to Premium on Forward Contract, $600.
   d. Credit to Foreign Currency Receivable from Exchange Broker, $12,600.
4. The entries on January 30, 20X9, include a
   a. Debit to Financial Expense, $400.
   b. Debit to Dollars Payable to Exchange Broker, $12,600.
   c. Credit to Foreign Currency Units (renminbi), $12,600.
   d. Debit to Foreign Currency Payable to Exchange Broker, $12,700.
5. The entries on January 30, 20X9, include a
   a. Debit to Foreign Currency Units (renminbi), $12,700.
   b. Debit to Dollars Payable to Exchange Broker, $12,700.
   c. Credit to Foreign Currency Transaction Gain, $100.
   d. Credit to Foreign Currency Receivable from Exchange Broker, $12,600.

LO 11-2, 11-3 P11-21 Foreign Sales

Tex Hardware sells many of its products overseas. The following are some selected transactions.

1. Tex sold electronic subassemblies to a firm in Denmark for 120,000 Danish kroner (Dkr) on June 6, when the exchange rate was Dkr 1 = $0.1750. Collection was made on July 3 when the rate was Dkr 1 = $0.1753.
2. On July 22, Tex sold copper fittings to a company in London for £30,000 with payment due on September 20. Also, on July 22, Tex entered into a 60-day forward contract to sell £30,000 at a forward rate of £1 = $1.630. The spot rates follow:

July 22	£1 = $1.580
September 20	£1 = $1.612

3. Tex sold storage devices to a Canadian firm for C$70,000 (Canadian dollars) on October 11, with payment due on November 10. On October 11, Tex entered into a 30-day forward contract to sell Canadian dollars at a forward rate of C$1 = $0.730. The forward contract is not designated as a hedge. The spot rates were as follows:

October 11	C$1 = $0.7350
November 10	C$1 = $0.7320

Required

Prepare journal entries to record Tex's foreign sales of its products, use of forward contracts, and settlements of the receivables.

LO 11-2, 11-3 P11-22 Foreign Currency Transactions

Globe Shipping, a U.S. company, is an importer and exporter. The following are some transactions with foreign companies.

1. Globe sold blue jeans to a South Korean importer on January 15 for $7,400, when the exchange rate was South Korean won (KRW)1 = $0.185. Collection, in dollars, was made on March 15, when the exchange rate was $0.180.
2. On March 8, Globe purchased woolen goods from Ireland for €7,000. The exchange rate was €1 = $0.622 on March 8, but the rate was $0.610 when payment was made on May 1.

3. On May 12, Globe signed a contract to purchase toys made in Taiwan for 80,000 Taiwan dollars (NT$). The toys were to be delivered 80 days later on August 1, and payment was due on September 9, which was 40 days after delivery. On May 12, Globe also entered into a 120-day undesignated forward contract to buy NT$80,000 at a forward rate of NT$1 = $0.0376. On August 1, the forward rate for a September 9 exchange is NT$1 = $0.0378. The spot rates were as follows:

May 12	NT$1 = $0.0370
August 1	NT$1 = 0.0375
September 9	NT$1 = 0.0372

4. Globe sold microcomputers to a German enterprise on June 6 for €150,000. Payment was due in 90 days on September 4. On July 6, Globe entered into a 60-day undesignated forward contract to sell €150,000 at a forward rate of €1 = $0.580. The spot rates follow:

June 6	€1 = $0.600
July 6	€1 = 0.590
September 4	€1 = 0.585

Required

Prepare all necessary journal entries for Globe to account for the foreign transactions, including the sales and purchases of inventory, forward contracts, and settlements.

LO 11-3 P11-23A Comprehensive Problem: Four Uses of Forward Exchange Contracts without and with Time Value of Money Considerations

On December 1, 20X1, Micro World Inc. entered into a 120-day forward contract to purchase 100,000 Australian dollars (A$). Micro World's fiscal year ends on December 31. The direct exchange rates follow:

Date	Spot Rate	Forward Rate for March 31, 20X2
December 1, 20X1	$0.600	$0.609
December 31, 20X1	0.610	0.612
January 30, 20X2	0.608	0.605
March 31, 20X2	0.602	

Required

Prepare all journal entries for Micro World Inc. for the following *independent* situations:

a. The forward contract was to manage the foreign currency risks from the purchase of furniture for A$100,000 on December 1, 20X1, with payment due on March 31, 20X2. The forward contract is not designated as a hedge.

b. The forward contract was to hedge a firm commitment agreement made on December 1, 20X1, to purchase furniture on January 30, with payment due on March 31, 20X2. The derivative is designated as a fair value hedge.

c. The forward contract was to hedge an anticipated purchase of furniture on January 30. The purchase took place on January 30 with payment due on March 31, 20X2. The derivative is designated as a cash flow hedge. The company uses the forward exchange rate to measure hedge effectiveness.

d. The forward contract was for speculative purposes only.

Note: Requirement (e) uses the material in Appendix 11A.

e. Assume that interest is significant and the time value of money is considered in valuing the forward contract. Use a 12 percent annual interest rate. Prepare all journal entries required if, as in requirement (*a*), the forward contract was to manage the foreign currency–denominated payable from the purchase of furniture for 100,000 Australian dollars on December 1, 20X1, with payment due on March 31, 20X2.

LO 11-2, 11-3 P11-24 Foreign Purchases and Sales Transactions and Hedging

Advanced StudyGuide .com

Part I

Maple Company had the following export and import transactions during 20X5:

1. On March 1, Maple sold goods to a Canadian company for C$30,000, receivable on May 30. The spot rates for Canadian dollars were C$1 = $0.65 on March 1 and C$1 = $0.68 on May 30.
2. On July 1, Maple signed a contract to purchase equipment from a Japanese company for ¥500,000. The equipment was manufactured in Japan during August and was delivered to Maple on August 30 with payment due in 60 days on October 29. The spot rates for yen were ¥1 = $0.102 on July 1, ¥1 = $0.104 on August 30, and ¥1 = $0.106 on October 29. The 60-day forward exchange rate on August 30, 20X5, was ¥1 = $0.1055.
3. On November 16, Maple purchased inventory from a London company for £10,000, payable on January 15, 20X6. The spot rates for pounds were £1 = $1.65 on November 16, £1 = $1.63 on December 31, and £1 = $1.64 on January 15, 20X6. The forward rate on December 31, 20X5, for a January 15, 20X6, exchange was £1 = $1.645.

Required

a. Prepare journal entries to record Maple's import and export transactions during 20X5 and 20X6.

b. What amount of foreign currency transaction gain or loss would Maple report on its income statement for 20X5?

Part II

Assume that Maple used forward contracts to manage the foreign currency risks of all of its export and import transactions during 20X5.

1. On March 1, 20X5, Maple, anticipating a weaker Canadian dollar on the May 30, 20X5, settlement date, entered into a 90-day forward contract to sell C$30,000 at a forward exchange rate of C$1 = $0.64. The forward contract was not designated as a hedge.
2. On July 1, 20X5, Maple, anticipating a strengthening of the yen on the October 29, 20X5, settlement date, entered into a 120-day forward contract to purchase 500,000 at a forward exchange rate of ¥1 = $0.105. The forward contract was designated as a fair value hedge of a firm commitment.
3. On November 16, 20X5, Maple, anticipating a strengthening of the pound on the January 15, 20X6, settlement date, entered into a 60-day undesignated forward exchange contract to purchase £10,000 at a forward exchange rate of £1 = $1.67.

Required

a. Prepare journal entries to record Maple's foreign currency activities during 20X5 and 20X6.

b. What amount of foreign currency transaction gain or loss would Maple report on its income statement for 20X5 if Parts I and II of this problem were combined?

c. What amount of foreign currency transaction gain or loss would Maple report on its income statement for 20X6 if Parts I and II of this problem were combined?

LO 11-1, 11-2 P11-25 Understanding Foreign Currency Transactions

Dexter Inc. had the following items in its unadjusted and adjusted trial balances at December 31, 20X5:

	Trial Balances	
	Unadjusted	**Adjusted**
Accounts Receivable (denominated in Australian dollars)	$42,000	$41,700
Dollars Receivable from Exchange Broker	40,600	?
Foreign Currency Receivable from Exchange Broker	82,000	81,000
Accounts Payable (denominated in South Korean won)	80,000	?
Dollars Payable to Exchange Broker	?	?
Foreign Currency Payable to Exchange Broker	40,600	?

Additional Information

1. On December 1, 20X5, Dexter sold goods to a company in Australia for A$70,000. Payment in Australian dollars is due on January 30, 20X6. On the transaction date, Dexter entered into a 60-day forward contract to sell 70,000 Australian dollars on January 30, 20X6. The 30-day forward rate on December 31, 20X5, was A$1 = $0.57.
2. On October 2, 20X5, Dexter purchased equipment from a South Korean company for KRW400,000, payable on January 30, 20X6. On the transaction date, Dexter entered into a 120-day forward contract to purchase KRW400,000 on January 30, 20X6. On December 31, 20X5, the spot rate was KRW1 = $0.2020.

Required

Using the information contained in the trial balances, answer each of the following questions:

a. What was the indirect exchange rate for Australian dollars on December 1, 20X5? What was the indirect exchange rate on December 31, 20X5?

b. What is the balance in the account Foreign Currency Payable to Exchange Broker in the adjusted trial balance?

c. When Dexter entered into the 60-day forward contract to sell A$70,000, what was the direct exchange rate for the 60-day forward contract?

d. What is the amount of Dollars Receivable from Exchange Broker in the adjusted trial balance?

e. What was the indirect exchange rate for South Korean won on October 2, 20X5? What was the indirect exchange rate on December 31, 20X5?

f. What is the balance in the account Dollars Payable to Exchange Broker in both the unadjusted and the adjusted trial balance columns?

g. When Dexter entered into the 120-day forward contract to purchase KRW400,000, what was the direct exchange rate for the 120-day forward contract?

h. What was the Accounts Payable balance at December 31, 20X5?

LO 11-1, 11-2, 11-3

P11-26 Matching Key Terms

Match the items in the left-hand column with the descriptions/explanations in the right-hand column.

Items	Descriptions/Explanations
1. Direct exchange rate	A. Exchange rate for immediate delivery of currencies.
2. Indirect exchange rate	B. Imports and exports whose prices are stated in a foreign currency.
3. Managing an exposed net asset position	C. The primary currency used by a company for performing its major financial and operating functions.
4. Spot rates	D. U.S. companies prepare their financial statements in U.S. dollars.
5. Current rates	E. 1 European euro equals $0.65.
6. Foreign currency transaction gain	F. A forward contract is entered into when receivables denominated in European euros exceed payables denominated in that currency.
7. Foreign currency transaction loss	G. Accounts that are fixed in terms of foreign currency units.
8. Foreign currency transactions	H. 1 U.S. dollar equals 99 Japanese yen.
9. Hedging a firm commitment	I. Spot rate on the entity's balance sheet date.
10. Functional currency	J. In an export or import transaction, the date that foreign currency units are received or paid, respectively.
11. Speculating in a foreign currency	K. A forward contract is entered into when payables denominated in British pounds exceed receivables denominated in that currency.
12. Managing an exposed net liability position	L. Reported when receivables are denominated in European euros and the euro strengthens compared to the U.S. dollar.
13. Settlement date	M. A forward contract is entered into on May 1 that hedges an import transaction to occur on July 1.
14. Denominated	N. Forward contract in which no hedging is intended.
15. Reporting currency	O. Reported when payables are denominated in Swiss francs and the franc strengthens compared to the U.S. dollar.

LO 11-3

P11-27B Multiple-Choice Questions on Derivatives and Hedging Activities

Select the correct answer for each of the following questions.

1. According to **ASC 815,** which of the following is *not* an underlying?
   a. A security price.
   b. A monthly average temperature.
   c. The price of a barrel of oil.
   d. The number of foreign currency units.
2. The intrinsic value of a cash flow hedge has increased since the last balance sheet date. Which of the following accounting treatments is appropriate for this increase in value?
   a. Do not record the increase in the value because it has not been realized in an exchange transaction.
   b. Record the increase in value to current earnings.
   c. Record the increase to Other Comprehensive Income.
   d. Record the increase in a deferred income account.
3. The requirements for a derivative instrument include all but which of the following?
   a. Has one or more underlyings.
   b. Has one or more notional amounts.
   c. Requires an initial net investment equal to that required for other types of contracts that would be expected to have a similar response to changes in market factors.
   d. Requires or permits net settlement.
4. A decrease in the intrinsic value of a fair value hedge is accounted for as
   a. A decrease of current earnings.
   b. Not recorded because the exchange transaction has not yet occurred.
   c. A decrease of Other Comprehensive Income.
   d. A liability to be offset with subsequent increases in the fair value of the hedge.
5. Changes in the fair value of the effective portion of a hedging financial instrument are recognized as a part of current earnings of the period for which of the following?

	Cash Flow Hedge	Fair Value Hedge
a.	Yes	Yes
b.	No	Yes
c.	Yes	No
d.	No	No

6. According to **ASC 815,** for which of the following is hedge accounting not allowed?
   a. A forecasted purchase or sale.
   b. Available-for-sale securities.
   c. Trading securities.
   d. An unrecognized firm commitment.

LO 11-3

P11-28B A Cash Flow Hedge: Use of an Option to Hedge an Anticipated Purchase

Advanced StudyGuide .com

Mega Company believes the price of oil will increase in the coming months. Therefore, it decides to purchase call options on oil as a price-risk-hedging device to hedge the expected increase in prices on an anticipated purchase of oil.

On November 30, 20X1, Mega purchases call options for 10,000 barrels of oil at $30 per barrel at a premium of $2 per barrel with a March 1, 20X2, call date. The following is the pricing information for the term of the call:

"B" indicates that the item relates to Appendix 11B.

Date	Spot Price	Futures Price (for March 1, 20X2, delivery)
November 30, 20X1	$30	$31
December 31, 20X1	31	32
March 1, 20X2	33	

The information for the change in the fair value of the options follows:

Date	Time Value	Intrinsic Value	Total Value
November 30, 20X1	$20,000	$ 0	$20,000
December 31, 20X1	6,000	10,000	16,000
March 1, 20X2		30,000	30,000

On March 1, 20X2, Mega sells the options at their value on that date and acquires 10,000 barrels of oil at the spot price. On June 1, 20X2, Mega sells the oil for $34 per barrel.

Required

a. Prepare the journal entry required on November 30, 20X1, to record the purchase of the call options.

b. Prepare the adjusting journal entry required on December 31, 20X1, to record the change in time and intrinsic value of the options.

c. Prepare the entries required on March 1, 20X2, to record the expiration of the time value of the options, the sale of the options, and the purchase of the 10,000 barrels of oil.

d. Prepare the entries required on June 1, 20X2, to record the sale of the oil and any other entries required as a result of the option.

LO 11-3 P11-29B A Fair Value Hedge: Use of an Option to Hedge Available-for-Sale Securities

On November 3, 20X2, PRD Corporation acquired 100 shares of JRS Company at a cost of $12 per share. PRD classifies them as available-for-sale securities. On this same date, PRD decides to hedge against a possible decline in the value of the securities by purchasing, at a cost of $100, an at-the-money put option to sell the 100 shares at $12 per share. The option expires on March 3, 20X3. The fair values of the investment and the options follow:

	November 3, 20X2	December 31, 20X2	March 3, 20X3
JRS Company shares			
Per share	$ 12	$ 11	$ 10.50
Put option (100 shares)			
Market value	$100	$140	$150
Intrinsic value	0	100	150
Time value	$100	$ 40	$ 0

Required

a. Prepare the entries required on November 3, 20X2, to record the purchase of the JRS stock and the put options.

b. Prepare the entries required on December 31, 20X2, to record the change in intrinsic value and time value of the options, as well as the revaluation of the available-for-sale securities.

c. Prepare the entries required on March 3, 20X3, to record the exercise of the put option and the sale of the securities at that date.

LO 11-3 P11-30B Matching Key Terms

Match the items in the left-hand column with the descriptions/explanations in the right-hand column.

Items	Descriptions/Explanations
1. Put option	A. Hedge of the exposure to changes in the fair value of a recognized asset or liability or an unrecognized firm commitment.
2. Notional amount	B. Hedge of the exposure to variable cash flows of a forecasted transaction.
3. Intrinsic value	C. Derivative instrument that is part of a host contract.
4. Underlying	D. Specified interest rate, security price, or other variable.
5. Gains or losses on cash flow hedges	E. Number of currency units, shares, bushels, or other units specified in the contract in U.S. dollars.
6. Foreign currency hedge	F. Recognized in current earnings in the period of the change in value.
7. Fair value hedge	G. Recognized in Other Comprehensive Income in the period of the change in value.
8. Call option	H. Measure of the extent to which the derivative offsets the changes in the fair values or cash flows of the hedged item.
9. Effectiveness	I. Hedge of the net investment in foreign operations.
10. Time value	J. Conversion of a company's fixed-rate debt to a variable-rate debt.
11. Gains or losses on fair value hedges	K. Option that provides the right to acquire an underlying at an exercise or strike price.
12. Cash flow hedge	L. Option that provides the right to sell an underlying at an exercise or strike price.
13. Interest rate swap	M. Value of an option due to the spread between the current market price of the hedged item and the option's strike price.
14. Bifurcation	N. Value of an option due to the opportunity to exercise the option over the term of the option period.
15. Embedded derivative	O. Process of separating the value of an embedded derivative from its host contract.

LO 11-2, 11-3 **P11-31**

Determining Financial Statement Amounts

Kiwi Painting Company engages in a number of foreign currency transactions in euros (€). For each of the following independent transactions, determine the dollar amount to be reported in the December 31, 2004, financial statements for the items presented in the following requirements. The relevant direct exchange rates for the euro follow:

	September 1, 2004	November 30, 2004	December 31, 2004
Spot rate	$0.95	$1.05	$0.98
Forward rate for exchange on February 1, 2005	0.97	1.03	1.01

These are the independent transactions:

1. Kiwi entered into a forward exchange contract on September 1, 2004, to be settled on February 1, 2005, to hedge a firm foreign currency commitment to purchase inventory on November 30, 2004, with payment due on February 1, 2005. The forward contract was for €20,000, the agreed-upon cost of the inventory. The derivative is designated as a fair value hedge of the firm commitment.
2. Kiwi entered into a forward exchange contract on September 1, 2004, to be settled on February 1, 2005, to hedge a forecasted purchase of inventory on November 30, 2004. The inventory was purchased on November 30 with payment due on February 1, 2005. The forward contract was for €20,000, the expected cost of the inventory. The derivative is designated as a cash flow hedge to be continued through to payment of the euro-denominated account payable.
3. Kiwi entered into a forward contract on November 30, 2004, to be settled on February 1, 2005, to manage the financial currency exposure of a euro-denominated accounts payable in the amount of €20,000 from the purchase of inventory on that date. The payable is due on February 1, 2005. The forward contract is not designated as a hedge.

4. Kiwi entered into a forward contract on September 1, 2004, to speculate on the possible changes in exchange rates between the euro and the U.S. dollar between September 1, 2004, and February 1, 2005. The forward contract is for speculation purposes and is not a hedge.

Required

Enter the dollar amount that would be shown for each of the following items as of December 31, 2004. Compute the statement amounts net. For example, if the transaction generated both a foreign currency exchange gain and a loss, specify just the net amount that would be reported in the financial statements. If no amount would be reported for an item, enter NA for Not Applicable in the space.

	Transaction			
	1	2	3	4
Forward contract receivable	____	____	____	____
Inventory	____	____	____	____
Accounts payable (€)	____	____	____	____
Foreign currency exchange gain (loss), net	____	____	____	____
Other comprehensive income gain (loss), net	____	____	____	____

KAPLAN CPA REVIEW

Kaplan CPA Review Simulation on Comprehensive Consolidation Procedures

Please visit the *Connect Library* for the online Kaplan CPA Review task-based simulation.

Situation

The Tee Corporation is a golfing equipment manufacturer based in Savannah, Georgia. A foreign subsidiary of the Tee Corporation, Club Corporation, located in South America, also manufactures golf equipment. Consolidated financial statements are being prepared for Year One. Tee Corp. and Club Corp. both have a December 31 year-end.

Topics Covered in the Simulation

a. Translation.

b. Remeasurement.

c. Foreign currency reporting.

Note to instructors: Parts *a* and *b* should be used after students have covered Chapter 12. Part *c* is appropriate after students have covered Chapter 11.

12 Multinational Accounting: Issues in Financial Reporting and Translation of Foreign Entity Statements

Multicorporate Entities

Multinational Entities

Foreign Currency Transactions

Translation of Foreign Statements

Reporting Requirements

Partnerships

Governmental and Not-for-Profit Entities

Corporations in Financial Difficulty

McDONALD'S—THE WORLD'S FAST FOOD FAVORITE

McDonald's was founded in 1940 by two brothers, Dick and Mac McDonald, in San Bernardino, California. The McDonald brothers introduced the "Speedee Service System" in 1948, which laid the groundwork for modern fast-food restaurants.

In 1954, the brothers were using four Multimixer milkshake machines in their San Bernardino location. This piqued the interest of Ray Kroc, one of Multimixer's distributors, so he headed to San Bernardino to see "what the devil was going on." Kroc was so impressed with the McDonald brothers' operation that he convinced them to allow him to franchise their restaurants throughout the country. In 1955, Kroc opened his first McDonald's franchise in Des Plaines, Illinois.

The chain grew slowly at first, operating 79 restaurants at the end of 1958. However, in 1959, Kroc expanded aggressively, opening 66 new restaurants. Two years later, he bought out the McDonald brothers' interest for $2.7 million. And just four years later he took the company public. Success continued for McDonald's for the rest of the 1960s. In 1963, the company sold its one billionth hamburger and, in 1968, it introduced the famous Big Mac and opened its 1,000th restaurant.

The 1970s were not much different. By 1971, McDonald's was operating restaurants in all 50 states. The company introduced the Egg McMuffin and the Happy Meal in 1975 and 1979, respectively. The McDonald's drive-thru was introduced in 1975 and in 1976 McDonald's sold its 20 billionth hamburger. The 1980s started out strong with the unveiling of the McChicken sandwich in 1983. In 1985, McDonald's became one of the 30 companies composing the Dow Jones Industrial Average.

The 1990s was a time of international growth for McDonald's. In 1992, 66 percent of McDonald's revenue came from U.S. sales. That number dropped to about 43 percent in 1998 and then to about 32 percent in 2011. In 1991, only 3,600 international locations were in operation, but by 1998, that number had more than tripled to 11,000. As of 2014, McDonald's is operating 35,429 stores in 119 countries; 21,162 of these stores are located outside of the United States. Clearly, McDonald's has become a symbol of globalization. With locations in virtually every country in the world, McDonald's is the epitome of a multinational corporation. Managing such a widespread global empire requires a detailed understanding of accounting and the effects of currency changes on the company's financial statements.

Differences in accounting standards across countries and jurisdictions can cause significant difficulties for multinational firms such as McDonald's. In fact, one of the significant challenges McDonald's faces is the preparation of financial statements according to the differing standards in countries where its subsidiaries are located and the subsequent consolidation of these foreign-based financial statements. These and other significant problems that result from differences in accounting standards have generated significant interest in the harmonization of accounting standards globally.

In addition, because of its global presence, McDonald's has to constantly monitor fluctuations in foreign currencies. For example, the company reports in its 2013 Form 10-K that "in 2013, foreign currency translation had a negative impact on consolidated operating results due to the weaker Australian Dollar, Japanese Yen and many other foreign currencies, partly offset by the stronger Euro." The following table from McDonald's 2013 Form 10-K shows the effects of translating subsidiaries' financial statements from foreign currencies to U.S. dollars.

	Reported Amount			Currency Translation Benefit/(Cost)		
In millions, except per share data	**2013**	**2012**	**2011**	**2013**	**2012**	**2011**
Revenues	**$28,106**	$27,567	$27,006	**$ (29)**	$(726)	$ 944
Company-operated margins	**3,296**	3,379	3,455	**(7)**	(97)	134
Franchised margins	**7,607**	3,437	7,232	**(43)**	(204)	213
Selling, general & administrative expenses	**2,386**	2,455	2,394	**(5)**	40	(55)
Operating income	**8,764**	8,605	8,530	**(66)**	(261)	301
Net income	**5,586**	5,465	5,503	**(52)**	(178)	195
Earnings per common share—diluted	**5.55**	5.36	5.27	**(0.05)**	(0.17)	0.19

Accountants preparing financial statements of global companies must consider (1) differences across national boundaries in accounting principles and (2) differences in currencies used to measure the operations of companies operating in different countries. Translation or restatement into U.S. dollars is necessary before a foreign subsidiary's financial statements can be consolidated with the U.S. parent company's statements, which are already reported in dollars. This chapter summarizes current efforts to develop a global set of high-quality accounting standards and explores the translation of financial statements of a foreign business entity into U.S. dollars.

LEARNING OBJECTIVES

When you finish studying this chapter, you should be able to:

LO 12-1 Understand and explain the benefits and ramifications of convergence to International Financial Reporting Standards (IFRS) and the expected timeline to global convergence.

LO 12-2 Determine the functional currency and understand the ramifications of different functional currency designations.

LO 12-3 Understand and explain the differences between translation and remeasurement.

LO 12-4 Make calculations and translate financial statements of a foreign subsidiary.

LO 12-5 Prepare consolidated financial statements including a foreign subsidiary after translation.

LO 12-6 Make calculations and remeasure financial statements of a foreign subsidiary.

LO 12-7 Prepare consolidated financial statements including a foreign subsidiary after remeasurement.

LO 12-8 Understand other issues related to foreign operations including the hedging of a net investment in a foreign subsidiary.

CONVERGENCE OF ACCOUNTING PRINCIPLES

LO 12-1

Understand and explain the benefits and ramifications of convergence to International Financial Reporting Standards (IFRS) and the expected timeline to global convergence.

Methods used to measure economic activity differ around the world. Many factors influence the development of accounting standards in a country, including its economic, legal, educational, and political systems; its stage of technological development; its culture and traditions; and other socioeconomic factors. These differences have led to significant diversity in accounting standards from one nation to another. The lack of a uniform set of accounting standards creates problems for companies, preparers, and users. Some countries develop their accounting principles based on the information needs of the taxing authorities. Other countries have accounting principles designed to meet the needs of central government economic planners. U.S. accounting standards focus on the information needs of the common stockholder or the creditors.

Arthur Levitt, former chairman of the Securities and Exchange Commission (SEC), noted in 1999 that the world economy was in a period of profound change because the notion of distance as a barrier was no longer a relevant impediment to business growth and development. Levitt noted that the flow of capital is a critical factor in global economic development, which had created a compelling need for a common business-reporting language. Indeed, Levitt stated that "new business opportunities demand financial reporting standards that supersede national borders and cultural customs. These standards are not merely an ideal for a better global marketplace—they are fundamental to its very existence."[1]

Since Levitt's statement, significant strides have been taken to move toward a single set of globally accepted reporting standards. Many feel that important benefits can be realized from the adoption of globally consistent accounting standards. These expected benefits include continued expansion of capital markets across national borders. Countries in which accounting principles do not currently focus on the needs of investors could more quickly achieve stable, liquid, capital markets, which in turn should drive economic growth. Another expected benefit is that the use of a single set of accounting standards should help investors to better evaluate opportunities across national borders, which also should facilitate a more efficient use of global capital. Benefits to reporting companies include the belief that a set of global standards also should reduce reporting costs that corporations currently incur if they attempt to access capital in markets outside their home country because they will no longer need to produce multiple sets of financial statements using different sets of accounting standards. And financial statement users are likely to have more confidence in financial reporting if it conforms to standards that have gained wide global acceptance.

One of the most significant steps the SEC has taken toward supporting and accepting ***International Financial Reporting Standards (IFRS)*** occurred on January 4, 2008, when the SEC issued new rules that allow foreign private issuers to file statements prepared in accordance with IFRS as issued by the International Accounting Standards Board (IASB) without reconciliation to United States Generally Accepted Accounting Principles (U.S. GAAP.[2]) Removing the Form 20-F requirement for companies strictly following IFRS reduces costs to foreign private issuers and encourages their continued participation in the U.S. public capital market, which is a benefit to investors by increasing investment possibilities and furthering the efficient allocation of capital.

While significant progress has been made in moving toward a single set of globally consistent accounting standards in the years following Levitt's statement, based on statements from the SEC in late 2012 it appears that the SEC currently has no timetable for allowing U.S. companies to file statements in accordance with IFRS for the

[1] Arthur Levitt, "Remarks to the American Council on Germany: Corporate Governance in a Global Arena," Speech by SEC Chairman, October 7, 1999, http://www.sec.gov/news/speech/speecharchive/1999/spch302.htm.

[2] Securities and Exchange Commission, "Acceptance from Foreign Private Issuers of Financial Statements Prepared in Accordance with International Financial Reporting Standards without Reconciliation to U.S. GAAP," Federal Register 73, no. 3 (January 4, 2008), pp. 986–1012, www.sec.gov/rules/final/2008/33-8879fr.pdf.

foreseeable future.[3,4] One of the many reasons for the continued delay in convergence or adoption of IFRS centers around the complexities that exist in allowing the ISAB to be a regulatory authority in the United States. Speaking on the Final Staff Report on the SEC Work Plan at the 2012 AICPA Conference on Current SEC and PCAOB Developments, Jenifer Minke-Girard, the senior associate chief accountant of the SEC, stated, "Looking directly to IASB, by designating the standards of the IASB as authoritative, would be challenging and was not supported by the vast majority of participants in the U.S. capital markets."[5]

There is still hope for a set of comparable accounting standards in the future. However, the SEC does not appear to be inclined to hurry toward adopting IFRS until it is clear that it provides the same level of protection that U.S. GAAP currently provides to investors. In 2012 Mary Schapiro, former chairperson of the SEC, made the following statement concerning U.S. GAAP-IFRS convergence: "I don't feel any pressure at all to go along with anybody. I feel pressured to do the right thing for the US markets and US investors."[6] This statement echoes what former SEC chief accountant, James Kroeker, said in 2009: I believe the fundamental focus of our evaluation of implementing a single set of high quality standards must be on the impact to investors. I believe that implementing a set of global accounting standards for U.S. issuers can and must be done only in a manner that is beneficial to U.S. capital markets and consistent with the SEC's mission of protecting investors.[7]

In late 2012, then-current SEC chief accountant, Paul Beswick, best summarized the SEC's current stance and situation in regards to IFRS adoption:

> The consideration of incorporating IFRS may be the single most important accounting determination for the Commission since the determination to look to the private sector to establish accounting standards in the 1930's. We understand individuals' interest in this topic and the potential uncertainty that may exist, but the staff is working to ensure that the Commission is properly informed on the issue. Obviously, we will work with our new Chairman and our existing Commissioners on determining the next steps in this process. So please stay tuned.[8]

While the world may have to "stay tuned" a little longer for a single set of global accounting standards, there was renewed hope in January of 2014 when current SEC Chairperson Mary Jo White stated: "I am gratified by the Financial Accounting Foundation's announcement that the FAF will provide a substantial contribution to the IFRS Foundation."[9] The FAF—in consultation with the SEC—announced that it would contribute $3 million to the IFRS foundation, prompting many in the accounting and finance world to believe that the SEC could be returning to its IFRS roadmap in the near future.[10]

[3] J. McEnroe and M. Sullivan, "The Rise and Stall of U.S. GAAP and IFRS," *The CPA Journal,* http://viewer.zmags.com/publication/56adc02d#/56adc02d/20.

[4] P. Harris, E. Jermakowicz, and B. Epstein, "Converting Financial Statements from U.S. GAAP to IFRS," *The CPA Journal,* http://viewer.zmags.com/publication/56adc02d#/56adc02d/20.

[5] Jenifer Minke-Girard, "Remarks Before the 2012 AICPA Conference on Current SEC and PCAOB Developments," December 3, 2012, http://www.sec.gov/News/Speech/Detail/Speech/1365171491876#.U2RJ-l6wS6E.

[6] S. Lynch and D. Clark, "SEC Chief Resists Pressure on Global Accounting," http://www.reuters.com/article/2012/02/24/us-sec-accounting-idUSTRE81N1GJ20120224.

[7] M. Lamoreaux, "SEC Chief Accountant Remains Mum on Specifics of Possible IFRS Adoption," *Journal of Accountancy,* http://www.journalofaccountancy.com/Web/20092393.

[8] Paul A. Beswick, "Remarks Before the 2012 AICPA Conference on Current SEC and PCAOB Developments," December 3, 2012, http://www.sec.gov/News/Speech/Detail/Speech/1365171491922#.U2RILF6wS6E.

[9] Mary Jo White, "Statement on Financial Accounting Foundation Announcement," January 29, 2014, http://www.sec.gov/News/PublicStmt/Detail/PublicStmt/1370540688889#.U2RqLl6wS6E.

[10] S. Burkholder, "FASB Parent's $3 Million Pledge to IASB's Parent Raises Concerns in Rulemaking Circles," Bloomberg BNA, http://www.bna.com/fasb-parents-million-n17179882071/.

In short, it is safe to assume that while there will be ongoing discussion of IFRS convergence and adoption by the SEC in the coming years, no single set of global accounting standards will be used by U.S. companies until the SEC can ensure that these standards provide the maximum amount of protection and transparency to investors.

ACCOUNTING FOR DIFFERENCES IN CURRENCIES AND EXCHANGE RATES

Currency Definitions

Before discussing international transactions in detail, it is helpful to first understand some of the terms commonly used to describe different currencies. The ***local currency unit*** is the legal tender in the country or jurisdiction where an affiliated subsidiary is located. The ***recording currency*** is the currency in which the company records its transactions. Finally, the ***reporting currency*** is the currency in which the financial reports will be presented to stakeholders. If a subsidiary is located in the United States, the local currency is the U.S. dollar. Transactions are recorded in dollars and the financial statements are reported in U.S. dollars. However, if for example, a U.S.-based parent company (which reports in U.S. dollars) owns a subsidiary located in Italy (where the local currency is the euro), it is likely that the subsidiary's recording currency will also be the euro. In order to consolidate this Italian subsidiary, the parent company domiciled in the United States will have to restate the Italian subsidiary's financial statements in dollars to facilitate the consolidation process. This chapter explains this process. The first step is to determine the functional currency.

DETERMINATION OF THE FUNCTIONAL CURRENCY

LO 12-2

Determine the functional currency and understand the ramifications of different functional currency designations.

Imagine that you received 100 British pounds sterling (£) in payment on an account in your London subsidiary on December 31, 20X1, and deposited it in a London bank. Assume that at the end of 20X1, the exchange rate is $1.80. To report the deposit on your 20X1 balance sheet stated in dollars, you would translate the deposit at the current rate and report an asset of $180. At the end of 20X2, assume you still have the £100 in the bank, but now the exchange rate is $1.70. To report the deposit on your 20X2 balance sheet, using the exchange rate at the end of 20X2, this amount would now translate into $170 and you would have an imbalance, also referred to as a *translation adjustment,* of $10 to deal with. If you translated at the historical rate, you would still translate into $180 and there would be no imbalance. Which is the correct exchange rate to use?

Date	Currency on Deposit	Current Exchange Rate	Dollar Equivalent
12/31/20X1	£100	$1.80	$180
12/31/20X2	100	1.70	170

Two major issues that must be addressed when financial statements are translated from a foreign currency into U.S. dollars are

1. Which exchange rate should be used to translate foreign currency balances to domestic currency?
2. How should translation gains and losses be accounted for? Should they be included in income?

Three possible exchange rates may be used in converting foreign currency values to the U.S. dollar. The ***current rate*** is the exchange rate at the end of the trading day on the balance sheet date. The ***historical rate*** is the exchange rate that existed when an initial transaction took place, such as the exchange rate on the date an asset was acquired or a liability was incurred. The ***average rate*** for the period is usually a simple average for a period of time and is usually the exchange rate used to measure revenues and expenses.[11] Translation methods may employ a single rate or multiple rates. The translation adjustment created by the application of these exchange rates also must be reflected in the financial statements, as either a component of net income or a component of comprehensive income. The disposition of the translation adjustment will be discussed later in this chapter.

ASC 830 provides specific guidelines for translating a foreign currency into U.S. dollars to allow preparation of consolidated financial statements measured, or denominated, in dollars. The purpose of **ASC 830** is to present results that are directionally sympathetic to the real economic effects of exchange rate movements. Additionally, **ASC 830** seeks to preserve financial results and relationships in the foreign financial statements through the translation process. For instance, if the gross margin on sales is positive when measured in the foreign currency, it should still be positive when sales and cost of goods sold are translated into dollars. The FASB adopted the concept of the ***functional currency,*** which is defined as "the currency of the primary economic environment in which the entity operates; normally that is the currency of the environment in which an entity primarily generates and receives cash."[12] The functional currency is used to differentiate between two types of foreign operations, those that are self-contained and integrated into a local environment and those that are an extension of the parent and integrated with the parent. A U.S. company may have foreign affiliates in many different countries. Each affiliate must be analyzed to determine its individual functional currency.

Refer to Figure 12–1 for the six indicators that must be assessed to determine an entity's functional currency: cash flows, sales prices, sales markets, expenses, financing, and intercompany transactions. If a foreign affiliate uses the local currency for most of its transactions, and if the cash generated is not regularly returned to the parent in the United States, the local currency is usually the functional currency. Also, the foreign affiliate usually has active sales markets in its own country and obtains financing from local sources.

Some foreign-based entities, however, use a functional currency different from the local currency. For example, a U.S. company's subsidiary in Venezuela may conduct virtually all of its business in Brazil, or a branch or a subsidiary of a U.S. company operating in Britain may well use the U.S. dollar as its major currency although it maintains its accounting records in British pounds sterling. The following factors indicate that the U.S. dollar is the functional currency for the British subsidiary: Most of its cash transactions are in U.S. dollars; its major sales markets are in the United States; production components are generally obtained from the United States; and the U.S. parent is primarily responsible for financing the British subsidiary.

The FASB adopted the functional currency approach after considering the following objectives of the translation process (**ASC 830**):

a. Provide information that is generally compatible with the expected economic effects of a rate change on an enterprise's cash flows and equity.
b. Reflect in consolidated statements the financial results and relationships of the individual consolidated entities as measured in their functional currencies in conformity with U.S. generally accepted accounting principles.

[11] If exchange rates change gradually during an accounting period and if a company's revenues and expenses are generated evenly throughout the period, a simple average is likely to provide an accurate conversion of financial statements from one currency to another. However, if exchange rates change rapidly or if a company experiences seasonal fluctuations in its income statement (e.g., if most of the revenues or expenses are recorded in a single quarter), then a weighted average rate would provide a more accurate conversion of financial statements from one currency to another. Accountants must use professional judgment to decide whether a simple average rate is sufficient or whether a weighted average rate is more appropriate. We provide examples of both in this chapter.

[12] **ASC 830-10-45 to 830-10-55.**

FIGURE 12–1 Functional Currency Indicators

Indicator	Factors Indicating Foreign Currency (Local Currency) Is the Functional Currency	Factors Indicating U.S. Dollar (Parent's Currency) Is the Functional Currency
Cash flows	Primarily in foreign currency and do not affect parent's cash flows	Directly impact the parent's current cash flows and are readily available to the parent company
Sales prices	Primarily determined by local competition or local government regulation; not generally responsive to changes in exchange rates	Responsive to short-term changes in exchange rates and worldwide competition
Sales markets	Active local sales markets for company's products; possibly, significant amounts of exports	Sales markets mostly in parent's country, or sales contracts are denominated in parent's currency
Expenses	Labor, materials, and other costs are primarily local costs	Production components generally obtained from the parent company's country
Financing	Primarily obtained from, and denominated in, local currency units; entity's operations generate funds sufficient to service financing needs	Primarily from the parent, or other dollar-denominated financing
Intercompany transactions and arrangements	Few intercompany transactions with parent	Frequent intercompany transactions with parent, or foreign entity is an investment or financing arm for the parent

FYI

Hyperinflation in Zimbabwe

On April 18, 1980, the Republic of Zimbabwe was created from what was then the British colony of Southern Rhodesia. As part of the formation of the Republic of Zimbabwe, the Rhodesian dollar was replaced by the Zimbabwean dollar at par value. At this time, the Zimbabwe dollar was more valuable than the U.S. dollar. When the country was formed in 1980, the inflation rate was 7 percent. By mid-November of 2008, the inflation rate was estimated to be 79,600,000,000 percent per month and the exchange rate was 1 U.S. dollar to 2,621,984,228 Zimbabwean dollars. The Zimbabwean government did not attempt to combat inflation with fiscal or monetary policy. Rather, it continued to print money in continually larger denominations. In fact, before hyperinflation reached its peak, Zimbabwe issued its largest denominated bank note, a 100 trillion dollar bank note. One could argue that such large denominated bills were needed considering that in any given day the price of bread could fluctuate anywhere between 550 million Zimbabwean dollars to 10 billion Zimbabwean dollars. In 2009 Zimbabwe abandoned its currency, rendering it worthless and as of 2014, the Republic of Zimbabwe still has no official national currency. Instead, foreign currencies, such as the dollar and the euro, are used.

The obverse of the 2009 Zimbabwe $100 trillion banknote.

The functional currency approach requires the foreign entity to translate all of its transactions into its functional currency. If an entity has transactions denominated in other than its functional currency, the foreign transactions must be adjusted to their equivalent functional currency value before the company may prepare financial statements.

Functional Currency Designation in Highly Inflationary Economies

An exception to the criteria for selecting a functional currency is specified when the foreign entity is located in countries such as Argentina and Peru, which have experienced severe inflation. *Severe inflation* is defined as inflation exceeding 100 percent over a three-year period. The FASB concluded that the volatility of hyperinflationary currencies distorts the financial statements if the local currency is used as the foreign entity's functional currency. Therefore, in cases of operations located in highly inflationary economies, the reporting currency of the U.S. parent—the U.S. dollar—should be used as the foreign entity's functional currency. This exception prevents unrealistic asset values and income statement charges if the hyperinflation is ignored and normal translation procedures are used. For example, assume that a foreign subsidiary constructed a building that cost 1,000,000 pesos when the exchange rate was $0.05 = 1 peso. Further assume that because of hyperinflation in the foreign subsidiary's country, the exchange rate becomes $0.00005 = 1 peso. The translated values of the building at the time it was constructed and after the hyperinflation follow:

	Date of Construction		After Hyperinflation	
Amount (pesos)	Rate	Translated Amount	Rate	Translated Amount
1,000,000	$0.05	$50,000	$0.00005	$50

The translated values after the hyperinflation do not reflect the building's market value or historical cost. Thus, the FASB required the use of the U.S. dollar as the functional currency in cases of hyperinflation to give some stability to the financial statements.

Once a foreign affiliate's functional currency is chosen, it should be used consistently. However, if changes in economic circumstances necessitate a change in the designation of the foreign affiliate's functional currency, the accounting change should be treated as a change in estimate: current and prospective treatment only, no restatement of prior periods.

TRANSLATION VERSUS REMEASUREMENT OF FOREIGN FINANCIAL STATEMENTS[13]

LO 12-3

Understand and explain the differences between translation and remeasurement.

Advanced StudyGuide .com

Two different methods are used (in different circumstances) to restate foreign entity statements to U.S. dollars: (1) the ***translation*** of the foreign entity's functional currency statements into U.S. dollars and (2) the ***remeasurement*** of the foreign entity's statements into its functional currency. After remeasurement, the statements must then be translated if the functional currency is *not* the U.S. dollar. No additional work is needed if the functional currency is the U.S. dollar.

Translation is the most common method used and is applied when the local currency is the foreign entity's functional currency. This is the normal case in which, for example, a U.S. company's French subsidiary uses the euro as its recording and functional currency. The subsidiary's statements must be translated from euros into U.S. dollars. To translate the financial statements, the company will use the current rate, which is the exchange rate on the balance sheet date, to convert the local currency balance sheet account balances into U.S. dollars. Because revenues and expenses are assumed to occur uniformly over the period, revenues and expenses on the income statement are translated using the average rate for the reporting period. Any translation adjustment that occurs is a component of comprehensive income. The method used to translate financial statements from the local currency to U.S. dollars is called the ***current rate method.***

Remeasurement is the restatement of the foreign entity's financial statements from the local currency that the entity used into the foreign entity's functional currency. Remeasurement is required only when the functional currency is different from the currency used to maintain foreign entity's the books and records. For example, a relatively self-contained Canadian sales branch of a U.S. company may use the U.S. dollar as its functional currency but may select the Canadian dollar as its recording and reporting currency. Of course, if the Canadian branch uses the U.S. dollar for both its functional and reporting currency, no translation or remeasurement is necessary: Its statements are already measured in U.S. dollars and are ready to be combined with the U.S. home office statements.

The method used to remeasure the financial statements from the local currency to the functional currency is called the ***temporal method.*** Monetary assets and liabilities are

[13] To view a video explanation of this topic, visit advancedstudyguide.com.

those that represent rights to receive or obligations to pay a fixed number of foreign currency units in the future. Under the temporal method, the current rate is usually used to translate these monetary amounts to the functional currency. Nonmonetary items include fixed assets, long-term investments, and inventories. These items are usually translated at the historical rate that existed when the assets originally were purchased or the liability originally was incurred. Revenues and expenses on the income statement are translated using the average rate for the reporting period. Any imbalance that occurs because of the application of the temporal method is included in the calculation of net income on the income statement.

The application of the temporal method converts a foreign currency to the functional currency. If the functional currency is the U.S. dollar, no additional adjustments are needed. If the functional currency is something other than the U.S. dollar, the current rate method must be applied to restate the financial information in U.S. dollars.

One application of remeasurement is for affiliates located in countries experiencing hyperinflation. For example, an Argentinean subsidiary of a U.S. parent records and reports its financial statements in the local currency, the Argentine peso. However, because the Argentine economy experiences inflation exceeding 100 percent over a three-year period, the U.S. dollar is specified as the functional currency for reporting purposes and the subsidiary's statements must then be remeasured from Argentine pesos into U.S. dollars.

Three possible scenarios may require the restatement of financial statements from one currency to another via translation and/or remeasurement.

Case 1: The local currency is the functional currency. Simply translate the financial statements from the functional currency to the reporting currency. No further work is necessary because the consolidation and financial reports can now be prepared in the reporting currency.

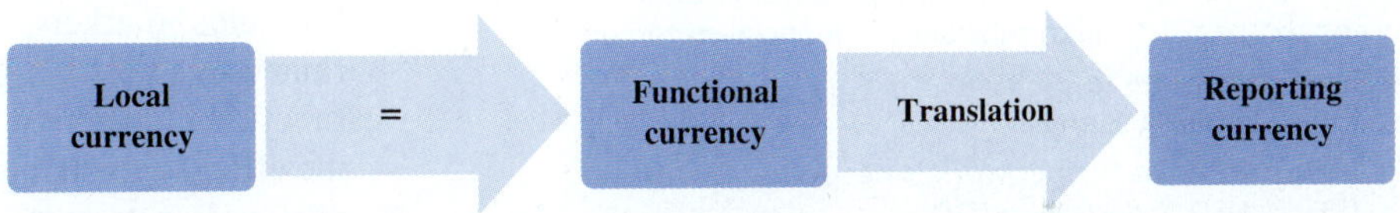

Case 2: The local currency is not the functional currency, but the functional currency is the reporting currency. Simply remeasure the financial statements from the local currency to the functional currency. No further work is necessary because the consolidation and financial reports can now be prepared in the functional currency (because it is the reporting currency).

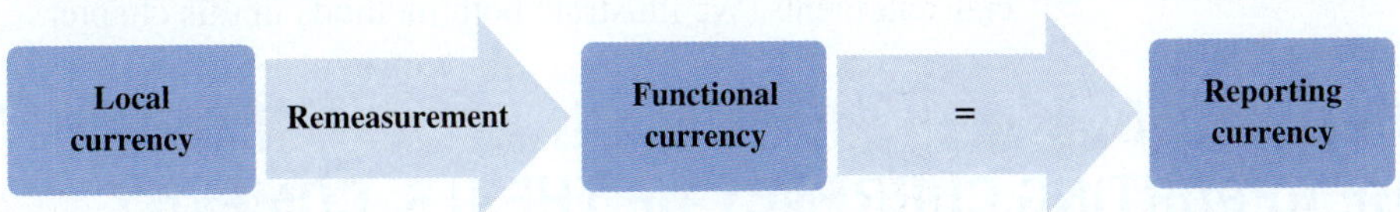

Case 3: The local currency is not the functional currency, and the functional currency is different from the reporting currency. First, remeasure the financial statements from the local currency to the functional currency. Second, translate the financial statements from the functional currency to the reporting currency so that the consolidation and financial statements can be prepared in the reporting currency.

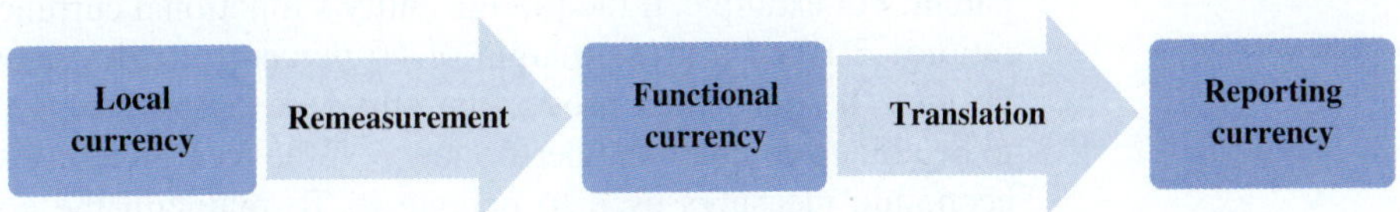

The following examples illustrate a situation for each of these three cases in which restatement of the financial statements is necessary.

Local Currency	Functional Currency	Reporting Currency	Restatement Method (s)
U.S. dollar (USD)	USD	USD	None
Case 1: Mexican peso (MP)	MP	USD	Translate from MP to USD
Case 2: British pound (BP)	USD	USD	Remeasure from BP to USD
Case 3: Uruguayan peso (UP)	Brazilian real (BRL)	USD	Remeasure from UP to BRL then translate from BRL to USD

The conceptual reasons for the two different methods, translation and remeasurement, come from a consideration of the primary objective of the restatement process: to provide information that shows the expected impact of exchange rate changes on the U.S. company's cash flows and equity. Foreign affiliates fall into two groups. Those in the first group are relatively self-contained entities that generate and spend local currency units. The local currency is the functional currency for this group of entities. These foreign affiliates may reinvest the currency they generate or may distribute funds to their home office or parent company in the form of dividends. Exchange rate changes do not directly affect the U.S. parent company's cash flows but do affect the foreign affiliate's net assets (assets minus liabilities) and, therefore, the U.S. parent company's net investment in the entity. Translation is appropriate for these firms' financial statements.

The second group of foreign affiliates is made up of entities that are extensions of the U.S. company. These affiliates operate in a foreign country but are directly affected by changes in exchange rates because they depend on the U.S. economy for sales markets, production components, or financing. For this group, the U.S. dollar is the functional currency. There is a presumption that the effect of exchange rate changes on the foreign affiliate's net assets will directly affect the U.S. parent company's cash flows, so the exchange rate adjustments are reported in the U.S. parent's income. Remeasurement is appropriate for these firms' financial statements.

Translation and remeasurement include different adjustment procedures and may result in significantly different consolidated financial statements. We illustrate both methods in this chapter.

CAUTION

Knowing when to translate and when to remeasure can be difficult. To ensure that you do not become confused, the following rule of thumb can be useful in determining how to restate a U.S.-based parent company's foreign subsidiary's financial statements:

If LC = FC, translate to USD
If LC ≠ FC, remeasure to FC

- If FC = USD, no further work is needed
- If FC ≠ USD, translate to USD

Where:

LC = local currency
FC = functional currency
USD = U.S. dollars

TRANSLATION OF FUNCTIONAL CURRENCY STATEMENTS INTO THE REPORTING CURRENCY OF THE U.S. COMPANY

LO 12-4

Make calculations and translate financial statements of a foreign subsidiary.

Most business entities transact and record business activities in the local currency. Therefore, the foreign entity's local currency is its functional currency. The translation of the foreign entity's statement into U.S. dollars is a relatively straightforward process.

The FASB believes that the underlying economic relationships presented in the foreign entity's financial statements should not be distorted or changed during the translation process from the foreign entity's functional currency into the currency of the U.S. parent. For example, if the foreign entity's functional currency statements report a current ratio of 2:1 and a gross margin of 60 percent of sales, these relationships should pass through the translation process into the U.S. parent's reporting currency. It is important to be able to evaluate the performance of the foreign entity's management with the same economic measures used to operate it. To maintain the economic relationships in the functional currency statements, the account balances must be translated by a comparable exchange rate.

The translation is made by using the current exchange rate for *all* assets and liabilities. This rate is the spot rate on the balance sheet date. The income statement items—revenue, expenses, gains, and losses—should be translated at the exchange rate on the dates on which the underlying transactions occurred, although for practical purposes, an average exchange rate for the period may be used for these items with the assumption that revenues and expenses are recognized evenly over the period. However, if a material gain or loss results from a specific event, the exchange rate on the date of the event rather than the average exchange rate should be used to translate the transaction results.

The stockholders' equity accounts, other than retained earnings, are translated at historical exchange rates. The appropriate historical rate is the rate on the latter of the date the parent company acquired the investment in the foreign entity or the date the subsidiary had the stockholders' equity transaction. This is necessary to complete the elimination of the parent company's investment account against the foreign subsidiary's capital accounts in the consolidation process. The subsidiary's translated retained earnings are carried forward from the previous period with additions for this period's income and deductions for dividends declared during the period. Dividends are translated at the exchange rate on the date of declaration. It is interesting to observe that if the foreign entity has not paid its declared dividend by the end of its fiscal period, it has a dividends payable account that is translated at the current rate. Nevertheless, the dividend deduction from retained earnings is translated using the exchange rate on the date of dividend declaration.

In summary, the translation of the foreign entity's financial statements from its functional currency into the reporting currency of the U.S. company is made as follows:

Income statement accounts:	
Revenue and expenses	Generally, average exchange rate for period covered by statement
Balance sheet accounts:	
Assets and liabilities	Current exchange rate on balance sheet date
Stockholders' equity	Historical exchange rates

Because various rates are used to translate the foreign entity's individual accounts, the trial balance debits and credits after translation generally are not equal. The balancing item to make the translated trial balance debits equal the credits is called the ***translation adjustment.***

Financial Statement Presentation of Translation Adjustment

Advanced StudyGuide .com

The translation adjustment resulting from the translation process is part of the entity's comprehensive income for the period. **ASC 220** defines comprehensive income to include all changes in equity during a period except those resulting from investments by owners and distributions to owners. ***Comprehensive income*** includes net income and ***other comprehensive income*** items that are part of the changes in the net assets of a business enterprise from nonowner sources (e.g., not additional capital investments and dividends) during a period. **ASC 220** requires the reporting of comprehensive income as part of the entity's primary financial statements. The major items of the other comprehensive income items are the changes during the period in foreign currency translation adjustments, unrealized gains or losses on available-for-sale securities, and deferred gains and losses from certain derivative contracts.

Each period's other comprehensive income (OCI) is closed to ***accumulated other comprehensive income*** (AOCI), which is displayed separately from other stockholders' equity items (e.g., capital stock, additional paid-in capital, and retained earnings). The statement of changes in stockholders' equity opens with the accumulated balance of the other comprehensive income items at the beginning of the period, then includes the change in the translation adjustment and the additional other comprehensive income items during the period that were included in the period's comprehensive income, and ends with the accumulated other comprehensive income balance at the end of the period. The accumulated ending balance of the other comprehensive income items is then reported in the entity's balance sheet as part of the stockholders' equity section, usually after retained earnings. The discussion of the disclosure requirements presented later in this chapter demonstrates the financial statements for the Peerless Products Corporation example presented in the chapter.

LO 12-5

Prepare consolidated financial statements including a foreign subsidiary after translation.

Illustration of Translation and Consolidation of a Foreign Subsidiary

To examine the consolidation of a foreign subsidiary, assume the following facts:[14]

1. On January 1, 20X1, Peerless, a U.S. company, purchased 100 percent of the outstanding capital stock of German Company, a firm located in Berlin, Germany, for $63,000, which is $3,000 above book value. (The proof of the differential is shown at the end of the next section of the chapter.) The excess of cost over book value is attributable to a patent amortizable over 10 years. Balance sheet accounts in a trial balance format for both companies immediately *before* the acquisition are presented in Figure 12–2.
2. The local currency for German Company is the euro (€), which is also its functional currency.
3. On October 1, 20X1, the subsidiary declared and paid dividends of €6,250.
4. The subsidiary received $4,200 in a sales transaction with a U.S. company when the exchange rate was $1.20 = €1. The subsidiary still has this foreign currency on December 31, 20X1.
5. Relevant direct spot exchange rates ($/€1) are:

Date	Rate
January 1, 20X1	$1.20
October 1, 20X1	1.36
December 31, 20X1	1.40
20X1 average	1.30

Date-of-Acquisition Translation Worksheet

Figure 12–3 presents the translation of German Company's trial balance on January 1, 20X1. This illustration assumes that the subsidiary's books and records are maintained in European euros, the subsidiary's functional currency.

The translation of the subsidiary's trial balance from the functional currency (€) into dollars, the U.S. parent's reporting currency, is made using the *current rate method.* Under acquisition accounting, the subsidiary's stockholders' equity accounts are translated using the current rate on the date the parent company purchased the subsidiary's stock.

Peerless Products makes this entry to record the purchase of 100 percent of German Company's stock:

	January 1, 20X1		
(1)	Investment in German Company Stock	63,000	
	Cash		63,000
	Purchase of German Company Stock.		

[14] The Chapter 11 examples illustrate the effects of a dollar that strengthens against the euro during 20X1. In the examples for the remainder of this chapter, the dollar weakens against the euro during 20X1. Thus, in Chapters 11 and 12, changes in exchange rates in both directions will have been illustrated.

FIGURE 12–2
Balance Sheet Accounts for the Two Companies on January 1, 20X1 (immediately before acquisition of 100 percent of German Company's stock by Peerless Products, a U.S. company)

	Peerless Products	German Company
Cash	$ 350,000	€ 2,500
Receivables	75,000	10,000
Inventory	100,000	7,500
Land	175,000	0
Plant & Equipment	800,000	50,000
Total Debits	$1,500,000	€70,000
Accumulated Depreciation	$ 400,000	€ 5,000
Accounts Payable	100,000	2,500
Bonds Payable	200,000	12,500
Common Stock	500,000	40,000
Retained Earnings, 12/31/X0	300,000	10,000
Total Credits	$1,500,000	€70,000

FIGURE 12–3
Worksheet to Translate Foreign Subsidiary on January 1, 20X1 (date of acquisition)

Functional Currency Is the European Euro

Item	Trial Balance, €	Exchange Rate, $/€	Trial Balance, $
Cash	2,500	1.20	3,000
Receivables	10,000	1.20	12,000
Inventory	7,500	1.20	9,000
Plant & Equipment	50,000	1.20	60,000
Total Debits	70,000		84,000
Accumulated Depreciation	5,000	1.20	6,000
Accounts Payable	2,500	1.20	3,000
Bonds Payable	12,500	1.20	15,000
Common Stock	40,000	1.20	48,000
Retained Earnings	10,000	1.20	12,000
Total Credits	70,000		84,000

Note: $1.20 is the direct exchange rate on January 1, 20X1.

The differential on January 1, 20X1, the date of acquisition, is computed as follows:

(P)	Fair value of consideration		$63,000
	Book value of shares acquired:		
1/1/X1	Common stock—German Co.	$48,000	
100%	Retained earnings—German Co.	12,000	
	Total	$60,000	
(S)	Percent of German Company's stock acquired by Peerless Corporation	× 1.00	
	Book value acquired by Peerless Corporation		60,000
	Difference between fair value and book value		$ 3,000

A graphic representation of the acquisition is as follows:

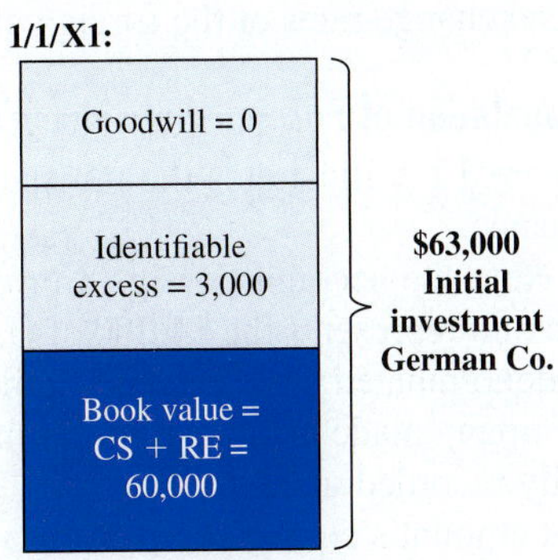

Advanced StudyGuide .com

Date-of-Acquisition Consolidated Balance Sheet

To prepare the elimination entries, we begin by analyzing the book value of the investment in German Company:

Book Value Calculations:

	Peerless 100%	=	Common Stock	+	Retained Earnings
Book Value at Acquisition Date	60,000		48,000		12,000

This leads to the basic elimination entry:

Basic Elimination Entry:

Common Stock	48,000		←Common stock balance
Retained Earnings	12,000		←Beginning balance in retained earnings
Investment in German Co.		60,000	←Net book value in investment account

The differential is entirely attributable to the patent, $3,000, so the excess value reclassification entry is as follows:

Excess Value Reclassification Entry:

Patent	3,000		←Excess value assigned to patent
Investment in German Co.		3,000	←Reclassify excess acquisition price

These two worksheet entries eliminate the balance in Peerless' investment account and the second entry assigns the differential to the patent account.

	Investment in German Co.		
Acquisition Price	63,000		
		60,000	Basic elimination entry
		3,000	Excess value reclassification entry
	0		

Finally, we include the optional accumulated depreciation elimination entry:

Optional Accumulated Depreciation Elimination Entry:

Accumulated Depreciation	6,000		←Accumulated depreciation at the time of the acquisition netted against cost
Buildings & Equipment		6,000	

Figure 12–4 presents the consolidation worksheet on the acquisition date.

Subsequent to Date of Acquisition

The accounting subsequent to the date of acquisition is very similar to the accounting used for domestic subsidiaries. The major differences are due to the effects of changes in the exchange rates of the foreign currency.

Translation of Foreign Subsidiary's Postacquisition Trial Balance

Figure 12–5 illustrates the translation of German Company's December 31, 20X1, trial balance.

Note the account Foreign Currency Units on German Company's trial balance. This account represents the $4,200 of U.S. dollars held by the subsidiary. Because this account is denominated in a currency other than the subsidiary's reporting currency, German Company made an adjusting journal entry to revalue the account from the amount originally recorded using the exchange rate on the date the company received the currency to that amount's equivalent exchange value at the end of the year.

FIGURE 12–4 January 1, 20X1, Worksheet for Consolidated Balance Sheet, Date of Acquisition

100 Percent Purchase at More Than Book Value

	Peerless Products	German Company	Elimination Entries DR	Elimination Entries CR	Consolidated
Balance Sheet					
Cash	287,000	3,000			290,000
Receivable	75,000	12,000			87,000
Inventory	100,000	9,000			109,000
Investment in German Co. Stock	63,000			60,000	0
				3,000	
Patent			3,000		3,000
Land	175,000				175,000
Plant & Equipment	800,000	60,000		6,000	854,000
Less: Accumulated Depreciation	(400,000)	(6,000)	6,000		(400,000)
Total Assets	**1,100,000**	**78,000**	**9,000**	**69,000**	**1,118,000**
Accounts Payable	100,000	3,000			103,000
Bonds Payable	200,000	15,000			215,000
Common Stock	500,000	48,000	48,000		500,000
Retained Earnings	300,000	12,000	12,000		300,000
Total Liabilities & Equity	**1,100,000**	**78,000**	**60,000**	**0**	**1,118,000**

FIGURE 12–5
December 31, 20X1, Translation of Foreign Subsidiary's Trial Balance

European Euro Is the Functional Currency

Advanced StudyGuide .com

Item	Balance, €	Exchange Rate	Balance, $
Cash	10,750	1.40	15,050
Foreign Currency Units	3,000	1.40	4,200
Receivables	10,500	1.40	14,700
Inventory	5,000	1.40	7,000
Plant & Equipment	50,000	1.40	70,000
Cost of Goods Sold	22,500	1.30	29,250
Operating Expenses	14,500	1.30	18,850
Foreign Currency Transaction Loss	500	1.30	650
Dividends Paid	6,250	1.36	8,500
Total Debits	123,000		168,200
Accumulated Depreciation	7,500	1.40	10,500
Accounts Payable	3,000	1.40	4,200
Bonds Payable	12,500	1.40	17,500
Common Stock	40,000	1.20	48,000
Retained Earnings (1/1)	10,000	(*a*)	12,000
Sales	50,000	1.30	65,000
Total	123,000		157,200
Accumulated Other Comprehensive Income—Translation Adjustment			11,000
Total Credits			168,200

(*a*) From the January 1, 20X1, translation worksheet.

The subsidiary made the following entry on its books when it received the U.S. dollars:

(2)			
	Foreign Currency Units ($)	3,500	
	Sales		3,500

Record sales and receipt of 4,200 U.S. dollars at spot exchange rate on the date of receipt: €3,500 = $4,200/$1.20 exchange rate.

At the end of the period, the subsidiary adjusted the foreign currency units (the U.S. dollars) to the current exchange rate ($1.40 = €1) by making the following entry:

(3)	Foreign Currency Transaction Loss	500	
	Foreign Currency Units ($)		500

Adjust account denominated in foreign currency units to current exchange rate:

$4,200/$1.40	€3,000
Less: Preadjusted balance	(3,500)
Foreign currency transaction loss	€ (500).

The foreign currency transaction loss is a component of the subsidiary's net income, and the Foreign Currency Units account is classified as a current asset on the subsidiary's balance sheet. The subsidiary's net income consists of the following elements:

Sales	€ 50,000
Cost of Goods Sold	(22,500)
Operating Expenses	(14,500)
Foreign Currency Transaction Loss	(500)
Net Income	€ 12,500

Because the European euro is the foreign entity's functional currency, the subsidiary's statements must be translated into U.S. dollars using the current rate method. The assets and liabilities are translated using the current exchange rate at the balance sheet date ($1.40), the income statement accounts are translated using the average rate for the period ($1.30), and the common stock account is translated using the appropriate historical exchange rate ($1.20). The dividends are translated at the October 1 rate ($1.36), which was the exchange rate on the date the dividends were declared. The example assumes the dividends were paid on October 1, the same day they were declared. If the dividends had not been paid by the end of the year, the liability dividends payable would be translated at the current exchange rate of $1.40 = €1.

One of the analytical features provided by the current rate method is that many of the ratios management uses to manage the foreign subsidiary are the same in U.S. dollars as they are in the foreign currency unit. This relationship is true for the assets and liabilities of the balance sheet and the revenue and expenses of the income statement because the translation for these accounts uses the same exchange rate—the current rate for the assets and liabilities, and the average exchange rate for the income statement accounts. Thus, the *scale* of these accounts has changed but not their *relative amounts* within their respective statements. This relationship is not true when the ratio includes numbers from both the income statement and the balance sheet or when a stockholders' equity account is included with an asset or liability. The following table illustrates the relative relationships within the financial statements using the data in Figure 12–5:

	Measured in €	Measured in U.S. $
Current ratio:		
Current assets	€29,250	$40,950
Current liabilities	3,000	4,200
Current ratio	9.75	9.75
Cost of goods sold as a percentage of sales:		
Cost of goods sold	€22,500	$29,250
Sales	50,000	65,000
Percent	45%	45%

FIGURE 12–6
Proof of Translation Adjustment as of December 31, 20X1

European Euro Is the Functional Currency

PEERLESS PRODUCTS AND SUBSIDIARY
Proof of Translation Adjustment
Year Ended December 31, 20X1

	€	Translation Rate	$
Net assets at beginning of year	50,000	1.20	60,000
Adjustment for changes in net assets position during year:			
Net income for year	12,500	1.30	16,250
Dividends paid	(6,250)	1.36	(8,500)
Net assets translated at:			
Rates during year			67,750
Rates at end of year	56,250	1.40	78,750
Change in other comprehensive income—net translation adjustment during year			11,000
Accumulated other comprehensive income—translation adjustment, 1/1			0
Accumulated other comprehensive income—translation adjustment, 12/31 (credit)			11,000

The translation adjustment in Figure 12–5 arises because the investee's assets and liabilities are translated at the current rate whereas other rates are used for the stockholders' equity and income statement account balances. Although the translation adjustment may be thought of as a balancing item to make the trial balance debits equal the credits, the effects of changes in the exchange rates during the period should be calculated to prove the accuracy of the translation process. This proof for 20X1, the acquisition year, is provided in Figure 12–6.

The proof begins with the determination of the effect of changes in the exchange rate on the beginning investment and on the elements that alter the beginning investment. Note that only events affecting the stockholders' equity accounts will change the net assets investment. In this example, the changes to the investment account occurred from income of €12,500 and dividends of €6,250. No changes occurred in the stock outstanding during the year. The beginning net investment is translated using the exchange rate at the beginning of the year. The income and dividends are translated using the exchange rate at the date the transactions occurred. The income was earned evenly over the year; thus, the average exchange rate for the period is used to translate income. The ending net assets position is translated using the exchange rate at the end of the year. The cumulative translation adjustment at the beginning of the year is zero in this example because the subsidiary was acquired on January 1, 20X1.

The Accumulated Other Comprehensive Income—Translation Adjustment account has a credit balance because the spot exchange rate at the end of the first period of ownership is higher than the exchange rate at the beginning of the period or the average for the period. If the exchange rate had decreased during the period, the translation adjustment would have had a debit balance. Another way of determining whether the accumulated translation adjustment has a debit or credit balance is to use balance sheet logic. For example, the subsidiary's translated balance sheet at the beginning of the year would be

Translated Balance Sheet, 1/1/X1			
Net assets	$60,000	Common stock	$48,000
		Retained earnings	12,000
Total	$60,000	Total	$60,000

The translated balance sheet at the end of the year would be

Translated Balance Sheet, 12/31/X1			
Net assets	$78,750	Common stock	$48,000
		Retained earnings	19,750
		Accumulated other comprehensive income—translation adjustment	11,000
Total	$78,750	Total	$78,750

Note that the $11,000 is a credit balance in order to make the balance sheet "balance."

Entries on Parent Company's Books

The parent company makes entries on its books to recognize the dollar equivalent values of its share of the foreign subsidiary's dividend, income, a cumulative translation adjustment for the parent's differential, and amortization of the excess of cost over book value. In addition, the parent company must recognize its share of the translation adjustment arising from the translation of the subsidiary's financial statements. The periodic change in the parent company's translation adjustment from the foreign investment is reported as a component of the parent company's other comprehensive income.

The entries that Peerless Products makes to account for its investment in German Company follow. Peerless Products received the dividend on October 1, 20X1, and immediately converted it to U.S. dollars as follows:

	October 1, 20X1		
(4)	Cash	8,500	
	Investment in German Company Stock		8,500
	Dividend received from foreign subsidiary: €6,250 × $1.36 exchange rate.		

	December 31, 20X1		
(5)	Investment in German Company Stock	16,250	
	Income from Subsidiary		16,250
	Equity in net income of German Co.: €12,500 × $1.30 average exchange rate.		

(6)	Investment in German Company Stock	11,000	
	Other Comprehensive Income—Translation Adjustment		11,000
	Parent's share of change in translation adjustment from translation of subsidiary's accounts: $11,000 × 1.00.		

If some time passed between the declaration and payment of dividends, the parent company would record dividends receivable from the foreign subsidiary on the declaration date. This account would be denominated in a foreign currency and would be adjusted to its current exchange rate on the balance sheet date and on the payment date, just like any other account denominated in a foreign currency. Any foreign transaction gain or loss resulting from the adjustment procedure would be included in the parent's income for the period.

The Differential

The allocation and amortization of the excess of cost over book value require special attention in the translation of a foreign entity's financial statements. The differential does not exist on the foreign subsidiary's books; it is part of the parent's investment account. However, the translated book value of the foreign subsidiary is a major component of the investment account on the parent's books and is directly related to a foreign-based asset. **ASC 830** requires that the allocation and amortization of the difference between the investment cost and its book value be made in terms of the foreign subsidiary's functional currency and that these amounts then be translated at the appropriate exchange rates on the worksheet balance sheet date. The periodic amortization affects the income statement and is therefore measured at the average exchange rate used to translate other income statement accounts. On the other hand, the remaining unamortized balance of the differential is reported in the balance sheet and is translated at the current exchange rate used for balance sheet accounts. The effect of this difference in rates is shown in the parent company's translation adjustment as a revision of part of its original investment in the subsidiary.

Peerless Products amortizes the patent over a five-year period. The patent amortization follows.

	European Euros (€)	Translation Rate	U.S. Dollars ($)
Income Statement			
Differential at beginning of year	2,500	1.20	3,000
Amortization this period (€5,000/5 years)	(500)	1.30	(650)
Remaining balances	2,000		2,350
Balance Sheet			
Remaining balance on 12/31/X1 translated at year-end exchange rates	2,000	1.40	2,800
Difference to other comprehensive income—translation adjustment (credit)			450

Another way to view the $450 differential adjustment is that it adjusts the parent company's differential, which is currently part of the investment account, to the amount necessary to prepare the consolidated balance sheet. In this example, if no differential adjustment is made, the patent on the consolidated balance sheet would be $2,350, which is incorrect. Because the balance sheet must report the patent translated at the end-of-period exchange rate of $2,800, the differential adjustment is made to properly report the amount in the consolidated balance sheet. Thus, the adjustment may be thought of as an adjustment necessary to obtain the correct amount of the differential to prepare the consolidated balance sheet. Depending on the direction of the changes in the exchange rate, the differential adjustment could be a debit or credit amount. In this case, the differential must be increased from $2,350 to $2,800, necessitating a $450 debit to the investment account and a corresponding credit to the Other Comprehensive Income—Translation Adjustment account.

Entry (7) recognizes the amortization of the patent for the period. Entry (8) records the portion of the translation adjustment on the increase in the differential for the investment in the foreign subsidiary.

		Debit	Credit
(7)	Income from Subsidiary	650	
	Investment in German Company Stock		650

Amortization of patent: $650 = €500 × $1.30 average exchange rate.

		Debit	Credit
(8)	Investment in German Company Stock	450	
	Other Comprehensive Income—Translation Adjustment		450

Recognize translation adjustment on increase in differential.

This $450 translation adjustment is attributable to the excess of cost paid over the book value of the assets and therefore is added to the differential, which is a component of the investment in the foreign subsidiary, thereby resulting in a debit to the investment account on the parent company's books.

The December 31, 20X1, balance in the Investment in German Company Stock account is $81,550 and the balance in Income from German Company is $15,600, as shown in the following T-accounts. A series of four worksheet entries (explained below) eliminates both accounts in the consolidation process.

	Investment in German Company (Debit)	Investment in German Company (Credit)	
Acquisition 1/1/X1	63,000		
100% Net Income	16,250		
		8,500	100% Dividends
German Co. Translation	11,000	650	Excess Value Amortization
Differential Translation	450		
Balance 12/31/X1	81,550		
		67,750	Basic
		2,800	Excess Reclass.
		11,000	OCI
	0		

Income from German Company (Debit)	Income from German Company (Credit)	
	16,250	100% Net Income
650		
	15,600	Balance 12/31/X1
16,250		Basic
	650	Excess Value Reclass.
	0	

Note that the $11,450 Other Comprehensive Income—Translation Adjustment account balance in the parent company's books is composed of its share of the translation adjustment from translating the subsidiary's trial balance ($11,000) plus the parent company's adjustment ($450) due to the differential it paid for the investment.

During the parent company's closing entries process, the following two entries would be included to separately close net income from the subsidiary and the other comprehensive income arising from its investment in the subsidiary.

		Debit	Credit
(9)	Income from Subsidiary	15,600	
	Retained Earnings		15,600
	To close net income from subsidiary: $15,600 = $16,250 − $650.		
(10)	Other Comprehensive Income—Trans. Adjustment	11,450	
	Accumulated OCI—Translation Adjustment		11,450
	To close other comprehensive income resulting from the investment in the German subsidiary: $11,450 = $11,000 + $450.		

Subsequent Consolidation Worksheet

The consolidation worksheet is prepared after the translation process is completed. The consolidation process is the same as for a domestic subsidiary except for two major differences: (1) The parent company will record its share of the translation adjustment arising from the translation of the foreign subsidiary's accounts. In this example, the parent owns 100 percent of the subsidiary, but, in cases of a less-than-wholly-owned subsidiary, the noncontrolling interest would be assigned its percentage share of the translation adjustment and (2) as shown previously, the patent amortization for the period is translated at the income statement rate (average for the period) whereas the ending patent balance is translated at the balance sheet rate (current exchange rate).Thus, a translation adjustment must be computed on the differential and assigned as part of the parent company's investment in the foreign subsidiary.

To prepare the elimination entries, we begin by analyzing the book value of the investment in German Company:

Book Value Calculations:

	Peerless 100%	=	Common Stock	+	Retained Earnings
Beginning Book Value	60,000		48,000		12,000
+ Net Income	16,250				16,250
− Dividends	(8,500)				(8,500)
Ending Book Value	67,750		48,000		19,750

This leads to the basic elimination entry:

Basic Elimination Entry:

Common Stock	48,000		← Common stock balance
Retained Earnings	12,000		← Beginning balance in retained earnings
Income from German Co.	16,250		← German Company's reported income
Dividends Declared		8,500	← 100% of German's dividends declared
Investment in German Co.		67,750	← Net book value in investment account

The $3,000 differential is entirely attributable to the patent; nevertheless, because it arises from the acquisition of a foreign subsidiary, we provide these calculations that illustrate the translation adjustment for the differential:

Excess Value (Differential) Calculation:

	Total Excess	=	Patent
Beginning Excess Value	3,000		3,000
− Amortization of Differential	(650)		(650)
+ Differential Translation Adjustment	450		450
Ending Excess Value	2,800		2,800

Note that the adjustments for $650 and $450 were already explained in entries (7) and (8).

Amortized Excess Value Reclassification Entry:

Operating Expense	650		← Amortization of patent
Income from German Co.		650	← Elimination of patent amortization

Excess Value (Differential) Reclassification Entry:

Patent	2,800		← Excess value assigned to patent
Investment in German Co.		2,800	← Reclassify excess acquisition price

In addition, we record the other comprehensive income entry illustrated in Chapter 5:

Other Comprehensive Income Entry:

OCI from German Co.	11,000	
Investment in German Co.		11,000

Finally, we include the optional accumulated depreciation elimination entry:

Optional Accumulated Depreciation Elimination Entry:

Accumulated Depreciation	6,000		← Accumulated depreciation at the time of the acquisition netted against cost
Buildings & Equipment		6,000	

See Figure 12–7 for the worksheet. The trial balance for German Company is obtained from the translated amounts computed earlier in Figure 12–5. The worksheet entries follow in journal entry form. These entries are *not* made on either company's books; they are only in the worksheet elimination columns.

When the parent company uses the equity method and no intercompany revenue transactions occur, the parent's net income and retained earnings equal the consolidated net income and consolidated retained earnings. This makes it possible to verify the amounts reported on the consolidated financial statements.

FIGURE 12–7 December 31, 20X1, Consolidation Worksheet, Prepared after Translation of Foreign Statements

	Peerless Products	German Company	Elimination Entries DR	Elimination Entries CR	Consolidated
Income Statement					
Sales	400,000	65,000			465,000
Less: COGS	(170,000)	(29,250)			(199,250)
Less: Operating Expenses	(90,000)	(18,850)	650		(109,500)
Less: Foreign Currency Transaction Loss		(650)			(650)
Income from German Co.	15,600		16,250	650	0
Net Income	**155,600**	**16,250**	**16,900**	**650**	**155,600**
Statement of Retained Earnings					
Beginning Balance	300,000	12,000	12,000		300,000
Net Income	**155,600**	**16,250**	**16,900**	**650**	155,600
Less: Dividends Declared	(60,000)	(8,500)		8,500	(60,000)
Ending Balance	**395,600**	**19,750**	**28,900**	**9,150**	**395,600**
Balance Sheet					
Cash	425,500	15,050			440,550
Dollars Held by German Company		4,200			4,200
Receivables	75,000	14,700			89,700
Inventory	100,000	7,000			107,000
Investment in German Company Stock	81,550			67,750 2,800 11,000	0
Land	175,000				175,000
Patent			2,800		2,800
Plant & Equipment	800,000	70,000		6,000	864,000
Less: Accumulated Depreciation	(450,000)	(10,500)	6,000		(454,500)
Total Assets	**1,207,050**	**100,450**	**8,800**	**87,550**	**1,228,750**
Accounts Payable	100,000	4,200			104,200
Bonds Payable	200,000	17,500			217,500
Common Stock	500,000	48,000	48,000		500,000
Retained Earnings	**395,600**	**19,750**	**28,900**	**9,150**	395,600
Accumulated Other Comprehensive Income	11,450	11,000	**11,000**	**0**	11,450
Total Liabilities & Equity	**1,207,050**	**100,450**	**87,900**	**9,150**	**1,228,750**
Other Comprehensive Income					
Accumulated Other Comprehensive Income, 1/1/X1	0	0			0
Other Comprehensive Income Translation Adjustment	11,450	11,000	11,000		11,450
Accumulated Other Comprehensive Income, 12/31/X1	**11,450**	**11,000**	**11,000**	**0**	**11,450**

Figure 12–8's consolidated statement of changes in stockholder's equity shows how the income statement and other comprehensive income accounts flow to the balance sheet's equity ending balances.

Noncontrolling Interest of a Foreign Subsidiary

Most U.S. companies prefer to own 100 percent of their foreign subsidiaries. Doing so provides for more efficient management of the subsidiary and no requirement to prepare separate financial statements of the subsidiary for a noncontrolling interest. If

FIGURE 12–8 Consolidated Statement of Changes in Stockholders' Equity

PEERLESS PRODUCTS AND SUBSIDIARY
Consolidated Statement of Changes in Equity
Year Ended December 31, 20X1

	Total	Comprehensive Income	Retained Earnings	Accumulated Other Comprehensive Income	Capital Stock
Beginning Balance	$800,000		$300,000	$ 0	$500,000
Comprehensive Income:					
Net Income	155,600	$155,600	155,600		
Other Comprehensive Income:					
Foreign Currency Translation Adjustment	11,450	11,450		11,450	
Comprehensive Income		$167,050			
Dividends Declared on Common Stock	(60,000)		(60,000)		
Ending Balance	$907,050		$395,600	$11,450	$500,000

a foreign subsidiary was less than wholly owned, however, the noncontrolling interest would be computed and accounted for just as it was in Chapter 3 of this text. The only difference is the allocation of the translation adjustment that arises from the translation of the foreign subsidiary's trial balance accounts. Thus, for example, if Peerless had an 80 percent interest in German Company and another investor owned a 20 percent noncontrolling interest, the noncontrolling interest would be allocated its percentage share of the translation adjustment through the elimination entry process. The noncontrolling interest on the consolidated balance sheet at year-end would include its share of the accumulated other comprehensive income from the translation adjustment, as follows:

Common stock ($48,000 × 0.20)		$ 9,600
Retained earnings:		
Beginning retained earnings ($12,000 × 0.20)	$2,400	
Add: Net income ($16,250 × 0.20)	3,250	
Less: Dividends ($8,500 × 0.20)	(1,700)	
Total retained earnings		3,950
Accumulated other comprehensive income—translation adjustment ($11,000 × 0.20)		2,200
Total noncontrolling interest		$15,750

REMEASUREMENT OF THE BOOKS OF RECORD INTO THE FUNCTIONAL CURRENCY

LO 12-6

Make calculations and remeasure financial statements of a foreign subsidiary.

A second method of restating foreign affiliates' financial statements in U.S. dollars is remeasurement. Although remeasurement is not as commonly used as translation, some situations in which the foreign affiliate's functional currency is not its local currency exist. Remeasurement is similar to translation in that its goal is to obtain equivalent U.S. dollar values for the foreign affiliate's accounts so they may be combined or consolidated with the U.S. company's statements. The exchange rates used for remeasurement, however, are different from those used for translation, resulting in different dollar values for the foreign affiliate's accounts.

The FASB provided examples of several situations requiring remeasurement:[15]

1. A foreign sales branch or subsidiary of a U.S. manufacturer that primarily takes orders from foreign customers for U.S.-manufactured goods, that bills and collects from foreign customers, and that might have a warehouse to provide for timely delivery of the product to those foreign customers. In substance, this foreign operation may be the same as the export sales department of a U.S. manufacturer.
2. A foreign division, branch, or subsidiary that primarily manufactures a subassembly shipped to a U.S. plant for inclusion in a product that is sold to customers located in the United States or in different parts of the world.
3. A foreign shipping subsidiary that primarily transports ore from a U.S. company's foreign mines to the United States for processing in a U.S. company's smelting plants.
4. A foreign subsidiary that is primarily a conduit for euro borrowings to finance operations in the United States.

In most cases, the foreign affiliate may be thought of as a direct production or sales arm of the U.S. company, but it uses the local currency to record and report its operations. In addition, foreign entities located in highly inflationary economies, defined as economies having a cumulative three-year inflation rate exceeding 100 percent, must use the dollar as their functional currency, and their statements are remeasured into U.S. dollars. Many South American countries have experienced hyperinflation with some countries having annual inflation rates in excess of 100 percent. If the foreign affiliate uses the U.S. dollar as both its functional and its reporting currency, no remeasurement is necessary because its operations are already reported in U.S. dollars.

The remeasurement process should produce the same end result as if the foreign entity's transactions had been initially recorded in dollars. For this reason, certain transactions and account balances are restated to their U.S.–dollar equivalents using a historical exchange rate, the spot exchange rate at the time the transaction originally occurred. The remeasurement process divides the balance sheet into monetary and nonmonetary accounts. Monetary assets and liabilities such as cash, short-term or long-term receivables, and short-term or long-term payables have their amounts fixed in terms of the units of currency. They represent amounts that will be received or paid in a fixed number of monetary units. Note that an exception to the general statement in Figure 12–9 about marketable securities applies to trading and available-for-sale securities. Because they are marked to market at each reporting date, they are considered monetary assets and are remeasured using current rates. These accounts are subject to gains or losses from changes in exchange rates. Nonmonetary assets are accounts such as inventories and plant and equipment, which are not fixed in relation to monetary units.

The monetary accounts are remeasured using the current exchange rate. The appropriate historical exchange rate is used to remeasure nonmonetary balance sheet account balances and related revenue, expense, gain, and loss account balances. A list of the accounts to be remeasured with the appropriate historical exchange rate is provided in Figure 12–9 **(ASC 830-10-45-18)**.

Because of the variety of rates used to remeasure the foreign currency trial balance, the debits and credits of the U.S. dollar–equivalent trial balance will probably not be equal. In this case, the balancing item is a ***remeasurement gain or loss,*** which is included in the period's income statement (i.e., not in other comprehensive income).

Statement Presentation of Remeasurement Gain or Loss

Any exchange gain or loss arising from the remeasurement process is included in the current period income statement, usually under "Other Income." Various account titles

[15] These examples were provided in the exposure draft of **ASC 830** but were not included in its final draft. The FASB did not want the examples to limit remeasurement to those cases in which the U.S. dollar is the functional currency.

FIGURE 12–9
Accounts to Be Remeasured Using Historical Exchange Rates

Examples of Balance Sheet Nonmonetary Items
Marketable securities:
  Equity securities
  Debt securities not intended to be held until maturity
Inventories
Prepaid expenses such as insurance, advertising, and rent
Property, plant, and equipment
Accumulated depreciation on property, plant, and equipment
Patents, trademarks, licenses, and formulas
Goodwill
Other intangible assets
Deferred charges and credits except deferred income taxes and policy acquisition costs for life insurance companies
Deferred income
Common stock
Preferred stock carried at issuance price

Examples of Revenue and Expenses Related to Nonmonetary Items
  Cost of goods sold
  Depreciation of property, plant, and equipment
  Amortization of intangible items such as patents, licenses, etc.
  Amortization of deferred charges or credits, except deferred income taxes and policy acquisition costs for life insurance companies

are used, such as Foreign Exchange Gain (Loss), Currency Gain (Loss), Exchange Gain (Loss), or Remeasurement Gain (Loss). The title Remeasurement Gain (Loss) is used here because it is most descriptive of the item's source. The remeasurement gain or loss is included in the period's income because if the transactions had originally been recorded in U.S. dollars, the exchange gains and losses would have been recognized this period as part of the adjustments required for valuation of foreign transactions denominated in a foreign currency. Upon completion of the remeasurement process, the foreign entity's financial statements are presented as they would have been had the U.S. dollar been used to record the transactions in the local currency as they occurred.

Illustration of Remeasurement of a Foreign Subsidiary

German Company again is used, this time to present remeasurement of financial statements. The only difference between the previous example of translation and the current example is that the foreign subsidiary's functional currency is now assumed to be the U.S. dollar rather than the European euro. German Company maintains its books and records in euros to provide required reports to the German government. Because the dollar is the functional currency, German Company's financial statements will be remeasured into dollars. Once the foreign affiliate's statements are remeasured, the consolidation process is the same as for a domestic subsidiary.

Remeasurement of Foreign Subsidiary's Postacquisition Trial Balance

The subsidiary's trial balance must be remeasured from the European euro into the U.S. dollar as shown in Figure 12–10. The current exchange rate is used to remeasure the monetary accounts, and the appropriate historical exchange rates are used for each of the nonmonetary accounts.

Three items need special attention. First, the plant and equipment are remeasured using the historical rate on the date the parent company acquired the foreign subsidiary. If the subsidiary purchases any additional plant or equipment after the parent has acquired the subsidiary's stock, the additional plant or equipment will be remeasured using the exchange rate on the date of the purchase of the additional plant. The same cautionary note is applicable to the other nonmonetary items. It is important to maintain a record of the subsidiary's acquisition or disposition of nonmonetary assets and equities after the

FIGURE 12–10
December 31, 20X1, Remeasurement of the Foreign Subsidiary's Trial Balance

U.S. Dollar Is the Functional Currency

Item	Balance, €	Exchange Rate	Balance, $
Cash	10,750	1.40	15,050
Foreign Currency Units	3,000	1.40	4,200
Receivables	10,500	1.40	14,700
Inventory	5,000	1.38	6,900
Plant & Equipment	50,000	1.20	60,000
Cost of Goods Sold	22,500	(*a*)	28,100
Operating Expenses	14,500	(*b*)	18,600
Foreign Currency Transaction Loss	500	1.30	650
Dividends Paid	6,250	1.36	8,500
Total Debits	123,000		156,700
Accumulated Depreciation	7,500	1.20	9,000
Accounts Payable	3,000	1.40	4,200
Bonds Payable	12,500	1.40	17,500
Common Stock	40,000	1.20	48,000
Retained Earnings	10,000	(*c*)	12,000
Sales	50,000	1.30	65,000
Total	123,000		155,700
Remeasurement Gain			1,000
Total Credits			156,700

	In Euros	Exchange Rate	In Dollars
(*a*) Cost of Goods Sold:			
Beginning Inventory	7,500	1.20	9,000
Purchases	20,000	1.30	26,000
Goods Available	27,500		35,000
Less: Ending Inventory	(5,000)	1.38	(6,900)
Cost of Goods Sold	22,500		28,100
(*b*) Operating Expenses:			
Cash Expenses	12,000	1.30	15,600
Depreciation Expense	2,500	1.20	3,000
	14,500		18,600

(*c*) Carry forward from January 1, 20X1, worksheet.

foreign subsidiary's stock is acquired to ensure use of the proper exchange rates to remeasure these items. Recall that the business combination was accounted for as a purchase; therefore, the appropriate historical rate is the spot rate on the date the parent purchased the foreign subsidiary's stock.

Second, the cost of goods sold consists of transactions that occurred at various exchange rates. The beginning inventory was acquired when the rate was $1.20 = €1. Inventory purchases were made at different times during the year, so the average rate of $1.30 was used for the remeasurement exchange rate. For purposes of illustration, the example assumes that ending inventory was acquired when the direct exchange rate was $1.38 = €1 and the FIFO inventory method is used.

Third, the operating expenses are also incurred at different exchange rates. The depreciation expense is remeasured at $1.20 = €1 because it is associated with a nonmonetary account, Plant and Equipment, which is remeasured at the historical exchange rate of $1.20 = €1. The average exchange rate is used to remeasure the remaining operating expenses because they are assumed to be incurred evenly throughout the period.

The remeasurement gain is recognized in this period's income statement. The remeasurement exchange gain is a balancing item to make total debits and total credits equal, but it can be proved by analyzing changes in the monetary items during the period.

FIGURE 12–11
Proof of the Remeasurement Exchange Gain for the Year Ended December 31, 20X1

Functional Currency Is the U.S. Dollar

Schedule 1
Statement of Net Monetary Positions

	End of Year	Beginning of Year
Monetary assets:		
Cash	€10,750	€ 2,500
Foreign currency units	3,000	0
Receivables	10,500	10,000
Total	€24,250	€12,500
Less: Monetary equities:		
Accounts payable	€ 3,000	€ 2,500
Bonds payable	12,500	12,500
Total	€15,500	€15,000
Net monetary liabilities		€ (2,500)
Net monetary assets	€ 8,750	
Increase in net monetary assets during year	€11,250	

Schedule 2
Analysis of Changes in Monetary Accounts

	€	Exchange Rate	U.S. $
Exposed net monetary liability position, 1/1	(2,500)	1.20	(3,000)
Adjustments for changes in net monetary position during year:			
Increases:			
From operations:			
Sales	50,000	1.30	65,000
From other sources	0		0
Decreases:			
From operations:			
Purchases	(20,000)	1.30	(26,000)
Cash expenses	(12,000)	1.30	(15,600)
Foreign currency transaction loss	(500)	1.30	(650)
From dividends	(6,250)	1.36	(8,500)
From other uses	0		0
Net monetary position prior to remeasurement at year-end rates			11,250
Exposed net monetary asset position, 12/31	8,750	1.40	12,250
Remeasurement gain			1,000

Proof of Remeasurement Exchange Gain

Peerless Products Corporation

Figure 12–11 provides a proof of this balancing item. The analysis primarily involves the monetary items because they are remeasured from the exchange rate at the beginning of the period or on the date of the generating transaction to the current exchange rate at the end of the period. The increase or decrease in net monetary assets resulting from remeasurement is recognized as an exchange gain or loss in the current period.

Schedule 1 presents the net monetary positions at the beginning and end of the year. The €11,250 change in the net monetary position is the change from a net liability opening balance of €2,500 to a net monetary asset position ending balance of €8,750. Schedule 2 presents the detailed effects of exchange rate changes on the foreign entity's net monetary position during this period. The beginning net monetary position is included using the exchange rate at the beginning of the year. Then all increases and decreases in the net monetary accounts are added or deducted using the exchange rates at the time the transactions occurred. Other sources of increases or decreases in the monetary accounts would include financing and investing transactions such as purchases of plant or equipment, issuance of long-term debt, or selling stock. The computed net monetary position at the end of the year using the transaction date exchange rates ($11,250) is then compared with the year-end net monetary position using the year-end exchange rate ($12,250). Because of the increasing exchange rate, the net asset position at the year-end was higher when remeasured using the December 31, 20X1, exchange rate of $1.40. This means that the U.S. dollar–equivalent value of the net monetary assets at year-end increased from $11,250 to $12,250 and that a remeasurement gain of $1,000 should be recognized. If the U.S. dollar–equivalent value of the December 31, 20X1, exposed net monetary assets position, as remeasured with the December 31 exchange rate, would have been lower than the computed value of $11,250, then a remeasurement loss would have been recognized for the reduction in the U.S. dollar–equivalent value of the net assets.

Remeasurement Case: Subsequent Consolidation Worksheet

LO 12-7

Prepare consolidated financial statements including a foreign subsidiary after remeasurement.

Figure 12–12 presents the consolidation worksheet for the remeasurement case. The accounts used for German Company in the consolidation worksheet come from the remeasured accounts computed in Figure 12–10. The remeasurement gain is included in the German subsidiary's trial balance because the source of this account is the remeasurement of the subsidiary's accounts.

In the consolidated income statement, the Remeasurement Gain account is usually offset against the foreign currency transaction loss account, generating, in this example, a net gain of $350 ($1,000 − $650). This gain is reported in the other income section of the income statement. The remaining consolidation process is identical to the process for a domestic subsidiary. Note that the $2,400 patent shown on the consolidated balance sheet is the unamortized portion of the initial $3,000 amount ($2,400 = $3,000 − $600). No special adjustments are required for the patent when using the remeasurement process.

To prepare the elimination entries, we begin by analyzing the book value of the investment in German Company:

Advanced StudyGuide .com

Book Value Calculations:

	Peerless 100%	=	Common Stock	+	Retained Earnings
Beginning Book Value	60,000		48,000		12,000
+ Net Income	18,650				18,650
− Dividends	(8,500)				(8,500)
Ending Book Value	70,150		48,000		22,150

This leads to the basic elimination entry:

Basic Elimination Entry:

Common Stock	48,000		← Common stock balance
Retained Earnings	12,000		← Beginning balance in retained earnings
Income from German Co.	18,650		← German Company's reported income
Dividends Declared		8,500	← 100% of German's dividends declared
Investment in German Co.		70,150	← Net book value in investment account

The differential is entirely attributable to the patent, $3,000; nevertheless, because it arises from the acquisition of a foreign subsidiary, we provide the following calculations to illustrate the translation adjustment for the differential (amortized over a five-year period):

Excess Value (Differential) Calculations:

	Total Excess	=	Patent
Beginning Excess Value	3,000		3,000
− Amortization of Differential ($3,000/5 years)	600		600
Ending Excess Value	2,400		2,400

FIGURE 12–12 December 31, 20X1, Consolidation Worksheet, Prepared after Remeasurement of Foreign Statements

	Peerless Products	German Company	Elimination Entries DR	Elimination Entries CR	Consolidated
Income Statement					
Sales	400,000	65,000			465,000
Less: COGS	(170,000)	(28,100)			(198,100)
Less: Operating Expenses	(90,000)	(18,600)	600		(109,200)
Less: Foreign Currency Transaction Loss		(650)			(650)
Remeasurement Gain		1,000			1,000
Income from German Co.	18,050		18,650	600	0
Net Income	**158,050**	**18,650**	**19,250**	**600**	**158,050**
Statement of Retained Earnings					
Beginning Balance	300,000	12,000	12,000		300,000
Net Income	**158,050**	**18,650**	19,250	600	**158,050**
Less: Dividends Declared	(60,000)	(8,500)		8,500	(60,000)
Ending Balance	**398,050**	**22,150**	**31,250**	**9,100**	**398,050**
Balance Sheet					
Cash	425,500	15,050			440,550
Dollars Held by German Company		4,200			4,200
Receivables	75,000	14,700			89,700
Inventory	100,000	6,900			106,900
Investment in German Company Stock	72,550			70,150	0
				2,400	
Land	175,000				175,000
Patent			2,400		2,400
Plant & Equipment	800,000	60,000		6,000	854,000
Less: Accumulated Depreciation	(450,000)	(9,000)	6,000		(453,000)
Total Assets	**1,198,050**	**91,850**	**8,400**	**78,550**	**1,219,750**
Accounts Payable	100,000	4,200			104,200
Bonds Payable	200,000	17,500			217,500
Common Stock	500,000	48,000	48,000		500,000
Retained Earnings	**398,050**	**22,150**	31,250	9,100	**398,050**
Total Liabilities & Equity	**1,198,050**	**91,850**	**79,250**	**9,100**	**1,219,750**

Amortized Excess Value Reclassification Entry:

Operating Expense	**600**		←Amortization of patent
Income from German Co.		**600**	←Elimination of patent amortization

Excess Value (Differential) Reclassification Entry:

Patent	**2,400**		←Excess value assigned to patent
Investment in German Co.		**2,400**	←Reclassify excess acquisition price

Finally, we include the optional accumulated depreciation elimination entry:

Optional Accumulated Depreciation Elimination Entry:

Accumulated Depreciation	**6,000**		← Accumulated depreciation at the time of the acquisition netted against cost
Buildings & Equipment		**6,000**	

A comparison of Figures 12–7 and 12–12 shows that the foreign subsidiary's reported income between translation and remeasurement differs. The primary reason that the subsidiary's reported income is approximately 15 percent higher when the dollar is the functional currency ($18,650 versus $16,250 under translation) is that the U.S. dollar weakened against the European euro during the year. This results in a remeasurement gain for the subsidiary because it was transacting in the stronger currency (the euro) during the period. Furthermore, the subsidiary's cost of goods sold and operating expenses also are remeasured at a lower exchange rate, resulting in a higher income.

The following T-accounts illustrate the calculation of the ending balances for Peerless' Investment in German Company and Income from German Company accounts and how the worksheet entries eliminate their balances:

	Investment in German Company			Income from German Company		
Acquisition 1/1/X1	63,000					
100% Net Income	18,650				18,650	100% Net Income
		8,500	Dividends			
		600	Excess Price Amortization	600		
Balance 12/31/X1	72,550				18,050	Balance 12/31/X1
		70,150	Basic	18,650		
		2,400	Excess Reclass.		600	Excess Value Reclass.
	0				0	

Summary of Translation versus Remeasurement

When the functional currency is the dollar, the nonmonetary items on the balance sheet are remeasured using historical exchange rates. In this example, the direct exchange rate has increased during the period; therefore, the nonmonetary accounts are lower when remeasured than when translated. See Figure 12–13 for a summary of the differences between the translation and remeasurement methods.

ADDITIONAL CONSIDERATIONS IN ACCOUNTING FOR FOREIGN OPERATIONS AND ENTITIES

LO 12-8

Understand other issues related to foreign operations including hedging of a net investment in a foreign subsidiary.

This section covers special topics in accounting for multinational enterprises. Although many of these additional considerations are very technical, study of this section will complement your understanding of the many issues of accounting for foreign entities. For example, Figure 12–14 illustrates the two-statement approach to display comprehensive income.

FOREIGN INVESTMENTS AND UNCONSOLIDATED SUBSIDIARIES

Most companies consolidate their foreign subsidiaries in conformity with **ASC 810 and ASC 840**. In some cases, these operations are not consolidated because of criteria that apply to foreign subsidiaries. Generally, a parent company consolidates a foreign subsidiary except when one of the following conditions becomes so severe that the U.S. company owning a foreign company may not be able to exercise the necessary level of economic control over the foreign subsidiary's resources and financial operations to warrant consolidation:

1. Restrictions on foreign exchange in the foreign country.
2. Restrictions on transfers of property in the foreign country.
3. Other governmentally imposed uncertainties.

FIGURE 12–13 Summary of the Translation and Remeasurement Processes

Item	Translation Process	Remeasurement Process
Foreign entity's functional currency	Local currency unit	U.S. dollar
Method used	Current rate method	Temporal method
Income statement accounts:		
Revenue	Weighted-average exchange rate	Weighted-average exchange rate except revenue related to nonmonetary items (historical exchange rate)
Expenses	Weighted-average exchange rate	Weighted-average exchange rate except costs related to nonmonetary items (historical exchange rate)
Balance sheet accounts:		
Monetary accounts	Current exchange rate	Current exchange rate
Nonmonetary accounts	Current exchange rate	Historical exchange rate
Stockholders' equity capital accounts	Historical exchange rate	Historical exchange rate
Retained earnings	Prior-period balance plus income less dividends	Prior-period balance plus income less dividends
Exchange rate adjustments arising in process	Translation adjustment accumulated in stockholders' equity	Remeasurement gain or loss included in period's income statement

FIGURE 12–14 Two-Statement Approach to Display Comprehensive Income

PEERLESS PRODUCTS AND SUBSIDIARY
Consolidated Income Statement
Year Ended December 31, 20X1

Sales	$465,000
Cost of Goods Sold	(199,250)
Gross Profit	265,750
Operating Expenses	(109,500)
Foreign Currency Transaction Loss	(650)
Consolidated Net Income to Controlling Interest	$155,600

PEERLESS PRODUCTS AND SUBSIDIARY
Consolidated Statement of Comprehensive Income
Year Ended December 31, 20X1

Consolidated Net Income to Controlling Interest	$155,600
Other Comprehensive Income: Foreign Currency Translation Adjustment	11,450
Comprehensive Income to Controlling Interest	$167,050

An unconsolidated foreign subsidiary is reported as an investment on the U.S. parent company's balance sheet. The U.S. investor company must use the equity method if it has the ability to exercise "significant influence" over the investee's financial and operating policies. If the equity method cannot be applied, the cost method is used to account for the foreign investment, recognizing income only as dividends are received.

When the equity method is used for an unconsolidated foreign subsidiary, the investee's financial statements are either remeasured or translated, depending on the determination of the functional currency. If remeasurement is used, the foreign entity's statements are remeasured in dollars and the investor records its percentage of the investee's income and makes necessary amortizations or impairments of any differential. A shortcut approach is available for translation: Multiply the foreign affiliate's net income measured in foreign currency units by the average exchange rate during the period and then recognize the parent company's percentage share of the translated net income. In addition, the investor must recognize its share of the translation adjustment arising from the translation of the foreign entity's financial statements. The investor's share of the translation adjustment from its foreign investees is reported on the investor's balance sheet as a separate component of stockholders' equity and as an adjustment of the carrying value of the investment account. The entries on the investor's books are the same under the equity method whether the subsidiary is consolidated or reported as an unconsolidated investment.

Liquidation of a Foreign Investment

The translation adjustment account is directly related to a company's investment in a foreign entity. If the investor sells a substantial portion of its stock investment, **ASC 830** requires that the pro rata portion of the accumulated translation adjustment account attributable to that investment be included in computing the gain or loss on the disposition of the investment. For example, if the parent company sold 30 percent of its investment in a foreign subsidiary, 30 percent of the related cumulative translation adjustment would be removed from the translation adjustment account and included in determining the gain or loss on the disposition of the foreign investment.

HEDGE OF A NET INVESTMENT IN A FOREIGN SUBSIDIARY

ASC 815 permits the hedging of a net investment in foreign subsidiaries. For example, Peerless has a net investment of €50,000 in its German subsidiary for which it paid $66,000. Peerless could decide to hedge all, some, or none of this investment by accepting a liability in euros. Peerless could hedge its net asset investment by contracting for a forward exchange contract to sell euros, or the company could incur a euro-based liability. **ASC 815** states that the gain or loss on the effective portion of a hedge of a net investment is taken to other comprehensive income as part of the translation adjustment. However, the amount of offset to comprehensive income is limited to the translation adjustment for the net investment. For example, if the forward exchange rate is used to measure effectiveness, the amount of offset is limited to the change in spot rates during the period. Any excess on the ineffective portion of the hedge must be recognized currently in earnings.

For example, on January 1, 20X1, Peerless decides to hedge the portion of its investment that it just made in German Company that is related to the book value of German Company's net assets. Peerless is unsure whether the direct exchange rate for euros will increase or decrease for the year and wishes to hedge its net asset investment. On January 1, 20X1, Peerless' 100 percent ownership share of German Company's net assets is equal to €50,000 (€40,000 capital stock plus €10,000 retained earnings). Peerless borrows €50,000 at a 5 percent rate of interest to hedge its equity investment in German Company, and the principal and interest are due and payable on January 1, 20X2.

The entries on Peerless' books to account for this hedge of a net investment follow:

January 1, 20X1

		Debit	Credit
(11)	Cash	60,000	
	Loan Payable (€)		60,000

Borrow a euro-denominated loan to hedge net investment in German subsidiary:
$60,000 = €50,000 × $1.20 spot rate.

December 31, 20X1

		Debit	Credit
(12)	Other Comprehensive Income	10,000	
	Loan Payable (€)		10,000

Revalue foreign currency–denominated payable to end-of-period spot rate:
$10,000 = €50,000 × ($1.40 − $1.20).

		Debit	Credit
(13)	Interest Expense	3,250	
	Foreign Currency Transaction Loss	250	
	Interest Payable (€)		3,500

Accrue interest expense and payable on euro loan:
$3,250 = €50,000 × 0.05 interest × $1.30 average exchange rate
$3,500 = €50,000 × 0.05 interest × $1.40 ending spot rate.

(14)	Accumulated OCI—Translation Adjustment	10,000	
	Profit and Loss Summary (or Retained Earnings)	250	
	Foreign Currency Transaction Loss		250
	Other Comprehensive Income		10,000

Close nominal accounts related to hedge of net investment in foreign subsidiary.

Then, when the principal and interest are paid on January 1, 20X2, Peerless makes the following entry:

	January 1, 20X2		
(15)	Interest Payable (€)	3,500	
	Loan Payable (€)	70,000	
	Cash		73,500

Pay principal and interest due on euro-denominated hedge: $70,000 = $60,000 + $10,000.

During 20X1, Peerless hedged a portion of its net asset investment in the foreign subsidiary. The dollar weakened against the euro (the direct exchange rate increased) and Peerless recognized a gain on a net asset investment in euros and a loss on a liability payable in euros. Without this hedge of the net investment, Peerless would have reported a $11,450 credit balance in the cumulative translation portion of accumulated other comprehensive income ($11,450 = $11,000 + $450 differential adjustment). With the hedge of its net investment, Peerless will report just $1,450 ($11,450 − $10,000 effect of hedge) as its change in the cumulative translation adjustment for 20X1. Thus, Peerless has balanced a portion of its net exposure on its January 1, 20X1, net asset investment in German Company.

Note also that the amount of the offset to other comprehensive income is limited to the effective portion of the hedge based on the revaluation of the net assets. Any excess, in this case the $250 loss on the revaluation of the interest payable in entry (14), is taken directly to current earnings on the income statement.

DISCLOSURE REQUIREMENTS

ASC 830 requires the aggregate foreign transaction gain or loss included in income to be separately disclosed in the income statement or in an accompanying note. This includes gains or losses recognized from foreign currency transactions, forward exchange contracts, and any remeasurement gain or loss. If not disclosed as a one-line item on the income statement, this disclosure is usually a one-sentence footnote summarizing the company's foreign operations.

Under the translation method, the periodic change in the translation adjustment is reported as an element of other comprehensive income as required by **ASC 220.** Figure 12–14 presents the two-statement approach to displaying comprehensive income. The consolidated statement of comprehensive income details the parent's other comprehensive income of $11,450. Review Figure 12–8 for the statement of changes in equity that reconciles all of the elements of stockholders' equity. The balance sheet would then display the capital stock, retained earnings, and accumulated other comprehensive income in the stockholders' equity section. In addition, **ASC 830** requires footnote disclosure of exchange rate changes that occur after the balance sheet date and their effect on unsettled foreign currency transactions, if significant.

Statement of Cash Flows

The statement of cash flows is a link between two balance sheets. Individual companies have some latitude and flexibility in preparing the statement of cash flows. A general rule is that accounts reported in the statement of cash flows should be restated in U.S. dollars using the same rates as used for balance sheet and income statement purposes. Because the average exchange rate is used in the income statement and the ending spot exchange rate (current rate) is used in the balance sheet, a balancing item for the differences in exchange rates appears in the statement of cash flows. This balancing item can be analyzed and traced to the specific accounts that generate the difference, but it does not affect the net change in the cash flow for the period.

Lower-of-Cost-or-Market Inventory Valuation under Remeasurement

The application of the lower-of-cost-or-market rule to inventories requires special treatment when the recording currency is not the entity's functional currency and, therefore, the foreign entity's financial statements must be remeasured into the functional currency. The historical cost of inventories must first be remeasured using historical exchange rates to determine the functional currency historical cost value. Then these remeasured costs are compared with the market value of the inventories translated using the current rate. The final step is to compare the cost and market, now both in the functional currency, and to recognize any appropriate write-downs to market. The comparison is made in functional currency values, not local or recording currency values; therefore, it is possible to have a write-down appear in the functional currency statements but not on the subsidiary's books, or on the subsidiary's books but not in the consolidated statements.

To illustrate the application of the lower-of-cost-or-market method, assume that a German subsidiary acquired €5,000 of inventory when the direct exchange rate was \$1.38 = €1. At the end of the year, the direct exchange rate had decreased to \$1.20 = €1. The estimated net realizable value of the inventory (ceiling) is €5,500; its replacement cost is €5,000; and the net realizable value less a normal profit margin (floor) is €4,000. The inventory valuation is first specified in the local currency unit (euro) and then evaluated after remeasurement into its functional currency, the U.S. dollar, using the end-of-period exchange rate, as follows:

	€	Exchange	U.S. $
Historical cost	5,000	$1.38	6,900
Net realizable value (ceiling)	5,500	$1.20	6,600
Replacement cost	5,000	1.20	6,000
Net realizable value less normal profit (floor)	4,000	1.20	4,800

The market value of the inventory is €5,000, or \$6,000. Note that the subsidiary recorded no write-down because the inventory's historical cost was the same as market. However, the comparison in functional currency (U.S. dollar) values shows that the U.S. parent requires a \$900 write-down to write the inventory down from its functional currency historical cost of \$6,900 to its functional currency market value of \$6,000.

Intercompany Transactions

A U.S. parent or home office may have many intercompany sales or purchases transactions with its foreign affiliate that create intercompany receivables or payables. The process of translating receivables or payables denominated in a foreign currency was discussed in Chapter 11. For example, assume that a U.S. company has a foreign currency–denominated receivable from its foreign subsidiary. The U.S. company would first revalue the foreign currency–denominated receivable to its U.S. dollar–equivalent value as of the date of the financial statements. After the foreign affiliate's statements have been translated or remeasured, depending on the foreign affiliate's functional currency, the intercompany payable and receivable should be at the same U.S. dollar value and can be eliminated.

ASC 830 provides an exception when the intercompany foreign currency transactions will not be settled within the foreseeable future. These intercompany transactions may be considered part of the net investment in the foreign entity. The translation adjustments on these long-term receivables or payables are deferred and accumulated as part of the cumulative translation adjustment account. For example, a U.S. parent company may loan its German subsidiary $10,000 for which the parent does not expect repayment for the foreseeable future. Under the translation method, the subsidiary's dollar-denominated loan payable account would first be adjusted for the effects of any changes in exchange rates during the period. Any exchange gain or loss adjustment relating to this intercompany note should be classified as part of the cumulative translation adjustment account in stockholders' equity, not in the subsidiary's net income for the period. The same result would occur whether the long-term intercompany financing was denominated in U.S. dollars or the local currency—in our example, the euro. Thus, when financing is regarded as part of the long-term investment in the foreign entity, any exchange gain or loss adjustments on that financing are accumulated in the cumulative translation adjustment account in stockholders' equity.

A particularly interesting problem arises when unrealized intercompany profits occur from transactions between the parent and foreign subsidiary. The problem is how to eliminate the profit across currencies that are changing in value relative to each other. For example, assume that the parent, Peerless Products Corporation, made a downstream sale of inventory to its German subsidiary. The goods cost the parent $10,000 but were sold to the subsidiary for €10,000 when the exchange rate was $1.30 = €1, resulting in an intercompany profit of $3,000 ($13,000 − $10,000). The goods are still in the subsidiary's inventory at the end of the year when the current exchange rate is $1.40 = €1. The relevant facts are summarized as follows:

	Measured in U.S. Dollars	Measured in European Euros
Initial inventory transfer date ($1.30 = €1):		
Selling price (€10,000 × $1.30)	13,000	10,000
Cost to parent	(10,000)	
Intercompany profit	3,000	
Balance sheet date ($1.40 = €1):		
Inventory translation ($14,000 = €10,000 × $1.40)	14,000	10,000

There are two issues here:

1. At what amount should the ending inventory be shown on the consolidated balance sheet—the original intercompany transfer price of $13,000 (€10,000 × $1.30), the present equivalent exchange value of $14,000 (€10,000 × $1.40 current exchange rate), or some other amount?
2. What amount should be eliminated for the unrealized intercompany gain—the original intercompany profit of $3,000 or the balance sheet date exchange equivalent of the intercompany profit of $4,000 ($14,000 present exchange value less $10,000 original cost to parent)?

ASC 830 provides the following guidance to answer these questions (**ASC 830-30-45-10**):

> The elimination of intra-entity profits that are attributable to sales or other transfers between entities that are consolidated, combined, or accounted for by the equity method in the reporting entity's financial statements shall be based on the exchange rates at the dates of the sales or transfers. The use of reasonable approximations or averages is permitted.

Therefore, for the example, the elimination entry for the intercompany profit is

Cost of Goods Sold	3,000	
Ending Inventory		3,000

The inventory is shown on the consolidated balance sheet at $11,000, which is a $1,000 increase over the initial cost to the parent company. This increase will result in a corresponding increase in a credit to the translation adjustment component of stockholders' equity. The FASB has stated that changes in exchange rates occurring *after* the date of the intercompany transaction are independent of the initial inventory transfer.

Income Taxes

Interperiod tax allocation is required whenever temporary differences exist in the recognition of revenue and expenses for income statement purposes and for tax purposes. Exchange gains and losses from foreign currency transactions require the recognition of a deferred tax asset or liability if they are included in income but not recognized for tax purposes in the same period.

A deferral is required for the portion of the translation adjustment related to the subsidiary's undistributed earnings that are included in the parent's income. **ASC 740** presumes that a temporary difference exists for undistributed earnings of a subsidiary unless the earnings are indefinitely reinvested in it. Deferred taxes need not be recognized if the undistributed earnings will be indefinitely reinvested in the subsidiary. However, if the parent expects eventually to receive the presently undistributed earnings of a foreign subsidiary, deferred tax recognition is required, and the tax entry recorded by the parent should include a debit to Other Comprehensive Income rather than to additional income tax, as follows:

(16)	Other Comprehensive Income—Translation Adjustment	X,XXX	
	Deferred Taxes Payable		X,XXX

Translation When a Third Currency Is the Functional Currency

In a few cases, the foreign subsidiary maintains its books and records in the local currency unit but has a third currency as its functional currency. For example, assume that our subsidiary, German Company, maintains its records in its local currency, the euro. If the subsidiary conducts many of its business activities in the Swiss franc, management may conclude that the Swiss franc is the subsidiary's functional currency. If the entity's books and records are *not* expressed in its functional currency, the following two-step process must be used:

1. Remeasure the subsidiary's financial statements into the functional currency. In our example, the financial statements expressed in euros would be remeasured into Swiss francs. The remeasurement process would be the same as illustrated earlier in the chapter. The statements would now be expressed in the entity's functional currency, the Swiss franc.
2. The statements expressed in Swiss francs are then translated into U.S. dollars using the translation process illustrated in the chapter.

As indicated, this occurrence is not common in practice but is a consideration for foreign subsidiaries that have very significant business activities in a currency other than the currency of the country in which the subsidiary is physically located. This discussion indicates that it is important first to determine the foreign entity's functional currency before beginning the translation process.

SUMMARY OF KEY CONCEPTS

The restatement of a foreign affiliate's financial statements in U.S. dollars may be made using the translation or remeasurement method, depending on the foreign entity's functional currency. Most foreign affiliates' statements are translated using the current rate method because the local currency unit is typically the functional currency. If the U.S. dollar is the functional currency, remeasurement is used to convert the foreign entity's statements from the local currency into dollars. The choice of functional currency affects the valuations of the foreign entity's accounts reported on the consolidated financial statements.

Because translation or remeasurement is performed with different exchange rates applied to balance sheet and income statement accounts, a balancing item called a "translation adjustment" or "remeasurement gain or loss" is created in the process. The translation adjustment is proportionally divided between the parent company and the noncontrolling interest. The parent company's share, adjusted for the effects from the differential paid for the investment, is reported as a component of other comprehensive income and then accumulated in the stockholders' equity section of the consolidated balance sheet. The noncontrolling interest's share is a direct adjustment to noncontrolling interest reported in the consolidated balance sheet. The remeasurement gain or loss is reported in the consolidated income statement.

KEY TERMS

accumulated other comprehensive income, *629*
average rate, *623*
comprehensive income, *629*
current rate, *623*
current rate method, *626*
functional currency, *624*
historical rate, *623*
International Financial Reporting Standards (IFRS), *621*
local currency unit, *623*
other comprehensive income, *629*
recording currency, *623*
remeasurement, *626*
remeasurement gain or loss, *642*
reporting currency, *623*
temporal method, *626*
translation, *626*
translation adjustment, *629*

QUESTIONS

LO 12-1 **Q12-1** Why is there increasing interest in the adoption of a single set of high-quality accounting standards?

LO 12-1 **Q12-2** Briefly discuss the International Accounting Standards Board (IASB). What is its mission? What is the composition of its membership and how long do members serve? Where is the IASB located?

LO 12-1 **Q12-3** The IASB promulgates International Financial Reporting Standards (IFRS). Briefly describe the standard-setting process used by the IASB.

LO 12-1 **Q12-4** How widely used are IFRS? Can IFRS be used for listings on U.S. stock exchanges?

LO 12-1 **Q12-5** What is the attitude toward the possible use of IFRS in the United States?

LO 12-1 **Q12-6** What potential benefits might be achieved if U.S. firms are allowed to use IFRS?

LO 12-2 **Q12-7** Define the following terms: (*a*) *local currency unit,* (*b*) *recording currency,* and (*c*) *reporting currency.*

LO 12-2 **Q12-8** What factors are used to determine a reporting entity's functional currency? Provide at least one example for which a company's local currency may not be its functional currency.

LO 12-1 **Q12-9** Some accountants are seeking to harmonize international accounting standards. What is meant by the term *harmonize?* How might harmonization result in better financial reporting for a U.S. parent company with many foreign investments?

LO 12-3 **Q12-10** A Canadian-based subsidiary of a U.S. parent uses the Canadian dollar as its functional currency. Describe the methodology for translating the subsidiary's financial statements into the parent's reporting currency.

LO 12-3 **Q12-11** A U.S. company has a foreign sales branch located in Spain. The Spanish branch has selected the U.S. dollar for its functional currency. Describe the methodology for remeasuring the branch's financial statements into the U.S. company's reporting currency.

LO 12-4, 12-5 **Q12-12** Discuss the accounting treatment and disclosure of translation adjustments. When does the translation adjustment account have a debit balance? When does it have a credit balance?

LO 12-6 **Q12-13** Where is the remeasurement gain or loss shown in the consolidated financial statements?

LO 12-4 **Q12-14** When the functional currency is the foreign affiliate's local currency, why are the stockholders' equity accounts translated at historical exchange rates? How is retained earnings computed?

LO 12-4 **Q12-15** Comment on the following statement: "The use of the current exchange rate method of translating a foreign affiliate's financial statements allows for an assessment of foreign management by the same ratio criteria used to manage the foreign affiliate."

LO 12-5 **Q12-16** A U.S. company paid more than book value in acquiring a foreign affiliate. How is this excess reported in the consolidated balance sheet and income statement in subsequent periods when the functional currency is the local currency unit of the foreign affiliate?

LO 12-5 **Q12-17** What is the logic behind the parent company's recognizing on its books its share of the translation adjustment arising from the translation of its foreign subsidiary?

LO 12-8 **Q12-18** Are all foreign subsidiaries consolidated? Why or why not?

LO 12-8 **Q12-19** Describe the accounting for a foreign investment that is not consolidated with the U.S. company.

LO 12-8 **Q12-20** Describe the basic problem of eliminating intercompany transactions with a foreign affiliate.

CASES

LO 12-1 **C12-1** **Comparison of U.S. GAAP and IFRS**

Research

PricewaterhouseCoopers offers a publication on its website entitled "IFRS and US GAAP: Similarities and Differences that provides a topic-based comparison. Access this publication on the web at http://www.pwc.com/us/en/issues/ifrs-reporting/publications/ifrs-and-us-gaap-similarities-and-differences.jhtml. On page 17 of this publication, there is a table of contents by reporting issue. Select any three of the items and read about the nature of the differences. Prepare a short paper approximately 2–3 pages long that defines the nature of the differences and discusses what you have found.

LO 12-1 **C12-2** **Structure of the IASB**

Research

The IASB website can be found at www.ifrs.org. At the top of the page, click on the link "About Us." Briefly describe the structure of the IASB.

LO 12-1 **C12-3** **IASB Deliberations**

Research

The IASB website can be found at www.ifrs.org. Access the website and click on the link at the top of the page for Standards development/Work plan for IFRSs. You may also access this page by going directly to www.ifrs.org/Current+Projects/IASB+Projects/IASB+Work+Plan.htm. What are three projects currently on the active agenda that are being addressed by the IASB? What is the timetable identified for milestones on each of the projects? What is the status of the Conceptual Framework project?

LO 12-2 **C12-4** **Determining a Functional Currency**

Following are descriptions of several independent situations.

Judgment

1. Rockford Company has a subsidiary in Argentina. The subsidiary does not have much debt because of the high interest costs resulting from the average annual inflation rate exceeding 100 percent. Most of its sales and expense transactions are denominated in Argentinean pesos, and the subsidiary attempts to minimize its receivables and payables. Although the subsidiary owns a warehouse, the primary asset is inventory that it receives from Rockford. The Argentinean government requires all companies located in Argentina to provide the central government with a financial report using the Argentinean system of accounts and government-mandated forms for financial statements.
2. JRB International, located in Dallas, Texas, is the world's largest manufacturer of electronic stirrups. The company acquires the raw materials for its products from around the world and begins the assembly process in Dallas. It then sends the partially completed units to its subsidiary in Mexico for assembly completion. Mexico has been able to hold its inflation rate under 100 percent over the last three years. The subsidiary is required to pay its employees and local

vendors in Mexican pesos. The parent company provides all financing for the Mexican subsidiary, and the subsidiary sends all of its production back to the warehouse in Dallas, from which it is shipped as orders are received. The subsidiary provides the Mexican government with financial statements.

3. Huskie Inc. maintains a branch office in Great Britain. The branch office is fairly autonomous because it must find its own financing, set its own local marketing policies, and control its own costs. The branch receives weekly shipments from Huskie Inc., which it then conveys to its customers. The pound sterling is used to pay the subsidiary's employees and to pay for the weekly shipments.
4. Hola Company has a foreign subsidiary located in a rural area of Switzerland, right next to the Swiss–French border. The subsidiary hires virtually all its employees from France and makes most of its sales to companies in France. The majority of its cash transactions are maintained in the European euro. However, it is required to pay local property taxes and sales taxes in Swiss francs and to provide annual financial statements to the Swiss government.

Required

For each of these independent cases, determine

a. The foreign entity's recording currency in which its books and records are maintained.
b. The foreign entity's functional currency.
c. The process to be used to restate the foreign entity's financial statements into the reporting currency of the U.S.-based parent company.

LO 12-4, 12-5, 12-8

C12-5 Principles of Consolidating and Translating Foreign Accounts [AICPA Adapted]

Understanding

Petie Products Company was incorporated in Wisconsin in 20X0 as a manufacturer of dairy supplies and equipment. Since incorporating, Petie has doubled in size about every three years and is now considered one of the leading dairy supply companies in the country.

During January 20X4, Petie established a subsidiary, Cream Ltd., in the emerging nation of Kolay. Petie owns 90 percent of Cream's outstanding capital stock; Kolay citizens hold the remaining 10 percent of Cream's outstanding capital stock as Kolay law requires. The investment in Cream, accounted for by Petie using the equity method, represents about 18 percent of Petie's total assets at December 31, 20X7, the close of the accounting period for both companies.

Required

a. What criteria should Petie use in determining whether it would be appropriate to prepare consolidated financial statements with Cream Ltd. for the year ended December 31, 20X7? Explain.
b. Independent of your answer to part *a,* assume it has been appropriate for Petie and Cream to prepare consolidated financial statements for each year, 20X4 through 20X7. Before they can be prepared, the individual account balances in Cream's December 31, 20X7, adjusted trial balance must be translated into dollars. The kola (K) is the subsidiary's functional currency. For each of the following 10 accounts taken from Cream's adjusted trial balance, specify what exchange rate (e.g., average exchange rate for 20X7, current exchange rate on December 31, 20X7) should be used to translate the account balance into dollars and explain why that rate is appropriate. Number your answers to correspond with these accounts.

(1) Cash in Kolay National Bank.
(2) Trade Accounts Receivable (all from 20X7 revenue).
(3) Supplies Inventory (all purchased during the last quarter of 20X7).
(4) Land purchased in 20X4.
(5) Short-term note payable to Kolay National Bank.
(6) Capital Stock (no par or stated value and all issued in January 20X4).
(7) Retained Earnings, January 1, 20X7.
(8) Sales Revenue.
(9) Depreciation Expense (on buildings).
(10) Salaries Expense.

LO 12-2, 12-4, 12-5, 12-6

C12-6 Translating and Remeasuring Financial Statements of Foreign Subsidiaries [AICPA Adapted]

Communication

Wahl Company's 20X5 consolidated financial statements include two wholly owned subsidiaries, Wahl Company of Australia (Wahl A) and Wahl Company of France (Wahl F). Functional currencies are the U.S. dollar for Wahl A and the European euro for Wahl F.

Required

a. What are the objectives of translating a foreign subsidiary's financial statements?

b. How are gains and losses arising from the translation or remeasurement of each subsidiary's financial statements measured and reported in Wahl's consolidated financial statements?

c. **ASC 830** identifies several economic indicators to be considered both individually and collectively in determining the functional currency for a consolidated subsidiary. List three of these indicators.

d. What exchange rate is used to incorporate each subsidiary's equipment cost, accumulated depreciation, and depreciation expense in Wahl's consolidated financial statements?

LO 12-5

C12-7 Translation Adjustment and Comprehensive Income

Analysis

Dundee Company owns 100 percent of a subsidiary located in Ireland. The parent company uses the Euro as the subsidiary's functional currency. At the beginning of the year, the debit balance in the Accumulated Other Comprehensive Income—Translation Adjustment account, which was the only item in accumulated other comprehensive income, was $80,000. The subsidiary's translated trial balance at the end of the year is as follows:

	Debit	Credit
Cash	$ 50,000	
Receivables	24,700	
Inventories	60,300	
Property, Plant, & Equipment (net)	328,000	
Cost of Sales	285,000	
Operating Expenses (including depreciation)	140,000	
Dividends	12,000	
Current Payables		$ 16,000
Long-Term Payables		181,000
Capital Stock		100,000
Retained Earnings (1/1 balance)		135,000
Sales		560,000
Accumulated Other Comprehensive Income—Translation Adjustment	92,000	
	$992,000	$992,000

Required

a. Prepare the subsidiary's income statement, ending in net income, for the year.

b. Prepare the subsidiary's statement of comprehensive income for the year.

c. Prepare a year-end balance sheet for the subsidiary.

d. **ASC 220** allows for alternative operating statement displays of the other comprehensive income items. Discuss the major differences between the one-statement format of the income statement and comprehensive income versus the two-statement format of the income statement with a separate statement of comprehensive income.

LO 12-5

C12-8 Changes in the Cumulative Translation Adjustment Account

Understanding

The following footnote was abstracted from a recent annual report of Johnson & Johnson Company:

> Footnote 7: Foreign Currency Translation
> For translation of its international currencies, the Company has determined that the local currencies of its international subsidiaries are the functional currencies except those in highly inflationary economies, which are defined as those which have had compound cumulative rates of inflation of 100 percent or more during the last three years.

In consolidating international subsidiaries, balance sheet currency effects are recorded as a separate component of stockholders' equity. This equity account includes the results of translating all balance sheet assets and liabilities at current exchange rates, except those located in highly inflationary economies, principally Brazil, which are reflected in operating results. These translation adjustments do not exist in terms of functional cash flows; such adjustments are not reported as part of operating results since realization is remote unless the international businesses were sold or liquidated.

An analysis of the changes during 20X3 and 20X2 in the separate component of stockholders' equity for foreign currency translation adjustments follows (with debit amounts in parentheses):

(Dollars in Millions)	20X3	20X2
Balance at beginning of year	$(146)	$ 134
Change in translation adjustments	(192)	(280)
Balance at end of year	$(338)	$(146)

Required

a. What is the main point of the footnote?

b. How is the footnote related to the concepts covered in the chapter?

c. List some possible reasons the company's translation adjustment decreased from a $134 million credit balance at the end of 20X1 to a $338 million debit balance at the end of 20X3.

d. Assume that the translated stockholders' equities of the foreign subsidiaries, other than the cumulative translation adjustment, remained constant from 20X1 through 20X3 at a balance of $500 million. What were the translated balances in the net assets (assets minus liabilities) of the foreign subsidiaries in each of the three years? What factors might cause the changes in the balances of the net assets over the three-year period?

e. How would changes in the local currency unit's exchange rate in the countries in which the company has subsidiaries affect the cumulative translation adjustment?

f. How could you verify the actual causal factors for the changes in the cumulative translation adjustment of Johnson & Johnson Company for the years presented? Be specific!

LO 12-8

Judgment

C12-9 Pros and Cons of Foreign Investment

Many larger U.S. companies have significant investments in foreign operations. For example, McDonald's Corporation, the food service company, obtains 47 percent of its consolidated revenues and 44 percent of its operating income from, and has 45 percent of its invested assets in, non-U.S. locations. Unisys, the information systems company, obtains 51 percent of its consolidated revenues and 65 percent of its operating income from, and has 40 percent of its invested assets in, non-U.S. locations. Foreign operations impose additional types of operating risks to companies, including the risks from changes in the exchange rates for currencies, statutory acts by the foreign governments, and producing and marketing goods in an environment outside the United States.

With the passage of the North American Free Trade Agreement (NAFTA), more companies are confronted with the decision of whether or not to expand their production and marketing investments to Canada and Mexico.

Required

Using NAFTA as a discussion focus, address the following questions:

a. Explain why a U.S. company might find it advantageous to increase its production capacity of its subsidiaries in Mexico. Describe some circumstances under which it would be disadvantageous for a U.S. company to increase its investment in production subsidiaries located in Mexico.

b. In your opinion, would an increase in U.S. companies' investments in Mexico and Canada be good or bad for U.S. consumers?

c. What are some possible solutions to the possible problem of an increase in the U.S. unemployment rate if U.S. companies shift their production facilities to non-U.S. locations? Select one and discuss the pros and cons of that possible solution.

d. What conclusion can you draw from the attempts of the U.S. government to decrease barriers to international trade and investment? In your opinion, is this a good effort on the part of the government, or do you feel this effort should be changed?

LO 12-2 **C12-10 Determining an Entity's Functional Currency**

Research

Maxima Corporation, a U.S. company, manufactures lighting fixtures and ceiling fans. Eight years ago, it set up a subsidiary in Mexico to manufacture three of its most popular ceiling fan models. When the subsidiary, Luz Maxima, was set up, it did business exclusively with Maxima, receiving shipments of materials from U.S. suppliers selected by Maxima and selling all of its production to Maxima. Maxima's management made a determination that its subsidiary's functional currency was the U.S. dollar.

During the past five years, changes in Luz Maxima's operations have occurred. The subsidiary has developed relationships with suppliers within Mexico and is obtaining a significant percentage of its materials requirements from these suppliers. In addition, Luz Maxima has expanded its production by introducing a new product line marketed within Mexico and Central America. These products now make up a substantial percentage of the subsidiary's sales. Luz Maxima obtained long-term debt financing and a line of credit from several Mexican banks to expand its operations.

Prior to the preparation of Maxima's consolidated financial statements for the current year, Luz Maxima's financial statements, reported in Mexican pesos, had to be converted into U.S. dollars. Maxima's CFO, Garry Parise, is concerned that Luz Maxima's functional currency may no longer be the U.S. dollar and that remeasurement of its financial statements may not be appropriate.

Required

Research the most current accounting standards on determining an entity's functional currency using the Accounting Standards Codification. Garry has asked you, as an accountant in the controller's department, to research the functional currency issue. Write a memo to him, reporting the results of your research. Support your recommendations with citations and quotations from the authoritative financial reporting standards.

LO 12-5 **C12-11 Accounting for the Translation Adjustment**

Research

Sonoma Company has owned 100 percent of the outstanding common stock of Valencia Corporation, a Spanish subsidiary, for the past 15 years. The Spanish company's functional currency is the euro, and its financial statements are translated into U.S. dollars prior to consolidation.

In the current year, Sonoma sold 30 percent of Valencia's voting common stock to a nonaffiliated company. Sonoma's controller, Renee Voll, calculated a gain on the sale of this portion of its investment in Valencia. The consolidated balance sheet at the end of last year contained a debit balance cumulative translation adjustment related to the Spanish subsidiary. Voll believes that the decrease in Sonoma's share of Valencia's translation adjustment will be automatically included in other comprehensive income as the year-end translation adjustment is calculated and that Sonoma's share is included in the consolidated financial statements. However, she has asked you, as an accountant in her department, to research the accounting for the translation adjustment as a result of the sale of a part of the investment in the Spanish subsidiary.

Required

Research the most current standards on accounting for the translation adjustment resulting from translating the trial balance of a foreign affiliate using the Accounting Standards Codification. Write a memo to Renee reporting the results of your research. Support your recommendations with citations and quotations from the authoritative financial reporting standards.

EXERCISES

LO 12-4, 12-6 **E12-1 Multiple-Choice Questions on Translation and Remeasurement [AICPA Adapted]**

For each of the following seven cases, work the case twice and select the best answer. First assume that the foreign currency is the functional currency; then assume that the U.S. dollar is the functional currency.

1. Certain balance sheet accounts in a foreign subsidiary of Shaw Company on December 31, 20X1, have been restated in U.S. dollars as follows:

	Restated at	
	Current Rates	**Historical Rates**
Accounts Receivable, Current	$100,000	$110,000
Accounts Receivable, Long-Term	50,000	55,000
Prepaid Insurance	25,000	30,000
Patents	40,000	45,000
Total	$215,000	$240,000

What total should be included in Shaw's balance sheet for December 31, 20X1, for these items?

a. $215,000.
b. $225,000.
c. $230,000.
d. $240,000.

2. A wholly owned foreign subsidiary of Nick Inc. has certain expense accounts for the year ended December 31, 20X4, stated in local currency units (LCU) as follows:

	LCU
Depreciation of Equipment (related assets were purchased January 1, 20X2)	120,000
Provision for Uncollectible Accounts	80,000
Rent	200,000

The exchange rates at various dates were as follows:

	Dollar Equivalent of 1 LCU
January 1, 20X2	0.50
December 31, 20X4	0.40
Average, 20X4	0.44

What total dollar amount should be included in Nick's income statement to reflect the preceding expenses for the year ended December 31, 20X4?

a. $160,000.
b. $168,000.
c. $176,000.
d. $183,200.

3. Linser Corporation owns a foreign subsidiary with 2,600,000 local currency units (LCU) of property, plant, and equipment before accumulated depreciation on December 31, 20X4. Of this amount, 1,700,000 LCU were acquired in 20X2 when the rate of exchange was 1.5 LCU = $1, and 900,000 LCU were acquired in 20X3 when the rate of exchange was 1.6 LCU = $1. The rate of exchange in effect on December 31, 20X4, was 1.9 LCU = $1. The weighted average of exchange rates that were in effect during 20X4 was 1.8 LCU = $1. Assuming that the property, plant, and equipment are depreciated using the straight-line method over a 10-year period with no salvage value, how much depreciation expense relating to the foreign subsidiary's property, plant, and equipment should be charged in Linser's income statement for 20X4?

a. $144,444.
b. $162,000.
c. $169,583.
d. $173,333.

4. On January 1, 20X1, Pat Company formed a foreign subsidiary. On February 15, 20X1, Pat's subsidiary purchased 100,000 local currency units (LCU) of inventory. Of the original inventory purchased on February 15, 20X1, 25,000 LCU made up the entire inventory on December 31,

20X1. The exchange rates were 2.2 LCU = $1 from January 1, 20X1, to June 30, 20X1, and 2 LCU = $1 from July 1, 20X1, to December 31, 20X1. The December 31, 20X1, inventory balance for Pat's foreign subsidiary should be restated in U.S. dollars in the amount of

a. $10,500.
b. $11,364.
c. $11,905.
d. $12,500.

5. At what rates should the following balance sheet accounts in the foreign currency financial statements be restated into U.S. dollars?

Equipment	Accumulated Depreciation of Equipment
a. Current	Current
b. Current	Average for year
c. Historical	Current
d. Historical	Historical

6. A credit-balancing item resulting from the process of restating a foreign entity's financial statement from the local currency unit to U.S. dollars should be included as a(an)

a. Separate component of stockholders' equity.
b. Deferred credit.
c. Component of income from continuing operations.
d. Extraordinary item.

7. A foreign subsidiary of the Bart Corporation has certain balance sheet accounts on December 31, 20X2. Information relating to these accounts in U.S. dollars is as follows:

	Restated at	
	Current Rates	**Historical Rates**
Marketable (AFS and Trading) securities	$ 75,000	$ 85,000
Inventories, carried at average cost	600,000	700,000
Refundable deposits	25,000	30,000
Goodwill	55,000	70,000
	$755,000	$885,000

What total should be included in Bart's balance sheet on December 31, 20X2, as a result of the preceding information?

a. $755,000.
b. $780,000.
c. $870,000.
d. $880,000.

LO 12-4, 12-5 **E12-2 Multiple-Choice Questions on Translation and Foreign Currency Transactions [AICPA Adapted]**

The following information should be used for questions 1, 2, and 3.

Select the best answers under each of two alternative assumptions: (*a*) the LCU is the functional currency and the translation method is appropriate or (*b*) the U.S. dollar is the functional currency and the remeasurement method is appropriate.

1. Refer to the preceding requirements. Gate Inc. had a $30,000 credit adjustment for the year ended December 31, 20X2, from restating its foreign subsidiary's accounts from their local currency units into U.S. dollars. Additionally, Gate had a receivable from a foreign customer payable in the customer's local currency. On December 31, 20X1, this receivable for 200,000 local currency units (LCU) was correctly included in Gate's balance sheet at $110,000. When

the receivable was collected on February 15, 20X2, the U.S. dollar equivalent was $120,000. In Gate's 20X2 consolidated income statement, how much should be reported as foreign exchange gain in computing net income?

a. $0.
b. $10,000.
c. $30,000.
d. $40,000.

2. Refer to the preceding requirements. Bar Corporation had a realized foreign exchange loss of $13,000 for the year ended December 31, 20X2, and must also determine whether the following items will require year-end adjustment:

(1) Bar had a $7,000 credit resulting from the restatement in dollars of the accounts of its wholly owned foreign subsidiary for the year ended December 31, 20X2.

(2) Bar had an account payable to an unrelated foreign supplier to be paid in the supplier's local currency. The U.S. dollar equivalent of the payable was $60,000 on the October 31, 20X2, invoice date and $64,000 on December 31, 20X2. The invoice is payable on January 30, 20X3.

What amount of the net foreign exchange loss in computing net income should be reported in Bar's 20X2 consolidated income statement?

a. $6,000.
b. $10,000.
c. $13,000.
d. $17,000.

3. Refer to the preceding requirements. The balance in Simpson Corp.'s foreign exchange loss account was $15,000 on December 31, 20X2, before any necessary year-end adjustment relating to the following:

(1) Simpson had a $20,000 debit resulting from the restatement in dollars of the accounts of its wholly owned foreign subsidiary for the year ended December 31, 20X2.

(2) Simpson had an account payable to an unrelated foreign supplier, payable in the supplier's local currency on January 27, 20X3. The U.S. dollar equivalent of the payable was $100,000 on the November 28, 20X2, invoice date, and $106,000 on December 31, 20X2.

In Simpson's 20X2 consolidated income statement, what amount should be included as foreign exchange loss in computing net income?

a. $41,000.
b. $35,000.
c. $21,000.
d. $15,000.

4. When remeasuring foreign currency financial statements into the functional currency, which of the following items would be remeasured using a historical exchange rate?

a. Inventories carried at cost.
b. Trading securities carried at market values.
c. Bonds payable.
d. Accrued liabilities.

5. A foreign subsidiary's functional currency is its local currency, which has not experienced significant inflation. The weighted-average exchange rate for the current year would be the appropriate exchange rate for translating

	Sales to Customers	Wages Expense
a.	No	No
b.	Yes	Yes
c.	No	Yes
d.	Yes	No

6. The functional currency of Dahl Inc.'s subsidiary is the European euro. Dahl borrowed euros as a partial hedge of its investment in the subsidiary. In preparing consolidated financial statements, Dahl's debit balance of its translation adjustment exceeded its exchange gain on the borrowing. How should the translation adjustment and the exchange gain be reported in Dahl's consolidated financial statements?

   a. The translation adjustment should be netted against the exchange gain, and the excess translation adjustment should be reported in the stockholders' equity section of the balance sheet.
   b. The translation adjustment should be netted against the exchange gain, and the excess translation adjustment should be reported in the income statement in computing net income.
   c. The translation adjustment is reported as a component of other comprehensive income and then accumulated in the stockholders' equity section of the balance sheet, and the exchange gain should be reported in the income statement in computing net income.
   d. The translation adjustment should be reported in the income statement, and the exchange gain should be reported separately in the stockholders' equity section of the balance sheet.

LO 12-1–12-8

E12-3 Matching Terms

Match the items in the left-hand column with the descriptions/explanations in the right-hand column.

Items

1. Financial Accounting Standards Board
2. Remeasurement gain or loss
3. Translation adjustment
4. Current rate method
5. Remeasurement method
6. U.S. dollar
7. Functional currency
8. International Accounting Standards Board
9. International Managerial Accounting Society
10. Functional currency indicators
11. Historical rate method
12. Cumulative transaction gain or loss

Descriptions/Explanations

A. The group that has attempted to harmonize the world's many different accounting methods.
B. The currency of the primary economic environment in which the entity operates.
C. The functional currency for a U.S. subsidiary located in a country with > 100 percent inflation over the last three years.
D. Translation of all assets and liabilities of a foreign subsidiary using the foreign exchange rate at the balance sheet date.
E. Restatement of the fixed assets and inventories of a foreign subsidiary into U.S. dollars using historical exchange rates.
F. Inclusion of this gain or loss on the U.S. company's income statement as part of net income.
G. The item that balances the debits and credits of the foreign subsidiary's adjusted trial balance in U.S. dollars, assuming the functional currency is the currency of the foreign subsidiary's country.
H. The item that balances the debits and credits of the foreign subsidiary's adjusted trial balance in U.S. dollars, assuming the functional currency is the U.S. dollar.
I. Translation of the income statement accounts of a foreign subsidiary using the average exchange rate for the year.
J. Restatement of depreciation expense and cost of goods sold of a foreign subsidiary using historical exchange rates.
K. An analysis of a foreign subsidiary's cash flows, sales prices, sales markets, expenses, and financing.
L. The periodic change in this item reported as a component of other comprehensive income.

LO 12-4, 12-5

E12-4 Multiple-Choice Questions on Translation and Remeasurement

Use the following information for questions 1, 2, and 3.

Bartell Inc., a U.S. company, acquired 90 percent of the common stock of a Malaysian company on January 1, 20X5, for $160,000. The net assets of the Malaysian subsidiary amounted to 680,000 ringgit (RM) on the date of acquisition. On January 1, 20X5, the book values of the Malaysian subsidiary's identifiable assets and liabilities approximated their fair values. Exchange rates at various dates during 20X5 follow:

	RM	$
January 1	1 =	0.21
December 31	1 =	0.24
Average for 20X5	1 =	0.22

1. Refer to the preceding information. On January 1, 20X5, how much goodwill was acquired by Bartell?

   a. $17,200.
   b. $31,480.
   c. $11,400.
   d. $25,360.

2. Refer to the preceding exchange rate information. Assume that Bartell acquired $10,500 of goodwill on January 1, 20X5, and the goodwill suffered a 10 percent impairment loss in 20X5. If the functional currency is the Malaysian ringgit, how much goodwill impairment loss should be reported on Bartell's consolidated income statement for 20X5?

   a. $1,050.
   b. $1,200.
   c. $1,100.
   d. $1,175.

3. Refer to the preceding information but now assume that the U.S. dollar is the functional currency. How much goodwill impairment loss should be reported on Bartell's consolidated income statement in this situation?

   a. $1,050.
   b. $1,200.
   c. $1,100.
   d. $1,175.

Use the following information for questions 4, 5, 6, and 7.

Mondell Inc., a U.S. company, acquired 100 percent of the common stock of a German company on January 1, 20X5, for $402,000. The German subsidiary's net assets amounted to €300,000 on the date of acquisition. On January 1, 20X5, the book values of its identifiable assets and liabilities approximated their fair values. As a result of an analysis of functional currency indicators, Mondell determined that the euro was the functional currency. On December 31, 20X5, the German subsidiary's adjusted trial balance, translated into U.S. dollars, contained $12,000 more debits than credits. The German subsidiary reported income of €25,000 for 20X5 and paid a cash dividend of €5,000 on November 30, 20X5. Included on the German subsidiary's income statement was depreciation expense of €2,500. Mondell uses the fully adjusted equity method of accounting for its investment in the German subsidiary and determined that goodwill in the first year had an impairment loss of 10 percent of its initial amount. Exchange rates at various dates during 20X5 follow:

	€	$
January 1	1 =	1.20
November 30	1 =	1.30
December 31	1 =	1.32
Average for 20X5	1 =	1.24

4. Refer to the preceding information. What amount should Mondell record as "income from subsidiary" based on the German subsidiary's reported net income?

   a. $31,000.
   b. $26,660.

c. $33,000.

d. $28,660.

5. Refer to the preceding information. The receipt of the dividend will result in

   a. A credit to the investment account for $6,200.

   b. A debit to the income from subsidiary account for $6,600.

   c. A credit to the investment account for $6,600.

   d. A credit to the investment account for $6,500.

6. Refer to the preceding information. On Mondell's consolidated balance sheet at December 31, 20X5, what amount should be reported for the goodwill acquired on January 1, 20X5?

   a. $37,660.

   b. $37,800.

   c. $41,580.

   d. $39,880.

7. Refer to the preceding information. In the stockholders' equity section of Mondell's consolidated balance sheet at December 31, 20X5, Mondell should report the translation adjustment as a component of other comprehensive income of

   a. $12,000.

   b. $15,920.

   c. $13,400.

   d. $8,080.

LO 12-4, 12-5

E12-5 Translation

Advanced StudyGuide .com

On January 1, 20X1, Popular Creek Corporation organized RoadTime Company as a subsidiary in Switzerland with an initial investment cost of Swiss francs (SFr) 60,000. RoadTime's December 31, 20X1, trial balance in SFr is as follows:

	Debit	Credit
Cash	SFr 7,000	
Accounts Receivable (net)	20,000	
Receivable from Popular Creek	5,000	
Inventory	25,000	
Plant & Equipment	100,000	
Accumulated Depreciation		SFr 10,000
Accounts Payable		12,000
Bonds Payable		50,000
Common Stock		60,000
Sales		150,000
Cost of Goods Sold	70,000	
Depreciation Expense	10,000	
Operating Expense	30,000	
Dividends Paid	15,000	
Total	SFr 282,000	SFr 282,000

Additional Information

1. The receivable from Popular Creek is denominated in Swiss francs. Popular Creek's books show a $4,000 payable to RoadTime.
2. Purchases of inventory goods are made evenly during the year. Items in the ending inventory were purchased November 1.
3. Equipment is depreciated by the straight-line method with a 10-year life and no residual value. A full year's depreciation is taken in the year of acquisition. The equipment was acquired on March 1.

4. The dividends were declared and paid on November 1.
5. Exchange rates were as follows:

	SFr $
January 1	1 = 0.73
March 1	1 = 0.74
November 1	1 = 0.77
December 31	1 = 0.80
20X1 average	1 = 0.75

6. The Swiss franc is the functional currency.

Required

Prepare a schedule translating the December 31, 20X1, trial balance from Swiss francs to dollars.

LO 12-4, 12-5

E12-6 Proof of Translation Adjustment

Refer to the data in Exercise E12-5.

Required

a. Prepare a proof of the translation adjustment computed in Exercise E12-5.

b. Where is the translation adjustment reported on Popular Creek's consolidated financial statements and its foreign subsidiary?

LO 12-6, 12-7

E12-7 Remeasurement

Refer to the data in Exercise E12-5, but assume that the dollar is the functional currency for the foreign subsidiary.

Required

Prepare a schedule remeasuring the December 31, 20X1, trial balance from Swiss francs to dollars.

LO 12-6, 12-7

E12-8 Proof of Remeasurement Gain (Loss)

Refer to the data in Exercises E12-5 and E12-7.

Required

a. Prepare a proof of the remeasurement gain or loss computed in Exercise E12-7.

b. How should this remeasurement gain or loss be reported on Popular Creek's consolidated financial statements and the financial statements of its foreign subsidiary?

LO 12-4, 12-5

Advanced StudyGuide .com

E12-9 Translation with Strengthening U.S. Dollar

Refer to the data in Exercise E12-5, but now assume that the exchange rates were as follows:

	SFr $
January 1	1 = 0.80
March 1	1 = 0.77
November 1	1 = 0.74
December 31	1 = 0.73
20X1 average	1 = 0.75

The receivable from Popular Creek Corporation is denominated in Swiss francs. Popular Creek's books show a $3,650 payable to RoadTime.

Assume the Swiss franc is the functional currency.

Required

a. Prepare a schedule translating the December 31, 20X1, trial balance from Swiss francs to dollars.

b. Compare the results of Exercise E12-5, in which the dollar is weakening against the Swiss franc during 20X1, with the results in this exercise (E12-9), in which the dollar is strengthening against the Swiss franc during 20X1.

LO 12-6, 12-7 **E12-10** **Remeasurement with Strengthening U.S. Dollar**

Advanced StudyGuide .com

Refer to the data in Exercise E12-5, but now assume that the exchange rates were as follows:

	SFr	$
January 1	1 =	0.80
March 1	1 =	0.77
November 1	1 =	0.74
December 31	1 =	0.73
20X1 average	1 =	0.75

The receivable from Popular Creek is denominated in Swiss francs. Its books show a $3,650 payable to RoadTime.

Assume that the U.S. dollar is the functional currency.

Required

a. Prepare a schedule remeasuring the December 31, 20X1, trial balance from Swiss francs to dollars.

b. Compare the results of Exercise E12-7, in which the dollar weakens against the Swiss franc during 20X1, with the results in this exercise (E12-10), in which the dollar strengthened against the Swiss franc during 20X1.

LO 12-5, 12-7 **E12-11** **Remeasurement and Translation of Cost of Goods Sold**

Advanced StudyGuide .com

Duff Company is a subsidiary of Rand Corporation and is located in Madrid, Spain, where the currency is the euro (€). Data on Duff's inventory and purchases are as follows:

Inventory, January 1, 20X7	€220,000
Purchases during 20X7	846,000
Inventory, December 31, 20X7	180,000

The beginning inventory was acquired during the fourth quarter of 20X6, and the ending inventory was acquired during the fourth quarter of 20X7. Purchases were made evenly over the year. Exchange rates were as follows:

	€	$
Fourth quarter of 20X6	1 =	1.29015
January 1, 20X7	1 =	1.32030
Average during 20X7	1 =	1.39655
Fourth quarter of 20X7	1 =	1.45000
December 31, 20X7	1 =	1.47280

Required

a. Show the remeasurement of cost of goods sold for 20X7, assuming that the U.S. dollar is the functional currency.

b. Show the translation of cost of goods sold for 20X7, assuming that the euro is the functional currency.

LO 12-4 **E12-12** **Equity-Method Entries for a Foreign Subsidiary**

Thames Company is located in London, England. The local currency is the British pound (£). On January 1, 20X8, Dek Company purchased an 80 percent interest in Thames for $400,000, which resulted in an excess of cost-over-book value of $48,000 due solely to a trademark having a remaining life of 10 years. Dek uses the equity method to account for its investment.

Thames's December 31, 20X8, trial balance has been translated into U.S. dollars, requiring a translation adjustment debit of $6,400. Thames's net income translated into U.S. dollars is $60,000. It declared and paid a £15,000 dividend on May 1, 20X8.

Relevant exchange rates are as follows:

	€ $
January 1, 20X8	1 = 1.60
May 1, 20X8	1 = 1.64
December 31, 20X8	1 = 1.65
Average for 20X8	1 = 1.63

Required

a. Record the dividend received by Dek from Thames.

b. Prepare the entries to record Dek's equity in the net income of Thames and the parent's share of the translation adjustment.

c. Show a calculation of the differential reported on the consolidated balance sheet of December 31, 20X8, and the translation adjustment from differential.

d. Record the amortization of the trademark on Dek's books.

e. Calculate the amount of the translation adjustment reported on the statement of comprehensive income as an element of other comprehensive income.

LO 12-5

E12-13 Effects of a Change in the Exchange Rate—Translation and Other Comprehensive Income

Bentley Company owns a subsidiary in India whose balance sheets in rupees (R) for the last two years follow:

	December 31, 20X6	December 31, 20X7
Assets:		
Cash	R 100,000	R 80,000
Receivables	450,000	550,000
Inventory	680,000	720,000
Fixed Assets, net	1,000,000	900,000
Total Assets	R2,230,000	R2,250,000
Equities:		
Current Payables	R 260,000	R 340,000
Long-Term Debt	1,250,000	1,100,000
Common Stock	500,000	500,000
Retained Earnings	220,000	310,000
Total Equities	R2,230,000	R2,250,000

Bentley formed the subsidiary on January 1, 20X6, when the exchange rate was 30 rupees for 1 U.S. dollar. The exchange rate for 1 U.S. dollar on December 31, 20X6, and December 31, 2007, had increased to 35 rupees and 40 rupees, respectively. Income is earned evenly over the year, and the subsidiary declared no dividends during its first two years of existence.

Required

a. Present both the direct and the indirect exchange rate for the rupees for the three dates of (1) January 1, 20X6, (2) December 31, 20X6, and (3) December 31, 20X7. Did the dollar strengthen or weaken in 20X6 and in 20X7?

b. Prepare the subsidiary's translated balance sheet as of December 31, 20X6, assuming the rupee is the subsidiary's functional currency.

c. Prepare the subsidiary's translated balance sheet as of December 31, 20X7, assuming the rupee is the subsidiary's functional currency.

d. Compute the amount that 20X7's other comprehensive income would include as a result of the translation.

LO 12-4,12-6 **E12-14 Computation of Gain or Loss on Sale of Asset by Foreign Subsidiary**

On December 31, 20X2, your company's Mexican subsidiary sold land at a selling price of 3,000,000 pesos. The land had been purchased for 2,000,000 pesos on January 1, 20X1, when the exchange rate was 10 pesos to 1 U.S. dollar. The exchange rate for 1 U.S. dollar was 11 pesos on December 31, 20X1, and 12 pesos on December 31, 20X2. Assume that the subsidiary had no other assets and no liabilities during the two years that it owned the land.

Required

a. Prepare all entries regarding the purchase and sale of the land that would be made on the books of the Mexican subsidiary whose recording currency is the Mexican peso.

b. Determine the amount of the gain or loss on the transaction that would be reported on the subsidiary's remeasured income statement in U.S. dollars, assuming the U.S. dollar is the functional currency. Determine the amount of the remeasurement gain or loss that would be reported on the remeasured income statement in U.S. dollars.

c. Determine the amount of the gain or loss on the transaction that would be reported on the subsidiary's translated income statement in U.S. dollars, assuming the Mexican peso is the functional currency. Determine the amount of the other comprehensive income that would be reported on the consolidated statement of other comprehensive income for 20X2.

LO 12-8 **E12-15* Intercompany Transactions**

Hawk Company sold inventory to United Ltd., an English subsidiary. The goods cost Hawk $8,000 and were sold to United for $12,000 on November 27, payable in British pounds. The goods are still on hand at the end of the year on December 31. The British pound (£) is the functional currency of the English subsidiary. The exchange rates follow:

	€ $
November 27	1 = 1.60
December 31	1 = 1.70

Required

a. At what dollar amount is the ending inventory shown in the trial balance of the consolidated worksheet?

b. What amount is eliminated for the unrealized intercompany gross profit, and at what amount is the inventory shown on the consolidated balance sheet?

PROBLEMS

LO 12-4 **P12-16 Parent Company Journal Entries and Translation**

On January 1, 20X1, Par Company purchased all the outstanding stock of North Bay Company, located in Canada, for $120,000. On January 1, 20X1, the direct exchange rate for the Canadian dollar (C$) was C$1 = $0.80. North Bay's book value on January 1, 20X1, was C$90,000. The fair value of North Bay's plant and equipment was C$10,000 more than book value, and the plant and equipment are being depreciated over 10 years with no salvage value. The remainder of the differential is attributable to a trademark, which will be amortized over 10 years.

During 20X1, North Bay earned C$20,000 in income and declared and paid C$8,000 in dividends. The dividends were declared and paid in Canadian dollars when the exchange rate was C$1 = $0.75. On December 31, 20X1, Par continues to hold the Canadian currency received from the dividend. On December 31, 20X1, the direct exchange rate is C$1 = $0.70. The average exchange rate during 20X1 was C$1 = $0.75. Management has determined that the Canadian dollar is North Bay's appropriate functional currency.

*Indicates that the item relates to "Additional Considerations."

Required

a. Prepare a schedule showing the differential allocation and amortization for 20X1. The schedule should present both Canadian dollars and U.S. dollars.

b. Par uses the fully adjusted equity method to account for its investment. Provide the entries that it would record in 20X1 for its investment in North Bay for the following items:

(1) Purchase of investment in North Bay.

(2) Equity accrual for Par's share of North Bay's income.

(3) Recognition of dividend declared and paid by North Bay.

(4) Amortization of differential.

(5) Recognition of translation adjustment on differential.

c. Prepare a schedule showing the proof of the translation adjustment for North Bay as a result of the translation of the subsidiary's accounts from Canadian dollars to U.S. dollars. Then provide the entry that Par would record for its share of the translation adjustment resulting from the translation of the subsidiary's accounts.

d. Provide the entry required by Par to restate the C$8,000 in the Foreign Currency Units account into its year-end U.S. dollar–equivalent value.

LO 12-4, 12-5 P12-17 Translation, Journal Entries, Consolidated Comprehensive Income, and Stockholders' Equity

On January 1, 20X5, Taft Company acquired all of the outstanding stock of Vikix Inc., a Norwegian company, at a cost of $151,200. Vikix's net assets on the date of acquisition were 700,000 kroner (NKr). On January 1, 20X5, the book and fair values of the Norwegian subsidiary's identifiable assets and liabilities approximated their fair values except for property, plant, and equipment and patents acquired. The fair value of Vikix's property, plant, and equipment exceeded its book value by $18,000. The remaining useful life of Vikix's equipment at January 1, 20X5, was 10 years. The remainder of the differential was attributable to a patent having an estimated useful life of 5 years. Vikix's trial balance on December 31, 20X5, in kroner, follows:

	Debits	Credits
Cash	NKr 150,000	
Accounts Receivable (net)	200,000	
Inventory	270,000	
Property, Plant & Equipment	600,000	
Accumulated Depreciation		NKr 150,000
Accounts Payable		90,000
Notes Payable		190,000
Common Stock		450,000
Retained Earnings		250,000
Sales		690,000
Cost of Goods Sold	410,000	
Operating Expenses	100,000	
Depreciation Expense	50,000	
Dividends Paid	40,000	
Total	NKr1,820,000	NKr1,820,000

Additional Information

1. Vikix uses the FIFO method for its inventory. The beginning inventory was acquired on December 31, 20X4, and ending inventory was acquired on December 15, 20X5. Purchases of NKr420,000 were made evenly throughout 20X5.
2. Vikix acquired all of its property, plant, and equipment on July 1, 20X3, and uses straight-line depreciation.

3. Vikix's sales were made evenly throughout 20X5, and its operating expenses were incurred evenly throughout 20X5.
4. The dividends were declared and paid on July 1, 20X5.
5. Taft's income from its own operations was $275,000 for 20X5, and its total stockholders' equity on January 1, 20X5, was $3,500,000. Taft declared $100,000 of dividends during 20X5.
6. Exchange rates were as follows:

	NKr $
July 1, 20X3	1 = 0.15
December 30, 20X4	1 = 0.18
January 1, 20X5	1 = 0.18
July 1, 20X5	1 = 0.19
December 15, 20X5	1 = 0.205
December 31, 20X5	1 = 0.21
Average for 20X5	1 = 0.20

Required

a. Prepare a schedule translating the trial balance from Norwegian kroner into U.S. dollars. Assume the krone is the functional currency.

b. Assume that Taft uses the fully adjusted equity method. Record all journal entries that relate to its investment in the Norwegian subsidiary during 20X5. Provide the necessary documentation and support for the amounts in the journal entries, including a schedule of the translation adjustment related to the differential.

c. Prepare a schedule that determines Taft's consolidated comprehensive income for 20X5.

d. Compute Taft's total consolidated stockholders' equity at December 31, 20X5.

LO 12-6, 12-7

P12-18 Remeasurement, Journal Entries, Consolidated Net Income, and Stockholders' Equity

Refer to the information in Problem P12-17. Assume the U.S. dollar is the functional currency, not the krone.

Required

a. Prepare a schedule remeasuring the trial balance from Norwegian kroner into U.S. dollars.

b. Assume that Taft uses the fully adjusted equity method. Record all journal entries that relate to its investment in the Norwegian subsidiary during 20X5. Provide the necessary documentation and support for the amounts in the journal entries.

c. Prepare a schedule that determines Taft's consolidated net income for 20X5.

d. Compute Taft's total consolidated stockholders' equity at December 31, 20X5.

LO 12-5

P12-19 Proof of Translation Adjustment

Refer to the information presented in Problem P12-17 and your answer to part *a* of Problem P12-17.

Required

Prepare a schedule providing a proof of the translation adjustment.

LO 12-6

P12-20 Remeasurement Gain or Loss

Refer to the information given in Problem P12-17 and your answer to part *a* of Problem P12-18.

Required

Prepare a schedule providing a proof of the remeasurement gain or loss. For this part of the problem, assume that the Norwegian subsidiary had the following monetary assets and liabilities at January 1, 20X5:

Monetary Assets	
Cash	NKr 10,000
Accounts Receivable (net)	140,000
Monetary Liabilities	
Accounts Payable	NKr 70,000
Notes Payable	140,000

On January 1, 20X5, the Norwegian subsidiary has a net monetary liability position of NKr60,000.

LO 12-4, 12-5 **P12-21** **Translation and Calculation of Translation Adjustment**

On January 1, 20X4, Alum Corporation acquired DaSilva Company, a Brazilian subsidiary, by purchasing all its common stock at book value. DaSilva's trial balances on January 1, 20X4, and December 31, 20X4, expressed in Brazilian reals (BRL), follow:

	January 1, 20X4		**December 31, 20X4**	
	Debit	**Credit**	**Debit**	**Credit**
Cash	BRL 62,000		BRL 57,700	
Accounts Receivable (net)	83,900		82,000	
Inventories	95,000		95,000	
Prepaid Insurance	5,600		2,400	
Plant & Equipment	250,000		350,000	
Accumulated Depreciation		BRL 67,500		BRL 100,000
Intangible Assets	42,000		30,000	
Accounts Payable		20,000		24,000
Income Taxes Payable		30,000		27,000
Interest Payable		1,000		1,100
Notes Payable		20,000		20,000
Bonds Payable		120,000		120,000
Common Stock		80,000		80,000
Additional Paid-In Capital		150,000		150,000
Retained Earnings		50,000		50,000
Sales				500,000
Cost of Goods Sold			230,000	
Insurance Expense			3,200	
Depreciation Expense			32,500	
Amortization Expense			12,000	
Operating Expense			152,300	
Dividends Paid			25,000	
Total	BRL538,500	BRL538,500	BRL1,072,100	BRL1,072,100

Additional Information

1. DaSilva uses FIFO inventory valuation. Purchases were made uniformly during 20X4. Ending inventory for 20X4 is composed of units purchased when the exchange rate was $0.25.
2. The insurance premium for a two-year policy was paid on October 1, 20X3.
3. Plant and equipment were acquired as follows:

Date	Cost
January 1, 20X1	BRL200,000
July 10, 20X2	50,000
April 7, 20X4	100,000

4. Plant and equipment are depreciated using the straight-line method and a 10-year life, with no residual value. A full month's depreciation is taken in the month of acquisition.

5. The intangible assets are patents acquired on July 10, 20X2, at a cost of BRL60,000. The estimated life is five years.
6. The common stock was issued on January 1, 20X1.
7. Dividends of BRL10,000 were declared and paid on April 7. On October 9, BRL15,000 of dividends were declared and paid.
8. Exchange rates were as follows:

	BRL $
January 1, 20X1	1 = 0.45
July 10, 20X2	1 = 0.40
October 1, 20X3	1 = 0.34
January 1, 20X4	1 = 0.30
April 7, 20X4	1 = 0.28
October 9, 20X4	1 = 0.23
December 31, 20X4	1 = 0.20
20X4 average	1 = 0.25

Required

a. Prepare a schedule translating the December 31, 20X4, trial balance of DaSilva from reals to dollars assuming the real is the functional currency.

b. Prepare a schedule calculating the translation adjustment as of the end of 20X4. The net assets on January 1, 20X4, were BRL280,000.

LO 12-6, 12-7 P12-22 Remeasurement and Proof of Remeasurement Gain or Loss

Refer to the information in Problem P12-21. Assume that the dollar is the functional currency.

Required

a. Prepare a schedule remeasuring DaSilva Company's December 31, 20X4, trial balance from reals to dollars.

b. Prepare a schedule providing a proof of the remeasurement gain or loss.

LO 12-4, 12-5 P12-23 Translation

Alamo Inc. purchased 80 percent of the outstanding stock of Western Ranching Company, located in Australia, on January 1, 20X3. The purchase price in Australian dollars (A$) was A$200,000, and A$40,000 of the differential was allocated to plant and equipment, which is amortized over a 10-year period. The remainder of the differential was attributable to a patent. Alamo Inc. amortizes the patent over 10 years. Western Ranching's trial balance on December 31, 20X3, in Australian dollars is as follows:

	Debits	Credits
Cash	A$ 44,100	
Accounts Receivable (net)	72,000	
Inventory	86,000	
Plant & Equipment	240,000	
Accumulated Depreciation		A$ 60,000
Accounts Payable		53,800
Payable to Alamo Inc.		10,800
Interest Payable		3,000
12% Bonds Payable		100,000
Premium on Bonds		5,700
Common Stock		90,000
Retained Earnings		40,000
Sales		579,000

(continued)

Cost of Goods Sold	330,000	
Depreciation Expense	24,000	
Operating Expenses	131,500	
Interest Expense	5,700	
Dividends Paid	9,000	
Total	A$942,300	A$942,300

Additional Information

1. Western Ranching uses average cost for cost of goods sold. Inventory increased by A$20,000 during the year. Purchases were made uniformly during 20X3. The ending inventory was acquired at the average exchange rate for the year.
2. Plant and equipment were acquired as follows:

Date	Cost
January 20X1	A$180,000
January 1, 20X3	60,000

3. Plant and equipment are depreciated using the straight-line method and a 10-year life with no residual value.
4. The payable to Alamo is in Australian dollars. Alamo's books show a receivable from Western Ranching of $6,480.
5. The 10-year bonds were issued on July 1, 20X3, for A$106,000. The premium is amortized on a straight-line basis. The interest is paid on April 1 and October 1.
6. The dividends were declared and paid on April 1.
7. Exchange rates were as follows:

	A$ $
January 20X1	1 = 0.93
August 20X1	1 = 0.88
January 1, 20X3	1 = 0.70
April 1, 20X3	1 = 0.67
July 1, 20X3	1 = 0.64
December 31, 20X3	1 = 0.60
20X3 average	1 = 0.65

Required

a. Prepare a schedule translating the December 31, 20X3, trial balance of Western Ranching from Australian dollars to U.S. dollars.

b. Prepare a schedule providing a proof of the translation adjustment.

LO 12-4 **P12-24 Parent Company Journal Entries and Translation**

Refer to the information given in Problem P12-23 for Alamo and its subsidiary, Western Ranching. Assume that the Australian dollar (A$) is the functional currency and that Alamo uses the fully adjusted equity method for accounting for its investment in Western Ranching.

Required

a. Prepare the entries that Alamo would record in 20X3 for its investment in Western Ranching. Your entries should include the following:

(1) Record the initial investment on January 1, 20X3.

(2) Record the dividend received by the parent company.

(3) Recognize the parent company's share of the equity income of the subsidiary.

(4) Record the amortizations of the differential.

(5) Recognize the translation adjustment required by the parent from the adjustment of the differential.

(6) Recognize the parent company's share of the translation adjustment resulting from the translation of the subsidiary's accounts.

b. Provide the necessary documentation and support for the amounts recorded in the journal entries, including a schedule of the translation adjustment related to the differential.

LO 12-5

P12-25 Consolidation Worksheet after Translation

Refer to the information given in Problems P12-23 and P12-24 for Alamo and its subsidiary, Western Ranching. Assume that the Australian dollar (A$) is the functional currency and that Alamo uses the fully adjusted equity method for accounting for its investment in Western Ranching. A December 31, 20X3, trial balance for Alamo Inc. follows. Use this translated trial balance for completing this problem.

Item	Debit	Credit
Cash	$ 38,000	
Accounts Receivable (net)	140,000	
Receivable from Western Ranching	6,480	
Inventory	128,000	
Plant & Equipment	500,000	
Investment in Western Ranching	152,064	
Cost of Goods Sold	600,000	
Depreciation Expense	28,000	
Operating Expenses	204,000	
Interest Expense	2,000	
Dividends Declared	50,000	
Translation Adjustment	22,528	
Accumulated Depreciation		$ 90,000
Accounts Payable		60,000
Interest Payable		2,000
Common Stock		500,000
Retained Earnings, January 1, 20X3		179,656
Sales		1,000,000
Income from Subsidiary		39,416
Total	$1,871,072	$1,871,072

Required

a. Prepare a set of elimination entries, in general journal form, for the entries required to prepare a comprehensive consolidation worksheet (including other comprehensive income) as of December 31, 20X3.

b. Prepare a comprehensive consolidation worksheet as of December 31, 20X3.

LO 12-7

P12-26 Remeasurement

Refer to the information in Problem P12-23. Assume the U.S. dollar is the functional currency.

Required

a. Prepare a schedule remeasuring the December 31, 20X3, trial balance of Western Ranching from Australian dollars to U.S. dollars.

b. Prepare a schedule providing a proof of the remeasurement gain or loss. The subsidiary's net monetary liability position on January 1, 20X3, was A$80,000.

LO 12-6

P12-27 Parent Company Journal Entries and Remeasurement

Refer to the information given in Problems P12-23 and P12-26 for Alamo and its subsidiary, Western Ranching. Assume that the U.S. dollar is the functional currency and that Alamo uses the fully adjusted equity method for accounting for its investment in Western Ranching.

Advanced StudyGuide .com

Required

a. Prepare the entries that Alamo would record in 20X3 for its investment in Western Ranching. Your entries should do the following:

(1) Record the initial investment on January 1, 20X3.

(2) Record the dividend the parent company received.

(3) Recognize the parent company's share of the equity income from the subsidiary.

(4) Record the amortizations of the differential.

b. Provide the necessary documentation and support for the amounts recorded in the journal entries.

LO 12-7

P12-28 Consolidation Worksheet after Remeasurement

Refer to the information given in Problems P12-23 and P12-27 for Alamo and its subsidiary, Western Ranching. Assume that the U.S. dollar is the functional currency and that Alamo uses the fully adjusted equity method for accounting for its investment in Western Ranching. A December 31, 20X3, trial balance for Alamo follows. Use this remeasured trial balance for completing this problem.

Item	Debit	Credit
Cash	$ 38,000	
Accounts Receivable (net)	140,000	
Receivable from Western Ranching	6,480	
Inventory	128,000	
Plant & Equipment	500,000	
Investment in Western Ranching	178,544	
Cost of Goods Sold	600,000	
Depreciation Expense	28,000	
Operating Expenses	204,000	
Interest Expense	2,000	
Dividends Declared	50,000	
Accumulated Depreciation		$ 90,000
Accounts Payable		60,000
Interest Payable		2,000
Common Stock		500,000
Retained Earnings, January 1, 20X3		179,656
Sales		1,000,000
Income from Subsidiary		43,368
Total	$1,875,024	$1,875,024

Required

a. Prepare a set of elimination entries, in general journal form, for the entries required to prepare a three-part consolidation worksheet as of December 31, 20X3.

b. Prepare a three-part consolidation worksheet as of December 31, 20X3.

LO 12-6, 12-7

P12-29 Foreign Currency Remeasurement [AICPA Adapted]

On January 1, 20X1, Kiner Company formed a foreign subsidiary that issued all of its currently outstanding common stock on that date. Selected accounts from the balance sheets, all of which are shown in local currency units, are as follows:

	December 31	
	20X2	20X1
Accounts Receivable (net of allowance for uncollectible accounts of 2,200 LCU on December 31, 20X2, and 2,000 LCU on December 31, 20X1)	LCU 40,000	LCU 35,000
Inventories, at cost	80,000	75,000

(continued)

	December 31	
	20X2	**20X1**
Property, Plant & Equipment (net of allowance for accumulated depreciation of 31,000 LCU on December 31, 20X2, and 14,000 LCU on December 31, 20X1)	163,000	150,000
Long-Term Debt	100,000	120,000
Common Stock, authorized 10,000 shares, par value 10 LCU per share; issued and outstanding, 5,000 shares on December 31, 20X2, and December 31, 20X1	50,000	50,000

Additional Information

1. Exchange rates are as follows:

	LCU $
January 1, 20X1–July 31, 20X1	2.0 = 1
August 1, 20X1–October 31, 20X1	1.8 = 1
November 1, 20X1–June 30, 20X2	1.7 = 1
July 1, 20X2–December 31, 20X2	1.5 = 1
Average monthly rate for 20X1	1.9 = 1
Average monthly rate for 20X2	1.6 = 1

2. An analysis of the accounts receivable balance is as follows:

	20X2	**20X1**
Accounts Receivable:		
Balance at beginning of year	LCU 37,000	
Sales (36,000 LCU per month in 20X2 and 31,000 LCU per month in 20X1)	432,000	LCU 372,000
Collections	(423,600)	(334,000)
Write-offs (May 20X2 and December 20X1)	(3,200)	(1,000)
Balance at end of year	LCU 42,200	LCU 37,000

	20X2	**20X1**
Allowance for Uncollectible Accounts:		
Balance at beginning of year	LCU 2,000	
Provision for uncollectible accounts	3,400	LCU 3,000
Write-offs (May 20X2 and December 20X1)	(3,200)	(1,000)
Balance at end of year	LCU 2,200	LCU 2,000

3. An analysis of inventories, for which the first-in, first-out inventory method is used, follows:

	20X2	**20X1**
Inventory at beginning of year	LCU 75,000	
Purchases (June 20X2 and June 20X1)	335,000	LCU375,000
Goods available for sale	LCU410,000	LCU375,000
Inventory at end of year	(80,000)	(75,000)
Cost of goods sold	LCU330,000	LCU300,000

4. On January 1, 20X1, Kiner's foreign subsidiary purchased land for 24,000 LCU and plant and equipment for 140,000 LCU. On July 4, 20X2, additional equipment was purchased for 30,000 LCU. Plant and equipment is being depreciated on a straight-line basis over a 10-year period with no residual value. A full year's depreciation is taken in the year of purchase.
5. On January 15, 20X1, 7 percent bonds with a face value of 120,000 LCU were issued. These bonds mature on January 15, 20X7, and the interest is paid semiannually on July 15 and January 15. The first interest payment was made on July 15, 20X1.

Required

Prepare a schedule remeasuring the selected accounts into U.S. dollars for December 31, 20X1, and December 31, 20X2, respectively, assuming the U.S. dollar is the functional currency for the foreign subsidiary. The schedule should be prepared using the following form:

Item	Balance in LCU	Appropriate Exchange Rate	Remeasured into U.S. Dollars
December 31, 20X1:			
Accounts Receivable (net)			
Inventories			
Property, Plant & Equipment (net)			
Long-Term Debt			
Common Stock			
December 31, 20X2:			
Accounts Receivable (net)			
Inventories			
Property, Plant & Equipment (net)			
Long-Term Debt			
Common Stock			

LO 12-4, 12-5 **P12-30** **Foreign Currency Translation**

Refer to the information in Problem P12-29 for Kiner Company and its foreign subsidiary.

Required

Prepare a schedule translating the selected accounts into U.S. dollars as of December 31, 20X1, and December 31, 20X2, respectively, assuming that the local currency unit is the foreign subsidiary's functional currency.

LO12-1–12-8 **P12-31** **Matching Terms**

Match the items in the left-hand column with the descriptions/explanations in the right-hand column.

Items	Descriptions/Explanations
1. Current exchange rate	A. Method used to restate a foreign entity's financial statement when the local currency unit is the functional currency.
2. Foreign entity goodwill under translation	B. Method used to restate a foreign entity's financial statements when the U.S. dollar is the functional currency.
3. Credit translation adjustment for the year	C. Currency of the environment in which an entity primarily generates and expends cash.
4. Other comprehensive income—translation adjustment	D. Always the local currency unit of the foreign entity.
5. Translation	E. Exchange rate at the end of the period.
6. Historical exchange rate	F. Exchange rate at the date of the asset acquisition or at the date of dividend declaration.
7. Foreign entity goodwill under remeasurement	
8. Remeasurement	
9. Debit translation adjustment for the year	
10. Functional currency	

(continued)

Items	Descriptions/Explanations
	G. Average exchange rate during the period.
	H. Periodic change in the cumulative translation adjustment.
	I. Method under which goodwill must be adjusted to the current exchange rate at the balance sheet date.
	J. Method under which goodwill is restated using the historical exchange rate.
	K. Increase in the Investment in Sub account.
	L. Decrease in the Investment in Sub account.

LO 12-4

P12-32 Translation Choices

The U.S. parent company is preparing its consolidated financial statements for December 31, 20X4. The foreign company's local currency (LCU) is the functional currency. Information is presented in Data Set A and Data Set B.

Data Set A:

	Exchange Rate	Date
1.	LCU 0.74	June 16, 20X1: date foreign company purchased
2.	0.80	January 1, 20X4: beginning of current year
3.	0.87	March 31, 20X4
4.	0.86	June 12, 20X4
5.	0.85	Average for year 20X4
6.	0.84	November 1, 20X4
7.	0.83	December 31, 20X4: end of current year
8.	No translation rate is applied	

Data Set B:

a. Accounts receivable outstanding from sales on March 31, 20X4.
b. Sales revenue earned during year.
c. Dividends declared on November 1, 20X4.
d. Ending inventory balance from acquisitions through the year.
e. Equipment purchased on March 31, 20X4.
f. Depreciation expense on equipment.
g. Common stock outstanding.
h. Dividends payable from dividends declared on June 12, 20X4.
i. Accumulated Other Comprehensive Income balance from prior fiscal year.
j. Bond payable issued January 1, 20X4.
k. Interest expense on the bond payable.

Required

a. Select the appropriate exchange rate from the amounts presented in Data Set A to prepare the translation worksheet for each of the accounts presented in Data Set B.
b. Determine the direct exchange rate for January 1, 20X4.
c. Determine whether the U.S. dollar strengthened or weakened against the LCU during 20X4.

LO 12-5

P12-33 Proof of Translation Adjustment

MaMi Co. Ltd. located in Mexico City is a wholly owned subsidiary of Special Foods, a U.S. company. At the beginning of the year, MaMi's condensed balance sheet was reported in Mexican pesos (MXP) as follows:

Assets	3,425,000	Liabilities	2,850,000
		Stockholders' Equity	575,000

During the year, the company earned income of MXP270,000 and on November 1 declared dividends of MXP150,000. The Mexican peso is the functional currency. Relevant exchange rates between the peso and the U.S. dollar follow:

January 1 (beginning of year)	$0.0870
Average for year	0.0900
November 1	0.0915
December 31 (end of year)	0.0930

Required

a. Prepare a proof of the translation adjustment, assuming that the beginning credit balance of the Accumulated Other Comprehensive Income—Translation Adjustment was $3,250.

b. Did the U.S. dollar strengthen or weaken against the Mexican peso during the year?

KAPLAN CPA REVIEW

KAPLAN CPA REVIEW

Kaplan CPA Review Simulation on Comprehensive Consolidation Procedures

Please visit the *Connect Library* for the online Kaplan CPA Review task-based simulation.

Situation

The Montana Corporation, based in Billings, transacts business in the United States and Mexico. Its wholly owned subsidiary (Cabo Inc.) is located in Mexico. Both companies assume the United States dollar as their functional currency.

Consolidated financial statements are being prepared for Year One. Montana Corp. and Cabo Inc. have a December 31 year-end. The currency exchange rates are as follows for the current year (Year One):

January 1, Year One:	1 peso equals $.088
Average for Year One:	1 peso equals $.090
November 1, Year One:	1 peso equals $.092
December 1, Year One:	1 peso equals $.094
December 31, Year One:	1 peso equals $.095
January 31, Year Two:	1 peso equals $.098

Topics covered in the simulation

a. Foreign currency translation.

b. Foreign currency remeasurement.

13 Segment and Interim Reporting

Multicorporate Entities

Multinational Entities

Reporting Requirements

Segment and Interim Reporting

SEC Reporting

Partnerships

Governmental and Not-for-Profit Entities

Corporations in Financial Difficulty

SEGMENT REPORTING AT WALMART

In 1962, Sam Walton opened the first Walmart store in Rogers, Arkansas. By 1967, the company had expanded to 24 stores, and it recorded more than $12 million in sales that year. In 1968, Walmart opened its first store outside of Arkansas. Then, in 1969, it incorporated, going public the following year. The company continued to expand during the 1970s and 1980s and, by its 25th anniversary, had 1,198 stores, employed more than 200,000 employees, and achieved $15.9 billion in annual sales. Finally, Walmart opened its first "Supercenter" in 1998.

Walmart jumped into the international market in 1991, opening a store in Mexico City. Three years later, it purchased Woolco to expand its operations into Canada. At the end of 1995, Walmart had nearly 2,000 stores and was just shy of $100 billion in revenues. The company's rapid expansion has continued into the 21st century. During fiscal 2012, Walmart operated 10,130 stores in 27 countries, employed approximately 2.2 million people, and had more than $443 billion in revenues.

Walmart divides its operations into three main segments: U.S. Walmart stores, International Walmart stores, and Sam's Club stores. Each segment reports stand-alone financial information. These individual segment financial disclosures reveal differences in operations. For example, in 2014, Sam's Club stores derived 12 percent of its revenues from auto fuel sales, which is unique to this segment. The aggregate numbers reported in the consolidated financial statements do not afford investors and other interested parties the ability to distinguish among the different segments. Hence, these detailed segment disclosures provide a way for financial statement users to better understand the operations of the company.

Walmart

LEARNING OBJECTIVES

When you finish studying this chapter, you should be able to:

LO 13-1 Understand accounting issues associated with segment reporting both in the United States and internationally.

LO 13-2 Understand and be able to calculate threshold tests for segment reporting.

LO 13-3 Understand the requirements for enterprisewide disclosures.

LO 13-4 Understand the rules for interim financial reporting.

REPORTING FOR SEGMENTS

LO 13-1

Understand accounting issues associated with segment reporting both in the United States and internationally.

Diversification into new products and multinational markets during the 1960s and early 1970s created the need for disaggregated information about the individual segments or components of an enterprise. This information need was addressed by the Accounting Principles Board, the Financial Executives Institute, the Institute of Management Accountants, the Securities and Exchange Commission, and, finally, the Financial Accounting Standards Board.

Large, diversified companies can be viewed as a portfolio of assets operated as divisions or subsidiaries, often multinational in scope. The various components of a large company may have different profit rates, different degrees and types of risk, and different opportunities for growth. A major issue for accountants is how to develop and disclose the information necessary to reflect these essential differences. The following discussion presents the accounting standards for reporting an entity's operating components, foreign operations, and major customers.

SEGMENT REPORTING ACCOUNTING ISSUES

ASC 280 defines an operating segment as having three characteristics:

1. The component unit's business activities generate revenue and incur expenses, including any revenue or expenses in transactions with the company's other business units.
2. The component unit's operating results are regularly reviewed by the entity's chief operating decision maker, who then determines the resources to assign to the segment and evaluates its performance.
3. Separate financial information is available for the component unit.

Generally, the corporate headquarters is not a separate operating segment. Also, the company may choose to aggregate several individual operating segments that have very similar economic characteristics (i.e., products and services, production processes, type or class of customer, methods used to distribute products or provide for services). Management also may believe that the aggregation will provide more meaningful information to the users of the financial statements.

Whenever the issue of defining the income for an enterprise's segment arises, one problem is the allocation of costs to specific segments. For example, should a segment's income include directly traceable costs only, or should it also include an allocation of common costs, such as companywide advertising or a central purchasing department? One accounting researcher has stated that all allocations are arbitrary, that is, not completely verifiable with empirical evidence, and, therefore, net income after deducting any allocated costs is arbitrary.[1] **ASC 280** states that the allocations of revenues and costs should be included for a reported segment only if they are included in the segment's profit or loss that the chief operating decision maker uses. Also, only those assets included in the measure of the segment's assets that the chief operating decision maker uses should be reported for that segment. Thus, the FASB desires to align the segments' external financial disclosures with the internal reporting used by the company's management to make resource allocations and other decisions regarding the operating segments.

International Financial Reporting Standards for Operating Segments

Segment reporting is also specified in **International Financial Reporting Standard No. 8,** "Operating Segments" (IFRS 8). This standard requires disclosure of information

[1] A. Thomas, *The Allocation Problem: Part Two* (Sarasota, FL: American Accounting Association, 1974).

about an entity's reportable operating segments in both its annual and its interim financial statements. The international standards are generally similar to those prescribed by U.S. GAAP.

INFORMATION ABOUT OPERATING SEGMENTS

LO 13-2

Understand and be able to calculate threshold tests for segment reporting.

Many entities are diversified across several lines of business. Each line may be subject to unique competitive factors and may react differently to changes in the economic environment. For example, a large company such as Johnson & Johnson operates in several major lines: consumer, pharmaceutical, and professional. Its products include disposable contact lenses, baby products, surgical products, antibody therapies, and cold and flu medications. A conglomerate may operate in several consumer markets, each with different characteristics. In addition, a company is exposed to different risks in each of the markets in which it acquires its production factors. Consolidated statements present all of these heterogeneous factors in a single-entity context. The purpose of segment reporting is to allow financial statement users to look behind the consolidated totals to the individual components that constitute the entity.

Advanced StudyGuide .com

Defining Reportable Segments[2]

The process of determining separately ***reportable operating segments,*** that is, segments for which separate supplemental disclosures must be made, is based on management's specification of those operating segments that are used internally for evaluating the enterprise's financial position and operating performance.

10 Percent Quantitative Thresholds

The FASB specified three ***10 percent significance rules*** to determine which of the operating segments shall have separately reported information. The separate disclosures are required for segments meeting at least one of the following tests:

1. The segment's revenue, including both external sales and intersegment sales or transfers, is 10 percent or more of the total revenues from external sales plus intersegment transactions of all operating segments.
2. The absolute value of the segment's profit or loss is 10 percent or more of the higher, in absolute value, of (*a*) the total profit of all operating segments that did not report a loss or (*b*) the total loss of all operating segments that did report a loss.
3. The segment's assets are 10 percent or more of the total assets of all operating segments.

Note that the revenue test includes intersegment sales or transfers. The FASB found that the full impact of a particular segment on the entire enterprise should be measured. Also, the FASB believed that the definition of an operating segment should include components of an enterprise that sell primarily or exclusively to other components of the enterprise. Information about these "vertically integrated" operations provides insight into the enterprise's production and operations.

FYI

Walmart reported the following operating segments in fiscal year 2014 (with sales in parentheses): Walmart U.S. ($279.4 billion), Walmart International ($136.5 billion), and Sam's Club ($57.2 billion). Clearly, the majority of the company's net sales come from Walmart US.

ASC 280 states that the segment disclosure should include the reportable segments' measures of profit or loss. Thus, the report should be the same as that used for internal decision-making purposes. Some companies allocate operating expenses arising from shared facilities such as a

[2] To view a video explanation of this topic, visit advancedstudyguide.com.

common warehouse. Other companies allocate items such as interest costs, income taxes, or income from equity investments to specific segments. Whatever is used for internal decision-making purposes to measure the operating segment's profit or loss should be reported in the external disclosure.

Although an enterprise is required to report the assets of the separately reportable operating segments, **ASC 280** also allows companies to report their segments' liabilities if the company finds that the fuller disclosure would be meaningful. The assets to be reported are those used by the chief operating decision maker in making decisions about the segment and might include intangible assets such as goodwill or other intangibles. If commonly used assets are allocated to the segments, then these should be included in the reported amounts. The assets also might include financing items such as investments in equity securities or intersegment loans. The key point is that the revenues, profit or loss, and assets should be reported on the same basis as used for internal decision-making purposes.

If the total external revenue of the separately reportable operating segments is less than 75 percent of the total consolidated revenue, then management must select and disclose information about additional operating segments until at least 75 percent of consolidated revenue is included in reportable segments. The choice of which additional operating segments to report is left to management.

Information about the operating segments that are not separately reportable is combined and disclosed in the "All Other" category. The sources of the revenue in the All Other category must be described, but the level of disclosure for this category is significantly less than for the separately reportable segments. Again, note that the corporate headquarters (or corporate administration) is not typically included as an operating segment of an enterprise.

Illustration of 10 Percent Tests

Peerless Products Corporation

Special Foods Inc.

See Figure 13–1 for the consolidated financial statements for Peerless Products Corporation and Special Foods Inc. Assume the following information for this example:

1. Peerless owns 80 percent of Special Foods' common stock. Special Foods reports a profit of $50,000 for 20X1 and pays dividends of $30,000. The December 31, 20X1, balances in Special Foods' stockholders' equity accounts total $300,000, of which the noncontrolling interest is 20 percent.
2. Peerless acquires 40 percent of Barclay Company stock on January 1, 20X1, for a cost of $160,000, which is equal to the stock's book value on that date. The equity method is used to account for this investment. Barclay earns $80,000 in profit during 20X1 and pays $20,000 in dividends. This investment is managed by the corporate office and is not assigned to any operating segment.

Segment disclosure provides a breakdown of the consolidated totals into their constituent parts. The items that appear in the consolidated statements and must be disaggregated are sales of $572,000 and total assets of $1,450,000. In the segment analysis, segment profit is also used; however, this figure is not usually presented directly on the consolidated income statement and is computed separately.

Figure 13–2 is a worksheet used to perform the disaggregation from the consolidated totals into the various operating segments. It also includes additional data necessary for preparing the annual report footnote disclosure presented later in this chapter.

Additional information for this illustration is as follows:

1. The consolidated entity of Peerless Products and Special Foods comprises five different operating segments as well as a central corporate administration. The operating segments are defined by management as Food Products, Plastic and Packaging, Consumer and Commercial, Health and Scientific, and Chemicals.
2. On January 1, 20X1, the Food Products segment of Special Foods issues a $100,000, 12 percent note payable to the Plastic and Packaging segment of Peerless Products. The intercompany interest is $12,000 for the year and is properly eliminated from the consolidated statements.

FIGURE 13–1
Consolidated Financial Statements for Peerless Products Corporation and Subsidiary

PEERLESS PRODUCTS CORPORATION AND SUBSIDIARY
Consolidated Statement of Income and Retained Earnings
Year Ended December 31, 20X1

Revenues:	
Sales	$572,000
Income from Investment in Barclay	32,000
Expenses and Deductions:	
Cost of Goods Sold	(267,000)
Depreciation & Amortization	(70,000)
Other Expenses	(15,000)
Interest Expense	(30,000)
Income to Noncontrolling Interest	(10,000)
Income Taxes	(62,000)
Net Income	$150,000
Retained Earnings, January 1	300,000
Less: Dividends	(60,000)
Retained Earnings, December 31	$390,000

PEERLESS PRODUCTS CORPORATION AND SUBSIDIARY
Consolidated Balance Sheet
December 31, 20X1

Cash		$ 131,000
Accounts Receivable		125,000
Inventory		165,000
Investment in Barclay Stock		184,000
Land		215,000
Building & Equipment	$1,400,000	
Less: Accumulated Depreciation	(770,000)	630,000
Total Assets		$1,450,000
Accounts Payable		$ 200,000
Bonds Payable		300,000
Noncontrolling Interest		60,000
Common Stock		500,000
Retained Earnings		390,000
Total Liabilities & Stockholders' Equity		$1,450,000

3. Each operating segment makes sales to unaffiliated customers. In addition, $28,000 of intersegment sales are made during the year by the Food Products, the Plastic and Packaging, and the Consumer and Commercial segments. The cost of these intersegment sales is $18,000. These goods are still in the ending inventories of the purchasing operating segments, and the unrealized inventory profit of $10,000 must be eliminated from both cost of goods sold and inventories in preparing the consolidated financials. Specific revenue information is presented in Figure 13–2.
4. Figure 13–2 also includes the profit and loss information for each segment as it is defined by the entity. The entity uses a concept it terms "controllable earnings" to measure segment performance. As the company defines it, controllable earnings include interest revenue and interest expense in the entity's definition of segment profit or loss. Therefore, interest is reported on a segment basis. Depreciation is separately reported because if depreciation, depletion, or amortization expenses are included in the measure of segment profit or loss, **ASC 280** requires that these cost elements be disclosed separately to provide information to financial statement users to approximate the cash flow for each segment.
5. The company acquires a computer costing $30,000 during the year. The computer is used for production scheduling and control and is depreciated using the straight-line method over a three-year period ($30,000 ÷ 3 years = $10,000 per year). The computer's annual depreciation expense is allocated based on use as monitored by the computer. Figure 13–2 presents these allocated costs below the other costs for each operating segment.

FIGURE 13–2 Worksheet to Analyze Peerless Products and Subsidiary's Operating Segments

PEERLESS PRODUCTS CORPORATION AND SPECIAL FOODS INC.
Segmental Disclosure Worksheet

Item	Operating Segments								
	Food Products	Plastic and Packaging	Consumer and Commercial	Health and Scientific	Chemicals	Corporate Administration	Combined	Intersegment Eliminations	Consolidated
Revenue:									
Sales to unaffiliated customers	317,000	95,000	41,000	86,000	33,000		572,000		572,000
Intersegment sales	6,000	18,000	4,000	—	—	—	28,000	(28,000)	—
Total revenue	323,000	113,000	45,000	86,000	33,000		600,000	(28,000)	572,000
Profit:									
Directly traceable operating costs	(103,000)	(31,000)	(63,000)	(55,000)	(37,000)		(289,000)	18,000	(271,000)
Depreciation of segment's assets	(7,000)	(4,000)	(5,000)	(6,000)	(4,000)		(26,000)		(26,000)
Allocated depreciation	(3,000)	(1,000)	(2,000)	(3,000)	(1,000)		(10,000)		(10,000)
Other items:									
Interest revenue—intersegment		12,000					12,000	(12,000)	
Interest expense—to unaffiliates		(30,000)					(30,000)		(30,000)
Interest expense—intersegment	(12,000)	—	—	—	—	—	(12,000)	12,000	—
Segment profit (loss)	198,000	59,000	(25,000)	22,000	(9,000)		245,000	(10,000)	235,000
General corporate expenses						(45,000)	(45,000)		(45,000)
Income from equity investment	—	—	—	—	—	32,000	32,000	—	32,000
Income from continuing operations, before taxes	198,000	59,000	(25,000)	22,000	(9,000)	(13,000)	232,000	(10,000)	222,000
Assets:									
Operating segments:									
Segment (other than intersegment)	411,000	275,000	100,000	310,000	80,000		1,176,000	(10,000)	1,166,000
Intersegment notes	—	100,000	—	—	—	—	100,000	(100,000)	—
Total of operating segments	411,000	375,000	100,000	310,000	80,000		1,276,000	(110,000)	1,166,000
General corporate						100,000	100,000		100,000
Equity investments						184,000	184,000		184,000
Total assets	411,000	375,000	100,000	310,000	80,000	284,000	1,560,000	(110,000)	1,450,000
Total expenditures made during year for long-term assets	48,000	21,000	10,000	29,000	12,000		120,000		

6. The intersegment interest expense from the intercompany note is attributable to the Food Products segment, and the intercompany interest income is earned by the Plastic and Packaging segment.
7. The company's policy on determining segment performance does not include income from the investment in any of its operating segment's profit or loss. Rather, this item is assigned to corporate administration. This information is collected in the worksheet to reconcile the consolidated totals.
8. The assets section of Figure 13–2 presents the assets for the operating segments as well as for the corporate administration center. Included in the segments' assets is an allocation of the production computer's $20,000 book value ($30,000 less $10,000 of accumulated depreciation). Note also that the intersegment notes are assigned to a specific segment for internal decision-making purposes, but these notes are eliminated in the preparation of the consolidated financials.

We next present each of Peerless Products' specific significance tests.

Advanced StudyGuide .com

10 Percent Revenue Test The first 10 percent test is applied to each operating segment's total revenue as a percentage of the combined revenue of all segments before elimination of intersegment transfers and sales. If an operating segment's total revenue is 10 percent or more of the combined revenue of all segments, then the segment is separately reportable, and supplementary disclosures must be provided for it in the annual report.

The 10 percent revenue tests are applied as follows:

Segment	Segment Revenue	Percent of Combined Revenue of $600,000	Reportable Segment
Food Products	$323,000	53.8%	Yes
Plastic and Packaging	113,000	18.8	Yes
Consumer and Commercial	45,000	7.5	No
Health and Scientific	86,000	14.3	Yes
Chemicals	33,000	5.5	No
Total	$600,000	100.0%*	

Unrounded percents for segments total to 100 percent.

The revenue test shows that the following operating segments are separately reportable: Food Products, Plastic and Packaging, and Health and Scientific. A common shortcut is to compute 10 percent of the denominator of the test (for Peerless and its subsidiary, $600,000 × 0.10) and then compare each segment's total revenue with that fraction. In this case, reportable segments are those with $60,000 or more in total revenue.

10 Percent Profit (Loss) Test The profit or loss test is the second test to determine which operating segments are separately reportable. The test is to determine whether a segment's profit or loss is equal to or more than 10 percent of the absolute value of either the combined operating profits or the combined operating losses of the segments, whichever is higher.

Because two segments had operating losses for the year, we present two separate tabulations as follows:

Segment	Segment Profits	Segment Losses
Food Products	$198,000	
Plastic and Packaging	59,000	
Consumer and Commercial		$(25,000)
Health and Scientific	22,000	
Chemicals		(9,000)
Total	$279,000	$(34,000)

The higher absolute total is the $279,000 of profits. This amount becomes the denominator for the 10 percent operating profit or loss test. Because this test is based on absolute amounts, all numbers are treated as positive numbers. The test data follow:

Segment	Profit (Loss)	Percent of Test Amount of $279,000	Separately Reportable
Food Products	$198,000	71.0%	Yes
Plastic and Packaging	59,000	21.1	Yes
Consumer and Commercial	(25,000)	9.0	No
Health and Scientific	22,000	7.9	No
Chemicals	(9,000)	3.2	No

The Food Products and Plastic and Packaging segments are separately reportable using the profit or loss test.

Advanced StudyGuide .com

10 Percent Assets Test The last of the tests to determine whether a segment is separately reportable is the 10 percent assets test. Note that management defines the items composing each segment's assets as used for internal decision-making purposes. Management may include intangibles, receivables, and even intercompany items as defined by management. Assume that Peerless' management defines the segment assets to include intercompany items such as the intercompany notes. Recognize that it really is up to management to define what is, and what is not, included in each of the definitions of segment profit or loss and the segment assets.

The combined assets of all operating segments ($1,276,000) are used for this test. The difference of $110,000 between the combined assets of the operating segments ($1,276,000) and the amount included ($1,166,000) in the consolidated assets is due to (1) the $10,000 unrealized intercompany profit from intersegment inventory transactions that has not been realized in sales to third parties and (2) the $100,000 of intersegment notes. These intercompany amounts must be eliminated in the consolidation process.

The 10 percent significance rule is applied to segment assets as follows:

Segment	Assets	Percent of Test Amount of $1,276,000	Separately Reportable
Food Products	$ 411,000	32.2%	Yes
Plastic and Packaging	375,000	29.4	Yes
Consumer and Commercial	100,000	7.8	No
Health and Scientific	310,000	24.3	Yes
Chemicals	80,000	6.3	No
Total	$1,276,000	100.0%	

The Food Products, Plastic and Packaging, and Health and Scientific operating segments are separately reportable using the 10 percent assets test; that is, their assets are equal to or more than 10 percent of the combined assets of the operating segments ($127,600 = $1,276,000 × 0.10).

FYI

GE is one of the most diversified companies in the world. It reports segment information from these segments: Power & Water, Oil & Gas, Energy Management, Aviation, Healthcare, Transportation, Appliance & Lighting, and GE Capital. GE Capital had the highest revenue ($44.1 billion) in 2013.

Figure 13–3 is a summary of the results of the three tests. Recall that a segment is separately reportable if it meets any one of the three 10 percent tests. The following segments are separately reportable under the three tests: Food Products, Plastic and Packaging, and Health and Scientific. The remaining segments, Consumer and Commercial and Chemicals, are not separately

FIGURE 13–3
Summary of Reportable Industry Segments: 10 Percent Tests

	Food Products	Plastic and Packaging	Consumer and Commercial	Health and Scientific	Chemicals
Revenue test	Yes	Yes	No	Yes	No
Operating profit (loss) test	Yes	Yes	No	No	No
Assets test	Yes	Yes	No	Yes	No

reportable under any of the three tests. Specific segment information must therefore be reported in the annual report for the three separately reportable segments, and summary information for the remaining two nonreportable segments must be combined under the heading "All Other."

Comprehensive Disclosure Test

After determining which of the segments is reportable under any of the three 10 percent tests, the company must apply a comprehensive test. The comprehensive test is the ***75 percent consolidated revenue test.***

75 Percent Consolidated Revenue Test

The total revenue from external sources by all separately reportable operating segments must equal at least 75 percent of the total consolidated revenue. The reporting company must identify additional operating segments as reportable until this test is met. Peerless Products and Special Foods, with three reportable segments, compute the 75 percent test as follows:

Sales to unaffiliated customers by reportable segments:		
Food Products	$317,000	
Plastic and Packaging	95,000	
Health and Scientific	86,000	
Total of reportable segments		$498,000
Consolidated revenue		$572,000
Reportable segments' percentage of consolidated revenue ($498,000 ÷ $572,000)		87.1%

Because this percentage is equal to or higher than 75 percent, no further operating segments must be separately reported. Had the percentage been less than 75 percent, additional individual operating segments would have been required to be treated as reportable until the 75 percent test was met.

STOP & THINK

What sales number is appropriate here? The comprehensive disclosure test uses only sales to unaffiliated customers in contrast to the test for determining reportable operating segments, which uses all sales (both external and intersegment sales).

Other Considerations

For practicality, about 10 is used as an upper limit on the number of reportable segments because more than that number can make the supplemental information overly detailed. A company having more than about 10 reportable segments should consider aggregating the most closely related segments. Peerless Products and Special Foods have just three reportable segments.

In addition, companies must exercise judgment to determine the individual segments to be reported. For example, a segment may meet or fail a specific test because of some unusual situation, such as an abnormally high profit or loss on a one-time contract. The concept of interperiod comparability should be followed in deciding whether the segment should be disclosed in the current period. Companies should separately report segments that have been reported in prior years but fail the current period's significance tests because of abnormal occurrences. Similarly, companies need not separately report a segment that has met a 10 percent test on a one-time basis only because of abnormal circumstances. A company is required, however, to indicate why a reportable segment is not disclosed.

Finally, if a segment becomes reportable in the current period that was not reported separately in earlier periods, the prior-years comparative segment disclosures, which are included in the current year's annual report, should be restated to obtain comparability of financial data.

Reporting Segment Information

ASC 280 defines the specific disclosures required for each reportable segment. In segment reporting, the following quantitative and descriptive information must be disclosed for *each* segment determined to be separately reportable:

1. *General information.* Information must be disclosed regarding (*a*) how the company identifies each separately reportable segment, including information about the company's organizational structure (i.e., whether the company organizes along product lines, geographic areas, or some other factor), and (*b*) the types of products or services from which each reportable segment earns its revenues.
2. *Amounts for each separately reportable segment.* Segment disclosures must include amounts for (*a*) each segment's profit or loss and the measurement procedures used to determine the profit or loss, including how the company accounts for intersegment transactions, and (*b*) each segment's assets.
3. *Measures of segment profit or loss.* Each of the following must be disclosed if the company's chief operating decision maker reviews it to measure the segment profit or loss: (*a*) revenues from external sales, (*b*) revenues from transactions with other operating segments of the company, (*c*) interest revenue, (*d*) interest expense, (*e*) depreciation and amortization expense, (*f*) equity in the income of investees accounted for by the equity method, (*g*) income tax expense or benefit, (*h*) extraordinary items, and (*i*) other significant noncash items.
4. *Segment assets.* The following information on each separately reportable segment's assets must be disclosed if the company's chief operating decision maker includes it in computing: (*a*) the amount of investment in equity-method investees and (*b*) the total expenditures for increases to long-term productive assets through the capital budget because these expenditures often indicate which segments the company is building for the future.
5. *Reconciliations to consolidated totals.* Finally, the segment disclosures must include reconciliations between the reportable segments' total revenues, total profits or losses, and total assets and the related consolidated totals for those items. If the company decides to disclose liabilities for each reportable segment, a reconciliation required also is between the reportable segments' total liabilities and the consolidated total liabilities.

Companies are allowed to present these disclosures in separate schedules or in the footnotes. Most companies present footnote disclosures with accompanying schedules. An example of a commonly used disclosure format is presented in Figure 13–4 for Peerless Products and Special Foods. The figure presents only the current year's data for the operating segments used in the example. In practice, however, companies provide comparative data for each of the three fiscal years ending on the balance sheet date.

ASC 280 specifies that segment disclosures also must be made in interim statements such as the quarterly financial statements. The interim reports must disclose the following about each reportable segment: (1) revenues from external customers, (2) intersegment revenues, (3) a measure of segment profit or loss, (4) total assets for which there has been a material change from the most recent annual report, (5) any differences from the most recent annual report in the definition of operating segments or in how segment profit or loss is computed, and (6) a reconciliation of the total of segment profit or loss to the entity's consolidated totals.

FIGURE 13–4 Required Footnote Disclosures for Peerless Products Corporation and Subsidiary's Operating Segments

Footnote X
Information about the Company's Operations in Different Operating Segments

	Operating Segments				
Item	Food Products	Plastic and Packaging	Health and Scientific	All Others	Combined
Revenue to unaffiliated customers	317,000	95,000	86,000	74,000	572,000
Intersegment revenue	6,000	18,000		4,000	28,000
Interest revenue—intersegment		12,000			12,000
Interest expense—unaffiliated		30,000			30,000
Interest expense—intersegment	12,000				12,000
Depreciation	10,000	5,000	9,000	12,000	36,000
Segment profit (loss)	198,000	59,000	22,000	(34,000)	245,000
Segment assets	411,000	375,000	310,000	180,000	1,276,000
Expenditures for segment assets	48,000	21,000	29,000	22,000	120,000

Reconciliation of reportable segment revenue to consolidated revenue	
Total revenues for reportable segments	$ 522,000
Other revenues	78,000
Elimination of intersegment revenues	(28,000)
Total consolidated revenues	$ 572,000
Reconciliation of reportable segment profit and loss to consolidated profit or loss	
Total profit and loss for reportable segments	$ 279,000
Other profits or loss	(34,000)
Elimination of intersegment profit	(10,000)
General corporate expense	(45,000)
Income from equity investment	32,000
Income before income taxes and extraordinary items	$ 222,000
Reconciliation of reportable segment assets to consolidated assets	
Total assets for reportable segments	$1,096,000
Other assets	180,000
Elimination of intersegment profits in assets	(10,000)
Intersegment notes	(100,000)
General corporate assets	100,000
Equity investments	184,000
Consolidated total assets	$1,450,000

ENTERPRISEWIDE DISCLOSURES

LO 13-3

Understand the requirements for enterprisewide disclosures.

The focus in **ASC 280** is to provide financial statement users information by which they may determine an entity's risks and potential returns applying the same basis of information aggregation as the company's management used. Certainly, the risks of doing business in one country may be quite different from the risks of doing business in another country. Today's large multinational entities have operations in many countries and foreign markets. In addition, a company that obtains a significant percentage of its revenue from just one customer has a different risk profile than a company that has many smaller customers. Thus, **ASC 280** established what it termed ***enterprisewide disclosure*** standards to provide users more information about the company's risks. These enterprisewide disclosures are typically made in a footnote to the financial statements.

Information about Products and Services

Three categories of required information are included under enterprisewide disclosures. The first is that the company is required to report the revenues from external customers for each major product and service or each group of similar products and services unless doing so is impracticable. The reason for this requirement is that the company may have organized its operating segments on a basis different from the organization of its product lines. However, if the company does establish its operating segments by product line, then the segment disclosures discussed earlier in this chapter meet this first, enterprisewide disclosure requirement.

Information about Geographic Areas

The second category is information about the geographic areas in which the company operates. The company must report the following unless doing so is impracticable:

1. Revenues from external customers attributed to the company's home country of domicile (the United States for U.S. firms) and the revenue from external customers attributed to all foreign countries in which the enterprise generates revenues. If revenues from external customers generated in an individual country are material, then that country's revenues also must be separately disclosed.
2. Long-lived productive assets located in the entity's home country and the total assets located in all foreign countries in which the entity holds assets. As with revenue, if assets in an individual country are material, then that country's assets must also be separately disclosed.

ASC 280-50-41 excludes financial instruments, long-term customer relationships of a financial institution, mortgage and other servicing rights, deferred policy acquisition costs, and certain deferred tax assets from long-term assets. The FASB believes that companies typically maintain accounting records on a country-by-country basis because of the political, economic, and other specific factors that differ across countries. Thus, if the company generates a material amount of revenue in a specific country or has made a material long-lived asset investment in a specific country, this information should be readily available for management to include in the enterprisewide disclosures. Although **ASC 280** specified no materiality threshold for specific country disclosures, the 10 percent guideline for disaggregated disclosures seems to have gained acceptance.

Note that the revenues for the geographic information are those only to unaffiliated, external customers. Intersegment revenues are not included. The assets for the geographic information are only long-lived, productive assets and exclude current assets and several types of noncurrent assets as noted above. All companies must disclose domestic versus total foreign revenues and long-lived assets unless doing so is impracticable. For purposes of the following disclosure, assume that $840,000 of the total consolidated assets of $1,450,000 are determined to be long-lived, productive assets meeting the specifications of **ASC 280-50-41.** Separate country disclosures would be provided for material amounts. Assume that Peerless uses a 10 percent materiality threshold for assessing its foreign operations. Therefore, separate disclosure is presented for any country having more than or equal to 10 percent of the consolidated revenue or the total long-lived assets. An example of the footnote disclosure that Peerless Products could make follows:

Geographic Information

	Revenue	Long-Lived Asset
United States	$380,000	$471,000
Total foreign	192,000	369,000
Total	$572,000	$840,000
Significant countries:		
Canada	$116,000	$220,000
Mexico	28,000	102,000

The company also must disclose the basis for attributing revenues from external customers to the individual countries. For example, one method may be to assign revenues based on the customer's location.

Information about Major Customers

The third and final category of enterprisewide disclosures required by **ASC 280** is information about major customers. An important issue is how to define an individual customer. For applying the disclosure test, each of the following is considered to be an individual customer: any single customer (including a group of customers or companies under common control), the federal government, a state government, a local government, or a foreign government. Materiality is not defined for this disclosure, but again, the 10 percent guideline seems to have gained the support of practice. The disclosures include the amount of revenue from each significant customer and the identity of the segment or segments reporting the revenues. The names of the individual customers need not be disclosed. The following is an example of the type of footnote disclosure that Peerless Products could use:

> Revenues from one customer of the Food Products segment represent approximately $64,000 of the company's consolidated revenues.

This concludes the discussion of segment reporting. The remainder of the chapter presents another major area of financial disclosure: interim financial reporting.

INTERIM FINANCIAL REPORTING

LO 13-4

Understand the rules for interim financial reporting.

Interim reports, which cover a time period of less than one year, provide timely information on the entity's operating progress throughout the year. Interim reports can be for a week, a month, a quarter, or several quarters. Many companies prepare monthly financial statements for internal management purposes. Publicly held companies are required to publish quarterly reports, and the rapid stock market reaction to the public release of quarterly information indicates that investors and other financial statement users look closely at these reports. The quarterly report is, in many ways, a smaller version of the annual report. It includes an abbreviated income statement, balance sheet, statement of cash flows, and selected footnotes and other disclosures for the quarter being reported, as well as comparative data for prior quarters.

Form 10-Q is the SEC's quarterly report and, for most companies, this quarterly report must be filed within 35 days after the end of each of the first three quarters. The annual report may be used in place of the interim report for the fourth quarter. The 35-day requirement is for publicly owned companies classified as "accelerated filers," which are companies with at least $75 million in aggregate market value that have been subject to the periodic and annual reporting requirements for at least one year, including the filing of at least one annual report. Most companies traded on the major stock exchanges are in the accelerated filers category. Those companies not meeting the accelerated filers criteria have 45 days after the end of each of the first three quarters to file their quarterly reports.

The SEC does not require quarterly financial statements to be audited, but selected quarterly financial data must be reported in a footnote in the annual financial report. This annual disclosure requirement means that the independent registered public accounting firm performing the company's annual audit must review the company's quarterly reports made during the fiscal year and note any errors or restatements. Because of the wide use of interim reports, including monthly and quarterly reports, accountants must be aware of the principles and procedures used in preparing these reports.

THE FORMAT OF THE QUARTERLY FINANCIAL REPORT

Quarterly financial reports generally contain the following items:

1. An income statement for the most recent quarter of the current fiscal period and a comparative income statement for the same quarter for the prior fiscal year.
2. Income statements for the cumulative year-to-date time period and for the corresponding period of the prior fiscal year.

3. A condensed balance sheet at the end of the current quarter and a condensed balance sheet at the end of the prior fiscal year. However, companies should include the balance sheet as of the end of the corresponding interim period of the previous year if it is necessary for an understanding of the impact of seasonal fluctuations on the company's financial condition.
4. A statement of cash flows as of the end of the current cumulative year-to-date period and for the same time span for the prior year.
5. Footnotes that update those in the last annual report. These interim footnotes include summaries of material changes in measurement or major economic events that have occurred since the end of the most recent fiscal year.
6. A report by management analyzing and discussing the results for the latest interim period.

ACCOUNTING ISSUES

Interim reporting presents accountants several technical and conceptual measurement issues. Most of these center on the accounting concept of periodicity and the division of the annual period into interim periods. Note that interim reporting includes financial statements for any period less than one year, including monthly reports, quarterly reports, or any other portion of an annual period.

The use of quarterly reports to provide timely information is a fairly recent development. Many firms began publishing quarterly reports voluntarily in the late 1940s. These early reports raised substantive accounting issues because no standards existed to guide their presentation. Some firms' first three quarterly reports suggested a significant profit for the year and then arbitrary and questionable fourth-quarter adjustments reconciled to an actual loss for the year. The lack of established guidelines led to experimentation with a variety of cost allocations among periods, resulting in unrealistic patterns of quarterly income. It was not until 1973 that guidelines were finally standardized (**ASC 270**).

Accounting Pronouncements on Interim Reporting

ASC 270 standardized the preparation and reporting of interim income statements. The standard defines the income elements and the measurement of costs on an interim basis. The standard also provides guidance for the annual report footnote summarizing the published interim disclosures and explaining any adjustments required to make the interim figures total the annual figures. This conformance to the annual report increases the reliability of the published interim statements and brings interim reporting under the view of the external auditors who review the footnotes in the annual report as part of the audit.

ASC 250 specifies that a change in an accounting principle made in an interim period is reported using the retrospective application to the prechange interim periods for the direct effects of the change. The financial statements for the earliest period presented, either annual or interim, are adjusted for the effects of the change at that point in time and all subsequent financial statements, again both annual and interim, are adjusted for the newly adopted accounting principle. A change in estimate in an interim period is reported currently and prospectively, and no prior periods are restated. A change in entity in an interim period requires retrospective application.

ASC 740 tackles the difficult problem of measuring the tax provision for interim reports when the actual tax expense is based on annual income. The interpretation allows estimates and judgments in order to obtain a reasonable relationship between the reported interim operating income and the related income tax provision. Examples of accounting for taxes in interim statements are presented later in this chapter.

International Financial Reporting Standards for Interim Reporting

The minimum content for an interim financial report to be in accordance with IFRS is defined in **International Accounting Standard 34,** "Interim Financial Reporting" (IAS 34). The international standards for interims are very similar to those of U.S. GAAP and explicitly recognize that more estimates may be used in determining interim amounts than for measurements of annual financial data. Materiality tests for interim reporting are made based on the relation to the interim period data, not on an estimate of annual data. **IAS 34** requires year-to-date disclosures in addition to the specific interim period disclosures, just as required by U.S. GAAP.

REPORTING STANDARDS FOR INTERIM INCOME STATEMENTS

The form of the interim income statement is the same as the form of the annual income statement. Some differences exist in the measurement of specific components of income because of the shorter time period. In general, the accounting standards used for interim statements are the same as those used for the annual statements, although **ASC 270 and ASC 740** provide an abundance of technical assistance to measure and report on an interim basis. Figure 13–5 presents an overview of the major accounting principles used for the interim income statement. The technical requirements relevant to interim reporting are discussed in the following sections.

Revenue

One of the most significant elements of the interim income statement is revenue from sales. Investors wish to assess the entity's revenue-generating capability, so they compare revenue of the current interim period with revenue of the corresponding interim period of the prior year. The measurement basis used to determine revenue earned in an interim period should be the same as that used for the full fiscal year.

FIGURE 13–5 Overview of Interim Income Statement Accounting Principles

Revenue	Recognize as earned during an interim period on same basis as used for annual reporting.
Cost of goods sold	Product costs for interim period recognized on same basis as used for annual reporting, except: • Estimated gross profit rates may be used to determine interim cost of goods sold. • Temporary liquidations of LIFO-based inventories are charged to cost of goods sold using expected replacement cost of the items. • Lower-of-cost-or-market valuation method allows for loss recoveries for increases in market prices in later interim periods of the same fiscal year. • Standard cost systems should use the same procedures as for annual reporting except that price variances or volume or capacity variances expected to be absorbed by end of the year should be deferred.
All other costs and expenses	Expense as incurred or allocated among interim periods' expenses based on benefits received or other systematic and rational basis.
Income taxes	Based on estimated annual effective tax rate with recognition of tax benefits of an operating loss if benefits are assured beyond a reasonable doubt; second and subsequent quarters are based on changes in cumulative amount of tax computed, including changes in estimates.
Disposal of a component of the entity, or extraordinary, unusual, infrequently occurring, and contingent items	Recognize in interim period in which they occur.
Accounting changes:	
1. Change in accounting principle	Retrospective application to all prechange interim periods reported.
2. Change in an accounting estimate	Apply to current and prospective interim periods only.
3. Change in a reporting entity	Retrospective application to all prechange interim periods reported.

Thus, revenue must be recognized and reported in the period in which it is earned and cannot be deferred to other periods to present a more stable revenue stream. Revenue from seasonal businesses, such as in agriculture, food products, wholesale or retail outlets, and amusements, cannot be manipulated to eliminate seasonal trends.

Businesses that experience material seasonal variations in their revenue are encouraged to supplement their interim reports with information for 12-month periods ending at the interim date for the current and preceding years. Such disclosures reduce the possibility that users of the reports might make unwarranted inferences about the annual results from an interim report with material seasonal variation.

Cost of Goods Sold and Inventory

Cost of goods sold is generally the largest single expense on the interim income statement. A general rule is that interim cost of goods sold should be computed with the direct and allocated cost elements on the same basis as used to compute the annual cost of goods sold. However, **ASC 270** and **ASC 740** permit the following practical modifications to this general rule:

1. *Use estimated gross profit rates.* Estimated gross profit rates may be used to compute the interim cost of goods sold. Thus, a physical inventory count does not need to be made in each interim period.
2. *LIFO temporary liquidations.* Due to seasonality and other factors, companies using the LIFO method of inventory valuation sometimes have temporary liquidations of the LIFO-based inventory during one or more interim periods. These temporary liquidations are expected to be replenished by the end of the fiscal year. In these cases, the interim cost of goods sold is charged for the expected replacement cost of the liquidated inventory, not the LIFO historical cost of the inventory. If, by the end of the year, the LIFO inventory base is not replaced, then the liquidated inventory is charged to cost of goods sold at its LIFO cost base.
3. *Lower-of-cost-or-market valuations.* Inventory losses from decreases in market value below cost are recognized in the period of the decline. Recoveries of market price in subsequent interim periods should be recognized in the period of recovery as recoveries of losses that were recognized in prior interim periods of that fiscal year. No gains are recognized for increases of market value above cost. Temporary market price declines that are expected to be reversed by the end of the fiscal year do not have to be recognized in the interim period because no loss is expected for the full fiscal year.
4. *Standard cost systems.* Manufacturers that use standard cost systems to compute cost of goods sold and ending inventory should use the same procedures for determining variances for an interim period as are used for the fiscal year. However, variances that are anticipated to be absorbed by the end of the fiscal year are usually not included in computing interim income.

Illustration of Temporary LIFO Liquidation

Advanced StudyGuide .com

The reason that the interim treatment of LIFO inventory liquidations differs from the annual treatment of LIFO liquidations is that the inventory is often likely to be replaced by the end of the fiscal year. Interim income for the period of the temporary liquidation would be overstated if cost of goods sold were charged with the lower LIFO inventory costs in a time of rising prices. The following example illustrates this point:

1. During the third quarter of its fiscal year, Special Foods experienced a temporary liquidation of 2,000 units in its LIFO base owing to seasonal fluctuations. The LIFO unit cost is $25. The liquidation is normal, and the company plans to replace the liquidated inventory during the early part of the next (fourth) interim period.
2. The estimated replacement cost of the inventory is $35 per unit.

The entry in the third interim period to account for the temporary inventory liquidation is

(1)			
	Cost of Goods Sold	70,000	
	Inventory		50,000
	Excess of Replacement Cost over LIFO Cost of Inventory Liquidated		20,000

Record temporary LIFO inventory liquidation:
$70,000 = 2,000 units × $35
$50,000 = 2,000 units × $25 LIFO cost.

The interim income statement presents cost of goods sold at the expected replacement cost. The Excess of Replacement Cost over LIFO Cost of Inventory Liquidated should be shown as a current liability on the interim balance sheet, although some accountants net this against the inventory reported on the interim balance sheet.

When the inventory is replaced at $36 per unit during the fourth quarter, the following entry is made:

(2)			
	Cost of Goods Sold	2,000	
	Inventory	50,000	
	Excess of Replacement Cost over LIFO Cost of Inventory Liquidated	20,000	
	Accounts Payable		72,000

Record replacement of LIFO inventory liquidation:
$50,000 = 2,000 × $25 LIFO cost
$72,000 = 2,000 × $36.

The actual replacement price of $36 is different from the estimated replacement price of $35. The difference is an adjustment to cost of goods sold in the replacement period. The third quarter's interim report is not retroactively restated. If the liquidated inventory is not replaced by the end of the fiscal year, the liability account is written off to Cost of Goods Sold, decreasing the reported annual cost of goods sold to its correct amount.

Illustration of Market Write-Down and Recovery

Advanced StudyGuide .com

The following example illustrates the use of the lower-of-cost-or-market (LCM) method for interim reports:

1. At the beginning of its fiscal year, Peerless Products has 10,000 units of inventory on hand with a FIFO cost of $10 each.
2. It makes no additional purchases during the year.
3. The sales and market values at the end of each quarter during the fiscal year are as follows:

Peerless Products Corporation

Quarter	Units Sold in Quarter	Unit Market Values at End of Quarter
1	2,000	$ 7
2	2,000	6
3	2,000	7
4	2,000	11

Peerless considers the reductions in market value to be permanent; therefore, it recognizes the reductions in the quarters in which they occur. *No recognition is required* if the reductions are anticipated to be temporary with recovery by year-end.

Refer to Figure 13–6 for the calculations needed to adjust Peerless' inventory account to the lower of cost or market. At the end of the first quarter, the ending inventory of the quarter is written down by $24,000, and a loss is recognized on the interim income statement. Many companies report this write-down as part of their cost of goods sold because it is associated with inventory. By the end of the second quarter, a $6,000 write-down of

FIGURE 13–6
Interim Lower-of-Cost-or-Market Analysis of the Inventory Account of Peerless Products Corporation

Quarter	Item	Inventory Units	Inventory Unit Price	Inventory Dollars
	Balance, beginning of year	10,000	$10	$100,000
1	Inventory sold, first quarter	(2,000)	$10	(20,000)
	Adjustment to market: [8,000 units × ($10 − $7)]	8,000	(3)	(24,000)
	Balance, end of first quarter	8,000	$ 7	$ 56,000
2	Inventory sold, second quarter	(2,000)	$ 7	(14,000)
	Adjustment to market: [6,000 units × ($7 − $6)]	6,000	(1)	(6,000)
	Balance, end of second quarter	6,000	$ 6	$ 36,000
3	Inventory sold, third quarter	(2,000)	$ 6	(12,000)
	Market price recovery: [4,000 units × ($6 − $7)]	4,000	1	4,000
	Balance, end of third quarter	4,000	$ 7	$ 28,000
4	Inventory sold, fourth quarter	(2,000)	$ 7	(14,000)
	Market price recovery: [2,000 units × ($7 − $10)]	2,000	3	6,000
	Balance, end of fourth quarter	2,000	$10(*a*)	$ 20,000

(*a*) Note that although market value is $11, inventory valuation cannot exceed cost.

the ending inventory is required. The third-quarter interim report shows a loss recovery of $4,000 due to an increase in inventory replacement costs. Note that this is a recovery of valuation losses recognized in prior quarters. In quarter 4, the $11 market price is $1 higher than the initial cost of the inventory. A $6,000 loss recovery on the fourth-quarter ending inventory of the 2,000 units is recognized to bring the inventory valuation from $7 per unit to its original cost of $10 per unit. Note that the inventory may not be valued at an amount in excess of cost.

A graphical representation of the market prices during the year is presented in Figure 13–7. Note that after decreasing during the first two quarters, the market price increases during the third and fourth quarters. At year-end, the price is $11 per unit, which is above the initial cost for the inventory.

FIGURE 13–7
Graph of Market Prices of Inventory

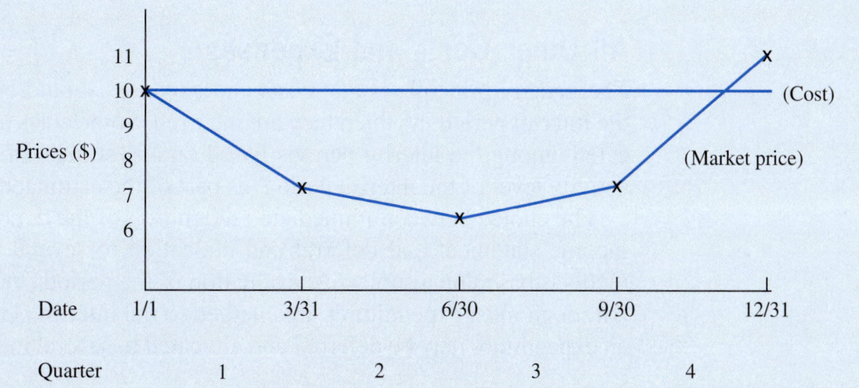

Another way to view the effects of the write-downs is to compute the amount that would be reported in each quarter's cost of goods sold that would include the costs assigned to the goods sold during the quarter plus the effects of any inventory write-downs and less the effects of any recoveries of losses recognized in prior interim periods. These market adjustments are normally treated as adjustments of cost of goods sold to represent all product costs in one location on the income statement. The following table shows the computation of cost of goods sold for each quarter:

Quarter	Costs Assigned to Goods Sold	Ending Inventory Write-Down to Market (or loss recovery)	Total
1	2,000 units × $10	8,000 units × $3	$44,000
2	2,000 units × $7	6,000 units × $1	20,000
3	2,000 units × $6	(4,000 units × $1)	8,000
4	2,000 units × $7	(2,000 units × $3)	8,000

If the reductions in market value in quarters 1 and 2 were considered temporary at the time, no write-downs would need to be recognized and therefore no loss recoveries would be recognized in quarters 3 and 4. The total of the cost of goods sold reported for the interims must reconcile to the amount reported on the annual financial statements. Note that the year-end market price ($11) is higher than the market price at the beginning of the year ($10). On the annual statement:

$$8{,}000 \text{ units} \times \$10 \text{ unit price} = \$80{,}000$$

On the interim statements:

Quarter 1	$44,000
Quarter 2	20,000
Quarter 3	8,000
Quarter 4	8,000
Total	$80,000

To be able to focus on the main points of the example, it was assumed that no additional inventory was acquired during the year. Of course, in actual practice, most companies make continuous inventory acquisitions. These purchases would be added to inventory at whatever cost flow method the company uses. The lower-of-cost-or-market valuation method would be applied at the end of each quarter in the same manner as in the example, and the losses or loss recoveries would be recognized.

All Other Costs and Expenses

The general principle is that costs and expenses should be charged to interim income in the interim period in which they are incurred. Some costs and expenses, however, are allocated among the interim periods based on an estimate of time used, benefit received, or activity level of the interim period, as part of the estimated amount for the full fiscal year.

The choice between immediate recognition of the expenditure on the interim period's income statement and deferral and allocation to several periods' interim income statements is based on a subjective evaluation of the periods that benefit from the expenditure. Although most expenditures are charged to the interim period in which they are incurred, an expenditure may be deferred and allocated to several interim periods as illustrated here:

1. Some companies concentrate their major equipment repairs in a plant shut-down time in one interim period. For interim reporting, these repair costs should be deferred (prepaid asset) or accrued (estimated liability) and allocated to repair expense in each of the interim periods that benefit from the repair costs.

2. Property taxes should be deferred or accrued in each interim period rather than recognized fully as an expense of the interim period in which they are paid.
3. Major advertising campaign costs should be allocated to the interim periods that benefit from them rather than recognized solely in the interim period in which they are incurred. A typical allocation procedure is to estimate the anticipated sales volume for each of the interim periods that will benefit from the advertising campaign. Generally, the total advertising costs are expensed for determining annual income and no deferral is made beyond the fiscal year-end.

Note that a company can accrue probable and estimable costs in earlier interim periods than the period in which the cash is paid. For example, Peerless has a management policy of closing its main production plant each August for a two-week repairs period. On January 1, the company estimates that a total of $60,000 will be incurred for this plant rehabilitation effort and that it will benefit all four quarters of the year. The company will allocate this cost to each quarter, even the two quarters preceding the actual shutdown. In this case, an accrual for the repair expense will be made in the first and second quarters. When the actual cost is incurred in the third quarter, the accrual liability will be eliminated, but the repair expense will still be shown for each quarter. The remaining repair expense for the year will then be allocated to the third and fourth quarters. The key point is that the repair expense can be allocated to each quarter that benefits even though the cash flow for the item does not occur until later in the fiscal year. Accruals (estimated liabilities) and deferrals (prepaid assets) are used for these applications.

Illustration of Deferral and Allocation of Advertising Costs

On April 1, the beginning of the second quarter of Peerless Products and Subsidiary's consolidated fiscal year, a $20,000 cost was incurred for an advertising campaign expected to benefit the last three quarters of the current year. Consolidated sales for the second, third, and fourth quarters are expected to total $400,000. In this case, Peerless determined that the advertising campaign would not benefit the first quarter; therefore, no advertising expense was accrued in the first quarter ending March 31, and the only advertising expenditure during the year is the $20,000 incurred on April 1.

The $20,000 cost is recorded as a prepaid asset when incurred and then charged to Advertising Expense in each of the interim periods benefited, as shown in Figure 13–8. The allocation base selected is the quarterly sales in the periods benefited as a percentage of the estimated total sales for the period of benefit.

At the beginning of the third quarter (July 1), $15,000 of advertising cost remains in Prepaid Advertising. If actual quarterly sales differ from the estimated amounts, the allocation procedure is revised for the change in estimate. For example, if on September 30, management determines the consolidated sales for the third quarter, ending on September 30, to be $120,000 and estimates that fourth-quarter sales will be $180,000, then a portion of the remaining $15,000 balance in Prepaid Advertising is allocated to the third quarter as follows:

$$\$6{,}000 = \frac{\$120{,}000}{\$300{,}000} \times \$15{,}000$$

The fourth quarter is charged for any remaining balance in the Prepaid Advertising account.

FIGURE 13–8
Accounting for Advertising Costs That Benefit More than One Interim Period

Date	Quarterly Sales	Debit Advertising Expense	Credit Prepaid Advertising	Balance in Prepaid Advertising
April 1				$20,000
June 30	$100,000	$ 5,000(*a*)	$ 5,000	15,000(*b*)
September 30	100,000	5,000	5,000	10,000
December 31	200,000	10,000	10,000	0
Totals	$400,000	$20,000	$20,000	

(*a*) $5,000 = ($100,000/$400,000) × $20,000.
(*b*) $15,000 = $20,000 − $5,000.

Advanced StudyGuide .com

Accounting for Income Taxes in Interim Periods

The ***interim income tax*** computation poses a particularly troublesome problem for accountants because the actual tax burden is computed on income for the entire fiscal year. In addition, temporary differences between tax accounting and GAAP accounting require the recognition of deferred taxes. Nevertheless, the interim tax provision is a significant item and requires estimates and a number of subjective evaluations based on the anticipated annual tax. The first step is to determine the effective annual tax rate for use in computing the interim income tax provision.

Estimating the Effective Annual Tax Rate

Estimates are a normal part of the accounting cycle, and the interim income tax provision is based on an estimate of the effective annual tax rate on income from continuing operations. The estimated annual tax rate includes all anticipated tax credits, state income taxes, foreign income taxes, capital gains taxes, and other tax-planning efforts that are expected for the full fiscal period. The estimate is updated each interim period and the interim tax provision or benefit is then determined.

Items such as unusual or infrequent events, discontinued operations, and extraordinary items are not included in the estimate because the income statement reports these separately along with their related net-of-tax effects. Also, extraordinary items often have specific tax treatments that differ from those for operating income. For example, a fire loss of a building may involve depreciation recapture and other capital loss tax considerations.

Differences between Book and Tax Income There typically will be differences between the amount of operating income computed for financial statement (book) purposes and the operating income computed for tax purposes. **ASC 740** discusses two major categories of differences. The first category is most often referred to as "permanent" or nontemporary differences. Permanent differences are not included in determining the amount of taxable income for a period. Examples of these permanent differences include

1. Life insurance premiums paid by the company on executive policies for which the company is the beneficiary (not tax deductible).
2. Proceeds of life insurance collected (not taxable).
3. Dividends received deduction on dividends received from U.S. corporation stock investments (not taxable).
4. Interest income received on state or local government bonds classified as not taxable.
5. Certain types of fines or court penalties designated as not tax deductible.

These items are included in the determination of financial statement (book) income, but they are not included in the computation of taxable income. Thus, book income is adjusted for these items in order to determine the taxable income for the interim period.

The second category of differences is usually referred to as *temporary*. Temporary differences between the recognition of a transaction for book versus tax income result in deferred taxes. For example, a revenue may be recognized for tax either before or after the period in which it is recognized for book purposes. Or an expense may be recognized for tax purposes in a period other than the one used for book purposes. Examples of temporary differences include

1. Rent collected in advance (reported on tax return in period collected but as revenue on books in period earned).
2. Estimated expenses and losses (reported on books at time of accrual but on tax return in period paid).
3. Accelerated depreciation on tax return and straight-line depreciation on the income statement (difference of depreciation expense on books versus tax).
4. Revaluing inventory to lower of cost or market on financial statements (loss shown on books in period of write-down but on tax return in period sold).

The deferred tax asset or deferred tax liability created by these temporary differences is reported on the balance sheet. The income tax expense shown on the income statement is the sum of the income tax actually payable in the period plus (or minus for a deferred tax asset) the amount of the tax deferral for the period. We now illustrate the reporting process.

Illustration of Estimating Effective Annual Tax Rate

Refer to Figure 13–9 for an illustration of the computation of the tax rate. While proceeding through the example, note the necessary adjustments, such as the differences between tax accounting and GAAP accounting, to determine the annual rate. Following are data for the illustration:

1. Peerless Products and its subsidiary expect to earn $225,000 consolidated income from continuing operations for the 20X1 fiscal year.
2. Permanent differences between accounting income and tax income are expected to be $2,000 for premiums paid for life insurance the company carried on key officers (company is beneficiary) and an exclusion of $27,000 for dividends received from investments in stocks of other companies.
3. The combined federal and state income tax rate is estimated to be 38 percent (30 percent federal and 8 percent state), and the company expects to be eligible for a $22,000 business tax credit related to new job development expenditures and employee retraining costs.

The estimated effective tax rate of 24 percent computed in Figure 13–9 is used to determine the income tax provision for the first quarter. Assuming that the first-quarter earnings were $20,000, the following entry records the tax provision:

(3)	Income Tax Expense	4,800	
	Income Taxes Payable		4,800

Record first-quarter tax provision:
$4,800 = $20,000 × 0.24 effective tax rate.

Updating the Estimated Annual Rate in Subsequent Interim Periods

Assume that the amount of second-quarter actual earnings is $25,000, for a cumulative total for the year to date $45,000 ($20,000 + $25,000). The consolidated entity must first recompute its estimate of its effective annual tax rate based on the updated information it has at the end of the second quarter, such as additional differences between taxable and accounting income or a better estimate of projected annual earnings. Assuming the new estimated effective annual tax rate is 34 percent because of changes in the estimated amount of the available business tax credit and other changes in estimates, this rate replaces the 24 percent rate used at the end of the first quarter.

FIGURE 13–9
Estimation of Effective Annual Tax Rate

	Estimated Annual Amounts
Income from continuing operations	$225,000
Adjust for permanent differences:	
Add premiums on key officers' life insurance	2,000
Deduct dividends received exclusion	(27,000)
Estimated annual taxable income	$200,000
Combined federal and state income taxes	× 38%
Estimated annual taxes before tax credits	$ 76,000
Deduct business tax credit	(22,000)
Estimated income taxes for year	$ 54,000
Divide by estimated annual income from continuing operations	$225,000
Estimated effective annual tax rate on continuing operations ($54,000 ÷ $225,000)	24%

The new estimated tax rate is used to compute the estimated year-to-date income tax provision at the end of the second interim period, as follows:

Actual cumulative income for first two quarters ($20,000 + $25,000)	$45,000
Updated estimated effective annual tax rate	× 34%
Cumulative income tax provision (expense)	$15,300
Less: Income tax provision made in first quarter	(4,800)
Income tax provision required in second quarter	$10,500

Peerless Products and its subsidiary report an income tax expense of $10,500 on the second-quarter consolidated income statement. The tax provision is cumulative, and the first-quarter provision is *not* retroactively restated for the change in the estimate of the annual tax rate.

The example does not include any temporary differences between accounting income and taxable income that result in deferred taxes. Temporary differences generally do not affect the estimate of the tax provision. Instead, the recognition of any temporary difference is normally made in the entry to record the tax provision and associated tax liability. For example, if $2,000 of the second-quarter income of $25,000 is due to a temporary difference in which accounting income is higher than tax income, the following entry is made to recognize the provision and deferral:

(4)			
	Income Tax Expense	10,500	
	Deferred Tax Liability		680
	Income Taxes Payable		9,820

Record second-quarter tax provision:
$10,500 = Income taxes payable plus deferred tax liability
$ 680 = Computation of deferred tax liability effect from temporary difference between tax and book income.

Losses and Operating Loss Carrybacks and Carryforwards

Accountants face an interesting problem when a company has a year-to-date loss as of the end of an interim period. Normally, an operating loss creates a tax benefit (that is, reduces tax payable) because the loss can be carried back against the operating income shown in the previous two years and the company may file a claim for a refund of taxes paid in those prior years. After the carryback portion of an operating loss is depleted, any remaining operating loss is carried forward against future operating income for up to 20 years. These carryback and carryforward provisions, however, apply only to annual results, not to interim results.

ASC 740 discusses these and other special tax problems. The first part of the guidance deals with the numerous alternative income trends possible, such as an operating loss for year to date but income anticipated for the year, or operating income for year to date but loss expected for the year. The possible combinations of interim and annual results are too numerous to show here, but one special case is covered: the determination of the tax benefit for a company with a year-to-date operating loss but with the expectation of an annual income. The issue is how to determine and report the income tax for the interim periods.

ASC 740 affirms the general rule that the realization of a tax benefit must be assured beyond a reasonable doubt before the benefit may be recognized in the financial statements. For interim reporting purposes, the most common reason for allowing the recognition of a tax benefit for a company with a year-to-date operating loss is that the company has had consistent seasonal trends in income during the year. Thus, the company has generally had income in the later interim periods that has offset the losses in the earlier interim periods. **ASC 740** establishes a more-likely-than-not criterion of having a likelihood of more than 50 percent as the threshold for beyond a reasonable doubt. Therefore, a company with an operating loss in the early interim periods with consistent experience of seasonality and income for the year can recognize a tax benefit of a to-date operating loss in the early interim periods. If the realization of a tax benefit of an interim operating loss is not assured by the end of the fiscal period, the company cannot show any tax benefit on the interim statements.

Illustration of Interim Operating Loss

See Figure 13–10 for the computation of the tax or benefit that should be shown on the interim statements if a company experiences a year-to-date loss but anticipates an annual income. For example, assume that the consolidated entity of Peerless Products Corporation and Special Foods Inc. has an actual first-quarter loss of $40,000 but expects an annual income of $222,000. The estimated annual tax rate is 24 percent. The consolidated entity has a normal seasonal variation of losses in the first quarter followed by profits in subsequent quarters. Therefore, the tax benefit of the operating loss of $9,600 ($40,000 × 0.24) is assured beyond a reasonable doubt, and the tax benefit is shown in the loss quarter.

A partial income statement for the first quarter follows. Note how the tax benefit reduces the reported net loss:

PEERLESS PRODUCTS AND SPECIAL FOODS
Partial Interim Consolidated Income Statement First Quarter Ended March 31, 20X1

Operating Loss before Income Tax Effect	$(40,000)
Less: Tax Benefit of Operating Loss	9,600
Net Loss	$(30,400)

At the end of 20X1, Peerless Products and its subsidiary computed its actual annual income tax provision for 20X1 as $62,000. The year-to-date tax provision in the fourth quarter should equal the total actual annual provision, and the amount of tax reported in the fourth quarter is the balance necessary to reach the amount of the annual provision. Therefore, the actual annual income tax rate on continuing income for 20X1 was 27.9 percent ($62,000 annual tax provision ÷ $222,000 annual income from continuing operations before the deduction for income to noncontrolling interest).

If the realizability of the tax benefit from the operating loss is not assured beyond a reasonable doubt, no tax benefit should be shown. This case is presented in Figure 13–11. Note that the actual annual provisions are identical; the differences are in the interim presentations.

FIGURE 13–10
Interim Analysis When Tax Benefit of Operating Loss Is Assured

	Continuing Income (Loss) before Taxes		Estimated	Tax (Benefit)		
Reporting Period	Reporting Period	Year to Date	Effective Annual Tax Rate, %	Year to Date (*a*)	Less Previously Provided	Reported in Period
First quarter	$ (40,000)	$(40,000)	24.0%	$(9,600)		$ (9,600)
Second quarter	20,000	(20,000)	34.0	(6,800)	$ (9,600)	2,800
Third quarter	80,000	60,000	34.0	20,400	(6,800)	27,200
Fourth quarter	162,000	222,000	27.9(*b*)	62,000	20,400	41,600
Fiscal year	$222,000					$62,000

(*a*) Year to date: Year-to-date continuing income (loss) × Updated estimated effective annual tax rate.
(*b*) Rounded.

FIGURE 13–11
Interim Analysis When Operating Loss Benefit Is Not Assured

	Continuing Income (Loss) before Taxes			Tax (Benefit)		
Reporting Period	Reporting Period	Year to Date	Estimated Effective Annual Tax Rate, %	Year to Date (*a*)	Less Previously Provided	Reported in Period
First quarter	$ (40,000)	$ (40,000)	24.0%	$ 0		$ 0
Second quarter	20,000	(20,000)	34.0	0	$ 0	0
Third quarter	80,000	60,000	34.0	20,400	0	20,400
Fourth quarter	162,000	222,000	27.9	62,000	20,400	41,600
Fiscal year	$222,000					$62,000

(*a*) Year to date: Year-to-date continuing income (loss) × Updated estimated effective annual tax rate.

Disposal of a Component of the Entity or Extraordinary, Unusual, Infrequently Occurring, and Contingent Items

ASC 270 and **ASC 740** require the measurement and reporting of major nonoperating items on the same bases as used to prepare the annual report. Extraordinary items, discontinued operations, and unusual and infrequently occurring items should be reported in the interim period in which they occur, not allocated to the other interim periods of the year. The materiality test for extraordinary items should be based on the estimate of income for the entire fiscal year. The materiality test for discontinued operations and unusual and infrequent transactions should be based on the operating income of the interim period in which the discontinued operations are first reported.

Contingencies or other major uncertainties that could affect the company also must be disclosed on the same basis as that used in the annual report. This disclosure is required to provide information on items that might affect the fairness of the interim report. **ASC 450** presents the procedures for measuring and reporting contingencies in both interim and annual reports.

ACCOUNTING CHANGES IN INTERIM PERIODS

ASC 250 specifies three categories of accounting changes, as follows: (1) change in an accounting principle, (2) change in an accounting estimate, and (3) change in a reporting entity. The statement noted that a correction of an error in previously issued financial statements is not an accounting change and the entity must restate all prior financial statements presented to correct the error(s) in those financials. **ASC 250** does not alter the transition provisions presented in other areas of the codification for applying changes in specific accounting requirements covered in an existing standard.

Change in an Accounting Principle (Retrospective Application)

An entity may make a change in accounting principle only if a new accounting standard requires the change or if the company can justify that the new accounting principle is preferable to the previously used accounting principle. A change from a generally accepted accounting principle to another generally accepted accounting principle for measurement or valuation purposes requires that the *retrospective application* process be applied to all prior periods' financial statements, including the financial statements for interim periods. Only the direct effects of the change in accounting principle, including any related tax effects, are included in the retrospective application to the prior periods.

A change from an accounting principle *not* generally accepted to a generally accepted accounting principle is a correction of an error, requiring restatement of all prior financial statements. However, accounting for changes in the method of depreciation, amortization, or depletion for long-lived, nonfinancial assets, such as from the straight-line to the accelerated method of depreciation for equipment, are treated as changes in estimates effected by a change in accounting principle. Changes in accounting estimates are discussed in the next section of this chapter.

FYI

Effective January 1, 2010, Freddie Mac prospectively adopted amendments to the accounting standards for transfers of financial assets and consolidation of variable interest entities (VIEs). Upon adoption, the company added $1.5 trillion of assets and liabilities to its consolidated balance sheet. The cumulative effect of these changes in accounting principles as of January 1, 2010, was a net decrease of $11.7 billion to total equity (deficit), which includes the changes to the opening balances of retained earnings (accumulated deficit) and accumulated other comprehensive income (AOCI), net of taxes.

Retrospective Application

Direct effects are those adjustments necessary to make the change in accounting principle in the immediately affected assets or liabilities. *Indirect effects* are those affecting current or future cash flows that result from making the change in accounting principle. These indirect effects are reported in the period the change is made. An adjusted balance sheet to reflect the retrospective application of the new accounting principle is provided for the earliest period presented. All financial statements for each subsequent annual and interim period are adjusted for the effects of the change in accounting principle. For example, if a company makes a change from the weighted-average method to the FIFO method of accounting for inventories in the current year, the company would retrospectively apply the FIFO method to all prior periods for which financial statements are provided. The beginning inventory amount for the earliest period presented would be adjusted to reflect the new accounting principle with a corresponding adjustment to retained earnings, and the new method would be reflected in all subsequent financial statements presented.

If the cumulative amount of the effect of the change can be determined but determining its period-by-period effects is impracticable, the company should report the cumulative amount of the change on the financial statements as of the beginning of the earliest period practicable and then revise the subsequent financial statements presented. However, if a company wishes to make an accounting change in principle in an interim period but is not able to determine the effects of the change on the current fiscal year's previous interim periods, the entity must wait until the beginning of a subsequent fiscal year to make the change in accounting principle.

Change in an Accounting Estimate (Current and Prospective Application)

Changes in accounting estimates are the result of new information that becomes available to the entity. These changes are reported on a current and prospective basis only; that is, the changes are reported only in the current period in which the change is made and in the future periods affected by the change. Previously issued financial statements are *not* adjusted. An example of a change in accounting estimate is a change in the method of computing the allowance for uncollectibles of accounts receivable because more recent information indicates the prior provisions were inadequate.

Changes in Depreciation, Amortization, or Depletion

ASC 250 requires a change in the method of accounting for depreciation, amortization, or depletion of long-lived, nonfinancial assets because of new information, such as current usage patterns that differ from expectations, as a change in accounting estimate effected by a change in accounting principle. The current and prospective application is used to report this change and prior financial statements are not restated.

Change in a Reporting Entity (Retrospective Application)

A change in reporting entity requires a retrospective application to all prior periods presented to reflect the new reporting entity. The primary examples of changes in reporting entity are (1) presenting consolidated or combined financial statements rather than individual statements for the separate entities, (2) changing the specific subsidiaries that comprise the consolidated entity for which consolidated financials are presented, and (3) changing the entities that are included in combined financial statements.

An entity making an accounting change is also required to make a number of disclosures in the period of the change, including effect of the change on income from continuing operations and net income. In the case of a change in accounting principle, the entity also must disclose the nature and justification for the change and the cumulative effect of the change on retained earnings or other components of equity as of the beginning of the earliest period presented.

International Financial Reporting Standards for Accounting Changes

International Accounting Standard No. 8, "Accounting Policies, Changes in Accounting Estimates and Errors" (IAS 8), provides the accounting treatment and disclosures for changes in accounting policies, changes in accounting estimates, and corrections of errors. The international standards for these changes are very similar to U.S. GAAP. **IAS 8** specifies that changes in accounting policy be applied retrospectively unless the change was made in initial application of a standard, in which case the specific transitional provisions presented in that standard will be applied. Changes in accounting estimates are recognized in the period of the change and future periods (prospectively). Prior-period errors are included in the international standard and are accounted for retrospectively, just as in U.S. GAAP.

SUMMARY OF KEY CONCEPTS

Segment disclosures about an entity's component operations and foreign areas in which an entity operates provide information about the different risks and profitability of each of the individual components that the entity comprises. These additional disclosures are useful in assessing past performance and prospects of future performance. A critical issue is the definition of a segment. The FASB allows management the flexibility it needs to disaggregate its operations but imposes several significance tests to determine which segments are separately reportable.

Interim reports must be issued by publicly held corporations so users of the information can assess corporate performance and make predictions about results for the annual fiscal period. The major issues are the measurement and disclosure problems of breaking down the annual reporting period into smaller parts. Many of the technical problems revolve around cost of goods sold and income taxes. Estimates based on expected annual results are allowed when determining both of these costs. Even with the estimation and measurement problems, interim reports are primary disclosure vehicles that investors and other users of financial statements quickly and carefully evaluate.

KEY TERMS

enterprisewide disclosure, *692*
interim income tax, *702*
interim reports, *694*
reportable operating segments, *684*
75 percent consolidated revenue test, *690*
10 percent significance rules, *684*

QUESTIONS

LO 13-1, 13-2 **Q13-1** How might information on a company's operations in different industries be helpful to investors?

LO 13-2 **Q13-2** What is the relationship between the FASB's requirements for segment-based disclosures and a company's profit centers?

LO 13-2 **Q13-3** What are the three 10 percent significance tests used to determine reportable segments under ASC 280? Give the numerator and denominator for each test.

LO 13-2 **Q13-4** Specifically, what items are in the determination of a segment's profit or loss?

LO 13-2 **Q13-5** A company has 10 industry segments, of which the largest 5 account for 80 percent of the combined revenues of the company. What considerations are important in determining the number of segments that are separately reportable? How are the remaining segments reported?

LO 13-3 **Q13-6** Only two materiality tests are used to determine separately reportable foreign operations. What are these two tests?

LO 13-3 **Q13-7** What information must be disclosed about a company's major customers? Are the names of customers disclosed?

LO 13-4 **Q13-8** How can investors use interim reports to identify a company's seasonal trends?

LO 13-4 **Q13-9** How is revenue recognized on an interim basis?

LO 13-4 **Q13-10** Describe the basic rules for computing cost of goods sold and inventory on an interim basis. In what circumstances are estimates permitted to determine costs?

LO 13-4 **Q13-11** What is the difference in the application of the lower-of-cost-or-market valuation method for inventories for interim statements and annual statements?

LO 13-4 **Q13-12** Describe the process of updating the estimate of the effective annual tax rate in the second quarter of a company's fiscal year.

LO 13-4 **Q13-13** How is the tax benefit of an interim period's operating loss treated if the future realizability of the tax benefit is *not* assured beyond a reasonable doubt?

LO 13-4 **Q13-14** How are extraordinary items reported on an interim basis?

LO 13-4 **Q13-15** Maness Company made a change in accounting for its inventories during the third quarter of its fiscal year. The company switched from the LIFO method to the average cost method. Describe the reporting of this accounting change on prior interim financial statements and on third-quarter interim financial statements.

CASES

LO 13-2 **C13-1**

Segment Disclosures [CMA Adapted]

Judgment

Chemax Inc. manufactures a wide variety of pharmaceuticals, medical instruments, and other medical supplies. Eighteen months ago the company developed and began to market a new product line of antihistamine drugs under various trade names. Sales and profitability of this product line during the current fiscal year greatly exceeded management's expectations. The new product line will account for 10 percent of the company's total sales and 12 percent of the company's operating income for the fiscal year ending June 30, 20X0. Management believes sales and profits will be significant for several years.

Chemax is concerned that its market share and competitive position could suffer if it discloses the volume and profitability of its new product line in its annual financial statements. Management is not sure how **ASC 280** applies in this case.

Required

a. What is the purpose of requiring segment information in financial statements?

b. Identify and explain the factors that should be considered when attempting to decide how products should be grouped to determine a single business segment.

c. What options, if any, does Chemax Inc. have with the disclosure of its new antihistamine product line? Explain your answer.

LO 13-4 **C13-2**

Matching Revenue and Expenses for Interim Periods

Understanding

Periodic reporting adds complexity to accounting by requiring estimates, accruals, deferrals, and allocations. Interim reporting creates even greater difficulties in matching revenue and expenses.

Required

a. Explain how revenue, product costs, gains, and losses should be recognized for interim periods.

b. Explain how determination of cost of goods sold and inventory differs for interim period reports versus annual reports.

c. Explain the interim accounting treatment of period costs such as depreciation.

d. Explain the treatment of the following items for interim financial statements:

(1) Long-term contracts
(2) Advertising
(3) Seasonal revenue
(4) Flood loss
(5) Annual major repairs and maintenance to plant and equipment during the last two weeks in December

LO 13-2

C13-3 Segment Disclosures in the Financial Statements [CMA Adapted]

Analysis

Bennett Inc. is a publicly held corporation whose diversified operations have been separated into five industry segments. Bennett is in the process of preparing its annual financial statements for the year ended December 31, 20X5. The following information has been collected for the preparation of the segment reports required by **ASC 280.**

BENNETT INC.
Selected Data
For the Year Ended December 31, 20X5
(in thousands)

Item	Power Tools	Fastening Systems	Household Products	Plumbing Products	Security Systems
Sales to Unaffiliated Customers	$32,000	$ 4,500	$ 4,800	$3,000	$2,000
Intersegment Sales	10,000	5,500	200	1,000	
Total Revenue	$42,000	$10,000	$5,000	$4,000	$2,000
Cost of Goods Sold	30,000	8,000	4,500	3,100	1,700
Operating Profit	4,500	1,000	(600)	700	(100)
Net Income	2,600	800	(750)	(100)	(200)
Segment Assets	50,000	23,000	17,000	6,000	4,000

Required

a. Determine which of the operating segments are reportable segments for Bennett. Your determination should include all required tests and the results of those tests for each of Bennett's five segments.

b. The reportable segments determined in (*a*) must represent a substantial portion of Bennett's total operations when taken together. Describe how to determine whether a substantial portion of Bennett's operations is explained by its segment information.

LO 13-3

C13-4 Determining Industry and Geographic Segments

Research

A major producer of cereal breakfast foods had been reporting in its annual reports just one dominant product line (cereals) in only the U.S. domestic geographic area. The company had no other separately reportable segments. For several years, the U.S. company has had a Canadian subsidiary that produces a variety of pasta. In 20X5, one brand of pasta, "Healthcare," suddenly became very popular with the health-conscious public in both the United States and Canada, and the Canadian subsidiary more than tripled its sales and profits within the year.

The management of the U.S. parent company did not want to disclose to its competitors how profitable the Canadian subsidiary was because the company wanted to maintain its strong economic position without additional competition.

You have been able to determine the following (in millions):

	Cereal Products	Pasta Products
Net sales	$3,885	$834
Operating profit	445	151
Segment assets	1,565	147

All cereal product operations are located in the United States, and all pasta product operations are located in Canada. The Standard Industrial Classification (SIC) number is 2043 for cereal products and 2098 for the Canadian subsidiary's pasta products. (The Standard Industrial Classification Index is prepared by the U.S. Office of Management and Budget and is used widely to define a company's major industrial groups.)

Required

a. Why would management be reluctant to disclose information about very successful—and very unsuccessful—operations in the segmental disclosure footnote in the annual report?

b. Present both theoretical and applied arguments for including the pasta products segment with the cereal products segment as one internal operating segment, thus not requiring separate disclosure under **ASC 280.** How does the fact that the pasta products have suddenly become popular affect the disclosure requirements under **ASC 280?**

c. Present the **ASC 280** requirements for reporting the cereal products and pasta products by geographic area. Must the Canadian operations be disclosed separately in a geographic disclosure footnote?

LO 13-1

C13-5 Segment Reporting

Research

The manager you work for has asked you to perform some research to determine what types of information public companies are providing on their Internet home pages. The public company you work for is considering establishing its own home page. In particular, the manager wants you to note how these companies describe their products and services on their home pages. After researching the home pages, the manager wants you to review each company's Form 10-K by using the Electronic Data Gathering, Analysis, and Retrieval (EDGAR) database. While looking at the Form 10-Ks, the manager wants you to observe how the companies describe the segments of their business. For example, are the segments as described in the Form 10-K similar to the products and services mentioned on the same company's home page?

Required

a. Using an Internet search engine, find the home page of a *public company.* (*Hint:* A helpful search term is "Company Home Pages.") Then write a brief summary about what you find on the company's home page discussing the following:

(1) What type of information related to the company's products or services is provided?

(2) What other information is presented on the home page?

b. Using the EDGAR database, locate the most recent Form 10-K for the company you selected. (*Note:* The EDGAR database collects and maintains the forms that are required to be filed by public companies to the U.S. Securities and Exchange Commission [SEC]. *Hint:* The Internet URL for the EDGAR database is http://www.sec.gov/.)

(1) Review the Form 10-K and locate the segment disclosure information. Print off this segment information.

(2) Write a brief report summarizing what you find in the company's Form 10-K regarding segment disclosures. Include the following information:

(a) Describe the company's segments as displayed in the Form 10-K. Discuss the basis on which the segments are presented.

(b) Discuss which segment(s) has (have) the highest revenues, is (are) the most profitable, and has (have) the most assets.

LO 13-4

C13-6 Interim Reporting

Research

The company you work for is considering going public. Your current position is in the external financial reporting group. The manager you work for wants you to review some public company quarterly reports, Form 10-Qs, to see what type of information is disclosed. The manager does not want you to perform technical research to determine what the exact reporting requirements are for the Form 10-Q but to understand generally what information other companies seem to be supplying in their Form 10-Qs.

Required

a. Determine the name of two public companies you would like to use in your review of Form 10-Qs. (*Hint:* There are various ways to determine the public companies you want to research. For example, you could use an Internet search engine to find a home page of a *public* company. A helpful search term is "Company Home Pages." Another method would be to select public companies you already know of or you find through the use of a newspaper or periodical.)

b. Using the EDGAR database, locate the most recent Form 10-Qs for the two companies you selected. (*Hint:* The Internet URL for the SEC's home page is http://www.sec.gov/. The SEC provides a company search engine for its EDGAR database.) In addition, for one of these companies, locate the Form 10-Q for the same period in the prior year. Prepare a one- to two-page summary for the following:

(1) Write a brief summary of the contents of one company's recent Form 10-Q. Discuss how the Form 10-Q information compares with the information you know is included in a Form 10-K, which is the annual report to the SEC.

(2) Review the same company's Form 10-Q from the previous year and discuss the similarities and differences you notice in the Form 10-Qs for different time periods.

(3) Review the other company's Form 10-Q from the current year and discuss the similarities and differences you notice in the Form 10-Qs for the two companies.

LO 13-2

C13-7 Defining Segments for Disclosure

Research

Randy Rivera, CFO of Stanford Corporation, a manufacturer of packaged retail food products, has reviewed the company's segment disclosures for the current year. In the first draft of the disclosures, the company reports information about four segments: cheese, snacks and crackers, pizza, and desserts and confectionery. He has suggested that the segment disclosures be expanded to include additional segments.

Randy notes that the cereals segment, included in the segment disclosures last year, is not included in the current year. Although the cereals segment reported a loss for the current year and suffered a significant decline in revenues as a result of a prolonged labor dispute, he believes that Stanford should continue to provide information about this segment. In addition, Stanford recently introduced a new product line, sports beverages. This operating segment is expected to expand rapidly and is highly profitable. Randy believes that shareholders would view its profitability positively if the sports beverage segment were included in the segment disclosures.

The accountant who prepared the segment information has reviewed the segment data with Randy. Revenues of the cereals segment and the sports beverage segment account for 9 percent and 6 percent of combined revenues of all segments, respectively. Each segment's assets are approximately 8 percent of the combined assets of all segments. The cereals segment was the only segment to record a loss, which amounted to 5 percent of the combined profit of all segments reporting profits. The sports beverage segment profit was 9 percent of this total.

After reviewing the data, Randy still believes that the inclusion of the two segments would improve the segment disclosures and has asked you to research the appropriateness of his suggestion.

Required

Obtain the most current accounting standards on accounting for segments. Write a memo to Randy responding to his suggestion that the segment disclosures be expanded to include the cereals and sports beverage segments. Support your recommendations with citations and quotations from the authoritative financial reporting standards.

LO 13-4

C13-8 Income Tax Provision in Interim Periods

Research

Andrea Meyers, a supervisor in the controller's department at Vanderbilt Company, is reviewing the calculation of the income tax provision to be included in the financial statements for the first quarter of 20X5. She is questioning the estimate of the effective tax rate expected to be applicable for fiscal year 20X5 because it is significantly lower than Vanderbilt's actual effective tax rate for 20X4.

Bob Graber, who prepared the income tax calculation, explains to Andrea that the estimate of the effective annual tax rate reflects the anticipated enactment of a new business energy tax credit that will provide substantial tax benefits to Vanderbilt. This credit has the approval of the president, has been passed by the House of Representatives, and is under consideration in the Senate. It is expected to be enacted no later than the third quarter of 20X5, and its benefits should be available beginning with 20X5 tax returns.

Required

Obtain the most current accounting standards for interim reporting. Andrea has asked you, an accountant in the controller's department, to research the computation of the estimated effective annual tax rate for interim reporting. Write a memo to her reporting your research results. Support your recommendations with citations and quotations from the authoritative financial reporting standards.

LO 13-4

C13-9 Questions about Interim Reporting

Application

Required

Prepare a brief answer to each of the following questions about interim reporting, assuming the company is preparing its Form 10-Q for the third quarter of its fiscal year.

a. How many different income statements would the company present? Describe the reporting periods presented in the income statements.

b. How would the company report a change in accounting principle for depreciation of its building that was made effective the first day of the third quarter? The change was made as a result of an accounting study that concluded that the estimated future benefits from the equipment will be different from those previously expected.

c. How many different balance sheets would the company present? What is the balance sheet date (as of what date) for each balance sheet?

d. Must interim financial statements filed with the SEC be audited by an independent public accountant who would provide an audit opinion on those statements? Explain your answer.

e. Is a company required to present segment information in the interim report? If yes, are the interim segment disclosures different from the annual segment disclosures? Explain your answers.

f. Within what period of time after the end of the quarter must a Form 10-Q be filed with the SEC?

g. May a company use one accounting method for computing interim total revenues and a different accounting method for computing its annual total revenues?

h. Is the company required to physically count its ending inventory each quarter so that it can accurately determine its ending inventory for the balance sheet and its cost of goods sold for the income statement? If not, explain how ending inventory is computed for interim reporting.

i. The company shuts down each year for two weeks during its third quarter to retool its manufacturing lines for the next year's products. Can the company allocate the costs of retooling incurred in its third quarter to the other three quarters (1, 2, and 4) during the year? If yes, explain how this allocation would be made.

j. How would the company report a change in accounting principle from the completed contract method of revenue recognition to the percentage-of-completion method of revenue recognition on its long-term construction contracts? The change was made on the last day of the third quarter.

k. The company had assumed during the first two quarters of the year that it would receive a material income tax credit from the federal government. However, during the third quarter, the company was informed that it would not be receiving the expected tax credit this year. The company had included the estimated tax credit in the computation of its income tax rate for the first two quarters of the year. Should the company retroactively restate the first two quarters of tax expense because of the change in information received in the third quarter? Explain your answer.

EXERCISES

LO 13-2

E13-1 Reportable Segments

Advanced StudyGuide .com

Data for the seven operating segments of Amalgamated Products follow:

Segments	Revenues	Segment Profit (Loss)	Segment Assets
Electronics	$ 42,000	$ (8,600)	$ 73,000
Bicycles	105,000	30,400	207,000
Sporting Goods	53,000	(4,900)	68,000
Home Appliances	147,000	23,000	232,000
Gas and Oil Equipment	186,000	11,700	315,000
Glassware	64,000	(19,100)	96,000
Hardware	178,000	38,600	194,000
Total	$775,000	$71,100	$1,185,000

Included in the $105,000 revenue of the Bicycles segment are sales of $25,000 made to the Sporting Goods segment.

Required

a. Which segments are separately reportable?

b. Do the separately reportable segments include a sufficient portion of total revenue? Explain.

LO 13-2, 13-3

E13-2 Multiple-Choice Questions on Segment Reporting [AICPA Adapted]

Select the correct answer for each of the following questions.

1. Barbee Corporation discloses supplementary operating segment information for its two reportable segments. Data for 20X5 are available as follows:

	Segment E	Segment W
Sales	$750,000	$250,000
Traceable operating expenses	325,000	130,000

Additional 20X5 expenses are as follows:

Indirect operating expenses	$120,000

Appropriately selected common indirect operating expenses are allocated to segments based on the ratio of each segment's sales to total sales. The 20X5 operating profit for Segment E was

a. $260,000.
b. $335,000.
c. $395,000.
d. $425,000.

2. Dutko Company has three lines of business, each of which is a significant industry segment. Company sales aggregated $1,800,000 in 20X6, of which Segment 3 contributed 60 percent. Traceable costs were $600,000 for Segment 3 from a total of $1,200,000 for the company as a whole. In addition, $350,000 of common costs are allocated in the ratio of a segment's income before common costs to the total income before common costs. For Segment 3, Dutko should report a 20X6 segment profit of

a. $200,000.
b. $270,000.
c. $280,000.
d. $480,000.

3. Stein Company is a diversified company that discloses supplemental financial information on its industry segments. The following information is available for 20X2:

	Sales	Traceable Costs	Allocable Costs
Segment A	$400,000	$225,000	
Segment B	300,000	240,000	
Segment C	200,000	135,000	
Totals	$900,000	$600,000	$150,000

Allocable costs are assigned based on the ratio of a segment's income before allocable costs to total income before allocable costs. This is an appropriate method of allocation. Segment B's profit for 20X2 is

a. $0.
b. $10,000.
c. $30,000.
d. $50,000.
e. None of the above.

4. Selected data for a segment of a business enterprise are to be reported separately in accordance with **ASC 280** when the revenue of the segment exceeds 10 percent of the

a. Combined net income of all segments reporting profits.
b. Total revenue obtained in transactions with outsiders.
c. Total revenue of all the enterprise's industry segments.
d. Total combined revenue of all segments reporting profits.

5. Kimber Company operates in four different industries, each of which is appropriately regarded as a reportable segment. Total sales for 20X2 for all segments combined were $1,000,000. Sales for Segment 2 were $400,000, and the traceable costs were $150,000. Total common costs for all segments combined were $500,000. Kimber allocates common costs based on the ratio of a segment's sales to total sales, an appropriate method of allocation. The segment profit to be reported for Segment 2 for 20X2 is

a. $50,000.
b. $125,000.
c. $200,000.
d. $250,000.
e. None of the above.

6. The following information pertains to Reding Corporation for the year ended December 31, 20X6.

Sales to unaffiliated customers	$2,000,000
Intersegment sales of products similar to those sold to unaffiliated customers	600,000

All of Reding's segments are engaged solely in manufacturing operations. Reding has a reportable segment if that segment's revenue exceeds

a. $264,000.
b. $260,000.
c. $204,000.
d. $200,000.

7. Snow Corporation's revenue for the year ended December 31, 20X2, was as follows:

Consolidated revenue per income statement	$1,200,000
Intersegment sales	240,000
Combined revenue of all industry segments	$1,440,000

Snow has a reportable operating segment if that segment's revenue exceeds

a. $6,000.
b. $24,000.
c. $120,000.
d. $144,000.

8. Porter Corporation is engaged solely in manufacturing operations. The following data (consistent with prior-years data) pertain to the industries in which operations were conducted for the year ended December 31, 20X5:

Industry Segment	Total Revenue	Segment Profit	Assets at 12/31/X5
A	$10,000,000	$1,750,000	$20,000,000
B	8,000,000	1,400,000	17,500,000
C	6,000,000	1,200,000	12,500,000
D	3,000,000	550,000	7,500,000
E	4,250,000	675,000	7,000,000
F	1,500,000	225,000	3,000,000
Totals	$32,750,000	$5,800,000	$67,500,000

In its segment information for 20X5, how many reportable segments does Porter have?

a. Three.
b. Four.
c. Five.
d. Six.

9. Boecker is a multidivisional corporation that has both intersegment sales and sales to unaffiliated customers. Boecker should report segment financial information for each segment meeting which of the following criteria?

a. Segment profit or loss is 10 percent or more of consolidated profit or loss.
b. Segment profit or loss is 10 percent or more of combined profit or loss of all company segments.
c. Segment revenue is 10 percent or more of combined revenue of all company segments.
d. Segment revenue is 10 percent or more of consolidated revenue.

Note: Use the following information for questions 10 and 11.

Ward Corporation, a publicly owned corporation, is subject to the requirements for segment reporting. In its income statement for the year ending December 31, 20X5, Ward reported revenues of $50,000,000, operating expenses of $47,000,000, and net income of $3,000,000. Operating expenses included payroll costs of $15,000,000. Ward's combined assets of all industry segments at December 31, 20X5, were $40,000,000.

10. In its 20X5 financial statements, Ward should disclose major customer data if sales to any single customer amount to at least
    a. $300,000.
    b. $1,500,000.
    c. $4,000,000.
    d. $5,000,000.
11. In its 20X5 financial statements, Ward should disclose foreign revenues in a specific country if revenues from foreign operations in that country are at least
    a. $5,000,000.
    b. $4,700,000.
    c. $4,000,000.
    d. $1,500,000.

LO 13-4

E13-3 Multiple-Choice Questions on Interim Reporting [AICPA Adapted]

Select the correct answer for each of the following questions.

1. Which of the following is an inherent difficulty in determining the results of operations on an interim basis?
    a. Cost of sales reflects only the amount of product expense allocable to revenue recognized as of the interim date.
    b. Depreciation on an interim basis is a partial estimate of the actual annual amount.
    c. Costs expensed in one interim period may benefit other periods.
    d. Revenue from long-term construction contracts accounted for by the percentage-of-completion method is based on annual completion, and interim estimates may be incorrect.
2. Which of the following reporting practices is permissible for interim financial reporting?
    a. Use of the gross profit method for interim inventory pricing.
    b. Use of the direct costing method for determining manufacturing inventories.
    c. Deferral of unplanned variances under a standard cost system until the following year.
    d. Deferral of nontemporary inventory market declines until year-end.
3. On January 1, 20X2, Harris Inc. paid $40,000 in property taxes on its plant for the calendar year 20X2. In March 20X2, Harris made $120,000 in annual major repairs to its machinery. These repairs will benefit the entire calendar year's operations. How should these expenses be reflected in Harris's quarterly income statements?

	Three Months Ended			
	March 31, 20X2	**June 30, 20X2**	**September 30, 20X2**	**December 31, 20X2**
a.	$ 22,000	$46,000	$46,000	$46,000
b.	40,000	40,000	40,000	40,000
c.	70,000	30,000	30,000	30,000
d.	160,000	0	0	0

4. Wenger Company experienced a $420,000 inventory loss from market decline in April 20X2. The company recorded this loss in April 20X2 after its March 31, 20X2, quarterly report was issued. None of this loss was recovered by the end of the year. How should this loss be reflected in Wenger's quarterly income statements?

	Three Months Ended			
	March 31, 20X2	**June 30, 20X2**	**September 30, 20X2**	**December 31, 20X2**
a.	$ 0	$ 0	$ 0	$420,000
b.	0	140,000	140,000	140,000
c.	0	420,000	0	0
d.	105,000	105,000	105,000	105,000

5. A company that uses the last-in, first-out (LIFO) method of inventory costing finds at an interim reporting date that there has been a partial liquidation of the base-period inventory level. The decline is considered temporary, and the base inventory will be replaced before year-end. The amount shown as inventory on the interim reporting date should
   a. Not consider the LIFO liquidation, and cost of sales for the interim reporting period should include the expected cost of replacement of the liquidated LIFO base.
   b. Be shown at the actual level, and cost of sales for the interim reporting period should reflect the decrease in LIFO base-period inventory level.
   c. Not consider the LIFO liquidations, and cost of sales for the interim reporting period should reflect the decrease in LIFO base-period inventory level.
   d. Be shown at the actual level, and the decrease in inventory level should not be reflected in the cost of sales for the interim reporting period.
6. During the second quarter of 20X5, Camerton Company sold a piece of equipment at a $12,000 gain. What portion of the gain should Camerton report in its income statement for the second quarter of 20X5?
   a. $12,000.
   b. $6,000.
   c. $4,000.
   d. $0.
7. On March 15, 20X1, Burge Company paid property taxes of $180,000 on its factory building for calendar year 20X1. On April 1, 20X1, Burge made $300,000 in unanticipated repairs to its plant equipment. The repairs will benefit operations for the remainder of the calendar year. What total amount of these expenses should be included in Burge's quarterly income statement for the three months ended June 30, 20X1?
   a. $75,000.
   b. $145,000.
   c. $195,000.
   d. $345,000.
8. SRB Company had an inventory loss from a market price decline that occurred in the first quarter. The loss was not expected to be restored in the fiscal year. However, in the third quarter, the inventory had a market price recovery that exceeded the first-quarter decline. For interim financial reporting, the dollar amount of net inventory should
   a. Decrease in the first quarter by the amount of the market price decline and increase in the third quarter by the amount of the market price recovery.
   b. Decrease in the first quarter by the amount of the market price decline and increase in the third quarter by the amount of the decrease in the first quarter.
   c. Not be affected in the first quarter and increase in the third quarter by the amount of the market price recovery that exceeded the amount of the market price decline.
   d. Not be affected in either the first quarter or the third quarter.

9. For external reporting purposes, it is appropriate to use estimated gross profit rates to determine the cost of goods sold for

	Interim Financial Reporting	Year-End Financial Reporting
a.	Yes	Yes
b.	Yes	No
c.	No	Yes
d.	No	No

10. On June 30, 20X5, Park Corporation incurred a $100,000 net loss from disposal of a business component. Also, on June 30, 20X5, Park paid $40,000 for property taxes assessed for calendar year 20X5. What amount of the preceding items should be included in the determination of Park's net income or loss for the six-month interim period ended June 30, 20X5?
    a. $140,000.
    b. $120,000.
    c. $90,000.
    d. $70,000.

LO 13-4

E13-4 LIFO Liquidation

Advanced StudyGuide .com

During July, Laesch Company, which uses a perpetual inventory system, sold 1,240 units from its LIFO-based inventory, which had originally cost $18 per unit. The replacement cost is expected to be $27 per unit.

Required

Respond to the following two independent scenarios as requested.

a. *Case 1:* In July, the company is planning to reduce its inventory and expects to replace only 900 of these units by December 31, the end of its fiscal year.
   (1) Prepare the entry in July to record the sale of the 1,240 units.
   (2) Discuss the proper financial statement presentation of the valuation account related to the 1,240 units sold.
   (3) Prepare the entry for the replacement of the 900 units in September at an actual cost of $31 per unit.

b. *Case 2:* In July, the company is planning to reduce its inventory and expects to replace only 300 of its units by December 31, the end of its fiscal year.
   (1) Prepare the entry in July to record the sale of the 1,240 units.
   (2) In December, the company decided not to replace any of the 1,240 units. Prepare the entry required on December 31 to eliminate any valuation accounts related to the inventory that will not be replaced.

LO 13-4

E13-5 Inventory Write-Down and Recovery

Cub Company, a calendar-year entity, had 2,100 geothermal heating pumps in its beginning inventory for 20X1. On December 31, 20X0, the heating pumps had been adjusted down to $850 per unit from an actual cost of $920 per unit. It was the lower of cost or market. Cub purchased no additional units during 20X1. The following additional information is provided for 20X1:

Quarter	Date	Inventory (units)	Unit Market Value
1	March 31, 20X1	1,700	$845
2	June 30, 20X1	1,400	860
3	September 30, 20X1	1,300	830
4	December 31, 20X1	900	840

Required

Respond to the following two independent scenarios as requested.

a. *Case 1:* The company does not have sufficient experience with the seasonal market for geothermal pumps and assumes that any reductions in market value during the year will be permanent.

(1) Determine the cost of goods sold for each quarter.

(2) Verify the total cost of goods sold by computing annual cost of goods sold on a lower-of-cost-or-market basis.

b. *Case 2:* The company has prior experience with the seasonal market for geothermal pumps and expects that any reductions in market value during the year will be only temporary and will recover by year-end.

(1) Determine the cost of goods sold for each quarter.

(2) Verify the total cost of goods sold by computing annual cost of goods sold on a lower-of-cost-or-market basis.

LO 13-4

E13-6 Multiple-Choice Questions on Income Taxes at Interim Dates [AICPA Adapted]

Select the correct answer for each of the following questions.

1. According to **ASC 270 and 740,** income tax expense in an income statement for the first interim period of an enterprise's fiscal year should be computed by

   a. Applying the estimated income tax rate for the full fiscal year to the pretax accounting income for the interim period.

   b. Applying the estimated income tax rate for the full fiscal year to the taxable income for the interim period.

   c. Applying the statutory income tax rate to the pretax accounting income for the interim period.

   d. Applying the statutory income tax rate to the taxable income for the interim period.

2. Neil Company, which has a fiscal year ending January 31, had the following pretax accounting income and estimated effective annual income tax rates for the first three quarters of the year ended January 31, 20X2:

Quarter	Pretax Accounting Income	Estimated Effective Annual Income Tax Rate at End of Quarter, %
First	$60,000	40%
Second	70,000	40
Third	40,000	45

   Neil's income tax expenses in its interim income statement for the third quarter are

   a. $18,000.

   b. $24,500.

   c. $25,500.

   d. $76,500.

   e. None of the above.

3. Beckett Corporation expects to sustain an operating loss of $100,000 for the full year ending December 31, 20X3. Beckett operates entirely in one jurisdiction where the tax rate is 40 percent. Anticipated tax credits for 20X3 total $10,000. No permanent differences are expected. Realization of the full tax benefit of the expected operating loss and realization of anticipated tax credits are assured beyond any reasonable doubt because they will be carried back. For the first quarter ended March 31, 20X3, Beckett reported an operating loss of $20,000. How much of a tax benefit should Beckett report for the interim period ended March 31, 20X3?

   a. $0.

   b. $8,000.

   c. $10,000.

   d. $12,500.

   e. None of the above.

4. The computation of a company's third-quarter provision for income taxes should be based on earnings
   a. For the quarter at an expected effective annual income tax rate.
   b. For the quarter at the statutory rate.
   c. To date at an expected effective annual income tax rate less prior quarters' provisions.
   d. To date at the statutory rate less prior-quarters provisions.
5. During the first quarter of 20X5, Stahl Company had income before taxes of $200,000, and its effective income tax rate was 15 percent. Stahl's 20X4 effective annual income tax rate was 30 percent, but Stahl expects its 20X5 effective annual income tax rate to be 25 percent. In its first-quarter interim income statement, what amount of income tax expense should Stahl report?
   a. $0.
   b. $30,000.
   c. $50,000.
   d. $60,000.
6. Which of the following items will result in the recognition of a deferred tax asset or liability in the second quarter of 20X7 for Nelson Company:
   a. The portion of dividends received this quarter on an investment in stock of a U.S. corporation that qualifies for the dividend exclusion.
   b. A provision of an expected loss from a lawsuit that is finally settled in 20X8.
   c. Expenses related to the acquisition of a municipal bond whose income is not taxable for income tax purposes.
   d. Life insurance payments made on policies for executives for which the company is the beneficiary.

LO 13-3

E13-7 Significant Foreign Operations

Advanced StudyGuide .com

Information about the domestic and foreign operations of Radon Inc. is as follows:

	Geographic Area					
	United States	Britain	Brazil	Israel	Australia	Total
Sales to unaffiliated customers	$364,000	$252,000	$72,000	$58,000	$47,000	$ 793,000
Interarea sales between affiliates	38,000	19,000	6,000			63,000
Total revenue	$402,000	$271,000	$78,000	$58,000	$47,000	$ 856,000
Profit	34,500	22,500	11,300	3,200	4,500	76,000
Long-lived assets	509,000	439,000	93,000	66,000	75,000	1,182,000

Required

Prepare schedules showing appropriate tests to determine which countries are material using a 10 percent materiality threshold.

LO 13-3

E13-8 Major Customers

Sales by Knight Inc. to major customers are as follows:

Customer	Sales	Reporting Segment
State of Illinois	$2,700,000	Computer hardware
Cook County, Illinois	3,500,000	Computer software
U.S. Treasury Department	3,900,000	Service contract
U.S. Department of Defense	2,200,000	Service contract
Bank of England	4,650,000	Computer software
Philips NV	2,850,000	Computer hardware
Honda	5,400,000	Computer hardware

Required

If worldwide sales total $43,000,000 for the year, which of Knight's customers should be disclosed as major customers?

LO 13-4

E13-9 Estimated Annual Tax Rate

Supra Inc. estimates total federal and state tax rates to be 40 percent. Expected annual pretax earnings from continuing operations are $1,200,000. Differences between tax income and financial statement income are expected to be the following:

Dividend exclusion for dividends received on the company's stock investments	$70,000
Tax-exempt income received	20,000
Premiums for life insurance on officers for which the company is the beneficiary	12,000

A business tax credit of $40,000 should be available. Supra's first-quarter pretax earnings is $170,000, which includes an extraordinary loss of $30,000 before any tax effect of the extraordinary loss.

Required

a. Estimate Supra's effective combined federal and state tax rate on income from continuing operations for the year.

b. Prepare the entry to record the tax provision for the income from continuing operations for the first quarter.

LO 13-4

E13-10 Operating Loss Tax Benefits

Tem Technology has a first-quarter operating loss of $100,000 and expects the following income for the other three quarters:

Second quarter	$ 80,000
Third quarter	160,000
Fourth quarter	400,000

Tem estimated the effective annual tax rate at 40 percent at the end of the first quarter and changed it to 45 percent at the end of the third quarter. The company has a normal seasonal pattern of losses in the first quarter and income in the other quarters.

Required

Prepare a schedule computing the tax obligations or benefits that should be shown on the interim statements.

LO 13-3

E13-11 Industry Segment and Geographic Area Revenue Tests

Symbiotic Chemical Company has four major industry segments and operates both in the U.S. domestic market and in several foreign markets. Information about its revenue from the specific industry segments and its foreign activities for the year 20X2 is as follows:

Sales to Unaffiliated Customers (in thousands)

Industry Segment	Domestic	Foreign	Total
Ethical Drugs	$300		$300
Nonprescription Drugs	325	$100	425
Generic Drugs	125	245	370
Industrial Chemicals	70		70

Sales to Affiliated Customers (in thousands)

Industry Segment	Domestic	Foreign	Total
Ethical Drugs	$20		$ 20
Nonprescription Drugs	50	$40	90
Generic Drugs	40	60	100
Industrial Chemicals	10		10

All the Nonprescription Drugs segment's foreign revenues, both from unaffiliated and intersegment customers, were attributable to a Taiwanese division of the company. This division operated exclusively in Taiwan except for a $10,000 sale to a U.S. subsidiary of the company. All other foreign operations of the company take place exclusively within Mexico.

Required

a. Determine which of the company's operating segments are separately reportable under the revenue test for segment reporting.

b. Determine which of the foreign countries are separately reportable under the revenue test for reporting foreign operations using a 10 percent materiality threshold.

c. Prepare a schedule for disclosing the company's revenue by industry segment for 20X2.

d. Prepare a schedule for disclosing the company's revenue by geographic area for 20X2.

LO 13-4

E13-12 Different Reporting Methods for Interim Reports [CMA Adapted]

Following are seven independent cases on how accounting facts might be reported on an individual company's interim financial reports.

1. Bean Company was reasonably certain it would have an employee strike in the third quarter. As a result, the company shipped heavily during the second quarter but plans to defer the recognition of the sales in excess of the normal sales volume until the third quarter when the strike is in progress. Bean management thinks this is more nearly representative of normal second- and third-quarter operations.
2. Green Inc. takes a physical inventory at year-end for annual financial statement purposes. Inventory and cost of sales reported in the interim quarterly statements are based on estimated gross profit rates because a physical inventory would result in a cessation of operations.
3. ER Company is planning to report one-fourth of its annual pension expense each quarter.
4. Fair Corporation wrote down inventory to reflect the lower of cost or market in the first quarter of 20X1. At year-end, the market price exceeds the original acquisition cost of this inventory. Consequently, management plans to write the inventory back up to its original cost as a year-end adjustment.
5. Carson Company realized a large gain on the sale of investments at the beginning of the second quarter. The company wants to report one-third of the gain in each of the remaining quarters.
6. Ring Corporation has estimated its annual audit fee. Management plans to prorate this expense equally over all four quarters.
7. Mega Corporation made a change in the depreciation of its warehouse building during the third quarter of 20X1. The change was from the accelerated method to the straight-line method to better match the depreciation expense to the current levels of usage of the warehouse. The company plans to use the cumulative effect approach to present the effects of the change as of the beginning of the third quarter.

Required

For each of the seven cases, state whether the method proposed for interim reporting is acceptable under generally accepted accounting principles applicable to interim financial data. Support each answer with a brief explanation.

PROBLEMS

LO 13-2

P13-13 Segment Reporting Worksheet and Schedules

West Corporation reported the following consolidated data for 20X2:

Sales	$ 810,000
Consolidated income before taxes	128,000
Total assets	1,200,000

Data reported for West's four operating divisions are as follows:

	Division A	Division B	Division C	Division D
Sales to outsiders	$280,000	$130,000	$340,000	$60,000
Intersegment sales	60,000		18,000	12,000
Traceable costs	245,000	90,000	290,000	82,000
Assets	400,000	105,000	500,000	75,000

Intersegment sales are priced at cost, and all goods have been subsequently sold to nonaffiliates. Some joint production costs are allocated to the divisions based on total sales. These joint costs were $45,000 in 20X2. The company's corporate center had $20,000 of general corporate expenses and $120,000 of assets that the chief operating decision maker did not use in making the decision regarding the operating segments.

Required

Each of the following items is unrelated to the others.

a. The divisions are industry segments.

(1) Prepare a segmental disclosure worksheet for the company.

(2) Prepare schedules showing which segments are reportable.

b. Assume that each division operates in an individual geographic area, Division A is in the domestic area, and each of the other divisions operates in a separate foreign country. Assume that one-half of the assets in each geographic area represents long-lived, productive assets as defined in **ASC 280.** Prepare schedules showing which geographic areas are reportable using a 10 percent materiality threshold.

c. Determine the amount of sales to an outside customer that would cause that customer to be classified as a major customer under the criteria of **ASC 280.**

LO 13-2

P13-14 Segment Reporting Worksheet and Schedules

Advanced StudyGuide .com

Calvin Inc. has operating segments in five different industries: apparel, building, chemical, furniture, and machinery. Data for the five segments for 20X1 are as follows:

	Apparel	Building	Chemical	Furniture	Machinery
Sales to nonaffiliates	$870,000	$750,000	$55,000	$95,000	$180,000
Intersegment sales			5,000	15,000	140,000
Cost of goods sold	480,000	450,000	42,000	78,000	150,000
Selling expenses	160,000	40,000	10,000	20,000	30,000
Other traceable expenses	40,000	30,000	6,000	12,000	18,000
Allocated general corporate expenses	80,000	75,000	7,000	13,000	25,000
Other information:					
Segment assets	610,000	560,000	80,000	90,000	140,000
Depreciation expense	60,000	50,000	10,000	11,000	25,000
Capital expenditures	20,000	30,000			15,000

Additional Information

1. The corporate headquarters had general corporate expenses totaling $235,000. For internal reporting purposes, $200,000 of these expenses were allocated to the divisions based on their cost of goods sold. The chief operating decision maker does not use the other corporate expenses for making segmental decisions.
2. The company has an intercorporate transfer pricing policy that all intersegment sales shall be priced at cost. All intersegment sales were sold to outsiders by December 31, 20X1.
3. Corporate headquarters had assets of $125,000 that the chief operating decision maker did not use for making segmental decisions.
4. The depreciation expense (listed in the section titled "Other Information") has already been added into cost of goods sold in accordance with the company's cost measurement policies.

Required

a. Prepare a segmental disclosure worksheet for Calvin Inc.

b. Prepare schedules to show which segments are separately reportable.

c. Prepare the information about the company's operations in different industry segments as required by **ASC 280.**

d. Would there be any differences in the specification of reportable segments if the building segment had $460,000 in assets instead of $560,000 and the furniture segment had $190,000 in assets instead of $90,000? Justify your answer by preparing a schedule showing the percentages for each of the three 10 percent segment tests for each of the five segments using these new amounts for segment assets.

LO 13-4

P13-15 Interim Income Statement

Advanced StudyGuide .com

Chris Inc. has accumulated the following information for its second-quarter income statement for 20X2:

Sales	$850,000
Cost of goods sold	420,000
Operating expenses	230,000

Additional Information

1. First-quarter income before taxes was $100,000, and the estimated effective annual tax rate was 40 percent. At the end of the second quarter, expected annual income is $600,000, and a dividend exclusion of $30,000 and a business tax credit of $15,000 are anticipated. The combined state and federal tax rate is 50 percent.
2. The $420,000 cost of goods sold is determined by using the LIFO method and includes 7,500 units from the base layer at a cost of $12 per unit. However, you have determined that these units are expected to be replaced at a cost of $26 per unit.
3. The operating expenses of $230,000 include a $60,000 factory rearrangement cost incurred in April. You have determined that the second quarter will receive about 25 percent of the benefits from this project with the remainder benefiting the third and fourth quarters.

Required

a. Calculate the effective annual tax rate expected at the end of the second quarter for Chris Inc.

b. Prepare the income statement for the second quarter of 20X2. Your solution should include a computation of income tax (or benefit) with the following headings:

	Operating Income (Loss) before Taxes			Tax (Benefit)		
Interim Period	**Current Period**	**Year to Date**	**Estimated Effective Annual Tax Rate**	**Year to Date**	**Less Previously Provided**	**Reported in This Period**

LO 13-4

P13-16 Interim Income Statement

At the end of the second quarter of 20X1, Malta Corporation assembled the following information:

1. The first quarter resulted in a $90,000 loss before taxes. During the second quarter, sales were $1,200,000; purchases were $650,000; and operating expenses were $320,000.
2. Cost of goods sold is determined using the FIFO method. The inventory at the end of the first quarter was reduced by $4,000 to a lower-of-cost-or-market figure of $78,000. During the second quarter, replacement costs recovered, and by the end of the period, market value exceeded the ending inventory cost by $1,250.
3. The ending inventory is estimated using the gross profit method. The estimated gross profit rate is 46 percent.
4. At the end of the first quarter, the effective annual tax rate was estimated at 45 percent. At the end of the second quarter, expected annual income is $600,000. An investment tax credit of $15,000 and dividends received deduction of $75,000 are expected for the year. The combined state and federal tax rate is 40 percent.
5. The tax benefits from operating losses are assured beyond a reasonable doubt. Prior-years income totaling $50,000 is available for operating loss carrybacks.

Required

a. Calculate the expected effective annual tax rate at the end of the second quarter for Malta.

b. Prepare the income statement for the second quarter of 20X1. Your solution should include a computation of income tax (or benefit) for the first and second quarters.

LO 13-3

P13-17 Evaluating Foreign Operations

Advanced StudyGuide .com

For many years, Clark Company operated exclusively in the United States but recently expanded its operations to the Pacific Rim countries of New Zealand, Singapore, and Australia. After a modest beginning in these countries, recent successes have resulted in an increased level of operations in each country. Operating information (in thousands of U.S. dollars) for the company's domestic and foreign operations follows.

	United States	New Zealand	Singapore	Australia
Sales to unaffiliated	$2,500	$320	$ 60	$120
Interarea sales	100		10	
Operating expenses	1,820	290	70	30
Long-lived assets	2,200	280	140	80

In addition, common costs of $120,000 are to be allocated to operations on the basis of the ratio of an area's sales to nonaffiliates to total company sales to nonaffiliates.

Required

a. Determine the profit or loss for each geographic segment.

b. Discuss the general reporting requirements related to the company's geographic areas.

c. Determine which, if any, of the three individual foreign geographic segments is separately reportable using a 10 percent materiality threshold.

LO 13-4

P13-18 Interim Accounting Changes

During the third quarter of its 20X7 fiscal year, Press Company is considering the different methods of reporting accounting changes on its interim segments. Preliminary data are available for the third quarter of 20X7, ending on September 30, 20X7, prior to any adjustments required for any accounting changes. The company's tax rate is 40 percent of income. Selected interim data for the company, in thousands of dollars, follow:

Quarter Ended	Net Sales	Gross Profit	Earnings from Operations, before Tax	Net Earnings
20X7:				
March 31	$388	$133	$27	$16.2
June 30	406	135	30	18.0
September 30 (preliminary)	428	151	32	19.2
20X6:				
March 31	394	139	27	16.2
June 30	416	151	32	19.2
September 30	403	148	31	18.6
December 31	385	134	31	18.6

Required

For each of the following *independent* cases, present the company's interim financial data for the three quarters of 20X7 and the comparative data for 20X6, assuming that in a meeting on the last day of the third quarter of 20X7, the company decides to make the specified accounting change.

a. The company decides to change from the FIFO method of accounting for inventory to the LIFO method. The accounting department has prepared the following schedule of data, in thousands of dollars, showing the cost of goods sold each quarter under the LIFO method. The preceding selected interim data are based on the FIFO method. The accounting department has determined that there will be no difference in cost of goods sold prior to January 1, 20X6.

Quarter Ended	LIFO
20X7:	
March 31	$265
June 30	283
September 30	291
20X6:	
March 31	267
June 30	278
September 30	280
December 31	260

b. The company decides to switch from the straight-line method of depreciation to the accelerated method because of a change in the estimated future benefits from the asset. The company has determined that the accumulated depreciation would have been $42,000 higher as of January 1, 20X6, if the accelerated method had been used. The depreciation expense determined under the two methods follows:

Quarter Ended	Depreciation Expense—Accelerated Method	Depreciation Expense—Straight-Line Method
20X7:		
March 31	$45	$45
June 30	44	45
September 30	42	45
20X6:		
March 31	50	40
June 30	48	40
September 30	47	40
December 31	45	40

c. The company decides to change its method of accounting for recognizing sales revenue on its long-term contracts. The company had been using the completed contract method but changed to the percentage-of-completion method. The accounting department has prepared an analysis of the sales and gross profit recognition under each of the two methods, in thousands of dollars, as follows:

	Completed Contract		Percentage of Completion	
Quarter Ended	Sales	Gross Profit	Sales	Gross Profit
20X7:				
March 31	$ 80	$ 20	$60	$30
June 30	0	0	55	30
September 30	100	50	70	40
20X6:				
March 31	0	0	60	40
June 30	150	100	40	20
September 30	0	0	50	30
December 31	60	40	50	30

LO 13-2

P13-19 Segment Disclosures in the Financial Statements

Multiplex Inc., a public company whose stock is traded on a national stock exchange, reported the following information on its consolidated financial statements for 20X5:

From the consolidated income statement:	
Sales revenues	$564,000,000
Rental revenues	34,000,000
Income before income taxes	65,000,000
Income taxes	20,000,000
From the consolidated balance sheet:	
Total assets	$475,000,000

Multiplex management determined that it had the following operating segments during 20X5: (1) car rental, (2) aerospace, (3) communications, (4) health and fitness products, and (5) heavy equipment manufacturing. The company assembled the following information for these industry segments for 20X5 (dollar amounts stated in millions):

Item	Car Rental	Aerospace	Communications	Health/ Fitness	Heavy Equipment
Sales		$204	$60	$50	$250
Rentals	$34				
Intersegment sales	5				25
Cost of goods sold		141			177
Selling expenses	16	42	29	23	37
Other traceable expenses	4	8	11	5	10
Allocation of common costs	2	7	2	2	7
Assets	20	107	70	80	195
Other information:					
Depreciation expense (included above)	4	15	4	5	25
Capital expenditures	3	30		15	40

Additional Information

1. The corporate headquarters had general corporate expenses totaling $33,000,000 and assets of $25,000,000 (the chief operating decision maker used neither piece of information in defining operating segment performance).
2. The car rental segment's $5,000,000 of intersegment sales consisted of rentals to the aerospace ($2,000,000) and communications ($3,000,000) segments. The intersegment sales of $25,000,000 of the heavy equipment segment were made to the aerospace segment to use in its manufacturing operations. The heavy equipment segment realized a profit of $8,000,000 from this sale. At December 31, 20X5, $7,000,000 of this profit was unrealized from a consolidated viewpoint.
3. At December 31, 20X5, no intercompany receivables or payables were related to the intersegment car rentals. However, the heavy equipment segment had a $15,000,000 receivable from the intersegment sale to the aerospace segment. The company's policy is to include intersegment receivables in a segment's assets for purposes of evaluating segment performance.

Required

a. Prepare schedules for each of the three 10 percent tests: (1) the revenue test, (2) the profit-or-loss test, and (3) the assets test. Each schedule should indicate which of Multiplex's industry segments are reportable segments for 20X5.

b. Indicate whether Multiplex's reportable segments meet the 75 percent revenue test.

c. Prepare the information about the company's operations in different industry segments as required by **ASC 280.**

LO 13-3 **P13-20**

Reporting Operations in Different Countries

Watson Inc., a multinational company, has operating divisions in France, Mexico, and Japan as well as in the United States. The company reported the following information on its consolidated financial statements for 20X5:

From the consolidated income statement:	
Sales revenues	$856,000,000
Net income	60,000,000
From the consolidated balance sheet:	
Total assets	750,000,000

The following additional information was assembled for Watson's domestic and international operations for 20X5 (dollars stated in millions):

Item	Domestic	France	Mexico	Japan
Sales to unaffiliated customers	$430	$300	$36	$90
Intracompany sales between geographic areas	50			10
Operating profit	7	40	2	18
General corporate expenses	30			
Long-lived assets	235	160	29	81

Additional Information

1. The domestic intracompany sales of $50,000,000 were made to Watson's French division. A total gross profit of $20,000,000 was realized by Watson's domestic operations on these sales. At December 31, 20X5, $10,000,000 of the total gross profit was unrealized from a consolidated viewpoint. At December 31, 20X5, Watson's French division owed domestic operations $15,000,000 related to these sales.
2. The intracompany sales made by Watson's Japanese division were made to Watson's Mexican division. The Japanese division realized a gross profit of $2,000,000 on the sales. At December 31, 20X5, all of the goods sold to the Mexican division remained in its inventory. At December 31, 20X5, the Japanese division had an $8,000,000 receivable related to these sales.

Required

a. Determine whether Watson Inc. must separately report its foreign operations.

b. Determine which of the three individual foreign geographic segments is separately reportable using a 10 percent materiality threshold.

c. Prepare the information about the company's domestic and foreign operations as required by **ASC 280.**

LO 13-2, 13-3 P13-21 Matching Terms

Match the items in the left-hand column with the descriptions/explanations in the right-hand column.

Items

1. Reportable operating segment
2. 10 percent significance rules
3. Revenue test for material foreign country disclosure
4. Asset test for reportable operating segments
5. Asset test for material foreign country disclosure
6. Comprehensive segment disclosure test
7. Enterprisewide disclosures
8. Recovery of prior write-down for interim inventory valuations
9. Interim LIFO liquidations to be replaced by year-end
10. Effective annual tax rate

Descriptions/Explanations

A. Based on all assets used by management to assess that business unit's performance.
B. Not computed until tax is paid.
C. Includes intercorporate sales and transfers.
D. Annual statutory tax rate.
E. Based on long-lived assets used in that business unit only.
F. Values cost of goods sold at the LIFO cost of the goods sold.
G. Values cost of goods sold at the expected replacement cost.
H. Requires sales to unaffiliated units for separately disclosed segments to be higher than or equal to 75 percent of total consolidated revenue.
I. Segment that must meet each of the three 10 percent segment significance tests.
J. Product revenues, geographic areas, and information about major customers.
K. Recovery allowed by **ASC 270 and ASC 740.**
L. Based on sales to unaffiliated entities only.
M. Not permitted under **ASC 270 and ASC 740.**
N. Estimate of the income tax rate that will actually be paid for the year.
O. Segment that has met at least one of the three 10 percent segment significance tests.

14 SEC Reporting

Multicorporate Entities

Multinational Entities

Reporting Requirements

Segment and Interim Reporting

SEC Reporting

Partnerships

Governmental and Not-for-Profit Entities

Corporations in Financial Difficulty

THE GENESIS OF SECURITIES REGULATION

The need for regulation has gone hand in hand with the offering of securities to the general public. In the 13th century, King Edward I of England established a Court of Aldermen to regulate security trades in London. In the latter part of the 18th century, England's Parliament passed several acts, termed the *Bubble Acts,* to control questionable security schemes that had become popular. In 1792, the New York Stock Exchange was created to serve as a clearinghouse for securities trades between its members. The need for additional sources of capital paralleled the advent of the industrial revolution and the growth of commerce in the United States. Some individuals took advantage of this situation and offered securities of fictitious companies for sale to the general public or used financial reports that were not factual about the offering company's financial picture. In 1911, because of the lack of any federal security regulatory laws, several states began passing what were called *blue sky laws* to regulate the offering of securities by companies made up only of "blue sky," that is, that did not have a sound financial base.

The era of the 1920s was one of heavy stock speculation by many individuals. Business executives, cab drivers, and assembly-line workers all wanted to participate in the many stock opportunities that existed at that time. Unfortunately, a number of abuses were occurring in the marketplace. For example, certain speculators sought to manipulate selected stock prices by issuing untrue press releases about companies' operations or managements. Companies were not required to be audited, and some of them issued false and misleading financial statements. Investors were using excessive amounts of margin; that is, they were borrowing heavily to invest in stocks. Some employees of companies were using inside information—information that had not been released to the public—to purchase or sell their company's stock for personal advantage.

The month of October 1929 is often viewed as the beginning of the Great Depression. Stock prices plunged to record lows within just a few weeks as panic took over the market. It became obvious that some form of federal regulation was necessary to restore confidence in the stock market. The Federal Securities Acts of 1933 and 1934 were part of President Franklin D. Roosevelt's New Deal legislation. The Securities Act of 1933 regulated the initial distribution of security issues by requiring companies to make "full and fair" disclosure of their financial affairs before their securities could be offered to the public. The Securities Exchange Act of 1934 required all companies whose stocks were traded on a stock exchange to periodically update their financial information. In addition, the 1934 act created the Securities and Exchange Commission and assigned it the responsibility of administering both the 1933 and 1934 acts.

The SEC has the legal responsibility to regulate trades of securities and to determine the types of financial disclosures that a publicly held company must make. Although the SEC has the ultimate legal authority to establish the disclosure requirements, it has worked closely with the accounting profession to prescribe the accounting principles and standards used to measure and report companies' financial conditions and results of operations. The SEC's role is to ensure full and fair disclosure; it does not guarantee the investment merits of any security. Stock markets still operate on a *caveat emptor* ("let the buyer beware") basis. The SEC has consistently taken the position that investors must have the necessary information to make their own assessments of the risk and return attributes of a security.

The present role of the SEC is particularly complex. In 1935, its first year of full activity, only 284 new securities were registered for sale to the general public. Now the number of new securities being registered for sale is more than 5,000 per year. The SEC also regulates more than 10,000 securities brokers and dealers and must monitor stock exchange volumes often surpassing a billion shares a day.

LEARNING OBJECTIVES

When you finish studying this chapter, you should be able to:

LO 14-1 Understand the SEC's structure and regulatory authority.

LO 14-2 Understand the process of registering securities with the SEC.

LO 14-3 Understand periodic reporting requirements.

LO 14-4 Understand requirements for management reporting laws.

LO 14-5 Understand disclosure requirements.

INTERNATIONAL HARMONIZATION OF ACCOUNTING STANDARDS FOR PUBLIC OFFERINGS[1]

Advanced StudyGuide .com

The global economy has a number of major securities exchanges in which business entities can seek equity or debt capital. The SEC wants to preserve the international prestige of the U.S. capital markets by providing financial markets for multinational and non-U.S. companies. With the encouragement of the SEC and the International Organization of Securities Commissions (IOSCO), the International Accounting Standards Board (IASB) is working with the Financial Accounting Standards Board (FASB) to converge on a uniform set of accounting and financial reporting standards that can be used by all companies seeking financing through any of the world's major stock markets, including those of the United States.

In 2007, the SEC took two actions regarding its roadmap toward a uniform global set of financial reporting standards. In its first action, the SEC published **Securities Act Release No. 33-8879,** "Acceptance from Foreign Private Issuers of Financial Statements Prepared in Accordance with International Financial Reporting Standards without Reconciliation to U.S. GAAP," under which the SEC will accept financial statements from foreign private issuers[2] without reconciliation to U.S. GAAP if they are prepared using International Financial Reporting Standards (IFRSs) as issued by the IASB. Previously, foreign companies using IFRSs in their SEC filings were required to present a reconciliation schedule that reconciled foreign financial statement items to U.S. GAAP. This schedule, Form 20-F, had been a cause of concern for a number of foreign companies that felt it was an unnecessary requirement and an indirect criticism of the IFRSs. By removing the requirement for the reconciliation schedule, the SEC felt that it would show support for the IASB-approved version of IFRSs and encourage the development of IFRSs as a uniform global standard, not as a divergent set of standards that can be applied differently in each country. This rule became applicable to financial statements for fiscal years ending after November 15, 2007, and to interim financial statements after that date.

[1] To view a video explanation of this topic, visit advancedstudyguide.com.

[2] Rule 205 of the Securities Act of 1933 defines *foreign private issuer* (FPI) as any foreign issuer, other than a foreign government, *except* an issuer that meets the following conditions: (1) more than 50 percent of its outstanding voting securities are directly or indirectly owned by residents of the United States and (2) any of the following: (a) the majority of its executive officers or directors are U.S. citizens or residents; (b) more than 50 percent of the issuer's assets are located in the United States; or (c) the business of the issuer is administered principally in the United States.

The second action taken by the SEC to support the use of IFRSs in U.S. capital markets was the issuance of **Securities Act Release No. 33-8831,** "Concept Release on Allowing U.S. Issuers to Prepare Financial Statements in Accordance with International Financial Reporting Standards." However, due to the financial crisis beginning in 2008, the SEC backed off temporarily on the transition toward the adoption of IFRS in the United States. The FASB and IASB will continue to work toward convergence of U.S. and international reporting standards, but it appears that much is still to be done. As of this writing, the SEC still has not definitely decided whether or when it will allow U.S. registrants to use IFRS.

SECURITIES AND EXCHANGE COMMISSION

LO 14-1

Understand the SEC's structure and regulatory authority.

Organizational Structure of the Commission

The SEC's five commissioners are appointed by the president of the United States with the advice and consent of the Senate. Figure 14–1 is an organizational chart of the Commission showing the five separate divisions and the major offices that must report directly to the Commission. The five divisions, and their primary responsibilities, are as follows:

FYI

As an example, the Division of Enforcement recently reached a settlement with Peter Siris, the New York investment manager of a hedge fund, who was found guilty of illegally helping a Chinese company go public in the United States while concealing his position as the company's consultant and his resulting commission. Siris and two firms he controls (Guerrilla Capital Management and Hua Mei 21st Century) were accused of conducting a reverse merger to obtain the Chinese food company China Yingxia. Siris paid US$1.1 million for the settlement without any comment on the charge.

1. *Division of Corporation Finance.* Develops and administers the disclosure requirements for the securities acts and reviews all registration statements and other issue-oriented disclosures. This is the division with which accountants are most familiar because all registration forms are submitted to it.
2. *Division of Enforcement.* Directs the SEC's enforcement actions. This division has several options for enforcement ranging from persuasion to *administrative proceedings* to litigation. An administrative proceeding often is used to gather evidence and present findings on a specific issue, such as a significant shareholder not filing proper reports with the SEC. Many of the administrative proceedings result in a consent action by a registrant, stock market participant, or professional practicing before the SEC in which the party accepts the SEC's judgment. *Litigation* is used for serious infractions of SEC-administered laws, such as a securities broker engaging in the fraudulent sale of securities. Litigation can result in injunctions to discontinue actions as well as civil or criminal sanctions.

FIGURE 14–1
Organizational Structure of the Securities and Exchange Commission

Divisions	Offices	

▪ Corporation Finance
▪ Enforcement
▪ Investment Management
▪ Economic and Risk Analysis
▪ Trading and Markets
	▪ Chief Operating Officer
	  ▪ Acquisitions
	  ▪ Financial Management
	  ▪ Human Resources
	  ▪ Information Technology
	  ▪ Support Operations
	▪ Administrative Law Judges
	▪ Chief Accountant
	▪ Compliance Inspections and Examinations
	▪ Credit Ratings
	▪ Municipal Securities
	▪ Investor Advocate
		▪ Equal Employment Opportunity
		▪ Ethics Counsel
		▪ General Counsel
		▪ Inspector General
		▪ International Affairs
		▪ Investor Education and Advocacy
		▪ Legislative and Intergovernmental Affairs
		▪ Minority and Women Inclusion
		▪ Public Affairs
		▪ Secretary

3. *Division of Investment Management.* Regulates investment advisers and investment companies.
4. *Division of Economic and Risk Analysis.* Integrates financial economics and rigorous data analytics into the core mission of the SEC.
5. *Division of Trading and Markets.* Regulates national securities exchanges, brokers, and dealers of securities.

Several offices support these divisions; one of the most important for accountants is the Office of the Chief Accountant. This office assists the Commission by studying current accounting issues and preparing position papers for the SEC to consider. The other major offices listed offer the Commission advice on a variety of economic and regulatory matters.

Laws Administered by the SEC

In addition to the Securities Acts of 1933 and 1934, the SEC is responsible for administering other laws established to regulate companies or individuals involved with the securities markets. The laws are

1. *Trust Indenture Act of 1939.* Requires a trustee to be appointed for sales of bonds, debentures, and other debt securities of public corporations, thus bringing in a bonded expert to administer the debt.
2. *Investment Company Act of 1940.* Controls companies such as mutual funds that invest funds for the public. These companies must be audited annually with the auditor reporting directly to the SEC.
3. *Investment Advisors Act of 1940.* Requires complete disclosure of information about investment advisers, including their backgrounds, business affiliations, and bases for compensation.
4. *Securities Investor Protection Act of 1970.* Created the Securities Investor Protection Corporation (SIPC), an entity responsible for insuring investors from possible losses if an investment house enters bankruptcy. A small fee is added to the cost of each stock trade to cover the costs of the SIPC.
5. *Sarbanes-Oxley Act of 2002.* Created the Public Company Accounting Oversight Board (PCAOB) and a number of responsibilities for audit committees of publicly held companies and for public accounting firms.
6. *Dodd-Frank Wall Street Reform and Consumer Protection Act of 2010.* Reshaped the U.S. regulatory system in a number of areas including, but not limited to, consumer protection, trading restrictions, credit ratings, regulation of financial products, corporate governance and disclosure, and transparency.
7. *Jumpstart Our Business Startups (JOBS) Act of 2012.* Helps businesses raise funds in public capital markets by minimizing regulatory requirements.

The SEC is often asked for assistance in the administration of two other major laws, as follows:

8. *Foreign Corrupt Practices Act of 1977.* Amended the 1934 Securities Exchange Act. It requires accurate and fair recording of financial activities and requires management to maintain an adequate system of internal control.
9. *Federal Bankruptcy Acts.* Provides SEC assistance to the courts when a publicly held company declares bankruptcy. The SEC's primary concern in these cases is to protect security holders.

The Regulatory Structure

Many people beginning a study of the regulatory structure of the SEC are overwhelmed by the myriad of regulations, acts, guides, and releases it uses to perform its tasks. It is easier to understand how the SEC operates after obtaining a basic understanding of these public documents and the nature of the SEC's pronouncements. Refer to Figure 14–2 for an overview of this regulatory structure.

FIGURE 14–2 The Regulatory Structure

Item	Contents
Securities Act of 1933	Statute regulating initial registration and sale of securities.
Securities Act rules	Basic definitions of Securities Act terms such as *offers, distribution, participation,* and *accredited investor.*
Securities Act regulations	Detailed requirements of registration. At the present time, there are six regulations (Regulations A, B, C, D, E, F) of which two (A and D) specify exemptions from registration requirements for small or private stock offerings.
Securities Act forms	Content of registration forms. The most frequently used forms are Form 1-A for small offerings of securities and Forms S-1, S-2, and S-3, which are general registration forms.
Securities Act industry guides	Specifications of additional disclosures required in registration statements of companies in special industries such as oil and gas, banking, and real estate.
Securities Act releases (SRs)	Announcements amending or adopting new rules, guides, forms, or policies under the 1933 act. Approximately 6,000 releases have been published. These are noted with a prefix, for example, for release number 6,000, Release 33-6000.
Securities Exchange Act of 1934	Regulation of security trading and requirements for periodic reports by publicly held companies.
Exchange Act rules	Specific reporting requirements of over-the-counter securities, special reports required by stockholders who own 5 percent or more of a company's outstanding stock, and prohibition of manipulative and deceptive devices or contrivances.
Exchange Act forms	Specification of the content of periodic reports. The most commonly used forms are Form 10-K (annual report), Form 10-Q (quarterly report), and Form 8-K (current events report).
Exchange Act industry guides	Additional periodic reporting requirements of companies in specialized industries such as electric and gas utilities, oil and gas, and banking.
Securities Exchange Act releases (SRs)	Announcements of amendments or adoptions of new rules, guides, forms, or policy statements pertaining to the 1934 act. More than 15,000 have been issued, and are identified with a prefix, for example, for number 15,000, Release 34-15000.
Regulation S-X (Reg. S-X)	Articles specifying the form and content of financial disclosures: financial statements, schedules, footnotes, reports of accountants, and pro forma disclosures.
Regulation S-K (Reg. S-K)	Articles specifying disclosure rules of nonfinancial items to be included in registration statements, annual reports, and proxy statements. Major items are descriptions of business, management's discussion and analysis, disagreements with accountants, and required information about new stock issues.
Accounting and Auditing Enforcement Releases (AAERs)	Announcements of enforcement actions involving accountants practicing before the SEC. Includes discussion of the findings and opinions (including sanctions against the accountants involved) of enforcement hearings held by the Commission. *AAER No. 1* is a codification of all enforcement topics previously included in the Accounting Series Releases.
Staff Accounting Bulletins (SABs)	New or revised administrative practices and interpretations used by the Commission's staff in reviewing financial statements.

The Securities Act of 1933 and the Securities Exchange Act of 1934 are broken down into rules, regulations, forms, guides, and releases. The rules generally provide specific definitions for complying with the acts. The regulations establish compliance requirements; for example, the regulations of the 1933 act detail specific reporting requirements for special cases such as small companies. The forms specify the format of the reports to be made under each of the acts. The guides provide specified additional disclosure requirements for selected industries such as oil and gas as well as banks. The releases are used for amendments or adoptions of new requirements under the acts.

Two major regulations, ***Regulation S-X*** and ***Regulation S-K,*** govern the preparation of financial statements and associated disclosures made in reports to the SEC. Specifically, Regulation S-X presents the rules for preparing financial statements, footnotes, and the auditor's report. Regulation S-K covers all nonfinancial items, such as management's discussion and analysis of the company's operations and financial position.

The SEC needed some reporting vehicle to inform accountants about changes made in disclosure requirements, regulatory changes in the auditor–client relationship, and the results of enforcement actions taken against participants in the financial disclosure or securities trading process. Before 1982, the SEC used Accounting Series Releases (ASRs) for this purpose and had issued 307 ASRs covering a wide range of topics. In 1982, these ASRs were classified as covering either financial accounting topics or enforcement actions. Regulatory actions of the SEC are now provided on its website. Those governing reporting and financial accounting requirements are identified by a release number that begins with the number of the securities act being changed or amended (e.g., Release No. 33-8545, Release No. 34-51293, and so on).

The ***Accounting and Auditing Enforcement Releases (AAERs)*** present the results of enforcement actions taken against accountants, brokers, and other participants in the filing process. Most of these actions result from the filing of a false or misleading statement. The SEC can use administrative proceedings, in which case the hearings take place before an administrative law judge (ALJ) who is independent of the Commission. Both the SEC and the defendant are allowed to present evidence. The administrative law judge then issues a report that includes the findings of fact and a recommended sanction, such as barring a person from further participation in auditing publicly traded companies or from employment as a broker or a member of management of a publicly traded company. In more serious cases, the SEC may file a complaint with a federal court seeking injunctions prohibiting illegal acts or practices, or other court orders seeking civil monetary penalties or other forms of sanctions.

An interesting example of a civil action is presented in Litigation Release No. 17588, issued June 27, 2002. It is also identified as Accounting and Auditing Release No. 1585. The title of the release is "SEC Charges WorldCom with $3.8 Billion Fraud. Commission Action Seeks Injunction, Money Penalties, Prohibitions on Destroying Documents and Making Extraordinary Payments to WorldCom Affiliates, and the Appointment of a Corporate Monitor." This litigation release presents the initial SEC action against WorldCom for its massive accounting fraud in which the company capitalized and deferred, rather than properly expensing, approximately $3.8 billion of costs. This fraud eventually led to the bankruptcy of WorldCom and the indictments of several of the company's top management.

The ***Staff Accounting Bulletins (SABs)*** allow the Commission's staff to make announcements on technical issues with which it is concerned as a result of reviews of SEC filings. The SABs are not formal actions of the Commission; nevertheless, most preparers follow these bulletins because they represent the views of the staff that will be reviewing their companies' filings.

An example of a Staff Accounting Bulletin is SAB No. 101, "Revenue Recognition in Financial Statements," issued in 1999. SAB No. 101 focused on the several revenue recognition procedures the SEC staff found inconsistently applied by registrants. One special item was the discussion of revenue recognition by the "New Economy" Internet firms. These companies focus on revenue growth, and many do not report any positive income. Analysts and stock market investors gauge these companies based on their revenue growth. For example, Company A, an Internet company, may offer another company's products (Company T) on Company A's website. Customers place their orders and provide a credit card number to A's Internet site. Company A then forwards the order to Company T, which ships the goods to the customer. The goods normally cost $200, for which Company A receives $20 for facilitating the sale. The question is this: Can Company A record the $200 gross sale and a $180 cost of goods sold to report its profit of $20, or should Company A record just the net $20 sales commission as its revenue? SAB No. 101 states that the revenue should be reported on the net basis, not the gross basis that the SEC staff believes inflates both the reported revenue and cost of goods sold. As viewed by the SEC staff, Company A did not take title to the goods, did not incur the risks and rewards of ownership of the goods, and was only an agent or broker for Company T for which it received a commission or fee.

The 1933 and 1934 securities acts gave the SEC broad regulatory powers to determine the accounting and reporting standards for publicly traded companies. The SEC has customarily relied on the accounting profession to establish accounting standards through creation and support for a standard-making body, for example, the APB and the FASB. The cooperation between the SEC and the FASB has worked with varying levels of success. The FASB is sensitive to the changes in the business world and attempts to react quickly to them by promulgating new accounting standards when needed. The SEC, however, continues to fulfill its responsibility by issuing releases on subjects that it believes must be addressed.

ISSUING SECURITIES: THE REGISTRATION PROCESS

LO 14-2

Understand the process of registering securities with the SEC.

The Securities Act of 1933 typically required companies wishing to sell debt or stock securities in interstate offerings to the general public to register those securities with the SEC. The registration process requires extensive disclosure about the company, its management, and the intended use of the proceeds from the issue. The registrant also must provide audited financial statements. The basic financial statements required in the annual report are (1) two years of balance sheets, (2) three years of income statements, (3) three years of statements of cash flows, and (4) three years of statements of shareholders' equity. Prior-years statements are presented on a comparative basis with those for the current period. In addition, the SEC requires at least five years of selected financial information presenting key numbers from the four basic financial statements.

A number of types' of securities and securities transactions are exempt from registration under the 1933 act. Although the SEC may exempt these from full registration requirements, the antifraud provisions of the securities acts still apply to all offerings. The exempt securities are commercial paper (i.e., notes) with a maturity of nine months or less; issues in which the securities are offered and sold only within one state; securities exchanged by an issuer exclusively with its existing shareholders with no commission charged (e.g., a stock split or a stock dividend issued by a corporation); issuances of securities by governments, banks, savings and loan associations, farmers, co-ops, and common carriers regulated by the Interstate Commerce Commission; and securities of nonprofit religious, educational, or charitable organizations. Under the SEC's ***Regulation A,*** issuances up to $5,000,000 within a 12-month period can be exempt if the entity files a notice with the SEC and an "offering circular" containing financial and other information provided to the persons to whom the offer is made (the financial statements in the offering circular do not have to be audited). Thus, some required disclosures of financial statements and other financial information fall under Regulation A.

Regulation D of the SEC presents three important exemptions from full registration requirements for private placements (i.e., not offered to the general public) of securities, as follows:

1. Rule 504 of Regulation D exempts small issuances up to $1,000,000 within a 12-month period to any number of investors. No specific disclosures are required, but the offerer must send a notice of the offering to the SEC within 15 days of the first sale of the securities.
2. Rule 505 of Regulation D exempts issuances up to $5,000,000 within a 12-month period. The sales can be made to up to 35 "unaccredited investors" and to an unlimited number of "accredited investors." *Accredited investors* include banks, credit unions, insurance companies, partnerships and corporations, and individuals having a net worth exceeding $1,000,000 or individual income of $200,000 for the two most recent years. *Unaccredited investors* are persons who do not meet the income or net worth requirements. An unaccredited investor who purchases the securities must be supplied audited balance sheets along with other financial statements. If the sales are only to accredited investors, no disclosures are required. Under Rule 505, the SEC must be notified within

15 days of the first sale, and the issuer must restrict the purchasers' rights to resell the securities, generally for a period of two years. The securities typically state the nature of their restriction and the fact that they have not been registered with the SEC.

3. Rule 506 of Regulation D allows private placements of an unlimited amount of securities and applies, in general, the same rules as Rule 505 except that the maximum of 35 unaccredited investors must be sophisticated investors who have knowledge and experience in financial affairs.

The offering process usually begins with the selection of an investment banker, also called an *underwriter,* who assists the company in the registration process by providing marketing information and ultimately directing the distribution of the securities. The *underwriting agreement* is a contract between the company and the underwriter and specifies such items as the underwriter's responsibilities and the final disposition of any unsold securities remaining at the end of the public offering. In some cases, the underwriter agrees to purchase any remaining securities; in others, the company is required to withdraw any unsold securities. An offering team includes the company, the underwriter, the company's independent auditor, the company's legal counsel, and experts such as appraisers or engineers who may be required. Typically, the underwriter requires a *comfort letter* from the auditor to indicate that the company has fulfilled all accounting requirements in the registration process.

The Registration Statement

The process of public offerings of securities begins with the preparation of the ***registration statement.*** The company must select one from among approximately 20 different forms the SEC currently has for registering securities. The most common are ***Form S-1, Form S-2,*** and ***Form S-3.*** Others are required when registering stock option plans, foreign issues, limited issuances under Regulation D, and special types of offerings. Form S-1, the most comprehensive registration statement, is for registering first-time offerings by companies that have never issued publicly traded stock. Form S-2 is an abbreviated form for present registrants who have other publicly traded stock; Form S-3 is a brief form available for large, established registrants whose stock has been trading for several years.

Form S-1 has two different levels of disclosure. Part I, often referred to as the *prospectus,* is intended primarily for investors and includes the basic information package as well as information about the intended use of the proceeds, a description of the securities being offered, and the plan of distribution, including the name of the principal underwriter. Filings for bond issues must include summary information about the ratio of earnings to fixed charges so investors are informed about some of the financial risk the new bond issue adds to the company. Part II of Form S-1 includes more detailed information, such as a list of the expenses of issuing and distributing the new security, additional information about directors and officers and additional financial statement schedules. The registration statement must be signed by the principal executive, financial, and accounting officers as well as a majority of the company's board of directors. The company then submits its registration statement to an SEC review by the Division of Corporation Finance.

SEC Review and Public Offering

The SEC seeks to provide potential investors full and fair disclosure of all material information necessary for assessing the securities' risk and return expectations. The SEC does not, however, guarantee the value of the stock or bond security.

Most first-time registrants receive a "customary review," which is a thorough examination by the SEC that may result in acceptance, or, alternatively, a ***comment letter*** specifying the deficiencies that must be corrected before the securities may be offered for sale. Established companies that already have stock widely traded generally are subject to a summary review or a cursory review. Once the registration statement becomes effective, the company may begin selling securities to the public. This review period is 20 days unless the company receives a comment letter from the SEC.

Between the time the registration statement is presented to the SEC and its effective date, the company may issue a ***preliminary prospectus,*** referred to as a *red herring prospectus,* which provides tentative information to investors about an upcoming issue. The name "red herring" comes from the red ink used on the cover of this preliminary prospectus, indicating that it is not an offering statement and that the securities being discussed are not yet available for sale. In addition, the company generally prepares a "tombstone ad" in the business press to inform investors of the upcoming offering. These ads are bordered in black ink, hence the title.

The time period between the initial decision to offer securities and the actual sale may not exceed 120 days. In the interim, many factors can affect the stock market and decrease the company's ability to obtain capital. In 1982, the SEC devised the ***shelf registration*** rule for large, established companies with other issues of stock already actively traded. These companies may file a registration statement with the SEC for a stock issue that may be "brought off the shelf" and, with the aid of an underwriter, updated within a very short time, usually two to three days. A shelf registration is limited to 10 percent of the company's currently outstanding stock but allows large companies to select the optimal time to sell their stock.

Accountants' Legal Liability in the Registration Process

Accountants play a key role in the registration statement's preparation. The company's own accountants prepare the initial financial disclosures, which the company's independent accountants then audit. The 1933 act created a very broad legal liability for all participants in the registration process, which is particularly high for accountants because financial disclosures make up the majority of the registration statement. Under section 11 of the 1933 act, accountants are liable for any materially false or misleading information *to the effective date* of the registration statement. The underwriters handling the sale of the securities often require a *comfort letter* from the registrant's public accountants for the period between the filing date and the effective date. This comfort letter provides additional evidence that the public accountant has not found any adverse financial changes since the filing date. Plaintiffs suing the accountant are not required to show they relied on the registration statement, only that the statement was wrong at the effective date! Accountants have a "due diligence" defense, the result of interpretations by the courts as to what is generally required in a reasonable investigation of the company's financial position; however, the broad legal exposure causes many anxieties for accountants involved with the offering of securities.

STOP & THINK

Accountants are not only responsible for their own actions but also must endeavor to discover their clients' fraudulent actions. A recent civil fraud case against Ernst & Young LLP held that it stood by while Lehman Brothers used accounting gimmickry to mask its shaky finances. The lawsuit said that Lehman ran "a massive accounting fraud," but it did not name any former top executives at the investment bank as defendants. Lehman's September 2008 collapse helped spark the global financial crisis. In 2013, Ernst & Young settled this class-action lawsuit for $99 million.

PERIODIC REPORTING REQUIREMENTS

LO 14-3

Understand periodic reporting requirements.

The Securities Exchange Act of 1934 regulates the trading of securities and imposes reporting requirements on companies whose securities trade on one of the stock exchanges. Companies with more than $10 million in assets and whose securities are held by more than 500 persons must file annual and other periodic reports as updates on their economic activities. The three basic ***periodic reporting forms*** used for this updating are Form 10-K, Form 10-Q, and Form 8-K.

Form 10-K is the annual filing to the SEC. In 2002, the SEC changed the filing deadlines of the Form 10-K for *accelerated filers,* which are defined as those companies having at least $75 million in aggregate market value that have been subject to the periodic and annual reporting requirements for at least one year, including the filing of at least one annual report. Accelerated filers must file their Form 10-K within 60 days after the end of the company's fiscal year. Small businesses and others who do not meet the requirements for an accelerated filer have until 90 days after the end of their fiscal years.

Form 10-K has four parts and the general format is similar to the company's annual report to shareholders (ARS). Parts I, II, and III include the management's discussion and analysis, the audited financial statements and footnotes, the report by management on the internal control structure and the assessment of the effectiveness of those controls, the auditor's opinion, and at least five years of condensed financial information disclosures. Some of this information is sometimes "incorporated by reference" to other ARS or other filings made to the SEC. Also included must be a statement signed by the CEO and CFO that certifies that the financials and disclosures in the report are appropriate and that those financial statements and disclosures fairly present, in all material respects, the issuer's operations and the financial condition.

Part IV of the Form 10-K contains additional schedules and exhibits. Form 10-K differs from the annual report to shareholders by providing specific information relevant to the security holders, such as descriptions of any matters submitted to a vote of security holders; discussion of any disagreements with external auditors; management compensation and major ownership blocks; and schedules detailing selected asset and liability accounts, including accounts receivable, property, plant, and equipment, the company's investments in other enterprises, and indebtedness of the company and its affiliates. The SEC also requires disclosure in the annual report as to where investors can obtain access to a company's SEC periodic filings, including whether it provides access to its filings on its website, free of charge, as soon as possible after the filings are made to the SEC.

Form 10-Q is the quarterly report to the SEC. Accelerated filers must submit a Form 10-Q within 35 days after the end of each of their first three quarters. No Form 10-Q is filed for the fourth quarter because that is when the Form 10-K is filed. Companies not classified as accelerated filers must file within 45 days after the end of each of their first three quarters.

Part I of Form 10-Q includes comparative financial statements prepared in accordance with **ASC 270** and **740;** these interim statements need not be audited. Essentially, the company provides financial statements for the most recent quarter, cumulative statements from the beginning of the fiscal period, and comparative statements for the equivalent quarters in the preceding fiscal year. Selected data from the interim statements also must be disclosed in a footnote in the company's annual report, and the independent auditors, on an ex post basis, review the previously issued interims for the year as part of the year-end annual audit.

Part II of Form 10-Q is an update on significant matters occurring since the last quarter. These include new legal proceedings, changes in the rights of securities, defaults on senior securities, increases or decreases in the number of securities outstanding, and other materially important events affecting security holders.

Form 8-K is used to disclose unscheduled material events. In 2004, the SEC issued final rules that increased the number of reportable items to be disclosed on Form 8-K filings and accelerated the timing of the filing requirement. Companies must file a Form 8-K within four business days of the occurrence of a "triggering event." Many of the triggering events involve the company's board of directors or an authorizing officer of the company making a commitment or conclusion regarding one or more of the reportable items. A number of these events involve accountants, and it is important that accountants understand which events require a Form 8-K filing. Because of the expansion of the number of reportable items, the SEC reorganized Form 8-K items into nine topical sections, each with a subnumbering system used for specific items in that section.

1. *Registrant's Business and Operations.* The four reportable events in this section are (1.01) entry into a material agreement, (1.02) termination of a material agreement, (1.03) the bankruptcy or receivership of the company, and (1.04) mine safety violations.
2. *Financial Information.* This section contains the following six items: (2.01) the completion of the acquisition or disposition of assets, (2.02) the public announcement of material results of operations and financial condition, (2.03) the creation of

a direct financial obligation under an off-balance sheet arrangement, (2.04) an event that accelerates or increases a direct financial obligation under an off-balance sheet arrangement, (2.05) costs associated with exit or disposal activities when the board commits the company to an exit or disposal of a material part of the business, and (2.06) material impairments of a company's assets.

3. *Securities and Trading Markets.* The three items in this section are (3.01) notice of delisting or failure to satisfy a continuing listing rule, (3.02) an unregistered sale of equity securities, and (3.03) material modifications to the rights of security holders.
4. *Matters Related to Accountants and Financial Statements.* The two items in this section are (4.01) changes in the registrant's certifying accountant and (4.02) nonreliance on previously issued financial statements or a related audit report.
5. *Corporate Governance and Management.* The eight items in this section are (5.01) changes in control of the registrant, (5.02) the departure of directors or principal officers, or the election or appointment of principal officers, (5.03) amendments to the articles of incorporation or bylaws, including any change in the registrant's fiscal year, (5.04) the temporary suspension of trading under the registrant's employee benefit plans, (5.05) amendments to the registrant's code of ethics, or waiver of a provision of the code of ethics, (5.06) a change in shell company status,[3] (5.07) the submission of matters to a vote of security holders, and (5.08) shareholder director nominations.
6. *Asset-Based Securities.* This section requires disclosure of material items related to asset-backed securities such as a bond issue. Disclosures are required for a change of servicer or trustee of the security, a change in the credit enhancement or other external support for the securities, or a failure to make a distribution required by the security agreement.
7. *Regulation FD.* (Item 7.01) This section requires filing a Form 8-K to broadly report material information that is being provided to securities analysts, selected institutional investors, or others. Regulation FD seeks to eliminate the informational advantages of having access to officers or other management members through public channels. For example, if the CEO of a registrant spoke to a group of financial analysts at a lunch meeting during which the general future of the company and its industry was discussed, the company would file a Form 8-K disclosing the meeting and include major informational items the CEO presented.
8. *Other Events.* (Item 8.01) This section is unstructured and flexible to allow management to disclose items it believes may be of material importance to security holders.
9. *Financial Statements and Exhibits.* (Item 9.01) This section includes a list of the financial statements, pro forma financial information, and exhibits required to be filed as part of Form 8-K.

For changes in the registrant's certifying accountant (Item 4.01), Form 8-K must include the following: the date the former auditor resigned or was dismissed, a statement describing and fully discussing any material disagreements with the former auditors over accounting or auditing standards over the past 24 months, a statement stating whether the former auditor's opinion was qualified in any way for the past two years and describing the nature of any qualification, and a letter from the former auditor as an exhibit to Form 8-K that states whether the former auditor agrees or disagrees with the facts as stated in the Form 8-K as presented by the registrant.

Schedule 13D is filed by any person or persons in a group who acquire a beneficial ownership of more than 5 percent of a class of registered equity securities and must be filed within 10 days after such an acquisition. *Beneficial ownership* is defined as directly or indirectly having the power to vote the shares or investment power to sell the security. In addition, any time there are material changes in the facts set forth in the schedule, the

[3] A shell company has very limited operations and holds only minor amounts of assets. The company is essentially a legal shell under which other companies operate.

investor must file an amendment on Schedule 13D. Thus, any investor making an acquisition of 5 percent or more of any class of equity securities of a publicly held company must promptly report the investment to the SEC.

Proxy statements are materials submitted to shareholders for votes on corporate matters such as the election of directors, changes in the corporate charter, issuance of new securities or modification of outstanding securities, or plans for a major business combination. In many cases, voting on these matters takes place at the annual meeting but sometimes at a special meeting. A proxy card soliciting the shareholder's vote is often in the form of a checkoff ballot that management encourages the shareholder to return to be voted at the meeting. The proxy solicitation materials must include the specific proposals being presented to the shareholders accompanied by supporting statements of facts and circumstances to explain the proposals. The materials also include information about the committees of the board of directors and executive compensation and share ownership. If there will be an election of directors, the SEC also requires that the registrant's annual report to shareholders be included with the proxy materials. An increasing number of companies are using the Internet to provide their proxy materials, annual report, and proxy cards to shareholders who request the electronic form. The company must send printed materials to all other shareholders. A copy of a registrant's proxy statement is available on the SEC's EDGAR database of filings for that company under the title "DEF 14A" to identify it as the definitive, or final, proxy statement filed under section 14A of the Securities Exchange Act of 1934.

Individual shareholders or a group of shareholders may sometimes use proxy solicitations for proposals that management opposes. Rule 14-8 of the Securities Exchange Act of 1934 presents detailed rules and regulations that must be met in order to have these shareholder proposals included on a company's proxy card and included with any supporting statements in the proxy statement. The rules are quite specific with regard to who is eligible to submit a proposal, the content and subject matter of a proposal, and deadlines for submitting a proposal. At times, the business press carries news of proxy battles between management and nonmanagement groups in which each side is soliciting shareholders' support.

Accountants' Legal Liability in Periodic Reporting

The 1934 Securities Exchange Act allows a limited level of legal exposure from involvement in preparing and filing periodic reports. Civil liability is imposed for filing materially false or misleading statements. The accountant's liability for registration statements under the 1933 act extends to the date the registration becomes effective. Plaintiffs suing accountants under the 1934 act must show that a periodic report contains a misleading material fact and that they suffered a loss because they relied on that report. Accountants have due diligence defenses to combat any lawsuits brought under the 1934 act.

ELECTRONIC DATA GATHERING, ANALYSIS, AND RETRIEVAL (EDGAR) SYSTEM

The SEC continues to work to facilitate the registration and filing process and has developed an electronic filing system known as EDGAR (Electronic Data Gathering, Analysis, and Retrieval). Under this system, firms electronically file directly by using computers, facilitating the data transfer and making public data more quickly available. EDGAR filings may be found on the Internet, on the SEC's home page (www.sec.gov) within 24 hours of filing. All public companies are now required to use EDGAR, although some hardship exemptions are allowed for small firms.

The SEC believes that EDGAR is accomplishing its primary purpose of increasing the efficiency and fairness of the securities markets by expediting the receipt, acceptance, dissemination, and analysis of time-sensitive data filed with it. Any individual with access to the Internet can easily download and print the documents from EDGAR, which has become an important data source for corporate researchers, investors, and all other participants in the securities markets.

FOREIGN CORRUPT PRACTICES ACT OF 1977

LO 14-4

Understand requirements of management reporting laws.

In the mid-1970s, Congress held a number of public hearings that identified the payment of millions of dollars in bribes to high government officials of other countries by U.S.-based companies seeking to win defense or consumer product contracts. Alarmed by the size and scope of these activities, Congress passed the ***Foreign Corrupt Practices Act of 1977 (FCPA)*** as a major amendment to the Securities Exchange Act of 1934. The FCPA has two major sections: Part I prohibits foreign bribes, and Part II requires publicly held companies to maintain an adequate system of internal control and accurate records.

Under Part I, individuals associated with U.S. companies are prohibited from bribing foreign governmental or political officials for the purpose of securing a contract or otherwise increasing the company's business. Small compensating or agents' fees to low-level civil servants are allowed if the purpose of these fees is to facilitate a transaction that is already in process, such as to obtain shipping permits or to acquire local licenses in a foreign country. Both civil and criminal sanctions can be imposed on individuals making bribes to foreign officials.

Part II of the FCPA has had a significant impact on both corporate accountants and independent auditors. This part requires all public companies, whether operating internationally or not, to keep detailed records that accurately and fairly reflect their financial transactions and to develop and maintain an adequate internal control system. An internal control system should ensure that all major transactions are fully authorized, transactions are properly recorded and reported, the company's assets are safeguarded, and management's policies are properly carried out.

Although the FCPA was not specific about the types of internal controls necessary, it defined the following as important aspects of a good internal control system: (1) strong budgetary controls, (2) an objective internal audit function that helps develop, document, and then monitor the control system, (3) an active audit committee of nonmanagement members of the company's board of directors, and (4) a review of the internal control system by the independent auditors. The FCPA allows for the development of "tailored" control procedures that best serve the company. In addition, the FCPA indicated that the cost of an internal control procedure should not outweigh its benefit to the firm.

The FCPA also had a significant effect on independent auditors by requiring them to evaluate a company's internal controls and to communicate any material weaknesses in them to the company's top management and board of directors. The total impact of the FCPA is still unclear. Subsequent proposals offered by the SEC itself have somewhat softened the foreign bribery section of the act; however, Part II of the FCPA, dealing with internal control, certainly increased the interest of companies in maintaining strong internal control systems.

SARBANES-OXLEY ACT OF 2002

Advanced StudyGuide .com

A major law affecting auditors and publicly traded companies was signed into law on July 30, 2002. The proposed law gained impetus after the revelations about accounting and financial mismanagement at Enron, WorldCom, and others. Named after its two sponsors, Senator Paul Sarbanes and Congressman Michael Oxley, the ***Sarbanes-Oxley Act*** (broadly known as SOX) has a number of major implications for accountants. Its supporters hoped that the act would minimize corporate governance accounting and financial reporting abuses and help restore investor confidence in the financial reports of publicly traded companies. The following discussion summarizes the major sections of SOX.

Title I: Public Company Accounting Oversight Board

Section 101 of Title I of SOX established a new accounting oversight board to regulate accounting firms and be responsible for establishing or modifying auditing and attestation standards. The SEC administers the ***Public Company Accounting Oversight Board (PCAOB)*** and is responsible for appointing its five full-time members. Two board members must be or must have been CPAs; however, the other three cannot have been CPAs. The PCAOB chair may be a CPA but must not have practiced accounting during the five years prior to being appointed as chair. The board's funding includes mandatory fees from public companies. Accounting firms with publicly held audit clients must be registered with the PCAOB and are subject to continuing quality inspections for compliance to the requirements of the act.

The PCAOB, which many accountants refer to by the nickname "Peekaboo," has the authority to establish or to adopt standards for audit firm quality controls. The range of its authority includes auditing and related attestation standards, quality control, ethics, independence, and other areas necessary to protect the public interest. The board also manages the regular inspection of the registered accounting firms' operations and auditing processes. Any accounting firm that does not cooperate can be prohibited from auditing public companies. If the PCAOB finds any violations of its standards, it can refer the accounting firm involved to the SEC and possibly to the Department of Justice for prosecution.

Title II: Auditor Independence

SOX made a major change that prohibits auditors from offering certain nonaudit services to their audit clients. These services include information systems design and implementations, appraisals or valuation services, internal audits, human resources services, legal or expert services not related to audit services, and bookkeeping services. Tax services provided by an auditor for a publicly held company require preapproval of the company's audit committee. Thus, accounting firms must determine whether to provide audit or nonaudit services to a company; they cannot provide both to the same company.

Title II requires that both the lead audit partner and the audit review partner for publicly held companies be rotated at least every five years. To avoid a conflict of interest, the company's CEO, controller, CFO, chief accounting officer, or person in an equivalent position cannot have been employed by the company's audit firm during the one-year period preceding the audit.

Title III: Corporate Responsibility

Title III specifies that ***audit committees*** be composed of nonmanagement members of a company's board of directors. Generally, the chair of the audit committee has financial experience. SOX requires the auditor to report directly to, and have its work overseen by, the company's audit committee, not the company's management. The audit committee is responsible for the appointment, compensation, and oversight of the work of the public accounting firm employed by the company. Furthermore, the audit committee must approve all services provided by the auditor, and the auditor must report the following additional information to the audit committee: critical accounting policies and practices, alternative treatments within GAAP that have been discussed with the company's management, accounting disagreements between the auditor and management, and any other important issues arising between the auditor and management.

Section 302 of the act requires both the CEO and the CFO of each publicly traded company to provide a signed statement to accompany each annual and quarterly financial report. These two officers are required to certify that the financial statements and disclosures fairly present, in all material respects, the issuer's operations and conditions. Furthermore, their signed statement must include declarations that they are responsible for establishing and maintaining internal controls and that these controls have been evaluated as to their effectiveness within 90 days prior to the report.

In the case of accounting restatements due to the issuer's material noncompliance, the CEO and CFO must forfeit bonuses and incentive compensation provided on the basis of the incorrect accounting information.

Title IV: Enhanced Financial Disclosures

Financial reports filed with the SEC must reflect all material correcting adjustments that the registered accounting firm has identified and all material off-balance sheet transactions and relationships that may have a material effect on the issuer's financial status. Section 402 prohibits a company from making personal loans to any director or executive officer. However, consumer credit companies may make home improvement and consumer credit loans to its officers if these loans are made on the same terms as those made to the general public.

A major requirement of SOX is specified in section 404, which requires that each annual filing of a stock issuer must contain an ***internal control report*** by management that reports on the existence and effectiveness of the company's internal control over financial reporting. A company's internal control over financial reporting is a process designed to provide reasonable assurance of the reliability of the financial reporting and preparation of financial statements for external purposes in accordance with generally accepted accounting principles. In May 2003, the SEC released rules (Release No. 33-8238) that established specific requirements for the content of this report. Management's internal control report must include the following items: (1) a statement that management is responsible for establishing and maintaining an adequate system, (2) the identification of the framework used to evaluate the internal controls, (3) a statement as to whether the internal control is effective as of year-end, and (4) the disclosure of any material weaknesses in the internal control system.

In May 2005, the SEC released a statement on the first year's implementation of section 404, suggesting that there had been significant start-up costs from this new requirement. However, the SEC feels that benefits have been produced from section 404's requirements and that the section 404 implementation process will become more efficient over time. The annual filings of publicly held companies now include both the management report on internal control over financial reporting and the expanded independent auditor's report on its audit of that internal control system.

Title V: Analyst Conflicts of Interest

Research analysts and brokers and dealers must report if they hold securities in any company for which they prepare a research report, if any compensation was received from the company that was the subject of a research report, and if a company that is the subject of a research report was a client of the broker or dealer.

Title VI: Commission Resources and Authority

Title VI increased the funding for the SEC and its disciplinary and litigation authority over auditors, attorneys, brokers and dealers, and others who practice in the securities markets and who have engaged in illegal, unethical, or improper professional conduct.

Title VII: Studies and Reports

The Government Accountability Office (GAO) and SEC are charged with conducting various studies, including of the factors leading to the consolidation of public accounting firms since 1989 and the impacts of that consolidation, the role of credit rating agencies in the securities markets, and whether investment banks and financial advisers assisted public companies in earnings manipulation and obfuscation of financial conditions.

Title VIII: Corporate and Criminal Fraud Accountability

SOX established severe penalties for anyone who destroys records, commits securities fraud, or fails to report fraud. The penalty for willfully failing to maintain all audit or review workpapers for at least five years is a felony punishable by up to 10 years. Section 802 of the act specifies that persons destroying documents in a federal or bankruptcy investigation are punishable by up to 20 years in prison. The criminal penalty for securities fraud was increased to 25 years.

The statute of limitations for the discovery of fraud was increased to two years from the date of discovery and five years after the actual fraud. Previously, it had been only one year from the date of discovery and three years after the actual fraud. Section 806 provides "whistle-blower protection" to employees of the company or the accounting firm who lawfully assist in an investigation of fraud or other criminal conduct by federal regulators, Congress, or supervisors.

Title IX: White-Collar Crime Penalty Enhancements

This title increases the minimum penalty for mail and wire fraud from 5 to 10 years, makes it a crime to tamper with a record or impede any official proceeding, and allows the SEC to prohibit anyone convicted of securities fraud from being an officer or director of any publicly traded company. In addition, this section of SOX includes criminal liability up to five years for corporate officers who fail to certify financial reports or who willfully certify financial statements knowing they do not comply with the act.

Title X: Sense of Congress Regarding Corporate Tax Returns

Congress felt that the chief executive officer should sign the corporation's federal income tax return.

Title XI: Corporate Fraud and Accountability

This section increased the penalties for persons using deceptive devices, engaging in fraudulent transactions, or otherwise acting to impede an official proceeding. It also increased the penalties for violations of the Securities Exchange Act of 1934 up to $25 million and up to 20 years in prison.

SOX has had a significant impact on financial reporting, auditing, and corporate governance. The SEC provides a link to the complete act on its website (www.sec.gov).

DODD-FRANK WALL STREET REFORM AND CONSUMER PROTECTION ACT

The financial crisis of 2008–2009 resulted in widespread calls to reform financial market practices. As a result, a bill introduced by Senator Chris Dodd and revised by Congressman Barney Frank was passed by the Senate on May 20, 2010, and approved by the House on July 30, 2010. The law became effective on July 21, 2010.

The Dodd-Frank Act establishes a number of new government agencies to oversee various components of the act. For example, the Financial Stability Oversight Council and Orderly Liquidation Authority oversees the financial stability of firms that have a significant influence on the economy (i.e., companies described as being "too big to fail"). It oversees liquidations or restructurings if these firms become too weak. It also has the responsibility to ensure that tax dollars are not used to sustain these firms. Moreover, it has the authority to break up banks that are so large that they pose systemic risk to the economy. It can also force them to increase their reserve requirements. In a similar way, the Federal Insurance Office is charged with identifying and monitoring insurance companies that are deemed to be "too big to fail."

The Consumer Financial Protection Bureau (CFPB) is responsible for preventing predatory mortgage lending and ensuring that consumers understand the mortgage terms prior to finalizing their paperwork. It prevents mortgage brokers from receiving higher commissions for closing loans with higher interest rates or fees. Finally, it ensures that mortgage originators cannot guide borrowers to the loan that will lead to higher originator profits. The CFPB also oversees other types of consumer lending, including credit and debit cards, and addresses consumer complaints. It ensures that lenders disclose information in a form that is easiest for consumers to read and understand; an example is the simplified terms you'll find on credit card applications.

The Dodd-Frank Act establishes the SEC Office of Credit Ratings because credit rating agencies were accused of giving overly favorable investment ratings that contributed to the financial crisis. This office must also ensure that agencies provide meaningful and reliable credit ratings of the entities they evaluate.

JUMPSTART OUR BUSINESS STARTUPS (JOBS) ACT

The Jumpstart Our Business Startups (JOBS) Act was signed into law on April 5, 2012. The act increases job creation and economic growth in the United States by improving access to the public capital markets for emerging growth companies. The JOBS Act contains a number of provisions designed to ease the raising of capital for private companies in ways such as: (1) increasing the maximum number of shareholders of record that a private company can have before it is required to register with the SEC as a public company from 500 to 2,000 and (2) allowing companies to advertise broadly when conducting private placements.

The JOBS Act also includes a financial statement requirement. Specifically, raising amounts up to $100,000 annually requires the certification of the principal financial officer that the financial statements are true and correct. Raising amounts between $100,000 and $500,000 annually will require the review of an independent public accountant, which is significantly smaller in scope than an audit. However, raising amounts above $500,000 annually will require audited financial statements. The JOBS Act also includes specific provisions about how those funds can be raised.

Finally, the JOBS Act creates a category of issuer called an *emerging growth company,* which is a company that has under $1.0 billion in annual revenue. These companies can remain an emerging growth company for five years after the IPO or until they (1) become a "large accelerated filer," (2) issue large amounts of nonconvertible debt, or (3) achieve $1.0 billion in annual revenue. Under the JOBS Act, these emerging growth companies are permitted to include only two years of audited financial statements (and two years of MD&A and selected financial information) in their IPO registration statements, rather than the normal three years for regular filers. They are not required to provide an auditor attestation of management's assessment of internal controls for financial reporting created under Sarbanes Oxley, and they are exempt from certain accounting requirements, including the audit firm rotation and the supplemental information by audit firm requirements. Finally, an emerging growth company is exempt from shareholder approval requirements of executive compensation.

DISCLOSURE REQUIREMENTS

LO 14-5

Understand disclosure requirements.

Virtually every SEC accounting release reminds registrants of the commitment to full and fair disclosure of financial information needed by investors. The SEC has taken the lead in requiring management to provide its analysis of the company's operations.

Management Discussion and Analysis

The ***management discussion and analysis (MD&A)*** of a company's financial condition and results of operations is part of the basic information package (BIP) required in all major filings with the SEC. The SEC has taken the leadership role in requiring management to analyze and discuss the financial statements for investors, and this discussion often extends to four or more pages of the annual report. The financial statements are, after all, management's expressions of the economic consequences of their decisions made during the period. Management has the clearest picture of the company's financial environment. A key element in the MD&A is a view that looks both historically and forward at the company's liquidity and solvency. The SEC recognizes that investors are particularly concerned with a company's ability to generate adequate amounts of cash to meet short-term and long-term cash needs.

Because it believes the information presented in the MD&A is important for investors, the SEC continually monitors it. In response to the requirement in section 401 of the Sarbanes-Oxley Act and new section 13(j) of the Securities Exchange Act of 1934, the SEC examined the items in its MD&A rules and with Release No. 33-8182 revised the list of required items in the MD&A, effective April 7, 2003. The items now required in the MD&A are

1. *Liquidity.* Identify trends, commitments, events, or uncertainties that are reasonably likely to materially change the registrant's liquidity. Indicate the course of action that is proposed to remedy any deficiency identified. Also, identify and describe the internal and external sources of liquidity with a brief discussion of any material unused sources of liquid assets.
2. *Capital resources.* Discuss material commitments for capital expenditures, their general purposes, and the expected sources of funds to fulfill those commitments. Also discuss trends and expected material changes in the mix of equity, debt, and any off-balance sheet financing arrangements.
3. *Results of operations.* Describe and discuss unusual or infrequent events or transactions affecting revenues, expenses, and the reported income from continuing operations. Discuss trends or expectations of material impacts on future revenues and expenses. For material increases in net sales, discuss the impact of an increase in price versus the impact of an increase in volume and discuss the impact of the introduction of new products. Then, for each of the most recent three years, discuss the impact of inflation and changing prices on net sales and revenue and on income from continuing operations.
4. *Off-balance sheet arrangements.* A separately identified section that includes discussion of off-balance sheet arrangements that have or are likely to have a material effect on the company's financial condition, changes in financial condition, results of operations, liquidity, capital expenditures, or capital resources. Required disclosures for these off-balance sheet arrangements include the nature and business purpose of the arrangements; the impact of the arrangements on revenues, expenses, and cash flows; and a description of events or other items that would materially change the benefits of the arrangement and the actions the company has taken or would take if those circumstances were to occur.
5. *Tabular disclosure of contractual obligations.* A table in the following format must be provided, listing the aggregated amount of each type of contractual obligation (if present):

	Payments Due by Period				
Contractual Obligations	**Total**	**Less than 1 Year**	**1–3 Years**	**3–5 Years**	**More than 5 Years**
Long-term debt obligations					
Capital lease obligations					
Operating lease obligations					
Purchase obligations for goods or services					
Other long-term liabilities reflected on the registrant's balance sheet under GAAP					
Total					

The MD&A should cover the financial statements and other statistical data for the most recent three-year time span and make year-to-year comparisons of material changes in the line items. Management should attempt to explain the cause(s) of the material changes. Section 401 of SOX specifies the required disclosure of material off-balance sheet transactions, arrangements, and obligations in each annual and each quarterly report. The MD&A in the quarterly reports should be viewed as updating the annual information. Thus, the MD&A in quarterly reports is generally much shorter than that in the annual report.

Pro Forma Disclosures

Pro forma disclosures are essentially "what-if" financial presentations often taking the form of summarized financial statements. Pro forma statements are used to show the effects of major transactions that occur after the end of the fiscal period or that have occurred during the year but are not fully reflected in the company's historical cost financial statements. The SEC requires these to be presented whenever the company has made a significant business combination or disposition, a corporate reorganization, an unusual asset exchange, or a restructuring of existing indebtedness. A pro forma condensed income statement presented in the footnotes shows the impact of the transaction on the company's income from continuing operations, thereby helping investors to focus on the specific effects of the major transaction. The pro forma balance sheet includes all adjustments reflecting the full impact of the transaction. Investors therefore have (1) the historical cost primary financial statements and (2) the pro forma statements, which more fully present and illustrate the effects of the transaction on the company's financial condition.

SUMMARY OF KEY CONCEPTS

Since its creation in 1934, the SEC has played a significant role in the development of financial disclosures necessary for investor confidence in the capital formation process. The Commission has consistently worked for full and fair disclosure of information it considers necessary so investors can assess the risks and returns of companies wishing to offer their securities to the public. The SEC has taken the leadership in a myriad of reporting issues, predominantly in reporting liquidity and solvency measures, thereby ensuring that investors have access to a management narrative of the company's performance.

Although the SEC has the statutory responsibility to develop and maintain accounting principles used for financial reporting, it has permitted the rule-making bodies of the accounting profession to take the initiative in establishing accounting principles and reporting standards. The cooperation has worked with varying success over the years. The SEC has shown its willingness and capacity to assume the lead in those areas in which it feels the private sector is not moving rapidly enough. It is expected that this arrangement will continue in the future.

KEY TERMS

Accounting and Auditing Enforcement Releases (AAERs), *734*
audit committees, *742*
comment letter, *736*
Foreign Corrupt Practices Act of 1977 (FCPA), *741*
internal control report, *743*
management discussion and analysis (MD&A), *745*
periodic reporting forms: Form 10-K, Form 10-Q, Form 8-K, *737–738*
preliminary prospectus, *737*
pro forma disclosures, *747*
proxy statements, *740*
Public Company Accounting Oversight Board (PCAOB), *742*
registration statements: Form S-1, Form S-2, Form S-3, *736*
Regulation A, *735*
Regulation D, *735*
Regulation S-K, *733*
Regulation S-X, *733*
Sarbanes-Oxley Act, *741*
Schedule 13D, *739*
shelf registration, *737*
Staff Accounting Bulletins (SABs), *734*

QUESTIONS

Note: These questions are designed to help students become familiar with the SEC website and other sources. Hence, answering some of these questions may require additional research beyond what is stated in the chapter.

LO 14-1 **Q14-1** What is the basis of the SEC's legal authority to regulate accounting principles?

LO 14-1 **Q14-2** Which securities act—1933 or 1934—regulates the initial registration of securities? Which regulates the periodic reporting of publicly traded companies?

LO 14-1 **Q14-3** Which division of the SEC receives the registration statements of companies wishing to make public offerings of securities? Which division investigates individuals or firms that may be in violation of a security act?

LO 14-1, 14-4 **Q14-4** Which law requires that companies maintain accurate accounting records and an adequate system of internal control? What is meant by an "adequate system of internal control"?

LO 14-1 **Q14-5** What does Regulation S-X cover? What is included in Regulation S-K?

LO 14-2 **Q14-6** What types of public offerings of securities are exempted from the SEC's comprehensive registration requirements?

LO 14-2 **Q14-7** When must a company use a Form S-1 registration form? In what circumstances may a company use a Form S-3 registration form?

LO 14-2 **Q14-8** Define the following terms, which are part of the SEC terminology: *(a) customary review, (b) comment letter, (c) red herring prospectus,* and *(d) shelf registration.*

LO 14-3 **Q14-9** What is included in Form 10-K? When must a 10-K be filed with the SEC?

LO 14-3 **Q14-10** Must interim reports submitted to the SEC be audited? What is the role of the public accountant in the preparation of Form 10-Q?

LO 14-3 **Q14-11** What types of items that specifically involve the accounting function are reported on Form 8-K?

LO 14-3 **Q14-12** What is a proxy? What must be included in the proxy material submitted to security holders?

LO 14-4 **Q14-13** Describe Parts I and II of the Foreign Corrupt Practices Act. What is this act's impact on companies and public accountants?

LO 14-5 **Q14-14** What types of information must be disclosed in the management discussion and analysis?

LO 14-4 **Q14-15** Describe the major requirements of the Sarbanes-Oxley Act of 2002.

CASES

LO 14-1, 14-4 **C14-1**

Objectives of Securities Acts [CMA Adapted]

Research

During the late 1920s, approximately 55 percent of all personal savings in the United States was used to purchase securities. Public confidence in the business community was extremely high as stock values doubled and tripled in short periods of time. The road to wealth was believed to be through the stock market, and everyone who was able to participated. Thus, the public was severely affected when the Dow Jones Industrial Average fell 89 percent between 1929 and 1933. The public outcry arising from this decline in stock prices motivated the passage of major federal laws regulating the securities industry.

Required

a. Describe the investment practices of the 1920s that contributed to the erosion of the stock market.

b. Explain the basic objectives of each of the following:

(1) Securities Act of 1933.

(2) Securities Exchange Act of 1934.

c. More legislation has resulted from abuses in the securities industry. Explain the provisions of the Foreign Corrupt Practices Act of 1977.

LO 14-1, 14-2

C14-2 **Roles of SEC and FASB [CMA Adapted]**

Understanding

The development of accounting theory and practice has been influenced directly and indirectly by many organizations and institutions. Two of the most important institutions have been the Financial Accounting Standards Board (FASB) and the Securities and Exchange Commission (SEC).

The FASB is an independent body established in 1973. It is composed of seven persons who represent public accounting and fields other than public accounting.

The SEC is a governmental regulatory agency created in 1934 to administer the Securities Act of 1933 and the Securities Exchange Act of 1934. These acts and the creation of the SEC resulted from the widespread collapse of business and the securities markets in the early 1930s.

Required

a. What official role does the SEC have in the development of financial accounting theory and practice?

b. What is the interrelationship between the FASB and the SEC with respect to the development and establishment of financial accounting theory and practice?

LO 14-3

C14-3 **Information Content of Proxy**

Application

The proxy contains an abundance of information the SEC believed to be necessary for stockholders to make an informed vote on the items the company presents for their voting consideration. This case provides opportunities to analyze the proxy of a publicly held company and to survey the types of information presented in the proxy.

Required

Using EDGAR or another source, obtain the most recent proxy for Caterpillar Inc. or a different company specified by your instructor. Answer the following questions regarding the information presented in the proxy.

a. Summarize the proposals that are being placed before the shareholders for their voting consideration and state the board of directors' recommendation on each proposal.

b. List and briefly describe the duties of each of the standing committees of the board of directors.

c. For the most recent year presented in your proxy, what was the total annual compensation received by the chairman and CEO of the company?

LO 14-3

C14-4 **Form 10-K Disclosures**

Application

Form 10-K is the annual filing required of publicly traded entities. The form contains the financial information for the year as well as a number of other disclosures the SEC requires.

Required

Using EDGAR or another source, obtain the most recent Form 10-K (the annual report) for Caterpillar Inc. or a different company specified by your instructor. Answer the following questions regarding information presented in the Form 10-K.

a. Identify the categories and major information presented in management's discussion and analysis.

b. Summarize the information presented in management's Report on Internal Control over Financial Reporting.

c. What does the Report of Independent Registered Public Accounting Firm include with regard to its evaluation of the company's internal control over financial reporting?

d. Who has to sign the section 302 certifications? What do these certifications include with regard to the company's internal control over financial reporting?

LO 14-2

C14-5 **Registration Process [CMA Adapted]**

Advanced StudyGuide .com

Bandex Inc. has been in business for 15 years and has compiled a record of steady but not spectacular growth. Bandex's engineers have recently perfected a product that has an application in the small computer market. Initial orders have exceeded the company's capacity, and the company has made the decision to expand.

Bandex has financed past growth from internally generated funds, and since the initial stock offering 15 years ago, it has sold no further shares. Bandex's finance committee has been discussing methods of financing the proposed expansion. Both short-term and long-term notes were ruled out because of high interest rates. Mel Greene, the chief financial officer, said, "It boils down to

Research

either bonds, preferred stock, or additional common stock." Alice Dexter, a consultant employed to help in the financing decision, stated, "Regardless of your choice, you will have to file a registration statement with the SEC."

Bob Schultz, Bandex's chief accountant for the past five years, stated, "I've coordinated the filing of all the periodic reports required by the SEC—10-Ks, 10-Qs, and 8-Ks. I see no reason I can't prepare a registration statement also."

Required

a. Identify the circumstances under which a firm must file a registration statement with the SEC.

b. Explain the objectives of the registration process required by the Securities Act of 1933.

c. Identify and explain the SEC publications that Bob Schultz would use to guide him in preparing the registration statement.

LO 14-3

Communication

C14-6 Change in Auditors and Form 8-K [CMA Adapted]

Jerford Company is a well-known manufacturing company with several wholly owned subsidiaries. The company's stock is traded on the New York Stock Exchange, and the company files all appropriate reports with the SEC. Jerford's financial statements are audited by a public accounting firm. Jerford changed independent auditors during 20X6. Consequently, the financial statements were certified by a different public accounting firm in 20X6 than in 20X5.

Required

a. What information is Jerford responsible for filing with the SEC with respect to this change in auditors? Explain your answer completely. (*Hint:* Item 304 of Regulation S-K provides guidance on reporting a change in auditor.)

b. Identify a company that has made a change in its auditor during the last two years. Summarize the reason(s) for the change and the major items reported in its Form 8-K regarding the change, and then compare those items with the requirements listed in Item 304 of Regulation S-K.

LO 14-3

Advanced StudyGuide .com

Understanding

C14-7 Form 8-K [CMA Adapted]

The purpose of the Securities Act of 1933 is to regulate the initial offering of a firm's securities by ensuring that investors are given full and fair disclosure of all pertinent information about the firm. The Securities Exchange Act of 1934 was passed to regulate the trading of securities on secondary markets and to eliminate abuses in the trading of securities after their initial distribution. To accomplish these objectives, the 1934 act created the SEC. Under its auspices, public companies must not only register their securities but also periodically prepare and file Forms 8-K, 10-K, and 10-Q.

Required

a. With regard to Form 8-K, discuss

(1) The report's purpose.

(2) The report's timing.

(3) The report's format.

(4) The role of financial statements in filing the report.

b. Identify five circumstances under which the SEC requires the filing of Form 8-K.

LO 14-4

Understanding

C14-8 Audit Committees [CMA Adapted]

An early event leading to the establishment of audit committees as a regular subcommittee of boards of directors occurred in 1940 as part of the consent decree relative to the McKesson-Robbins scandal. (A *consent decree* is the formal statement issued in an enforcement action when a person agrees to terms of a disciplinary nature without admitting to the allegations in the complaint.) An audit committee composed of outside directors was required as part of the consent decree.

Title III of SOX specifies requirements for the membership of the audit committee and its authority. All publicly traded firms must follow SOX.

Required

a. Explain the role of the audit committee as SOX specifies, with regard to the annual audit conducted by the company's external auditors.

b. Discuss the relationship that should exist between the audit committee and a company's internal audit staff.

c. Explain why the members of the audit committee should be outside (independent of management) board members.

LO 14-1 **C14-9 SEC**

Research

The company that employs you is a U.S. publicly traded corporation that manufactures chemicals. You are in the external financial reporting department, and your position requires that you keep current on all the new accounting requirements. Although you realize that Staff Accounting Bulletins (SABs) are not formal SEC actions, you like to review the new SABs periodically to see whether any are relevant to your company.

Today you decided to perform some research to ascertain whether any new SABs have been issued. In addition, your boss, the manager in charge of the department, recently mentioned something to you about the SEC's Division of Enforcement. You do not know a lot about this particular division; however, because you will be doing some SEC research today anyway, you have decided you will find out more about the SEC's Division of Enforcement.

Required

a. Prepare a one-page memo summarizing a recent SAB.

b. Research the SEC's Division of Enforcement. Answer or perform the following:

(1) What year was the division formed?

(2) Discuss various actions the division may take.

(3) Prepare a one-paragraph summary of a recent litigation proceeding.

(4) Prepare a one-paragraph summary of a recent administrative proceeding.

LO 14-3 **C14-10 EDGAR Database**

Research

Currently, you are an experienced senior working at a public accounting firm. For the upcoming busy season, you have a new client, a publicly traded corporation. You have not worked with the manager of this client assignment before. You hope to impress this manager because you hear that she strongly supports those seniors who work for her if she considers them to be excellent employees. At the end of this busy season, you will be up for promotion to manager and would like her support.

Next week you have an internal planning meeting with the manager. Today you will be working in the office, and you have decided to devote the day to performing some background reading to become acquainted with this client. When you get to the office today, you learn that the manager is at a client location and unreachable. Because you will not be able to get any background information on your client from her today, you decide to get information using the Internet.

Required

a. Using the SEC's browser, select a company from the EDGAR database with a name beginning with the first letter of your last name. The company selected will be your new client as discussed.

b. Prepare a one- to two-page summary listing the types of reports your client made to the SEC over the last year. Include a brief description of the contents of each of these reports. Select one of the reports and print its first page.

LO 14-4 **C14-11 Discovery Case**

Research

This case provides learning opportunities using available databases and/or the Internet to obtain contemporary information about the topics in advanced financial accounting. Note that the Internet is dynamic and any specific website listed may change its address. In that case, use a good search engine to locate the current address for the website.

Required

Find two recent articles on the Sarbanes-Oxley Act of 2002. Then review and summarize the major information items reported in the articles. Prepare a one- to two-page report presenting your summary.

To locate the two articles, use a good search engine to explore the Internet, access an index of business articles such as that for *The Wall Street Journal,* or use a database of business articles such as ABI/INFORM® or LEXIS-NEXIS®.

EXERCISES

LO 14-1

E14-1 Organization Structure and Regulatory Authority of the SEC [CMA Adapted]

Select the correct answer for each of the following questions.

1. Two interesting and important topics concerning the SEC are the role it plays in the development of accounting principles and the impact it has had and will continue to have on the accounting profession and business in general. Which of the following statements about the SEC's authority on accounting practice is *false?*
   a. The SEC has the statutory authority to regulate and to prescribe the form and content of financial statements and other reports it receives.
   b. Regulation S-X of the SEC is the principal source of the form and content of financial statements to be included in registration statements and financial reports filed with the Commission.
   c. The SEC has little if any authority over disclosures in corporate annual reports mailed to shareholders with proxy solicitations. The type of information disclosed and the format to be used are left to the discretion of management.
   d. If the Commission disagrees with some presentation in the registrant's financial statements, but the principles used by the registrant have substantial authoritative support, the SEC often accepts footnotes to the statements in lieu of correcting the statements to the SEC view, provided the SEC has not previously expressed its opinion on the matter in published material.
2. The Securities and Exchange Commission was established in 1934 to help regulate the U.S. securities market. Which of the following statements is *true* about the SEC?
   a. The SEC prohibits the sale of speculative securities.
   b. The SEC regulates securities offered for public sale.
   c. Registration with the SEC guarantees the accuracy of the registrant's prospectus.
   d. The SEC's initial influences and authority have diminished in recent years as the stock exchanges have become more organized and better able to police themselves.
   e. The SEC's powers are broad with respect to enforcement of its reporting requirements as established in the 1933 and 1934 acts but narrow with respect to new reporting requirements because these require confirmation by Congress.
3. The SEC is organized into several divisions and principal offices. The organization unit that reviews registration statements, annual reports, and proxy statements filed with the Commission is
   a. The Office of the Chief Accountant.
   b. The Division of Corporation Finance.
   c. The Division of Enforcement.
   d. The Division of Market Regulation.
   e. The Office of the Comptroller.
4. Regulation S-X
   a. Specifies the information that can be incorporated by reference from the annual report into the registration statement filed with the SEC.
   b. Specifies the regulation and reporting requirements of proxy solicitations.
   c. Provides the basis for generally accepted accounting principles.
   d. Specifies the general form and content requirements of financial statements filed with the SEC.
   e. Provides explanations and clarifications of changes in accounting or auditing procedures used in reports filed with the SEC.
5. Which of the following is *not* a purpose of the Securities Exchange Act of 1934?
   a. To establish federal regulation over securities exchanges and markets.
   b. To prevent unfair practices on securities exchanges and markets.
   c. To discourage and prevent the use of credit in financing excessive speculation in securities.
   d. To improve the securities of corporations that are to be traded publicly.
   e. To control unfair use of information by corporate insiders.

6. Regulation S-K disclosure requirements of the SEC deal with the company's business, properties, and legal proceedings; selected five-year summary financial data; management's discussion and analysis of financial condition and results of operations; and
   a. The form and content of the required financial statements.
   b. The requirements for filing interim financial statements.
   c. Unofficial interpretations and practices regarding securities laws disclosure requirements.
   d. Supplementary financial information such as quarterly financial data and information on the effects of changing prices.
   e. The determination of the proper registration statement form to be used in any specific public offering of securities.

LO 14-2

E14-2 Registration of New Securities [CMA Adapted]

Select the correct answer for each of the following questions.

1. In the registration and sales of new securities issues, the SEC
   a. Endorses a security's investment merit by allowing its registration to "go effective."
   b. Provides a rating of the investment quality of the security.
   c. Disallows the registration to "go effective" if it judges the security's investment risk to be too great.
   d. Allows all registrations to "go effective" if the issuing company's external accountant is satisfied that disclosures and representations are not misleading.
   e. Does not make any guarantees regarding the material accuracy of the registration statement.
2. The 1933 Securities Act provides for a 20-day review period between the filing and the effective date of the registration. During this review period, the registrant is prohibited from
   a. Preparing any amendments to the registration statement.
   b. Announcing the prospective issue of the securities being registered.
   c. Accepting offers to purchase the securities being registered from potential investors.
   d. Placing an advertisement indicating by whom orders for the securities being registered will be accepted.
   e. Issuing a prospectus in preliminary form.
3. Before turning over the proceeds of a securities offering to a registrant, the underwriters frequently require a comfort letter from the public accountant. The comfort letter's purpose is to
   a. Remove the public distrust of a red herring by converting the letter into a prospectus.
   b. Indicate whether the public accountant found any adverse financial change between the date of audit and the effective date of the securities offering.
   c. Provide assurance from the public accountant's audit of the stub-period financial statements contained in the registration statement.
   d. State that SEC regulations requiring the public accountant to give an opinion as an expert on the registrant's financial statements have been met.
   e. Indicate that the offering conforms to New York Stock Exchange (NYSE) member requirements that a comfort letter from a public accountant be obtained before public sale of securities.

LO 14-3

E14-3 Reporting Requirements of the SEC [CMA Adapted]

Select the correct answer for each of the following questions.

1. Form 10-K is filed with the SEC to update the information a company supplied when filing a registration statement under the Securities and Exchange Act of 1934. Form 10-K is a report that is filed
   a. Annually within 60 days of the end of a company's fiscal year.
   b. Semiannually within 30 days of the end of a company's second and fourth fiscal quarters.
   c. Quarterly within 45 days of the end of each quarter.
   d. Monthly within two weeks of the end of each month.
   e. Within 15 days of the occurrence of significant events.

2. The SEC's Regulation S-X disclosure requirements address
   a. Changes in and disagreements with accountants on accounting and financial disclosure.
   b. Management's discussion and analysis of the financial condition and the results of operations.
   c. The requirements for filing interim financial statements and pro forma financial information.
   d. Summary information, risk factors, and the ratio of earnings to fixed charges.
   e. Information concerning recent sales of unregistered securities.
3. Form 10-Q is filed with the SEC to keep both investors and experts apprised of a company's operations and financial position. Form 10-Q is a report that is filed within
   a. 90 days after the end of the fiscal year the report covered.
   b. 35 days after the end of each of the first three quarters of each fiscal year.
   c. 90 days after the end of an employee stock purchase plan fiscal year.
   d. 15 days after the occurrence of a significant event.
   e. 60 days after the end of the fiscal year covered by the report.
4. A company registered under the Securities and Exchange Act of 1934 should report a significant event affecting it on
   a. Form 10-K.
   b. Form 10-Q.
   c. Form S-1.
   d. Form 8-K.
   e. Form 11-K.
5. Within four days after the occurrence of any event that is of material importance to the stockholders, a company must file a Form 8-K information report with the SEC to disclose the event. An example of the type of event required to be disclosed is
   a. A salary increase to the officers.
   b. A contract to continue to employ the same certified public accounting firm as in the prior year.
   c. A change in projected earnings per share from $12.00 to $12.11 per share.
   d. The purchase of bank certificates of deposit.
   e. The acquisition of a large subsidiary other than in the ordinary course of business.
6. Form 8-K must generally be submitted to the SEC within four days after the occurrence of a significant event. Which one of the following is *not* an event that would be reported by Form 8-K?
   a. The replacement of the registrant company's external auditor.
   b. A change in accounting principle.
   c. The resignation of one of the directors of the registrant company.
   d. A significant acquisition or disposition of assets.
   e. A change in control of the registrant company.
7. Which one of the following items is *not* required to be included in a company's periodic 8-K report filed with the SEC when significant events occur?
   a. Acquisition or disposition of a significant amount of assets.
   b. Instigation or termination of material legal proceedings other than routine litigation incidental to the business.
   c. Change in certifying public accountant.
   d. Election of a new vice president of finance to replace the retiring incumbent.
   e. Default in the payment of principal, interest, or sinking fund installment.

LO 14-2, 14-3 **E14-4 Corporate Governance [CMA Adapted]**

Select the correct answer for each of the following questions.

1. A major impact of the Foreign Corrupt Practices Act of 1977 is that registrants subject to the Securities Exchange Act of 1934 are required to
   a. Keep records that reflect the transactions and dispositions of assets and maintain a system of internal accounting controls.
   b. Provide authorized agencies of the federal government access to records.

c. Record all correspondence with foreign nations.

d. Prepare financial statements in accordance with international accounting standards.

e. Produce full, fair, and accurate periodic reports on foreign commerce, foreign political party affiliations, or both.

2. Shareholders may ask or allow others to enter their vote at a shareholders' meeting that they are unable to attend. The document furnished to shareholders to provide background information for their vote is a

   a. Registration statement.

   b. Proxy statement.

   c. 10-K report.

   d. Prospectus.

3. Formation and meaningful utilization of an audit committee of the board of directors is required of publicly traded companies that are subject to the rules of the

   a. Securities and Exchange Commission.

   b. Financial Accounting Standards Board.

   c. National Association of Securities Dealers.

   d. American Institute of Certified Public Accountants.

4. An external auditor's involvement with a Form 10-Q that is being prepared for filing with the SEC would most likely consist of

   a. An audit of the financial statements included in Form 10-Q.

   b. A compilation report on the financial statements included in Form 10-Q.

   c. The issuance of a comfort letter that covers stub-period financial data.

   d. The issuance of an opinion on the internal controls under which the Form 10-Q data were developed.

   e. A review of the interim financial statements included in Form 10-Q.

LO 14-2

E14-5 Application of Securities Act of 1933 [AICPA Adapted]

Various Enterprises Corporation is a medium-size conglomerate listed on the American Stock Exchange. It is constantly in the process of acquiring small corporations and invariably needs additional money. Among its diversified holdings is a citrus grove that it purchased eight years ago as an investment. The grove's current fair market value is in excess of $2 million. Various also owns 800,000 shares of Resistance Corporation, which it acquired in the open market over a period of years. These shares represent a 17 percent minority interest in Resistance and are worth approximately $2.5 million. Various does its short-term financing with a consortium of banking institutions. Several of these loans are maturing; in addition to renewing these loans, it wishes to increase its short-term debt from $3 to $4 million.

Because of these factors, Various is considering resorting to one or all of the following alternatives to raise additional working capital.

1. An offering of 500 citrus grove units at $5,000 per unit. Each unit would give the purchaser a 0.2 percent ownership interest in the citrus grove development. Various would furnish management and operation services for a fee under a management contract, and net proceeds would be paid to the unit purchasers. The offering would be confined almost exclusively to the state in which the groves are located or in the adjacent state in which Various is incorporated.
2. An increase in the short-term borrowing by $1 million from the banking institution that currently provides short-term funds. The existing debt would be consolidated, extended, and increased to $4 million and would mature over a nine-month period. This would be evidenced by a short-term note.
3. Sale of the 17 percent minority interest in Resistance in the open market through its brokers in an orderly manner in their ordinary course of business over a period of time and in such a way as to avoid decreasing the stock's value.

Required

In separate paragraphs discuss the impact of the registration requirements of the Securities Act of 1933 on each of the proposed alternatives.

LO 14-2

E14-6 Federal Securities Acts [AICPA Adapted]

Select the correct answer for each of the following questions.

1. Which of the following statements concerning the prospectus required by the Securities Act of 1933 is correct?
   a. The prospectus is a part of the registration statement.
   b. The prospectus should enable the SEC to pass on the merits of the securities.
   c. The prospectus must be filed after an offer to sell.
   d. The prospectus is prohibited from being distributed to the public until the SEC approves the accuracy of the facts embodied therein.
2. Which of the following securities would be regulated by the provisions of the Securities Act of 1933?
   a. Securities issued by not-for-profit, charitable organizations.
   b. Securities guaranteed by domestic governmental organizations.
   c. Securities issued by savings and loan associations.
   d. Securities issued by insurance companies.
3. Which of the following securities is exempt from registration under the Securities Act of 1933?
   a. Shares of nonvoting common stock provided their par value is less than $1.
   b. A class of stock given in exchange for another class by the issuer to its existing stockholders without the issuer paying a commission.
   c. Limited partnership interests sold for the purpose of acquiring funds to invest in bonds issued by the United States.
   d. Corporate debentures that were previously subject to an effective registration statement provided they are convertible into shares of common stock.
4. Pix Corp. is making a $6,000,000 stock offering. Pix wants the offering exempt from registration under the Securities Act of 1933. Which of the following provisions of the act would Pix have to comply with for the offering to be exempt?
   a. Regulation A.
   b. Regulation D, Rule 504.
   c. Regulation D, Rule 505.
   d. Regulation D, Rule 506.
5. An offering made under the provisions of Regulation A of the Securities Act of 1933 requires that the issuer
   a. File an offering circular with the SEC.
   b. Sell only to accredited investors.
   c. Provide investors the prior four years' audited financial statements.
   d. Provide investors a proxy registration statement.
6. Which of the following factors by itself requires a corporation to comply with the reporting requirements of the Securities Exchange Act of 1934?
   a. 600 employees.
   b. Shares listed on a national securities exchange.
   c. Total assets of $2 million.
   d. 400 holders of equity securities.
7. Which of the following persons is *not* an insider of a corporation subject to the Securities Exchange Act of 1934 registration and reporting requirements?
   a. An attorney for the corporation.
   b. An owner of 5 percent of the corporation's outstanding debentures.
   c. A member of the board of directors.
   d. A stockholder who owns 10 percent of the outstanding common stock.

15 Partnerships: Formation, Operation, and Changes in Membership

Multicorporate Entities
Multinational Entities
Reporting Requirements
Partnerships
Formation, Operation, Changes
Liquidation
Governmental and Not-for-Profit Entities
Corporations in Financial Difficulty

THE EVOLUTION OF PRICEWATERHOUSECOOPERS (PwC)

All of today's "Big 4" accounting firms are partnerships and all have evolved over time through continual mergers of existing accounting firms. PricewaterhouseCoopers (PwC) has a long history dating back to the mid-1800s. Samuel Price set up his own accounting practice in London in 1849. A few years later in 1854, William Cooper established his accounting practice in London as well. It would take nearly 150 years for these two firms to eventually come together. In fact, they competed with one another during most of this time.

Price, Holyland and Waterhouse joined forces in 1865 to form what would eventually become Price, Waterhouse & Co. Not until 1957 did several large accounting firms come together to form Coopers & Lybrand. These two firms became two of the "Big 8" accounting firms. Throughout most of the 20th century, the profession was dominated by these Big 8 accounting firms:

1. Arthur Andersen
2. Arthur Young
3. Coopers & Lybrand
4. Ernst & Whinney
5. Deloitte Haskins & Sells
6. Peat Marwick Mitchell
7. Price Waterhouse
8. Touche Ross

In 1989 due to intense competition, Ernst & Whinney merged with Arthur Young to form Ernst & Young. That same year, Deloitte, Haskins & Sells merged with Touche Ross to form Deloitte & Touche, narrowing the field to the "Big 6." Finally, in 1998, one of the largest mergers in the history of the public accounting profession occurred when Price Waterhouse merged with Coopers & Lybrand to form PricewaterhouseCoopers. This merger brought about the brief reign of the "Big 5" before the demise of Arthur Andersen in 2002 in the wake of the Enron scandal, which limited the playing field to the current "Big 4" accounting firms.

Most of the early mergers in the accounting profession were general partnerships. Not until the 1990s did a new type of legal entity, the limited liability partnership (LLP), emerge, allowing some protection to partners for liabilities incurred by other partners. Although only two states in the United States allowed LLPs in 1992, by the end of the decade, most had passed laws allowing LLPs. All of the Big 4 accounting firms are now LLPs.

According to the U.S. Census Bureau, as of 2008, 3.1 million partnerships filed tax returns compared to 22.6 million proprietorships and 5.8 million corporations. Accountants are often called on to aid in the formation and operation of partnerships to ensure proper measurement and valuation of the partnership's transactions. This chapter focuses on the formation and operation of partnerships, including accounting for the addition of new partners and the retirement of an existing partner. Chapter 16 presents the accounting for the termination and liquidation of partnerships.

LEARNING OBJECTIVES

When you finish studying this chapter, you should be able to:

LO 15-1 Understand and explain the nature and regulation of partnerships.

LO 15-2 Understand and explain the differences among different types of partnerships.

LO 15-3 Make calculations and journal entries for the formation of partnerships.

LO 15-4 Make calculations and journal entries for the operation of partnerships.

LO 15-5 Make calculations and journal entries for the allocation of partnership profit or loss.

LO 15-6 Make calculations and journal entries to account for changes in partnership ownership.

THE NATURE OF THE PARTNERSHIP ENTITY

LO 15-1

Understand and explain the nature and regulation of partnerships.

The *partnership* is a popular form of business because it is easy to form and allows several individuals to combine their talents and skills in a particular business venture. In addition, partnerships provide a means of obtaining more equity capital than a single individual can obtain and allow the sharing of risks for rapidly growing businesses.

Accounting for partnerships requires recognition of several important factors. First, from an accounting viewpoint, the partnership is a separate business entity. The Internal Revenue Code, however, views the partnership as a conduit only, not separable from the business interests of the individual partners. Therefore, tax and financial accounting rules for specific partnership events differ from those for other forms of business in several ways, such as the value assigned to assets contributed in the formation of the partnership. This chapter presents the generally accepted accounting principles of partnership accounting. We present a brief discussion of the tax aspects of a partnership in Appendix 15A.

Second, although many partnerships account for their operations using accrual accounting, others use the cash basis or modified cash basis of accounting. These alternatives are allowed because partnership records are maintained for the partners and must reflect their information needs. The partnership's financial statements are usually prepared only for the partners but occasionally for the partnership's creditors. Unlike publicly traded corporations, most partnerships are not required to have annual audits of their financial statements. Although many partnerships adhere to generally accepted accounting principles (GAAP), deviations from GAAP are found in practice. The partners' specific needs should be the primary criteria for determining the accounting policies to be used for a specific partnership.

Legal Regulation of Partnerships

The partnership form of business has several unique elements because of its legal and accounting status. Each state regulates the partnerships that are formed in it. Accountants advising partnerships must be familiar with partnership laws because these laws describe many of the rights of each partner and of creditors during the creation, operation, and liquidation of the partnership. Each state tends to begin with a uniform or model act and then modifies it to fit that state's business culture and history. The Uniform Partnership Act of 1914 served for many years as the model for defining the rights and responsibilities of the partners to each other and to the creditors of the partnership. In 1994, the National Conference of Commissioners on Uniform State Laws (NCCUSL) approved the first major revision of the model act to better reflect current business practices while retaining many of the original act's valuable provisions. This 1994 revision was titled the Revised Uniform Partnership Act (RUPA). During the next three years, the NCCUSL continued to make small revisions to the model act and in 1997, it approved the final model as the ***Uniform Partnership Act of 1997 (UPA 1997).*** Most states have now adopted the UPA 1997 model because, although the UPA 1997 includes many features of the Uniform Partnership Act of 1914, the UPA 1997 reflects today's more complex partnership events and transactions, and stresses the fiduciary responsibilities of the partners to each other. We use the UPA 1997 for discussion and illustration in this and the next chapter on partnerships.

Definition of a Partnership

Section 202 of the UPA 1997 states that ". . . the association of two or more persons to carry on as co-owners of a business for profit forms a partnership. . . ." This definition encompasses three distinct factors:

1. *Association of two or more persons.* The "persons" are usually individuals; however, they also may be corporations or other partnerships.
2. *To carry on as co-owners.* This means that each partner has the apparent authority, unless restricted by the partnership agreement, to act as an agent of the partnership for transactions in the ordinary course of business of the kind carried on by the partnership. These transactions can legally bind the partnership to third parties.
3. *Business for profit.* A partnership may be formed to perform any legal business, trade, profession, or other service. However, the partnership must attempt to make a profit; therefore, not-for-profit entities such as fraternal groups may not be organized as partnerships.

Formation of a Partnership

A primary advantage of the partnership form of entity is ease of formation. The agreement to form a partnership may be as informal as a handshake or as formal as a many-paged partnership agreement. Each partner must agree to the formation agreement, and partners are strongly advised to have a formal written agreement to avoid potential problems that could arise during the operation of the business. It is usually true that if the potential partners cannot agree on the various operating aspects before a partnership is formed, many future disputes that could cause severe management problems and seriously imperil the partnership's operations might arise. Each partner should sign the partnership agreement to indicate acceptance of its terms. A carefully prepared partnership agreement can prevent many of these problems in operations.

The partnership agreement should include the following items:

1. The name of the partnership and the names of the partners.
2. The type of business to be conducted by the partnership and the duration of the partnership agreement.
3. The initial capital contribution of each partner and the method by which to account for future capital contributions.
4. A complete specification of the profit or loss distribution, including salaries, interest on capital balances, bonuses, limits on withdrawals in anticipation of profits, and the percentages used to distribute any residual profit or loss.
5. Procedures used for changes in the partnership, such as admission of new partners and the retirement of a partner.
6. Other aspects of operations the partners decide on, such as each partner's management rights and the election procedures and accounting methods to use.

Other Major Characteristics of Partnerships

After a state adopts the provisions of the UPA 1997, the act regulates all partnerships formed in that state. For partnerships that do not have a formal partnership agreement, the act provides the legal framework that governs the relationships among the partners and the rights of creditors of the partnership; in essence, the UPA 1997 becomes the partnership agreement for those partnerships that do not have one. The following list presents the sections of the UPA 1997 applicable to the formation and operation of a partnership. Chapter 16 will present the sections of the UPA 1997 applicable to the dissolution and liquidation of a partnership.

1. *Partnership agreement.* The UPA 1997 governs in those partnership relations that are not specifically presented in the partnership agreement; thus, the courts use the UPA 1997 when there is no partnership agreement. Several provisions of the UPA 1997 are not waivable by partnership agreement. For example, a partnership may not restrict a partner's rights of access to the partnership's books and records, eliminate the obligations of partners for good faith and fair dealing with the other partners and the partnership, restrict any rights of third parties under the UPA 1997, or reduce any legal rights of individual partners.
2. *Partnership as a separate entity.* A partnership is a separate business entity distinct from its partners. This ***entity concept*** means that a partnership can sue or be sued and that its property belongs to the partnership, not to any individual partner. Thus, there is no new partnership entity when a membership change in the partners occurs (a new partner is admitted or a partner leaves).
3. *Partner as an agent of the partnership.* Each partner is an agent of the partnership for transactions carried on in the ordinary course of the partnership business unless the partner did not have the authority to act for the partnership in that specific matter and the third party knew or had received a notification that the partner lacked authority. This agency relationship among the partners is very important. If the partnership determines that only specific partners have the authority for conducting specific business transactions, then the partnership must make third parties aware of the limitations of authority of other partners. This notice should be in a public form either as a formal filing of a statement of partnership authority (discussed in the next point) or in direct communications with third parties. Otherwise, third parties may presume a partner has the authority to act as an agent for the partnership in those normal business transactions engaged in for the business the partnership operates.
4. *Statement of partnership authority.* A ***statement of partnership authority*** describes the partnership and identifies the specific authority of partners to transact specific types of business on behalf of the partnership. This voluntary statement is filed with the secretary of the state. The statement is a notice of any limitations on the rights of specific partners to enter into specific types of transactions. Partnerships should file these statements particularly for the firm's real estate transactions. The UPA 1997 states that a filed statement of partnership authority is sufficient constructive notice to third parties for partnership real estate transactions, but it is not necessarily sufficient notice for other types of partnership transactions.
5. *Partner's liability is joint and several.* All partners are liable jointly and severally for all obligations of the partnership unless otherwise provided by law. In the event a partnership fails and its assets are not sufficient to pay its obligations, partners are required to make contributions to the partnership in the proportion to which they share partnership losses. If a partner fails to make a contribution of the amount required, all other partners must contribute in the proportion to which those partners share partnership losses. Partnership creditors must first be satisfied from partnership assets, and additional partner contributions are classified as partnership assets. However, a partner is liable for partnership liabilities incurred prior to that partner's admission into the partnership only to the extent of the partner's capital credit. A new partner is not personally liable for partnership debts incurred prior to his or her admission to the firm. If a partnership creditor takes legal action against an individual partner for a partnership obligation, the creditor does not have any superior rights to the partner's individual assets. In this case, the partnership creditor joins with the other personal creditors.
6. *Partner's rights and duties.* Each partner is to have a capital account showing the amount of his or her contributions to the partnership, net of any liabilities, and the partner's share of the partnership profits or losses, less any distributions. The partner is entitled to an equal share of the profits or losses unless otherwise agreed to in the partnership agreement. New partners can be admitted only with the consent of all of the partners. Each partner has a right of access to the partnership's books and records, and each partner has a duty to act for the partnership in good faith and fair dealing.

7. *Partner's transferable interest in the partnership.* Under the entity approach to a partnership stated in the act, a partner is not a co-owner of any partnership property. This means that the only ***transferable interest*** of a partner is his or her share of the profits and losses of the partnership and the right to receive distributions, including any liquidating distribution. A partner may not transfer any rights of management or authority to transact any of the partnership's business operations. Thus, the partner's individual creditors may not attach any of the partnership's assets, but a partner's personal creditor may obtain a legal judgment for attachment of the partner's transferable interest.
8. *Partner's disassociation.* A ***partner's disassociation*** means that the partner can no longer act on the firm's behalf. A partner is disassociated from a partnership when any of the following events occurs: (*a*) he or she gives notice to the partnership of his or her express will to withdraw as a partner, (*b*) the firm expels him or her from the firm in accordance with the partnership agreement, typically for violating some part of the partnership agreement or his or her continuance becomes unlawful, (*c*) one of several judicial determinations occurs (such as the partner's committing a material breach of the partnership agreement or engaging in serious conduct that materially and adversely affects the partnership), (*d*) the partner becomes a debtor in bankruptcy, or (*e*) the partner dies.

LO 15-2

Understand and explain the differences among different types of partnerships.

Types of Limited Partnerships

Many persons view the possibility of personal liability for a partnership's obligations as a major disadvantage of the general partnership form of business. For this reason, sometimes people become limited partners in one of the several limited partnership forms. A limited partnership (LP) differs from a limited liability partnership (LLP) and a limited liability limited partnership (LLLP). The variations are based on the degree of liability shield provided to the partners.

Limited Partnerships (LP) A limited partnership (LP) has at least one general partner and one or more limited partners. The general partner is personally liable for the partnership's obligations and has management responsibility. Limited partners are liable only to the extent of their capital contribution but do not have any management authority. The Uniform Limited Partnership Act of 2001 (ULPA 2001) is the model law regulating limited partnerships and has been adopted in many states. Accounting for the investment in a limited partnership is based on an evaluation of control. Typically, the general partner has the necessary elements of operational control of the limited partnership and consolidates the investment on her or his books. The limited partners typically use the equity method to account for their investments. However, **ASC 810** indicates that in cases in which the limited partners have either (1) the ability to dissolve the limited partnership or to remove the general partners without cause (the so-called kick-out right) or (2) substantive participating rights to be actively engaged in the significant decisions of the LP's business, the presumption of the general partners' control could be overcome and then each would account for its investment in the LP using the equity method of accounting. The identifier, LP or Limited Partnership, must be included in the name or identification of the limited partnership.

Limited Liability Partnerships (LLP) A limited liability partnership (LLP) is one in which each partner has some degree of liability shield. An LLP has no general or limited partners; thus, each partner has the rights and duties of a general partner but limited legal liability. A partner in a limited liability partnership is not personally liable for a partnership obligation. However, several states have determined that each partner in an LLP is fully liable for the partnership's obligations, though not for acts of professional negligence or malpractice committed by other partners. Some legal support for the LLP came as a result of the fact that most professional service partnerships, such as accounting firms, have significant amounts of insurance to cover judgments in lawsuits and other losses from offering services. An LLP must identify itself as such by adding the LLP letters following the partnership's name in all correspondence or other means of identifying the firm. Virtually all large public accounting firms are LLPs. This designation has not changed the nature of accounting services provided to clients and has been generally accepted in the business market.

Limited Liability Limited Partnership (LLLP) In most states, a limited partnership may elect to become a limited liability limited partnership. Each partner in an LLLP is liable only for the business obligations of the partnership, not for acts of malpractice or other wrongdoing by the other partners in the normal course of the partnership's business. The ULPA 2001 includes the regulatory guidance for LLLPs. The advantage of an LLLP is that general partners, even though responsible for management of the partnership, have no personal liability for partnership obligations, similar to the shield provided to limited partners. The identifier LLLP or the phrase Limited Liability Limited Partnership must be included in the entity's name or identification.

Accounting and Financial Reporting Requirements for Partnerships

Most partnerships are small or medium-size entities, although some are large. Partnerships do not issue stock; thus, their information needs typically differ from those of corporations that have stockholders. A partnership has much more flexibility to select specific accounting measurement and recognition methods and specific financial reporting formats.

If a partnership wishes to issue general-purpose financial statements for external users such as credit grantors, vendors, or others, it should use GAAP as promulgated by the FASB and other standard-setting bodies, and the independent auditor can issue an opinion that the statements are in accordance with GAAP. The FASB created the Private Company Financial Reporting Committee in June 2006 to provide input to the FASB on proposed and existing accounting standards as to their impact on nonpublic business entities. Thus, the FASB has a vehicle by which GAAP standards can be adapted to meet the cost/benefit perspective of nonpublic entities.

If a partnership has only internal reporting needs, the accounting and financial reporting should meet the partners' internal information needs. In this case, the partnership may use non-GAAP accounting methods and have financial reports in a format different from those required under GAAP. For example, some partnerships use the accounting methods prescribed by tax laws, thereby generating tax-based financial reports. Some partnerships use the cash-based accounting system, often with some adjustments, so the financial reports provide specific cash flow and cash positions. Other partnerships may use accounting methods that are proximate to GAAP with some adjustments that fit the partners' information needs, such as recognizing increases in the fair value of nonfinancial assets at the time of admission of a new partner. In these cases, if the financial statements are presented to users external to the partnership, such as banks, vendors, or regulatory bodies, the statements should clearly identify the specific accounting methods the entity used so that the users understand that the information presented does not conform to GAAP. An independent accountant's opinion on these financial statements also would have to disclose the specific accounting methods used or the deviations from GAAP that affected the amounts reported. It is up to the partners to determine their financial information needs, and then the partnership accountant applies the necessary accounting measurement, recognition, and reporting methods that meet the partners' financial information needs.

International Financial Reporting Standards for Small and Medium-Size Entities and Joint Ventures

In 2009, the International Accounting Standards Board issued "International Financial Reporting Standard for Small and Medium-sized Entities," more commonly known as International Financial Reporting Standards (IFRS) for small and medium-size enterprises (SMEs). *SMEs* are defined as those entities that (1) do not have public accountability (i.e., do not have stock or issue bonds in a public capital market) and (2) publish general-purpose financial statements for external users. This standard presents the definitions of items and accounting concepts that are quite similar to those already in the international financial accounting and reporting standards except that less detail and fewer disclosures are mandated and more flexibility is provided for the formats of the financial statements. Moreover, **International Accounting Standards (IAS) 31** on the accounting for joint ventures, many of which are accounted as partnerships, also became effective in January 2011. Thus, the International Accounting Standards Board (IASB) is addressing the specific accounting and financial reporting requirements for SMEs and joint ventures that are required to provide general-purpose financial statements to external users. However, these standards do not apply to partnerships that do *not* have public accountability *and* do *not* issue general-purpose financial statements to external users.

ACCOUNTING FOR THE FORMATION OF A PARTNERSHIP[1]

LO 15-3

Make calculations and journal entries for the formation of partnerships.

Advanced StudyGuide .com

At the formation of a partnership, it is necessary to assign a proper value to the noncash assets and liabilities contributed by the partners. Section 201 of the UPA 1997 specifies that a partnership is an entity distinct from its partners. Thus, an item contributed by a partner becomes partnership property. The partnership must clearly distinguish between capital contributions and loans made to the partnership by individual partners. Loan arrangements should be evidenced by promissory notes or other legal documents necessary to show that a loan arrangement exists between the partnership and an individual partner. Also, it is important to clearly distinguish between tangible assets that the partnership owns and those specific assets that individual partners own but are used by the partnership. Accurate records of the partnership's tangible assets must be maintained.

ASC 820 continues the long-held accounting concept that the contributed assets should be valued at their fair values, which may require appraisals or other valuation techniques. Liabilities assumed by the partnership should be valued at the present value of the remaining cash flows.

The individual partners must agree to the percentage of equity that each will have in the partnership's net assets. Generally, the capital balance is determined by the proportionate share of each partner's capital contribution. For example, if A contributes 70 percent of the net assets in a partnership with B, then A will have a 70 percent capital share and B will have a 30 percent capital share. In recognition of intangible factors, such as a partner's special expertise or necessary business connections, however, partners may agree to any proportional division of capital. Therefore, before recording the initial capital contribution, all partners must agree on the valuation of the net assets and on each partner's capital share.

Illustration of Accounting for Partnership Formation

The following illustration is used as the basis for the remaining discussion in this chapter. Alt, a sole proprietor, has been developing software for several types of computers. The business has the following account balances as of December 31, 20X0:

Cash	$ 3,000	Liabilities	$10,000
Inventory	7,000	Alt, Capital	15,000
Equipment	20,000		
Less: Accumulated Depreciation	(5,000)		
Total Assets	$25,000	Total Liabilities & Capital	$25,000

Alt needs additional technical assistance to meet increasing sales and offers Blue an interest in the business. Alt and Blue agree to form a partnership. Alt's business is audited, and its net assets are appraised. The audit and appraisal disclose that $1,000 of liabilities have not been recorded, inventory has a market value of $9,000, and the equipment has a fair value of $19,000.

[1] To view a video explanation of this topic, visit advancedstudyguide.com.

Alt and Blue prepare and sign a partnership agreement that includes all significant operating policies. Blue will contribute $10,000 cash for a one-third capital interest. The AB Partnership is to acquire all of Alt's business and assume its debts.

The entry to record the initial capital contribution on the partnership's books is

	January 1, 20X1		
(1)	Cash	13,000	
	Inventory	9,000	
	Equipment	19,000	
	Liabilities		11,000
	Alt, Capital		20,000
	Blue, Capital		10,000
	Record the formation of AB Partnership by capital contributions of Alt and Blue.		

Key Observations from Illustration

Note that the partnership is an accounting entity separate from each of the partners and that the assets and liabilities are recorded at their market values at the time of contribution. No accumulated depreciation is carried forward from the sole proprietorship to the partnership. All liabilities are recognized and recorded.

The partnership's capital is $30,000. This is the sum of the individual partners' capital accounts and is the value of the partnership's assets less liabilities. The fundamental accounting equation—assets less liabilities equals capital—is used often in partnership accounting. Blue is to receive a one-third capital interest in the partnership with a contribution of $10,000. In this case, his capital interest equals his capital contribution.

Each partner's capital amount recorded does not necessarily have to equal his or her capital contribution. The partners could decide to divide the total capital equally regardless of the source of the contribution. For example, although Alt contributed $20,000 of the $30,000 partnership capital, he could agree to $15,000 as his initial capital balance and permit Blue the remaining $15,000 as a capital credit. On the surface, this may not seem to be a reasonable action by Alt, but it is possible that Blue has some particularly important business experience the partnership needs, and Alt agrees to the additional credit to Blue in recognition of her experience and skills. The key point is that the partners may allocate the capital contributions in any manner they desire. The accountant must be sure that all partners agree to the allocation and then record it accordingly.

ACCOUNTING FOR THE OPERATIONS OF A PARTNERSHIP

LO 15-4

Make calculations and journal entries for the operation of partnerships.

A partnership provides services or sells products in pursuit of profit. These transactions are recorded in the appropriate journals and ledger accounts. Many partnerships use accrual accounting and GAAP to maintain their books because its use provides better measures of income over time. Some creditors, such as banks, and some vendors, such as large suppliers to the partnership, may periodically require audited financial statements, and if GAAP is used, the financial statements can then receive a "clean" or unqualified audit opinion. Furthermore, the partners can compare the GAAP-based financial statements of their business to published financial profiles, such as Moody's or many published by the U.S. government, or those of other companies in the same line of business so that the partners can evaluate their respective financial performance and position.

But some partnerships use alternative non-GAAP methods, such as the cash-basis method or the modified cash-basis method. These two methods have simplified recordkeeping requirements and can continuously provide the partners the current cash position of their partnership. A few partnerships revalue all their assets at the end of each fiscal period in order to estimate the market value of their business as a whole at year-end. Some partnerships use federal income tax rules to account for transactions so the partners can determine the effects of transactions that will be reportable on their personal income tax returns. The accountant works with the partners to determine their specific information needs regarding the partnership and then applies the appropriate accounting and financial reporting methods to meet those needs.

Partners' Accounts

The partnership may maintain several accounts for each partner in its accounting records. These ***partners' accounts*** are capital, drawing, and loan accounts.

Capital Accounts

A partner's initial investment, any subsequent capital contributions, profit or loss distributions, and any withdrawals of capital are ultimately recorded in the partner's capital account. Each partner has one capital account, which usually has a credit balance. On occasion, a partner's capital account may have a debit balance, called a *deficiency* or sometimes a *deficit,* which occurs because the partner's share of losses and withdrawals exceeds his or her capital contribution and share of profits. A deficiency is usually eliminated by additional capital contributions. The balance in the capital account represents the partner's share of the partnership's net assets.

Drawing Accounts

Partners generally withdraw assets from the partnership during the year in anticipation of profits. A separate drawing account often is used to record the periodic withdrawals and is then closed to the partner's capital account at the end of the period. For example, the following entry is made in the AB Partnership's books for a $3,000 cash withdrawal by Blue on May 1, 20X1:

	May 1, 20X1		
(2)	Blue, Drawing	3,000	
	Cash		3,000
	Record Blue's withdrawal of $3,000.		

Noncash drawings should be valued at their market values at the date of the withdrawal, and the related gain or loss should be recognized by the partnership. A few partnerships make an exception to the rule of market value for partners' withdrawals of inventory and record withdrawals of inventory at cost, thereby not recording a gain or loss on these drawings.

Loan Accounts

A partnership may look to its present partners for additional financing. Any loans between a partner and the partnership should always be accompanied by proper loan documentation such as a promissory note. A loan from a partner is shown as a payable on the partnership's books, the same as for any other loan. Unless all partners agree otherwise, the partnership is obligated to pay interest on the loan to the individual partner. Note that interest is *not* required to be paid on capital investments unless the partnership agreement states that capital interest is to be paid. The partnership records interest on loans as an operating expense. Alternatively, the partnership may lend money to a partner in which case it records a loan receivable from the partner. Again, unless all partners agree otherwise, these loans should bear interest, and the interest income should be recognized on the partnership's income statement. The following entry is made to record a $4,000, 10 percent, one-year loan from Alt to the partnership on July 1, 20X1:

	July 1, 20X1		
(3)	Cash	4,000	
	Loan Payable to Alt		4,000
	Record loan agreement with partner Alt.		

The loan payable to Alt is reported in the partnership's balance sheet. A loan from a partner is a related-party transaction for which separate footnote disclosure is required, and it must be reported as a separate balance sheet item, not included with other liabilities.

ALLOCATING PROFIT OR LOSS TO PARTNERS

LO 15-5

Make calculations and journal entries for the allocation of partnership profit or loss.

Profit or loss is allocated to the partners at the end of each period in accordance with the partnership agreement. If the entity does not have a formal partnership agreement, section 401 of the UPA 1997 indicates that all partners should share profits and losses equally. Virtually all partnerships have a profit or loss allocation agreement that must be followed precisely, and if it is unclear, the accountant should make sure that all partners agree to the profit or loss distribution. Many problems and later arguments can be avoided by carefully specifying the profit or loss distribution in the partnership agreement.

A wide range of ***profit distribution plans*** is found in the business world. Some partnerships have straightforward distribution plans; others have extremely complex ones. It is the accountant's responsibility to distribute the profit or loss according to the partnership agreement regardless of how simple or complex that agreement is. Profit distributions are similar to a corporation's dividends: These distributions should not be included on the partnership's income statement regardless of how the profit is distributed. Profit distributions are recorded directly into the partner's capital accounts, not treated as expense items.

Most partnerships use one or more of the following distribution methods:

1. Preselected ratio.
2. Interest on capital balances.
3. Salaries to partners.
4. Bonuses to partners.

! CAUTION

Note that the titles for these distribution methods can be deceiving. They simply describe different ways to allocate a fixed amount of partnership profit. For example, if a partnership earns $100,000 in profit for a given period, these methods are simply four different ways to divide the $100,000 among the partners.

Preselected ratios are usually the result of negotiations between the partners. Ratios for profit distributions may be based on the percentage of total partnership capital, time, and effort invested in the entity, or a variety of other factors. Small partnerships often split profits evenly among the partners. In addition, some partnerships have different ratios if the firm suffers a loss rather than earns a profit. The partnership form of business allows a wide selection of profit distribution ratios to meet the partners' individual desires.

Distributing partnership income based on ***interest on capital balances*** simply means that the partners divide some or all of the $100,000 among themselves based on the relative balances they have maintained in their capital accounts. This method recognizes the contribution of the partners' capital investments to the partnership's profit-generating capacity and requires the allocation of profits based on a fixed rate multiplied by the partner's capital account balance. This allocation of profits based on capital balances is generally not an expense of the partnership (like interest on a loan from a bank). It is simply a method for distributing profits.

If one or more of the partners' services are important to the partnership, the profit distribution agreement may provide for salaries or bonuses. Again, these represent fixed amounts allocated to partners from the $100,000 earned during the period. They are simply a form of profit distribution, not a partnership expense. Think of a ***salary*** as a fixed amount of company profits allocated to a given partner and a ***bonus*** as a portion of profits allocated to a partner based on a predetermined performance formula. Occasionally, the distribution process may depend on the size of the profit or may differ if the partnership has a loss for the period. For example, salaries to partners might be paid only if revenue exceeds expenses by a certain amount. The accountant must carefully read the partnership agreement to determine the precise profit distribution plan for the specific circumstances at the time.

The profit or loss distribution is recorded with a closing entry at the end of each period. The revenue and expenses are often closed into an income summary account that is then allocated to the partners' capital accounts based on the formula prescribed in the partnership agreement (which could include one or more of the four methods described earlier).

If the partnership earns $100,000 for the period, the formula provided in the partnership agreement tells the accountant how to allocate this amount to the partners' capital accounts. Sometimes partnerships bypass the income summary account and close revenue and expense accounts directly to the partners' capital accounts. In the following examples, we use an income summary account. Its balance (either net income or net loss) is closed and distributed to the partners' capital accounts.

Illustrations of Profit Allocation

During 20X1, the AB Partnership earned $45,000 of revenue and incurred $35,000 in expenses, leaving a profit of $10,000 for the year. Alt maintains a capital balance of $20,000 during the year, but Blue's capital investment varies during the year as follows:

Date	Debit	Credit	Balance
January 1			$10,000
May 1	$3,000		7,000
September 1		$500	7,500
November 1	1,000		6,500
December 31			6,500

The debits of $3,000 and $1,000 are recorded in Blue's drawing account; the additional investment is credited to her capital account.

Arbitrary Profit-Sharing Ratio

Alt and Blue could agree to share profits in a ratio unrelated to their capital balances or to any other operating feature of the partnership. For example, assume the partners agree to share profits or losses in the ratio of 60 percent to Alt and 40 percent to Blue. Some partnership agreements specify this ratio as 3:2 (i.e., 3/5 to Alt and 2/5 to Blue). The following schedule illustrates how the net income is distributed using a 3:2 profit-sharing ratio:

	Alt	Blue	Total
Profit-sharing percentage	60%	40%	100%
Net income			$10,000
Allocate 60:40	$6,000	$4,000	(10,000)
Total	$6,000	$4,000	$ 0

This schedule shows how net income is distributed to the partners' capital accounts. The actual distribution is accomplished by closing the Income Summary account. In addition, the drawing accounts are closed to the capital accounts at the end of the period.

	December 31, 20X1		
(4)	Blue, Capital	4,000	
	Blue, Drawing		4,000
	Close Blue's drawing account.		

(5)	Revenue	45,000	
	Expenses		35,000
	Income Summary		10,000
	Close revenue and expenses.		

(6)	Income Summary	10,000	
	Alt, Capital		6,000
	Blue, Capital		4,000
	Distribute profit in accordance with partnership agreement.		

Interest on Capital Balances

The partnership agreement may provide for interest to be credited on the partners' capital balances as part of the distribution of profits. The rate of interest is often a stated percentage, but some partnerships use a rate determined by reference to current U.S. Treasury rates or current money market rates.

As stated earlier, interest calculated on partners' capital is generally a form of profit distribution. The calculation is made after net income has been determined in order to decide how to distribute the income.

Particular caution must be exercised when interest on capital balances is included in the profit distribution plan. For example, the amount of the distribution can be significantly different depending on whether the interest is computed on beginning capital balances, ending capital balances, or average capital balances for the period. Most provisions for interest on capital specify that a weighted-average capital should be used. This method explicitly recognizes the time span for which each capital level is maintained during the period. For example, Blue's weighted-average capital balance for 20X1 is computed as follows:

Date	Debit	Credit	Balance	Months Maintained	Months Times Dollar Balance
January 1			$10,000	4	$40,000
May 1	$3,000		7,000	4	28,000
September 1		$500	7,500	2	15,000
November 1	1,000		6,500	2	13,000
Total				12	$96,000
Average capital ($96,000 ÷ 12 months)					$ 8,000

Assume Alt and Blue agree to allocate profits first based on 15 percent of the weighted-average capital balances and then to any remaining profit based on a 60:40 ratio; the distribution of the $10,000 profit would be calculated as follows:

	Alt	Blue	Total
Profit percentage	60%	40%	100%
Average capital	$20,000	$8,000	
Net income			$10,000
Interest on average capital (15%)	$ 3,000	$1,200	(4,200)
Residual income			$ 5,800
Allocate 60:40	3,480	2,320	(5,800)
Total	$ 6,480	$3,520	$ 0

Salaries

Recall that salaries to partners are simply fixed amounts allocated to partners as part of the regular allocation of profits. They are generally included as part of the profit distribution plan to recognize and compensate partners for differing amounts of personal services provided to the business.

Section 401 of the UPA 1997 states that a partner is not entitled to compensation for services performed for the partnership except for reasonable compensation for services in winding up the partnership business. Some partnership agreements, however, do specify a management fee to be paid to a partner who provides very specific administration responsibilities.

As mentioned previously, a general precept of partnership accounting is that salaries to partners are not operating expenses but are part of the profit distribution plan. This precept is closely related to the proprietary concept of owner's equity. According to the proprietary theory, the proprietor invests capital and personal services in pursuit of income.

STOP & THINK

What if the partnership experiences losses? Can salaries to the partners during the year be treated as a distribution of profits? Although any amounts actually paid to partners during the year are really drawings made in anticipation of profits, the agreed salary amounts usually are added to the loss, and that total is then distributed to the partners' capital accounts. Caution should be exercised if the partnership experiences a loss during the year. Some partnership agreements specify different distributions for profit than for losses. The accountant must be especially careful to follow precisely the partnership agreement when distributing the period's profit or loss to the partners.

The earnings are a result of those two investments. The same logic applies to the partnership form of organization. Some partners invest capital, and others invest personal time. Those who invest capital are typically rewarded with interest on their capital balances; those who invest personal time are rewarded with salaries. However, both interest and salaries result from the respective investments and are used not to determine income but to determine the proportion of income to credit to each partner's capital account.

To illustrate the allocation of partnership profit based on salaries, assume that the partnership agreement provides for fixed allocations of \$2,000 to Alt and \$5,000 to Blue. Any remainder is to be distributed in the profit and loss–sharing ratio of 60:40 percent. The profit distribution is calculated as follows:

	Alt	Blue	Total
Profit percentage	60%	40%	100%
Net income			\$10,000
Salary	\$2,000	\$5,000	(7,000)
Residual income			\$ 3,000
Allocate 60:40	1,800	1,200	(3,000)
Total	\$3,800	\$6,200	\$ 0

Bonuses

Bonuses are sometimes used to provide additional compensation to partners who have provided services to the partnership, and are typically stated as a percentage of income either before or after subtracting the bonus. Sometimes the partnership agreement requires a minimum income to be earned before a bonus is calculated, which is easily done by deriving and solving an equation. To illustrate the difference between a bonus based on partnership profits *before* and a bonus *after* subtracting the bonus, we provide the following example. Assume that a bonus of 10 percent of income in excess of \$5,000 is to be credited to Blue's capital account before distributing the remaining profit. In Case 1, the bonus is computed as a percentage of income *before* subtracting the bonus amount. In Case 2, the bonus is computed as a percentage of income *after* subtracting it.

Case 1:

$$\begin{aligned}\text{Bonus} &= X\,\%\,(\text{NI} - \text{MIN})\\ \text{where: } X &= \text{The bonus percentage}\\ \text{NI} &= \text{Net income before bonus}\\ \text{MIN} &= \text{Minimum amount of income before bonus}\\ \text{Bonus} &= 0.10\,(\$10{,}000 - \$5{,}000)\\ &= \$500\end{aligned}$$

Case 2:

$$\begin{aligned}\text{Bonus} &= X\,\%\,(\text{NI} - \text{MIN} - \text{Bonus})\\ &= 0.10\,(\$10{,}000 - \$5{,}000 - \text{Bonus})\\ &= 0.10\,(\$5{,}000 - \text{Bonus})\\ &= \$500 - 0.10\ \text{Bonus}\\ 1.10\ \text{Bonus} &= \$500\\ \text{Bonus} &= \$454.55\\ &\approx \$455\end{aligned}$$

The distribution of net income based on Case 2 is calculated as follows:

	Alt	Blue	Total
Profit percentage	60%	40%	100%
Net income			$10,000
Bonus to partner		$ 455	(455)
Residual income			$ 9,545
Allocate 60:40	5,727	3,818	(9,545)
Total	$5,727	$4,273	$ 0

Multiple Profit Allocation Bases

Advanced StudyGuide .com

A partnership agreement may provide a formula describing several allocation procedures to be used to distribute profit. For example, assume the AB Partnership profit and loss agreement of specifies the following allocation process:

1. Interest of 15 percent on weighted-average capital balances.
2. Salaries of $2,000 for Alt and $5,000 for Blue.
3. A bonus of 10 percent of profits to be paid to Blue on partnership income exceeding $5,000 before subtracting the bonus, partners' salaries, and interest on capital balances.
4. Any residual to be allocated in the ratio of 60 percent to Alt and 40 percent to Blue.

The partnership agreement also should specify the allocation process in the event that partnership income is not sufficient to satisfy all allocation procedures. Some partnerships specify a profit distribution to be followed but only to the extent possible (i.e., stop following the formula once profits are exhausted). Most agreements specify that the entire process is to be completed and any remainder at each step of the process (whether positive or negative) is to be allocated in the profit and loss ratio as illustrated in the following schedule:

	Alt	Blue	Total
Profit percentage	60%	40%	100%
Average capital	$20,000	$8,000	
Net income:			$10,000
Step 1:			
Interest on average capital (15 percent)	$ 3,000	$1,200	(4,200)
Remaining after step 1			$ 5,800
Step 2:			
Salary	2,000	5,000	(7,000)
Deficiency after step 2			$ (1,200)
Step 3:			
Bonus		500	(500)
Deficiency after step 3			$ (1,700)
Step 4:			
Allocate 60:40	(1,020)	(680)	1,700
Total	$ 3,980	$6,020	$ 0

In this case, the first two distribution steps created a deficiency. The AB Partnership agreement provided that the entire profit distribution process must be completed and any deficiency distributed in the profit and loss ratio. A partnership agreement could specify that the profit distribution process should stop at any point in the event of an operating loss or the creation of a deficiency. Again, it is important for the accountant to have a thorough knowledge of the partnership agreement before beginning the profit distribution process.

Special Profit Allocation Methods

Some partnerships distribute net income on the basis of other criteria. For example, most public accounting partnerships distribute profit on the basis of partnership "units." A new partner acquires a certain number of units, and a firmwide compensation committee assigns additional units for obtaining new clients, providing the firm specific areas of industrial expertise, serving as a local office's managing partner, or accepting a variety of other responsibilities.

Other partnerships may devise profit distribution plans that reflect the firms' earnings. For example, some medical or dental partnerships allocate profit on the basis of billed services. Other criteria may be number or size of clients, years of service with the firm, or the partner's position within it. An obvious advantage of the partnership form of organization is the flexibility it allows partners for profits distribution.

PARTNERSHIP FINANCIAL STATEMENTS

A partnership is a separate reporting entity for accounting purposes, and the three financial statements—income statement, balance sheet, and statement of cash flows—typically are prepared for the partnership at the end of each reporting period. Interim statements also may be prepared to meet the partners' information needs. In addition to the three basic financial statements, a ***statement of partners' capital*** is usually prepared to present the changes in the partners' capital accounts for the period. The statement of partners' capital for the AB Partnership for 20X1 under the multiple-base profit distribution plan illustrated in the prior section follows:

AB PARTNERSHIP
Statement of Partners' Capital
For the Year Ended December 31, 20X1

	Alt	Blue	Total
Balance, January 1, 20X1	$20,000	$10,000	$30,000
Add: Additional investment		500	500
Net income distribution	3,980	6,020	10,000
	$23,980	$16,520	$40,500
Less: Withdrawal		(4,000)	(4,000)
Balance, December 31, 20X1	$23,980	$12,520	$36,500

CHANGES IN MEMBERSHIP

LO 15-6

Make calculations and journal entries to account for changes in partnership ownership.

Changes in the membership of a partnership occur with the addition of new partners or the disassociation of present partners. New partners are often a primary source of additional capital or needed business expertise. The legal structure of a partnership requires that the ***admission of a new partner*** be subject to the unanimous approval of the existing partners. Furthermore, public announcements are typically made about new partner additions so that third parties transacting business with the partnership are aware of the change. Section 306 of the UPA of 1997 states that a person admitted as a new partner of an existing partnership is not personally liable for any partnership obligation incurred before the new partner was admitted. Thus, a new partner can be charged for partnership liabilities existing prior to admission only up to the amount of his or her capital contribution at the time of admission.

The retirement or withdrawal of a partner from a partnership is a ***disassociation*** of that partner. A partner's disassociation does not necessarily mean a dissolution and winding up of the partnership. Many partnerships continue in business and, under section 701 of the UPA 1997, the partnership may purchase the disassociated partner's interest at a

buyout price. The buyout price is the estimated amount if (1) the assets were sold for a price equal to the higher of the liquidation value or the value based on a sale of the entire business as a going concern without the disassociated partner and (2) the partnership was wound up at that time with payment of all the partnership's creditors and termination of the business. Partners who simply wish to leave a partnership may be liable to the partnership for damages to the partnership caused by a *wrongful disassociation*, which occurs when the disassociation is in breach of an express provision of the partnership agreement or, for partnerships formed for a definite term or specific undertaking before the term or undertaking has been completed. Some events require judicial dissolution and winding up of the partnership. These will be discussed in Chapter 16.

General Concepts to Account for a Change in Membership in the Partnership

The Partnership as an Entity Separate from the Individual Partners and the Use of GAAP

The UPA of 1997 clearly defines a partnership as an entity separate from the individual partners. As such, the partnership entity does not change because of an individual partner's addition or withdrawal. This is similar to the concept of the entity for the corporate form of business in which the business is not necessarily revalued each time there is a change in stockholders.

Some partnerships choose to comply with GAAP in their accounting and financial reporting. These partnerships follow the same standards established by the FASB and other regulatory bodies as those for public companies. Often venture capital firms or other credit suppliers may require that the private partnership company comply with GAAP so that financials can be compared with those of other public companies. Venture capital firms have a goal of eventually taking their investees public. Thus, a partnership that follows GAAP and is audited by external auditors can receive an audit opinion stating that it is in conformity with GAAP.

A partnership following GAAP and defining its company as an entity separate from the individual partners would account for a change in membership in the same manner as a corporate entity would account for changes in its investors. Additional investments would be recognized at their fair values along with the related increase in the company's total capital.[2]

Frequently, a partnership's existing assets are undervalued when a partner joins the partnership. The difficulty lies in recording the admission of additional partners in a manner that is fair and equitable to all parties involved. Two main methods for recording the admission of a new partner to a partnership are

1. The bonus method (follows GAAP).
2. The revaluation method (does not follow GAAP).

Both methods require the partnership to make journal entries based on fair value estimates. The problem with making journal entries based on estimates is that should the estimates not materialize in the future, inequalities among the partners can arise.[3]

[2] In a few situations, GAAP allows for the recognition of decreases in the fair value of specific nonfinancial assets. One of these allowed decreases may be triggered by a change in partnership membership. For example, ASC 350 presents procedures for recognizing impairments of currently held goodwill. ASC 360 presents the accounting standards for recognizing impairment losses on long-lived assets. Net asset revaluations performed using the appropriate accounting standards are in accordance with GAAP. However, no GAAP standards provide for *increases* in the value of nonfinancial assets or recognition of new goodwill solely due to a change in partnership membership.

[3] An alternative to these methods is to appraise assets and liabilities when a new partner joins the partnership and make special provisions in the partnership agreement on how gains or losses on existing assets and liabilities should be allocated to the partners. In this way, the partnership can avoid making journal entries based on estimates but wait until assets and liabilities have been disposed to make journal entries. The benefit of this approach is that the partnership agreement specifies how to deal with the admission date differential so that no inequalities arise in the future.

Bonus Method Partners sometimes agree to use the ***bonus method*** to record the admission of a new partner. This method records an increase in the partnership's total capital only for the capital amount the new partner invests, in accordance with GAAP. However, the bonus method assigns partners' capital account balances based on the partners' agreement, which is often based on the value of the new partner's investment. In some cases, the existing partners assign some of their capital to a new partner; in others, a new partner agrees to assign a portion of his or her capital interest to the existing partners. Thus, the bonus method does not violate GAAP because partners may legally assign any or all of their transferable partnership capital interest to other partners.

Revaluation Method The partners in a private company may choose to follow non-GAAP accounting methods that meet their specific information needs. These partnerships may use the transactions surrounding the change of members as an opportunity for recognizing increases in the fair value of the partnership's existing nonfinancial assets or for recording previously unrecognized goodwill.

The practices of recognizing increases in a partnership's existing net assets using the ***revaluation method,*** or recognizing previously unrecorded goodwill (sometimes called the ***goodwill recognition method)*** are *not* in compliance with GAAP. Partnerships using these non-GAAP methods argue that revaluing all assets and liabilities at the time of the change in partnership membership states fully the true economic condition at that point in time and properly assigns the partnership's changes in asset and liability values and goodwill to the partners who have been managing the business during the time the changes in value occurred.

Partners in private companies have free choice as to how they may account for changes in partnership membership. As noted, a private partnership may use either GAAP or non-GAAP methods based on the partners' information needs. Because some partnerships record increases in value by applying the revaluation (or goodwill recognition) method, the following sections of this chapter discuss these non-GAAP methods of accounting for the change in the partnership membership.

New Partner Purchases Partnership Interest Directly from an Existing Partner

An individual may acquire a partnership interest directly from one or more of the existing partners. In this type of transaction, cash or other assets are exchanged outside the partnership, and the only entry necessary on its books is a reclassification of the partnership's total capital. For example, a new partner, Cha, could purchase Blue's partnership interest directly from her (as depicted in the diagram). This simple example would result in an entry to remove Blue's capital account from the books with a debit and transfer the balance to Cha's new capital account with a credit.

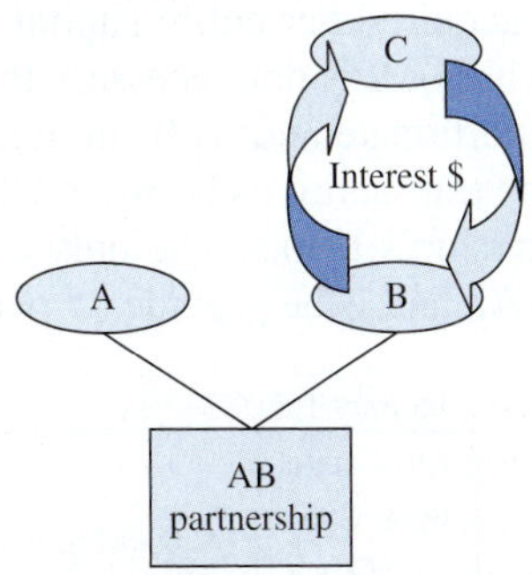

This type of transaction focuses solely on a transfer of the selling partner's share of the partnership's book value to the new partner. The ***book value of a partnership*** is simply the total amount of partnership capital, which is just another name for the partnership's

FYI

Note that the bonus and revaluation methods mentioned previously do not apply when the new partner simply purchases a partnership interest directly from an existing partner and the journal entry simply transfers the investment's book value from the existing partner to the new partner.

net assets (total assets minus total liabilities). Book value is important because it serves as a basis for asset and liability revaluations or goodwill recognition.

To provide a more complex example, assume that after operations and partners' withdrawals during 20X1 and 20X2, AB Partnership has a book value of $30,000 and profit percentages on January 1, 20X3, as follows:

	Capital Balance	Profit Percentage
Alt	$20,000	60
Blue	10,000	40
Total	$30,000	100

The following information describes the case:

1. On January 1, 20X3, Alt and Blue invite Cha to become a partner in their business. The resulting partnership will be called the ABC Partnership.
2. Cha purchases a 25 percent interest in the partnership capital directly from Alt and Blue for a total cost of $9,000, paying $5,900 to Alt and $3,100 to Blue. Cha will have a capital credit of $7,500 ($30,000 × 0.25) in a proportionate reclassification from Alt and Blue's capital accounts.
3. Cha will be entitled to a 25 percent interest in the partnership's profits or losses. The remaining 75 percent interest will be divided between Alt and Blue in their previous profit ratio of 60:40 percent. The resulting profit and loss percentages after Cha's admission follow:

Partner	Profit Percentage
Alt	45 (75% of 0.60)
Blue	30 (75% of 0.40)
Cha	25
Total	100

In this example, Cha's 25 percent share of partnership profits or losses is the same as her 25 percent capital interest. These two percentage shares do not have to be the same. As described previously, a partner's capital interest may change over time because of profit distributions, withdrawals, or additional investments in capital. Furthermore, Cha could have acquired her entire capital interest directly from either partner (or proportionately from both). It is not necessary that a new partner directly purchasing an interest do so in a proportionate reclassification from each of the existing partners.

The transaction is between Cha and the individual partners and is not reflected on the partnership's books. The only entry in this case is to reclassify the partnership capital. Both Alt and Blue provide 25 percent of their capital to Cha, as follows:

	January 1, 20X3		
(7)	Alt, Capital	5,000	
	Blue, Capital	2,500	
	Cha, Capital		7,500
	Reclassify capital to new partner: From Alt: $5,000 = $20,000 × 0.25 From Blue: $2,500 = $10,000 × 0.25.		

In this case, the capital credit to Cha is only \$7,500, although \$9,000 is paid for the 25 percent interest. The \$9,000 payment implies that the fair value of the partnership is \$36,000, calculated as follows:

$$\$9{,}000 = \text{Fair value} \times 0.25$$
$$\$36{,}000 = \text{Fair value}$$

The partnership's book value is \$30,000 before Cha's investment. The \$9,000 payment is made directly to the individual partners, but it does not become part of the firm's assets. The \$6,000 difference between the partnership's fair value and its new book value could be due to understated assets or to unrecognized goodwill.

Recognizing Fair Value Increases in the Partnership's Net Assets (Non-GAAP)

Up to this point, the partnership has followed GAAP because the partners may legally assign any or all of their transferable partnership capital interest to other persons or among themselves as they agree. If the partners wish to be in accordance with GAAP, they must follow the appropriate recognition and measurement methods for the net assets as prescribed in GAAP.

Assume that Alt and Blue decide to use the evidence from Cha's investment to recognize increases in fair values of the nonfinancial long-lived assets that have taken place before Cha's admission. The partnership's accountant has informed the members that this type of revaluation is not in accordance with GAAP. For example, if the partnership has land undervalued by \$6,000 and sells it after Cha is admitted to the partnership, she will share in the gain on the sale according to the profit ratio. To avoid this possible problem, some partnerships revalue the assets at the time a new partner is admitted even if the new partner purchases the partnership interest directly from the present partners. In this case, Alt and Blue could recognize the increase in the value of the land immediately before Cha's admission and allocate the increase to their capital accounts in their 60:40 profit ratio, as follows:

(8)			
	Land	6,000	
	Alt, Capital		3,600
	Blue, Capital		2,400

Revaluation of land before admission of new partner:
To Alt: \$3,600 = \$6,000 × 0.60
To Blue: \$2,400 = \$6,000 × 0.40.

Note that the partnership's total resulting capital is \$36,000 (\$30,000 prior plus the \$6,000 revaluation). The transfer of a 25 percent capital credit to Cha is recorded as follows:

(9)			
	Alt, Capital	5,900	
	Blue, Capital	3,100	
	Cha, Capital		9,000

Reclassify capital to new partner:
Cha = (\$30,000 + \$6,000) × 0.25 = \$9,000
From Alt = (\$20,000 + \$3,600) × 0.25 = \$5,900
From Blue = (\$10,000 + \$2,400) × 0.25 = \$3,100.

The partnership's accountant should ensure that sufficient evidence exists for any revaluation of assets and liabilities to prevent valuation abuses. Corroborating evidence such as appraisals or an extended period of excess earnings helps support asset valuations.

Advanced StudyGuide .com

New Partner Invests in Partnership

A new partner may acquire a share of the partnership by investing in the business. In this case, the partnership receives the cash or other assets.

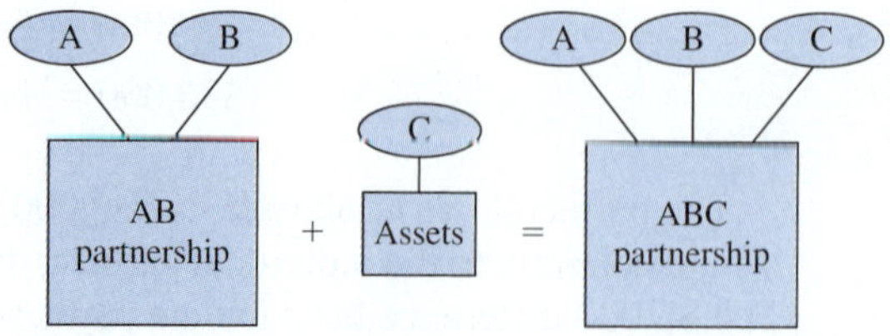

Three cases are possible when a new partner invests in a partnership:

Case 1: The new partner's investment equals the new partner's proportion of the partnership's book value.

Case 2: The investment is for *more* than the new partner's proportion of the partnership's book value. This indicates that the partnership's prior net assets are undervalued on the books or that unrecorded goodwill exists.

Case 3: The investment is for *less* than the new partner's proportion of the partnership's book value. This suggests that the partnership's prior net assets are overvalued on its books or that the new partner may be contributing goodwill in addition to other assets.

The first step in determining how to account for the admission of a new partner is to compute the ***new partner's proportion of the partnership's net book value*** as follows:

$$\begin{array}{c}\text{New partner's}\\\text{proportion of}\\\text{the partnership's}\\\text{net book value}\end{array} = \left(\begin{array}{c}\text{Prior}\\\text{capital of}\\\text{existing}\\\text{partners}\end{array} + \begin{array}{c}\text{Investment}\\\text{of new}\\\text{partner}\end{array}\right) \times \begin{array}{c}\text{Percentage}\\\text{of capital}\\\text{to new}\\\text{partner}\end{array}$$

The new partner's proportion of the partnership's book value of net assets is compared with the new partner's investment to determine the procedures to follow in accounting for his or her admission. See Figure 15–1 for an overview of the three possible cases. Step 1 compares the new partner's investment with his or her proportion of the partnership's book value. Note that this is done before any revaluations or recognition of goodwill. Step 2 determines the specific admission method. As explained previously, two methods are available to the partnership to account for the admission of a new partner when a difference exists between the new partner's investment and his or her proportion of the partnership's book value. The two methods are to (1) revalue existing net assets or recognize goodwill and (2) use the bonus method. Under the revaluation of net assets and goodwill recognition method, the historical cost bases of the partnership's net assets are adjusted at the time of the new partner's admission. Some partners object to this departure from historical cost and prefer the bonus method, which uses capital interest transfers among the partners to align the partnership's total resulting capital. Under the bonus method, net assets remain at their historical cost bases to the partnership. The choice of accounting method for the admission of a new partner is up to the partners.

The accounting for the admission of a new partner parallels the accounting for an investment in the stock of another company. If a new partner pays more than book value, the excess of cost over book value—that is, the positive differential—may be due to unrecognized goodwill or to undervalued assets, the same cases as in accounting for the differential for stock investments. If book value equals the investment cost, no differential exists, indicating that the book values of the net assets equal their fair values. If the new partner's investment is less than the proportionate book value—that is, an excess of book value over cost exists—the assets of the partnership may be overvalued. A concept unique to partnership accounting is the use of the bonus method. Figure 15–1 serves as a guide through the following discussion.

FIGURE 15–1 Overview of Accounting for Admission of a New Partner

Step 1: Compare Investment of New Partner and Proportionate Book Value	*Step 2: Alternative Methods to Account for Admission*	*Key Observations*
Investment cost > Book value (Case 2)	1. Revalue net assets up to market value and/or record unrecognized goodwill, and allocate to existing partners.	• Existing partners receive asset valuation increase, goodwill, or bonus indicated by the excess of new partner's investment over book value of the capital share initially assignable to new partner.
	2. Assign bonus to existing partners.	• Recording asset valuation increase or existing partners' goodwill increases total resulting partnership capital.
Investment cost = Book value (Case 1)	1. No revaluations, bonus, or goodwill.	• No additional allocations necessary because new partner will receive a capital share equal to the amount invested.
		• Total resulting partnership capital equals existing partners' capital plus investment of new partner.
Investment cost < Book value (Case 3)	1. Revalue existing net assets down to market value and allocate to existing partners and/or recognize goodwill brought in by new partner.	• Existing partners are assigned the reduction of asset values occurring before admission of the new partner. Alternatively, new partner is assigned goodwill or bonus as part of admission incentive.
	2. Assign bonus to new partner.	• Recording the decrease in asset valuation reduces total resulting capital, and recording new partner goodwill increases total resulting capital.

We again use the AB Partnership example presented earlier to illustrate the three cases. A review of the major facts for this example follows:

1. The January 1, 20X3, capital of the AB Partnership is $30,000. Alt's balance is $20,000, and Blue's balance is $10,000. Alt and Blue share profits in the ratio of 60:40.
2. Cha is invited into the partnership. Cha will have a 25 percent capital interest and a 25 percent share of profits. Alt and Blue will share the remaining 75 percent of profits in the ratio of 60:40, resulting in Alt having a 45 percent share of any profits and Blue having a 30 percent share.

Case 1: Investment Equals Proportion of the Partnership's Book Value

The partnership's total book value before the admission of the new partner is $30,000, and the new partner, Cha, is buying a 25 percent capital interest for $10,000.

The amount of a new partner's investment is often the result of negotiations between the existing partners and the prospective partner. As with any acquisition or investment, the investor must determine its market value. In a partnership, the prospective partner attempts to ascertain the market value and earning power of the partnership's net assets. The new partner's investment is then a function of the percentage of partnership capital being acquired. In this case, Cha must believe that the $10,000 investment required is a fair price for a 25 percent interest in the resulting partnership; otherwise, she would not make the investment.

After the amount of investment is agreed on, it is possible to calculate the new partner's proportionate book value. For a $10,000 investment, Cha will have a 25 percent interest in the partnership, as follows:

Investment in partnership	$10,000
New partner's proportionate book value: ($30,000 + $10,000) × 0.25	(10,000)
Difference (Investment = Book value)	$ 0

Because the amount of the investment ($10,000) equals the new partner's 25 percent proportionate book value ($10,000 = $40,000 × 0.25), there is an implication that the net assets are fairly valued. Total resulting capital equals the original partners' capital

($30,000) plus the new partner's tangible investment ($10,000). Note that the capital credit assigned to the new partner is her share of the total resulting capital of the partnership after her admission as partner. The entry on the partnership's books is

	January 1, 20X3		
(10)	Cash	10,000	
	Cha, Capital		10,000
	Admission of Cha for 25 percent interest upon investment of $10,000.		

The following schedule presents the key concepts in Case 1:

	Prior Capital	New Partner's Tangible Investment	New Partner's Proportion of Partnership's Book Value (25%)	Total Resulting Capital	New Partner's Share of Total Resulting Capital (25%)
Case 1					
New partner's investment equals proportionate book value	$30,000	$10,000	$10,000		
No revaluations, bonus, or goodwill				$40,000	$10,000

Case 2: New Partner's Investment More than Proportion of the Partnership's Book Value

In some cases, a new partner may invest more in an existing partnership than his or her proportionate share of the partnership's book value. This means that the new partner perceives some value in the partnership that the books do not reflect.

For example, assume Cha invests $11,000 for a 25 percent capital interest in the ABC Partnership. The first step is to compare her investment with her proportionate book value, as follows:

Investment in partnership	$11,000
New partner's proportionate book value: ($30,000 + $11,000) × 0.25	(10,250)
Difference (Investment > Book value)	$ 750

Cha has invested $11,000 for an interest with a book value of $10,250, thus paying an excess of $750 over the present book value.

Generally, an excess of investment over the respective book value of the partnership interest indicates that the partnership's prior net assets are undervalued or that the partnership has some unrecorded goodwill. Two alternative accounting treatments can be used in this case:

1. *Revaluation method.* Under this alternative:
   a. Increase the book values of existing net assets to their market values.
   b. Record unrecognized goodwill.
   c. Increase the existing partners' capital accounts for their respective shares of the increase in the book values of the net assets and the recorded goodwill.
   d. The partnership's total resulting capital reflects the existing capital balances plus the amount of asset revaluation plus the new partner's investment.

Under the revaluation method, the partnership's assets (tangible and/or intangible) are revalued upward either to recognize unrecorded excess value or to record previously unrecorded goodwill. Thus, the size of the "pie" the partners are to divide among themselves becomes larger, so that the "slice" for each becomes proportionately larger.

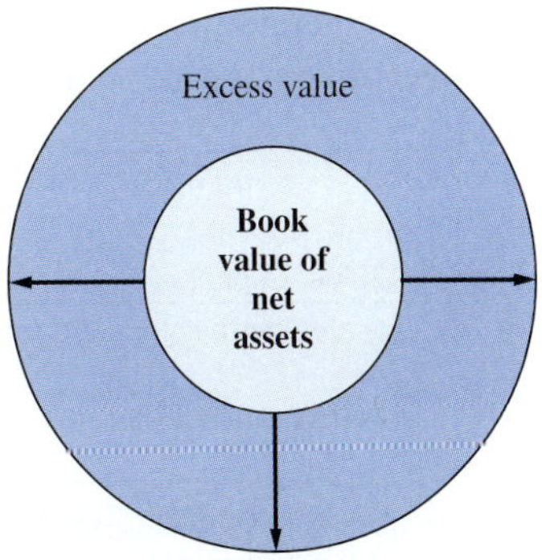

2. *Bonus method.* Essentially, the bonus method is a transfer of capital balances among the partners. This method is used when the partners do not wish to record adjustments in asset and liability accounts or recognize goodwill. Thus, the size of the pie stays the same (the book value of existing equity plus the contribution of the new partner), but one or more partners will give some of his or her "slice" to the other partners.

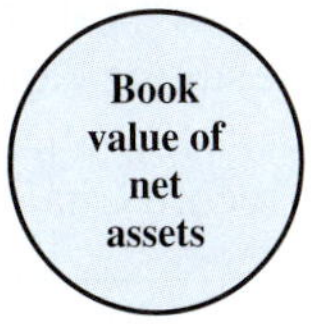

Under this method:

a. The existing partners' capital accounts are increased for their respective shares of the bonus paid by the new partner.

b. The partnership's total resulting capital reflects the existing capital balances plus the new partner's investment.

The partnership may use either of the two alternatives. The decision is usually a result of negotiations between the existing partners and the prospective partner. Some accountants criticize the revaluation of net assets or recognition of goodwill because it results in a marked departure from the historical cost principle and differs from the accepted accounting principles in **ASC 350,** which prohibits corporations from recognizing goodwill that has not been acquired by purchase. Accountants who use the goodwill or asset revaluation methods argue that the goal of partnership accounting is to state fairly the relative capital equities of the partners, and this may require accounting procedures that differ from those that corporate entities use.

The accountant's function is to ensure that any estimates used in the valuation process are based on the best evidence available. Subjective valuations that could impair the fairness of the presentations made in the partnership's financial statements should be avoided or minimized.

Illustration of Revaluation Approach (Non-GAAP) Assume that Cha paid a $750 *excess* ($11,000 − $10,250) over her proportionate book value because the partnership owns land on which it has constructed warehouse buildings. The land has a book value of $4,000, but a recent appraisal indicates that it has a market value of $7,000. The partnership expects to continue using the land for warehouse space for as long as the business operates. The accountant has informed the original partners that GAAP does not allow *increasing* the value of nonfinancial, long-lived assets held and used in the operations of the business. But the original partners decide to use the admission of the new partner to recognize the increase in the land's value and to assign this increase to their capital accounts. The increase in land value is allocated to the partners' capital accounts in the profit and loss ratio that existed during the time of the increase. Alt's capital increases by $1,800 (60 percent of the $3,000 increase), and Blue's capital increases by $1,200 (40 percent of the $3,000). The partnership makes the following entry for the revaluation of the land:

(11)			
	Land	3,000	
	Alt, Capital		1,800
	Blue, Capital		1,200
	Revalue partnership land to market value.		

Cha's $11,000 investment brings the partnership's total resulting capital to $44,000, as follows:

Prior capital of AB Partnership	$30,000
Revaluation of land to market value	3,000
Cha's investment	11,000
Total resulting capital of ABC Partnership	$44,000

Cha is acquiring a 25 percent interest in ABC Partnership's total resulting capital. Her capital credit, after revaluing the land, is calculated as follows:

$$\text{New partner's share of total resulting capital} = (\$30,000 + \$3,000 + \$11,000) \times 0.25 = \$11,000$$

The entry to record Cha's admission into the partnership follows:

(12)			
	Cash	11,000	
	Cha, Capital		11,000
	Admission of Cha for 25 percent capital interest in ABC Partnership.		

When the land is eventually sold, Cha will participate in the gain or loss calculated on the basis of the new $7,000 book value, which is the land's market value at the time of her admission into the partnership. The entire increase in the land value before Cha's admission belongs to the original partners.

An important key to remember is that the new partner's capital account balance should be equal to her respective ownership percentage multiplied by either the book value of net assets (the small pie) under the bonus method or the revalued net assets (the large pie) under the revaluation (or goodwill) method. In this case, the partners decided to revalue the balance sheet upward by recording the land's excess fair value at the time of Cha's admission. Thus, Cha's capital account balance upon admission is 25 percent of the newly expanded "pie," or $11,000.

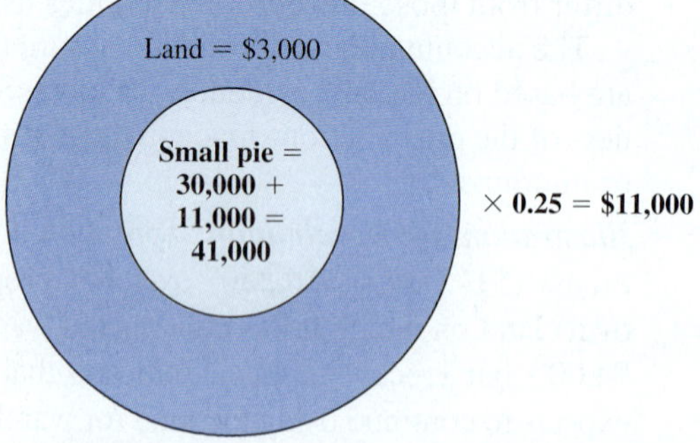

Illustration of Goodwill Recognition (Non-GAAP) An entering partner may pay an extra amount to compensate the existing partners for unrecognized goodwill, indicated by the partnership's high profitability. Some partnerships use the change in membership as an opportunity to record unrecognized goodwill created by the existing partners. Recording unrecognized goodwill is used for partnership accounting to establish appropriate capital equity among the partners. As noted earlier, this is not in accordance with the rule established in **ASC 350,** but the partners' information needs and the specific purposes of the partnership's financial statements could serve to support the use of this non-GAAP method.

Generally, the amount of goodwill is determined by negotiations between the current and prospective partners and is based on estimates of future earnings. For example, the current and new partners may agree that, due to the existing partners' efforts, the partnership has superior earnings potential and that $3,000 of goodwill should be recorded to recognize this fact. The new partner's negotiated investment cost will be based partly on the partnership's earnings potential. Alternatively, goodwill may be estimated from the amount of the new partner's investment. For example, in this case, Cha is investing $11,000 for a 25 percent interest; therefore, she must believe the total resulting partnership capital is $44,000 ($11,000 ÷ 0.25). The estimated goodwill is $3,000:

Step 1	
25% of estimated total resulting capital	$ 11,000
Estimated total resulting capital ($11,000 ÷ 0.25)	$ 44,000
Step 2	
Estimated total resulting capital	$ 44,000
Total net assets not including goodwill ($30,000 prior plus $11,000 invested by Cha)	(41,000)
Estimated goodwill	$ 3,000

Another way to view the creation of goodwill at the time of a new partner's admission is to use a T-account form for the partnership's balance sheet. Any additional net assets, such as goodwill recognition, must be balanced with additional capital, as follows:

	Balance Sheet			
Prior to admission of new partner Cha	Net assets	$30,000	Partners' capital	$30,000
New partner's cash investment	Cash	11,000	New tangible capital	11,000
Capital prior to recognizing goodwill		41,000		41,000
Estimated new goodwill	Goodwill	3,000	Capital from goodwill	3,000
Total resulting capital	Net assets	$44,000	Total resulting capital	$44,000

Once the new ABC Partnership's total resulting capital is estimated ($44,000), the new goodwill ($3,000) is the balance sheet balancing difference between the tangible capital ($41,000), which includes the new partner's cash investment and the estimated total resulting capital of ABC Partnership ($44,000).

The unrecorded goodwill is recorded, and the original partners' capital accounts are credited for the increase in assets. The adjustments to the capital accounts are in the profit and loss ratio that existed during the periods the goodwill was developed. This increased Alt's capital by 60 percent of the goodwill and Blue's by 40 percent. The entries to record goodwill and the admission of Cha are as follows:

(13)	Goodwill	3,000	
	Alt, Capital		1,800
	Blue, Capital		1,200
	Recognize unrecorded goodwill.		
(14)	Cash	11,000	
	Cha, Capital		11,000
	Admission of Cha to partnership for a 25 percent capital interest: $44,000 × 0.25.		

Another reason for recording goodwill is that the new partner may want her capital balance to equal the amount of investment made. The investment is based on the partnership's market value, and for this equality to occur, the partnership must restate its previous net assets to their fair values.

Again, it is important to note that the $11,000 credit to Cha's capital account is 25 percent of ABC Partnership's total resulting capital of $44,000. Again, because the partners elected to revalue the balance sheet upward by recording goodwill, Cha's capital account balance is 25 percent of the larger pie (the newly expanded net assets).

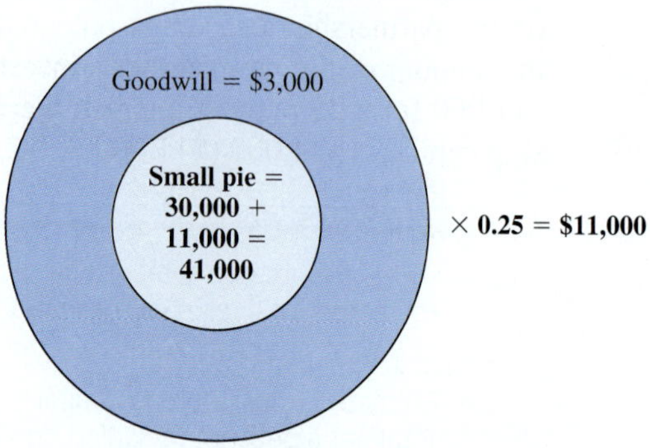

In future periods, any goodwill impairment loss will be charged against partnership earnings before net income is distributed to the partners. Consequently, Cha's future profit distribution may be affected by the goodwill recognized at the time of her admission into the partnership.

Illustration of Bonus Method (GAAP) Some partnerships are averse to recognizing asset revaluations or unrecorded goodwill when a new partner is admitted. Instead, they record a portion of the new partner's investment as a bonus to the existing partners to align the capital balances properly at the time of the new partner's admission. In this case, the $750 excess Cha paid is a bonus allocated to the original partners in their profit and loss ratio of 60 percent to Alt and 40 percent to Blue. ABC Partnership's total resulting capital consists of $30,000 existing capital of Alt and Blue plus the $11,000 investment of Cha. No additional capital is recognized by revaluing assets. Because the partners do not revalue the balance sheet, they simply divide the existing (small) pie based on their relative ownership percentages. Thus, Cha's capital account balance will be 25 percent of the small pie, $10,250.

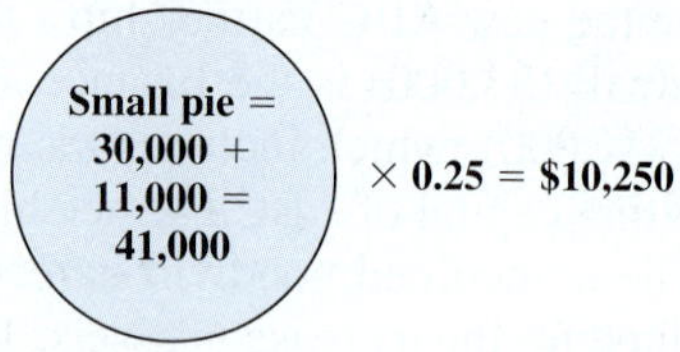

The entry to record Cha's admission under the bonus method is as follows:

(15)			
(15)	Cash	11,000	
	Alt, Capital		450
	Blue, Capital		300
	Cha, Capital		10,250

Admission of Cha with bonus to Alt and Blue.
Alt = $750 × 0.60 = $450
Blue = $750 × 0.40 = $300.

Cha may dislike the bonus method because her capital balance is $750 less than her investment in the partnership. This is a disadvantage of the bonus method.

The following schedule presents the key concepts for Case 2:

	Prior Capital	New Partner's Tangible Investment	New Partner's Proportion of Partnership's Book Value (25%)	Total Resulting Capital	New Partner's Share of Total Resulting Capital (25%)
Case 2					
New partner's investment of more than proportionate book value	$30,000	$11,000	$10,250		
1. Revalue assets by increasing land $3,000				$44,000	$11,000
2. Recognize $3,000 goodwill for original partners				44,000	11,000
3. Bonus of $750 to original partners				41,000	10,250

Case 3: New Partner's Investment Less than Proportion of the Partnership's Book Value

It is possible that a new partner may pay less than his or her proportionate share of the partnership's book value. For example, assume Cha invests $8,000 for a 25 percent capital interest in the ABC Partnership. The first step is to compare the new partner's investment with her proportionate book value, as follows:

Investment in partnership	$ 8,000
New partner's proportionate book value: ($30,000 + $8,000) × 0.25	(9,500)
Difference (Investment < Share of book value)	$(1,500)

The fact that Cha's investment is less than the book value of a 25 percent interest in the partnership indicates that the partnership has overvalued net assets or the original partners recognize that Cha is contributing additional value in the form of her expertise or skills that the partnership needs. In this case, Cha is investing $8,000 in cash and an additional amount that may be viewed as goodwill.

As with Case 2, in which the investment is more than the book value acquired, there are two alternative approaches to account for the differential when the investment is less than the book value acquired. The two approaches are

1. *Revaluation method.* Under this alternative:

   a. Decrease book values of net assets to recognize the reduction in their values.

   b. Decrease the original partners' capital accounts for their respective share of the decrease in the values of the net assets.

   c. Record goodwill or other intangible benefits brought in by the new partner and record the increase in the new partner's capital account.

   d. Recognize that the partnership's total resulting capital reflects the prior capital balances less the amount of the net asset valuation write-down plus the new partner's investment and new goodwill.

2. *Bonus method.* Under the bonus method:

   a. The new partner is assigned a bonus from the original partners' capital accounts, which are decreased for their respective shares of the bonus paid to the new partner.

   b. The partnership's total resulting capital reflects the prior capital balances plus the new partner's investment.

Illustration of Revaluation of Net Assets Approach (GAAP) Almost all of an entity's assets and liabilities have one or more generally accepted accounting principles for recognizing impairment losses or write-downs to fair value. Several examples of these GAAP are recognition of a valuation loss on inventory valued using the lower-of-cost-or-market method, impairment losses on goodwill, impairment losses on long-lived assets used in the business, and losses on financial assets such as investments. Thus, GAAP allows the recognition of decreases in the values of many assets. The process of admitting a new partner is a common time for evaluating the fair values of the partnership's net assets and comparing those values with the book values.

Assume that the reason Cha paid only $8,000 for a 25 percent interest in the partnership is that equipment used in current production is recorded at a book value of $14,000 but has a fair value of only $8,000. The partners agree to recognize the impairment loss and write down the equipment to its fair value before the new partner's admission. The write-down is allocated to the original partners in the profit and loss ratio that existed during the period of the decline in the equipment's fair value: 60 percent to Alt and 40 percent to Blue. The write-down is recorded as follows:

(16)			
	Alt, Capital	3,600	
	Blue, Capital	2,400	
	Equipment		6,000
	Recognize impairment loss on equipment.		

Note that the partnership's total capital has now been reduced from $30,000 to $24,000 as a result of the $6,000 write-down. The value of Cha's share of ABC Partnership's total resulting capital, *after the write-down,* is calculated as follows:

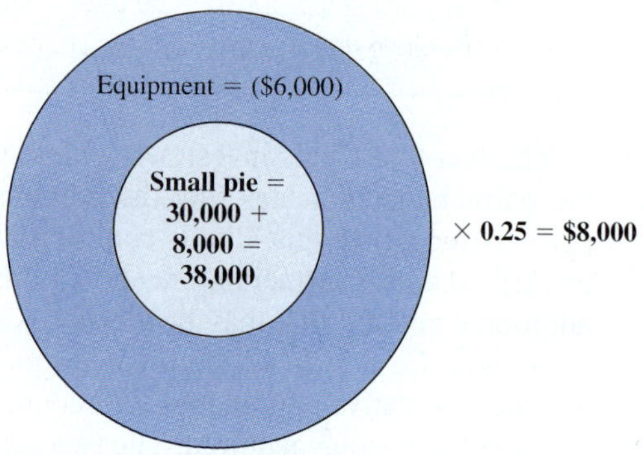

In this case, the revaluation actually reduces the size of the pie. Cha's capital account is credited for 25 percent of $32,000 for $8,000.

Note that because the "excess value" portion is really negative, the size of the pie is actually shrinking, not growing. The entry to record the admission of Cha as a partner in the ABC Partnership is

(17)			
	Cash	8,000	
	Cha, Capital		8,000
	Admission of Cha to partnership.		

Cha's recorded capital credit is equal to her investment because the total partnership capital of $32,000 ($24,000 + $8,000) now represents the partnership's fair value.

Illustration of Recording Goodwill for New Partner (Non-GAAP) The original partners may offer Cha a 25 percent capital interest in the ABC Partnership for an $8,000 investment because she has essential business experience, skills, customer contacts, reputation, or other aspects of goodwill that she will bring into the partnership. The amount of goodwill the new partner brings in is usually determined through negotiations between the original partners and the prospective partner. For example, Alt, Blue, and Cha may agree that Cha's abilities will generate excess earnings for the resulting ABC Partnership.

They agree that Cha should be given $2,000 of goodwill recognition when she joins the partnership in recognition of her anticipated excess contribution to the partnership's future earnings. The negotiated goodwill is recognized and added to her tangible investment to determine the amount of capital credit.

Alternatively, the amount of goodwill the new partner brings in may be estimated from the amount of the total capital being retained by the original partners. In this case, they are retaining a 75 percent interest in the partnership and allowing the new partner a 25 percent capital interest. The dollar amount of the original partners' 75 percent interest is $30,000. Cha's investment of $8,000 plus goodwill makes up the remaining 25 percent. The amount of goodwill that Cha brought into the partnership is determined as follows:

Step 1	
75% of estimated total resulting capital	$30,000
Estimated total resulting capital ($30,000 ÷ 0.75)	$40,000
Step 2	
Estimated total resulting capital	$40,000
Total net assets not including goodwill ($30,000 + $8,000)	(38,000)
Estimated goodwill	$ 2,000

Note that the goodwill estimate for the new partner is made using the information from the original partners' interests. In Case 2, the estimate of goodwill to the original partners was made using the information from the new partner's investment. The reason for this difference is that the best available information should be used for the goodwill estimates. If the new partner's goodwill is being estimated, it is not logical to use his or her tangible investment to estimate the total investment he or she made, including goodwill. This is circular reasoning that involves using a number to estimate itself. Furthermore, when goodwill is being assigned to the original partners, it is not logical to use their existing capital to estimate their goodwill. A useful way to remember how to estimate goodwill is to use the opposite partner's information for the estimate. Use the new partner to estimate goodwill to original partners; use them to estimate goodwill to the new partner. Cha's capital account balance will be 25 percent of the newly revalued partnership balance sheet, $10,000.

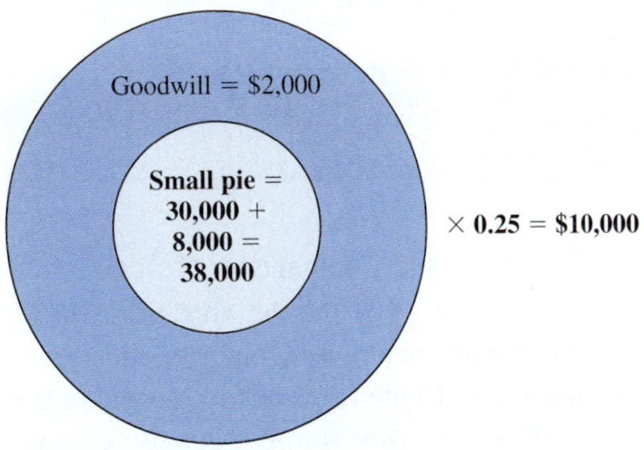

The entry to record Cha's admission into the ABC Partnership is

(18)	Cash	8,000	
	Goodwill	2,000	
	Cha, Capital		10,000
	Admission of Cha to partnership.		

Note that the ABC Partnership's total resulting capital is now $40,000 with Alt and Blue together having a 75 percent interest and Cha having a 25 percent interest.

Illustration of Bonus Method (GAAP) Cha's admission as a new partner with a 25 percent interest in the ABC Partnership for an investment of only $8,000 may be accounted for by recognizing a bonus the original partners give Cha. The $1,500 bonus is the difference between Cha's $9,500 book value and her $8,000 investment. The original partners' capital accounts are reduced by $1,500 in their profit and loss ratio of 60 percent for Alt and 40 percent for Blue, and Cha's capital account is credited for $9,500, as follows:

(19)		Debit	Credit
	Cash	8,000	
	Alt, Capital	900	
	Blue, Capital	600	
	Cha, Capital		9,500

Admission of Cha to partnership.
Alt = $1,500 × 0.60 = $900
Blue = $1,500 × 0.40 = $600.

Note that the amount of the capital credit assigned to the new partner is her share of the total resulting capital (the small pie) because the partners did not elect to revalue the balance sheet other than to record Cha's capital contribution.

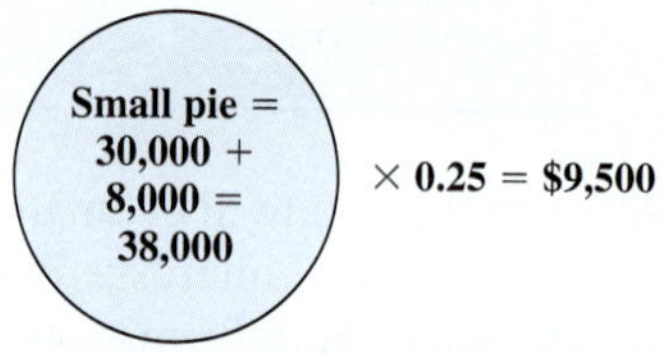

The following schedule presents the key concepts for Case 3:

	Prior Capital	New Partner's Tangible Investment	New Partner's Proportion of Partnership's Book Value (25%)	Total Resulting Capital	New Partner's Share of Total Resulting Capital (25%)
Case 3					
New partner's investment less than proportionate book value	$30,000	$8,000	$9,500		
1. Revalue assets by decreasing equipment by $6,000				$32,000	$ 8,000
2. Recognize goodwill of $2,000 for new partner				40,000	10,000
3. Bonus of $1,500 to new partner				38,000	9,500

Summary and Comparison of Accounting for Investment of New Partner

See Figure 15–2 for the entries made in each of the three cases discussed. In addition, the capital balance of each of the three partners immediately after Cha's admission is presented to the right of the journal entries.

The following summarizes the alternative methods of accounting for the investment of a new partner:

Case 1: New partner's investment equals his or her proportion of the partnership's book value.

1. The new partner's capital credit equals his or her investment.
2. This case recognizes no goodwill or bonus.

FIGURE 15–2
Summary of Accounting for Investment of New Partner: Journal Entries and Capital Balances after Admission of New Partner

Case 1: New partner's investment equals proportionate book value. Cha invests $10,000 cash for 25 percent capital interest.

Entry	Debit	Credit
Cash	10,000	
Cha, Capital		10,000

Partner	Capital
Alt	$20,000
Blue	10,000
Cha	10,000
Total	$40,000

Case 2: New partner's investment is more than proportionate book value. Cha invests $11,000 cash for 25 percent capital interest.

(a) *Revalue net assets (upward):*

Entry	Debit	Credit
Land	3,000	
Alt, Capital		1,800
Blue, Capital		1,200

Entry	Debit	Credit
Cash	11,000	
Cha, Capital		11,000

Partner	Capital
Alt	$21,800
Blue	11,200
Cha	11,000
Total	$44,000

(b) *Recognize goodwill for original partners:*

Entry	Debit	Credit
Goodwill	3,000	
Alt, Capital		1,800
Blue, Capital		1,200

Entry	Debit	Credit
Cash	11,000	
Cha, Capital		11,000

Partner	Capital
Alt	$21,800
Blue	11,200
Cha	11,000
Total	$44,000

(c) *Bonus to original partners:*

Entry	Debit	Credit
Cash	11,000	
Alt, Capital		450
Blue, Capital		300
Cha, Capital		10,250

Partner	Capital
Alt	$20,450
Blue	10,300
Cha	10,250
Total	$41,000

Case 3: New partner's investment is less than proportionate book value. Cha invests $8,000 cash for a 25 percent capital interest.

(a) *Revalue net assets (downward)*

Entry	Debit	Credit
Alt, Capital	3,600	
Blue, Capital	2,400	
Equipment		6,000

Entry	Debit	Credit
Cash	8,000	
Cha, Capital		8,000

Partner	Capital
Alt	$16,400
Blue	7,600
Cha	8,000
Total	$32,000

(b) *Recognize goodwill for new partner:*

Entry	Debit	Credit
Cash	8,000	
Goodwill	2,000	
Cha, Capital		10,000

Partner	Capital
Alt	$20,000
Blue	10,000
Cha	10,000
Total	$40,000

(c) *Bonus to new partner:*

Entry	Debit	Credit
Cash	8,000	
Alt, Capital	900	
Blue, Capital	600	
Cha, Capital		9,500

Partner	Capital
Alt	$19,100
Blue	9,400
Cha	9,500
Total	$38,000

Case 2: New partner's investment is more than his or her proportion of the partnership's book value.

1. The revaluation of an asset (or recognition of goodwill) increases the partnership's total resulting capital. The increase is allocated to the existing partners in their profit and loss ratio.
2. After recognition of the asset revaluation or unrecorded goodwill, the new partner's capital credit equals his or her investment and his or her percentage of the total resulting capital.
3. Under the bonus method, the partnership's total resulting capital is the sum of the existing partnership's capital plus the new partner's investment. The capital credit recorded for the new partner is less than the investment but equals his or her percentage of the resulting partnership capital.

Case 3: New partner's investment is less than his or her proportion of the partnership's book value.

1. Under the revaluation of assets approach, the write-down of the assets reduces the existing partners' capital in their profit and loss ratio. The new partner's capital is then credited for the amount of the investment. Moreover, the goodwill is assigned to the new partner, increasing the partnership's total resulting capital. The new partner's capital is credited for his or her percentage interest in the partnership's total resulting capital.
2. The bonus method results in a transfer of capital from the existing partners to the new partner. The new partnership's total resulting capital equals the prior capital plus the new partner's investment. The new partner's capital credit is more than the investment made but equals his or her percentage of the total resulting capital.

Determining a New Partner's Investment Cost

Advanced StudyGuide .com

The previous sections have provided the amount of the new partner's contribution. In some instances, accountants are requested to determine the amount of cash investment by asking the new partner to contribute. The basic principles of partnership accounting provide the means to answer this question. For example, let's continue the basic example of partners Alt and Blue wishing to admit Cha as a new partner. The original partnership capital was $30,000, and the partners wish to invite Cha into the partnership for a 25 percent interest.

Assume that the original partners, Alt and Blue, agree that the partnership's assets should be revalued up by $3,000 to recognize the increase in value of the land the partnership holds. The question is how much Cha, the new partner, should be asked to invest for her 25 percent interest.

When determining the new partner's investment cost, it is important to note the partnership's total resulting capital and the percentage of ownership interest the existing partners retain. In this example, they retain a 75 percent interest in the resulting partnership, for which their 75 percent capital interest is $33,000, the $30,000 of existing capital plus the $3,000 from the revaluation of the land, as follows:

75% of total resulting capital	$33,000
	÷ 0.75
Total resulting capital (100%)	$44,000
Less existing partners' capital	(33,000)
Cash contribution required of new partner	$11,000

Note that this is simply another way to evaluate the admission process as discussed in the net asset revaluation illustration under Case 2.

In some cases, the bonus amount may be determined prior to determining the new partner's required cash contribution. For example, assume that Alt and Blue agree to give Cha a bonus of $1,500 for joining the partnership. The following schedule determines the cash investment amount required of Cha, the new partner:

Prior capital of Alt and Blue	$30,000
Less bonus given to Cha upon admission	(1,500)
Capital retained by Alt and Blue (75%)	$28,500
Total resulting capital ($28,500 ÷ 0.75)	$38,000
Less original partners' capital	(28,500)
Capital credit required of new partner	$ 9,500
Less bonus to new partner from original partners	(1,500)
Cash contribution required of new partner	$ 8,000

This second example is another way to view the bonus-to-new-partner method under Case 3 as presented. The key is to determine the amount of capital that the existing partners will retain for their percentage share in the partnership's total resulting capital after admitting the new partner. The new partner's cash contribution can be computed simply by determining the amount of the capital credit that will be assigned to him or her and then recognizing any bonuses that will be used to align the capital balances.

Disassociation of a Partner from the Partnership

When a partner retires or withdraws from a partnership, that partner is disassociated from the partnership. In most cases, the partnership purchases the disassociated partner's interest in the partnership for a buyout price. Section 701 of the UPA 1997 states that the buyout price is the estimated amount if (1) the partnership's assets were sold at a price equal to the higher of the liquidation value or the value based on a sale of the entire business as a going concern without the disassociated partner and (2) the partnership was wound up at that time with all partnership obligations settled. Note that goodwill may be included in the valuation. The partnership must pay interest to the disassociated partner from the date of disassociation to the date of payment. In cases of wrongful disassociation, the partnership may sue the partner for damages the wrongful disassociation causes the partnership.

In the case in which the partnership agrees to the disassociation and it is not wrongful, the accountant can aid in computing the buyout price. It is especially important to determine all existing liabilities on the disassociation date. The partnership agreement may include other procedures to use in the case of a partner disassociation, such as the specifics of valuation, the process of the acquisition of the disassociated partner's transferable value, and other aspects of the change in membership process.

Some partnerships have an audit performed when a change in partners is made. This audit establishes the existence of and the accuracy of the book values of the assets and liabilities. On occasion, accounting errors are found during an audit. Errors should be corrected and the partners' capital accounts adjusted based on the profit and loss ratio that existed in the period in which the errors were made. For example, if an audit disclosed that three years ago depreciation expense was charged for $4,000 less than it should have been, the error is corrected retroactively, and the partners' capital accounts are charged with their respective shares of the adjustment based on their profit and loss ratio of three years ago.

Generally, the continuing partners buy out the retiring partner either by making a direct acquisition or by having the partnership acquire the retiring partner's interest. If the continuing partners directly acquire the retiring partner's interest, the only entry on the partnership's books is to record the reclassification of capital among the partners. If the partnership acquires the retiring partner's interest, the partnership must record the reduction of total partnership capital and the corresponding reduction of assets paid to the retiring partner. Computation of the buyout price when a partner disassociates from the partnership can take the form of three possible scenarios. These are discussed next.

1. Buyout Price Equal to Partner's Capital Credit

Assume Alt retires from the ABC Partnership when his capital account has a balance of $55,000 after recording all increases in the partnership's net assets including income earned up to the date of the retirement. All partners agree to $55,000 as the buyout price of Alt's partnership interest. The entry made by the ABC Partnership is

(20)			
	Alt, Capital	55,000	
	Cash		55,000
	Retirement of Alt.		

If the partnership is unable to pay the total of $55,000 to Alt at the time of retirement, it must recognize a liability for the remaining portion.

2. Buyout Price Higher than Partner's Capital Credit

Assume Alt has a capital credit of $55,000 and all the partners agree to a buyout price of $65,000. Most partnerships would account for the $10,000 payment above Alt's capital credit ($65,000 paid – $55,000) as a capital adjustment bonus to Alt from the capital accounts of the remaining partners. In this case, the $10,000 would be allocated against the capital accounts of Blue and Cha in their profit ratio. Blue has a 30 percent interest, and Cha has a 25 percent interest in ABC Partnership's net income. The sum of their respective shares is 55 percent (30 percent + 25 percent), and their relative profit percentages, rounded to the nearest percentage, are 55 percent for Blue and 45 percent for Cha, computed as follows:

	Prior Profit Percentage	Remaining Profit Percentage
Alt	45	0
Blue	30	55 (30/55)
Cha	25	45 (25/55)
Total	100	100

The entry to record Alt's retirement is

(21)			
	Alt, Capital	55,000	
	Blue, Capital	5,500	
	Cha, Capital	4,500	
	Cash		65,000
	Retirement of Alt.		

The $10,000 bonus paid to Alt is allocated to Blue and Cha in their respective profit ratios. Blue is charged for 55 percent, and Cha is charged for the remaining 45 percent.

Occasionally, a partnership uses the retirement of a partner to record unrecognized goodwill. In this case, the partnership may record the retiring partner's share only, or it may impute the entire amount of goodwill based on the retiring partner's profit percentage. If it imputes total goodwill, the remaining partners also receive their respective shares of the total goodwill recognized. Many accountants criticize recording goodwill on the retirement of a partner on the same theoretical grounds as they criticize recording unrecognized goodwill on the admission of a new partner. Nevertheless, partnership accounting sometimes recognizes all of the imputed goodwill at this event.

For example, if $65,000 is paid to Alt and only his share of unrecognized goodwill is to be recorded, the partnership makes the following entries at the time of his retirement:

(22)	Goodwill	10,000	
	Alt, Capital		10,000
	Recognize Alt's share of goodwill.		

(23)	Alt, Capital	65,000	
	Cash		65,000
	Retirement of Alt.		

3. Buyout Price Less than Partner's Capital Credit

Sometimes, the buyout price is less than a partner's capital credit. This could result if liquidation values of net assets are less than their book values or because the disassociating partner wishes to leave the partnership badly enough to accept less than his or her current capital balance. For example, Alt agrees to accept $50,000 as the buyout price for his partnership interest. The partnership should evaluate its net assets to determine whether any impairments or write-downs should be recognized and the related losses should be allocated to the partners immediately before the buyout. If no revaluations of the net assets are necessary, then the $5,000 difference ($50,000 cash paid less $55,000 capital credit) is distributed as a capital adjustment to Blue and Cha in their respective profit and loss ratio.

(24)	Alt, Capital	55,000	
	Blue, Capital		2,750
	Cha, Capital.		2,250
	Cash		50,000
	Retirement of Alt.		

SUMMARY OF KEY CONCEPTS

Accounting for partnerships recognizes the unique aspects of this form of business organization. Most states have enacted the major provisions of the Uniform Partnership Act of 1997 (UPA 1997), which delineates the rights and responsibilities of the partners, both with third parties and among the partners, and the rights of third parties, such as creditors, with the partnership. A partnership agreement is very important because many sections of the UPA 1997 can be waived with a formal partnership agreement. The partnership also should file a statement of partnership authority with the secretary of the state and the clerk of the county in which the partnership business takes place. The UPA 1997 includes sections stating that the partnership is an entity distinct from its partners, that partners are the partnership's agents, that partners are personally liable for the partnership obligations that exceed its assets, that partnership profits or losses are shared equally, and that a partner may disassociate, in which case that partner no longer may share in the partnership's management.

Partnerships use a wide variety of profit or loss distribution methods, and accountants must ensure that the partnership agreement is followed closely. Most partnerships continue in business when a partner disassociates (leaves the partnership) by purchasing that partner's interest at a buyout price based on the partnership's value were it to wind up its business. Several accounting methods are used to account for changes in partnership membership. Some partnerships use a net asset revaluation approach, sometimes including goodwill recognition. The other major accounting approach used to account for changes in membership is the bonus method, which uses a reclassification of partner capital. Partnerships provide four financial statements: the income statement, the balance sheet, the statement of cash flows, and a statement of partners' capital that presents the changes in the partners' capital accounts during the period.

KEY TERMS

admission of a new partner, *771*
bonus, *766*
bonus method, *773*
book value of a partnership, *773*
buyout price, *772*
disassociation, *771*
entity concept, *760*
goodwill recognition method, *773*
interest on capital balances, *766*
new partner's proportion of the partnership's net book value, *776*
partners' accounts, *765*
partner's disassociation, *761*
preselected ratio, *766*
profit distribution plans, *766*
revaluation method, *773*
salary, *766*
statement of partners' capital, *771*
statement of partnership authority, *760*
transferable interest, *761*
Uniform Partnership Act of 1997 (UPA 1997), *758*

Appendix 15A Tax Aspects of a Partnership

The Internal Revenue Service views the partnership form of organization as a temporary aggregation of some of the individual partners' rights. The partnership is not a separate taxable entity. Therefore, the individual partners must report their share of the partnership income or loss on their personal tax returns, whether withdrawn or not. This sometimes creates cash flow problems for partners who leave their share of income in the partnership and permit the firm to use their share for growth. In such cases, the partners must pay income tax on income that was not distributed to them. However, this tax conduit feature also offers special tax features to the individual partners. For example, charitable contributions made by the partnership are reported on the partners' individual tax returns. Also, any tax-exempt income earned by the partnership is passed through to the individual partners.

This pass-through benefits individual partners when the business has an operating loss. The individual partners can recognize their shares of the partnership loss on their own tax returns, thereby offsetting other taxable income. If the business is incorporated, the loss does not pass through to the stockholders.

TAX BASIS OF ASSET INVESTMENTS

For capital investments, the accounting basis and the tax basis are computed differently. For tax purposes, a partnership must value the assets invested in it at the tax basis of the individual partner who invests the assets. For example, assume that partner A contributes a building to the AB Partnership. The building originally cost $6,000 and has been depreciated $2,000, leaving a book value of $4,000. The building has a market value of $10,000. For tax purposes, the partnership records the building at $4,000, partner A's adjusted basis.

This tax valuation differs from the amount that is recognized under generally accepted accounting principles. A basic GAAP concept is to value asset transfers between separate reporting entities at their respective fair market values. In this case, the partnership records the building at its $10,000 fair value for accounting purposes. Most partnerships maintain their accounting records and financial statements using GAAP, and they use a separate adjusting schedule at the end of each period to report the results for tax purposes on Form 1065, the partnership tax information form.

In addition to asset transfers, a partnership also may assume the liabilities associated with an asset. For example, if the building was subject to a $2,000 mortgage, which the AB Partnership assumed with the building, partner A benefits because the other partners have assumed a portion of the mortgage that A originally owed entirely.

A partner's tax basis in a partnership is the sum of the following:

The partner's tax basis of any assets contributed to the partnership.

Plus: The partner's share of other partners' liabilities assumed by the partnership.

Less: The amount of the partner's liabilities assumed by the other partners.

To illustrate, A contributes the building discussed, which has an adjusted tax basis of $4,000 ($6,000 cost less $2,000 depreciation) and is subject to a mortgage of $2,000. The building's market value is $10,000. B contributes machinery that has a book value of $15,000 and a market value of $20,000 and is subject to a note payable of $5,000. The partners agree to share equally in the liabilities assumed by the AB Partnership. The tax basis of each partner in the partnership is calculated as follows:

	Partner A	Partner B
Tax basis of assets contributed	$4,000	$15,000
Partner's share of other partner's liabilities assumed by partnership:		
Partner A: (1/2 of $5,000)	2,500	
Partner B: (1/2 of $2,000)		1,000
Partner's liabilities assumed by other partners:		
Partner A: (1/2 of $2,000)	(1,000)	
Partner B: (1/2 of $5,000)		(2,500)
Tax basis of partner's interest	$5,500	$13,500

Each partner's tax basis is used for tax recognition of gains or losses on subsequent disposals of the partner's investment in the partnership.

For GAAP purposes, each partner's investment is based on the fair value of the assets less liabilities assumed. Thus, in the preceding case, partner A's accounting basis is $8,000 ($10,000 market value of the building less $2,000 mortgage), and partner B's accounting basis is $15,000 ($20,000 market value of the equipment less $5,000 note payable). Any asset disposal gain or loss in the accounting financial statements is based on the valuations made using GAAP. A separate schedule of tax bases for each of the partners is typically maintained in case the information is required for a partner's individual tax return.

Appendix 15B Joint Ventures

A *joint venture* usually is a business entity owned and operated by a small group of investors as a separate and specific business project organized for the mutual benefit of the ownership group. Many joint ventures are short-term associations of two or more parties to fulfill a specific project, such as the development of real estate, joint oil or gas drilling efforts, the financing of a joint production center, or the financing of a motion picture effort. Many international efforts to expand production or markets involve joint ventures either with foreign-based companies or with foreign governments. A recent phenomenon is the formation of research joint ventures in which two or more corporations agree to share the costs and eventual research accomplishments of a separate research laboratory. The venturers might not have equal ownership interests; a venturer's share could be as low as 5 or 10 percent or as high as 90 or 95 percent. Many joint ventures of only two venturers, called *50 percent–owned ventures,* divide the ownership share equally.

A joint venture may be organized as a corporation, partnership, or undivided interest. A corporate joint venture is usually formed for long-term projects such as developing and sharing of technical knowledge among a small group of companies. The incorporation of the joint venture formalizes the legal relationships between the venturers and limits each investor's liability to the amount of her or his investment in the venture. The venture's stock is not traded publicly, and the venturers usually have other business transactions between them. Accounting for a corporate joint venture is guided by **ASC 323** which requires that investors use the equity method to account for their investments in the common stock of corporate joint ventures.

When one corporation controls another, the controlled corporation is considered a subsidiary rather than a corporate joint venture even if it has a small number of other owners. A subsidiary should be consolidated by the controlling owner, and a noncontrolling interest recognized for the interests of other owners.

A partnership joint venture is accounted for as any other partnership. All facets of partnership accounting presented in the chapter apply to these partnerships, each of which has its own accounting records. Some joint ventures are accounted for on one of the venturer's books; however, this combined accounting does not fully reflect the fact that the joint venture is a separate reporting entity. Each partner, or venturer, maintains an investment account on its books for its share of the partnership venture capital. The investment in the partnership account is debited for the initial investment and for the investor's share of subsequent profits. Withdrawals and shares of losses are credited to the investment account; its balance should correspond to the balance in the partner's capital account shown on the joint venture partnership's statements.

ASC 323, states that intercompany profits should be eliminated and the investor-partners should record their shares of the venture's income or loss in the same manner as with the equity method. For financial reporting purposes, if one of the investor-venturers in fact controls the joint venture, she or he should consolidate the joint venture into its financial statements. If all investor-venturers maintain joint control, then the one-line equity method should be used to report the investment in the joint venture.

Accounting for unincorporated joint ventures that are undivided interests usually follows the accounting method used by partnerships. An *undivided interest* exists when each investor-venturer owns a proportionate share of each asset and is proportionately liable for its share of each liability. Some established industry practices, especially in oil and gas venture accounting, provide for a pro rata recognition of a venture's assets, liabilities, revenue, and expenses. For example, assume that both A Company and B Company are 50 percent investors in a joint venture, called JTV, for the purposes of oil exploration. The JTV venture has plant assets of $500,000 and long-term liabilities of $200,000. Therefore, both A Company and B Company have an investment of $150,000 ($300,000 × 0.50). Under the method, the balance sheets of both A and B companies report the investment as a $150,000 investment in joint venture.

International Accounting Standard No. 31, "Interests in Joint Ventures" (IAS 31), specifies the reporting of joint ventures under international accounting financial reporting standards. **IAS 31** identifies three types of joint ventures: (1) *jointly controlled operations,* for which each venturer recognizes the assets that it controls and the liabilities and the expenses it incurs and its share of the joint venture's income, (2) *jointly controlled assets,* for which each venturer recognizes its share of the jointly controlled assets, any liabilities it has incurred plus its share of any liabilities the joint venture incurred, and its share of the income together with its share of the expenses incurred from the joint venture's operations plus any expenses that the individual venturer has incurred from its interest in the joint venture, and (3) *jointly controlled entities,* for which each venturer recognizes its interest in the joint venture using proportionate consolidation or the equity method.

Under the proportionate consolidation method, each venturer recognizes a pro rata share of the assets, liabilities, income, and expenses of the jointly controlled entity. This approach is illustrated in the JTV example. In this case, assets of $250,000 ($500,000 × 0.50) and liabilities of $100,000 ($200,000 × 0.50) are added to the present assets and liabilities of each investor-venturer. The proportionate share of the assets and liabilities should be added to similar items in the investor's financial statements. The same pro rata method is also used for the joint venture's revenue and expenses. A comparison of the equity method and the proportionate consolidation for venturer A Company is presented in Figure 15–3.

Joint ventures provide their investors flexibility as to management, operations, and the division of profits or losses. However, companies need to be aware of **ASC 810.** When an investor does not have a majority stock ownership, contractual or other agreements may specify the allocation of the entity's profits or losses. **ASC 810** specifies that consolidation of a variable interest entity (VIE) is required if an investor will absorb a majority of its expected losses or receive a majority of the entity's expected return. Therefore, an equity investor not having a controlling financial interest may be determined to be the primary beneficiary of the VIE and thus be required to fully consolidate that entity.

FIGURE 15–3
Comparative Balance Sheets for Reporting a Joint Venture

	Balance Sheets of A Company		
	Before Joint Venture	**Equity Method**	**Proportionate Consolidation**
Current Assets	$250	$100	$100
Property, Plant & Equipment	400	400	650
Investment in Joint Venture	0	150	0
Total	$650	$650	$750
Current Liabilities	$100	$100	$100
Long-Term Debt	300	300	400
Stockholders' Equity	250	250	250
Total	$650	$650	$750

Real estate development is often conducted through joint ventures. Accounting for noncontrolling interests in real estate joint ventures is guided by **ASC 970**, which recommends the use of the equity method to account for noncontrolling investments in corporate or noncorporate real estate ventures.

A joint venture also makes footnote disclosures to present additional details about the its formation and operation, its methods of accounting, and a summary of its financial position and earnings.

Another form of business association is the *syndicate*, which is usually short term and has a defined single purpose, such as developing a financing proposal for a corporation. Syndicates are typically very informal; nevertheless, the legal relationships between the parties should be clearly specified before beginning the project.

QUESTIONS

LO 15-1 **Q15-1** Why is the partnership form of business organization sometimes preferred over the corporate or sole proprietorship forms?

LO 15-1 **Q15-2** What is the Uniform Partnership Act of 1997 and what is its relevance to partnership accounting?

LO 15-1 **Q15-3** What items are typically included in the partnership agreement?

LO 15-1 **Q15-4** Define the following features of a partnership: (*a*) separate business entity, (*b*) agency relationship, and (*c*) partner's joint and several liability.

LO 15-4 **Q15-5** Under what circumstances would a partner's capital account have a debit, or deficiency, balance? How is the deficiency usually eliminated?

LO 15-5 **Q15-6** A partnership agreement specifies that profits will be shared in the ratio of 4:6:5. What percentage of profits will each partner receive? Allocate a profit of $60,000 to each of the three partners.

LO 15-5 **Q15-7** The Good-Nite partnership agreement includes a provision for profit distribution of interest on capital balances. Unfortunately, the provision does not state the specific capital balance to be used in computing the profit share. What choices of capital balances are available to the partners? What is the preferred capital balance to be used in an interest allocation? Why?

LO 15-4 **Q15-8** Are salaries to partners a partnership expense? Why or why not?

LO 15-6 **Q15-9** Does a partner leaving the partnership require the partnership to dissolve and wind up its business? Explain how the partnership may purchase the disassociated partner's interest in the partnership.

LO 15-6 **Q15-10** What is the book value of a partnership? Does book value also represent its market value?

LO 15-6 **Q15-11** Present the arguments for and against the bonus method of recognizing the admission of a new partner.

LO 15-6 **Q15-12** In which cases of a new partner's admission does the credit to capital equal the new partners' investment? In which cases of a new partner's admission is his or her capital credit less than or more than the amount of the investment?

LO 15-5 **Q15-13** Aabel, a partner in the ABC Partnership, receives a bonus of 15 percent of income. If income for the period is $20,000, what is Aabel's bonus, assuming that it is computed as a percentage of income *before* the bonus? What is the bonus if it is computed as a percentage of income *after* deducting the bonus?

LO 15-6 **Q15-14** Caine, a new partner in the ABC Partnership, has invested $12,000 for a one-third interest in a partnership with capital of $21,000 before Caine's admission. What is the ABC Partnership's implied fair value? If the partners agree to recognize goodwill for the difference between the book value and fair value, present the entries the ABC Partnership should make upon Caine's admission.

Q15-15A S. Horton contributes assets with a book value of $5,000 to a partnership. The assets have a market value of $10,000 and a remaining liability of $2,000 that the partnership assumes. If the liability is shared equally with the other three partners, what is the basis of Horton's contribution for tax purposes? For GAAP purposes?

Q15-16B What is a joint venture? How are corporate joint ventures accounted for on the books of the investor companies?

"A" and "B" indicate that the item relates to Appendix 15A and Appendix 15B, respectively.

CASES

LO 15-1, 15-5

C15-1 Partnership Agreement

Judgment

Nitty and Gritty are considering the formation of a partnership to operate a crafts and hobbies store. They have come to you to obtain information about the basic elements of a partnership agreement. These agreements usually specify an income and loss–sharing ratio. They also may provide for additional income and loss–sharing features such as salaries, bonuses, interest allowances on invested capital.

Required

a. Discuss why a partnership agreement may need features in addition to the income and loss–sharing ratio.

b. Discuss the arguments in favor of recording salary and bonus allowances to partners as expenses included in computing net income.

c. What are the arguments against recording salary and bonus allowances to partners as partnership expenses?

d. Some partnership agreements provide for interest on invested capital in distributing income to the individual partners. List the additional provisions that should be included so the interest amounts can be computed.

LO 15-6

C15-2 Comparisons of Bonus, Goodwill, and Asset Revaluation Methods

Communication

Bill, George, and Anne are partners in the BGA Partnership. A difference of opinion exists among the partners as to how to account for Newt's admission as a new partner. The three present partners have the following positions:

Bill wants to use the bonus method.

George believes the goodwill method is best.

Anne wants to revalue the existing tangible assets.

You have been called in to advise the three partners.

Required

Prepare a memo discussing the three different methods of accounting for the admission of a new partner, including consideration of the effects on partnership capital in the year Newt is admitted and on the capital balances in future years.

LO 15-1

C15-3 Uniform Partnership Act Issues

Research

(*Note:* Obtain a copy of the Uniform Partnership Act of 1997 [UPA 1997] for answering this case question. The UPA 1997 can be obtained from your university's general library, law library, or the Internet.)

You are in a group that is considering forming a partnership to purchase a coffee shop located near your campus. The coffee shop offers freshly brewed coffee and rolls in the morning and soup and sandwiches the remainder of the day. During your preliminary discussions, several issues have emerged for which your group needs additional information.

Required

Research and provide a written summary for the following:

a. Does every partner in fact have the right to serve as an agent of the partnership and bind the partnership by that individual partner's actions in carrying out the partnership business?

b. If a new partner is admitted after the partnership operates for a time, what is the new partner's liability for partnership obligations arising before his or her admission? What is the new partner's liability for obligations of the partnership incurred after his or her admission?

c. Should all partners be able to examine the accounting records (the partnership's books) at any time?

d. What happens if the term of the partnership is set at one year and the partners decide to continue doing business? Is a new partnership agreement necessary at that time?

e. What happens if an individual partner wishes to leave the partnership? Can that person just announce to the other partners that he or she no longer wishes to be in the partnership and will not be liable for any future partnership obligations? What are the rights of the other partners in this matter?

f. What items do you believe should be in the partnership agreement prepared before actually agreeing to form the partnership?

LO 15-1

Understanding

C15-4 Defining Partners' Authority

Adam, Bob, and Cathy are planning to form a partnership to create a business that will retail cell phones in a new shopping center just completed in their city. They have been able to reach agreement on many issues, but Cathy is still concerned that Adam might become a little irresponsible and use his position as a partner and the partnership's name in business transactions that Cathy would not approve for the partnership. Cathy feels that Adam has superb marketing skills that will benefit the business, but she wonders what he might do in regard to transactions with third parties on behalf of the partnership.

Required

Prepare a memo to Cathy discussing each partner's rights to engage in transactions on behalf of the partnership and how a partnership can restrict a partner's authority to engage in specific types of transactions.

LO 15-4, 15-5

Understanding

C15-5 Preferences for Using GAAP for Partnership Accounting

You are providing accounting services for the JR Company partnership. The two partners, Jason and Richard, are thinking of adding a third partner to their business, and they have several questions regarding the use of GAAP for their partnership.

Required

Prepare a memo for the partners addressing each of their questions.

a. Why are salaries to partners not shown on the partnership's income statement prepared using GAAP?

b. Why should the partnership use GAAP to account for the admission of a new partner? Why is it not preferable for the partnership to recognize holding gains on its long-lived assets at the time of admitting the third partner? (The two partners argue that recognizing these gains now would allocate them to the partners who were growing the business prior to a new partner's admission.)

c. Why should the partners and the partnership fully analyze all the partnership's liabilities to ensure that there are no unrecognized liabilities when a new partner is admitted? (The two partners feel this is an unnecessary cost because an unpaid supplier will simply send another bill in the future.)

EXERCISES

LO 15-3

E15-1 Multiple-Choice on Initial Investment [AICPA Adapted]

Select the correct answer for each of the following questions.

1. On May 1, 20X1, Cathy and Mort formed a partnership and agreed to share profits and losses in the ratio of 3:7, respectively. Cathy contributed a parcel of land that cost her $10,000. Mort contributed $40,000 cash. The land was sold for $18,000 immediately after the partnership's formation. What amount should be recorded in Cathy's capital account at the time the partnership is formed the partnership's?
   a. $18,000.
   b. $17,400.
   c. $15,000.
   d. $10,000.
2. On July 1, 20X1, James and Short formed a partnership. James contributed cash. Short, previously a sole proprietor, contributed property other than cash, including realty subject to a mortgage, which the partnership assumed. Short's capital account on July 1, 20X1, should be recorded at
   a. Short's book value of the property on July 1, 20X1.
   b. Short's book value of the property less the mortgage payable on July 1, 20X1.

c. The property's fair value less the mortgage payable on July 1, 20X1.

d. The property's fair value on July 1, 20X1.

3. Two individuals who were previously sole proprietors form a partnership. Property other than cash that is part of the initial investment in the partnership is recorded for financial accounting purposes at the

   a. Proprietors' book values or the property's fair value on the date of the investment, whichever is higher.

   b. Proprietors' book values or the property's fair value on the date of the investment, whichever is lower.

   c. Proprietors' book values of the property on the date of the investment.

   d. Property's fair value at the date of the investment.

4. Mutt and Jeff formed a partnership on April 1 and contributed the following assets:

	Mutt	Jeff
Cash	$150,000	$ 50,000
Land		310,000

   The land was subject to a $30,000 mortgage, which the partnership assumed. Under the partnership agreement, Mutt and Jeff share profit and loss in the ratio of one-third and two-thirds, respectively. Jeff's capital account at April 1 should be

   a. $300,000.

   b. $330,000.

   c. $340,000.

   d. $360,000.

5. On July 1, Mabel and Pierre formed a partnership, agreeing to share profits and losses in the ratio of 4:6, respectively. Mabel contributed a parcel of land that cost her $25,000. Pierre contributed $50,000 cash. The land was sold for $50,000 on July 1, four hours after formation of the partnership. How much should be recorded in Mabel's capital account on the partnership formation?

   a. $10,000.

   b. $20,000.

   c. $25,000.

   d. $50,000.

LO 15-5

E15-2 Division of Income—Multiple Bases

Advanced StudyGuide .com

The partnership agreement of Angela and Dawn has the following provisions:

1. The partners are to earn 10 percent on the average capital.
2. Angela and Dawn are to earn salaries of $25,000 and $15,000, respectively.
3. Any remaining income or loss is to be divided between Angela and Dawn using a 70:30 ratio.

Angela's average capital is $50,000 and Dawn's is $30,000.

Required

Prepare an income distribution schedule assuming the income of the partnership is (*a*) $80,000 and (*b*) $20,000. If no partnership agreement exists, what does the UPA 1997 prescribe as the profit or loss distribution percentages?

LO 15-5

E15-3 Division of Income—Interest on Capital Balances

Left and Right are partners. Their capital accounts during 20X1 were as follows:

Left, Capital			
8/23	6,000	1/1	30,000
		4/3	8,000
		10/31	6,000

Right, Capital			
3/5	9,000	1/1	50,000
		7/6	7,000
		10/7	5,000

Partnership net income is $50,000 for the year. The partnership agreement provides for the division of income as follows:

1. Each partner is to be credited 8 percent interest on his or her average capital (calculated after rounding to the nearest number of whole months).
2. Any remaining income or loss is to be divided equally.

Required

Prepare an income distribution schedule.

LO 15-5

E15-4 Distribution of Partnership Income and Preparation of a Statement of Partners' Capital

Advanced StudyGuide .com

The income statement for the Apple-Jack Partnership for the year ended December 31, 20X5, follows:

APPLE-JACK PARTNERSHIP
Income Statement
For the Year Ended December 31, 20X5

Net Sales	$300,000
Cost of Goods Sold	(190,000)
Gross Margin	$110,000
Operating Expenses	(30,000)
Net Income	$ 80,000

Additional Information for 20X5

1. Apple began the year with a capital balance of $40,800.
2. Jack began the year with a capital balance of $112,000.
3. On April 1, Apple invested an additional $15,000 into the partnership.
4. On August 1, Jack invested an additional $20,000 into the partnership.
5. Throughout 20X5, each partner withdrew $400 per week in anticipation of partnership net income. The partners agreed that these withdrawals are *not* to be included in the computation of average capital balances for purposes of income distributions.

Apple and Jack have agreed to distribute partnership net income according to the following plan:

	Apple	Jack
1. Interest on average capital balances	6%	6%
2. Bonus on net income before the bonus but after interest on average capital balances	10%	
3. Salaries	$25,000	$30,000
4. Residual (if positive)	70%	30%
Residual (if negative)	50%	50%

Required

a. Prepare a schedule that discloses the distribution of partnership net income for 20X5. Show supporting computations in good form. Round to the nearest dollar.

b. Prepare the statement of partners' capital at December 31, 20X5.

c. How would your answer to part *a* change if all of the provisions of the income distribution plan were the same except that the salaries were $30,000 to Apple and $35,000 to Jack?

LO 15-1–15-6

E15-5 Matching Terms

Required

Match the items in the left-hand column with the descriptions/explanations in the right-hand column.

Items	Descriptions/Explanations
1. General partner	A. Item that occurs when the new partner's investment exceeds the new partner's capital credit.
2. Note payable to a partner	B. Partner who cannot actively participate in the management of the partnership.
3. Recognition of neither bonus nor goodwill	C. A allocation of partnership profits and losses when nothing is stated in the partnership agreement.
4. Drawing account	D. Item that occurs when the new partner's investment equals the new partner's capital credit and no change occurs in the existing partners' capital balances.
5. Limited partner	E. Cost not deducted to determine the partnership's net income for the period.
6. Bonus to existing partners	F. Partner who actively participates in the partnership management and who is personally liable for the partnership's debts.
7. Interest on capital accounts	G. Item that occurs when the new partner's capital credit exceeds his or her investment and no change occurs in the existing partners' capital balances.
8. Partnership income or loss shared equally	H. Account that increases when a partner takes assets out of the partnership in anticipation of partnership net income.
9. New partner's goodwill recognized	I. Account that increases for the fair value of noncash assets invested by a partner.
10. Existing partners' goodwill recognized	J. Related-party transaction that must be disclosed in the notes to the financial statements.
11. Partnership agreement	K. Item that occurs when the new partner's investment equals his or her capital credit and an increase occurs in the existing partners' capital balances.
12. Bonus to new partner	L. Item that occurs when the new partner's capital credit exceeds his or her investment and a decrease occurs in the existing partners' capital balances.
13. Capital account	M. Recognition of an intangible asset upon a new partner's admission to the partnership that results in increases in the existing partners' capital balances.
	N. Account closed to the capital account at year-end.
	O. Deduction of interest expense on this payable to determine the partnership's net income.

LO 15-6

E15-6 Admission of a Partner

In the GMP partnership (to which Elan seeks admittance), the capital balances of Mary, Gene, and Pat, who share income in the ratio of 6:3:1, are

Mary	$240,000
Gene	120,000
Pat	40,000

Required

a. If no goodwill or bonus is recorded, how much must Elan invest for a one-third interest?

b. Prepare journal entries for the admission of Elan if she invests $80,000 for a 20 percent interest and goodwill is recorded.

c. Prepare journal entries for the admission of Elan if she invests $200,000 for a 20 percent interest. Total capital will be $600,000; the partners use the bonus method.

d. Elan is concerned that she may be held liable for the partnership liabilities existing on the day she is admitted to the GMP partnership. She found nothing in the partnership agreement on this item. What does the UPA 1997 state with regard to the liability of a new partner for partnership obligations incurred prior to admission?

LO 15-6

E15-7 Admission of a Partner

Pam and John are partners in PJ's partnership, having capital balances of $120,000 and $40,000, respectively, and share income in a ratio of 3:1. Gerry is to be admitted into the partnership with a 20 percent interest in the business.

Required

For each of the following independent situations, first record Gerry's admission into the partnership and then specify and briefly explain why the accounting method used in that situation is GAAP or non-GAAP.

a. Gerry invests $50,000, and goodwill is to be recorded.
b. Gerry invests $50,000. Total capital is to be $210,000; the partners use the bonus method.
c. Gerry purchases the 20 percent interest by directly paying Pam $50,000. Gerry is assigned 20 percent interest in the partnership solely from Pam's capital account.
d. Gerry invests $35,000. Total capital is to be $195,000; the partners use the bonus method.
e. Gerry invests $35,000, and goodwill is to be recorded.
f. Gerry invests $35,000. During the valuation process made as part of admitting the new partner, the partnership's inventory is determined to be overvalued by $20,000 because of obsolescence. PJ's partnership uses the lower-of-cost-or-market value method for inventories.

LO 15-6

E15-8 Multiple-Choice Questions on the Admission of a Partner

Select the correct answer for each of the following questions.
(*Note:* The following balance sheet is for the partnership of Alex, Betty, and Claire in questions 1 and 2.)

Cash	$ 20,000
Other Assets	180,000
	$200,000
Liabilities	$ 50,000
Alex, Capital (40%)	37,000
Betty, Capital (40%)	65,000
Claire, Capital (20%)	48,000
Total Liabilities & Capital	$200,000

(*Note:* Figures shown parenthetically reflect agreed-upon profit and loss–sharing percentages.)

1. If the assets are fairly valued on this balance sheet and the partnership wishes to admit Denise as a new one-sixth-interest partner without recording goodwill or bonus, Denise should contribute cash or other assets of
   a. $40,000.
   b. $36,000.
   c. $33,333.
   d. $30,000.
2. If assets on the initial balance sheet are fairly valued, Alex and Betty give their consent, and Denise pays Claire $51,000 for her interest, the revised capital balances of the partners would be
   a. Alex, $38,000; Betty, $66,500; Denise, $51,000.
   b. Alex, $38,500; Betty, $66,500; Denise, $48,000.
   c. Alex, $37,000; Betty, $65,000; Denise, $51,000.
   d. Alex, $37,000; Betty, $65,000; Denise, $48,000.
3. On December 31, 20X4, Alan and Dave are partners with capital balances of $80,000 and $40,000, and they share profit and losses in the ratio of 2:1, respectively. On this date, Scott invests $36,000 cash for a 20 percent interest in the capital and profit of the new partnership.

The partners agree that the implied partnership goodwill is to be recorded simultaneously with Scott's admission. The firm's total implied goodwill is

a. $4,800.
b. $6,000.
c. $24,000.
d. $30,000.

4. Boris and Richard are partners who share profits and losses in the ratio of 6:4. On May 1, 20X9, their respective capital accounts were as follows:

Boris	$60,000
Richard	50,000

On that date, Lisa was admitted as a partner with a one-third interest in capital and profits for an investment of $40,000. The new partnership began with a total capital of $150,000. Immediately after Lisa's admission, Boris's capital should be

a. $50,000.
b. $54,000.
c. $56,667.
d. $60,000.

5. At December 31, Rod and Sheri are partners with capital balances of $40,000 and $20,000, and they share profits and losses in the ratio of 2:1, respectively. On this date, Pete invests $17,000 in cash for a 20 percent interest in the new partnership's capital and profit. Assuming that the bonus method is used, how much should be credited to Pete's capital account on December 31?

a. $12,000.
b. $15,000.
c. $15,400.
d. $17,000.

6. The capital accounts of the partnership of Ella, Nick, and Brandon follow with their respective profit and loss ratios:

Ella	$139,000	(.500)
Nick	209,000	(.333)
Brandon	96,000	(.167)

Tony was admitted to the partnership when he purchased directly, for $132,000, a proportionate interest from Ella and Nick in the partnership's net assets and profits. As a result, Tony acquired a 20 percent interest in the firm's net assets and profits. Assuming that implied goodwill is not to be recorded, what is the combined gain realized by Ella and Nick upon the sale of a portion of their partnership interests to Tony?

a. $0.
b. $43,200.
c. $62,400.
d. $82,000.

7. Fred and Ralph are partners who share profits and losses in the ratio of 7:3, respectively. Their respective capital accounts are as follows:

Fred	$35,000
Ralph	30,000

They agreed to admit Lute as a partner with a one-third interest in the capital and profits and losses upon an investment of $25,000. The new partnership will begin with total capital of $90,000. Immediately after Lute's admission, what are the capital balances of Fred, Ralph, and Lute, respectively?

a. $30,000, $30,000, $30,000.
b. $31,500, $28,500, $30,000.
c. $31,667, $28,333, $30,000.
d. $35,000, $30,000, $25,000.

8. If A is the total capital of a partnership before the admission of a new partner, B is the total capital of the partnership after the new partner's investment, C is the amount of the new partner's investment, and D is the amount of capital credit to the new partner, then there is

a. A bonus to the new partner if $B = A + C$ and $D < C$.
b. Goodwill to the old partners if $B > (A + C)$ and $D = C$.
c. Neither bonus nor goodwill if $B = A - C$ and $D > C$.
d. Goodwill to the new partner if $B > (A + C)$ and $D < C$.

LO 15-6

E15-9 Withdrawal of a Partner

In the LMK partnership, Luis's capital is $40,000, Marty's is $50,000, and Karl's is $30,000. They share income in a 4:1:1 ratio, respectively. Karl is retiring from the partnership.

Advanced StudyGuide .com

Required

Prepare journal entries to record Karl's withdrawal according to each of the following independent assumptions:

a. Karl is paid $38,000, and no goodwill is recorded.
b. Karl is paid $42,000, and only his share of the goodwill is recorded.
c. Karl is paid $35,000, and all implied goodwill is recorded.
d. Prepare a one-paragraph note summarizing the guidance the UPA 1997 offers on computing the buyout price for a partner who is retiring from the partnership.

LO 15-6

E15-10 Retirement of a Partner

On January 1, 20X1, Eddy decides to retire from the partnership of Cobb, Davis, and Eddy. The partners share profits and losses in the ratio of 3:2:1, respectively. The following condensed balance sheets present the account balances immediately before and, for six independent cases, after Eddy's retirement.

Accounts	Balances prior to Eddy's Retirement	Balances after Eddy's Retirement					
		Case 1	Case 2	Case 3	Case 4	Case 5	Case 6
Assets:							
Cash	$ 90,000	$ 10,000	$ 16,000	$ 25,000	$ 16,000	$ 50,000	$ 90,000
Other Assets	200,000	200,000	200,000	200,000	200,000	220,000	200,000
Goodwill	10,000	10,000	14,000	10,000	34,000	10,000	10,000
Total Assets	$300,000	$220,000	$230,000	$235,000	$250,000	$280,000	$300,000
Liabilities & Capital:							
Liabilities	$ 60,000	$ 60,000	$ 60,000	$ 60,000	$ 60,000	$ 60,000	$ 60,000
Cobb, Capital	80,000	74,000	80,000	83,000	92,000	110,000	80,000
Davis, Capital	90,000	86,000	90,000	92,000	98,000	110,000	160,000
Eddy, Capital	70,000	0	0	0	0	0	0
Total Liabilities & Capital	$300,000	$220,000	$230,000	$235,000	$250,000	$280,000	$300,000

Required

Prepare the necessary journal entries to record Eddy's retirement from the partnership for each of the six independent cases.

PROBLEMS

LO 15-6

P15-11 Admission of a Partner

Debra and Merina sell electronic equipment and supplies through their partnership. They wish to expand their computer lines and decide to admit Wayne to the partnership. Debra's capital is $200,000, Merina's capital is $160,000, and they share income in a ratio of 3:2, respectively.

Required

Record Wayne's admission for each of the following independent situations:

a. Wayne directly purchases half of Merina's investment in the partnership for $90,000.

b. Wayne invests the amount needed to give him a one-third interest in the partnership's capital if no goodwill or bonus is recorded.

c. Wayne invests $110,000 for a 25 percent interest. Goodwill is to be recorded.

d. Debra and Merina agree that some of the inventory is obsolete. The inventory account is decreased before Wayne is admitted. Wayne invests $100,000 for a 25 percent interest.

e. Wayne directly purchases a 25 percent interest by paying Debra $80,000 and Merina $60,000. The land account is increased before Wayne is admitted.

f. Wayne invests $80,000 for a 20 percent interest in the total capital of $440,000.

g. Wayne invests $100,000 for a 20 percent interest. Goodwill is to be recorded.

LO 15-5

P15-12 Division of Income

C. Eastwood, A. North, and M. West are manufacturers' representatives in the architecture business. Their capital accounts in the ENW partnership for 20X1 were as follows:

C. Eastwood, Capital				A. North, Capital				M. West, Capital			
9/1	8,000	1/1	30,000	3/1	9,000	1/1	40,000	8/1	12,000	1/1	50,000
		5/1	6,000			7/1	5,000			4/1	7,000
						9/1	4,000			6/1	3,000

Required

For each of the following independent income-sharing agreements, prepare an income distribution schedule.

a. Salaries are $15,000 to Eastwood, $20,000 to North, and $18,000 to West. Eastwood receives a bonus of 5 percent of net income after deducting his bonus. Interest is 10 percent of ending capital balances. Eastwood, North, and West divide any remainder in a 3:3:4 ratio, respectively. Net income was $78,960.

b. Interest is 10 percent of weighted-average capital balances. Salaries are $24,000 to Eastwood, $21,000 to North, and $25,000 to West. North receives a bonus of 10 percent of net income after deducting the bonus and her salary. Any remainder is divided equally. Net income was $68,080.

c. West receives a bonus of 20 percent of net income after deducting the bonus and the salaries. Salaries are $21,000 to Eastwood, $18,000 to North, and $15,000 to West. Interest is 10 percent of beginning capital balances. Eastwood, North, and West divide any remainder in an 8:7:5 ratio, respectively. Net income was $92,940.

LO 15-6

P15-13 Determining a New Partner's Investment Cost

Advanced StudyGuide .com

The following condensed balance sheet is presented for the partnership of Der, Egan, and Oprins, who share profits and losses in the ratio of 4:3:3, respectively.

Cash	$ 40,000	Accounts Payable	$150,000
Other Assets	710,000	Der, Capital	260,000
		Egan, Capital	180,000
		Oprins, Capital	160,000
Total Assets	$750,000	Total Liabilities & Capital	$750,000

Assume that the partnership decides to admit Snider as a new partner with a 25 percent interest.

Required

For each of the following independent cases, determine the amount that Snider must contribute in cash or other assets.

a. No goodwill or bonus is to be recorded.

b. Goodwill of $30,000 is to be recorded and allocated to the original partners.

c. A bonus of $24,000 is to be paid by Snider and allocated to the original partners.

d. The original partners, Der, Egan, and Oprins, agree to give Snider $10,000 of goodwill upon admission to the partnership.

e. Other assets are revalued for an increase of $20,000, and goodwill of $40,000 is recognized and allocated to the original partners at the time of Snider's admission.

f. The partners agree that total resulting capital should be $820,000 and no goodwill should be recognized.

g. Other assets are revalued down by $20,000 and a bonus of $40,000 is paid to Snider at the time of admission.

LO 15-5

P15-14 Division of Income

Advanced StudyGuide .com

Champion Play Company is a partnership that sells sporting goods. The partnership agreement provides for 10 percent interest on invested capital, salaries of $24,000 to Luc and $28,000 to Dennis, and a bonus for Luc. The 20X3 capital accounts were as follows:

Luc, Capital				Dennis, Capital			
8/1	15,000	1/1	50,000	7/1	10,000	1/1	70,000
		4/1	5,000			9/1	22,500

Required

For each of the following independent situations, prepare an income distribution schedule.

a. Interest is based on weighted-average capital balances. The 5 percent bonus is calculated on net income after deducting the bonus. In 20X3, net income was $64,260. Any remainder is divided between Luc and Dennis in a 3:2 ratio, respectively.

b. Interest is based on ending capital balances after deducting salaries, which the partners normally withdraw during the year. The 8 percent bonus is calculated on net income after deducting the bonus and salaries. Net income was $108,700. Any remainder is divided equally.

c. Interest is based on beginning capital balances. The 12.5 percent bonus is calculated on net income after deducting the bonus. Net income was $76,950. Any remainder is divided between Luc and Dennis in a 4:2 ratio, respectively.

LO 15-6

P15-15 Withdrawal of a Partner under Various Alternatives

The partnership of Ace, Jack, and Spade has been in business for 25 years. On December 31, 20X5, Spade decided to retire. The partnership balance sheet reported the following capital balances for each partner at December 31, 20X5:

Ace, Capital	$150,000
Jack, Capital	200,000
Spade, Capital	120,000

The partners allocate partnership income and loss in the ratio 20:30:50, respectively.

Required

Record Spade's withdrawal under each of the following independent situations.

a. Jack acquired Spade's capital interest for $150,000 in a personal transaction. Partnership assets were not revalued, and partnership goodwill was not recognized.

b. Assume the same facts as in part *a* except that partnership goodwill applicable to the entire business was recognized by the partnership.

c. Spade received $180,000 of partnership cash upon retirement. Capital of the partnership after Spade's retirement was $290,000.

d. Spade received $60,000 of cash and partnership land with a fair value of $120,000. The carrying amount of the land on the partnership books was $100,000. Capital of the partnership after Spade's retirement was $310,000.

e. Spade received $150,000 of partnership cash upon retirement. The partnership recorded the portion of goodwill attributable to Spade.

f. Assume the same facts as in part *e* except that partnership goodwill attributable to all partners was recorded.

g. Because of limited cash in the partnership, Spade received land with a fair value of $100,000 and a partnership note payable for $50,000. The land's carrying amount on the partnership books was $60,000. Capital of the partnership after Spade's retirement was $360,000.

LO 15-5, 15-6 **P15-16 Multiple-Choice Questions—Initial Investments, Division of Income, Admission and Retirement of a Partner [AICPA Adapted]**

Select the correct answer for each of the following questions.

1. When property other than cash is invested in a partnership, at what amount should the noncash property be credited to the contributing partner's capital account?
   a. Contributing partner's tax basis.
   b. Contributing partner's original cost.
   c. Assessed valuation for property tax purposes.
   d. Fair value at the date of contribution.

2. William and Martha drafted a partnership agreement that lists the following assets contributed at the partnership's formation:

	Contributed by	
	William	**Martha**
Cash	$20,000	$30,000
Inventory		15,000
Building		40,000
Furniture & Equipment	15,000	

The building is subject to a $10,000 mortgage, which the partnership has assumed. The partnership agreement also specifies that profits and losses are to be distributed evenly. What amounts should be recorded as capital for William and Martha at the partnership's formation?

	William	Martha
a.	$35,000	$85,000
b.	$35,000	$75,000
c.	$55,000	$55,000
d.	$60,000	$60,000

3. Smith and Duncan are partners with capital balances of $60,000 and $20,000, respectively. Profits and losses are divided in the ratio of 60:40. Smith and Duncan decided to form a new partnership with Johnson, who invested land valued at $15,000 for a 20 percent capital interest in the new partnership. Johnson's cost of the land was $12,000. The partnership elected to use the bonus method to record Johnson's admission into the partnership. Johnson's capital account should be credited for
   a. $12,000.
   b. $15,000.
   c. $16,000.
   d. $19,000.

4. On April 30, 20X5, Apple, Blue, and Crown formed a partnership by combining their separate business proprietorships. Apple contributed $50,000 cash. Blue contributed property with a $36,000 carrying amount, a $40,000 original cost, and $80,000 fair value. The partnership accepted responsibility for the property's $35,000 mortgage. Crown contributed equipment with a $30,000 carrying amount, a $75,000 original cost, and $55,000 fair value. The partnership agreement specifies that profits and losses are to be shared equally but is silent regarding capital contributions. Which partner's capital account has the largest April 30, 20X5, balance?
   a. Apple.
   b. Blue.
   c. Crown.
   d. All capital account balances are equal.

(*Note:* The following information is for questions 5 and 6.)

The Moon-Norbert Partnership was formed on January 2, 20X5. Under the partnership agreement, each partner has an equal initial capital balance accounted for under the goodwill method. Partnership net income or loss is allocated 60 percent to Moon and 40 percent to Norbert. To form the partnership, Moon originally contributed assets costing $30,000 with a fair value of $60,000 on January 2, 20X5, and Norbert contributed $20,000 in cash. Partners' drawings during 20X5 totaled $3,000 by Moon and $9,000 by Norbert. Moon-Norbert's net income for 20X5 was $25,000.

5. Norbert's initial capital balance in Moon-Norbert is
   a. $20,000.
   b. $25,000.
   c. $40,000.
   d. $60,000.
6. Moon's share of Moon-Norbert's net income is
   a. $15,000.
   b. $12,500.
   c. $12,000.
   d. $7,800.
7. In the Crowe-Dagwood partnership, Crowe and Dagwood had a capital ratio of 3:1 and a profit and loss ratio of 2:1. They used the bonus method to record Elman's admittance as a new partner. What ratio should be used to allocate to Crowe and Dagwood the excess of Elman's contribution over the amount credited to Elman's capital account?
   a. Crowe and Dagwood's new relative capital ratio.
   b. Crowe and Dagwood's new relative profit and loss ratio.
   c. Crowe and Dagwood's previous capital ratio.
   d. Crowe and Dagwood's previous profit and loss ratio.
8. Blue and Green formed a partnership in 20X4. The partnership agreement provides for annual salary allowances of $55,000 for Blue and $45,000 for Green. The partners share profits equally and losses in a 60:40 ratio, respectively. The partnership had earnings of $80,000 for 20X5 before any allowance to partners. What amount of these earnings should be credited to each partner's capital account?

	Blue	Green
a.	$40,000	$40,000
b.	$43,000	$37,000
c.	$44,000	$36,000
d.	$45,000	$35,000

9. When Jill retired from the partnership of Jill, Bill, and Hill, the final settlement of her interest exceeded her capital balance. Under the bonus method, the excess
   a. Was recorded as goodwill.
   b. Was recorded as an expense.

c. Reduced the capital balances of Bill and Hill.

d. Had no effect on the capital balances of Bill and Hill.

LO 15-3–15-6 **P15-17 Partnership Formation, Operation, and Changes in Ownership**

The partnership of Jordan and O'Neal began business on January 1, 20X7. Each partner contributed the following assets (the noncash assets are stated at their fair values on January 1, 20X7):

	Jordan	O'Neal
Cash	$ 60,000	$ 50,000
Inventories	80,000	0
Land	0	130,000
Equipment	100,000	0

The land was subject to a $50,000 mortgage, which the partnership assumed on January 1, 20X7. The equipment was subject to an installment note payable that had an unpaid principal amount of $20,000 on January 1, 20X7. The partnership also assumed this note payable. Jordan and O'Neal agreed to share partnership income and losses in the following manner:

	Jordan	O'Neal
Interest on beginning capital balances	3%	3%
Salaries	$12,000	$12,000
Remainder	60%	40%

During 20X7, the following events occurred:

1. Inventory was acquired at a cost of $30,000. At December 31, 20X7, the partnership owed $6,000 to its suppliers.
2. Principal of $5,000 was paid on the mortgage. Interest expense incurred on the mortgage was $2,000, all of which was paid by December 31, 20X7.
3. Principal of $3,500 was paid on the installment note. Interest expense incurred on the installment note was $2,000, all of which was paid by December 31, 20X7.
4. Sales on account amounted to $155,000. At December 31, 20X7, customers owed the partnership $21,000.
5. Selling and general expenses, excluding depreciation, amounted to $34,000. At December 31, 20X7, the partnership owed $6,200 of accrued expenses. Depreciation expense was $6,000.
6. Each partner withdrew $200 each week in anticipation of partnership profits.
7. The partnership's inventory at December 31, 20X7, was $20,000.
8. The partners allocated the net income for 20X7 and closed the accounts.

Additional Information

On January 1, 20X8, the partnership decided to admit Hill to the partnership. On that date, Hill invested $99,800 of cash into the partnership for a 20 percent capital interest. Total partnership capital after Hill was admitted totaled $450,000.

Required

a. Prepare journal entries to record the formation of the partnership on January 1, 20X7, and to record the events that occurred during 20X7.

b. Prepare the income statement for the Jordan-O'Neal Partnership for the year ended December 31, 20X7.

c. Prepare a balance sheet for the Jordon-O'Neal Partnership at December 31, 20X7.

d. Prepare the journal entry for the admission of Hill on January 1, 20X8.

P15-18A Initial Investments and Tax Bases [AICPA Adapted]

The DELS partnership was formed by combining individual accounting practices on May 10, 20X1. The initial investments were as follows:

	Current Value	Tax Basis
Delaney:		
Cash	$ 8,000	$ 8,000
Building	60,000	32,000
Mortgage payable, assumed by DELS	36,000	36,000
Engstrom:		
Cash	9,000	9,000
Office furniture	23,000	17,000
Note payable, assumed by DELS	10,000	10,000
Lahey:		
Cash	12,000	12,000
Computers and printers	18,000	21,000
Note payable, assumed by DELS	15,000	15,000
Simon:		
Cash	21,000	21,000
Library (books and periodicals)	7,000	5,000

Required

a. Prepare the journal entry to record the initial investments using GAAP accounting.

b. Calculate the tax basis of each partner's capital if Delaney, Engstrom, Lahey, and Simon agree to assume equal amounts for the payables.

LO 15-3–15-5

P15-19 Formation of a Partnership and Allocation of Profit and Loss

Haskins and Sells formed a partnership on January 2, 20X3. Each had been a sole proprietor before forming their partnership.

Part I

Each partner's contributions follow. The amounts under the cost column represent the amounts reported on the books of each sole proprietorship immediately before the formation of the partnership.

	Cost	Fair Value
Haskins:		
Cash	$ 45,000	$ 45,000
Inventories (FIFO)	48,000	49,000
Trade accounts receivable	40,000	40,000
Allowance for uncollectible accounts	(1,500)	(2,000)
Building	550,000	370,000
Accumulated depreciation	(200,000)	
Mortgage on building assumed by partnership	(175,000)	(175,000)
Sells:		
Cash	$ 10,000	$ 10,000
Trade accounts receivable	30,000	30,000
Allowance for uncollectible accounts	(2,000)	(2,500)
Inventories (FIFO)	15,000	13,500
Note receivable due in 6 months	50,000	50,000
Temporary investments	100,000	81,500
Customer lists	0	60,000

Required

Using the preceding information, prepare a classified balance sheet as of January 2, 20X3, for the Haskins and Sells partnership. Assume that $25,000 of the mortgage is due in 20X3 and that the customer lists are accounted for as an intangible asset to be amortized over a five-year period.

Part II

During 20X3, the Haskins and Sells Partnership reported the following information:

Revenues	$650,000
Cost of goods sold	320,000
Selling, general, and administrative expenses	70,000
Salaries paid to each partner (not included in selling, general, and administrative expenses):	
Haskins	90,000
Sells	70,000
Bonus paid to Haskins (not included in selling, general, and administrative expenses)	10% of net income
Withdrawals made during the year in addition to salaries:	
Haskins	10,000
Sells	5,000
Residual profit and loss–sharing ratio:	
Haskins	20%
Sells	80%

Required

a. Prepare an income statement for the Haskins and Sells partnership for the year ended December 31, 20X3.

b. Prepare a schedule that shows how to allocate the partnership net income for 20X3.

c. What is the capital balance for each partner that will appear on the December 31, 20X3, balance sheet?

d. Assume that the distribution of partnership net income remains the same (i.e., Haskins will continue to receive a 10 percent bonus and salaries will continue to be $90,000 and $70,000 to Haskins and Sells, respectively) and the residual profit and loss–sharing ratio will continue to be 20:80. What would partnership net income have to be for each partner to receive the same amount of income?

16 Partnerships: Liquidation

Multicorporate Entities
Multinational Entities
Reporting Requirements
Partnerships
Formation, Operation, Changes
Liquidation
Governmental and Not-for-Profit Entities
Corporations in Financial Difficulty

THE DEMISE OF LAVENTHOL & HORWATH

In 1990, when the "Big Six" accounting firms dominated the profession, Laventhol & Horwath was the seventh-largest accounting firm with more than 3,400 employees and a firm record revenue of $345.2 million. The Philadelphia-based accounting partnership had been in operation since 1915 and its prospects could not have seemed brighter. However, serious problems had begun in October 1989 when Laventhol was forced to pay more than $30 million to nine banks that had relied on Laventhol's audit of a real estate corporation. Five months later, the firm negotiated a $13 million settlement with another group of plaintiffs. As the lawsuits continued to pile up, the strain on Laventhol increased.

In an effort to stay afloat following these large settlements, Laventhol announced a 10 percent across-the-board salary cut in October 1990. In fact, in a press release accompanying the cut, the firm was said it was "optimistic" about the future. Sadly, "the future" lasted only about a month. In November 1990, the firm fired the majority of its employees and filed for Chapter 11 bankruptcy protection in New York. At the time of the filing, Laventhol had 110 pending lawsuits and $75 million in debt.

LAVENTHOL & HORWATH

Because of the normal risks of doing business, the majority of partnerships begun in any year fail within three years and require dissolution and liquidation. The ending of a partnership's business is often an emotional event for the partners. They may have had high expectations and invested a large amount of personal resources and time in the business. The end of the partnership often is the end of those business dreams. Accountants usually assist in the winding-up and liquidation process and must recognize the legitimate rights of and any amounts due to the many parties involved in the partnership: its individual partners, creditors, and customers as well as others doing business with it.

The Uniform Partnership Act of 1997 has 71 sections, 7 of which deal specifically with the dissolution and winding-up of a partnership. Several sections discuss the specific rights of the partnership's creditors. They have first claim to the partnership's assets. After the creditors are fully satisfied, any remaining assets are distributed to the partners based on the balances in their capital accounts. This chapter presents the concepts that accountants must know if they offer professional services to partnerships undergoing winding-up and liquidation.

LEARNING OBJECTIVES

When you finish studying this chapter, you should be able to:

LO 16-1 Understand and explain terms associated with partnership liquidations.

LO 16-2 Make calculations related to lump-sum partnership liquidations.

LO 16-3 Make calculations related to installment partnership liquidations.

OVERVIEW OF PARTNERSHIP LIQUIDATIONS

LO 16-1

Understand and explain terms associated with partnership liquidations.

Most states have adopted the major provisions of the UPA 1997, which is used for the illustrations in this chapter. The chapter first presents the UPA 1997's major provisions regarding events and processes associated with partnership liquidations. After this overview, the chapter illustrates the winding-up process in both a lump-sum liquidation and an installment liquidation.

Disassociation, Dissolution, Winding-Up, and Liquidation of a Partnership

As discussed in Chapter 15, disassociation is the legal description of a partner's withdrawal, including the following:

1. A partner's death.
2. A partner's voluntary withdrawal (i.e., a retirement).
3. A judicial determination, including (*a*) the partner engaged in wrongful conduct that materially and negatively affected the partnership, (*b*) the partner willfully committed a material breach of the partnership agreement, (*c*) the partner became a debtor in bankruptcy, or (*d*) a partner cannot perform his or her duties under the partnership agreement.

Not all disassociations result in a partnership liquidation. Many involve only a buyout of the withdrawing partner's interest rather than a winding-up and liquidation of the partnership's business.

Dissolution is the termination of a partnership. Events that cause its dissolution and winding-up are presented in section 801 of the UPA 1997, as follows:

1. A partner gives notice of his or her intention to leave the partnership. An *at-will partnership* is one in which there is, at most, only an oral understanding among the partners and no definite term or specific task undertaking. A partnership agreement can eliminate this event as a cause for dissolution by including, for example, a provision for a buyout of that partner's interest in the partnership.
2. A dissolution of a partnership created for a definite term or specific undertaking takes place when (*a*) after a partner's death or wrongful disassociation, at least half of the remaining partners decide to wind up the partnership business, (*b*) all partners agree to wind up the partnership business, or (*c*) the term or specific undertaking has expired or been completed.
3. An event occurs that makes carrying on a substantial part of the partnership business unlawful.
4. A judicial determination that (*a*) the partnership's economic purpose is unlikely to be achieved, (*b*) a partner has engaged in conduct relating to the partnership that makes continuing the business impracticable, or (*c*) carrying on the partnership in conformity with the partnership agreement is not reasonably practicable.

On dissolution, the partnership begins the winding-up of its business.

Winding-Up and Liquidation

Winding-up and liquidation of the partnership begin after its dissolution. The partnership continues for the limited purpose of winding-up the business and completing work in process. The winding-up process includes the transactions necessary to liquidate the partnership, such as the collection of receivables, including any receivables from partners; conversion of the noncash assets to cash; payment of the partnership's obligations; and the distribution of any remaining net balance to the partners, in cash, according to their capital interests. If the partnership agreement does not provide for a special liquidation ratio, profits or losses are distributed during liquidation in the normal profit and loss ratio used during the partnership's operation.

Some terminating partnerships change to the liquidation basis of accounting once they no longer consider the business to be a going concern. When the liquidation basis of accounting is adopted, the partnership's assets are valued at their estimated net realizable liquidation values and liabilities at their estimated settlement amounts. Because of the apparent uncertainties in practice of specifically defining the point at which an entity is no longer a going concern, the FASB, decided (in March 2010) not to specifically define a going concern. Instead, the Board decided to require detailed disclosures when management, applying commercially reasonable business judgment, is aware of conditions and events that indicate, based on current facts and circumstances, that it is reasonably foreseeable that an entity may not be able to meet its obligations as they become due.

Loans to or from Partners Under the UPA 1997, liabilities to partners for loans they have made to the partnership ("inside debt") have the same status as liabilities to the partnerships' third-party creditors ("outside debt"). In effect, UPA 1997 removes previous rules formally subordinating inside debt to outside debt. However, a partner ultimately is personally liable for any outside debt that is still unsatisfied if the partnership has insufficient funds to satisfy all claims of outside creditors. The result is that the obligation to satisfy partnership debts effectively ends in the equitable subordination of inside debt to outside debt when the partnership assets are insufficient to satisfy all obligations to nonpartners. Even though the UPA 1997 indicates that partnership obligations to the individual partners must normally be paid during its winding-up on the same proportional basis as the firm's other liabilities, outside creditors frequently require partners to subordinate their receivables from the partnership. Thus, in all examples, we assume partners have agreed to subordinate their receivables from the partnership to outside debt. Therefore, we typically illustrate examples in which liquidation payments are made in the following order: (1) outside debt, (2) inside debt, and (3) partners' capital.

Deficits in Partners' Capital Accounts As part of the liquidation process, each partner with a deficit in his or her capital account must make a contribution to the partnership to remedy that capital deficit. The partnership makes a liquidating distribution, in cash, to each partner with a capital credit balance. The UPA 1997 specifies cash for these liquidating distributions. If a partner fails to make a required contribution to remedy his or her capital deficit, all other partners must contribute the additional amount necessary to pay the partnership's obligations in the proportion to which those partners share partnership losses.

Although the UPA 1997 does not provide for a formal offset of a loan payable to an individual partner with a deficit in his or her capital account, a failure to do so can result in inequalities. For example, assume a partnership owes a partner $10,000. If it pays the partner the $10,000, he or she could spend the money and subsequently become personally insolvent. Then, if the allocation of losses incurred on the sale of assets later results in a deficit balance in that partner's capital account, the other partners would have to absorb the deficit. Therefore, the legal doctrine of setoff effectively treats loans from partners to the partnership as additional capital investments that can be offset against a deficit capital account balance to avoid inequities in the liquidation process.

STOP & THINK

Assume partner Z lends $10,000 to the XYZ Partnership during a time when the partnership is short on cash to pay its obligations. At a subsequent date, the partnership sells some of its assets at a loss and allocates the loss to the partners' capital accounts, resulting in a deficit balance in Z's $2,000 capital account of $2,000. Assume Z's only source of additional cash to remedy her deficit balance is the savings account she established years before to fund her son's college education. Should Z be required to remove the $2,000 in her son's college savings account to wipe out the deficit in her capital account?

Although the UPA 1997 states that Z would need to contribute cash to dispose of her deficit balance, the courts have dealt with similar situations. As a result, the legal doctrine of setoff suggests that Z's deficit balance can be offset against her loan balance. Instead of making her write a check to pay the partnership $2,000 so that it can then write a check to pay her $10,000, the partnership can simply write off her deficit against the loan balance so that it will only have to pay her $8,000 to satisfy her loan.

Statement of Partnership Realization and Liquidation

To guide and summarize the partnership liquidation process, a ***statement of partnership realization and liquidation*** may be prepared. The statement, often called a "statement of liquidation," is the basis of the journal entries made to record the liquidation.

It presents in worksheet form the effects of the liquidation on the partnership's balance sheet accounts. The statement summarizes the conversion of assets into cash, the allocation of any gains or losses to the partners, and the distribution of cash to creditors and partners. This statement is a basic feature of accounting for a partnership liquidation and is presented and illustrated in the remainder of the chapter.

LUMP-SUM LIQUIDATIONS

LO 16-2

Make calculations related to lump-sum partnership liquidations.

Advanced StudyGuide .com

A ***lump-sum liquidation*** of a partnership is one in which all assets are converted into cash within a very short time, creditors are paid, and a single, lump-sum payment is made to the partners for their capital interests. Although most partnership liquidations take place over an extended period, as illustrated later, the lump-sum liquidation is an excellent focal point for presenting the major concepts of partnership liquidation.

Realization of Assets[1]

Typically, a partnership experiences losses on the disposal of its assets. It may have a "Going Out of Business" sale in which its inventory is marked down well below normal selling price to encourage immediate sale. Often the firm sells the remaining inventory to companies that specialize in acquiring assets of liquidating businesses. The partnership's furniture, fixtures, and equipment also may be offered at a reduced price or sold to liquidators. Any goodwill on the partnership's books is generally written off when the partnership begins a liquidation because it is no longer a going concern.

The partnership attempts to collect its accounts receivable. Sometimes it offers a large cash discount for the prompt payment of any remaining receivables whose collection may otherwise delay terminating the partnership. Alternatively, the receivables may be sold to a *factor,* a business that specializes in acquiring accounts receivable and immediately paying cash to the seller. The partnership records the sale of the receivables as it would any other asset. Typically, the factor acquires only the best of a business's receivables at a price below face value, but some factors are willing to buy all receivables at a price significantly lower than face value.

A partnership's assets, including any receivables from the partners and any contributions required of partners to remedy their capital deficits, are applied to pay the firm's creditors. Loans to or from partners must be settled during the winding-up process. Any remaining amount is then paid, in cash, as required by Section 807 of the UPA 1997 to the partners in accordance with their rights to liquidating distributions.

Liquidation Expenses

The liquidation process usually begins with scheduling the partnership's known assets and liabilities. The names and addresses of creditors and the amounts owed to each are specified. As diligent as the effort usually is, additional, unscheduled creditors may become known during the liquidation process, which also involves some expenses, such as additional legal and accounting costs. The partnership also may incur costs of disposing of the business, such as special advertising and locating specialized equipment dealers. These expenses are allocated to partners' capital accounts in the profit and loss distribution ratio.

Illustration of a Lump-Sum Liquidation

The following illustration presents the liquidation of the ABC Partnership, whose partners, Alt, Blue, and Cha, decide to terminate the business on May 1, 20X5. The AB Partnership was formed on January 1, 20X1. Cha was admitted into the partnership on January 1, 20X3, and the name of the business was changed to the ABC Partnership. For purposes of this illustration, assume that Alt remained in the partnership, and in 20X4,

[1] To view a video explanation of this topic, visit advancedstudyguide.com.

the partners agreed to a realignment of their profit and loss–sharing percentages to more closely conform with each partner's efforts. The profit and loss–sharing percentages after realignment in 20X4 were as follows: Alt, 40 percent; Blue, 40 percent; and Cha, 20 percent. The company's condensed trial balance on May 1, 20X5, the day the partners decide to liquidate the business, follows:

ABC PARTNERSHIP
Trial Balance
May 1, 20X5

Cash	$ 10,000	
Noncash Assets	90,000	
Liabilities		$ 42,000
Alt, Capital (40%)		34,000
Blue, Capital (40%)		10,000
Cha, Capital (20%)		14,000
Total	$100,000	$100,000

The basic accounting equation, Assets − Liabilities = Owners' equity, applies to partnership accounting. In this case, owners' equity is the sum of the partners' capital accounts, as follows:

$$\text{Assets} - \text{Liabilities} = \text{Partners' equity}$$
$$\$100{,}000 - \$42{,}000 = \$58{,}000$$

The following three cases illustrate the partnership liquidation concepts used most commonly. Each case begins with ABC's May 1, 20X5, trial balance. The amount of cash realized from the disposal of the noncash assets is different for each of the three cases, and the effects of the different realizations are shown in the statement of partnership realization and liquidation presented for each case.

Case 1: Partnership Solvent and No Deficits in Partners' Capital Accounts

The noncash assets are sold for $80,000 on May 15, 20X5, at a $10,000 loss. The partnership's creditors are paid their $42,000 on May 20, and the remaining $48,000 cash is distributed to the partners on May 30, 20X5.

Refer to Figure 16-1 for the statement of realization and liquidation for Case 1. The statement includes only balance sheet accounts across the columns, with all noncash assets presented together as a single total. Note that each row in the spreadsheet must balance (i.e., Assets = Liabilities + Partners' equity). Once a business has entered liquidation, the balance sheet accounts are the only relevant ones; the income statement is for a going concern. The liquidation process is presented in the order of occurrence in the rows of the worksheet. Thus, the worksheet includes the entire realization and liquidation process and is the basis for the journal entries to record the liquidation.

Other important observations are as follows:

1. The preliquidation balances are obtained from the May 1, 20X5, trial balance.
2. When the partnership's noncash assets are sold, the $10,000 loss is allocated to the partners' capital accounts.
3. Creditors, including individual partners who have made any loans to the partnership, are paid before any cash is distributed to partners.
4. Payments to partners are made for their positive capital balances.
5. The postliquidation balances are all zero, indicating the accounts are all closed and the partnership is fully liquidated and terminated.

FIGURE 16–1 Case 1: Partnership Solvent; No Deficits in Partners' Capital Accounts

ABC PARTNERSHIP
Statement of Partnership Realization and Liquidation
Lump-Sum Liquidation

							Capital Balance				
	Cash	+	Noncash Assets	=	Liabilities	+	Alt, 40%	+	Blue, 40%	+	Cha, 20%
Preliquidation balances, May 1	10,000		90,000		42,000		34,000		10,000		14,000
Sales of assets and distribution of $10,000 loss	80,000		(90,000)				(4,000)		(4,000)		(2,000)
	90,000		0		42,000		30,000		6,000		12,000
Payment to creditors	(42,000)				(42,000)						
	48,000		0		0		30,000		6,000		12,000
Lump-sum payment to partners	(48,000)						(30,000)		(6,000)		(12,000)
Postliquidation balances	0		0		0		0		0		0

The statement of partnership realization and liquidation is the basis for the following journal entries to record the liquidation process:

	May 15, 20X5		
(1)	Cash	80,000	
	Alt, Capital	4,000	
	Blue, Capital	4,000	
	Cha, Capital	2,000	
	Noncash Assets		90,000
	Realization of all noncash assets of the ABC Partnership and distribution of $10,000 loss using profit and loss ratio.		

	May 20, 20X5		
(2)	Liabilities	42,000	
	Cash		42,000
	Pay creditors.		

	May 30, 20X5		
(3)	Alt, Capital	30,000	
	Blue, Capital	6,000	
	Cha, Capital	12,000	
	Cash		48,000
	Lump-sum payments to partners.		

Case 2: Partnership Solvent and Deficit Created in Partner's Capital Account

Advanced StudyGuide .com

A deficit in a partner's capital account can occur if its credit balance is too low to absorb his or her share of losses. A capital deficit may be created at any time in the liquidation process. Such deficits may be remedied by either of the following means:

1. The partner invests cash or other assets to eliminate the capital deficit.
2. The partner's capital deficit is distributed to the other partners in their resulting loss-sharing ratio.

The approach used depends on the solvency of the partner with the capital deficit. A partner who is personally solvent and has sufficient net worth to eliminate the capital deficit must make an additional investment in the partnership to cover the deficit. On the other hand, if the partner is personally insolvent—that is, personal liabilities exceed personal assets—section 807 of the UPA 1997 requires the remaining partners to absorb the insolvent partner's deficit by allocating it to their capital accounts in their resulting loss-sharing ratio.

The following lump-sum distribution illustrates these points:

1. The three partners' personal financial statements are as follows:

	Alt	Blue	Cha
Personal assets	$150,000	$ 12,000	$ 42,000
Personal liabilities	(86,000)	(16,000)	(14,000)
Net worth (deficit)	$ 64,000	$ (4,000)	$ 28,000

   Blue is personally insolvent; Alt and Cha are personally solvent.
2. The partnership's noncash assets are sold for $35,000 on May 15, 20X5, and the $55,000 loss is allocated to the partners' capital accounts.
3. The partnership pays its creditors $42,000 on May 20, 20X5.
4. Because Blue is personally insolvent, her $12,000 capital deficit is allocated to the other partners.
5. The remaining $4,000 cash is distributed as a lump-sum payment on May 30, 20X5.

Review the statement of partnership realization and liquidation for Case 2 in Figure 16–2. Note the following from this illustration:

1. The $55,000 loss on the realization of noncash assets is allocated in the partners' loss-sharing ratio of 40 percent for Alt, 40 percent for Blue, and 20 percent for Cha. Blue's $22,000 share of the loss on disposal creates a $12,000 deficit in her capital account. Blue is personally insolvent and is unable to make an additional investment to remove the capital deficit.

FIGURE 16–2 Case 2: Partnership Solvent; Deficit Created in Personally Insolvent Partner's Capital Account

ABC PARTNERSHIP
Statement of Partnership Realization and Liquidation
Lump-Sum Liquidation

				Capital Balance		
	Cash +	Noncash Assets	= Liabilities +	Alt, 40% +	Blue, 40% +	Cha, 20%
Preliquidation balances, May 1	10,000	90,000	42,000	34,000	10,000	14,000
Sales of assets and distribution of $55,000 loss	35,000	(90,000)		(22,000)	(22,000)	(11,000)
	45,000	0	42,000	12,000	(12,000)	3,000
Payment to creditors	(42,000)		(42,000)			
	3,000	0	0	12,000	(12,000)	3,000
Allocation of insolvent partner's deficit:					12,000	
40/60 × $12,000				(8,000)		
20/60 × $12,000						(4,000)
	3,000	0	0	4,000	0	(1,000)
Contribution by Cha to remedy capital deficit	1,000					1,000
	4,000	0	0	4,000	0	0
Lump-sum payment to partners	(4,000)			(4,000)		
Postliquidation balances	0	0	0	0	0	0

2. The partnership pays its creditors before making any distributions to the partners.
3. Blue's $12,000 deficit is distributed to Alt and Cha in their resulting loss-sharing ratio. Note that the UPA 1977 specifies use of the loss-sharing ratio for this allocation. Alt absorbs two-thirds (40/60) of Blue's deficit, and Cha absorbs one-third (20/60).
4. The distribution of Blue's deficit creates a deficit in Cha's capital account. Because Cha is personally solvent, she must contribute $1,000 to remedy her capital deficit.
5. Alt receives a lump-sum payment for his $4,000 capital balance.
6. All postliquidation balances are zero, indicating the completion of the liquidation process.

Advanced StudyGuide .com

Case 3: Partnership Is Insolvent and Deficit Created in Partner's Capital Account

A partnership is insolvent when existing cash and cash generated by the sale of the assets are not sufficient to pay the partnership's liabilities. In this case, the individual partners are liable for the remaining unpaid partnership liabilities. The following illustration presents an insolvent partnership and a deficit in one of the partner's capital accounts.

1. Alt and Cha are personally solvent, and Blue is personally insolvent as in Case 2.
2. The firm sells noncash assets for $20,000 on May 15, 20X5.
3. The partnership pays creditors $42,000 on May 20, 20X5.

See Figure 16–3 for the statement of partnership realization and liquidation for Case 3. The following observations are made from this illustration:

1. The $70,000 loss is allocated to the partners in their loss-sharing ratio. This allocation creates a deficit of $18,000 in Blue's capital account.
2. Because Blue is personally insolvent, her $18,000 deficit is distributed to Alt and Cha in their loss-sharing ratio of 40:60 for Alt and 20:60 for Cha. The distribution of Blue's deficit results in a $6,000 deficit for both Alt and Cha.
3. Because Alt and Cha are personally solvent, they make additional capital contributions to remedy their respective capital deficits of $6,000 and $6,000.

FIGURE 16–3 Case 3: Partnership Insolvent; Deficit Created in Personally Insolvent Partner's Capital Account

ABC PARTNERSHIP
Statement of Partnership Realization and Liquidation
Lump-Sum Liquidation

				Capital Balance		
	Cash +	Noncash Assets =	Liabilities +	Alt, 40% +	Blue, 40% +	Cha, 20%
Preliquidation balances, May 1	10,000	90,000	42,000	34,000	10,000	14,000
Sales of assets and distribution of $70,000 loss	20,000	(90,000)		(28,000)	(28,000)	(14,000)
	30,000	0	42,000	6,000	(18,000)	0
Allocation of insolvent partner's deficit:					18,000	
40/60 × $18,000				(12,000)		
20/60 × $18,000						(6,000)
	30,000	0	42,000	(6,000)	0	(6,000)
Contributions by Alt and Cha to remedy capital deficits	12,000			6,000		6,000
	42,000	0	42,000	0	0	0
Payment to creditors	(42,000)		(42,000)			
Postliquidation balances	0	0	0	0	0	0

4. The $42,000 partnership cash now available is used to pay its creditors.
5. The postliquidation balances are zero, indicating completion of the partnership liquidation.

In Case 3, both Alt and Cha made additional capital contributions to eliminate their capital deficits. When a partner must remedy another partner's capital deficit, the partner making the remedy has cause to bring suit against the failing partner. Blue's failure in the amount of $12,000 in Case 2 and $18,000 in Case 3 required Alt and Cha to remedy Blue's deficit. Alt and Cha can sue Blue and be included in the list of her personal liabilities. Although Blue is personally insolvent, Alt and Cha may obtain a partial recovery of their amounts.

INSTALLMENT LIQUIDATIONS

LO 16-3

Make calculations related to installment partnership liquidations.

An ***installment liquidation*** typically requires several months to complete and includes periodic, or installment, payments to the partners during the liquidation period because they require funds for personal purposes. Most partnership liquidations take place over an extended period in order to obtain the largest possible amount from the realization of the assets.

Some partnerships using installment liquidations prepare a Plan of Liquidation and Dissolution prior to beginning the liquidation. This plan sets out the intended liquidation of its assets and the winding-up of its affairs. The partners discuss and perhaps modify the plan, but their agreement is expected. And some partnerships, upon obtaining the consent of the partners to proceed with the installment liquidation, adopt the liquidation basis of accounting under which assets are stated at their estimated net realizable value, and liabilities, including projected costs of liquidation, are stated at their estimated settlement amounts. These partnerships may prepare a statement of net assets in liquidation and a statement of changes in net assets in liquidation. However, partnerships using GAAP apply **ASC 360** to value their long-lived assets to be disposed of by sale. **ASC 360** states that these assets are to be classified separately and valued at the lower of carrying amount or fair value less costs to sell. And **ASC 20** requires that costs associated with an exit activity be recognized and measured at fair value in the period in which the liability is incurred, not in earlier periods when, for example, a restructuring plan is adopted. Most partnerships use the statement of partnership realization and liquidation during the installment liquidation process and recognize gains or losses from the liquidation events.

Installment liquidations involve distributing cash to partners before complete liquidation of the assets occurs. The accountant must be especially cautious when distributing available cash because future events may change the amounts to be paid to each partner. We illustrate two methods for ensuring fairness and equality in making cash distributions in an installment liquidation: (1) the ***schedule of safe payments to partners*** and (2) the ***cash distribution plan***. A new schedule of safe payments must be prepared each time cash becomes available for distribution to the partners whereas the cash distribution plan is prepared only once at the beginning of the liquidation process. We first demonstrate the use of schedules of safe payments and later illustrate the use of a cash distribution plan. Either method is acceptable. The following practical guidelines should be followed in preparing schedules of safe payments to the partners:

1. Distribute no cash to the partners until all outside liabilities and actual plus potential liquidation expenses have been paid or provided for by reserving the necessary cash.
2. Anticipate the worst, or most restrictive, possible case before determining the amount of cash installment each partner receives. Make the following *hypothetical* assumptions to determine how much excess capital (if any) the partners have in their capital accounts:

a. Assume that all remaining noncash assets will be written off as a loss; that is, assume that nothing will be realized on future asset disposals.

b. Assume that any deficits created in the partners' capital accounts by the hypothetical assumption that all noncash assets are worthless will be absorbed by the remaining partners with positive hypothetical capital balances; that is, assume that hypothetical deficits will not be eliminated by additional partner capital contributions.

3. After the accountant has assumed these two hypothetical worst possible cases, the remaining credit balances in capital accounts represent safe distributions of cash that may be distributed to partners in those amounts.

STOP & THINK

Why would these hypothetical "worst-case" assumptions lead to the optimal cash distributions to partners at any particular point in time? Picture the accounting equation after all outside loans have been paid (and assuming no inside loans):

Cash + Noncash assets = Partners' capital accounts

By hypothetically assuming that the noncash assets are worthless, we are essentially assuming this is the last cash we'll ever collect. To whom should it be distributed? The hypothetical loss would be written off to the partners' capital accounts, leaving the following accounting equation:

Cash = Partners' capital accounts

Once hypothetical deficits created by the assumed write-off of the noncash assets have been absorbed by partners with positive capital balances, the cash on hand equals the amount of "extra capital" remaining in partner's accounts after absorbing the most extreme losses possible. Partners with this much "extra" capital deserve to receive the cash that is available.

Illustration of Installment Liquidation

Advanced StudyGuide .com

We now use the same illustration in the lump-sum liquidation of the ABC Partnership to illustrate liquidation in installments. Alt, Blue, and Cha decide to liquidate their business over a period of time and to receive installment distributions of available cash during the liquidation process.

ABC Partnership's condensed trial balance on May 1, 20X5, the day the partners decide to liquidate the business, follows. Each partner's profit and loss–sharing percentage is also shown.

ABC PARTNERSHIP
Trial Balance
May 1, 20X5

Cash	$ 10,000	
Noncash Assets	90,000	
Liabilities		$ 42,000
Alt, Capital (40%)		34,000
Blue, Capital (40%)		10,000
Cha, Capital (20%)		14,000
Total	$100,000	$100,000

The following information describes this case in more detail.

1. The partners' net worth statements on May 1, 20X5, are as follows:

	Alt	Blue	Cha
Personal assets	$150,000	$12,000	$42,000
Personal liabilities	(86,000)	(16,000)	(14,000)
Net worth (deficit)	$ 64,000	$ (4,000)	$28,000

Blue is personally insolvent; Alt and Cha are personally solvent.

2. The noncash assets are sold as follows:

Date	Book Value	Proceeds	Loss
5/15/X5	$55,000	$45,000	$10,000
6/15/X5	30,000	15,000	15,000
7/15/X5	5,000	5,000	

FIGURE 16–4 Installment Liquidation Worksheet

ABC PARTNERSHIP
Statement of Partnership Realization and Liquidation
Installment Liquidation

	Cash	+	Noncash Assets	=	Liabilities	+	Capital Balance Alt, 40%	+	Blue, 40%	+	Cha, 20%
Preliquidation balances, May 1	10,000		90,000		42,000		34,000		10,000		14,000
May 20X5:											
Sale of assets and distribution of $10,000 loss	45,000		(55,000)				(4,000)		(4,000)		(2,000)
	55,000		35,000		42,000		30,000		6,000		12,000
Payment to creditors	(42,000)				(42,000)						
	13,000		35,000		0		30,000		6,000		12,000
Payment to partners (Schedule 1, Figure 16–5)	(3,000)						(3,000)				
	10,000		35,000		0		27,000		6,000		12,000
June 20X5:											
Sale of assets and distribution of $15,000 loss	15,000		(30,000)				(6,000)		(6,000)		(3,000)
	25,000		5,000		0		21,000		0		9,000
Payment to partners (Schedule 2, Figure 16–5)	(15,000)						(11,000)				(4,000)
	10,000		5,000		0		10,000		0		5,000
July 20X5:											
Sale of assets at book value	5,000		(5,000)								
	15,000		0		0		10,000		0		5,000
Payment of $7,500 in liquidation costs	(7,500)						(3,000)		(3,000)		(1,500)
	7,500		0		0		7,000		(3,000)		3,500
Distribution of deficit of insolvent partner:									3,000		
40/60 × $3,000							(2,000)				
20/60 × $3,000											(1,000)
	7,500		0		0		5,000		0		2,500
Payment to partners	(7,500)						(5,000)				(2,500)
Postliquidation balances, July 31	0		0		0		0		0		0

3. The partnership pays the creditors $42,000 on May 20. Note that, given our assumption of subordination of all loans received from partner to outside liabilities, outside creditors must always be paid in full before any cash is distributed to the partners.
4. The partners agree to maintain a $10,000 cash reserve during the liquidation process to pay for any liquidation expenses.
5. The partners agree to distribute the available cash at the end of each month; that is, installment liquidations will be made on May 31 and June 30. The final cash distributions to partners will be made on July 31, 20X5, the end of the liquidation process. The amounts to be distributed at the end of each month must be calculated using a schedule of safe payments to partners, as seen in Figure 16–5.

Refer to Figure 16–4 for the statement of partnership realization and liquidation for the ABC Partnership installment liquidation.

FIGURE 16–5 Schedule of Safe Payment to Partners for an Installment Liquidation

ABC PARTNERSHIP
Schedule of Safe Payment to Partners

	Partner		
	Alt 40%	**Blue 40%**	**Cha 20%**
Schedule 1, May 31, 20X5			
Computation of distribution of cash available on May 31, 20X5:			
Capital balances, May 31, before cash distribution	30,000	6,000	12,000
Assume full loss of $35,000 on remaining noncash assets and $10,000 in possible future liquidation expenses	(18,000)	(18,000)	(9,000)
	12,000	(12,000)	3,000
Assume Alt and Cha must absorb Blue's potential deficit:		12,000	
40/60 × $12,000	(8,000)		
20/60 × $12,000			(4,000)
	4,000	0	(1,000)
Assume Alt must absorb Cha's potential deficit	(1,000)		1,000
Safe payment to partners, May 31	3,000	0	0
Schedule 2, June 30, 20X5			
Computation of distribution of cash available on June 30, 20X5:			
Capital balances, June 30, before cash distribution	21,000	0	9,000
Assume full loss of $5,000 on remaining noncash assets and $10,000 in possible future liquidation expenses	(6,000)	(6,000)	(3,000)
	15,000	(6,000)	6,000
Assume Alt and Cha must absorb Blue's potential deficit:		6,000	
40/60 × $6,000	(4,000)		
20/60 × $6,000			(2,000)
Safe payment to partners, June 30	11,000	0	4,000

Transactions during May 20X5

The events during May 20X5 result in a distribution of $3,000 to the partners. The procedure to arrive at this amount is as follows:

1. The sale of $55,000 of assets results in a loss of $10,000, which is distributed to the three partners in their loss-sharing ratio.
2. Payments of $42,000 are made to the partnership's outside creditors for the known liabilities.
3. Available cash is distributed to the partners on May 31, 20X5, as calculated by the schedule of safe payments to partners (Figure 16–5).

Advanced StudyGuide .com

To determine the safe payment of cash to be distributed to partners, the accountant must make some assumptions about the future liquidation of the remaining assets. Under the assumption of the worst possible situation, the remaining $35,000 of assets will result in a total loss. Before making a cash distribution to the partners, the accountant prepares a schedule of safe payments to partners using the worst-case assumptions. See Schedule 1 in Figure 16–5 for the schedule of safe payments to partners as of May 31, 20X5.

The schedule of safe payments begins with the partners' capital balances as of May 31. The logic of using just the capital accounts comes from the accounting equation: Assets − Liabilities = Partners' capital balances. Thus, for example, if

FYI

When a partner has a loan outstanding to the partnership, the legal doctrine of setoff essentially treats the loan as an additional cash contribution. Thus, loans to the partnership are added to the partner's capital balance at the start of the schedule of safe payments to accurately reflect the partner's total contributions.

Conversely, if a partner has borrowed from the partnership (i.e., the partnership has a receivable from that partner), the loan is subtracted from the partner's capital balance at the commencement of the schedule of safe payments.

there were an increase in a liability that reduced the net assets, the equality of the accounting equation would also result in a decrease in the total of partners' capital balances. Because the partners' capital accounts are the focus of the payments to partners, it is unnecessary to include the assets and liabilities in the schedule of safe payments to partners. The schedule includes all information partners need to know how much cash they will receive at each cash distribution date.

Alt, Blue, and Cha agree to withhold $10,000 for possible liquidation expenses. In addition, the noncash assets have a remaining balance of $35,000 on May 31. A worst-case assumption is a complete loss on the noncash assets and $10,000 of liquidation expenses, totaling $45,000 of charges to be distributed to the partners' capital accounts. The capital accounts of Alt, Blue, and Cha would be charged for $18,000, $18,000, and $9,000, respectively, for their shares of the $45,000 assumed loss. These assumptions result in a pro forma deficit in Blue's capital account. This is not an actual deficit that must be remedied! It is merely the result of applying the worst-case assumptions.

Continuing such worst-case planning, the accountant assumes that Blue is insolvent (which happens to be true in this example) and distributes the pro forma deficit in Blue's capital account to Alt and Cha in their *loss-sharing ratio* of 40:60 to Alt and 20:60 to Cha. The resulting credit balances indicate the amount of cash that may be safely distributed to the partners. Refer to Figure 16–4 for the May 31 cash distribution. The available cash of $3,000 is distributed to Alt. The ending balances should satisfy the equality of assets and equities of the accounting equation. If the equality has been destroyed, an error has occurred that must be corrected before proceeding. As of May 31, after the installment distribution, the accounting equation is

$$\text{Assets} - \text{Liabilities} = \text{Partners' equity}$$
$$\$45{,}000 - \$0 = \$45{,}000$$

Transactions during June 20X5

Transactions for June 20X5 continue in Figure 16–4 as follows:

1. The company sells noncash assets of $30,000 on June 15 for a $15,000 loss, which is distributed to the partners in their loss-sharing ratio, resulting in a zero capital balance for Blue.
2. On June 30, 20X5, available cash is distributed as an installment payment to the partners.

The schedule of safe payments to partners as of June 30, 20X5, in Figure 16–5 shows how to calculate the distribution amounts. A worst-case plan assumes that the remaining noncash assets of $5,000 must be written off as a loss and that the $10,000 cash in reserve will be completely used for liquidation expenses. This $15,000 pro forma loss is allocated to the partners in their loss-sharing ratio, which creates a $6,000 deficit in Blue's capital account. Continuing the worst-case scenario, it is assumed Blue will not eliminate this debit balance. Therefore, the $6,000 potential deficit is allocated to Alt and Cha in their resulting loss-sharing ratio of 40/60 to Alt and 20/60 to Cha. The resulting credit balances in the partners' capital accounts show the amount of cash that can be distributed safely. Only $15,000 of the available cash is distributed to Alt and Cha on June 30 (Figure 16–4).

Transactions during July 20X5

The last part of Figure 16–4 shows the completion of the liquidation transactions during July 20X5:

1. The firm sells its remaining assets at their book value of $5,000.
2. The partnership pays actual liquidation costs of $7,500 and allocates them to the partners in their loss-sharing ratio, creating a deficit of $3,000 in Blue's capital account. The remaining $2,500 of the $10,000 reserved for the expenses is released for distribution to the partners.

3. Because Blue is personally insolvent and cannot contribute to the partnership, the \$3,000 deficit is distributed to Alt and Cha in their loss-sharing ratio. Note that this is an actual, not a pro forma, deficit.
4. The \$7,500 of remaining cash is paid to Alt and Cha to the extent of their capital balances. After this last distribution, all account balances are zero, indicating the completion of the liquidation process.

Cash Distribution Plan

At the beginning of the liquidation process, accountants commonly prepare a cash distribution plan, which gives the partners an idea of the installment cash payments each will receive as cash becomes available. The actual installment distributions are determined using the statement of realization and liquidation supplemented with the schedule of safe payments to partners as presented in the preceding section. The cash distribution plan is a pro forma projection of the application of cash as it becomes available.

Loss Absorption Potential

A basic concept of the cash distribution plan at the beginning of the liquidation process is ***loss absorption potential (LAP).*** An individual partner's LAP is defined as the maximum loss that the partnership can realize before that partner's capital account balance is extinguished. The LAP is a function of two elements, as follows:

$$\text{LAP} = \frac{\text{Partner's capital account balance}}{\text{Partner's loss share}}$$

FYI

When a partner has a loan outstanding to the partnership, the legal doctrine of setoff essentially treats the loan as an additional cash contribution. Thus, loans to the partnership are added to the numerator of the LAP calculation, effectively increasing that partner's loss absorption potential. In other words, that partner is assumed to have "more skin in the game."

Conversely, if a partner has borrowed from the partnership (i.e., the partnership has a receivable from that partner), the loan is subtracted from the partner's capital in the numerator, decreasing that partner's loss absorption potential.

For example, on May 1, 20X5, Alt has a capital account credit balance of \$34,000 and a 40 percent share in the losses of ABC Partnership. Alt's LAP is

$$\text{LAP} = \frac{\$34{,}000}{0.40} = \$85{,}000$$

This means that \$85,000 in losses on disposing of noncash assets or from additional liquidation expenses would eliminate the credit balance in Alt's capital account, as follows:

$$\$85{,}000 \times 0.40 = \$34{,}000$$

Illustration of Cash Distribution Plan

The following illustration is based on the ABC Partnership example. A trial balance of its balance sheet accounts on May 1, 20X5, the day the partners decide to liquidate the business, is prepared.

ABC PARTNERSHIP
Trial Balance
May 1, 20X5

Cash	\$ 10,000	
Noncash Assets	90,000	
Liabilities		\$ 42,000
Alt, Capital (40%)		34,000
Blue, Capital (40%)		10,000
Cha, Capital (20%)		14,000
Total	\$100,000	\$100,000

FIGURE 16–6 Cash Distribution Plan for Liquidating Partnership

ABC PARTNERSHIP
Cash Distribution Plan
May 1, 20X5

	Loss Absorption Potential			Capital Balance		
	Alt	Blue	Cha	Alt	Blue	Cha
Loss-sharing percentages				40%	40%	20%
Preliquidation capital balances, May 1, 20X5				34,000	10,000	14,000
Loss absorption potential (LAP)						
(Capital balance/Loss ratio)	85,000	25,000	70,000			
Decrease highest LAP to next-highest LAP:						
Decrease Alt by $15,000						
(cash distribution: $15,000 × 0.40 = $6,000)	(15,000)			(6,000)		
	70,000	25,000	70,000	28,000	10,000	14,000
Decrease LAPs to next-highest level:						
Decrease Alt by $45,000						
(cash distribution: $45,000 × 0.40 = $18,000)	(45,000)			(18,000)		
Decrease Cha by $45,000						
(cash distribution: $45,000 × 0.20 = $9,000)			(45,000)			(9,000)
	25,000	25,000	25,000	10,000	10,000	5,000
Decrease LAPs by distributing cash in the loss-sharing percentages	40%	40%	20%			

Summary of Cash Distribution Plan

	Alt	Blue	Cha
Step 1: First $42,000 to outside creditors			
Step 2: Next $10,000 to liquidation expenses			
Step 3: Next $6,000 to Alt	6,000		
Step 4: Next $45,000 to Alt and Cha in their respective loss ratios ($27,000 now available)	18,000		9,000
Step 5: Any additional distributions in the partners' loss-sharing ratios	40%	40%	20%

The partners ask for a cash distribution plan as of May 1, 20X5, to determine the distributions of cash as it becomes available during the liquidation process. Such a plan always provides for paying the partnership's outside creditors before making any distributions to the partners. See Figure 16–6 for the cash distribution plan as of May 1, the beginning date of the liquidation process.

The important observations from this illustration are as follows:

1. Each partner's loss absorption potential is computed as his or her capital balance divided by that partner's *loss-sharing percentage.* Alt has the highest LAP ($85,000), Cha has the next-highest ($70,000), and Blue has the lowest ($25,000). Each partner's LAP is the amount of loss that would completely eliminate his or her net capital credit balance. Alt is the least vulnerable to a loss, and Blue is the most vulnerable.
2. The least vulnerable partner is the first to receive any cash distributions after paying creditors. Alt is the only partner to receive cash until his LAP is decreased to the level of the next-highest partner, Cha. To decrease Alt's LAP by $15,000 requires paying Alt $6,000 ($15,000 × 0.40). After payment of $6,000 to Alt, his new loss absorption potential will be the same as Cha's, calculated as Alt's remaining capital balance of $28,000 divided by his loss-sharing percentage of 40 percent ($28,000/0.40 = $70,000).
3. Alt's and Cha's LAPs are now equal, and they will receive cash distributions until the LAP of each decreases to the next-highest level, the $25,000 of Blue. Multiplying the loss absorption potential of $45,000 ($70,000 − $25,000) by the two partners' loss-sharing ratios shows how much of the next available cash can be safely paid to

FIGURE 16–7 Confirmation of Cash Distribution Plan

ABC PARTNERSHIP
Capital Account Balances
May 1, 20X5, through July 31, 20X5

	Partner		
	Alt 40%	**Blue 40%**	**Cha 20%**
Preliquidation balances, May 1	34,000	10,000	14,000
May loss of $10,000 on disposal of assets	(4,000)	(4,000)	(2,000)
	30,000	6,000	12,000
May 31 distribution of $3,000 available cash to partners:			
First $3,000 (of $6,000 priority to Alt)	(3,000)		
	27,000	6,000	12,000
June loss of $15,000 on disposal of assets	(6,000)	(6,000)	(3,000)
	21,000	0	9,000
June 30 distribution of $15,000 available cash to partners:			
Next $3,000 (to complete Alt's $6,000 priority)	(3,000)		
Remaining $12,000:			
40/60 to Alt	(8,000)		
20/60 to Cha			(4,000)
	10,000	0	5,000
Liquidation cost of $7,500	(3,000)	(3,000)	(1,500)
	7,000	(3,000)	3,500
Allocation of Blue's actual deficit	(2,000)	3,000	(1,000)
	5,000	0	2,500
Final payment of $7,500 to partners on July 31, 20X5:			
40/60 to Alt	(5,000)		
20/60 to Cha			(2,500)
Postliquidation balances, July 31	0	0	0

each partner. Alt and Cha will receive cash distributions according to their loss-sharing ratios. As the next $27,000 of cash becomes available, it will be distributed to Alt and Cha in the ratio of 40:60 to Alt and 20:60 to Cha.

4. Finally, when all three partners have the same LAPs, any remaining cash is distributed according to their loss-sharing ratios.

The summary of the cash distribution plan at the bottom of Figure 16–6 is provided to the partners. From this summary, they are able to determine the relative amounts each will receive as cash becomes available to the partnership.

See Figure 16–7 for the capital balances for each partner in the ABC Partnership during the installment liquidation period from May 1, 20X5, through July 31, 20X5. The installment payments to partners are computed on the statement of partnership realization and liquidation (Figure 16–4) using a schedule of safe distributions to partners (Figure 16–5). The actual distributions of available cash conform to the cash distribution plan prepared at the beginning of the liquidation process (Figure 16–7), with adjustment because of Blue's actual deficit that Alt and Cha absorb.

ADDITIONAL CONSIDERATIONS

Incorporation of a Partnership

As a partnership continues to grow, the partners may decide to incorporate the business to have access to additional equity financing, to limit their personal liability, to obtain selected tax advantages, or to achieve other sound business purposes. At the incorporation, the partnership is terminated, and the assets and liabilities are revalued to their fair values. The gain or loss on revaluation is allocated to the partners' capital accounts in the profit and loss–sharing ratio.

Capital stock in the new corporation is then distributed in proportion to the partners' capital accounts. The separate business entity of the partnership should now close its accounting records and the corporation, as a new business entity, should open its own new accounting records to record the issuance of its capital stock to the partnership's previous partners.

We use the ABC Partnership's trial balance on May 1, 20X5, as shown previously, to illustrate incorporation of a partnership. Instead of liquidating the partnership as shown throughout the chapter, assume the partners agree to incorporate it.

The new corporation is to be called Peerless Products Corporation. At the time of conversion from a partnership to a corporation, all assets and liabilities should be appraised and valued at their fair values. Any gain or loss must be distributed to the partners in their profit and loss–sharing ratios. Assume that the noncash assets have an $80,000 fair value. The $10,000 loss to fair value is allocated to the partners' capital accounts before the incorporation, as follows:

(4)	Alt, Capital	4,000	
	Blue, Capital	4,000	
	Cha, Capital	2,000	
	Noncash Assets		10,000
	Recognize loss on reduction of assets to fair values.		

Of course, in practice, specific asset accounts are used instead of the general classification of noncash assets. Gains on asset revaluations also may occur when a successful partnership elects to incorporate.

The partnership's net assets have a fair value of $48,000 ($90,000 of assets less $42,000 of liabilities). The corporation issues 4,600 shares of $1 par common stock in exchange for ABC Partnership's assets and liabilities. Peerless Products Corporation makes this entry to acquire the partnership's assets and liabilities in exchange for the issuance of the 4,600 shares of stock

(5)	Cash	10,000	
	Noncash Assets	80,000	
	Liabilities		42,000
	Common Stock		4,600
	Paid-in Capital in Excess of Par		43,400
	Issuance of stock for partnership's assets and liabilities.		

The partners make the following entry on the partnership's books:

(6)	Investment in Peerless Products	48,000	
	Liabilities	42,000	
	Cash		10,000
	Noncash Assets		80,000
	Receipt of stock in Peerless Products in exchange for partnership's net assets.		

Recall that the noncash assets were reduced to their fair values in entry (4). To distribute the stock to the partners and close the partnership's books, the final entry is:

(7)	Alt, Capital	30,000	
	Blue, Capital	6,000	
	Cha, Capital	12,000	
	Investment in Peerless		48,000
	Distribution of Peerless Products stock to partners.		

SUMMARY OF KEY CONCEPTS

The process of terminating and liquidating a partnership is often traumatic for partners. The Uniform Partnership Act of 1997 provides guidance for the liquidation process and specifies the legal rights of the partners and of partnership creditors.

Disassociation of a partner is his or her withdrawal, either voluntarily or involuntarily, from the partnership. Dissolution is the ending of a partnership. Not all disassociations and dissolutions require termination, which is the cessation of normal business functions, or liquidation with the disposal of assets, payment of liabilities, and distribution of remaining cash to the partners. UPA 1997 defines a partnership as a legal entity apart from the individual partners. Therefore, unless required by judicial determination, termination and liquidation often can be avoided by carefully preparing the partnership agreement to allow continuation of the business when a partner retires or leaves the partnership. The most common reasons for involuntary liquidation are court decrees or the bankruptcy of the partnership.

Liquidation can involve a single lump-sum payment to partners. Most liquidations, however, take several months and involve installment payments to partners during the process. Items that facilitate liquidations are the statement of partnership realization and liquidation, and a worksheet summarizing the liquidation process and serving as a basis for the journal entries to record the events. Installment payments to partners are determined on a worst-case basis using a schedule of safe payments to partners, which assumes that all noncash assets will be written off and that partners with debit balances in their capital accounts will not be able to remedy the deficiencies.

A cash distribution plan provides information to partners about the installment payments they will receive as cash becomes available to the partnership. The plan is prepared at the beginning of the liquidation process. Actual cash distributions during the liquidation are determined with the statement of partnership realization and liquidation. The concept of loss absorption potential (LAP) is central to the development of the cash distribution plan. LAP is the amount of partnership loss required to eliminate a given partner's capital credit balance. The LAP is determined by dividing a partner's net capital credit balance by his or her loss-sharing percentage.

KEY TERMS

cash distribution plan, *819*
dissolution (of a partnership), *812*
installment liquidation, *819*
loss absorption potential (LAP), *824*
lump-sum liquidation, *814*
schedule of safe payments to partners, *819*
statement of partnership realization and liquidation, *813*

Appendix 16A Partners' Personal Financial Statements

At the beginning of the liquidation process, partners are usually asked for personal financial statements to determine each partner's personal solvency. Guidelines for preparing personal financial statements are found in **ASC 274.**

Personal financial statements consist of the following:

1. Statement of financial condition, or personal balance sheet, that presents the partner's assets and liabilities at a point in time.
2. Statement of changes in net worth, or personal income statement, that presents the primary sources of changes in the partner's net worth.

In addition to presenting a partner's assets and liabilities, the statement of financial condition should include an estimate of the income taxes incurred as if all the assets were converted and the liabilities extinguished. The partner's net worth would then be computed as assets less liabilities less estimated taxes (see Figure 16–8). In general, the accrual basis of accounting should be used to determine the partner's assets and liabilities, and comparative statements are usually provided. However, unlike a balance sheet of a business that is based on historical cost, the assets in the personal statement of financial condition are stated at their estimated current values. The liabilities are stated at the lower of the discounted value of future cash payments or the current cash settlement amount. Included immediately below the liabilities are the estimated taxes that would be paid if all assets were converted to cash and all the liabilities were paid.

FIGURE 16–8
Personal Statement of Financial Condition

C. ALT
Statement of Financial Condition
May 1, 20X5 and 20X4

	Year	
	20X5	**20X4**
Assets		
Cash	$ 4,000	$ 2,500
Receivables	3,500	4,000
Investments:		
Marketable securities	5,000	4,000
ABC Partnership	34,000	26,000
Cash surrender value of life insurance	3,100	3,000
Residence	84,000	76,000
Personal effects	16,400	12,500
Total assets	$150,000	$128,000
Liabilities and Net Worth		
Charge accounts	$ 2,000	$ 3,000
Income taxes—current-year balance	1,200	800
10 percent note payable	6,000	10,000
Mortgage payable	60,000	62,000
Estimated income taxes on the difference between the estimated current values of assets & liabilities & their tax bases	16,800	12,200
Net worth	64,000	40,000
Total liabilities & net worth	$150,000	$128,000

Assets and liabilities are presented in their order of liquidity and maturity, not as current and noncurrent. **ASC 274** provides guidelines for determining the current value of a person's assets and liabilities. The primary valuation methods are the discounted value of future cash flows, current market prices of marketable securities or other investments, and appraisals of properties. An investment in a separate business entity (e.g., a partnership) should be reported as a one-line, combined amount valued at the net investment's market value. The liabilities are stated at their discounted cash flow value or current liquidation value. The accountant uses applicable tax laws, carryover provisions, and other regulations to compute the estimated tax liability from the assumed conversion of assets and the assumed extinguishment of liabilities.

The statement of changes in net worth presents the major sources of income. It recognizes both realized and unrealized income. The income statement of a commercial business may not recognize holding gains on some marketable securities, but an individual's statement of changes in net worth recognizes such gains.

ILLUSTRATION OF PERSONAL FINANCIAL STATEMENTS

The following illustration presents Alt's personal financial condition as of May 1, 20X5, the day the partners decide to liquidate the ABC Partnership. His net worth on this date is as follows:

Personal assets	$150,000
Personal liabilities	(86,000)
Net worth	$ 64,000

Statement of Financial Condition

Figure 16–8 included Alt's statement of financial condition on May 1, 20X5, as well as the prior-year statement. The 20X5 statement illustrates the following:

1. Receivables due to Alt from other people have a present value of $3,500.
2. Alt has two investments, one of which is his interest in the ABC Partnership, valued at estimated current market value, which in this case also equals its book value of $34,000. The marketable security investments are shown at market value.

FIGURE 16–9
Personal Statement of Changes in Net Worth

C. ALT
Statement of Changes in Net Worth
For the Years Ended May 1, 20X5 and 20X4

	Year Ended May 1	
	20X5	**20X4**
Realized increases in net worth:		
Salary	$ 36,900	$ 34,900
Dividends & interest income	800	400
Distribution from ABC Partnership	3,000	1,000
Cash surrender value of life insurance	100	100
Gains on sales of marketable securities	1,400	1,200
	$ 42,200	$ 37,600
Realized decreases in net worth:		
Income taxes	$ 8,200	$ 7,800
Interest expense	1,400	700
Real estate taxes	2,400	2,200
Insurance payments (including $100 for increase in cash surrender value of life insurance)	400	300
Personal expenditures	18,800	18,600
	$(31,200)	$(29,600)
Net realized increase in net worth	$ 11,000	$ 8,000
Unrealized increases in net worth:		
Marketable securities	$ 1,600	$ 400
ABC Partnership	8,000	5,000
Residence	8,000	4,000
	$ 17,600	$ 9,400
Unrealized decreases in net worth:		
Increase in estimated income taxes on the difference between the estimated current values of assets & liabilities & their tax bases	(4,600)	(4,400)
Net unrealized increase in net worth	$ 13,000	$ 5,000
Net increase in net worth:		
Realized & unrealized	$ 24,000	$ 13,000
Net worth at beginning of period	40,000	27,000
Net worth at end of period	$ 64,000	$ 40,000

3. The cash surrender value of life insurance is presented net of any loans payable on the policies.
4. Alt's residence and personal effects are presented at their appraised values.
5. Liabilities are presented at their estimated current liquidation value or the discounted value of the future cash flows.
6. The estimated income taxes on the difference between the estimated current values of assets and liabilities and their tax bases represent the amount of income tax Alt would be liable for if all assets were converted to cash and all liabilities were paid.
7. Net worth is the difference between the estimated current value of Alt's assets and liabilities, including estimated tax.

Statement of Changes in Net Worth

Alt's statement of changes in net worth, shown in Figure 16–9, illustrates the following:

1. The statement separates the realized and unrealized changes in net worth. *Realized changes* are cash flows to or from Alt that have already taken place. *Unrealized changes* are equivalent to holding gains or losses. They have not yet been converted to cash. For example, Alt received $3,000 from the ABC Partnership during the year ended May 1, 20X5. In addition, Alt's partnership interest increased by $8,000 during the year.
2. Alt had $42,200 of realized increases in net worth during the year ended May 1, 20X5. The primary source was a salary of $36,900 from full-time employment outside the ABC Partnership.

3. The major realized decrease in net worth during the year ended May 1, 20X5, was for personal expenditures of $18,800.
4. Unrealized increases of $17,600 during the year were primarily from an increase in the value of Alt's personal residence ($8,000) and an increase in the investment value of his partnership interest in the ABC Partnership ($8,000). Unrealized holding gains of $1,600 are available in Alt's investments in marketable securities.
5. The change in the estimated tax liability is an unrealized decrease because this amount is due only if Alt converts these assets to cash.
6. The net unrealized changes in net worth are added to the net realized changes in net worth to obtain the total change in Alt's net worth for each year. His net worth increased by $13,000 during the year ended May 1, 20X4, and by $24,000 during the year ended May 1, 20X5.

Footnote Disclosures

Sufficient footnote disclosures should accompany the two personal financial statements. The footnotes should describe the following:

1. The methods used to value the major assets.
2. The names and the nature of businesses in which the person has major investments.
3. The methods and assumptions used to compute the estimated tax bases and a statement that the tax provision in an actual liquidation will probably differ from the estimate because the actual tax burden will then be based on actual realizations determined by market values at the point of liquidation.
4. Maturities, interest rates, and other details of any receivables and debt.
5. Any other information needed to present fully the person's net worth.

QUESTIONS

LO 16-1 **Q16-1** What are the major causes of a dissolution? What are the accounting implications of a dissolution?

LO 16-1 **Q16-2** During a partnership liquidation, do a partnership's liabilities to individual partners have a lower priority than the partnership's obligations to other, third-party creditors? Explain.

LO 16-1 **Q16-3** X, Y, and Z are partners. The partnership is liquidating, and Partner Z is personally insolvent. What implications may this have for Partners X and Y?

LO 16-1 **Q16-4** May an individual partner simply decide to leave a partnership? Does the partnership have any legal recourse against that partner? Explain.

LO 16-2, 16-3 **Q16-5** Contrast a lump-sum liquidation with an installment liquidation.

LO 16-1 **Q16-6** How is a deficit in a partner's capital account eliminated if he or she is personally insolvent?

LO 16-2 **Q16-7** The DEF Partnership has total assets of $55,000. Partner D has a capital credit of $6,000, Partner E has a capital deficit of $20,000, and Partner F has a capital credit of $8,000. Is the DEF Partnership solvent or insolvent?

LO 16-1 **Q16-8** Assume that, because of a new law recently passed, the types of significant transactions in which a partnership engages are no longer lawful. Two of the five partners wish to wind up and terminate the partnership. Can these two partners require the partnership to terminate? Explain.

LO 16-3 **Q16-9** How are a partner's personal payments to partnership creditors accounted for on the partnership's books?

LO 16-3 **Q16-10** What is the purpose of the schedule of safe payments to partners?

LO 16-1 **Q16-11** In what ratio are losses during liquidation assigned to the partners' capital accounts? Is this ratio used in all instances?

LO 16-3 **Q16-12** The installment liquidation process uses a worst-case assumption in computing the payments to partners. What does *worst-case assumption* mean?

LO 16-3 **Q16-13** Define *loss absorption potential* and explain its importance in determining cash distributions to partners.

LO 16-3 **Q16-14** Partner A has a capital credit of $25,000. Partner B's capital credit is also $25,000. Partners A and B share profits and losses in a 60:40 ratio. Which partner will receive the first payment of cash in an installment liquidation?

LO 16-3 **Q16-15*** Explain the process of incorporating a partnership.

CASES

LO 16-3

C16-1 Cash Distributions to Partners

Analysis

The partnership of Bull and Bear is in the process of termination. The partners have disagreed on virtually every decision and have decided to liquidate the present business with each partner taking his own clients from the partnership. Bull wants cash distributed as it becomes available; Bear wants no cash distributed until all assets have been sold and all liabilities settled. You are called in to aid in the termination and liquidation process.

Required

How would you respond to each of the partners' requests?

LO 16-1, 16-2

C16-2 Cash Distributions to Partners

Analysis

Adam and Bard agreed to liquidate their partnership. Having been asked to assist them in this process, you prepare the following balance sheet for the date of the beginning of the liquidation. The loss-sharing percentages are in parentheses next to the capital account balances.

Cash	$ 40,000
Loan Receivable from Adam	10,000
Other Assets	200,000
Total	$250,000
Accounts Payable	$ 30,000
Loan Payable to Bard	100,000
Adam, Capital (50%)	80,000
Bard, Capital (50%)	40,000
Total	$250,000

Bard is demanding that the loan from him be paid before any cash is distributed to Adam. Adam believes the available cash should be paid to him until his capital account is reduced to $40,000, the same as Bard's. Adam will then pay the loan receivable to the partnership with the cash received. You have been asked to reconcile the argument.

Required

What would you advise in this case?

LO 16-3

C16-3* Incorporation of a Partnership

After successfully operating a partnership for several years, the partners have proposed to incorporate the business and admit another investor. The original partners will purchase at par an amount of preferred stock equal to the book values of their capital interests in the partnership and common stock for the amount of the market value, including unrecognized goodwill, of the business that exceeds book value. The new investor will make an investment at a 5 percent premium over par value in both preferred and common stock equal to one-third of the total number of shares the original partners purchased. The corporation will acquire all the partnership's assets, assume its liabilities, and employ the original partners and the new investor.

Required

a. Discuss the differences in accounts used and valuations expected in comparing the balance sheets of the proposed corporation and the partnership.

b. Discuss the differences that would be expected in a comparison of the income statements of the proposed corporation with that of the partnership.

*Indicates that the item relates to "Additional Considerations."

LO 16-1

C16-4 Sharing Losses during Liquidation

Research

Hiller, Luna, and Welsh are attempting to form a partnership to operate a travel agency. They have agreed to share profits in a ratio of 4:3:2 but cannot settle on the terms of the partnership agreement relating to possible liquidation. Hiller believes that it is best not to get into any arguments about potential liquidation now because the partnership will be a success and it is not necessary to think negatively now. Luna believes that in the event of liquidation, any losses should be shared equally because each partner would have worked equally for the partnership's success, or lack thereof. Welsh believes that any losses during liquidation should be distributed in the ratio of capital balances at the beginning of any liquidation because then the losses will be distributed based on a capital ability to bear the losses.

You have been asked to help resolve the differences and to prepare a memo to the three individuals including the following items.

Required

a. Specify the procedures for allocating losses among partners stated in the Uniform Partnership Act of 1997 to be used if no partnership agreement terms are agreed upon regarding liquidation. (You may wish to access a copy of the UPA 1997 for this requirement.)

b. Critically assess each partner's viewpoint, discussing the pros and cons of each.

c. Specify another option for allocating potential liquidation losses not included in the positions the three individuals currently take. Critically assess the pros and cons of your alternative.

LO 16-1

C16-5 Analysis of a Court Decision on a Partnership Liquidation

Application

The *Mattfield v. Kramer Brothers* court case presents a number of the interesting legal issues that often arise from the dissolution of a partnership. The case was heard in the Supreme Court of the State of Montana in 2005 and decided on May 31, 2005, as Case 03-796. The court's decision includes a summary of the disputes and lower court decisions.

The legal briefs that each side presented to the Supreme Court may be obtained at the State Law Library of Montana website (http://courts.mt.gov/) via "Quicklinks," "Supreme Court," "Home Page," "Opinions/Briefs Search," and then searching for case number 03-796 or a text term such as Mattfield. The briefs will then be made available.

Required

Obtain a copy of the Montana Supreme Court decision in the *Mattfield v. Kramer Brothers* case. Then answer each of the following questions regarding it.

a. Prepare a short summary of the history of the Kramer Brothers Co-Partnership from formation through the appeal to the Montana Supreme Court.

b. What type of partnership agreement existed? Recommend several provisions that you feel should have been included in a formal, written partnership agreement.

c. When the case was appealed to the Supreme Court, did Bill Kramer still have an economic interest in the partnership? Explain.

d. What legal recourse did the other partners have when Don Kramer disassociated from the partnership in 1994?

e. In February 1997, why did Don Kramer's attorney, Floyd Brower, request copies of Ray Kramer's and Doug Kramer's personal tax returns?

f. Select and discuss two key points regarding partnership liquidations that this case illustrates and that you feel are important.

EXERCISES

LO 16-2, 16-3

E16-1 Multiple-Choice Questions on Partnership Liquidations

Select the correct answer for each of the following questions.

(*Note:* The following information is for questions 1, 2, and 3.)

The balance sheet for the partnership of Joan, Charles, and Thomas, whose shares of profits and losses are 40, 50, and 10 percent, respectively is as follows:

Cash	$ 50,000	Accounts Payable	$150,000
Inventory	360,000	Joan, Capital	160,000
		Charles, Capital	45,000
		Thomas, Capital	55,000
Total Assets	$410,000	Total Liabilities & Equities	$410,000

Assume Charles is insolvent.

1. If the inventory is sold for $300,000, how much should Joan receive upon liquidation?
   a. $48,000.
   b. $100,000.
   c. $136,000.
   d. $160,000.
2. If the inventory is sold for $180,000, how much should Thomas receive upon liquidation?
   a. $28,000.
   b. $32,500.
   c. $37,000.
   d. $55,000.
3. The partnership will be liquidated in installments. As cash becomes available, it will be distributed to the partners. If inventory costing $200,000 is sold for $140,000, how much cash should be distributed to each partner at this time?

Joan	Charles	Thomas
a. $56,000	$70,000	$14,000
b. $16,000	$20,000	$ 4,000
c. $32,000	$ 0	$ 8,000
d. $20,000	$ 0	$20,000

4. In accounting for partnership liquidation, cash payments to partners after all creditors' claims have been satisfied but before the final cash distribution should be according to
   a. The partners' relative profit and loss–sharing ratios.
   b. The final balances in partner capital accounts.
   c. The partners' relative share of the gain or loss on liquidations.
   d. Safe payments computations.
5. After all noncash assets have been converted into cash in the liquidation of the Adam and Kay Partnership, the ledger contains the following account balances:

	Debit	Credit
Cash	$47,000	
Accounts Payable		$32,000
Loan Payable to Adam		15,000
Adam, Capital	7,000	
Kay, Capital		7,000

Available cash should be distributed with $32,000 going to accounts payable and then
   a. $15,000 to the loan payable to Adam.
   b. $7,500 each to Adam and Kay.
   c. $8,000 to Adam and $7,000 to Kay.
   d. $7,000 to Adam and $8,000 to Kay.

(*Note:* The following information is for questions 6 and 7.)

F, A, S, and B are partners sharing profits and losses equally. The insolvent partnership is to be liquidated. The status of the partnership and each partner is as follows:

	Partnership Capital Balance	Personal Assets (exclusive of partnership interest)	Personal Liabilities (exclusive of partnership interest)
F	$(15,000)	$100,000	$40,000
A	(10,000)	30,000	60,000
S	20,000[a]	80,000	5,000
B	30,000[a]	1,000	28,000
Total	$ 25,000[a]		

[a] Deficit

6. The partnership creditors
   - *a.* Must first seek recovery against S because she is personally solvent and has a negative capital balance.
   - *b.* Will *not* be paid in full regardless of how they proceed legally because the partnership assets are less than its liabilities.
   - *c.* Will have to share A's interest in the partnership on a pro rata basis with A's personal creditors.
   - *d.* Have first claim to the partnership assets before any partner's personal creditors have rights to those assets.
7. The partnership creditors should seek recovery of their claims
   - *a.* From the partnership, including additional contributions from F and S.
   - *b.* From the personal assets of either F or A.
   - *c.* From the personal assets of either S or B.
   - *d.* From the personal assets of any of the partners for all or some of their claims.

LO 16-3

E16-2 Multiple-Choice Questions on Partnership Liquidation [AICPA Adapted]

Select the correct answer for each of the following questions.

1. On January 1, 20X7, the partners of Casey, Dithers, and Edwards, who share profits and losses in the ratio of 5:3:2, decided to liquidate their partnership. On this date, its condensed balance sheet was as follows:

Assets		Liabilities and Capital	
Cash	$ 50,000	Liabilities	$ 60,000
Other Assets	250,000	Casey, Capital	80,000
		Dithers, Capital	90,000
		Edwards, Capital	70,000
Total	$300,000	Total	$300,000

On January 15, 20X7, the first cash sale of other assets with a carrying amount of $150,000 realized $120,000. Safe installment payments to the partners were made on the same date. How much cash should be distributed to each partner?

	Casey	Dithers	Edwards
a.	$15,000	$51,000	$44,000
b.	$40,000	$45,000	$35,000
c.	$55,000	$33,000	$22,000
d.	$60,000	$36,000	$24,000

2. In a partnership liquidation, the final cash distribution to the partners should be made in accordance with the
   - *a.* Partners' profit and loss–sharing ratio.
   - *b.* Balances of the partners' capital accounts.

c. Ratio of the capital contributions by the partners.

d. Ratio of capital contributions less withdrawals by the partners.

(*Note:* The following information is for questions 3 through 5.)

The balance sheet for the Art, Blythe, and Cooper Partnership is as follows. Figures shown parenthetically reflect agreed profit and loss–sharing percentages.

Assets		Liabilities and Capital	
Cash	$ 20,000	Liabilities	$ 50,000
Other Assets	180,000	Art, Capital (40%)	37,000
		Blythe, Capital (40%)	65,000
		Cooper, Capital (20%)	48,000
Total	$200,000	Total	$200,000

3. If the firm, as shown on the balance sheet, is dissolved and liquidated by selling assets in installments and if the first sale of noncash assets having a book value of $90,000 realizes $50,000 and all cash available after settlement with creditors is distributed, the respective partners would receive (to the nearest dollar)

	Art	Blythe	Cooper
a.	$8,000	$ 8,000	$ 4,000
b.	$6,667	$ 6,667	$ 6,666
c.	$ 0	$13,333	$ 6,667
d.	$ 0	$ 3,000	$17,000

4. If the facts are as in question 3 except that $3,000 cash is to be withheld, the respective partners would then receive (to the nearest dollar)

	Art	Blythe	Cooper
a.	$6,800	$ 6,800	$ 3,400
b.	$5,667	$ 5,667	$ 5,666
c.	$ 0	$11,333	$ 5,667
d.	$ 0	$ 1,000	$16,000

5. If each partner properly received some cash in the distribution after the second sale, if the cash to be distributed amounts to $12,000 from the third sale, and if unsold assets with an $8,000 book value remain, ignoring questions 3 and 4, the respective partners would receive

	Art	Blythe	Cooper
a.	$ 4,800	$ 4,800	$ 2,400
b.	$ 4,000	$ 4,000	$ 4,000
c.	37/150 of $12,000	65/150 of $12,000	48/150 of $12,000
d.	$ 0	$ 8,000	$ 4,000

6. The following condensed balance sheet is for the partnership of Arnie, Bart, and Kurt, who share profits and losses in the ratio of 4:3:3, respectively:

Assets		Liabilities and Capital	
Cash	$100,000	Liabilities	$150,000
Other Assets	300,000	Arnie, Capital	40,000
		Bart, Capital	180,000
		Kurt, Capital	30,000
Total	$400,000	Total	$400,000

The partners agreed to dissolve the partnership after selling the other assets for $200,000. On dissolution of the partnership, Arnie should receive

a. $0.
b. $40,000.
c. $60,000.
d. $70,000.

LO 16-2

E16-3 Computing Alternative Cash Distributions to Partners

Bracken, Louden, and Menser, who share profits and losses in a ratio of 4:3:3, respectively are partners in a home decorating business that has not been able to generate the income the partners had hoped for. They have decided to liquidate the business and have sold all assets except for their decorating equipment. All partnership liabilities have been settled and all the partners are personally insolvent. The decorating equipment has a book value of $40,000, and the partners have capital account balances as follows:

Bracken, capital	$25,000
Louden, capital	5,000
Menser, capital	10,000

Required

Determine the amount of cash each partner will receive as a liquidating distribution if the decorating equipment is sold for the amount stated in each of the following independent cases:

a. $30,000.
b. $21,000.
c. $7,000.

LO 16-2

Advanced StudyGuide .com

E16-4 Lump-Sum Liquidation

Matthews, Mitchell, and Michaels are partners in BG Land Development Company and share losses in a 5:3:2 ratio, respectively. The balance sheet on June 30, 20X1, when they decide to liquidate the business, is as follows:

Assets		Liabilities and Capital	
Cash	$ 20,000	Accounts Payable	$ 30,000
Noncash Assets	150,000	Mitchell, Loan	10,000
		Matthews, Capital	80,000
		Mitchell, Capital	36,000
		Michaels, Capital	14,000
Total Assets	$170,000	Total Liabilities & Equities	$170,000

The noncash assets are sold for $110,000.

Required

a. Prepare a statement of partnership realization and liquidation.
b. Prepare the required journal entries to account for the liquidation of BG Land Development Company.

LO 16-3

E16-5 Schedule of Safe Payments

After working for In the Kitchen remodeling business for several years, Terry and Phyllis decided to go into business for themselves and formed the Kitchens Just for You Partnership. Three years ago, they admitted Connie as a partner and recognized goodwill at that time because of her good client list for planned kitchen makeovers. However, they were not able to gain a sufficient market for new customers and on September 1, 20X9, they agreed to dissolve and liquidate the business. They decided on an installment liquidation to complete the projects already initiated.

The balance sheet, with profit and loss–sharing percentages at the beginning of liquidation, is as follows:

KITCHENS JUST FOR YOU
Balance Sheet
September 1, 20X9

Assets		Liabilities and Equities	
Cash	$ 12,000	Accounts Payable	$ 43,000
Receivables	63,000	Connie, Loan	15,000
Terry, Loan	9,000	Terry, Capital (30%)	12,000
Inventory	48,000	Phyllis, Capital (50%)	36,000
Goodwill	28,000	Connie, Capital (20%)	54,000
Total Assets	$160,000	Total Liabilities & Equities	$160,000

Connie's loan was for working capital; the loan to Terry was for his unexpected personal medical bills.

During September 20X9, the first month of liquidation, the partnership collected $41,000 in receivables and decided to write off $12,000 of the remaining receivables. Sales of one-half of the book value of the inventory realized a loss of $4,000. The partners estimate that the costs of liquidating the business (newspaper ads, signs, etc.), are expected to be $6,000 for the remainder of the liquidation process.

Required

Prepare a schedule of safe payments to partners as of September 30, 20X9, to show how the available cash should be distributed to the partners.

LO 16-3

Advanced StudyGuide .com

E16-6 Schedule of Safe Payments to Partners

Partners Maness and Joiner have decided to liquidate their business. The ledger shows the following account balances:

Cash	$ 25,000	Accounts Payable	$15,000
Inventory	120,000	Maness, Capital	65,000
		Joiner, Capital	65,000

Maness and Joiner share profits and losses in an 8:2 ratio. During the first month of liquidation, half the inventory was sold for $40,000, and $10,000 of the accounts payable was paid. During the second month, the rest of the inventory was sold for $30,000, and the remaining accounts payable were paid. Cash was distributed at the end of each month, and the liquidation was completed at the end of the second month.

Required

Prepare a statement of partnership realization and liquidation with a schedule of safe payments for the two-month liquidation period.

LO 16-2

E16-7 Alternative Profit and Loss–Sharing Ratios in a Partnership Liquidation

Nelson, Osman, Peters, and Quincy have decided to terminate their partnership because of recurrent arguments among the partners. The partnership's balance sheet when they decide to wind up follows:

Cash	$ 17,000	Accounts Payable	$ 12,000
Noncash Assets	190,000	Nelson, Capital	15,000
		Osman, Capital	75,000
		Peters, Capital	75,000
		Quincy, Capital	30,000
Total Assets	$207,000	Total Liabilities & Equities	$207,000

During the winding-up of the partnership, the other assets were sold for $100,000 and the accounts payable were paid. Osman and Peters are personally solvent, but Nelson and Quincy are personally insolvent.

Required

Determine the amount of cash each partner will receive from the final distributions of the partnership for each of the following independent cases of profit and loss ratios for Nelson, Osman, Peters, and Quincy respectively, *a.* The partners share profits and losses in the ratio of 3:3:2:2.

b. The partners share profits and losses in the ratio of 3:1:3:3.

c. The partners share profits and losses in the ratio of 3:1:2:4.

LO 16-2

E16-8 Cash Distribution Plan

Adams, Peters, and Blake share profits and losses for their APB Partnership in a ratio of 2:3:5. When they decide to liquidate, the balance sheet is as follows:

Assets		Liabilities and Equities	
Cash	$ 40,000	Liabilities	$ 50,000
Adams, Loan	10,000	Adams, Capital	55,000
Other Assets	200,000	Peters, Capital	75,000
		Blake, Capital	70,000
Total Assets	$250,000	Total Liabilities & Equities	$250,000

Liquidation expenses are expected to be negligible. No interest accrues on loans with partners after termination of the business.

Required

Prepare a cash distribution plan for the APB Partnership.

LO 16-3

E16-9 Confirmation of Cash Distribution Plan

Refer to the data in exercise E16-8. During the liquidation process for the APB Partnership, the following events occurred:

1. During the first month of liquidation, noncash assets with a book value of $85,000 were sold for $65,000, and $21,000 of the liabilities were paid.
2. During the second month, the remaining noncash assets were sold for $79,000. The loan receivable from Adams was collected, and the rest of the creditors were paid.
3. Cash is distributed to partners at the end of each month.

Required

Prepare a statement of partnership realization and liquidation with a schedule of safe payments to partners for the liquidation period.

LO 16-3

E16-10* Incorporation of a Partnership

When Alice and Betty decided to incorporate their partnership, its trial balance was as follows:

	Debit	Credit
Cash	$ 8,000	
Accounts Receivable (net)	22,400	
Inventory	36,000	
Equipment (net)	47,200	
Accounts Payable		$ 17,200
Alice, Capital (60%)		62,400
Betty, Capital (40%)		34,000
Total	$113,600	$113,600

The partnership's books will be closed, and new books will be used for A & B Corporation. The following additional information is available:

1. The estimated fair values of the assets follow:

Accounts Receivable	$21,600
Inventory	32,800
Equipment	40,000

*Indicates that the item relates to "Additional Considerations."

2. All assets and liabilities are transferred to the corporation.
3. The common stock is $10 par. Alice and Betty receive a total of 7,100 shares.
4. The partners' profit and loss–sharing ratio is shown in the trial balance.

Required

a. Prepare the entries on the partnership's books to record (1) the revaluation of assets, (2) the transfer of the assets to A & B Corporation and the receipt of the common stock, and (3) the closing of the books.

b. Prepare the entries on A & B Corporation's books to record the assets and the issuance of the common stock.

LO 16-3 E16-11A Multiple-Choice on Personal Financial Statements [AICPA Adapted]

Select the correct answer for each of the following questions:

1. On December 31, 20X7, Judy is a fully vested participant in a company-sponsored pension plan. According to the plan's administrator, Judy has at that date the nonforfeitable right to receive a lump sum of $100,000 on December 28, 20X8. The discounted amount of $100,000 is $90,000 at December 31, 20X7. The right is not contingent on Judy's life expectancy and requires no future performance on her part. In her December 31, 20X7, personal statement of financial condition, the vested interest in the pension plan should be reported at

   a. $0.
   b. $90,000.
   c. $95,000.
   d. $100,000.

2. On December 31, 20X7, Mr. and Mrs. McManus owned a parcel of land held as an investment. They had purchased it for $95,000 in 20X0, and the mortgage on it had a principal balance of $60,000 at December 31, 20X7. On this date, the land's fair value was $150,000. In the McManuses' December 31, 20X7, personal statement of financial condition, at what amount should the land investment and mortgage payable be reported?

	Land Investment	Mortgage Payable
a.	$150,000	$60,000
b.	$ 95,000	$60,000
c.	$ 90,000	$ 0
d.	$ 35,000	$ 0

3. Rich Drennen's personal statement of financial condition at December 31, 20X6, shows net worth of $400,000 before consideration of employee stock options owned on that date. Information relating to the stock options is as follows:

   - Options are to purchase 10,000 shares of Oglesby Corporation stock.
   - Options' exercise price is $10 a share.
   - Options expire on June 30, 20X7.
   - Market price of the stock is $25 a share on December 31, 20X6.
   - The exercise of the options in 20X7 would result in ordinary income taxable at 35 percent.

   After giving effect to the stock options, Drennen's net worth at December 31, 20X6, would be

   a. $497,500.
   b. $550,000.
   c. $562,500.
   d. $650,000.

"A" indicates that the item relates to Appendix 16A.

4. Nancy Emerson owns 50 percent of the common stock of Marks Corporation. She paid $25,000 for this stock in 20X3. At December 31, 20X8, her 50 percent stock ownership in Marks had a current value of $185,000. Marks's cumulative net income and cash dividends declared for the five years ended December 31, 20X8, were $300,000 and $30,000 respectively. In Nancy's personal statement of financial condition at December 31, 20X8, what amount should she report as her net investment in Marks?
   a. $25,000.
   b. $160,000.
   c. $175,000.
   d. $185,000.

5. In a personal statement of financial condition, which of the following should be reported at estimated current values?

	Investments in Closely Held Business	Investments in Leaseholds
a.	Yes	Yes
b.	Yes	No
c.	No	No
d.	No	Yes

6. Personal financial statements should include which of the following statements?

	Financial Condition	Changes in Net Worth	Cash Flows
a.	No	Yes	Yes
b.	Yes	No	No
c.	Yes	Yes	No
d.	Yes	Yes	Yes

7. A business interest that constitutes a large part of an individual's total assets should be presented in a personal statement of financial condition as
   a. A single amount equal to the proprietorship equity.
   b. A single amount equal to the estimated current value of the business interest.
   c. A separate list of the individual assets and liabilities, at cost.
   d. Separate line items of both total assets and total liabilities, at cost.

8. Personal financial statements should report assets and liabilities at
   a. Historical cost.
   b. Historical cost and, as additional information, at estimated current values at the date of the financial statements.
   c. Estimated current values at the date of the financial statements.
   d. Estimated current values at the date of the financial statements and, as additional information, at historical cost.

9. The following information pertains to Kent's marketable equity securities:

	Fair Value at December 31		
Stock	**20X3**	**20X2**	**Cost in 20X0**
City Manufacturing Inc.	$95,500	$93,000	$89,900
Tri Corporation	3,400	5,600	3,600
Zee Inc.		10,300	15,000

Kent sold the Zee stock in January 20X3 for $10,200. In his personal statement of financial condition at December 31, 20X3, what amount should he report for marketable equity securities?

a. $93,300.
b. $93,500.
c. $94,100.
d. $98,900.

10. Personal financial statements should report an investment in life insurance at the
    a. Face amount of the policy less the amount of premiums paid.
    b. Cash value of the policy less the amount of any loans against it.
    c. Cash value of the policy less the amount of premiums paid.
    d. Face amount of the policy less the amount of any loans against it.

11. Mrs. Taft owns a $150,000 insurance policy on her husband's life. The policy's cash value is $125,000, and there is a $50,000 loan against it. The Tafts' personal statement of financial condition at December 31, 20X3, should show what amount as an investment in life insurance?
    a. $150,000.
    b. $125,000.
    c. $100,000.
    d. $75,000.

LO 16-3 **E16-12A** **Personal Financial Statements**

Leonard and Michelle have asked you to prepare their statement of changes in net worth for the year ended August 31, 20X3. They have prepared the following comparative statement of financial condition based on estimated current values as required by **ASC 274:**

LEONARD AND MICHELLE
Statement of Financial Condition
August 31, 20X3 and 20X2

		20X3		20X2
Assets				
Cash		$ 3,600		$ 6,700
Marketable securities		4,900		16,300
Residence		94,800		87,500
Personal effects		10,000		10,000
Cash surrender value of life insurance		3,200		5,600
Investment in farm business:				
Farmland	$42,000		$32,100	
Farm equipment	22,400		9,000	
Note payable on farm equipment	(10,000)		0	
Net investment in farm		54,400		41,100
Total assets		$170,900		$167,200
Liabilities & Net Worth				
Credit card		$ 2,400		$ 1,500
Income taxes payable		11,400		12,400
Mortgage payable on residence		71,000		76,000
Estimated income taxes on the difference between the estimated current values of assets & liabilities and their tax bases		19,700		16,500
Net worth		66,400		60,800
Total liabilities & net worth		$170,900		$167,200

Additional Information

1. Leonard and Michelle's total salaries during the fiscal year ended August 31, 20X3, were $44,300; farm income was $6,700; personal expenditures were $43,500; and interest and dividends received were $1,400.

2. They purchased marketable securities in 20X1 at a cost of $11,000 and with a market value of $11,000 on August 31, 20X2, and sold them on March 1, 20X3, for $10,700. Leonard and Michelle neither purchased nor sold additional marketable securities during the fiscal year.
3. The values of the residence and farmland are based on year-end appraisals.
4. On August 31, 20X3, Leonard purchased a used combine at a cost of $14,000. He made a $4,000 down payment and signed a five-year, 10 percent note payable for the $10,000 balance owed. He did not purchase or sell other farm equipment during the fiscal year.
5. The cash surrender value of the life insurance policy increased during the fiscal year by $1,600. However, Leonard had borrowed $4,000 against the policy on September 1, 20X2. Interest at 15 percent for this loan's first year was paid when due on August 31, 20X3.
6. Leonard and Michelle paid federal income taxes of $12,400 during the 20X3 fiscal year.
7. Mortgage payments made during the year totaled $9,000, which included payments of principal and interest.

Required

Using the comparative statement of financial condition and additional information provided, prepare the statement of changes in net worth for the year ended August 31, 20X3. (*Hint:* It will be helpful to use T-accounts to determine several realized and unrealized amounts. An analysis of the cash, personal effects, and credit card accounts should not be required to properly complete the statement.)

PROBLEMS

LO 16-2 **P16-13** **Lump-Sum Liquidation**

Advanced StudyGuide .com

The CDG Carlos, Dan, and Gail Partnership has decided to liquidate as of December 1, 20X6. A balance sheet on the date follows:

CDG PARTNERSHIP
Balance Sheet
At December 1, 20X6

Assets		
Cash		$ 25,000
Accounts Receivable (net)		75,000
Inventories		100,000
Property, Plant & Equipment (net)		300,000
Total Assets		$500,000
Liabilities & Capital		
Liabilities:		
Accounts Payable		$270,000
Capital:		
Carlos, Capital	$120,000	
Dan, Capital	50,000	
Gail, Capital	60,000	
Total Capital		230,000
Total Liabilities & Capital		$500,000

Additional Information

1. Each partner's personal assets (excluding partnership capital interests) and personal liabilities as of December 1, 20X6, follow:

	Carlos	Dan	Gail
Personal assets	$250,000	$300,000	$350,000
Personal liabilities	(230,000)	(240,000)	(325,000)
Personal net worth	$ 20,000	$ 60,000	$ 25,000

2. Carlos, Dan, and Gail share profits and losses in the ratio 20:40:40.
3. CDG sold all noncash assets on December 10, 20X6, for $260,000.

Required

a. Prepare a statement of realization and liquidation for the CDG Partnership on December 10, 20X6.

b. Prepare a schedule of the net worth of each of the three partners as of December 10, 2006, after the partnership liquidation is completed.

LO 16-3

P16-14 Installment Liquidation [AICPA Adapted]

Advanced StudyGuide .com

On January 1, 20X1, partners Art, Bru, and Chou, who share profits and losses in the ratio of 5:3:2, respectively, decide to liquidate their partnership. The partnership trial balance at this date follows:

	Debit	Credit
Cash	$ 18,000	
Accounts Receivable	66,000	
Inventory	52,000	
Machinery & Equipment (net)	189,000	
Accounts Payable		$ 53,000
Art, Capital		88,000
Bru, Capital		110,000
Chou, Capital		74,000
Total	$325,000	$325,000

The partners plan a program of piecemeal conversion of assets to minimize liquidation losses. All available cash, less an amount retained to provide for future expenses, is to be distributed to the partners at the end of each month. A summary of the liquidation transactions follows:

January 20X1

1. Collected $51,000 on accounts receivable; the balance is uncollectible.
2. Received $38,000 for the entire inventory.
3. Paid $2,000 liquidation expenses.
4. Paid $50,000 to creditors, after offset of a $3,000 credit memorandum received on January 11, 20X1.
5. Retained $10,000 cash in the business at the end of the month for potential unrecorded liabilities and anticipated expenses.

February 20X1

6. Paid $4,000 liquidation expenses.
7. Retained $6,000 cash in the business at the end of the month for potential unrecorded liabilities and anticipated expenses.

March 20X1

8. Received $146,000 on sale of all items of machinery and equipment.
9. Paid $5,000 liquidation expenses.
10. Retained no cash in the business.

Required

Prepare a statement of partnership liquidation for the partnership with schedules of safe payments to partners.

LO 16-3

P16-15 Cash Distribution Plan

Advanced StudyGuide .com

The Pen, Evan, and Torves Partnership has asked you to assist in winding-up its business affairs. You compile the following information.

1. The partnership's trial balance on June 30, 20X1, is

	Debit	Credit
Cash	$ 6,000	
Accounts Receivable (net)	22,000	
Inventory	14,000	
Plant & Equipment (net)	99,000	
Accounts Payable		$ 17,000
Pen, Capital		55,000
Evan, Capital		45,000
Torves, Capital		24,000
Total	$141,000	$141,000

2. The partners share profits and losses as follows: Pen, 50 percent; Evan, 30 percent; and Torves, 20 percent.
3. The partners are considering an offer of $100,000 for the firm's accounts receivable, inventory, and plant and equipment as of June 30. The $100,000 will be paid to creditors and the partners in installments, the number and amounts of which are to be negotiated.

Required

Prepare a cash distribution plan as of June 30, 20X1, showing how much cash each partner will receive if the partners accept the offer to sell the assets.

LO 16-3

P16-16 Installment Liquidation

Refer to the facts in Problem 16-15. The partners have decided to liquidate their partnership by installments instead of accepting the $100,000 offer. Cash is distributed to the partners at the end of each month. A summary of the liquidation transactions follows:

July

1. Collected $16,500 on accounts receivable; balance is uncollectible.
2. Received $10,000 for the entire inventory.
3. Paid $1,000 liquidation expense.
4. Paid $17,000 to creditors.
5. Retained $8,000 cash in the business at the end of the month.

August

6. Paid $1,500 in liquidation expenses.
7. As part payment of his capital, Torves accepted an item of special equipment that he developed, which had a book value of $4,000. The partners agreed that a value of $10,000 should be placed on this item for liquidation purposes.
8. Retained $2,500 cash in the business at the end of the month.

September

9. Received $75,000 on sale of remaining plant and equipment.
10. Paid $1,000 liquidation expenses, retaining no cash in the business.

Required

Prepare a statement of partnership realization and liquidation with supporting schedules of safe payments to partners.

LO 16-3

P16-17 Installment Liquidation

The DSV Partnership decided to liquidate as of June 30, 20X5. Its balance sheet as of this date follows:

DSV PARTNERSHIP
Balance Sheet
At June 30, 20X5

Assets		
Cash		$ 50,000
Accounts Receivable (net)		95,000
Inventories		75,000
Property, Plant & Equipment (net)		500,000
Total Assets		$720,000
Liabilities & Partners' Capital		
Liabilities:		
Accounts Payable		$405,000
Partners' Capital:		
D, Capital	$100,000	
S, Capital	140,000	
V, Capital	75,000	
Total Capital		315,000
Total Liabilities & Capital		$720,000

Additional Information

1. The personal assets (excluding partnership loan and capital interests) and personal liabilities of each partner as of June 30, 20X5, follow:

	D	S	V
Personal assets	$250,000	$450,000	$300,000
Personal liabilities	(270,000)	(420,000)	(240,000)
Personal net worth	$ (20,000)	$ 30,000	$ 60,000

2. The DSV Partnership was liquidated during the months of July, August, and September. The assets sold and the amounts realized follow:

Month	Assets Sold	Carrying Amount	Amount Realized
July	Inventories	$ 50,000	$ 45,000
	Accounts receivable (net)	60,000	40,000
	Property, plant & equipment	400,000	305,000
August	Inventories	25,000	18,000
	Accounts receivable (net)	10,000	4,000
September	Accounts receivable (net)	25,000	10,000
	Property, plant & equipment	100,000	45,000

Required

Prepare a statement of partnership realization and liquidation for the DSV Partnership for the three-month period ended September 30, 20X5. D, S, and V share profits and losses in the ratio 50:30:20, respectively. The partners wish to distribute available cash at the end of each month after reserving $10,000 of cash at the end of both July and August to meet unexpected liquidation expenses. Actual liquidation expenses incurred and paid each month amounted to $2,500. Support each cash distribution to the partners with a schedule of safe installment payments.

LO 16-3

P16-18 Cash Distribution Plan

Refer to the information in problem 16-17. Assume the following cash amounts were received during the months of July, August, and September from the sale of DSV Partnership's noncash assets:

July	$390,000
August	22,000
September	55,000

The partnership wishes to keep $10,000 of cash on hand at the end of both July and August to pay for unexpected liquidation expenses.

It paid liquidation expenses of $2,500 at the end of each month, July, August, and September.

Required

a. Prepare a statement as of June 30, 20X5, showing how cash will be distributed among partners as it becomes available.

b. Prepare schedules showing how cash is distributed at the end of July, August, and September 20X5.

LO 16-1–16-3

P16-19 Matching Terms

Match the items in the left-hand column with the descriptions/explanations in the right-hand column.

Items	Descriptions/Explanations
1. Dissolution	A. Sale of partnership assets, payment of its creditors, and distribution of any remaining assets to partners.
2. Partner's loss absorption potential	B. Allocation to other partners in their profit and loss–sharing ratio if the partner is personally insolvent.
3. Liquidation	C. Schedule that shows how cash is to be distributed as it becomes available during liquidation process.
4. Statement of partnership realization and liquidation	D. Amount computed by dividing a partner's capital balance by that partner's loss-sharing ratio.
5. Installment liquidation	E. Revaluation of a partnership's assets and liabilities to their market values.
6. Cash distribution plan	F. Change in the legal relationship between partners.
7. Incorporation of a partnership	G. End of the normal business function of the partnership.
8. Partner's deficit in capital	H. Liquidation in which all assets are converted into cash over a short time period, enabling all creditors to be paid, with any remaining cash being distributed according to the partners' capital balance.
9. Lump-sum liquidation	I. Cash payments to partners computed on the assumption that all noncash assets will be sold for nothing.
10. Safe payments to partners	J. Presentation, in worksheet form, of the effects of the liquidation process on the balance sheet accounts of the partnership.
	K. Liquidation in which cash is periodically distributed to partners during the liquidation process.

LO 16-1

P16-20 Partnership Agreement Issues [AICPA Adapted]

A partnership involves an association between two or more persons to carry on a business as co-owners for profit. Items 1 through 10 relate to partnership agreements.

The statement of facts for Parts A and B are followed by numbered sentences that state legal conclusions relating to those facts. Determine whether each legal conclusion is correct or not and mark it with the letter Y for yes, correct, or N for no, not correct.

Part A

Adams, Webster, and Coke were partners in a construction business. Coke decided to retire and found Black, who agreed to purchase his interest. Black was willing to pay Coke $20,000 and promised to assume Coke's share of all firm obligations.

Required (Use Y for yes and N for no)

1. Unless the partners agree to admit Black as a partner, she could not become a member of the firm.
2. The retirement of Coke would cause a dissolution of the firm.
3. The firm's creditors are third-party beneficiaries of Black's promise to Coke.
4. If Black purchased Coke's interest and promised to pay his share of the firm's debts, Coke would be released from all liability for those debts.
5. If the other partners refused to accept Black as a partner, Coke could retire, thereby causing a dissolution.

Part B

Carson, Crocket, and Kitt were partners in an importing business. They needed additional capital to expand and located White who agreed to purchase a one-quarter interest in the partnership by contributing $50,000 in capital. Before White became a partner, several creditors had loaned money to the partnership. The partnership subsequently failed, and the creditors are now attempting to assert personal liability against White.

Required (Use Y for yes and N for no)

6. White is personally liable on all of the firm's debts contracted subsequent to his entry into the firm.
7. Creditors of the partnership prior to White's admission automatically continue to be creditors of the partnership after the admission of the new partner.
8. Creditors of the partnership that existed prior to White's entry can assert rights against his capital contribution.
9. White has personal liability for firm debts existing prior to his entry into the firm.
10. White must remain in the partnership for at least one year to be subject to personal liability.

17 Governmental Entities: Introduction and General Fund Accounting

Multicorporate Entities

Multinational Entities

Reporting Requirements

Partnerships

Governmental and Not-for-Profit Entities

Governmental Entities

Special Funds

Not-For-Profit

Corporations in Financial Difficulty

ACCOUNTING FOR THE BUSTLING CITY OF SAN DIEGO

The City of San Diego, California, is one of the most popular places to visit in the United States. The city has everything from beaches, lakes, and parks to a world-class zoo and pro sports teams. Because of its beauty and nearly perfect climate, San Diego is a popular location for visitors to hold meetings and conventions year-round. It is also a very desirable place to live and work. With a population of 1.33 million, it is the eighth-largest city in the United States and the second-largest in California.

Have you ever considered what it takes to run a city of this size and diversity? In addition to maintaining the popular tourist attractions such as beaches and parks, the city manages public pools, a cemetery, libraries, public transportation, youth recreation programs, law enforcement, emergency services, public utilities, airports, social services, schools, and countless other activities. To facilitate all of these programs, services, and activities, San Diego City has a long list of departments from Police to Lifeguard Services and from Engineering to Environmental Services, to name a few. Naturally, the city has to report on its stewardship of these many activities, services, and programs to its citizens. This chapter and Chapter 18 explore the financial reporting aspects of governmental units such as San Diego City, San Diego County, and the State of California.

Each of the 50 states follows relatively uniform accounting standards; however, some states have unique statutory provisions for selected items. Local governments are political subdivisions of state government. The 89,000-plus local governmental units in the United States are classified as (1) general-purpose local governments, such as counties, cities, towns, villages, and townships, (2) special-purpose local governments, such as soil conservation districts, and (3) authorities and agencies, such as the Port Authority of New York and New Jersey and local housing authorities. Authorities and agencies differ from other governmental units because they typically do not have taxing power and may sell only revenue bonds, not general obligation bonds.

The first part of this chapter introduces the accounting and reporting requirements for state and local governmental units. We first discuss and illustrate the major concepts of governmental accounting. In the last part of this chapter, we present a comprehensive illustration of accounting for a city's general fund. The comprehensive illustration reviews and integrates the concepts presented in the first part of the chapter. Chapter 18 continues the comprehensive illustration to complete the discussion of state and local governmental accounting and reporting.

LEARNING OBJECTIVES

When you finish studying this chapter, you should be able to:

LO 17-1 Understand and explain the basic differences between governmental and private sector accounting.

LO 17-2 Understand and explain major concepts of governmental accounting.

LO 17-3 Understand and explain the differences between the various governmental fund types.

LO 17-4 Understand and explain basic concepts for financial reporting in governmental accounting.

LO 17-5 Understand and explain the basic differences in the measurement focus and basis of accounting between governmental and private sector accounting.

LO 17-6 Understand and explain basic budgeting concepts in governmental accounting.

LO 17-7 Make calculations and record journal entries for the general fund.

LO 17-8 Make calculations and record journal entries for basic interfund activities.

DIFFERENCES BETWEEN GOVERNMENTAL AND PRIVATE SECTOR ACCOUNTING

LO 17-1

Understand and explain the basic differences between governmental and private sector accounting.

During the last decade, the combined annual spending of federal, state, and local governments exceeded $4.0 trillion. Governmental purchases of goods and services constitute approximately 20 percent of the total gross national product of the United States.[1]

Governmental entities have operating objectives that differ from those of commercial entities; therefore, governmental accounting is different from accounting for commercial enterprises. The major differences between governmental and for-profit entities are as follow:

1. Governmental accounting must recognize that governmental units collect resources and make expenditures to fulfill societal needs. Society expects governmental units to develop and maintain an infrastructure of highways, streets, and sewer and sanitation systems as well as to provide public protection, recreation, and cultural services.
2. Except for some proprietary activities such as utilities, governmental entities do not have a general profit motive. Police and fire departments do not have a profit motive; instead these units must be evaluated on their abilities to provide for society's needs.
3. Governmental operations have legal authorization for their existence, raise revenue through the power of taxation, and have mandated expenditures they must make to provide their services. The governmental accounting system must make possible the determination and demonstration of compliance with finance-related legal and contractual provisions. Governmental units are subject to extensive regulatory oversight through laws, grant restrictions, bond indentures, and a variety of other legal constraints.
4. Governmental entities use comprehensive budgetary accounting, which serves as a significant control mechanism and provides the basis for comparing actual operations against budgeted amounts. The budget is a legally established control vehicle.
5. The primary emphasis in governmental fund accounting is to measure and report on management's stewardship of the financial resources committed to the objectives of the governmental unit. Accountability for the flow of financial resources is a chief objective of governmental accounting. The managers of the governmental unit must be able to show that they are in compliance with the many legal regulations governing its operations.
6. Governmental entities typically are required to establish separate funds to carry out their various missions. Each fund is an independent accounting and fiscal entity and is responsible for using its own resources to accomplish its specific responsibilities.
7. Many fund entities do not record fixed assets or long-term debt in their funds. These fund entities record the purchase of assets such as equipment and buildings as

[1] Annual reports of the national income and product accounts, including aggregate revenues and expenditures of governmental entities, are presented in the *Survey of Current Business,* published periodically by the U.S. Department of Commerce.

expenditures of the period. The governmental unit maintains a separate record of fixed assets and long-term debt.

8. An important objective of governmental financial reporting is accountability. Governments must be able to explain and justify to citizens and to other governments the raising and using of public resources. A key element of accountability is *interperiod equity* in which it is determined whether current year revenues are sufficient to pay for services provided during that year or if future taxpayers will be required to assume burdens for services previously provided or deficits created in prior years.

HISTORY OF GOVERNMENTAL ACCOUNTING

Before 1984, the Municipal Finance Officers Association (MFOA) directed the development of accounting principles for local governmental units. In 1934, the National Committee on Municipal Accounting, a committee of the MFOA, published the first statement on local governmental accounting, *A Tentative Outline—Principles of Municipal Accounting.* In 1968, the National Committee on Governmental Accounting, the successor committee, published *Governmental Accounting, Auditing, and Financial Reporting* (GAAFR). Some governmental accountants call it the "blue book" after the color of its cover. The GAAFR is periodically updated to include the most recent governmental financial reporting standards.

In 1974, the American Institute of Certified Public Accountants (AICPA) published an industry audit guide, *Audits of State and Local Governmental Units,* stating that "except as modified in this guide, the standards outlined in the GAAFR constitute generally accepted accounting principles."[2] In March 1979, the National Council on Governmental Accounting (NCGA) issued its **Statement No. 1,** "Governmental Accounting and Financial Reporting Principles" (NCGA 1), which establishes a set of accounting principles for governmental reporting.

In 1984, the Financial Accounting Foundation created a companion group to the Financial Accounting Standards Board. The Governmental Accounting Standards Board (GASB) is now responsible for maintaining and developing accounting and reporting standards for state and local governmental entities. In **GASB 1**, released in July 1984, the GASB stated that all NCGA statements and interpretations issued and in effect on that date were accepted as generally accepted accounting principles for governmental accounting. In 1985, the GASB published a codification of the existing GAAP for state and local governments, *Codification of Governmental Accounting and Financial Reporting Standards.* The first section of the codification is virtually identical to **NCGA 1** as amended by subsequent NCGA statements. The focus of Section 2 is on the financial reporting issues for governmental entities. Sections 3 and 4 address specific balance sheet and operating statement topics. The GASB continues to publish updated codifications periodically. The codification is an authoritative source for accounting and financial reporting principles for governmental units.

A very significant change in the governmental reporting model for governmental units was required by **GASB Statement 34,** "Basic Financial Statements—and Management's Discussion and Analysis—for State and Local Governments" (GASB 34), issued in 1999. **GASB 34** establishes governmentwide financial statements to be prepared on the accrual basis of accounting and an array of fund-based financial statements. This standard also requires several new footnote and schedule disclosures that increase the transparency of governmental reporting. The GASB continues to issue new standards to meet the information needs of citizens, creditors, and other users of governmental units' financial reports.

Accounting for governmental entities is given the general name of *fund accounting* to distinguish it from accounting for commercial entities. This chapter first presents an overview of fund accounting, including accounting for typical transactions and providing required financial statements for a governmental entity. After introducing the major

[2] Committee on Governmental Accounting and Auditing, *Audits of State and Local Governmental Units* (New York: American Institute of Certified Public Accountants, 1974), pp. 8–9.

concepts of governmental accounting, we present a comprehensive illustration of accounting and financial reporting for the general fund, typically the most important fund of most governmental entities. Chapter 18 presents the accounting for a governmental entity's remaining funds and its required financial statements. The comprehensive illustration provides integrated examples of the governmental accounting and financial reporting concepts that the first part of this chapter discusses. Some students may initially find governmental accounting to be quite different from the financial accounting learned in earlier accounting courses. However, after studying the concepts and working through the comprehensive illustration, the reasons and logic for fund accounting and the content and form of governmental financial statements become more focused.

MAJOR CONCEPTS OF GOVERNMENTAL ACCOUNTING

LO 17-2

Understand and explain major concepts of governmental accounting.

Governmental entities use a fund-based accounting system in which some of the funds use a modified-accrual accounting method as opposed to the accrual method used by commercial entities. Also, the financial statements of governmental entities have a foundation in the individual funds but aggregate to a governmentwide level. The following section discusses the major concepts for governmental accounting.

Elements of Financial Statements

Concepts Statement No. 4, "Elements of Financial Statements" (CON 4), defines each of the seven elements of financial statements of state and local governments (five elements of statements of financial condition and two elements of resource flows statements.) Each definition uses the central focus of a *resource,* which is an item having a present capacity to provide, directly or indirectly, services for the governmental entity. This present service capacity may be in the form of direct provision of services as well as those items having the ability to affect cash flows in the future.

The *five elements of a statement of financial condition* are

1. *Assets.* Resources with present service capacity that the entity presently controls.
2. *Liabilities.* Present obligations to sacrifice resources that the entity has little or no discretion to avoid.
3. A *deferred outflow of resources.* A consumption of net assets that is applicable to a future reporting period.
4. A *deferred inflow of resources.* An acquisition of net assets that is applicable to a future reporting period.[3]
5. *Net position.* The residual of all other elements presented in a statement of financial condition.

The *two elements of the resource flows statements* are

1. An *outflow of resources.* A consumption of net assets that is applicable to the current reporting period.
2. An *inflow of resources.* An acquisition of net assets that is applicable to the current reporting period.

The central focus of present service capacity for defining the elements of governmental financial statements is different from the FASB's focus in its **Concepts Statement No. 6,** "Elements of Financial Statements" (CON 6). The FASB developed its definitions of the elements of financial statements based on the usefulness of financial reporting information to investors and creditors in making economic decisions for allocating scarce resources among alternative uses.

[3] GASB 55 amends the financial statement element classification of certain items previously reported as assets and liabilities to be reported as deferred outflows and inflows of resources, consistent with the definitions in Concepts Statement 4.

The GASB felt that its concepts statement provides a framework that will enhance consistency in setting future governmental accounting standards and serve as guidance for preparers and auditors when evaluating transactions that are not explicitly included in existing governmental accounting standards.

Expendability of Resources versus Capital Maintenance Objectives

The major differences between commercial and governmental accounting and reporting stem from the entities' objectives. In commercial, profit-seeking enterprises, the measurement focus is on the flow of *all economic resources* of the firm. The accrual method of accounting is used to record the revenues and expenses during a period with the purpose of measuring profitability. The company's balance sheet contains both current and noncurrent assets and liabilities, and the change in retained earnings reflects the company's ability to maintain its capital investment.

In contrast, the measurement focus for the governmental funds of a government entity is on changes in *current financial resources* available to provide services to the public in accordance with the governmental entity's legally adopted budget. The modified accrual method of accounting is used to measure the revenues that are available to finance current expenditures and the expenditures made during the period. The balance sheet reports only current assets, current liabilities, and a fund balance. The legislative governing body initiates the operating authorization for a fiscal period's transactions when it passes a budget. Managers of governmental units must be fiscally accountable to show that resources are expended in compliance with the legal and financial restrictions placed on the governmental entity by its legislative body.

In 2006, the GASB published a white paper that identified a number of key differences between financial reporting for governments and for-profit businesses.[4] The white paper argued that users of governmental financial reports and users of business financial reports require substantially different financial and economic information to evaluate fiscal and operational performance. The white paper expands on the differences stated in the preceding list and presents the GASB's perspective on the need for separate governmental accounting and financial reporting standards.

Definitions and Types of Funds

LO 17-3

Understand and explain the differences between the various governmental fund types.

Fund accounting must recognize the unique aspects of governmental operations. Governmental units must provide a large range of services such as fire and police protection, water and sewerage, legal courts, and construction of public buildings and other facilities. In addition, governmental units receive their resources from many different sources and must make expenditures in accordance with legal restrictions.

The operations of a governmental unit also must be separated into periodic reporting intervals of fiscal years because the management of these public operations may change as a result of elections or new appointments. Thus, governmental accounting must recognize the governmental unit's many different purposes, its different sources of revenue, mandated expenditures, and its fiscal periodicity. To accomplish the governmental unit's objectives, the unit establishes a variety of ***funds*** as that unit's fiscal and accounting entities. A fund is a separate accounting group with accounts to record the transactions and prepare the financial statements of a defined part of the governmental entity that is responsible for specific activities or objectives. Each fund records those transactions affecting its assets, related liabilities, and residual fund balance.

Different funds are established for the specific functions that a government must provide. Most funds obtain resources from taxes on property, income, or commercial sales; they also may obtain resources from grants provided by other governmental agencies, fines or licenses, and charges for services. Each fund must make its expenditures in accordance with its specified purposes. For example, a fund established for fire protection cannot be

[4] Governmental Accounting Standards Board, *Why Governmental Accounting and Financial Reporting Is—and Should Be—Different* (Norwalk, CT: GASB, 2006).

used to provide school buses for the local school. The fire department may make expenditures only as directly related to its function of providing fire protection.

Each governmental fund has its own asset and liability accounts and its own revenue and expenditures accounts. The term ***expenditures*** refers to decreases in net financial resources available under the current financial resources measurement focus. The governmental unit makes expenditures in accordance with its budget established by that unit's governing body, and the internal control structure of a vouchers payable system is generally used prior to paying external vendors. Upon receipt and acceptance of the goods or services from the external vendor, the journal entry to recognize the approved expenditure is a debit to expenditures and a credit to vouchers payable. The increase in the payables decreases the net financial resources available. The unit's governing body then must approve the payment of the vouchers payable.

Separate fund-based financial statements must be prepared for each fiscal period. In this manner, governing bodies or other interested parties may assess the fiscal and operating performance of each fund in fulfillment of the specific purposes for which each fund was established.

Governmental accounting systems are established on a fund basis in three major categories: governmental, proprietary, and fiduciary. Refer to Figure 17–1 for an overview of each fund and a brief description of the types of activities each fund accounts for.

Governmental Funds

Five types of ***governmental funds*** account for basic governmental services to the public. They are (1) the general fund, (2) special revenue funds, (3) capital projects funds, (4) debt service funds, and (5) permanent funds (see Figure 17–1). The number of governmental funds the entity maintains is based on its legal and operating requirements. Each governmental entity creates only one general fund, but it may create more than one of each of the other types of governmental funds based on the entity's specific needs. For example, some governmental entities establish a separate capital projects fund for each major capital project.

FYI

In its 2013 comprehensive annual financial report, the City of San Diego indicates that it has many separate capital project funds in use to separately track the financial resources dedicated to specific projects.

Proprietary Funds

Some of a governmental unit's activities, such as the operation of a public swimming pool or a municipal water system, are similar to those of commercial enterprises. The governmental unit's objective is to recover its costs in these operations through a system of user charges. The two types of ***proprietary funds*** that governmental entities typically use are enterprise funds and internal service funds (see Figure 17–1). Accounting and reporting for a proprietary fund are similar to accounting for a commercial operation. The balance sheet of each proprietary fund reports all assets, including long-term capital assets, and all liabilities, including long-term liabilities. Chapter 18 presents a complete discussion of proprietary funds.

Fiduciary Funds

The two main types of ***fiduciary funds,*** trust and agency funds, account for resources that are maintained by but do not belong to a governmental unit. Specifically, the three types of trust funds that account for financial resources maintained in trust by the government are (1) pension and other employee benefit trust funds, (2) investment trust funds, and (3) private-purpose trust funds. Agency funds are used to account for resources the government holds solely in a custodial capacity (see Figure 17–1). Note that the permanent fund, which is a governmental fund, includes resources that are legally restricted so that the entity must maintain the principal and can use only the earnings from the fund's resources to benefit the government's programs for all of its citizens. The private-purpose trust funds include trusts under which the principal may or may not be expendable but for which the trust agreement specifies that the principal, if expendable, and the earnings may be used only for the benefit of specific individuals, organizations, or other governments. Chapter 18 presents examples of fiduciary funds.

FIGURE 17–1 Fund Structure

Governmental Fund Types	
1. General fund	Accounts for all financial resources except for those accounted for in another fund. Includes transactions for general governmental services provided by the entity's executive, legislative, and judicial operations.
2. Special revenue fund	Accounts for the proceeds of specific revenue sources that are restricted for specified purposes. Includes resources and expenditures for operations, such as public libraries, when a separate tax is levied for their support.
3. Capital projects fund	Accounts for financial resources for the acquisition or construction of major capital facilities that benefit many citizens, such as parks and municipal buildings. This fund exists only during the acquisition or construction of the facilities and is closed once the project is completed.
4. Debt service fund	Accounts for the accumulation of resources for, and the payment of, general long-term debt principal and interest. This fund is used for servicing the government's long-term debt.
5. Permanent fund	Accounts for resources that are restricted such that only earnings, but not principal, may be used in support of governmental programs that benefit the government or its citizenry.
Proprietary Fund Types	
6. Enterprise fund	Accounts for operations of governmental units that charge for services provided to the general public. Includes activities financed in a manner similar to private business enterprises regarding the governing body's intent to recover the costs of providing goods or services to the general public on a continuing basis through user charges. Also includes operations that the governing body intends to operate at a profit. Examples include sports arenas, municipal electric utilities, and municipal bus companies.
7. Internal service fund	Accounts for the financing of goods or services provided by one governmental unit's department or agency to other of its departments or agencies. The services are usually provided on a cost-reimbursement basis and are offered only to other governmental agencies, not the general public. Examples are municipal motor vehicle pools, city print shops, and central purchasing operations.
Fiduciary Fund Types and Similar Component Units	
8. Trust funds	
a. Pension (and other employee benefit) trust fund	Accounts for resources required to be held in trust for the members and beneficiaries of pension plans, other postemployment benefit plans, or other employee benefit plans.
b. Investment trust fund	Accounts for the external portion of investment pools reported by the sponsoring government.
c. Private-purpose trust fund	Accounts for all other trust arrangements under which the fund's resources are to be used to benefit specific individuals, private organizations, or other governments as the trust agreement specified.
9. Agency fund	Accounts for assets held by a governmental unit in an agency capacity for employees or for other governmental units. An example is the city employees' payroll withholding for health insurance premiums.

FINANCIAL REPORTING OF GOVERNMENTAL ENTITIES[5]

LO 17-4

Understand and explain basic concepts for financial reporting in governmental accounting.

Advanced StudyGuide .com

A governmental unit may control a variety of boards, commissions, authorities, or other component units. Its financial statements are presented for the ***reporting entity,*** which consists of

1. The *primary government* such as a state government, a general-purpose local government, or a special-purpose local government that has a separately elected governmental body.
2. *Component units,* legally separate organizations for which the primary unit has financial accountability.
3. Other organizations that have a significant relationship with the primary government and need to be included in its financial statements to avoid misleading or incomplete financial representations. (We present more on these "other organizations" in Chapter 18.)

[5] To view a video explanation of this topic, visit advancedstudyguide.com.

GASB 14 states that financial accountability exists for those component units if the primary governmental unit appoints a majority of an organization's governing body and

(*a*) is able to impose its will on the organization, or

(*b*) possesses a financial benefit or assumes a financial burden for the organization.

GASB 61 modifies the definition of a component unit. For organizations that previously were required to be included as component units by meeting the fiscal dependency criterion, a financial benefit or burden relationship would also need to be present between the primary government and that organization for it to be included in the reporting entity as a component unit. Moreover, GASB 61 clarifies situations where organizations that do not meet the financial accountability criteria as a component unit should be included because the primary government's management determines that it would be misleading to exclude them.

GASB 34 specifies the use of the ***governmental financial reporting model.*** See Figure 17–2 for the names of the financial statements and the other major information **GASB 34** specifies. The reporting model has two integrated levels of financial statements.

1. The first level is the ***fund-based financial statements*** because governments continue to use fund-based accounting to record transactions in accordance with the legal or budgetary requirements established by their governing body. These fund-based financial statements demonstrate fiscal accountability of the management of each fund.
2. The second level is the ***governmentwide financial statements.*** After preparing the fund-based financial statements, the government prepares reconciliation schedules to go from the governmental fund financial statements to the governmentwide financial statements. In addition to the governmental funds, the reporting entity includes other funds in the governmentwide financial statements. These statements also include the governmental entity's capital assets, such as buildings and equipment, and long-term debt. The governmentwide financial statements demonstrate the operational accountability of the governmental unit's management as a whole.

This chapter and the first part of Chapter 18 focus on the fund-based financial statements. After completing our discussion of each fund type in Chapter 18, we present the governmentwide financial statements.

FIGURE 17–2
The Government Reporting Model

1. Independent auditors' report
2. Management's Discussion and Analysis (required supplementary information)
3. Governmentwide financial statements
   a. Statement of Net Assets
   b. Statement of Activities
4. Fund-based financial statements
   a. Governmental funds
      (1) Balance Sheet
      (2) Statement of Revenues, Expenditures, and Changes in Fund Balances
      (3) Reconciliation Schedules (of each of the two governmental fund-based statements to their related governmentwide financial statements, either at the bottom of each of the two fund-based financial statements or in an accompanying schedule)
   b. Proprietary funds
      (1) Statement of Net Assets
      (2) Statement of Revenues, Expenses, and Changes in Fund Net Assets
      (3) Statement of Cash Flows
   c. Fiduciary funds
      (1) Statement of Fiduciary Net Assets
      (2) Statement of Changes in Fiduciary Net Assets
5. Notes to the financial statements
6. Required Supplementary Information (RSI) (in addition to the MD&A)
   a. Budgetary Comparison Schedules
   b. Information about Infrastructure Assets
   c. Information about Pensions

Fund-Based Financial Statements: Governmental Funds

Two financial statements are required for governmental funds: (1) balance sheet and (2) statement of revenues, expenditures, and changes in fund balance.

Balance Sheet for Governmental Funds

The balance sheet format with added parenthetical guidance for learning assistance for each of the governmental funds is

Balance Sheet for Governmental Funds

Assets (financial resources available for current use; presented in order of liquidity)		$X,XXX
Total Assets		$X,XXX
Liabilities & Fund Balances		
Liabilities (due and expected to be paid from current financial resources; presented in order of due date)		$ XXX
Fund Balances		
Nonspendable	$XX	
Spendable:		
Restricted	XX	
Limited	XX	
Assigned	XX	
Unassigned	XX	XX
Total Liabilities & Fund Balances		$X,XXX

The five governmental funds use the ***current financial resources measurement focus.*** Under this method, the asset section of the balance sheet reports only financial assets such as cash or other assets that will convert into cash (e.g., receivables) in the normal course of operations over the near future, which has been determined to mean within 60 days after the reporting period end. Some governments report inventories or other prepayments because they save the entity from incurring future outflows of current financial resources. Long-term capital items such as equipment or buildings are not reported on the fund-based balance sheet because these amounts are no longer currently available for expenditure. However, the long-term capital assets of the governmental entity are scheduled and reported in the governmentwide financial statements as illustrated in Chapter 18.

The liability section of the balance sheet reports only those liabilities that have become due and will require current financial resources to liquidate, such as vouchers payable or the current portion of long-term debt. A short-term debt often used in governmental funds is a tax-anticipation note that represents loans obtained using future taxes as collateral. Most states restrict these borrowings to taxes that have been levied but not yet collected. Notes payable are paid from the first tax collections of the tax levy to which the notes are related. The principal of long-term debt not due within the next year is not reported on the balance sheet because it will not be settled in the near term with current financial resources. However, the governmental unit's long-term debt is scheduled and is reported in the governmentwide financial statements.

The third section of the balance sheet for the five governmental funds reports the net fund balance, which is the amount of the difference between reported assets and reported liabilities. **GASB 54** specifies that the fund balances for the governmental funds should be segregated into two categories:

1. *Nonspendable fund balances.* Amounts that are *(a)* not in spendable form, such as amounts related to inventories and prepaid items, or *(b)* required by legal or contractual provisions to be maintained intact, such as the principal of a permanent fund.
2. *Spendable fund balances.* Amounts that are available for spending. Amounts in this portion of the fund balance would be further classified as *(a)* restricted, *(b)* limited,

(c) assigned, or *(d)* unassigned. The classification would be based on an examination of requirements imposed by legal or contractual provisions and then of any constraints established by the entity's governing body.[6]

Statement of Revenues, Expenditures, and Changes in Fund Balance for Governmental Funds

This is often called the *operating statement* of the governmental funds, but the financial statements for the governmental funds use the full title. The statement of revenues, expenditures, and changes in fund balance has four major sections:

1. *Operating section.* The top section contains the revenues less expenditures for the period with the difference indicated as the excess (or deficiency) of revenues over expenditures.
2. *Other financing sources or uses.* This section includes nonrevenue items such as bond issue proceeds and interfund transfers. (Note that issuance of bonds and debt refundings of governmental long-term debt are included in the other financing sources and uses section although the long-term debt is not shown on the fund's balance sheet.)
3. *Special and extraordinary items.* This section lists extraordinary items that are both unusual and infrequent, such as losses due to a hurricane. Special items are transactions or events within management's control that are either unusual or infrequent in occurrence. An example of a special item is the one-time sale of county park land.
4. *Fund balance.* The bottom portion includes the fund balances at both the beginning and the end of the year.

The format of the statement of revenues, expenditures, and changes in fund balance, with added parenthetical guidance, is

Statement of Revenues, Expenditures, and Changes in Fund Balance	
Revenues (recognized when both measurable and available; presented by source of revenue)	$XX,XXX
Expenditures (approved decreases in net financial resources; presented by function and character)	X,XXX
Excess of Revenues over Expenditures	$ XXX
Other Financing Sources or Uses (other increases or decreases in net financial resources available, such as bond issue proceeds and interfund transfers)	XX
Special Items & Extraordinary Items	(X)
Net Change in Fund Balance	$ XX
Fund Balance—Beginning	XXX
Fund Balance—Ending (reconciles to total fund balance on balance sheet)	$ XXX

Revenues: Under the current financial resources measurement focus, revenues are recognized when they become both *measurable* and *available* to finance expenditures of the fiscal period. Profit-seeking businesses measure revenue by the accrual basis as it is earned, but the current financial resources measurement focus requires that the expected timing of the revenue-related inflow be evaluated. The word *available* means that the

[6] **GASB 54** modifies the definitions of some governmental funds to make the definitions consistent across all governmental units. Furthermore, the standard establishes a fund balance classification system for the governmental fund types. Note that this statement applies only to the governmental fund types, not to proprietary or fiduciary fund types. The governmental fund balance classification system uses a hierarchy based on the extent to which a government is required to comply with constraints placed upon the use of resources reported in governmental funds. The hierarchy separates the fund balance into nonspendable and spendable resources. Note that the statement changed only the presentation of the fund balances for the governmental funds, not the accounting.

transaction will result in financial resources collectible within the current period or soon enough thereafter to be used to pay liabilities of the current period.

Expenditures: The expenditure portion of the operating statement reports reductions in available current financial assets. Only when the governmental entity receives approved services or goods does it recognize the expenditure. Vouchers Payable or some other payable is credited when the expenditure is recognized. The increase in liabilities decreases the net financial resources still available for spending to meet the public purposes established by the governing body. Expenditures also include amounts to purchase capital assets such as trucks or buildings because they result in a net outflow of current financial assets. Note that once the expenditure has been made for a capital asset, that amount is no longer currently available to spend. Thus, although an expenditure is recognized for the purchase of a capital asset, that asset (e.g., truck) is not reported on the governmental fund's balance sheet.

Other Financing Sources and Uses: The second section of the operating statement, other financing sources and uses, reports changes in current financial resources from nonrevenue items, such as sales of bonds or interfund transfers with other funds of the governmental entity. Note that under the current financial resources focus, the proceeds from a sale of bonds are reported in the operating statement, but the long-term bond payable is not reported in the liabilities on the governmental fund's balance sheet. Interfund transfers are discussed in depth later in this chapter.

Special Items: The special items section includes unusual or infrequent items that affect the fund balance but are not revenue or expenditure items. Finally, the fund balance section indicates the change in the fund balance to obtain its ending balance, which should reconcile to the total fund balance shown on the balance sheet.

After each governmental fund prepares its financial statements, it prepares a combined balance sheet and a combined operating statement. These combined statements include all governmental funds. The format for the combined governmental funds statements is multicolumnar with a separate column for each of the major governmental funds and a separate column for the aggregated nonmajor (small) governmental funds. The columns are then added together horizontally and shown in a total column for each line item in the governmental funds. We will illustrate combined governmental financial statements in Chapter 18.

MEASUREMENT FOCUS AND BASIS OF ACCOUNTING (MFBA)

LO 17-5

Understand and explain the basic differences in the measurement focus and basis of accounting between governmental and private sector accounting.

Because the concepts of *measurement focus* and *basis of accounting* are so important in understanding accounting for the various funds of state and local governments, we first present a brief review of these two concepts. Then we provide additional detail about the accounting measurement and recognition requirements applicable to revenues and expenditures in the governmental funds.

The ***measurement focus*** refers to the flows that should be measured for operations. For example, most businesses focus on the flow of all economic resources in and out of the company whereas governmental funds focus solely on the flow of current financial resources.

The ***basis of accounting*** refers to the timing of recognizing a transaction for financial reporting purposes. In other words, the basis of accounting tells us when we should recognize transactions in the financial statements. For example, the cash basis recognizes revenue or expenditures when cash is received or paid. The accrual basis recognizes revenue or expenditures when the transaction or event takes place. The ***modified accrual basis*** is a hybrid system that includes some aspects of accrual accounting and some aspects of cash basis accounting. The modified accrual basis is used in funds that have a flow of *current financial resources measurement focus.* This measurement focus concentrates on the flow of current financial resources and their proper expendability for designated purposes and determination of the available resources remaining to be expended. Expenditures recognized under the modified accrual basis are the amounts that would

Advanced StudyGuide .com

normally be liquidated with expendable available financial resources. The five governmental funds maintain this focus.

The accrual basis is used in funds that have a flow of ***economic resources measurement focus.*** This measurement focus concerns all economic resources available to a fund during a particular time period, thereby allowing for a comparison of revenues and expenses and a focus on maintenance of capital. The proprietary funds and fiduciary funds have this focus.

In addition, as is presented in Chapter 18, the governmentwide financial statements are based on the accrual basis. This necessitates a reconciliation schedule for those items accounted for under the modified accrual basis for governmental fund accounting to obtain the accrual basis amount that is reported on the governmentwide financials. The reconciliation schedule is discussed in more detail in Chapter 18.

Basis of Accounting—Governmental Funds

The current financial resources measurement focus and the modified accrual basis of accounting are used for the governmental funds financial statements. The modified accrual basis is applied as follows:

1. *Revenue.* Recorded in the accounting period in which it is both *measurable* and *available* to finance expenditures made during the current fiscal period.
2. *Expenditures.* Recognized in the period in which the liabilities are both *measurable* and *incurred* and are payable out of current financial resources.

Measurable means that the amount of the revenue or expenditure can be objectively determined. *Available* means that income is due or past due and receivable within the current period and collected within the current period or expected to be collected soon enough thereafter to be used to pay current-period liabilities. The definition of "soon enough thereafter" has been stated for property taxes as a period of not more than 60 days after the end of the current fiscal period.

Recognition of Revenue—Exchange and Nonexchange Transactions

The accrual method of accounting recognizes revenues from exchange transactions (sales of goods or services) and from nonexchange transactions in which the government gives or receives value without directly receiving or giving equal value in exchange. Private sector accrual accounting recognizes revenue almost exclusively from exchange transactions (i.e., sales of goods or services). A government's authority to levy taxes gives it the ability to receive value without directly giving equal value in exchange. This is called *revenue from nonexchange transactions.* **GASB 33,** classifies nonexchange transactions into four categories. How revenues are recognized depends on the category. We discuss the four categories next.

1. *Derived tax revenues.* From assessments on exchange transactions. Examples are income taxes and sales taxes.
   a. The *asset (cash or receivable).* Recognized when the underlying transaction occurs or resources are received, whichever comes first.
   b. *Revenue recognition.* Depends on the accounting basis used to measure the transaction. Under accrual accounting (proprietary and fiduciary funds), revenue is recognized when the underlying exchange transaction occurs. Under modified accrual accounting (governmental funds), revenue is recognized when the underlying exchange has occurred and the resources are available.

Resources received prior to the exchange transaction is reported as deferred revenue (reported as a liability) until the revenue recognition requirement is met for the fund receiving the resources.

2. *Imposed nonexchange revenues.* From assessments on nongovernmental entities, including individuals. Examples include property taxes and fines.
   a. The *asset (cash or receivable).* Recognized when the government has an enforceable legal claim to the resources or has received them, whichever comes first.
   b. *Revenue recognition.* Made in the period when use of the resources for current expenditures is first permitted or required or when the asset is recorded if no time restriction on the fund's use of the resources exists.

Resources received or recorded as receivables prior to the period in which they can be recognized as revenue should be reported as deferred revenues.

Providers of financial resources often impose additional eligibility requirements for the next two categories. These requirements must be met before the transaction can be completed, that is, before the receiving governmental unit can recognize an asset and the associated revenue. The four types of eligibility requirements are typically (1) the recipient's characteristics as specified by the provider of the financial resources (e.g., the receiving entity must be a school district), (2) the time for expending the resources (e.g., within a specific fiscal period), (3) the reimbursements for only those costs determined to be allowable and incurred in conformity with the program, and (4) contingencies in which the recipient has met all conditions the provider stipulated. If the recipient has met all eligibility requirements the provider imposed, the provider should recognize the liability (or decrease in assets) and expense, and the recipient should recognize the receivable (or increase in assets) and revenue at that time. The two categories are as follows:

3. *Government-mandated nonexchange transactions.* From one governmental unit's provision of resources to a governmental unit at another level and the requirement that the recipient use the resources for a specific purpose. An example of this type is federal programs that state or local governments are required to perform.
4. *Voluntary nonexchange transactions.* From legislative or contractual agreements other than exchanges. Examples include certain grants and private donations.

GASB 36 amends **GASB 33** for government-mandated and voluntary nonexchange situations in which a government provides part of its own derived tax units to recipients. Typically, the government provides a periodic report of the amount of shared revenues the recipients should anticipate. **GASB 36** states that if the notification from the providing government is not available in a timely manner, the recipient government should use a reasonable estimate of the amount to be accrued, to avoid waiting to record the transaction after the actual receipt of the cash resources.

The following examples present the accounting, under the modified accrual basis of accounting as used in preparing the governmental funds financial statements.

1. *Property taxes.* Property taxes involve a series of steps that guide the recognition of the property tax asset and the property tax revenue. A typical process is as follows:

Year 1:

Step 1: Levy filed for enforceable claims to property taxes for year 1.

Step 2: Assessment notice presenting assessed value as of levy date mailed to each property owner and any appeals heard.

Step 3: Property tax bills for year 1 mailed to each property owner. (Each property's tax is based on assessed value multiplied by the tax rate that is determined based on the requirements specified in the levy request filed by each unit of government within the taxing district.)

Year 2:

Step 4: First installment of property taxes for year 1 are due.

Step 5: Second (and last) installment of property taxes for year 1 are due.

The levy creates an enforceable claim to the future collection of property taxes and a property tax receivable should be recorded at that date along with a deferred property tax revenue credit. As explained, the property tax bill is mailed to each property owner in one fiscal period and the property taxes applicable to that fiscal period are then collected in the next fiscal period. There normally is a legally imposed time restriction on the use of the property tax resources until, in this example, year 2, at which time the resources become available for expenditure. In this example, property tax revenue would not be recognized until year 2 when the time restriction is extinguished. The year 2 entry would include a debit to deferred property tax revenue and a credit to property tax revenue. Although this example presents the levy date in year 1 and the collection in year 2, some governmental entities make the levy and the collection within the same fiscal period. The key to the timing of recognizing revenue from property taxes is to determine the fiscal period in which the use of the resources for current expenditures is permitted, not necessarily when the property taxes are levied or collected.

NCGA Interpretation No. 3 specifies that property taxes must be collectible within a maximum of 60 days after the end of the current fiscal period to be recognized as revenue in that period. Taxes collectible 60 or more days after the current period ends are recorded as deferred revenue for that period and then accounted for as next period's revenue.

Revenue from another governmental unit or tax-exempt entity in lieu of taxes, such as a university's payment to a city for police and fire protection, should be accrued and recorded as revenue when it becomes billable.

Revenue from property taxes should be recorded *net* of any uncollectibles or abatements. The Property Taxes Receivable account is debited for the full amount of the taxes levied with estimated uncollectibles recorded separately in an allowance account reported as a contra account to the receivable.

2. *Interest on investments and delinquent taxes.* Interest on investments or delinquent property taxes is accrued in the period in which it is earned and available to finance that period's expenditures. The governmental funds may temporarily invest available cash in interest-generating financial instruments such as certificates of deposit and federal or state securities. Governmental entities should carefully determine the credit and market risks of possible investments to minimize their potential loss. Governmental funds report their own current and long-term financial investments and any accrued interest receivable as assets of the funds.

3. *Income taxes and sales taxes.* These derived tax revenues are recognized as assets under the modified accrual basis of accounting in the period in which the tax is imposed or when the resources are received, whichever comes first. These taxes must be available to finance expenditures made during the current fiscal period before recognition as revenue for the period. Income tax revenue should be reported net of any anticipated refunds to taxpayers. Sales taxes collected by another governmental unit (e.g., the state government) but not yet distributed should be accrued prior to receipt by the governmental unit to which they will be distributed (e.g., a city) if the taxes are both measurable and available for expenditure. Measurability in this case is based on an estimate of the sales taxes to be received, and availability is based on the ability of the governing entity (the city) to obtain current resources through credit by using future sales tax collections as collateral for the loan.

4. *Miscellaneous revenue.* Miscellaneous revenues such as license fees, fines, parking meter revenue, and charges for services are generally recorded when the cash is received because these amounts cannot be predicted accurately. Often states take custody of private property when its legal owner cannot be found as with unclaimed estates or abandoned bank accounts. The property is said to *escheat* (or revert) to the state government. The government should record the property as revenue at its fair market value less a liability for any anticipated claims from possible heirs or other claimants. States generally record the net revenue in the general fund, but some states prefer to account for these resources in a separate, private-purpose trust fund.

5. *Grants, entitlements, and shared revenue.* These resources are received from other governmental units. *Grants* are contributions from another governmental unit to be used for a specified purpose, activity, or facility. *Entitlements* are payments local governments are authorized to receive as determined by the federal government. *Shared revenue* is levied by one governmental unit but shared with others on some predetermined basis (e.g., revenue from taxes on the retail sale of gasoline collected by the state). Grants are recognized as revenue in the period in which all eligibility requirements have been met. This may be at the point the grant is authorized, but, in practice, some governmental units wait until the cash is received because the grantor might withdraw the grant. Some grants are made to reimburse a governmental unit for expenditures made in accordance with legal requirements. The revenue from such grants should be recognized only when the expenditure is made and all other eligibility requirements have been met. For example, a state government might agree to provide a grant for a local government's purchase of firefighting vehicles. Typically, the local government must meet all the grant's requirements before it receives the monies from the state government. In these cases, the local government would record the grant revenue when it is received. In a few cases, such as a state grant of reimbursement for the purchase of the firefighting vehicles, the local government may receive grant monies before all the steps of the required expenditure are completed. In those few cases, the local government may be required to record the receipt of the grant monies as an unearned revenue (liability) until all requirements have been met and the grant is expendable—at which time the unearned revenue is reclassified as earned revenue.

Proceeds from the sale of bonds are not revenue! These proceeds are reported as other financing sources on the statement of revenues, expenditures, and changes in fund balance. Although bond sales do increase the resources available for expenditure, bonds must be repaid whereas revenue of the governmental unit does not need to be repaid.

Recognition of Expenditures

Under the modified accrual basis of accounting, expenditures are recorded in the period in which the related liability is both *measurable* and *incurred.* Specific examples are as follows:

1. Costs for personal services, such as wages and salaries, are generally recorded in the period paid because they are a governmental unit's normal, recurring expenditures.
2. Goods and services obtained from outside the governmental entity are recorded as expenditures in the period in which they are received.
3. Capital outlays for equipment, buildings, and other long-term facilities are recorded as expenditures in the period of acquisition.
4. Interest on long-term debt is recorded in the period in which it is legally payable.

Basis of Accounting—Proprietary Funds

The two major proprietary funds are the internal service fund and the enterprise fund. Proprietary funds are established for governmental operations that have a management focus of income determination and capital maintenance; therefore, the accrual method as used by profit-seeking corporate entities is used to account for these funds. Proprietary funds record their own long-term assets and recognize depreciation on these assets. Long-term debt is recorded and interest is accrued as it is for commercial operations.

Basis of Accounting—Fiduciary Funds

The accrual basis of accounting is used for all fiduciary funds. Agency funds are for those resources for which the governing unit is the temporary custodian. Agency funds have only assets and liabilities; no fund equity, revenue, or expenditures are used. An example of an agency fund is a county's billing and collecting taxes on behalf of other governmental entities, such as a city and a school district. After collection is completed on the "tax roll," the county properly distributes the taxes in accordance with each governmental entity's approved levy.

For fiduciary trust funds, the economic resources measurement focus and the accrual basis of accounting are used. Note that the fiduciary trust funds include funds in which both the principal and income may be used for the benefit of specific individuals, organizations, or other governments, in accordance with the terms under which the trust fund was established. Agency and trust funds are discussed in depth in Chapter 18.

BUDGETARY ASPECTS OF GOVERNMENTAL OPERATIONS

LO 17-6

Understand and explain basic budgeting concepts in governmental accounting.

Governmental accounting uses ***budgets*** to assist in management control and to provide the legal authority to levy taxes, collect revenue, and make expenditures in accordance with the budget. A budget establishes the governmental units' objectives and priorities.

Governors propose budgets for state governments, and legislative bodies debate elements in the budgets. Governing boards such as the city council, county board, or township board hold public hearings and discussions prior to adopting the final budget. After passage, the budget usually becomes legally binding. The mayor or the major administrator may propose a local government's budget.

A governmental unit may have several types of budgets, including the following:

1. *Operating budgets.* These budgets specify expected revenue from the various sources provided by law. The operating budget includes expected expenditures for various line items, such as employee payrolls, supplies, and goods and services to be obtained from outside the governing unit. Operating budgets are used in the general fund, special revenue funds, and sometimes debt service funds.
2. *Capital budgets.* These budgets are prepared to provide information about proposed construction projects such as new buildings or street projects. Capital budgets are used in the capital projects funds.

FYI

In its fiscal 2013 budget, the City of San Diego budgeted total revenues of $1,077,794, total expenditures of $1,075,573, and total other net financing uses of ($14,948) (all numbers in thousands).

Although budgets may be prepared for proprietary funds, these budgets do not serve as a primary control vehicle. Budgets in the proprietary funds are advisory in much the same way that commercial entities use them.

Recording the Operating Budget

Budgets are such an important control vehicle that governmental funds with legally adopted annual operating budgets should enter their budgets into the formal accounting records, although capital budgets are not normally entered. Recording the operating budgets permits better management control and facilitates a year-end comparison of budgeted and actual amounts. This comparison is part of the required supplementary information for the government reporting model for the funds that must have operating budgets. A budget-to-actual comparison provides an assessment of management's stewardship of the governmental entity and allows citizens and others to determine whether the governmental entity remained within its operating budgetary limits.

To help understand the process of accounting for operating budgets, this text uses the technique illustrated in *Governmental Accounting, Auditing, and Financial Reporting* (GAAFR)[7] that identifies the budgetary accounts with all capital letters. Capitalization of the budgetary accounts clearly separates the budgetary nominal accounts from the governmental unit's operating accounts. Although budgetary accounts are not capitalized in actual practice, this convention is helpful in learning the following material.

The following example demonstrates the recording of the operating budget for the general fund. Assume that at January 1, 20X1, the first day of the new fiscal period, the city council of Barb City approves the operating budget for the general fund, providing for $900,000 in revenue and $850,000 in expenditures. Approval of the budget provides the legal authority to levy the local property taxes and to appropriate resources for the

[7] *Governmental Accounting, Auditing, and Financial Reporting* is updated periodically by the Government Finance Officers Association (Chicago).

expenditures. The term ***appropriation*** is the legal description of the authority to expend resources. The entry made in the general fund's accounting records on this date follows:

	January 1, 20X1		
(1)	ESTIMATED REVENUES CONTROL	900,000	
	APPROPRIATIONS CONTROL		850,000
	BUDGETARY FUND BALANCE—UNASSIGNED		50,000
	Record general fund budget for year.		

Note the word CONTROL used as part of the account titles. Governmental accounting often use control accounts in the major journals with subsidiary accounts recording the detail behind each control account. This method is similar to a commercial entity's using a control account for its accounts receivable and then using subsidiary ledgers for the specific customer transactions. Throughout this chapter, the control account level is illustrated to focus on the major issues.

The ESTIMATED REVENUES CONTROL account is an *anticipatory asset;* that is, the governmental unit anticipates receiving resources from the revenue sources listed in the budget. The APPROPRIATIONS CONTROL account is an *anticipatory liability;* that is, the governmental unit anticipates incurring expenditures and liabilities for the budgeted amount. The excess of estimated revenues over anticipated expenditures is the budget surplus and is recorded to BUDGETARY FUND BALANCE—UNASSIGNED. Some approved budgets have deficits in which expected expenditures exceed anticipated revenue. These budgets are recorded with a debit to BUDGETARY FUND BALANCE—UNASSIGNED.

FYI

In practice, detailed accounting is maintained for each separate classification of revenue and appropriation, either in the major journal or in a subsidiary ledger. The AICPA uses both control-level accounts and budgetary accounts on the Uniform CPA Examination, although it does not capitalize the letters of the budgetary accounts used in the exam.

Recording the budget in the governmental entity's books makes it a formal accounting control mechanism for the fiscal period. In addition, having the budget in the accounting records provides the necessary information for the budgetary comparison schedules that are part of the required supplementary information (RSI) footnotes that **GASB 34** imposes on the government reporting model. At the end of the year, after the appropriate financial statements have been prepared, all the budgetary accounts are closed.

ACCOUNTING FOR EXPENDITURES

LO 17-7

Make calculations and record journal entries for the general fund.

Advanced StudyGuide .com

The governmental funds use a variety of controls over expenditures to ensure that each expenditure is made in accordance with any legal restrictions on the fund.

The Expenditure Process

The expenditure process in governmental accounting comprises the following sequential steps: appropriation, encumbrance, expenditure, and disbursement.

Step 1. Appropriation

The budget enables the appropriating authority to make future expenditures. Operating budgets are prepared for the general, special revenue, and often the debt service funds. Because appropriations originate in the operating budget, it is always the starting point for making all expenditures. The capital projects fund prepares capital budgets.

The appropriation was recorded in entry (1) made previously for Barb City's general fund. Recall that a total of $850,000 in anticipated expenditures was approved in the budget.

Step 2. Encumbrance

An ***encumbrance*** is a reservation of part of the budgetary appropriation and is recognized at the time an order is placed for goods or services. An encumbrance is a unique element of governmental accounting. Its purpose is to ensure that the expenditures within a period do not exceed the budgeted appropriations. The approved budget establishes the appropriation level and sets the legal maximum that may be expended for each budgeted item. The managers of the governmental unit must be sure that they do not exceed this budgetary authority. Thus, encumbrances provide a control system and safeguard for governmental unit administrators.

When an order is placed for goods or services to be received from outside the governmental unit, the budgeted appropriation is encumbered for the order's estimated cost. Encumbrances are of greatest use when an order is placed and a period of time expires before delivery. Payroll costs, immaterial costs, and costs for goods acquired from within the governmental entity typically are not encumbered because they are normal and recurring and the managers of the governmental unit are able to predict these costs based on past experiences and other administrative controls, such as employment agreements.

A sensible approach should be used with an encumbrance system. For example, it is not necessary to establish an individual encumbrance when an employee orders a pad of paper. Rather, a blanket purchase order with a maximum dollar amount, for example, a total of $500, should be prepared and encumbered, and then can serve as the control for small, routine supply purchases. Encumbrances provide unit administrators an important accounting control to fulfill their management responsibilities within an approved budget.

To illustrate encumbrance accounting, assume that on August 1, 20X1, Barb City completed a purchase order (PO) to buy goods estimated to cost $15,000 from an outside vendor. The entry to record this application of the budgeted appropriation authority for the period follows:

	August 1, 20X1		
(2)	ENCUMBRANCES	15,000	
	BUDGETARY FUND BALANCE—ASSIGNED FOR ENCUMBRANCES		15,000
	Record order for goods estimated to cost $15,000.		

Note that the ENCUMBRANCES account is a budgetary account that reserves part of the budget's appropriation authority. For detailed accounting, governmental entities often maintain a subsidiary ledger including accounts for specific types of encumbrances to correspond to each specific type of appropriation. For purposes of this illustration, we use the single title ENCUMBRANCES to indicate a control-level account to focus attention on the major aspects of governmental accounting. In practice, very detailed account titles and classification numbers are used to fully account for each type of transaction. It is important to note that the BUDGETARY FUND BALANCE—ASSIGNED FOR ENCUMBRANCES is a ***reservation (or restriction) of the budgetary fund balance,*** not an actual liability.

Step 3. Expenditure

An expenditure and a corresponding liability are recorded when the governmental entity receives the goods or services ordered in step 2. When the goods are received, the encumbrance entry is reversed for the amount encumbered and the expenditure is recorded for the actual cost to the governmental entity. Although the actual cost is typically very close to the encumbered amount, some differences may exist because of partially completed orders, less expensive replacements, or unforeseen costs. Assume that the goods are received on September 20, 20X1, at an actual cost of $14,000. The entries to reverse the encumbrance for the goods and to record the actual expenditures are as follows:

	September 20, 20X1		
(3)	BUDGETARY FUND BALANCE—ASSIGNED FOR ENCUMBRANCES	15,000	
	ENCUMBRANCES		15,000
	Reverse encumbrances for goods received.		
(4)	Expenditures	14,000	
	Vouchers Payable		14,000
	Receive goods at cost of $14,000.		

At any time, the remaining appropriating authority available to the fund managers can be determined by the following equation:

$$\begin{array}{c}\text{Appropriating}\\ \text{authority}\\ \text{remaining}\\ \text{available}\end{array} = \text{APPROPRIATIONS} - (\text{ENCUMBRANCES} + \text{Expenditures})$$

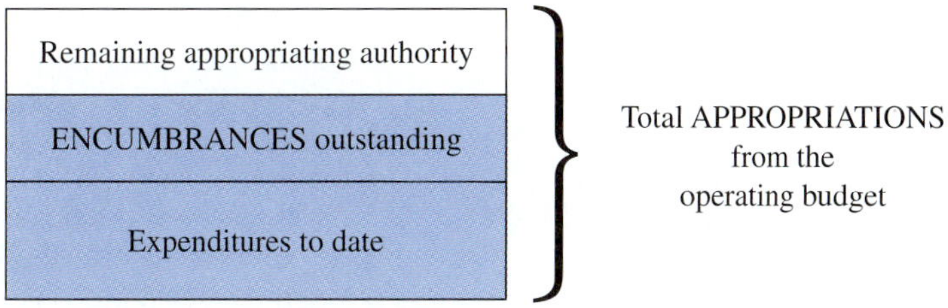

Step 4. Disbursement

A ***disbursement*** is the payment of cash for expenditures. The governing board or council usually must approve disbursements as an additional level of control over them.

Virtually all governmental entities use a comprehensive voucher system to control cash outflows. The governing board receives a schedule of vouchers to be approved for payment by vote of the board. This is usually one of the early agenda items in any board or council meeting as a vote is taken to "pay all bills." Checks are then written and delivered to the supplier of the specified goods. If the Barb City council approved the voucher at its October 8 meeting and a check was prepared in the amount of $14,000 and mailed on October 15, 20X1, the following entry records the disbursement:

	October 15, 20X1		
(5)	Vouchers Payable	14,000	
	Cash		14,000
	Payment of voucher for goods received.		

Classification of Expenditure Transactions and Accounts

Governmental accounting places many controls over expenditures, and much of the financial reporting focuses on the various aspects of an expenditure. Expenditures should be classified by fund, character, function (or program), organizational unit, activity, and principal classes of objects. See Figure 17–3 for a description of the major expenditure classifications.

Many governmental units have a comprehensive chart of accounts with specific coding digits that provide the basis for classifying each expenditure. For example, an expenditure journal entry might specify the expenditure account to be charged as number 421.23-110. The chart of accounts shows that the 421.23 account is for public safety: police—crime control and investigation—patrol, as follows:

420. Public safety
    421. Police
        421.2 Crime control and investigation
            421.23 Patrol

The -110 suffix indicates that this expenditure is for personal services in the form of salaries and wages for regular employees. It is not unusual for some accounting systems to have 11- to 14-digit accounts classifying each individual transaction. The level of specificity in the chart of accounts depends on the particular governing entity's information needs. Classifying information with such specificity allows the governing entity to maintain complete database control over the expenditure information, which it can use

FIGURE 17–3
Major Expenditure Classifications for Governmental Funds

Classification	Description
Fund	The fund is identified to show the specific source of the expenditure. For example, the general fund would be noted for expenditures from that fund.
Character	Character classifications are based primarily on the period the expenditures are anticipated to benefit. Four major character classifications are current, capital outlay, debt service, and intergovernmental.
Function (or program)	Functions are group-related activities directed at accomplishing a major service or regulatory responsibility. Standard classifications of function include general governmental, public safety, highway and streets, sanitation, health and welfare, culture and recreation, and education.
Organizational unit	Classifying by organizational unit maintains each unit director's accountability. The organizational unit is determined by the governmental unit's organization chart. For example, public safety could be separated into police, fire, corrections, protective inspection (such as plumbing and electrical code inspections), and other protection (such as flood control, traffic engineering, and examination of licensed occupations).
Activity	Activities within a function are recorded to maintain a record of the efficiency of each activity. For example, the police function could be classified in the following activities: police administration, crime control and investigation, traffic control, police training, support service (such as communication services and ambulance services), special detail services, and police station and building maintenance. Each of these activities could be categorized further, if desired.
Object class	Object class groups types of items purchased or services obtained. For example, operating expenditures include personal services, purchased and contractual services, and commodities. Each of these objects could be further categorized, depending on the governmental entity's information needs. For example, purchased services could include utility services, cleaning services (such as custodial, lawn care, and snow plowing), repair and maintenance services, rentals, construction services, and other purchased services, such as insurance or printing.

at any time in aggregate or relational analysis. For the examples in this chapter, only the expenditure control level is presented; in practice, a complete specification of the expenditure is made.

Outstanding Encumbrances at the End of the Fiscal Period

Advanced StudyGuide .com

In the previous example, Barb City received the goods within the same fiscal period in which they were ordered. What happens if the goods are ordered in one fiscal year and received in the next year? In this case, the encumbrance is not reversed before the end of the fiscal period.

Accounting for these outstanding encumbrances depends on the governmental unit's policy. The government may allow outstanding encumbrances to lapse; that is, the unit is not required to honor these encumbrances carried over to the new year, and the new year's budget must rebudget them. In virtually all cases, the encumbrances will be rebudgeted and honored; however, this policy specifically recognizes the legal authority of the new governing board to determine its own expenditures. A second method is to carry over the encumbrances as nonlapsing spending authority. This method recognizes the practical aspects of encumbrances outstanding at the end of a fiscal period. Either method may be used in governmental accounting.

FIGURE 17–4 Comparison of Accounting for Lapsing and Nonlapsing Encumbrances at Year-End

Item	Outstanding Encumbrances Lapse at Year-End			Outstanding Encumbrances Nonlapsing at Year-End		
December 31, 20X1						
Close remaining budgetary encumbrances	BUDGETARY FUND BALANCE—ASSIGNED FOR ENCUMBRANCES	15,000		BUDGETARY FUND BALANCE—ASSIGNED FOR ENCUMBRANCES	15,000	
	ENCUMBRANCES		15,000	ENCUMBRANCES		15,000
Reserve actual fund balance for outstanding encumbrances at end of 20X1 expected to be honored in 20X2	Fund Balance—Unassigned	15,000		Fund Balance—Unassigned	15,000	
	Fund Balance—Assigned for Encumbrances		15,000	Fund Balance—Assigned for Encumbrances		15,000
January 1, 20X2						
Reverse prior year encumbrance reserve	Fund Balance—Assigned for Encumbrances	15,000				
	Fund Balance—Unassigned		15,000			
Establish budgetary control over encumbrances renewed from prior period	ENCUMBRANCES	15,000				
	BUDGETARY FUND BALANCE—ASSIGNED FOR ENCUMBRANCES		15,000			
Reclassify reserve from prior year				Fund Balance—Assigned for Encumbrances	15,000	
				Fund Balance—Assigned for Encumbrances—20X1		15,000
February 1, 20X2						
Receive goods and remove budgetary reserve for encumbrances	BUDGETARY FUND BALANCE—ASSIGNED FOR ENCUMBRANCES	15,000				
	ENCUMBRANCES		15,000			
Record actual expenditure for goods received	Expenditures	14,000		Expenditures—20X1	14,000	
	Vouchers Payable		14,000	Vouchers Payable		14,000
December 31, 20X2						
Close expenditures account	Fund Balance—Unassigned	14,000		Fund Balance—Assigned for Encumbrances—20X1	15,000	
	Expenditures		14,000	Expenditures—20X1		14,000
				Fund Balance—Unassigned		1,000

To illustrate the differences between the lapsing and nonlapsing methods of accounting for encumbrances, assume the following:

1. On August 1, 20X1, the unit ordered $15,000 of goods and made an appropriate entry to record the encumbrance.
2. The unit had not received the goods on December 31, 20X1, the end of the fiscal period.
3. It receives the goods on February 1, 20X2, at an actual cost of $14,000.

Refer to Figure 17–4 for a comparison of the journal entries that would be required under each of the two methods of accounting for unfilled encumbrances at year-end.

Lapse of Outstanding Encumbrances at Year-End

The entries on December 31, 20X1, close the remaining budgetary encumbrances and establish a reserve of the actual fund balance on the December 31, 20X1, balance sheet. Although the GAAFR recommends that a reserve for lapsing encumbrances be reported on the balance sheet, the GASB's codification allows the alternative of only footnote disclosure of lapsing orders at year-end that are expected to be honored in the next fiscal period. If only footnote disclosure is used, the governmental entity would have only the first closing entry on December 31, 20X1, to close out the budgetary accounts related to the encumbrance. No balance sheet reserve is established if the footnote disclosure alternative is used.

Normal procedure for many governmental entities is for the next year's governing board to meet after elections or appointments for the next year. This meeting is generally held shortly before the beginning of the next fiscal year so that the budget is effective beginning on January 1 of the next year. Thus, the incoming governing board typically decides during the budget process whether to honor year-end outstanding encumbrances in the next fiscal period. If the new governing board decides not to honor the 20X1 year-end outstanding encumbrances, only the closing entry to close the remaining budgetary encumbrances would be made on December 31, 20X1. If the governmental entity uses the footnote disclosure alternative, no footnote disclosure in the 20X1 financial statements would be made for those outstanding encumbrances not expected to be renewed in the next fiscal year.

If the new governing board decides to honor the outstanding encumbrances from 20X1, they must be included in the 20X2 budgeted appropriations. An entry is made as of January 1, 20X2, to establish budgetary control over the expected expenditure. A "fresh start," new spending authority is established, and the sequence of entries continues as if this is a new purchase order effective for 20X2.

In the unusual case that the new governing board decides as of January 1, 20X2, not to honor the outstanding encumbrances and the December 31, 20X1, entry had already been recorded, the following entry is made as of January 1, 20X2, to record the cancellation of the outstanding encumbrance from 20X1:

	January 1, 20X2		
(6)	Fund Balance—Assigned for Encumbrances	15,000	
	Fund Balance—Unassigned		15,000
	Eliminate reserve for outstanding encumbrances not being renewed.		

If the January 1, 20X2, entries had already been made and the governing board later decides not to honor the outstanding encumbrance from 20X1, reversing entries would be made to eliminate the actual fund balance reserve and the budgetary fund balance reserve that had been created on January 1, 20X2. If the governmental entity used only footnote disclosure in its 20X1 financial statements for the year-end outstanding encumbrances expected to be honored, only a reversing entry is required to reverse the January 1, 20X2, entry that had established the budgetary encumbrances and budgetary fund balance reserve. The governmental entity then simply cancels the order with the external vendor.

Nonlapsing Outstanding Encumbrances at Year-End

Some governing entities carry over prior-year appropriations authority as nonlapsing encumbrances. In this case, the budget for the second fiscal period does not show these carryovers because they arose from the prior-year appropriations authority. The nonlapsing encumbrances are dated for the prior year to indicate they arose from that year's appropriating authority. Some governmental accountants believe this method is realistic for many situations in which orders placed with outside vendors cannot easily be canceled.

The 20X1 year-end closing entries in Figure 17–4 show the required reservation of the actual fund balance. Note that these are the same two entries made under the lapsing method with balance sheet recognition of the reserve of the fund balance. The differences between the two methods become apparent during the second fiscal period. Under the

FYI

The City of San Diego follows a nonlapsing encumbrances policy.

nonlapsing method, separately identifying expenditures made from spending authority carried over from prior periods is important. Typically this is done in a reclassification entry on the first day of the second fiscal period, which dates the Fund Balance—Assigned for Encumbrances. No budgetary entry is made in the second year because the appropriation authority comes from the first year's budget. When the goods are received, the expenditures account is also dated to indicate that the expenditure authority emanated from 20X1.

At the end of 20X2, the Expenditures—20X1 account is closed directly to the Fund Balance—Assigned for Encumbrances—20X1. Note that the $1,000 difference between the actual $14,000 cost and the $15,000 assigned amount is closed to Fund Balance—Unassigned because the actual cost is less than the amount encumbered from the prior-year appropriation authority. If the actual cost is more than the reserve, the difference must be approved as part of the appropriation authority for 20X2.

Key Observations from the Illustrations

As a practical matter, almost all a governmental unit's outstanding encumbrances at year-end are honored and completed in the next fiscal period. The method of accounting for open encumbrances at year-end is based on the unit's budgetary policy, which may be affected by legal statutes controlling carryover of appropriating ability from one fiscal period to the next. Both methods are used in practice. It is important to note that, in this example, the 20X1 statement of revenues, expenditures, and changes in fund balance will report no expenditures relating to this item. In 20X2, $14,000 of expenditures will be recognized. Under the nonlapsing method, expenditures made in 20X2 but carried over from 20X1 encumbrances are dated to note that they arose from 20X1's appropriations. The comprehensive illustration presented later in this chapter uses the lapsing method because of its widespread use.

Reporting of Encumbrances under the Recent Standard on Fund Balance Reporting

GASB 54 does not report any reserves of fund balance on the balance sheet. Rather, it includes the amount of encumbrances as part of the spendable fund balance, usually in the assigned category. Only footnote disclosure is now used to report the aggregate amount of encumbrances along with the required disclosures about other significant commitments. Because governments will continue to use encumbrance accounting because of the control and management information an encumbrance system provides, we continue to show encumbrance accounting even though encumbrances are no longer reported in the balance sheet. **GASB 54** does not restrict the accounting systems used by governments.

Expenditures for Inventory

Most governmental units maintain a small amount of inventory in office supplies. A first issue is to determine which of two methods should be followed to account for the expenditure of inventories. The first method recognizes the entire expenditure for inventory in the period the supplies are acquired. This is called the *purchase* method. The second method is the *consumption* method; it recognizes expenditures for only the amount of inventory used in the period. The specific method to follow depends on the governing unit's policy and how inventory expenditures are included in the budget.

A second issue is whether to show inventory as an asset on the governmental funds' balance sheet. Inventory is not an expendable asset; that is, it may not be spent as the governing entity wishes. **NCGA 1** states that inventory should be shown on the balance sheets for governmental funds if the inventory amount is material. Immaterial inventories need not be shown on the balance sheet. If the inventory is material, it is presented as an asset on the balance sheet; an amount equal to the inventory also should be shown as a reservation of the fund balance, indicating that that amount is no longer expendable.

The entries to account for inventories under both the purchase method and the consumption method appear in Figure 17–5. The illustration assumes that Barb City

FIGURE 17–5 Comparison of Accounting for Inventories—Purchase versus Consumption Method

Item	Purchase Method of Accounting			Consumption Method of Accounting		
November 1, 20X1						
Record acquisition of $2,000 of inventory.	Expenditures	2,000		Expenditures	2,000	
	Vouchers Payable		2,000	Vouchers Payable		2,000
December 31, 20X1						
Recognize ending inventory of $1,400.	Inventory of Supplies	1,400		Inventory of Supplies	1,400	
	Fund Balance—Nonspendable		1,400	Expenditures		1,400
				Fund Balance—Unassigned	1,400	
				Fund Balance—Nonspendable		1,400
December 31, 20X2						
Record remaining inventory of $500, with $900 of supplies having been consumed during 20X2.	Fund Balance—Nonspendable	900		Expenditures	900	
	Inventory of Supplies		900	Inventory of Supplies		900
				Fund Balance—Nonspendable	900	
				Fund Balance—Unassigned		900

acquires $2,000 of inventory on November 1, 20X1, having held no inventory previously. On December 31, 20X1, the end of Barb City's fiscal year, a physical count shows $1,400 still in stock. During 20X2, $900 of this inventory is used, resulting in a $500 remaining balance of supplies on December 31, 20X2.

Purchase Method of Accounting for Inventories

Under the purchase method, the entire amount of inventory acquired is charged to Expenditures in the period acquired. On December 31, 20X1, the end of the fiscal year, an adjusting entry is made to recognize the $1,400 remaining inventory as an asset and to restrict the fund balance for the nonexpendable portion applicable to inventories.

The $2,000 expenditure is closed into Fund Balance—Unassigned for 20X1 in a closing entry made at the end of the fiscal year. The December 31, 20X1, balance sheet includes the inventory of supplies as an asset in the amount of $1,400, and Fund Balance—Nonspendable for $1,400 to indicate that the inventory cannot be used to pay for current obligations. The 20X1 operating statement shows a $2,000 expenditure for supplies.

At the end of 20X2, an adjusting entry is made to recognize the use of the $900 of supplies of the $1,400 remaining from the 20X1 purchase. This entry reduces the reservation of the fund balance and decreases inventory. At the end of 20X2, Inventory of Supplies is $500, and Fund Balance—Assigned for Inventories is $500 for the remaining unused supplies.

In summary, the $2,000 expenditure is recognized in the period in which the supplies are purchased. No expenditures are recognized in subsequent periods although some of the supplies are used in those periods.

Consumption Method of Accounting for Inventories

Under the consumption method, expenditures for a period are reported only for the amount consumed. In this case, the budget for the period should be based on the expected amount of use so that the budgeted and actual amounts compared at year-end are on the same basis.

A net expenditure of $600 ($2,000 – $1,400) for supplies used is reported in 20X1, the year the supplies were acquired. With $500 of inventory remaining at the end of 20X2, an expenditure of $900 is reported in the 20X2 operating

FYI

The City of San Diego uses the consumption method to account for inventory.

statement to show the amount of supplies consumed during 20X2. The consumption method relates the expenditures with the use of the inventory.

A comparison of selected account balances under the purchase method and consumption method shows the different amounts reported under these two methods:

	Purchase Method	Consumption Method
20X1:		
Expenditures	$2,000	$ 600
Inventory of Supplies	1,400	1,400
20X2:		
Expenditures	0	900
Inventory of Supplies	500	500

Note that the choice of methods has no effect on the balance sheet amounts; the only effect is on the period in which the expenditures for inventory are reported.

Both inventory methods are used in practice. The method a specific governmental unit uses depends on its budgeting policy. If the unit includes all inventory acquisitions in its appropriations for the period, it should use the purchase method. If the governmental unit includes only the expected amount of inventory to be used during a period in that period's appropriations, it should use the consumption method.

Reporting of Inventory under the New Standard on Fund Balance Reporting

If they are material in amount, inventories are reported as an asset on the balance sheet. Under **GASB 54,** reserves of fund balance are not reported on the face of the balance sheet. But the fund balance associated with inventories is reported in the nonspendable fund balance category.

Accounting for Fixed Assets

Governmental entities may acquire equipment that has an economic life of more than one year. Accounting for this acquisition depends on which fund expends the resources for it. Governmental funds are concerned with the expendability and control over available resources and account for equipment acquisitions as expenditures. Governmental funds recognize the entire amount of the cost of the acquisition of equipment and other capital assets as an expenditure in the year the asset is acquired. No capital assets are recorded in the general fund; they are treated as expenditures of the period.

Proprietary funds are concerned with capital maintenance and account for acquisitions of capital assets in the same manner as commercial entities. Thus, accounting for the purchase of a capital asset differs in the five governmental funds from the accounting used in the proprietary funds.

For example, assume that Barb City acquires a truck from the resources of, and is accounted for in, the general fund. The encumbrance is $12,000, but the actual cost is $12,500 because of minor modifications required by the city.

The general fund makes the following entries to account for the truck's acquisition:

		Debit	Credit
(7)	ENCUMBRANCES	12,000	
	BUDGETARY FUND BALANCE—ASSIGNED FOR ENCUMBRANCES		12,000
	Order truck at estimated cost of $12,000.		

		Debit	Credit
(8)	BUDGETARY FUND BALANCE—ASSIGNED FOR ENCUMBRANCES	12,000	
	ENCUMBRANCES		12,000
	Cancel reserve for truck received.		

		Debit	Credit
(9)	Expenditures	12,500	
	Vouchers Payable		12,500
	Receive truck at actual cost of $12,500.		

The truck is not recorded as an asset in the general fund but as an expenditure in it. Sales of capital assets are recorded as a debit to Cash (or receivable) and a credit to Other Financing Sources—Sales of General Capital Assets for the amount received from the sale. If the amount from the sale is immaterial, the governmental entity may elect to record the credit to other revenues. Governmental entities should maintain a schedule or ledger to track the acquisition or sale of capital assets by any governmental fund, but that record is only used in preparing the governmentwide financial statements, which do report a governmental unit's long-term assets.

Works of Art and Historical Treasures

For the purposes of governmentwide financial statements, governments should capitalize works of art, historical treasures, and similar types of assets at their historical costs at acquisition or at their fair values at the date of the contribution. For example, if the general fund expended $10,000 for a work of art, it reports an expenditure for that amount. However, when preparing the governmentwide financial statements, the cost of the work of art is reported as an asset of the government. If the assets are donated, contribution revenue is recognized in the governmentwide financial statements.

The GASB provided practical guidance to the general rule of capitalizing works of art and historical treasures. For example, many collections have a very large number of items collected over long periods of time, and it is virtually impossible to determine the cost or fair value at the times of acquisition. A provision in **GASB 34** states that the government is not required but is still encouraged to capitalize a collection of art or historical treasures if the government meets all three of the following provisions: (1) holds the collection for public exhibition, education, or research, (2) protects and preserves the collection, and (3) has an organizational policy that requires the proceeds from sales of collection items to be used to acquire other items for collections. If contributed items are not capitalized, the governmentwide financial statements report both a program expense and a contribution revenue for the item's fair market value the time of its donation.

Capitalized collections that are exhaustible, such as displays of works whose useful lives are reduced due to display, or used for education or research should be depreciated over their estimated useful lives. Collections or individual items whose lives are inexhaustible are not depreciated.

Long-Term Debt and Capital Leases

Commercial, profit-seeking businesses recognize long-term debt and capital leases as noncurrent liabilities. Businesses take on debt or enter into capital leases in order to earn income. As a result, they recognize a liability under the flow of economic resources measurement focus model. However, the flow of current financial resources measurement focus model directly affects the accounting for long-term liabilities in governmental funds.

The governmental funds, which include the general fund, record the proceeds from a bond issue as a debit to Cash and a credit to Bond Issue Proceeds, an other-financing source. Bond issue proceeds are not revenue because the bonds must be repaid. Other financing sources are shown in the middle section of the statement of revenues, expenditures, and other changes in fund balances. Bonds are not reported on the governmental funds' balance sheets but only on the governmentwide financial statements.

Capital leases are accounted for in a manner similar to long-term debt. If a proprietary fund (e.g., internal service or enterprise fund) enters into a capital lease, the lease is accounted for using methods similar to those that commercial, profit-seeking entities use by recording an asset

FYI

In an effort to spur economic growth in the region, Hamilton County, Ohio, issued more than $1 billion in bonds to fund stadiums for the Cincinnati Bengals and Cincinnati Reds. In 2012, the county sold a hospital valued in 2006 at $30 million for just $15 million, presumably to cover financing costs related to investments in the stadiums.

and a lease liability. However, if a governmental fund (e.g., general fund) enters into a capital lease, it accounts for the capital lease in a manner similar to a bond's accounting.

Investments

Some entities maintain investments in stock or bond securities. The purpose of doing this typically is to obtain an investment return on available resources. **GASB 31** establishes a general rule of fair market valuation for investments held by a governmental entity. The following investments are to be valued at fair value, if determinable, in the asset section of the balance sheet for the governmental entity: (1) investments in debt securities, (2) investments in equity securities (other than those accounted for under the equity method as provided for in **ASC 325**), including option contracts, stock warrants, and stock rights, (3) investments in open-end mutual funds, (4) investment pools in which a governmental entity combines with other investors, and (5) interest-earning investment contracts in which the value is affected by market (interest rate) changes. **GASB 52** extends the general rule of using fair value to real estate investments by endowments. The periodic changes in the fair value of all the types of investments included in **GASB 31** and **GASB 52** should be recognized as an element of investment income in the operating statement (or statement of activities) of each fund making the investment. For financial reporting purposes, an internal investment pool that combines the resources of several of the governmental entity's funds allocates the pool's assets and its income to each individual fund based on its percentage of the total amount invested.

Many state and local governments have deposits and make investments that are open to a variety of risks. **GASB 40** establishes detailed note disclosure requirements related to the following types of investment risks: credit risk (including concentrations of credit risk), interest rate risk, foreign currency risk, and deposit risks of custodial credit risk and foreign currency risk. The main objective of **GASB 40** is to require footnote disclosures of the policies and the profiles of the government's investment portfolios, such as the credit quality ratings of debt securities and other fixed-income securities and the terms of investments whose fair value is highly sensitive to changes in the interest rate.

INTERFUND ACTIVITIES

LO 17-8

Make calculations and record journal entries for basic interfund activities.

Advanced StudyGuide .com

A basic concept in governmental accounting is that each fund is a separate entity and has separate sources of resources, sometimes including the power to levy and collect taxes. Each fund's revenues must then be expended in accordance with the budget and legal restrictions. Because a single governmental entity has a number of separate funds, it sometimes becomes necessary to transfer resources from one fund to another. ***Interfund activities*** are resource flows between fund entities. In a consolidated financial statement for a commercial entity, intercompany transactions are eliminated to report only the effect of transactions with external entities. Governmental accounting, on the other hand, requires the separate maintenance and reporting of interfund items. The governing body must approve any interfund transfers and transactions to provide a public record and to prevent distortion of fund uses. Many governmental entities include in their operating budgets for the year interfund activities anticipated during a fiscal year. The comprehensive example of Sol City presented later in this chapter illustrates budgetary entries for interfund activities. Interfund transfers must be accounted for carefully to ensure that the legal and budgetary restrictions are followed and that resources intended for one fund are not used in another.

GASB 34 establishes four types of interfund activities: (1) interfund loans, (2) interfund services provided and used, (3) interfund transfers, and (4) interfund reimbursements. A discussion of the four interfund items follows; they are illustrated in Figure 17–6.

FIGURE 17–6 Interfund Transactions and Transfers

Item	Entry in General Fund			Entry in Other Fund		
				INTERNAL SERVICE FUND:		
1. Interfund loan	Due from Internal Service Fund	4,000		Cash	4,000	
	Cash		4,000	Due to General Fund		4,000
	Cash	4,000		Due to General Fund	4,000	
	Due from Internal Service Fund		4,000	Cash		4,000
				INTERNAL SERVICE FUND:		
2. Interfund service provided and used	Expenditures	100		Due from General Fund	100	
	Due to Internal Service Fund		100	Charge for Services		100
	Due to Internal Service Fund	100		Cash	100	
	Cash		100	Due from General Fund		100
				CAPITAL PROJECTS FUND:		
3. Interfund transfer	Other Financing Uses—Transfer Out to Capital Projects Fund	10,000		Cash	10,000	
	Cash		10,000	Other Financing Sources—Transfer In from General Fund		10,000
				CAPITAL PROJECTS FUND:		
4. Interfund reimbursement	Cash	3,000		Expenditures	3,000	
	Expenditures		3,000	Cash		3,000

(1) Interfund Loans

State law may allow lending or borrowing activities between funds. The loans must be repaid, usually within one year or before the end of the fiscal period. Loans and advances are not shown on a fund's statement of revenues, expenditures, and changes in fund balance; however, all outstanding loans or advances must be shown on the balance sheet as payables or receivables. Interest usually is not charged on interfund financing arrangements. If interest is charged, it is accounted for in the funds in the same manner as for other interest income or expense.

Some governmental entities distinguish between short-term and long-term financing arrangements by using the term "Advances to (or from)" to denote a long-term agreement and "Due to (or from)" for a short-term agreement.

The illustration of an interfund financing transaction in Figure 17–6 assumes that Barb City's general fund loans the internal service fund $4,000 for two months. The general fund reports a receivable for the amount of the loan until it is repaid.

(2) Interfund Services Provided and Used

These interfund activities are transactions that would be treated as revenue, expenditures, or expenses if they involved parties external to the governmental unit. These activities are still reported as revenue, expenditures, or expenses but differently because they are entirely within the governmental unit. These interfund activities are often normal and recurring items, usually involving at least one proprietary fund. Three examples follow:

1. The general fund purchases goods or services from an internal service or enterprise fund.
2. Payments are made to the general fund from the enterprise fund for fire and police protection.
3. A transfer of resources from the general fund to the pension trust fund is made to pay for the city's cost of pension benefits for its employees. This is a cost associated with employee services provided to the city and is therefore an expenditure of the general fund.

Usually these transfers involve the recognition of a receivable or payable because of the time lag between the purchase of the services and the disbursement of funds. A "Due to (or from)" account is used for short-term interfund receivables and payables rather than a formal Vouchers Payable account.

The illustration of this type of interfund activity in Figure 17–6 assumes that Barb City's general fund uses an auto from the city motor pool. The motor pool operates as an internal service fund. The general fund is billed $100 based on mileage and pays the bill 30 days later.

(3) Interfund Transfers

The general fund often transfers resources into another fund for the receiving fund to use for its own operations; occasionally, the general fund receives resources from other funds. These interfund transfers are not expected to be repaid. Such transfers are not fund revenues or expenditures but are instead called *interfund transfers*. These transfers are classified under "Other Financing Sources or Uses" in the operating financial statements of the funds. The reason that the receiving fund does not recognize these transfers as revenue is that the issuing fund has already properly recognized these resources as revenue. Thus, recording these transfers as other financing sources eliminates the possibility of double-counting the same resources as revenue in two different funds of the combined governmental entity. Examples include the following:

1. A transfer of resources, such as cash or other assets, is made from the general fund to an enterprise fund or internal service fund that has an operating deficit that must be eliminated.
2. A transfer of resources from the general fund to a capital projects fund is made to help finance new construction.
3. A transfer of resources from the general fund to the debt service fund is made to pay principal and interest.

The illustration of an interfund transfer in Figure 17–6 assumes that Barb City's general fund agrees to provide $10,000 to the capital projects fund toward the construction of a new library. The Transfer Out account in the general fund is closed to its Unassigned Fund Balance at the end of the fiscal period. The capital projects fund also closes its Transfer In account at the end of the fiscal period to its Unassigned Fund Balance. These interfund transfers are not expected to be repaid.

(4) Interfund Reimbursements

A reimbursement transaction is for reimbursing a fund's expenditure or expense that was initially made from the fund but that is properly chargeable to another fund. These initial payments are sometimes made either because of improper classification to the wrong fund or for expediency within the governmental entity. The reimbursement from one fund to another is recorded as a reduction of the expenditure in the fund initially recording the expenditure and a recording of the expenditure in the proper fund for the appropriate amount. Two examples as follow:

1. The general fund initially records and pays an expenditure properly chargeable to the special revenue fund, and the special revenue fund subsequently reimburses the general fund.
2. The general fund records and pays for an expenditure to provide preliminary architectural work on the planning for a new sports arena. The sports arena enterprise fund later reimburses the general fund.

The illustration of an interfund reimbursement in Figure 17–6 assumes that Barb City's general fund recorded a $3,000 expenditure for a bill from outside consultants that is later discovered to be properly chargeable to the capital projects fund. Upon notification, the capital projects fund reimbursed the general fund and properly recorded the expenditure in its fund.

FIGURE 17–7
Overview of General Fund

Item	Description
Measurement focus	Flow of current financial resources—expendability.
Accounting basis	Modified accrual.
Budgetary basis	Operating budget.
Financial statements	1. Balance sheet. 2. Statement of revenues, expenditures, and changes in fund balance.
Balance Sheet	
Current assets	Includes current financial resources such as cash, certificates of deposit, accrued property taxes receivable, and estimated allowance for uncollectible taxes. Interfund loans receivable included as assets. Material inventories reported.
Long-term productive assets (buildings, etc.)	Fixed assets not reported in general fund.
Current liabilities	Vouchers payable are the primary current liabilities. Interfund loans payable also included as liabilities.
Long-term debt	Governmental unit long-term debt not reported in general fund.
Fund balance	Unassigned fund balance and reservations of fund balance (e.g., encumbrances and inventories).
Statement of Revenues, Expenditures, and Changes in Fund Balance	
Revenue	Recorded when measurable and available under the modified accrual basis of accounting. Interfund services provided and used included in revenues (or expenditures).
Expenditures	Recognized in period when measurable and fund liability arises.
Other financing sources and uses	Includes bond issue proceeds and interfund transfers.
Changes in fund balance	Reconciles changes in fund balance during period, including changes in reservations of fund balance.

OVERVIEW OF ACCOUNTING AND FINANCIAL REPORTING FOR THE GENERAL FUND

Review Figure 17–7 for an overview of the accounting for the general fund, including accounting for the interfund activities on the general fund's operating statement, the statement of revenues, expenditures, and changes in fund balance. Note that the interfund loans are reported only on the fund's balance sheet.

Chapter 18 presents an example of the fund balance reporting for the governmental fund types.

COMPREHENSIVE ILLUSTRATION OF ACCOUNTING FOR THE GENERAL FUND

The following example illustrates the accounting for Sol City's general fund for the January 1, 20X2, to December 31, 20X2, fiscal year. The entries are presented by topic, not necessarily in chronological order. The balance sheet for the general fund as of December 31, 20X1 (Figure 17–8), represents the opening balances for fiscal 20X2.

Adoption of the Budget

The city council adopts the budget for fiscal 20X2 (Figure 17–9). Charles Alt, a Sol City alderman, voted in favor of adopting the budget, which summarizes the city's four major

FIGURE 17–8
General Fund Balance Sheet at the Beginning of 20X2

SOL CITY
General Fund Balance Sheet
December 31, 20X1

Assets:		
Cash		$ 50,000
Property Taxes Receivable—Delinquent	$100,000	
Less: Allowance for Uncollectibles—Delinquent	(5,000)	95,000
Inventory of Supplies		14,000
Total Assets		$159,000
Liabilities & Fund Balance:		
Vouchers Payable		$ 30,000
Fund Balance:		
Nonspendable:		
Supplies Inventory	$ 14,000	
Spendable:		
Assigned to:		
General Government Services	11,000	
Unassigned	104,000	129,000
Total Liabilities & Fund Balance		$159,000

FIGURE 17–9
General Fund Operating Budget for Fiscal 20X2

SOL CITY
General Fund Operating Budget
For Period of January 1, 20X2, to December 31, 20X2

Estimated Revenue:		
Property Taxes	$775,000	
Grants	55,000	
Sales Taxes	25,000	
Miscellaneous	20,000	
Total Estimated Revenue		$875,000
Appropriations:		
General Government	$200,000	
Streets and Highways	75,000	
Public Safety	400,000	
Sanitation	150,000	
Total Appropriations		(825,000)
Excess of Estimated Revenue over Appropriations		$ 50,000
Other Financing Uses:		
Transfer Out to Capital Projects Fund	$ (20,000)	
Transfer Out to Initiate Internal Service Fund	(10,000)	
Total Other Financing Uses		(30,000)
Excess of Estimated Revenue and Interfund Transfers over Appropriations and Interfund Transfers		$ 20,000

functions: general government, streets and highways, public safety (fire and police), and sanitation. In the complete budget used by the city council, the expenditures in each of the four functions are separated into the following categories: personal services, supplies, other services and charges, and capital outlay. The public safety budget includes a budgeted capital outlay of $50,000 for a new fire truck.

The city elects the following accounting policies:

1. *Consumption method for inventories.* The city budgets the supplies inventory on the consumption method, including only the costs of expected inventory use during the year.
2. *Lapsing method of accounting for encumbrances.* The city uses the lapsing method for accounting for any encumbrances outstanding at the end of fiscal periods. The APPROPRIATIONS CONTROL for fiscal 20X2 includes a reappropriation of the $11,000 of outstanding encumbrances as of December 31, 20X1.

3. *Use of control accounts.* The city uses a comprehensive system of control accounts for its major journals. The following accounts have extensive subsidiary ledgers that correspond to the entries made in the journal: ESTIMATED REVENUES CONTROL, APPROPRIATIONS CONTROL, ENCUMBRANCES, and Expenditures. The subsidiary records maintain the specific details supporting each control account. To focus on the major aspects of governmental accounting, the Sol City illustration includes the control-level entries only.
4. *Budgeted interfund activities.* The city includes in the budget all anticipated interfund activities during the fiscal year. The general fund is expected to have the following interfund transfers:

OTHER FINANCING USES:	
Transfer Out to Capital Projects Fund	$20,000
Transfer Out to Internal Service Fund	10,000

The interfund transfer out to the capital projects fund is to pay for the city's share of a municipal courthouse addition project, and the transfer out to the internal service fund is to initiate the internal service fund.

The following entries are made to record the budget and to renew the lapsing encumbrances from the prior period:

	January 1, 20X2		
(10)	ESTIMATED REVENUES CONTROL	875,000	
	APPROPRIATIONS CONTROL		825,000
	ESTIMATED OTHER FINANCING USES—TRANSFER OUT TO CAPITAL PROJECTS		20,000
	ESTIMATED OTHER FINANCING USES—TRANSFER OUT TO INTERNAL SERVICE		10,000
	BUDGETARY FUND BALANCE—UNASSIGNED		20,000
	Record budget for fiscal 20X2.		
(11)	Fund Balance—Assigned for Encumbrances	11,000	
	Fund Balance—Unassigned		11,000
	Reverse prior-year encumbrances reserve.		
(12)	ENCUMBRANCES	11,000	
	BUDGETARY FUND BALANCE—ASSIGNED FOR ENCUMBRANCES		11,000
	Renew encumbrances from prior period as included in budgeted appropriations in 20X2.		

(*Note:* The technique of capitalizing the account titles of all budgetary accounts continues through the comprehensive illustration. This technique is used in the text to differentiate the budgetary from the operating accounts. In practice, the budgetary accounts are not capitalized.)

Property Tax Levy and Collection

Most municipalities obtain resources from property taxes, which are recorded as a receivable when an enforceable legal claim arises. Revenue is recorded if the property taxes are measurable and available for current expenditures. Recall that the 60-day rule for property taxes allows the recognition of revenue for the current fiscal period if the property taxes are expected to be collected within 60 days of the end of the current fiscal period. A deferred revenue account is credited if the property taxes are not available for current expenditures. Sol City's property taxes are due and available for use within the fiscal period and therefore are recorded as revenue as of the levy date. Note that a provision for uncollectibles must be recorded as a reduction of property tax revenue, not a bad debts expense as in commercial accounting. Governmental funds have no such account as bad debts expense. The receivables are classified as current, collectible within this period, or delinquent for past due accounts.

The entries in Sol City's general fund for the transactions relating to property taxes follow:

(13)	Property Taxes Receivable—Current	785,000	
	Allowance for Uncollectible Taxes—Current		10,000
	Revenue—Property Tax		775,000
	Property taxes levied for this fiscal year with a reduction from revenues for the estimated uncollectibles.		
(14)	Cash	791,000	
	Property Taxes Receivable—Current		695,000
	Property Taxes Receivable—Delinquent		96,000
	Collect portion of property taxes including $96,000 of past due accounts.		
(15)	Allowance for Uncollectible Taxes—Delinquent	4,000	
	Property Taxes Receivable—Delinquent		4,000
	Write off remaining $4,000 of delinquent property taxes.		
(16)	Allowance for Uncollectible Taxes—Delinquent	1,000	
	Allowance for Uncollectible Taxes—Current	5,000	
	Revenues—Property Tax		6,000
	Revise estimate of uncollectibles from $10,000 to $5,000 and close remaining $1,000 balance of allowance account for delinquent accounts.		
(17)	Property Taxes Receivable—Delinquent	90,000	
	Allowance for Uncollectible Taxes—Current	5,000	
	Property Taxes Receivable—Current		90,000
	Allowance for Uncollectible Taxes—Delinquent		5,000
	Reclassify remaining receivables and allowance account from current to delinquent.		

Other Revenue

Other sources of income are grants from other governmental units, a portion of the sales tax collected on retail sales made within the city, and miscellaneous revenue from parking meters, fines, and licenses. The city should recognize grants from other governmental units as revenue when the grants become available and measurable. The city's policy is to recognize these grants as the monies are received because the grantor might withdraw the grants at any time up to the actual transmittal of the monies. In our example, the city receives only 60 percent of the expected grant that had been budgeted at $55,000. Sales tax revenue may be accrued if the city can make a good estimate of the amount to be received and if the sales tax revenue is available for current expenditures. The city's policy is to recognize the sales taxes when received. Miscellaneous revenue is recognized as received.

The entries to record the other sources of income follow:

(18)	Cash	33,000	
	Revenue—Grant		33,000
	Receive only 60 percent of expected grant.		
(19)	Cash	32,000	
	Revenue—Sales Tax		32,000
	Receive sales tax revenue from state.		
(20)	Cash	18,000	
	Revenue—Miscellaneous		18,000
	Receive miscellaneous revenue from fines, license fees, minor disposals of equipment, and other sources.		

Expenditures

The appropriations were recorded in the budget entry [entry (10)] with a renewal of the encumbrances carried over from the prior period under the lapsing method of accounting for encumbrances [entries (11) and (12)]. Orders for goods and services from outside vendors are encumbered, and a voucher system is used. Recall that a governmental entity typically does not encumber internal payroll.

Sol City makes the following entries for the encumbrances, expenditures, and disbursements made in the general fund during the year:

(21)	ENCUMBRANCES	210,000	
	BUDGETARY FUND BALANCE—ASSIGNED FOR ENCUMBRANCES		210,000
	Encumber for purchase orders for goods and services ordered from outside vendors.		
(22)	BUDGETARY FUND BALANCE—ASSIGNED FOR ENCUMBRANCES	5,000	
	ENCUMBRANCES		5,000
	Reverse encumbrance for portion of order that is not deliverable because item has been discontinued.		
(23)	BUDGETARY FUND BALANCE—ASSIGNED FOR ENCUMBRANCES	190,000	
	ENCUMBRANCES		190,000
	Reverse reserve for partial order of goods received.		
(24)	Expenditures	196,000	
	Vouchers Payable		196,000
	Receive goods at actual cost of $196,000 that had been encumbered for $190,000. Difference due to increase in cost of items. Includes supplies for inventory.		
(25)	BUDGETARY FUND BALANCE—ASSIGNED FOR ENCUMBRANCES	11,000	
	ENCUMBRANCES		11,000
	Reverse reserve for goods received that were ordered in prior year.		
(26)	Expenditures	9,000	
	Vouchers Payable		9,000
	Receive goods ordered in prior year. Actual cost is $9,000 on encumbered amount of $11,000. Difference due to price reduction as part of special sale.		
(27)	Expenditures	550,000	
	Vouchers Payable		550,000
	Payroll costs to employees for period.		
(28)	Vouchers Payable	730,000	
	Cash		730,000
	Vouchers approved by city council and paid during period.		

Acquisition of Capital Asset

The fire department's budget includes $50,000 for a new fire truck. This capital outlay is accounted for as any other expenditure of available resources. The resources for the fire truck are encumbered when the order is placed with the manufacturer. The entries in the general fund for the fire truck acquisition follow:

(29)	ENCUMBRANCES	50,000	
	BUDGETARY FUND BALANCE—ASSIGNED FOR ENCUMBRANCES		50,000
	Order fire truck at estimated cost of $50,000		
(30)	BUDGETARY FUND BALANCE—ASSIGNED FOR ENCUMBRANCES	50,000	
	ENCUMBRANCES		50,000
	Reverse reserve for fire truck received.		

(31)	Expenditures	58,000	
	Vouchers Payable		58,000
	Receive fire truck at actual cost of $58,000 due to approved additional items required to meet new fire code.		

(32)	Vouchers Payable	58,000	
	Cash		58,000
	Voucher approved and disbursement made for fire truck.		

Interfund Activities

The anticipated interfund items are included in the budget for the fiscal period. They include the estimated transfer out of $10,000 to initiate the internal service fund and the estimated transfer out of $20,000 for capital improvements to a capital projects fund. In addition to these transfers, the general fund also has an interfund transaction with the internal service fund for services received in the amount of $1,000, and it lends the enterprise fund $3,000.

The following entries in the general fund record its side of the interfund activities during the year. Chapter 18 continues the comprehensive example of Sol City and presents the entries for these interfund transactions and transfers in each of the related funds so that both sides of accounting for interfund items are illustrated for the Sol City example:

(33)	Other Financing Uses—Transfer Out to Internal Service Fund	10,000	
	Due to Internal Service Fund		10,000
	Recognize the transfer out and associated liability to the internal service fund as included in the budget.		

(34)	Other Financing Uses—Transfer Out to Capital Projects Fund	20,000	
	Due to Capital Projects Fund		20,000
	Recognize the transfer out and associated liability to the capital projects fund as included in the budget.		

(35)	Due to Internal Service Fund	10,000	
	Cash		10,000
	Pay cash to internal service fund for payable from interfund transfer out previously recognized.		

(36)	Due to Capital Projects Fund	20,000	
	Cash		20,000
	Pay cash to capital projects fund for payable from interfund transfer out previously recognized.		

(37)	Expenditures	1,000	
	Due to Internal Service Fund		1,000
	Recognize payable for interfund supplies provided and used (received from the internal service fund).		

(38)	Due to Internal Service Fund	1,000	
	Cash		1,000
	Pay cash to eliminate payable.		

(39)	Due from Enterprise Fund	3,000	
	Cash		3,000
	City Council approves loan to enterprise fund to be repaid in 90 days.		

Adjusting Entries

Certain adjusting entries are required to state the year's balance sheet items correctly. Assume that a physical count of the inventory shows an ending balance of $17,000 on December 31, 20X2. This is a net increase of $3,000 from the beginning balance of $14,000.

The policy of the general fund is to recognize inventory as an asset and to report a reserve against fund balance for the ending balance. Recall that the city is using the consumption method of accounting for inventories. The entries required to adjust the ending balance of the supplies inventory follow:

(40)	Inventory of Supplies	3,000	
	Expenditures		3,000

Adjust ending inventory to $17,000 and reduce expenditures to net amount consumed during the period.

(41)	Fund Balance—Unassigned	3,000	
	Fund Balance—Assigned for Inventories		3,000

Adjust the reserve for inventories from beginning balance of $14,000 to its ending balance of $17,000.

Closing Entries

The final set of entries closes the nominal accounts. The format presented first reverses the budget entry and then closes the operating revenues and expenditures. Some governmental entities close the accounts in a slightly different order by closing budgeted revenue against actual revenue and budgeted appropriations against actual expenditures. The specific order of closing the accounts has no impact on the final effect; all budgetary accounts and nominal operating accounts must be closed at year-end.

Refer to the preclosing trial balance in Figure 17–10. Recall that the city is using the lapsing method of accounting for encumbrances open at the end of the fiscal year. The closing entries for Sol City's general fund for fiscal 20X2 follow:

	December 31, 20X2		
(42)	APPROPRIATIONS CONTROL	825,000	
	ESTIMATED OTHER FINANCING USES—TRANSFER OUT TO CAPITAL PROJECTS	20,000	
	ESTIMATED OTHER FINANCING USES—TRANSFER OUT TO INTERNAL SERVICES	10,000	
	BUDGETARY FUND BALANCE—UNASSIGNED	20,000	
	ESTIMATED REVENUES CONTROL		875,000

Close budgetary accounts.

(43)	BUDGETARY FUND BALANCE—ASSIGNED FOR ENCUMBRANCES	15,000	
	ENCUMBRANCES		15,000

Close remaining encumbrances by reversing remaining budgetary balance.

(44)	Fund Balance—Unassigned	15,000	
	Fund Balance—Assigned for Encumbrances		15,000

Reservation of fund balance for encumbrances that lapse but are expected to be honored in 20X3.

(45)	Revenue—Property Tax	781,000	
	Revenue—Grant	33,000	
	Revenue—Sales Tax	32,000	
	Revenue—Miscellaneous	18,000	
	Expenditures		811,000
	Other Financing Uses—Transfer Out to Capital Projects Fund		20,000
	Other Financing Uses—Transfer Out to Internal Service Fund		10,000
	Fund Balance—Unassigned		23,000

Close operating statement accounts.

FIGURE 17–10
Preclosing Trial Balance for General Fund

SOL CITY
General Fund
Preclosing Trial Balance December 31, 20X2

	Debit	Credit
Cash	$ 102,000	
Property Taxes Receivable—Delinquent	90,000	
Allowance for Uncollectible Taxes—Delinquent		$ 5,000
Due from Enterprise Fund	3,000	
Inventory of Supplies	17,000	
Vouchers Payable		55,000
Fund Balance—Nonspendable		17,000
Fund Balance—Unassigned		112,000
Revenue—Property Tax		781,000
Revenue—Grant		33,000
Revenue—Sales Tax		32,000
Revenue—Miscellaneous		18,000
Expenditures	811,000	
Other Financing Uses—Transfer Out to Capital Projects Fund	20,000	
Other Financing Uses—Transfer Out to Internal Service Fund	10,000	
ESTIMATED REVENUES CONTROL	875,000	
APPROPRIATIONS CONTROL		825,000
ESTIMATED OTHER FINANCING USES—TRANSFER OUT TO CAPITAL PROJECTS		20,000
ESTIMATED OTHER FINANCING USES—TRANSFER OUT TO INTERNAL SERVICE		10,000
ENCUMBRANCES	15,000	
BUDGETARY FUND BALANCE—ASSIGNED FOR ENCUMBRANCES		15,000
BUDGETARY FUND BALANCE—UNASSIGNED		20,000
Total	$1,943,000	$1,943,000

The following reconciliation explains the calculation of the Fund Balance—Unassigned account balance:

Fund Balance—Unassigned

		Bal. 1/1/X2	104,000
(41)	3,000	(11)	11,000
		Bal. Preclosing	112,000
(44)	15,000	(45)	23,000
		Bal. 12/31/X2	120,000

General Fund Financial Statement Information

The general fund is always specified as a major governmental fund type. The two required statements for a major governmental fund are (1) the balance sheet and (2) the statement of revenues, expenditures, and changes in fund balance. For purposes of illustration, we provide the financial statements for the general fund, applying the requirements of **GASB 34,** and then we present the fund balance section of the balance sheet under the proposed governmental accounting statement on fund balance reporting and governmental fund type definitions.

The Balance Sheet

See Figure 17–11 for the balance sheet required under **GASB 34.** It includes the supplies inventory for $17,000 and the associated reservation of fund balance, reflecting that the portion of the fund balance already applied to inventory is not expendable. The $3,000 receivable from the interfund loan transaction with the enterprise fund is shown as a current asset. The $15,000 outstanding encumbrances are a reservation of fund

FIGURE 17–11
General Fund Balance Sheet Information at the End of the Fiscal Period

SOL CITY General Fund Balance Sheet Information December 31, 20X2		
Assets:		
Cash		$102,000
Property Taxes Receivable—Delinquent	$ 90,000	
Less: Allowance for Uncollectibles—Delinquent	(5,000)	85,000
Due from Enterprise Fund		3,000
Inventory of Supplies		17,000
Total Assets		$207,000
Liabilities & Fund Balance:		
Vouchers Payable		$ 55,000
Fund Balance:		
Nonspendable:		
Supplies Inventory	$ 17,000	
Spendable:		
Assigned to:		
General Government Services	15,000	
Unassigned	120,000	152,000
Total Liabilities & Fund Balance		$207,000

balance indicating that a portion of the year's appropriation has been used but that the ordered goods or services have not yet been received.

The General Fund's Balance Sheet under GASB 54

The recent statement on fund balance reporting and governmental fund type definitions does not change the reporting of assets or liabilities. The statement affects only the reporting of the fund balance for governmental fund types that includes the general fund. The fund balance section of the balance sheet could report only aggregate amounts for the nonspendable and spendable categories with detail presented in the footnotes. Alternatively, the balance sheet can report the detailed items within each category of the general fund balance. The nonspendable category includes the two classifications of amounts not in spendable form, such as inventories, or amounts that are legally or contractually required to be maintained. The spendable category includes resources that are in spendable form and are considered to be available for spending, such as fund balance related to cash, investments, and receivables. Amounts in the spendable fund balance category can then be classified as restricted, limited, assigned, or unassigned based on a hierarchy of the level of control over the spending of the resources.

Under **GASB 54,** reserves are not reported on the balance sheet; rather, the amount of encumbrances is reported in a footnote along with other commitments. The Sol City government has no restricted or limited spendable fund balances, but it does have an assigned amount for resources the government intends to use for the specific purpose of paying currently outstanding encumbrances from goods and services ordered to be used for general government functions.

The Statement of Revenues, Expenditures, and Changes in Fund Balance

Refer to Figure 17–12 for the required statement of revenues, expenditures, and changes in fund balance, which has the following sections:

1. *Operating section.* This section reports revenues less expenditures, resulting in an excess of revenues over expenditures for the period. Expenditures include the interfund services provided and used, and separate reporting of outlays for capital assets.
2. *Other financing sources (uses).* This section includes interfund transfers and nonrevenue proceeds such as bond issues.

FIGURE 17–12
General Fund Statement of Revenues, Expenditures, and Changes in Fund Balance Information for Fiscal 20X2

SOL CITY Statement of Revenues, Expenditures, and Changes in Fund Balance Information General Fund For the Year Ended December 31, 20X2		
Revenues:		
Property Taxes	$781,000	
Grants	33,000	
Sales Taxes	32,000	
Miscellaneous	18,000	
Total Revenues		$864,000
Expenditures:		
General Government	$206,000	
Streets & Highways	71,000	
Public Safety	335,000	
Sanitation	141,000	
Capital Outlay:		
Public Safety	58,000	
Total Expenditures		811,000
Excess of Revenues over Expenditures		$ 53,000
Other Financing Sources (Uses):		
Transfer Out to Capital Projects Fund	$ (20,000)	
Transfer Out to Internal Service Fund	(10,000)	
Total Other Financing Sources (Uses)		(30,000)
Net Change in Fund Balances		$ 23,000
Fund Balance, January 1		129,000
Fund Balance, December 31		$152,000

3. *Reconciliation of fund balance.* The ending balance in fund balances, including both assigned and unassigned, is reconciled for (*a*) the results of operations, (*b*) other financing sources or uses, and (*c*) special or extraordinary items in the period.

Revenues should be classified by major sources and expenditures by character and major functions. Although the entries in the illustrations for Sol City did not categorize the expenditures by function (general government, streets and highways, public safety, and sanitation), the actual governmental accounting process does categorize them so each expenditure can be classified by both function and object (personal services, supplies, and other services and charges). The amounts in the expenditures section in Figure 17–12 are the assumed amounts from a comprehensive accounting system. Total expenditures do reconcile to the expenditures recorded in the Sol City illustration.

The statement of revenues, expenditures, and changes in fund balance presents the total fund balance, including both assigned and unassigned. Note that in this example, Sol City reported no extraordinary items or special items. Special items would include significant transactions or other events within the control of management that were either unusual in nature or infrequent in occurrence. An example of a special item could be a one-time sale of some city park land. If the city did have a special or extraordinary item, the city would report it below the other financing sources (uses) section.

The General Fund's Statement of Revenues, Expenditures, and Changes in Fund Balance

GASB 54 on governmental fund type balances does not require any changes in the statement of revenues, expenditures, and changes in fund balance. The reconciliation in this financial statement is to total fund balance, not to a specific classification of the fund balance. Therefore, this financial statement is the same under **GASB 54** as was previously required under **GASB 34.**

SUMMARY OF KEY CONCEPTS

Accounting for state and local governmental units requires the use of fund accounting to recognize properly the governmental unit's variety of services and objectives. Funds are separate fiscal and accounting entities established to segregate, control, and account for resource flows. Governmental units use three types of funds: governmental funds, of which the general fund is usually the most important; proprietary funds; and fiduciary funds. The basis of accounting for each fund depends on the fund's objective. Governmental financial statements use the current financial resources measurement focus and the modified accrual basis of accounting. The economic resources measurement focus and accrual basis of accounting are used for the governmentwide statements, the proprietary fund statements, and the fiduciary fund statements.

The modified accrual basis recognizes revenue when it is both measurable and available for financing expenditures of the period. A major source of revenue is property tax levies, but other sources may include sales taxes; grants from other governmental units; and fines, licenses, or permits. Note that in the five governmental funds, the estimated uncollectible property taxes are a reduction of the property tax revenue, not an expense as in commercial accounting. Expenditures are recognized in the period in which the related liability is both measurable and incurred. The expenditure process usually begins with a budget, which establishes the fund's spending authority. Encumbrances are used for purchases outside the governmental entity to recognize the use of a portion of the spending authority for the period and to avoid overspending the expenditure authority. Under current GAAFR, encumbrances outstanding at the end of a fiscal period are reported as a reserve of the fund balance and may be accounted for as lapsing or nonlapsing. Another type of fund balance reserve is a reserve for inventories, which is used if the amount of inventory is material.

The general fund is responsible for offering many of the usual services of governmental units. Fire and police protection, the local government's administrative and legislative functions, and many other basic governmental services are administered through the general fund. It will provide balance sheet information and statement of revenues, expenditures, and changes in fund balances information to the governmental funds financial statements.

The government reporting model, as established by **GASB 34,** specifies that both fund-based financial statements and governmentwide financial statements must be presented. The general fund uses the modified accrual basis of accounting to recognize revenue and expenditure transactions. Furthermore, no long-term capital assets or general long-term debt is recorded in the general fund. However, a reconciliation schedule will be required to go from the governmental fund types financial statements to the governmentwide financial statements. The governmentwide financial statements use the accrual basis of accounting and report all capital assets and all long-term debt. Governmentwide financial statements are presented in Chapter 18 after the conclusion of that chapter's discussion of the remaining funds.

Interfund activities must be evaluated carefully to ensure that the governmental unit's legal and budgetary controls are not violated. Four types of interfund activities exist: (1) interfund loans, (2) interfund services provided and used, (3) interfund transfers, and (4) interfund reimbursements. Outstanding interfund loans are presented as receivables or payables on the fund's balance sheet information. Interfund services provided and used are reported as part of the revenues and expenditures on the operating statements. Interfund transfers are reported separately in the other financing sources (uses) section of the operating statement. Interfund reimbursements are not reported separately on the fund's financial statements.

KEY TERMS

appropriation, *865*
basis of accounting, *859*
budgets, *864*
current financial resources measurement focus, *857*
disbursement, *867*
economic resources measurement focus, *860*
encumbrance, *865*
expenditure, *854*
fiduciary funds, *854*
fund-based financial statements, *856*
funds, *853*
governmental financial reporting model, *856*
governmental funds, *854*
governmentwide financial statements, *856*
interfund activities, *875*
measurement focus, *859*
modified accrual basis, *859*
proprietary funds, *854*
reporting entity, *855*
reservation (or restriction) of the budgetary fund balance, *866*

QUESTIONS

LO 17-1 **Q17-1** What is a fund? How does a fund receive resources?

LO 17-1 **Q17-2** What are the nine funds that local and state governments generally use? Briefly state the purpose of each fund.

LO 17-1 **Q17-3** Compare the modified accrual basis with the accrual basis of accounting.

LO 17-3 **Q17-4** Which of the two, the modified accrual basis or the accrual basis, is used for funds for which expendability is the concern? Why?

LO 17-5 **Q17-5** When are property taxes recognized as revenue in the general fund?

LO 17-4 **Q17-6** How are taxpayer-assessed income and sales taxes recognized in the general fund? Why?

LO 17-6 **Q17-7** What is meant by *budgetary accounting*? Explain the accounting for expected revenue and anticipated expenditures.

LO 17-6 **Q17-8** Are all expenditures encumbered?

LO 17-5 **Q17-9** Why do some governmental units not report small amounts of supply inventories in their balance sheets?

LO 17-6 **Q17-10** What are the main differences between the lapsing and nonlapsing methods of accounting for encumbrances outstanding at the fiscal year-end? What are the differences in accounting between the lapsing and nonlapsing methods when accounting for the actual expenditure in the subsequent year?

LO 17-4 **Q17-11** When is the expenditure for inventories recognized under the purchase method? Under the consumption method?

LO 17-6 **Q17-12** Explain the difference between an interfund service provided and used and an interfund transfer. Give examples of each.

LO 17-4 **Q17-13** Where is an interfund transfer reported on the general fund's financial statements?

LO 17-4 **Q17-14** The general fund agrees to lend the enterprise fund $2,000 for three months. How is this interfund loan reported on the general fund's financial statements?

LO 17-4 **Q17-15** Explain how an expenditure may be classified by (1) function, (2) activity, and (3) object within a governmental unit's financial statements.

CASES

LO 17-6 **C17-1** **Budget Theory**

Understanding

Governmental accounting gives substantial recognition to budgets, which are being recorded in the governmental unit's accounts.

Required

a. What is the purpose of a governmental accounting system, and why is the budget recorded in the accounts of a governmental unit? Include in your discussion the purpose and significance of appropriations.

b. Describe when and how a governmental unit (1) records its budget and (2) closes out the budgetary accounts.

LO 17-1 **C17-2** **Municipal versus Financial Accounting**

Judgment

Wilma Bates is executive vice president of Mavis Industries Inc., a publicly held industrial corporation. She has just been elected to Gotham City's council. Before assuming office, she asks you to explain the major differences in accounting and financial reporting for a large city compared with accounting and reporting for a large industrial corporation.

Required

a. Describe the major differences that exist in the purpose of accounting and financial reporting and in the type of financial reports of a large city when compared with that of a large industrial corporation.

b. Why are inventories often ignored in accounting for local governmental units? Explain.

LO 17-4

C17-3 Revenue Issues

Communication

The bookkeeper for the community of Spring Valley has asked for your assistance regarding the following items.

Required

Prepare a memo discussing the proper accounting and financial reporting in the general fund for each of the following items.

a. Property taxes receivable are recognized at the levy date. One percent of the levy is not expected to be collected.

b. Spring Valley collects property taxes in advance of the year in which they are expendable.

c. Spring Valley receives sales tax revenues from the state, but the state still owes the city another $15,000 that will not be received until the next month.

d. Spring Valley receives an unexpected state grant to finance the purchase of fire prevention equipment. One-half of the grant is expended in this fiscal period, and the remainder is expected to be expended in the next fiscal period.

e. Interest is earned on short-term investments made from the general fund's resources.

f. A gift from a local citizen was given to be used for a new city park once it has been completed. If the park is not constructed within two years, the gift must be returned to the grantor. The park's completion is expected in the next fiscal period.

LO 17-4

C17-4 Examining the General Fund Disclosures in a Comprehensive Annual Financial Report (CAFR)

Analysis

This case focuses on a governmental unit's general fund.

Required

Using the CAFR for a governmental entity chosen by your instructor, answer the following questions that relate to the overall government and governmental funds:

a. Find the budgetary comparison schedules for the general fund. Using them, what were the estimated revenues and appropriations for the most recent fiscal year?

b. Using the same information as in part *a*, list the amounts of any transfers in and transfers out that were budgeted for the most recent year.

c. Based on the notes following the financial statements, what is the policy of the general fund with respect to outstanding encumbrances at the fiscal year-end?

d. On the balance sheet of the general fund at the most recent fiscal year-end what is the total amount reported for assets and for fund balance? Of the total amount reported for fund balance, how much is unassigned?

e. On the balance sheet of the general fund at the most recent fiscal year-end what is the amount reported for inventories? If inventories are reported, does the government use the purchase method or the consumption method?

f. Based on the notes following the financial statements, what is the government's revenue recognition policy with respect to property taxes in the general fund? What percentage of the property tax levy is estimated to be uncollectible?

g. Read the CAFR section that contains management's discussion and analysis. What reasons were given for the increase or decrease in general fund revenues for the most recent year?

h. Examine the statement of revenues, expenditures, and changes in fund balance for the most recent year. Compare the change in fund balance for the general fund with the amount of change in fund balance that was budgeted for the year. Were the government's general fund actual results better or worse than expected?

i. After revenue from taxes, what was the next most significant source of revenue for the general fund for the most recent year?

j. Has the general fund engaged in any interfund loans and advances? If yes, show the amounts that are owed to or by the general fund as of the most recent year-end.

LO 17-2

C17-5 Examining Deposit and Investment Risk Disclosures of a Governmental Entity

Discovery

The financial reports of governmental entities must provide footnote disclosure of the deposit and investment risks the entity faces. **GASB 40** amended **GASB 3.**

The GASB requires disclosures of (1) the nature of the deposits and of investment risks the governmental entity faces, (2) the governmental entity's policies regarding each of those risks, and (3) specific ones such as credit ratings of investments in fixed income securities and a schedule of their maturity dates and fair values; the types of other investment securities held and their amounts and fair values; any concentrations of investments, other than those in U.S. government securities or in mutual or pooled investment funds, consisting of 5 percent or more of total investments; and the risks from changing interest rates and changing foreign exchange rates.

Required

First, go to the GASB's website (www.gasb.org) and obtain the summaries of **GASB 40** and **GASB 3** (the GASB does not provide online access to their complete publications). Second, using an online search engine such as Google, locate the most recent annual report of a local government near your college or university. Then complete parts *a* through *e*.

a. List the types of deposit and investment risks addressed in **GASB 3** and **GASB 40.**

b. Explain why disclosures of information about these risks are important to the users of the government's financial statements.

Complete the following instructions using the footnote information for Deposits and Investments from your local government's most recent annual report.

c. Describe the types of deposit and investment risks of your local government.

d. Describe the policies your local government has for each type of risk identified.

e. Describe the types of specific disclosures of information for each type of risk identified.

EXERCISES

LO 17-7

E17-1 Multiple-Choice Questions on the General Fund [AICPA Adapted]

Select the correct answer for each of the following questions.

1. One difference between accounting for a governmental (not-for-profit) unit and a commercial (for-profit) enterprise is that a governmental unit should

   a. *Not* record depreciation expense in any of its funds.
   b. Always establish and maintain complete self-balancing accounts for each fund.
   c. Use only the cash basis of accounting.
   d. Use only the modified accrual basis of accounting.

2. Belle Valley incurred $100,000 of salaries and wages for the month ended March 31, 20X2. How should this be recorded on that date?

		Debit	Credit
a.	Expenditures—Salaries and Wages	100,000	
	Vouchers Payable		100,000
b.	Salaries and Wages Expense	100,000	
	Vouchers Payable		100,000
c.	Encumbrances—Salaries and Wages	100,000	
	Vouchers Payable		100,000
d.	Fund Balance	100,000	
	Vouchers Payable		100,000

3. Which of the following accounts of a governmental unit is credited when taxpayers are billed for property taxes?

   a. Estimated Revenue.
   b. Revenue.

c. Appropriations.

d. Fund Balance—Assigned for Encumbrances.

4. Fixed assets purchased from general fund revenue were received. What account, if any, should have been debited in the general fund?

    a. None.

    b. Fixed Assets.

    c. Expenditures.

    d. Fund Balance—Unassigned.

5. The initial transfer of cash from the general fund to establish an internal service fund requires the general fund to credit Cash and debit

    a. Accounts Receivable—Internal Service Fund.

    b. Transfers Out.

    c. Budgetary Fund Balance—Assigned for Encumbrances.

    d. Expenditures.

LO 17-7

E17-2 Matching for General Fund Transactions [AICPA Adapted]

For each general fund transaction in items 1 through 12, select its appropriate recording next to letters A through O. A letter may be selected once, more than once, or not at all.

Transactions	Recording of Transactions
1. Made an interfund transfer out to the capital projects fund.	A. Credit Revenues
2. Issued approved purchase orders for supplies.	B. Debit Expenditures
3. Received the above-mentioned supplies whose invoices were approved.	C. Debit Encumbrances
4. Incurred salaries and wages.	D. Debit Inventories
5. Transferred cash to establish an internal service fund.	E. Debit Interfund Services Provided and Used
6. Sent tax bills to property owners after city council passed the property tax levy.	F. Credit Budgetary Fund Balance—Unassigned
7. Collected property taxes for the current year.	G. Debit Appropriations Control
8. Recorded appropriations upon adoption of the budget.	H. Credit Property Taxes Receivable—Current
9. Recorded estimated revenues upon adoption of the budget.	I. Credit Appropriations Control
10. Recorded excess of estimated inflows over estimated outflows.	J. Credit Residual Equity Transfer Out
11. Received invoices for computer equipment.	K. Debit Interfund Transfer Out
12. Received billing from water and sewer fund (enterprise fund) for using city water and sewer.	L. Credit Interfund Transfer Out
	M. Debit Estimated Revenues Control
	N. Debit Budgetary Fund Balance—Unassigned
	O. Debit Computer Equipment

LO 17-6, 17-7

E17-3 Multiple-Choice Questions on Budgets, Expenditures, and Revenue [AICPA Adapted]

Select the correct completion of each of the following items.

1. Which of the following steps in the acquisition of goods and services occurs first?

    a. Appropriation.

    b. Encumbrance.

    c. Budget.

    d. Expenditure.

2. What account is used to earmark the fund balance to recognize the contingent obligations of goods ordered but not yet received?
   a. Appropriations.
   b. Encumbrances.
   c. Obligations.
   d. Fund Balance—Assigned for Encumbrances.
3. When a governmental unit's Estimated Revenues Control account is closed out at the end of the fiscal year, the excess of estimated revenues over estimated appropriations is
   a. Debited to Fund Balance—Unassigned.
   b. Debited to Fund Balance—Assigned for Encumbrances.
   c. Debited to Budgetary Fund Balance—Unassigned.
   d. Credited to Fund Balance—Assigned for Encumbrances.
4. Carson City's general fund issued purchase orders of $630,000 to vendors for supplies. Which of the following entries should the city make to record this transaction?

		Debit	Credit
a.	ENCUMBRANCES	630,000	
	BUDGETARY FUND BALANCE—ASSIGNED FOR ENCUMBRANCES		630,000
b.	Expenditures	630,000	
	Vouchers Payable		630,000
c.	Expenses	630,000	
	Accounts Payable		630,000
d.	BUDGETARY FUND BALANCE—ASSIGNED FOR ENCUMBRANCES	630,000	
	ENCUMBRANCES		630,000

5. The following balances are included in the subsidiary records of Dogwood's Parks and Recreation Department on March 31, 20X2:

Appropriations—Supplies	$7,500
Expenditures—Supplies	4,500
Encumbrances—Supply Orders	750

   How much does the department have available to purchase additional supplies?
   a. $0.
   b. $2,250.
   c. $3,000.
   d. $6,750.
6. The board of commissioners of the City of Elgin adopted its budget for the year ending July 31, 20X2, which indicated revenue of $1,000,000 and appropriations of $900,000. If the budget is formally integrated into the accounting records, what is the required journal entry?

a.	Memorandum entry only		
b.	APPROPRIATIONS CONTROL	900,000	
	BUDGETARY FUND BALANCE—UNASSIGNED	100,000	
	ESTIMATED REVENUES CONTROL		1,000,000
c.	ESTIMATED REVENUES CONTROL	1,000,000	
	APPROPRIATIONS CONTROL		900,000
	BUDGETARY FUND BALANCE—UNASSIGNED		100,000
d.	REVENUE RECEIVABLE	1,000,000	
	EXPENDITURES PAYABLE		900,000
	BUDGETARY FUND BALANCE—UNASSIGNED		100,000

7. Which of the following accounts of a governmental unit is credited when the budget is recorded?
   a. Encumbrances.
   b. Budgetary Fund Balance—Assigned for Encumbrances.
   c. Estimated Revenue Control.
   d. Appropriations Control.
8. Which of the following accounts of a governmental unit is debited when supplies previously ordered are received?
   a. Encumbrances.
   b. Budgetary Fund Balance—Assigned for Encumbrances.
   c. Vouchers Payable.
   d. Appropriations Control.
9. Which of the following situations will increase a governmental unit's fund balance at the fiscal year-end?
   a. Appropriations are less than expenditures and budgetary fund balance assigned for encumbrances.
   b. Appropriations are less than expenditures and encumbrances.
   c. Appropriations are more than expenditures and encumbrances.
   d. Appropriations are more than estimated revenue.
10. Which of the following accounts of a governmental unit is credited to close it out at the fiscal year-end?
   a. Appropriations Control.
   b. Revenue—Property Tax.
   c. Budgetary Fund Balance—Assigned for Encumbrances.
   d. Encumbrances.

LO 17-2, 17-7

E17-4 Multiple-Choice Questions on the General Fund

Select the correct answer for each of the following items.

1. The primary focus in accounting and reporting for governmental funds is
   a. Income determination.
   b. Flow of financial resources.
   c. Capital maintenance.
   d. Transfers relating to proprietary activities.
2. The governmental fund measurement focus is the determination of

	Income	Financial Position	Flow of Financial Resources
a.	Yes	Yes	No
b.	No	Yes	No
c.	No	No	Yes
d.	No	Yes	Yes

3. A Budgetary Fund Balance—Assigned for Encumbrances in excess of a balance of Encumbrances Control indicates
   a. An excess of vouchers payable over encumbrances.
   b. An excess of purchase orders over invoices received.
   c. A recording error.
   d. An excess of appropriations over encumbrances.
4. The Encumbrances Control account of a governmental unit is debited when
   a. Goods are received.
   b. A voucher payable is recorded.

c. A purchase order is approved.

d. The budget is recorded.

5. The following pertains to property taxes levied by Cedar City for the calendar year 20X6:

Expected collections during 20X6	$500,000
Expected collections during the first 60 days of 20X7	100,000
Expected collections during the remainder of 20X7	60,000
Expected collections during January 20X8	30,000
Estimated to be uncollectible (3/1/X7 through 1/1/X8)	10,000
Total levy	$700,000

City Cedar should report revenues from property taxes for 20X6 of

a. $700,000.

b. $600,000.

c. $690,000.

d. $500,000.

6. Oak City issued a purchase order for supplies with an estimated cost of $5,000. When the supplies and accompanying invoice were received, the invoice indicated a $4,950 actual price. What amount should Oak City debit (credit) to Budgetary Fund Balance—Assigned for Encumbrances?

a. $5,000.

b. $(50).

c. $4,950.

d. $50.

7. For the budgetary year ending December 31, 20X6, Johnson City expects the following inflows of resources in its general fund:

Property taxes, licenses, and fines	$9,000,000
Transfer in from internal service fund	500,000
Transfer in from debt service fund	1,000,000

In the budgetary entry, what amount should Johnson City record for estimated revenues?

a. $9,000,000.

b. $9,500,000.

c. $10,500,000.

d. $10,000,000.

8. Encumbrances outstanding at year-end in a state's general fund should be reported as a

a. Liability in the general fund.

b. Fund balance designation in the general fund.

c. Fund balance reserve in the general fund.

d. Liability in the general long-term debt account group.

9. Interperiod equity is an objective of financial reporting for governmental entities. According to the Governmental Accounting Standards Board, is interperiod equity fundamental to public administration? Is it a component of accountability?

	Fundamental to Public Administration	Component of Accountability
a.	Yes	Yes
b.	No	No
c.	Yes	No
d.	No	Yes

10. Which of the following statements is correct regarding comparability of governmental financial reports?
    a. Comparability is not relevant in governmental financial reporting.
    b. Differences between financial reports should be due to substantive differences in underlying transactions or the governmental structure.
    c. Selection of different alternatives in accounting procedures or practices account for the differences between financial reports.
    d. Similarly designated governments perform the same functions.

LO 17-7

E17-5 Encumbrances at Year-End

Advanced StudyGuide .com

The City of Batavia ordered new computer equipment for $21,000 on November 3, 20X2. The equipment had not been received by December 31, 20X2, Batavia's fiscal year-end.

Required

a. Assume that the city has a policy that outstanding encumbrances lapse at year-end.
(1) Prepare the entry to record the encumbrance on November 3, 20X2.
(2) Prepare the entries required on December 31, 20X2.
(3) Assuming that the city council accepts outstanding encumbrances in its budget for the next fiscal period (20X3), prepare entries on January 1, 20X3.
(4) Prepare entries on January 18, 20X3, when the equipment was received with an invoice cost of $21,800 and accepted by the city.
(5) Prepare the entry on December 31, 20X3, to close the expenditures account.

b. Assume the city's policy is that outstanding encumbrances are nonlapsing.
(1) Prepare the entry to record the encumbrance on November 3, 20X2.
(2) Prepare the entries required on December 31, 20X2.
(3) Prepare the entry on January 1, 20X3, to classify the expenditure in 20X2, the year the encumbrance was initiated.
(4) Prepare the entry on January 18, 20X3, when the equipment was received for $21,800. The City Council approved the additional $800 equipment cost as an addition to 20X3's expenditures.
(5) Prepare the entries on December 31, 20X3, to close the expenditures accounts.

c. Now assume the city has a policy that outstanding encumbrances are nonlapsing, but the 20X3 City Council decided, during its budget hearings for 20X3, not to accept the encumbrance for the computer equipment that had been ordered on November 3, 20X2.
(1) Prepare the entry required on January 1, 20X3, to cancel the encumbrance reserve for the equipment ordered on November 3, 20X2.

LO 17-7

E17-6 Accounting for Inventories of Office Supplies

Advanced StudyGuide .com

Georgetown purchased supplies on August 8, 20X2, for $3,600. At the fiscal year-end on September 30, the inventory of supplies was $2,800.

Required

a. Assume that Georgetown uses the consumption method of accounting for inventories.
(1) Prepare the entry for the purchase on August 8, 20X2.
(2) Prepare the entries required on September 30, 20X2, including the closing of the Expenditures account.
(3) Assuming the supplies were used during 20X3, prepare the entries on September 30, 20X3.

b. Assume that Georgetown uses the purchase method of accounting for inventories.
(1) Prepare the entry for the purchase on August 8, 20X2.
(2) Prepare the entries required on September 30, 20X2, including the closing of the Expenditures account.
(3) Assuming the supplies were used during 20X3, prepare the entry on September 30, 20X3.

LO 17-7

E17-7 Accounting for Prepayments and Capital Assets

Required

Prepare journal entries for Iron City's general fund for the following, including any adjusting and closing entries on December 31, 20X1:

Advanced StudyGuide .com

a. Acquired a three-year fire insurance policy for $5,400 on September 1, 20X1.

b. Ordered new furniture for the city council meeting room on September 17, 20X1, at an estimated cost of $15,600. The furniture was delivered on October 1; its actual cost was $15,200, its estimated life is 10 years, and it has no residual value.

c. Acquired supplies on November 4, 20X1, for $1,800. Iron City uses the consumption method of accounting. Supplies on hand on December 31, 20X1, were $1,120.

LO 17-7

E17-8 Computation of Revenues Reported on the Statement of Revenues, Expenditures, and Changes in Fund Balance for the General Fund

Gilbert City had the following transactions involving resource inflows into its general fund for the year ended June 30, 20X8:

1. The general fund levied $2,000,000 of property taxes in July 20X7. The city estimated that 2 percent of the levy would be uncollectible and that $100,000 of the levy would not be collected until after August 31, 20X8.
2. On April 1, 20X8, the general fund received $50,000 repayment of an advance made to the internal service fund. Interest on the advance of $1,500 also was received.
3. During the year ended June 30, 20X8, the general fund received $1,800,000 of the property taxes levied in transaction (1).
4. The general fund received $250,000 in grant monies from the state to be used solely to acquire computer equipment. During March 20X8, the general fund acquired computer equipment using $235,000 of the grant. The city has not yet determined the use of the remainder of the grant.
5. During the year ended June 30, 20X8, the general fund received $125,000 from the state as its portion of the sales tax. At June 30, 20X8, the state owed the general fund an additional $25,000 of sales taxes. The general fund does not expect to have the $25,000 available until early August 20X8.
6. In July 20X7, the general fund borrowed $800,000 from a local bank using the property tax levy as collateral. The loan was repaid in September 20X7 with the proceeds from property tax collections.
7. In February 20X8, a terminated debt service fund transferred $30,000 to the general fund. The $30,000 represented excess resources left in the debt service fund after a general long-term debt obligation had been paid in full.
8. On July 1, 20X7, the general fund estimated that it would receive $75,000 from the sale of liquor licenses during the fiscal year ended June 30, 20X8. For the year ended June 30, 20X8, $66,000 had been received from liquor license sales.
9. The general fund received $15,000 in October 20X7 from one of the city's special revenue funds. The amount received represented a reimbursement for an expenditure of the special revenue fund that the city's general fund paid.
10. In July 20X7, the general fund collected $80,000 of delinquent property taxes that had been classified as delinquent on June 30, 20X7. In the entry to record the property tax levy in July 20X6, the general fund estimated that it would collect all property tax revenues by July 31, 20X7.

Required

Prepare a schedule showing the amount of revenue that should be reported by Gilbert City's general fund on the statement of revenues, expenditures, and changes in fund balance for the year ended June 30, 20X8.

LO 17-7

Advanced StudyGuide .com

E17-9 Computation of Expenditures Reported on the Statement of Revenues, Expenditures, and Changes in Fund Balance for the General Fund

Benson City had the following transactions involving resource outflows from its general fund for the year ended June 30, 20X8:

1. During March 20X8, the general fund transferred $150,000 to a capital projects fund to help pay for the construction of a new police station.
2. During August 20X7, the general fund ordered computer equipment at $200,000 estimated cost. The equipment arrived in September 20X7, and a $202,000 invoice was paid.

3. In November 20X7, the city authorized the establishment of an internal service fund for the maintenance of city-owned vehicles. The general fund was authorized to transfer $500,000 to the internal service fund in late November. Of this amount, the internal service fund will repay $200,000 in two years with interest at 6 percent; the remaining $300,000 represents a permanent transfer to the internal service fund.
4. In May 20X8, the general fund paid $15,000 to one of the city's special revenue funds. The amount paid represented a reimbursement to the special revenue fund for expending $15,000 of its resources on behalf of the general fund.
5. During the year ended June 30, 20X8, the general fund received bills from the city's water department totaling $12,000. Of this amount, the general fund had paid all but $500 by June 30, 20X8.
6. During the year ended June 30, 20X8, the general fund acquired supplies costing $35,000 and paid the salaries and wages of its employees totaling $900,000. The general fund uses the purchase method of accounting for its supplies. At June 30, 20X8, unused supplies in the general fund amounted to $5,000.
7. At June 30, 20X8, outstanding encumbrances for goods ordered in the general fund amounted to $25,000. Outstanding encumbrances do not lapse at the end of the fiscal year.
8. On March 15, 20X8, the general fund repaid a local bank $265,000 for a loan of which $250,000 represented the principal borrowed. The general fund borrowed the money in July 20X7 and used collections of the property tax levy to repay the loan.
9. For the year ended June 30, 20X8, the general fund transferred $95,000 to the city's pension trust fund. The amount transferred represented the employer's contribution to the pension trust on behalf of the employees of the general fund.
10. During May 20X8, the general fund decided to lease several copying machines instead of purchasing them. The lease arrangement was properly accounted for as an operating lease. By June 30, 20X8, the general fund had made lease payments of $10,000 to the owner.

Required

Prepare a schedule showing the amount of expenditures that Benson's general fund should reported on the statement of revenues, expenditures, and changes in fund balance for the year ended June 30, 20X8.

LO 17-7

E17-10 Closing Entries and Balance Sheet

The preclosing trial balance at December 31, 20X1, for Lone Wolf's general fund follows.

	Debit	Credit
Cash	$ 90,000	
Property Taxes Receivable—Delinquent	100,000	
Allowance for Uncollectibles—Delinquent		$ 7,200
Due from Other Funds	14,600	
Vouchers Payable		65,000
Due to Other Funds		8,400
Fund Balance—Unassigned		119,000
Property Tax Revenue		1,130,000
Miscellaneous Revenue		40,000
Expenditures	1,140,000	
Other Financing Uses—Transfer Out	25,000	
Estimated Revenues Control	1,200,000	
Appropriations Control		1,145,000
Estimated Other Financing Uses—Transfer Out		25,000
Encumbrances	32,000	
Budgetary Fund Balance—Assigned for Encumbrances		32,000
Budgetary Fund Balance—Unassigned		30,000
Total	$2,601,600	$2,601,600

Lone Wolf uses the purchase method of accounting for inventories and the lapsing method of accounting for encumbrances.

Required

a. Prepare the closing entries for the general fund.

b. Prepare a general fund–only balance sheet at December 31, 20X1.

LO 17-7

E17-11 Statement of Revenues, Expenditures, and Changes in Fund Balance

Refer to the preclosing trial balance in Exercise 17-10. Assume that the balances on December 31, 20X0, were as follows:

Fund Balance—Assigned for Encumbrances	$28,000
Fund Balance—Unassigned	91,000

Required

Prepare a general fund–only statement of revenues, expenditures, and changes in fund balance for fiscal 20X1.

LO 17-8

E17-12 Matching Items Involving Interfund Transactions and Transfers

Mattville's general fund had several interfund activities during the fiscal year ended June 30, 20X9 (see the left-hand column of the following table). The right-hand column lists the types of interfund activities that occur in state and local governmental accounting. For each general fund transaction/transfer, select a letter from the list on the right that best describes the interfund activity.

General Fund Transactions and Transfers	Type of Interfund Transactions and Transfers
1. Received bills from an internal service fund for using city-owned vehicles.	A. Interfund loan
2. Transferred cash to start an enterprise fund that does not have to return the cash to the general fund.	B. Interfund service provided and used
3. Received cash from a discontinued special revenue fund.	C. Interfund transfer
4. Transferred cash to a capital projects fund to help construct a building.	D. Interfund reimbursement
5. Transferred cash to a debt service fund to pay interest and principal of general long-term debt.	
6. Transferred cash to the pension trust fund representing the employer's contribution for the pension of general fund employees.	
7. Transferred resources to an enterprise fund that is expected to repay these resources with interest.	
8. Transferred cash to a special revenue fund that incurred and paid expenditures on behalf of the general fund.	
9. Received from an internal service fund cash that represented repayment of an advance made during the previous year.	
10. Received bills from an enterprise fund for using public parking facilities.	

PROBLEMS

LO 17-7

P17-13 General Fund Entries [AICPA Adapted]

The following information was abstracted from the accounts of the general fund of the City of Noble after the books had been closed for the fiscal year ended June 30, 20X2.

Advanced StudyGuide .com

	Postclosing Trial Balance, June 30, 20X1	Transactions July 1, 20X1–June 30, 20X2 Debit	Credit	Postclosing Trial Balance, June 30, 20X2
Cash	$700,000	$1,820,000	$1,852,000	$668,000
Taxes Receivable	40,000	1,870,000	1,828,000	82,000
Total	$740,000			$750,000
Allowance for Uncollectible Taxes	$ 8,000	8,000	10,000	$ 10,000
Vouchers Payable	132,000	1,852,000	1,840,000	120,000
Fund Balance:				
Assigned for Encumbrances			70,000	70,000
Unassigned	600,000	70,000	20,000	550,000
Total	$740,000			$750,000

Additional Information

The budget for the fiscal year ended June 30, 20X2, provided for estimated revenue of $2,000,000 and appropriations of $1,940,000. Encumbrances of $1,070,000 were made during the year.

Required

Prepare proper journal entries to record the budgeted and actual transactions for the fiscal year ended June 30, 20X2. Include closing entries.

LO 17-7, 17-8 **P17-14 General Fund Entries [AICPA Adapted]**

The following trial balances were taken from the accounts of Omega City's general fund before the books had been closed for the fiscal year ended June 30, 20X2:

	Trial Balance July 1, 20X1	Trial Balance June 30, 20X2
Cash	$400,000	$ 700,000
Taxes Receivable	150,000	170,000
Allowance for Uncollectible Taxes	(40,000)	(70,000)
Estimated Revenues Control	—	3,000,000
Expenditures	—	2,900,000
Encumbrances	—	91,000
Total	$510,000	$6,791,000
Vouchers Payable	$ 80,000	$ 408,000
Due to Other Funds	210,000	142,000
Fund Balance—Assigned for Encumbrances	60,000	—
Fund Balance—Unassigned	160,000	220,000
Revenue from Taxes	—	2,800,000
Miscellaneous Revenues	—	130,000
Appropriations Control	—	2,980,000
Budgetary Fund Balance—Assigned for Encumbrances	—	91,000
Budgetary Fund Balance—Unassigned	—	20,000
Total	$510,000	$6,791,000

Additional Information

1. The estimated taxes receivable for the year ended June 30, 20X2, were $2,870,000, and the taxes collected during the year totaled $2,810,000. Miscellaneous revenue of $130,000 also was collected during the year.
2. Encumbrances in the amount of $2,700,000 were recorded. In addition, the $60,000 of lapsed encumbrances from the 20X1 fiscal year was renewed.
3. During the year, the general fund was billed $142,000 for services performed on its behalf by other city funds (debit Expenditures).

4. An analysis of the transactions in the Vouchers Payable account for the year ended June 30, 20X2, follows:

	Debit (Credit)
Current expenditures (liquidating all encumbrances to date except for renewed 20X1 commitment)	$(2,700,000)
Expenditures applicable to previous year	(58,000)
Vouchers for payments to other funds	(210,000)
Cash payments during year	2,640,000
Net change	$ (328,000)

5. On May 10, 20X2, encumbrances were recorded for the purchase of next year's supplies at an estimated cost of $91,000.

Required

On the basis of the data presented, reconstruct the original detailed journal entries that were required to record all transactions for the fiscal year ended June 30, 20X2, including the recording of the current year's budget. Do not prepare closing entries for June 30, 20X2.

LO 17-7, 17-8 P17-15 General Fund Entries and Statements

The postclosing trial balance of the general fund of the town of Pine Ridge on December 31, 20X1, is as follows:

	Debit	Credit
Cash	$111,000	
Property Taxes Receivable—Delinquent	90,000	
Allowance for Uncollectibles—Delinquent		$ 9,000
Vouchers Payable		31,000
Fund Balance—Assigned for Encumbrances		21,000
Fund Balance—Unassigned		140,000
Total	$201,000	$201,000

Additional Information Related to 20X2

1. Estimated revenue consisted of property taxes, $1,584,000 from a tax levy of $1,600,000 of which 1 percent was estimated uncollectible; sales taxes, $250,000; and miscellaneous, $43,000. Appropriations totaled $1,840,000, and estimated transfers out were $37,000. Appropriations included outstanding purchase orders from 20X1 of $21,000. Pine Ridge uses the lapsing method for outstanding encumbrances.
2. Cash receipts consisted of property taxes, $1,590,000, including $83,000 from 20X1; sales taxes, $284,000; licenses and fees, $39,000; and a loan from the motor pool, $10,000. The remaining property taxes from 20X1 were written off, and those remaining from 20X2 were reclassified.
3. Orders were issued for $1,800,000 in addition to the acceptance of the $21,000 outstanding purchase orders from 20X1. A total of $48,000 of purchase orders still was outstanding at the end of 20X2. Actual expenditures were $1,788,000, including $42,000 for office furniture. Vouchers paid totaled $1,793,000.
4. Other cash payments and transfers follow:

Loan to central stores	$13,000
Transfer out	37,000

Required

a. Prepare entries to summarize the general fund budget and transactions for 20X2.

b. Prepare a preclosing trial balance.

c. Prepare closing entries for the general fund.

d. Prepare a balance sheet for the general fund as of December 31, 20X2.

e. Prepare a statement of revenues, expenditures, and changes in fund balance for 20X2 for the general fund.

LO 17-2, 17-6 **P17-16 Matching Terms**

Match the items in the left-hand column with the descriptions/explanations in the right-hand column.

Items	Descriptions/Explanations
1. Proprietary funds	A. Trust and agency funds.
2. Modified accrual method	B. Fiscal and accounting entities of a government.
3. Estimated revenues	C. Basis of accounting used by proprietary funds.
4. Appropriations	D. Example of this transaction when the general fund uses the services of an internal service fund.
5. Encumbrances	E. Expenditures for inventories representing the amount of inventories consumed during the period.
6. Expenditures	F. General, special revenue, debt service, capital projects funds, and permanent funds.
7. Budgetary fund balance—unassigned	G. Legal authority to make expenditures.
8. Consumption method for supplies inventories	H. Budgeted resource inflows.
9. Nonlapsing encumbrances	I. Revenues recognized when they are both measurable and available to finance expenditures made during the current period.
10. Interfund services provided or used	J. Internal service and enterprise funds.
11. Governmental funds	K. Expenditures for inventories representing the amount of inventories acquired during the current period.
12. Interfund transfers	L. Reports governmental unit's infrastructure assets.
13. Fiduciary funds	M. Recorded when the general fund orders goods and services.
14. Funds	N. Appropriation authority that carries over to the next fiscal year for these orders.
15. Governmentwide financials	O. Appropriation authority that does not carry over to the next fiscal year for these orders.
16. Accrual method	P. Type of transaction that occurs when the general fund makes a cash transfer to establish an internal service fund.
	Q. Account debited in the general fund when an invoice for computer equipment is received.
	R. Account that would indicate a budget surplus or deficit in the general fund.

LO 17-2, 17-8 **P17-17 Identification of Governmental Accounting Terms**

Give the term(s) that is (are) described in each of the following numbered statements.

1. This is the set of financial statements that presents the governmental unit's infrastructure assets and long-term debt.
2. At the present time, this body has the authority to prescribe generally accepted accounting principles for state and local governmental entities.
3. This is a fiscal and an accounting entity with a self-balancing set of accounts recording cash and other financial resources with all related liabilities and residual equities or balances and changes therein segregated for the purpose of carrying on specific activities or attaining certain objectives in accordance with special regulations, restrictions, or limitations.
4. This type of interfund activity is accounted for as an expenditure or revenue.
5. These are the proprietary funds.
6. These are assets of the governmental unit and include roads, municipal buildings, sewer systems, sidewalks, and so forth.
7. These are the fiduciary funds.
8. This basis is used in funds that have a flow of financial resources measurement focus.
9. This is the measurement focus of governmentwide financials.

10. This gives the governmental entity the legal right to collect property taxes.
11. These are the governmental funds.
12. This is subtracted from Property Taxes Receivable—Current to determine the revenue from property taxes for the year.
13. This account is credited in the budget entry for the general fund if expected resource inflows exceed expected resource outflows.
14. This account is debited when the general fund records a purchase order for goods or services.
15. This method of accounting for supplies inventories in the general fund reports expenditures for supplies for only the amount used during the year.
16. This account is debited in the general fund when a transfer out is made to another fund.
17. This account is debited in the general fund when it records a billing from another fund for services that were provided to the general fund.
18. This is reported on the general fund balance sheet when assets exceed liabilities and assigned fund balance.
19. This account is debited in the general fund when fixed assets are acquired. Assume that a purchase order to acquire the fixed assets was not recorded.

20 This is the legal term that allows the general fund to make expenditures.

21. Under this method of accounting for encumbrances outstanding at year-end, expenditures are dated in the following year when the orders are received.

LO 17-2, 17-7 **P17-18** **General Fund Entries [AICPA Adapted]**

DeKalb City Council approved and adopted its 20X2 budget that contained the following amounts:

Estimated revenues	$700,000
Appropriations	660,000
Authorized transfer out to the library debt service fund	30,000

During 20X2, various transactions and events occurred that affected the general fund.

Required

For items 1 through 39, indicate whether the item should be debited (D), credited (C), or is not affected (N).

Items 1 through 5 involve recording the adopted budget in the general fund.

1. Estimated Revenues.
2. Budgetary Fund Balance.
3. Appropriations.
4. Estimated Transfer Out.
5. Expenditures.

Items 6 through 10 involve recording the 20X2 property tax levy in the general fund. It was estimated that $5,000 would be uncollectible.

6. Property Tax Receivable.
7. Bad Debts Expense.
8. Allowance for Uncollectibles—Current.
9. Revenues.
10. Estimated Revenues.

Items 11 through 15 involve recording encumbrances in the general fund at the time purchase orders are issued.

11. Encumbrances.
12. Budgetary Fund Balance—Assigned for Encumbrances.
13. Expenditures.
14. Vouchers Payable.
15. Purchases.

Items 16 through 20 involve the recording in the general fund of expenditures that had been encumbered earlier in the current year.

16. Encumbrances.
17. Budgetary Fund Balance—Assigned for Encumbrances.
18. Expenditures.
19. Vouchers Payable.
20. Purchases.

Items 21 through 25 involve the recording in the general fund of the transfer out of $30,000 made to the library debt service fund. (No previous entries were made regarding this transaction.)

21. Interfund Services Provided and Used.
22. Due from Library Debt Service Fund.
23. Cash.
24. Other Financing Uses—Transfer Out.
25. Encumbrances.

Items 26 through 35 involve the recording in the general fund of the closing entries (other than encumbrances) for 20X2.

26. Estimated Revenues.
27. Budgetary Fund Balance.
28. Appropriations.
29. Estimated Transfer Out.
30. Expenditures.
31. Revenues.
32. Other Financing Uses—Transfer Out.
33. Allowance for Uncollectibles—Current.
34. Bad Debt Expense.
35. Depreciation Expense.

Items 36 through 39 involve the recording in the general fund of the closing entry relating to the $12,000 of outstanding encumbrances at the end of 20X2 and an adjusting entry to reflect the intent to honor these commitments in 20X3.

36. Encumbrances.
37. Budgetary Fund Balance—Assigned for Encumbrances.
38. Fund Balance—Unassigned.
39. Fund Balance—Assigned for Encumbrances.

LO 17-7, 17-8 **P17-19 Questions on Fund Items [AICPA Adapted]**

The following information relates to actual results from Central Town's general fund for the year ended December 31, 20X1:

	Revenues	Expenditures and Transfers
Property tax collections:		
Current year taxes collected	$630,000	
Prior-year taxes due 12/1/X0, collected 2/1/X1	50,000	
Current year taxes due 12/1/X1, collection expected by 2/15/X2	70,000	
Other cash receipts	190,000	
General government expenditures:		
Salaries & wages		$160,000
Other		100,000
Public safety & welfare expenditures:		
Salaries & wages		350,000
Other		150,000
Capital outlay		140,000
Transfer out to debt service fund		30,000

- Other cash receipts include a county grant of $100,000 for a specified purpose, of which $80,000 was expended; $50,000 in fines; and $40,000 in fees.
- General Government Expenditures—Other includes employer contributions to the pension plan and $20,000 in annual capital lease payments for computers over three years; the fair value and present value at lease inception are $50,000.
- Capital outlay is for police vehicles.
- Debt service represents annual interest payments due December 15 of each year on $500,000 face value, 6 percent, 20-year term bonds.

Capital Projects Fund

Central Town's council approved $750,000 for construction of a fire station to be financed by $600,000 in general obligation bonds and a $150,000 state grant. Construction began during 20X1, but the fire station was not completed until April 20X2. During 20X1, the following transactions were recorded:

State grant	$150,000
Bond proceeds	610,000
Expenditures	500,000
Unpaid invoices at year-end	30,000
Outstanding encumbrances at year-end, which do not lapse and are to be honored the following year	25,000

The unassigned fund balance in the capital projects fund at January 1, 20X1, was $110,000.

Required

For questions *(a)* through *(i)*, determine the December 31, 20X1, year-end amounts to be recognized in the particular fund. If the item is not reported in a particular fund but is reported on the governmentwide financial statements, specify the amount that would be reported on the financials. Select your answer from the list of amounts following the questions. An amount may be selected once, more than once, or not at all.

a. What amount was recorded for property tax revenues in the general fund?
b. What amount was recorded for other revenues in the general fund?
c. What amount was reported for capital leases of computers in the governmentwide statement of net assets?
d. What amount was reported for the new police vehicles in the governmentwide statement of net assets?
e. What amount was reported for the debt service interest payment in the debt service fund?
f. What was the total amount recorded for function expenditures in the general fund?
g. What amount was recorded for revenues in the capital projects fund?
h. What amount was reported for construction in progress in the governmentwide statement of net assets?
i. What amount was reported as the Fund Balance—Unassigned at December 31, 20X1, in the capital projects fund?

Amounts
1. $ 0
2. $ 30,000
3. $ 50,000
4. $ 55,000
5. $ 60,000
6. $140,000
7. $150,000
8. $170,000
9. $190,000
10. $315,000

(continued)

Amounts
11. $345,000
12. $370,000
13. $500,000
14. $525,000
15. $630,000
16. $700,000
17. $710,000
18. $760,000

LO 17-7, 17-8 **P17-20 Identifying Types of Revenue Transactions**

Required

Using the requirements of **GASB 33,** classify each of the following independent transactions for the community of Fair Lake into the proper category of revenue presented in the right-hand column.

Transactions	Types of Revenue
1. Property taxes were levied by the general fund.	A. Derived tax revenue
2. The electric utility (enterprise) fund billed the general fund for power usage.	B. Imposed nonexchange revenue
3. The city received a state grant for training its police force in additional security measures of public property.	C. Government-mandated nonexchange transaction
4. The city estimated its share of locally generated sales taxes that it expects to receive within the next month.	D. Voluntary nonexchange transaction
5. The city collected various fines it imposed during the period.	E. None of the above
6. The city sold excess office equipment from its municipal headquarters.	
7. The city received resources from the state that must be used to pay for local welfare costs.	
8. The city received a bequest from a local citizen to buy children's recreational items for the city park.	
9. The city collects its share of the local hotel taxes whose proceeds are legislatively required to be used for a new community convention center.	
10. The state reimburses the city for specific costs related to extra security training of the city's fire department employees.	
11. The city receives its share of funds for environmental improvement resources under a state-required program.	
12. The city receives resources from the federal government to acquire new fire-prevention equipment that it has not yet acquired.	
13. The city receives grant monies under a state program encouraging cities to make their infrastructure assets wheelchair accessible.	
14. A company that manufactures road-repaving materials gives the city a grant for the company to conduct a research project on the durability of various types of road repair materials.	

18 Governmental Entities: Special Funds and Governmentwide Financial Statements

Multicorporate Entities
Multinational Entities
Reporting Requirements
Partnerships
Governmental and Not-for-Profit Entities
Governmental Entities
Special Funds
Not-for-Profit
Corporations in Financial Difficulty

GOVERNMENTAL ACCOUNTING IN MARYLAND

In 1498, John Cabot was the first to explore the area that is now the state of Maryland. One of the original 13 colonies, Maryland began its provincial government after receiving its charter from King Charles I in 1632. The various governments of this geographical area have kept accounting records for nearly 400 years. The evolution from province to colony to state along with a growing population has led to increasingly more complex governmental functions and programs, which, in turn, have led to more complex accounting. However, not until the 20th century did accounting standards for governmental entities become widely accepted.

Chapter 17 discussed the various public services provided by the City of San Diego, but those of the State of Maryland are even more complex and diverse. Consider the following representative sample of the varied activities the State of Maryland administers:

- **Public safety** (state police, prisons, crime prevention, firearms control)
- **Housing and home ownership** (public housing, construction regulation, energy programs)
- **Children and parenting** (adoption, child care assistance, foster parenting)
- **Disabilities** (Special Olympics, transportation for people with disabilities, disability programs)
- **Assistance programs** (food assistance, energy assistance, homelessness prevention)
- **Senior citizens** (assisted living programs, home nursing programs, Senior Olympics)
- **Business** (environmental permits, agriculture licenses, unemployment programs)
- **Employment** (employment of minors, equal opportunity programs, injured workers programs)
- **Youth education** (Pre-K through Grade 12, public schools)
- **Adult learning** (literacy programs, rehabilitation services, English language schools)
- **Higher education** (colleges and universities, online learning)
- **Financial aid** (college savings programs, grant and loan programs)
- **Travel and tourism** (maps and travel guides, welcome centers and rest areas, state parks)
- **Recreation and sports** (camping information, fisheries services, golf courses)
- **Arts and culture** (museums, historical locations, Maryland Science Center)

Although this list is not exhaustive, it illustrates the diverse activities and programs the state oversees. The disclosure of these many activities is a major part of the state's fiscal responsibility to its citizens. Maryland's 2013 comprehensive annual financial report (CAFR) is 166 pages long. It summarizes all activities of the different departments, programs, and entities affiliated with the state government. In addition to the general fund, discussed in Chapter 17, governments usually have a number of other funds. Maryland's 2013 CAFR contains governmentwide financial statements similar to consolidated financial statements in the private sector as well as financial statements of these individual funds. This chapter presents the accounting and financial reporting requirements for (1) the four remaining governmental fund types, (2) the two proprietary fund types, and (3) the two fiduciary fund types.

LEARNING OBJECTIVES

When you finish studying this chapter, you should be able to:

LO 18-1 Understand and explain the differences in financial reporting requirements of the different fund types and understand the basics of the special revenue fund.

LO 18-2 Make calculations and record journal entries for capital projects funds.

LO 18-3 Make calculations and record journal entries for debt service funds.

LO 18-4 Make calculations and record journal entries for permanent funds.

LO 18-5 Understand and explain how governmental funds are reported and rules for separate reporting as major funds.

LO 18-6 Make calculations and record journal entries for enterprise funds.

LO 18-7 Understand and explain the financial reporting of proprietary funds.

LO 18-8 Make calculations and record journal entries for internal service funds.

LO 18-9 Make calculations and record journal entries for trust funds.

LO 18-10 Make calculations and record journal entries for agency funds.

LO 18-11 Understand and explain the preparation of governmentwide financial statements.

LO 18-12 Understand and explain the additional disclosures that accompany governmentwide financial statements.

SUMMARY OF GOVERNMENTAL FUND TYPES

LO 18-1

Understand and explain the differences in financial reporting requirements of the different fund types and understand the basics of the special revenue fund.

See Figure 18–1 for the typical fund organization for a local government. In practice, the funds are often identified with the acronyms from the first letters of their titles, as follows:

Governmental Fund Types

GF	General fund
SRF	Special revenue funds
DSF	Debt service funds
CPF	Capital projects funds
PF	Permanent funds

FIGURE 18–1
Funds for a Governmental Entity

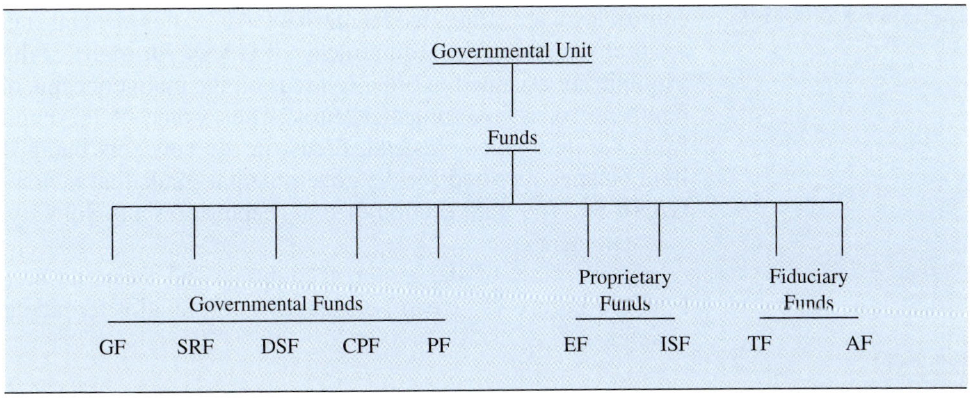

Proprietary Fund Types

EF Enterprise funds
ISF Internal service funds

Fiduciary Fund Types

TF Trust funds
AF Agency funds

A government should establish those funds required by law and the governmental entity's specific operating and management needs. Unnecessary, additional funds add unneeded complexity and do not enhance the government's operational efficiency. Many governmental units follow the general rule that all activities should be accounted for in the general fund unless specifically required by law or the different measurement focus used for proprietary and fiduciary funds. This rule does not prohibit the creation of additional funds but places a reasonable restraint on their proliferation. Most state and local governmental systems typically use the structure of funds discussed in this chapter.

One event may require entries in several funds. For example, the construction of a new municipal building through the issuance of general obligation bonds may require entries in both a capital project fund and a debt service fund. In addition, interfund activities require entries in two or more funds.

Governmental funds use the modified accrual basis of accounting, and proprietary and fiduciary funds use the accrual basis. Governmental entities recognize estimated uncollectible amounts as a reduction of revenue, not as an expense. The five governmental funds do not report long-term assets or long-term debt, but the governmentwide statements do report them. Investments are reported in the appropriate funds and are valued at their fair market values at each balance sheet date. The governmental entity's financial report includes both fund-based and governmentwide financial statements. The governmentwide statements are prepared using the accrual basis of accounting. Reconciliation schedules are required to show the differences in the amounts reported in the governmental fund's financial statements presented using the modified accrual basis of accounting and the amounts reported in the governmentwide financial statements presented using the accrual basis.

Some governmental units have pension trust funds for their employees. Accounting and reporting for pension trust funds is quite complex and beyond the scope of an advanced financial accounting course.

This chapter continues the Sol City example started in Chapter 17, which presented the entries and financial reports for the general fund for 20X2. Sol City uses the lapsing method of accounting for encumbrances and the consumption method for inventories and records all expected budgetary accounts including anticipated interfund transactions. The techniques of capitalizing all budgetary accounts and recording journal entries at the control level are continued from Chapter 17. The financial statements for the illustration are prepared using the requirements of **GASB 34.** Many of the numbers for the Sol City example are assumed in order to focus on the main concepts of accounting and financial reporting for a governmental entity. Thus, some of the numbers cannot be computed from the data given. Instead, focus on the concepts being discussed. We present the fund balance reported for the governmental funds that is now required under the recent **GASB 54.** The final section of this chapter presents Sol City's governmentwide financial statements.

An overview of the major accounting and financial standards for the individual funds in Figure 18–2 can be used as a continual reference point during study of this chapter.

GOVERNMENTAL FUNDS WORKSHEETS

Each of the five governmental funds reports two ***fund-based financial statements:*** the balance sheet and the statement of revenues, expenditures, and changes in fund balance. Rather than presenting each of the separate governmental funds' financial statements in the chapter, we provide worksheets to summarize all governmental funds' financial statements. Specifically, refer to Figure 18–3 for the individual fund information that is used to prepare the governmental funds' balance sheet and to Figure 18–4 for the individual governmental funds information used to prepare the governmental funds' statement of revenues, expenditures, and changes in fund balance. The amounts for the general fund are taken from the information in Chapter 17. The amounts for the other funds will be developed throughout this chapter. We use these two worksheets, which also include major funds tests, throughout the chapter as the basis for preparing the governmental funds' financial statements that will be presented later in the chapter. Thus, we develop the two worksheets through the discussions of each fund type in this chapter.

SPECIAL REVENUE FUNDS

Current governmental resources may be restricted to expenditures for specific purposes, such as the development of a state highway system, the maintenance of public parks, or the operation of the public school system, city libraries, and museums. The necessary revenue often comes from special tax levies or federal or state governmental grants. Some minor revenue may be earned through user charges, but they are usually not sufficient to fully fund the service. ***Special revenue funds*** are used to account for such restricted resources. The governmental entity usually has a separate special revenue fund for each different activity of this type. Thus, a city may have several special revenue funds.

FYI

The State of Maryland uses a special revenue fund to account for resources related to the Maryland Department of Transportation.

The accounting for special revenue funds is identical to the accounting for the general fund. Special revenue funds use the modified accrual basis of accounting, they do not report fixed assets or depreciation, their operating budgets are typically recorded in the accounts, and they do not record long-term debt.

We do not illustrate special revenue fund accounting in the chapter because its principles are the same as those for the general fund as covered in Chapter 17. For purposes of the governmental funds statements, assume that $62,000 of property taxes was collected for the special revenue fund and that $49,000 was expended for the designated culture and recreation purposes for which the special revenue fund was established. This chapter focuses on the unique or interesting aspects of governmental accounting and financial reporting. Review Figure 18–3 for the assumed numbers for the special revenue fund's balance sheet and Figure 18–4 for the revenues ($62,000) and expenditures ($49,000) assumed for the special revenue fund.

FIGURE 18–2 Overview of Accounting and Financial Reporting for Governments

	Governmental Funds					Proprietary Funds		Fiduciary Funds		
	General Fund	Special Revenue Funds	Capital Projects Funds	Debt Service Funds	Permanent Funds	Enterprise Funds	Internal Service Funds	Trust Funds	Agency Funds	Government wide Financials
Basis of accounting	Modified accrual	Modified accrual	Modified accrual	Modified accrual	Modified accrual	Accrual	Accrual	Accrual	Accrual	Accrual
Budgetary basis recorded (budgetary accounts are typically used when a legally adopted annual operating budget is passed)	Operating budget often recorded	Operating budget often recorded	Capital budget usually not recorded	Not required	Not required	No	No	No		
Long-term productive assets (buildings, equipment, etc.) reported	No	No	No	No	No	Yes	Yes	Yes	No	Yes
Long-term debt reported	No	No	No	No	No	Yes	Yes	Yes	No	Yes
Encumbrances recorded	Yes	Yes	Possibly	Possibly	Possibly	No	No	No	No	
Financial Statements										
Balance sheet	X	X	X	X	X					
Statement of net position						X	X			X
Statement of revenues, expenditures, and changes in fund balance	X	X	X	X	X					
Statement of revenues, expenses, and changes in fund net position						X	X			
Statement of activities										X
Statement of cash flows						X	X			
Statement of fiduciary net position								X	X	
Statement of changes in fiduciary net position								X	X	

FIGURE 18–3 Worksheet for the Balance Sheet for the Governmental Funds

	Governmental Funds					Total Governmental Funds	Enterprise Fund	Total Governmental and Enterprise
	General	Special Revenue	Capital Projects	Debt Service	Permanent			
Assets								
Current								
Cash	102,000	15,000	16,000	2,000	13,000			
Property Taxes (net of allowances)	85,000	1,000		3,000				
Due from Enterprise Fund	3,000							
Inventory of Supplies	17,000							
Noncurrent								
Investment in Government Bonds					90,000			
Total Assets	207,000	16,000	16,000	5,000	103,000	347,000	140,000	487,000
Liabilities & Fund Balances								
Vouchers Payable	55,000	3,000						
Contract Payable—Retainage			10,000					
Total Liabilities	55,000	3,000	10,000	0	0	68,000	112,000	180,000
Fund Balances								
Nonspendable:								
Inventories	17,000							
Permanent Fund					103,000			
Spendable:								
Assigned to:								
General Governmental Services	15,000	6,000						
Debt Service				5,000				
Unassigned, reported in:								
General Fund	120,000							
Special Revenue Fund		7,000						
Capital Projects Fund			6,000					
Total Fund Balances	152,000	13,000	6,000	5,000	103,000	279,000		
Total Liabilities & Fund Balances	207,000	16,000	16,000	5,000	103,000	347,000		
Major Fund Tests on Total Assets:								
10% Test of Total Governmental or Enterprise		4.61%	4.61%	1.44%	29.68%		100.00%	
5% Test of Governmental Plus Enterprise		3.29%	3.29%	1.03%	21.15%		28.75%	
Major Fund Test (Yes or No)	Yes	No	No	No	Yes		Yes	
Major Fund Tests on Total Liabilities:								
10% Test of Total Governmental or Enterprise		4.41%	14.71%	0.00%	0.00%		100.00%	
5% Test of Governmental Plus Enterprise		1.67%	5.56%	0.00%	0.00%		62.22%	
Major Fund Test (Yes or No)	Yes	No	Yes	No	No		Yes	

FIGURE 18–4 Worksheet for the Statement of Revenues, Expenditures, and Changes in Fund Balances for the Governmental Funds

	Governmental Funds					Total Governmental Funds	Enterprise Fund	Total Governmental and Enterprise
	General	Special Revenue	Capital Projects	Debt Service	Permanent			
Revenues								
Property Taxes	781,000	62,000		33,000				
Sales Taxes	32,000							
Grants	33,000		10,000					
Miscellaneous	18,000				8,000			
Total Revenues	864,000	62,000	10,000	33,000	8,000	977,000	37,000	1,014,000
Expenditures								
Current								
General Government	206,000							
Streets & Highways	71,000							
Public Safety	335,000							
Sanitation	141,000							
Culture & Recreation		49,000			5,000			
Miscellaneous								
Debt Service								
Principal Retirement				20,000				
Interest Charges				10,000				
Capital Outlay	58,000		124,000					
Total Expenditures/Expenses	811,000	49,000	124,000	30,000	5,000	1,019,000	35,000	1,054,000
Excess (Deficiency) of Revenues over Expenditures	53,000	13,000	(114,000)	3,000	3,000	(42,000)		
Other Financing Sources (Uses)								
Proceeds of Bond Issue			102,000					
Transfers In			20,000	2,000				
Transfers Out	(30,000)		(2,000)					
Total Other Financing Sources & Uses	(30,000)	0	120,000	2,000	0	92,000		
Special Item								
Contribution					100,000	100,000		
Net Change in Fund Balances	23,000	13,000	6,000	5,000	103,000	150,000		
Fund Balances—Beginning	129,000	0	0	0	0	129,000		
Fund Balances—Ending	152,000	13,000	6,000	5,000	103,000	279,000		
Major Fund Tests on Total Revenues:								
10% Test of Total Governmental or Enterprise		6.35%	1.02%	3.38%	0.82%		100.00%	
5% Test of Governmental and Enterprise		6.11%	0.99%	3.25%	0.79%		3.65%	
Major Fund Test (Yes or No)	Yes	No	No	No	No		No	
Major Fund Tests on Total Expenditures/Expenses:								
10% Test of Total Governmental or Enterprise		4.81%	12.17%	2.94%	0.49%		100.00%	
5% Test of Governmental and Enterprise		4.65%	11.76%	2.85%	0.47%		3.32%	
Major Fund Test (Yes or No)	Yes	No	Yes	No	No		No	

CAPITAL PROJECTS FUNDS[1]

LO 18-2

Make calculations and record journal entries for capital projects funds.

Advanced StudyGuide .com

Capital projects funds account for financial resources specified for the acquisition or construction of major capital facilities or improvements that benefit the public. Typical examples are the construction of libraries, civic centers, fire stations, courthouses, bridges, major streets, and city municipal buildings. A separate capital projects fund is created when the project is approved and ceases at its completion. Each project or group of related projects usually is accounted for in a separate capital projects fund.

Accounting for capital projects funds is similar to accounting for the general fund. Capital projects funds use the modified accrual basis of accounting. Moreover, they do not record fixed assets, depreciation, or long-term debt. Capital projects funds, however, typically do not have annual operating budgets. Instead, the entity must prepare a capital budget as a basis for selling bonds to finance a project, and the capital budget is the control mechanism for the project's length. The capital budget for the project may or may not be formally recorded in the accounts. Theoretically, encumbrances are part of the budgetary system and should flow from the budget's appropriating authority. However, the entity may record encumbrances even if it does not record the capital project budget. Encumbrances maintain an ongoing accounting record of the expenditure commitments that have been made on a project, and Sol City has a policy to use encumbrances in its capital projects funds and chooses not to formally enter the project budget into the accounts.

The capital projects fund records capital outlays as expenditures. Thus, this fund does not record fixed assets. A record of the construction in progress, however, may be maintained in memorandum format. Finally, completed fixed assets are transferred to a general capital assets ledger or schedule so that these assets may be included in the governmentwide financial statements.

Illustration of Transactions

On January 1, 20X2, Sol City establishes a capital projects fund to account for a capital addition to the municipal courthouse. The expected cost of the addition is $120,000. A $100,000, 10 percent general obligation bond issue is sold at 102 for total proceeds of $102,000. The bond is a five-year serial bond with equal amounts of $20,000 to be paid each year, beginning on December 31, 20X2, until the debt is extinguished. The bond proceeds are not revenue to the capital projects fund; they are reported in the other financing sources section of the fund's statement of revenues, expenditures, and changes in fund balance. Any debt issue costs such as underwriting fees or attorney fees are recognized as expenditures when the liabilities are both measurable and incurred and are payable out of current financial resources.

The capital projects fund is not entitled to the $2,000 premium on the sale of bonds. This premium is transferred out to the debt service fund immediately upon receipt. The debt service fund records the receipt of the transfer as a transfer in [see entry (15) later in this chapter]. The premium is viewed as an adjustment of the interest rate, not as a part of the funds expendable by the capital projects fund. If bonds are sold at a discount, either the amount expended for the improvement must be decreased or the general fund must make up the difference to the face value of the bonds.

In addition, the city receives a federal grant for $10,000 as financial support for part of the capital addition, and the capital projects fund receives an interfund transfer in of $20,000 from the city's general fund. Recall that an interfund transfer is an interfund transaction in which resources are moved from one fund, usually from the general fund, to another fund to be used for the operations of the receiving fund. The general fund records this transfer of $20,000 as an interfund transfer out [see entry (34) in Chapter 17]. The following entries are recorded for the 20X2 fiscal year.

[1] To view a video explanation of this topic, visit advancedstudyguide.com.

Capital Projects Revenue and Bond Proceeds

The sale of the bonds and receipt of the federal grant and operating transfer in are recorded as follows:

		Debit	Credit
(1)	Cash	102,000	
	Other Financing Sources—Bond Issue		100,000
	Other Financing Sources—Bond Premium		2,000
	Issue $100,000 of bonds at 102.		

		Debit	Credit
(2)	Other Financing Uses—Transfer Out to Debt Service Fund	2,000	
	Cash		2,000
	Forward bond premium to debt service fund.		

		Debit	Credit
(3)	Cash	10,000	
	Revenue—Federal Grant		10,000
	Receive federal grant to be applied to courthouse addition.		

		Debit	Credit
(4)	Due from General Fund	20,000	
	Other Financing Sources—Transfer In from General Fund		20,000
	Establish receivable for interfund transfer in from general fund.		

		Debit	Credit
(5)	Cash	20,000	
	Due from General Fund		20,000
	Receive transferred resources from general fund.		

Entry (3) recognizes the $10,000 grant from the federal government as revenue when the grant is received. Some grants from the federal government are termed "expenditure-driven" grants for which revenue can be recognized only as expenditures are incurred in conformity with the grant agreement. The local governmental entity recognizes revenue from expenditure-driven grants only after it has met the eligibility requirements for the government-mandated nonexchange transaction: that is, the allowable expenditures have been made.

Capital Projects Fund Expenditures

The following encumbrances, expenditures, and disbursements are recorded in 20X2:

		Debit	Credit
(6)	ENCUMBRANCES	110,000	
	BUDGETARY FUND BALANCE—ASSIGNED FOR ENCUMBRANCES		110,000
	Budgetary entry to record the issuance of a construction contract for $110,000.		

		Debit	Credit
(7)	BUDGETARY FUND BALANCE—ASSIGNED FOR ENCUMBRANCES	110,000	
	ENCUMBRANCES		110,000
	Budgetary entry to record the completion of the construction project. Reverse reserve for encumbrances.		

		Debit	Credit
(8)	Expenditures	118,000	
	Contract Payable		108,000
	Contract Payable—Retained Percentage		10,000
	Actual construction cost of courthouse addition is $118,000. Additional cost is approved. Contract terms include retained percentage of $10,000 until full and final acceptance of project.		

		Debit	Credit
(9)	Expenditures	6,000	
	Vouchers Payable		6,000
	Additional items for courthouse addition.		

		Debit	Credit
(10)	Vouchers Payable	6,000	
	Contract Payable	108,000	
	Cash		114,000
	Pay current portion of construction contract and vouchers.		

Entry (8) credits Contract Payable $108,000 for the current portion due, and Contract Payable—Retained Percentage for $10,000. Entry (10) indicates the payment in full of the $108,000 current portion of the contract liability. A normal practice of governmental units is to hold back a retained percentage of the total amount due under a construction contract to ensure that the contractor fully completes the project to the unit's satisfaction. For example, a city may stipulate that 10 percent of the total contract price be retained until the project is fully completed and accepted. The governmental unit releases and pays this retainage payable upon it final acceptance of the project.

Closing Entries in the Capital Projects Fund

The following entries close the nominal accounts:

(11)	Revenue—Federal Grant	10,000	
	Fund Balance—Unassigned	114,000	
	Expenditures		124,000
	Close operating accounts of revenue and expenditures.		
(12)	Other Financing Sources—Bond Issue	100,000	
	Other Financing Sources—Bond Premium	2,000	
	Fund Balance—Unassigned		102,000
	Close other financing sources.		
(13)	Other Financing Sources—Transfer In from General Fund	20,000	
	Other Financing Uses—Transfer Out to Debt Service Fund		2,000
	Fund Balance—Unassigned		18,000
	Close interfund transfers.		

No encumbrances are outstanding as of the end of the fiscal year. At this point, the Fund Balance—Unassigned account has a credit balance of $6,000. Depending on its policy, the governmental unit transfers the remaining fund balance upon the capital project's completion and final approval either to the general fund or to the debt service fund. It is a transfer out for the capital projects fund and a transfer in for the receiving fund because it involves the one-time transfer of the remaining resources in the capital projects fund. In the preceding example, Sol City decided that the fund should remain open through the first part of the next fiscal year in case any minor modifications of the new courthouse addition are required. If no further modifications are required, the city officially accepts the courthouse addition project and pays the contractor the $10,000 in the Contract Payable—Retained Percentage account. Any remaining resources in the capital projects fund are then transferred and the capital projects fund is closed.

Financial Statement Information for the Capital Projects Fund

The financial statement information for the capital projects funds is presented in Figure 18–3 for the balance sheet and in Figure 18–4 for the statement of revenues, expenditures, and changes in fund balances. Sol City created its capital projects fund on January 1, 20X2, the date the capital addition was approved and the serial bonds were sold. The only asset remaining in this fund on December 31, 20X2 (Figure 18–3), is $16,000 of cash, which includes the $10,000 for the contract payable–retainage. The capital projects fund column (Figure 18–4) presents the $102,000 of proceeds from the bond issue, which is reported among other financing sources with a reduction for the transfer out of the $2,000 premium to the debt service fund and the transfer in of $20,000, netting against the large excess of expenditures over revenue in the amount of $114,000. The statement of revenues, expenditures, and changes in fund balance reconciles to the $6,000 fund balance at the end of the fiscal period.

DEBT SERVICE FUNDS

LO 18-3

Make calculations and record journal entries for debt service funds.

Advanced StudyGuide .com

Debt service funds account for the accumulation and use of resources for the payment of general long-term debt principal and interest. A government may have several types of general long-term debt obligations, as follows:

1. *Serial bonds.* Serial bonds are the most common form of debt issued by governments. The bonds are repaid in installments over the life of the debt. A serial bond is called *regular* if the installments are equal and *irregular* if they are not equal.
2. *Term bonds.* This form of debt is less frequent now than in the past. The entire principal of the debt is due at the maturity date.
3. *Special assessment bonds.* Tax liens on the property located within the special assessment tax district secure special assessment bonds. The governmental unit also may become obligated in some manner to assume the debt payment in the event the property owners default. Special assessment bonds may finance capital projects or acquire other assets such as ambulances or fire engines necessary to operate the governmental unit. Special assessment bonds sold to acquire enterprise fund assets, however, should be accounted for within the enterprise fund. The special assessment feature simply states the source of financing and means of repayment.
4. *Notes and warrants.* These consist of debt typically issued for one or two years. These debts are usually secured by specific tax revenue, which must first be used to repay the debt. The property tax anticipation warrant is an example.
5. *Capital leases.* Governmental entities must record capital leases in accordance with generally accepted accounting principles. These leases then become the governmental unit's long-term liabilities.

Some governmental entities service long-term debt directly from the general fund, thereby eliminating the need for a debt service fund as a separate fiscal, accounting, and reporting entity. However, if a governmental entity has several long-term general obligations outstanding, bond indentures or other regulations may require it to establish a separate debt service fund for each obligation to account for properly servicing each debt obligation.

FYI

As of 2013, the State of Maryland maintained two debt service fund accounts: general obligation bonds and transportation bonds.

The accounting and financial reporting for debt service funds is the same as for the general fund. The modified accrual basis of accounting is used, and only that portion of the long-term debt that has matured and is currently payable is recorded in the debt service funds.

Interest payable on long-term debt is not accrued; interest is recognized as a liability only when it comes due and payable. The "when-due" recognition of interest matches the debt service expenditures with the resources accumulated to repay the debt. This approach prevents an understatement of the debt service fund balance. For example, if interest is accrued before it is actually due, the fund balance may show a deficit because of the excess of liabilities over assets. The function of the debt service fund is to accumulate resources to pay debt principal and interest as they become due. Thus, the when-due recognition of interest is consistent with the fund's objectives. Entities usually record long-term debt in a general long-term liabilities ledger or schedule so that they may be included in the governmentwide financial statements. Many municipal governments maintain a general capital assets and general long-term liabilities (GCA-GLTL) ledger to record all long-term items because the governmental financial statements have a current focus.

Illustration of Transactions

Sol City establishes a debt service fund to service the $100,000, five-year, 10 percent serial bond issued on January 1, 20X2, to finance the capital project courthouse addition.

The city initially sold the bond at a premium of $2,000. A property tax levy specifically for debt service will provide the resources to pay the bond principal and interest as they become due.

Adoption of Debt Service Fund Budget

Debt service funds are not required to adopt annual operating budgets because bond agreements generally mandate the fund's expenditures and an operating budget may be viewed as unnecessarily redundant. Nevertheless, there is no restriction against having an operating budget for the debt service fund as part of a comprehensive budgeting system for a governmental entity as illustrated here.

Sol City adopts its annual operating budget for the debt service fund when it creates the fund to service the serial bonds sold for the courthouse addition. The city budgets appropriations of $30,000 to pay $20,000 of maturing principal and $10,000 of interest for the year. Sol City budgets all expected interfund transactions and records the anticipated interfund transfer in of the $2,000 premium on the serial bonds sold with the budget:

(14)	ESTIMATED REVENUES CONTROL	30,000	
	ESTIMATED OTHER FINANCING SOURCES—TRANSFER IN	2,000	
	APPROPRIATIONS CONTROL		30,000
	BUDGETARY FUND BALANCE		2,000
	Adopt budget for 20X2.		

The budgetary accounts ESTIMATED REVENUES CONTROL and APPROPRIATIONS CONTROL are used to account for servicing serial bonds.

Debt Service Fund Revenue and Other Financing Sources

In this example, the debt service fund obtains revenue from a specified property tax levy. The bond premium received from the capital projects fund is recognized as a transfer in. Note that the capital projects fund records this transfer as an interfund transfer out [see entry (2) earlier in this chapter]. The entries to record the receipt of the bond premium and the levy and collection of taxes follow:

(15)	Cash	2,000	
	Other Financing Sources—Transfer In from Capital Projects Fund		2,000
	Receive bond premium from capital projects fund.		
(16)	Property Taxes Receivable	35,000	
	Allowance for Uncollectible Taxes		5,000
	Revenue—Property Tax		30,000
	Levy property taxes and provide for allowance for uncollectible taxes. Estimated uncollectible property taxes reduce revenue.		
(17)	Cash	30,000	
	Property Taxes Receivable		30,000
	Receive portion of property taxes.		
(18)	Property Taxes Receivable—Delinquent	5,000	
	Allowance for Uncollectible Taxes	5,000	
	Property Taxes Receivable		5,000
	Revenue—Property Tax		3,000
	Allowance for Uncollectible Taxes—Delinquent		2,000
	Reclassify remaining property taxes as delinquent and reduce allowance for uncollectible taxes from $5,000 to $2,000.		

Debt Service Fund Expenditures

The primary expenditures of the debt service fund are for the first annual payment of principal and interest on the serial bonds payable. Governmental entities typically do not use an encumbrance system for matured principal and interest because the debt agreement serves as the expenditure control mechanism:

(19)	Expenditures—Principal	20,000	
	Matured Bonds Payable		20,000
	Recognize matured portion of serial bond: $100,000 ÷ 5 years.		

(20)	Expenditures—Interest	10,000	
	Matured Interest Payable		10,000
	Recognize interest due this period: $100,000 × 0.10 × 1 year.		

(21)	Matured Bonds Payable	20,000	
	Matured Interest Payable	10,000	
	Cash		30,000
	Pay first year's installment plus interest on bond.		

Closing Entries in the Debt Service Fund

The nominal accounts are closed as follows:

(22)	APPROPRIATIONS CONTROL	30,000	
	BUDGETARY FUND BALANCE	2,000	
	ESTIMATED REVENUES CONTROL		30,000
	ESTIMATED OTHER FINANCING SOURCES—TRANSFER IN		2,000
	Close budgetary accounts.		

(23)	Revenue—Property Tax	33,000	
	Expenditures—Principal		20,000
	Expenditures—Interest		10,000
	Fund Balance—Assigned for Debt Service		3,000
	Close operating revenue and expenditures.		

(24)	Other Financing Sources—Transfer In from Capital Projects Fund	2,000	
	Fund Balance—Assigned for Debt Service		2,000
	Close interfund transfer.		

If the debt service fund services term bonds, a different budgetary account system is used. The following budgetary entry would be made for term bonds for the periods prior to the maturity date:

REQUIRED CONTRIBUTIONS	XXX	
REQUIRED EARNINGS	XXX	
BUDGETARY FUND BALANCE		XXX

The budgetary amounts are determined based on a computation of the contributions needed each period to be invested, earning a given return to accumulate to the amount required for the bonds payment. The debt service fund may then receive resources from the general fund or from a tax levy, which it would invest until the term bonds became due. In the period that the term bonds reach maturity, the debt service fund pays the matured principal and interest from its available resources. The debt service fund may make temporary investments of excess cash to maximize the return from its resources. The debt service fund reports these investments as an asset. Most temporary investments are made in low-risk U.S. Treasury securities or in certificates of deposit from large banks. Interest income is accrued as earned. The investments are valued in accordance with **GASB 31**. The general valuation standard in **GASB 31** is fair value for most investments made by a governmental entity. However, an exception is allowed for governmental entities other than external investment pools in order to report market investments at amortized cost, provided the investment has a remaining maturity of one year or less from the date of purchase. Unrealized gains or losses on investments are combined with realized gains or losses, and the governmental entity's operating statements report them as net investment income or loss.

Financial Statement Information for the Debt Service Fund

The financial statement information for the debt service fund for the governmental funds is presented in Figure 18–3 for the balance sheet and Figure 18–4 for the governmental funds statement of revenues, expenditures, and changes in fund balance.

PERMANENT FUNDS

LO 18-4

Make calculations and record journal entries for permanent funds.

Advanced StudyGuide .com

Government entities establish ***permanent funds*** when a donor restriction stipulates that the fund principal must be preserved and that the income from these permanent funds be used to benefit the government's programs or its general citizenry. The donor-restricted donation may be from individuals, estates, and public or private organizations. Permanent funds are classified in the governmental funds category because the income resources in these funds are to be used toward the government's programs and services for its general citizenry. Permanent funds use the modified accrual basis of accounting and the financial statements for the permanent funds are the same as for all other governmental funds.

Illustration of Transactions

On January 1, 20X2, Sol City receives a $100,000 bequest from a long-term city resident. The will stipulates that the $100,000 be invested and the income be used to provide for maintenance and improvement of the city park. Note that a private-purpose fund, which would be a fiduciary fund, requires the government to use the principal or earnings for the benefit of specific individuals, private organizations, or other designated governments, as stated in the trust agreement. This bequest is for the benefit of the general citizenry, however, and is established as a permanent fund that is a governmental fund type. Entries (25)–(29) in this permanent fund during 20X2 follow:

(25)	Cash	100,000	
	Contributions		100,000

Accept permanent fund resources.

This contribution will be reported as a special item after other financing sources and uses toward the bottom of the statement of revenues, expenditures, and changes in fund balance.

Investment and Interest

Sol City uses the fund's resources to acquire $100,000 face value, high-grade, 8 percent governmental securities at 90 to yield an effective interest rate of 10 percent. The fund uses the modified accrual method for interest income, which means that the revenue recognition may be for only the interest amount that is both measurable and available to finance expenditures made during the current fiscal period. Therefore, only the $8,000 of accrued interest receivable is available for expenditures this period, and the modified accrual basis financial statements would not show the discount amortization.

(26)	Investment in Bonds	90,000	
	Cash		90,000

Acquire $100,000 face value government securities at 90.

(27)

Accrued Interest Receivable	8,000	
Interest Revenue		8,000

Accrue interest:
$8,000 = $100,000 × 0.08, nominal (coupon) rate.

(28)

Cash	8,000	
Accrued Interest Receivable		8,000

Collect accrued interest on securities.

Expenditures

The permanent trust fund expends $5,000 during the period for maintenance of the city park and recognizes the following entry:

(29)

Expenditures	5,000	
Cash		5,000

Expenditures made for maintenance of the city park.

See Figure 18–3 for the permanent fund's balance sheet information as of December 31, 20X2. The entire amount of the fund balance for the permanent fund is classified as nonspendable because the principal must be preserved and its income is required to be used for specified purposes. The information for the statement of revenues, expenditures, and changes in fund balance for the permanent fund is in Figure 18–4. Note that the $100,000 contribution is not part of operations but is reported at the bottom of the operating statement.

GOVERNMENTAL FUNDS FINANCIAL STATEMENTS

LO 18-5

Understand and explain how governmental funds are reported and rules for separate reporting as major funds.

Advanced StudyGuide .com

GASB Statement No. 34, requires two financial statements for the governmental funds: (1) the governmental funds balance sheet (Figure 18–5) and (2) the governmental statement of revenues, expenditures, and changes in fund balance (Figure 18–6). The worksheets in Figures 18–3 and 18–4 are the basis for preparing these two financial statements. In practice, the governmental entity prepares the two financial statements for each individual governmental fund and these individual fund statements serve as the foundation for the financial statements. However, the fund-based financial statements in the governmental entity's CAFR only report major governmental funds individually, not necessarily each of the five governmental funds. **GASB 34** specifies that the general fund is always a major fund. But some of the other governmental funds may not be determined to be major funds and are aggregated and reported in a single column as other governmental funds. **GASB 34** establishes criteria that also encompass the enterprise funds. To determine which of the other governmental or specific enterprise funds are major, **GASB 34** specifies that *both* of the following criteria must be met:

1. *10 percent criterion.* Total assets, liabilities, revenues, or expenditures/expenses of that individual governmental or enterprise fund are at least 10 percent of the corresponding total (assets, liabilities, revenues, or expenditures/expenses) for all funds of that category or type (i.e., total governmental funds or total enterprise funds).
2. *5 percent criterion.* Total assets, liabilities, revenues, or expenditures/expenses of the individual governmental fund or enterprise fund are at least 5 percent of the corresponding total for all governmental *plus* enterprise funds combined.

FIGURE 18–5 Governmental Funds Balance Sheet

SOL CITY
Balance Sheet
Governmental Funds
December 31, 20X2

	General	Capital Projects	Permanent	Other Governmental Funds	Total Governmental Funds
Assets					
Current					
Cash	$102,000	$16,000	$ 13,000	$17,000	$148,000
Property Taxes (net of allowances)	85,000			4,000	89,000
Due from Enterprise Fund	3,000				3,000
Inventory of Supplies	17,000				17,000
Noncurrent					
Investment in Government Bonds			90,000		90,000
Total Assets	$207,000	$16,000	$103,000	$21,000	$347,000
Liabilities & Fund Balances					
Vouchers Payable	55,000			3,000	$ 58,000
Contract Payable—Retainage		$10,000			10,000
Total Liabilities	$ 55,000	$10,000		$ 3,000	$ 68,000
Fund Balances:					
Nonspendable:					
Inventory	$ 17,000				$ 17,000
Permanent Fund Principal			$100,000		100,000
Spendable:					
Restricted for:					
Maintain City Park			3,000		3,000
Limited to:					
Culture & Recreation				$13,000	13,000
Assigned to:					
General Government	15,000				15,000
Courthouse Project		$ 6,000			6,000
Debt Service				5,000	5,000
Unassigned	120,000				120,000
Total Fund Balances	$152,000	$ 6,000	$103,000	$18,000	$279,000
Total Liabilities & Fund Balances	$207,000	$16,000	$103,000	$21,000	$347,000

Note that the major fund reporting requirements apply to a governmental or enterprise fund only if the same element (e.g., assets, liabilities, revenues, or expenditures/expenses) exceeds both the 10 percent and the 5 percent criteria. We present these major funds tests at the bottom of Figures 18–3 and 18–4. To prepare the tests, information is also required for the enterprise funds. The underlying transactions for Sol City's enterprise fund are presented in the next section of this chapter. We obtain the information for the total assets, liabilities, revenues, and expenses of Sol City's enterprise fund from the enterprise fund's financial statement information. For now, we present the information for the enterprise fund solely to discuss the major funds tests. Immediately after the following discussion of the two major funds tests, we present more detail on the enterprise fund.

10 Percent Criterion Tests

To compute the 10 percent criterion tests for the five governmental funds, the denominators of the four tests (assets, liabilities, revenues, and expenditures) are the totals from the five governmental funds. For example, the assets of the governmental funds in Figure 18–3 total $347,000. Note again that the general fund is always a major fund, so no percentages need be computed for that fund. The 10 percent asset test shows that the permanent

FIGURE 18–6 Governmental Funds Statement of Revenues, Expenditures, and Changes in Fund Balance

SOL CITY
Statement of Revenues, Expenditures, and Changes in Fund Balance
Governmental Funds
For the Year Ended December 31, 20X2

	General	Capital Projects	Permanent	Other Governmental Funds	Total Governmental Funds
Revenues					
Property Taxes	$781,000			$95,000	$ 876,000
Sales Taxes	32,000				32,000
Grants	33,000	$ 10,000			43,000
Miscellaneous	18,000		$ 8,000		26,000
Total Revenues	$864,000	$ 10,000	$ 8,000	$95,000	$ 977,000
Expenditures					
Current					
General Government	$206,000				$ 206,000
Streets & Highways	71,000				71,000
Public Safety	335,000				335,000
Sanitation	141,000				141,000
Culture & Recreation			$ 5,000	$49,000	54,000
Debt Service					
Principal Retirement				20,000	20,000
Interest Charges				10,000	10,000
Capital Outlay	58,000	$ 124,000			182,000
Total Expenditures	$811,000	$ 124,000	$ 5,000	$79,000	$1,019,000
Excess (deficiency) of Revenues over Expenditures	$ 53,000	$(114,000)	$ 3,000	$16,000	$ (42,000)
Other Financing Sources (Uses)					
Proceeds of Bond Issue		$ 102,000			$ 102,000
Transfers In		20,000		$ 2,000	22,000
Transfers Out	$ (30,000)	(2,000)			(32,000)
Total Other Financing Sources & Uses	$ (30,000)	$ 120,000	$ 0	$ 2,000	$ 92,000
Contributions, Special Items & Extraordinary Items:					
Contribution			100,000		$ 100,000
Net Change in Fund Balances	$ 23,000	$ 6,000	$103,000	$18,000	$ 150,000
Fund Balances—Beginning	129,000	0	0	0	129,000
Fund Balances—Ending	$152,000	$ 6,000	$103,000	$18,000	$ 279,000

fund meets the 10 percent criterion for total assets (29.68% = $103,000 ÷ $347,000). Continuing down to the liabilities, only the capital projects fund meets the 10 percent criterion for total liabilities (14.71% = $10,000 ÷ $68,000). Information in Figure 18–4 indicates that none of the nongeneral governmental funds meets the 10 percent criterion for revenues. For expenditures, the capital projects fund meets the 10 percent criterion for total expenditures (12.17% = $124,000 ÷ $1,019,000). Thus, the only two nongeneral governmental funds that meet the 10 percent criterion tests for a major fund are (1) the permanent fund (for total assets) and (2) the capital projects fund (for both total liabilities and total expenditures).

5 Percent Criterion Tests

To compute the 5 percent criterion tests, the second group of major fund tests, the GASB specifies that the denominator of each of the four tests (assets, liabilities, revenues, and expenditures/expenses) be the combined total of each of these items for the five governmental funds *plus* the enterprise funds. For example, in Figure 18–3, the combined assets for the 5 percent asset test total \$487,000 (\$347,000 from the governmental funds plus \$140,000 from the enterprise fund). For the nongeneral governmental funds, the permanent fund is the only one that meets the 5 percent criterion for total assets (21.15% = \$103,000 ÷ \$487,000). For total liabilities, the capital projects fund meets the 5 percent criterion (5.56% = \$10,000 ÷ \$180,000). For revenues, the special revenue fund meets the 5 percent criterion (6.11% = \$62,000 ÷ \$1,014,000) (Figure 18–4). For expenditures/expenses, only the capital projects fund meets the 5 percent criterion (11.76% = \$124,000 ÷ \$1,054,000).

Note that to be classified as a major fund, a governmental fund other than the general fund must meet *both* the 10 percent and the 5 percent criterion tests for at least one of the four financial statement items. Thus, the following governmental funds are classified as major funds: (1) the general fund—always a major fund, (2) the capital projects fund (for liabilities and expenditures), and (3) the permanent fund (for assets). As in Figures 18–5 and 18–6, the governmental funds financial statements present details on these three funds. The two nonmajor funds, special revenue and debt service, are combined into a single Other Governmental Funds column. However, the governmental unit's management may elect to disclose separately any nonmajor fund that it believes is important for users of the financial statements to fully understand. **GASB 34** requires that a total for all governmental funds be provided. Note that enterprise funds are not governmental-type funds.

Governmental units are permitted to disclose designations of unassigned funds on the governmental funds' balance sheet. A designation is not a legal reservation or restriction but is similar to an appropriation of retained earnings for a commercial entity. The designation represents management's plans for the intended use of the resources and is a communication to users of the financial statements. However, designations are not permitted to be reported on the governmentwide financial statements.

GASB 34 requires a reconciliation schedule to the governmentwide financial statements to be presented either at the bottom of each of the two fund financial statements or in accompanying schedules. These two schedules reconcile the modified accrual basis of accounting used for the governmental funds to the accrual basis of accounting used for reporting in the two governmentwide financial statements. We present the reconciliation schedules later in this chapter within the discussion of presenting the governmentwide financial statements.

ENTERPRISE FUNDS

LO 18-6

Make calculations and record journal entries for enterprise funds.

Governments sometimes offer goods or services for sale to the public. The amounts charged to customers are intended to recover all or most of the cost of these goods or services. For example, a city may operate electric, gas, and water utilities; transportation systems such as buses, trains, and subways; airports; sports arenas; parking lots and garages; and public housing. Such operations are accounted for in ***enterprise funds,*** which differ from special revenue funds in that user charges reimburse the costs of enterprise fund activities. Therefore, the primary difference between establishing a special revenue fund and an enterprise fund is the revenue source.

The enterprise fund is one of the two proprietary fund types and has a measurement focus on all economic resources and uses the accrual basis of accounting. Proprietary funds report fixed assets, which are depreciated, and long-term debt, if issued, and focus on income determination and capital maintenance as do commercial entities. The financial statements for proprietary funds are very similar to those for commercial entities: (1) the statement of net position (balance sheet), (2) the statement of revenues, expenses, and changes in fund net position (income statement), and (3) the statement of cash flows.

Budgeting in the proprietary funds also has the same role as in commercial entities. A budget may be prepared for management planning purposes; however, it is normally not entered into the accounts.

Illustration of Transactions

Sol City operates a municipal water utility as an enterprise fund. The utility's trial balance as of January 1, 20X2, the first day of the 20X2 fiscal year, follows:

SOL CITY
Trial Balance for Water Utility Enterprise Fund
January 1, 20X2

Cash	$ 9,000	
Machinery & Equipment	94,000	
Buildings	40,000	
Accumulated Depreciation—Machinery and Equipment		$ 15,000
Accumulated Depreciation—Buildings		2,000
Bonds Payable, 5%		100,000
Net Position:		
Invested in Capital Assets, Net of Related Debt		17,000
Unrestricted		9,000
Totals	$143,000	$143,000

One difference between balance sheet accounts for commercial entities and those for proprietary funds is the absence of a stockholders' equity section in governmental accounting. The general public is the theoretical owner of all governmental assets. Furthermore, proprietary funds issue no stock certificates; therefore, a net position section is used instead of common stock and additional paid-in capital. **GASB 34** requires the separate disclosure of the net position invested in capital assets, net of related debt. Proprietary funds report the book value (cost basis less accumulated depreciation) invested in capital assets such as land, buildings, machinery, equipment, and other tangible and intangible assets having expected useful lives exceeding one year. These resources are not readily available for other unrestricted uses as are the current assets. The related debt is that directly associated with the capital assets and is typically long term in nature. For our example, assume the $100,000 of bonds payable is related to the $117,000 of net capital assets ($134,000 cost less $17,000 of accumulated depreciation). Other interesting differences are the large relative amounts of fixed assets and long-term debt because enterprise funds typically require large investments in productive assets in order to provide the necessary level of service to the public, and long-term revenue bonds these investments usually service.

The water utility sells its product to the residents of Sol City based on a user charge. In addition to water revenue, the utility receives a $3,000 short-term interfund loan from the general fund and obtains its office supplies from the city's centralized purchasing operation, which is accounted for as an internal service fund. During the year, the water utility acquires a new pump costing $6,000.

Enterprise Fund Revenues

The water utility provides service during the period and bills its customers for the amount of water used. The utility estimates that 7.5 percent of its billings will not be collected. Note that revenues are reported net of uncollectibles. These transactions are recorded as follows:

(30)	Accounts Receivable	40,000	
	Allowance for Uncollectibles		3,000
	Revenue—Water Sales		37,000

Bill customers for water used as indicated by meter readings.
Estimate $3,000 of billings will be uncollectible.

(31)	Cash	32,000	
	Accounts Receivable		32,000
	Collect portion of accounts receivable.		

Capital Asset Acquisition

The water utility acquires a new pump during the year.

(32)	Equipment	6,000	
	Vouchers Payable		6,000
	Receive new pump for well house.		

(33)	Vouchers Payable	6,000	
	Cash		6,000
	Pay voucher for new pump.		

FYI

In its 2013 comprehensive annual financial report, the State of Maryland reported almost $14 billion of total assets on its statement of fund net position for enterprise funds.

Interfund Activities

Several interfund transactions occur during the year. First, in an interfund financing transaction, the water utility receives $3,000 from the general fund as a short-term loan to be repaid within 90 days. The general fund records this as a short-term receivable, Due from Enterprise Fund [see entry (39) in Chapter 17]. Second, the utility acquires its office supplies from the internal service fund in an interfund services provided and used transaction. The internal service fund reports this as a revenue transaction [see entry (48) later in this chapter]:

(34)	Cash	3,000	
	Due to General Fund		3,000
	Recognize payable for loan from general fund.		

(35)	Supplies Inventory	3,000	
	Due to Internal Service Fund		3,000
	Receive office supplies from centralized purchasing department at a cost of $3,000.		

(36)	Due to Internal Service Fund	2,000	
	Cash		2,000
	Approve payment of $2,000 to centralized purchasing department for supplies received.		

Enterprise Fund Expenses

The water utility fund incurs $9,000 of operating expenses during the period. Several adjusting journal entries are required at the end of the fiscal year to recognize additional expenses. Note that these adjusting entries are similar to those of a commercial entity:

(37)	General Operating Expenses	9,000	
	Vouchers Payable		9,000
	Incur operating expenses during year.		

(38)	Vouchers Payable	6,000	
	Cash		6,000
	Pay approved vouchers for operating expenses.		

(39)	General Operating Expenses	3,000	
	Supplies Inventory		3,000
	Adjust for $3,000 of supplies consumed.		

		Debit	Credit
(40)	Depreciation Expense	18,000	
	Accumulated Depreciation—Buildings		3,000
	Accumulated Depreciation—Machinery and Equipment		15,000
	Recognize depreciation expense for year.		

		Debit	Credit
(41)	Interest Expense	5,000	
	Accrued Interest Payable		5,000
	Accrue interest on bond payable: $100,000 × 0.05 × 1 year.		

Closing and Reclassification Entries in the Enterprise Fund

The enterprise fund's nominal accounts are closed, the period's profit or loss is determined, and, at the close of the fiscal year, the government reclassifies the various components of net position based on the year-end amount invested in capital assets, net of related debt:

		Debit	Credit
(42)	Revenue—Water Sales	37,000	
	General Operating Expenses		12,000
	Depreciation Expense		18,000
	Interest Expense		5,000
	Profit and Loss Summary		2,000
	Close nominal accounts into profit and loss summary.		

		Debit	Credit
(43)	Profit and Loss Summary	2,000	
	Net Position—Unrestricted		2,000
	Close profit and loss summary into net position.		

		Debit	Credit
(44)	Net Position—Invested in Capital Assets, Net of Related Debt	12,000	
	Net Position—Unrestricted		12,000

To reclassify net position as of end of fiscal period:
12/31/X1 balance: $ 5,000 = $105,000 capital assets − $100,000 of related debt
1/1/X1 balance: 17,000 = $117,000 capital assets − $100,000 of related debt
$12,000 = Decrease during period in net position invested in capital assets, net of related debt.

LO 18-7

Understand and explain the financial reporting of proprietary funds.

Advanced StudyGuide .com

Financial Statements for the Proprietary Funds

Three financial statements are required for the proprietary funds. A governmental entity that has more than one enterprise fund must individually assess each using both the 10 percent criterion and the 5 percent criterion tests to determine whether it is a major fund. Sol City has only one enterprise fund. See Figure 18–7 for the statement of net position for the enterprise proprietary fund and for the internal service proprietary fund that will be discussed in the next section of this chapter. Figure 18–8 is the statement of revenues, expenses, and changes in fund net position for Sol City's two proprietary funds. Figure 18–9 is the statement of cash flows for these two proprietary funds.

The statement of net position in Figure 18–7 is similar to that required for commercial entities. Proprietary funds report their own fixed assets, investments, and long-term liabilities. **GASB 34** specifies that the net position section for the proprietary funds, which is presented below liabilities, be separated into three components: (1) invested in capital assets, net of related debt, (2) restricted because of restrictions beyond the government's control, such as externally imposed restrictions or legal requirements, and (3) unrestricted. **GASB 46** amends **GASB 34** with regard to net position restricted by legally enforceable actions such as enabling legislation, which specifies that a government use resources only for the purposes stated in the enabling legislation.

FIGURE 18–7
Proprietary Funds Statement of Net Position

SOL CITY
Statement of Net Position
Proprietary Funds
December 31, 20X2

	Enterprise Fund	Internal Service Fund
Assets:		
Current Assets:		
Cash	$ 30,000	$ 4,000
Accounts Receivable (net)	5,000	
Due from Other Funds		1,000
Inventory of Supplies		6,000
Total Current Assets	$ 35,000	$11,000
Noncurrent Assets:		
Capital Assets:		
Machinery & Equipment	$100,000	$ 3,000
Less: Accumulated Depreciation	(30,000)	(1,000)
Buildings	40,000	
Less: Accumulated Depreciation	(5,000)	
Total Noncurrent Assets	$105,000	$ 2,000
Total Assets	$140,000	$13,000
Liabilities:		
Current Liabilities:		
Vouchers Payable	$ 3,000	$ 6,000
Accrued Interest Payable	5,000	
Due to Other Funds	4,000	
Total Current Liabilities	$ 12,000	$ 6,000
Noncurrent Liabilities:		
Bonds Payable, 5%	100,000	
Total Liabilities	$112,000	$ 6,000
Net Position:		
Invested in Capital Assets, Net of Related Debt	$ 5,000	$ 2,000
Unrestricted	23,000	5,000
Total Net Position	$ 28,000	$ 7,000

GASB 46 provides guidance for reporting the restricted net position and accounting for changes when new enabling legislation replaces the prior legislation. The key point is that **GASB 46** confirms the **GASB 34** requirement for separate disclosure of net position restricted by legal requirements. Our example has no externally imposed or legal restrictions on net position. The amount of the net position invested in capital assets, net of related debt, is computed as capital assets less accumulated depreciation, less outstanding principal of related debt. For purposes of this example, assume that the information in Figure 18–7 shows that the enterprise fund has $5,000 of net position invested in capital assets, net of related debt ($105,000 − $100,000), and the internal service fund has $2,000 invested in capital assets, net of related debt ($2,000 − $0).

The statement of revenues, expenses, and changes in fund net position is similar to the income statement for commercial entities. A separation of operating and nonoperating revenues and expenses is made to provide more information value regarding the operations of the proprietary funds. Contributions and transfers in or out are reported below the income (loss) line in the statement of revenues, expenses, and changes in fund net position. Contributions would include any capital asset transfers from a governmental fund to a proprietary fund. For example, the general fund may transfer equipment to an enterprise

FIGURE 18–8
Proprietary Funds Statement of Revenues, Expenses, and Changes in Fund Net Position

SOL CITY
Statement of Revenues, Expenses, and Changes in Fund Net Position
Proprietary Funds
For the Year Ended December 31, 20X2

	Enterprise Fund	Internal Service Fund
Operating Revenues:		
Charges for Services	$37,000	$ 4,000
Total Operating Revenues	$37,000	$ 4,000
Operating Expenses:		
General Operating	$12,000	$ 4,000
Cost of Goods Sold		2,000
Depreciation	18,000	1,000
Total Operating Expenses	$30,000	$ 7,000
Nonoperating Revenue (Expenses):		
Interest Expense	$ (5,000)	
Total Nonoperating Expense	$ 5,000	
Income (Loss) before Contributions & Transfers	$ 2,000	$(3,000)
Transfer In		10,000
Change in Net Position	$ 2,000	$ 7,000
Net Position—Beginning	26,000	0
Net Position—Ending	$28,000	$ 7,000

fund. Note that the governmental funds describe the interfund transfers as other financing sources or uses, but the proprietary funds use only the terms *transfer in* or *transfer out* to describe these nonoperating interfund transactions. And both interest income and interest expense are reported as nonoperating items.

GASB 9, requires the statement of cash flows for enterprise funds. This standard provides a format that differs somewhat from the three-section format of the statement of cash flows for commercial entities. Because of the large number of capital asset acquisition and financing transactions in proprietary funds, the GASB specified four sections of the statement of cash flows, as follows:

1. *Cash flows from operating activities.* This first section includes all transactions from providing services and delivering goods. **GASB 34** requires the use of the direct method of computing cash flows from operating activities. This section includes cash flows from interfund operating transactions and reimbursements from other funds.
2. *Cash flows from noncapital financing activities.* This second section includes activities such as borrowing or repaying money for purposes other than to acquire, construct, or improve capital assets. It includes cash for financing activities received from, or paid to, other funds except that specified for capital asset use.
3. *Cash flows from capital and related financing activities.* This third section includes all activities clearly related to, or attributable to, the acquisition, disposition, construction, or improvement of capital assets. This section also includes the interest paid on borrowings for capital assets.
4. *Cash flows from investing activities.* This fourth section includes all investing activities, interest and dividend revenue, and acquisition and disposition of debt or equity instruments.

In addition to the statement of cash flows, the GASB also requires proprietary funds to provide a supplementary schedule that reconciles the cash flow from operating activities with the operating income or loss reported on the statement of revenues, expenses, and changes in fund net position.

FIGURE 18–9 Proprietary Funds Statement of Cash Flows

SOL CITY
Statement of Cash Flows
Proprietary Funds
For the Year Ended December 31, 20X2

	Enterprise Fund	Internal Service Fund
Cash Flows from Operating Activities:		
Receipts from Customers	$32,000	$ 3,000
Cash Payments for Goods and Services	(6,000)	(6,000)
Cash Paid to Internal Service Fund for Supplies	(2,000)	
Net Cash Provided (Used) by Operating Activities	$24,000	$(3,000)
Cash Flows from Noncapital Financing Activities:		
Cash Received from General Fund for Noncapital Loan	$ 3,000	$ 7,000
Net Cash Provided by Noncapital Financing Activities	$ 3,000	$ 7,000
Cash Flows from Capital & Related Financing Activities:		
Acquisition of Capital Asset	$ (6,000)	$(3,000)
Cash Received from General Fund for Capital Activity		3,000
Net Cash Provided (Used) for Capital Financing Activities	$ (6,000)	$ 0
Cash Flows from Investing Activities	$ 0	$ 0
Net Increase in Cash	$21,000	$ 4,000
Balances—Beginning of Year	9,000	0
Balances—End of Year	$30,000	$ 4,000
Reconciliation of Operating Income to Net Cash Provided by Operating Activities:		
Operating Income	$ 7,000	$(3,000)
Adjustments to Reconcile Operating Income to Net Cash Provided (Used) by Operating Activities:		
Depreciation	18,000	1,000
Change in Assets & Liabilities:		
Increase in Net Accounts Receivable	(5,000)	
Increase in Due from Other Funds from Billings		(1,000)
Increase in Inventory of Supplies		(6,000)
Increase in Vouchers Payable	3,000	6,000
Increase in Due to Internal Service Fund	1,000	
Net Cash Provided (Used) by Operating Activities	$24,000	$(3,000)

INTERNAL SERVICE FUNDS

LO 18-8

Make calculations and record journal entries for internal service funds.

Internal service funds account for the financing of goods or services provided by one department or agency to other departments or agencies on a cost-reimbursement basis. These services are not available to the general public, making the internal service fund different from the enterprise fund. Examples are motor vehicle pools, central computer facilities, printing shops, and centralized purchasing and storage facilities. Separate internal service funds are established for each of these functions the local governmental unit maintains.

Accounting and financial reporting for internal service funds is the same as for enterprise funds or for commercial entities. The accrual basis is used to measure revenue and expenses, and the balance sheet may include fixed assets, which are depreciated, and long-term debt, if issued. The statement of revenue, expenses, and changes in fund net position reports the fund's income for the period. The statement of cash flows also is required.

Illustration of Transactions

Sol City decides to establish a centralized purchasing and storage function as an internal service fund. This centralized purchasing department provides office supplies to all other funds of the local government on a user-charge basis. After acquiring the necessary supplies, the centralized purchasing department makes the following sales:

Buying Fund	Selling Price	Cost to Internal Service Fund
General fund	$1,000	$ 500
Enterprise fund	3,000	1,500

Sol City makes entries (45), (46), and (47) during the year to record the activities of the centralized purchasing and storage department.

Establishment of Internal Service Fund and Acquisition of Inventories

An entity starts its internal service fund with a transfer in from the general fund in the amount of $10,000, which the internal service fund then uses to acquire inventory and equipment. The general fund records this interfund transfer as a transfer out [see entry (33) in Chapter 17]:

		Debit	Credit
(45)	Cash	10,000	
	Transfer In		10,000

Receive interfund transfer in from general fund to initiate centralized purchasing and storage function.

		Debit	Credit
(46)	Inventory	8,000	
	Vouchers Payable		8,000

Acquire inventory of supplies.

		Debit	Credit
(47)	Machinery and Equipment	3,000	
	Vouchers Payable		3,000

Acquire equipment.

Internal Service Fund Revenue

The internal service fund earns revenue by selling supplies to other funds and billing them for the value of the supplies. The billing rate is typically established at more than the operating costs of the internal service fund so that the fund may acquire replacement assets or new assets:

		Debit	Credit
(48)	Due from General Fund	1,000	
	Due from Enterprise Fund	3,000	
	Charges for Services		4,000

Recognize revenue from providing supplies to general fund and enterprise fund.

		Debit	Credit
(49)	Cash	3,000	
	Due from General Fund		1,000
	Due from Enterprise Fund		2,000

Collect portion of receivables.

The general fund records the $1,000 for supplies as an interfund expenditures transaction [see entry (37) in Chapter 17]. The enterprise fund records the $3,000 as an interfund inventory purchase transaction [see entry (35) earlier in this chapter].

Internal Service Fund Expenses

The internal service fund incurs $4,000 of operating expenses, including payroll, during the period. In addition, the fund recognizes cost of goods sold of $2,000 and $1,000 of depreciation expense in adjusting entries. The $9,000 of vouchers paid include a voucher in the amount of $3,000 for the equipment acquired in entry (47) above:

		Debit	Credit
(50)	General Operating Expenses	4,000	
	Vouchers Payable		4,000

Incur operating expenses.

		Debit	Credit
(51)	Vouchers Payable	9,000	
	Cash		9,000
	Pay approved vouchers.		

		Debit	Credit
(52)	Cost of Goods Sold	2,000	
	Inventory		2,000
	Recognize cost of supplies sold.		

		Debit	Credit
(53)	Depreciation Expense	1,000	
	Accumulated Depreciation		1,000
	Depreciation of equipment.		

Closing Entries in the Internal Service Fund

The closing and reclassifying entries for the internal service fund follow. In this example, we use Profit and Loss Summary in the closing process; however, some governmental units use the account Excess of Net Revenues over Costs to perform the same function.

		Debit	Credit
(54)	Charges for Services	4,000	
	Profit and Loss Summary	3,000	
	Cost of Goods Sold		2,000
	General Operating Expenses		4,000
	Depreciation Expense		1,000
	Close revenue and expenses.		

		Debit	Credit
(55)	Transfer In	10,000	
	Profit and Loss Summary		3,000
	Net Position—Unrestricted		7,000
	Close profit and loss summary and transfer in to net position.		

		Debit	Credit
(56)	Net Position—Unrestricted	2,000	
	Net Position—Invested in Capital Assets, Net of Related Debt		2,000
	To reclassify net position as of end of fiscal period: $2,000 = $2,000 net capital assets − $0 related debt.		

Financial Statements for Internal Service Funds

The financial statements required for internal service funds are the same as those required for the enterprise fund. See Figure 18–7 for the statement of net position, Figure 18–8 for the statement of revenues, expenses, and changes in fund net position for the internal service fund, and Figure 18–9 for the statement of cash flows for the internal service fund.

TRUST FUNDS

LO 18-9

Make calculations and record journal entries for trust funds.

A ***trust fund*** is a fiduciary fund type that accounts for resources held by a governmental unit in a trustee capacity. The unit acts as a fiduciary for monies or properties held on behalf of individuals, employees, or other governmental agencies. The three main types of fiduciary trust funds are (1) pension and other employee benefit trust funds, (2) investment trust funds, and (3) private-purpose trust funds.

Fiduciary funds use the accrual basis of accounting, and the financial statements required for fiduciary funds are the statement of fiduciary net position (Figure 18–10) and the statement of changes in fiduciary net position (Figure 18–11). The statement of fiduciary net position includes all trusts and agency funds. The statement of changes in fiduciary net position includes only the trust funds because agency funds do not have a net asset balance; their assets must equal their liabilities. We discuss agency funds after trust funds.

Private-purpose trust funds account for trust agreements for which the principal and/or income benefits specific individuals, private organizations, or other governments. Note that the benefit is limited to private, rather than general public, purposes. The trust agreement may require the principal to be preserved (i.e., nonexpendable principal), in which

FIGURE 18–10
Fiduciary Funds Statement of Fiduciary Net Position

SOL CITY
Statement of Fiduciary Net Position
Fiduciary Funds
December 31, 20X2

	Private-Purpose Funds	Agency Funds
Assets:		
Cash	$ 1,600	$1,000
Investments, at Fair Value:		
Municipal Bonds	26,200	
Total Assets	$27,800	$1,000
Liabilities:		
Due to Insurance Company		$1,000
Total Liabilities	$ 0	$1,000
Net Position Held in Trust	$27,800	

FIGURE 18–11
Fiduciary Funds Statement of Changes in Fiduciary Net Position

SOL CITY
Statement of Changes in Fiduciary Net Position
Fiduciary Funds
For the Year Ended December 31, 20X2
Private-Purpose Fund

Additions:		
Contributions		$50,000
Investment Earnings:		
Increase in Fair Value of Investments	$1,200	
Interest	600	
Total Investment Earnings		1,800
Total Additions		$51,800
Deductions:		
Benefits		$23,000
Administrative Costs		1,000
Total Deductions		$24,000
Change in Net Position		$27,800
Net Position—Beginning of Year		0
Net Position—End of Year		$27,800

case an endowment is created. In other trust agreements, both the principal and income may be used for the specific purposes for which the trust was created. The governmental entity does not have to accept the donation if it is not consistent with the government's objectives. However, in many cases, a governmental entity accepts the donation and agrees to its provisions because of the benefits that the resources can achieve. For example, a citizen group may donate money to a city to be used for award recognition for businesses located in the downtown area that update and improve the appearances of their storefronts. The governmental entity is typically allowed to charge the private-purpose trust fund a fee for managing the trust's resources, which would include investing the resources and making the allowed expenditures from the resources. An example of a private-purpose trust fund is illustrated in the next section of this chapter.

Illustration of Private-Purpose Trust Fund

On January 1, 20X2, Sol City received a $50,000 donation from Charles Alt, a citizen of Sol City. The terms of the trust agreement specify that the city is to use about $25,000 each year for the next two years to help alleviate the cost of transporting senior citizens to and from the senior citizens' center. The city accepts the donation and, as allowed by the trust agreement, invests $25,000 in highly rated bonds. It deposited the remaining $25,000 in a bank account that earns 4 percent interest. The terms of the trust agreement allow the city to deduct $1,000 per year for its administrative costs of managing the trust and the transportation services. During the first year, 20X2, the fund paid $23,000 for transportation services. The fund pays the remaining resources in 20X3.

(57)	Cash	50,000	
	Additions—Contributions		50,000
	The city accepts a private-purpose trust fund of $50,000.		
(58)	Investment in Bonds	25,000	
	Cash		25,000
	The city invests half of the trust funds, as allowed by the trust agreement.		
(59)	Cash	600	
	Additions—Interest		600
	Interest earned during the year on the monies deposited in the bank is recognized from bank statements.		
(60)	Deductions—Transportation Benefits	23,000	
	Cash		23,000
	Transportation costs during the year are paid.		
(61)	Deductions—Administration Costs	1,000	
	Cash		1,000
	The $1,000 of administrative costs allowed to the city are recognized and paid.		

An adjusting journal entry made on December 31, 20X2, revalues the investment in bonds to their fair values, as follows:

(62)	Investment in Bonds	1,200	
	Additions—Investment Revalued		1,200
	The fair value of the investment in bonds increased by $1,200 by the end of the year.		

Note that this private-purpose trust fund had an expendable principal as well as earnings. The requirement for a private-purpose trust fund is that its resources are to be used only for specific individuals, organizations, or other governmental units as the donor specified. Some private-purpose trust funds specify that the principal is nonexpendable and that only the earnings are to be used for the private purpose. A private-purpose trust fund is differentiated from a permanent fund, which is part of the governmental funds, in the following manner. A permanent fund must maintain its principal but may use the earnings to support the government's programs that benefit all citizens. A private-purpose trust fund must be used only for the purposes the donor or grantor of the trust fund specified and is not available to support the government's general programs.

Sol City reports the statement of fiduciary net position for the fiduciary funds, including the private-purpose fund and agency fund (Figure 18–10). Refer to Figure 18–11 for the statement of changes in fiduciary net position for the private-purpose trust fund. The next section of the chapter discusses Agency funds.

AGENCY FUNDS

LO 18-10

Make calculations and record journal entries for agency funds.

An ***agency fund*** is a fiduciary fund type that accounts for resources held by a governmental unit as a custodial agent for individuals, private organizations, other funds, or other governmental units. Examples are tax collection funds that collect property taxes and then distribute them to local governmental units and employee benefit funds for such items as dental insurance or charitable contributions that employees authorize as withholdings from their paychecks.

Accounting for agency funds uses the accrual basis of accounting. Because agency funds are custodial in nature, assets always equal liabilities and there is no fund equity. The financial statement for agency funds is the statement of fiduciary net position presented in Figure 18–9. Note that agency funds cannot have any net position balance; therefore, no statement of changes in fiduciary net position is required for them. As a result, the accounting equation for agency funds is rather unique: Assets = Liabilities.

Illustration of Transactions in an Agency Fund

Sol City has established an agency fund to account for employees' share of health insurance, which is deducted from their monthly paychecks and then forwarded to the insurance company on a quarterly basis. For this example, the city deducted a total of $9,000 from the employees' paychecks and paid $8,000 to the insurance company in 20X2. The remaining $1,000 will be paid to the insurance company in the first quarter of 20X3.

Agency Fund Receipts and Disbursements

The receipts and disbursements in the agency fund during 20X2 follow:

(63)	Cash	9,000	
	Due to Insurance Company		9,000
	Employees' contributory share of health insurance deducted from payroll checks.		

(64)	Due to Insurance Company	8,000	
	Cash		8,000
	Pay liability to insurance company for employees' share of insurance cost.		

THE GOVERNMENT REPORTING MODEL

LO 18-11

Understand and explain the preparation of governmentwide financial statements.

GASB 34 specifies the reporting model for governmental entities. All general-purpose units such as states, counties, and municipalities must provide all financial statements required by this standard. These statements are both the fund-based financial statements presented earlier in this chapter and the governmentwide financial statements that we discuss in a following section of this chapter. Some special-purpose governmental units such as cemetery associations engaged in a single governmental activity are not required to provide the governmentwide financial statements but still must provide fund-based financial statements. We now discuss four major issues that arise in the governmental reporting model.

Four Major Issues

Issue 1: What Organizations Compose the Reporting Entity?

The first issue to address is the determination of the ***reporting entity*** for which the statements will be provided. The primary government is part of the reporting entity, but this issue concerns what other boards, commissions, agencies, or authorities should be included with the reporting entity. **GASB 34** defines the reporting entity as (1) the primary government, such as a city, county, or state, (2) a component unit for which the primary government is financially accountable, and (3) any organization that has a significant relationship with the primary government and should be included to avoid misleading or incomplete financial statements.

Issue 2: What Constitutes Financial Accountability?

GASB 14 states that the primary government's financial accountability for the component organization is evidenced by either *board appointment* or *fiscal dependence*. Financial accountability is evidenced when the primary government appoints a majority of the organization's governing board. Thus, the primary government has effective control over the organization, which in turn may provide specific benefits to, or may impose specific financial burdens on, the primary government. Financial accountability also may exist if the organization has a separately elected or appointed board but depends on the primary government for the financial resources required to operate.

The primary government's ability to impose its will on an organization is evidenced by such things as its ability to (1) remove appointed members of the organization's governing board, (2) approve or modify the organization's budget or approve rates or fee changes, (3) veto or overrule the decisions of the organization's governing body, or (4) appoint, hire, reassign, or dismiss those persons responsible for the organization's day-to-day operations. The potential for an organization to impose specific burdens on the primary government is evidenced by such things as its legal obligation or assumption of the obligation to finance the deficits or otherwise provide financial support to the organization or the primary government's obligation in some manner for the debt of the organization. These criteria indicate that when the primary governmental unit is financially accountable for legally separate organizations, those organizations should be included in the primary government's financial statements as ***component units.***

Issue 3: What Other Organizations Should Be Included in the Reporting Entity?

GASB 14 specifies a third category of organizations to be evaluated to determine whether they are part of the reporting entity with the primary government. These are legally separate, tax-exempt entities for which the primary government is *not* financially accountable. **GASB 39** and **GASB 61** amend parts of **GASB 14** to more fully define what other organizations should be included in a government's reporting entity. In general, a legally separate, tax-exempt organization is reported as a component unit of the primary government if *all three* of the following characteristics are met:

1. The resources of the separate organization are held for the benefit of the primary government, its component units, or the persons served by the primary government or it component units.
2. The primary government or its component units are entitled to, or can use, a majority of the economic resources of the separate organization.
3. The economic resources of the separate organization that the primary government or its component units can use are significant to the primary government.

GASB 61 modifies the definition of a component unit. For organizations that previously were required to be included as component units by meeting the fiscal dependency criterion, a financial benefit or burden relationship also would need to be present between the primary government and that organization for it to be included in the reporting entity as a component unit. Examples of other organizations that should be included in the reporting entity include university foundations and university alumni associations.

Issue 4: How Should the Financial Results of the Component Units Be Reported?

The fourth issue is how to report component units' financial results. A choice between two methods must be made: (1) ***discrete presentation*** in a separate column of the primary government's financial statements or (2) ***blended presentation*** by combining the organization's results into the primary government's financial results.

Most component units are discretely presented; however, the blending method should be used when the component unit is so intertwined with the primary government that, in essence, they are the same governmental unit. Blending should be used when either (1) the component unit's governing body is substantively the same as the primary government's governing body or (2) the component unit provides services entirely, or almost entirely, to the primary government or almost exclusively benefits it. Some of these organizations are similar to the internal services fund. Component units may use governmental fund accounting or proprietary fund accounting, depending on their types of activities. Neither discretely presenting nor blending should change the measurement basis of the type of accounting the component unit; however, a general fund of a blended component unit should be reported as a special revenue fund for the primary government.

FIGURE 18–12 The Comprehensive Annual Financial Report (CAFR)

Section 1: Introductory Section This section contains organizational information and other preliminary items.

Section 2: Financial Section The financial section contains the following items:

1. Independent auditors' report.
2. Management's discussion and analysis (required supplementary information) (**GASB 34**).
3. Governmentwide financial statements.
   a. Statement of net position (Figure 18–13).
   b. Statement of activities (Figure 18–14).
4. Fund-based financial statements.
   a. Governmental funds.
      (1) Balance sheet (Figure 18–5).
      (2) Statement of revenues, expenditures, and changes in fund balances (Figure 18–6).
      (3) Reconciliation schedules (Figures 18–15 and 18–16).
   b. Proprietary funds.
      (1) Statement of net position (Figure 18–7).
      (2) Statement of revenues, expenses, and changes in fund position (Figure 18–8).
      (3) Statement of cash flows (Figure 18–9).
   c. Fiduciary funds.
      (1) Statement of fiduciary position (Figure 18–10).
      (2) Statement of changes in fiduciary position (Figure 18–11).
5. Notes to the financial statements (**GASB 34 and 38**).
6. Required supplementary information (RSI).
   a. Budgetary comparison schedules (Figure 18–17) (**GASB 41**).
   b. Information about infrastructure assets (**GASB 34** for modified approach).
   c. Information about pension funding progress and employer contributions to retirement and pension funds (**GASB 25, 27, 43, 45, 50, 57, 67, and 68**).

Section 3: Combining and Individual Fund Financial Statements This section contains the financial statements of each individual fund as well as financial statements showing the combining of individual funds as a fund type (e.g., combining all individual special projects fund into one fund).

Section 4: Statistical Section This section presents the economic condition reporting that **GASB 44** requires to be presented in the statistical section of the annual report.

For purposes of the Sol City example, assume that the city has a separate library board responsible for managing the city library. The mayor appoints the library board, and the mayor and council must approve its budget and tax levy. In this case, the library is a component unit that will be discretely presented in a separate column of Sol City's two governmentwide financial statements.

Government Financial Reports

The annual report of a governmental entity is termed the ***comprehensive annual financial report*** (**CAFR**). Refer to Figure 18–12 for the components of the CAFR and parenthetical information noting the figure number in the text, or the number of the GASB standard providing guidance on the information to be included in that item.

The GASB has continued to develop the reporting standards for the statistical section to make it more useful and comparative for users of the annual report. In 2004, the GASB issued **GASB 44,** which specifies the types of information that should be reported in each of the five sections of the statistical section: (1) financial trends information, (2) revenue capacity information, (3) debt capacity information, (4) demographic and economic information, and (5) operating information. The intent of this statement is to further improve the understandability and usefulness of this section by also requiring the governmental unit to add information about the sources of the data and the major assumptions used and expand explanations for any unusual information presented. Thus, the statistical section is an important part of the CAFR.

The fund-based financial statements were discussed previously in this chapter. The following discussion centers on the governmentwide financials and the required supplementary information (RSI).

Governmentwide Financial Statements

The ***governmentwide financial statements*** include (1) the statement of net position and (2) the statement of activities. **GASB 34** requires that governmentwide financial statements be prepared on the *economic resources measurement focus* with the accrual basis of accounting. *Note:* The fiduciary funds (e.g., private-purpose trust funds and agency funds) are *not* included in the two governmentwide financial statements because fiduciary funds are not available to support government programs. **GASB 63** adds additional requirements related to the reporting of deferred outflows and inflows of resources and it changes the focus from net assets to "net position."

Statement of Net Position

Some important points regarding Sol City's statement of net position (Figure 18–13) follow:

1. *Format.* The format of the statement is Assets − Liabilities = Net Position. This focuses attention on the governmental entity's net position.
2. *Columnar presentation.* A columnar presentation is used because it emphasizes that the primary government has two different categories of activities, each needing a net asset base to support that category's activities, and the reporting entity's component units have their own net asset base.
   a. The primary government's activities are assigned to either governmental activities or business-type activities.
   b. The internal service funds are included as part of the governmental activities because internal service funds provide service to only the governmental entity, not to external parties.
   c. The enterprise funds are presented as business-type activities of the primary government because the enterprise funds offer services to the public, and thus they are more business oriented.
3. *Assets.* Reported assets include all types of the governmental entity's assets, including infrastructure such as roads, sewers, and so on. These capital assets are not reported in the governmental funds that, under the current financial resources measurement focus, record costs of capital assets as expenditures of the period. **GASB 34** requires that all capital and infrastructure assets be reported on the governmentwide financial statements. Capital assets, such as buildings and equipment, are depreciated and that depreciation appears as an expense on the governmentwide statement of activities. Infrastructure assets are, by their definition, long-lived assets that can be maintained for a much longer time than capital assets. Roads can be paved over, bridges can be repaired, and water and sewer systems can be maintained.

   Because of the difficulty in determining any reasonable estimated useful life for the infrastructure assets, **GASB 34** provides two methods to account for the depreciating attribute of these infrastructure assets:

   a. Report estimated depreciation expense. The first method requires governments to estimate depreciation expense and report that estimated expense on the governmentwide statement of activities.
   b. Use the modified approach. The second approach allows governments to avoid estimating depreciation expense on infrastructure assets that are part of a network or a network subsystem as long as the government manages those assets using an asset management system and can document that the assets are preserved

FIGURE 18–13 Governmentwide Statement of Net Position

SOL CITY
Statement of Net Position
December 31, 20X2

	Primary Government			
	Governmental Activities	**Business-Type Activities**	**Total**	**Component Unit**
Assets:				
Cash & Cash Equivalents	$ 153,500	$ 33,150	$186,650	$ 3,000
Receivables, Net	89,000	5,000	94,000	0
Internal Balances	4,000	(4,000)	0	0
Inventories	23,000	0	23,000	1,000
Investment in Government Bonds	91,000	0	91,000	0
Capital Assets:				
Land & Infrastructure	3,000,000		3,000,000	
Depreciable Assets, Net	1,202,000	105,000	1,307,000	870,000
Total Assets	$4,562,500	$139,150	$4,701,650	$874,000
Deferred Outflows of Resources:				
Accumulated decrease in fair value of hedging derivatives	0	7,650	7,650	0
Liabilities:				
Vouchers Payable	$ 64,000	$ 3,000	$ 67,000	0
Accrued Interest Payable	0	5,000	5,000	0
Contract Payable—Retainage	10,000	0	10,000	0
Noncurrent Liabilities:				
Due in More than 1 Year	80,000	100,000	180,000	120,000
Total Liabilities	$ 154,000	$108,000	$ 262,000	$120,000
Deferred Inflows of Resources:				
Accumulated increase in fair value of hedging derivatives	$ 1,500	$ 0	$ 1,500	0
Deferred service concession arrangement receipts	0	10,800	10,800	0
Total deferred inflows of resources	$ 1,500	$ 10,800	$ 12,300	$ 0
Net Position:				
Invested in Capital Assets, Net of Related Debt	$4,122,000	$ 5,000	$4,127,000	$750,000
Restricted for:				
Debt Service	5,000	0	5,000	0
Permanent Funds	103,000	0	103,000	0
Unrestricted	177,000	23,000	200,000	4,000
Total Net Position	$4,407,000	$ 28,000	$4,435,000	$754,000

approximately at, or above, a condition level the government established. Under the modified approach, the governmental entity annually expenses actual renewal costs associated with the infrastructure assets. Additions and improvements are added to the cost basis of the infrastructure asset. Required footnote disclosures include (1) an estimate of the cost required to maintain or preserve the infrastructure assets as well as the actual costs for each of the last five years and (2) the presentation of condition assessments of the infrastructure assets for the last three years to show that these assets are indeed being maintained.

Many governments use the modified approach rather than the estimated depreciation expense method. Regardless of the method used for depreciation, the government must report the infrastructure assets in the asset section of the governmentwide statement of net position.

Note that Sol City distinguishes between its infrastructure assets and its buildings and equipment. Sol City has chosen to use the modified approach in recognizing the depreciating factors in its infrastructure assets. Thus, the depreciation expense reported on the statement of activities is from only the Depreciable Assets category, which includes items such as buildings and equipment. The asset Internal Balances represents interfund receivables/payables between the primary government's funds composing the governmental activities (governmental funds plus internal service funds) and the funds composing the business-type activities (the enterprise funds). These internal balances cancel out each other for the total column. Prior to 2001, state and local governments were required to capitalize construction-period interest on capital assets used in governmental activities. In the Sol City example, the enterprise fund owes a total of $4,000 to other funds: $3,000 to the general fund for a loan and $1,000 to the internal service fund for supplies purchases. Note again that the internal service fund is considered a governmental activity because the fund provides services and supplies only to other entities within the government's reporting entity.

4. *Categories of net position.* Net position is separated into three categories:
   a. Invested in capital assets, net of related debt.
   b. Restricted (by external requirements of creditors, grantors, contributors, or other governmental entities).
   c. Unrestricted.

Note that restricted and unrestricted do not mean the same things as assigned and unassigned as used for the fund-based statements.

Since **GASB 63** requires the disclosure of deferred outflows and inflows of resources, Figure 18-13 provides three examples of these items. While the technical nature of these transactions is beyond the scope of this brief overview, assume that Sol City is involved in two derivative contracts, both of which qualify under **GASB 53** as hedging derivatives. First, it has entered into an interest rate swap that is reported in the city's governmental activities. As of December 31, 20X2, the fair value of the derivative is determined to be $1,500. The city has also entered into a forward contract reported in the city's business-type activities. The contract currently has a negative fair value of $7,650. Finally, assume that the city has 5 years remaining on a 10-year service concession arrangement with a nongovernmental operator who manages the city's parking garages. The arrangement is reported in the city's business-type activities. The terms of the arrangement include a substantial upfront payment from the operator. The entire amount of the upfront payment is recognized as a deferred inflow of resources at the agreement inception date, $10,800.

Statement of Activities

Important observations regarding the statement of activities for Sol City (Figure 18–14) follow:

1. *Accrual basis.* The full accrual basis of accounting is used to measure revenues and expenses for the governmentwide statements. A reconciliation between the modified accrual basis of accounting for the governmental funds and the accrual basis of the governmentwide statements is required.
2. *Format.* The format of the statement of activities is based on the governmental unit's functions or programs.
   a. Program revenues are categorized by type, and the net expenses (revenues) are shown separately for each of the governmental and business-type activities.
   b. The internal service fund is blended into the Governmental Activities because this fund provides service solely within the governmental entity.
   c. The enterprise funds are presented in the Business-Type Activities column because this fund includes resources obtained by user charges to the public.
   d. Fiduciary funds are not reported on the statement of activities because these funds are not available for providing governmental services.
   e. Note that the component unit, the city library, is discretely presented in its own column.

FIGURE 18–14 Governmentwide Statement of Activities

		Program Revenues			Net (Expenses) Revenue and Changes in Net Position			
					Primary Government			
	Expenses	Charges for Services	Operating Grants and Contributions	Capital Grants and Contributions	Governmental Activities	Business-Type Activities	Total	Component Unit
Functions/Programs								
Primary Government								
Governmental Activities:								
General Government	$212,000	$ 4,000	$23,000	$20,000	$(165,0000)		$ (165,000)	
Streets & Highways	71,000				(71,000)		(71,000)	
Public Safety	335,000				(335,000)		(335,000)	
Sanitation	141,000				(141,000)		(141,000)	
Culture & Recreation	54,000				(54,000)		(54,000)	
Depreciation of Capital Assets	120,000				(120,000)		(120,000)	
Interest on Long-Term Debt	10,000				(10,000)		(10,000)	
Total Government Activities	$943,000	$ 4,000	$23,000	$20,000	$ (896,000)		$ (896,000)	
Business-Type Activities:								
Water	$ 38,000	$40,000				$ 2,000	$ 2,000	
Total Business-Type Activities	$ 38,000	$40,000						
Total Primary Government	$981,000	$44,000	$23,000	$20,000	$ (896,000)	$ 2,000	$ (894,000)	
Component Unit:								
Library	$ 6,000							
Total Component Unit	$ 6,000	$ 0						$ (6,000)
	General Revenues:							
	Taxes:							
	Property Taxes, Levied for General Purposes				$ 781,000			
	Property Taxes, Levied for Special Purposes				62,000			$ 12,000
	Property Taxes, Levied for Debt Service				33,000			
	Sales Taxes				32,000			
	Investment Earnings				9,000			
	Miscellaneous Revenues				18,000			
	Contribution				100,000			
	Transfers between Governmental & Business-Type Funds				0			
	Total General Revenues, Special Items, & Transfers				$1,035,000		$1,035,000	
	Change in Net Position				$ 139,000	$ 2,000	$ 141,000	$ 6,000
	Net Position—Beginning				4,268,000	26,000	4,294,000	748,000
	Net Position—Ending				$4,407,000	$28,000	$4,435,000	$754,000

FIGURE 18–15
Reconciliation Schedule for the Statement of Net Position

SOL CITY
Reconciliation of the Balance Sheet of Governmental Funds to the Statement of Net Position
December 31, 20X2

Fund balances reported in the governmental funds	$ 279,000
Amounts reported for the governmental activities in the statement of net position are different because:	
Capital assets used in governmental activities are not financial resources and therefore are not reported in the governmental funds.	4,200,000
Management uses internal service funds to charge the costs of certain activities, such as centralized purchasing and storage functions, to individual funds. The assets and liabilities of the internal service fund are included in governmental activities in the statement of net position.	7,000
Long-term liabilities, including bonds payable, are not due and payable in the current period and therefore are not reported in the funds.	(80,000)
Interest on bonds in the permanent fund is recognized in that fund under the modified accrual basis but must be adjusted to the accrual basis for the governmentwide financial statements.	1,000
Net position of governmental activities	$4,407,000

3. *Expenses.* The expenses include depreciation of the capital assets and expenses for any infrastructure assets. However, the expenses would not include any expenditures in the governmental funds that were made for long-term capital assets. For governmentwide statements, these expenditures must be included as increases to long-term capital assets on the balance sheet.
4. *General revenues.* General revenues are reported separately on the bottom of the statement. These are revenues not directly tied to any specific program. **GASB 34** requires that contributions to permanent endowments, special items, and extraordinary items be reported in this section for the governmentwide statements. Special items are events within management control that are either unusual in nature or infrequent in occurrence. Sol City has no special or extraordinary items, and the only contribution to a permanent endowment was the $100,000 received by the permanent fund. Note that the amount of ending net position reported in this statement articulates with the amount of ending net position presented on the statement of net position.

LO 18-12

Understand and explain the additional disclosures that accompany governmentwide financial statements.

Reconciliation Schedules

GASB 34 requires that two ***reconciliation schedules*** be presented to reconcile the net change in the total amounts reported on the governmental funds statements with the amounts reported on the governmentwide statements. These reconciliation schedules may be presented as part of the governmental funds statements or in an accompanying schedule on the page immediately following the governmental fund financial statement it supports. The two required reconciliation schedules are as follows:

1. *Reconciliation schedule for statement of net position.* See Figure 18–15 for the first reconciliation schedule, the reconciliation between the fund balances reported for the governmental funds to the net position for the governmentwide financials. This schedule describes the adjustments necessary to move from the modified accrual basis used in the governmental funds to the accrual basis used for the governmentwide statements. For example, the balance sheets of the governmental funds do not include infrastructure and capital assets. These costs are recognized as expenditures in the periods in which they are made. However, the governmentwide statement of net position must report the balance sheet date cost less depreciation of these infrastructure and capital assets. In addition, the governmentwide statements must include the accounts of the internal service funds, which are reported separately from the governmental funds in the fund-based financial statements.

FIGURE 18–16
Reconciliation Schedule for the Statement of Revenues, Expenditures, and Changes in Fund Balances

SOL CITY
Reconciliation of the Statement of Revenues, Expenditures, and Changes in Fund Balances of Governmental Funds to the Statement of Activities
For the Year Ended December 31, 20X2

Net change in fund balances—governmental funds	$150,000
Governmental funds report capital outlays as expenditures. However, in the statement of activities, the costs of those assets are capitalized and depreciated over their estimated useful lives. This is the amount by which capital outlays in the governmental funds ($182,000) exceeded depreciation of the governmental assets ($119,000).	63,000
Bond proceeds provide current financial resources for the governmental funds. However, the issuance of debt increases long-term liabilities in the statement of net position. Repayment of debt principal is an expenditure in the governmental funds, but the repayment reduces the long-term liabilities in the statement of net position. This is the amount by which bond proceeds ($102,000) exceeded the net repayments of principal ($20,000).	(82,000)
Revenues in the statement of activities are recorded on the accrual basis. Interest revenue in the governmental funds is recorded on the modified accrual basis. This is the amount that accrual interest exceeded the interest recognized in the permanent funds.	1,000
Management used internal service funds to charge the costs of certain services, such as a centralized purchasing function, to individual funds. The net revenue (expense) of the internal service funds is reported with governmental activities.	7,000
Change in net position of governmental activities	$139,000

2. *Reconciliation schedule for Statement of Activities.* The second reconciliation schedule (Figure 18–16), requires the reconciliation between the net change in fund balances reported in the governmental funds' statement of revenues, expenditures, and changes in fund balance to the change in net position reported in the governmentwide financials. For example, interest revenue on the investment in bonds in the permanent fund was presented in that fund under the modified accrual basis for the amount of $8,000. However, under the accrual basis, the interest revenue would be computed based on the effective interest rate with amortization of the discount in the amount of $9,000 ($90,000 × 0.10). The difference of $1,000 is an adjustment to the change in net position.

Budgetary Comparison Schedule

GASB 34 requires that a ***budgetary comparison schedule*** be presented as required supplementary information for the general fund and for each special revenue fund that has a legally adopted annual budget. This schedule may be presented as a separate financial statement after the governmental funds financials or in the footnotes of the annual report. The budgetary comparison schedule for Sol City's general fund is in Figure 18–17.

Important observations regarding the budgetary comparison schedule follow:

1. **GASB 34** requires that both the original budget and the final budget be presented. The original budget is the first budget for the fiscal period adopted by the governmental entity. Through the year, many governmental entities modify the original budget because of new events or changes in expectations. These changes must go through the legislative process of the government, such as the city council. For our example, no changes were made to the formal budget during the year.
2. The budgetary comparison schedule should be presented in the same format with the same terminology and classifications as the original budget.
3. A separate column for the variance between the final budget and the actual amounts is encouraged but not required. It is presented here to provide a complete presentation of the possible disclosures of a governmental entity.

FIGURE 18–17 Budgetary Comparison Schedule

SOL CITY
Budgetary Comparison Schedule
General Fund
For the Year Ended December 31, 20X2

	Budgeted Amount			
	Original	**Final**	**Actual Amounts (Budgetary Basis)**	**Variance with Final Budget Positive (Negative)**
Budgetary fund balance, January 1	$129,000	$129,000	$129,000	$ 0
Resources (inflows):				
Property taxes	775,000	775,000	781,000	6,000
Grants	55,000	55,000	33,000	(22,000)
Sales taxes	25,000	25,000	32,000	7,000
Miscellaneous	20,000	20,000	18,000	(2,000)
Amounts available for appropriation	$875,000	$875,000	$864,000	$(11,000)
Charges to appropriations (outflows):				
General government	$200,000	$200,000	$206,000	$ (6,000)
Streets & highways	75,000	75,000	71,000	4,000
Public safety	400,000	400,000	393,000	7,000
Sanitation	150,000	150,000	141,000	9,000
Nondepartmental:				
Transfers out to other funds	30,000	30,000	30,000	0
Total charges to appropriations	$855,000	$855,000	$841,000	$ 14,000
Budgetary fund balance, December 31	$149,000	$149,000	$152,000	$ 3,000

Management's Discussion and Analysis

GASB 34 specifies that Management's Discussion and Analysis (MD&A) be included in the ***required supplementary information (RSI)*** of the governmentwide financial statements. MD&A comes before the financial statements and provides an analytical overview of the government's financial and operating activities.

MD&A discusses current period operations and financial position and then compares those with the same information for prior periods. The purpose of this RSI item is to provide financial statement users an objective discussion of whether the government's financial position has improved or deteriorated during the year. **GASB 37** states that MD&A should be limited to the items specified in **GASB 34** rather than present an abundance of other topics not specifically required. The GASB believes that additional discussions beyond those required might result in information that is not objective and cannot be directly analyzed. Governments that wish to provide additional information may do so in other supplementary information such as footnotes or transmittal letters.

Notes to the Governmentwide Financial Statements

GASB 34 specifies a number of required note disclosures in the governmentwide financial statements that include the following:

1. Accounting and measurement policies that the primary governmental entity uses.
2. Information about capital assets, including beginning and ending balances as well as capital acquisitions and sales during the year and depreciation expense and accumulated depreciation.
3. For collections not capitalized, disclosures describing the collection and the reasons for not capitalizing them.
4. Note disclosures about long-term liabilities, including a schedule of the beginning and ending balances and increases or decreases during the year, for each long-term debt item; the current portion of each long-term item; and the amount of annual debt service required.

5. Disclosures about donor-restricted endowments, including net increases in investments for which the income is available for expenditure, and the policy for spending investment income.
6. Segment information for the enterprise funds included in the governmentwide financial statements.

GASB 38 states that the required footnotes should be modified as follows:

1. Provide in the summary of significant accounting policies descriptions of the activities accounted for in the major funds, internal service fund type, and fiduciary fund types. This change is a result of **GASB 34**'s focus on major funds rather than all funds.
2. Delete the requirement to disclose the accounting policy for encumbrances in the summary of significant accounting policies (i.e., the lapsing or nonlapsing method).
3. Disclose the period of availability used for recording revenues in governmental funds.
4. Disclose debt service requirements to maturity, separately identifying principal and interest for each of the subsequent five years and in five-year increments thereafter and changes in variable-rate debt. In addition, governments should disclose the future minimum payments for capital and noncancelable operating leases for each of the five succeeding years.
5. Provide a schedule of changes in short-term debt during the year including the purposes for which the debt was issued.
6. Add a disclosure of actions taken to address any significant violations of finance-related legal or contractual provisions to the footnote describing these violations.
7. Disclose details of the payable and receivable amounts for interfund balances and the purposes of the interfund transfers. In addition, disclosures should be made regarding the amounts of interfund transfers during the period as well as a description and amount of significant transfers that are not expected to occur on a routine basis.
8. Provide details of the components of accounts payable so that the financial statement users can understand the payables' timeliness and payment priorities.
9. Provide details about significant individual accounts when aggregation obscures their nature. For example, more disclosure could be made for receivables that contain a myriad of different credit risks or liquidity attributes.

Other Financial Report Items

Governments may choose to provide additional information beyond that required as discussed previously. For example, some governmental entities present comprehensive annual financial reports (CAFRs), which include additional statistical information about the sources of revenues, property tax levies and property values, demographic statistics, and other miscellaneous statistics that the entity's management believes will aid financial report users. Some governmental entities additionally disclose financial statements for individual funds or combined by fund type. Some governments go beyond the required footnote disclosures and provide additional schedules and information. As with commercial enterprises, it is up to the entity's management to determine how much additional disclosure it wishes to provide in its annual report.

Interim Reporting

Governmental entities generally are not required to publish interim reports although many prepare monthly or quarterly reports to determine the current progress of compliance with legal and budgetary limitations and to plan for changes in events or developments that were not foreseen when the annual budget was prepared. Interim reports are a valuable internal management control instrument; they typically are not made available to the general public.

Auditing Governmental Entities

Most governmental entities are audited annually because of state or federal requirements or because long-term creditors demand audited statements as part of the debt agreements.

The audit of a governmental entity is different from the audit of a commercial entity. The auditor not only must express an opinion on the fairness of the audited entity's financial statements in conformity with applicable accounting principles but also must assess the audited entity's compliance with legal or contractual provisions of state law, debt covenants, terms of grants from other governmental entities, and other restrictions on the entity. The AICPA publishes the "State and Local Governments—Audit and Accounting Guide" that provides guidance relevant to audits of state and local governments. The guide includes planning the audit under the Risk Assessment Statements of Auditing Standards (SAS) in eight recent standards, numbers 104 through 111. In addition, the guide defines internal control deficiencies for state and local governments.

The Single Audit Act of 1984 is a federal law specifying the audit requirements for all state and local governments receiving federal financial assistance. The audit act requires auditors to determine whether (1) the financial statements fairly present the government's financial condition, (2) the governmental entity has an internal control system to provide reasonable assurance that it is managing federal financial assistance programs in compliance with applicable laws and regulations, and (3) the governmental entity has complied with laws and regulations that may have a material effect on each federal program. The auditors issue not only the standard audit report but also special reports on items (2) and (3).

The Single Audit Act does not apply to all governmental entities receiving federal assistance. Governmental entities that expend $500,000 or more in federal awards in a year must have either a single or a program-specific audit for that year. A governmental entity is eligible for a program-specific audit only if the federal award is expended under a single federal program and that federal program's laws, regulations, or grant agreements do not require the entity to have a financial statement audit. Otherwise a single audit is required. Governmental entities that expend less than $500,000 in federal awards in a year are exempt from the single audit requirement for that year. However, their records must be available for review or audit by officials from the federal agency, the pass-through entity providing the award, or the Government Accountability Office (GAO).

ADDITIONAL CONSIDERATIONS

Special-Purpose Governmental Entities

This chapter and Chapter 17 discuss the accounting and financial reporting standards for general-purpose governments such as states, counties, and municipalities. However, a number of governments are ***special-purpose governments,*** which are legally separate entities. They may be component units of a general-purpose government or stand-alone governments apart from a general-purpose government. Special-purpose governments include governmental entities such as cemetery districts, levee districts, park districts, tollway authorities, and school districts. Some of these special-purpose entities may be engaged in governmental activities that generally are financed through taxes, intergovernmental revenues, and other nonexchange revenues. Governmental or internal service funds usually report these activities. Some of these entities are engaged in business-type activities financed by fees charged for goods or services. Enterprise funds usually report these activities. **GASB 34** establishes specific reporting requirements for each of the following types of special-purpose governments:

1. *Engaged in more than one governmental program or in both governmental and business-type activities.* These governmental entities must provide both fund financial statements and governmentwide financial statements as presented earlier in this chapter and in Chapter 17.
2. *Engaged in a single governmental program (such as cemetery districts or drainage districts).* These governmental entities may present a simplified set of governmentwide and fund-based financial statements, often combining the two statements.

3. *Engaged in only business-type activities.* These governmental entities must present only the financial statements required for enterprise funds. Many public universities and public hospitals are included in this category.
4. *Engaged in only fiduciary-type activities.* These governmental entities are not required to present the governmentwide financials but must provide only the financial statements required for fiduciary funds. This category includes special-purpose governmental entities responsible for managing pension funds.

Regardless of the category of special-purpose governmental entity, all governments must include in their financial reports (1) MD&A, (2) footnotes, and (3) any required supplementary information.

SUMMARY OF KEY CONCEPTS

This chapter completes the discussion of accounting and financial reporting principles that local and state governments use. Governments may use five governmental fund types, two proprietary fund types, and two fiduciary fund types (including agency funds). The governmental funds use the modified accrual basis of accounting; the other funds use the accrual basis.

GASB 34 generally specifies the current governmental reporting model with modifications indicated by subsequent statements. It requires both fund-based financial statements and governmentwide financial statements. The governmentwide statements are based on the accrual basis and present both long-term capital assets, including infrastructure assets, and long-term debt. Governmental entities also must include required supplementary information (RSI) in their annual financial reports. This RSI includes reconciliation schedules and a budgetary comparison schedule. **GASB 54** specifies changes for fund balance reporting in the governmental fund types.

KEY TERMS

agency funds, *934*
blended presentation, *936*
budgetary comparison schedule, *943*
capital projects funds, *914*
component units, *936*
comprehensive annual financial report (CAFR), *937*
debt service funds, *917*
discrete presentation, *936*
enterprise funds, *924*
fund-based financial statements, *910*
governmentwide financial statements, *938*
internal service funds, *930*
permanent funds, *920*
reconciliation schedules, *942*
reporting entity, *935*
required supplementary information (RSI), *944*
special-purpose governments, *946*
special revenue funds, *910*
trust funds, *932*

Appendix 18A Other Governmental Entities—Public School Systems and the Federal Government

In addition to local and state governmental entities, two other governmental entities—public schools and the federal government—have pervasive influences on the lives of citizens. This appendix presents a brief overview of the basic accounting and financial reporting requirements for these two governmental entities.

PUBLIC SCHOOL SYSTEMS

In the United States today, approximately 50 million students attend nearly 94,000 public elementary and secondary school systems employing about 3.3 million teachers and expending more than $571 billion annually. Many other students attend one of the myriad of private schools formed by religious or other groups.[2]

[2] These statistics are compiled by the National Center for Education Statistics: http://nces.ed.gov/fastfacts/display.asp?id=372.

Accounting and Financial Reporting for Public School Systems

Accounting for public schools is similar to accounting for local or state governments. Most funds use the modified accrual basis of accounting, and the financial statements for a school district are similar to those of a local government. More than half of school district revenue is obtained from local property taxes; the remaining sources are fees for services, state education aid, and federal grants to education. Most school districts have an elected school board that serves as a public policy-making body.

The fund structure for a school district is similar to the fund structure for a local or state government. School district funds include the general fund, special revenue funds, capital projects funds, debt service funds, enterprise funds, internal service funds, and trust and agency funds.

The school district expends general fund resources for costs directly associated with the education process: teachers' salaries, books and supplies, and other costs. Special revenue funds may include specific funds for operations, building, and maintenance (OBM) of the school district's physical facilities as well as the transportation special revenue fund, which is responsible for acquiring and maintaining the buses for transporting children to and from the schools.

Public school systems have a public hearing on the annual budget, which is then approved by the school board or other governing body. The budget specifies the revenue from the three basic sources: local property taxes and fees, state school aid, and federal sources. The expenditures are categorized into the following three dimensions: *program,* such as gifted, vocational, elementary, secondary, and adult/continuing education; *function,* such as guidance counselors, instructional staff, school administration, and student transportation; and *object,* such as salaries, employee benefits, purchased services, and supplies and materials.

Each state department of education receives the annual reports from that state's school districts. Typically independent auditors must audit these financial statements. Many school districts are legally separate, fiscally independent, special-purpose governmental entities engaged in both governmental and business-type activities. These school districts have their own legally mandated budget process and tax levy authority, and they do not depend financially on another governmental entity. In these cases, school districts present their financial statements in accordance with **GASB 34,** which requires governmentwide financial statements as well as fund financial statements. **GASB 34** also requires an MD&A, footnotes, and specified supplementary information. School districts that are fiscally dependent and component units of a primary governmental entity, such as the city government in which the school is located, present their financial information within the primary government's financial statements, usually discretely in a column separate from the primary government's financial data. Other required statements are the same as for other governmental units. In addition, the comprehensive annual financial report for a school district includes a variety of other disclosures relevant to the district, such as the cost per student, the district's debt capacity, and the assessed valuation of all property included in the school district.

Federal Government Accounting

An accounting structure for the federal government has been part of the U.S. statutes since 1789. The following individuals or entities have significant roles in the federal budgeting and expending process:

Executive Branch	Legislative Branch
President	Congress
Office of Management and Budget (OMB)	Government Accountability Office (GAO)
Secretary of the Treasury	Congressional Budget Office (CBO)
Federal agencies	

The fiscal period for the U.S. federal government is from October 1 to September 30 of the next calendar year. The president of the United States directs that the annual budget be prepared by the director of the Office of Management and Budget, who is a member of the president's staff. The director of the OMB then consults the various federal agencies and the secretary of the treasury and prepares the budget that the president presents to Congress. The Congressional Budget Office then evaluates the executive budget and may propose that Congress present one of its own. After the legislative process runs its course and the budget is approved, Congress provides the authority for the executive branch to obtain revenue through taxation or other charges. The primary agency responsible for obtaining revenue is the Internal Revenue Service, which is an agency of the Department of the Treasury.

The appropriation-expenditure process is a little different for the federal government than for local governmental units. The federal budget provides the appropriation authority for the federal government. This appropriation authority is then allocated to the various agencies through a process of apportionments made by the OMB. The apportionment is then divided among the agency's programs and activities by a process of allotments. The agency then makes obligations by incurring costs for services provided. These obligations are then liquidated through the preparation of vouchers, which are submitted to the Department of the Treasury for payment.

The Federal Accounting Standards Advisory Board (FASAB) establishes the generally accepted accounting principles for federal financial reporting entities. In 1990, three federal government officials created the FASAB as a federal advisory committee. The three officials were the secretary of the treasury, the director of the OMB, and the comptroller general of the United States. The FASAB has issued more than 43 statements and several technical releases establishing federal financial accounting standards. These standards are quite different from those for either profit-seeking entities (FASB) or state and local governmental entities (GASB) because of the many unique aspects of the federal government's operations.

The Department of the Treasury annually issues the "Financial Report of the United States Government," which includes the auditor's report from the comptroller general of the United States. The financial report presents information on the federal government and its agencies, including a stewardship report and a statement of net cost by agency. The financial report is available on the Department of the Treasury's website.

Audits of Federal Agencies

The comptroller general of the United States is the head of the Government Accountability Office (GAO), an agency of the legislative branch of the federal government that works with the Department of the Treasury, an executive department, to develop and maintain the federal government's accounting system. The GAO reviews the accounting systems of each executive agency each year from both financial and compliance perspectives. The compliance part of the audit ensures that the agency fulfilled all legal and budgetary restrictions. Exceptions are reported to Congress, which then communicates them to the executive branch, thus completing the cycle that began when the executive branch first proposed the annual budget to Congress.

QUESTIONS

LO 18-1 **Q18-1** In what circumstances would a governmental unit use a special revenue fund rather than a general fund?

LO 18-1 **Q18-2** Which governmental funds use operating budgets? Which use capital budgets?

LO 18-3 **Q18-3** How is interest on long-term debt accounted for in the debt service fund?

LO 18-1 **Q18-4** What are the major differences between a special revenue fund and an enterprise fund?

LO 18-7 **Q18-5** What is the basis of accounting in the proprietary funds? Why?

LO 18-5, 18-6 **Q18-6** What financial statements must be prepared for the governmental funds? For the enterprise funds?

LO 18-2 **Q18-7** How are the proceeds from a bond issue accounted for in governmental funds? Where are these proceeds reported on the governmental funds' statement of revenues, expenditures, and changes in fund balance?

LO 18-4, 18-9 **Q18-8** What are the primary differences between a permanent fund (governmental) and a private-purpose trust fund (fiduciary)?

LO 18-5 **Q18-9** Not all governmental funds need to be separately presented on the governmental funds financial statements. What are the two tests for determining major governmental funds for which separate disclosure is required?

LO 18-11 **Q18-10** How are contributions to governmental funds as well as special or extraordinary items reported on the governmental funds' statement of revenues, expenditures, and changes in fund balance?

LO 18-10 **Q18-11** Do agency funds have a net fund balance? Why or why not?

LO 18-11 **Q18-12** What are component units of a government, and how are they reported on the governmentwide financial statements?

LO 18-12 **Q18-13** A reconciliation schedules is a required disclosure in the governmentwide financial statements. What are the purpose and content of these reconciliation schedules?

LO 18-12 **Q18-14** **GASB 34** requires a budgetary comparison schedule for each governmental fund that has a legally adopted budget. What information does this budgetary comparison schedule present?

LO 18-11 **Q18-15** How are infrastructure and other long-term assets as well as general long-term debt reported on the governmentwide financial statements?

CASES

LO 18-1 **C18-1** **Basis of Accounting and Reporting Issues**

Judgment

The accounting system of Barb City is organized and operated on a fund basis. Among the types of funds used are a general fund, a special revenue fund, and an enterprise fund.

Required

a. Explain the basic differences in revenue recognition between the accrual basis of accounting and the modified accrual basis of accounting in relation to governmental accounting.

b. What basis of accounting should be used for each of the following: (1) general fund, (2) special revenue fund, and (3) enterprise fund?

LO 18-2, 18-3, 18-8 **C18-2** **Capital Projects, Debt Service, and Internal Service Funds**

The funds of Lake City include a debt service fund, a capital projects fund, and an internal service fund.

Required

Understanding

a. Explain the use of capital projects funds. Include what they account for, the basis of accounting used, unusual entries and accounts, and their financial statements.

b. Explain the use of debt service funds. Include what they account for, the basis of accounting used, unusual entries and accounts, and their financial statements.

c. Explain the use of internal service funds. Include what they account for, the basis of accounting used, unusual entries and accounts, and their financial statements.

C18-3A **Discovery**

Research

This case provides learning opportunities using available databases and/or the Internet to obtain contemporary information about the topics in advanced financial accounting. Note that the Internet is dynamic and the specific address of the website listed may change. In that case, use a good search engine to locate its current address.

Required

Access the U.S. Department of the Treasury's website and scroll through until you locate the most recent "Financial Report of the United States Government" (http://fms.treas.gov/fr/index.html). Look over the report, especially the comptroller general's statement and the auditor's report, and then prepare a one- to two-page memo summarizing the major information items reported in the report.

LO 18-11 **C18-4** **Becoming Familiar with a Local Government's Comprehensive Annual Financial Report (CAFR)**

Analysis

Using the Internet, find the comprehensive annual financial report (CAFR) of a local government selected by your instructor. At a minimum, a CAFR includes (1) MD&A, (2) the basic financial statements—governmentwide and fund-based financial statements, (3) notes to the basic financial statements, (4) RSI, and (5) the external auditor's opinion on the basic financial statements.

Required

Using the CAFR chosen by your instructor, answer the following questions that relate to the overall government and to the governmental funds:

a. Read the section of the report that contains MD&A. Is your government a general-purpose government? If yes, what types of services does it provide?

b. What type of opinion did the external auditor give on the basic financial statements? What responsibility did the auditor take with regard to MD&A and the other RSI?

"A" indicates that the item relates to Appendix 18A.

c. Examine the financial statements for the funds. List the fund types your government uses.

d. From reading the notes that follow the governmentwide and fund-based financial statements, what are the measurement focus and basis of accounting the governmental funds use?

e. List the government's financial statements that use the economic resources measurement focus and the accrual basis of accounting.

f. In addition to the general fund, list your government's other major governmental and proprietary funds.

g. Examine the governmentwide financial statements. List any component units over which your government has fiscal accountability.

h. Examine the balance sheet of the governmental funds. What are the total assets and the total fund balance as of the most recent balance sheet date? How much of the total fund balance is assigned?

i. Examine the statement of revenues, expenditures, and changes in fund balance for the most recent year. How much of the total revenue came from taxes?

j. Examine the statement of revenues, expenditures, and changes in fund balance for the most recent year. How are expenditures classified?

k. Examine the statement of revenues, expenditures, and changes in fund balance for the most recent year. How much of the other financing sources resulted from transfers in?

l. Examine the statement of revenues, expenditures, and changes in fund balance for the most recent year. List any special items reported. What was the increase or decrease in fund balance for the year?

LO 18-11

C18-5 The GASB's Decision-Making Process

Discovery

The Statements of Governmental Accounting Standards are the final step in the GASB's decision-making process. Standard setting has a number of specific steps with open and thorough study of the issues and public participation and input encouraged throughout the process.

Required

Access the GASB's website at www.gasb.org; click on the "Reference Library" tab and then on "How Standards are Set." Then read through the process described in the links on this page and prepare a one-page memorandum summarizing the steps the GASB takes before adopting a new governmental accounting standard.

LO 18-11

C18-6 Summarizing a Recent GASB Exposure Draft

Discovery

The Governmental Accounting Standards Board places exposure drafts (EDs) of proposed future standards on its website. These exposure drafts provide an early view of the GASB's consensus viewpoints on a project. Accountants wishing to remain current in governmental accounting and auditing need to be aware of proposed governmental standards and their potential impacts on the accounting and reporting of the governmental entities with which the accountants are associated.

Required

Access the GASB's website at www.gasb.org; locate the most recent exposure draft of a proposed statement. Read through the Summary presented at the front of the exposure draft and then prepare a one-page memorandum on the issues the proposed statement is addressing; why the GASB feels the proposed statement is needed; and the key provisions it proposes. Toward the bottom of your memorandum, place the expected effective date of the proposed statement and, if included in the ED, the proposed transition implementation from current standards to the new standard.

EXERCISES

LO 18-1, 18-11

E18-1 Multiple-Choice Items on Government Financial Reporting

Select the correct response to each of the following.

1. The governmentwide financial statements use the
   a. Economic resources measurement focus and the accrual basis of accounting.
   b. Current financial resources measurement focus and the accrual basis of accounting.
   c. Economic resources measurement focus and the modified accrual basis of accounting.
   d. Current financial resources measurement focus and the modified accrual basis of accounting.

2. The financial statements for the governmental funds use the
   a. Economic resources measurement focus and the accrual basis of accounting.
   b. Current financial resources measurement focus and the accrual basis of accounting.
   c. Economic resources measurement focus and the modified accrual basis of accounting.
   d. Current financial resources measurement focus and the modified accrual basis of accounting.
3. According to **GASB 34,** infrastructure fixed assets
   a. Must be capitalized and depreciated.
   b. Must be capitalized, but governments do *not* have to depreciate them.
   c. May be capitalized and depreciated.
   d. Must be reported using the modified approach.
4. On which of the following governmentwide financial statements would you find all liabilities of a state or local government?
   a. Statement of net position.
   b. Statement of financial condition.
   c. Statement of activities.
   d. Statement of financial position.
5. On which of the following financial statements would you find all of the capital assets of a local government?
   a. Statement of net position.
   b. Statement of financial condition.
   c. Statement of activities.
   d. Statement of financial position.
6. For which fund category is a statement of cash flows prepared?
   a. Governmental.
   b. Proprietary.
   c. Fiduciary.
   d. None of the above.

(*Note:* Use the information below to answer questions 7 through 9.)

The Village of Hampton reported the following data for its governmental activities for the year ended June 30, 20X5:

Item	Amount
Cash & cash equivalents	$ 1,880,000
Receivables	459,000
Capital assets	14,250,000
Accumulated depreciation	1,750,000
Accounts payable	650,000
Long-term liabilities	5,350,000

Additional data:
All of the long-term debt was used to acquire capital assets.
Cash of $654,000 is restricted for debt service.

7. On the statement of net position prepared at June 30, 20X5, what amount should be reported for total net position?
   a. $8,839,000.
   b. $7,804,000.
   c. $7,150,000.
   d. $8,189,000.

8. On the statement of net position prepared at June 30, 20X5, what amount should be reported for net position invested in capital assets net of related debt?
   a. $8,839,000.
   b. $7,804,000.
   c. $7,150,000.
   d. $8,189,000.
9. On the statement of net position prepared at June 30, 20X5, what amount should be reported for net position, unrestricted?
   a. $1,685,000.
   b. $1,689,000.
   c. $1,035,000.
   d. $1,031,000.
10. Which of the following funds can be major assuming they meet the appropriate tests?
    a. The parking meter special revenue fund and the water utility enterprise fund.
    b. The fire station capital projects fund and a property tax agency fund.
    c. The fire station bonds debt service fund and the city teachers pension trust fund.
    d. The local symphony permanent fund and the Edwina Williams private-purpose trust fund.
11. Where in the basic financial statements would you find a description of the measurement focus and the basis of accounting used in the governmentwide financial statements?
    a. In the statement of net position.
    b. In the statement of activities.
    c. In MD&A.
    d. In the notes to the financial statements.
12. Where in the financial section of a CAFR would you find an analysis of the balances and transactions of individual funds?
    a. In the governmentwide financial statements.
    b. In the fund financial statements.
    c. In MD&A.
    d. In the notes to the financial statements.

LO 18-1, 18-3 **E18-2 Multiple-Choice Items on Governmental Funds [AICPA Adapted]**

Select the correct answer for each of the following.

1. On December 31, 20X1, Tiffin Township paid a contractor $2,000,000 for the total cost of a new firehouse built in 20X1 on township-owned land. Financing was by means of a $1,500,000 general obligation bond issue sold at face amount on December 31, 20X1, with the remaining $500,000 transferred from the general fund. What should be reported on Tiffin's financial statements for the capital projects fund?
   a. Revenue, $1,500,000; Expenditures, $1,500,000.
   b. Revenue, $1,500,000; Other Financing Sources, $500,000; Expenditures, $2,000,000.
   c. Revenue, $2,000,000; Expenditures, $2,000,000.
   d. Other Financing Sources, $2,000,000; Expenditures, $2,000,000.
2. A municipality's debt service fund is an example of which of the following types of funds?
   a. Fiduciary.
   b. Governmental.
   c. Proprietary.
   d. Internal service.
3. Revenue of a governmental unit's special revenue fund should be recognized in the period in which the
   a. Revenue becomes available and measurable.
   b. Revenue becomes available for appropriation.

c. Revenue is billable.
d. Cash is received.

4. Taxes collected and held by a municipality for a school district would be accounted for in a(n)
   a. Enterprise fund.
   b. Intragovernmental (internal) service fund.
   c. Agency fund.
   d. Special revenue fund.
5. Interest expense on bonds payable should be recorded in a debt service fund
   a. At the end of the fiscal period if the interest due date does not coincide with the end of the fiscal period.
   b. When issued.
   c. When legally payable.
   d. When paid.
6. Which of the following funds does *not* have a fund balance?
   a. General fund.
   b. Agency fund.
   c. Special revenue fund.
   d. Capital projects fund.

LO 18-6, 18-8 **E18-3 Multiple-Choice Items on Proprietary Funds [AICPA Adapted]**

Select the correct response for each of the following.

1. Which of the following accounts could be included in an enterprise fund's statement of net position?

	Reserve for Encumbrances	Revenue Bonds Payable	Net Position
a.	No	No	Yes
b.	No	Yes	Yes
c.	Yes	Yes	No
d.	No	No	No

2. Customers' meter deposits that cannot be spent for normal operating purposes would most likely be classified as restricted cash in the balance sheet of which fund?
   a. Internal service.
   b. Private-purpose trust.
   c. Agency.
   d. Enterprise.
3. Which fund is *not* an expendable fund?
   a. Capital projects.
   b. General.
   c. Special revenue.
   d. Internal service.
4. If a governmental unit established a data processing center to service all agencies within the unit, the center should be accounted for as a(n)
   a. Capital projects fund.
   b. Internal service fund.
   c. Agency fund.
   d. Trust fund.

5. Recreational facilities run by a governmental unit and financed on a user-charge basis would be accounted for in which fund?
   a. General.
   b. Trust.
   c. Enterprise.
   d. Capital projects.

6. The Underwood Electric Utility Fund, which is an enterprise fund, had the following during its 20X1 fiscal year, ending at December 31, 20X1:

Prepaid insurance paid in December 20X1	$ 43,000
Depreciation for 20X1	129,000

   What amount should be reflected in the fund's statement of revenues, expenses, and changes in fund net position for these items?
   a. $(43,000).
   b. $0.
   c. $129,000.
   d. $172,000.

7. Which of the following funds of a governmental unit uses the same basis of accounting as an enterprise fund?
   a. Special revenue.
   b. Internal service.
   c. Permanent fund.
   d. Capital projects.

8. Fixed assets utilized in a city-owned utility are accounted for in which of the following?

	Enterprise Fund	General Fund
a.	No	No
b.	No	Yes
c.	Yes	No
d.	Yes	Yes

9. Which of the following funds of a governmental unit would account for long-term debt in the fund's accounts?
   a. Special revenue.
   b. Capital projects.
   c. Internal service.
   d. General.

LO 18-8, 18-9 **E18-4** **Multiple-Choice Items on Various Funds**

(*Note:* Use the information below to answer questions 1 and 2.)

On August 1, 20X6, the City of Rockhaven received $1,000,000 from a prominent citizen to establish a private-purpose trust fund. The donor stipulated that the cash be permanently invested and that the earnings from the investments be spent to support local artists. During the year ended June 30, 20X7, the fund received $50,000 of dividends from stock investments and earned $35,000 of interest from bond investments. At June 30, $5,000 of the interest earned had not yet been received. During the year ended June 30, 20X7, the trust fund spent $75,000 to support local artists.

1. For the year ended June 30, 20X7, the trust fund should report investment earnings of
   a. $80,000.
   b. $50,000.

c. $85,000.

d. $35,000.

2. For the year ended June 30, 20X7, the trust fund should report the $75,000 spent to support local artists as a

   a. Deduction.

   b. Contra contribution.

   c. Transfer out.

   d. Direct adjustment from fund balance.

3. Which of the following statements is (are) correct about agency funds?

   I. Agency funds should report investment earnings only when they are both measurable and available.

   II. Agency funds are reported on the proprietary funds' statement of cash flows.

   a. I only.

   b. II only.

   c. I and II.

   d. Neither I nor II.

(*Note:* Use the following information to answer questions 4 through 8.)

On July 2, 20X6, the Village of Westbury established an internal service fund to service the data processing needs of the other village departments. The internal service fund received a transfer of $600,000 from the general fund and a $100,000 long-term advance from the water utility enterprise fund to acquire computer equipment. During July 20X6, computer equipment costing $650,000 was acquired. The following events occurred during the year ended June 30, 20X7:

Charges for services to other departments for data processing services rendered	$100,000
Operating expenses (exclusive of depreciation expense)	45,000
Depreciation expense	40,000
Interest expense on the advance	5,000

At June 30, 20X7, all but $7,000 of the billings had been collected, and all operating expenses and the interest expense except for $3,000 of operating expenses had been paid.

4. For the year ended June 30, 20X7, what was the income of Westbury's internal service fund?

   a. $13,000.

   b. $6,000.

   c. $3,000.

   d. $10,000.

5. At June 30, 20X7, what total assets amount would appear on the internal service fund balance sheet?

   a. $700,000.

   b. $710,000.

   c. $713,000.

   d. $708,000.

6. Assume that the mayor's office and the police department were billed $55,000 for data processing work during the year ended June 30, 20X7. What account in the general fund should be debited to record these billings?

   a. Other Financing Use—Transfers Out.

   b. Expenditures.

   c. Due to Internal Service Fund.

   d. Operating Expenses.

7. Assume that the water utility, an enterprise fund, was billed $25,000 for data processing work during the year ended June 30, 20X7. What account in the enterprise fund should be debited to record these billings?
   a. Operating expenses.
   b. Other Financing Use—Transfers Out.
   c. Expenditures.
   d. Due to Internal Service Fund.
8. Assume that the income for Westbury's internal service fund was $10,000 for the year ended June 30, 20X7. What net position should be reported on the internal service fund's statement of net position at June 30, 20X7?
   a. $713,000.
   b. $610,000.
   c. $710,000.
   d. $613,000.

LO 18-11

E18-5 Multiple-Choice Questions on Financial Reporting Issues for Governmentwide and Fund-Based Financial Statements

Select the correct answer for each of the following questions.

1. Which of the following statements is correct?
   I. In the governmentwide financial statements, internal service fund activities are reported in the Governmental Activities column.
   II. The total balance for the governmental funds that is reported on the governmental funds balance sheet will not equal the total net position of governmental activities that is reported on the governmentwide statement of net position.
   a. I only.
   b. II only.
   c. I and II.
   d. Neither I nor II.
2. For the year ended June 30, 20X5, Stanton Township's internal service funds reported an increase in net position of $300,000 and ending net position of $4,500,000 at June 30, 20X5. On the reconciliation of the balance sheet of the governmental funds to the statement of net position, what amount should be added as of June 30, 20X5?
   a. $300,000.
   b. $4,200,000.
   c. $4,500,000.
   d. $4,800,000.
3. For the year ended June 30, 20X5, Stanton Township's enterprise funds reported an increase in net position of $300,000 and ending net position of $4,500,000 at June 30, 20X5. The enterprise fund also reported net position—unrestricted of $1,200,000 at June 30, 20X5, on its statement of net position. On the reconciliation of the balance sheet of the governmental funds to the statement of net position as of June 30, 20X5, what amount should be added?
   a. $4,200,000.
   b. $5,700,000.
   c. $4,800,000.
   d. $0.
4. Which of the following is true regarding permanent funds?
   a. They use modified accrual accounting.
   b. Their principal cannot be expended.
   c. Dividend and interest income from their investments are used to benefit the government and its citizens.
   d. All of the above.

(*Note:* Use the information below to answer questions 5 through 7.)

A water and sewer enterprise fund provided you the following information for the year ended June 30, 20X5:

Customer receipts	$ 500,000
Dividends received from investments in common and preferred stock	25,000
Proceeds from issuance of revenue bonds (used for plant construction)	1,000,000
Proceeds of short-term notes (used to pay operating expenses)	30,000
Capital grant received from state (used for wastewater plant addition)	300,000
Interest on revenue bonds paid	40,000
Interest on short-term notes paid	1,000
Proceeds from sale of Dell common stock received	20,000
Investments in corporate bonds acquired	8,000
Capital expenditures made	600,000
Operating expenses paid	350,000
Depreciation expense for period determined	50,000

Answer the following questions about the amounts reported on the statement of cash flows for the water and sewer enterprise fund.

5. What amount should be reported for cash flows provided by operating activities?
   a. $150,000.
   b. $175,000.
   c. $134,000.
   d. $100,000.
6. What amount should be reported for cash flows provided by investing activities?
   a. $12,000.
   b. $45,000.
   c. $17,000.
   d. $37,000.
7. What amount should be reported for cash flows provided by capital and related financing activities?
   a. $700,000.
   b. $360,000.
   c. $660,000.
   d. $400,000.
8. Smith donated cash of $1,000,000 to Elizabeth City with the stipulation that the contribution be invested and that the investment's earnings be spent for salaries for the city's symphony orchestra. The contribution was received on June 30, 20X4, and was invested in bonds on July 1, 20X4. The bonds were acquired at face value and pay interest at 6 percent on January 1 and July 1. At June 30, 20X5, the fair value of the bonds was $995,000. During the year ended June 30, 20X5, $20,000 was provided to the symphony orchestra to help pay salaries. On the statement of fiduciary net position at June 30, 20X5, what would be the amount reported for net position held in trust for the symphony orchestra?
   a. $1,060,000.
   b. $1,055,000.
   c. $1,025,000.
   d. $1,035,000.

LO 18-2

Advanced StudyGuide .com

E18-6 Capital Projects Fund Entries and Statements

The City of Waterman established a capital projects fund for the construction of an access ramp from the parking garage to the city's office building to be used by individuals with disabilities. The estimated cost of the ramp is $200,000. On January 1, 20X2, a 10 percent, $150,000 bond issue was sold at 104.0 with the premium transferred to the debt service fund. At that date, the county board provided a $50,000 grant. After a period of negotiation, the city council awarded a construction contract for $182,000 on April 5, 20X2. The ramp was completed on August 8, 20X2; its actual cost was $189,000. The city council approved payment of the total actual cost of $189,000. In addition to the $189,000, the ramp was carpeted with all-weather material at a cost of $5,500.

On November 3, 20X2, the city council gave the final approval to pay for the ramp and the carpeting. After all bills were paid, the remaining fund balance was transferred to the debt service fund.

Required

a. Prepare entries for the capital projects fund for 20X2.

b. Prepare a statement of revenues, expenditures, and changes in fund balance for the capital projects fund for 20X2.

LO 18-3

E18-7 Debt Service Fund Entries and Statements

Advanced StudyGuide.com

The City of Waterman established a debt service fund to account for the financial resources used to service the bonds issued to finance the ramp (see Exercise 18-6). The 10 percent, $150,000 bond issue was sold at 104.0 on January 1, 20X2. It is a 10-year serial bond issue. The resources to pay the interest and annual principal will be from a property tax levy.

Additional Information

1. The operating budget for 20X2 included estimated revenue of $35,000. Budgeted appropriations included $15,000 for principal, $15,000 for interest, and $4,000 for other items. The budget also included an estimated transfer in of $5,000 from the capital projects fund.
2. The property tax levy was for $40,000 and an allowance for uncollectibles of $4,000 was established. Collections totaled $35,000. The remaining taxes were reclassified as delinquent and the allowance was reduced to $1,000. The bond premium was received from the capital projects fund.
3. The current portion of the serial bonds and the interest due this year were recorded and paid. Other expenses charged to the debt service fund totaled $1,700, of which $1,200 was paid.
4. The nominal accounts were closed.

Required

a. Prepare entries for the debt service fund for 20X2.

b. Prepare a balance sheet for the debt service fund as of December 31, 20X2.

c. Prepare a statement of revenues, expenditures, and changes in fund balance for the debt service fund for 20X2.

LO 18-6, 18-7

E18-8 Enterprise Fund Entries and Statements

Augusta has a municipal water and gas utility district (MUD). The trial balance on January 1, 20X1, follows:

	Debit	Credit
Cash	$ 92,000	
Accounts Receivable	25,000	
Inventory of Supplies	8,000	
Land	120,000	
Plant & Equipment	480,000	
Accumulated Depreciation		$ 80,000
Vouchers Payable		15,000
Bonds Payable, 6%		500,000
Net Position:		
Invested in Capital Assets, Net of Related Debt		20,000
Unrestricted		110,000
Total	$725,000	$725,000

Advanced StudyGuide.com

Additional Information for 20X1

1. Charges to customers for water and gas were $420,000; collections were $432,000.
2. A loan of $30,000 for two years was received from the general fund.
3. The water and gas lines were extended to a new development at a cost of $75,000. The contractor was paid.

4. Supplies were acquired from central stores (internal service fund) for $12,400. Operating expenses were $328,000, and interest expense was $30,000. Payment was made for the interest and the payable to central stores, and $325,000 of the vouchers were paid.
5. Adjusting entries were as follows: estimated uncollectible accounts receivable, $6,300; depreciation expense, $32,000; and supplies expense, $15,200.

Required

a. Prepare entries for the MUD enterprise fund for 20X1 and closing entries.

b. Prepare a statement of net position for the fund for December 31, 20X1.

c. Prepare a statement of revenues, expenses, and changes in fund net position for 20X1. Assume that the $500,000 of the 6 percent bonds is related to the net capital assets of land and of plant and equipment.

d. Prepare a statement of cash flows for 20X1.

LO 18-1

E18-9 Interfund Transfers and Transactions

During 20X8, the following transfers and transactions between funds took place in the City of Matthew.

1. On March 1, a $12,000 transfer was made from the general fund to establish a building maintenance internal service fund. Matthew uses transfer accounts for this type of transfer.
2. On April 1, the general fund made an $8,000, six-month loan to the building maintenance service fund.
3. On April 15, $2,400 was transferred from the general fund to the debt service fund to pay interest.
4. On May 5, Matthew's transportation service fund billed the general fund $825 for April services.

Required

a. Prepare journal entries for the general fund and the other fund involved at the time of each transfer or transaction.

b. For each transfer or transaction, prepare the appropriate closing entries for the general fund and the other fund involved for the year ended June 30, 20X8.

LO 18-8

E18-10 Internal Service Fund Entries and Statements

Bellevue City's printing shop had the following trial balance on January 1, 20X2:

	Debit	Credit
Cash	$ 24,600	
Due from Other Funds	15,600	
Inventory of Supplies	9,800	
Furniture & Equipment	260,000	
Accumulated Depreciation		$ 50,000
Vouchers Payable		12,000
Net Position:		
Invested in Capital Assets (no related debt)		210,000
Unrestricted		38,000
Total	$310,000	$310,000

Additional Information for 20X2

Advanced StudyGuide .com

1. During 20X2, the printing shop acquired supplies for $96,000, furniture for $1,500, and a copier for $3,200.
2. Printing jobs billed to other funds amounted to $292,000; cash received from other funds, $287,300; costs of printing jobs, $204,000, including $84,000 of supplies; operating expenses, $38,000, including $8,400 of supplies; depreciation expense, $23,000; and vouchers paid, $243,000.

Required

a. Prepare entries for the printing shop for 20X2, including closing entries.

b. Prepare a statement of net position for the fund on December 31, 20X2. No debt is related to the year-end amount of the fund's capital assets.

c. Prepare a statement of revenues, expenses, and changes in fund net position for 20X2.

d. Prepare a statement of cash flows for 20X2.

LO 18-11

E18-11 Multiple-Choice Questions on Governmentwide Financial Statements

(*Note:* Items 1 and 2 are based on the following.)

Mountain View City is preparing its governmentwide financial statements for the year. As of the year-end, the city has determined the following information for its capital assets, exclusive of its infrastructure assets:

Cost of capital assets acquired by governmental funds	$1,450,000
Accumulated depreciation on the capital assets	120,000
Outstanding debt related to the capital assets	780,000

1. On the governmentwide statement of net position for the year-end, what amount should be reported for capital assets in the Governmental Activities column?

   a. $550,000.

   b. $780,000.

   c. $1,330,000.

   d. $1,450,000.

2. On the governmentwide statement of net position for the year-end, what amount should be reported for the capital assets in the net position section?

   a. $550,000.

   b. $780,000.

   c. $1,330,000.

   d. $1,450,000.

3. In accordance with **GASB 34,** which of the following is correct regarding the reporting of internal service funds?

   I. The internal service fund should be discretely presented as part of the government's business-type activities.

   II. The internal service fund should be blended into the governmental activities.

   a. I only.

   b. II only.

   c. I and II.

   d. Neither I nor II.

(*Note:* Items 4 and 5 are based on the following.)

At the beginning of the year, the City of Vero Beach sold bonds in its capital projects fund. The 6 percent, $500,000 par bonds were sold for 102. The effective interest rate was 5 percent.

4. How should the bonds be reported in the reconciliation schedule for the statement of revenues, expenditures, and changes in fund balance?

   a. A decrease of $500,000 for the par value of the bonds.

   b. A decrease of $30,000 for the interest paid on the bonds.

   c. A decrease of $510,000 for the selling price of the bonds.

   d. Not shown in this reconciliation schedule.

5. How should an interest adjustment be shown in the reconciliation of the balance sheet of governmental funds to the statement of net position for the year?
   a. A decrease of $30,000.
   b. A decrease of $25,000.
   c. A decrease of $5,000.
   d. Not shown in this reconciliation schedule.

6. For which of the following should the accrual basis of accounting be used to measure financial performance?

	General Fund	Internal Service Fund	Governmentwide Financial Statements
a.	Yes	Yes	Yes
b.	Yes	No	Yes
c.	No	No	No
d.	No	Yes	Yes

7. The City of Hastings has a separately elected school board that administers the city's schools. The city council must approve the school district's budget and tax levy. Its financial results should be reported in Hastings's financial statements in which way?
   a. Included only as schedules in the footnotes of Hastings's financial reports.
   b. Blended into Hastings's financial reports.
   c. Discretely presented in Hastings's financial reports.
   d. Not required to be presented in Hastings's financial reports.

8. Glen Valley City has properly adopted the modified approach to account for its infrastructure assets. Which of the following statements is correct about accounting for these assets on the governmentwide statement of activities?
   I. Depreciation expense should be computed based on the assets' estimated useful lives and reported under the Governmental Activities column of the city's statement of activities.
   II. The amount of the expenditures made for the infrastructure assets except for additions and improvements should be expensed in the period incurred.
   a. I only.
   b. II only.
   c. I and II.
   d. Neither I nor II.

9. For which of these funds is a statement of cash flows required

	General Fund	Internal Service Fund	Governmentwide Entity
a.	Yes	Yes	Yes
b.	No	Yes	Yes
c.	No	Yes	No
d.	Yes	No	No

10. Which of the following is reported as a restriction of net position in the net position section of the statement of net position?
    a. A reservation of the fund balance in the general fund for $10,000 of encumbrances.
    b. A requirement in the permanent funds that the $100,000 principal of a bequest be maintained.
    c. A governing board's decision that $15,000 of general fund resources should be assigned for planning for a city park.
    d. A governing board allocation of $4,000 to establish an internal services fund.

PROBLEMS

LO 18-1

P18-12 Adjusting Entries for General Fund [AICPA Adapted]

On June 30, 20X2, the end of the fiscal year, the Wadsworth Park District prepared the following trial balance for the general fund:

	Debit	Credit
Cash	$ 47,250	
Taxes Receivable—Current	31,800	
Allowance for Uncollectibles—Current		$ 1,800
Temporary Investments	11,300	
Inventory of Supplies	11,450	
Buildings	1,300,000	
ESTIMATED REVENUES CONTROL	1,007,000	
APPROPRIATIONS CONTROL		1,000,000
Revenue—State Grants		300,000
Bonds Payable		1,000,000
Vouchers Payable		10,200
Expenditures	848,200	
Debt Service from Current Funds	130,000	
Capital Outlays (Equipment)	22,000	
Revenue—Taxes		1,008,200
Fund Balance—Unassigned		81,800
BUDGETARY FUND BALANCE—UNASSIGNED		7,000
Total	$3,409,000	$3,409,000

An examination of the records disclosed the following information:

1. The recorded estimate of losses for the current year taxes receivable was considered to be adequate.
2. The local governmental unit gave the park district 20 acres of land to be used for a new community park. The unrecorded estimated value of the land was $50,000. In addition, the unit received a state grant of $300,000, and used the full amount in payment of contracts pertaining to the construction of the park buildings. Purchases of playground equipment costing $22,000 were paid from general funds.
3. Five years ago, a 4 percent, 10-year sinking fund bond issue in the amount of $1,000,000 for constructing park buildings was sold; it is still outstanding. Interest on the issue is payable at maturity. Budgetary requirements of a contribution of $130,000 to the debt service fund were met. Of this amount, $100,000 represents the fifth equal contribution for principal repayment.
4. Outstanding purchase orders not recorded in the accounts at year-end totaled $2,800.
5. A physical inventory of supplies at year-end revealed $6,500 of the supplies on hand.
6. Except where indicated to the contrary, all recordings were made in the general fund.

Required

Prepare the adjusting entries to correct the general fund records.

LO 18-1, 18-2, 18-3, 18-8, 18-9

P18-13 Entries for Funds [AICPA Adapted]

Olivia Village was recently incorporated and began financial operations on July 1, 20X2, the beginning of its fiscal year. The following transactions occurred during this first fiscal year, July 1, 20X2, to June 30, 20X3:

1. The village council adopted a budget for general operations for the fiscal year ending June 30, 20X3. Revenue was estimated at $400,000. Legal authorizations for budgeted expenditures totaled $394,000.
2. Property taxes of $390,000 were levied; 2 percent of this amount was estimated to be uncollectible. These taxes are available to finance current expenditures as of the date of levy.

3. During the year, a village resident donated marketable securities valued at $50,000 to the village under the terms of a trust agreement that stipulated that the principal amount be kept intact. The use of revenue generated by the securities is restricted to financing college scholarships for needy students. Revenue earned and received on these marketable securities amounted to $5,500 through June 30, 20X3.
4. A general fund transfer of $5,000 was made to establish an internal service fund to provide for a permanent investment in inventory.
5. The village decided to install lighting in the village park financed through an authorized special assessment project at a cost of $75,000. The city is obligated if the property owners default on their special assessments. The village issued special assessment bonds in the amount of $72,000 and levied the first year's special assessment of $24,000 against the village's property owners. The remaining $3,000 for the project will be contributed from the village's general fund.
6. The special assessments for the lighting project are due over a three-year period, and the first year's assessments of $24,000 were collected. The $3,000 transfer from the village's general fund was received by the lighting capital projects fund.
7. A contract for $75,000 was let for the lighting installation. The capital projects fund was encumbered for the contract. On June 30, 20X3, the contract was completed, and the contractor was paid.
8. During the year, the internal service fund purchased various supplies at a cost of $1,900.
9. The general fund cash collections recorded during the year as follows:

Current property taxes	$386,000
Licenses and permit fees	7,000

   The allowance for estimated uncollectible taxes is adjusted to $4,000.

10. The village council decided to build a village hall at an estimated cost of $500,000 to replace space occupied in rented facilities. The village does not record project authorizations. The council decided to issue general obligation bonds bearing interest at 6 percent. On June 30, 20X3, the bonds were issued at face value of $500,000, payable in 20 years. No contracts have been signed for this project, no expenditures have been made, nor has an annual operating budget been prepared.
11. The voucher for purchasing a fire truck for $15,000 was approved and paid by the general fund. This expenditure previously had been encumbered for $15,000.

Required

Prepare journal entries to record properly each of these transactions in the appropriate fund or funds of Olivia Village for the fiscal year ended June 30, 20X3.

Use the following funds: general fund, capital projects fund, debt service fund, internal service fund, and private-purpose trust fund. Each journal entry should be numbered to correspond to the transactions. Do *not* prepare closing entries for any fund. Your answer sheet should be organized using the following format:

Fund	Journal Entry

LO 18-11

P18-14 Entries to Adjust Account Balances [AICPA Adapted]

The town of Papillion has assigned you to examine its June 30, 20X1, balance sheet. You are the first CPA to be engaged by the town, and you find that acceptable methods of municipal accounting have not been employed. The town clerk stated that the books had not been closed and presented the following preclosing trial balance of the general fund as of June 30, 20X1:

	Debit	Credit
Cash	$150,000	
Taxes Receivable—Current Year	59,200	
Allowance for Uncollectibles—Current		$ 18,000
Taxes Receivable—Delinquent	8,000	
Allowance for Uncollectibles—Delinquent		10,200
ESTIMATED REVENUES CONTROL	310,000	
APPROPRIATIONS CONTROL		348,000
Donated Land	27,000	
Expenditures—Building Addition Constructed	50,000	
Expenditures—Serial Bonds Paid	16,000	
Other Expenditures	280,000	
Special Assessment Bonds Payable		100,000
Revenue		354,000
Accounts Payable		26,000
Fund Balance—Unassigned		82,000
BUDGETARY FUND BALANCE—UNASSIGNED	38,000	
Total	$938,200	$938,200

Additional Information

1. The estimated losses of $18,000 for current year taxes receivable were determined to be a reasonable estimate. The delinquent taxes allowance account should be adjusted to $8,000, the amount of the remaining delinquent taxes.
2. Included in the Revenue account is a credit of $27,000, representing the value of land donated by the state as a grant-in-aid for construction of a municipal park.
3. Operating supplies ordered in the prior fiscal year and chargeable to that year had been received, recorded, and consumed in July 20X0. The outstanding purchase orders for these supplies, which had not been recorded in the accounts on June 30, 20X0, amounted to $8,800. The vendors' invoices for these supplies totaled $9,400. Appropriations lapse one year after the end of the fiscal year for which they are made.
4. Outstanding purchase orders for operating supplies totaled $2,100 on June 30, 20X1. These purchase orders had not been recorded on the books.
5. The special assessment bonds were sold in June 20X1 to finance a street-paving project. No contracts have been signed for this project, and no expenditures have been made from the capital projects fund. The city is obligated for the bonds if the property owners default.
6. The balance in the Revenue account includes credits for $20,000 for a note issued to a bank to obtain cash in anticipation of tax collections and for $1,000 for the sale of scrap iron from the town's water plant. The note was still outstanding on June 30, 20X1. The operations of the water plant are accounted for in the water fund.
7. The Expenditures—Building Addition Constructed account balance is the cost of an addition to the town hall building constructed and completed in June 20X1. The general fund recorded the payment as authorized.
8. The Expenditures—Serial Bonds Paid account reflects the annual retirement of general obligation bonds issued to finance the construction of the town hall. Interest payments of $7,000 for the bond issue are included in other expenditures.

Required

a. Prepare the formal adjusting and closing journal entries for the general fund for the fiscal year ended June 30, 20X1.

b. The preceding information disclosed by your examination was recorded only in the general fund even though other funds were involved. Prepare the formal adjusting journal entries for any other funds involved.

LO 18-2

P18-15 Capital Projects Fund Entries and Statements

During the fiscal year ended June 30, 20X3, West City Council authorized construction of a new city hall building and the sale of serial bonds to finance the construction. The following transactions related to financing and constructing the city hall occurred during fiscal 20X3:

1. On August 1, 20X2, West issued $5,000,000 of serial bonds for $5,080,000. Interest is payable annually, and the first retirement of $500,000 is due on July 31, 20X7. The premium is transferred to the debt service fund.
2. The old city hall, which had a recorded cost of $650,000, was torn down. The cost of razing the old building was $45,000, net of salvage value. This cost was included in the capital budget but was not encumbered. The cost is vouchered and paid.
3. West signed a contract with Roth Construction Company to build the city hall for $4,500,000. The contract cost is to be encumbered. Construction is to be completed during fiscal 20X4.
4. Roth Construction Company bills West $2,000,000 for construction completed during fiscal 20X3. Ten percent of the billings will be retained until final acceptance of the new city hall. The billing less the retainage had been paid during the fiscal year.

Required

a. For each of these transactions, prepare the necessary journal entries for all funds involved. Indicate the fund in which the entry is made by giving its initials in the left margin: CPF (capital projects fund) or DSF (debt service fund). Give the closing entries for the capital projects fund.

b. Prepare a balance sheet for the capital projects fund at June 30, 20X3.

c. Prepare a statement of revenues, expenditures, and changes in fund balance for the capital projects fund for the fiscal year ended June 30, 20X3.

LO 18-2, 18-10

Advanced StudyGuide .com

P18-16 Recording Entries in Various Funds [AICPA Adapted]

The following information relates to Vane City during the year ended December 31, 20X8:

1. On October 31, 20X8, to finance the construction of a city hall annex, Vane issued 8 percent, 10-year general obligation bonds at their face value of $800,000. A contractor's bid of $750,000 was accepted for the construction. By year-end, one-third of the contract had been completed at a cost of $246,000, all of which was paid on January 5, 20X9.
2. Vane collected $109,000 from hotel room taxes restricted for tourist promotion in a special revenue fund. The fund incurred and paid $81,000 for general promotions and $22,000 for a motor vehicle. Estimated revenues for 20X8 were $112,000; appropriations were expected to be $108,000.
3. General fund revenues of $313,500 for 20X8 were transferred to a debt service fund and used to repay $300,000 of 9 percent, 15-year term bonds, which matured in 20X8, and to repay $13,500 of matured interest. The bond proceeds were used to construct a citizens' center.
4. At December 31, 20X8, Vane was responsible for $83,000 of outstanding encumbrances in its general fund. The city uses the nonlapsing method to account for its outstanding encumbrances.
5. Vane uses the purchases method to account for supplies in the general fund. At December 31, 20X8, an inventory indicated that the supplies inventory was $42,000. At December 31, 20X7, the supplies inventory was $45,000.

Required

For each numbered item above, make all the journal entries in all funds affected for the year ended December 31, 20X8. Before each journal entry, identify the fund in which it is made. *Do not make any adjusting/closing entries for items (1), (2), and (3).*

LO 18-2, 18-3, 18-6, 18-8 18-10

P18-17 Matching Items Involving Various Funds

The numbered items on the left consist of a variety of transactions that occur in a municipality. The lettered items on the right consist of various ways to record the transactions. Select the appropriate method for recording each transaction. Some transactions have more than one correct answer. Lettered items may be used once, more than once, or not at all.

Transactions	Recording of Transactions
1. Term bond proceeds of $100,000 were received by the capital projects fund.	A. Debit Expenditures in the general fund
2. Equipment costing $50,000 was acquired by the water utility, an enterprise fund.	B. Debit General Operating Expenses in the general fund
3. Land with a fair value of $500,000 was donated to the city to be used as a municipal park.	C. Debit Equipment in the enterprise fund
4. Central stores, an internal service fund, received a transfer in of $750,000 from the general fund.	D. Debit Equipment in the general fund
5. General obligation serial bonds of $250,000 matured and were paid by the debt service fund.	E. Debit Building in the capital projects fund
6. Expenditures of $5,000,000 were incurred by the capital projects fund to construct a new city hall annex. The project was started and completed within the fiscal year.	F. Debit General Operating Expenses in the enterprise fund
7. The water utility, an enterprise fund, billed the mayor's office $200 for water usage.	G. Debit Expenditures in the capital projects fund
8. The mayor's office received the billing in item 7.	H. Credit building in the capital projects fund
9. The tax agency fund received $250,000 of tax revenues that are to be distributed to the school districts within the municipality.	I. Debit Expenditures in the debt service fund
10. Salaries and wages of $25,000 were incurred by the water utility enterprise fund.	J. Credit Revenue in the private-purpose trust fund
	K. Credit Revenue in the capital projects fund
	L. Credit Other Financing Sources in the capital projects fund
	M. Credit Transfers in the internal services fund
	N. Debit Revenue in the agency fund
	O. Credit Due to Other Governmental Units in the agency fund
	P. Credit Revenue in the agency fund
	Q. Credit Revenue in the enterprise fund
	R. Reported only on the governmentwide financial statements

LO 18-1, 18-2, 18-3, 18-11

P18-18 Questions on Fund Transactions [AICPA Adapted]

The following information relates to Dane City during its fiscal year ended December 31, 20X2:

1. On October 31, 20X2, to finance the construction of a city hall annex, Dane issued 8 percent, 10-year general obligation bonds at their face value of $600,000. Construction expenditures during the period equaled $364,000.
2. Dane reported $109,000 from hotel room taxes restricted for tourist promotion in a special revenue fund. The fund paid $81,000 for general promotions and $22,000 for a motor vehicle.
3. Dane transferred 20X2 general fund revenues of $104,500 to a debt service fund and used them to repay $100,000 of 9 percent, 15-year term bonds and to pay $4,500 of interest. The bonds were used to acquire a citizens' center.
4. At December 31, 20X2, as a consequence of past services, city firefighters had accumulated entitlements for compensated absences of $86,000. General fund resources available at December 31, 20X2, are expected to be used to settle $17,000 of this amount, and $69,000 is expected to be paid out of future general fund resources.
5. At December 31, 20X2, Dane was responsible for $83,000 of outstanding general fund encumbrances, including the $8,000 for supplies in the following table.

6. Dane uses the purchases method to account for supplies. The following information relates to supplies:

Inventory—1/1/X2	$ 39,000
—12/31/X2	42,000
Encumbrances outstanding—1/1/X2	6,000
—12/31/X2	8,000
Purchase orders during 20X2	190,000
Amount credited to vouchers payable during 20X2	181,000

Required

For items 1 through 10, determine the amounts based solely on the preceding information.

1. What is the amount of 20X2 general fund transfers out?
2. How much should be reported in 20X2 as general fund liabilities from entitlements for compensated absences?
3. What is the 20X2 assigned amount of the general fund balance?
4. What is the 20X2 capital projects fund balance?
5. What is the 20X2 fund balance on the special revenue fund for tourist promotion?
6. What is the amount of 20X2 debt service fund expenditures?
7. What amount should be included in the governmentwide financial statements for the cost of long-term assets acquired in 20X2?
8. What amount stemming from the 20X2 transactions and events decreased the long-term debt liabilities reported in the governmentwide financial statements?
9. Using the purchases method, what is the amount of 20X2 supplies expenditures?
10. What was the total amount of 20X2 supplies encumbrances?

LO 18-6, 18-7 P18-19 Matching Items Involving the Statement of Cash Flows for a Proprietary Fund

The numbered items on the left consist of a variety of transactions that occurred in Jeffersen City's water utility enterprise fund for the year ended June 30, 20X9. Items A, B, C, and D on the right represent the four categories of cash flows that are reported on the statement of cash flows for proprietary funds. Item E is for transactions that are not reported on the statement of cash flows. Assume that the direct method is used for disclosing cash flows from operating activities. Select the appropriate letter to indicate where each transaction should be disclosed on the statement of cash flows or whether that item would not be reported on the statement of cash flows.

Transactions

1. Received $5,000,000 from revenue bonds to be used for construction of water treatment plant.
2. Paid $500,000 of salaries to employees of the water utility.
3. Received $1,000,000 state grant restricted for construction of water treatment plant.
4. Collected $2,500,000 of accounts receivable from households for use of city water.
5. Determined that depreciation expense for the year amounted to $300,000.
6. Received $75,000 state grant restricted to the maintenance of fixed assets.
7. Paid $250,000 of interest on the revenue bonds issued in item 1.

Categories of Disclosure

A. Operating activities
B. Noncapital financing activities
C. Capital and related financing
D. activities
E. Investing activities
Not reported on the statement of cash flows

(continued)

8. Borrowed $125,000 from a local bank on revenue anticipation notes payable.
9. Paid $5,000 of interest on the notes payable in item 8.
10. Spent $1,200,000 of the revenue bonds for construction of the water treatment plant.
11. Paid $5,000 fire insurance premium on June 30, 20X9, for next year's insurance coverage.
12. Determined that uncollected accounts receivable amounted to $135,000 on June 31, 20X9.
13. Acquired $250,000 of state bonds as an investment of idle funds.
14. Received $7,500 of interest on the state bonds in item 13.
15. Received a $375,000 contribution from the city's general fund to be used for the construction of water treatment plant.

LO 18-2, 18-3 **P18-20** **Matching Items Involving the Statement of Revenues, Expenditures, and Changes in Fund Balance for a Capital Projects Fund and a Debt Service Fund**

The numbered items on the left consist of a variety of transactions and events that occurred in the capital projects and debt service funds of Walton City for the year ended June 30, 20X9. Items A, B, and C on the right represent three categories that are reported on the statement of revenues, expenditures, and changes in fund balance for capital projects and debt service funds. Item D is for transactions that are not reported on the statement of revenues, expenditures, and changes in fund balance for either debt service or capital projects funds. For each transaction, select the appropriate letter to indicate where that transaction should be reported on the statement of revenues, expenditures, and changes in fund balance or whether that item would not be reported on the statement.

Transactions/Events

1. The capital projects fund received the proceeds of general obligation bonds to be used for construction of a new courthouse.
2. The capital projects fund accepted the lowest bid for the construction of the courthouse.
3. The capital projects fund received resources from the city's general fund to be used in the construction of the courthouse.
4. The bonds in item 1 were sold at a premium. The capital projects fund transferred the premium to the debt service fund. Indicate how the capital projects fund should report this transaction.
5. During the year ended June 30, 20X9, courthouse construction was completed.
6. In addition to the resources provided by the general obligation bonds and the general fund, the capital projects fund also received a state grant to construct the courthouse.
7. The city's general fund transferred a portion of the property tax collections to the debt service fund to be used to pay the principal and interest of the general obligation bonds issued in item 1.
8. The debt service fund acquired investments with part of the resources provided by the general fund.
9. The investments acquired in item 8 earned interest.
10. The debt service fund received the bond premium from the capital projects fund.

Categories of Disclosure

A. Revenues
B. Expenditures
C. Other financing sources and uses
D. Not reported on the statement of revenues, expenditures, and changes in fund balance

(continued)

Transactions/Events	Categories of Disclosure
11. The debt service fund paid semiannual interest on the general obligation bonds on March 1, 20X9.	
12. The debt service fund used a local bank to be its fiscal agent with regard to the recordkeeping activities related to the general obligation bonds issued in item 1. The bank charged a fee for this service.	
13. As of June 30, 20X9, unmatured interest for four months was due on the general obligation bonds issued in item 1. Resources to pay this interest will be transferred to the debt service fund in the next fiscal year.	

LO 18-1–18-4, 18-6–18-8

P18-21 Matching Items on Fund Transactions [AICPA Adapted]

Items 1 through 10 in the left-hand column represent various transactions pertaining to a municipality that uses encumbrance accounting. Items 11 through 20, also listed in the left-hand column, represent the funds and accounts used by the municipality. To the right of these items is a list of possible accounting and reporting methods.

Required

a. For the municipality, select the appropriate method to record each transaction (items 1 through 10). A method of recording the transactions may be selected once, more than once, or not at all.

b. Select the appropriate method of accounting and reporting for each of the municipality's funds, accounts, and other items (items 11 to 20). An accounting and reporting method may be selected once, more than once, or not at all.

Transactions	Recording of Transactions
1. General obligation bonds were issued at par.	A. Credit Appropriations Control
2. Approved purchase orders were issued for supplies.	B. Credit Budgetary Fund Balance—Unassigned
3. Supplies in item 2 were received and the related invoices were approved.	C. Credit Expenditures Control
4. General fund salaries and wages were incurred.	D. Credit Deferred Revenues
5. The internal service fund had interfund billings.	E. Credit Interfund Revenues
6. Revenues were earned from a previously awarded grant.	F. Credit Tax Anticipation Notes Payable
7. Property taxes were collected in advance.	G. Credit Other Financing Sources
8. Appropriations were recorded on adoption of the budget.	H. Credit Other Financing Uses
9. Short-term financing secured by the city's taxing power was received from a bank.	I. Debit Appropriations Control
10. Estimated inflows exceeded estimated outflows.	J. Debit Deferred Revenues
	K. Debit Encumbrances Control
	L. Debit Expenditures Control

Funds and Accounts	Accounting and Reporting
11. Enterprise fund fixed assets.	A. Accounted for in a fiduciary fund
12. Capital projects fund.	B. Accounted for in a proprietary fund
13. Permanent fund.	C. Accounts for permanent endowments that can be used for government programs
14. Infrastructure fixed assets.	D. Reported as an other financing use
15. Enterprise fund cash.	E. Accounted for in a special assessment fund
16. General fund.	F. Accounts for major construction activities
17. Agency fund cash.	G. Accounts for property tax revenues
18. Transfer out from the general fund to the internal service fund.	H. Accounts for payment of interest and principal on tax-supported debt
19. Special revenue fund (a major fund).	I. Accounts for revenues from earmarked sources to finance designated activities
20. Debt service fund (a major fund).	J. Reported in governmentwide statements

LO 18-5 **P18-22** **Major Fund Tests**

The City of Somerset has the following fund information:

Fund	Assets	Liabilities	Revenues	Expenditures (Expenses)
General	$1,320,400	$ 878,300	$4,620,000	$4,550,000
Special revenue	27,000	19,000	327,000	328,000
Capital project—library	450,000	38,000	460,000	418,000
Capital project—arena	28,000	16,000	41,000	55,800
Debt service	41,000	0	331,000	290,000
Permanent	246,000	0	11,000	18,000
Enterprise—electric	2,640,000	1,800,700	289,000	245,000
Enterprise—water	1,356,000	1,100,000	329,000	298,000

Required

Apply the criteria specified in **GASB 34** to determine which of these funds meets the major fund reporting criteria.

LO 18-12 **P18-23** **Reconciliation Schedules**

The City of Sycamore is preparing its financial reports for the year and has requested that you prepare the reconciliation schedules to accompany its governmentwide financial statements based on the following information:

1. The fund balances reported in the five governmental funds as of the end of the fiscal year total $888,400. The fund balances in governmental funds at the beginning of the year totaled $379,000.
2. The city has estimated its depreciation on capital assets to be $187,000 for the period. The city expended a total of $287,000 in capital outlays from the governmental funds. At year-end, the capital assets, net of depreciation, totaled $4,329,000. The internal service fund reported $18,000 of net capital assets. Total accumulated depreciation at year-end was $1,208,000.
3. The internal service fund reports $178,000 in total assets and $141,000 in total liabilities. The internal service fund reported $48,000 of revenues and $39,000 of expenses during the year.
4. The debt service fund paid $40,000 in interest during the year. The city sold bonds with a face value of $500,000 and a coupon rate of 8 percent at the beginning of the year at $460,000 for an effective interest rate of 10 percent. Interest is paid annually on the last day of the fiscal year. The bonds were sold to provide current financial resources for the governmental funds.
5. The permanent fund recorded interest received of $4,000 under the modified accrual basis of measurement. If the accrual basis of measurement had been used in the fund, an additional $1,000 of interest revenue would have been earned.

Required

a. Prepare a reconciliation schedule of the balance sheet of the governmental funds to the statement of net position.

b. Prepare a reconciliation schedule of the statement of revenues, expenditures, and changes in fund balance of governmental funds to the statement of activities.

LO 18-11, 18-12 **P18-24** **True/False Statements**

1. The budgetary comparison schedule in the governmentwide financial statements for the period requires only the final budget and the actual amounts.
2. The accrual basis of accounting is used in the governmentwide financial statements.
3. A component unit of a primary government is a unit that is related to the primary government but is not financially accountable to it.

4. The statement of net position in the governmentwide financial statements requires the net position to be segregated as follows: assigned net position (for items such as encumbrances and inventories) and unassigned net position.
5. A major governmental fund that must be separately disclosed in the governmentwide financial statements would be a fund that composed 5 percent of the total of the governmental funds.
6. Permanent governmental funds account for resources that have a principal that must be maintained and whose earnings are available for any government program that benefits all citizens.
7. The governmental unit's infrastructure and other fixed assets are reported on the governmentwide statement of net position.
8. The internal service fund is a proprietary fund and is not, therefore, shown in the Governmental Activities column of the governmentwide statement of net position.
9. In the reconciliation schedule for the statement of net position, to reconcile from the net position reported in the governmental funds to the net position of governmental activities, capital assets used in governmental activities would be added.
10. In the reconciliation schedule for the statement of revenues, expenditures, and changes in fund balance, to reconcile from the net change in fund balances—governmental funds to the change in net position of governmental activities, bond proceeds would be added back.
11. In the governmentwide statement of activities, transfers between governmental and business-type funds must be reported as part of the change in net position.
12. In the governmentwide statement of activities, depreciation of fixed assets would equal the amount of the expenditures for assets made in the governmental funds.
13. MD&A is a recommended but voluntary disclosure in the governmentwide financial statements.
14. The governmentwide statement of net position includes the fiduciary funds of the governmental unit.
15. The format of the governmentwide statement of activities is based on the governmental entity's programs rather than the type of its revenues.

LO 18-5

P18-25 Determining Whether a Special Revenue Fund Is a Major Fund

The City of Elmtree is preparing its financial statements for the year ended December 31, 20X2, and has asked for your assistance in determining whether its special revenue fund is a major or a nonmajor fund for the financial statements of its governmental funds. The city has provided the following information:

Items	Totals for Governmental Funds	Totals for Governmental and Enterprise Funds
Assets	$50,000,000	$80,000,000
Liabilities	22,000,000	37,000,000
Revenues	70,000,000	95,000,000
Expenditures/expenses	60,000,000	82,000,000

The special revenue fund reported the following amounts at December 31, 20X2 (assets and liabilities), and for the year ended December 31, 20X2 (revenues and expenditures):

Assets	$4,100,000
Liabilities	3,900,000
Revenues	6,700,000
Expenditures	6,500,000

Required

Determine whether Elmtree's special revenue fund is a major fund for the 20X2 financial statements of the city's governmental funds.

LO 18-11

P18-26 Preparation of a Statement of Net Position for a Governmental Entity

Gibson City reported the following items at December 31, 20X2. It has no component units and does not depreciate its infrastructure fixed assets. It issued all bonds—general obligation bonds and revenue—to acquire capital assets. As of December 31, 20X2, net position of $25,000 were restricted for road maintenance in special revenue funds, and net position of $30,000 were restricted for debt service. Cash of $5,000 was restricted in business-type activities for plant maintenance.

	Governmental Activities	Business-Type Activities
Assets:		
Cash & cash equivalents	$ 68,000	$28,000
Taxes receivable (net)	52,000	
Accounts receivable (net)		12,000
Due from governmental activities		5,000
Inventories	10,000	7,000
Investments	25,000	15,000
Capital assets:		
Land	100,000	50,000
Infrastructure	60,000	
Other depreciable assets (net)	75,000	45,000
Liabilities:		
Vouchers payable	32,000	4,000
Accrued interest payable	1,500	2,000
Due to business-type activities	5,000	
Revenue bonds payable		80,000
General obligation bonds payable	60,000	

Required

Using the information provided, prepare in good form a statement of net position for Gibson City at December 31, 20X2.

19 Not-for-Profit Entities

Multicorporate Entities
Multinational Entities
Reporting Requirements
Partnerships
Governmental and Not-for-Profit Entities
Governmental Entities
Special Funds
Not-For-Profit
Corporations in Financial Difficulty

UNITED WAY WORLDWIDE

United Way traces its roots to an organization originally called "The Charity Organization Society," which began as a coordinated effort between many religious and community organizations in Denver, Colorado, in 1887. During the 20th century, more and more community service organizations continued to join together to form the American Association for Community Organizations. By 1963 many of these independent charitable organizations began using the name "United Way," but not until 1971 did the national organization officially adopt the title "United Way of America" and move its headquarters from New York City to Alexandria, Virginia. In 2009, United Way of America and United Way International merged to form United Way Worldwide with a network in more than 30 countries around the globe.

The stated mission of United Way is "[t]o improve lives by mobilizing the caring power of communities around the world to advance the common good." Its work is focused in three main areas, which United Way calls "the building blocks for a good quality of life":

1. Education—Helping Children and Youth Achieve Their Potential.
2. Income—Promoting Financial Stability and Independence.
3. Health—Improving People's Health and Safety.

United Way's role is "to recruit the people and organizations who bring the passion, expertise and resources needed to get things done." Among its many collaborative activities, United Way has had an ongoing partnership with the National Football League since 1973. Both organizations benefit from the arrangement; United Way has a viable platform for spreading awareness about youth health and fitness, and the NFL has the opportunity to serve its community while meeting one of its goals to help kids get more active.

United Way has become the largest privately funded charitable organization in the United States with more than $4.2 billion in contributions during 2007. In 2009, it was named the largest privately funded charity in the world. In 2011, United Way Worldwide signed a partnership agreement with The China Charity Federation, increasing the reach of the worldwide organization. It raised $5.27 billion worldwide in 2012. With such large contributions and nearly 1,800 local United Way organizations in 41 countries and territories, its accounting can be a daunting task. This chapter discusses the accounting and financial reporting principles used by both governmental (public) and nongovernmental (private) colleges and universities, health care providers such as hospitals and nursing homes, voluntary health and welfare organizations such as the Red Cross and United Way, and other not-for-profit organizations such as professional and fraternal associations.

LEARNING OBJECTIVES

When you finish studying this chapter, you should be able to:

LO 19-1 Understand financial reporting rules and make basic journal entries for private, not-for-profit entities.

LO 19-2 Understand financial reporting rules for not-for-profit colleges and universities.

LO 19-3 Understand financial reporting rules and make basic journal entries for not-for-profit health care providers.

LO 19-4 Understand financial reporting rules and make basic journal entries for not-for-profit voluntary health and welfare organizations.

LO 19-5 Understand financial reporting rules for other not-for-profit organizations.

FINANCIAL REPORTING FOR PRIVATE, NOT-FOR-PROFIT ENTITIES

LO 19-1

Understand financial reporting rules and make basic journal entries for private, not-for-profit entities.

The Governmental Accounting Standards Board (GASB) controls the accounting and financial reporting for governmental, not-for-profit entities, and the Financial Accounting Standards Board (FASB) controls the accounting and financial reporting for nongovernmental, not-for-profit entities. Thus, it is important to determine the role the government has in not-for-profit organizations to determine which reporting standards apply.

Private, not-for-profit entities must report their net assets in accordance with **ASC 958-205,** which specifies the financial display standards for private, not-for-profit entities. The three major financial statements are the (1) statement of financial position, (2) statement of activities, and (3) statement of cash flows. We identify the unique features of the statement of financial position and the statement of activities for not-for-profit organizations in more detail in the following discussions. Although **ASC 958** allows some flexibility in the format of financial statements a major feature of the statement of financial position is the combined presentation of all assets and equities in a single, simplified statement. In addition, **ASC 958-210** separates the net assets into those that are (1) unrestricted, (2) temporarily restricted, and (3) permanently restricted.

1. *Unrestricted net assets.* This class of net assets is not restricted by a donor and these assets are used for the entity's general operations. Unrestricted net assets include all assets and liabilities that do not have externally imposed restrictions on their use.

2. *Temporarily restricted net assets.* This net asset class reports net assets that have donor-imposed time or purpose restrictions, typically detailed in the contribution agreement between the donor and the organization. A *time restriction* means that the assets will not be available for use until after a specific time has passed. *Term endowments* that have limited lives are included in temporarily restricted net assets. A *purpose restriction* means that the resources may be used only for specified purposes. For example, the donor may specify that the contribution be used in a specific program or for specified building and equipment acquisitions.

3. *Permanently restricted net assets.* This class of net assets includes permanently restricted contributions such as regular endowments for which the principal must be preserved into perpetuity.

Properly accounting for and reporting each class of net assets is very important. Some not-for-profit entities use a fund structure to account for each type of net asset class because of the discipline that fund accounting provides. These entities would have funds such as the general fund, specific-purpose fund, building fund, endowment fund, and so on. Other not-for-profit entities maintain only an accounting record to show the amounts in each net asset class. The specific identification of any restricted asset must be made when the asset comes into the entity, generally by donation or bequest. The gifting agreement must be examined fully to determine whether the gift has any donor-imposed restrictions on its principal and/or the income it generates. The entity records revenue in only one net asset class when the contribution is made. Then, as restrictions are eliminated or met, the resources are released and transferred from the restricted net asset class to the unrestricted net asset class.

For example, if Charles Alt donates $40,000 to a not-for-profit organization to be used specifically for a research program, it makes the following entry in the *temporarily restricted class of net assets* because of the donor-imposed use restriction:

(1)	Cash	40,000	
	Contribution Revenue		40,000
	Receipt of $40,000 donor-restricted contribution for a specified research program.		

Note that the contribution revenue is recorded in the temporarily restricted net asset class when the not-for-profit receives the restricted contribution.

When the research program costs have been approved in the unrestricted net asset class, the organization makes a reclassification entry in the temporarily restricted net asset class to record the transfer of the resources to the unrestricted net asset class. Note that the reclassification entry is not an expense of the restricted class.

(2)	Reclassification from Temporarily Restricted Net Assets—Satisfaction of Program Restriction	40,000	
	Cash		40,000
	Reclassification of temporarily restricted resources to the unrestricted fund upon satisfaction of the use restriction.		

The organization then makes entries in the unrestricted net asset class to show the receipt of the cash and reclassification to satisfy the program restriction. The reclassification is not a revenue in the unrestricted net asset class because the revenue from the contribution has already been recognized once in the temporarily restricted net asset class. A key concept is that the appropriate receiving net asset class should recognize revenue once and only once. The entries in the *unrestricted net asset class* follow:

(3)	Cash	40,000	
	Reclassification into Unrestricted Net Assets—Satisfaction of Program Restriction		40,000
	Receipt of resources from the temporarily restricted net asset class due to satisfaction of use restriction.		
(4)	Expenses	40,000	
	Cash		40,000
	Expenses for research program.		

Some not-for-profit entities use the term *net assets released from restriction* instead of *reclassification*. The purpose is the same; the resources are released from a restricted net asset class and assigned or transferred to another net asset class.

It is very important to note that the restricted net asset classes, either temporarily or permanently, do not report expenses on the organization's statement of activities. The (temporarily or permanently) restricted net asset classes report restricted contribution revenue and any restricted investment income/losses but cannot report any expenses. Expenses are reported *only* in the unrestricted net asset class. Thus, the reclassification entry records the transfer of the resources from a restricted to the unrestricted net asset class. The reclassification and transfer are made when appropriate evidence is provided to the restricted net asset class that the cash can be released because the temporary restriction has been satisfied or the permanent restriction is no longer valid. The reclassification entry ensures that the unrestricted net asset class is spending the resources according to the donor's wishes.

Additional Standards for Not-for-Profit Entities

ASC 958 provides additional guidance specific to not-for-profit entities. It covers several important accounting issues including, but not limited to: (1) depreciation, (2) accounting for investments, (3) accounting for general contributions, (4) accounting for transfers of assets to a not-for-profit organization that raises or holds contributions for others, and (5) mergers and acquisitions of not-for-profit organizations.

Accounting for Depreciation

ASC 958-360 requires that private, not-for-profit entities must show depreciation for long-lived tangible assets other than works of art or historical treasures that have cultural, aesthetic, or historical value worth preserving perpetually and whose holders have the ability to preserve that value and are doing so. The depreciation is reported as an expense for the period. **ASC 958-360** also requires disclosure of (1) depreciation for the period, (2) the total of each of the major classes of depreciable assets, (3) the accumulated depreciation at the balance sheet date, and (4) the method used to compute depreciation for the major classes of depreciable assets.

Accounting for Investments

ASC 958-320 and **958-325** extend to not-for-profit organizations the basic standard of fair value for investments that is presented in **ASC 320** on investments. **ASC 958** specifies that fair value should be the measurement basis for investments in all debt securities and in equity securities that have readily determinable fair values other than those accounted for under the equity method in accordance with **ASC 323 and 325.** Note that **ASC 958** requires that debt securities be valued at fair value. Investment income for the period includes interest or dividends and the changes in fair value. Changes in the fair value of investments in temporarily or permanently restricted net assets are recognized in accordance with donor specifications as to the income. Otherwise, investment income is reported as a change in unrestricted net assets.

Accounting for General Contributions

ASC 958-605 establishes the guidelines for private, not-for-profit entities to account for contributions. They can be of cash, other assets, or a promise to give (a pledge). The general rule is that contributions are measured at their fair value and are recognized as revenues or gains in the period pledged. The contributions are reported as unrestricted support or, if there are donor-imposed restrictions, as restricted support. A private, not-for-profit entity does not need to recognize contributions of works of art, historical treasures, and similar assets if the donated items are added to collections that (1) are held for public exhibition, education, or research, (2) are protected, cared for, and preserved, and (3) have an organizational policy that proceeds from the sales of collection items are to be used to acquire other items for collections.

Contributions of services are recognized as revenue with an equivalent amount recorded as an expenditure if the services received (1) create or enhance nonfinancial assets or (2) require specialized skills, are provided by individuals possessing those skills, and typically need to be purchased if not donated. Examples of contributed services are specialized skills provided by accountants, architects, doctors, teachers, and other professionals. Some religious-based colleges record revenue with an offsetting amount to an expense for the fair value of contributed lay teaching services. This recognition is made to report the full cost of the teaching mission of these private colleges.

Accounting for Asset Transfers to a Not-for-Profit That Raises or Holds Others' Contributions

ASC 958-605 also establishes the accounting for contributions made to foundations or other similar organizations that raise resources for not-for-profit entities. It defines three parties to the typical contribution process. The *donor* initially provides the resources. The *recipient organization* receives the assets from the donor. The *beneficiary* eventually receives the assets through the recipient organization as specified by the donor.

Many not-for-profit, private colleges and universities have a foundation that is responsible for raising financial support from alumni and other donors. Typically, these foundations are institutionally related to the college or university and use its assets for the organization's benefit. In most cases, when the donor contributes the assets to the foundation (the recipient), it records an increase in assets and a contribution revenue for the fair value of the donation. Usually these assets are temporarily restricted until the foundation transfers them to the college or university. When the foundation does transfer the assets to the university (the beneficiary), the foundation records an expense and a decrease in its assets. The college or university normally has an interest in the foundation's net assets and at the time of the donation to the foundation, recognizes the change in its interest in the university foundation, usually as a temporarily restricted net asset, unless the donor specified a permanent restriction on the donation. Then when the college or university actually receives the assets, it increases the specific assets received and decreases its interest in the net assets of the foundation. The institutionally related foundation recognizes the contribution revenue when it receives the donation.

> **FYI**
>
> Some recipient organizations, such as United Way, fund-raise to benefit a number of not-for-profits. Donors may name the specific recipient of their gifts or they may give to United Way without a restriction as to how to use the gift. When the donor restricts a contribution to a specific beneficiary, United Way acts as an agent and recognizes an increase in its assets and records a liability to the specified beneficiary. The donor-specified organization records an increase in net assets, usually as a receivable, and records contribution revenue at the time of the donation. When transferring the assets to the specified beneficiaries, United Way decreases its liabilities and assets. For unrestricted donations for which United Way may determine their best uses, it records an increase in its assets and records unrestricted gifts as contribution revenue. When it distributes the assets, United Way records the expense and the decrease in its assets, and the beneficiary records contribution revenue for the fair value of the assets transferred.

Finally, **ASC 958** states that in the case of nonfinancial assets such as artwork, the recipient organization (for example, the university foundation or United Way) may choose whether to record the fair value of these nonfinancial assets in its books. Typically, they will be transferred to the beneficiary, which must record all contributed nonfinancial assets at their fair values when received.

Mergers and Acquisitions of Not-for-Profit Organizations

ASC 958-805 provides guidance to not-for-profit entities for the initial accounting for a merger or acquisition of either another not-for-profit entity or a business. It also indicates that when two not-for-profit entities merge, the newly formed entity should account for the merger using the carryover method. Thus, the new not-for-profit entity measures the assets and liabilities in its financial statements on the merger date at the amounts reported in the merging entities' financial statements prepared in accordance with GAAP. The standard allows the new entity to adjust the amounts of those assets and liabilities as necessary to reflect a consistent method of accounting if the two merging entities previously used different ones. **ASC 958-805-20** provides guidance for a not-for-profit entity's acquisition of another entity. It requires the recognition of identifiable assets acquired and liabilities assumed at their fair values at the date of the acquisition.[1] Goodwill would be the excess of the sum of (1) the value of the consideration transferred, (2) the fair value of any noncontrolling interest, and (3) any equity interest in the entity previously held over the net amount assigned to identifiable assets acquired and liabilities assumed.

[1] Certain exceptions to the fair value approach are applied to identifiable assets or liabilities for which other GAAP methods of valuation are required: certain inexhaustible collection items, conditional promises to give, operating leases, assets held for sale, deferred taxes, and pension and other postemployment benefits. Identifiable assets include intangible assets apart from goodwill.

ASC 958-805-35 requires that goodwill and intangible assets other than goodwill be assigned to reporting units that are acquired. Moreover, it specifies that an identifiable intangible asset that has a finite useful life be amortized over that useful life. An identifiable intangible asset that has an indefinite useful life must be tested at least annually for impairment by comparing its fair value with its carrying value.

COLLEGES AND UNIVERSITIES[2]

LO 19-2

Understand financial reporting rules for not-for-profit colleges and universities.

Advanced StudyGuide .com

The United States has more than 4,000 colleges and universities. Some offer two-year programs, some offer four-year programs, and others offer a wide selection of both undergraduate and graduate programs. Public and private institutions provide a large variety of liberal arts, science, and professional programs for our society. Public colleges and universities receive a significant portion of their operating resources from federal and state governments. Private, not-for-profit colleges and universities receive most of their resources from tuition and fees.

Special Conventions of Revenue and Expenditure Recognition

Both public and private colleges and universities follow several conventions of recognizing revenue and expenses as follows:

1. *Tuition and fee remissions/waivers and uncollectible accounts.* Tuition and fees are important revenue sources for colleges and universities. In their account, they recognize the full amount of the standard rate for tuition and fees as revenue. The accounting for university-sponsored scholarships, fellowships, tuition and fee remissions, or waivers depends on whether the recipient provides any services in exchange. For example, if a student receives a university-sponsored scholarship that does not require any employment-type work as a result, the university accounts for this as a deduction from revenue. On the other hand, if the student must provide employment-type work, the university accounts for the scholarship as an expense. Another example is the tuition remission (reduction) often given to graduate students who accept teaching assistantships. The university records revenue for the graduate student's tuition at the standard rate and then records the tuition remission as an expense of the year in which the graduate student is a teaching assistant.

FYI

In 2011, the University of Washington received 38.8 percent of its operating revenues from federal, state and local, and nongovernmental grants. Tuition and fees constituted 17.5 percent of its operating revenues.

2. *Tuition and fee reimbursements for withdrawals from coursework.* Students withdrawing from classes after the beginning of the class term may be able to collect a reimbursement or return of some of the tuition and fees paid at the beginning of the term. Colleges and universities account for these reimbursements of tuition and fees as a reduction of revenue. When the check to the student is approved, the university debits revenue from tuition and fee reimbursements and credits cash or accounts payable.

3. *Academic terms that span two fiscal periods.* Some academic terms may begin in one fiscal year of the university and be completed in another. This is often true for summer school sessions. For example, many universities end their fiscal years on June 30 of each year. The College and University Audit Guide (published by the AICPA) recommends that colleges and universities recognize tuition fees as revenue in the fiscal year in which (1) the term is predominantly conducted and (2) expenses are incurred to finance that term. However, more recent practices by the National Association of College and University Business Officers (NACUBO) recommend the use of the accrual basis of accounting, which requires that the tuition revenue and costs be allocated proportionately

[2] To view a video explanation of this topic, visit advancedstudyguide.com.

to the two fiscal years based on the relative portions of the academic term. Many colleges and universities are electing to follow the NACUBO recommendation.

For example, if an institution collects tuition and fees at the beginning of summer school in which two weeks occur in the first fiscal year and the remaining six weeks fall in the second fiscal year, the AICPA audit guide's approach would result in recording the collections as a debit to Cash and a credit to Deferred Revenue for their entire amount. The institution would then recognize the deferred revenue and any deferred expenses as revenue and expenses of the next fiscal period in which most of the term is conducted. Under the NACUBO approach, the institution would recognize revenue in the first fiscal period for two-eighths of the tuition and fees and record the remaining six-eighths as a deferred revenue. The NACUBO method also would recognize the related expenses that correspond with the first two weeks of the summer session in the first fiscal period and the remaining six-eighths of the revenue and related expenses in the second fiscal period for the last six weeks of the summer session. NACUBO feels its approach follows the principles of accrual accounting.

Board-Designated Funds

The governing board, sometimes termed *regents* or *trustees,* may designate unrestricted current fund resources for specific purposes in future periods. These *board-designated funds* are internal designations similar to appropriations of retained earnings for a commercial entity. The governing board may make any designation at its own volition. For example, it might designate $50,000 of future spending in the unrestricted current fund for the development of a foreign student counseling office. Such designations are usually reported in the footnotes to the financial statements but also may be shown as allocations of part of the fund balance in the unrestricted current fund balance sheet. However, **ASC 958** specifies that these board-designated funds may not be reported as restricted net assets because only external, donor-imposed restrictions can result in restricted net assets.

Public Colleges and Universities

The GASB specifies the accounting and reporting for public colleges and universities. **GASB Statement No. 35,** "Basic Financial Statements—and Management's Discussion and Analysis—for Public Colleges and Universities" (GASB 35), issued in 1999, requires that these institutions follow the standards for governmental entities as specified in **GASB 34.** Most public institutions are special-purpose governmental entities engaged in only business-type activities because most do not have their own taxing authority. These special-purpose governmental entities present only the financial statements required for enterprise funds and then are included as the state government's component units. However, some community colleges do have their own taxing authority because they are special-purpose governmental entities engaged in both governmental and business-type activities. These community colleges provide both fund-based and governmentwide financial statements.

Private Colleges and Universities

The FASB specifies the accounting and financial reporting standards for private colleges and universities. Although many of them are not-for-profit entities, some, such as the University of Phoenix, are profit seeking. Accounting for profit-seeking educational entities is similar to accounting for any commercial entity and is not covered in this chapter.

The three financial statements required for private, not-for-profit colleges and universities are the (1) statement of financial position, (2) statement of activities, and (3) statement of cash flows. Private colleges and universities are free to select any account structure that best serves their management and financial reporting needs, but some choose to use fund accounting similar to that of governmental entities. Fund accounting creates an accounting discipline and provides an accounting vehicle to track revenues and expenses related to specific programs (see Figure 19–1 for an overview of the accounting and financial reporting of colleges and universities.) We discussed the financial reporting for public, special-purpose governmental entities in Chapters 17 and 18 of this textbook.

The statement of financial position for Sol City College, a private, not-for-profit college (Figure 19–2) presents all assets and equities in a single statement. Note that the net assets are separated into three categories: (1) unrestricted, (2) temporarily restricted, and (3) permanently restricted. The unrestricted category includes all assets, including property, plant, and equipment whose use the provider or donor did not restrict. Temporarily restricted assets include those that the donor has designated for specific use or for use in subsequent periods. Term endowments and funds donated to support special activities and for unrestricted (or other) use in future periods are included as temporarily restricted net assets. Permanently restricted assets typically include only the principal balance of permanent endowments.

The statement of activities in Figure 19–3 presents separately the revenues and expenses of the unrestricted, temporarily restricted, and permanently restricted net asset categories. It also shows the transfer of assets among the three categories during the period. For example, contributions received in 20X1 and available for use in 20X2 are shown as a transfer from temporarily restricted to unrestricted net assets in the statement of activities for 20X2. Auxiliary enterprises include activities such as operating a student union bookstore, cafeterias, and residence halls.

The statement of cash flows in Figure 19–4 is similar to that used for commercial entities. Either the direct or indirect method may be used to compute cash flows from operating activities. Activities in the restricted funds are noted separately from those in the unrestricted funds.

HEALTH CARE PROVIDERS

LO 19-3

Understand financial reporting rules and make basic journal entries for not-for-profit health care providers.

The health care environment is currently undergoing a revolution. Rapidly increasing costs of providing medical care are forcing hospitals to merge at an increasing rate in order to consolidate the types of services offered. The cost of new technology also is requiring health care providers to reevaluate their missions to the communities they serve.

Although the major focus of this section is on hospitals, the accounting and financial reporting guidelines for them are the same as those used by all health care providers included within the scope of the AICPA's Audit and Accounting Guide for Health Care Organizations,[3] which applies to the following health care entities:

1. Clinics, medical group practices, individual practice associations, individual practitioners, emergency care facilities, laboratories, surgery centers, and other ambulatory care organizations.
2. Continuing-care retirement communities (CCRCs).
3. Health maintenance organizations (HMOs) and similar prepaid health care plans.
4. Home health agencies.
5. Hospitals.
6. Nursing homes that provide skilled, intermediate, and less intensive levels of health care.
7. Drug and alcohol rehabilitation centers and other rehabilitation facilities.

The AICPA audit guide serves as an important authoritative source in selecting accounting and financial reporting procedures for health care providers. The hospital financial statements illustrated in this chapter incorporate the disclosure standards of **ASC 958** as presented and amplified in the AICPA's Audit and Accounting Guide for Health Care Organizations.

[3] The AICPA periodically revises its audit and accounting guides for specialized industries. It was most recently updated in 2011.

FIGURE 19–1 Overview of the Accounting and Reporting of Colleges and Universities

	Public, Special-Purpose Governmental Entities		Private Entities	
	Engaged in Both Governmental and Business-Type Activities	**Engaged in Only Business-Type Activities**	**Not for Profit**	**Profit Seeking**
Accounting and reporting standards	GASB	GASB	FASB	FASB
Accounting structure	Funds	Funds	Not required but many use fund-based structure	Account-based, same as for commercial businesses
Distinguishing features	Separate governmental entity with own taxing authority	Generally reported as a component unit of a state government	Net assets classified into three classes: 1. Unrestricted 2. Temporarily restricted 3. Permanently restricted	Same as for profit-seeking businesses
Financial statements	Both fund-based and governmentwide financial statements as presented in Chapters 17 and 18	Same as for an enterprise fund as presented in Chapter 18	Three basic financial statements: 1. Statement of Financial Position 2. Statement of Activities 3. Statement of Cash Flows	Same as for profit-seeking businesses

FIGURE 19–2
Statement of Financial Position for a Private College

SOL CITY COLLEGE
Statement of Financial Position
June 30, 20X2 and 20X1

	20X2	20X1
Cash	$ 579,000	$ 514,000
Investments, at Fair Value	10,763,000	9,536,000
Deposits with Trustees	125,000	122,000
Accounts Receivable	161,000	182,000
Less: Allowance for Uncollectibles	(13,000)	(14,000)
Loans to Students, Faculty & Staff	275,000	190,000
Inventories	45,000	40,000
Prepaid Expenses	14,000	10,000
Property, Plant & Equipment (net)	20,330,000	19,970,000
Total Assets	$32,279,000	$30,550,000
Accounts Payable	$ 70,000	$ 53,000
Accrued Liabilities	10,000	8,000
Students' Deposits	15,000	18,000
Deferred Credits	15,000	10,000
Annuities Payable	1,080,000	1,155,000
Notes Payable	50,000	—
Bonds Payable	1,300,000	1,200,000
Mortgage Payable	200,000	100,000
Deposits Held in Custody	55,000	45,000
Total Liabilities	$ 2,795,000	$ 2,589,000
Net Assets:		
Unrestricted	$20,221,000	$20,294,000
Temporarily Restricted by Donors	5,363,000	4,307,000
Permanently Restricted by Donors	3,900,000	3,360,000
Total Net Assets	$29,484,000	$27,961,000
Total Liabilities & Net Assets	$32,279,000	$30,550,000

Hospital Accounting

Advanced StudyGuide .com

The United States has about 5,700 hospitals. Some are not-for-profit hospitals managed by charities, and government agencies manage a large number of them. For example, many universities operate an affiliated hospital. The federal government operates several hundred hospitals, including those offering health care to veterans. More than 1,000 hospitals are investor-owned, for-profit companies. The guidelines that each type follows are:

1. The not-for-profit hospitals use the FASB's accounting and reporting requirements for not-for-profit organizations.
2. The governmental hospitals follow the GASB's accounting and reporting requirements.
3. The investor-owned, for-profit hospitals follow the FASB's accounting and reporting requirements that are the same for other profit-seeking business entities.

Investor-owned hospitals seek additional financial resources by selling stocks and issuing large amounts of debt. These profit-seeking hospitals provide the same types of financial reports as commercial entities. Not-for-profit hospitals present their financial results using a specific format required by the FASB; they often affiliated with a religious group or a civic association. Governmental hospitals managed by or affiliated with a governmental unit follow the GASB's accounting and reporting requirements. They are considered special-purpose entities engaged in business-type activities. As such, they present financial statements that are required for enterprise funds as presented in Chapter 18 of this textbook. Governmental hospitals then are included in the governmental entity's governmentwide financial statements.

FIGURE 19–3 Statement of Activities for a Private College

SOL CITY COLLEGE
Statement of Activities
For the Year Ended June 30, 20X2

	Unrestricted	Temporarily Restricted	Permanently Restricted	Total
Revenues, Gains, & Other Support:				
Tuition & Fees	$ 1,290,000			$ 1,290,000
Government Appropriations	650,000	$ 40,000		690,000
Government Grants & Contracts	20,000	300,000		320,000
Contributions	425,000	1,063,000	$ 495,000	1,983,000
Auxiliary Enterprises	1,100,000			1,100,000
Investment Income	265,000	139,000	15,000	419,000
Gain on Investments		69,000	25,000	94,000
Net Assets Transferred or Released from Restriction:				
Program Use Restriction	601,000	(601,000)		
Transferred to Restricted Funds	(101,000)	101,000		
Expired Term Endowment	50,000	(50,000)		
Transferred to Endowment		(5,000)	5,000	
Total Revenue, Gains & Other Support	$ 4,300,000	$1,056,000	$ 540,000	$ 5,896,000
Expenditures & Other Deductions:				
Instruction	$ 1,725,000			$ 1,725,000
Research	250,000			250,000
Public Service	77,000			77,000
Academic Support	125,000			125,000
Student Services	100,000			100,000
Scholarships & Fellowships	95,000			95,000
Institutional Support	275,000			275,000
Operation & Maintenance	110,000			110,000
Depreciation Expense	500,000			500,000
Interest Expense	106,000			106,000
Auxiliary Enterprises	915,000			915,000
Other Operating Costs	95,000			95,000
Total Expenses	$ 4,373,000	$ 0	$ 0	$ 4,373,000
Change in Net Assets	$ (73,000)	$1,056,000	$ 540,000	$ 1,523,000
Net Assets at Beginning of Year	20,294,000	4,307,000	3,360,000	27,961,000
Net Assets at End of Year	$20,221,000	$5,363,000	$3,900,000	$29,484,000

Two professional associations, the American Hospital Association (AHA) and the Hospital Financial Management Association (HFMA), are active in developing and improving hospital management, accounting, and financial reporting. Publications of both organizations can be useful to individuals seeking additional information on hospital accounting and reporting practices.

In this chapter, we assume that the hospital is a separate, not-for-profit reporting entity, not a component unit of any government. This chapter's focus is not-for-profit hospitals because of the large number of such hospitals and their special accounting and financial reporting issues.

Hospital Fund Structure

Although not required to do so, many hospitals have used a fund accounting structure for accounting purposes. In general, operating activities are carried on in the general fund, and a series of restricted funds can be used to account for assets whose use the donor has restricted. If separate funds are not maintained, all transactions are recorded in the general fund, and memorandum records show restricted amounts in the general fund. The presentation of financial statement information under **ASC 958** requires a

FIGURE 19–4 Statement of Cash Flows for a Private College

SOL CITY COLLEGE
Statement of Cash Flows
For the Year Ended June 30, 20X2

Cash flows from Operating Activities:			
Change in Net Assets			$1,523,000
Adjustments to Reconcile Changes in Net Assets to Net Cash Provided by Operating Activities:			
Depreciation		$ 500,000	
Increase in Deposits with Trustees		(3,000)	
Decrease in Accounts Receivable		20,000	
Increase in Loans to Students, Faculty & Staff		(85,000)	
Increase in Inventories		(5,000)	
Increase in Prepaid Expenses		(4,000)	
Increase in Accounts Payable		17,000	
Increase in Accrued Liabilities		2,000	
Decrease in Students' Deposits		(3,000)	
Increase in Deferred Credits		5,000	
Restricted Contributions & Investment Income:			
Contributions, Grants & Investment Income in Temporarily Restricted Funds	$(1,611,000)		
Contributions, Grants & Investment Income in Permanently Restricted Funds	(535,000)		
Total Restricted Contributions & Investment Income	$(2,146,000)	(2,146,000)	
Total Adjustments		$(1,702,000)	(1,702,000)
Net Cash Provided by Operating Activities			$ (179,000)
Cash Flows from Investing Activities:			
Acquisition of Property, Plant & Equipment		$ (920,000)	
Sale of Used Equipment		60,000	
Net Acquisition of Investments		(65,000)	
Flows Related to Restricted Items:			
Net Acquisition of Temporarily Restricted Investments	$ (112,000)		
Net Acquisition of Permanently Restricted Investments	(1,050,000)		
Net Cash Flow Related to Restricted Items	$(1,162,000)	(1,162,000)	
Net Cash Provided by Investing Activities			(2,087,000)
Cash Flows from Financing Activities:			
Decrease in Annuities Payable		$ (75,000)	
Increase in Notes Payable		50,000	
Increase in Bonds Payable		100,000	
Increase in Mortgage Payable		100,000	
Increase in Deposits Held in Custody		10,000	
Flows Related to Restricted Items:			
Contributions, Grants & Investment Income in Temporarily Restricted Funds	$ 1,611,000		
Contributions, Grants & Investment Income in Permanently Restricted Funds	535,000		
Cash Flows Related to Restricted Items	$ 2,146,000	$ 185,000	
Net Cash Provided by Financing Activities			2,331,000
Net Change in Cash			$ 65,000
Cash at the Beginning of the Year			514,000
Cash at the End of the Year			$ 579,000

distinction between net assets that are unrestricted, temporarily restricted, and permanently restricted. The following discussion of accounting and financial reporting for hospitals assumes that unrestricted net assets are accounted for in the general fund and that one or more separate funds are used to account for temporarily restricted and permanently restricted net assets.

All transactions involving the use of unrestricted net assets are recorded in the general fund. As such, it is the hospital's primary operating fund. Assets restricted as to the period of use or particular purposes are accounted for in restricted funds until the restriction is satisfied. When that happens, the hospital transfers (reclassifies) the assets from the restricted fund to the general (unrestricted) fund. It reports any expenses incurred in satisfying the restrictions as expenses in the general fund.

Restricted funds account for assets received from donors or other third parties who restricted their use. The restricted funds are often termed *holding* funds because they must hold the restricted assets and transfer expendable resources to the general fund for expenditure. See Figure 19–5 for an overview of the fund structure and the typical financial reporting for hospitals.

General Fund The ***general fund*** accounts for the resources received and expended in the hospital's primary health care mission using the accrual method to measure fully all expenses of providing services during the period. Depreciation is included in the operating expenses. Fixed assets are included in the fund based on the theory that the governing board may use these assets in any manner desired.

The governing board may establish ***board-designated resources*** within the general fund for such purposes as hospital expansion and debt retirement. Funds designated in this manner are considered to be part of the unrestricted funds, but this designation provides information on the intended use of the resources.

Donor-Restricted Funds All ***restricted funds*** account for resources whose use the donor restricts. For financial reporting purposes, a distinction is made between temporarily and permanently restricted funds. The major *temporarily restricted* funds are (1) specific-purpose funds, (2) time-restricted funds, and (3) plant replacement and expansion funds. *Permanently restricted funds* are assets that must be held into perpetuity and generally are included in an endowment fund. Hospitals also may have restricted loan funds and annuity and life income funds; however, few hospitals use them, and they are not discussed in this chapter.

Specific-purpose funds are restricted for ***specific operating purposes.*** For example, a donor may specify that a $25,000 donation be used for maternity care. The donation is held in the specific-purpose fund until the maternity expenditure is approved in the general fund. Once approved, the specific-purpose fund transfers the resources to the general fund.

Time-restricted funds account for assets received or pledged by donors for use in future periods. The passage of time satisfies the donor's restriction. A pledge received in 20X1 to contribute a stated amount in 20X2 for unrestricted purposes is included in the time-restricted fund in the balance sheet prepared at December 31, 20X1.

FIGURE 19–5
Overview of Hospital Accounting and Reporting

	Fund Groups				
		Restricted			
	General	**Specific-Purpose**	**Time-Restricted**	**Plant Replacement and Expansion**	**Endowment**
Distinguishing features		Resources restricted for specific operating purposes	Resources not available until date specified by donor	Resources restricted for additions to plant assets	Principal preserved as specified by donor
Financial statements	Balance Sheet				
	Statement of Operations				
	Statement of Changes in Net Assets				
	Statement of Cash Flows				

Plant replacement and expansion restricted funds account for contributions to be used only for additions to fixed assets. When the general fund approves or makes the appropriate expenditures for the fixed assets, the plant replacement and expansion fund transfers the resources to the general fund.

Endowment funds account for resources when the principal must be preserved. Their income is usually available for either a restricted or a general purpose. Endowments may be either permanent or term. Term endowments are for limited time periods, for example, 5 or 10 years, or until a specific event occurs, such as the donor's death. After the term expires, the governing board uses the principal of the fund in accordance with the gift agreement.

Financial Statements for a Not-for-Profit Hospital

Separate, not-for-profit hospitals issue four basic financial statements: (1) balance sheet, (2) statement of operations, (3) statement of changes in net assets, and (4) statement of cash flows. Comparative data for prior fiscal periods are normally presented within each statement. Each of the four statements is demonstrated in the comprehensive illustration presented later in this chapter.

Balance Sheet

The *balance sheet* presents the total assets, liabilities, and net assets of the organization as a whole.

Receivables Receivables may include amounts due from patients, third-party payers, other insurers of health care, pledges or grants, and interfund transactions. Receivables should be reported at the anticipated realizable amount. Thus, these amounts may include reductions due to contractual agreements with third-party payers or provider practices, such as allowing courtesy discounts to medical staff members and employees. An allowance for uncollectibles is recognized for estimated bad debts. Note that not-for-profit hospitals recognize estimated uncollectibles from providing services as bad debts expense. Charity care occurs when hospitals provide health care services to a patient who has demonstrated in accordance with the hospital's established criteria an inability to pay. In these cases, charity care does not qualify for recognition as either receivables or revenue in the hospital's financial statements. The determination of a charity care case may not be possible when the patient is admitted, but before reducing the amount owed, the hospital must determine that the person does meet the necessary qualifications for charity care. Receivables from pledges of future contributions are reported in the period the pledge is made, net of an allowance for uncollectible amounts.

Investments Investments are initially recorded at cost if purchased or at fair value at the date of receipt if received as a gift. Subsequently, investor-owned, *profit-seeking hospitals* report equity and debt securities in accordance with **ASC 320,** which establishes three portfolios of investments: trading securities, available-for-sale securities, and held-to-maturity debt securities. The accounting and reporting of the investment differ according to the category. For *nonprofit hospitals,* equity securities with readily determinable fair values and all investments in debt securities are measured at fair value in accordance with **ASC 958.** The Audit and Accounting Guide for Health Care Organizations states that the investment return (including realized and unrealized gains and losses) not restricted by donors should be classified as changes in unrestricted net assets in the hospital's statement of operations. The investment return designated for current operations is included above the operation performance indicator line (Excess of Revenues, Gains, and Other Support over Expenses) reflecting operations; the investment return in excess of amounts designated for current operations is reported in the statement of operations below the operating performance indicator line. Investment returns restricted by donors or by law are reported as changes in net assets in the appropriate restricted funds. For *governmental health care entities,* **GASB Statement No. 31,** "Accounting and Financial Reporting for

Certain Investments and for External Investment Pools" (GASB 31), specifies the general rule of fair value accounting for investments.

For these three types of hospitals, investments in stock accounted for under the equity method are reported in accordance with **ASC 323 and 325.** Some hospitals receive income from trusts that donors have established with fiduciaries such as banks. If the hospital does not own the trust or its investments, the independent trusts are not the hospital's assets and are not reported on its balance sheet. Footnote disclosure of major independent endowments or trust agreements that benefit the hospital may be made.

Plant Assets Property, plant, and equipment is reported with any accumulated depreciation. Depreciation is recorded in the general fund because the use of assets is part of the cost of providing medical services. The assets are reported in the general fund because they are available for use in any manner the governing board deems necessary.

Assets Whose Use Is Limited Separate disclosure should be made for assets whose donor has restricted their use or the board of directors has designated for special use. Such funds may come from a variety of sources. For example, grant monies received for cancer research are reported as funds restricted for specific purposes and classified as temporarily restricted until used in support of research. Funds contributed to assist in constructing a new children's wing of the hospital are reported as restricted for plant replacement and expansion and classified as temporarily restricted until used in construction. Funds received for permanent investment in the principal of an endowment fund are reported as permanently restricted. Only those donor-restricted funds are classified as restricted; thus, assets set aside for identified purposes by the governing board and over which the board retains control are not classified as restricted but are regarded as ***assets whose use is limited.***

Long-Term Debt The hospital also must account for its long-term debt and pay the principal and interest as they become due. The debt is shown in the balance sheet. This practice differs from that used by most governmental entities that establish a separate debt service fund to service debt.

Net Assets The hospital segregates its net assets into (1) ***unrestricted net assets*** available for use at the discretion of the hospital staff and board of directors, (2) ***temporarily restricted net assets*** available for use when specific events established by the donor are satisfied, and (3) ***permanently restricted net assets*** whose donor has restricted their use.

Statement of Operations

The results of not-for-profit hospitals' operations are reported in a *statement of operations,* which is termed the *statement of activities.* It includes the revenues, expenses, gains and losses, and other transactions affecting the unrestricted net assets during the period. Note that only those transactions in the general fund are reported on the statement of operations. Transactions affecting only the restricted funds are *not* shown on it but are reported on the statement of changes in net assets. Gains and losses from transactions that are peripheral or ancillary to the provision of health care services are reported separately from net patient service revenue. The statement of operations should report an operating ***performance indicator*** of the results of the hospital's operating activities for the period. This performance indicator should include both operating income (loss) for the period and other income available for current operations. **ASC 958** requires that net assets released from restrictions for use in operations be included before the performance indicator line on the statement of activities, generally termed *above the line.* This is so because the transfer of net assets from the restricted group of assets for entity's operations in the unrestricted group of net assets can then be matched with the expenses incurred to fulfill the operating restriction. The title of the performance indicator should be descriptive, such as the "Excess of Operating Revenues, Gains, and Other Support over Operating Expenses."

Other changes in the unrestricted net assets during the period should be reported after the performance indicator, generally termed *below the line.* These changes include investment return in excess of amounts designated for current operations as defined by **ASC 958.** For example, a hospital's board of directors could reserve a portion of the investment return from the revaluation of investments for use in future periods, thus making them unavailable for current operations. The AICPA's audit guide for hospitals indicates that the investment return from other than trading securities should be presented below the operating performance indicator line, and the investment return from trading securities should be presented above it. However, an audit guide is lower than an FASB standard in the hierarchy of generally accepted accounting principles. Other changes reported below the operating performance indicator line include transfers from restricted net assets of resources used to purchase property and equipment. Note that the statement of operations must separately report those items related to the acquisition of property or equipment from those related to operating activities.

Net Patient Service Revenue Net patient service revenue represents the hospital's revenue from inpatient and outpatient care excluding charity care and contractual adjustments. Net patient service revenue represents the billings for services provided and the hospital's earning capacity. Many hospitals are required to perform a certain amount of charity care for which they recognize no revenue. The charity cases are imposed by terms of certain federal medical care grant programs. Charity care helps ensure that indigent persons living in the region served by the hospital obtain adequate medical services. When a hospital provides charity care, it recognizes no revenue but presents disclosure of the estimated amount in the footnotes to the financial statements.

Contractual Adjustments Contractual adjustments constitute a major deduction from gross patient service revenue. They result from the involvement of third-party payers in the medical reimbursement process. Insurance companies or governmental units (especially the federal government) reimburse less than the full standard rate for medical services provided to patients covered by insurance or government-provided services such as Medicare. These third-party payers may stipulate limits on the amount of costs they will pay. A hospital may have a standard rate for a specific service but may contract with the third-party payer to accept a lower amount for that service. For example, Medicare establishes specific reimbursement rates for various services, termed a "diagnosis-related group" (DRG). The hospital makes a contractual adjustment from its normal service charge as a deduction from gross Patient Service Revenue.

Income from Ancillary Programs Income from ancillary programs represents the income earned from nonpatient sources such as a hospital's television rentals, sales in cafeterias and gift shops, parking fees, and tuition on hospital-provided educational programs. The income reported typically represents the net earnings from such operations rather than the gross receipts.

Interfund Transfers Holding assets in a restricted fund when the donor-specified requirements have been satisfied is not appropriate. For example, when contributions received to purchase plant and equipment have been used to purchase new assets or contributions received for use in educational programs have been used for their stated purposes, the funds should be transferred from the restricted fund to the general fund. For financial reporting purposes, this transfer is reported as Net Assets Released in the statement of operations and is shown as an addition to the general fund. If the interfund transfer to the general fund is to be used for operations, the general fund reports it above the operating performance indicator line in the statement of operations. If the interfund transfer to the general fund is to be used for acquiring long-term assets, the general fund reports it below the performance indicator line in the statement of operations.

General Fund Expenses The major expenses in the general fund are for nursing services, other professional services, depreciation, bad debts, and the general and administrative costs of the hospital. These costs are recognized on the accrual basis of accounting similar to their recognition by commercial entities. Hospitals that self-insure for such costs should recognize an expense and a liability for such costs in the period during which the incidents that give rise to the claims occur if it is probable that liabilities have been incurred and the amounts of the losses can be reasonably estimated. Any expenses related to fund-raising should be classified separately.

Donations Hospitals often receive a wide variety of services from volunteers. For example, retired physicians and pharmacists may voluntarily work part-time in their professional roles. In addition, the hospital may receive donations of supplies or equipment. The rules on accounting for donations and contributions to hospitals follow:

1. *Donated services.* Because placing a value on donated services is often difficult, their values are usually not recorded. However, if the following conditions exist, the estimated value of the donated services is reported as an expense and a corresponding amount is reported as contributions. **ASC 958** specifies that a contribution of services should be recognized if the services received (*a*) create or enhance nonfinancial assets or (*b*) require specialized skills, are provided by individuals possessing those skills, and would typically be purchased if not donated.
2. *Donated assets.* Donated assets are reported at fair market value at the date of the contribution:

   a. Donated assets are reported as contributions in the statement of operations if unrestricted. For example, a donation of medical supplies is recorded as a contribution in the general fund in the period received.

   b. Donated assets that the donor restricts in use are recognized as contribution revenue in the temporarily restricted or permanently restricted fund upon receipt. Note that contribution revenue is recognized in the appropriate restricted fund when the restricted donation is received. When the restriction no longer applies, the hospital transfers donated assets to the general fund. For example, when the general fund purchases assets with resources restricted for that purpose, the transfer is made from the restricted fund as a debit to Net Assets Released from Restriction and a credit to Cash. The general fund accounts for the transfer of cash with a debit to Cash and a credit to Net Assets Released from Restriction, which is reported in the general fund's statement of operations.

   If the hospital does not use a fund structure for restricted assets, it accounts for their contribution as a debit to Cash and a credit to Net Assets Restricted, which is reported on the hospital's balance sheet. However, the general fund's statement of operations reports the donated assets only after the restriction is no longer applicable and the assets have become available for use in the general fund. When the assets become available for use in the general fund, it reports their transfer for use in the hospital's operations on the general fund's statement of operations and reclassifies them from the restricted net asset class to the unrestricted net asset class.

Appropriate expense accounts are charged as the donated assets are consumed. For example, donated supplies such as medicines, linen, and disposable medical items are charged to an expense as used from inventory. For donated physical plant or equipment having an estimated economic life of more than one year, depreciation is charged to each period in which the plant or equipment is used.

Statement of Changes in Net Assets

The third of the four financial statements for a not-for-profit hospital is the *statement of changes in net assets.* It presents the changes in all three categories of net assets: unrestricted, temporarily restricted, and permanently restricted. Donor-restricted contributions are reported in the appropriate category of restricted net assets. Net assets released from restrictions are shown as deductions from restricted net assets and as transfers to the unrestricted net assets. The reason for this release could be the completion of a time restriction, the fulfillment of a use restriction, or the satisfaction of any other donor-specified restriction.

Statement of Cash Flows

The fourth, and final, financial statement for a not-for-profit hospital is the *statement of cash flows.* Its format is similar to that for commercial entities and is presented as part of the comprehensive illustration in the next section of this chapter.

Comprehensive Illustration of Hospital Accounting and Financial Reporting

Sol City Community Hospital, a not-for-profit hospital operated by a community group, provides medical care for the surrounding region. The hospital has established the following funds: (1) general, (2) specific-purpose, (3) time-restricted, (4) plant replacement and expansion, and (5) endowment.

Entries to record transactions in each of the funds during the 20X2 fiscal year, ending December 31, 20X2, are provided in the next section. First we present the financial statements for the period and then the transactions from which these statements resulted. Note that the balance sheet for both the general and the restricted funds in Figure 19–6 is presented in what is generally termed an *aggregated style* rather than a *columnar* or *layered style* that would show each fund's financial position separately. The selection of display formats is the choice of the hospital's governing board, but the aggregated format for the entity as a whole is more in keeping with the recommendations of **ASC 958.** An analysis of the composition of the net assets held as temporarily and permanently restricted at December 31, 20X2 and 20X1, provides the following amounts:

	Dec. 31, 20X2	Net Change	Dec. 31, 20X1
Temporarily restricted:			
Plant replacement and expansion fund			
Cash	$ 50,000	$(150,000)	$200,000
Pledges receivable	15,000	(105,000)	120,000
Investments	140,000	122,000	18,000
Net assets	$ 205,000	$(133,000)	$338,000
Specific-Purpose fund			
Cash	$ 3,000	$ 1,000	$ 2,000
Investments	20,000	0	20,000
Net assets	$ 23,000	$ 1,000	$ 22,000
Time-Restricted fund			
Cash	$ 2,000	$ 0	$ 2,000
Contributions receivable	0	(12,000)	12,000
Investments	196,000	0	196,000
Net assets	$ 198,000	$ (12,000)	$210,000
Permanently restricted:			
Endowment fund			
Cash	$ 25,000	$ 15,000	$ 10,000
Investments	1,190,000	400,000	790,000
Net assets	$1,215,000	$ 415,000	$800,000

The specific-purpose fund and the time-restricted fund contain resources that will be available for operations as the restrictions are met.

We present the statement of operations in Figure 19–7, the statement of changes in net assets in Figure 19–8, and the statement of cash flows in Figure 19–9 after we discuss the journal entries for 20X2 for Sol City Community Hospital.

General Fund

The hospital presents the transactions in the general fund for 20X2 in accordance with their relative degree of importance in its operations. The first series of entries are for the period's revenues generated from patient care and associated operating expenses.

Net Patient Care Revenue The hospital provides patient services of $2,600,000 measured by standard rates. From this amount, it deducts $240,000 for contractual adjustments with third-party payers, which results in a net patient revenue of $2,360,000. It does not

FIGURE 19–6
Balance Sheet for a Not-for-Profit Hospital

SOL CITY COMMUNITY HOSPITAL
Balance Sheet
December 31, 20X2 and 20X1

	20X2	20X1
Assets		
Current:		
Cash	$ 295,000	$ 14,000
Receivables	460,000	400,000
Less: Estimated Uncollectibles	(40,000)	(30,000)
Contributions Receivable	0	12,000
Inventories	50,000	60,000
Prepaid Expenses	15,000	20,000
Total Current Assets	$ 780,000	$ 476,000
Assets Limited as to Use:		
Cash Restricted as to Use for Plant Expansion & Endowment	$ 75,000	$ 210,000
Pledges Receivable Restricted for Plant Expansion & Replacement	15,000	120,000
Investments Restricted as to Use for Plant Expansion & Endowment	1,330,000	808,000
Total Limited Assets	$1,420,000	$1,138,000
Investments (at fair value)	$ 681,000	$ 716,000
Property, Plant & Equipment	$3,375,000	$3,200,000
Less: Accumulated Depreciation	(1,150,000)	(1,000,000)
Net Property, Plant & Equipment	$2,225,000	$2,200,000
Total Assets	$5,106,000	$4,530,000
Liabilities & Net Assets		
Current:		
Notes Payable to Bank	$ 65,000	$ 70,000
Current Portion of Long-Term Debt	50,000	60,000
Accounts Payable	50,000	90,000
Accrued Expenses	30,000	25,000
Estimated Malpractice Costs Payable	30,000	0
Advances from Third Parties	160,000	125,000
Deferred Revenue	5,000	5,000
Total Current Liabilities	$ 390,000	$ 375,000
Long-Term Debt:		
Mortgage Payable	1,050,000	1,100,000
Total Liabilities	$1,440,000	$1,475,000
Net Assets:		
Unrestricted	$2,025,000	$1,685,000
Temporarily Restricted by Donors	426,000	570,000
Permanently Restricted by Donors	1,215,000	800,000
Total Net Assets	$3,666,000	$3,055,000
Total Liabilities & Net Assets	$5,106,000	$4,530,000

recognize costs of Charity care as a revenue or reduction in revenue but recognizes related costs as operating expenses. Although the hospital does not explicitly recognize charity care on the statement of operations, footnote disclosures in the financial reports should provide the amount of charity care.

		Debit	Credit
(5)	Accounts Receivable	2,600,000	
	Patient Services Revenue		2,600,000
	Gross charges at standard rates.		

		Debit	Credit
(6)	Patient Services Revenue	240,000	
	Accounts Receivable		240,000
	Deduction from gross patient services revenue for contractual adjustments.		

Revenue from Ancillary Programs The hospital receives income in 20X2 from providing nonpatient services that include operating a cafeteria and gift shop and from vending machine commissions.

(7)	Cash	30,000	
	Revenue from Cafeteria Sales		20,000
	Revenue from Gift Shop Sales		4,000
	Revenue from Vending Machine Commissions		6,000
	Income from ancillary services.		

Operating Expenses The hospital incurs $2,600,000 in operating expenses for nursing and other professional care, general and administrative expenses, bad debts expense, and depreciation. Not-for-profit hospitals account for estimated uncollectibles from services provided as an operating expense. Fiscal Services Expense includes interest expense on the hospital's debt. The hospital recognized $30,000 in estimated malpractice costs that are probable and reasonably estimated and made cash payments for $2,125,000 of the total operating expenses, and the remainder is consumption of Prepaid Assets, Allowance for Uncollectibles, Depreciation, and increases in liabilities. The hospital receives donated services valued at $10,000, which are recognized in entry (9):

(8)	Nursing Services Expense	800,000	
	Other Professional Services Expense	620,000	
	General Services Expense	700,000	
	Fiscal Services Expense	100,000	
	Administrative Services Expense	80,000	
	Medical Malpractice Costs	30,000	
	Bad Debts Expense	60,000	
	Depreciation Expense	200,000	
	Cash		2,125,000
	Allowance for Uncollectibles		60,000
	Inventories		90,000
	Prepaid Expenses		5,000
	Accumulated Depreciation		200,000
	Accounts Payable		50,000
	Accrued Expenses		30,000
	Estimated Medical Malpractice Costs Payable		30,000
	Record operating expenses.		

(9)	Other Professional Services Expense	10,000	
	Donated Services—Revenue		10,000
	Receive donated services.		

Entry (9) records the fair value of donated services both as a debit for the operating expense and as a credit for operating revenue. Therefore, donated services do not affect the bottom line of the hospital's statement of revenue and expenses, but they do affect the amounts shown for the expenses and revenue sections.

Contribution Revenue During 20X2, Sol City Community Hospital received unrestricted cash gifts of $63,000 and donated medicines and medical supplies with a market value of $30,000:

(10)	Cash	63,000	
	Contributions—Unrestricted		63,000
	Unrestricted contributions received.		

(11)	Inventory	30,000	
	Contributions—Unrestricted		30,000
	Donated supplies received.		

Other Revenues and Gains Also during 20X2, the unrestricted fund earned $10,000 income that is available for current operations. In addition, a $5,000 gain was realized on the sale of equipment:

(12)	Cash	10,000	
	Investment Income—Designated for Current Operations		10,000
	Investment earnings available for current operations.		

(13)	Cash	55,000	
	Accumulated Depreciation	50,000	
	Property, Plant, and Equipment		100,000
	Gain on Disposal of Equipment		5,000
	Sale of hospital equipment. The cash will be used in the operations of the hospital.		

Net Assets Released from Restriction Assets were released for unrestricted use from a variety of sources in 20X2, as follows:

Amount	From Restricted Fund	Description
$120,000	Specific purpose	Resources for education and research
60,000	Specific purpose	Income from endowment investment
200,000	Plant expansion and replacement	Resources to acquire equipment
25,000	Plant expansion and replacement	Donated assets placed into use
12,000	Time restricted	Collection of pledges receivable

Entries in the unrestricted fund to record these transactions follow:

(14)	Cash	120,000	
	Net Assets Released from Program Use Restrictions		120,000
	Record payment for reimbursement of operating expenses incurred in accordance with restricted gift.		

(15)	Cash	60,000	
	Net Assets Released from Program Use Restrictions		60,000
	Receipt of endowment earnings from specific-purpose fund upon approval and completion of specified purpose.		

(16)	Cash	200,000	
	Net Assets Released from Equipment Acquisition Restriction		200,000
	Transfer from temporarily restricted plant replacement and expansion fund for use in acquiring plant assets.		

(17)	Property, Plant, and Equipment	25,000	
	Net Assets Released from Equipment Acquisition Restriction		25,000
	Transfer from temporarily restricted plant replacement and expansion fund of donated assets placed in service.		

(18)	Cash	12,000	
	Net Assets Released from Passage of Time		12,000
	Transfer from temporarily restricted funds restricted for use in 20X2.		

Each transfer from temporarily restricted funds involves one or more journal entries in those funds. These amounts are not included among 20X2 contributions or income in the unrestricted fund because they were recorded as contributions or income upon receipt in the temporarily restricted or permanently restricted funds. The transfer of donated equipment initially is recorded in the temporarily restricted plant fund until the hospital begins using the asset. When the assets are placed in service, the donated equipment's value is transferred to the unrestricted fund.

Other Transactions in the General Fund The remaining transactions during the 20X2 fiscal year affect the balance sheet accounts. Transactions affecting only the asset accounts include collecting receivables, acquiring inventory, selling an investment, and purchasing additional physical plant assets as follows:

(19)	Cash	2,250,000	
	Allowance for Uncollectibles	50,000	
	Accounts Receivable		2,300,000
	Collect some receivables and write off $50,000 as uncollectible		
(20)	Inventories	50,000	
	Cash		50,000
	Acquire inventories.		
(21)	Cash	50,000	
	Investments		50,000
	Sell investment at cost.		
(22)	Property, Plant, and Equipment	250,000	
	Cash		250,000
	Purchase new plant with cash of $50,000 from sale of investments and $200,000 from transfer in from temporarily restricted plant replacement and expansion fund.		

Transactions affecting the current liability accounts include paying current liabilities and recording the receipt of cash in advance of billings from third parties. The hospital reclassified the portion of the long-term mortgage that is currently due and revalued the general fund's investment securities to fair value.

ASC 958 requires that not-for-profit organizations value their investment securities other than equity investments accounted for under **ASC 323 and 325** at fair value at each balance sheet date. The total investment income during a period is from dividends, interest, and realized and unrealized holding gains or losses. After the total investment income is determined, a not-for-profit hospital reports the portion of investment income designated for current operations above the operating performance indicator line on its statement of activities. The hospital separately reports on its statement of activities the investment return in excess of the amount designated for current operations below the operating performance indicator line its statement of activities. The not-for-profit's management is permitted to establish a policy as to the separation of total investment return for current operations or for other purposes that should be described in the footnotes to the financial statements. For our example, assume that Sol City Community Hospital's board of directors has a policy to set aside the recognition of unrealized holding gains of unrestricted investments for possible future operations. Therefore, the hospital recognizes the entire $15,000 of unrealized holding gain on its year-end revaluation of its investment securities separately below the operating performance indicator line on its statement of activities.

(23)	Notes Payable to Bank	5,000	
	Current Portion of Long-Term Debt	60,000	
	Accounts Payable	90,000	
	Accrued Expenses	25,000	
	Cash		180,000
	Pay liabilities outstanding at beginning of period.		
(24)	Cash	35,000	
	Advances from Third Parties		35,000
	Increase in cash received from third parties for deposits in advance of service billings.		
(25)	Mortgage Payable	50,000	
	Current Portion of Long-Term Debt		50,000
	Reclassify current portion of long-term debt.		

(26)	Investments	15,000	
	Unrealized Holding Gain on Investment Securities		15,000
	Revalue securities to fair value and report as not designated for current operations.		

FIGURE 19–7
Statement of Operations for a Not-for-Profit Hospital

SOL CITY COMMUNITY HOSPITAL
Statement of Operations
For the Year Ended December 31, 20X2

Unrestricted Revenue, Gains & Other Support:	
Net Patient Service Revenue	$2,360,000
Ancillary Programs	30,000
Unrestricted Gifts Used in Operations	93,000
Disposal of Hospital Assets	5,000
Donated Services	10,000
Investment Income Designated for Current Operations	10,000
Net Assets Released from Restrictions for Use in Operations	192,000
Total Revenue, Gains & Other Support	$2,700,000
Expenses:	
Nursing Services	$ 800,000
Other Professional Services	630,000
General Services	700,000
Fiscal Services	100,000
Administrative Services	80,000
Medical Malpractice Costs	30,000
Bad Debts	60,000
Depreciation	200,000
Total Expenses	$2,600,000
Excess of Operating Revenues over Operating Expenses	$ 100,000
Other Items:	
Investment Return in Excess of Amounts Designated for Current Operations	15,000
Net Assets Released from Restrictions Used for Acquisition of Equipment	225,000
Increase in Unrestricted Net Assets	$ 340,000

FIGURE 19–8
Statement of Changes in Net Assets for a Not-for-Profit Hospital

SOL CITY COMMUNITY HOSPITAL
Statement of Changes in Net Assets
For the Year Ended December 31, 20X2

Unrestricted Net Assets:	
Excess of Operating Revenues over Operating Expenses	$ 100,000
Investment Return in Excess of Amounts Designated for Current Operations	15,000
Net Assets Released from Equipment Acquisition Restrictions	225,000
Increase in Unrestricted Net Assets	$ 340,000
Temporarily Restricted Net Assets:	
Contributions	$ 200,000
Investment Gains	73,000
Net Assets Released from:	
Program Use Restrictions	(180,000)
Equipment Acquisition Restrictions	(225,000)
Passage of Time	(12,000)
Decrease in Temporarily Restricted Net Assets	$ (144,000)
Permanently Restricted Net Assets:	
Contributions	$ 415,000
Increase in Permanently Restricted Net Assets	$ 415,000
Increase in Net Assets	$ 611,000
Net Assets at Beginning of Year	3,055,000
Net Assets at End of Year	$3,666,000

FIGURE 19–9 Statement of Cash Flows for a Not-for-Profit Hospital (Indirect Method)

SOL CITY COMMUNITY HOSPITAL
Statement of Cash Flows
For the Year Ended December 31, 20X2

Cash Flows from Operating Activities:			
Change in Total Net Assets			$ 611,000
Adjustments to Reconcile Changes in Net Assets to Net Cash Provided by Operating Activities:			
Depreciation		$ 200,000	
Investment Unrealized Holding Gain (not available for current operations)		(15,000)	
Contribution of Property, Plant & Equipment		(25,000)	
Gain on Disposal of Equipment		(5,000)	
Increase in Advances from Third Parties		35,000	
Increase in Malpractice Costs		30,000	
Increase in Accrued Expenses		5,000	
Decrease in Accounts Payable		(40,000)	
Increase in Receivables, Net		(50,000)	
Decrease in Pledges Receivable—Current		12,000	
Decrease in Prepaid Expenses		5,000	
Decrease in Inventories		10,000	
Restricted Contributions & Investment Income:			
Contribution for Permanent Endowment	$(415,000)		
Contributions Restricted for Plant Acquisition	(60,000)		
Investment Income Restricted for Plant Acquisition	(7,000)		
Total Restricted Contributions & Investment Income		(482,000)	
Total Adjustments			(320,000)
Net Cash Provided by Operating Activities			$ 291,000
Cash Flows from Investing Activities:			
Sale of Used Hospital Assets			$ 55,000
Sale of Investments			50,000
Acquisition of Plant, Property & Equipment			(250,000)
Flows Related to Restricted Items:			
Purchase of Investments in Endowment & Plant Replacement Funds		$(522,000)	
Remainder of Contributions to Endowment Fund Restricted to Investing		(15,000)	
Remainder of Contributions to Plant Fund Restricted to Plant Purchases		(50,000)	
Cash Transferred from Plant Fund for Plant Expansion		200,000	
Total Investing Flows Related to Restricted Items			(387,000)
Net Cash Used by Investing Activities			$(532,000)
Cash Flows from Financing Activities:			
Paid Notes Payable			$ (5,000)
Paid Current Portion of Long-Term Debt			(60,000)
Proceeds from Restricted Contributions:			
Contributions Restricted for Permanent Endowment		$ 415,000	
Contributions Restricted for Acquiring Fixed Assets		172,000	
Total Restricted Proceeds			587,000
Net Cash Provided by Financing Activities			$ 522,000
Net Increase in Cash			$ 281,000
Cash at the Beginning of Year			14,000
Cash at the End of Year (unrestricted)			$ 295,000

We do not show closing entries, which are required for all nominal accounts, because the focus is on other aspects of hospital accounting and the closing process for hospitals is the same as for any other accounting entity. The statement of changes in net assets (Figure 19–8) includes a reconciliation of net assets between the beginning and end of the year.

The statement of cash flows (Figure 19–9) is required. Either the direct or the indirect method may be used to display net cash flows from operations. The direct method presents the specific inflows and outflows from operations. Under the indirect method, the statement begins with the change in net assets as on the statement of changes in net assets and then presents the adjustments necessary to reconcile the net amount shown on the statement of changes in net assets with the cash flow provided by operating activities. Because of its popularity and wide use, we present the indirect method in Figure 19–9. The statement of cash flows is similar to that required of commercial, profit-seeking entities. The three categories of operating activities, investing activities, and financing activities are the same as for commercial entities. A not-for-profit hospital's statement of cash flows has an important feature, however; it reconciles to the change in cash and cash equivalents the hospital reports as a current asset on the hospital's balance sheet. This cash amount does not include the cash balances in the restricted accounts not available for operations (the plant fund and the endowment fund in the Sol City Community Hospital example). For example, the hospital received a $415,000 cash contribution to the endowment fund in transaction (40) (presented later in this chapter). The $415,000 must first be subtracted from the change in net assets in the operating section of the statement of cash flows because the endowment fund does not constitute operating activities. The $415,000 is reported as an increase in financing activities on the statement of cash flows. Of the $415,000, the hospital used $400,000 to acquire investments (transaction [41] presented later in this chapter) and included this amount in the $522,000 as an investing activity on the statement of cash flows. The $15,000 of contributions not used to acquire investments in 20X2 is reported on the statement of cash flows as an investing activity, "Remainder of Contributions to Endowment Fund Restricted to Investing" because the amount of financing resources from the restricted endowment fund must equal the amount of investing resources from that restricted fund. Thus, the statement of cash flows reconciles only to the change in cash and cash equivalents shown as a current asset on the hospital's balance sheet.

In addition to the primary financial statements for the present fiscal period with comparatives for the prior period, hospitals are required to present extensive footnotes similar to those of a commercial entity. A specific footnote disclosure is required to report the estimated value of charity care services the hospital provided during the period.

Temporarily Restricted Funds

Sol City Community Hospital uses three funds to account for temporarily restricted funds. The specific-purpose fund is for contributions designated for a particular use by the donor other than plant replacement and expansion. The time-restricted fund is for contributions pledged or received in advance that will be available for unrestricted use in the future. The plant replacement and expansion fund is for contributions to be used in acquiring additional land, buildings, and equipment.

Specific-Purpose Fund

The specific-purpose fund is used to account for contributions for which a donor-specific use has been designated. For the most part, such contributions support particular hospital operating activities, such as educational or research programs, or provide a particular service to patients. The specific-purpose fund does not directly spend the resources; it holds the restricted resources until the general fund satisfies the terms of the restriction, usually by making the appropriate operating cost or by having the restricted cost approved by the governing board, upon which the specific-purpose fund transfers the resources to the general fund to pay for the operating cost.

The specific-purpose restricted fund typically invests its cash and receives interest or dividends from its investments. A variety of investment transactions can affect the fund balance. Nevertheless, the specific fund is only a holding fund for temporarily restricted resources until they are released for hospital use.

The following entries record the transactions in Sol City Community Hospital's specific-purpose fund during the 20X2 fiscal year and are reflected in the balance sheet in Figure 19–6 and the statement of changes in net assets in Figure 19–8.

Additions to Specific-Purpose Fund The specific-purpose fund receives $6,000 of interest income from its investment of funds from a restricted gift to support the hospital's research activity. The fund receives restricted gifts of $115,000 in response to a community fund-raising effort. The restricted gifts are allocated based on the donors' specifications. In addition, endowment fund earnings of $60,000 were deposited directly in the temporarily restricted fund:

(27)	Cash	6,000	
	Investment Income—Research		6,000
	Interest on investment of research gift resources.		

(28)	Cash	115,000	
	Contributions—Education		60,000
	Contributions—Research		55,000
	Receive restricted gifts.		

(29)	Cash	60,000	
	Investment Income—Endowment Earnings		60,000
	Earnings of endowment fund deposited in temporarily restricted funds until released for specified purposes.		

Entry (29) shows the earnings generated by the permanently restricted endowment fund's investments as reported by the temporarily restricted fund. **ASC 958** specifies that dividend, interest, and other investment income be reported in the period earned as increases in unrestricted net assets unless their use has donor-imposed restrictions. However, Sol City Community Hospital reports the earnings as investment income of the temporarily restricted fund because they have a donor-imposed restriction. After clearance is given, the hospital then transfers the resources to the general fund to be expended for the donor-specified purposes. If permanently restricted, the investment income is reported in the permanently restricted net assets.

Gains or losses from valuation adjustments to fair value or from sales of securities also must be applied in accordance with any donor restrictions. For example, if the donor specifies that an investment be held for perpetuity, any valuation or sales transaction gain or loss on it is reported in the permanently restricted net asset class. The important point is to follow any restrictions imposed by the donor or applicable laws. If no restrictions are applicable, the investment income and gains or losses are reported in the unrestricted net asset class.

Deductions from Specific-Purpose Fund The specific-purpose fund is notified that the general fund fulfilled the terms of agreements for specific restricted grants totaling $120,000. In addition to the $120,000, the specific-purpose fund also transferred $60,000 from endowment income to the general fund.

(30)	Net Assets Released from Program Use Restriction—Research	61,000	
	Net Assets Released from Program Use Restriction—Education	59,000	
	Net Assets Released from Program Use Restriction—Endowment Income	60,000	
	Cash		180,000
	Funds released from temporary restriction.		

This interfund transaction also was recorded in the general fund (see entries [14] and [15] earlier in the chapter).

Time-Restricted Fund

ASC 958 changed procedures for recording contributions. Earlier recognition of contribution revenue generally is now required for most not-for-profit organizations, including hospitals. Because of the critical nature of contributions to the operations of voluntary health and welfare organizations, a thorough treatment of this topic is included later in the chapter as part of the discussion of these organizations. For purposes of illustration in the hospital setting, we assume that in 20X1, the hospital received pledges for $12,000 to be collected in 20X2. During 20X2, this $12,000 was collected and immediately transferred to the general fund for unrestricted use (see entry [18] earlier in the chapter).

(31)	Cash	12,000	
	Pledges Receivable		12,000
	Collection of prior period pledge.		

(32)	Net Assets Released from Time Restrictions	12,000	
	Cash		12,000
	Funds released from time restrictions.		

Plant Replacement and Expansion Fund

Hospitals use the plant replacement and expansion fund, sometimes called the *plant fund,* to account for restricted resources given to them only for additions or major modifications to the physical plant. This is a holding fund until the governing board approves the transfer of the expenditures to the general fund.

A primary source of resources for the plant replacement and expansion fund is from fund-raising efforts in the communities the hospital serves. A hospital often asks potential donors to sign pledges specifying a giving level for a period of time, for example, $100 per month for the next 12 months. The pledges become receivables of the fund and typically require a substantial allowance for uncollectibles. The fund records contribution revenue when the pledge is received.

The entries recorded in Sol City Community Hospital's plant replacement and expansion fund during 20X2 are presented next and are reflected in the balance sheet in Figure 19–6.

Additions to Plant Fund Increases in the plant replacement and expansion fund during the period are a donation of equipment with a fair value of $25,000 that is recorded in the restricted plant fund until the equipment is placed into service; a donation of $60,000 to acquire additional equipment; and the receipt of $7,000 of interest on the plant fund's investments restricted to purchase plant assets. Entries to record these events follow:

(33)	Property, Plant & Equipment	25,000	
	Contributions—Plant		25,000
	Receive donated equipment with fair value of $25,000.		

(34)	Cash	60,000	
	Contributions—Plant		60,000
	Receive restricted gifts for use to acquire equipment.		

(35)	Cash	7,000	
	Investment Income—Plant		7,000
	Receive interest on fund's investments.		

Deductions from Plant Fund Deductions from the plant fund during the year occur in two interfund transfers to the general fund. The first transfers $25,000 of donated equipment in service, and the second transfers $200,000 to the general fund for expenditures for fixed assets. These two interfund transfers also are recorded in the general fund (see entries [16] and [17] earlier in the chapter):

(36)	Net Assets Released—Plant Acquisition	25,000	
	Property, Plant & Equipment		25,000
	Transfer donated equipment to general fund at time of placement into service.		

(37)	Net Assets Released—Plant Acquisition	200,000	
	Cash		200,000
	Transfer cash to general fund for use in acquiring plant assets.		

Other Transactions in Plant Fund Other transactions affecting only the plant fund's asset or liability accounts represent a collection of pledges made by individual donors during the last capital fund-raising drive as well as the acquisition of additional investments in the fund. Entries for these transactions follow:

(38)	Cash	105,000	
	Pledges Receivable		105,000
	Collect pledges receivable.		

(39)	Investments	122,000	
	Cash		122,000
	Increase investments.		

Endowment Fund

An endowment fund is a collection of cash, securities, or other assets. The use of its assets may be permanently restricted, temporarily restricted, or unrestricted based on the donor's wishes. Generally, donors establish endowment funds to permanently restrict the capital of the donation and specify the use(s) of any income from those investments. The classification of an endowment fund is based, however, on the terms of the donor's contribution. If the fund is temporarily restricted for a stated period of time after which the principal becomes available for the specified uses, it is normally described as a *term endowment.* If permanently restricted into perpetuity, an endowment fund is normally described as a *regular* or *permanent endowment.*

Sol City Community Hospital has a permanently restricted endowment fund to account for resources whose donors have specified that the principal be maintained in perpetuity. The income from the investments in the endowment fund is recorded in the appropriate fund based on the donor's specifications. If the investment income is restricted, it is recorded in the appropriate restricted fund. If no donor-imposed restriction is present, the investment income should be recorded and reported in the unrestricted net asset fund.

The balance sheet in Figure 19–6 and the statement of changes in net assets in Figure 19–8 include the entries in Sol City Community Hospital's endowment fund for 20X2.

Additions to Endowment Fund The endowment fund earns $60,000 interest and dividends from its permanent investments deposited directly in the temporarily restricted fund (see entry [29]). In addition, the hospital receives $415,000 in new permanent endowments and uses $400,000 from them to acquire additional investments:

(40)	Cash	415,000	
	Contributions—Permanent Endowment		415,000
	Receive additional endowments.		

(41)	Investments	400,000	
	Cash		400,000
	Acquire additional investments.		

Summary of Hospital Accounting and Financial Reporting

A hospital's major operating activities take place in the general fund. Restricted funds are holding funds that transfer resources to the general fund for expenditures upon satisfaction of their respective restrictions. The general fund uses the accrual basis of accounting to fully measure the revenue and costs of providing health care and reports patient services revenue at gross amounts measured at standard billing rates. A deduction for contractual adjustments is then made to arrive at net patient services revenue. Other revenue is recognized for ongoing nonpatient services, such as sales of cafeteria food, television rentals, and donated supplies and medicines. A hospital presents charity care services only in the footnotes and recognizes no revenue for them. Operating expenses in the general fund include depreciation, bad debts, and the value of recognized donated services that support the hospital's basic services; however, it does not recognize all donated services. A hospital typically records donated property and equipment in a restricted fund, such as the plant fund, until placed into service when it transfers them to the general fund. Donated assets are recorded at their fair market values at the date of gift.

The financial statements of a hospital are the (1) balance sheet, (2) statement of operations, (3) statement of changes in net assets, and (4) statement of cash flows.

VOLUNTARY HEALTH AND WELFARE ORGANIZATIONS

LO 19-4

Understand financial reporting rules and make basic journal entries for not-for-profit voluntary health and welfare organizations.

Voluntary health and welfare organizations (VHWOs) provide a variety of social services. Examples are United Way, the American Heart Association, the March of Dimes, the American Cancer Society, the Red Cross, and the Salvation Army. These organizations solicit funds from the community at large and typically provide their services for no fee, or they may charge a nominal fee to those with the ability to pay. The federal government normally provides tax-exempt status to these organizations.

ASC 958 summarizes the accounting and financial reporting principles for VHWOs. Additional information may be obtained from a variety of sources. The AICPA Audit and Accounting Guide for Not-for-Profit Organizations requires the use of generally accepted accounting principles for VHWOs. They are typically audited and make their audited financial statements available to contributors and others interested in knowing about the organization's financial condition and how it uses its resources. Another source for accounting and reporting guidelines for VHWOs is the *Standards of Accounting and Financial Reporting for Voluntary Health and Welfare Organizations* published by the combined group of the National Health Council, the National Assembly of National Voluntary Health and Social Welfare Organizations, and United Way Worldwide. The standards book, known as the "black book" for the color of its cover, represents an effort to incorporate in one manual accounting and financial reporting standards as well as the actual experiences of the largest VHWOs in the United States.

Advanced StudyGuide .com

Accounting for a VHWO

The accrual basis of accounting is required for a VHWO to measure fully the resources available to it. It reports depreciation as an operating expense each period because its omission would result in an understatement of the costs of providing the organization's services. Therefore, accounting for a VHWO is similar to that for other not-for-profit organizations except for special financial statements that report on a VHWO's important aspects. This section presents an overview of the accounting and financial reporting principles for a VHWO.

Even though not required to do so, VHWOs have been free to use fund accounting in their accounting and reporting processes. In the past, the typical VHWO has been portrayed as using a fund structure with (1) a current unrestricted fund, (2) a current restricted fund, (3) a land, building, and equipment fund, and (4) an endowment fund. Many VHWOs are considerably smaller in size and scope of activity than hospitals and may find it convenient to convert from the traditional fund structure to a single accounting entity or a fund structure that distinguishes between unrestricted, temporarily restricted, and permanently restricted assets. The journal entries for Voluntary Health and Welfare Service presented in this section assume the use of a single fund or accounting entity. When appropriate, designations have been added to the journal entry captions to show which of the three classes of assets (unrestricted, temporarily restricted, or permanently restricted) is affected. Thus, the entries could be used equally well if separate funds were established for each of the three asset classifications. Journal entries are presented in the following discussion for only a portion of the transactions of Voluntary Health and Welfare Service in 20X2.

Financial Statements for a VHWO

ASC 958 requires that a VHWO provide the following financial statements: (1) statement of financial position, (2) statement of activities, (3) statement of cash flows, and (4) statement of functional expenses.

The financial statements are designed primarily for users interested in the organization as "outsiders," not management. These include contributors, beneficiaries of services, creditors and potential creditors, and related organizations. A clear distinction should be maintained between restricted resources and those resources available for expenditure for the organization's major missions. As outlined in **FASB Concepts Statement No. 6,** "Elements of Financial Statements" (FAC 6), a not-for-profit organization divides its net assets into three mutually exclusive classes: permanently restricted, temporarily restricted, and unrestricted. Restricted resources are subject to externally imposed constraints, not internal or board-designated decisions that may be changed by the VHWO's governing board. In addition, readers of the general-purpose financial statements should be able to clearly evaluate management's performance in accomplishing the VHWO's objectives.

Statement of Financial Position for a VHWO

Refer to Figure 19–10 for a VHWO's statement of financial position. The format is similar to the one in the hospital illustration. Although not required by existing standards, the assets and liabilities are segregated into current and noncurrent classifications. The net assets section of a VHWO's statement of financial position must be segregated into unrestricted, temporarily restricted, and permanently restricted as illustrated.

Pledges from Donors Pledges to give may be unconditional or conditional. Conditional promises, which depend on the occurrence of a specified future and uncertain event, are recognized only after the conditions on which they depend have been substantially met (i.e., when the conditional promise becomes unconditional). The pledges may be unrestricted, temporarily restricted, or permanently restricted based on the circumstances of the pledge and the donor's specifications.

For the VHWO example, the current unrestricted fund includes net ***pledges receivable*** of $78,400 in 20X2. The accrual basis of accounting recognizes the receivable and associated revenue when the VHWO receives the unconditional pledge. If the contribution is available to support current period activities, there is no restriction. An adequate allowance for uncollectibles for the pledges receivable is recognized by a debit to Contributions as a direct reduction from the contribution revenue account and as a credit to Allowance for Uncollectible Pledges, which is a contra account to the pledges receivable asset account. Note that a VHWO does not have a bad debts expense account; it charges the revenue account directly for estimated uncollectible amounts. Pledges or other contributions applicable to future periods should be reported in temporarily restricted net assets as "Contributions—Temporarily Restricted" to show that these resources are not currently available for the entity's operations. Further accuracy could be attained by identifying the temporary restriction as "Contributions—Temporarily Restricted—Time Restrictions." Conditional pledges are not recognized until the conditions on which they depend have been substantially met.

FIGURE 19–10
Statement of Financial Position for a Voluntary Health and Welfare Organization

VOLUNTARY HEALTH AND WELFARE SERVICE Statement of Financial Position December 31, 20X2 and 20X1	20X2	20X1
Assets		
Current:		
Cash	$ 68,000	$ 47,600
Short-Term Investments	39,000	48,000
Accounts Receivable	1,200	1,000
Inventories	6,400	8,300
Net Pledges Receivable	78,400	61,600
Prepaid Expenses	8,000	7,200
Total Current Assets	$201,000	$173,700
Cash Restricted for Long-Term Use	1,000	0
Long-Term Investments	383,000	351,900
Property, Plant & Equipment	125,500	121,600
Total Assets	$710,500	$647,200
Liabilities & Net Assets		
Current:		
Accounts Payable	$ 16,100	$ 12,400
Accrued Expenses	4,800	4,300
Total Current Liabilities	$ 20,900	$ 16,700
Noncurrent:		
Mortgage Payable	$ 21,000	$ 23,000
Capital Leases	8,000	7,000
Total Liabilities	$ 49,900	$ 46,700
Net Assets:		
Unrestricted	$498,200	$437,800
Temporarily Restricted by Donors	22,900	24,100
Permanently Restricted by Donors	139,500	138,600
Total Net Assets	$660,600	$600,500
Total Liabilities & Net Assets	$710,500	$647,200

The following illustrates the entries Voluntary Health and Welfare Service used in accounting for a portion of the pledges in 20X2. Note that this discussion is for only a part of the pledges, not all of those received in the year, nor does the following discussion attempt to reconcile to the $78,400 balance in net pledges receivable at the end of the year. The discussion includes the accounting for the pledges from only one of the organization's several pledge campaigns during the year.

A special pledge campaign resulted in $100,000 of new pledges. Of this total, $5,000 is to be received in the current period but is to be held for use for unrestricted purposes in the following period. Experience shows that 20 percent of pledges to this organization are uncollectible. An allowance for uncollectibles is recognized in the amount of $20,000. Note that both the current and deferred pledges are reported as contribution revenue in the period the unconditional pledges are received and that provisions for estimated uncollectibles are then recorded as reductions of contribution revenue.

		Debit	Credit
(42)	Pledges Receivable—Unrestricted	95,000	
	Pledges Receivable—Temporarily Restricted	5,000	
	Contributions—Unrestricted		95,000
	Contributions—Temporarily Restricted		5,000

Receive pledges and recognize receivables.

(43)			
	Contributions—Unrestricted	19,000	
	Contributions—Temporarily Restricted	1,000	
	Allowance for Uncollectible Pledges—Unrestricted		19,000
	Allowance for Uncollectible Pledges—Restricted		1,000
	Provide for estimated uncollectible pledges as a reduction of contributions.		

Note that there is no separate bad debt expense recognition. Instead, the contributions accounts are reduced for the estimated amount of uncollectible pledges. **ASC 958** states that unconditional promises to give that are expected to be collected in less than one year may be measured at net realizable value (net settlement value). Pledged contributions expected to be collected in the future beyond one year can be valued at the present value of their estimated future cash flows. Subsequent increases in the present value of the future cash flows due to the reduction of the present value discount are accounted for as contribution income in the fund for which the pledge was received.

All $5,000 of the funds pledged for use the following year and $85,000 of unrestricted pledges are collected in the current period, requiring an adjustment to both unrestricted and temporarily restricted contribution revenue. Temporarily restricted contribution revenue increased by $1,000 to the full $5,000 received, and $9,000 is added to unrestricted contribution revenue due to collections of $85,000 in pledges versus the initial estimate of $76,000 ($95,000 × 0.80). Of the remaining balance, $3,000 is written off as uncollectible, and the remainder is carried over to the following period:

(44)			
	Cash—Unrestricted	85,000	
	Cash—Temporarily Restricted	5,000	
	Allowance for Uncollectible Pledges—Unrestricted	9,000	
	Allowance for Uncollectible Pledges—Restricted	1,000	
	Pledges Receivable—Unrestricted		85,000
	Pledges Receivable—Temporarily Restricted		5,000
	Contribution Revenue—Unrestricted		9,000
	Contribution Revenue—Temporarily Restricted		1,000
	Collect pledges including $10,000 above initial estimate of collectability.		

(45)			
	Allowance for Uncollectible Pledges—Unrestricted	3,000	
	Pledges Receivable—Unrestricted		3,000
	Write off uncollectible pledges in unrestricted net asset class.		

In the following period when the $5,000 is available for unrestricted use, the balance is reclassified as unrestricted. Some organizations would use the terms *net assets released* instead of *reclassification,* but the terms are synonymous, and both are used in this chapter to show their equality.

(46)			
	Cash—Unrestricted	5,000	
	Reclassification of Contributions to Unrestricted		5,000
	Reclassify time-restricted funds to unrestricted.		

(47)			
	Reclassification of Contributions from Temporarily Restricted	5,000	
	Cash—Temporarily Restricted		5,000
	Reclassify time-restricted funds from temporarily restricted.		

ASC 958 also prescribes appropriate treatment for unconditional pledges to be received over a long period of time. In general, contribution revenue is recognized at the present value of future cash receipts. As is the normal practice in utilizing present value procedures in the corporate sector, the present value is used to record contributions to be received in following accounting periods. For example, if a donor agrees to contribute

$10,000 per year at the end of each of the next five years, the stream of the payments is discounted at an appropriate rate (e.g., 8 percent), and the present value is recognized when the pledge is received:

(48)	Pledges Receivable—Temporarily Restricted	39,927	
	Contributions—Temporarily Restricted		39,927
	Receipt of pledge.		

At the end of the first year when the first payment of $10,000 is received, that amount is reclassified from temporarily restricted to unrestricted, and the increase in present value of the contributions receivable is recognized as an increase in temporarily restricted contributions and contributions receivable:

(49)	Cash—Unrestricted	10,000	
	Reclassification of Contributions to Unrestricted		10,000
	Reclassify time-restricted funds to unrestricted.		
(50)	Reclassification of Contributions from Temporarily Restricted	10,000	
	Pledges Receivable—Temporarily Restricted		10,000
	Reclassify time-restricted funds from temporarily restricted.		

Note that after the receipt of the first $10,000 contribution, the balance in the Pledges Receivable—Temporarily Restricted account decreases from $39,927 to $29,927. However, recalculating the present value of the next four payments yields a present value of $33,121. Thus, a $3,194 adjustment must be made to the account to increase its balance to the new present value of future contributions receivable ($33,121 – $29,927 = $3,194).

(51)	Pledges Receivable—Temporarily Restricted	3,194	
	Contributions—Temporarily Restricted		3,194
	Increase in the present value of contributions receivable.		

Investments The VHWO may obtain investments through purchase or donation and should record purchased investments at acquisition cost. The organization should record donated securities at their fair values at the dates of the gifts. Subsequently, it reports equity investments (other than **ASC 323 and 325** equity investments) and all investments in bonds at fair value. The organization's statement of activity should separately identify appreciation gains (or reductions in value) as unrealized gains (losses) in accordance with **ASC 958.** Transfers of investments from one portfolio to another should be made at fair value with any gains or losses in valuation recorded.

The VHWO should report investment earnings or losses as unrestricted, temporarily restricted, or permanently restricted, depending on how they are to be used. For example, the donor of a restricted endowment fund may not specify any limitations on the uses of its income or losses. In that case, the income or losses on the investments are reported on the statement of activities as changes in unrestricted net assets. However, the stipulated treatment of the income or losses from a donor-restricted endowment fund must be implemented. In some cases, the donor may impose some time or dollar requirement on the earnings, such as requiring that the income for the first five years be added to the permanent endowment or that income only above some dollar amount be transferred to an unrestricted fund and the income below that amount be added to the permanent endowment's principal. The key point is that the VHWO must follow the donor's specifications as presented in the contribution agreement between it and the donor and any applicable law regarding a not-for-profit association's management of restricted resources.

Land, Buildings, and Equipment Land, buildings, and equipment; depreciation expense; and the accumulated depreciation on the fixed assets generally are reported as unrestricted unless donor restricted. The VHWO may have an accounting policy of retaining long-lived, restricted buildings and equipment in the restricted net asset class even though the assets are used in the entity's operations. As the VHWO uses the buildings and equipment in the operations, it reclassifies an allowance for depreciation from the restricted net asset class to the unrestricted net asset class. This provides for depreciation and maintains the net book value of the restricted buildings and equipment in the restricted net asset class. The basis of fixed assets is cost, and donated assets are recorded at their fair values at the dates of the gifts. Donations of fixed assets that the organization will sell in the near future are equivalent to other contributions and should be separately reported as unrestricted assets until sold. For example, assume that the VHWO receives land as a donation and plans to sell it and use the proceeds to support the entity's program services. It should record the land at fair value as an unrestricted asset and report it as land held for resale until sold.

A VHWO may use any one of the depreciation methods available to commercial entities. A not-for-profit entity is not required to depreciate assets such as works of art or other historically valuable assets when the entity has made a commitment to preserve the value of the art or historical assets and has shown the capacity to do so.

Liabilities The VHWO records liabilities in the normal manner under the accrual model. In most situations, it reports liabilities as part of the unrestricted net assets. For example, the mortgage payment made by Voluntary Health and Welfare Service in 20X2 was recorded as a $2,000 debit to Mortgage Payable and a $2,000 credit to Cash. In this illustration, the VHWO classifies property, plant, and equipment as an unrestricted asset. In some cases, the entity makes mortgage payments on assets classified as restricted from unrestricted funds. The following entries are needed in the latter case:

(52)	Reclassification to Restricted Assets	2,000	
	Cash (Unrestricted)		2,000
	Mortgage payment made from unrestricted assets.		

(53)	Mortgage Payable—Restricted Assets	2,000	
	Reclassification from Unrestricted Assets		2,000
	Reduction of carrying value of mortgage.		

Net Assets The VHWO should disclose separately the amounts of net assets designated as unrestricted, temporarily restricted, and permanently restricted. Its governing board also may show its intent to use unrestricted resources for specific needs in the future by creating one or more board-designated categories. For example, the $498,200 of unrestricted net assets at December 31, 20X2, in Figure 19–10 could be separated into board designated and undesignated. Board-designated purposes might be for purchases of new equipment, research, construction of new facilities, or other asset acquisitions. Although the statement of financial position could reflect the designation of resources, the governing board may change it at any time.

Statement of Activities

Refer to Figure 19–11 for Voluntary Health and Welfare Service's major operating statement for Voluntary Health and Welfare Service, the statement of activities. The statement's overall structure for VHWOs and other not-for-profit entities should be very similar as a result of **ASC 958.** A number of organizations have issued standards relating to VHWOs as they have for other types of not-for-profit entities (see the later discussion of other not-for-profit organizations [ONPOs]). Both the National Health Council's black book of standards for VHWOs and the AICPA Audit and Accounting Guide for Not-for-Profit Organizations contain recommendations for accounting for them. We discuss several unique aspects of VHWOs next.

Public Support Historically, a distinction has been made in the sources of funding VHWOs receive. Nonprofit organizations generally provide services to those who cannot afford to pay for the benefits received or support programs for which little compensation is received.

FIGURE 19–11 Statement of Activities for a Voluntary Health and Welfare Organization

VOLUNTARY HEALTH AND WELFARE SERVICE
Statement of Activities
For the Year Ended December 31, 20X2

	Unrestricted	Temporarily Restricted	Permanently Restricted	Total
Revenues, Gains, & Other Support:				
Contributions	$627,000	$42,300	$ 9,900	$679,200
Legacies & Bequests	15,000			15,000
Collections through Affiliates	2,800			2,800
Allocated from Federated Fund-Raising Effort	45,300			45,300
Memberships	6,100			6,100
Program Fees	700			700
Sale of Materials	200			200
Investment Income	36,400	500		36,900
Gain on Investments	12,000		1,000	13,000
Donated Services	3,000			3,000
Net Assets Released from Restriction:				
Program Use Restrictions	25,000	(25,000)		
Passage of Time	8,100	(8,100)		
Equipment Acquisition	10,900	(10,900)		
Endowment Transfers	10,000		(10,000)	
Total Revenues, Gains & Other Support	$802,500	$ (1,200)	$ 900	$802,200
Program Services & Operating Costs:				
Research	$274,300			$274,300
Public Health Education	92,000			92,000
Professional Training	106,000			106,000
Community Services	98,600			98,600
Management & General	91,700			91,700
Fund-Raising	64,500			64,500
Payments to National Offices	15,000			15,000
Total Expenses	$742,100	$ 0	$ 0	$742,100
Change in Net Assets	$ 60,400	$ (1,200)	$ 900	$ 60,100
Net Assets at Beginning of Year	437,800	24,100	138,600	600,500
Net Assets at End of Year	$498,200	$22,900	$139,500	$660,600

The primary source of funds for VHWOs is likely to be contributions from individuals or organizations that do not derive any direct benefit from the VHWO for their gifts. The magnitude of funds received and the diversity of contributors are important in evaluating the effectiveness of VHWOs. Four sources of resources included in the 20X2 statement of activities for Voluntary Health and Welfare Service in Figure 19–11 are considered to fall in the category of support. They include contributions, legacies and bequests, collections through affiliates (other organizations in the same community or with similar goals), and contributions received from a federated (national or regional) organization's fund-raising efforts.

Under the guidelines of **ASC 958,** total proceeds from a sponsored event such as a dance gala or marathon are reported as support from special events, and the costs of sponsoring the event are reported as fund-raising costs. Even though many of the necessary items for such activities are contributed, the costs of sponsoring an event can be rather substantial. The frequency of such events undoubtedly was a factor in the change in the tax laws that now require not-for-profit organizations sponsoring a special event to provide participants a statement detailing the portion of the cost of a ticket or other contribution that may be treated as a charitable contribution for tax purposes.

Revenues Funds received in exchange for services provided or other activities are classified as revenues. Although the majority of a VHWO's resources come from public support, memberships, fees charged to program participants, sales of supplies and services, and investment income also provide funds.

Gains A VHWO may sell investments and other assets from time to time and incudes the difference between the sale price and the carrying value in its statement of activities as a gain or loss. Much of the time, the entity reinvests gains received from sales of investments in anticipation of future earnings; nevertheless, all gains and losses should be included in the period's statement of activities.

Donated Materials and Services A VHWO often relies heavily on ***donated materials and services.*** Donated materials are recorded at fair value when received. If a VHWO uses the donated materials in one of its program services, it should record their value as an expense in the period used. If the donated materials simply pass through the VHWO to its charitable beneficiaries, it is acting as an agent and does not record the materials as a contribution or an expense.

Donated services are essential to a VHWO. Because of the difficulty of valuing these services, they often are not recorded as contributions. However, if donated services are significant, the VHWO should recognize them if they (1) create or enhance nonfinancial assets or (2) require specialized skills, are provided by individuals possessing those skills, and typically need to be purchased if not donated. If these conditions are satisfied, the entity should report the value of donated services as part of public support and as an expense in the period in which it provides the services. As an example of donated services, assume that a CPA donates audit services with an estimated value of $3,000. The VHWO makes the following entry in the current unrestricted fund to recognize the donated services:

(54)			
	Expenses—Supporting Services	3,000	
	Support—Donated Services		3,000
	CPA donates audit.		

Donated services that are directly related to restricted assets should be reported in the restricted net assets class. For example, an architect may donate services for planning the construction of a new building that is restricted for a specific purpose. In this case, the value of the donated services is capitalized to the construction in progress in the restricted net asset class and becomes part of the basis of the new building.

Expenses The statement of activities should contain information about the major costs of providing services to the public, fund-raising, and general and administrative costs to provide contributors and others useful information in assessing the VHWO's effectiveness. Those costs of providing goods and services to beneficiaries, customers, or members in fulfilling the primary VHWO mission are referred to as *program service costs.* A VHWO's statement of activities normally should include the total costs of providing each major class of program services. The primary activities for Voluntary Health and Welfare Service are research, public health education, professional training, and community services (Figure 19–11). **ASC 958** requires that all not-for-profit entities report total entity expenses—even those financed by restricted fund resources—in the unrestricted fund. The restricted fund will report no expenses but a transfer out for the amount expended, and the unrestricted fund will report a transfer in.

The statement of activities also provides information on the costs of other activities needed for the organization to operate effectively but that may not be directly assignable to a particular program. These costs generally are reported either as management and general administrative costs or as fund-raising costs. Management and general activities include the costs of maintaining the general headquarters, recordkeeping, business management, and other management and administrative activities not directly assignable to program services or fund-raising activities. Fund-raising activities include the costs of special mailings, compiling potential donor lists, conducting campaigns through contacts with foundations and governmental agencies, and other similar costs. Those organizations whose membership contributions are important sources of funds separately disclose the costs of soliciting members and providing special benefits to current members.

Depreciation costs for 20X2 totaled $9,500. An allocation is made to each program service and supporting service based on square footage used or some other reasonable basis. For example, an allocation of the $9,500 of depreciation based on square footage occupied to each of the program and supporting services is recorded with the following entry:

(55)	Research—Depreciation	4,300	
	Public Health—Depreciation	1,000	
	Professional Training—Depreciation	2,000	
	Community Services—Depreciation	1,200	
	Management and General—Depreciation	500	
	Fund-Raising—Depreciation	500	
	Accumulated Depreciation		9,500
	Record depreciation for 20X2.		

Costs of Informational Materials That Include a Fund-Raising Appeal Not-for-profit entities often prepare informational materials that include a direct or indirect message soliciting funds. The issue is how to record the cost of these materials. Should they be program or fund-raising expenses? Many VHWOs prefer to classify them as program rather than fund-raising costs to highlight the fulfillment of their basic service mission and to present a better ratio of program expenses to total expenses. Users of the general-purpose financial statements are concerned with the amounts that VHWO organizations spend to solicit contributions as opposed to the amounts they spend for program services. If a not-for-profit entity cannot show that it conducted a program or management function in conjunction with the appeal for funds, it should report the entire cost of the informational materials or activities as a fund-raising expense. However, if it can demonstrate that it conducted a bona fide program or management function in conjunction with the appeal for funds, it should allocate the ***costs of informational materials*** between programs and fund-raising. Evidence of a bona fide program intent in a brochure would be an appeal designed to motivate its audience to action other than provide financial support to the organization. The informational content of a brochure might include a description of the symptoms of a disease and the actions an individual should take if one or more of the symptoms occur. Thus, the content of the message and the intended audience are significant factors.

Statement of Cash Flows

The third required financial statement for VHWOs is the statement of cash flows (Figure 19–12). The statement's format is similar to that for hospitals discussed earlier in the chapter. Note that under the indirect approach, the statement begins with the change in net assets and reconciles to the net cash provided by operating activities.

Statement of Functional Expenses

The fourth statement **ASC 958** specifies for VHWOs is the ***statement of functional expenses*** that details the items reported in the expenses section of the statement of activities in Figure 19–11. Figure 19–13 is a standard format for the statement of functional expenses that presents the expense categories across the columns. The rows provide the specific nature of the items composing these expense categories from the various funds.

Bad Debts Expense is from estimated uncollectibles directly related to program services and operations, including membership fees. Note that any estimated uncollectible pledges are deducted directly from contribution revenue.

The statement of functional expenses includes depreciation of $9,500 for the year allocated among the various programs and supporting services. Total expenses of $742,100 in Figure 19–11 are analyzed and reconciled on the statement of functional expenses in Figure 19–13.

Summary of Accounting and Financial Reporting for VHWOs

The accounting and financial reporting requirements for VHWOs are specified in **ASC 958** and the AICPA Audit and Accounting Guide for Not-for-Profit Organizations. The accrual basis of accounting is used. The VHWO reports its primary activities in the unrestricted asset class. Donor-restricted resources for specific operating purposes or future periods are reported as temporarily restricted assets. Assets contributed by the donor with permanent restrictions are reported as permanently restricted assets.

A VHWO provides four financial statements: (1) statement of financial position, (2) statement of activities, (3) cash flow statement, and (4) statement of functional expenses. All VHWOs must provide an analysis of all of their expenses, including depreciation, on its statement of functional expenses. Expenses are separated into types, such as salaries, supplies, and travel, and are summarized by individual program services and individual supporting services.

FIGURE 19–12
Statement of Cash Flows for a Voluntary Health and Welfare Organization

VOLUNTARY HEALTH AND WELFARE SERVICE
Statement of Cash Flows
For the Year Ended December 31, 20X2

Change in Net Assets		$ 60,100
Adjustments to Reconcile Changes in Net Assets to Net Cash Provided by Operating Activities:		
Depreciation	$ 9,500	
Gain on Sale of Investments	(13,000)	
Decrease in Short-Term Investments	9,000	
Increase in Accounts Receivable	(200)	
Increase in Pledges Receivable (net)	(16,800)	
Decrease in Inventories	1,900	
Increase in Prepaid Expenses	(800)	
Increase in Accounts Payable	3,700	
Increase in Accrued Expenses	500	
Contributions Restricted for Equipment Acquisition	(10,900)	
Endowment Contributions Restricted for Acquisition of Investments	(9,900)	(27,000)
Net Cash Provided by Operating Activities		$ 33,100
Cash Flows from Investing Activities:		
Purchase of Property, Plant & Equipment	$(13,400)	
Proceeds from Sale of Investments	40,000	
Purchase of Investments	(59,100)	
Investment Gain Restricted to Purchase of Investments	(1,000)	
Net Cash Used by Investing Activities		(33,500)
Cash Flows from Financing Activities:		
Mortgage Payments	$ (2,000)	
Capital Lease Agreements	1,000	
Contributions Restricted to Acquiring Fixed Assets	10,900	
Endowment Gain Restricted to Acquiring Investments	1,000	
Contributions Restricted for Permanent Endowment	9,900	
Net Cash Used in Financing Activities		20,800
Net Increase in Cash		$ 20,400
Cash at the Beginning of Year		47,600
Cash at the End of Year		$ 68,000

FIGURE 19–13 Statement of Functional Expenses for a Voluntary Health and Welfare Organization

VOLUNTARY HEALTH AND WELFARE SERVICE
Statement of Functional Expenses
Year Ended December 31, 20X2
(with comparative totals for 20X1)

	Program Services					Supporting Services			Total Program and Supporting Services Expenses	
	Research	Public Health Education	Professional Training	Community Services	Total	Management and General	Fund-Raising	Total	20X2	20X1
Salaries	$ 49,000	$58,200	$ 51,100	$53,800	$212,100	$66,100	$34,100	$100,200	$312,300	$347,000
Employee Benefits	2,800	2,900	2,900	2,900	11,500	4,100	1,000	5,100	16,600	16,800
Payroll Taxes, etc.	2,400	3,100	2,600	2,900	11,000	3,600	1,800	5,400	16,400	15,500
Total Salaries & Related Expenses	$ 54,200	$64,200	$ 56,600	$59,600	$234,600	$73,800	$36,900	$110,700	$345,300	$379,300
Professional Fees	200	1,000	5,200	1,600	8,000	3,000	1,500	4,500	12,500	12,000
Supplies	400	600	1,000	1,000	3,000	2,100	3,000	5,100	8,100	7,900
Telephone	400	1,400	1,200	4,300	7,300	2,500	7,200	9,700	17,000	16,800
Bad Debts & Other	400	3,200	900	2,800	7,300	2,600	6,000	8,600	15,900	14,300
Occupancy	1,000	3,400	6,000	9,000	19,400	3,000	1,000	4,000	23,400	20,500
Rental of Equipment	200	800	3,400	400	4,800	600	100	700	5,500	4,800
Printing & Publications	600	11,200	6,500	1,400	19,700	900	7,400	8,300	28,000	23,000
Travel	1,600	2,000	10,800	4,200	18,600	1,100	200	1,300	19,900	21,500
Conferences & Meetings	800	1,800	10,500	1,600	14,700	1,400	600	2,000	16,700	16,300
Awards & Grants	209,300	1,200	600	10,300	221,400				221,400	157,500
Postage & Shipping	900	200	1,300	1,200	3,600	200	100	300	3,900	4,200
Total Expenses before Depreciation	$270,000	$91,000	$104,000	$97,400	$562,400	$91,200	$64,000	$155,200	$717,600	$678,100
Depreciation of Buildings & Equipment	4,300	1,000	2,000	1,200	8,500	500	500	1,000	9,500	6,500
Total Functional Expenses	$274,300	$92,000	$106,000	$98,600	$570,900	$91,700	$64,500	$156,200	$727,100	$684,600
Payments to National Office									15,000	12,000
Total Expenses									$742,100	$696,600

OTHER NOT-FOR-PROFIT ENTITIES

LO 19-5

Understand financial reporting rules for other not-for-profit organizations.

There are many types of not-for-profit entities in addition to colleges and universities, hospitals, and voluntary health and welfare organizations. Our society depends heavily on such organizations for religious, educational, social, and recreational needs. Examples of other not-for-profit organizations (ONPOs) include the following:

Cemetery organizations	Private and community foundations
Civic organizations	Private elementary and secondary schools
Fraternal organizations	Professional associations
Labor unions	Public broadcasting stations
Libraries	Religious organizations
Museums	Research and scientific organizations
Other cultural institutions	Social and country clubs
Performing arts organizations	Trade associations
Political parties	Zoological and botanical societies

Accounting for an ONPO

The issuance of **ASC 958** has done much to bring the financial reporting standards of hospitals, voluntary health and welfare organizations, and other not-for-profit organizations into agreement. In addition to the FASB standards, the AICPA Audit Guide for Not-for-Profit Organizations provides guidance for accounting and financial reporting standards for ONPOs.

FYI

Beta Alpha Psi with which many accounting students are familiar is an example of an other not-for-profit organization (ONPO). In 2012, this ONPO reported total unrestricted revenue and support of more than $1.5 million and total expenses of almost $1.3 million.

ONPOs vary significantly in size and scope. Although accrual accounting is required for all ONPOs, some small organizations operate on a cash basis during the year and convert to an accrual basis at year-end. Other ONPOs have thousands or even millions of members and hold assets worth substantial sums of money. From the viewpoint of asset management and control procedures, such organizations may be virtually identical to a large business entity. The fact that they are not in business to earn profits from selling goods and services continues to distinguish some aspects of financial reporting for ONPOs from those of business entities, however.

Financial Statements of an ONPO

The principal purpose of an ONPO's financial statements is to explain how it has used available resources to carry out its activities. Therefore, the statements should disclose the nature and source of the resources acquired, any restrictions on the resources, and the principal programs and their costs; they also should provide information on the organization's ability to continue to carry out its objectives. **ASC 958** requires that an ONPO provide the following financial statements: (1) statement of financial position, (2) statement of activities, and (3) statement of cash flows. Although the statement of functional expenses is not required, it may be appropriate for an ONPO to prepare a statement providing information on expenses by function for each major program when the entity is involved in a broad range of activities or conducts activities that are very distinct from one another.

Statement of Financial Position for an ONPO

A statement of financial position for Ellwood Historical Society, a not-for-profit organization that renovates and preserves historical buildings in Sol City, appears in Figure 19–14. The society has its own governing board and is not associated with a government. The illustrated statement of financial position is a very simple one in light of the organization's well-defined mission.

FIGURE 19–14
Statement of Financial Position for an Other Not-for-Profit Organization

ELLWOOD HISTORICAL SOCIETY
Statement of Financial Position
June 30, 20X2 and 20X1

	20X2	20X1
Cash	$ 32,000	$ 16,800
Accounts Receivable	17,500	1,500
Contributions Receivable	48,000	30,000
Inventories	3,000	1,000
Prepaid Expenses	6,500	6,500
Cash Restricted for Long-Term Investments	2,000	0
Long-Term Investments (at fair value)	184,000	87,000
Property, Plant & Equipment (net)	242,000	246,000
Total Assets	$535,000	$388,800
Accounts Payable	$ 28,000	$ 28,000
Mortgage Payable	178,000	187,000
Net Assets:		
Unrestricted	179,000	130,800
Temporarily Restricted by Donors	48,000	43,000
Permanently Restricted by Donors	102,000	0
Total Liabilities & Net Assets	$535,000	$388,800

Land, Buildings, and Equipment Land, buildings, and equipment owned by an ONPO and used in its activities generally are recorded at historical cost and depreciated in the normal manner. Donated operating assets should be recorded at fair market value at the date of contribution. Unless the donor restricts the asset's use, the ONPO should include land, buildings, and equipment in unrestricted net assets reported on the statement of financial position.

Inexhaustible Collections Libraries, museums, art galleries, and similar entities often hold collections of works of art or other historical items for public viewing or research. Some organizations recognize such works of art or other historical treasures as assets, but most do not. Moreover, when individual works of art or historical holdings are recorded, the Financial Accounting Standards Board in **ASC 958** concludes that not-for-profit organizations are not required to record depreciation on those collections. **ASC 958** discusses specific rules for disclosure of the costs of items purchased and funds generated from their sale.

Statement of Activities

A statement of activities for Ellwood Historical Society presented in Figure 19–15 reports the support, revenue, expenses, transfers, and changes in fund balance during the fiscal period.

The format for the statement of activities is comparable to the statement of activities for a VHWO. For the Ellwood Historical Society, contributions are the primary source of support. However, both membership dues and admissions provide higher revenue than they do in the voluntary health and welfare setting. Memberships often provide free or reduced-rate admission to a museum, art gallery, or library. Thus, memberships and admissions may be interrelated in these organizations. Other types of organizations may have very different sources of funds and major expense categories. The financial statement categories and presentation should be adjusted to focus on these attributes in such cases.

As with VHWOs, depreciation charges for the period have been apportioned to the ONPO's primary programmatic activities and reported as expenses in the unrestricted assets section of the statement of activities. The ONPO's financial statements or the footnotes to them should disclose depreciation charges for the period and the

FIGURE 19–15 Statement of Activities for an Other Not-for-Profit Organization

ELLWOOD HISTORICAL SOCIETY
Statement of Activities
For the Year Ended June 30, 20X2

	Unrestricted	Temporarily Restricted	Permanently Restricted	Total
Revenues, Gains & Other Support:				
Contributions	$130,000	$ 78,000	$100,000	$308,000
Donated Services	3,000			3,000
Membership Dues	16,000			16,000
Admissions	12,000			12,000
Investment Income	12,200	2,600	12,000	26,800
Gain on Investments	5,000			5,000
Net Assets Released from Restriction:				
Program Use Restrictions	62,600	(62,600)		
Equipment Acquisition	13,000	(13,000)		
Endowment Transfers	10,000		(10,000)	
Total Revenues, Gains & Other Support	$263,800	$ 5,000	$102,000	$370,800
Program Services & Support:				
Community Education	$139,400			$139,400
Research	24,200			24,200
Auxiliary Activities	19,000			19,000
General & Administrative	20,000			20,000
Fund-Raising	13,000			13,000
Total Expenses	$215,600	$ 0	$ 0	$215,600
Change in Net Assets	$ 48,200	$ 5,000	$102,000	$155,200
Net Assets at Beginning of Year	130,800	43,000	0	173,800
Net Assets at End of Year	$179,000	$ 48,000	$102,000	$329,000

balance of accumulated depreciation to assist financial statement readers in assessing the ONPO's operating effectiveness and financial position.

An ONPO shows assets released from restriction during the period as reclassifications in the statement of activities. Thus, a contribution of $21,000 for research on Civil War activities would be included in the $78,000 reported as temporarily restricted contributions in Figure 19–15. If the organization spends $19,500 of the contribution during 20X2, that amount is part of the $62,600 reclassified from temporarily restricted to unrestricted assets (net assets released from program use restrictions) in 20X2. The $19,500 expense incurred in conducting the research is included in the $24,200 total reported as research expense in 20X2.

Statement of Cash Flows

The statement of cash flows for Ellwood Historical Society in Figure 19–16 begins with the net change in assets for the combined entity taken from the statement of activities. Adjustments are made for noncash revenues and expenses and changes in account balances to determine the amount of cash provided by operating activities. Net cash flows from investing activities and financing activities are added (deducted) to get the net increase (decrease) in cash for the period. The net cash flow for the period is added to the beginning cash balance in unrestricted assets to determine the balance the end of the period.

Summary of Accounting and Financial Reporting for an ONPO

Accounting for an ONPO is similar to that for a VHWO. An ONPO uses the accrual basis of accounting for financial reporting purposes and must provide a statement of financial

FIGURE 19–16
Statement of Cash Flows for an Other Not-for-Profit Organization

ELLWOOD HISTORICAL SOCIETY Statement of Cash Flows For the Year Ended June 30, 20X2		
Change in Net Assets		$ 155,200
Adjustments to Reconcile Changes in Net Assets to Net Cash Provided by Operating Activities:		
Depreciation	$ 17,000	
Gain on Sale of Equipment	(5,000)	
Increase in Accounts Receivable	(16,000)	
Increase in Contributions Receivable	(18,000)	
Increase in Inventories	(2,000)	
Contribution for Permanent Endowment	(100,000)	
Contribution Restricted for Plant	(13,000)	
Permanently Restricted Endowment Income	(2,000)	(139,000)
Net Cash Provided by Operating Activities		$ 16,200
Cash Flows from Investing Activities:		
Purchase of Property Plant, & Equipment	$ (16,000)	
Proceeds from Sale of Investments	3,000	
Purchase of Additional Investments	(100,000)	
Investment Income Restricted for Investments	(2,000)	
Proceeds from Sale of Equipment	8,000	
Net Cash Used by Investing Activities		(107,000)
Cash Flows from Financing Activities:		
Contributions Restricted for Permanent Endowment	$100,000	
Investment Income Restricted for Permanent Endowment	2,000	
Contributions Restricted for Acquiring Fixed Assets	13,000	
Mortgage Payments	(9,000)	
Net Cash Provided by Financing Activities		106,000
Net Increase in Cash		$ 15,200
Cash at Beginning of Year		16,800
Cash at End of Year		$ 32,000

position, statement of activities, and statement of cash flows for financial reporting purposes. When a large number of programs or a number of very different types of programs are part of the operations of an ONPO, it may be desirable to prepare a statement of expenses by functional area or major program as well. As a result of **ASC 958,** an ONPO's reporting requirements are substantially the same as those for a VHWO.

SUMMARY OF KEY CONCEPTS

Colleges and universities may be public or private. The GASB specifies the accounting and financial reporting standards for public (governmental) colleges and universities in **GASB 34** and **GASB 35. ASC 958** specifies accounting and reporting for private colleges and universities. This standard requires (1) charging depreciation to operations, (2) reporting the balance of net assets, (3) presenting the standards for accounting for contributions, (3) displaying standards for not-for-profit entities, and (4) specifying the accounting for investments held by not-for-profit entities. Private not-for-profit colleges and universities must provide three financial statements: (a) statement of financial position, (b) statement of activities, and (c) statement of cash flows. The net assets must be separated into three categories: (1) unrestricted, (2) temporarily restricted, and (3) permanently restricted based on restrictions imposed by donors, law, or contract.

Health care providers, voluntary health and welfare organizations (VHWOs), and other not-for-profit organizations (ONPOs) use the accrual basis of accounting and account for a majority of transactions in the unrestricted assets class. Health care providers and other not-for-profit entities report restricted funds as temporarily or permanently restricted, depending on the terms the donor established. Such funds are classified as restricted until the those conditions have been met and then are reclassified to the unrestricted net asset category. Hospitals deduct contractual adjustments from gross billings in arriving at net patient services revenue in the statement of operations. Hospitals include donated medical supplies and medicines as revenue in the period of receipt. Not-for-profit hospitals provide a statement of financial position, a statement of operations, a statement of changes in net assets, and a statement of cash flows. The statement of operations for a hospital must present a performance indicator, called something such as *Excess of Revenues over Expenses,* that includes both operating income and other income such as investments from trading securities in the general fund's investment portfolio. Below this operating indicator, hospitals present unrealized gains or losses on the general fund's other-than-trading securities, amounts for net assets released from restrictions used for purchase of property and equipment, and other nonoperating items.

VHWOs and ONPOs recognize contribution revenue, investment income, and gains and losses on investments for unrestricted, temporarily restricted, and permanently restricted net assets classes. They report contributions in the unrestricted net assets class unless the donor specifies their use in future periods or for a designated use, in which case they are included as contributions in the temporarily or permanently restricted net assets classes. When donor-imposed temporarily restricted contributions have been satisfied, a reclassification to unrestricted net assets is shown in the statement of activities, and any expenses associated with the release from restricted funds are included in expenses for unrestricted net assets for the period. Earnings of permanently restricted funds available for temporarily restricted or unrestricted purposes are shown as income in those net assets classes in the statement of activities for the period as well.

VHWOs and ONPOs prepare a statement of financial position, statement of activities, and statement of cash flows. VHWOs also must prepare a statement of functional expenses. Because of differences in the types and scope of activities of the various organizations, the statements may have differences in account titles and items included.

KEY TERMS

- assets whose use is limited, *988*
- board-designated resources, *986*
- costs of informational materials, *1010*
- donated materials and services, *1009*
- general fund, *986*
- performance indicator, *988*
- permanently restricted net assets, *988*
- pledges receivable, *1003*
- restricted funds, *986*
- specific operating purposes, *986*
- statement of functional expenses, *1010*
- temporarily restricted net assets, *988*
- unrestricted net assets, *988*

QUESTIONS

LO 19-2 **Q19-1** How are tuition scholarships reported by a private college or university?

LO 19-2 **Q19-2** What are the classifications of net assets reported in the statement of financial position by private colleges? Identify the types of assets assigned to each classification.

LO 19-1, 19-2 **Q19-3** What are the major differences in financial reporting for a public university and a private university?

LO 19-3 **Q19-4** What is the basis of accounting in a hospital's general fund? In its restricted funds?

LO 19-3 **Q19-5** How does a hospital account for donated services, equipment, and medical supplies?

LO 19-3 **Q19-6** A donor contributes $15,000 to a hospital to use for operating costs in the intensive care unit. How does it account for this contribution? How does it account for the expenditure of the $15,000?

LO 19-3 **Q19-7** What are the components of a hospital's net patient service revenue?

LO 19-3 **Q19-8** Where is a gain on the sale of hospital properties recorded by a hospital? How is the gain reported in the hospital's financial statements?

LO 19-3 **Q19-9** Is depreciation accounted for by a hospital? Why or why not?

LO 19-4 **Q19-10** What is a VHWO's basis of accounting for unrestricted assets and restricted assets?

LO 19-4 **Q19-11** Where does a VHWO record fixed assets? Does it record depreciation?

LO 19-4 **Q19-12** An individual contributes $10,000 to a VHWO for restricted use in a public health education service. How does the VHWO account for this contribution and for the $10,000 expenditure?

LO 19-4 **Q19-13** How does a VHWO account for pledges from donors?

LO 19-4 **Q19-14** Why do VHWOs not report all pledges received in the period in the unrestricted assets section of the statement of activities? Identify what is not included.

LO 19-4 **Q19-15** How do VHWOs account for donated services?

LO 19-4 **Q19-16** Describe the statement of functional expenses. What organizations must prepare it?

LO 19-5 **Q19-17** An alumna of a sorority donates $12,000 to it for restricted use in its community service activity. How does this ONPO account for the contribution? How does it account for the $12,000 expenditure?

LO 19-5 **Q19-18** Are donated services received by an ONPO accounted for in the same manner as those received by hospitals? Why or why not?

LO 19-5 **Q19-19** Should a rotary club, an ONPO, report depreciation expense? Why or why not?

LO 19-5 **Q19-20** Describe the statement of activities for an ONPO. How does it compare with a VHWO's statement of activities?

LO 19-5 **Q19-21** What are two examples of contributions to an ONPO that should be reported as temporarily restricted and two that should be reported as permanently restricted?

CASES

LO 19-3, 19-4, 19-5

Judgment

C19-1 Accounting for Donations

Hospitals, voluntary health and welfare organizations, and other not-for-profit organizations often rely heavily on donations of volunteers' time and equipment, supplies, or other assets.

Required

a. Specify the criteria to be used to determine the accounting for donated services to (1) hospitals, (2) VHWOs, and (3) ONPOs. Discuss the reasons for any differences in the accounting criteria.

b. How are donations of capital assets such as equipment accounted for by hospitals? Is depreciation recorded on these donations? Why or why not?

c. How are cash contributions accounted for by (1) hospitals, (2) VHWOs, and (3) ONPOs?

LO 19-5

Understanding

C19-2 Public Support to an Other Not-for-Profit Organization

Dawnes has just been elected treasurer of the local professional association of registered nurses. The association provides public health messages for the community as well as services for members. Dawnes is now preparing financial statements for the year and comes to you for advice on accounting for the proceeds from a major fund drive that occurred during the year. The nursing association received $25,000 in unrestricted donations and $15,000 in donations that are restricted to public health advertisements. A total of $6,000 has been incurred for public health advertising since the restricted donations were received.

The former treasurer accounted for the $40,000 of donations as revenue in the unrestricted fund, but Dawnes believes that this may not be correct because the association does not disclose the restricted nature of the donations for the advertisements.

Required

a. Discuss the accounting and financial statement disclosure to account for the $25,000 of unrestricted donations to the professional association.

b. How should the $15,000 of restricted contributions have been accounted for at the time of the donation? How should it have been reported on this year's financial statements?

LO 19-4

Analysis

C19-3 A Brief Analysis of the Financial Disclosures of United Way of America

Access the website for United Way Worldwide (www.unitedway.org) and then look through the site until you locate the most recent consolidated financial statements and supplemental schedule and the Form 990. Review the statements and Form 990 and then prepare a two- to three-page memo presenting your summary of the following items that refer to consolidated amounts for the most recent year available:

a. Briefly describe the reporting units that compose the consolidated entity of United Way of America. How are they operationally interrelated?

b. Using the consolidated statement of financial position, identify and briefly explain the consolidation eliminations. Then describe the components and amounts of each of the major items composing the consolidated net assets and equity. Finally, using the statement of financial position information along with the footnote information, describe the components of the custodial funds asset and custodial funds liability in the consolidated columns.

c. Using the consolidated statement of activities, what are the four largest revenue sources? What are the four largest expenses? What is the consolidated total of fund-raising expenses?

d. Using the supplemental schedule, the statement of functional expenses, and the footnotes, describe the four largest program services categories. What are the three largest expense categories?

e. Accessing the Form 990, briefly describe the major types of information required on this Internal Revenue Service form.

LO 19-5

C19-4 Conditional Gift to a Not-for-Profit Organization

Research

Gardner is the treasurer for the Central Illinois chapter of a national not-for-profit organization, the Alzheimer's Association. The chapter sends some of the money it raises to the national organization to support research into Alzheimer's disease. The chapter also provides information about the disease and sponsors support programs for families of patients within the community. The chapter has just received a significant pledge from a donor who has offered to contribute $20,000 a year for the next five years on the condition that the chapter sponsor a series of annual educational programs about the disease. If it does not do so, the donor will direct future contributions elsewhere.

The donor has already contributed the first $20,000, and the chapter has made the arrangements for the first educational workshop, which will take place in six weeks, shortly after the chapter's fiscal year-end.

Gardner is aware that the chapter intends to continue the educational workshops and has asked you, as a public accountant who volunteers to audit the chapter's financial statements each year, to research the appropriate accounting for the donor $20,000 contribution and $80,000 pledge in the chapter's financial statements for the current fiscal year.

Required

Obtain the most current accounting standards for accounting for conditional gifts to not-for-profit organizations. You can obtain access to accounting standards through the *Accounting Standards Codification*®. Write a memo to Gardner reporting your research findings. Support your recommendations with citations and quotations from the authoritative financial reporting standards.

LO 19-4

C19-5 Accounting for Contributions to and Activities of a Not-for-Profit Organization

Research

Finley, a manager in a public accounting firm, has volunteered to audit the financial statements of the Community Chest, a not-for-profit organization that raises funds to assist people in central Illinois who are homeless or have low incomes. In reviewing the statement of activities, Finley notices the revenue item Auction Extravaganza. The Community Chest treasurer indicates that this amount is the net proceeds for this event, which is the organization's largest fund-raising event for the year.

The Auction Extravaganza combines a black-tie dinner, entertainment, and an auction of numerous donated items. Supporters buy tickets to the event and bid on the auction items. The treasurer informs Finley that the dollar amount reported in the statement of activities is the total raised from ticket sales and from the auction, net of the expenses incurred for the event. These expenses include advertising and part of the cost of the dinner. The expenses, however, are comparatively low because a local hotel donates the ballroom and part of the cost of the dinner. A local auctioneer volunteers her time for the auction, the state university's music department provides the entertainment, and local businesses donate all auction items.

Required

Obtain the most current accounting standards for accounting for gifts to not-for-profit organizations. You can obtain access to accounting standards through the *Accounting Standards Codification*. Finley has asked you, as a staff accountant in the public accounting firm, to research the appropriate accounting for the Auction Extravaganza. Write a memo reporting your research findings. Support your recommendations with citations and quotations from the authoritative financial reporting standards.

LO 19-4

C19-6 An Analysis of the Financial Statements for the American Red Cross, a Voluntary Health and Welfare Organization

Analysis

Answer the following questions by reading the most recent consolidated financial statements of the American Red Cross (ARC) at its website, www.redcross.org. (The financial statements may be accessed through the Publications link on the website's home page.)

a. Why does the U.S. Army Audit Agency audit the ARC's financial statements?

b. For the most recent year, what was the ratio of program services expenses to total expenses? According to the Better Business Bureau, a ratio of program expenses to total expenses of 60 percent is considered acceptable. How does the ratio for the ARC compare with this benchmark?

c. What is the ARC's policy with respect to recognizing contribution revenue? Of the total contributions receivable at June 30 of the most recent year, what amount is temporarily restricted?

d. What interest rate was used to determine the present value for contributions receivable in years after June 30 of the most recent year?

e. For the most recent year ended June 30, what was the amount of net assets reclassified due to satisfaction of purpose and/or time restrictions?

f. Of all program services provided, which one had the highest total cost for salaries, wages, and employee benefits?

g. How does the ARC define *temporarily restricted net assets?*

h. At June 30 of the most recent year, what was the amount of conditional contributions? Did the ARC report these contributions in revenue for that year?

i. Of the total amount of unrestricted investment income reported for the most recent year, what amount came from dividends and interest?

j. What does the ARC report when donor-imposed purpose restrictions are accomplished or donor-imposed time restrictions expire?

k. Assume the ARC received a cash contribution during the most recent year that the donor restricted for disaster relief. Also assume that the ARC spent the amount donated in the year for disaster relief. Specify whether the ARC would report this donation on its statement of activities for the most recent year as (1) an increase in unrestricted net assets when the donation was received or (2) an increase in temporarily restricted net assets when the donation was received and as a reclassification of net assets from temporarily restricted to unrestricted when the donation was used.

l. Assume the ARC received a donation of equipment in the most recent year from a donor who did not place any restrictions on the donated assets. Specify whether the ARC would report this donation in its statement of activities for the current year as (1) an increase in unrestricted net assets when the equipment was received or (2) an increase in temporarily restricted net assets when the equipment was received and as a reclassification of net assets from temporarily restricted to unrestricted when the equipment is depreciated.

LO 19-1

C19-7 An Analysis of the Financial Statements of the University of Notre Dame, a Private University

Analysis

Answer the following questions by reading the most recent annual report of the University of Notre Dame that can be accessed by going to www.nd.edu.

a. For the most recent year, how much cash did donors contribute for the acquisition of buildings and equipment?

b. On the statement of changes in unrestricted net assets, how does the university decide what information to disclose in the nonoperating section?

c. On the statement of changes in unrestricted net assets for the most recent year, how much of the net assets released were for operations?

d. What is the university's accounting policy for its art collection?

e. What interest rate did the university use to determine the present value of multiyear pledges?

f. On the statement of financial position at June 30 for the most recent year, how much of the amount reported for contributions receivable is unrestricted?

g. At June 30 of the most recent year, what amount of unrestricted net assets is designated by the board?

h. True or false: Operating expenses on the statement of changes in unrestricted net assets for the most recent year are reported by functional categories.

i. True or false: Land, buildings, and equipment, net of accumulated depreciation, are reported in unrestricted net assets on the university's statement of financial position.

j. For the most recent year, what was the total investment return on investments reported in all three net asset categories? How much of this amount represented an increase in unrestricted net assets?

k. On the statement of financial position at June 30 of the most recent year, what amount of investments in endowments is reported in the permanently restricted net asset class?

LO 19-4

C19-8 Profiles of Large Charitable Organizations

Analysis

The BBB Wise Giving Alliance is widely known for presenting profiles of nationally soliciting charitable organizations. The BBB Wise Giving Alliance website provides information to donors and to assist charities to operate responsibly.

Required

Go to www.bbb.org/us/charity/ and provide answers for each of the following questions.

a. Briefly describe the standards for charity accountability used by the BBB Wise Giving Alliance. Explain why a charity might seek to be recognized as a BBB accredited charity.

b. Use the List of National BBB Wise Giving Reports to obtain information for the American Red Cross. Provide an overview of the types of information provided for it, including its governance and fund-raising.

c. Select another charity from the same location. You can select one with its name beginning with the same letter as your last name or a charity of your interest. Provide an overview of the types of information provided for your selected charity, including its governance and fund-raising. How does your selected charity compare with the ARC?

EXERCISES

LO 19-2

E19-1 Multiple-Choice Items on Colleges and Universities [AICPA Adapted]

Select the correct response for each of the following.

1. For the summer session of 20X2, Pacific University assessed its students $1,700,000 (net of refunds) covering tuition and fees for educational and general purposes. However, only $1,500,000 was expected to be realized because scholarships totaling $150,000 had been granted to students, and tuition remissions of $50,000 had been allowed to faculty members' children attending Pacific. What amount should Pacific include as revenues from student tuition and fees?

   a. $1,500,000.
   b. $1,550,000.
   c. $1,650,000.
   d. $1,700,000.

2. Tuition remissions for graduate student teaching assistantships should be classified by a university as

	Revenue	Expenditures
a.	No	No
b.	No	Yes
c.	Yes	Yes
d.	Yes	No

3. For the fall semester of 20X1, Dover University assessed its students $2,300,000 for tuition and fees. The net amount realized was only $2,100,000 because of the following revenue reductions:

Refunds occasioned by class cancellations and student withdrawals	$ 50,000
Tuition remissions granted to faculty members' families	10,000
Scholarships and fellowships (for which no services are rendered)	140,000

How much should Dover report for the period for revenue from tuition and fees?

a. $2,100,000.
b. $2,150,000.
c. $2,250,000.
d. $2,300,000.

(*Note:* Items 4 through 6 are based on the following information pertaining to Global University, a private institution, as of June 30, 20X1, and for the year then ended.)

Unrestricted net assets comprised $7,500,000 of assets and $4,500,000 of liabilities (including deferred revenues of $150,000). Among the receipts recorded during the year were unrestricted gifts of $550,000 and restricted grants totaling $330,000, of which $220,000 was expended during the year for current operations and $110,000 remained unexpended at the close of the year.

Volunteers from the surrounding communities regularly contribute their services to Global, which normally purchases them; it pays the volunteers nominal amounts to cover their travel costs. During the year, the amount for travel paid to these volunteers aggregated to $18,000. The gross value of services performed by them, determined by reference to equivalent wages available in that area for similar services, amounted to $200,000. The university believes the contributed services enhance its assets.

4. At June 30, 20X1, Global's unrestricted net asset balance was

   a. $7,500,000.
   b. $3,150,000.
   c. $3,000,000.
   d. $2,850,000.

5. For the year ended June 30, 20X1, what amount should be included in Global's revenue for the unrestricted gifts and restricted grants?

   a. $550,000.
   b. $660,000.
   c. $770,000.
   d. $880,000.

6. For the year ended June 30, 20X1, what amount should Global record as contribution revenue for the volunteers' services?

   a. $218,000.
   b. $200,000.
   c. $18,000.
   d. $0.

LO 19-3

E19-2 Multiple-Choice Items on Hospital Accounting [AICPA Adapted]

Select the correct response for each of the following.

(*Note:* The following data are for items 1 through 3.)

Under its established rate structure, Dodge Hospital would have earned patient service revenue of $5,000,000 for the year ended December 31, 20X3. However, Dodge did not expect to collect this amount because of contractual adjustments of $500,000 to third-party payers. In May 20X3, Dodge purchased bandages from Hunt Supply Company at a cost of $1,000. However, Hunt notified Dodge that the invoice was being canceled and that the bandages were being donated. On December 31, 20X3, Dodge had board-designated assets consisting of $40,000 in cash and investments of $700,000.

1. For the year ended December 31, 20X3, how much should Dodge report as net patient service revenue?

   a. $4,500,000.
   b. $5,000,000.
   c. $5,500,000.
   d. $5,740,000.

2. For the year ended December 31, 20X3, Dodge should record the donation of bandages as

   a. A $1,000 reduction in operating expenses.
   b. A decrease in net assets released from restrictions.

c. An increase in unrestricted revenue, gains, and other support.
d. A memorandum entry only.

3. How much of Dodge's board-designated assets should be included in unrestricted net assets?
   a. $0.
   b. $40,000.
   c. $700,000.
   d. $740,000.
4. Donated medicines that a hospital normally would purchase should be recorded at fair value and should be credited directly to
   a. Unrestricted revenue.
   b. Expense of medicines.
   c. Fund balance.
   d. Deferred revenue.
5. Which of the following would normally be included as revenue of a not-for-profit hospital?
   a. Unrestricted interest income from an endowment fund.
   b. An unrestricted gift.
   c. Tuition received from an educational program.
   d. All of the above.
6. An unrestricted gift pledge from an annual contributor to a not-for-profit hospital made in December 20X1 and paid in March 20X2 would generally be credited to
   a. Contribution revenue in 20X1.
   b. Contribution revenue in 20X2.
   c. Other income in 20X1.
   d. Other income in 20X2.
7. An organization of high school seniors assists patients at Lake Hospital. These student volunteers perform services that the hospital would not otherwise provide, such as wheeling patients in the park and reading to them. Lake has no employer–employee relationship with these volunteers, who donated 5,000 hours of service to Lake in 20X2. Assuming a minimum wage of $7.50, these services would amount to $18,750, and the estimated fair value of these services was $25,000. In Lake's 20X2 statement of operations, what amount should it report as donated services?
   a. $25,000.
   b. $18,750.
   c. $6,250.
   d. $0.
8. Which of the following would be included in the unrestricted funds of a not-for-profit hospital?
   a. Permanent endowments.
   b. Term endowments.
   c. Board-designated funds originating from previously accumulated income.
   d. Funds designated by the donor for plant expansion and replacement funds.
9. During the year ended December 31, 20X1, Greenacre Hospital received the following donations stated at their respective fair values:

Essential specialized employee-type services from members of a religious group	$100,000
Medical supplies restricted for indigent care from an association of physicians and used for such purpose in 20X1	30,000

   How much total revenue from donations should Greenacre report in 20X1?
   a. $0.
   b. $30,000.
   c. $100,000.
   d. $130,000.

10. Johnson Hospital's property, plant, and equipment (net of depreciation) consists of the following:

Land	$ 500,000
Buildings	10,000,000
Movable equipment	2,000,000

What amount should it report as restricted assets?

a. $0.
b. $2,000,000.
c. $10,500,000.
d. $12,500,000.

11. Depreciation should be recognized in the financial statements of

a. Proprietary (for-profit) hospitals only.
b. Both proprietary and not-for-profit hospitals.
c. Both proprietary and not-for-profit hospitals only when they are affiliated with a college or university.
d. All hospitals, in a memorandum entry not affecting the statement of revenue and expenses.

12. On March 1, 20X1, Rowe established a $100,000 endowment fund, the income from which is to be paid to Central Hospital for general operating purposes. Central does not control the fund's principal. The donor appointed Sycamore National Bank as trustee of this fund. What journal entry is required by Central to record the establishment of the endowment?

		Debit	Credit
a.	Cash	100,000	
	Nonexpendable Endowment Fund		100,000
b.	Cash	100,000	
	Endowment Fund Balance		100,000
c.	Nonexpendable Endowment Fund	100,000	
	Endowment Fund Balance		100,000
d.	Memorandum entry only	—	—

LO 19-3

Advanced StudyGuide .com

E19-3 Entries for a Hospital's Unrestricted (General) Fund

The following are transactions and events of the general fund of Sycamore Hospital, a not-for-profit entity, for the 20X6 fiscal year ending December 31, 20X6.

1. Provided a total of $6,200,000 in patient services.
2. Had total operating expenses of $5,940,000, as follows:

Nursing services	$2,070,000
Other professional expenses	1,250,000
Fiscal services	225,000
General services	1,510,000
Bad debts	125,000
Administration	260,000
Depreciation	500,000

Accounts credited for operating expenses other than depreciation:

Cash	$4,785,000
Allowance for Uncollectibles	125,000
Accounts Payable	210,000
Inventories	240,000
Donated Services	80,000

3. Allowed contractual adjustments of $220,000 as deductions from gross patient revenue.
4. Received a transfer of $180,000 from specific-purpose funds for payment of approved operating costs in accordance with the terms of the restricted gift.
5. Received a transfer of $200,000 from the temporarily restricted plant fund to purchase new equipment for the hospital.
6. Received $155,000 of unrestricted gifts.
7. Collected accounts receivable except for $75,000 written off.
8. Reported a $70,000 increase in the market value of the investment securities portfolio of the general fund from the beginning of the period. The board designated this entire income for other than current operations.

Required

a. Prepare journal entries in the general fund for each of the transactions and events.

b. Prepare the statement of operations for the general, unrestricted fund of Sycamore Hospital.

LO 19-3

E19-4 Entries for Other Hospital Funds

The following are selected transactions of the specific-purpose fund, the plant fund, and the endowment fund of Toddville Hospital, a not-for-profit entity:

1. Received in the endowment fund new permanent endowments totaling $150,000 and new term endowments totaling $120,000.
2. Received in the plant replacement and expansion fund pledges of $1,500,000 for the new wing and estimated uncollectibles at 10 percent.
3. Received in the specific-purpose fund gifts of $50,000 for research and $30,000 for education.
4. Received the following interest and dividends on investments:

Endowment fund (permanent)	$100,000
Plant fund	45,000
Specific-purpose fund (research)	31,000

This year's interest and dividends in the endowment fund have a donor-imposed permanent restriction.

5. Notified that the specific-purpose fund in the general fund had fulfilled the agreements related to restricted gifts as follows:

Research	$55,000
Education	32,000

Transferred cash of $70,000 to the general fund with the balance to be sent later.

6. Made the following investments:

Endowment fund	$270,000
Plant fund	160,000
Specific-purpose fund	75,000

Required

Prepare appropriate journal entries for the transactions in the specific-purpose fund, plant fund, and endowment fund.

LO 19-4

E19-5 Multiple-Choice Questions on Voluntary Health and Welfare Organization Accounting [AICPA Adapted]

Select the correct answer for each of the following questions.

1. Which basis of accounting should a voluntary health and welfare organization use?
   a. Cash basis for all funds.
   b. Modified accrual basis for all funds.

c. Accrual basis for all funds.

d. Accrual basis for some funds and modified accrual basis for other funds.

(*Note:* The following data are for questions 2 and 3.)

Town Service Center is a voluntary health and welfare organization funded by contributions from the general public. During 20X6, it received unrestricted pledges of $800,000, half of which were payable in 20X6 with the other half payable in 20X7 for use in 20X7. It was estimated that 10 percent of these pledges would be uncollectible. In addition, Ladd, a social worker on Town's permanent staff earning $30,000 annually for a normal workload of 1,500 hours, contributed an additional 600 hours of time to Town at no charge.

2. How much should Town report as unrestricted contribution revenue for 20X6 with respect to the pledges?

   a. $0.

   b. $360,000.

   c. $720,000.

   d. $800,000.

3. How much should Town record in 20X6 for contributed service expenses?

   a. $0.

   b. $1,200.

   c. $10,000.

   d. $12,000.

4. A voluntary health and welfare organization received a pledge in 20X1 from a donor specifying that the amount pledged be used in 20X3. The donor paid the pledge in cash in 20X2. For what amount should it be accounted?

   a. Contribution revenue in 20X3.

   b. Contribution revenue in 20X2.

   c. Contribution revenue in 20X1.

   d. Contribution revenue in the period in which the funds are spent.

5. Turner Fund, a voluntary health and welfare organization funded by contributions from the general public, received unrestricted pledges of $300,000 during 20X4. It was estimated that 10 percent of these pledges would be uncollectible. By the end of 20X4, $240,000 of them had been collected. It was expected that $35,000 more would be collected in 20X5 and the balance of $25,000 would be written off as uncollectible. What amount should Turner include as contribution revenue in 20X4?

   a. $300,000.

   b. $275,000.

   c. $270,000.

   d. $240,000.

(*Note:* The following data are for questions 6 through 9.)

On January 1, 20X2, State Center Health Agency, a voluntary health and welfare organization, received a bequest of a $200,000 certificate of deposit maturing on December 31, 20X6. The contributor's only stipulations were that the certificate be held to maturity and the interest revenue received annually be used to purchase books for children in the preschool program run by the agency to read. Interest revenue each of the years was $9,000, and the full $9,000 was spent for books each year. When the certificate was redeemed, the board of trustees adopted a formal resolution designating $150,000 of the proceeds for future purchase of playground equipment for the preschool program.

6. What should the temporarily restricted fund report in the 20X2 statement of activities?

   a. Legacies and bequests of $200,000.

   b. Investment income of $9,000.

   c. Transfers to unrestricted fund of $9,000.

   d. All of the above.

7. What amounts should the 20X2 statement of activities for the unrestricted fund report?
   a. Legacies and bequests of $200,000.
   b. Investment income of $9,000.
   c. Transfers from the restricted fund of $9,000.
   d. Contributions of $209,000.
8. What should be reported for the unrestricted fund in the 20X6 statement of activities?
   a. Transfers from restricted fund of $209,000.
   b. Board designated funds of $150,000.
   c. Playground equipment of $150,000.
   d. Transfers to plant and equipment fund of $150,000.
9. What should be reported for the unrestricted fund in the December 31, 20X6, statement of financial position?
   a. Liability for purchase of playground equipment, $150,000.
   b. Due to plant and equipment fund, $150,000.
   c. Board-designated funds, $150,000.
   d. Temporarily restricted funds, $200,000.

LO 19-4

Advanced StudyGuide .com

E19-6 Entries for Voluntary Health and Welfare Organizations

The following are the 20X2 transactions of the Midwest Heart Association, which has the following funds and fund balances on January 1, 20X2:

Unrestricted net assets	$281,000
Temporarily restricted net assets	87,000
Permanently restricted (endowment) net assets	219,000

1. Had Unrestricted pledges totaling $700,000, of which $150,000 is for 20X3 and uncollectible pledges estimated at 8 percent.
2. Had restricted use grants totaling $150,000.
3. Collected a total of $520,000 of current pledges and wrote off $30,000 of remaining uncollected current pledges.
4. Purchased office equipment for $15,000.
5. Used unrestricted funds to pay the $3,000 mortgage payment due on the buildings.
6. Received interest and dividends of $27,200 on unrestricted investments and $5,400 on temporarily restricted investments. An endowment investment with a recorded value of $5,000 was sold for $6,000, resulting in a realized transaction gain of $1,000. A donor-imposed restriction specified that gains on sales of endowment investments must be maintained in the permanently restricted endowment fund.
7. Recorded and allocated depreciation as follows:

Community services	$12,000
Public health education	7,000
Research	10,000
Fund-Raising	15,000
General and administrative	9,000

8. Had other operating costs of the unrestricted current fund:

Community services	$250,600
Public health education	100,000
Research	81,000
Fund-Raising	39,000
General and administrative	61,000

9. Received clerical services totaling $2,400 donated during the fund drive. These are not part of the expenses reported in item 8. It has been determined that these donated services should be recorded.

Required

a. Prepare journal entries for the transactions in 20X2.

b. Prepare a statement of activities for 20X2.

LO 19-4

E19-7 Determination of Contribution Revenue

Atwater Health Services, a voluntary health and welfare organization, has provided support for families with low income in the town of Atwater for approximately 20 years. In 20X6, it conducted a major funding campaign to help replace facilities that are no longer adequate and to generate operating and endowment funds.

The community of Atwater ran a number of special events, and the chamber of commerce made the fund-raising campaign a major activity for 20X6. In 20X6, Atwater Health Services received the following gifts and pledges:

1. The Plentiful family donated a lot adjacent to the current building for future use as a playground and parking lot. The family had purchased the lot for $22,000 several years ago. It had a current value of $42,000 at the date contributed.
2. A number of new pledges were received and many were partially or fully paid in 20X6. The following information was compiled:

Unrestricted pledges for use in 20X6	$120,000
Unrestricted pledges for use in 20X7	70,000
Pledges to support screening tests for children's hearing abilities	90,000
Pledge to assist in construction of addition to building; donor agrees to make eight annual payments of $50,000 each	400,000
	$680,000

3. Also during 20X6, $45,000 was spent in providing free vision tests for all grade school children in the community. A total of $38,000 collected in 20X4 and 20X5 for this purpose were used to help pay for the costs of providing the tests.

Required

a. Prepare the journal entries for 20X6 for these activities, including receipt of the first installment on the pledge for building construction, which was received at the end of 20X6. Atwater currently earns an 8 percent return on its investments. The present value of the seven future payments of $50,000 is $260,318.

b. Prepare the journal entry or entries recorded at the end of 20X7 upon receipt of the second payment on the pledge for building construction.

LO 19-5

E19-8 Multiple-Choice Items on Other Not-for-Profit Organizations [AICPA Adapted]

Select the correct response for each of the following.

1. On January 2, 20X2, a not-for-profit botanical society received a gift of an exhaustible fixed asset with an estimated useful life of 10 years and no salvage value. The donor's cost of this asset was $20,000, and its fair market value at the date of the gift was $30,000. What amount of depreciation of this asset should the society recognize in its 20X2 financial statements?

   a. $3,000.

   b. $2,500.

   c. $2,000.

   d. $0.

2. In 20X1, a not-for-profit trade association enrolled five new member companies, each of which was obligated to pay nonrefundable initiation fees of $1,000. The association received these fees in 20X1. Three of the new members paid the initiation fees in 20X1, and the other two paid them in 20X2. The association received from all members annual dues (excluding initiation fees) that have always covered the costs of services provided to members. Future dues can be reasonably expected to cover all costs of the organization's future services to members. Average membership

duration is 10 years because of mergers, attrition, and economic factors. What amount of initiation fees from these five new members should the association recognize as revenue in 20X1?

a. $5,000.
b. $3,000.
c. $500.
d. $0.

3. Roberts Foundation received a nonexpendable endowment of $500,000 in 20X3 from Multi Enterprise and invested it in publicly traded securities. Multi did not specify how gains and losses from dispositions of endowment assets were to be treated. No restrictions were placed on the use of dividends received and interest earned on fund resources. In 20X4, Roberts realized gains of $50,000 on sales of fund investments and received total interest and dividends of $40,000 on fund securities. The amount of these capital gains, interest, and dividends available for expenditure by Roberts's unrestricted current fund is

   a. $0.
   b. $40,000.
   c. $50,000.
   d. $90,000.

4. In July 20X2, Ross donated $200,000 cash to a church with the stipulation that the revenue generated from this gift be paid to him during his lifetime. The conditions of this donation are that after Ross dies, the church may use the principal for any purpose voted on by its elders. The church received interest of $16,000 on the $200,000 for the year ended June 30, 20X3, and remitted the interest to Ross. In the church's June 30, 20X3, annual financial statements should report

   a. $200,000 as temporarily restricted net assets in the balance sheet.
   b. $184,000 as revenue in the activity statement.
   c. $216,000 as revenue in the activity statement.
   d. Both *a* and *c*.

5. The following expenditures were among those a not-for-profit botanical society incurred during 20X4:

Printing of annual report	$15,000
Unsolicited merchandise sent to encourage contributions	35,000

   What amount should be classified as fund-raising costs in the society's activity statement?

   a. $0.
   b. $5,000.
   c. $35,000.
   d. $40,000.

6. Trees Forever, a community foundation, incurred $5,000 in expenses during 20X3 putting on its annual fund-raising talent show. In its statement of activities, Trees Forever should report the $5,000 as

   a. A contra asset account.
   b. A contra revenue account.
   c. A reduction of fund-raising costs.
   d. Part of fund-raising costs.

7. In 20X3, Burr Foundation's board of trustees designated $100,000 from its current funds for college scholarships. Also in 20X3, the foundation received a bequest of $200,000 from the estate of a benefactor who specified that it be used for hiring teachers to tutor students with disabilities. What amount should be accounted for as temporarily restricted funds?

   a. $0.
   b. $100,000.
   c. $200,000.
   d. $300,000.

(*Note:* The following information is for questions 8 through 10.)

United Together, a labor union, had the following receipts and expenses for the year ended December 31, 20X2:

Receipts:	
Per capita dues	$680,000
Initiation fees	90,000
Sales of organizational supplies	60,000
Nonexpendable gift restricted by donor for loan purposes for 10 years	30,000
Nonexpendable gift restricted by donor for loan purposes in perpetuity	25,000
Expenses:	
Labor negotiations	500,000
Fund-Raising	100,000
Membership development	50,000
Administrative and general	200,000

The union's constitution provides that 10 percent of the per capita dues be designated for the strike insurance fund to be distributed for strike relief at the discretion of the union's executive board.

8. In United Together's statement of activities for the year ended December 31, 20X2, what amount should it report under the classification of revenue from unrestricted funds?
   a. $740,000.
   b. $762,000.
   c. $770,000.
   d. $830,000.
9. In United Together's statement of activities for the year ended December 31, 20X2, what amount should it report under the classification of program services?
   a. $500,000.
   b. $550,000.
   c. $600,000.
   d. $850,000.
10. In United Together's statement of activities for the year ended December 31, 20X2, what amounts should it report under the classifications of temporarily and permanently restricted net assets?
    a. $0 and $55,000, respectively.
    b. $55,000 and $0, respectively.
    c. $30,000 and $25,000, respectively.
    d. $25,000 and $30,000, respectively.

LO 19-5

E19-9 Statement of Activities for an Other Not-for-Profit Organization

The following is a list of selected account balances in the unrestricted operating fund for Pleasant School:

	Debit	Credit
Unrestricted Net Assets, July 1, 20X1		$ 420,000
Tuition & Fees		1,200,000
Contributions		165,000
Auxiliary Activities Revenue		40,000
Investment Income (for current operations)		32,000
Other Revenue		38,000
Instruction	$1,050,000	
Auxiliary Activities Expenses	37,000	
Administration	250,000	
Fund-Raising	28,000	
Transfer from Temporarily Restricted Assets		130,000
Transfer from Permanently Restricted Assets		12,000

Required

Prepare a statement of activities for Pleasant School's unrestricted operating fund for the year ended June 30, 20X2.

PROBLEMS

LO 19-2 **P19-10 Financial Statements for a Private, Not-for-Profit College**

Advanced StudyGuide .com

Friendly College is a small, privately supported liberal arts college. The college uses a fund structure; however, it prepares its financial statements in conformance with **ASC 958.**

	Debit	Credit
Unrestricted Items:		
Cash	$210,000	
Accounts Receivable (student tuition and fees, less allowance for doubtful accounts of $9,000)	341,000	
State Appropriation Receivable	75,000	
Accounts Payable		$ 45,000
Deferred Revenue		66,000
Unrestricted Net Assets		515,000
Restricted Items:		
Cash	$ 7,000	
Investments	60,000	
Temporarily Restricted Net Assets		$ 67,000

Partial balance sheet information as of June 30, 20X2, follows:
The following transactions occurred during the fiscal year ended June 30, 20X3:

1. Received a gift of $100,000 on July 7, 20X2, from an alumnus who stipulated that half the gift be restricted to purchase books for the university library and the remainder be used to establish an endowed scholarship fund. The alumnus further requested that the income generated by the scholarship fund be used annually to award a scholarship to a qualified disadvantaged student. On July 20, 20X2, the board of trustees resolved that the funds of the newly established scholarship endowment fund would be invested in savings certificates and purchased them on July 21, 20X2.
2. Collected $1,900,000 of revenue from student tuition and fees applicable to the year ended June 30, 20X3. Of this amount, $66,000 was collected in the prior year, and $1,686,000 was collected during the year ended June 30, 20X3. In addition, on June 30, 20X3, the college had received cash of $158,000 representing deferred revenue fees for the session beginning July 1, 20X3.
3. Collected $349,000 of outstanding accounts receivable at the beginning of the year ended June 30, 20X3. The balance was determined to be uncollectible and was written off against the allowance account, which on June 30, 20X3, was increased by $3,000 to $11,000.
4. Earned and collected interest charges of $6,000 on late student fee payments during the year.
5. Received the state appropriation during the year. The state made an additional unrestricted appropriation of $50,000 but had not paid the college as of June 30, 20X3.
6. Received an unrestricted gift of $25,000 cash from college alumni.
7. Sold restricted investments of $21,000 for $26,000 during the and received temporarily restricted investment interest income amounting to $1,900.
8. Recorded unrestricted operating expenses of $1,777,000 during the year, not including year-end accruals or transfers from other categories of net assets. On June 30, 20X3, $59,000 of these expenses remained unpaid.
9. Had restricted current funds of $13,000 released and spent them for authorized operating purposes during the year.

10. Paid the accounts payable on June 30, 20X2, during the year.
11. Earned and received during the $7,000 interest on the savings certificates purchased in accordance with the board of trustees' resolutions as discussed in transaction 1.

Required

a. Prepare a comparative balance sheet for Friendly College as of June 30, 20X2, and June 30, 20X3.

b. Prepare a statement of activities for Friendly College for the year ended June 30, 20X3.

LO 19-3

P19-11 Balance Sheet for a Hospital

Advanced StudyGuide .com

Brookdale Hospital hired an inexperienced controller early in 20X4. Near the end of 20X4, the board of directors decided to conduct a major fund-raising campaign. They wished to have the December 31, 20X4, statement of financial position for Brookdale fully conform with current generally accepted principles for hospitals. The trial balance prepared by the controller at December 31, 20X4, follows:

	Debit	Credit
Cash	$ 100,000	
Investment in Short-Term Marketable Securities	200,000	
Investment in Long-Term Marketable Securities	300,000	
Interest Receivable	15,000	
Accounts Receivable	55,000	
Inventory	35,000	
Land	120,000	
Buildings & Equipment	935,000	
Allowance for Depreciation		$ 260,000
Accounts Payable		40,000
Mortgage Payable		320,000
Fund Balance		1,140,000
Total	$1,760,000	$1,760,000

Additional Information

1. Your analysis of the contributions receivable as of December 31, 20X4, determined that there were unrecognized contributions for the following:

Unrestricted use	$ 40,000
Cancer research	10,000
Purchase of equipment	20,000
Permanently restricted endowment principal	30,000
Total	$100,000

2. Short-term investments at year-end consist of $150,000 of unrestricted funds and $50,000 of funds restricted for future cancer research. All of the long-term investments are held in the permanently restricted endowment fund.
3. Land is carried at its current market value of $120,000. The original owner purchased the land for $70,000, and at the time of donation to the hospital, it had an appraised value of $95,000.
4. Buildings purchased 11 years ago for $600,000 had an estimated useful life of 30 years. Equipment costing $150,000 was purchased 7 years ago and had an expected life of 10 years. The controller had improperly increased the reported values of the buildings and equipment to their current fair value of $935,000 and had incorrectly computed the accumulated depreciation.
5. The board of directors voted on December 29, 20X4, to designate $100,000 of unrestricted funds invested in short-term investments for developing a drug rehabilitation center.

Required

Prepare in good form a balance sheet for Brookdale Hospital at December 31, 20X4.

LO 19-5

P19-12 Entries and Statement of Activities for an Other Not-for-Profit Organization [AICPA Adapted]

A group of civic-minded merchants in Eldora organized the Committee of 100 for establishing the Community Sports Club, a not-for-profit sports organization for local youth. Each of the committee's 100 members contributed $1,000 toward the club's capital and, in turn, received a participation certificate. In addition, each participant agreed to pay dues of $200 a year for the club's operations. All dues have been collected in full by the end of each fiscal year ending March 31. Members who have discontinued their participation have been replaced by an equal number of new members through transfer of the participation certificates from the former members to the new ones. Following is the club's trial balance for April 1, 20X2:

	Debit	Credit
Cash	$ 9,000	
Investments (at market, equal to cost)	58,000	
Inventories	5,000	
Land	10,000	
Building	164,000	
Accumulated Depreciation—Building		$130,000
Furniture & Equipment	54,000	
Accumulated Depreciation—Furniture & Equipment		46,000
Accounts Payable		12,000
Participation Certificates (100 at $1,000 each)		100,000
Cumulative Excess of Revenue over Expenses		12,000
Total	$300,000	$300,000

Transactions for the year ended March 31, 20X3, follow:

Collections from participants for dues	$20,000
Snack bar and soda fountain sales	28,000
Interest and dividends received	6,000
Additions to voucher register:	
House expenses	17,000
Snack bar and soda fountain	26,000
General and administrative	11,000
Vouchers paid	55,000
Assessments for capital improvements not yet incurred (assessed on March 20, 20X3; none collected by March 31, 20X3; deemed 100% collectible during year ending March 31, 20X4)	10,000
Unrestricted bequest received	5,000

Adjustment Data

1. Investments are valued at market, which totaled $65,000 on March 31, 20X3. There were no investment transactions during the year.
2. Depreciation for year:

Building	$4,000
Furniture & equipment	8,000

3. Allocation of depreciation:

House expenses	$9,000
Snack bar & soda fountain	2,000
General and administrative	1,000

4. Actual physical inventory on March 31, 20X3, was $1,000 and pertains to the snack bar and soda fountain.

Required

a. Record the transactions and adjustments in journal entry form for the year ended March 31, 20X3. Omit explanations.

b. Prepare the appropriate all-inclusive statement of activities for the year ended March 31, 20X3.

LO 19-3

P19-13 Entries and Statements for General Fund of a Hospital

The postclosing trial balance of the general fund of Serene Hospital, a not-for-profit entity, on December 31, 20X1, was as follows:

	Debit	Credit
Cash	$ 125,000	
Accounts Receivable	400,000	
Allowance for Uncollectibles		$ 50,000
Due from Specific-Purpose Fund	40,000	
Inventories	95,000	
Prepaid Expenses	20,000	
Investments	900,000	
Property, Plant & Equipment	6,100,000	
Accumulated Depreciation		1,500,000
Accounts Payable		150,000
Accrued Expenses		55,000
Deferred Revenue—Reimbursement		75,000
Bonds Payable		3,000,000
Fund Balance—Unrestricted		2,850,000
Total	$7,680,000	$7,680,000

During 20X2 the following transactions occurred:

1. Provided the value of patient services, $6,160,000.
2. Approved contractual adjustments of $330,000 from patients' bills.
3. Had operating expenses totaling $5,600,000 as follows:

Nursing services	$1,800,000
Other professional services	1,200,000
Fiscal services	250,000
General services	1,550,000
Bad debts	120,000
Administration	280,000
Depreciation	400,000

Accounts credited for operating expenses other than depreciation:

Cash	$4,580,000
Allowance for Uncollectibles	120,000
Accounts Payable	170,000
Accrued Expenses	35,000
Inventories	195,000
Prepaid Expenses	30,000
Donated Services	70,000

4. Received $75,000 cash from specific-purpose fund for partial reimbursement of $100,000 for operating expenditures made in accordance with a restricted gift. The receivable increased by the remaining $25,000 to an ending balance of $65,000.
5. Had payments for inventories and prepaid expenses of $176,000 and $24,000, respectively.
6. Received $85,000 income from endowment fund investments.

7. Sold an X-ray machine that had cost $30,000 and had accumulated depreciation of $20,000 for $17,000.
8. Collected $5,800,000 in receivables and wrote off $132,000.
9. Acquired investments amounting to $60,000.
10. Had $72,000 income from board-designated investments.
11. Paid the beginning balance in Accounts Payable and Accrued Expenses.
12. Had a $20,000 increase in Deferred Revenue—Reimbursement.
13. Received $140,000 from the plant replacement and expansion fund for acquiring fixed assets.
14. Had $63,000 in net receipts from the cafeteria and gift shop.

Required

a. Prepare journal entries to record the transactions for the general fund. Omit explanations.
b. Prepare comparative balance sheets for only the general fund for 20X2 and 20X1.
c. Prepare a statement of operations for the unrestricted general fund for 20X2.
d. Prepare a statement of cash flows for 20X2.

LO 19-4

P19-14 Statements for Current Funds of a Voluntary Health and Welfare Organization [AICPA Adapted]

Following are the adjusted current funds trial balances of Community Association for Children With Disabilities, a voluntary health and welfare organization, on June 30, 20X4:

COMMUNITY ASSOCIATION FOR CHILDREN WITH DISABILITIES
Adjusted Current Funds Trial Balances
June 30, 20X4

	Unrestricted		Restricted	
	Debit	Credit	Debit	Credit
Cash	$ 40,000		$ 9,000	
Bequest Receivable			5,000	
Pledges Receivable	12,000			
Accrued Interest Receivable	1,000			
Investments (at market)	100,000			
Accounts Payable & Accrued Expenses		$ 50,000		$ 1,000
Deferred Revenue		2,000		
Allowance for Uncollectible Pledges		3,000		
Fund Balances, July 1, 20X3:				
Designated		12,000		
Undesignated		26,000		
Restricted				23,000
Transfers of Expired Endowment Fund Principal		20,000	20,000	
Contributions		300,000		15,000
Membership Dues		25,000		
Program Service Fees		30,000		
Investment Income		10,000		
Deaf Children's Program Expenses	120,000			
Blind Children's Program Expenses	150,000			
Management and General Services	45,000		4,000	
Fund-Raising Services	8,000		1,000	
Provision for Uncollectible Pledges	2,000			
Total	$478,000	$478,000	$39,000	$39,000

Required

a. Prepare a statement of activities for the year ended June 30, 20X4.
b. Prepare a statement of financial position as of June 30, 20X4.

LO 19-4

P19-15 Comparative Journal Entries for a Governmental Entity and a Voluntary Health and Welfare Organization [AICPA Adapted]

Following are four independent transactions or events that relate to a local government and a voluntary health and welfare organization:

1. Made a disbursement of $25,000 from the general fund unrestricted assets for the cash purchase of new equipment.
2. Received an unrestricted cash gift of $100,000 from a donor.
3. Sold investments in common stocks with a total carrying value of $50,000 of a permanently restricted endowment fund for $55,000 before any dividends were earned on them. The donor-restricted gain is to remain in the permanently restricted fund.
4. Sold general obligation bonds payable with a face amount of $1,000,000 at par with the proceeds required to be used for construction of a new building. This building was completed at a total cost of $1,000,000, and the total amount of bond issue proceeds was disbursed toward this cost. Disregard interest capitalization.

Required

a. For each of these transactions or events, prepare journal entries without explanations, specifying the affected funds and showing how these transactions or events should be recorded by a local government whose debt is serviced by general tax revenue.

b. For each of these transactions or events, prepare journal entries without explanations, specifying the affected funds and showing how a VHWO should record these transactions or events.

LO 19-3

P19-16 Matching Effects of Transactions on a Hospital's Financial Statements [AICPA Adapted]

DeKalb Hospital, a large not-for-profit organization, has adopted an accounting policy that does not imply a time restriction on gifts of long-lived assets.

For each of the six items presented, select the best match from the Match List.

Transactions	Match List
1. Received news that DeKalb's board had designated $1,000,000 to purchase investments whose income will be used for capital improvements.	A. Increase in unrestricted revenues, gains, and other support
2. Received income from investments in item 1, which was not previously accrued.	B. Decrease in an expense
3. Received benefactor-provided funds for building expansion.	C. Increase in temporarily restricted net assets
4. Used the funds in item 3 to purchase a building in the fiscal period following the period in which they funds were received.	D. Increase in permanently restricted net assets
5. Received annual financial statements prepared by an accounting firm without charge.	E. No required reportable event
6. Received investments subject to the donor's requirement that investment income be used to pay for outpatient services.	

LO 19-3

P19-17 Balance Sheet for a Hospital

The following information is for funds used to account for the transactions of the Hospital of Havencrest, which is operated by a religious organization. The balances in the accounts are as of June 30, 20X8, the end of the hospital's fiscal year.

	General Fund	Specific-Purpose Fund	Plant Replacement and Expansion Fund	Endowment Fund
Cash	$ 30,000	$32,000	$140,000	$ 20,000
Accounts Receivable	25,000			
Allowance for Uncollectibles	(5,000)			
Inventories	50,000			
Prepaid Expenses	10,000			
Long-Term Investments	100,000		60,000	500,000
Property, Plant & Equipment	300,000			
Accumulated Depreciation	(140,000)			
Accounts Payable	45,000			
Accrued Expenses	17,000			
Deferred Revenue	11,000			
Current Portion—Long-Term Debt	24,000			
Mortgage Payable	125,000			

Additional Information

The $32,000 in the specific-purpose fund is restricted for research activities to be conducted by the hospital.

Required

Prepare a balance sheet for Havencrest at June 30, 20X8.

LO19-3

P19-18 Matching Transactions to Effects on Statement of Changes in Net Assets for a Hospital

Match the transactions on the left with their effects on the statement of changes in net assets on the right for a private, not-for-profit hospital.

Transactions

1. Billed patients for services rendered.
2. Realized a gain from the sale of permanently invested securities.
3. Recorded depreciation expense for the year.
4. Designated assets for plant expansion.
5. Received restricted contributions for research activities received.
6. Restricted contributions for equipment acquisition.
7. Acquired equipment with all contributions in item 6 received.
8. Earned endowment income. The donor placed no restrictions on the investment earnings.
9. Expended 50 percent of the contributions in item 5 restricted for research.
10. Received cash contribution from donor who stipulated the contribution be permanently invested.
11. Acquired investments with cash received in item 10.
12. Received tuition revenue from hospital nursing program and cash from sales of goods in the hospital gift shop.

Effects of Transactions on Statement of Changes in Net Assets

A. Increases unrestricted net assets
B. Decreases unrestricted net assets
C. Increases temporarily restricted net assets
D. Decreases temporarily restricted net assets
E. Increases permanently restricted net assets
F. Decreases permanently restricted net assets
G. Does not affect the statement of changes in net assets

LO 19-4

P19-19 Matching Transactions to Effects on Statement of Activities for a Voluntary Health and Welfare Organization

Match the transactions on the left with their effects on the statement of activities on the right for a voluntary health and welfare organization. A transaction may have more than one effect.

Transactions	Effects of Transactions on Statement of Activities
1. Received cash contributions restricted by donors for research.	A. Increases unrestricted net assets
2. Incurred fund-raising costs.	B. Decreases unrestricted net assets
3. Recorded depreciation expense for the year.	C. Increases temporarily restricted net assets
4. Designated assets for plant expansion.	D. Decreases temporarily restricted net assets
5. Realized a gain from the sale of securities that were permanently restricted. The donor specified that any gains from sales of these securities be preserved and invested in other permanently restricted investments.	E. Increases permanently restricted net assets
6. Earned endowment income. The donor specified that the income be used for community service.	F. Decreases permanently restricted net assets
7. Received a multiyear pledge with cash being received this year and for the next four years. Donors did not place any use restrictions on how the pledges were to be spent.	G. Is not reported on the statement of activities
8. Earned income from investments of assets that the board designated in item 4.	
9. Received pledges from donors who placed no time or use restrictions on how the pledges were to be spent.	
10. Received cash contributions restricted by donors for equipment.	
11. Acquired equipment with all of the contributions received in item 10.	
12. Expended 75 percent of the contributions received in item 1 for research.	

LO 19-2

P19-20 Net Asset Identification for Transactions Involving a Private Not-for-Profit University

Buckwall University (BU), a private not-for-profit university, had the following transactions during the year ended June 30, 20X8:

1. Assessed students $2,000,000 for tuition for the winter semester, starting in January 20X8.
2. Received $1,000,000 from the federal government to be distributed to qualified students as loans and grants.
3. Recognized depreciation expense of $200,000 on university buildings and equipment for the fiscal year.
4. Received $1,500,000 in alumni contributions restricted to the construction of a new library building. Construction is expected to begin in September 20X8.
5. Invested the contributions received in item 4 in equity securities that had a market value of $1,650,000 on June 30, 20X8.
6. Received $75,000 of investment revenue from investments in a term endowment. The donor stipulated that the investment revenue be used to fund scholarships for qualified entering freshmen.
7. Used $60,000 of the investment revenue in item 6 to fund scholarships during the year ended June 30, 20X8.
8. Designated $250,000 of cash for refurbishing the steam tunnels used for heating the university during the winter.
9. Received from an alumnus a contribution of artwork with a fair value of $3,750,000. The donor has stipulated that the artwork be preserved, that it not be sold, and that it be on public

view in the university museum. The university has a policy of recording donations of works of art and historical treasures.

10. Acquired debt securities at a cost of $400,000 during the year that the governing board required to keep intact for the next five years and to use their interest revenue for funding summer research grants to faculty of BU.
11. Received during the year ended June 30, 20X8, interest revenue from the debt securities in item 10, which amounted to $18,000, of which $12,000 was used for research grants.

Required

Indicate for each numbered transactions the net asset class it affected for the year ended June 30, 20X8. The three net asset classes are (1) unrestricted, (2) temporarily restricted, and (3) permanently restricted. Your answer also should specify the dollar amount and whether the asset class increased or decreased.

LO 19-4

P19-21 Items on Voluntary Health and Welfare Organization [AICPA Adapted]

Items 1 through 6 represent various transactions pertaining to Crest Haven, a voluntary health and welfare organization, for the year ended December 31, 20X2. The information presented includes a list of how transactions could affect the statement of activities (List A Effects) and the statement of cash flows (List B Effects). Crest Haven follows **ASC 958.**

Transactions

1. Received pledges of $500,000 made by various donors to acquire new equipment in 20X3.
2. Received donor-stipulated dividends and interest of $40,000 from endowment investments whose earnings must be used for research in 20X3.
3. Received cash donations of $350,000 with no information regarding how they are to be used.
4. Acquired donor-stipulated investments of $250,000 from cash donated in 20X0 to be invested permanently.
5. Recorded Depreciation expense of $75,000 for 20X2.
6. Received $300,000 of the amount pledged in transaction 1.

Required

Indicate how Crest Haven should report each transaction on the (1) statement of activities and (2) statement of cash flows prepared for the year ended December 31, 20X2. Crest Haven reports separate columns for changes in unrestricted, temporarily restricted, and permanently restricted net assets on its statement of activities. In addition, Crest Haven uses the direct method of reporting its cash flows from operating activities. The items in List A Effects and List B Effects may be used once, more than once, or not at all.

Example

Cash paid to employees and suppliers: List A = D List B = I

Statement of Activities List A Effects	Statement of Cash Flows List B Effects
A. Increases unrestricted net assets	H. Increases cash flows from operating activities
B. Increases temporarily restricted net assets	I. Decreases cash flows from operating activities
C. Increases permanently restricted net assets	J. Increases cash flows from investing activities
D. Decreases unrestricted net assets	K. Decreases cash flows from investing activities
E. Decreases temporarily restricted net assets	L. Increases cash flows from financing activities
F. Decreases permanently restricted net assets	M. Decreases cash flows from financing activities
G. Is not reported on the statement of activities	N. Is not reported on the statement of cash flows

LO 19-3

P19-22 Contributions to a Hospital [AICPA Adapted]

Alpha Hospital, a large not-for-profit organization, has adopted an accounting policy that does not imply a time restriction on gifts of long-lived assets.

Required

For items 1 through 6, indicate the effect of the transaction on Alpha's financial statements by selecting the appropriate letter.

Transactions	Effect
1. Received information that Alpha's board had designated \$1,000,000 to purchase investments whose income will be used for capital improvements.	A. Increase in unrestricted revenues, gains, and other support
2. Received income from investments in item 1, which was not previously accrued.	B. Decrease in expense
3. Received benefactor-provided funds for a building expansion.	C. Increase in temporarily restricted net assets
4. Used funds in item 3 to purchase a building in the fiscal period following the period they were received.	D. Increase in permanently restricted net assets
5. Received annual financial statements prepared by an accounting firm without charge.	E. No required reportable event
6. Received investments subject to the donor's requirement that investment income be used to pay for outpatient services.	

LO 19-3

P19-23 Evaluating Items for a Hospital's Statement of Operations

Smallville Community Hospital, a not-for-profit hospital, needs to evaluate a number of items to determine their proper placement on its statement of operations (either above or below the performance measure of Excess of Revenues over Expenses.

Items	Where Reported
1. Bad debts expense.	A. Above the performance measure line
2. Donated supplies used in patient care.	B. Below the performance measure line
3. Unrestricted investment interest income.	C. Not reported on the statement of operations
4. Gain on sale of hospital assets.	
5. Net assets released from restriction for acquisition of equipment.	
6. Net assets released from restriction for use in hospital operations.	
7. Gain on sale of donor-required permanently restricted endowment investments.	
8. Investment interest income that donor restricted for use in medical care education programs, which the hospital plans to begin next year.	
9. Pledges for a new hospital building wing to be constructed next year.	
10. Revenue from sales of cafeteria items.	
11. Donations of specialized, professional-quality services.	
12. Depreciation expense on hospital equipment.	
13. Resources designated by the hospital board of directors to be set aside for the new hospital wing.	
14. Gift of new heart-monitoring equipment.	
15. Charity care provided by the hospital in accordance with its state charter.	
16. Contractual adjustment to the normal service charge for persons covered by an insurance company's health insurance.	
17. Proceeds of a bond issue for the new wing.	
18. Purchase of new operating tables.	
19. Recognition of unrealized holding gain for change in market value of investment securities. Income is in excess of amounts designated for current operations.	

Required

Select the proper letter from the Where Reported column to match each item in the left-hand column. If an item is presented in two or more places on the statement of operations, provide the correct answer for each placement. It is possible that an item need not be reported on the hospital's statement of operations.

LO 19-1–19-5 **P19-24** **True-False Questions about Not-for-Profit Accounting and Reporting**

Determine whether each of the following is true or false. Assume that each organization is a private, not-for-profit entity. It is possible that an item need not be reported on the hospital's statement of operations.

1. A statement of functional expenses is required for a musical arts association.
2. Pledges received by a research organization should result in recording revenue net of estimated uncollectible pledges.
3. A college should account for a donor-restricted contribution to support student scholarships for the next three years as contribution revenue in its unrestricted net assets.
4. A hospital should record an insurance provider's contractual adjustment on a patient bill as an operating expense for the period in which the services were provided to the patient.
5. A university should account for its governing board's designation of resources for the development of a fine arts academic program as a transfer to a temporarily restricted net asset class.
6. An environmental watch organization received a donor-restricted donation for the purchase of equipment and it properly accounted for the donation when it was received. When it acquired the equipment, the organization should record net assets released from temporarily restricted net assets and an addition to unrestricted net assets.
7. A hospital that used donated supplies for its patient services during the year should not record the donation because it incurred no cost to obtain the supplies.
8. An organization earned investment income on its endowment fund that is permanently donor restricted for use in a specific organizational program. The investment income should be recorded directly into the temporarily restricted net asset class.
9. A hospital has a portfolio of securities that decreased in fair market value during the year. Because the securities were not sold during the year, their change in market value should not be recognized on the hospital's statement of operations.
10. A not-for-profit art museum receives for public display a donation of historical artifacts to care for and preserve. If any item in the collection is ever sold, the museum has agreed to use the proceeds for additional items for the collection. The museum is not required to record the contribution revenue and increase in collection assets.
11. All of a hospital's building and equipment should be recorded in its restricted building fund.
12. A local accountant donated significant professional services to a local fraternal organization, which should recognize their value as both a contribution revenue and an operating expense.
13. A hospital has estimated uncollectibles on patient accounts that should be reported as a reduction of net patient service revenue.
14. A college received a conditional pledge based on the occurrence of a future event and should record it at its fair value if the future event is determined to be possible.
15. A hospital that received a donation restricted for a cancer awareness education program properly recorded it as contribution revenue in the temporarily restricted net asset class. The cost of the program that the hospital offered should be recorded as an expense in the temporarily restricted net asset class to offset the contribution revenue for the program.
16. A voluntary health and welfare organization received a contribution that the donor specified could not be spent until the next year. Because the organization received it in this year, the donation should be recorded as a debit to Cash and a credit to Deferred Revenue in the unrestricted net asset class.
17. Hospitals are required to use fund accounting, that specifies which funds are unrestricted, which are temporarily restricted, and which are permanently restricted.
18. Hospitals are required to report a performance measure in their statement of operations to separate the operating income from the nonoperating income.

19. A hospital's building fund transfers resources to the general fund for the purchase of new equipment. The building fund should record this as an expense of the period of the transfer, and the general fund should record this as an income of the period of the transfer.
20. A voluntary health and welfare organization conducted a major fund-raising effort that involved significant expenses. Because they were incurred to obtain contribution revenue, the fund-raising costs should be accounted for as a direct reduction of contribution revenue to obtain the net contribution revenue reported on the organization's statement of activities.

LO 19-4

P19-25 Statement of Activities for a Voluntary Health and Welfare Organization

The following information pertains to United Ways, a private voluntary health and welfare organization, for the year ended December 31, 20X3.

Balances in net assets at January 1, 20X3:	
Unrestricted	$3,000,000
Temporarily restricted	5,000,000
Permanently restricted	6,000,000

The following transactions occurred during the year ended December 31, 20X3:

1. Received cash donations of $500,000 from donors who did not place any time or purpose restrictions on them.
2. Received $1,000,000 of pledges from donors to be received in 20X4; it was estimated that 5 percent of the pledges would not be collected. Donors did not place any restrictions on the use of their pledges.
3. Earned investment income of $200,000 on endowment investments that donors permanently restricted for research activities.
4. Designated $225,000 of the $500,000 of cash donations received in 20X3 for computer acquisitions.
5. Spent $150,000 of the $200,000 of investment income earned on endowment investments on research during the year ended December 31, 20X3. (This amount is included in the $250,000 for research expenses shown in the following table.)
6. Acquired $100,000 of equipment from donations made in 20X2 that donors had restricted for that purchase. The governing board of United Ways reports acquisitions of capital assets as unrestricted.
7. Received donated audit services from the organization's accounting firm that would have cost $15,000.
8. Learned that the fair value of endowment investments was $600,000 higher at the end of 20X3 than at the beginning. United Ways did not acquire or sell any endowment investments during 20X3 and treats gains and losses on endowment investments as permanently restricted.
9. Incurred program and supporting services expenses during 20X3 as follows (depreciation expense for 20X3 has been properly allocated to the functional expenses):

Research	$250,000
Public health education	100,000
Community services	150,000
Management and general (does not include the audit that was donated)	125,000
Fund-Raising	115,000

Required

Prepare a statement of activities in good form for United Ways for the year ended December 31, 20X3.

LO 19-1

P19-26 Reporting Transactions on the Statement of Cash Flows for Private, Not-for-Profit Entities

Following is a list of transactions and events that may occur in private, not-for-profit entities. Indicate where each transaction or event should be reported on the entity's statement of cash flows.

Assume that the indirect method of reporting operating activities is used. If a transaction or event is reported as an adjustment to the change in net assets in the operating activities section, your answer should indicate whether the adjustment is added to or subtracted from the change in net assets. If a transaction or event is reported in more than one section on the statement of cash flows, you should include all sections in your answer.

Sample Question

A hospital recorded depreciation expense for the year of $50,000.

Answer

Report the depreciation expense of $50,000 as an addition to the change in net assets in the operating activities section.

Transactions and Events

1. A hospital's accounts receivable from patients increased $100,000 during the year.
2. A college received a $200,000 contribution that the donor restricted to acquiring fixed assets.
3. A voluntary health and welfare organization received $25,000 from a donor who stipulated that the amount be invested permanently.
4. A hospital's accounts payable for the purchase of medical supplies increased $20,000 during the year.
5. A botanical society borrowed $70,000 from First National Bank on a long-term note payable.
6. A professional trade association invested $50,000 to acquire investments in bonds that it intends to keep until their maturity.
7. A college received investment income of $45,000 from endowment investments. The donor stipulated that the income be used for the acquisition of fixed assets.
8. A hospital spent $850,000 to acquire equipment.
9. A college made loans of $100,000 to students and faculty.
10. A zoological society made a payment of $30,000 to a local bank to repay the principal of a short-term note payable.
11. A college's accrued interest receivable related to student and faculty loans increased $5,000 during the year.
12. A performing arts organization had an increase of $12,000 in deferred revenue for the year.
13. A college received $100,000 for the repayment of principal on loans made to students and faculty.
14. A hospital's prepaid assets increased $2,500 during the year.
15. A hospital's endowment investments increased in value by $35,000 during the year.

20 Corporations in Financial Difficulty

- Multicorporate Entities
- Multinational Entities
- Reporting Requirements
- Partnerships
- Governmental and Not-for-Profit Entities
- **Corporations in Financial Difficulty**

GM IN FINANCIAL DISTRESS

On June 1, 2009, General Motors Corporation (GM) filed for Chapter 11 bankruptcy protection in the Manhattan, New York, federal bankruptcy court. At its peak in terms of revenues (in 2006), GM employed roughly 280,000 people, operated 17 major manufacturing plants in various countries, and had more than $200 billion in revenues. At the time of the filing, GM reported $82.29 billion in assets and $172.81 billion in debt, leading some to argue that it was "too big to fail."

The business press often carries stories of companies in financial difficulty, including other well-known companies such as Kmart, United Airlines, Delta Airlines, Bethlehem Steel, Enron, and WorldCom. According to the American Bankruptcy Institute, approximately 50,000 businesses filed for bankruptcy in the United States during 2011. About 60 percent of these filed as Chapter 7 liquidations and the remaining 40 percent filed as Chapter 11 reorganizations. Each year, an untold number of other companies use alternate courses of action, such as debt restructuring agreements with creditors, to work through financial difficulty while avoiding filing for bankruptcy.

Companies find themselves in financial difficulty for a wide variety of reasons. For example, a company may have (1) continued to incur losses from operations, (2) overextended credit to customers, (3) had poor working capital management, (4) failed to react to changes in economic conditions, and (5) had inadequate financing, as well as a host of other factors that lead to a weak economic position. A company's liquidity problems accumulate over time and the path to bankruptcy often follows a downward spiral. For example, failure to achieve a sufficient level of sales can lead to consecutive losses, which can prevent a company from obtaining adequate short-term financing. Inadequate sales also can lead to restricted cash flows, which can cause the company to miss debt payments, and the downward spiral of financial difficulty accelerates. At this point, outside creditors may decide to exercise their claims and demand payment of their receivables. The debtor company has a number of alternative courses of action available. It may try to reach an agreement with its creditors to postpone required payments, to turn its assets over to its creditors for liquidation, or to seek bankruptcy protection from its creditors.

Poor operating performance does not always lead to a bankruptcy filing. For example, two decades earlier in 1991, GM incurred a large net loss but was able to return to profitability the following year. However, in 2009, GM was out of options. As illustrated by the following graphs, although revenues trended upward, net income was headed in the opposite direction. Moreover, bankruptcy did not happen overnight.

In 2006, under financial pressure due to pension liabilities, GM attempted to obtain help first from the U.S. government, which failed, and then through alliances with Nissan and Renault, which also failed. In November 2008, the company announced that it anticipated running out of cash by mid-2009. GM again petitioned the U.S. government for help but Congress declined the proposal. Having exhausted all other options, GM filed for Chapter 11 protection.

Finally, both the U.S. and Canadian governments did step up to help. As part of GM's reorganization, the U.S. government provided nearly $52 billion for a 60 percent stake in the new GM's stock. Moreover, the U.S. government also provided significant debtor in possession financing (loans), and the Canadian government provided an additional $3.9 billion of funding. The company also phased out its Hummer, Pontiac, and Saturn brands.

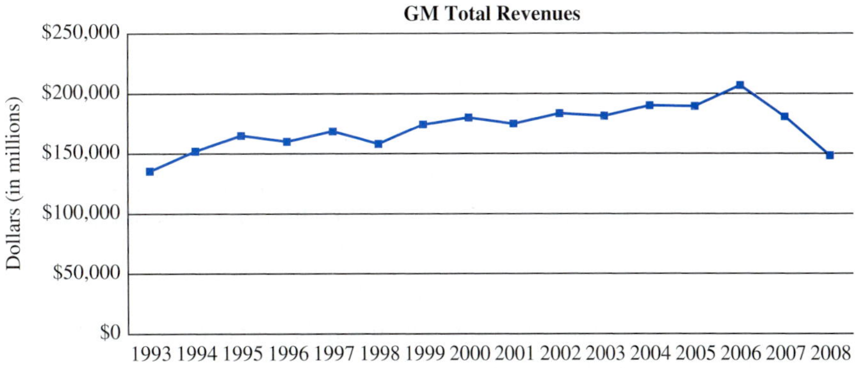

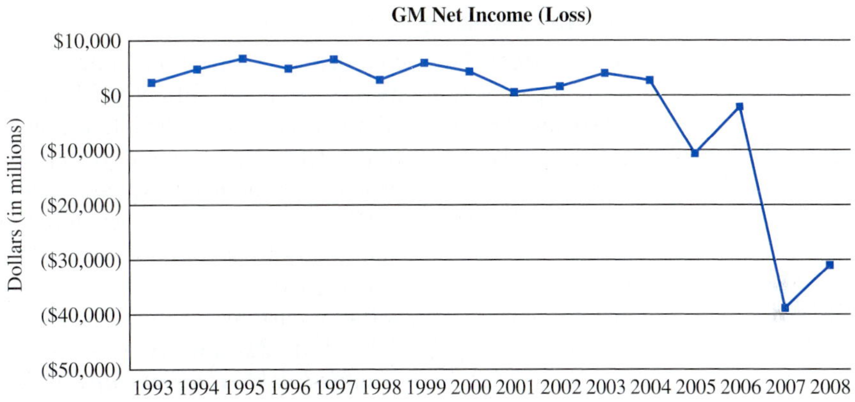

GM sold its SAAB brand to Spyker Cars in 2010. In addition, it laid off some 20,000 employees and completely reorganized its management. The newly reorganized GM had repaid the loan to the U.S. Government, with interest by mid-2010 and the U.S. Treasury began to sell its GM shares as GM began to return to health. In late 2013, the U.S. Treasury sold the last of its remaining GM stock, ending the government's ownership of the company.

This example illustrates the fact that dealing with financial difficulty can be a long and complicated process, especially for large corporations. Plans must be made and followed and a thorough understanding of accounting for these plans and their related transactions are keys to success. A company may petition the courts for bankruptcy for other reasons, such as to protect itself from an onslaught of legal suits. Several companies also have attempted to void union contracts by petitioning for bankruptcy. The courts are still defining the exact limits of bankruptcy, and each case must be decided individually.

Insolvency is defined as a condition in which a company is unable to meet debts as they mature. The insolvent company is unable to meet its liabilities. Before 1978, creditors had to show that the debtor was insolvent before they could force the debtor into bankruptcy. Because of changes in the bankruptcy law in 1978, insolvency is no longer a necessary precondition for bankruptcy. A company in financial difficulty has a large number of alternatives of which bankruptcy is only a final course. This chapter presents the range of major actions companies experiencing financial problems typically use.

LEARNING OBJECTIVES

When you finish studying this chapter, you should be able to:

LO 20-1 Understand the courses of action available to financially distressed firms.

LO 20-2 Understand Chapter 11 reorganizations and be able to prepare financial statements for debtors-in-possession as well as a plan of recovery.

LO 20-3 Understand Chapter 7 liquidations and be able to prepare a statement of affairs.

LO 20-4 Understand trustee accounting and reporting.

COURSES OF ACTION

LO 20-1

Understand the courses of action available to financially distressed firms.

Bankruptcy is the final step for a financially distressed business. Prior to that, however, management usually tries to work closely with the company's creditors to provide for their claims while attempting to ensure the firm's continuing existence. Various nonjudicial arrangements with creditors are available. If these fail, the company usually ends up in a judicial action under the direction of a bankruptcy court.

Nonjudicial Actions

Formal agreements between the company and its creditors are legally binding but are not administered by a court.

Debt Restructuring Arrangements

Arrangements between a debtor company and one or more of its creditors are common for companies in temporary financial difficulty. The debtor may solicit an extension of due dates of its debt, ask for a decrease of the interest rate on the debt, or ask for a modification of other terms of the debt contract. Creditors are usually willing to extend concessions to a debtor rather than risk the legal expense and ill will from legal action against a previously valuable debtor. Many banks, for example, prefer to continue to work with a customer who is in temporary financial difficulty rather than force it into bankruptcy. Experience has shown that banks eventually realize a larger portion of their receivables and continue to have a future customer if they assist the debtor with financial problems by restructuring the debt. **ASC 310 and ASC 470** provide guidance for the debtors' accounting for these ***troubled debt restructurings*** as well as the creditors' accounting for impairments in the values of notes and loans involved in the restructurings. **ASC 310** also provides guidance for creditor accounting for the income from impaired loans. We present examples of an impairment and a troubled debt restructuring as supplementary information on this text's website.

Another form of debt restructuring arrangement is the *composition agreement.* In this case, creditors agree to accept less than the face amount of their claims. The advantage to the creditors is that they receive an immediate cash payment and usually negotiate the timing of the remaining cash payments. Although creditors receive less than the full amount, they are assured of receiving most of their receivables. Composition agreements typically involve all creditors, although some may not be willing to agree to them. In some cases, the consenting group of creditors agrees to allow the dissenting creditors to be paid in full if it is highly probable the debtor can eventually return to profitable operations.

Creditors' Committee Management

Under ***creditors' committee management,*** the creditors may agree to assist the debtor in managing the most efficient payment of its claims. Most creditors' committees advise and closely counsel the debtor because the creditors do not want to assume additional liabilities and problems of the debtor's actual operation. Forming a creditors' committee is a nonjudicial action usually initiated with a *plan of settlement* proposed by the debtor. The plan of settlement is a detailed document that includes a schedule of payments listing the specific debts and the anticipated payments. The creditors then work closely with the debtor to implement the plan.

In some extreme cases, creditors may decide to assume operating control of the debtor company by appointing a trustee who assumes the company's management responsibility. The trustee reports to the creditors with recommendations for the eventual settlement of claims and may attempt to work out a payment schedule or recommend bankruptcy as the best alternative. The advantage of the creditors' committee management in these extreme cases is that creditors have operating control of the debtor and receive a full report of its financial condition. The disadvantage of assuming operating control to the creditors is that they incur an increased risk if the debtor enters bankruptcy because, as managers before the bankruptcy, they may be held responsible. The advantage to the debtor is that the creditors are attempting to assist it to overcome its financial difficulty and may return operating control once the financial problems have been solved without resorting to legal action.

Transfer of Assets

Some debtors in financial difficulty may transfer assets, such as receivables or other financial instruments, in an effort to obtain quick cash. For example, debtors that need cash may factor their trade receivables at a discount, and the contract may specify that the receivables be sold "with recourse" or "without recourse." The with recourse provision means that the debtor must accept the return of any uncollectible receivables that were initially transferred. The accounting issue is to determine whether these transfers should be accounted for as sales of the receivables or as a financing arrangement between the debtor company and the factor company. **ASC 860** provides the accounting and reporting guidelines for these transfers. It specifies that a transfer of financial assets is considered a sale only if the transferor (the debtor company) has surrendered control over the transferred assets. Surrendering control means that the transferred assets have been isolated from the transferor, that the transferee (i.e., recipient) obtains the right to pledge or exchange the these assets, and that the transferor does not maintain effective control over them such as through an agreement allowing the transferor to repurchase or redeem the transferred assets. **ASC 860** requires that separately recognized servicing assets or liabilities in transactions such as these asset transfers be initially measured at fair value.

Judicial Actions

Bankruptcy is a judicial action administered by bankruptcy courts and bankruptcy judges using the guidance provided in Title 11 of the U.S. Bankruptcy Code (Bankruptcy Code). This Bankruptcy Code provides the essential structure for bankruptcy proceedings, but periodically, U.S. Congress has amended it. For example, the Bankruptcy Reform Act of 1994 (Reform Act of 1994) attempts to improve the efficiency and administration of bankruptcy cases while increasing creditors' legal protections. The Reform Act of 1994 also created a National Bankruptcy Review Commission to periodically investigate, analyze, and review bankruptcy issues and to improve the Bankruptcy Code. The Bankruptcy Abuse Prevention and Consumer Protection Act of 2005 (Bankruptcy Reform Act of 2005) made several changes for business filings, but most of the act pertains to personal filings. For example, the Bankruptcy Reform Act of 2005 makes it more difficult for persons to file for bankruptcy under Chapter 7 liquidations, and it changed Chapter 11 for personal filings to require the payment of debts such as credit card balances and other common forms of consumer debt. Personal bankruptcy filings are beyond the scope of this chapter; however, individuals considering filing for bankruptcy should first seek appropriate legal guidance.

The Bankruptcy Code is composed of eight chapters, numbered as follows:

Chapter 1	General Provisions
Chapter 3	Case Administration
Chapter 5	Creditors, the Debtor, and the Estate
Chapter 7	Liquidation
Chapter 9	Adjustment of Debts of a Municipality
Chapter 11	Reorganization
Chapter 12	Adjustment of Debts of a Family Farmer with Regular Annual Income
Chapter 13	Adjustment of Debts of an Individual with Regular Income

Chapters 1, 3, and 5 present the definitions and operating provisions of the Bankruptcy Code. Chapters 7 and 11 deal with corporate bankruptcies. Chapter 9 covers municipal governments, and Chapters 12 and 13 provide guidance for individual bankruptcies.

Either the debtor or its creditors may decide that a judicial action is best in the individual circumstances. The debtor may file a *voluntary petition* seeking judicial protection in the form of an ***order of relief*** against the initiation or continuation of legal claims by the creditors against the debtor. Alternatively, creditors may file an *involuntary petition* against the debtor but first certain conditions must exist. The first condition is that the debtor has generally not been paying debts as they become due or within the last 120 days and has appointed a custodian to take possession of its assets or other creditors or some other agency has done so. Second, if more than 12 creditors exist, 3 or more must combine to file the petition and must have aggregate unsecured claims of at least $5,000. The debtor is permitted to file an answer to an involuntary petition.

Once a petition has been filed, the bankruptcy court evaluates the company and determines whether present management should continue to manage it or should appoint a trustee. Appointments of trustees are common when creditors make allegations of management fraud or gross management incompetence.

The Bankruptcy Code provides two major alternatives under the bankruptcy court's protection. These two alternatives are often known by the chapters of the Bankruptcy Code. The first is ***reorganization under Chapter 11,*** which provides the debtor judicial protection for a rehabilitation period during which it can eliminate unprofitable operations, obtain new credit, develop a new company structure with sustainable operations, and work out agreements with its creditors. The second alternative is a ***liquidation under Chapter 7*** of the Bankruptcy Code, which is often administered by a court-appointed trustee. The debtor's assets are sold and its liabilities extinguished as the business is liquidated. The major difference between a reorganization and a liquidation is that the debtor continues as a business after a reorganization whereas the business does not survive a liquidation. We illustrate both of these alternatives next.

CHAPTER 11 REORGANIZATIONS

LO 20-2

Understand Chapter 11 reorganizations and be able to prepare financial statements for debtors-in-possession as well as a plan of recovery.

Chapter 11 of the Bankruptcy Code allows for legal protection from creditors' actions during a time needed to reorganize the debtor company and return its operations to a profitable level. The bankruptcy court administers reorganizations and often appoints trustees to direct them. Reorganizations are typically described by four Ps. A company in financial distress *petitions* the bankruptcy court for *protection* from its creditors. If granted protection, the company receives an order of relief to suspend making any payments on its prepetition debt. The company continues to operate while it prepares a ***plan of reorganization,*** which serves as an operating guide during the reorganization. The *proceeding* includes the actions that take place from the time the petition is filed until the company completes the reorganization.

The petition must discuss the alternative of liquidating the debtor and distributing the expected receipts to creditors. The plan of reorganization is the essence of any reorganization and must include a complete description of the expected debtor actions during the reorganization period and the way these actions will be in the best interest of the debtor and its creditors. A *disclosure statement* is transmitted to all creditors and other parties eligible to vote on the plan of reorganization. The disclosure statement includes information that would enable a reasonable investor or creditor to make an informed judgment about the worthiness of the plan and how it will affect that person's financial interest in the debtor company. The bankruptcy court then evaluates the responses to the plan from creditors and other parties and

FYI

Lehman Brothers was the fourth largest U.S. investment bank before filing for Chapter 11 bankruptcy protection in 2008. With more than $600 billion in assets, this was the largest bankruptcy proceeding in U.S. history and it had a significant impact on the 2007–2009 financial crisis. Barclays, an international banking and financial services firm based in London, purchased Lehman Brothers North American businesses in September 2008, shortly after Lehman filed for Chapter 11 bankruptcy protection.

FYI

GM earned $5.3 billion and $6.2 billion in net income during fiscal years 2013 and 2012, respectively. It is a vastly different company than it was prior to the bankruptcy. It is smaller, has less debt, and its contract with the United Auto Workers is less costly. But it took a nearly $50 billion government bailout and bankruptcy protection in 2009 to cut its bloated costs. Thus, GM's reorganization as part of its Chapter 11 bankruptcy filing appears to have helped the company to shed less productive assets and operations.

either confirms or rejects the reorganization plan. Confirmation of the plan implies that the debtor, or an appointed trustee, will fully follow the plan. The reorganization period may be as short as a few months or as long as several years. Most reorganizations require more than one year; however, the time span of the proceeding depends on the complexity of the reorganization.

ASC 852 provides guidance for financial reporting for companies in reorganization. The financial statements issued by a company during Chapter 11 proceedings should distinguish transactions and events directly associated with the reorganization from those associated with ongoing operations. Companies in reorganization are required to present balance sheets, income statements, and statements of cash flows, but **ASC 852** requires these three statements to clearly reflect the unique circumstances related to the reorganization.

The balance sheet of a company in reorganization has the following special attributes:

1. Prepetition liabilities subject to compromise as part of the reorganization proceeding should be reported separately from liabilities not subject to compromise. Liabilities subject to compromise include unsecured debt and other payables that were incurred before the company entered reorganization. Liabilities that are not subject to change by the reorganization plan include fully secured liabilities incurred before reorganization and all liabilities incurred after the company enters its petition for reorganization relief.
2. The liabilities should be reported at the expected amount to be allowed by the bankruptcy court. If no reasonable estimation is possible, the claims should be disclosed in the footnotes.

The income statement of a company in reorganization has the following special requirements:

1. Amounts directly related to the reorganization, such as legal fees and losses on disposals of assets, should be reported separately as reorganization items in the period incurred. However, any gains or losses on discontinued operations or extraordinary items should be reported separately according to **ASC 225**.
2. Some of the interest income earned during reorganization is a result of not requiring the debtor to pay debt and thus investing the available resources in interest-bearing sources. Such interest income should be reported separately as a reorganization item. The extent to which reported interest expense differs from the contractual interest on the company's debt should be disclosed, either parenthetically on the face of the income statement or within the footnotes.
3. Earnings per share is disclosed as are any anticipated changes to the number of common shares or common stock equivalents outstanding as a result of the reorganization plan.

The statement of cash flows of a company in reorganization has the following special features:

1. **ASC 852** prefers the direct method of presenting cash flows from operations, but if the indirect method is used, the company also must disclose separately the operating cash flows associated with the reorganization.
2. Cash flows related to the reorganization should be reported separately from those from regular operations. For example, excess net interest received as a result of the company's not paying its debts during reorganization should be reported separately.

Fresh Start Accounting

The basic view of a reorganization is that it is a fresh start for the company. However, it is difficult to determine whether a Chapter 11 reorganization results in a new entity for which fresh start accounting should be used or if it results in a continuation of the prior entity. **ASC 852** states that fresh start reporting should be used as of the confirmation date of the plan of reorganization if both the following conditions occur:[1]

1. The reorganization value of the assets of the emerging entity immediately before the date of confirmation is less than the total of all postpetition liabilities and allowed claims.
2. Holders of existing voting shares immediately before confirmation receive less than 50 percent of the emerging entity's voting shares. This implies that the prior shareholders have lost control of the emerging company.

Fresh start accounting results in a new reporting entity. First, the company is required to compute the reorganization value of the emerging entity's assets. ***Reorganization value*** represents the fair value of the entity before considering liabilities and approximates the amount a willing buyer would pay for the entity's assets. The reorganization value is then allocated to the assets using the value method prescribed in **ASC 805.** A reorganization value in excess of amounts assignable to identifiable assets is reported as an intangible asset called Reorganization Value in Excess of Amounts Allocable to Identifiable Assets. This excess is then accounted for in conformity with **ASC 350.** The emerging company records its liabilities at the present values of the amounts to be paid. Any retained earnings or deficits are eliminated. A set of final operating statements is prepared just prior to emerging from reorganization. In essence, the company is a new reporting entity after reorganization.

Companies Not Qualifying for Fresh Start Accounting

Those companies not meeting the two conditions for fresh start accounting should determine whether their assets are impaired in value. In addition, they should report liabilities at the present values of the amounts to be paid with any gain or loss on the revaluation of the liabilities recorded in accordance with **ASC 225** as to extraordinary or ordinary events.

Many companies decide to restructure their operations as part of the reorganization plan. Those companies not qualifying for fresh start accounting account for restructuring costs such as those for closing a plant and reducing the workforce and combining some of the remaining operations in accordance with **ASC 420.** This standard establishes the recognition of a liability for a cost associated with an exit or disposal activity when the liability is incurred, not at the earlier time the company makes a commitment to an exit plan.

The accounting for long-lived assets should be performed in accordance with **ASC 360.** The long-lived assets are divided between (1) those to be held and used and (2) those to be sold. An impairment loss on a long-lived asset to be held and used is recognized only if its carrying value is less than the asset's estimated undiscounted cash flows from operations over its estimated useful life. The amount of the impairment loss is the difference between the asset's carrying amount and its fair value. Goodwill is not considered part of long-lived assets to be tested for impairment under **ASC 360.** Note that **ASC 350** guides the accounting for any impairment of goodwill.

Individual long-lived assets that will be sold are revalued to their lower of carrying amount or fair value less the selling costs. In addition, once the use of a long-lived asset is discontinued and set aside for sale, depreciation is stopped. A management decision to dispose of a component of the entity is accounted for as a discontinued segment under **ASC 225.**

[1] ASC 852-10-45-19.

ASC 310 and 470 do not apply to troubled debt restructurings in which debtors restate their liabilities generally under the purview of the bankruptcy court. **ASC 310 and 470** apply only to specific debt restructuring transactions. This exception is not an issue in the immediate settlement of debt in which the debtor's gain or loss is the difference between the fair value of the consideration given and the carrying value of the debt. The gain or loss is the same under **ASC 310 and 470** as under a general restatement of liabilities in a reorganization. However, in cases of modification of terms in a reorganization involving a general restatement of liabilities, the debtor's restructuring gain is computed as the difference between the debt's carrying value and the new principal after restructuring. The future cash flows from interest payments are not included in the computation of the new principal. Thus, in most cases of debt restructuring of companies in reorganization proceedings, the debtor's gain from the debt restructuring is higher than it would have been under **ASC 310 and 470.**

Plan of Reorganization

The plan of reorganization is typically a detailed document with a full discussion of all major actions to be taken during the reorganization period. In addition to these major actions, management also continues to manufacture and sell products, collect receivables, and pursue other day-to-day operations. Most plans include detailed discussions of the following:

1. Disposing of unprofitable operations through either sale or liquidation.
2. Restructuring of debt with specific creditors.
3. Revaluation of assets and liabilities.
4. Reductions or eliminations of original stockholders' claims and issuances of new shares to creditors or others.

The plan of reorganization must be approved by at least half of all creditors, who must hold at least two-thirds of the dollar amount of the debtor's total outstanding debt, although the court may still confirm a plan that the necessary number of creditors do not approve provided the court finds that the plan is in the best interests of all parties and is equitable and fair to those groups not voting approval.

Illustration of a Reorganization[2]

Figure 20–1 is a balance sheet for Peerless Products Corporation on December 31, 20X6. On January 2, 20X7, Peerless' management petitions the bankruptcy court for a Chapter 11 reorganization to obtain relief from debt payments and time to rehabilitate the company and return to profitable operations.

The following timeline presents the dates relevant for this example:

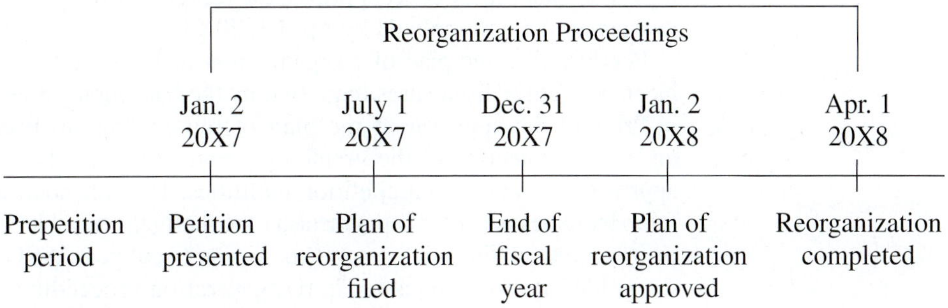

[2] To view a video explanation of this topic, visit advancedstudyguide.com.

FIGURE 20–1
Balance Sheet on the Date of Corporate Insolvency

PEERLESS PRODUCTS CORPORATION
Balance Sheet
December 31, 20X6

	Cost	Accumulated Depreciation	Undepreciated Cost	
Assets				
Cash				$ 2,000
Marketable Securities				8,000
Accounts Receivable			$ 20,000	
Less: Allowance for Uncollectible Accounts			(2,000)	18,000
Inventory				45,000
Prepaid Assets				1,000
Total Current Assets				$ 74,000
Property, Plant & Equipment:				
Land	$ 10,000	$ 0	$ 10,000	
Plant	75,000	20,000	55,000	
Equipment	40,000	4,000	36,000	
Total	$125,000	$24,000	$101,000	101,000
Total Assets				$175,000
Liabilities				
Accounts Payable				$ 26,000
Notes Payable:				
Partially Secured			$ 10,000	
Unsecured, 10% interest			80,000	90,000
Accrued Interest				3,000
Accrued Wages				14,000
Total Current Liabilities				$133,000
Mortgages Payable				50,000
Total Liabilities				$183,000
Shareholders' Equity				
Preferred Stock			$ 40,000	
Common Stock ($1 par)			10,000	
Retained Earnings (Deficit)			(58,000)	
Total Shareholders' Equity				(8,000)
Total Liabilities & Shareholders' Equity				$175,000

The bankruptcy court accepts the petition, and Peerless Products prepares its plan of reorganization. The plan is filed on July 1, 20X7, and the disclosure statement is sent to all creditors and other affected parties. On December 31, 20X7, the company presents its financial statements for the 20X7 fiscal period in which it was in Chapter 11 proceedings. The bankruptcy court approves the reorganization plan on January 2, 20X8, and the reorganization is completed by April 1, 20X8.

Peerless files the plan of reorganization in Figure 20–2 with audited financial statements and other disclosures requested by the bankruptcy court.

Prior to the approval of the plan of reorganization, Peerless continues to operate under the protection of the granted petition of relief. The company makes only court-approved payments on prepetition liabilities. The only court-approved payment on prepetition liabilities is a $2,000 payment on the mortgage payable. On December 31, 20X7, the company issues financial statements for the fiscal year. **ASC 852** prescribes the reporting guidelines for companies in reorganization proceedings. A most important reporting concern is that the reorganization amounts be reported separately from other operating amounts. Peerless Products prepares the following financial statements as of December 31, 20X7: balance sheet (Figure 20–3), income statement (Figure 20–4), and statement of cash flows (Figure 20–5). Note that Debtor-in-Possession indicates

FIGURE 20–2
Plan of Reorganization

PEERLESS PRODUCTS CORPORATION
Plan of Reorganization under Chapter 11 of the Bankruptcy Code
(Filed July 1, 20X7)

a. The accounts payable of $26,000 will be provided for as follows: (1) $6,000 will be eliminated, (2) $4,000 will be paid in cash, (3) $12,000 of the payables will be exchanged for subordinated debt, and (4) $4,000 of the payables are to be exchanged for 4,000 shares of newly issued common stock.
b. The partially secured notes payable of $10,000 will be provided for as follows: (1) $2,000 will be paid in cash and (2) the remaining $8,000 will be exchanged for senior debt secured by a lien on equipment.
c. The unsecured notes payable of $80,000 will be provided for as follows: (1) $12,000 is to be eliminated, (2) $14,000 is to be paid in cash, (3) $49,000 is to be exchanged into senior debt secured by a lien against fixed assets, and (4) $5,000 is to be exchanged into 5,000 shares of newly issued common stock.
d. The accrued interest of $3,000 will be provided as follows: (1) $2,000 will be eliminated and (2) the remaining $1,000 will be paid in cash.
e. The accrued wages of $14,000 will be provided as follows: (1) $12,000 will be paid in cash and (2) the remaining $2,000 will be exchanged into 2,000 shares of newly issued common stock.
f. The preferred shareholders will receive 8,000 shares of newly issued common stock in exchange for their preferred stock.
g. The present common stockholders will receive 1,000 shares of newly issued common stock in exchange for their present common stock

FIGURE 20–3
Balance Sheet for a Company in Reorganization Proceedings

PEERLESS PRODUCTS CORPORATION
(Debtor-in-Possession)
Balance Sheet
December 31, 20X7

Assets		
Cash		$ 40,000
Income Tax Refund Receivable		12,000
Marketable Securities		8,000
Accounts Receivable	$ 6,000	
Less: Allowance for Uncollectibles	(1,000)	5,000
Inventory		37,000
Total Current Assets		$102,000
Property, Plant & Equipment	$104,000	
Less: Accumulated Depreciation	(26,000)	78,000
Total Assets		$180,000
Liabilities		
Liabilities Not Subject to Compromise:		
Current Liabilities (postpetition):		
Short-Term Borrowings	$ 15,000	
Accounts Payable—Trade	10,000	
Noncurrent Liability:		
Mortgage Payable, Fully Secured	48,000	
Total Liabilities Not Subject to Compromise		$ 73,000
Liabilities Subject to Compromise (prepetition):		
Accounts Payable	$ 26,000	
Notes Payable, Partially Secured	10,000	
Notes Payable, Unsecured	80,000	
Accrued Interest	3,000	
Accrued Wages	14,000	
Total Liabilities Subject to Compromise		133,000
Total Liabilities		$206,000
Shareholders' Equity		
Preferred Stock	$ 40,000	
Common Stock ($1 par)	10,000	
Retained Earnings (deficit)	(76,000)	
Total Shareholders' Equity		(26,000)
Total Liabilities & Shareholders' Equity		$180,000

FIGURE 20–4
Income Statement for a Company in Reorganization Proceedings

PEERLESS PRODUCTS CORPORATION (Debtor-in-Possession) Income Statement For the Year Ended December 31, 20X7		
Revenue:		
Sales		$120,000
Cost and Expenses:		
Cost of Goods Sold	$110,000	
Selling, Operating & Administrative	21,000	
Interest (contractual interest $6,000)	3,000	134,000
Loss before Reorganization Items & Income Tax Benefit		$ (14,000)
Reorganization Items:		
Loss on Disposal of Assets	$ (10,000)	
Professional Fees	(8,000)	
Interest Earned on Accumulated Cash Resulting from Chapter 11 Proceeding	2,000	
Total Reorganization Items		(16,000)
Loss before Income Tax Benefit		$ (30,000)
Income Tax Benefit		12,000
Net Loss		$ (18,000)

FIGURE 20–5
Statement of Cash Flows for a Company in Reorganization Proceedings

PEERLESS PRODUCTS CORPORATION (Debtor-in-Possession) Statement of Cash Flows For the Year Ended December 31, 20X7	
Cash Flows Provided by Operating Activities:	
Cash Received from Customers	$133,000
Cash Paid to Suppliers & Employees	(109,000)
Interest Paid	(3,000)
Net Cash Provided by Operating Activities before Reorganization Items	$ 21,000
Operating Cash Flows Used by Reorganization Activities:	
Professional Fees	$ (8,000)
Interest Received on Cash Accumulated Due to Chapter 11 Proceeding	2,000
Net Cash Used by Reorganization Items	$ (6,000)
Net Cash Provided by Operating Activities & Reorganization Items	$ 15,000
Cash Flows Provided by Investing Activities:	
Proceeds from Sale of Assets Due to Chapter 11 Proceeding	$ 10,000
Net Cash Provided by Investing Activities	$ 10,000
Cash Flows Provided by Financing Activities:	
Net Borrowings under Short-Term Financing Plan	$ 15,000
Principal Payments on Prepetition Debt Authorized by Court (Mortgage Payable)	(2,000)
Net Cash Provided by Financing Activities	$ 13,000
Net Increase in Cash	$ 38,000
Cash at January 1, 20X7	2,000
Cash at December 31, 20X7	$ 40,000

that Peerless continues to manage its own assets rather than have a court-appointed trustee manage them.

On January 2, 20X8, the bankruptcy court approves the plan of reorganization as filed. Peerless carries out the plan as shown in the recovery analysis in Figure 20–6.

An important concept for determining the appropriate accounting for entities in reorganization is calculating reorganization value. Reorganization value is the fair value of the

FIGURE 20–6 Recovery Analysis for Plan of Reorganization

PEERLESS CORPORATION
Plan of Reorganization
Recovery Analysis

		Recovery								
							Common Stock		Total Recovery	
		Elimination of Debt and Equity	Surviving Debt	Cash	Senior Debt	Subordinated Debt	%	Value	$	%
Postpetition Liabilities	(73,000)		(73,000)						(73,000)	100%
Claims/Interest:										
Accounts Payable	(26,000)	6,000		(4,000)		(12,000)	20%	(4,000)	(20,000)	77
Notes Payable, partially secured	(10,000)			(2,000)	(8,000)				(10,000)	100
Notes Payable, unsecured	(80,000)	12,000		(14,000)	(49,000)		25	(5,000)	(68,000)	85
Accrued interest	(3,000)	2,000		(1,000)					(1,000)	33
Accrued wages	(14,000)			(12,000)			10	(2,000)	(14,000)	100
Total	(133,000)	20,000								
Preferred Shareholders	(40,000)	32,000					40	(8,000)	(8,000)	
Common Shareholders	(10,000)	9,000					5	(1,000)	(1,000)	
Retained Earnings Deficit	76,000	(76,000)								
Total	(180,000)	(15,000)	(73,000)	(33,000)	(57,000)	(12,000)	100%	(20,000)	(195,000)	

Note: Parentheses indicate credit amount.

entity's assets. Typical methods of determining reorganization value are discounting future cash flows or appraisals. After extensive analysis, a reorganization value of $195,000 is determined for Peerless' assets. Recall that fresh start accounting is appropriate only when both of the following conditions occur: (1) reorganization value is less than total postpetition liabilities and allowed claims and (2) holders of existing shares of voting stock immediately before the plan of reorganization is approved retain less than 50 percent of the voting shares of the emerging entity. To determine the first condition for Peerless, the following comparison approves the plan of reorganization:

Postpetition liabilities	$ 73,000
Liabilities deferred pursuant to Chapter 11 proceedings	133,000
Total postpetition liabilities & allowed claims	$206,000
Reorganization value	(195,000)
Excess of liabilities over reorganization value	$ 11,000

Note that the first condition for fresh start accounting is present. The second condition for fresh start accounting also occurs as shown in Figure 20–6. Immediately before the plan of reorganization is approved, the common shareholders hold only 5 percent of the common stock of the emerging entity. Therefore, fresh start accounting is used for Peerless.

After intensive study of risk-equivalent companies, the profit potential of the emerging company, and the present value of future cash flows, the capital structure of the emerging company is established as follows:

Postpetition current liabilities	$ 25,000
Postpetition mortgage payable	48,000
Senior debt	57,000
Subordinated debt	12,000
Common stock (new)	20,000
Total postreorganization capital structure	$162,000

Note that for purposes of the illustration, the newly issued common stock is no-par stock; therefore, no additional paid-in capital is carried forward to the emerging entity. If the assigned value of the newly issued stock is higher than its par value, an additional paid-in capital account is credited for the excess. The $162,000 of postreorganization capital is the reorganization value of $195,000 less the $33,000 paid for the prepetition liabilities as part of the plan of reorganization.

Peerless Products prepares entries to record the execution of the plan of reorganization as it transpires between January 1, 20X8, and April 1, 20X8. Figure 20–7 is a worksheet illustrating the effects of executing the plan of reorganization on Peerless' balance sheet accounts. The first journal entry (1) records the debt restructuring and the gain on the discharge of debt:

	January 1, 20X8–April 1, 20X8		
(1)	Liabilities Subject to Compromise	133,000	
	Cash		33,000
	Senior Debt		57,000
	Subordinated Debt		12,000
	Common Stock (new)		11,000
	Gain on Debt Discharge		20,000
	Record debt discharge.		

The second journal entry (2) records the exchange of stock for stock. The prior preferred shareholders receive 8,000 shares of newly issued common stock. The prior common shareholders receive 1,000 shares of the newly issued common stock:

	January 1, 20X8–April 1, 20X8		
(2)	Preferred Stock	40,000	
	Common Stock (old)	10,000	
	Common Stock (new)		9,000
	Additional Paid-In Capital		41,000
	Record exchange of stock for stock.		

The last journal entry (3) records the fresh start adjustments of the assigned values of the emerging entity's assets and the elimination of any retained earnings or deficit. A comparison between the company's book values and fair values follows. The fair values are determined according to the procedures in **ASC 360.** An ***impairment loss***

FIGURE 20–7 Effect of Plan of Reorganization on Company's Balance Sheet

		Adjustments to Record Confirmation of Plan			
	Pre-confirmation	Debt Discharge	Exchange of Stock	Fresh Start	Company's Reorganized Balance Sheet
Assets					
Cash	$ 40,000	$ (33,000)			$ 7,000
Income Tax Refund Receivable	12,000				12,000
Marketable Securities	8,000			$ 2,000	10,000
Accounts Receivable (net)	5,000				5,000
Inventory	37,000			(4,000)	33,000
Total	$ 102,000				$ 67,000
Property, Plant & Equipment (net)	78,000			7,000	85,000
Reorganization Value in Excess of Amounts Allocable to Identifiable Assets				10,000	10,000
Total Assets	$ 180,000	$ (33,000)		$ 15,000	$ 162,000
Liabilities					
Liabilities Not Subject to Compromise:					
Current Liabilities:					
Short-Term Borrowings	$ (15,000)				$ (15,000)
Accounts Payable	(10,000)				(10,000)
Noncurrent Liability:					
Mortgage Payable	(48,000)				(48,000)
Total	$ (73,000)				$ (73,000)
Liabilities Subject to Compromise:	(133,000)	$133,000			
Senior Debt		(57,000)			(57,000)
Subordinated Debt		(12,000)			(12,000)
Total Liabilities	$(206,000)	$ 64,000			$(142,000)
Shareholders' Equity					
Preferred Stock	$ (40,000)		$40,000		
Common Stock (old)	(10,000)		10,000		
Common Stock (new)		$ (11,000)	(9,000)		$ (20,000)
Additional Paid-In Capital			(41,000)	$ 41,000	
Retained Earnings (deficit)	76,000	(20,000)		20,000	
				(76,000)	0
Total Shareholders' Equity	$ 26,000	$ (31,000)	0	$(15,000)	$ (20,000)
Total Liabilities & Shareholders' Equity	$(180,000)	$ 33,000	0	$(15,000)	$(162,000)

Note: Parentheses indicate credit amount.

is measured by the amount that the carrying value of a long-lived asset (or asset group) exceeds its fair value. Note that Reorganization Value in Excess of Amounts Allocable to Identifiable Assets is debited for an amount not assignable to other assets. The reorganization value excess is reported as an intangible asset and accounted for according to **ASC 350,** which specifies that intangibles with finite useful lives should be amortized over their lives. However, for intangible assets determined to have an indefinite life, no amortization should be taken. Instead these indefinite life intangibles must be tested for impairment at least annually to determine whether they are impaired and a loss should be recognized for a reduction in their carrying amount.

Note that if prior to entering reorganization Peerless had goodwill that was judged to be impaired, it would recognize any impairment loss on the debtor-in-possession income statement. Typically, a company in reorganization proceedings is not expected to have goodwill because it is related to excess earnings potential. A case-by-case examination must be made, however, to determine whether the company's recognized goodwill was impaired.

	Book Value	Fair Value	Difference
Cash	$ 7,000	$ 7,000	$ 0
Income tax refund receivable	12,000	12,000	0
Marketable securities	8,000	10,000	2,000
Accounts receivable (net)	5,000	5,000	0
Inventory	37,000	33,000	(4,000)
Property, plant & equipment	78,000	85,000	7,000
Reorganization value in excess of amounts allocable to identifiable assets	0	10,000	10,000
Totals	$147,000	$162,000	$15,000

The entry to record the fresh start revaluation of assets and elimination of the deficit follows:

	April 1, 20X8		
(3)	Marketable Securities	2,000	
	Property, Plant, and Equipment	7,000	
	Reorganization Value in Excess of Amounts Allocable to Identifiable Assets	10,000	
	Gain on Debt Discharge	20,000	
	Additional Paid-In Capital	41,000	
	Inventory		4,000
	Retained Earnings—Deficit		76,000
	Record fresh start accounting and eliminate deficit.		

The last column in Figure 20–7 presents the postreorganization, new reporting entity's balance sheet.

Some reorganizations are unsuccessful, and the debtor must be liquidated. The major reason for unsuccessful reorganizations is continuing losses from operations and no reasonable likelihood of rehabilitation. Another common reason is the inability to consummate a reorganization plan because of the failure to dispose of an unprofitable subsidiary, a material default of the plan by either the debtor or a creditor, or the inability to effect part of the plan as a result of changes in the economic environment. The debtor company then moves from reorganization into liquidation; the latter is the topic of the next section of the chapter.

CHAPTER 7 LIQUIDATIONS

LO 20-3

Understand Chapter 7 liquidations and be able to prepare a statement of affairs.

Bankruptcy courts administer liquidations in the interests of the corporation's creditors and shareholders. The intent in liquidation is to maximize the net dollar amount recovered from disposal of the debtor's assets. Bankruptcy courts appoint accountants, attorneys, or experienced business managers as trustees to administer the liquidation. The liquidation process is often completed within 6 to 12 months during which the trustees must make periodic reports to the bankruptcy court. The entire liquidation process is governed by the Bankruptcy Code, which describes the specific procedures to be followed and reports to be made. A very important aspect of liquidation is determining the legal rights of each creditor and establishing priorities for those rights.

FYI

Circuit City initially filed for Chapter 11 bankruptcy in November 2008 in an effort to continue operating. However, the company ultimately converted to Chapter 7 bankruptcy and began liquidating its stores in January 2009.

CLASSES OF CREDITORS

The Bankruptcy Code specifies three classes of creditors whose claims have the following priorities: (1) secured creditors, (2) creditors with priority, and (3) general unsecured creditors. The priority of claims determines the order and source of payment to each creditor.

Secured Creditors

Secured creditors have liens, or security interests, on specific assets, often called *collateral*. A creditor with such a legal interest in a specific asset has the highest priority claim on that asset. For example, as noted in Figure 20–8, Peerless Products' $50,000 mortgage payable is secured by the company's land and plant. On December 31, 20X6, the land and plant have a combined net book value of $65,000 and a fair value of $55,000. The mortgage holders have first claim to the proceeds from the sale of the land and plant. Therefore, when the land and plant are sold for $55,000, $50,000 of the proceeds is used to discharge the Mortgage Payable account and the remaining $5,000 is available to the next-lower class of creditor.

Creditors with Priority

As defined by the Bankruptcy Code, ***creditors with priority*** are unsecured creditors—that is, those having no collateral claim against specific assets who have priority over other unsecured creditors. Creditors with priority are the first to be paid from any proceeds available to unsecured creditors. For businesses, the Bankruptcy Code presents the following as liabilities (listed in the order of their priority):

1. Costs of administering the bankruptcy, including accounting and legal costs for experts appointed by the bankruptcy court.
2. Liabilities arising in the ordinary course of business during the bankruptcy proceedings.
3. Wages, salaries, or commissions, including severance and sick pay earned within 180 days of the date the petition was filed but limited to $10,000 for each individual.
4. Contributions to employee benefit plans for the last 180 days remaining after elimination of compensation in item 3 but constrained by the remainder of the limit of $10,000 per individual.
5. Deposits of customers who made partial payments for the purchase or lease of goods or services that were not delivered. Priority is given to the first $1,800 per individual; any excess deposit is added to the unsecured claims.
6. Unsecured tax claims of governmental units, including income taxes, property taxes, excise taxes, and other taxes.

FIGURE 20–8 Accounting Statement of Affairs

PEERLESS PRODUCTS CORPORATION
Statement of Affairs
December 31, 20X6

Book Values		Estimated Current Values	Estimated Amount Available to Unsecured Claims	Estimated Gain (Loss) on Realization
Assets				
	(1) Assets pledged with fully secured creditors:			
$ 10,000	Land	$15,000		$ 5,000
55,000	Plant (net)	40,000		(15,000)
		$55,000		
	Less: Mortgage Payable	(50,000)	$ 5,000	
	(2) Assets pledged with partially secured creditors:			
8,000	Marketable Securities	$ 9,000		1,000
	Less: Notes Payable	(10,000)		
	(3) Free assets:			
2,000	Cash	$ 2,000	2,000	
18,000	Accounts Receivable (net)	18,000	18,000	
45,000	Inventory	26,000	26,000	(19,000)
1,000	Prepaid Assets	0	0	(1,000)
36,000	Equipment (net)	12,000	12,000	(24,000)
	Estimated amount available		$ 63,000	
	Less: Creditors with priority		(18,000)	
	Net estimated amount available to unsecured creditors (41 cents on the dollar: $45,000/$110,000)		$ 45,000	
	Estimated deficiency to unsecured creditors		65,000	
$175,000				$(53,000)
	Total unsecured debt (from liabilities)		$110,000	

Book Values			Estimated Amount Unsecured
Liabilities and Stockholders' Equity			
	(1) Fully secured creditors:		
$ 50,000	Mortgage Payable	$50,000	
	(2) Partially secured creditors:		
10,000	Notes Payable—Partially Secured	$10,000	
	Less: Marketable Securities	(9,000)	$ 1,000
	(3) Creditors with priority:		
0	Estimated liquidation expenses	$ 4,000	
14,000	Accrued wages	14,000	
		$18,000	
	(4) Remaining unsecured creditors:		
26,000	Accounts Payable		26,000
80,000	Notes Payable—Unsecured		80,000
3,000	Accrued Interest		3,000
	(5) Stockholders' equity:		
40,000	Preferred Stock		
10,000	Common Stock		
(58,000)	Retained Earnings (Deficit)		
$175,000	(Carry up to asset section)		$110,000

These six groups of creditors are paid from assets available to unsecured creditors. Any remaining monies are then distributed to the general unsecured creditors.

General Unsecured Creditors

The lowest priority is given to claims by ***general unsecured creditors*** who are paid only after secured creditors and unsecured creditors with priority have been satisfied to the extent of any legal limits. Often the general unsecured creditors receive less than the full amount of their claim. The amounts to be paid to these creditors are usually stated as a percentage of the total claim, such as 55 cents on the dollar, or whatever the specific percentage is. The payment to general unsecured creditors is often termed a *dividend*. It is not uncommon for these dividends to be as low as 20 to 25 percent of the total remaining unsecured claims.

Preference payments made by the debtor to one creditor to the detriment of all other creditors within 90 days before the bankruptcy petition was filed may usually be recovered from the specific creditor and returned to the cash available for all creditors. Sometimes a member of the debtor's management may assure a creditor that the debtor will pay any claim to that specific creditor. This often occurs during the latter phases of financial difficulty, just before filing a petition for bankruptcy. These management assurances are not binding and do not increase the level of the legal claim against the debtor's assets. The priority of the claims is determined solely in accordance with the Bankruptcy Code.

Statement of Affairs

The ***accounting statement of affairs*** is the basic accounting report made at the beginning of the liquidation process to present the expected realizable amounts from disposal of the assets, the order of creditors' claims, and the expected amount that unsecured creditors will receive as a result of the liquidation. A different report, also entitled the *statement of affairs*, is a list of questions the debtor must answer as part of the bankruptcy petition. The following discussion is about the accounting report, not the legal questionnaire.

The statement of affairs is not a going-concern report; it is an important planning report for a company's anticipated liquidation. The statement of affairs presents the book values of the debtor company's balance sheet accounts, the estimated fair market values of the assets, the order of the claims, and the estimated deficiency to the general unsecured creditors. Common stockholders rarely receive any monies from a liquidating company. The statement of affairs is a planning instrument.

Assume that rather than reorganizing, Peerless decided on December 31, 20X6, to enter Chapter 7 bankruptcy on that date. The following illustration begins with the December 31, 20X6, statement of affairs for Peerless Products shown in Figure 20–8:

1. The report presents the balance sheet accounts in order of priority for liquidation. Current versus noncurrent accounts no longer have importance for Peerless.
2. The report presents estimated current fair values and expected gains or losses on the disposal of the assets. These are only estimates at the point the bankruptcy petition is filed. Actual gains or losses will be recorded as realized.
3. In this example, fully secured creditors are expected to have their entire claims of \$50,000 satisfied with the proceeds from the disposal of the secured asset. The mortgage payable is expected to be fully satisfied with the proceeds of \$55,000 from the sale of the land and plant. The remaining \$5,000 will then be available to satisfy unsecured claims.
4. The claims of partially secured creditors will not be completely satisfied from the sale of the collateral asset. Marketable securities having an estimated fair value of \$9,000 are used to secure notes payable of \$10,000. The first \$9,000 of the notes payable is satisfied; the remaining \$1,000 is added to the general unsecured liabilities.

5. Free assets are available to unsecured creditors. The first unsecured creditors are those with priority as defined by the Bankruptcy Code. Peerless has accrued wages of $14,000 payable to its employees, none of whom has more than $2,000 due. In addition, the company expects to incur $4,000 of expenses to administer the liquidation.
6. All remaining claims are added to the general unsecured liabilities. The total of unsecured claims is $110,000, but only $45,000 is expected to be available to meet them. Therefore, the estimated dividend to general unsecured creditors is 41 cents on the dollar ($45,000/$110,000). The estimated deficiency to unsecured creditors is $65,000.
7. The stockholders will not receive anything upon Peerless' liquidation. Stock is a residual claim to be settled only after all creditors' claims have been fully settled. Stockholders typically do not receive anything from a bankruptcy liquidation.

The statement of affairs is a planning instrument prepared only at the beginning of the bankruptcy process. It provides important information to creditors and the bankruptcy court as to the expected monies available to each class of creditors. Once the bankruptcy is under way, the debtor records the transactions on its accounting records as they occur.

ADDITIONAL CONSIDERATIONS

LO 20-4

Understand trustee accounting and reporting.

We now present the accounting and reporting practices for trustees who act as fiduciaries for the creditors' committee or for the bankruptcy court. Trustees' reports are different from the traditional financial statements because the trustees' legal rights and responsibilities differ from those of the debtor company's management.

Trustee Accounting and Reporting

Bankruptcy courts appoint trustees to manage a company under Chapter 11 reorganization in cases of management fraud, dishonesty, incompetence, or gross mismanagement. The trustee then attempts to rehabilitate the business. In Chapter 7 liquidations, the trustee normally has the responsibility to expeditiously liquidate the bankrupt company and pay creditors in conformity with the legal status of their secured or unsecured interests. In some cases under Chapter 7, the court appoints a trustee to operate the company for a short time in an effort to obtain a better price for it in entirety rather than selling it piecemeal.

Trustees examine the proofs of all creditors' claims against the debtor's bankruptcy estate, that is, the debtor's net assets. Sometimes the trustee receives title to all assets as a ***receivership,*** becomes responsible for the debtor's actual management, and must direct a plan of reorganization or liquidation. A trustee who takes title to the debtor's assets in a liquidation must make a periodic financial report to the bankruptcy court on the progress of the liquidation and on the fiduciary relationship held. Upon accepting the assets, the trustee usually establishes a set of accounting records to account for the receivership. The trustee's accounting records include a liability of the trustee that is created to recognize the debtor's interest in the assets accepted by the trustee. This new account is credited for the book value of the assets accepted and is usually named for the debtor company in receivership. The trustee does not transfer the debtor's liabilities because these remain the debtor company's legal responsibility. The general form of the trustee's opening entry when accepting the assets of the debtor company follows:

Assets	XXX	
Debtor Company—In Receivership		XXX

The actual entry details the individual asset accounts and includes the debtor's company name.

Statement of Realization and Liquidation

Trustees prepare a monthly report, called a ***statement of realization and liquidation,*** for the bankruptcy court. It shows the results of the trustee's fiduciary actions beginning at the point the trustee accepts the debtor's assets. The statement has three major sections: assets, supplementary items, and liabilities. The debtor's liabilities are not transferred to the trustee, but the trustee may incur new liabilities that must be reported in the statement of realization and liquidation.

Assets	
Assets to be realized Assets acquired	Assets realized Assets not realized

Supplementary Items	
Supplementary charges	Supplementary credits

Liabilities	
Liabilities liquidated Liabilities not liquidated	Liabilities to be liquidated Liabilities incurred

Assets: The assets section of the statement is divided into the four groups shown above. The assets to be realized are those received from the debtor company. The assets acquired are those subsequently acquired by the trustee. The assets realized are those sold by the trustee; the assets not realized are those remaining under the trustee's responsibility as of the end of the period. Cash is usually not reported in the statement of realization and liquidation because a separate cash flow report is typically made.

Supplementary Items: The supplementary items section of the report consists of the two items shown above. Supplementary charges include the trustee's administration fees and any cash expenses paid by the trustee. Supplementary credits may include any unusual revenue items.

Liabilities: Although the trustee does not record the debtor's liabilities, the trustee settles some of the debtor's payables and may incur new payables during the receivership. The liabilities section of the statement is divided as shown above. The liabilities liquidated are creditors' claims settled during the period. The liabilities not liquidated are those outstanding at the end of the reporting period. The liabilities to be liquidated are those debts remaining on the books of the debtor company for whose liquidation the trustee is responsible as of the date of appointment. Finally, the liabilities incurred are new obligations the trustee incurred.

Illustration of Trustee Accounting and Reporting

Advanced StudyGuide .com

On December 31, 20X6, D. Able was appointed trustee in charge of liquidating Peerless Products Corporation. Able will be allowed to operate the company for a short period of time to determine whether it can be sold in entirety as opposed to piecemeal. During this time, the trustee must reduce Peerless' current short-term debts. If a sale in entirety is infeasible, Able is directed to liquidate the company. Able accepts the assets on December 31, 20X6, and makes several transactions during January 20X7. The transactions and the entries made on Peerless' books and on the trustee's books are presented in Figure 20–9 and discussed in the following pages.

1. Entry (4) records the transfer of assets from Peerless Products to D. Able. Able recognizes the assets at their book values as reported by Peerless. Accounts receivable are dated as "old" to note that these were part of the transferred assets. The credit for $175,000 to Peerless Products Corporation—In Receivership is a liability

FIGURE 20–9 Trustee and Debtor Company Entries during Liquidation

	Trustee D. Able's Books	Debit	Credit	Peerless Products Corporation's Books	Debit	Credit
(4)	Cash	2,000		D. Able—Receiver	175,000	
	Marketable Securities	8,000		Allowance for Uncollectibles	2,000	
	Accounts Receivable (old)	20,000		Accumulated Depreciation	24,000	
	Inventory	45,000		Cash		2,000
	Prepaid Assets	1,000		Marketable Securities		8,000
	Property, Plant, and Equipment	125,000		Accounts Receivable		20,000
	Allowance for Uncollectibles (old)		2,000	Inventory		45,000
	Accumulated Depreciation		24,000	Prepaid Assets		1,000
	Peerless Products Corporation—In Receivership		175,000	Property, Plant, and Equipment		125,000
	Transfer of Peerless' net assets to trustee.					
(5)	Inventory	20,000		(No entry)		
	Accounts Payable (new)		20,000			
	Purchases of inventory on account by trustee, $20,000.					
(6)	Accounts Receivable (new)	85,000		(No entry)		
	Sales		85,000			
	Sales on account by trustee, $85,000.					
(7)	Cost of Sales	50,000		(No entry)		
	Inventory		50,000			
	Cost of sales is $50,000, including all inventory transferred from Peerless Products Corporation.					
(8)	Cash	56,000		(No entry)		
	Accounts Receivable (old)		12,000			
	Accounts Receivable (new)		44,000			
	Receivables collected by trustee: Old receivables $12,000; New receivables 44,000.					
(9)	Peerless Products Corporation—In Receivership	30,000		Accounts Payable	20,000	
	Accounts Payable (new)	4,000		Notes Payable	10,000	
	Operating Expenses	13,000		D. Able—Receiver		30,000
	Trustee's Expenses	5,000				
	Cash		52,000			
	Disbursements by trustee: Old accounts payables $30,000; New accounts payables 4,000; Operating expenses 13,000; Trustee's expenses 5,000.					

(continued)

FIGURE 20–9 Trustee and Debtor Company Entries during Liquidation (*continued*)

	Trustee D. Able's Books			Peerless Products Corporation's Books		
(10)	Cash	9,000		(No entry)		
	Marketable Securities		8,000			
	Gain on Sale of Securities		1,000			
	Sales of marketable securities for $9,000.					
	Adjusting entries at end of the period:					
(11)	Uncollectibles Expense	3,000		(No entry)		
	Depreciation Expense	10,000				
	Allowance for Uncollectibles (old)		1,000			
	Allowance for Uncollectibles (new)		2,000			
	Accumulated Depreciation		10,000			
	Provision for bad debts:					
	Old receivables $ 1,000					
	New receivables 2,000					
	Recognize depreciation expense of $10,000 for period.					
(12)	Allowance for Uncollectibles (old)	2,000		(No entry)		
	Accounts Receivable (old)		2,000			
	Old receivables of $2,000 are written off.					
(13)	Prepaid Costs Expense	1,000		(No entry)		
	Prepaid Assets		1,000			
	Recognize prepaid costs of $1,000 expired during period.					
	Closing entry at end of the period:					
(14)	Sales	85,000		D. Able—Receiver	4,000	
	Gain on Sale of Securities	1,000		Retained Earnings		4,000
	Cost of Sales		50,000			
	Operating Expenses		13,000			
	Trustee's Expenses		5,000			
	Prepaid Costs Expense		1,000			
	Uncollectibles Expense		3,000			
	Depreciation Expense		10,000			
	Peerless Products Corporation—In Receivership		4,000			

of the trustee. On Peerless' books, the reciprocal account, D. Able—Receiver, is a receivable. Note that no liabilities are transferred but remain on Peerless' books because they are the corporation's legal responsibilities.

2. The trustee's transactions are recorded in the normal manner in entries (5) through (8). The only difference is the distinction between "old" accounts, which were part of the assets transferred, and "new" accounts, which result from the trustee's transactions.
3. The trustee pays $20,000 of Peerless' accounts payable and $10,000 for the partially secured note payable. In entry (9), the $30,000 debit is made to the liability account Peerless Products Corporation—In Receivership. Peerless makes a corresponding entry to reduce its accounts payable and notes payable and to reduce the receivable, D. Able—Receiver.
4. The remaining entries (10) through (14) complete the transactions, adjust the books, and close the books at the end of the first period of receivership. Operations resulted in a net income of $4,000 for the period. The closing entry transfers the net income to the receivership account on the trustee's books. A corresponding entry on Peerless' books increases the receiver's account and the retained earnings account.

The entries are the basis of the statement of realization and liquidation for the month of January 20X7. This statement is reported to the bankruptcy court to show the current state of the liquidation process and to report on the fiduciary responsibility of D. Able, the trustee. Figure 20-10 is the statement of realization and liquidation for Peerless Products Corporation as reported by Able.

FIGURE 20–10
Receiver's Statement of Realization and Liquidation

PEERLESS PRODUCTS CORPORATION
D. Able, Receiver
Statement of Realization and Liquidation
December 31, 20X6, to January 31, 20X7

	Assets		
Assets to Be Realized		**Assets Realized**	
Old receivables (net)	$ 18,000	Old receivables	$ 12,000
Marketable securities	8,000	New receivables	44,000
Old inventory	45,000	Marketable securities	9,000
Prepaid assets	1,000	Sales of inventory	85,000
Depreciable assets (net)	101,000		
Assets Acquired		**Assets Not Realized**	
New receivables	85,000	Old receivables (net)	5,000
New inventory purchased	20,000	New receivables (net)	39,000
		New inventory	15,000
		Depreciable assets (net)	91,000
	Supplementary Items		
Supplementary Charges		**Supplementary Credits**	
Operating expenses paid	$ 13,000		
Receiver's expenses	5,000		
Net gain from operations	4,000		
	Liabilities		
Debts Liquidated		**Debts to Be Liquidated**	
Old current payables	$ 30,000	Old current payables	$133,000
New current payables	4,000	Mortgage payable	50,000
Debts Not Liquidated		**Debts Incurred**	
Old current payables	103,000	New current payables	20,000
New current payables	16,000		
Mortgage payable	50,000		
	$503,000		$503,000

Note the following observations concerning this statement:

1. The statement begins with an accounting of the assets received from Peerless and those acquired by the trustee. The assets realized section reports the proceeds of the sale of assets. For example, the marketable securities were sold for $9,000, which is $1,000 more than their book value. Sales of inventory are also reported for the amount of the total proceeds. This is the traditional approach used most often in practice, although an alternative sometimes found recognizes the disposal of the assets at their book values with the profit or gain element recognized as a supplementary credit. Either method—using gross proceeds or book value—is allowed in practice. The assets not realized section shows the ending book values of remaining assets as of January 31, 20X7. Cash is not included on the statement because it is already a realized asset. The trustee reports cash in a separate statement.
2. Supplementary items include $13,000 of operating expenses paid, receiver's expenses of $5,000, and the net gain of $4,000 as a balancing item. It is important to note that cost allocations are not included in the supplementary items. For example, the trustee recognized depreciation expense of $10,000, bad debt expense of $3,000, and expiration of prepaid assets of $1,000. These do not appear directly in the statement but are shown indirectly. For example, under assets to be realized, depreciable assets, net, are reported as $101,000, and under the assets not realized, the depreciable assets, net, are shown as $91,000. The $10,000 difference is the depreciation expense for the period. Bad debts expense and prepaid expense are treated in a similar way.
3. The last part of the statement is a report on the liabilities. The trustee is responsible for liquidating the preexisting debts of $183,000 and has incurred additional debt of $20,000 during the month. A total of $34,000 of debts has been liquidated, leaving $169,000 still to be liquidated.
4. The statement balances at a total of $503,000, indicating that all items have been reported.

The trustee provides a statement of realization and liquidation to the bankruptcy court on a monthly basis. In addition, a short cash flow statement that summarizes the cash receipts and cash disbursements during the period is provided.

The fact that various bankruptcy courts are accepting alternative forms of the statement of realization may create some consternation for accountants providing professional services in several judicial districts. For example, should assets realized be shown at their gross proceeds, or should a net amount be shown with the gain or loss in supplementary items? The report format presented in this chapter is the traditional approach accepted by a large majority of courts.

SUMMARY OF KEY CONCEPTS

Various nonjudicial actions are available to companies in financial difficulty. A debtor may restructure its existing debt by agreeing to settle its obligation at less than current value or to modify some terms of the debt agreement. The debtor's payable may be settled with the transfer of equity or assets, or the terms of the debt may be modified. In some cases, creditors may form a committee to manage the debtor's business. In this nonjudicial action, the debtor agrees to comply with the creditors' decisions. The creditors' committee may attempt to rehabilitate the business or find that liquidation is the best course of action.

Two judicial remedies are available under the Bankruptcy Code. The first is Chapter 11 reorganization in which the debtor is given some relief from creditors' claims and can attempt to rehabilitate the business and return it to profitable operations. The bankruptcy court sometimes appoints a trustee to advise the debtor. **ASC 852** requires that financial statements produced during reorganization proceedings clearly separate the reorganization items from operating items. In addition, **ASC 852** prescribes the two conditions that must occur before firms emerging from reorganization proceedings may use fresh start accounting: (1) the postpetition liabilities plus prepetition liabilities allowed as claims by the court must be higher than the reorganization value assigned to the company's assets and (2) immediately prior to confirmation of the plan of reorganization, the holders of voting shares must have less than 50 percent of the voting shares of the emerging company. Fresh start accounting includes the revaluation of assets and the elimination of any retained earnings or deficit.

The second judicial remedy is a Chapter 7 liquidation. At the beginning of a judicial action, a statement of affairs is prepared as a planning document to show the expected amounts that will be realized on the liquidation of the business and the order of the creditors' claims against the debtor's assets. During liquidation, the debtor's assets are sold, and the creditors' claims are settled in the order of priority defined by the Bankruptcy Code. Secured claims are satisfied with proceeds of the sale of the corresponding collateral; unsecured claims with priority are then settled. Any remaining cash is distributed to the general unsecured creditors.

Bankruptcy courts sometimes appoint trustees to administer the reorganization or liquidation process. A trustee provides a statement of realization and liquidation to the bankruptcy court to report on the progress of the judicial action and the trustee's fiduciary actions. The statement presents the assets transferred to the trustee, the additional assets acquired by the trustee, and the ending balance of unrealized assets still to be converted into cash. The statement also reports the debtor's liabilities discharged by the trustee as well as the additional liabilities the trustee incurred. Some minor variations of the statement format are found in bankruptcy courts.

KEY TERMS

accounting statement of affairs, *1061*
creditors' committee management, *1046*
creditors with priority, *1059*
fresh start accounting, *1050*
general unsecured creditors, *1061*
impairment loss, *1057*
liquidation under Chapter 7, *1048*
order of relief, *1048*
plan of reorganization, *1048*
receivership, *1062*
reorganization under Chapter 11, *1048*
reorganization value, *1050*
secured creditors, *1059*
statement of realization and liquidation, *1063*
troubled debt restructurings, *1046*

QUESTIONS

LO 20-1 **Q20-1** What are the nonjudicial actions available to a financially distressed company? What judicial actions are available?

LO 20-1, 20-2, 20-3 **Q20-2** What is the difference between a Chapter 7 action and a Chapter 11 bankruptcy action?

LO 20-1 **Q20-3** Under what circumstances may an involuntary petition for relief be filed? Who files this petition?

LO 20-2 **Q20-4** What is usually included in the plan of reorganization filed as part of a Chapter 11 reorganization?

LO 20-2 **Q20-5** How is the account Reorganization Value in Excess of Amount Assigned to Identifiable Assets used during a Chapter 11 reorganization?

LO 20-2 **Q20-6** What conditions must occur for a company in reorganization to use fresh start accounting?

LO 20-2 **Q20-7** What financial statements must a company file during a Chapter 11 reorganization?

LO 20-3 **Q20-8** What are the rights of creditors with priority in a Chapter 7 liquidation?

LO 20-3 **Q20-9** How is the statement of affairs used in planning an anticipated liquidation?

LO 20-4 **Q20-10** What are the financial reporting responsibilities of a trustee who accepts the debtor company's assets in a Chapter 7 liquidation?

LO 20-4 **Q20-11** How are the sales of assets reported on the statement of realization and liquidation?

CASES

LO 20-1 **C20-1** **Creditors' Alternatives**

Communication

The creditors of Lost Hope Company have had several meetings with the company's management to discuss its financial difficulties. Lost Hope currently has a significant deficit in retained earnings and has defaulted on several of its debt issues. The options currently open to the creditors are to (1) form a creditors' committee, (2) work with the company in a Chapter 11 reorganization, or (3) go through a Chapter 7 liquidation. The creditors have come to you to seek your advice on the advantages and disadvantages of each of the three options from their viewpoint.

Required

Discuss the advantages and disadvantages of each of the three options available. Include a discussion of the probable recovery of each of the creditors' claims and the time period of that recovery.

LO 20-1

C20-2 Research Related to Bankruptcy

Research

You are working on a report regarding bankruptcies. You need to locate more information and have heard that the U.S. bankruptcy courts have a website that would be useful. Locate the website using a search engine. (*Hint:* A helpful search term may be "U.S. Bankruptcy Courts.") Locate the following information, and incorporate it into a one- to two-page report.

a. How are bankruptcy judges assigned to specific cases? (You might look under the frequently asked questions, FAQs, for guidance on this question.)

b. (1) How can a business obtain the appropriate filing forms for a voluntary petition for bankruptcy?
(2) Briefly summarize the types of information required on the voluntary petition.

c. Locate and summarize the following bankruptcy statistics:

(1) First determine total business filings and then determine the number of filings by type (e.g., Chapter 7, Chapter 11, and so on) for the most recent calendar year ending on December 31.

(2) Determine the number of filings by type for businesses in your specific federal judicial district. (*Hint:* Some circuits have several district courts, so select the one you feel is most appropriate based on the location of your educational institution.) Briefly discuss how the number of filings in your federal judicial district compares with those filed in other districts.

LO 20-4

C20-3 Selection of Bankruptcy Trustee and Trustee's Responsibilities

Research

The U.S. trustee in each of the federal judicial districts is an official appointed by the U.S. attorney general to oversee the administration of bankruptcy cases or private trustees in specific cases. You seek information on the selection of a trustee and the trustee's responsibilities in a Chapter 7 bankruptcy filing.

a. Access Title 11 of the U.S. Bankruptcy Code and locate the material for a Chapter 7 filing. Summarize the procedure by which an interim trustee is appointed to a bankruptcy case. Then briefly summarize how the creditors may elect a trustee.

b. Summarize the duties of the trustee under Chapter 7 of the Bankruptcy Code.

LO 20-2

C20-4 The Bankruptcy of WorldCom

Analysis

WorldCom Inc. was one of the largest companies to file for bankruptcy. This case requires the analysis of WorldCom's December 31, 2002, 10-K filed with the Securities and Exchange Commission. The 10-K can be obtained through EDGAR (www.sec.gov) or some other publicly available source. (*Note:* After its emergence from bankruptcy, WorldCom was merged into MCI, Inc.; however, that did not affect WorldCom's financial reporting for periods prior to the merger.)

Required

Provide responses to the following by referencing the section(s) of the 10-K where you found the information.

a. At what date and under which chapter of the Bankruptcy Code did WorldCom file?

b. Briefly discuss several reasons WorldCom filed for bankruptcy at that time.

c. Describe WorldCom's major accounting irregularities prior to its bankruptcy.

d. After the bankruptcy filing, WorldCom performed an extensive review and restatement of its consolidated financial statements for the two years prior to the bankruptcy. List the major categories and amounts of these restatements for each of the two years.

e. Describe the company's financial accounting and reporting during the reorganization period. Include in your answer a brief discussion of the meaning of the title Debtors-in-Possession at the top of each of the company's financial statements during the reorganization period.

f. Briefly discuss the form of accounting the company used as it emerged from bankruptcy.

EXERCISES

LO 20-1, 20-2

E20-1 Multiple-Choice Items on Chapter 11 Reorganizations [AICPA Adapted]

Select the correct response for each of the following.

1. A client has joined other creditors of Jet Company in a composition agreement seeking to avoid a bankruptcy proceeding against Jet. Which statement describes the composition agreement?
   a. It provides for the appointment of a receiver to take over and operate the debtor's business.
   b. It must be approved by all creditors.
   c. It provides that the creditors will receive less than the full amount of their claims.
   d. It provides a temporary delay, not to exceed six months, in the debtor's obligation to repay the debts included in the composition.
2. Hardluck Inc. is insolvent. Its liabilities exceed its assets by $13 million. Blank, its president, and other family members own Hardluck. Blank, whose assets are estimated at less than $1 million, guaranteed the corporation's loans. A consortium of banks is the principal creditor of Hardluck, having lent it $8 million, the bulk of which is unsecured. The banks have decided to seek reorganization of Hardluck, and Blank has agreed to cooperate. Regarding the proposed reorganization:
   a. Blank's cooperation is necessary for signing the petition for a reorganization.
   b. If a petition for bankruptcy is filed against Hardluck, Blank also will have personal bankruptcy status resolved and relief granted.
   c. Only a duly constituted creditors' committee may file a plan of reorganization of Hardluck.
   d. Hardluck will remain in possession of its assets unless a request is made to the court to appoint a trustee.
3. Among other provisions, a Chapter 11 plan of reorganization must
   a. Rank claims according to their liquidation priorities.
   b. Not impair claims of secured creditors.
   c. Provide adequate means for the plan's execution.
   d. Treat all claims alike.
4. A condition that must exist for filing an involuntary bankruptcy petition is
   a. The debtor must have debts of at least $10,000.
   b. If the debtor has 12 or more creditors, a majority of them must sign the petition.
   c. If the debtor has 12 or more creditors, only one need sign the petition, but that creditor must be owed at least $5,000.
   d. If the debtor has 12 or more creditors, the required number signing the petition must be owed at least $5,000 in total.
5. The plan of reorganization must be approved by
   a. At least one-third of all creditors who hold at least half of the total debt.
   b. At least half of all creditors who hold at least half of the total debt.
   c. At least half of all creditors who hold at least two-thirds of the total debt.
   d. At least two-thirds of all creditors who hold at least two-thirds of the total debt.

LO 20-2

E20-2 Recovery Analysis for a Chapter 11 Reorganization

The plan of reorganizing for Taylor Companies, Inc., was approved by the court, stockholders, and creditors on December 31, 20X1. The plan calls for a general restructuring of all of Taylor's debt. The company's liability and capital accounts on December 31, 20X1, are as follows:

Accounts Payable (postpetition)	$ 30,000
Liabilities Subject to Compromise:	
Accounts Payable	80,000
Notes Payable, 10%, unsecured	150,000
Interest Payable	40,000
Bonds Payable, 12%	200,000
Common Stock, $1 par	100,000
Additional Paid-In Capital	200,000
Retained Earnings (deficit)	(178,000)
Total	$622,000

A total of $30,000 of accounts payable has been incurred since the company filed its petition for relief under Chapter 11. No other liabilities have been incurred since the petition was filed. No payments have been made on the liabilities subject to the compromise that existed on the petition date. Under the terms of the reorganization plan:

1. The accounts payable creditors existing at the date the petition was filed agree to accept $72,000 of net accounts receivable in full settlement of their claims.
2. The holders of the 10 percent notes payable of $150,000 plus $16,000 of interest payable agree to accept land having a fair value of $125,000 and a book value of $85,000.
3. The holders of the 12 percent bonds payable of $200,000 plus $24,000 of interest payable agree to cancel accrued interest of $18,000, accept cash payment of the remaining $6,000 of interest, and accept a secured interest in the company's equipment in exchange for extending the term of the bonds for an additional year at no interest.
4. The common shareholders agree to reduce the deficit by changing the stock's par value to $2 per share and eliminating any remaining deficit after recognition of all gains or losses from the debt restructuring transactions specified in the plan of reorganization. The deficit will be eliminated by reducing additional paid-in capital.

Required

a. Prepare a recovery analysis for the plan of reorganization, concluding with the total recovery of each liability and capital component of Taylor Companies.

b. Prepare the journal entries to account for the discharge of the debt and the restructuring of the common equity in fulfillment of the plan of reorganization.

LO 20-1, 20-3

E20-3 Multiple-Choice Items on Chapter 7 Liquidations

Select the correct response for each of the following.

1. Lear Company ceased doing business and is in bankruptcy. Among the claimants are employees seeking unpaid wages. The following statements describe the possible status of such claims in a bankruptcy proceeding. Which is the *incorrect* statement?
   - *a.* They are entitled to priority.
   - *b.* If a priority is afforded such claims, it cannot exceed $5,000 per wage earner.
   - *c.* Such claims include wages earned within 180 days before the filing of the bankruptcy petition but not to exceed $10,000 in amount per wage earner.
   - *d.* The amounts of excess wages not entitled to a priority are mere unsecured claims.
2. The highest priority for payment of unsecured claims in a bankruptcy proceeding is
   - *a.* Administrative expenses of the bankruptcy.
   - *b.* Unpaid federal income taxes.
   - *c.* Wages of each employee up to $10,000 earned within 180 days before the petition.
   - *d.* Wages owed to an insolvent employee.
3. The order of payments for unsecured priority claims in a Chapter 7 bankruptcy case is such that
   - *a.* Tax claims of governmental units are paid before claims for administrative expenses incurred by the trustee.
   - *b.* Tax claims of governmental units are paid before claims of employees for wages.
   - *c.* Claims of employees for wages are paid before administrative expenses incurred by the trustee.
   - *d.* Claims incurred between the filing of an involuntary petition and appointment of a trustee are paid before the claims for contributions to employee benefit plans.
4. Narco is in serious financial difficulty and is unable to meet current unsecured obligations of $30,000 to some 14 creditors who are demanding immediate payment. Narco owes Johnson $5,000, and Johnson has decided to file an involuntary petition against Narco. Which of the following is necessary for Johnson to file validly?
   - *a.* Johnson must be joined by at least two other creditors.
   - *b.* Narco must have committed a fraudulent act within one year of the filing.

c. Johnson must allege and subsequently establish that Narco's liabilities exceed its assets upon fair valuation.

d. Johnson must be a secured creditor.

5. Your client is insolvent under the federal bankruptcy law. Under the circumstances

a. So long as the client can meet current debts or claims by its most aggressive creditors, a bankruptcy proceeding is *not* possible.

b. Your CPA firm need *not* disclose such information—that is, insolvency—in the financial statements so long as you are convinced that the problem is short-lived.

c. A transfer of assets to a creditor less than 90 days before filing a petition may be voidable.

d. Your client *cannot* file a voluntary petition for bankruptcy.

LO 20-3

Advanced StudyGuide .com

E20-4 Chapter 7 Liquidation

Penn Inc.'s assets have the carrying values and estimated fair values as follows:

	Carrying Value	Fair Value
Cash	$ 16,000	$ 16,000
Accounts Receivable	60,000	50,000
Inventory	90,000	65,000
Land	100,000	80,000
Building (net)	220,000	160,000
Equipment (net)	250,000	100,000
Total	$736,000	$471,000

Penn's debts follow:

Accounts Payable	$ 95,000
Wages Payable (all have priority)	9,500
Taxes Payable	14,000
Notes Payable (secured by receivables and inventory)	190,000
Interest on Notes Payable	5,000
Bonds Payable (secured by land and building)	220,000
Interest on Bonds Payable	11,000
Total	$544,500

Required

a. Prepare a schedule to calculate the net estimated amount available for general unsecured creditors.

b. Compute the percentage dividend to general unsecured creditors.

c. Prepare a schedule showing the amount to be paid each of the creditor groups upon distribution of the $471,000 estimated to be realizable.

LO 20-4

Advanced StudyGuide .com

E20-5 Statement of Realization and Liquidation

A trustee has been appointed for Pace Inc., which is being liquidated under Chapter 7 of the Bankruptcy Code. The following occurred after the assets were transferred to the trustee:

1. Sales on account by the trustee were $75,000. Cost of goods sold were $60,000, consisting of all inventory transferred from Pace.
2. The trustee sold all $12,000 worth of marketable securities for $10,500.
3. Receivables collected by the trustee:

Old:	$21,000 of the $38,000 transferred
New:	$47,000

4. Depreciation of $16,000 on the plant assets of $96,000 transferred from Pace recorded.
5. Disbursements by the trustee:

Old current payables:	$22,000 of the $48,000 transferred
Trustee's expenses:	$4,300

Required

Prepare a statement of realization and liquidation according to the traditional approach illustrated in the chapter.

PROBLEMS

LO 20-2

Advanced StudyGuide .com

P20-6 Chapter 11 Reorganization

During the recent recession, Polydorous Inc. accumulated a deficit in retained earnings. Although still operating at a loss, the company posted better results during 20X1. Polydorous is having trouble paying suppliers on time and is paying interest when it is due. The company files for protection under Chapter 11 of the Bankruptcy Code and has the following liabilities and stockholders' equity accounts at the time the petition is filed:

Accounts Payable	$160,000
Interest Payable	20,000
Notes Payable, 10%, unsecured	340,000
Preferred Stock	100,000
Common Stock, $5 par	150,000
Retained Earnings (deficit)	(80,000)
Total	$690,000

A plan of reorganization is filed with the court, which approves it after review and obtaining creditor and investor votes. The plan of reorganization includes the following actions:

1. The prepetition accounts payable will be restructured according to the following: (*a*) $40,000 will be paid in cash, (*b*) $20,000 will be eliminated, and (*c*) the remaining $100,000 will be exchanged for a five-year, secured note payable paying 12 percent interest.
2. The interest payable will be restructured as follows: elimination of $10,000 of the interest and payment of the remaining $10,000 in cash.
3. The 10 percent, unsecured notes payable will be restructured as follows: (*a*) $60,000 of them will be eliminated, (*b*) $10,000 of them will be paid in cash, (*c*) $240,000 of them will be exchanged for a five-year, 12 percent secured note, and (*d*) the remaining $30,000 will be exchanged for 3,000 shares of newly issued common stock having a par value of $10.
4. The preferred shareholders will exchange their stock for 5,000 shares of newly issued $10 par common stock.
5. The common shareholders will exchange their stock for 2,000 shares of newly issued $10 par common stock.

After extensive analysis, the company's reorganization value is determined to be $510,000 prior to any payments of cash required by the reorganization plan. An additional $10,000 in current liabilities have been incurred since the petition was filed. After the reorganization is completed, the capital structure of the company will be as follows:

Current liabilities (postpetition)	$ 10,000
Notes payable, 12%, secured	340,000
Common stock ($10 par)	100,000
Postreorganization capital structure	$450,000

An evaluation of the assets' fair values was made after the company completed its reorganization, immediately prior to the point the company emerged from the proceedings. The following information is available:

	Book Value	Fair Value
Cash	$ 30,000	$ 30,000
Accounts receivable (net)	140,000	110,000
Inventory	25,000	18,000
Property, plant & equipment (net)	445,000	262,000
Total	$640,000	$420,000

Required

a. Prepare a plan of reorganization recovery analysis for the liability and stockholders' equity accounts of Polydorous Inc. on the day the plan of reorganization is approved. (*Hint:* The liabilities on the plan's approval day are $530,000, which is $520,000 from prepetition payables plus $10,000 in additional accounts payable incurred postpetition.)

b. Prepare an analysis showing whether the company qualifies for fresh start accounting as it emerges from the reorganization.

c. Prepare journal entries for execution of the plan of reorganization with its general restructuring of debt and capital.

d. Prepare the balance sheet for the company on completion of the plan of reorganization.

LO 20-3

P20-7 Chapter 7 Liquidation, Statement of Affairs

Name Brand Company is to be liquidated under Chapter 7 of the Bankruptcy Code. The balance sheet on July 31, 20X1, follows:

Assets	
Cash	$ 5,000
Marketable Securities	30,000
Accounts Receivable (net)	105,000
Inventory	160,000
Prepaid Insurance	7,000
Land	80,000
Plant & Equipment (net)	412,000
Franchises	72,000
Total	$871,000
Liabilities and Equities	
Accounts Payable	$265,000
Wages Payable	20,000
Taxes Payable	12,000
Interest Payable	37,000
Notes Payable	280,000
Mortgages Payable	220,000
Common Stock ($20 par)	240,000
Retained Earnings (deficit)	(203,000)
Total	$871,000

Additional Information

1. Marketable securities consist of 1,000 shares of Wooly Inc. common stock. The stock's market value per share is $22. The stock was pledged against a $28,000, 10 percent note payable that has accrued interest of $1,400.

2. Accounts receivable of $50,000 are collateral for a $40,000, 12 percent note payable that has accrued interest of $4,000.

3. Inventory with a book value of $79,000 and a current value of $75,000 is pledged against accounts payable of $105,000. The appraised value of the remainder of the inventory is $76,000.

4. Only $1,500 will be recovered from prepaid insurance.

5. Land is appraised at $110,000 and plant and equipment at $340,000.
6. It is estimated that the franchises can be sold for $30,000.
7. All wages payable qualify for priority.
8. The mortgages are on the land and a building with a book value of $162,000 and an appraised value of $150,000. The accrued interest on the mortgages is $14,600.
9. Estimated legal and accounting fees for the liquidation are $13,000.

Required

a. Prepare a statement of affairs as of July 31, 20X1.

b. Compute the estimated percentage settlement to unsecured creditors.

LO 20-3

P20-8 Chapter 7 Liquidation, Statement of Affairs [AICPA Adapted]

Tower Inc. advises you that it is facing bankruptcy proceedings. As the company's CPA, you are aware of its condition. Tower's balance sheet on December 31, 20X1, and supplementary data follow:

Assets	
Cash	$ 2,000
Accounts Receivable (net)	70,000
Inventory, Raw Materials	40,000
Inventory, Finished Goods	60,000
Marketable Securities	20,000
Land	13,000
Buildings (net)	90,000
Machinery (net)	140,000
Prepaid Expenses	5,000
Total Assets	$440,000

Liabilities and Capital	
Accounts Payable	$ 80,000
Notes Payable	135,000
Wages	15,000
Mortgages Payable	130,000
Common Stock	100,000
Retained Earnings (deficit)	(20,000)
Total Liabilities & Capital	$440,000

Additional Information

1. Cash includes a $500 travel advance that has been expended.
2. Accounts receivable of $40,000 have been pledged in support of bank loans of $30,000. Credit balances of $5,000 are netted in the accounts receivable total.
3. Marketable securities consist of government bonds costing $10,000 and 500 shares of Dawson Company stock. The market value of the bonds is $10,000, and the stock is $18 per share. The bonds have $200 of accrued interest due. The securities are collateral for a $20,000 bank loan.
4. Appraised value of raw materials and finished goods is $30,000 and $50,000, respectively. For an additional cost of $10,000, the raw materials could realize $70,000 as finished goods.
5. The appraised value of fixed assets is $25,000 for land, $110,000 for buildings, and $75,000 for machinery.
6. Prepaid expenses will be exhausted during the liquidation period.
7. Accounts payable include $15,000 of withheld payroll taxes and $6,000 owed to creditors who have been reassured by the president of Tower that they will be paid. There are unrecorded employer's payroll taxes in the amount of $500.
8. Wages payable are not subject to any limitations under bankruptcy laws.

9. Mortgages payable consist of $100,000 on land and buildings and $30,000 for a chattel mortgage on machinery. Total unrecorded accrued interest for these mortgages amounts to $2,400.
10. Estimated legal fees and expenses in connection with the liquidation are $10,000.
11. The probable judgment on a pending damage suit is $50,000.
12. You have not rendered an invoice for $5,000 for last year's audit, and you estimate a $1,000 fee for liquidation work.

Required

a. Prepare a statement of affairs. (The Book Value column should reflect adjustments that properly should have been made as of December 31, 20X1, in the normal course of business.)

b. Compute the estimated settlement per dollar of unsecured liabilities.

LO 20-2

P20-9 Financial Statements for a Firm in Chapter 11 Proceedings

On January 2, 20X2, Hobbes Company files a petition for relief under Chapter 11 of the Bankruptcy Code. Hobbes had disastrous operating performance during the recent recession and needs time to reestablish profitable operations. The trial balance on January 2, 20X2, follows:

	Debit	Credit
Cash	$ 15,000	
Accounts Receivable (net)	65,000	
Inventory	102,000	
Property, Plant & Equipment	620,000	
Accumulated Depreciation		$140,000
Accounts Payable		138,000
Notes Payable, 10%		170,000
Bonds Payable, 12%		250,000
Interest Payable		47,000
Preferred Stock		50,000
Common Stock, $1 par		50,000
Additional Paid-In Capital		75,000
Retained Earnings (deficit)	118,000	
Total	$920,000	$920,000

The following information applies to the 20X2 fiscal year ending December 31, 20X2. Hobbes is in reorganization proceedings for the entire year, and the plan of reorganization has not been approved as of December 31, 20X2. The debtor retained possession of the company during the year.

Income Data for 20X2

1. Sales revenue of $246,000 is generated during the year.
2. Cost of goods sold is $170,000 as a result of cost reduction programs implemented during the year.
3. Selling, operating, and administrative expenses are $50,000 for the year.
4. Interest expense is $4,000. Contractual interest would have been $51,000 for the year.
5. Reorganization items include $15,000 in fees paid to professionals and $3,000 of interest earned on cash accumulated as a result of the Chapter 11 proceedings.
6. The income tax of $5,000 on operating income was paid during the year.
7. Discontinued operations included a $16,000 loss on operations, net of tax, and a $9,000 gain on the sale of assets, net of tax. The bankruptcy court administered the sale of the assets under the Chapter 11 proceedings.

Cash Flow Data for 20X2

1. A total of $264,000 is received from customers. This includes $18,000 received on the accounts receivable that were outstanding prior to filing the petition.
2. A total of $206,000 is paid to suppliers, employees, and others for operations.

3. The current interest expense of $4,000 on postpetition debt is paid during the year.
4. Professional fees of $15,000 are paid, and interest on cash accumulations of $3,000 is received.
5. Net cash used by discontinued operations, excluding the sale of assets, is $3,000.
6. The proceeds from the sale of the discontinued assets is $18,000. The bankruptcy court administered this sale.
7. Hobbes borrowed $10,000 in short-term debt as part of a financing plan administered by the court.
8. The court authorized a payment of $10,000 on the bonds payable. The ending cash balance of $72,000 represents an increase of $57,000 during the year.

Other Data for 20X2

1. Careful working capital management reduced the ending inventory to $88,000. Continued reduction is expected in 20X3.
2. The property, plant, and equipment, net of accumulated depreciation, at the end of 20X2 totaled $460,000.
3. In addition to the $10,000 short-term borrowings that are part of the court-approved financing plan, Hobbes has postpetition accounts payable of $7,000.

Required

a. Prepare the income statement for Hobbes for the year ending December 31, 20X2.
b. Prepare the statement of cash flows for the company for the year ending December 31, 20X2.
c. Prepare the balance sheet for the company as of December 31, 20X2.

Index

A

B

C

D

G

H

J

K

L

N

O

P

T

U

V

W

X

Y

Z